MANAGEMENT

Leading & Collaborating in a Competitive World

Thomas S. Bateman
McIntire School of Commerce,
University of Virginia

Scott A. Snell
Cornell University

Seventh Edition

 McGraw-Hill Irwin

Boston   Burr Ridge, IL   Dubuque, IA   Madison, WI   New York   San Francisco   St. Louis
Bangkok   Bogotá   Caracas   Kuala Lumpur   Lisbon   London   Madrid   Mexico City
Milan   Montreal   New Delhi   Santiago   Seoul   Singapore   Sydney   Taipei   Toronto

McGraw-Hill
Irwin

MANAGEMENT: LEADING & COLLABORATING IN A COMPETITIVE WORLD
Published by McGraw-Hill/Irwin, a business unit of The McGraw-Hill Companies, Inc., 1221 Avenue of
the Americas, New York, NY, 10020. Copyright © 2007 by The McGraw-Hill Companies, Inc. All rights
reserved. No part of this publication may be reproduced or distributed in any form or by any means, or
stored in a database or retrieval system, without the prior written consent of The McGraw-Hill
Companies, Inc., including, but not limited to, in any network or other electronic storage or transmission,
or broadcast for distance learning.

Some ancillaries, including electronic and print components, may not be available to customers outside
the United States.

This book is printed on acid-free paper.

1 2 3 4 5 6 7 8 9 0 DOW/DOW 0 9 8 7 6 5

ISBN-13: 978-0-07-110584-2
ISBN-10: 0-07-110584-0

www.mhhe.com

For my parents, Tom and Jeanine Bateman
and Mary Jo, Lauren, T.J., and James

and

My parents, John and Clara Snell,
and Marybeth, Sara, Jack and Emily

About the Authors

Thomas S. Bateman

Thomas S. Bateman is Bank of America Professor and management area coordinator in the McIntire School of Commerce at the University of Virginia. Prior to joining the University of Virginia, he taught organizational behavior at the Kenan-Flager Business School of the University of North Carolina to undergraduates, M.B.A. students, Ph.D. students, and practicing managers. He also recently returned from two years in Europe as a visiting professor at the Institute for Management Development (IMD), one of the world's leaders in the design and delivery of executive education. Professor Bateman completed his doctoral program in business administration in 1980 at Indiana University. Prior to receiving his doctorate, Dr. Bateman received his B.A. from Miami University. In addition to Virginia, UNC-Chapel Hill, and IMD, Dr. Bateman has taught at Texas A&M, Tulane, and Indiana universities.

Professor Bateman is an active management researcher, writer, and consultant. He has served on the editorial boards of major academic journals and has presented numerous papers at professional meetings on topics including managerial decision making, job stress, negotiation, employee commitment and motivation, group decision making, and job satisfaction. His articles have appeared in professional journals such as the *Academy of Management Journal, Academy of Management Review, Journal of Applied Psychology, Organizational Behavior and Human Decision Processes, Journal of Management, Business Horizons, Journal of Organizational Behavior, and Decision Sciences.*

Dr. Bateman's current consulting and research centers on practical wisdom in business executives, top management credibility and employee cynicism, and the successful pursuit of long-term work goals. He works with organizations including, Nokia, Singapore Airlines, USPS, the Brookings Institution, Virginia Bankers Association and the U.S. Chamber of Commerce.

Scott A. Snell

Scott A. Snell is Professor of Human Resource Studies in the School of Industrial and Labor Relations at Cornell University. He received a B.A. in Psychology from Miami University, as well as M.B.A. and Ph.D. degrees in Business Administration from Michigan State University. Dr. Snell has taught courses in human resource management and strategic management to undergraduates, graduates, and executives. He is actively involved in executive education and has conducted international programs in Europe and Asia as well as Australia and New Zealand.

Professor Snell has worked with companies such as AT&T, GE, IBM, Merck, and Shell to address the alignment of human resource systems with strategic initiatives such as globalization, technological change, and knowledge management. His research and teaching interests center on how leading companies manage their people to gain competitive advantage. This work focuses on the development and deployment of intellectual capital as a foundation of an organization's core competencies.

Dr. Snell's research has been published in a number of professional journals, including the *Academy of Management Journal, Academy of Management Review, Human Resource Management, Human Resource Management Review, Industrial Relations, Journal of Business Research, Journal of Management, Journal of Managerial Issues, Journal of Management Studies, Organizational Dynamics, Organization Studies, Personnel Psychology,* and *Strategic Management Journal.* He is also coauthor of *Managing Human Resources.* In addition, Dr. Snell has served on the editorial boards of *Journal of Managerial Issues, Digest of Management Research, Human Resource Management, Human Resource Management Review, Human Resource Planning,* and *Academy of Management Journal.*

Preface

When Ed Breen became CEO of Tyco International, he immediately got rid of the entire board of directors. Is this a stereotypic example of a ruthless, power-hungry corporate executive? No, it's not—Ed Breen is an ethical, courageous individual who was hired when Tyco's former CEO left due to mismanagement, financial improprieties, and legal charges. The Tyco case was one of a continuing string of highly-publicized business scandals that rocked the business world, harmed the public image of business, and brought on important regulatory reforms. Ed Breen's actions were those of a good manager doing the right thing, and leading a once-respected but struggling organization back toward greatness.

As things change in the world and in business, some unethical and ineffective management practices will continue—but good people will continue also, managing well and making things better, as they always have. In this book, you will read about many managers, some doing things brilliantly, others making mistakes (with some learning from their mistakes, and some not). The people will include not only company presidents and CEOs like Ed Breen of Tyco and Jeff Immelt of GE—Immelt was in the interesting position of succeeding Jack Welch, *Fortune* magazine's "Manager of the Century" (as one observer put it, "Who wants to follow Babe Ruth?"). You also will read about students like Jason Olim who started CDnow when he was in college, social entrepreneurs like Stella Ogiale who use their companies to help people who need help, and middle managers like Ken Kutaragi of Sony who create and pursue new visions within big organizations.

Management is about people, but it also is about organizations. You will read about companies ranging from Pixar to Land's End, eBay to Avon, Electronic Arts to Proctor and Gamble, MTV to the National Hockey League, and Google to Nissan. And that's just a small sample from Chapter 1.

Some organizations rise from the ashes, or come from seemingly nowhere, to become the next hot investment. Some organizations are high-flyers one day and come crashing down the next. Some achieve greatness, and have occasional downturns, but continue being great. These performance shifts occur in large part from the ways in which they are managed, and partly from how circumstances change. Business environments, like pendulums, swing from one extreme to another. By the time you read this, some things will have changed again. These changes will contribute to the fall of some currently successful companies and managers and the rise of others who currently struggle or are now just dreaming of new business ideas.

For you, as a businessperson as in life, uncertainty will be a constant state of affairs. That is, no one knows for certain what will happen, or what to do in pursuit of a successful future. Luck and the right circumstances can help companies (and people) succeed in the short run. But in the long run good management is essential.

Fortunately, you have access to current knowledge about how to manage. We have learned a lot from the people and companies that have succeeded and failed. The continuing experiment created by the vast array of management practices that exist in the business world, combined with sound research that helps tease out what works from what doesn't, helps us to learn from mistakes and identify the most important lessons and useful practices that managers can employ. We hope that you will not only learn as much as you can about this vital activity but also commit to applying it—by reading and learning, and by using it in the best possible ways.

This book and the course you are taking will help you face the managerial challenges of a changing world. In doing so, they will help you identify what's important and what's not, make good decisions, and take effective action on behalf of yourself, your colleagues, and the organizations for which you work.

Our Goals

Our mission with this text hasn't changed from that of our previous editions: to inform, instruct, and inspire. We hope to *inform* by providing descriptions of the important concepts and practices of modern management. We hope to *instruct* by describing how you can take action on the ideas discussed. We hope to *inspire* not only by writing in a positive, interesting, and optimistic way but also by providing a real sense of the unlimited opportunities ahead of you. Whether your goal is starting your own company, leading a team to greatness, building a strong organization, delighting your customers, or generally forging a positive future, we want to inspire you to take positive actions.

We hope to inspire you to be both a thinker and a doer. We want you to think about the issues, think about the impact of your actions, think before you act. But being a good thinker is not enough; you also must be a doer. Management is a world of action. It is a world that requires timely and appropriate action. It is a world not for the passive but for those who commit to positive accomplishments.

Keep applying the ideas you learn in this course, read about management in sources outside of this course, and certainly keep learning about management after you leave school and continue your career. Make no mistake about it, learning about management is a personal voyage that will last years, an entire career, your entire lifetime.

Competitive Advantage

Today's world is competitive. Never before has the world of work been so challenging. Never before has it been so imperative to your career that you learn the skills of management. Never before have people had so many opportunities with so many potential rewards.

You will compete with other people for jobs, resources, and promotions. Your organization will compete with other firms for contracts, clients, and customers. To survive the competition, and to thrive, you must perform in ways that give you an edge over your competitors, that make the other party want to hire you, buy from you, and do repeat business with you. You will want them to choose you, not your competitor.

To survive and thrive, today's managers have to think and act strategically. Today's customers are well educated, aware of their options, and demanding of excellence. For this reason, managers today must think constantly about how to build a capable workforce and manage in a way that delivers the goods and services that provide the best possible value to the customer.

By this standard, managers and organizations must perform. Four essential types of performance, on which the organization beats, equals, or loses to the competition, are *cost*, *quality*, *speed*, and *innovation*. These four performance dimensions, when done well, deliver value to the customer and competitive advantage to you and your organization. We will elaborate on all these topics throughout the book.

The idea is to keep you focused on a type of "bottom line," to make sure you think continually about "delivering the goods" that make both the manager (you) and the organization a competitive success. This results-oriented approach is unique among management textbooks.

Leading & Collaborating

Yes, business is competitive. But, it's not that simple. In fact, it is overly cynical to think strictly in terms of competition; such cynicism can sabotage your own performance. The other fundamental elements in the success equation are collaboration and leadership.

People working with one another, rather than against, is essential to competitive advantage. Put another way, you can't do it alone—the world is too complex, and business is too challenging.

You need to work with your teammates. Leaders and followers need to work as collaborators more than as adversaries. Work groups throughout your organization need to cooperate with one another. Business and government, often viewed as antagonists, can work productively together. And today more than ever, companies that traditionally were competitors engage in joint ventures and find other ways to collaborate on some things even as they compete in others. It takes leadership to make these collaborations happen.

How does an organization create competitive advantage through collaboration? It's all about the people, and it derives from good leadership. Three stereotypes of leadership are that it comes from the top of the company, that it comes from one's immediate boss, and that it means being decisive and issuing commands. There are grains of truth to these stereotypes, but the reality is much more complex. First, the person at the top may or may not provide effective leadership—in fact, many observers believe that good leadership is far too rare. Second, organizations need leaders at all levels, in every team and work unit. This includes you, beginning early in your career, and this is why leadership is an important theme in this book. Third, leaders should be capable of decisiveness and of giving commands, but relying too much on this traditional approach isn't enough. Great leadership is far more inspirational than this, and helps people to both think differently but also to work differently—including working collaboratively, with a focus on results.

Leadership—from your boss, as well as from you—generates collaboration, which in turn creates results which are good for the company and good for the people involved.

NEW and IMPROVED in the 7th edition

Topical Currency

It goes without saying that this textbook, in its seventh edition, remains on the cutting edge of topical coverage, as updated via both current business examples and recent management research. Chapters have been thoroughly updated, and students are exposed to a broad array of important current topics.

We have done our very best to draw from a wide variety of subject matter, sources, and personal experiences.

Below is just a sampling of the changes made to this edition.

Chapter 1
- New unfolding case: Ed Catmull and Pixar.
- Major themes remain the same, but all are supported by many new examples.
- The Internet section is now titled Technological Change.
- Additional historic material on Total Quality (per reviewer request).
- 2005 examples of *Business Week's* Best & Worst managers.
- New discussion of managerial roles.
- Emotional intelligence.
- Social capital (in careers sections).
- Peter Drucker on what makes an effective executive.

Chapter 2
- Title change: The External Environment and Organizational Culture.
- The material on organization culture, formerly in Chapter 16, has been expanded (particularly managing culture as a way of adapting and responding to the external environment), updated, and moved here.
- The effect of the stock market and Wall Street expectations on managerial behavior.
- A brand-new and extended discussion has been added on supply-chain management.
- The discussion on domain selection, diversification, merger or acquisition, and divesture has been expanded and clarified.
- Odds and ends: We opened the chapter with a figure on organizations as open systems. In the Laws and Regulations section, we noted that while many in the corporate community see government as an adversary, government can also be a source of competitive advantage. In the Social Issues discussion, we noted some of the new public relations and other difficulties Wal-Mart is experiencing.
- New exercises.

Chapter 3
- New unfolding case: Merck & Vioxx.
- New material on managerial risk-taking.
- New material on reasons for failed decision making.
- The "speed trap" (the dangers of pressure to make decisions quickly, plus remedies).

- Information technology as a source of crises.
- Plenty of new examples.

Chapter 4
- Put the early planning material in context.
- Presented new strategy map material in a clear way.
- More on the planning cycle.
- Examples and clarification of missions, visions, and goals.
- Expanded SWOT discussion (including a paragraph on students using the technique to find a job).

Chapter 5
- New unfolding case: Ethics at Citigroup.
- Many current examples.
- How (un)ethical are you?
- Added material on norms across cultures (relativism).
- Sarbanes-Oxley Act.
- Moral person versus moral manager (being moral versus influencing others to be moral).
- Moral awareness, moral judgment, and moral character.
- The "veil of ignorance" as a metaphor for guiding ethical decision making.
- A model for resolving ethical dilemmas.
- The costs of unethical behavior.
- Courage.
- Transcendent education: one that balances self-interest with responsibility to others.
- Sustainable growth and life cycle analysis now in chapter, not just in the appendix.

Chapter 6
- An extended treatment on China.
- A new section on offshoring.
- Ethnocentrism.
- Inpatriates.

Chapter 7
- Title change: Entrepreneurship.
- New unfolding case: Jeff Bezos and Amazon.com
- Lots of new examples.
- New material on immigrant entrepreneurs.
- Franchising.

- Five successful Internet business models.
- Causes of success and failure, common management challenges, and increasing your changes of success are reorganized.
- Initial public stock offerings.
- Updated Appendix on where to get information.

Chapter 8

- Moved the Network Organization material from Chapter 9 here.
- More on the importance of delegation.
- A heads-up on the informal organization discussion coming in future chapters.
- The matrix organization from Time Inc.

Chapter 9

- Title change: Organizational Agility.
- Value chain now here rather than Chapter 8.
- Strategy section now at the front of the chapter.
- Connection with organization design much clearer.
- Additional perspective on downsizing.
- New material on the value chain and Six Sigma.
- A better setup of the Baldridge award and an updated box of award criteria.

Chapter 10

- The growing shortage of highly skilled, educated workers.
- More on interview techniques.
- Rewritten legal discussion.
- Management training programs.
- Additional material on appraisal techniques.
- Expanded MBO discussion and 360 appraisal discussion.
- Executive pay and stock options.
- Changes in benefits companies are making.

Chapter 11

- More diversity history
- More on gender-related issues
- Hostile work environment
- Expanded discussion on the difference between affirmative action and diversity
- More on the challenges of diversity
- Added list of African-American CEOs.

Chapter 12

- New unfolding case: Andrea Jung and Avon's Extreme Makeover.
- Kouzes and Posner's exemplary leader behaviors.
- Level 5 leadership.
- Authentic leadership.
- Servant leaders.
- Bridge leaders.
- Lateral leadership.
- Shared leadership.
- Additional material on developmental experiences.

Chapter 13

- New unfolding case: Cleanup at the Rocky Flats Nuclear Facility.
- More on how goals affect (un)ethical behavior.
- Self-set goals.
- Managing mistakes.
- More on providing feedback.
- How Maslow applies, post-9/11.
- General employment contracts.

Chapter 14

- Title change: Teamwork.
- New unfolding case: John Mackey at Whole Foods.
- Group development in virtual teams.
- How to be an effective mediator.
- Conflict in virtual teams.
- Conflict in B2B commerce.

Chapter 15

- New unfolding case: David Neeleman and JetBLue.
- Q&A at a presidential press conference.
- IMing.
- Blogging.
- Added material on "town meetings" as a means of communicating.
- New table: 10 Ways to Add Power to Your Presentation.

Chapter 16

- Expanded treatment of Six Sigma in the section on feedback control.

- Fixed and variable costs.
- Top-down vs. bottom-up budgets.
- The importance of maintaining open communications with subordinates, as part of designing effective control systems.
- Progressive discipline.
- A revised discussed on market control of the CEO, to reflect both recent scandals and the more sophisticated treatment of the options issue in Chapter 10, which is referenced.
- The importance of building a culture of integrity.

Chapter 17

- More on the managerial implications of the concepts discussed (e.g., the fact that marketing managers promote heavily among early adopters and innovators to create buzz).
- Reinforced the importance of managers understanding the role of technology.
- Reinforced the importance of a careful cost/benefit analysis of new technology investment.
- The importance of taking into account the effect that new technology will have on employees, and referenced Chapter 18 in that context.
- Intellectual property theft.
- A better explanation of Figure 17.2.
- Additional important benefits of the CTO's role.
- The competition between cellphones and iPod.
- Next-generation e-commerce (with an opening paragraph on dating) and hydrogen-powered motorcycles.

Chapter 18

- New unfolding case: GE and Jeffrey Immelt.
- Current examples.
- Added feature: boxes featuring "change agents," people who made a positive difference in or through their companies.
- Organizational ambidexterity.
- New material on organization development.
- New material on how companies achieve greatness.
- How communities achieve greatness via business/government cooperation.
- Fanciful but informative examples of companies of the future.
- Blogging and the changing competitive landscape (box).

A Team Effort

This book is the product of a fantastic McGraw-Hill/Irwin team. Moreover, we wrote this book believing that we are part of a team with the course instructor and with students. The entire team is responsible for the learning process.

Our goal, and that of your instructor, is to create a positive learning environment in which you can excel. But in the end, the raw material of this course is just words. It is up to you to use them as a basis for further thinking, deep learning, and constructive action.

What you do with the things you learn from this course, and with the opportunities the future holds, *counts*. As a manager, you can make a dramatic difference for yourself and for other people. What managers do matters, *tremendously*.

Outstanding Pedagogy

Management: Leading & Collaborating in a Competitive World is pedagogically stimulating and is intended to maximize student learning. With this in mind, we used a wide array of pedagogical features—some tried and true, others new and novel:

- Learning Objectives, which open each chapter, identify what students will learn by reading and studying the chapter.
- Opening quotes provide a thought-provoking preview of chapter material. The quotes are from people like Peter Drucker (on management), Jack Welch (on strategy), Henry David Thoreau (on ethics), Julius Caesar (on leadership), and Charles Kettering (on change and the future).
- **New! "Unfolding" Case:** Each chapter begins with a *Prologue* which describing an actual leader, company, or situation. The case is then expanded within the chapter in *Connections* boxes, showing the student how the chapter content relates back to the company leader or situation highlighted in the Prologue. At the end of the chapter, the *Epilogue* ties up loose ends and brings the material full circle for the student.
- **New! Advantages of Collaboration boxes:** Managers must deliver results. An essential skill toward doing so is the ability to work effectively with others toward a goal. These boxes speak directly to the student, and highlight the advantages of collaboration.
- **New! Random Pop-ups:** Throughout the chapter, these marginal boxes highlight interesting factoids, statistics, and quotes relating to chapter content.

- **Updated! Bottom-line Practices Icons:** While the icons with their four running themes of Innovation, Cost, Speed, and Quality have been a hallmark of the text, this edition includes added text with the icon, furthering student understanding and reinforcing these important results-oriented themes.
- New boxed inserts describing current examples and controversial issues are found throughout the text.
- "From the Pages of *Business Week*" highlights recent *Business Week* articles.

End-of-Chapter Elements

- Key terms are page-referenced to the text and are part of the vocabulary-building emphasis. These terms are defined again in the glossary at the end of the book.
- A Summary of Learning Objectives provides clear, concise responses to the learning objectives, giving students a quick reference for reviewing the important concepts in the chapter.
- Discussion Questions, which follow the Summary of Learning Objectives, are thought-provoking questions on concepts covered in the chapter and ask for opinions on controversial issues.
- **New Concluding Cases!** Each chapter ends with a case based on disguised but real companies and people that reinforces key chapter elements and themes.
- **New Experiential Exercises!** Many exercises have been added to tried and true previous edition favorites. Some exercises allow for personality assessment, some are for use as group activities in the classroom, and some involve outside research.

End-of-Part Elements

- **Updated! Supplementary Cases:** At the end of each part, a new case is provided for professors who want students to delve further into part topics.

Comprehensive Supplements

For the Student

- **Online Learning Center (OLC)** at *www.mhhe.com/ bateman7e:* More and more students are studying online. As they do, they can refer to the OLC for such benefits as: Self-grading Quizzes (including mid-term and final exam practice), internet exer-

cises, and learning objectives. Management: Leading &Collaborating in a Competitive World also offers a Career Planning Exercise, and flash-based self-assessments and learning exercises called "Build Your Management Skills." Students are able to complete these exercises on their own and receive instant, comprehensive feedback to their responses. There are nearly 50 exercises to choose from, and a matrix for use is provided online and in the Instructor's Manual. The exercises include:

- Management's Historical Figures
- Ethics
- SWOT Analysis
- Characteristics of Managerial Control
- What is Your Primary Conflict-Handling Style?
- Assessing Your Emotional Intelligence
- Comparing Affirmative Action, Valuing Diversity, and Managing Diversity and many more!

For the Instructor

- **Instructor's Manual:** prepared by Carol Moore, California State University–Hayward, contains above and beyond the material you need to prepare an effective classroom experience. Utilizing her own students for feedback in preparing, Professor Moore has created a "road map" for each chapter, highlighting within the Lecture Outline not only where available supplements can be brought into the discussion, but also offering Teaching Tips and other useful facts that can be used to capture students' interest. In detail, the manual includes such features as:

-Key Student Questions - taken directly from her own classroom experience
-Class Prework Assignments
-Guidance for using the "Unfolding" cases - How to make these chapter-opening features important for students – additional comments on setting up the introductory case study, examples of how the concepts are important in the real world
Chapter Outline with Teaching Tips: a completely integrated overview of how to teach a class. It includes:
 -Chapter Content in Outline Form (Lecture Notes)
 -Exercises and Cases from text placed where they naturally fall in outline
 -Examples where appropriate (at least one for each major learning objective)
 -Common student questions, with answers

-Teaching Tips (how to handle large lecture sections, etc.)

-Extra Exercises as available from previous editions

-Concluding Case Notes

-Supplementary Case Notes

-Video Notes – for each chapter video

- **Test Bank:** prepared by Amy Sevier, University of Southern Mississippi, contains a variety of true/false, multiple choice, and essay questions. Also includes "Scenario-based" questions, which are application-based, and use a situation described in a narrative, with 3–5 multiple-choice test questions based on the situation described in the narrative.

- **PowerPoint Presentation slides:** prepared by Kris Blanchard, North Central University, the Power-Point presentation slides collection contains everything from an easy-to-follow outline, to additional slides with embedded video clips and weblinks, to figure downloads from the text. This versatility allows you to create a custom presentation suitable for your own classroom experience.

- All of the above can be found on the Instructor's CD-ROM.

- **NEW! The Group & Video Resource Manual: An Instructor's Guide to an Active Classroom.** Authored by Amanda Johnson and Angelo Kinicki of Arizona State University, the Group & Video Resource Manual was created to help instructors create a livelier and stimulating classroom environment. The manual contains interactive in-class group and individual exercises to accompany **Build Your Management Skills** assessments on the OLC, additional group exercises for each chapter, comprehensive notes and discussion questions to accompany the **Manager's Hot Seat DVD,** and information on how to use the **Team Learning Assistant** (see below for a further description of these products).

This valuable guide includes information and material to help instructors successfully execute additional group exercises and the Manager's Hot Seat DVD into their classrooms. For each exercises, the manual includes learning objectives, unique PowerPoint slides to accompany the exercises, and comprehensive discussion questions to facilitate enhanced learning. The manual also includes lecturettes and associated PowerPoint slides to supplement and expand material presented for each exercise.

- **The Manager's Hot Seat DVD:** The Manager's Hot Seat is an interactive DVD that allows students to watch 15 real managers apply their years of experience in confronting issues. Students assume the role of the manager as they watch the video and answer multiple-choice questions that pop up during the segment, forcing them to make decisions on the spot. Students learn from the manager's mistakes and successes, and then do a report critiquing the manager's approach by defending their reasoning. The Hot Seat DVD is an optional package with this text.

- **Team Learning Assistant (TLA):** TLA is a Web-based system to facilitate team learning no matter what course you teach. It was developed at Boston University's Center for Team Learning with a grant from The General Electric Fund. If you are interested in incorporating a team-centered environment in your classroom or online course, this system facilitates effective team learning. Students in teams learn more when they are held accountable for their behavior and for meeting team learning goals. This system of Web-based toolboxes for students, faculty, and program administrators enables a secure and reliable process of monitoring and maintaining team outcome data. Your Mc-Graw-Hill/Irwin sales representative can help you if you're interested in using the product with your Management course.

- **Videos** are available for each chapter. Corresponding video cases and a guide that ties the videos closely to the chapter can be found in the Instructor's Manual and Online.

Acknowledgments

This book could not have been written and published without the valuable contributions of many individuals.

First, Sheldon Czapnik. Sheldon has been extraordinarily helpful in so many ways. Sheldon has a wide array of KSAs (knowledge, skills, and abilities) that have contributed mightily to creating such a strong product. Many thanks!

Our reviewers over the last six editions contributed time, expertise, and terrific ideas that significantly enhanced the quality of the text. The reviewers of the seventh edition are:

Mark Brown
Bradley University

Nancy Bryant
Metropolitan State University

J. Charlene Davis
Trinity University

Jack Dustman
Northern Arizona University

Northern Arizona University

Vincent Enslein
Clinton Community College

Jonathon R. B. Halbesleben
University of Oklahoma

Dorothy Hetmer-Hinds
Trinity Valley Community College

Thomas Jay
Flathead Valley Community College

Scott A. Johnson
Southeast Missouri State University

Subodh P. Kulkarni
Howard University

Linda Keup
Concordia College

Dick Larkin
Central Washington University

Larry Maher
State University of New York—Oswego

Ken Murdock
University of Texas—Arlington

Tim O'Leary
University of Notre Dame

Monica Quattlebaum
Phillips Community College

Gary Roberts
Kennesaw State University

Marian Schultz
University of West Florida

Amy Sevier
University of Southern Mississippi

Linda Shonesy
Athens State University

James Swenson
Minnesota State University—Moorhead

Patricia Tadlock
Horry Georgetown Tech College

Barry L. Van Hook
Arizona State University

George Wagman
Texas A&M—Kingsville

John Wong
Neumann College

We also would like to thank those who reviewed for
us in previous editions:

Rathin Basu
Ferrum College

Anthony S. Marshall
Columbia College

James C. McElroy
Iowa State University

John W. Rogers
American International College

Christina Stamper
Western Michigan University

Ray Aldag
University of Wisconsin—Madison

Shawn Carraher
Indiana University—NW Campus

Al Crispo
Purdue University

Marya Leatherwood
University of Illinois—Springfield

MarySue Love
Maryville University

Granger Macy
Texas A&M—Corpus Christi

Michael Vijuk
William Rainey Harper College

Ben Weeks
St. Xavier University

Debra A. Arvanites
Villanova University

Robert J. Ash
Rancho Santiago College

Charles A. Beasley
State University of New York—Buffalo

Hrach Bedrosian
New York University

Charles Blalack
Kilgore College

Mary A. Bouchard
Bristol Community College

Eugene L. Britt
Grossmont College

Barbara Boyington
Brookdale Community College

Lyvonne Burleson
Rollins College—Brevard

Diane Caggiano
Fitchburg State College

Elizabeth A. Cooper
University of Rhode Island

Anne C. Cowden
California State University—Sacramento

Ron Dibattista
Bryant College

Dale Dickson
Mesa State College

Michael W. Drafke
College of DuPage

J. F. Fairbank
Pennsylvania State University

Janice Felbauer
Austin Community College

David Foote
Middle Tennessee State University

Alan J. Fredian
Loyola University—Chicago

Steve Garlick
DeVry Institute—Kansas City

John Hall
University of Florida

Donald E. Harris
Oakton Community College

Carolyn Hatton
Cincinnati State Tech Community College

Frederic J. Hebert
East Carolina University

Durward Hofler
Northeastern Illinois University

Thomas O. James
Benedictine College

William Jedlicka
William Rainey Harper College

Elias Kalman
Baruch College

Gus. L. Kotoulas
Morton College

Augustine Lado
Cleveland State University

Catherine C. McElroy
Bucks County Community College

Jim McElroy
Iowa State University

David L. McLain
Virginia State University

Dot Moore
The Citadel

Joseph B. Mosca
Monmouth College

Randy Nichols

Oakland City University

Bert Nyman
Rockford College

James J. Ravelle
Moravian College

Joseph C. Santora
Essex County College

Marc Siegall
California State University—Chico

Fred Slack
Indiana University of Pennsylvania

Carl Sonntag
Pikes Peak Community College

Christina Stamper
University of North Carolina—Wilmington

Jim Wachspress
New Jersey Institute of Technology

Many individuals contributed directly to our development as textbook authors. Dennis Organ provided one of the authors with an initial opportunity and guidance in textbook writing. John Weimeister has been a friend and adviser from the very beginning. The entire McGraw-Hill/Irwin team demonstrated continued and generous support for this book. John Biernat was a great champion for the project and is a talented publisher and a good friend. Kurt Strand is, too. Christine Scheid is the consummate developmental editor, doing all with great skill and professionalism. And Meg Beamer/Lisa Nicks, Marketing Managers, you *rock*. What a team!

Finally, we thank our families. Our parents, Jeanine and Tom Bateman and Clara and John Snell, provided us with the foundation on which we have built our careers. They continue to be a source of great support. Our wives, Mary Jo and Marybeth, demonstrated great encouragement, insight, and understanding throughout the process. Our children, Lauren (who also helped with clerical work), T. J., and James Bateman and Sara, Jack, and Emily Snell, inspire us in every way.

Thomas S. Bateman
Charlottesville, VA

Scott A. Snell
Ithaca, NY

LEARNING FEATURE HIGHLIGHTS

An important theme of this text is how to manage in ways that deliver *results*—how to deliver what customers want; how to be a "thinker and doer"; how to know when, and if, to act. Bateman and Snell have put together a rich selection of learning features that highlight companies' ups and downs, stimulate learning and understanding, and challenge students to respond.

Prologue

TELECOM MANAGERS FIGHT FOR MARKET SHARE

As recently as the early 1980s, Americans who wanted to talk over the phone dealt essentially with one company—AT&T—which owned both long-distance and local telephone companies. Managers at that company operated for years in a heavily regulated, low-competition, predictable business climate. Rates were set less by the market than by government-approved formulas. But court cases and efforts by the Federal Communications Commission (FCC) to deregulate the industry required AT&T in 1984 to divest, or sell off, its local telephone business. That change opened the market to aggressive new entrants. Other rulings since that time have accelerated the trend toward deregulation.

Today, a manager at a newer telecom company like Sprint, Nextel, or Verizon, or at any of the Baby Bells (the regional telephone companies AT&T divested), is

operating in an environment light-years removed from the calm telecom climate of the early 1980s. Now several players—and several technologies—are competing aggressively for business. Which will win and which will lose is far from clear. Every company offers local and long-distance telephone service, with some (like BellSouth) offering land lines, others (like Cingular) offering wireless, and others (like Verizon) offering both. And executives at Internet and cable companies (like Time Warner Cable) are elbowing into the business as well. Voice-over Internet Protocol (VoIP) is a technology that allows users to make phone calls over a high-speed Internet connection, like a cable or DSL line. Cable executives have already made this technology available in several areas of the country—in some cases free to their cable subscribers.

All of this activity is good news for consumers. They have many options for their personal and business communication needs, with prices and features that worldwide competition keeps affordable. New options and services are constantly emerging. But for telecom managers, their business environment is filled with risk, as a number of aggressive companies, and a number of different technologies, compete intensely for market share.

So far, telecom managers have decided to compete in all types of services. They want to provide voice *and* data transmission, consumer *and* business applications, wireless *and* Internet service, and even video. And all are keeping prices low to maintain market share. Yet it's far from clear that every telecom has the size and financial depth to continue this strategy for long. Many industry observers believe that, as the industry shakes out, *mergers* (companies combining) and industry consolidation are inevitable.

Should telecom managers continue to compete across-the-board, taking the risk that they will be spread too thin? Should they merge with other telecom companies to strengthen their position? Or should they go for a lower market share but reduce their risk by focusing on high-growth and high-profit services? Telecom managers in an era of deregulation will have to find the right business model for the new environment of intense competition, uncertainty, and technological change.

Sources for Prologue and Connections: Jonathan Byrnes, "Airline Deregulation: Lessons for Telecom," *HBS Working Knowledge*, June 7, 2004; Jeff Kagan, "Telecom's Future," *Intele-Card News*, September 1, 2002; Jim Jubak, "Only Some Will Survive the Telecom Shakeout," *thestreet.com*, May 1, 2002.

NEW! "UNFOLDING" CASE

The chapter begins with a *Prologue* which describes an actual organizational situation, leader, or company. The case is then referred back to within the chapter in *Connections* boxes, showing the student how the chapter material relates back to the company, situation, or leader highlighted in the Prologue. At the end of the chapter, the *Epilogue* ties up loose ends and brings the material full circle for the student.

Connection: TELECOM MANAGERS FIGHT FOR MARKET SHARE

Our Prologue mentioned the ongoing competition in the telecommunications industry. Different parts of the industry—cable, the Baby Bells, and cell-phone companies—are all competing to provide telephone service to their customers. Each is concerned about the threat of substitution. For example, the availability of cell phones has dramatically reduced consumer dependence on the traditionally wired home phone. Phone service provided by cable and Internet companies may do the same. Similarly, in many areas of the country satellite broadcasters like DirecTV provide customers with an alternative to cable. The effort by cable companies to enhance their appeal by offering telephone service in addition to TV programming is one response to this threat.

EPILOGUE

TELECOM MANAGERS FIGHT FOR MARKET SHARE

At the opening of this chapter, and throughout, we reviewed some of the environmental challenges faced by telecom managers. We will now close our discussion by mentioning that at the end of 2004 Sprint and Nextel announced that they would merge, turning the newly named Sprint Nextel into the country's third-largest wireless company.

Why did the management of these two companies decide to merge? The main answer lies in the difficult competitive environment they faced. Earlier that year, Cingular had acquired AT&T Wireless, making it the number 1 wireless operator, with 47 million subscribers. Verizon, with 42 million, was number 2. Compared to these two giants, Sprint and Nextel top managers feared that on their own they would be too small to compete. In addition, Nextel's main focus was on the business market. Its top managers felt that would leave the company vulnerable, as bigger companies offering a fuller range of services achieved higher revenues and economies of scale. By combining Sprint's consumer market and Nextel's business market, the merger strengthened both companies.

The merger was also driven by the technological environment the companies faced. Left on its own, Nextel would have had to upgrade its entire network to meet the demand for higher speed and other services. Now it can upgrade both more quickly and less expensively, by building on Sprint's more advanced technol-

ogy. In turn, Nextel offered Sprint access to newer and faster parts of the broadcast spectrum to which it had negotiated access from government regulators. Sprint also announced that it had entered into a deal with Time Warner Cable, allowing that company to offer Sprint's cell phone service on a trial basis.

The merger represented one response to the complex regulatory, competitive, and technological environment faced by telecom managers. But many uncertainties and challenges remain. Cable companies have already wired almost all American households and are in a very strong position to provide communication and entertainment options for the home. The Baby Bells have landlines installed and also own wireless companies; they have also begun to build high-speed fiber lines to compete with cable. And technological improvements may eventually allow wireless companies like Sprint Nextel to hold their own against their cable and Baby Bell competitors. Watching over it all are federal regulators, with the job of protecting consumers and maintaining a level playing field while at the same time encouraging competition and innovation. Telecom managers will need considerable skill to navigate the challenging external environment they confront.

SOURCES: Steve Rosenbush, "Nextel and Sprint: The Big Little Guy," *BusinessWeek online*, December 15, 2004; Roger O. Crockett and Catherine Yang, "Why Sprint and Nextel Got Hitched," *BusinessWeek online*, December 27, 2004

NEW! ADVANTAGES OF COLLABORATION BOX

Managers must deliver results. An essential skill toward doing so is the ability to work effectively with others toward a goal. These boxes speak directly to the student, and highlight the advantages of collaboration, not only with colleagues but other companies as well.

The first question to consider is: Who is the competition? Sometimes answers are obvious. Coca-Cola and PepsiCo are competitors, as are the Big Three automakers: General Motors, Ford, and DaimlerChrysler. But sometimes organizations focus too exclusively on traditional rivalries and miss the emerging ones. Historically, Sears & Roebuck focused on its competition with J.C. Penney. However, Sears' real competitors are Wal-Mart at the low end; Target in the middle; Nordstrom at the high end; and a variety of catalogers, such as L.L. Bean and Eddie Bauer. In fact, Kmart recently purchased Sears precisely to be able to compete in these other markets, which it could not do on its own. Similarly, United Airlines, Delta, American, and U.S.Airways have focused their attention on a battle over long haul and international routes. In the process, they all but ignored smaller carriers such as Southwest, Alaska Air, and Jet Blue that have grown and succeeded in regional markets.[6]

Thus, as a first step in understanding their competitive environment, organizations must identify their competitors. Competitors may include (1) small domestic firms, especially their entry into tiny, premium markets; (2) strong regional competitors; (3) big new domestic companies exploring new markets; (4) overseas firms, especially those that either try to solidify their position in small niches (a traditional Japanese tactic) or are able to draw on an inexpensive labor force on a large scale (as in China); and (5) newer entries, such as firms offering their products on the Web. The growth in competition from other countries has been especially significant in recent years, with the worldwide reduction in international trade barriers. For example, the North American Free Trade Agreement (NAFTA) sharply reduced tariffs on trade between the United States, Canada, and Mexico. Managers today confront a particular challenge from low-cost producers abroad (see Chapter 6).

Once competitors have been identified, the next step is to analyze how they compete. Competitors use tactics such as price reductions, new-product introductions, and advertising campaigns to gain advantage over their rivals. It's essential to understand what competitors are doing when you are honing your own strategy. Competition is most intense when there are many direct competitors (including foreign contenders), when industry growth is slow, and when the product or service cannot be differentiated in some way.

New, high-growth industries offer enormous opportunities for profits. When an industry matures and growth slows, profits drop. Then, intense competition causes an industry shakeout: Weaker companies are eliminated, and the strong companies survive.[7] We will be discussing the issue of competitors and strategy in further detail in Chapter 4.

Companies often compete through innovation, quality, and cost. We will be discussing the issue of competitors and strategy in further detail in Chapter 4.

Advantages of Collaboration:

It might surprise you to find that even strong competitors will sometimes collaborate. For example, it is common for companies to join in financing promotional campaigns for their industry ("Got milk?"), to agree on common product standards (in DVDs), or to engage in joint ventures. In 2004, for instance, General Motors and DaimlerChrysler, two very large and normally highly competitive automakers, announced that they would jointly produce new hybrid technology for their cars. They felt they had to collaborate to overcome the Japanese lead in hybrid vehicles. As a manager, similar concerns about some larger threat may one day cause you, too, to collaborate with competitors in some areas, even as you continue to compete in others.

Threat of New Entrants

New entrants into an industry compete with established companies. If many factors prevent new companies from entering the industry, the threat to established firms is less serious. If there are few such **barriers to entry,** the threat of new entrants is more serious. Some major barriers to entry are government policy, capital requirements, brand identification, cost disadvantages, and distribution channels. The government can limit or prevent entry, as occurs when the FDA forbids a new drug

barriers to entry
Conditions that prevent new companies from entering an industry.

NEW! RANDOM POP-UPS

Throughout the chapter, these marginal boxes highlight interesting factoids, statistics, and quotes relating to the chapter content.

Step 4: Goal and Plan Selection   Once managers have assessed the various goals and plans, they will select the one that's most appropriate and feasible. The evaluation process will identify the priorities and trade-offs among the goals and plans. For example, if your plan is to launch a number of new publications, and you're trying to choose among them, you might weigh the different up-front investment each requires, the size of each market, which one fits best with your existing product line or company image, and so on. Experienced judgment always plays an important role in this process. However, as you will discover later in the chapter, relying on judgment alone may not be the best way to proceed.

"Most discussions of decision making assume that only senior executives make decisions or that only senior executives' decisions matter. This is a dangerous mistake."
Peter Drucker

UPDATED! BOTTOM-LINE PRACTICES ICON

While the icons with their four running themes of Innovation, Cost, Speed, and Quality have been a hallmark of the text, this edition includes added text with the icon, furthering student understanding and reinforcing these important results-oriented themes.

Connections: DELTA AIR LINES

One of the key requirements in CEO Grinstein's strategic plan was the need to lower Delta's labor costs. In October 2004, Delta and its pilots union announced that they had reached agreement to cut flight-crew wages by a third. This change would save Delta $1 billion a year. The pilots also agreed to work-rule changes that would save still more. In return, the pilots were given the option to buy a 15 percent stake in the company. Grinstein had been helped in his efforts to reach a deal by being candid with the union about Delta's financial condition and about the very real threat of bankruptcy. In a series of "town hall" meetings with pilots and other employees, he discussed the details of the company's new plan, its goals, and why change was necessary. He also postponed high top-executive bonuses, including his own, until Delta became profitable. This sent a signal to the organization that sacrifices would be shared.

Finally, successful implementation requires that the plan be linked to other systems in the organization, particularly the budget and reward systems. If the budget does not provide the manager with sufficient financial resources to execute the plan, the plan is probably doomed. Similarly, goal achievement must be linked to the organization's reward system. Many organizations use incentive programs to encourage employees to achieve goals and to implement plans properly. Commissions, salaries, promotions, bonuses, and other rewards are based on successful performance.

Step 6: Monitor and Control   Although it is sometimes ignored, this step in the formal planning process is essential. Without it, you would have no way of knowing whether your plan is succeeding. As we mentioned earlier, planning works in a cycle;

Tying plans to a firm's financials is a key element of success.

NEW! CONCLUDING CASES

Each chapter ends with a case based on disguised but real companies and people that reinforces key chapter elements and themes.

CONCLUDING CASE
The Wallingford Bowling Center

A group of twelve lifelong friends put together $1,200,000 of their own funds and built a $6,000,000, 48-lane bowling alley, near Norfolk, Virginia. Two of the investors became employees of the corporation. Ned Flanders works full-time as General Manager and James Ahmad, a licensed CPA, serves as Controller on a part-time basis.

The beautiful, modern-day facility features a multilevel spacious interior with three rows of 16 lanes on two separate levels of the building, a full-service bar, a small restaurant, a game room (pool, video games, pinball), and two locker rooms. The facility sits on a spacious lot with plenty of parking and room to grow.

The bowling center is located in the small blue-collar town of Wallingford. There is no direct competition within the town. The surrounding communities include a wide-ranging mix of ethnic groups, professionals, middle- to upper-middle-class private homes, and apartment and condominium complexes ranging from singles to young married couples to senior citizen retirement units. Nearly 200,000 people live within 15 miles of Wallingford.

The bowling center is open 24 hours per day and has a staff of 27 part- and full-time employees. After four years of operation, the partners find themselves frustrated with the low profit performance of the business. While sales are covering expenses, the partners are not happy with the end-of-year profit sharing pool. The most recent income statement follows:

Sales	$ 1,844,000
CGS	315,000
GM	$ 1,529,000
Operating expenses	$ 1,466,000
Mortgage	$ 460,000
Depreciation	95,000
Utilities	188,000
Maintenance	70,000
Payroll	490,000
Supplies	27,000
Insurance	136,000
Taxable income	$ 63,000
Taxes	19,000
Net income	$ 44,000

The bowling center operates at 100 percent capacity on Sunday through Thursday nights from 6:00 P.M. until midnight. Two sets of men's leagues come and go on each of those nights, occupying each lane with mostly five-person teams. Bowlers from each league consistently spend money at both the bar and restaurant. In fact, the men's leagues combine to generate about 60 percent of total current sales.

The bowling center operates at about 50 percent capacity on Friday and Saturday nights and on Saturday morning. The Friday and Saturday "open bowling" nights include mostly teenagers, young couples, and league members who come to practice in groups of two or three. The Saturday morning group is a kid's league, ages 10 through 14.

There are four ladies leagues that bowl on Monday and Wednesday afternoons.

Business is extremely slow at the bowling center on Monday through Friday and Sunday mornings, and on the afternoons of Tuesday, Thursday, Friday, Saturday, and Sunday. It is not uncommon to have just three or four lanes in operation during those time periods.

The owners have taken a close look at the cost side of their business as a way to improve profitability. They concluded that while the total operating expense of $1,466,000 might appear to be high, there was in fact little room for expense cutting.

At a recent meeting of the partners, James Ahmad reported on the results of his three-month-long investigation into the operating cost side of other bowling alleys and discovered that the Wallingford Bowling Center was very much in keeping with their industry. James went on to report that bowling alleys were considered to be "heavy fixed cost operations" and that the key to success and profitability lies in maximizing capacity and sales dollars.

QUESTIONS

1. Apply the decision-making process described in the chapter to this case. What is the major problem facing Wallingford? List five specific alternative solutions that could be implemented to solve that major problem.

2. As general manager of this company, how could you utilize and manage the group decision-making process and technique to improve company profits? Which employees would you include in the group?

early in your career: Positive, proactive, motivated people can easily change majors and jobs; plenty of people in each of those venues will offer referrals, recommendations, and guidance.

Take a few minutes to review the chapter and its main topics one more time while thinking about yourself. Think about your personality, what you like and dislike, what you fear, and what you dream, and then address the following.

QUESTIONS

1. Generate a list of products, services, industries, and cultures that you are interested in. Generate a second list of your personal favorite activities and interests. From those two lists, name and describe three or four specific jobs that match up nicely.

2. Draw a time-line across a page and highlight the next 1–3, 5–10, and 15–30 years. Move across that line and draft/jot down a series of internships, part-time jobs, and full-time jobs that you would like to have. Be sure to incorporate travel, community service, and anything else that you want to do with your life.

Congratulations! You have just created a plan of action for yourself that ties in with the world of opportunities for a career in business management.

Creating a plan is easy (talking the talk). Making it happen can be easy too, but you must take action (walking the walk). And don't forget, you can change your mind and your plan; just stay on that positive track. Good luck!

EXPERIENTIAL EXERCISES
1.1 Personal Assessment of Management Skills (PAMS)

To get an overall profile of your level of skill competence, respond to the following statements using the rating scale below. Please rate your behavior as it is, not as you would like it to be. If you have not engaged in a specific activity, answer according to how you think you would behave based on your experience in similar activities. Be realistic; this instrument is designed to help you tailor your learning to your specific needs.

RATING SCALE

1 Strongly disagree
2 Disagree
3 Slightly disagree
4 Slightly agree
5 Agree
6 Strongly agree

In regard to my level of self-knowledge:

_____ 1. I seek information about my strengths and weaknesses from others as a basis for self-improvement.

_____ 2. In order to improve, I am willing to be self-disclosing to others (that is, to share my beliefs and feelings).

_____ 3. I am aware of my preferred style in gathering information and making decisions.

_____ 4. I understand how I cope with situations that are ambiguous and uncertain.

_____ 5. I have a well-developed set of personal standards and principles that guide my behavior.

When faced with stressful or time-pressured situations:

_____ 6. I use effective time-management methods such as keeping track of my time, making to-do lists, and prioritizing tasks.

_____ 7. I reaffirm my priorities so that less important things don't drive out more important things.

_____ 8. I maintain a program of regular exercise for fitness.

_____ 9. I maintain an open, trusting relationship with someone with whom I can share my frustrations.

_____ 10. I know and practice several temporary relaxation techniques such as deep breathing and muscle relaxation.

_____ 11. I maintain balance in my life by pursuing a variety of interests outside of work.

When I approach a typical, routine problem:

_____ 12. I state clearly and explicitly what the problem is. I avoid trying to solve it until I have defined it.

_____ 13. I generate more than one alternative solution to the problem, instead of identifying only one obvious solution.

_____ 14. I keep steps in the problem-solving process distinct; that is, I define the problem before proposing alternative solutions, and I generate alternatives before selecting a single solution.

When faced with a complex or difficult problem that does not have an easy solution:

_____ 15. I define a problem in multiple ways. I don't limit myself to just one problem definition.

_____ 16. I unfreeze my thinking by asking lots of questions about the nature of the problem before considering ways to solve it.

_____ 17. I think about the problem from both the left (logical) side of my brain and the right (intuitive) side of my brain.

_____ 18. I avoid selecting a solution until I have developed many possible alternatives.

_____ 19. I have specific techniques that I use to help develop creative and innovative solutions to problems.

When trying to foster more creativity and innovation among those with whom I work:

_____ 20. I make sure there are divergent points of view represented or expressed in every complex problem-solving situation.

NEW AND UPDATED! EXPERIENTIAL EXERCISES

Many new exercises have been added to tried and true previous edition favorites. Some exercises allow for personality assessment, some are for use as group activities in the classroom, and some involve outside research.

---

8. Interracial adoption
9. Premarital and extramarital sex
10. Prayer in schools
11. Diversity in the workplace
12. Pornography on the Internet

QUESTIONS

1. Did you arrive at a mutually agreeable solution? What helped you get there?

2. What were some factors that hindered this process?

3. How comfortable did you feel "arguing" the position you were given? How did this influence your ability to actively listen?

4. If the position you were given was exactly opposite your values or beliefs, did you see this topic differently now than before the exercise?

5. What steps can you take to improve your ability to listen actively to friends or associates, especially when you don't agree with their viewpoint?

PART 4 INTEGRATING CASE
Leadership at AIG: Does Style Matter?

"The King Is Dead, Long Live the King." These indeed may be the very words echoed by employees at American International Group, the world's largest insurance company, now that its legendary CEO Maurice "Hank" Greenberg, age 79, has been deposed by AIG's board of directors after Elliot Spitzer, New York State's attorney general, leveled charges against the company for possibly manipulating its earnings.

Headquartered in New York, AIG has been in business for nearly 90 years, has some $170 billion in market capitalization, and has approximately 80,000 employees worldwide. Greenberg, an attorney and a much heralded figure in the insurance business, has worked at AIG for more than four decades. In 1967, he became president, replacing company founder Cornelius Vander Starr. Greenberg transformed the company from a midlevel insurance company into a major international player. With a reputation as an autocratic leader, Greenberg was known to scream at employees. One source likened Greenberg's "tenure to a reign of terror." Another source offered insights to Greenberg's leadership and managerial style: He "calls employees with detailed questions about contracts and other minutiae." For example, at one meeting in the late 1990s, he told a high-ranking manager: "This is one of the worst presentations I've seen in years . . . Go back, get your stuff and don't come back until you can tell me something I don't already know."

Greenberg also had trouble with his sons, Jeffrey and Evan, when they worked for him at AIG. Jeffrey, the older of the two, worked there for 17 years before quitting in 1995; Evan, who had been designated as his father's successor at AIG, resigned a few years later, in 2000. In some circles people believed their father "pushed" his sons too much by expecting more from them than from other company executives. His sons—Evan, in particular—were concerned about their father's so-called succession plan. Apparently, the senior Greenberg had given only lip service to the idea of succession with no intention of retiring any time soon.

In early March 2005, AIG's board of directors replaced Greenberg with 50-year-old vice chairman and co-chief operating officer (COO) Martin Sullivan, who had worked at the company and for Greenberg in various capacities for more than 30 years. His years in the company make him the consummate insider to lead

the company. However, like Greenberg, he is considered a micromanager, known to get involved in some of the nitty-gritty detail-making instead of enabling subordinates to play their role. If he continues micromanaging instead of delegating, he may create some serious problems for himself and the company. Yet, despite any managerial similarities to his former boss, staff view him as more pleasant and more amicable. One source stated that his "greatest strength is the respect he gets from people who work for him . . . He doesn't scream and shout like Mr. Greenberg." Sullivan's leadership style may be exactly the breath of fresh air the troubled company needs.

This case was prepared by Joseph C. Santora, who is a professor of business administration at Essex County College, Newark, New Jersey.

QUESTIONS

1. AIG chairman and CEO Maurice "Hank" Greenberg was considered an autocratic leader and a micromanager by many employees, yet the company grew dramatically during his reign as CEO. Does leadership style matter as long as the company performs well and shareholders are satisfied with their return on investment?

2. AIG's new CEO Sullivan has been labeled a micromanager, but with a more pleasant personality. Can he, as a micromanager, develop a more participative leadership style? How?

3. Greenberg named his son Evan as the heir apparent. Yet Greenberg never set a departure date. Should a good leader set a date for departure once a successor is named? Why? Why not?

Sources: D. Brady, "AIG Needs New Policies," BusinessWeek online, March 1, 2005; E. Kelleher and A. Felsted, "New AIG Chief Has a Softer Touch," Financial Times, March 21, 2005, p. 18; I. McDonald, "Insurance Industry's First Family Fades," The Wall Street Journal March 15, 2005, p. C13; N. Scheiber, "Sins of the Son," New York Magazine, 2004; J. Weil, M. Langley, and N. Deogun, "AIG's Greenberg Plans to Depart as Woes Mount," The Wall Street Journal, March 14, 2005, pp. 1, 14.

UPDATED! SUPPLEMENTARY CASES

At the end of each part, a new case is provided for professors who want students to delve further into part topics.

"FROM THE PAGES OF *BUSINESS WEEK*"

Current *Business Week* articles spotlight key issues in the text.

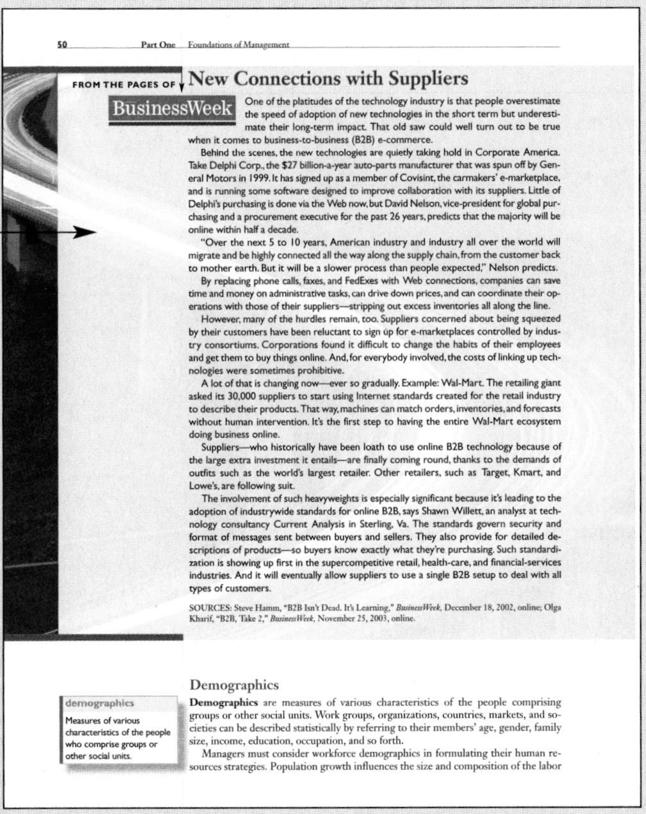

FROM THE PAGES OF BusinessWeek

New Connections with Suppliers

One of the platitudes of the technology industry is that people overestimate the speed of adoption of new technologies in the short term but underestimate their long-term impact. That old saw could well turn out to be true when it comes to business-to-business (B2B) e-commerce.

Behind the scenes, the new technologies are quietly taking hold in Corporate America. Take Delphi Corp., the $27 billion-a-year auto-parts manufacturer that was spun off by General Motors in 1999. It has signed up as a member of Covisint, the carmakers' e-marketplace, and is running some software designed to improve collaboration with its suppliers. Little of Delphi's purchasing is done via the Web now, but David Nelson, vice-president for global purchasing and a procurement executive for the past 26 years, predicts that the majority will be online within half a decade.

"Over the next 5 to 10 years, American industry and industry all over the world will migrate and be highly connected all the way along the supply chain, from the customer back to mother earth. But it will be a slower process than people expected," Nelson predicts.

By replacing phone calls, faxes, and FedExes with Web connections, companies can save time and money on administrative tasks, can drive down prices, and can coordinate their operations with those of their suppliers—stripping out excess inventories all along the line.

However, many of the hurdles remain, too. Suppliers concerned about being squeezed by their customers have been reluctant to sign up for e-marketplaces controlled by industry consortiums. Corporations found it difficult to change the habits of their employees and get them to buy things online. And, for everybody involved, the costs of linking up technologies were sometimes prohibitive.

A lot of that is changing now—ever so gradually. Example: Wal-Mart. The retailing giant asked its 30,000 suppliers to start using Internet standards created for the retail industry to describe their products. That way, machines can match orders, inventories, and forecasts without human intervention. It's the first step to having the entire Wal-Mart ecosystem doing business online.

Suppliers—who historically have been loath to use online B2B technology because of the large extra investment it entails—are finally coming round, thanks to the demands of outfits such as the world's largest retailer. Other retailers, such as Target, Kmart, and Lowe's, are following suit.

The involvement of such heavyweights is especially significant because it's leading to the adoption of industrywide standards for online B2B, says Shawn Willett, an analyst at technology consultancy Current Analysis in Sterling, Va. The standards govern security and format of messages sent between buyers and sellers. They also provide for detailed descriptions of products—so buyers know exactly what they're purchasing. Such standardization is showing up first in the supercompetitive retail, health-care, and financial-services industries. And it will eventually allow suppliers to use a single B2B setup to deal with all types of customers.

SOURCES: Steve Hamm, "B2B Isn't Dead. It's Learning," *BusinessWeek*, December 18, 2002, online; Olga Kharif, "B2B, Take 2," *BusinessWeek*, November 25, 2003, online.

Demographics

demographics
Measures of various characteristics of the people who comprise groups or other social units.

Demographics are measures of various characteristics of the people comprising groups or other social units. Work groups, organizations, countries, markets, and societies can be described statistically by referring to their members' age, gender, family size, income, education, occupation, and so forth.

Managers must consider workforce demographics in formulating their human resources strategies. Population growth influences the size and composition of the labor

SUMMARY OF LEARNING OBJECTIVES AND END-OF-CHAPTER MATERIAL

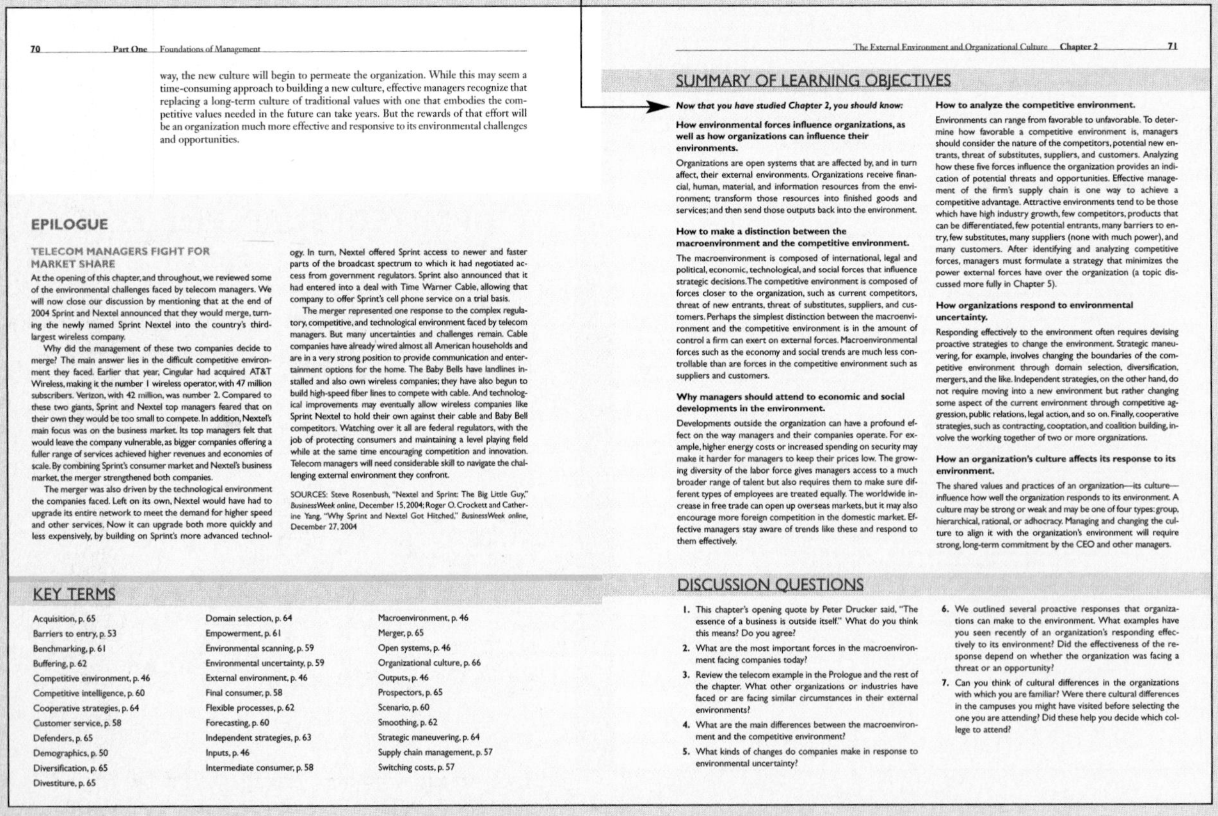

way, the new culture will begin to permeate the organization. While this may seem a time-consuming approach to building a new culture, effective managers recognize that replacing a long-term culture of traditional values with one that embodies the competitive values needed in the future can take years. But the rewards of that effort will be an organization much more effective and responsive to its environmental challenges and opportunities.

EPILOGUE

TELECOM MANAGERS FIGHT FOR MARKET SHARE

At the opening of this chapter, and throughout, we reviewed some of the environmental challenges faced by telecom managers. We will now close our discussion by mentioning that at the end of 2004 Sprint and Nextel announced that they would merge, turning the newly named Sprint Nextel into the country's third-largest wireless company.

Why did the management of these two companies decide to merge? The main answer lies in the difficult competitive environment they faced. Earlier that year, Cingular had acquired AT&T Wireless, making it the number 1 wireless operator, with 47 million subscribers. Verizon, with 42 million, was number 2. Compared to these two giants, Sprint and Nextel top managers feared that on their own they would be too small to compete. In addition, Nextel's main focus was on the business market. Its top managers felt that would leave the company vulnerable, as bigger companies offering a fuller range of services achieved higher revenues and economies of scale. By combining Sprint's consumer market and Nextel's business market, the merger strengthened both companies.

The merger was also driven by the technological environment the companies faced. Left on its own, Nextel would have had to upgrade its entire network to meet the demand for higher speed and other services. Now it can upgrade both more quickly and less expensively, by building on Sprint's more advanced technology. In turn, Nextel offered Sprint access to newer and faster parts of the broadcast spectrum to which it had negotiated access from government regulators. Sprint also announced that it had entered into a deal with Time Warner Cable, allowing that company to offer Sprint's cell phone service on a trial basis.

The merger represented one response to the complex regulatory, competitive, and technological environment faced by telecom managers. But many uncertainties and challenges remain. Cable companies have already wired almost all American households and are in a very strong position to provide communication and entertainment options for the home. The Baby Bells have landlines installed and also own wireless companies; they have also begun to build high-speed fiber lines to compete with cable. And technological improvements may eventually allow wireless companies like Sprint Nextel to hold their own against their cable and Baby Bell competitors. Watching over it all are federal regulators, with the job of protecting consumers and maintaining a level playing field while at the same time encouraging competition and innovation. Telecom managers will need considerable skill to navigate the challenging external environment they confront.

SOURCES: Steve Rosenbush, "Nextel and Sprint: The Big Little Guy," *BusinessWeek online*, December 15, 2004; Roger O. Crockett and Catherine Yang, "Why Sprint and Nextel Got Hitched," *BusinessWeek online*, December 27, 2004

KEY TERMS

Acquisition, p. 65
Barriers to entry, p. 53
Benchmarking, p. 61
Buffering, p. 62
Competitive environment, p. 46
Competitive intelligence, p. 60
Cooperative strategies, p. 64
Customer service, p. 58
Defenders, p. 65
Demographics, p. 50
Diversification, p. 65
Divestiture, p. 65
Domain selection, p. 64
Empowerment, p. 61
Environmental scanning, p. 59
Environmental uncertainty, p. 59
External environment, p. 46
Final consumer, p. 58
Flexible processes, p. 62
Forecasting, p. 60
Independent strategies, p. 63
Inputs, p. 46
Intermediate consumer, p. 58
Macroenvironment, p. 46
Merger, p. 65
Open systems, p. 46
Organizational culture, p. 66
Outputs, p. 46
Prospectors, p. 65
Scenario, p. 60
Smoothing, p. 62
Strategic maneuvering, p. 64
Supply chain management, p. 57
Switching costs, p. 57

SUMMARY OF LEARNING OBJECTIVES

Now that you have studied Chapter 2, you should know:

How environmental forces influence organizations, as well as how organizations can influence their environments.

Organizations are open systems that are affected by, and in turn affect, their external environments. Organizations receive financial, human, material, and information resources from the environment; transform those resources into finished goods and services; and then send those outputs back into the environment.

How to make a distinction between the macroenvironment and the competitive environment.

The macroenvironment is composed of international, legal and political, economic, technological, and social forces that influence strategic decisions. The competitive environment is composed of forces closer to the organization, such as current competitors, threat of new entrants, threat of substitutes, suppliers, and customers. Perhaps the simplest distinction between the macroenvironment and the competitive environment is in the amount of control a firm can exert on external forces. Macroenvironmental forces such as the economy and social trends are much less controllable than are forces in the competitive environment such as suppliers and customers.

Why managers should attend to economic and social developments in the environment.

Developments outside the organization can have a profound effect on the way managers and their companies operate. For example, higher energy costs or increased spending on security may make it harder for managers to keep their prices low. The growing diversity of the labor force gives managers access to a much broader range of talent but also requires them to make sure different types of employees are treated equally. The worldwide increase in free trade can open up overseas markets, but it may also encourage more foreign competition in the domestic market. Effective managers stay aware of trends like these and respond to them effectively.

How to analyze the competitive environment.

Environments can range from favorable to unfavorable. To determine how favorable a competitive environment is, managers should consider the nature of the competitors, potential new entrants, threat of substitutes, suppliers, and customers. Analyzing how these five forces influence the organization provides an indication of potential threats and opportunities. Effective management of the firm's supply chain is one way to achieve a competitive advantage. Attractive environments tend to be those which have high industry growth, few competitors, products that can be differentiated, few potential entrants, many barriers to entry, few substitutes, many suppliers (none with much power), and many customers. After identifying and analyzing competitive forces, managers must formulate a strategy that minimizes the power external forces have over the organization (a topic discussed more fully in Chapter 5).

How organizations respond to environmental uncertainty.

Responding effectively to the environment often requires devising proactive strategies to change the environment. Strategic maneuvering, for example, involves changing the boundaries of the competitive environment through domain selection, diversification, mergers, and the like. Independent strategies, on the other hand, do not require moving into a new environment but rather changing some aspect of the current environment through competitive aggression, public relations, legal action, and so on. Finally, cooperative strategies, such as contracting, cooptation, and coalition building, involve the working together of two or more organizations.

How an organization's culture affects its response to its environment.

The shared values and practices of an organization—its culture—influence how well the organization responds to its environment. A culture may be strong or weak and may be one of four types: group, hierarchical, rational, or adhocracy. Managing and changing the culture to align it with the organization's environment will require strong, long-term commitment by the CEO and other managers.

DISCUSSION QUESTIONS

1. This chapter's opening quote by Peter Drucker said, "The essence of a business is outside itself." What do you think this means? Do you agree?
2. What are the most important forces in the macroenvironment facing companies today?
3. Review the telecom example in the Prologue and the rest of the chapter. What other organizations or industries have faced or are facing similar circumstances in their external environments?
4. What are the main differences between the macroenvironment and the competitive environment?
5. What kinds of changes do companies make in response to environmental uncertainty?
6. We outlined several proactive responses that organizations can make to the environment. What examples have you seen recently of an organization's responding effectively to its environment? Did the effectiveness of the response depend on whether the organization was facing a threat or an opportunity?
7. Can you think of cultural differences in the organizations with which you are familiar? Were there cultural differences in the campuses you might have visited before selecting the one you are attending? Did these help you decide which college to attend?

FLEXIBLE APPENDICES

So that professors have flexibility in structuring their course, we offer seven topical appendices such as "Managing in Our Natural Environment," "Information for Entrepreneurs," and "Operations Management in the New Economy."

APPENDIX A

APPENDIX A

The Evolution of Management

For thousands of years, managers have wrestled with the same issues and problems confronting executives today. Around 1100 B.C., the Chinese practiced the four management functions—planning, organizing, leading, and controlling—discussed in Chapter 1. Between 350 and 400 B.C., the Greeks recognized management as a separate art and advocated a scientific approach to work. The Romans decentralized the management of their vast empire before the birth of Christ. During medieval times, the Venetians standardized production through the use of an assembly line, building warehouses and using an inventory system to monitor the contents.[2]

But throughout history most managers operated strictly on a trial-and-error basis. The challenges of the industrial revolution changed that. Management emerged as a formal discipline at the turn of the century. The first university programs to offer management and business education, the Wharton School at the University of Pennsylvania and the Amos Tuck School at Dartmouth, were founded in the late 19th century. By 1914, 25 business schools existed.[3]

Thus, the management profession as we know it today is relatively new. This appendix explores the roots of modern management theory. Understanding the origins of management thought will help you grasp the underlying contexts of the ideas and concepts presented in the chapters ahead.

Although this appendix is titled "The Evolution of Management," it might be more appropriately called "The Revolutions of Management," because it documents the wide swings in management approaches over the last 100 years. Out of the great variety of ideas about how to improve management, parts of each approach have survived and been incorporated into modern perspectives on management. Thus, the legacy of past efforts, triumphs, and failures has become our guide to future management practice.

EARLY MANAGEMENT CONCEPTS AND INFLUENCES

Communication and transportation constraints hindered the growth of earlier businesses. Therefore, improvements in management techniques did not substantially improve performance. However, the industrial revolution changed that. As companies grew and became more complex, minor improvements in management tactics produced impressive increases in production quantity and quality.[4]

The emergence of **economies of scale**—reductions in the average cost of a unit of production as the total volume produced increases—drove managers to strive for further growth. The opportunities for mass production created by the industrial revolution spawned intense and systematic thought about management problems and issues—particularly efficiency, production processes, and cost savings.[5]

Figure A.1 provides a timeline depicting the evolution of management thought through the decades. This historical perspective is divided into two major sections: classical approaches and contemporary approaches. Many of these approaches overlapped as they developed, and they often had a significant impact on one another. Some approaches were a direct reaction to the perceived deficiencies of previous approaches. Others developed as the needs and issues confronting managers changed over the years. All the approaches attempted to explain the real issues facing managers and provide them with tools to solve future problems.

Figure A.1 will reinforce your understanding of the key relationships among the approaches and place each perspective in its historical context.

The oldest company on the Fortune 500 list is the Bank of New York, founded in 1784 by Alexander Hamilton. The oldest industrial company is DuPont, begun in 1802 after E. I. du Pont fled persecution during the French Revolution.[1]

CLASSICAL APPROACHES

The classical period extended from the mid-19th century through the early 1950s. The major approaches that emerged during this period were systematic management, scientific management, administrative management, human relations, and bureaucracy.

Systematic Management During the 19th century, growth in U.S. business centered on manufacturing.[6] Early writers such as Adam Smith believed the management of these firms was chaotic, and their ideas helped to systematize it. Most organizational tasks were subdivided and performed by specialized labor. However, poor coordination caused frequent problems and breakdowns of the manufacturing process.

APPENDIX B

APPENDIX B

The Caux Round Table Principles of Ethics (see p. 154 for general description)

PRINCIPLE 1. THE RESPONSIBILITIES OF BUSINESSES: BEYOND SHAREHOLDERS TOWARD STAKEHOLDERS

The value of a business to society is the wealth and employment it creates and the marketable products and services it provides to consumers at a reasonable price commensurate with quality. To create such value, a business must maintain its own economic health and viability, but survival is not a sufficient goal.

Businesses have a role to play in improving the lives of all their customers, employees, and shareholders by sharing with them the wealth they have created. Suppliers and competitors as well should expect businesses to honor their obligations in a spirit of honesty and fairness. As responsible citizens of the local, national, regional, and global communities in which they operate, businesses share a part in shaping the future of those communities.

PRINCIPLE 2. THE ECONOMIC AND SOCIAL IMPACT OF BUSINESS: TOWARD INNOVATION, JUSTICE, AND WORLD COMMUNITY

Businesses established in foreign countries to develop, produce, or sell should also contribute to the social advancement of those countries by creating productive employment and helping to raise the purchasing power of their citizens. Businesses also should contribute to human rights, education, welfare, and vitalization of the countries in which they operate.

Businesses should contribute to economic and social development not only in the countries in which they operate, but also in the world community at large, through effective and prudent use of resources, free and fair competition, and emphasis upon innovation in technology, production, methods, marketing, and communications.

PRINCIPLE 3. BUSINESS BEHAVIOR: BEYOND THE LETTER OF LAW TOWARD A SPIRIT OF TRUST

While accepting the legitimacy of trade secrets, businesses should recognize that sincerity, candor, truthfulness, the keeping of promises, and transparency contribute not only to their own credibility and stability but also to the smoothness and efficiency of business transactions, particularly on the international level.

PRINCIPLE 4. RESPECT FOR RULES

To avoid trade friction and to promote freer trade, equal conditions for competition, and fair and equitable treatment for all participants, businesses should respect international and domestic rules. In addition, they should recognize that some behavior, although legal, may still have adverse consequences.

PRINCIPLE 5. SUPPORT FOR MULTILATERAL TRADE

Businesses should support the multilateral trade systems of GATT/World Trade Organization and similar international agreements. They should cooperate in efforts to promote the progressive and judicious liberalization of trade, and to relax those domestic measures that unreasonably hinder global commerce, while giving due respect to national policy objectives.

PRINCIPLE 6. RESPECT FOR THE ENVIRONMENT

A business should protect and, where possible, improve the environment, promote sustainable development, and prevent the wasteful use of natural resources.

PRINCIPLE 7. AVOIDANCE OF ILLICIT OPERATIONS

A business should not participate in or condone bribery, money laundering, or other corrupt practices; indeed, it should seek cooperation with others to eliminate them. It should not trade in arms or other materials used for terrorist activities, drug traffic, or other organized crime.

PRINCIPLE 8. CUSTOMERS

We believe in treating all customers with dignity, irrespective of whether they purchase our products and services directly from us or otherwise acquire them in the market. We therefore have a responsibility to:

- provide our customers with the highest quality products and services consistent with their requirements;
- treat our customers fairly in all respects of our business transactions, including a high level of service and remedies for their dissatisfaction;

175

INSTRUCTOR SUPPLEMENTS

Because time, both inside and outside of the classroom, is valuable to both you and your students, Management: Leading & Collaborating in a Competitive World comes complete with a full set of instructor supplementary material.

INSTRUCTOR'S RESOURCE GUIDE

New! Completely revamped Instructor's Manual: prepared by Carol Moore, California State University – Hayward, contains above and beyond the material you need to prepare an effective classroom experience. Utilizing her own students for feedback in preparing, Professor Moore has created a "road map" for each chapter, highlighting within the Lecture Outline not only where available supplements can be brought into the discussion, but also offering Teaching Tips and other useful facts that can be used to capture students' interest. In detail, the manual includes such features as:

- Key Student Questions - taken directly from her own classroom experience
- Class Prework Assignments
- Guidance for using the "Unfolding" cases - How to make these chapter-opening features important for students – additional comments on setting up the introductory case study, examples of how the concepts are important in the real world

Chapter Outline with Teaching Tips: a completely integrated overview of how to teach a class. It includes:

- Chapter Content in Outline Form (Lecture Notes)
- Exercises and Cases from text placed where they naturally fall in outline
- Examples where appropriate (at least one for each major learning objective.)
- Common student questions, with answers.
- Teaching Tips (how to handle large lecture sections, etc.)
- Extra Exercises as available from previous editions
- Concluding Case Notes
- Supplementary Case Notes
- Video Notes – for each chapter video

CLASS ROADMAP

I. **OBJECTIVE 1: HOW ENVIRONMENTAL FORCES INFLUENCE ORGANIZATIONS, AS WELL AS HOW ORGANIZATIONS CAN INFLUENCE THEIR ENVIRONMENTS**

  A. Organizations are open systems (Figure 2.1)

    1. Receive financial, human, material and information resources from the environment
    2. Transform resources into finished goods and services
    3. Send outputs back into the environment

  B. Organization/Environment Influences

    1. When resources change, environment influences the organization
    2. When outputs differ, organization influences the environment

    Student Discussion Question 1. This chapter's opening quote by Peter Drucker said, "The essence of a business is outside itself." What do you think this means? Do you agree?

    Example: In February, 2001, the last typewriter repair shop closed in New York City.[1] Did it close because its employees didn't do good work? Because of a poor organizational structure? No, the typewriter repair store simply fell victim to a changing environment - changes in technology decreased demand for services and finally shut the business down.

II. **OBJECTIVE 2: HOW TO MAKE A DISTINCTION BETWEEN THE MACROENVIRONMENT AND THE COMPETITIVE ENVIRONMENT. (Figure 2.2)**

  A. The Macroenvironment

    1. Macroenvironment is defined by the most general elements in the external environment that can potentially influence strategic decisions

    2. Laws and Regulations

      a. U.S. government policies both impose strategic constraints and provide opportunities.
      b. Government can affect business opportunities through tax laws, economic policies, and international trade rulings.
      c. Regulators are specific government organizations in a firm's more immediate task environment.
      d. Regulatory agencies have the power to investigate company practices and take legal actions to ensure compliance with the laws are:

        i. Occupational Safety and Health Administration (OSHA)
        ii. Interstate Commerce Commission (ICC)
        iii. Federal Aviation Administration (FAA)
        iv. Equal Employment Opportunity Commission (EEOC)
        v. National Labor Relations Board (NLRB)
        vi. Office of Federal Contract Compliance Programs (OFCCP)
        vii. Environmental Protection Agency (EPA)

[1] "TECH.Tuesday", February 20, 2001, Vol. 13, #23. Retrieved August 15, 2005 from http://web.dexter.k12.mi.us/tech_resource/tec_tue/tt110.html.

---

    1. Example: higher energy costs make it harder to keep prices low.

    Example: In 1999, Shawn Fanning thought that he had a great idea. He would create a software program that would allow anyone, anywhere to post and receive music downloads over the Internet. He called the program "Napster" - his own nickname. What Shawn didn't know is how much opposition he would encounter from the recording industry. Almost immediately, Shawn was sued by the Recording Industry Association of America. Today, Napster exists as a pay service, which allows people to download music for a fee.[1]

II. **OBJECTIVE 4: HOW TO ANALYZE THE COMPETITIVE ENVIRONMENT**

  A. Environmental scanning

    1. A process that involves searching out information that is unavailable to most people and sorting through that information in order to interpret what is important and what is not.
    2. Competitive intelligence is the information necessary to decide how best to manage in the competitive environment they have identified.

    Example: Life hasn't been easy for bread manufacturers since the Atkins diet craze started. For example, Wendy Born and James Barrett, who own the Metropolitan Bakery in Philadelphia, found that their business dropped 15% as everyone seemed to be fighting carbs. To compete in this environment, Born and Barrett trained their employees to discuss the health benefits of whole grain breads with their customers. As a result, business is better than ever. A different approach to dealing with this environmental problem was used by Stephen Lanzalotta. Through environmental scanning, Lanzalotta picked up on the popularity of the book, "The Da Vinci Code." Since Barrett uses Da Vinci's "golden ratio" in his breadmaking, he saw a first class sales opportunity. Now customers are flocking to his restaurant, Sophia's, for the "Da Vinci platter" a combination of carbs, fat, and grains that also form the basis for the diet that Lanzalotta promotes.[2]

  B. Scenario development (Table 2.2)

    1. Scenario is a narrative that describes a particular set of future conditions.
    2. Best-case scenario--events occur that are favorable to the firm.
    3. Worst-case scenario--events are all unfavorable.
    4. Scenario development helps managers develop contingency plans for what they might do given different outcomes.

    Teaching Tip: Ask students to image different scenarios that might impact your school, and to develop contingency plans that might address those scenarios. This can either be done as a discussion question with the entire class, or students can work in groups to answer the question, and report back. For example, a possible scenario might center around a population boom or bust. In a population boom, universities might respond by setting up satellite campuses, whereas in a bust, universities might look for additional students by setting up international programs and/or programs targeted to meet the needs of working professionals.

  C. Forecasting

[1] Time Magazine, retrieved August 15, 2005 at http://www.time.com/time/poy2000/pwm/fanning.html.
[2] Pennington, April Y. "On the rise." Entrepreneur, July 2005, pg. 30.

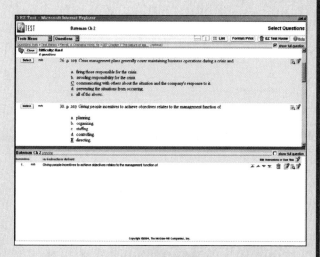

TEST BANK
COMPUTERIZED TEST BANK
Located on our instructor's CD-ROM,

New! Completely Revamped Test Bank: prepared by Amy Sevier, University of Southern Mississippi, contains a variety of true/false, multiple choice, and essay questions. Also includes "Scenario-based" questions, which are application-based, and use a situation described in a narrative, with 3–5 multiple-choice test questions based on the situation described in the narrative.

INSTRUCTOR'S CD-ROM
ISBN 007-292337-7

This CD-ROM allows professors to easily create their own custom presentation. They can pull from resources on the CD, like the Instructor's Manual, the Test Bank, figures downloaded from the text, and PowerPoint, or from their own PowerPoint slides or Web screen shots.

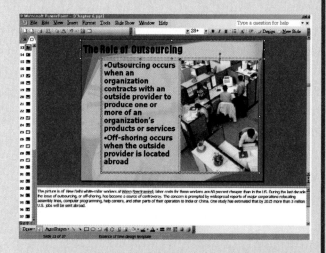

POWERPOINT®
Prepared by Kris Blanchard, North Central University, the PowerPoint presentation slide collection contains everything from an easy-to-follow outline, to additional slides with material from outside the text, to embedded video clips and weblinks, to figure downloads from the text. This versatility allows you to create a custom presentation suitable for your own classroom experience.

VIDEOS VHS: 007-292336-2 DVD: 007-325851-2
All new videos are included for this edition, in both VHS and DVD format, from BusinessWeek TV, NBC, and McGraw-Hill/Irwin's own Management Library. Chapter videos include such companies as: Circ du Soleil, Panera, Mini-Cooper, and The Container Store. They also include "Winning Advice–Jack Welch," "Fallen Star–Carly Fiorina," and "The Future Workforce."

INSTRUCTOR SUPPLEMENTS

ONLINE LEARNING CENTER

www.mhhe.com/bateman7e

The Online Learning Center (OLC) is a Web site that follows the text chapter by chapter, with additional materials and quizzing that enhance the text and/or classroom experience. As students read the book, they can go online to take self-grading quizzes, review material, or work through interactive exercises. OLCs can be delivered in multiple ways—professors and students can access them directly through the textbook Web site, through PageOut, or within a course management system (e.g., WebCT, Blackboard, TopClass, or eCollege).

NEW! The Group & Video Resource Manual: An Instructor's Guide to an Active Classroom. Authored by Amanda Johnson and Angelo Kinicki of Arizona State University, the Group & Video Resource Manual was created to help instructors create a livelier and stimulating classroom environment. The manual contains interactive in-class group and individual exercises to accompany **Build Your Management Skills** assessments on the OLC, additional group exercises for each chapter, comprehensive notes and discussion questions to accompany the **Manager's Hot Seat DVD,** and information on how to use the **Team Learning Assistant** (see the next page for a further description of these products).

This valuable guide includes information and material to help instructors successfully execute additional group exercises and the **Manager's Hot Seat DVD** into their classrooms. For each exercise, the manual includes learning objectives, unique PowerPoint slides to accompany the exercises, and comprehensive discussion questions to facilitate enhanced learning. The manual also includes lecturettes and associated PowerPoint slides to supplement and expand material presented in the text. You can ask your sales representative for a print copy, or you can access the online version through this text's Web site at www.mhhe.com/bateman7e.

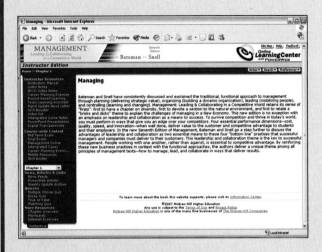

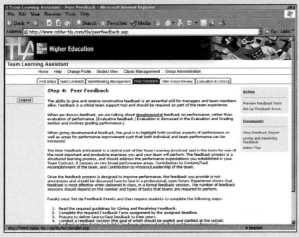

The Odyssey Corporation is influenced by factors from outside its close boundaries. These influencing factors include such things as governmental interference and economic recession. When these influences are present, it can be stated this corporation is being affected by its _____.

A. macroenvironment
B. competitive environment
C. global environment
D. external environment
E. microenvironment

Chapter Two: The External Environment and Organizational Culture   2-1

- **The Manager's Hot Seat DVD:** The Manager's Hot Seat is an interactive DVD that allows students to watch 15 real managers apply their years of experience in confronting issues. Students assume the role of the manager as they watch the video and answer multiple-choice questions that pop up during the segment, forcing them to make decisions on the spot. Students learn from the manager's mistakes and successes, and then do a report critiquing the manager's approach by defending their reasoning. The Hot Seat DVD is an optional package with this text.

- **Team Learning Assistant (TLA):** TLA is a Web-based system to facilitate team learning no matter what course you teach. It was developed at Boston University's Center for Team Learning with a grant from The General Electric Fund. If you are interested in incorporating a team-centered environment in your classroom or online course, this system facilitates effective team learning. Students in teams learn more when they are held accountable for their behavior and for meeting team learning goals. This system of web-based toolboxes for students, faculty, and program administrators enables a secure and reliable process of monitoring and maintaining team outcome data. Your McGraw-Hill/Irwin sales representative can help you if you're interested in using the product with your Management course.

CPS (wireless Classroom Performance System) by eInstruction

If you've ever asked yourself, "How can I measure class participation?" or "How do I encourage class participation?" then **CPS** might be the product for you. **CPS** enables you to record responses from students to questions posed in a PowerPoint slide, even record attendance, and offers a variety of reporting features, including easy export to WebCT or Blackboard grade books. For your students, it's as easy as using buttons on a remote control. Questions can be designed by you, or you can choose from a set of 20 per chapter written by Amit Shah, Frostburg State University, available with *Management: Leading and Collaborating in a Competitive World.* Ask your local McGraw-Hill/Irwin Sales Representative how to get **CPS** for your classroom.

STUDENT SUPPLEMENTS

ONLINE LEARNING CENTER (OLC)

at *www.mhhe.com/bateman7e:* More and more students are studying online. As they do, they can refer to the OLC for such benefits as: Self-grading Quizzes (including mid-term and final exam practice), internet exercises, and learning objectives. *Management: Leading & Collaborating in a Competitive World* also offers a Career Planning Exercise, and flash-based self-assessments and learning exercises called "Build Your Management Skills." Students are able to complete these exercises on their own and receive instant, comprehensive feedback to their responses. There are nearly 50 exercises to choose from, and a matrix for use is provided online and in the Instructor's Manual. The exercises include:

- Management's Historical Figures
- Ethics
- SWOT Analysis
- Characteristics of Managerial Control
- What is Your Primary Conflict-Handling Style?
- Assessing Your Emotional Intelligence
- Comparing Affirmative Action, Valuing Diversity, and Managing Diversity and many more!

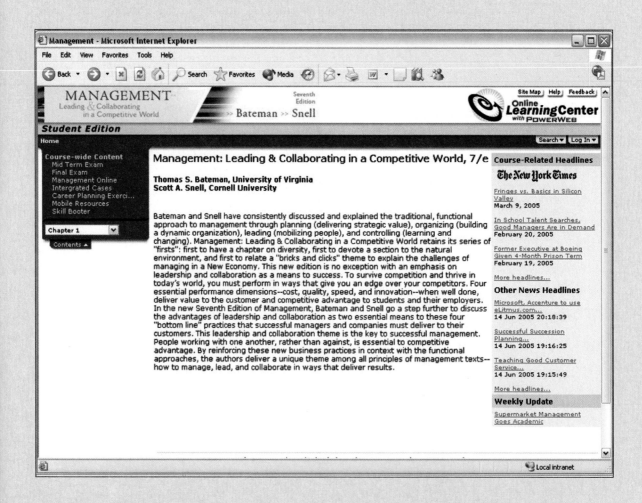

Contents in Brief

Contents

Part I
Foundations of Management   2

Part 2
Planning: Delivering Strategic Value   114

Part 3
Organizing: Building a Dynamic Organization   256

Chapter 11
Managing the Diverse Workforce   355

Part 3

Part 4
Leading: Mobilizing People   390

Chapter 12
Leadership   392

Appendix E:

Part 5
Controlling: Learning and Changing   516

MANAGEMENT

Leading & Collaborating
in a Competitive World

PART
ONE

Foundations of Management
- Managing
- The External Environment and Organizational Culture
- Managerial Decision Making

Planning: Delivering Strategic Value
- Planning and Strategic Management
- Ethics and Corporate Responsibility
- International Management
- Entrepreneurship

Strategy Implementation

Organizing: Building a Dynamic Organization
- Organization Structure
- Organizational Agility
- Human Resources Management
- Managing the Diverse Workforce

Leading: Mobilizing People
- Leadership
- Motivating for Performance
- Teamwork
- Communicating

Controlling: Learning and Changing
- Managerial Control
- Managing Technology and Innovation
- Creating and Managing Change

Foundations of Management

The three chapters in Part 1 describe the foundations of management. Chapter 1 discusses the imperatives of managing in today's business landscape and introduces the key functions, skills, and competitive goals of effective managers. In other words, it discusses what you need to do and accomplish to become a high-performing manager. Chapter 2 describes the external environment in which managers and their organizations operate—the context that both constrains and provides opportunities for managers. It also discusses what can be described as the organization's internal environment: its culture. Chapter 3 discusses the most fundamental managerial activity: decision making. Because managers make decisions constantly, sound decision-making skills are essential for good performance.

Chapter **1**

Managing

Management means, in the last analysis, the substitution of thought for brawn and muscle, of knowledge for folklore and tradition, and of cooperation for force.

—**Peter Drucker**

CHAPTER OUTLINE

LEARNING OBJECTIVES

After studying Chapter 1, you will know:

1. The major challenges of managing in the new competitive landscape.

2. The drivers of competitive advantage for your company.

3. The functions of management and how they are evolving in today's business environment.

4. The nature of management at different organizational levels.

5. The skills you need to be an effective manager.

6. What to strive for as you manage your career.

ED CATMULL AND PIXAR

Pixar came out of the gates hitting five-for-five: Every film Pixar created, from *Toy Story* to *The Incredibles,* was a blockbuster. Every one of its films was not just a commercial success; each was extraordinary in its innovation and quality.

The founder and president of Pixar is Ed Catmull, Pixar's unsung hero. Steve Jobs is Pixar's rock-star-famous CEO. Jobs (who actually spends most of his time with Apple), stated, "I'd trust Ed with my life. He runs the company day to day, and he doesn't get enough credit."

Catmull started dreaming about making computer-animated films in his 20s. Since then, he has created a new technology, turned it into a new art form, demonstrated impressive entrepreneurialism, and built one of the world's most distinctive business enterprises. *Fortune* magazine describes Catmull as a "geek's geek" who is "so down-to-earth that you'd never know by talking to him that he belongs in the ranks of Silicon Valley's most creative company builders."

Pixar doesn't just create great movies; it invents its own technologies, continually develops new production methods and organizational innovations, and is much more disciplined in its execution than its rivals in the movie-making industry. John Lasseter, the pioneering animator who directed Pixar's first three films, describes Catmull as "Pixar's heart and soul."

Sources: B. Schlender, "Incredible: The Man Who Built Pixar's Innovation Machine," *Fortune,* November 15, 2004, 206–12; P. Burrows, "Pixar's Unsung Hero," *BusinessWeek,* June 30, 2003, p. 68.

Pixar is a great success story as described in the Prologue. In contrast, consider the founder of the streaming media company Pseudo.com. During the height of the Internet gold rush, he brashly told *60 Minutes* and CBS, "Our business is to take you out. I'm in a race to take CBS out of business . . . That's why we're going to make the big bucks."[1] He said this before CBS was embarrassed by its failure to authenticate some documents about President Bush's years with the National Guard, and before Dan Rather's resignation. But CBS, of course, is still around, whereas Pseudo.com, like many other dot-com startups, is not.

Companies, like individuals, succeed or fail for a variety of reasons. Some of these reasons are circumstantial. Most are personal and human and include the decisions managers make and the actions they take.

In business, there is no replacement for effective management. Companies may fly high for a while, but they cannot do well for very long without good management. It's the same for individuals: *BusinessWeek*'s Managers of the Year succeed by focusing on fundamentals, knowing what's important, and managing well. The aim of this book is to help you succeed in those pursuits.

Managing in the New Competitive Landscape

When this decade began, the economy was soaring. Business seemed easy. Turns out, it's not easy. Even though the high-tech "new economy" heated up for a while, profits proved hard to come by, and many high-flying companies came crashing down.

Why did so many companies fall so far, so fast? In little more than one year, the business world changed dramatically. The dot-com bubble burst, a recession came, September 11, 2001, brought terrorist attacks, and economic uncertainties snowballed. But changing circumstances were only part of the story. During the good times, managers made a lot of bad decisions. Many grew arrogant, mistreated customers, didn't worry about costs, and gave away valuable services because profits didn't seem to matter. They misapplied management principles, in part because they lacked managerial experience and expertise.[2]

According to *BusinessWeek*, "The Darwinian struggle of daily business will be won by the people—and the organizations—that adapt most successfully to the new world that is unfolding."[3] What defines this "new world," and the competitive landscape of business? You will be reading about many relevant issues in the coming chapters, but we begin here by highlighting four key elements that make the current business landscape different from the past: globalization, technological change, the importance of knowledge and ideas, and collaboration across organizational "boundaries."

Globalization

Far more than in the past, enterprises are global, with offices and production facilities in countries all over the world. Corporations such as GE, Bertelsmann, ASEA Brown Boveri, and Nestlé are "stateless": They operate worldwide, transcending national borders.[4]

Founded in the United States, MTV has been extremely successful expanding overseas, reaching 400 million households in 164 countries in 18 languages. CEO Judy McGrath recently announced MTV's 100th channel: TV Base in Africa.[5] The movie industry also is grateful for expanding overseas markets.[6] The 2004 films *King Arthur, Troy,* and *The Terminal* all did poorly in the United States but did three times or more business internationally. Troy made more than $21 million in South Korea, which had virtually no theaters a few years ago. Russian companies are investing aggressively in theater building, and the third Harry Potter film opened in Italy during the summer—timing that used to be unthinkable, until theaters recently added air conditioning. Brad Pitt movies do particularly well in Japan, where women are the most frequent moviegoers, often going with girlfriends to Wednesday openings and then with their boyfriends on Saturdays.

Meg Whitman took a chance on eBay in Germany based on her hunch that the urge to trade is human nature.

Top CEOs know that the change from a local to a global marketplace is gaining momentum and is irreversible.[7] But some U.S. managers retain a U.S.-centric view of the business world. Some people told CEO Meg Whitman that eBay was uniquely American—for it to succeed, they said, buyers and sellers need optimism and mutual trust.[8] But Whitman suspected that the urge to trade is human nature. She moved into Europe and Australia. The best eBay franchise worldwide, she says, is Germany. And she entered China when the country had virtually no e-commerce. China is now eBay's fastest growing market. Whitman is now placing a long-term bet on India, where only about 2 percent of the population uses the Net.

Ideally, transnational companies have managers who specialize not only in particular businesses and functions but also in particular countries.[9] Managers throughout the company need to be enlightened to global realities. But the point isn't simply that global-

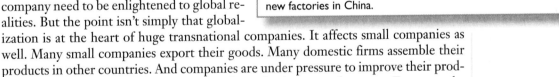

In a recent three-year period, foreign companies opened about 60,000 new factories in China.

ization is at the heart of huge transnational companies. It affects small companies as well. Many small companies export their goods. Many domestic firms assemble their products in other countries. And companies are under pressure to improve their products in the face of intense competition from foreign manufacturers. For example, Transmatic Manufacturing of Holland, Michigan, lost its most profitable contract to a Chinese firm.[10] Firms today must ask themselves, "How can we be the best in the world?"

For students, it's not too early to think about the personal ramifications. As CEO Jim Goodnight of SAS, the largest privately held software company in the world, put it, "The best thing business schools can do to prepare their students is to encourage them to look beyond their own backyards. Globalization has opened the world for many opportunities, and schools should encourage their students to take advantage of them" (p. 19).[11]

Technological Change

You know how important technology is in life. It is, of course, vitally important in the business world as well. Technology both complicates things and creates new opportunities. The challenges come from the rapid rate at which communication, transportation, information, and other technologies change.[12] For example, Robert Nardelli of Home Depot and Phil Knight of Nike were named two of *BusinessWeek*'s Best Managers of the Year.[13] Both were named for a variety of reasons, including good business results. But key decisions involved technology change. Nardelli invested in new technologies including cordless scan guns and self-checkout lanes. Knight not only changed some unpopular labor practices but also spent more time developing excellent information systems, logistics, and supply chains. In early 2005, Nike was in its strongest financial shape ever.

> Google search sites span the Internet in over 100 languages.

Later chapters will discuss technology further, but here we highlight the rise of the Internet and its effects. Why is the Internet so important to business?[14] It is a marketplace, a means for manufacturing goods and services, a distribution channel, an information service, and more. It drives down costs and speeds up globalization. It provides access to information, allows more informed decisions, and improves efficiency of decision making. It facilitates design of new products, from pharmaceuticals to financial services. Managers can watch and learn what other companies are doing, on the other side of the world. While these advantages create business opportunities, they also create threats as competitors sometimes capitalize more than you do.

At the beginning of this decade, technology was dazzling people with returns that seemed limitless. E-business (business conducted electronically) was all the rage. But when the overheated market crashed, "profitable Internet company" became an oxymoron.[15] The term *e-business* became discredited to the point where GM dropped it and started calling its e-business efforts "digitization."

But by mid-2002, 25 percent of the publicly held Internet companies had become profitable.[16] E-travel and e-finance (shining examples at the time: Expedia, Priceline, and Schwab) emerged as big winners. The health services company WebMD, once branded a loser, began making money. Even nonprofitable Net companies at least had potential as takeover targets for established companies, because they could provide the Internet services those companies needed.

When the dot-com bubble burst, many Internet-only companies died, making it seem that mixing the Internet with physical stores was the only way to make money online. But by 2002, most profitable Web companies were selling information-based products that don't require shipping, and so they didn't need physical stores[17] (as the jargon had it, "bricks" to go with their "clicks").

Will Wright of Electronic Arts helped develop the first Sims game in 2000, and also Sims2.

At the same time, old economy types, written off for dead during the heyday of the dot-com boom, have survived and are now using the Internet as a tool to solidify their future. Barnes & Noble sells successfully via the Net, not solely but as a complement to its real stores—people still like to browse the aisles, thumb through books, and have a cup of coffee.[18]

Some observers compare e-commerce to the automobile industry in the era of the Model T, Ford's original all-black model in the early 1900s.[19] The Net clearly is a powerful tool for doing and improving business. The industry may now be poised for a long, steady climb for decades.[20] The Internet revolution is definitely here, and the real wealth creation is yet to come.[21]

Knowledge Management

Companies and managers face a growing need for good, new ideas. Because companies in advanced economies have become so efficient at producing physical goods, most workers have been freed up to provide services or "abstract goods" like software, entertainment, data, and advertising. Efficient factories with fewer workers produce the cereals and cell phones the market demands; meanwhile, more and more workers create software and invent new products and services. As top consultant Gary Hamel puts it, "We have moved from an economy of hands to an economy of heads."[22]

Electronic Arts (EA) is a leader in a fad-driven, fast-moving business, and it has to work hard to stay on top. The company can't do that without utilizing the knowledge of world-class developers. Good developers are scarce. They must be able to create interesting stories, have the artistic talent to draw characters, and understand complex calculations to use cutting-edge graphics.[23] Electronic Arts has 12 studios around the world, in large part to capitalize on the knowledge held all over the globe.

Chief knowledge officer will be an important job in coming years.[24] **Knowledge management** is the set of practices aimed at discovering and harnessing an organization's intellectual resources—fully utilizing the intellects of the organization's people. Knowledge management is about finding, unlocking, sharing, and altogether capitalizing on the most precious resources of an organization: people's expertise, skills, wisdom, and relationships. Knowledge managers find these human assets, help people collaborate and learn, help people generate new ideas, and harness those ideas into successful innovations.

Production of tangible goods remains an essential part of the economy and of effective management, but companies like GE, Dell, Toyota, and ABB owe their success in large part to intellectual capital. Whereas "capital" used to be a purely financial concept, it now has an additional meaning. Intellectual capital is the collective knowledge and brainpower of the organization.[25] Today, managers must create a work environment that attracts good people, makes them want to stay, and inspires creative ideas from everyone. The goal is to turn the brainpower of their people into profitable products.

> **knowledge management**
>
> Practices aimed at discovering and harnessing an organization's intellectual resources.

Advantages of Collaboration

In business, you compete. Now more than ever, you must also collaborate to succeed. You collaborate with others in your work unit, other units in your organization, customers, and other companies including competitors. Because of the importance of collaboration in today's business world, we will highlight examples in every chapter so you don't lose sight of how essential it is.

Collaboration across "Boundaries"

One of the most important processes of knowledge management is to ensure that people in different parts of the organization collaborate effectively with one another. This requires productive communications among different departments, divisions, or other subunits of the organization. For example, British Petroleum tries to create "T-shaped" managers who break out of the traditional corporate hierarchy to share knowledge freely across the organization (the horizontal part of the T) while remaining fiercely committed to the bottom-line performance of their individual business units (the vertical part). This emphasis on dual responsibilities for performance and knowledge sharing occurs at GlaxoSmithKline (the pharmaceutical giant), Siemens (the large German industrial company), and Ispat International (a London-based steelmaker).[26]

For example, a huge recent success for Procter & Gamble has been Prilosec—which is someone else's product.[27] Priolosec is AstraZeneca's over-the-counter version of its prescription heartburn medicine, and P&G sells it. Think also about the cross-company collaboration required for Apple Computer to create the huge successes of the iPod portable music player and iTunes online music store.[28] To build the iPod, Apple worked with Toshiba to come up with a new hard disk, a little-known start-up to customize software, and contractors to assemble the product in Taiwan. Apple also persuaded all the major record labels—known for their rivalries and distrust—to make their music available for download. Apple's ability to line up partners was key to creating these runaway market leaders.

Collaboration across former "boundaries" occurs even between competing firms. For example, competitors dovetail electronic systems to purchase jointly, ship on shared semis, and store goods in commonly rented warehouses.[29] Companies today also must motivate and capitalize on the ideas of people outside the traditional company boundaries. How can a company best use the services of its consultants, ad agencies, and suppliers? What kinds of partnerships can it create with other companies in the same industry? And how about customers? Companies today still need to focus on delivering a product and making the numbers, but above all they must realize that the need to serve the customer drives everything else.

Best serving the customer can start with involving the customer more in company decisions. For example, companies like P&G are getting customers to think creatively and talk with one another online to come up with new product and service ideas.[30] Jim Goodnight of SAS requires that all customer suggestions for product improvements be recorded.[31] The suggestions are placed in an annual survey for customers to rank, and the 10 top suggestions usually are followed for the next product upgrade. This isn't about the occasional comment from a customer; it's about a strategic, systematic, active approach to achieve better customer service through managing relationships in such a way that customers contribute their best ideas.

Globalization, technological change, the monumental importance of new ideas, collaboration across disappearing boundaries . . . what are the repercussions of this tidal wave of new forces? The magazine *Fast Company* asked 17 business leaders to consider this question. Table 1.1 offers some of their comments.

TABLE 1.1   Comments on the Competitive Landscape of the 21st Century

Tom Peters, author and consultant: "Somebody once asked me what I wanted my epitaph to say. I want it to say, 'He was a player.' It wouldn't mean that I got rich . . . It would mean that I participated fully in these fascinating times . . . whatever this 'new economy' thing is, it is reinventing the world of commerce."
Jonathan Hoenig, founder of capitalistpig asset management: "The most valuable commodity isn't soybeans but service . . . The human touch is what's going to propel our 'commodified' business models into the next century and beyond. I feel terribly privileged to be alive at such an exciting time in history."
Patricia Seybold, author of customers.com: "A lot of people think the new economy is all about the Internet . . . it's really about customers. Customers are transforming entire industries . . . the customer is at the core of the business."
Nathan Myhrvold, cofounder and copresident of Intellectual Ventures: "The new economy is about rethinking and reshaping what has already happened. It's about producing fertile ground for radically new ideas. Workers with good ideas, or the ability to generate ideas, can write their own ticket."
Krishna Subramanian, chairwoman and CEO, Kovair Inc.: "Companies used to be structured around individual contribution. Now teamwork—presenting a seamless interface to the customer, across all points of contact and all business functions—is becoming more important.
Pehong Chen, chairman, president and CEO, Broadvision Inc.: "That's what is so awesome about the new economy. You have the ability to do something with your work and to know that you made a difference. You. Not your system. Not your company's policies. You."
Thomas Stewart, Fortune *magazine:* "We stand at the beginning of a new century, in the middle of a technological revolution, and at the end of a great stock market bubble—virgin territory, construction sites, and ruins, all at once. Let's go."

SOURCES: R. F. Maruca, "Voices," *Fast Company*, September 2000, pp. 105–44; T. Stewart, "Intellectual Capital: Ten Years Later, How Far We've Come," *Fortune*, May 28, 2001, pp. 192–93.

Connections: ED CATMULL AND PIXAR

One difference between animated and live-action film is that live-action uses what Hollywood calls a "gypsy" model: groups of actors, producers, and technicians who come together for a project and then scatter to new and different projects with new people. Animated films require far more collaboration, and Pixar doesn't disintegrate after each project—the organization remains, and the people keep working together. Most live-action films list 100 to 200 names in the credits; animated films require so much collaboration that *The Incredibles,* for example, credits about 800 people.

Pixar has world-class artists and world-class programmers. The organization has three groups: technology development (delivering computer-graphics tools); creative development (creating stories, characters, and animation), and production (coordinating the entire filmmaking process). It wouldn't work if they didn't collaborate well. Catmull insists that the three groups talk with one another, continually. Anyone can talk with anyone else, without having to go up and down a rigid hierarchy of bosses and subordinates. The U.S. Navy sent people to Pixar to learn how to improve its own organization and communication.

Ed Catmull has many patents to his name, but he is most proud of establishing Pixar University. Pixar U. offers 111 different courses, and everyone takes about half a dozen per year. Every person in Pixar receives enough training in cinema and the fine arts to think like a complete filmmaker. Goals like Catmull's are worthy of every other kind of business organization: to inspire people at all levels and in different units to work collaboratively, and to develop the depth and breadth of knowledge to think not only as specialists, but also like complete businesspeople.

Managing for Competitive Advantage

The rise of the Internet turned careers (and lives) upside down. People dropped out of school to join Internet start-ups or start their own. Managers in big corporations quit their jobs to do the same. Investors salivated, and invested heavily. The risks were often ignored, or downplayed—sometimes tragically, as companies went under.

Consider two earlier industries of similar transforming power: automobiles and aviation. There have been at least 2,000 car makers, but now there are only three car companies left in the United States—and even they have not been great investments. Similarly, hundreds of aircraft manufacturers have gone bankrupt, some very recently. In all of aviation history, up to the year 2000, the net amount of money made by all U.S. airline companies was zero.[32] That's right: all those companies in total had made no money whatsoever. And that was before American, United, Delta, and Northwest lost over $3.6 *billion* in 2003 alone.[33] In recent years, the largest airlines have laid off more than 10,000 pilots, some of whom made six-figure salaries and have had to start over with regional carriers for $20,000.[34]

What is the lesson to be learned from all the failures in these important transformational industries? A key to understanding the success of a company—whether traditional, Internet-based, or a combination of both—is not how much the industry in which it operates will affect society or how much it will grow. The key is the competitive advantage held by a particular company and how sustainable or renewable that advantage is.[35] Good managers know that they are in a competitive struggle to survive and win.

To survive and win, you have to gain advantage over your competitors and earn a profit. You gain competitive advantage by being better than your competitors at doing valuable things for your customers. But what does this mean, specifically? To succeed, what must managers deliver? The fundamental success drivers are innovation, quality, speed, and cost competitiveness.

Because it's easy for managers to get so caught up in being busy, get distracted, and lose sight of what really drives performance, you will periodically see this icon as a reminder of the need for innovation, quality, speed, and cost competitiveness.

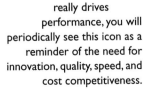

Innovation

Procter & Gamble under new CEO A. G. Lafley has become a hot growth company through innovation. According to Lafley, organic growth (from growing core businesses through innovation rather than buying new businesses) is "the most precious kind of growth . . . Organic growth exercises your innovation muscle. It *is* a muscle. If you use it, it gets stronger" (p. 168).[36]

innovation

The introduction of new goods and services.

Innovation is the introduction of new goods and services. Your firm must adapt to changes in consumer demands and to new competitors. When the Net allowed merchants to bypass traditional distribution channels and reach buyers directly, traditional marketers had to learn how to innovate to remain competitive.[37] Plus, products don't sell forever; in fact, they don't sell for nearly as long as they used to, because so many competitors are introducing so many new products all the time. Your firm must innovate, or it will die.

In contrast to Procter & Gamble, Kraft hasn't had a major new brand launch since DiGiorno pizza in 1995, and it recently had a string of quarterly profit declines. Historically, Kraft was an icon of business innovation—think Oreos and Mac & Cheese. Kraft brought the world Miracle Whip at the 1933 World's Fair, Minute Rice right after World War II, then Cheez Whiz, Shake 'N Bake, and Lunchables. Why the recent decline? Successes and failures have multiple sources, but after Kraft lost two top executives who were champions of new product development the company stopped taking risks and simply tried to milk aging brands.[38]

Your firm must innovate, or it will die. Tide took its well-established detergent into new directions including Tide for cold-water washing, and a scrub brush to get out stains—all branded with the Tide name.

A top consultant, Gary Hamel, notes that the real competition has always been between newcomers and the old guard.[39] The perpetual battle is between unconventional thinking and unthinking ritual. In recent years, newcomers battered incumbents with unconventional new approaches to business. Only the incumbents that keep innovating, like Wal-Mart and IBM, have continued to increase their share of wealth.

Not mincing words while speaking directly to successful executives, Hamel warns, "Odds are, over the next few years newcomers are going to capture most of the new wealth in your industry. Odds are, your company is going to get its ass kicked by a bunch of irreverent, tradition-defying rebels."[40]

Innovation is today's holy grail.[41] It is the most potent means of creating new wealth.[42] Like the other sources of competitive advantage, innovation comes from people; it must be a strategic goal; and it must be managed properly. You will learn how great companies innovate in later chapters.

Quality

A Los Angeles–based homebuilder, KB Home, had a bad reputation for quality a few years back. But chairman and CEO Bruce Karatz worked with the National Association of Home Builders to create training programs for builders and contractors aimed at improving quality.[43] He also created a "Say Yes" program to handle customer complaints faster. But until the Web site called kbhomesucks.com closes, KB Home will need to continue working to improve its quality reputation.[44]

quality

The excellence of your product (goods or services).

Quality is the excellence of your product. The importance of quality and standards for acceptable quality have increased dramatically in recent years. Customers now demand high-quality goods and services, and often they will accept nothing less. Bruce

McMillan of Electronic Arts states, "Ten years ago, you could get away with creating a mediocre game. Now, with competition, you don't have that luxury."[45]

Historically, quality pertained primarily to the physical goods that customers bought, and it referred to attractiveness, lack of defects, reliability, and long-term dependability. The traditional approach to quality was to check work after it was completed and then eliminate defects, using inspection and statistical data to determine whether products were up to standards. But then W. Edwards Deming, J. M. Juran, and other quality gurus convinced managers to take a more complete approach to achieving *total* quality. This includes *preventing* defects before they occur, *achieving zero defects* in manufacturing, and *designing* products for quality. The goal is to solve and eradicate from the beginning all quality-related problems and to live a philosophy of *continuous improvement* in the way the company operates. Deming and his ideas were actually rebuffed by U.S. managers; only when he found an audience in Japan, and Japan started grabbing big chunks of market share from the United States in autos, computer chips, and TVs, did U.S. managers start living his quality philosophy.[46]

Consumers are willing to spend more for Sony electronics because of Sony's consistent delivery of quality in its products.

Today, service quality is vital as well. For example, making things easy for customers is an important dimension of service quality; FedEx, Alamo, and Dell make it easy for customers to use their services. Compared to Wal-Mart, Target in some ways offers stronger quality not only in its products but also product selection (more products, unique products) and the shopping experience: aesthetics, less crowded aisles, video games not in locked cabinets, and no TVs or other products in the parking lots in tractor trailers (as Wal-Mart sometimes has to do).[47]

Quality is further provided when companies customize goods and services to the wishes of the individual consumer. Lands' End allows customers to create a "personal model" for testing the fit and look of swimwear. Chipshot.com allows golfers to configure clubs to their preferred specifications.[48] Cannondale of Bethel, Connecticut, allows customers to create personalized bicycles on a Web site.[49] Each customer is linked to a local dealer to place the final order and receive the product.

Providing world-class quality requires a thorough understanding of what quality really is.[50] Quality can be measured in terms of product performance, customer service, reliability (failure or breakdowns), conformance to standards, durability, and aesthetics. Only by moving beyond broad, generic concepts like "quality," to identifying specific quality requirements, can you identify problems, target needs, set performance standards more precisely, and deliver world-class value.

Speed

Google constantly improves its search product at a rapid rate.[51] Applebee's new computerized ordering system helped 98 percent of food orders to reach the table in less than 16 minutes, reducing the average length of a visit to the restaurant by seven minutes.[52] Right after digital images from Paris, Milan, and New York runway shows hit the Internet, knockoff houses reinterpret styles for the mass market and get them into stores within weeks.[53] For its athletic brand C9, Target has cut its product development cycle from over a year to between 10 weeks and nine months, depending on how trendy the item is.[54] Raymundo Hache of Interamericana Products International of the Dominican Republic, which ships pants to the U.S. market for Liz Claiborne, Tommy Hilfiger, and others, states, "If we're not fast enough, China will trample us."[55]

Speed often separates the winners from the losers. How fast can you develop and get a new product to market? How quickly can you respond to customer requests? You are far better off if you are faster than the competition—and if you can respond quickly to your competitors' actions.

Speed isn't everything—you can't get sloppy in your quest to be first. But other things being equal, faster companies are more likely to be the winners, slow ones the losers. Even pre-Internet, speed had become a vital requirement in the 1990s. Companies were getting products to market, and in the hands of customers, faster than ever. Now, the speed requirement has increased exponentially. Andy Grove, chairman of Intel Corporation, says the Internet is a tool, and the biggest impact of that tool is speed.[56] Everything, it seems, is on fast-forward.

Speed is no longer just a goal of some companies; it is a strategic imperative. Regarding quick delivery, Bruce Birnback, president of Rowe Furniture, said in November 2004, "Today it's not critical, but 18 to 24 months from now, I believe it will be the difference between being in business and not."[57]

Cost Competitiveness

Wal-Mart keeps driving hard to find new ways to cut billions of dollars from its already very low distribution costs. Mona Williams, VP of communications for Wal-Mart, states, "We are the low-price leader in retail and will not cede that ground to anyone."[58] While fuel and labor costs are high in the airline industry, LCCs (low-cost carriers, such as AirTran, Southwest, and JetBlue) keep expenditures 30 to 40 percent lower than the legacies, allowing them to offer lower fares and making all the major airlines suffer.[59] JetBlue and Southwest hold down repair costs by flying only one kind of jet. JetBlue's per-passenger-mile cost is lowest in the industry, and its market value is bigger than some of the big players.[60]

Cost competitiveness means that your costs are kept low enough so that you can realize profits and price your products (goods or services) at levels that are attractive to consumers. eBay set the standard for profitable Internet companies by having so few fixed costs—no inventory, sales force, or warehouses.[61] Marriott, hit hard by the drop in tourism and travel, cut costs every way it could and offered much lower room rates.[62] Needless to say, if you can offer a desirable product at a low price, it is more likely to sell.

Small businesses usually attend closely to costs at first, but then their owners start paying attention to other things.[63] The frugality habit slips, spending goes up, and costs escalate. If something goes wrong (things happen, unexpectedly), the company is strapped for cash. When a cash crisis comes, it's too late, and the owners have to think about laying off employees. Money can be wasted in countless ways, and savings can come from the most unexpected places. You want everyone in the company looking for new ways to keep costs under control.

Managing your costs and keeping them down requires being efficient: accomplishing your goals by using your resources wisely and minimizing waste. Little things can save big money, but cost cuts involve trade-offs. Lucent cut the number of lightbulbs per cubicle from four to one.[64] The BBC could save $400,000 per year by banning free biscuits from internal meetings. The Swedish navy, dealing with budget cuts, dropped round-the-clock operations in favor of Monday through Friday, 9 to 5.

Raw materials, equipment, capital, manufacturing, marketing, delivery, and labor are just some of the costs that need to be managed carefully. One reason so many dot-coms failed was that their huge, up-front advertising costs usually didn't translate into big sales; their customer acquisition costs were as much as four times higher than those of offline competitors.[65] And one reason every company must worry about cost is that consumers can now easily compare prices on the Net from thousands of competitors. If you can't cut costs and offer attractive prices, you can't compete.

As with the many dimensions of quality, understanding all specific costs is important. A chart making the e-mail rounds indicates that the cost of the active ingredients used in some of the most popular drugs in the United States is often under $1 while the consumer price is hundreds of dollars, indicating huge and arguably unfair percentage markups. Supporters of the pharmaceutical companies note that prices are less a function of the cost of ingredients than of the cost of funding R&D and the prices charged by pharmacies. The good news for consumers is that some pharmacies compete on the basis of cost and price: Costco, Sam's Club, and other discount volume stores often charge little over their cost for generic drugs. Although these are "membership" stores, nonmembers can buy prescriptions there because prescriptions are federally regulated.

Delivering All Four

Don't assume that you can settle for delivering just one of the four competitive advantages: low cost alone, or quality alone, for example. The best managers and companies deliver them all.

Rubbermaid used to be *Fortune*'s most admired company in the early 1990s, in large part because it was such a great innovator. But when it refused to meet Wal-Mart's requests for faster delivery and lower prices, it fell off the map.[66] A strong emphasis on speed hurt quality at Nissan; CEO Carlos Ghosn had to work hard to reverse the quality problem. He succeeded, and the brand got hot once again.[67] For MTV, rival music video channels have sprung up on every continent, and it has to respond quickly. The company is innovating with video-on-demand services, more new channels, expansion in the Internet and mobile entertainment markets, and a music download service to compete with Napster and Apple's iTunes. These moves are costly, and quality must be high to make these moves competitive and worthwhile.[68]

Trade-offs may occur among the four, but this doesn't need to be a zero-sum game where one has to suffer at the expense of another. Early on, Wal-Mart realized that constant innovation in inventory-control systems would get merchandise on and off the shelves faster. This added speed would result in lower prices.[69] Electronic Arts sets demanding deadlines for teams pursuing breakthrough innovation.[70] An important component is an intranet library through which developers share best practices and technologies. They work (much!) faster by working smarter. And low cost isn't the only thing at which Dell excels: Its quality ratings tend to be high, and it builds and ships PCs quickly after receiving an order (all of Dell's suppliers know they must deliver parts to Dell within one hour).[71]

Many of *BusinessWeek*'s worst managers were forced out due to ethics scandals.[72] You will read more about the importance of ethics in later chapters. But "best" and "worst" are also determined by results, as indicated by the following examples.

Don't forget: Don't focus on one aspect of performance and neglect the others. You might be better at or more interested in one than the others, but you should strive for all four.

Best and Worst

▼ **FROM THE PAGES OF**

BusinessWeek

When *BusinessWeek* announced in 2005 its Best and Worst Managers of the Year, the profiles describe the managers' business results and their major decisions and actions. As you read these examples, consider their relevance to the things described so far in the chapter. Among the best managers:

- Jeff Immelt, for embracing technology, generating innovation, and strengthening GE's global culture.
- Steve Jobs of Apple and Linus Torvalds of Open Source Development Labs, for their innovative iPod and Linux devices and software.
- Steven Reinemund of Pepsico, which is adding 200 product variations each year. Pepsico under Reinemund also is strong at developing people, especially leadership talent in the local teams that are key to its strength in India and China.

- John Henry of the Boston Red Sox, for adding seats to the oldest stadium in baseball, selling out all games, and routinely winning regional prime-time TV ratings after deciding to broadcast home games in high definition. His systems for mining baseball statistics to find undervalued players and avoiding long-term contracts for older stars whose performance might be on the decline kept costs down while forging a quality team. After 86 years without a championship, the Red Sox won it all in 2004.

BusinessWeek's "worst manager" picks for the year included:

- Franklin Raines of Fannie Mae, who gave his CFO free rein and tolerated "weak or nonexistent" financial controls. He employed improper bookkeeping, misstated earnings, and was forced out.
- Gary Bettman, who led the National Hockey League through years of unsustainable salary growth, culminating in a strike and then cancellation of the 2004–2005 season. NHL finances were in shambles. Salaries were 75 percent of revenues in 2004 versus 41 percent in 1991.
- Howard Pien of Chiron, one of only two major flu vaccine providers. Chiron was not allowed to release doses produced in the Liverpool, England, plant due to contamination problems. Pien increased production speed dramatically: Chiron produced 50 percent more vaccines than in the previous year and planned another 37 percent increase in 2005. But quality dropped. Chiron and its investors took a huge financial hit, and most of the rest of us went without flu vaccines.

SOURCE: Special Report, "The Best & Worst Managers of the Year," *BusinessWeek*, January 10, 2005, pp. 55–86.

The Functions of Management

> **management**
>
> The process of working with people and resources to accomplish organizational goals.

Management is the process of working with people and resources to accomplish organizational goals. Good managers do those things both effectively and efficiently. To be *effective* is to achieve organizational goals. To be *efficient* is to achieve goals with minimal waste of resources, that is, to make the best possible use of money, time, materials, and people. Some managers fail on both criteria, or focus on one at the expense of another. The best managers maintain a clear focus on both effectiveness *and* efficiency.

These definitions have been around for a long time. But as you know, business is changing radically. The real issue is what to *do*.[73]

The context of business and the specifics of doing business are changing,[74] but there are still plenty of timeless principles that make great managers, and great companies, great. While fresh thinking and new approaches are required now more than ever, much of what has already been learned about successful management practices remains relevant, useful, and adaptable, with fresh thinking, to the 21st-century business environment.

To use an analogy: Engineering practices evolve continually, but the laws of physics are relatively constant.[75] In the business world today, the great executives not only adapt to changing conditions but also apply—fanatically, rigorously, consistently, and with discipline—the fundamental management principles. These fundamentals include the four traditional functions of management: *planning, organizing, leading,* and *controlling*. They remain as relevant as ever, and they still provide the fundamentals that are needed in start-ups as much as in established corporations. But their form has evolved.

Planning: Delivering Strategic Value

> **planning**
>
> The management function of systematically making decisions about the goals and activities that an individual, a group, a work unit, or the overall organization will pursue.

Planning is specifying the goals to be achieved and deciding in advance the appropriate actions needed to achieve those goals. Planning activities include analyzing current situations, anticipating the future, determining objectives, deciding in what types of activities the company will engage, choosing corporate and business strategies, and determining the resources needed to achieve the organization's goals. Plans set the stage for action and for major achievements.

The planning function for the new business environment, discussed in Part 2 of this book, is more dynamically described as *delivering strategic value*. Historically, planning described a top-down approach in which top executives establish business plans and tell others to implement them. Now and in the future, delivering strategic value is a continual process in which people throughout the organization use their brains and the brains of customers, suppliers, and other stakeholders to identify opportunities to create, seize, strengthen, and sustain competitive advantage. This dynamic process swirls around the objective of creating more and more value for the customer. Effectively creating value requires fully considering a new and changing set of stakeholders and issues, including the government, the natural environment, globalization, and the dynamic economy in which ideas are king and entrepreneurs are both formidable competitors and potential collaborators. You will learn about these and related topics in Chapter 4 (planning and strategic management), Chapter 5 (ethics and corporate social responsibility), Chapter 6 (international management), and Chapter 7 (entrepreneurship).

Organizing: Building a Dynamic Organization

Organizing is assembling and coordinating the human, financial, physical, informational, and other resources needed to achieve goals. Organizing activities include attracting people to the organization, specifying job responsibilities, grouping jobs into work units, marshaling and allocating resources, and creating conditions so that people and things work together to achieve maximum success.

Part 3 of the book describes the organizing function as *building a dynamic organization*. Historically, organizing involved creating an organization chart by identifying business functions, establishing reporting relationships, and having a personnel department that administered plans, programs, and paperwork. Now and in the future, effective managers will be using new forms of organizing and viewing their people as perhaps their most valuable resources. They will build organizations that are flexible and adaptive, particularly in response to competitive threats and customer needs. Progressive human resource practices that attract and retain the very best of a highly diverse population will be essential aspects of the successful company. You will learn about these topics in Chapter 8 (organization structure), Chapter 9 (organizational agility), Chapter 10 (human resources management), and Chapter 11 (managing the diverse workforce).

Leading: Mobilizing People

Leading is stimulating people to be high performers. It includes motivating and communicating with employees, individually and in groups. Leading involves close day-to-day contact with people, helping to guide and inspire them toward achieving team and organizational goals. Leading takes place in teams, departments, and divisions, as well as at the tops of large organizations.

In earlier textbooks, the leading function was about how managers motivate workers to come to work and execute top management's plans by doing their jobs. Today and in the future, managers must be good at *mobilizing people* to contribute their ideas, to use their brains in ways never needed or dreamed of in the past. As described in Part 4, they must rely on a very different kind of leadership (Chapter 12) that empowers and motivates people (Chapter 13). Far more than in the past, great work must be done via great teamwork (Chapter 14), both within work groups and across group boundaries. Ideally, underlying these processes will be effective interpersonal and organizational communication (Chapter 15).

> **organizing**
>
> The management function of assembling and coordinating human, financial, physical, informational, and other resources needed to achieve goals.

> **leading**
>
> The management function that involves the manager's efforts to stimulate high performance by employees.

When Gert Boyle unexpectedly found herself at the helm of a debt-ridden company, she had no knowledge of how to run it. Change was needed. Thirty-two years later, she and her son Tim Boyle have turned Columbia Sportswear Company into a successful outerwear company. Her first decisions were difficult ones, including firing nearly all of her roughly 55 employees, but Gert and Tim focused on listening to customers and innovating. Since 1984, sales have grown from $3 million to nearly $1 billion. Change can sometimes lead to very good things.

Controlling: Learning and Changing

controlling

The management function of monitoring performance and making needed changes.

Planning, organizing, and leading do not guarantee success. The fourth function, **controlling,** monitors performance and implements necessary changes.

Monitoring is an essential aspect of control. If you have any doubts that this function is important, consider that after the terror attacks of September 11, 2001, many Department of Agriculture laboratories could not account for dangerous biological agents supposedly in their stockpiles, including 3 billion doses of a dangerous virus. The Department of Energy could not account fully for radioactive fuel rods and other nuclear materials lent to other countries.[76] On a different note, a man with a hatchet entered an Oklahoma City Wal-Mart. On his way in, the greeter not only failed to alert authorities but placed a sticker on the weapon so he would not be charged for it when he left. The man, who robbed the store, had claimed he was returning it.[77] Control failures can take many forms!

When managers implement their plans, they often find that things are not working out as planned. The controlling function makes sure that goals are met. It asks and answers the question, "Are our actual outcomes consistent with our goals?" It makes adjustments as needed.

Successful organizations, large and small, pay close attention to the controlling function. But Part 5 of the book makes it clear that today and for the future, the key managerial challenges are far more dynamic than in the past; they involve continually *learning and changing.* Controls must still be in place, as described in Chapter 16. But new technologies and other innovations (Chapter 17) make it possible to achieve controls in more effective ways, and to help all the people throughout the company, and across company boundaries (including customers and suppliers), to use their brains, learn, make a variety of new contributions, and help the organization change in ways that forge a successful future (Chapter 18).

The four management functions apply to you personally, as well. You must find ways to create value, organize for your own personal effectiveness, mobilize your own talents and skills as well as those of others, monitor performance, and constantly learn, develop, and change for the future. As you proceed through this book and this course, we encourage you to not merely do your "textbook learning" of an impersonal course subject, but to think about these issues from a personal perspective as well, using the ideas for your own personal development.

Performing All Four Management Functions

As a manager, your typical day will not be neatly divided into the four functions. You will be doing many things more or less simultaneously.[78] Your days will be busy and fractionated, spent dealing with interruptions, meetings, and firefighting. There will be plenty to do that you wish you could be doing but can't seem to get to. These activities will include all four management functions.

Some managers are particularly interested in, devoted to, or skilled in one or two of the four functions but not in the others. But you should devote adequate attention and resources to *all four* functions. You can be a skilled planner and controller, but if you organize your people improperly or fail to inspire them to perform at high levels, you will not be realizing your potential as a manager. Likewise, it does no good to be the kind of manager who loves to organize and lead, but who doesn't really understand where to go or how to determine whether you are on the right track. Good managers don't neglect any of the four management functions. Knowing what they are, you can periodically ask yourself if you are devoting adequate attention to *all* of them.

Management Levels and Skills

Organizations (particularly large organizations) have many levels. In this section, you will learn about the types of managers found at three different organizational levels: top-level, middle level, and frontline.

Top-Level Managers

Top-level managers are the senior executives of an organization and are responsible for its overall management. Top-level managers, often referred to as *strategic managers*, are supposed to focus on long-term issues and emphasize the survival, growth, and overall effectiveness of the organization.

Top managers are concerned not only with the organization as a whole but also with the interaction between the organization and its external environment. This interaction often requires managers to work extensively with outside individuals and organizations.

The chief executive officer (CEO) is one type of top-level manager found in large corporations. This individual is the primary strategic manager of the firm and has authority over everyone else. Others include the chief operating officer (COO), company presidents, vice presidents, and members of the top management team.

> Among 1,000 top executives in *Fortune* 100 companies, 48 percent went to public undergraduate schools, compared with only 32 percent two decades earlier. The number of top executives who went to Ivy League schools fell from 14 percent to 10 percent, and private non-Ivies from 54 percent to 42 percent.[79]

Traditionally, the role of top-level managers has been to set overall direction by formulating strategy and controlling resources. But now, top managers are more commonly called upon to be not only strategic architects but also true organizational leaders. As leaders they must create and articulate a broader corporate purpose with which people can identify, and one to which people will enthusiastically commit.

top-level managers

Senior executives responsible for the overall management and effectiveness of the organization.

Middle-Level Managers

As the name implies, **middle-level managers** are located in the organization's hierarchy below top-level management and above the frontline managers. Sometimes called *tactical managers*, they are responsible for translating the general goals and plans developed by strategic managers into more specific objectives and activities.

Traditionally, the role of the middle manager is to be an administrative controller who bridges the gap between higher and lower levels. Middle-level managers take corporate objectives and break them down into business unit targets; put together separate business unit plans from the units below them for higher-level corporate review; and serve as linchpins of internal communication, interpreting and broadcasting top management's priorities downward and channeling and translating information from the front lines, upward.

As a stereotype, the term *middle manager* connotes mediocrity: unimaginative people behaving like bureaucrats and defending the status quo. But middle managers are closer than top managers to day-to-day operations, customers, and frontline managers and employees—so they know the problems. They also have many creative ideas—often better than their bosses'. Good middle managers provide the operating skills and practical problem solving that keep the company working.[80]

middle-level managers

Managers located in the middle layers of the organizational hierarchy, reporting to top-level executives.

Frontline Managers

Frontline managers, or *operational managers*, are lower-level managers who supervise the operations of the organization. These managers often have titles such as supervisor or sales manager. They are directly involved with nonmanagement employees, implementing the specific plans developed with middle managers. This role is critical in the organization, because operational managers are the link between management and nonmanagement personnel. Your first management position probably will fit into this category.

Traditionally, frontline managers have been directed and controlled from above, to make sure that they successfully implement operations in support of company strategy. But in leading companies, the role has expanded. Whereas the operational execution aspect of the role remains vital, in leading companies frontline managers are increasingly called upon to be innovative and entrepreneurial, managing for growth and new business development.

frontline managers

Lower-level managers who supervise the operational activities of the organization.

TABLE 1.2

Transformation of Management Roles and Activities Roles

	Frontline Managers	Middle-Level Managers	Top-Level Managers
Changing Roles	• From operational implementers to aggressive entrepreneurs	• From administrative controllers to supportive coaches	• From resource allocators to institutional leaders
Key Activities	• Creating and pursuing new growth opportunities for the business	• Developing individuals and supporting their activities	• Establishing high performance standards
	• Attracting and developing resources	• Linking dispersed knowledge and skills across units	• Institutionalizing a set of norms and values to support cooperation and trust
	• Managing continuous performance improvement within the unit	• Managing the tension between short-term performance and long-term ambition	• Creating an overarching corporate purpose and ambition

SOURCE: Adapted from C. Bartlett and S. Goshal, "The Myth of the Generic Manager: New Personal Competencies for New Management Roles," *California Management Review* 40, no. 1, Fall 1997, pp. 92–116.

Managers on the front line—which usually means newer, younger managers—are crucial to creating and sustaining quality, innovation, and other drivers of financial performance.[81] In outstanding organizations, talented frontline managers are not only *allowed* to initiate new activities but are *expected* to by their top- and middle-level managers. And they are given freedom, incentives, and support to find ways to do so.[82]

Table 1.2 elaborates on the changing aspects of different management levels. You will learn about each of these aspects of management throughout this course.

Working Leaders with Broad Responsibilities

The trend today is toward less hierarchy and more teamwork. In small firms—and in those large companies that have adapted to the times—managers have strategic, tactical, *and* operational responsibilities. They are *complete* businesspeople; they have knowledge of all business functions, are accountable for results, and focus on serving customers both inside and outside their firms. All of this requires the ability to think strategically, translate strategies into specific objectives, coordinate resources, and do real work with lower-level people.

In short, today's best managers can do it all; they are "working leaders."[83] They focus on relationships with other people and on achieving results. They don't just make decisions, give orders, wait for others to produce, and then evaluate results. They get dirty, do hard work themselves, solve problems, and produce value.

What does all of this mean in practice? How do managers spend their time—what do they actually do? A classic study of top executives found that they spend their time engaging in 10 key activities or roles, falling into three categories: interpersonal, informational, and decisional.[84] Table 1.3 summarizes these roles. Even though the study was done decades ago, it remains highly relevant as a description of what executives do. And even though the study focused on top executives, managers at all levels engage in all these activities. As you study the table, you might ask yourself, Which of these activities do I enjoy most (and least)? Where do I excel (and not excel)? Which would I

Interpersonal Roles	*Leader:* Staffing, training, and motivating people
	Liaison: Maintaining a network of outside contacts who provide information and favors
	Figurehead: Performing symbolic duties (ceremonies and serving other social and legal demands)
Informational Roles	*Monitor:* Seeking and receiving information to develop a thorough understanding of the organization and its environment; serving as the "nerve center" of communication
	Disseminator: Transmitting information from source to source, sometimes interpreting and integrating diverse perspectives
	Spokesperson: Speaking on behalf of the organization about plans, policies, actions, and results
Decisional Roles	*Entrepreneur:* Searching for new business opportunities and initiating new projects to create change
	Disturbance handler: Taking corrective action during crises or other conflicts
	Resource allocator: Providing funding and other resources to units or people; includes making or approving significant organizational decisions
	Negotiator: Engaging in negotiations with parties outside the organization as well as inside (for example, resource exchanges)

TABLE 1.3
Managerial Roles: What Managers Do

SOURCE: Adapted from H. Mintzberg, *The Nature of Managerial Work* (New York: Harper & Row, 1973), pp. 92–93.

like to improve? Whatever your answers, you will be learning more about these activities throughout this course.

Management Skills

Performing management functions and roles, and achieving competitive advantage, are the cornerstones of a manager's job. However, understanding this does not ensure success. Managers need a variety of skills to *do* these things *well*. Skills are specific abilities that result from knowledge, information, practice, and aptitude. Although managers need many individual skills, which you will learn about throughout the text, consider three general categories: technical skills, interpersonal and communication skills, and conceptual and decision skills.[85]

First-timers greatly underestimate the challenges of the many technical, human, and conceptual competencies required.[86] But when the key management functions are performed by managers who have these critical management skills, the result is high performance.

A **technical skill** is the ability to perform a specialized task that involves a certain method or process. Most people develop a set of technical skills to complete the activities that are part of their daily work lives. The technical skills you learn in school will provide you with the opportunity to get an entry-level position; they will also help you as a manager. For example, your accounting and finance courses will develop the technical skills you need to understand and manage the financial resources of an organization.

Conceptual and decision skills involve the ability to identify and resolve problems for the benefit of the organization and everyone concerned. Managers use these skills when they consider the overall objectives and strategy of the firm, the interactions among different parts of the organization, and the role of the business in its external environment. As you acquire greater responsibility, you must exercise your conceptual and decision skills with increasing frequency. You will confront issues that involve all aspects of the organization and must consider a larger and more interrelated set of decision factors.

technical skill

The ability to perform a specialized task involving a particular method or process.

conceptual and decision skills

Skills pertaining to the ability to identify and resolve problems for the benefit of the organization and its members.

When Hewlett-Packard hired Carly Fiorina, the beleaguered computer company seemed to be on the upswing. But deteriorating leadership and interpersonal skills, not to mention a problematic Compaq merger, sealed her fate in early 2005.

Much of this text is devoted to enhancing your conceptual and decision skills, but remember that experience also plays an important part in their development.

Interpersonal and communication skills influence the manager's ability to work well with people. These skills are often called *people skills*. Managers spend the great majority of their time interacting with people,[87] and they must develop their abilities to lead, motivate, and communicate effectively with those around them. Your people skills often make the difference in how high you go.[88]

A *Fortune* article decried the lack of communication and other "people" skills among recent MBAs launching their management careers.[89] It is vital to realize the importance of these skills in getting a job, keeping it, and performing well in it. As one expert commented, "In many, many companies, the reason a manager fails is not because he doesn't have the technical skills. It's because he doesn't have the people skills."[90] Recruiters want good technical skills, of course, but the attribute they rank at the top of the list is communication and interpersonal skills.

The importance of these skills varies by managerial level. Technical skills are most important early in your career. Conceptual and decision skills become more important than technical skills as you rise higher in the company. But interpersonal skills are important throughout your career, at every level of management. Many high-potential, "fast-track" managers have had their careers "derailed" because of problems in the interpersonal arena.[91]

Hewlett-Packard CEO Carly Fiorina, a highly talented executive, was fired in early 2005. All three of these skills contributed in some way to her downfall.[92] She is courageous, decisive, and forceful, makes great presentations, and was widely admired outside the company. But she lacked a technical background and became interpersonally difficult when the Compaq merger which she conceived (and others doubted) didn't work well. She became more stubborn, handled confrontation poorly, and used a leadership style that most H-P employees didn't appreciate. A key task of her successor is to boost morale.

You and Your Career

At the beginning of your career, your contribution to your employer depends on your own performance; that's all you're responsible for. But upon becoming a manager, you are responsible for a whole group. To use an orchestra analogy, instead of playing an instrument, you're a conductor, coordinating others' efforts.[93] The challenge is much greater than most first-time managers expect it to be.

Throughout your career you'll need to lead teams effectively, as well as influence people over whom you have no authority; thus the human skills are especially important. These days, businesspeople talk about **emotional intelligence,**[94] or "EQ"—the skills of understanding yourself (including strengths and limitations), managing yourself (dealing with emotions, making good decisions, seeking and using feedback, exercising self-control), and dealing effectively with others (listening, showing empathy, motivating, leading, and so on). Andrea Jung, chair and CEO of Avon Products, says "Emotional intelligence is in our DNA here at Avon because relationships are critical at every stage of our business."[95]

A common complaint about leaders, especially newly promoted ones who had been outstanding individual performers, is that they lack what is perhaps the most fundamental of EQ skills: empathy. The issue is not lack of ability to change (you can), but the lack of motivation to change (you should decide to do so).[96] William George, former chair and CEO of Medtronic, says some people can go a long way in their careers based on sheer determination and aggressiveness, but personal development including EQ ultimately becomes essential.[97]

What should you do to forge a successful, gratifying career? You are well advised to be both a specialist and a generalist, to be self-reliant and connected, to actively manage your relationship with your organization, and to be fully aware of what is required to not only survive, but also to thrive, in today's world.

Be Both a Specialist and a Generalist

If you think your career will be as a specialist, think again. Chances are, you will not want to stay forever in strictly technical jobs with no managerial responsibilities. Accountants are promoted to accounting department heads and team leaders, sales representatives become sales managers, writers become editors, and nurses become nursing directors. As your responsibilities increase, you must deal with more people, understand more about other aspects of the organization, and make bigger and more complex decisions. Beginning to learn now about these managerial challenges may yield benefits sooner than you think.

So, it will help if you can become both a specialist and a generalist.[98] Seek to become a *specialist:* you should be an expert in something. This will give you specific skills that help you provide concrete, identifiable value to your firm and to customers. And over time, you should learn to be a *generalist*, knowing enough about a variety of business disciplines so that you can think strategically and work with different perspectives.

Be Self-Reliant

To be self-reliant means to take full responsibility for yourself, your actions, and your career.[99] You cannot count on your boss or your company to take care of you. A useful metaphor is to think of yourself as a business, with you as president and sole employee. Table 1.4 gives some specific advice about what this means in practice.

To make this point in another way: To add value, you must think and act like an entrepreneur.

Find new ways to make your overall performance better. Take responsibility for change; be an innovator.[100] Don't just do your work and wait for orders; look for opportunities to contribute in new ways, to develop new products and processes, and to generate constructive change that strengthens the company and benefits customers and colleagues.

TABLE 1.4
Keys to Career Management

Vicky Farrow of Sun Microsystems gave the following advice to help people assume responsibility for their own careers:
1. Think of yourself as a business.
2. Define your product: What is your area of expertise?
3. Know your target market: To whom are you going to sell this?
4. Be clear on why your customer buys from you. What is your "value proposition"— what are you offering that causes him to use you?
5. As in any business, strive for quality and customer satisfaction, even if your customer is just someone else in your organization—like your boss.
6. Know your profession or field and what's going on there.
7. Invest in your own growth and development, the way a company invests in research and development. What new products will you be able to provide?
8. Be willing to consider changing your career.

SOURCE: W. Kiechel III, "A Manager's Career in the New Economy," *Fortune*, April 4, 1994, pp. 68–72. Copyright © 1994 Times, Inc. All rights reserved. Reprinted by permission.

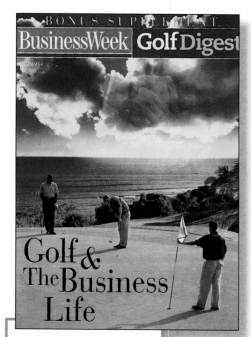

Playing golf is an excellent way to make contacts and build a network. *BusinessWeek* produced this supplement noting, "Business golf is very much a part of the modern world. Whether you're opening doors or closing deals, whether you're entertaining clients or being entertained, golf probably plays an important role."

social capital

Goodwill stemming from your social relationships.

Be Connected

Being *connected* means having many good working relationships and interpersonal contacts and being a team player with strong interpersonal skills.[101] For example, those who want to become partners in professional service organizations like accounting, advertising, and consulting firms strive constantly to build a network of contacts. Their "connectedness" goal is to work not only with lots of clients but also with a half dozen or more senior partners, including several from outside their home offices and some from outside their country. A recent study of new auditors[102] showed that social relationships improved newcomers' knowledge of the organization and their jobs, their social integration into the firm, and their commitment to the organization.

Social capital is the goodwill stemming from your social relationships, and can be mobilized on your behalf. It aids career success, compensation, employment, team effectiveness, successful entrepreneurship, and relationships with suppliers and other outsiders.[103] Just ask Jay Alix, a successful advisor to and acquirer of troubled companies. Believing that in his competitive business getting hired is not a function of competence alone, but also of whom you know, Mr. Alix prides himself on his networking prowess. He stays in constant touch with hundreds of people, and calls his network of contacts "the daisy chain."[104]

Look at this another way: All business is a function of human relationships.[105] Building competitive advantage depends not only on you but on other people. Management is personal. Commercial dealings are personal. Purchase decisions, repurchase decisions, and contracts all hinge on relationships. Even the biggest business deals—takeovers—are intensely personal and emotional. Without good work relationships, you are an outsider, not a good manager and leader.

Actively Manage Your Relationship with Your Organization

Many of the previous comments suggest the importance of taking responsibility for your own actions and your own career. Unless you are self-employed and your own boss, one way to do this is to think about the nature of the relationship between you and your employer. Figure 1.1 shows two possible relationships—and you have some control over which relationship you will be in.

Relationship #1 is one in which you view yourself as an employee, and passively expect your employer to tell you what to do and give you pay and benefits. Your employer is in charge, and you are a passive recipient of its actions. Your contributions are likely to be adequate but minimal—you won't make the added contributions that strengthen your organization, and if all organizational members take this perspective, the organization is not likely to be strong for the long run. Personally, you may lose your job, or keep your job in a declining organization, or receive few positive benefits from working there and either quit or become cynical and unhappy in your work.

FIGURE 1.1
Two Relationships: Which Will You Choose?

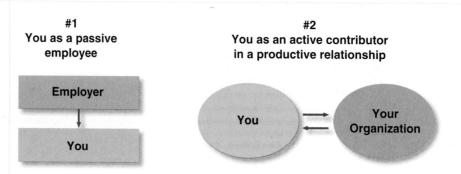

#1
You as a passive employee

Employer
↓
You

#2
You as an active contributor in a productive relationship

You ⇄ Your Organization

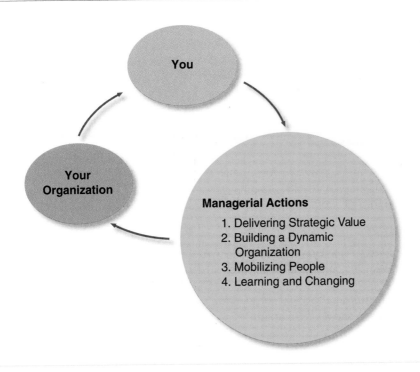

FIGURE 1.2
Managerial action is your opportunity to contribute

In contrast, relationship #2 is a two-way relationship in which you and your organization both benefit from one another. The mindset is different: Instead of doing what you are told, you think about how you can contribute—and you act accordingly. To the extent that your organization values your contributions, you are likely to benefit in return by receiving full and fair rewards, support for further personal development, and a more gratifying work environment. If you think in broad terms about how you can help your company, and if others think like this as well, there is likely to be continuous improvement in the company's ability to innovate, cut costs, and deliver quality products quickly to an expanding customer base. As the company's bottom line strengthens, benefits accrue to shareholders as well as to you and other employees.

What contributions can you make? You can do your basic work. But you can, and should, go further. You can also figure out new ways to add value—by thinking of and implementing new ideas that improve processes and results. You can do this by using your technical knowledge and skills, as in developing a better information system, accounting technique, or sales technique.

You also can contribute with your conceptual and human skills and your managerial actions (see Figure 1.2). You can execute the essential management functions and deliver competitive advantage. You can deliver strategic value (Part 2 of this book). You can take actions that help build a more dynamic organization (Part 3). You can mobilize people to contribute to their fullest potential (Part 4). And you can learn and change—and help your colleagues and company learn and change—in order to adapt to changing realities and forge a successful future (Part 5).

Survive and Thrive

Table 1.5 shows a résumé that might help a person to not just survive, but to thrive, in the 21st century.[106] Don't be discouraged if your résumé doesn't match this idealized résumé—it's tough to match, especially early in life! But do think about the messages. It indicates the kinds of skills that companies need now more than ever—and therefore the skills you should consider working to develop and the experiences you might want to accumulate.

TABLE 1.5

A Résumé for the
21st Century

Experience

- Multinational Corp—Worked with top-notch mentors in an established company with global operations. Managed a talented and fickle staff and helped tap new markets.
- Foreign Operation LLC—A stint at a subsidiary of a U.S. company, or at a foreign operation in a local market. Exposure to different cultures, conditions, and ways of doing business.
- Startup Inc.—Helped to build a business from the ground up, assisting with everything from product development to market research. Honed entrepreneurial skills.
- Major Competitor Ltd.—Scooped up by the competition and exposed to more than one corporate culture.

Education

- Liberal Arts University—Majored in economics, but took courses in psychology (how to motivate customers and employees), foreign language (the world is a lot bigger than the 50 states), and philosophy (to seek vision and meaning in your work).
- Graduate Studies—The subject almost doesn't matter, so long as you developed your thinking and analytical skills.

Extracurricular

- Debating (where you learned to market ideas and think on your feet).
- Sports (where you learned discipline and teamwork).
- Volunteer work (where you learned to step outside your own narrow world to help others).
- Travel (where you learned about different cultures).

SOURCE: D. Brady "Wanted: Eclectic Visionary with a Sense of Humor," *BusinessWeek.* August 28, 2000, p. 144.

Now—far more than ever—you will be accountable for your actions and for results.[107] In the past, people at many companies could show up, do an OK job, get a decent evaluation, and get a raise equal to the cost of living and maybe higher. Today, managers must do more, better. Eminent management scholar Peter Drucker, in considering what makes managers effective, notes that some are charismatic while some are not, and some are visionary while others are more numbers-oriented.[108] But successful executives do share some common practices:

- They asked "What needs to be done?" rather than "What do I want to do?"
- They write an action plan. They don't just think, they do, based on a sound, ethical plan.
- They take responsibility for decisions. This requires checking up, revisiting, and changing if necessary.
- They focus on opportunities rather than problems. Problems have to be solved, and problem solving prevents more damage. But exploiting opportunities is what creates great results.

A study of career success led one author to state, "In the current economic environment, people who fear competition, want security, and demand stability are often sinking like rocks in water."[109] Success requires high standards, self-confidence in competitive situations, and a willingness to keep growing and learning new things.[110] You will need to learn how to think strategically, discern and convey your business vision, make decisions, and work in teams. You will need to deliver competitive advantage and thrive on change. These and other topics, essential to your successful career, provide the focus for the following chapters.

EPILOGUE

ED CATMULL AND PIXAR

Because the last part of the chapter discussed careers, let's step back from the Pixar organization and describe its founder's career. When Ed Catmull was a kid, he drew crude animations and dreamed of working for Disney. He wasn't very good at art, but he was good at math, and he studied physics and computer science at the University of Utah. It so happened that the epicenter for the new discipline of computer graphics was Utah. After graduation, he worked for Boeing, returned to Utah for grad school, and met classmates including John Warnock (founder of Adobe Systems), Jim Clark (founder of Silicon Graphics and Netscape), and Alan Kay, who helped invent the graphical user interface.

One of Catmull's animation projects was used by one movie as a special effect—but he was disappointed to never land another. He and his computer-graphics research group did make one of the first rock music videos. Then he went to work for Lucasfilm. George Lucas said that he hired Ed because his credentials were right, he was a nice guy, he loved movies, and he had an ambition: to make a computer-animated movie. Lucas later told

Catmull he couldn't fund the group any longer and offered to let him keep the animation technology and go out on his own. Alan Kay, Catmull's friend from Utah, was now working at Apple, and he told Steve Jobs about Catmull. Jobs offered Catmull a position, but he was interested in using Catmull's technology only to build his computer company, not to make movies. The choice Catmull faced was to save his company (with Jobs's investment) or give up his dream (making computer-animated movies). Catmull said no thanks.

Fortunately, within a year, Jobs changed his mind and agreed to support Catmull's filmmaking. Catmull joined Apple, where he used animation to produce commercials and learned about budgets, deadlines, and dealing with customers. Disney noticed Catmull's work and offered to fund a full-length feature film. That film, *Toy Story*, launched an incredible run.

One analyst recently said about Pixar, "You show me another media company that generates 80% gross margins and 40% net margins. There aren't any." A rave review, and it came even before *The Incredibles* and its successors.

KEY TERMS

Conceptual and decision skills, p. 21

Controlling, p. 18

Cost competitiveness, p. 14

Emotional intelligence, p. 22

Frontline managers, p. 19

Innovation, p. 12

Interpersonal and communication skills, p. 22

Knowledge management, p. 9

Leading, p. 17

Management, p. 16

Middle-level managers, p. 19

Organizing, p. 17

Planning, p. 16

Quality, p. 12

Social capital, p. 24

Speed, p. 14

Technical skill, p. 21

Top-level managers, p. 19

SUMMARY OF LEARNING OBJECTIVES

Now that you have studied Chapter 1, you should know:

The major challenges of managing in the new competitive landscape.

Managers today must deal with dynamic forces that create greater and more constant change than ever before. Among many forces that are creating a need for managers to rethink their approaches, we highlighted four major waves of change: globalization, technological change including the Internet, knowledge management, and collaboration across organizational boundaries.

The drivers of competitive advantage for your company.

Because business is a competitive arena, you need to deliver value to customers in ways that are superior to your competitors. The four pillars of competitive advantage are innovation, quality, speed, and cost.

The functions of management and how they are evolving in today's business environment.

Despite massive change, management retains certain foundations that will not disappear. The primary functions of management are planning, organizing, leading, and controlling. Planning is analyzing a situation, determining the goals that will be pursued, and deciding in advance the actions needed to pursue these goals. Organizing is assembling the resources needed to complete the job and coordinating employees and tasks for maximum success. Leading is motivating people and stimulating high performance. Controlling is monitoring the progress of the organization or the work unit toward goals and then taking corrective action if necessary. In today's business environment, these functions more broadly require creating strategic value, building a dynamic organization, mobilizing people, and learning and changing.

The nature of management at different organizational levels.

Top-level, strategic managers are the senior executives and are responsible for the organization's overall management. Middle-level, tactical managers translate general goals and plans into more specific objectives and activities. Frontline, operational managers are lower-level managers who supervise operations. Today, managers at all levels must perform a variety of interpersonal, informational, and decisional roles. Even at the operational level, the best managers think strategically and operate like complete businesspeople.

The skills you need to be an effective manager.

To execute management functions successfully, managers need technical skills, conceptual and decision skills, and interpersonal and communication skills. A technical skill is the ability to perform a specialized task involving a certain method or process. Conceptual and decision skills help the manager recognize complex and dynamic issues, analyze the factors that influence those issues or problems, and make appropriate decisions. Interpersonal and communication skills enable the manager to interact and work well with people. As you rise to higher organizational levels, technical skills tend to become less important and conceptual skills become more important, while human skills remain extremely important at every level.

What to strive for as you manage your career.

To help you succeed in your career, keep in mind several goals: Be both a specialist and a generalist; be self-reliant but also connected; actively manage your relationship with your organization; and continuously improve your skills in order to perform in the ways demanded in the changing work environment.

DISCUSSION QUESTIONS

1. Identify and describe a great manager. What makes him or her stand out from the crowd?

2. Have you ever seen or worked for an ineffective manager? Describe the causes and the consequences of the ineffectiveness.

3. Describe in as much detail as possible how the Internet and globalization affect your daily life.

4. Identify some examples of how different organizations collaborate "across boundaries."

5. Name a great organization. How do you think management contributes to making it great?

6. Name an ineffective organization. What can management do to improve it?

7. Give examples you have seen of firms that are outstanding and weak on each of the four pillars of competitive advantage. Why do you choose the firms you do?

8. Describe your use of the four management functions in the management of your daily life.

9. Discuss the importance of technical, conceptual, and interpersonal skills at school and in jobs you have held.

10. What are your strengths and weaknesses as you contemplate your career? How do they correlate with the skills and behaviors identified in the chapter?

11. Devise a plan for developing yourself and making yourself attractive to potential employers. How would you go about improving your managerial skills?

12. Consider the managers and companies discussed in the chapter. Have they been in the news lately, and what is the latest? If their image, performance, or fortunes have gone up or down, what has changed to affect how they have fared?

13. Who are *BusinessWeek*'s most recent "best and worst managers," and why were they selected?

CONCLUDING CASE

The New Recruit—You!

The 21st century offers many challenges to every one of us. Just think about all that has happened and changed in your life already. The Internet, terrorism, major health issues, the development of third-world countries, hip-hop music, and even the Red Sox finally winning a World Series are all events of the recent past.

Chapter 1 introduced you to many business-related aspects of the new competitive landscape. You just read about topics ranging from eBay and globalization to knowledge and innovation to quality, speed, and cost control. The basic functions and levels of management were discussed, along with personal management styles and strategies.

Now enter you, the new recruit. How and where will you fit into all of this? Where will you live? What will you do? How will your business and personal careers evolve as the world continues to change at such a fast pace?

We highly recommend that you consider and adopt the following perspective, strategy, and action plan.

First and foremost, relax. Rarely, if ever, can or does a college student know exactly what lies ahead. The important thing is to just be doing something positive at all times. You are already doing that by attending college. Other positives include but are not limited to internships, part-time and summer jobs, travel, and community service. Try what you think you like. A steady diet of the above almost always leads to positive outcomes.

And the nice thing is that you can change your mind and your course at almost any time. Nothing is carved in stone, especially early in your career. Positive, proactive, motivated people can easily change majors and jobs; plenty of people at school and work will offer referrals, recommendations, and guidance.

Take a few minutes to review the chapter and its main topics one more time while thinking about yourself. Think about your personality, what you like and dislike, what you fear, and what you dream, and then address the following.

QUESTIONS

1. Generate a list of products, services, industries, and cultures in which you are interested. Generate a second list of your favorite activities and interests. From those two lists, name and describe three or four specific jobs that match up nicely.

2. Draw a time-line across a page and highlight the next 1–3, 5–10, and 15–30 years. Move across that line and draft/jot down a series of internships, part-time jobs, and full-time jobs that you would like to have. Be sure to incorporate travel, community service, and anything else that you want to do with your life.

Congratulations! You have just created a plan of action for yourself that ties in with the world of opportunities for a career in business management.

Creating a plan is easy (talking the talk). Making it happen is possible, too, but you must take action (walking the walk). And don't forget, you can change your mind and your plan; just stay on that positive track. Good luck!

EXPERIENTIAL EXERCISES

1.1 Personal Assessment of Management Skills (PAMS)

To get an overall profile of your level of skill competence, respond to the following statements using the rating scale below. Please rate your behavior as it is, not as you would like it to be. If you have not engaged in a specific activity, answer according to how you think you would behave based on your experience in similar activities. Be realistic; this instrument is designed to help you tailor your learning to your specific needs.

RATING SCALE

1 Strongly disagree
2 Disagree
3 Slightly disagree
4 Slightly agree
5 Agree
6 Strongly agree

In regard to my level of self-knowledge:

_____ 1. I seek information about my strengths and weaknesses from others as a basis for self-improvement.

_____ 2. In order to improve, I am willing to be self-disclosing to others (that is, to share my beliefs and feelings).

_____ 3. I am aware of my preferred style in gathering information and making decisions.

_____ 4. I understand how I cope with situations that are ambiguous and uncertain.

_____ 5. I have a well-developed set of personal standards and principles that guide my behavior.

When faced with stressful or time-pressured situations:

_____ 6. I use effective time-management methods such as keeping track of my time, making to-do lists, and prioritizing tasks.

_____ 7. I reaffirm my priorities so that less important things don't drive out more important things.

_____ 8. I maintain a program of regular exercise for fitness.

_____ 9. I maintain an open, trusting relationship with someone with whom I can share my frustrations.

_____ 10. I know and practice several temporary relaxation techniques such as deep breathing and muscle relaxation.

_____ 11. I maintain balance in my life by pursuing a variety of interests outside of work.

When I approach a typical, routine problem:

_____ 12. I state clearly and explicitly what the problem is. I avoid trying to solve it until I have defined it.

_____ 13. I generate more than one alternative solution to the problem, instead of identifying only one obvious solution.

_____ 14. I keep steps in the problem-solving process distinct; that is, I define the problem before proposing alternative solutions, and I generate alternatives before selecting a single solution.

When faced with a complex or difficult problem that does not have an easy solution:

_____ 15. I define a problem in multiple ways. I don't limit myself to just one problem definition.

_____ 16. I unfreeze my thinking by asking lots of questions about the nature of the problem before considering ways to solve it.

_____ 17. I think about the problem from both the left (logical) side of my brain and the right (intuitive) side of my brain.

_____ 18. I avoid selecting a solution until I have developed many possible alternatives.

_____ 19. I have specific techniques that I use to help develop creative and innovative solutions to problems.

When trying to foster more creativity and innovation among those with whom I work:

_____ 20. I make sure there are divergent points of view represented or expressed in every complex problem-solving situation.

_____ 21. I try to acquire information from individuals outside the problem-solving group who will be affected by the decision, mainly to determine their preferences and expectations.

_____ 22. I provide recognition not only for those who come up with creative ideas (the idea champions) but also for those who support others' ideas (supporters) and who provide resources to implement them (orchestrators).

_____ 23. I encourage informed rule-breaking in pursuit of creative solutions.

In situations where I have to provide negative feedback or offer corrective advice:

_____ 24. I help others recognize and define their own problems when I counsel them.

_____ 25. I am clear about when I should coach someone and when I should provide counseling instead.

_____ 26. When I give feedback to others, I avoid referring to personal characteristics and focus on problems or solutions instead.

_____ 27. When I try to correct someone's behavior, our relationship is strengthened.

_____ 28. I am descriptive in giving negative feedback to others. That is, I objectively describe events, their consequences, and my feelings about them.

_____ 29. I take responsibility for my statements and point of view, for example, "I have decided" instead of "They have decided."

_____ 30. I identify some area of agreement in a discussion with someone who has a different point of view.

_____ 31. I don't talk down to those who have less power or less information than I.

_____ 32. When discussing someone's problem, I respond with a reply that indicates understanding rather than advice.

In a situation where it is important to obtain more power:

_____ 33. I put forth more effort and take more initiative than expected in my work.

_____ 34. I am continually upgrading my skills and knowledge.

_____ 35. I support organizational ceremonial events and activities.

_____ 36. I form a broad network of relationships with people throughout the organization at all levels.

_____ 37. In my work I strive to generate new ideas, initiate new activities, and minimize routine tasks.

_____ 38. I send personal notes to others when they accomplish something significant or when I pass along important information to them.

_____ 39. I refuse to bargain with individuals who use high-pressure negotiation tactics.

_____ 40. I avoid using threats or demands to impose my will on others.

When another person needs to be motivated:

_____ 41. I determine if the person has the necessary resources and support to succeed in a task.

_____ 42. I use a variety of rewards to reinforce exceptional performances.

_____ 43. I design task assignments to make them interesting and challenging.

_____ 44. I make sure the person gets timely feedback from those affected by task performance.

_____ 45. I help the person establish performance goals that are challenging, specific, and time bound.

_____ 46. Only as a last resort do I attempt to reassign or release a poorly performing individual.

_____ 47. I discipline when effort is below expectations and capabilities.

_____ 48. I make sure that people feel fairly and equitably treated.

_____ 49. I provide immediate compliments and other forms of recognition for meaningful accomplishments.

When I see someone doing something that needs correcting:

_____ 50. I avoid making personal accusations and attributing self-serving motives to the other person.

_____ 51. I encourage two-way interaction by inviting the respondent to express his or her perspective and to ask questions.

_____ 52. I make a specific request, detailing a more acceptable option.

When someone complains about something I've done:

_____ 53. I show genuine concern and interest, even when I disagree.

_____ 54. I seek additional information by asking questions that provide specific and descriptive information.

_____ 55. I ask the other person to suggest more acceptable behaviors.

When two people are in conflict and I am the mediator:

_____ 56. I do not take sides but remain neutral.

_____ 57. I help the parties generate multiple alternatives.

_____ 58. I help the parties find areas on which they agree.

In situations where I have an opportunity to empower others:

_____ 59. I help people feel competent in their work by recognizing and celebrating their small successes.

_____ 60. I provide regular feedback and needed support.

_____ 61. I provide all the information that people need to accomplish their tasks.

_____ 62. I highlight the important impact that a person's work will have.

When delegating work to others:

_____ 63. I specify clearly the results I desire.

_____ 64. I specify clearly the level of initiative I want others to take (for example, wait for directions, do part of the task and then report, do the whole task and then report, etc.).

_____ 65. I allow participation by those accepting assignments regarding when and how work will be done.

_____ 66. I avoid upward delegation by asking people to recommend solutions, rather than merely asking for advice or answers, when a problem is encountered.

_____ 67. I follow up and maintain accountability for delegated tasks on a regular basis.

When I am in the role of leader in a team:

_____ 68. I know how to establish credibility and influence among team members.

_____ 69. I am clear and consistent about what I want to achieve.

_____ 70. I build a common base of agreement in the team before moving forward with task accomplishment.

_____ 71. I articulate a clear, motivating vision of what the team can achieve along with specific short-term goals.

When I am in the role of team member:

_____ 72. I know a variety of ways to facilitate task accomplishment in the team.

_____ 73. I know a variety of ways to help build strong relationships and cohesion among team members.

When I desire to make my team perform well, regardless of whether I am a leader or member:

_____ 74. I am knowledgeable about the different stages of team development experienced by most teams.

_____ 75. I help the team avoid groupthink by making sure that sufficient diversity of opinions is expressed in the team.

_____ 76. I diagnose and capitalize on my team's core competencies, or unique strengths.

_____ 77. I encourage exceptionally high standards of performance and outcomes that for exceed expectations.

When I am leading change:

_____ 78. I usually emphasize a higher purpose or meaning associated with the work I do.

_____ 79. I keep track of things that go right, not just things that go wrong.

_____ 80. I frequently give other people positive feedback.

_____ 81. I work to close abundance gaps—the difference between good performance and great performance.

_____ 82. I express gratitude frequently and conspicuously, even for small acts.

_____ 83. I know how to get people to commit to my vision of positive change.

_____ 84. I know how to unlock the positive energy in other people.

_____ 85. I express compassion toward people who are facing pain or difficulty.

Source: David A. Whetten and Kim S. Cameron, _Developing Management Skills,_ 6th ed. (Upper Saddle River, NJ: Pearson/Prentice Hall, 2005),. pp. 23–27.

1.2 Your Personal Network

1. See the figure on the next page. Working on your own, write down all of your primary contacts—individuals you know personally who can support you in attaining your professional goals. Then begin to explore their secondary connections. Make assumptions about possible secondary connections that can be made for you by contacting your primary connections. For example, through one of your teachers (primary), you might be able to obtain some names of potential employers (secondary). (10–15 min.)

2. Then meet with your partner or small group to exchange information about your primary and secondary networks and to exchange advice and information on how to best use these connections, as well as how you could be helpful to them. (about 5 min. per person; 10–30 min. total, depending on group size).

3. Add names or types of names to your list based on ideas you get by talking with others in your group. (2–5 min.)

4. Discuss with large group or class, using discussion questions below. (10 min.)

QUESTIONS

1. What were some of the best primary sources identified by your group?

2. What were some of the best sources for secondary contacts identified by your group?

3. What are some suggestions for approaching primary contacts?

4. What are some suggestions for approaching secondary contacts, and how is contacting secondary sources different from contacting primary contacts?

5. What did you learn about yourself and others from this exercise?

SOURCE: Suzanne C. de Janasz, Karen O. Dowd, and Beth Z. Schneider, _Interpersonal Skills in Organizations_ (New York: McGraw-Hill, 2002), p. 211.

Primary and Secondary
Connections

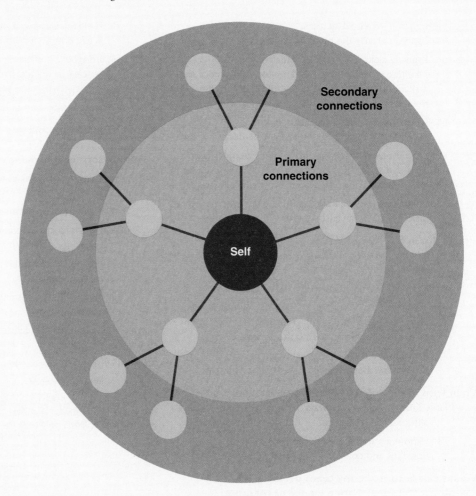

1.3 Effective Managers

OBJECTIVES

1. To better understand what behaviors contribute to effective management.

2. To conceive a ranking of critical behaviors that you personally believe reflects their importance to your success as a manager.

INSTRUCTIONS

1. Following is a partial list of behaviors in which managers may engage. Rank these items in terms of their importance for ef-

fective performance as a manager. Put a 1 next to the item that you think is most important, 2 for the next most important, down to 10 for the least important.

2. Bring your rankings to class. Be prepared to justify your results and rationale. If you can add any behaviors to this list that might lead to success or greater management effectiveness, write them in.

Effective Managers Worksheet

_____ Communicates and interprets policy so that it is understood by the members of the organization.

_____ Makes prompt and clear decisions.

_____ Assigns subordinates to the jobs for which they are best suited.

_____ Encourages associates to submit ideas and plans.

_____ Stimulates subordinates by means of competition among employees.

_____ Seeks means of improving management capabilities and competence.

_____ Fully supports and carries out company policies.

_____ Participates in community activities as opportunities arise.

_____ Is neat in appearance.

_____ Is honest in all matters pertaining to company property or funds.

SOURCE: Excerpted from Lawrence R. Jauch, Arthur G. Bedeian, Sally A. Coltrin, and William F. Glueck, _The Managerial Experience: Cases, Exercises, and Readings_, 5th ed. Copyright © 1989. Reprinted with permission of South-Western, a division of Thomson Learning, www.thomson-rights.com.

1.4 Career Planning

OBJECTIVES

1. To explore your career thinking.
2. To visualize your ideal job in terms as concrete as possible.
3. To summarize the state of your career planning, and to become conscious of the main questions you have about it at this point.

INSTRUCTIONS

Read the instructions for each activity, reflect on them, and then write your response. Be as brief or extensive as you like.

Career Planning Worksheet

1. Describe your ideal occupation in terms of responsibilities, skills, and how you would know if you were successful.

_____
_____
_____
_____
_____
_____
_____
_____
_____

2. Identify 10 statements you can make today about your current career planning. Identify 10 questions you need answered for career planning

10 statements

1._____
_____
_____

2._____
_____
_____

3._____
_____
_____

4._____
_____
_____

5._____
_____
_____

6._____
_____
_____

10 questions

1._____
_____
_____

2._____
_____
_____

3._____
_____
_____

4._____
_____
_____

5._____
_____
_____

6._____
_____
_____

7._____

_____

_____

8._____

_____

_____

9._____

_____

_____

10._____

_____

_____

7._____

_____

_____

8._____

_____

_____

9._____

_____

_____

10._____

_____

_____

The Evolution of Management

For thousands of years, managers have wrestled with the same issues and problems confronting executives today. Around 1100 B.C., the Chinese practiced the four management functions—planning, organizing, leading, and controlling—discussed in Chapter 1. Between 400 B.C. and 350 B.C., the Greeks recognized management as a separate art and advocated a scientific approach to work. The Romans decentralized the management of their vast empire before the birth of Christ. During medieval times, the Venetians standardized production through the use of an assembly line, building warehouses and using an inventory system to monitor the contents.[1]

But throughout history most managers operated strictly on a trial-and-error basis. The challenges of the industrial revolution changed that. Management emerged as a formal discipline at the turn of the century. The first university programs to offer management and business education, the Wharton School at the University of Pennsylvania and the Amos Tuck School at Dartmouth, were founded in the late 19th century. By 1914, 25 business schools existed.[2]

Thus, the management profession as we know it today is relatively new. This appendix explores the roots of modern management theory. Understanding the origins of management thought will help you grasp the underlying contexts of the ideas and concepts presented in the chapters ahead.

Although this appendix is titled "The Evolution of Management," it might be more appropriately called "The Revolutions of Management," because it documents the wide swings in management approaches over the last 100 years. Out of the great variety of ideas about how to improve management, parts of each approach have survived and been incorporated into modern perspectives on management. Thus, the legacy of past efforts, triumphs, and failures has become our guide to future management practice.

EARLY MANAGEMENT CONCEPTS AND INFLUENCES

Communication and transportation constraints hindered the growth of earlier businesses. Therefore, improvements in management techniques did not substantially improve performance. However, the industrial revolution changed that. As companies grew and became more complex, minor improvements in management tactics produced impressive increases in production quantity and quality.[3]

The emergence of **economies of scale**—reductions in the average cost of a unit of production as the total volume produced increases—drove managers to strive for further growth. The opportunities for mass production created by the industrial revolution spawned intense and systematic thought about management problems and issues—particularly efficiency, production processes, and cost savings.[4]

Figure A.1 provides a timeline depicting the evolution of management thought through the decades. This historical perspective is divided into two major sections: classical approaches and contemporary approaches. Many of these approaches overlapped as they developed, and they often had a significant impact on one another. Some approaches were a direct reaction to the perceived deficiencies of previous approaches. Others developed as the needs and issues confronting managers changed over the years. All the approaches attempted to explain the real issues facing managers and provide them with tools to solve future problems.

Figure A.1 will reinforce your understanding of the key relationships among the approaches and place each perspective in its historical context.

The oldest company on the *Fortune* 500 list is the Bank of New York, founded in 1784 by Alexander Hamilton. The oldest industrial company is DuPont, begun in 1802 after E. I. du Pont fled persecution during the French Revolution.[5]

CLASSICAL APPROACHES

The classical period extended from the mid-19th century through the early 1950s. The major approaches that emerged during this period were systematic management, scientific management, administrative management, human relations, and bureaucracy.

Systematic Management During the 19th century, growth in U.S. business centered on manufacturing.[6] Early writers such as Adam Smith believed the management of these firms was chaotic, and their ideas helped to systematize it. Most organizational tasks were subdivided and performed by specialized labor. However, poor coordination caused frequent problems and breakdowns of the manufacturing process.

FIGURE A.1
The Evolution of Management Thought

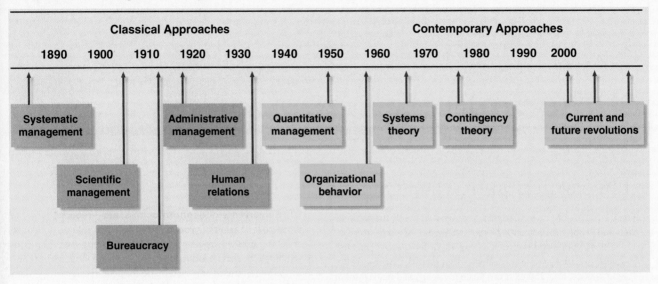

The **systematic management** approach attempted to build specific procedures and processes into operations to ensure coordination of effort. Systematic management emphasized economical operations, adequate staffing, maintenance of inventories to meet consumer demand, and organizational control. These goals were achieved through:

- Careful definition of duties and responsibilities.
- Standardized techniques for performing these duties.
- Specific means of gathering, handling, transmitting, and analyzing information.
- Cost accounting, wage, and production control systems to facilitate internal coordination and communications.

Systematic management emphasized internal operations because managers were concerned primarily with meeting the explosive growth in demand brought about by the industrial revolution. In addition, managers were free to focus on internal issues of efficiency, in part because the government did not constrain business practices significantly. Finally, labor was poorly organized. As a result, many managers were oriented more toward things than toward people.

Systematic management did not address all the issues 19th-century managers faced, but it tried to raise managers' awareness about the most pressing concerns of their job.

An Early Labor Contract

The following rules, taken from the records of Cocheco Company, were typical of labor contract provisions in the 1850s.

1. The hours of work shall be from sunrise to sunset, from the 21st of March to the 20th of September inclusively; and from sunrise until eight o'clock, P.M., during the remainder of the year. One hour shall be allowed for dinner, and half an hour for breakfast during the first mentioned six months; and one hour for dinner during the other half of the year; on Saturdays, the mill shall be stopped one hour before sunset, for the purpose of cleaning the machinery.

2. Every hand coming to work a quarter of an hour after the mill has been started shall be docked a quarter of a day; and every hand absenting him or herself, without absolute necessity, shall be docked in a sum double the amount of the wages such hand shall have earned during the time of such absence. No more than one hand is allowed to leave any one of the rooms at the same time—a quarter of a day shall be deducted for every breach of this rule.

3. No smoking or spiritous liquors shall be allowed in the factory under any pretense whatsoever. It is also forbidden to carry into the factory, nuts, fruits, etc., books, or papers during the hours of work.

SOURCE: W. Sullivan, "The Industrial Revolution and the Factory Operative in Pennsylvania," *The Pennsylvania Magazine of History and Biography* 78 (1954), pp. 478–79.

Production costs dropped as mass manufacturing lowered unit costs. Thus economies of scale was born, a concept that persists in the modern manufacturing era.

Scientific Management Systematic management failed to lead to widespread production efficiency. This shortcoming became apparent to a young engineer named Frederick Taylor, who was hired by Midvale Steel Company in 1878. Taylor discovered that production and pay were poor, inefficiency and waste were prevalent, and most companies had tremendous unused potential. He concluded that management decisions were unsystematic and that no research to determine the best means of production existed.

In response, Taylor introduced a second approach to management, known as **scientific management.**[7] This approach advocated the application of scientific methods to analyze work and to determine how to complete production tasks efficiently. For example, U.S. Steel's contract with the United Steel Workers of America specified that sand shovelers should move 12.5 shovelfuls per minute; shovelfuls should average 15 pounds of river sand composed of 5.5 percent moisture.[8]

Taylor identified four principles of scientific management:

1. Management should develop a precise, scientific approach for each element of one's work to replace general guidelines.

2. Management should scientifically select, train, teach, and develop each worker so that the right person has the right job.

3. Management should cooperate with workers to ensure that jobs match plans and principles.

4. Management should ensure an appropriate division of work and responsibility between managers and workers.

To implement this approach, Taylor used techniques such as time-and-motion studies. With this technique, a task was divided into its basic movements, and different motions were timed to determine the most efficient way to complete the task.

After the "one best way" to perform the job was identified, Taylor stressed the importance of hiring and training the proper worker to do that job. Taylor advocated the standardization of tools, the use of instruction cards to help workers, and breaks to eliminate fatigue.

Another key element of Taylor's approach was the use of the differential piecerate system. Taylor assumed workers were motivated by receiving money. Therefore, he implemented a pay system in which workers were paid additional wages when they exceeded a standard level of output for each job. Taylor concluded that both workers and management would benefit from such an approach.

Scientific management principles were widely embraced. Other proponents, including Henry Gantt and Frank and Lillian Gilbreth, introduced many refinements and techniques for applying scientific management on the factory floor. One of the most famous examples of the application of scientific management is the factory Henry Ford built to produce the Model T.[9]

The legacy of Taylor's scientific management approach is broad and pervasive. Most important, productivity and efficiency in manufacturing improved dramatically. The concepts of scientific methods

Scientific Management and the Model-T

At the turn of the century, automobiles were a luxury that only the wealthy could afford. They were assembled by craftspeople who put an entire car together at one spot on the factory floor. These workers were not specialized, and Henry Ford believed they wasted time and energy bringing the needed parts to the car. Ford took a revolutionary approach to automobile manufacturing by using scientific management principles.

After much study, machines and workers in Ford's new factory were placed in sequence so that an automobile could be assembled without interruption along a moving production line. Mechanical energy and a conveyor belt were used to take the work to the workers.

The manufacture of parts likewise was revolutionized. For example, formerly it had taken one worker 20 minutes to assemble a flywheel magneto. By splitting the job into 29 different operations, putting the product on a mechanical conveyor, and changing the height of the conveyor, Ford cut production time to 5 minutes.

By 1914 chassis assembly time had been trimmed from almost 13 hours to 1½ hours. The new methods of production required complete standardization, new machines, and an adaptable labor force. Costs dropped significantly, the Model-T became the first car accessible to the majority of Americans, and Ford dominated the industry for many years.

SOURCE: H. Kroos and C. Gilbert, *The Principles of Scientific Management* (New York: Harper & Row, 1911).

Frederick Taylor (left) and Dr. Lillian Gilbreth (right) were early experts in management efficiency.

and research were introduced to manufacturing. The piecerate system gained wide acceptance because it more closely aligned effort and reward. Taylor also emphasized the need for cooperation between management and workers. And the concept of a management specialist gained prominence.

> ✳ The first female executive to head a company on the *Fortune* 500 list was Katharine Graham of *The Washington Post* (first listed in 1972).[10]

Despite these gains, not everyone was convinced that scientific management was the best solution to all business problems. First, critics claimed that Taylor ignored many job-related social and psychological factors by emphasizing only money as a worker incentive. Second, production tasks were reduced to a set of routine, machinelike procedures that led to boredom, apathy, and quality control problems. Third, unions strongly opposed scientific management techniques because they believed management might abuse their power to set the standards and the piecerates, thus exploiting workers and diminishing their importance. Finally, although scientific management resulted in intense scrutiny of the internal efficiency of organizations, it did not help managers deal with broader external issues such as competitors and government regulations, especially at the senior management level.

Administrative Management The **administrative management** approach emphasized the perspective of senior managers within the organization, and argued that management was a profession and could be taught.

An explicit and broad framework for administrative management emerged in 1916, when Henri Fayol, a French mining engineer and executive, published a book summarizing his management experiences. Fayol identified five functions and 14 principles of management. The five functions, which are very similar to the four functions discussed in Chapter 1, include planning, organizing, commanding, coordinating, and controlling. Table A.1 lists and defines the 14 principles. Although some critics claim Fayol treated the principles as universal truths for management, he actually wanted them applied flexibly.[11]

A host of other executives contributed to the administrative management literature. These writers discussed a broad spectrum of management topics, including the social responsibilities of management, the philosophy of management, clarification of business terms and concepts, and organizational principles. Chester Barnard's and Mary Parker Follet's contributions have become classic works in this area.[12]

Barnard, former president of New Jersey Bell Telephone Company, published his landmark book *The Functions of the Executive* in 1938. He outlined the role of the senior executive: formulating the purpose of the organization, hiring key individuals, and maintaining organizational communications.[13] Mary Parker Follet's 1942 book *Dynamic Organization* extended Barnard's work by emphasizing the continually changing situations that managers face.[14] Two of her key contributions—the notion that managers desire flexibility and the differences between motivating groups and individuals—laid the groundwork for the modern contingency approach discussed later in the chapter.

TABLE A.1
Fayol's 14 Principles of Management

1. *Division of work*—divide work into specialized tasks and assign responsibilities to specific individuals.
2. *Authority*—delegate authority along with responsibility.
3. *Discipline*—make expectations clear and punish violations.
4. *Unity of command*—each employee should be assigned to only one supervisor.
5. *Unity of direction*—employees' efforts should be focused on achieving organizational objectives.
6. *Subordination of individual interest to the general interest*—the general interest must predominate.
7. *Remuneration*—systematically reward efforts that support the organization's direction.
8. *Centralization*—determine the relative importance of superior and subordinate roles.
9. *Scalar chain*—keep communications within the chain of command.
10. *Order*—order jobs and material so they support the organization's direction.
11. *Equity*—fair discipline and order enhance employee commitment.
12. *Stability and tenure of personnel*—promote employee loyalty and longevity.
13. *Initiative*—encourage employees to act on their own in support of the organization's direction.
14. *Esprit de corps*—promote a unity of interests between employees and management.

All the writings in the administrative management area emphasize management as a profession along with fields such as law and medicine. In addition, these authors offered many recommendations based on their personal experiences, which often included managing large corporations. Although these perspectives and recommendations were considered sound, critics noted that they might not work in all settings. Different types of personnel, industry conditions, and technologies may affect the appropriateness of these principles.

> **1955** Ray Kroc's first McDonald's opens. Bill Gates and Steve Jobs are born.[15]

Human Relations A fourth approach to management, **human relations,** developed during the 1930s. This approach aimed at understanding how psychological and social processes interact with the work situation to influence performance. Human relations was the first major approach to emphasize informal work relationships and worker satisfaction.

This approach owes much to other major schools of thought. For example, many of the ideas of the Gilbreths (scientific management) and Barnard and Follet (administrative management) influenced the development of human relations from 1930 to 1955. In fact, human relations emerged from a research project that began as a scientific management study.

Western Electric Company, a manufacturer of communications equipment, hired a team of Harvard researchers led by Elton Mayo and Fritz Roethlisberger. They were to investigate the influence of physical working conditions on workers' productivity and efficiency in one of the company's factories outside Chicago. This research project, known as the *Hawthorne Studies,* provided some of the most interesting and controversial results in the history of management.[16]

The Hawthorne Studies were a series of experiments conducted from 1924 to 1932. During the first stage of the project (the Illumination Experiments), various working conditions, particularly the lighting in the factory, were altered to determine the effects of those changes on productivity. The researchers found no systematic relationship between the factory lighting and production levels. In some cases, productivity continued to increase even when the illumination was reduced to the level of moonlight. The researchers concluded that the workers performed and reacted differently because the researchers were observing them. This reaction is known as the **Hawthorne Effect.**

This conclusion led the researchers to believe productivity may be affected more by psychological and social factors than by physical or objective influences. With this thought in mind, they initiated the other four stages of the project. During these stages, the researchers performed various work group experiments and had extensive interviews with employees. Mayo and his team eventually concluded that productivity and employee behavior were influenced by the informal work group.

Human relations proponents argued that managers should stress primarily employee welfare, motivation, and communication. They believed social needs had precedence over economic needs. Therefore, management must gain the cooperation of the group and promote job satisfaction and group norms consistent with the goals of the organization.

Another noted contributor to the field of human relations was Abraham Maslow.[17] In 1943, Maslow suggested that humans have five levels of needs. The most basic needs are the physical needs for food, water, and shelter; the most advanced need is for self-actualization, or personal fulfillment. Maslow argued that people try to satisfy their lower-level needs and then progress upward to the higher-level needs. Managers can facilitate this process and achieve organizational goals by removing obstacles and encouraging behaviors that satisfy people's needs and organizational goals simultaneously.

Although the human relations approach generated research into leadership, job attitudes, and group dynamics, it drew heavy criticism.[18] Critics believed that one result of human relations—a belief that a happy worker was a productive worker—was too simplistic. While scientific management overemphasized the economic and formal aspects of the workplace, human relations ignored the more rational side of the worker and the important characteristics of the formal organization. However, human relations was a significant step in the development of management thought, because it prompted

A Human Relations Pioneer

In 1837, William Procter, a ruined English retailer, and James Gamble, son of a Methodist minister, formed a partnership in Cincinnati to make soap and candles. Both were known for their integrity, and soon their business was thriving.

By 1883, the business had grown substantially. When William Cooper Procter, grandson of the founder, left Princeton University to work for the firm, he wanted to learn the business from the ground up. He started working on the factory floor. "He did every menial job from shoveling rosin and soap to pouring fatty mixtures into crutchers. He brought his lunch in a paper bag . . . and sat on the floor [with the other workers] and ate with them, learning their feelings about work."

By 1884, Cooper Procter believed, from his own experience, that increasing workers' psychological commitment to the company would lead to higher productivity. His passion to increase employee commitment to the firm led him to propose a scandalous plan: share profits with workers to increase their sense of responsibility and job satisfaction. The surprise was audible on the first "Dividend Day," when workers held checks equivalent to seven weeks' pay.

Still, the plan was not complete. Workers saw the profit sharing as extra pay rather than as an incentive to improve. In addition, Cooper Procter recognized that a fundamental issue for the workers, some of whom continued to be his good friends, was the insecurity of old age. Public incorporation in 1890 gave Procter a new idea. After trying several versions, by 1903 he had discovered a way to meet all his goals for labor: a stock purchase plan. For every dollar a worker invested in P&G stock, the company would contribute four dollars' worth of stock.

Finally, Cooper Procter had resolved some key issues for labor that paid off in worker loyalty, improved productivity, and an increasing corporate reputation for caring and integrity. He went on to become CEO of the firm, and P&G today remains one of the most admired corporations in the United States.

SOURCES: O. Schisgall, *Eyes on Tomorrow* (Chicago: J. G. Ferguson, 1981): T. Welsh, "Best and Worst Corporate Reputations," *Fortune,* February 7, 1994, pp. 58–66.

managers and researchers to consider the psychological and social factors that influence performance.

Bureaucracy   Max Weber, a German sociologist, lawyer, and social historian, showed how management itself could be more efficient and consistent in his book *The Theory of Social and Economic Organizations.*[19] The ideal model for management, according to Weber, is the **bureaucracy** approach.

Weber believed bureaucratic structures can eliminate the variability that results when managers in the same organization have different skills, experiences, and goals. Weber advocated that the jobs themselves be standardized so that personnel changes would not disrupt the organization. He emphasized a structured, formal network of relationships among specialized positions in an organization. Rules and regulations standardize behavior, and authority resides in positions rather than in individuals. As a result, the organization need not rely on a particular individual, but will realize efficiency and success by following the rules in a routine and unbiased manner.

 1962   The first Wal-Mart store opens in Rogers, Arkansas.
1964   Blue Ribbon Sports ships its first shoes. It's now called Nike.
1969   Don and Doris Fisher open the first Gap store in San Francisco.

According to Weber, bureaucracies are especially important because they allow large organizations to perform the many routine activities necessary for their survival. Also, bureaucratic positions foster specialized skills, eliminating many subjective judgments by managers. In addition, if the rules and controls are established properly, bureaucracies should be unbiased in their treatment of people, both customers and employees.

Many organizations today are bureaucratic. Bureaucracy can be efficient and productive. However, bureaucracy is not the appropriate model for every organization. Organizations or departments that need rapid decision making and flexibility may suffer under a bureaucratic approach. Some people may not perform their best with excessive bureaucratic rules and procedures.

Other shortcomings stem from a faulty execution of bureaucratic principles rather than from the approach itself. Too much authority may be vested in too few people; the procedures may become the ends rather than the means; or managers may ignore appropriate rules and regulations. Finally, one advantage of a bureaucracy—its permanence—can also be a problem. Once a bureaucracy is established, dismantling it is very difficult.

CONTEMPORARY APPROACHES

The contemporary approaches to management include quantitative management, organizational behavior, systems theory, and the contingency perspective. The contemporary approaches have developed at various times since World War II, and they continue to represent the cornerstones of modern management thought.

Quantitative Management   Although Taylor introduced the use of science as a management tool early in the 20th century, most organizations did not adopt the use of quantitative techniques for management problems until the 1940s and 1950s.[20] During World War II, military planners began to apply mathematical techniques to defense and logistic problems. After the war, private corporations began assembling teams of quantitative experts to tackle many of the complex issues confronting large organizations. This approach, referred to as **quantitative management,** emphasizes the application of quantitative analysis to management decisions and problems.

Quantitative management helps a manager make a decision by developing formal mathematical models of the problem. Computers facilitated the development of specific quantitative methods. These include such techniques as statistical decision theory, linear programming, queuing theory, simulation, forecasting, inventory modeling, network modeling, and break-even analysis. Organizations apply these techniques in many areas, including production, quality control, marketing, human resources, finance, distribution, planning, and research and development.

Despite the promise quantitative management holds, managers do not rely on these methods as the primary approach to decision making. Typically they use these techniques as a supplement or tool in the decision process. Many managers will use results that are consistent with their experience, intuition, and judgment, but they often reject results that contradict their beliefs. Also, managers may use the process to compare alternatives and eliminate weaker options.

Several explanations account for the limited use of quantitative management. Many managers have not been trained in using these techniques. Also, many aspects of a management decision cannot be expressed through mathematical symbols and formulas. Finally, many of the decisions managers face are nonroutine and unpredictable.

1971   Intel introduces the first microprocessor and IBM introduces the floppy disk.
1976   Steve Jobs and Steve Wozniak start Apple Computer in their garage.

Organizational Behavior   During the 1950s, a transition took place in the human relations approach. Scholars began to recognize that worker productivity and organizational success are based on more than the satisfaction of economic or social needs. The revised perspective, known as **organizational behavior,** studies and identifies management activities that promote employee effectiveness through an understanding of the complex nature of individual, group, and organizational processes. Organizational behavior draws from a variety of disciplines, including psychology and sociology, to explain the behavior of people on the job.

During the 1960s, organizational behaviorists heavily influenced the field of management. Douglas McGregor's Theory X and Theory Y marked the transition from human relations.[21] According to McGregor, Theory X managers assume workers are lazy and irresponsible and require constant supervision and external motivation to achieve organizational goals. Theory Y managers assume employees *want* to work and can direct and control themselves. McGregor advocated a Theory Y perspective, suggesting that managers who encourage participation and allow opportunities for individual challenge and initiative would achieve superior performance.

Other major organizational behaviorists include Chris Argyris, who recommended greater autonomy and better jobs for workers,[22] and Rensis Likert, who stressed the value of participative management.[23] Through the years, organizational behavior has consistently emphasized development of the organization's human resources to achieve individual and organizational goals. Like other approaches, it has been criticized for its limited perspective, although more recent contributions have a broader and more situational viewpoint. In the past few years, many of the primary issues addressed by organizational behavior have experienced a rebirth with a greater interest in leadership, employee involvement, and self-management.

1980   Microsoft licenses its operating system to IBM.
1981   MTV launches on cable.
1995   Netscape goes public and kicks off the dot-com boom.

Systems Theory   The classical approaches as a whole were criticized because they (1) ignored the relationship between the organization and its external environment, and (2) usually stressed one aspect of the organization or its employees at the expense of other considerations. In response to these criticisms, management scholars during the 1950s stepped back from the details of the organization to attempt to understand it as a whole system. These efforts were based on a general scientific approach called **systems theory.**[24] Organizations are open systems, dependent on inputs from the outside world, such as raw materials, human resources, and capital. They transform these inputs into outputs that (ideally) meet the market's needs for goods and services. The environment reacts to the outputs through a feedback loop; this feedback provides input for the next cycle of the system. The process repeats itself for the life of the system, and is illustrated in Figure A. 2.

Systems theory also emphasizes that an organization is one system in a series of subsystems. For instance, Southwest Airlines is a subsystem of the airline industry and the flight crews are a subsystem of Southwest. Systems theory points out that each subsystem is a component of the whole and is interdependent with other subsystems.

Contingency Perspective   Building on systems theory ideas, the **contingency perspective** refutes universal principles of management by stating that a variety of factors, both internal and external to the firm, may affect the organization's performance.[25] Therefore, there is no "one best way" to manage and organize, because circumstances vary.

Situational characteristics are called **contingencies.** Understanding contingencies helps a manager know which sets of circumstances dictate which management actions. You will learn recommendations for the major contingencies throughout this text. The contingencies include

1. Circumstances in the organization's external environment.

2. The internal strengths and weaknesses of the organization.

3. The values, goals, skills, and attitudes of managers and workers in the organization.

4. The types of tasks, resources, and technologies the organization uses.

With an eye to these contingencies, a manager may categorize the situation and then choose the proper competitive strategy, organization structure, or management process for the circumstances.

Researchers continue to identify key contingency variables and their effects on management issues. As you read the topics covered in each chapter, you will notice similarities and differences among management situations and the appropriate responses. This perspective should represent a cornerstone of your own approach to management. Many of the things you will learn about throughout this course apply a contingency perspective.

2000   AOL becomes the first pure Internet company to make the *Fortune* 500 list and merges with Time Warner the same year.
2001   Enron files for bankruptcy.
2002   United Airlines files for bankruptcy.
2003   AOL Time Warner posts a record $98.7 billion loss[26.]

AN EYE ON THE FUTURE

All of these historical perspectives have left legacies that affect contemporary management thought and practice. Their undercurrents continue to flow, even as the context and the specifics change.

Times do pass, and things do change. This may sound obvious, but it isn't to those managers who sit by idly while their firms fail to adapt to changing times. Business becomes global. New technologies change how we work, produce goods, and deliver services. Change continually creates both new opportunities and new demands for lowering costs and for achieving greater innovation, quality, and speed. Management knowledge and practices evolve accordingly.

The essential facts about change are these: First, change is happening more rapidly and dramatically than at any other time in history. Second, if you don't anticipate change and adapt to it, you and your firm will not thrive in a competitive business world. The theme of change—what is happening now, what lies ahead, how it

FIGURE A.2

Open-System Perspective of an Organization

EXTERNAL ENVIRONMENT

| Raw materials
Human resources
Energy
Financial resources
Information
Equipment | → Inputs → | **Organization**
Transformation process | → Outputs → | Goods
Services |

affects management, and how you can deal with it—permeates this entire book.

What are the implications of these changes for you and your career? How can you best be ready to meet the challenges? You must ask questions about the future, anticipate changes, know your responsibilities, and be prepared to meet them head-on. We hope you study the remaining chapters with these goals in mind.

KEY TERMS

administrative management A classical management approach that attempted to identify major principles and functions that managers could use to achieve superior organizational performance, p. 38.

bureaucracy A classical management approach emphasizing a structured, formal network of relationships among specialized positions in the organization, p. 39.

contingencies Factors that determine the appropriateness of managerial actions, p. 41.

contingency perspective An approach to the study of management proposing that the managerial strategies, structures, and processes that result in high performance depend on the characteristics, or important contingencies, or the situation in which they are applied, p. 41.

economies of scale Reductions in the average cost of a unit of production as the total volume produces increases, p. 35.

Hawthorne Effect People's reactions to being observed or studied resulting in superficial rather than meaningful changes in behavior, p. 39.

human relations A classical management approach that attempted to understand and explain how human psychological and social processes interact with the formal aspects of the work situation to influence performance, p. 38.

organizational behavior A contemporary management approach that studies and identifies management activities that promote employee effectiveness by examining the complex and dynamic nature of individual, group, and organizational processes, p. 40.

quantitative management A contemporary management approach that emphasizes the application of quantitative analysis to managerial decisions and problems, p. 40.

scientific management A classical management approach that applied scientific methods to analyze and determine the "one best way" to complete production tasks, p. 37.

systematic management A classical management approach that attempted to build into operations the specific procedures and processes that would ensure coordination of effort to achieve established goals and plans, p. 36.

systems theory A theory stating that an organization is a managed system that changes inputs into outputs, p. 41.

DISCUSSION QUESTIONS

1. How does today's business world compare with the one of 40 years ago? What is different about today, and what is not so different?

2. What is scientific management? How might today's organizations use it?

3. Table A.3 lists Fayol's 14 principles of management, first published in 1916. Are they as useful today as they were then? Why or why not? *When* are they most, and least, useful?

4. What are the advantages and disadvantages of a bureaucratic organization?

5. In what situations are quantitative management concepts and tools applicable?

6. Choose any organization and describe its system of inputs and outputs.

7. Why did the contingency perspective become such an important approach to management? Generate a list of contingencies that might affect the decisions you make in your life or as a manager.

8. For each of the management approaches discussed in the chapter, give examples you have seen. How effective or ineffective were they?

9. The margins in the appendix highlighted a few landmark events in recent business history. What additional landmarks during those decades would you include?

10. The final landmark was from 2003—what are the most important landmarks since then, and why?

Experiential Exercises

A.1 Approaches to Management

OBJECTIVES

1. To help you conceive a wide variety of management approaches.
2. To clarify the appropriateness of different management approaches in different situations.

INSTRUCTIONS

Your instructor will divide your class randomly into groups of four to six people each. Acting as a team, with everyone offering ideas and one person serving as official recorder, each group will be responsible for writing a one-page memo to your present class. Subject matter of your group's memo will be "My advice for managing people today is . . ." The fun part of this exercise (and

its creative element) involves writing the memo from the viewpoint of the person assigned to your group by your instructor.

Among the memo viewpoints your instructor may assign are:

- An ancient Egyptian slave master (building the great pyramids)
- Henri Fayol
- Frederick Taylor
- Mary Parker Follett
- Douglas McGregor
- A contingency management theorist
- A Japanese auto company executive
- The chief executive officer of IBM in the year 2030
- Commander of the Starship Enterprise II in the year 3001
- Others, as assigned by your instructor

Use your imagination, make sure everyone participates, and try to be true to any historical facts you've encountered. Attempt to be as specific and realistic as possible. Remember, the idea is to provide advice about managing people from another point in time (or from a particular point of view at the present time).

Make sure you manage your 20-minute time limit carefully. A recommended approach is to spend 2 to 3 minutes putting the exercise into proper perspective. Next, take about 10 to 12 min-utes brainstorming ideas for your memo, with your recorder jotting down key ideas and phrases. Have your recorder use the remaining time to write your group's one-page memo, with constructive comments and help from the others. Pick a spokesperson to read your group's memo to the class.

SOURCE: R. Krietner and A. Kinicki, *Organization Behavior,* 3d ed. (Burr Ridge, IL: Richard D. Irwin, 1994), pp. 30–31.

A.2 The University Grading System Analysis

OBJECTIVES

1. To learn to identify the components of a complex system.
2. To better understand organizations as systems.
3. To visualize how a change in policy affects the functioning of an organization system.

INSTRUCTIONS

1. Assume that your university has decided to institute a pass–fail system of grading instead of the letter-grade system it presently has. Apply the systems perspective learned from this chapter to understanding this decision.

2. Answer the questions on the Grading System Analysis Worksheet individually, or in small groups, as directed by your instructor.

DISCUSSION QUESTIONS

Share your own or your group's responses with the entire class. Then answer the following questions.

1. Did you diagram the system in the same way?
2. Did you identify the same system components?
3. Which subsystems will be affected by the change?
4. How do you explain differences in your responses?

Grading System Analysis Worksheet

DESCRIPTION

1. What subsystems compose the system (the university)? Diagram the system.

_____

_____

_____

2. Identify in this system: inputs, outputs, transformations.

_____

_____

_____

DIAGNOSIS

3. Which of the subsystems will be affected by the change; that is, what changes are likely to occur throughout the system as a result of the policy change?

_____

_____

_____

SOURCE: J. Gordon, A *Diagnostic Approach to Organizational Behavior* (Englewood Cliffs, NJ: Prentice-Hall, 1983), p. 38. Reprinted with permission of Prentice-Hall, Inc., Englewood Cliffs, NJ.

Chapter **2**

CHAPTER 2

The External Environment and Organizational Culture

The essence of a business is outside itself.

—Peter Drucker

LEARNING OBJECTIVES

After studying Chapter 2, you will know:

1. How environmental forces influence organizations, as well as how organizations can influence their environments.

2. How to make a distinction between the macroenvironment and the competitive environment.

3. Why managers and organizations should attend to economic and social developments.

4. How to analyze the competitive environment.

5. How organization's respond to environmental uncertainty.

6. How an organization's culture affects its response to its environment.

TELECOM MANAGERS FIGHT FOR MARKET SHARE

As recently as the early 1980s, Americans who wanted to talk over the phone dealt essentially with one company—AT&T—which owned both long-distance and local telephone companies. Managers at that company operated for years in a heavily regulated, low-competition, predictable business climate. Rates were set less by the market than by government-approved formulas. But court cases and efforts by the Federal Communications Commission (FCC) to deregulate the industry required AT&T in 1984 to *divest*, or sell off, its local telephone business. That change opened the market to aggressive new entrants. Other rulings since that time have accelerated the trend toward deregulation.

Today, a manager at a newer telecom company like Sprint, Nextel, or Verizon, or at any of the Baby Bells (the regional telephone companies AT&T divested), is operating in an environment light-years removed from the calm telecom climate of the early 1980s. Now several players—and several technologies—are competing aggressively for business. Which will win and which will lose is far from clear. Every company offers local and long-distance telephone service, with some (like BellSouth) offering land lines, others (like Cingular) offering wireless, and others (like Verizon) offering both. And executives at Internet and cable companies (like Time Warner Cable) are elbowing into the business as well. Voice-over Internet Protocol (VoIP) is a technology that allows users to make phone calls over a high-speed Internet connection, like a cable or DSL line. Cable executives have already made this technology available in several areas of the country—in some cases free to their cable subscribers.

All of this activity is good news for consumers. They have many options for their personal and business communication needs, with prices and features that worldwide competition keeps affordable. New options and services are constantly emerging. But for telecom managers, their business environment is filled with risk, as a number of aggressive companies, and a number of different technologies, compete intensely for market share.

So far, telecom managers have decided to compete in all types of services. They want to provide voice *and* data transmission, consumer *and* business applications, wireless *and* Internet service, and even video. And all are keeping prices low to maintain market share. Yet it's far from clear that every telecom has the size and financial depth to continue this strategy for long. Many industry observers believe that, as the industry shakes out, *mergers* (companies combining) and industry consolidation are inevitable.

Should telecom managers continue to compete across-the-board, taking the risk that they will be spread too thin? Should they merge with other telecom companies to strengthen their position? Or should they go for a lower market share but reduce their risk by focusing on high-growth and high-profit services? Telecom managers in an era of deregulation will have to find the right business model for the new environment of intense competition, uncertainty, and technological change.

Sources for Prologue and Connections: Jonathan Byrnes, "Airline Deregulation: Lessons for Telecom," *HBS Working Knowledge*, June 7, 2004; Jeff Kagan, "Telecom's Future," *Intele-Card News*, September 1, 2002; Jim Jubak, "Only Some Will Survive the Telecom Shakeout," *thestreet.com*, May 1, 2002.

Inputs

Outputs

Raw materials
Services
Equipment
Capital
Information
→
Organization
→
Products
Services

open systems

Organizations that are
affected by, and that affect,
their environment.

inputs

Goods and services
organizations take in and
use to create products or
services.

outputs

The products or services
organizations create.

external environment

All relevant forces outside a
firm's boundaries, such as
competitors, customers, the
government, and the
economy.

**competitive
environment**

The immediate
environment surrounding
a firm; includes suppliers,
customers, competitors,
and the like.

macroenvironment

The most general
environment; includes
governments, economic
conditions, and other
fundamental factors that
generally affect all
organizations.

The telecom companies mentioned in the Prologue are heavily influenced by factors outside their organizations, like competitors and changes in technology. In this chapter, we will discuss in detail how pressures from outside the organization help create the context in which managers and their companies must operate.

As we suggested in the first chapter, organizations are **open systems**—that is, they are affected by and in turn affect their external environments. For example, they take in **inputs** like goods or services from their environment and use them to create products or services that they **output** to their environment. (See Figure 2.1.) But when we use the term **external environment** here, we mean not only an organization's clients or customers, but *all* relevant forces outside the organization's boundaries.

Many of these factors are uncontrollable. Companies large and small are buffeted or battered by recession, government interference, competitors' actions, and so forth. But their lack of control does not mean that managers can ignore such forces, use them as excuses for poor performance, and try to just get by. Managers must stay abreast of external developments and react accordingly. Moreover, as we will discuss later in this chapter, it sometimes is possible to influence components of the external environment. We will examine ways in which organizations can do just that.

Figure 2.2 shows the external environment of a firm. The firm exists in its **competitive environment,** which is composed of the firm and competitors, suppliers, customers, new entrants, and substitutes. At the more general level is the **macroenvironment,** which includes legal, political, economic, technological, demographic, and social and natural factors that generally affect all organizations.

A Look Ahead

This chapter discusses the basic characteristics of an organization's environment and the importance of that environment for strategic management. We will also address the *internal environment,* or *culture,* of the organization, and how that culture may influence the organization's response to its environment. Later chapters will elaborate on many of the basic environmental forces introduced here. For example, technology will be discussed again in Chapter 17. The global environment gets a thorough treatment in Chapter 6, which is devoted entirely to international management. Other chapters focus on ethics, social responsibility, and the natural environment. Chapter 18 reiterates the theme that recurs throughout this text: Organizations must change continually because environments change continually.

The Macroenvironment

All organizations operate in a macroenvironment, which is defined by the most general elements in the external environment that potentially can influence strategic decisions. Although a top executive team may have unique internal strengths and ideas about its goals, it must consider external factors before taking action.

Laws and Regulations

U.S. government policies both impose strategic constraints and provide opportunities. For example, in the Prologue, we mentioned the Federal Communication Commis-

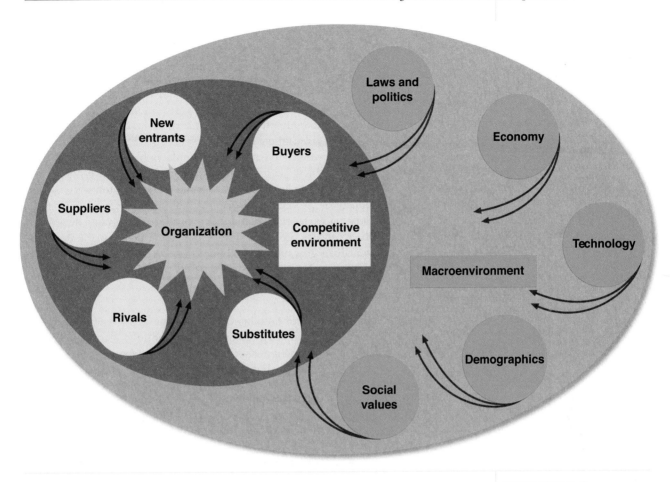

FIGURE 2.2
The External Environment

sion (FCC) and the profound effect it had on the telecom industry when it required AT&T to divest its local telephone business. In the 1970s and early 1980s, airline deregulation had a similarly powerful effect. New low-cost regional carriers, like Southwest Airlines, emerged to threaten the largest carriers' market share. Some of them (like Pan Am) even went bankrupt.

The government can affect business opportunities through tax laws, economic policies, and international trade rulings. An example of restraint on business action is the U.S. government's standards regarding bribery. In some countries, bribes and kickbacks are common and expected ways of doing business, but for U.S. firms these are illegal practices. Indeed, some U.S. businesses have been fined for using bribery when competing internationally.

Regulators are specific government organizations in a firm's more immediate task environment. Regulatory agencies such as the Occupational Safety and Health Administration (OSHA), the Interstate Commerce Commission (ICC), the Federal Aviation Administration (FAA), the Equal Employment Opportunity Commission (EEOC), the National Labor Relations Board (NLRB), the Office of Federal Contract Compliance Programs (OFCCP), and the Environmental Protection Agency (EPA) have the power to investigate company practices and take legal action to ensure compliance with the laws.

The Securities and Exchange Commission (SEC) regulates U.S. financial markets; since the insider-trading scandals, the SEC has changed investment houses' policies and practices dramatically. And the Food and Drug Administration (FDA) can prevent a company from selling an unsafe or ineffective product to the public.

Publicly traded pharmaceutical firms, for example, face regulation from the FDA, the SEC, and other government regulators. A study funded by the FDA found that some patients who took Merck's Vioxx, a highly profitable painkiller, had a greater risk of heart attacks. (A National Cancer Institute study found a similar effect for Pfizer's Celebrex.) Merck had to announce a worldwide withdrawal of its drug and its stock price fell sharply. The SEC and the Justice Department also launched separate inquiries into the matter.

In many cases, the corporate community sees government as an adversary. However, many organizations realize that government may be the source of competitive advantages for an individual company or an entire industry. For example, public policy may prevent or limit entry into an industry by new foreign or domestic competitors. Government may subsidize failing companies or provide tax breaks to some. Federal patents are used to protect innovative products or production process technologies. Legislation may be passed to support industry prices, thereby guaranteeing profits or survival. The government may also intervene to ensure the survival of certain key industries or companies. For example, government loan guarantees saved Chrysler Corporation from probable bankruptcy and gave it the opportunity to become a viable, profitable corporation.

The Economy

Although most Americans are used to thinking in terms of the U.S. economy, the economic environment is created by complex interconnections among the economies of different countries. Wall Street investment analysts begin their workday thinking not just about what the Dow Jones did yesterday but also about how the London and Tokyo exchanges did overnight. Growth and recessions occur worldwide as well as domestically.

With increased competition, managers must pay particular attention to costs.

The economic environment dramatically affects managers' ability to function effectively and influences their strategic choices. Interest and inflation rates affect the availability and cost of capital, the ability to expand, prices, costs, and consumer demand for products. Unemployment rates affect labor availability and the wages the firm must pay, as well as product demand. Steeply rising energy and health costs, and significantly increased spending on security after the events of September 11, 2001, have a great effect on companies' ability to hire and their cost of doing business. Changes in the value of the dollar on world exchanges may make American products cheaper or more expensive than their foreign competitors.

An important economic influence has centered on the stock market. Individuals and institutions looking for good returns had invested in promising companies, including start-ups and dot-coms. When technology-based firms during the 1990s provided better than 20 percent returns to investors, more individuals entered the capital markets (Figure 2.3). With the slide in technology stocks and the mistrust of corporate ac-

FIGURE 2.3
Twelve-Month Comparison of Stock Markets

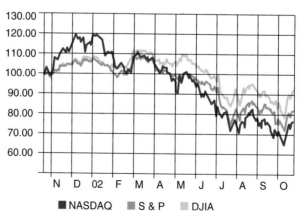

SOURCE: www.nasdaq.com.

counting, the returns fell to negative numbers in the early 2000s, although other economic indicators remained strong.[1]

We should add that the stock market may also have a profound effect on the behavior of individual managers. In publicly held companies, managers throughout the organization may feel required to meet Wall Street's earnings expectations. It is quite likely that you, too, at some point in your career, will be asked to improve a budget or estimate because your company does not want to disappoint "the Street." Such external pressures usually have a very positive effect—they help make many firms more efficient and profitable. But failure to meet those expectations can cause a company's stock price to drop, making it more difficult for the firm to raise additional capital for investment. The compensation of managers may also be affected, particularly if they have been issued stock options. The net effect may sometimes be that managers focus on short-term results at the expense of the long-term success of their organizations. Even worse, as was the case in the Enron scandal, a few managers may be tempted to engage in unethical or unlawful behavior in order to mislead investors. We will discuss managerial ethics in Chapter 5 and stock options in more detail in Chapter 10.[2]

Economic conditions change over time and are difficult to predict. Bull and bear markets come and go. Periods of dramatic growth may be followed by a recession. Every trend undoubtedly will end—but when? Even when times seem good, budget deficits or other considerations create concern about the future.

Technology

Today a company cannot succeed without incorporating into its strategy the astonishing technologies that exist and continue to evolve. Technological advances create new products, advanced production techniques, and better ways of managing and communicating. In addition, as technology evolves, new industries, markets, and competitive niches develop. For example, the advent of computers created a huge industry. Early entrants in biotechnology are trying to establish dominant positions, while later entrants work on technological advances that will give them a competitive niche. Advances in technology also permit companies to enter markets that would otherwise be unavailable to them. For example, the use of the Internet permits even small businesses to reach a much wider market, domestically and overseas. And, as we mentioned in our opening case, cable companies may leverage, or expand the use of, their cable technology to enter the telephone market.

In 2004, for the first time, sales of digital cameras were surpassed by sales of camera-equipped cell phones.

SOURCE: *The Wall Street Journal*, January 4, 2005, p. B11.

New technologies also provide new production techniques. In manufacturing, sophisticated robots perform jobs without suffering fatigue, requiring vacations or weekends off, or demanding wage increases. Until the U.S. steel industry began modernizing its plants, its productivity lagged far behind that of the technologically superior Japanese plants.

New technologies also provide new ways to manage and communicate. Computerized management information systems (MIS) make information available when needed. Computers monitor productivity and note performance deficiencies. Telecommunications allow conferences to take place without requiring people to travel to the same location. Consider the following discussion of how many companies are automating connections with their suppliers. As you can see, technological advances create innovations in business. Strategies developed around the cutting edge of technological advances create a competitive advantage; strategies that ignore or lag behind competitors in considering technology lead to obsolescence and extinction. This issue is so important that we devote an entire chapter (Chapter 17) to the topic.

Managers with ready access to information gain a significant competitive edge.

FROM THE PAGES OF ↓ # New Connections with Suppliers

BusinessWeek

One of the platitudes of the technology industry is that people overestimate the speed of adoption of new technologies in the short term but underestimate their long-term impact. That old saw could well turn out to be true when it comes to business-to-business (B2B) e-commerce.

Behind the scenes, the new technologies are quietly taking hold in Corporate America. Take Delphi Corp., the $27 billion-a-year auto-parts manufacturer that was spun off by General Motors in 1999. It has signed up as a member of Covisint, the carmakers' e-marketplace, and is running some software designed to improve collaboration with its suppliers. Little of Delphi's purchasing is done via the Web now, but David Nelson, vice-president for global purchasing and a procurement executive for the past 26 years, predicts that the majority will be online within half a decade.

"Over the next 5 to 10 years, American industry and industry all over the world will migrate and be highly connected all the way along the supply chain, from the customer back to mother earth. But it will be a slower process than people expected," Nelson predicts.

By replacing phone calls, faxes, and FedExes with Web connections, companies can save time and money on administrative tasks, can drive down prices, and can coordinate their operations with those of their suppliers—stripping out excess inventories all along the line.

However, many of the hurdles remain, too. Suppliers concerned about being squeezed by their customers have been reluctant to sign up for e-marketplaces controlled by industry consortiums. Corporations found it difficult to change the habits of their employees and get them to buy things online. And, for everybody involved, the costs of linking up technologies were sometimes prohibitive.

A lot of that is changing now—ever so gradually. Example: Wal-Mart. The retailing giant asked its 30,000 suppliers to start using Internet standards created for the retail industry to describe their products. That way, machines can match orders, inventories, and forecasts without human intervention. It's the first step to having the entire Wal-Mart ecosystem doing business online.

Suppliers—who historically have been loath to use online B2B technology because of the large extra investment it entails—are finally coming round, thanks to the demands of outfits such as the world's largest retailer. Other retailers, such as Target, Kmart, and Lowe's, are following suit.

The involvement of such heavyweights is especially significant because it's leading to the adoption of industrywide standards for online B2B, says Shawn Willett, an analyst at technology consultancy Current Analysis in Sterling, Va. The standards govern security and format of messages sent between buyers and sellers. They also provide for detailed descriptions of products—so buyers know exactly what they're purchasing. Such standardization is showing up first in the supercompetitive retail, health-care, and financial-services industries. And it will eventually allow suppliers to use a single B2B setup to deal with all types of customers.

SOURCES: Steve Hamm, "B2B Isn't Dead. It's Learning," *BusinessWeek*, December 18, 2002, online; Olga Kharif, "B2B, Take 2," *BusinessWeek*, November 25, 2003, online.

Demographics

demographics

Measures of various characteristics of the people who comprise groups or other social units.

Demographics are measures of various characteristics of the people comprising groups or other social units. Work groups, organizations, countries, markets, and societies can be described statistically by referring to their members' age, gender, family size, income, education, occupation, and so forth.

Managers must consider workforce demographics in formulating their human resources strategies. Population growth influences the size and composition of the labor force. By 2012, the U.S. civilian labor force, growing at a rate of 1.1 percent annually, is expected to reach approximately 162 million. The number of younger workers declined somewhat in recent decades, and many employers saw a shortage of entry-level workers. But the number of younger workers is expected to rise again as the children of the baby boom generation enter the workforce. At the same time the baby boomers are aging, and as they do the number of older workers (55 and above) will rise to about 19 percent of the labor force. Eventually, however, declining participation in work by older persons will require managers to find replacements for these highly experienced workers.

The education and skill levels of the workforce are another demographic factor managers must consider. For example, many companies find that they must invest heavily in training their entry-level workers, because they may not have been adequately prepared for some of the more complex tasks the modern workplace requires. (We discuss training in greater detail in Chapter 10.) Also, as education levels improve around the globe, more managers find that they are able to send even technical tasks to lower-priced but highly trained workers overseas. (We discuss this issue further in Chapter 6.)

Immigration is also a factor that significantly influences the U.S. population and labor force. Over the last decade immigrants have accounted for approximately 40 percent of the U.S. population growth, a trend that has an important impact on the labor force. Immigrants are frequently of working age but have different educational and occupational backgrounds from the rest of the labor force. By 2012, the labor force will be even more diverse than it is today. The biggest percentage employment increases will be by Asian-Americans and Hispanic or Latino populations, followed by African-Americans.

In the last quarter-century women joined the U.S. labor force in record numbers. In 1970, women made up only about one-third of the labor force. Today they make up a little over one-half. The professional training women receive has also increased markedly in recent years. Today, women make up about 30 percent of enrollment in MBA programs and about 50 percent of the enrollment in law and medical schools—figures far higher than they were only a few decades ago.[3]

A more diverse workforce has many advantages, but managers have to make certain they provide equality for women and minorities with respect to employment, advancement opportunities, and compensation. Strategic plans must be made for recruiting, retaining, training, motivating, and effectively utilizing people of diverse demographic backgrounds with the skills needed to achieve the company's mission. We discuss the issue of managing the diverse workforce in full detail in Chapter 11.

Social Issues and the Natural Environment

Societal trends regarding how people think and behave have major implications for management of the labor force, corporate social actions, and strategic decisions about products and markets.

During the 1980s and 1990s women in the workforce often chose to delay having children as they focused on their careers, but today more working women are having children and then returning to the workforce. As a result, companies have introduced more supportive policies, including family leave, flexible working hours, and child care assistance. Many firms also extend these benefits to all employees or allow them to design their own benefits packages, where they can choose from a menu of available benefits that suit their individual situations. Domestic partners, whether they are in a marital relationship or not, also are covered by many employee benefit programs. Firms provide these benefits as a way of increasing a source of competitive advantage: an experienced workforce.

A prominent issue today pertains to natural resources: drilling for oil in formerly protected areas in the United States. Firms in the oil industry face considerable public opinion both in favor of preserving the natural environment, and against the country's

The Honda FCX, the first hydrogen-powered fuel cell vehicle, was the first car in the world to be certified as a Zero-Emission Vehicle.

dependence on other countries for fuel. Automakers face similar concerns about air quality as they strive to create more fuel-efficient cars.[4] The protection of the natural environment is so important in managerial decisions that we devote Appendix C following Chapter 5 to it.

How companies respond to these and other social issues may also affect their reputation in the marketplace, which in turn may help or hinder their competitiveness. For example, Wal-Mart has traditionally not offered its employees high pay and benefits, in order to be able to keep its prices low. This low-price strategy has served its customers well and helped to make Wal-Mart the world's largest retailer. However, the strategy has recently generated resistance in many communities and labor organizations. In several locations its efforts to open new stores have been delayed or even blocked. Wal-Mart has had to engage in an expensive advertising and public-relations campaign to argue that it is a good and generous employer.[5]

The Competitive Environment

All managers are affected by the general components of the macroenvironment we just discussed. Each organization also functions in a closer, more immediate competitive environment. The competitive environment includes the specific organizations with which the organization interacts. As shown in Figure 2.4, the competitive environment includes rivalry among current competitors, threat of new entrants, threat of substitutes, power of suppliers, and power of customers. This model was originally developed by Michael Porter, a Harvard professor and a noted authority on strategic management. According to Porter, successful managers do more than simply react to the environment; they act in ways that actually shape or change the organization's environment. In strategic decision making, Porter's model is an excellent method for analyzing the competitive environment in order to help managers adapt to or influence the nature of their competition.

Competitors

Among the various components of the competitive environment, competitors within the industry must first deal with one another. When organizations compete for the same customers and try to win market share at the others' expense, all must react to and anticipate their competitors' actions.

FIGURE 2.4
The Competitive
Environment

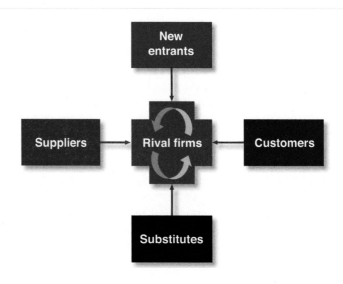

The first question to consider is: Who is the competition? Sometimes answers are obvious. Coca-Cola and PepsiCo are competitors, as are the Big Three automakers: General Motors, Ford, and DaimlerChrysler. But sometimes organizations focus too exclusively on traditional rivalries and miss the emerging ones. Historically, Sears & Roebuck focused on its competition with J.C. Penney. However, Sears' real competitors are Wal-Mart at the low end; Target in the middle; Nordstrom at the high end; and a variety of catalogers, such as L.L. Bean and Eddie Bauer. In fact, Kmart recently purchased Sears precisely to be able to compete in these other markets, which it could not do on its own. Similarly, United Airlines, Delta, American, and U.S.Airways have focused their attention on a battle over long haul and international routes. In the process, they all but ignored smaller carriers such as Southwest, Alaska Air, and Jet Blue that have grown and succeeded in regional markets.[6]

Thus, as a first step in understanding their competitive environment, organizations must identify their competitors. Competitors may include (1) small domestic firms, especially their entry into tiny, premium markets; (2) strong regional competitors; (3) big new domestic companies exploring new markets; (4) overseas firms, especially those that either try to solidify their position in small niches (a traditional Japanese tactic) or are able to draw on an inexpensive labor force on a large scale (as in China); and (5) newer entries, such as firms offering their products on the Web. The growth in competition from other countries has been especially significant in recent years, with the worldwide reduction in international trade barriers. For example, the North American Free Trade Agreement (NAFTA) sharply reduced tariffs on trade between the United States, Canada, and Mexico. Managers today confront a particular challenge from low-cost producers abroad (see Chapter 6).

Once competitors have been identified, the next step is to analyze how they compete. Competitors use tactics such as price reductions, new-product introductions, and advertising campaigns to gain advantage over their rivals. It's essential to understand what competitors are doing when you are honing your own strategy. Competition is most intense when there are many direct competitors (including foreign contenders), when industry growth is slow, and when the product or service cannot be differentiated in some way.

New, high-growth industries offer enormous opportunities for profits. When an industry matures and growth slows, profits drop. Then, intense competition causes an industry shakeout: Weaker companies are eliminated, and the strong companies survive.[7] We will be discussing the issue of competitors and strategy in further detail in Chapter 4.

> Companies often compete through innovation, quality, and cost. We will be discussing the issue of competitors and strategy in further detail in Chapter 4.

Advantages of Collaboration

It might surprise you to find that even strong competitors will sometimes collaborate. For example, it is common for companies to join in financing promotional campaigns for their industry ("Got milk?"), to agree on common product standards (as in DVDs), or to engage in joint ventures. In 2004, for instance, General Motors and DaimlerChrysler, two very large and normally highly competitive automakers, announced that they would jointly produce new hybrid technology for their cars. They felt they had to collaborate to overcome the Japanese lead in hybrid vehicles. As a manager, similar concerns about some larger threat may one day cause you, too, to collaborate with competitors in some areas, even as you continue to compete in others.

Threat of New Entrants

New entrants into an industry compete with established companies. If many factors prevent new companies from entering the industry, the threat to established firms is less serious. If there are few such **barriers to entry,** the threat of new entrants is more serious. Some major barriers to entry are government policy, capital requirements, brand identification, cost disadvantages, and distribution channels. The government can limit or prevent entry, as occurs when the FDA forbids a new drug

> **barriers to entry**
>
> Conditions that prevent new companies from entering an industry.

Was the iPod Shuffle a *barrier to entry* for new competitors to the iPod or a preemptive strike against *substitutes*?

entrant. Some industries, such as liquor retailing, are regulated; more subtle government controls operate in fields such as mining and ski area development. Patents are also entry barriers. When a patent expires, other companies can then enter the market. For example, when the pharmaceutical firm Eli Lilly and Co.'s patent on its antidepressant drug Prozac expired, it lost its U.S. monopoly on the drug and its sales plunged. Barr Laboratories Inc. won the right to be the exclusive seller of a generic version of Prozac for six months. After that period other copycats flooded the market, eroding Barr's sales of the drug.

Other barriers are less formal but can have the same effect. Capital requirements may be so high that companies won't risk or try to raise such large amounts of money. Brand identification forces new entrants to spend heavily to overcome customer loyalty. Imagine, for example, the costs involved in trying to launch a new cola against Coke or Pepsi. The cost advantages established companies hold—due to large size, favorable locations, existing assets, and so forth—also can be formidable entry barriers.

Finally, existing competitors may have such tight distribution channels that new entrants have difficulty getting their products or services to customers. For example, established food products already have supermarket shelf space. New entrants must displace existing products with promotions, price breaks, intensive selling, and other tactics.

Cost is often a major barrier to entry.

Threat of Substitutes

Technological advances and economic efficiencies are among the ways that firms can develop substitutes for existing products. For example, although Southwest Airlines has developed strong rivalries with other airlines, it also competes—as a substitute—with bus companies such as Greyhound and rental car companies such as Avis. Southwest has gotten its cost base down to such a low point that it is now cheaper to fly from Los Angeles to Phoenix than it is to take a bus or rent a car. This particular example shows that substitute products or services can limit another industry's revenue potential. Companies in those industries are likely to suffer growth and earnings problems unless they improve quality or launch aggressive marketing campaigns.[8]

Connections: TELECOM MANAGERS FIGHT FOR MARKET SHARE

Our Prologue mentioned the ongoing competition in the telecommunications industry. Different parts of the industry—cable, the Baby Bells, and cell-phone companies—are all competing to provide telephone service to their customers. Each is concerned about the threat of substitution. For example, the availability of cell phones has dramatically reduced consumer dependence on the traditionally wired home phone. Phone service provided by cable and Internet companies may do the same. Similarly, in many areas of the country satellite broadcasters like DirecTV provide customers with an alternative to cable. The effort by cable companies to enhance their appeal by offering telephone service in addition to TV programming is one response to this threat.

If the Product Is . . .	The Substitute Might Be . . .
Cotton	Polyester
Coffee	Soft drinks
Fossil fuels	Solar fusion
Movie theater	Home video/DVD
Music CD	Radio/MP3
Automobile	Train, bus, bicycle
Personal computer	Personal Digital Assistant (PDA)
Sugar	Nutrasweet
House	Apartment, condo, mobile home
Bricks	Aluminum siding
Trashy magazine	Internet
Local telephone	Cellular phone, pager

TABLE 2.1
Potential Substitutes
for Products

In addition to current substitutes, companies need to think about potential substitutes that may be viable in the near future. For example, as alternatives to fossil fuels, experts suggest that nuclear fusion, solar power, and wind energy may prove useful one day. The advantages promised by each of these technologies are many: inexhaustible fuel supplies, electricity "too cheap to meter," zero emissions, universal public acceptance, and so on. Yet while they may look good on paper (and give us a warm, fuzzy feeling inside), they often come up short in terms of economics and/or technical viability. Table 2.1 shows a list of products and potential substitutes.[9]

Suppliers

Recall from our earlier mention of open systems that organizations must acquire resources (inputs) from their environment and convert those resources into products or services (outputs) to sell. Suppliers provide the resources needed for production and may come in the form of people (supplied by trade schools and universities), raw materials (supplied by producers, wholesalers, and distributors), information (supplied by researchers and consulting firms), and financial capital (supplied by banks and other sources). But suppliers are important to an organization for reasons that go beyond the resources they provide. Suppliers can raise their prices or provide poor-quality goods and services. Labor unions can go on strike or demand higher wages. Workers may produce defective work. Powerful suppliers, then, can reduce an organization's profits, particularly if the organization cannot pass on price increases to its customers.

One particularly noteworthy set of suppliers to some industries is the international labor unions. Although unionization in the United States has dropped to about 10 percent of the private labor force, labor unions are still particularly powerful in industries such as steel, autos, and transportation. Even the Screen Actors Guild, the union representing workers in the entertainment industry, exerts considerable power on behalf of its members. For example, Tiger Woods was fined $100,000 for making a nonunion Buick commercial during a strike by the American Federation of Television and Radio Artists. Labor unions represent and protect the interests of their members with respect to hiring, wages, working conditions, job security, and due process appeals. Historically, the relationship between management and labor unions has been adversarial; however, both sides seem to realize that to increase productivity and competitiveness, management and labor must work together in collaborative relationships. Troubled labor relations can create higher costs and productivity declines and eventually lead to layoffs.[10]

Collaborative Wings

BusinessWeek

Major U.S. airlines have tried nearly everything to cope with the battering they got from the September 11 terrorist attacks and the economic slowdown. They cut routes, workers, and fares, grounded planes, renegotiated debt, and took bailout aid from Congress. But the bad news just keeps coming, from soaring jet-fuel prices to the rapid spread of low-cost carriers. At this point, a despairing industry has to ask: Can anything else be done that can turn all the red ink to black and restore the competitiveness of the country's largest airlines?

One answer may come from a dramatic experiment in labor relations under way at AMR's American Airlines. After years of labor turmoil every bit as rancorous as that at other carriers, new CEO Gerard J. Arpey has decided that motivated and involved employees can be a key competitive advantage. So he's pulling out all the stops to form a partnership with his workers and their unions.

This isn't a new concept, of course. And it's too early to tell if American's effort will succeed. But it's clear that the majors must find new ways to compete on efficiency and service—and joining hands with labor may be one of the few options left. If Arpey's strategy works, it could offer a much-needed model for other big airlines that are struggling to survive.

Arpey's plan is deceptively simple: Include employees in making and implementing decisions, big and small. "If you don't involve people in the decisions before they've already been made, then you're not really collaborating—you're just communicating. We're really trying to go to the next level," says Arpey, 45.

To that end, a "joint leadership team" of senior managers and union officials meets every month to discuss strategy and finances, while another team communicates with employees through the company and union Web sites. Union heads also meet monthly with American's chief financial officer. Similar joint teams are being created at airports and maintenance bases. "We've never in the history of American had this type of information flow before," says James C. Little, director of the Transport Workers Union's air-transport division, which represents mechanics.

Of course, in a 92,000-person company marred by decades of labor strife, change won't come easily. But there are signs of progress. Consider American's code-sharing deal with Alaska Air Group, the first such domestic partnership for American. In the past, American's pilots resisted efforts to sell seats on another U.S. carrier and market them as its own. This time, execs negotiated job protections with union leaders while they were talking to Alaska. "There was very little pushback from the employees because we had been involved in the process from the get-go," says Allied Pilots Assn. President John E. Darrah, whose union represents American's 11,000 active pilots.

Financial health, though, is still a long way off. Despite whacking costs by $4 billion, including $1.6 billion from its unions, much of the gains have been wiped out by record fuel prices and the need to slash fares to compete with a slew of low-cost carriers. American also faces massive debt and pension obligations. Some airline experts figure it needs to lop an additional billion or two off its costs to compete in the long term.

That's not likely to come from employees, who gave massive concessions to avoid bankruptcy. Arpey's make-nice ambitions won't easily win over this battle-hardened workforce, who have heard such promises before. But if Arpey gets anywhere with his peace efforts, American could be one of the first major airlines to fly out of the financial danger zone.

SOURCE: Wendy Zellner, "Collaborative Wings for America," *BusinessWeek*, May 28, 2004, online.

Organizations are at a disadvantage if they become overly dependent on any powerful supplier. A supplier is powerful if the buyer has few other sources of supply or if the supplier has many other buyers. For example, if computer companies can go only to Microsoft for software or only to Intel for microchips, those suppliers can exert a great deal of pressure. Similarly, certain critical industries, like oil or steel, have only a few suppliers, and thus are better able to dictate price. In many cases, even when alternatives are available, managers have to take switching costs into account.

Switching costs are fixed costs buyers face if they change suppliers. For example, once a buyer learns how to operate a supplier's equipment, such as computer software, the buyer faces both economic and psychological costs in changing to a new supplier.[11]

In recent years, supply chain management has become an increasingly important contributor to a company's competitiveness and profitability. By **supply chain management**, we mean the managing of the entire network of facilities and people that obtain raw materials from outside the organization, transform them into products, and distribute them to customers.[12] In the past, managers did not have to pay as much attention to supply chain management as they do today. Products tended to be standardized; overseas competition, particularly from Japan, was still years in the future; and the pace of change was slower. But increased competition has required managers to pay very close attention to their costs. For example, they could no longer afford to hold large and costly inventories, waiting for orders to come in. Furthermore, once orders did come in, some products still sitting in inventory might well be out of date.

With the emergence of the Internet, customers look for products built to their specific needs and preferences—and they want them delivered quickly, at the lowest available price. This requires the supply chain to be not only efficient but also *flexible*, so that the organization's output can quickly respond to changes in demand.

Today, the goal of effective supply chain management is to have *the right product in the right quantity available at the right place at the right cost*. Dell Inc., the computer company, provides a good example of effective supply chain management. Most of you are probably aware that Dell sells its products online. But the company also uses the Web for all the links in its supply chain. For example, Dell handles over 90 percent of its own component purchases online. Even more important, it has developed close working relationships with its suppliers and communicates with them several times a day. These relationships allow the firm not only to obtain good prices, but also to develop world-class production, quality, and delivery techniques. Any process improvements are shared with all suppliers. Dell's manufacturers, located in the United States, are price competitive with overseas plants and give Dell the benefit of faster shipping to the U.S. market. In addition, by automating much of Dell's supply chain and collaborating closely with its suppliers, Dell managers are able to build their products to order. A computer is built quickly only *after* an order is placed. Rather than having a huge amount of costly inventory on site, Dell typically has fewer than four days' worth of product inventory on hand at any given time.[13]

switching costs
Fixed costs buyers face when they change suppliers.

supply chain management
The managing of the network of facilities and people that obtain materials from outside the organization, transform them into products, and distribute them to customers.

Advantages of Collaboration

Many U.S. manufacturers are concerned about the cost advantage that overseas manufacturers gain through their low-wage structure. They may even decide to send some jobs or even entire plants to less expensive workers overseas. As a manager and an employee, you may one day experience such concerns, too. But you may also find that collaboration can help you remain price competitive without relocating jobs. You may collaborate *externally*, with suppliers who work with you on improving quality, automation, and delivery and on lowering costs. You may also collaborate *internally*, working together with other managers and employees in every area to eliminate inefficiency. By doing so, you may be able to remain close to your customers here—and profitable besides.

In sum, choosing the right supplier is an important strategic decision. Suppliers can affect manufacturing time, product quality, and inventory levels. The relationship between suppliers and the organization is changing in many companies. The close supplier relationship has become a new model for many organizations that are using a just-in-time manufacturing approach (discussed further in Chapters 16 and 17). And in some companies, innovative managers are forming strategic partnerships with their

The ability to manufacture even customized products quickly has become a competitive requirement.

key suppliers in developing new products or new production techniques. We describe this kind of strategic partnership in more detail in Chapter 9.

Customers

Customers purchase the products or services an organization offers. Without customers, a company won't survive. You are a **final consumer** when you buy a McDonald's hamburger or a pair of jeans from a retailer at the mall. **Intermediate consumers** buy raw materials or wholesale products and then sell to final consumers. Intermediate customers actually make more purchases than individual final consumers do. Examples of intermediate customers include retailers, who buy clothes from wholesalers and manufacturers' representatives before selling them to their customers, and industrial buyers, who buy raw materials (such as chemicals) before converting them into final products.

Like suppliers, customers are important to organizations for reasons other than the money they provide for goods and services. Customers can demand lower prices, higher quality, unique product specifications, or better service. They also can play competitors against one another, as occurs when a car customer (or a purchasing agent) collects different offers and negotiates for the best price. The Internet has further empowered customers, by making information about the lowest possible price available to everyone and by forcing organizations to compete with each other online.

> **final consumer**
>
> Those who purchase products in their finished form.
>
> **intermediate consumer**
>
> A customer who purchases raw materials or wholesale products before selling them to final customers.

Connections: **TELECOM MANAGERS FIGHT FOR MARKET SHARE**

In the Prologue we mentioned the crowded and competitive environment that telecom managers face. But they must also deal with a much-changed consumer environment. In the preregulation days consumers stayed with their phone companies for decades—there was, after all, no other choice. Today customer loyalty is quite low, for land-line as well as wireless services. Customer "churn" is now a daily feature of the business, with consumers constantly chasing after low prices and added telephone features. Wireless consumers can—and often do—carry their cell phone numbers from one provider to another after their contract period has elapsed. Land-line phone service can be changed even more frequently. Instead of the "old" days, when prices were controlled by regulation, today consumers often negotiate with their providers, insisting that they meet their competitors' latest offer. In other words, they have bargaining power. Telecom managers must constantly monitor competitor prices and consumer trends to keep from losing market share.

Customer service means giving customers what they want or need, the way they want it, the first time. This usually depends on the speed and dependability with which an organization can deliver its products or services. Actions and attitudes that mean excellent customer service include the following:

- Speed of filling and delivering normal orders.
- Willingness to meet emergency needs.
- Merchandise delivered in good condition.
- Readiness to take back defective goods and resupply quickly.
- Availability of installation and repair services and parts.
- Service charges (that is, whether services are "free" or priced separately).[14]

In all businesses—services as well as manufacturing—strategies that emphasize good customer service provide a critical competitive advantage. The organization is at a disadvantage if it depends too heavily on powerful customers. Customers are powerful if they make

> **customer service**
>
> The speed and dependability with which an organization can deliver what customers want.

> "Your most unhappy customers are your greatest source of learning."
> Bill Gates

large purchases or if they can easily find alternative places to buy. If you are the largest customer of a firm and there are other firms from which you can buy, you have power over that firm, and you are likely to be able to negotiate with it successfully. Your firm's biggest customers—especially if they can buy from other sources—will have the greatest negotiating power over you. Customer relationship management is discussed more fully in Chapter 9.

Environmental Analysis

If managers do not understand how the environment affects their organizations or cannot identify opportunities and threats that are likely to be important, their ability to make decisions and execute plans will be severely limited. For example, if little is known about customer likes and dislikes, organizations will have a difficult time designing new products, scheduling production, developing marketing plans, and the like. In short, timely and accurate environmental information is critical for running a business.

But information about the environment is not always readily available. For example, even economists have difficulty predicting whether an upturn or a downturn in the economy is likely. Moreover, managers do not find it easy to forecast how well their own products will sell, let alone how a competitor might respond. In other words, managers often operate under conditions of uncertainty. **Environmental uncertainty** means that managers do not have enough information about the environment to understand or predict the future. Uncertainty arises from two related factors: (1) complexity and (2) dynamism. Environmental *complexity* refers to the number of issues to which a manager must attend as well as their interconnectedness. For example, industries that have many different firms that compete in vastly different ways tend to be more complex—and uncertain—than industries with only a few key competitors. Similarly, environmental *dynamism* refers to the degree of discontinuous change that occurs within the industry. For example, high-growth industries with products and technologies that change rapidly tend to be more uncertain than stable industries where change is less dramatic and more predictable.[15]

> **environmental uncertainty**
> Lack of information needed to understand or predict the future.

As environmental uncertainty increases, managers must develop techniques and methods for collecting, sorting through, and interpreting information about the environment. We discuss some of these approaches below. (In the next chapter, we will also discuss how managers make decisions under conditions of uncertainty.) By analyzing environmental forces—in both the macroenvironment and the competitive environment—managers can identify opportunities and threats that might affect the organization.

Environmental Scanning

Perhaps the first step in coping with uncertainty in the environment is pinning down what might be of importance. Frequently organizations (and individuals) act out of ignorance, only to regret those actions in the future. IBM, for example, had the opportunity to purchase the technology behind xerography but turned it down. Xerox saw the potential, and the rest is history. However, Xerox researchers later developed the technology for the original computer mouse, but not seeing the potential, the company missed an important market opportunity.

To understand and predict changes, opportunities, and threats, organizations such as Monsanto, Weyerhaeuser, and Union Carbide spend a good deal of time and money monitoring events in the environment. **Environmental scanning** means both searching out information that is unavailable to most people and sorting through that information to interpret what is important and what is not. Managers can ask questions such as

- Who are our current competitors?
- Are there few or many entry barriers to our industry?

> **environmental scanning**
> Searching for and sorting through information about the environment.

- What substitutes exist for our product or service?
- Is the company too dependent on powerful suppliers?
- Is the company too dependent on powerful customers?[16]

competitive intelligence

Information that helps managers determine how to compete better.

Answers to these questions help managers develop **competitive intelligence,** the information necessary to decide how best to manage in the competitive environment they have identified. Porter's competitive analysis, discussed earlier, can guide environmental scanning and help managers evaluate the competitive potential of different environments. Table 2.2 describes two extreme environments: an attractive environment, which gives a firm a competitive advantage, and an unattractive environment, which puts a firm at a competitive disadvantage.[17]

Scenario Development

scenario

A narrative that describes a particular set of future conditions.

As managers attempt to determine the effect of environmental forces on their organizations, they frequently develop **scenarios** of the future. Scenarios combine alternative combinations of different factors into a total picture of the environment and the firm. For example, when Congress and the president must forecast the size of the federal budget deficit, they develop several different scenarios about what the economy is likely to do over the next decade or so. Frequently, organizations develop a *best-case scenario* (i.e., if events occur that are favorable to the firm), a *worst-case scenario* (i.e., if events are all unfavorable), and some middle-ground alternatives. The value of scenario development is that it helps managers develop contingency plans for what they might do given different outcomes.[18] For example, as a manager, you will quite likely be involved in budgeting for your area. You will almost certainly be asked to list initiatives that you would eliminate in case of an economic downturn, or new investments you would make if your firm does better than expected.

Effective managers regard the scenarios they develop as living documents, not merely prepared once and put aside. Instead, they are constantly updated to take into account relevant new factors that emerge, such as significant changes in the economy or actions by competitors.

Forecasting

forecasting

Method for predicting how variables will change the future.

Whereas environmental scanning is used to identify important factors and scenario development is used to develop alternative pictures of the future, **forecasting** is used to predict exactly how some variable or variables will change in the future. For example, in making capital investments, firms may try to forecast how interest rates will change. In deciding to expand or downsize a business, firms may try to forecast the demand for goods and services or forecast the supply and demand of labor they probably would use. Available publications such as *BusinessWeek's Business Outlook* provide forecasts to businesses both large and small.

TABLE 2.2
Attractive and Unattractive Environments

Environmental Factor	Unattractive	Attractive
Competitors	Many; low industry growth; equal size; commodity	Few; high industry growth; unequal size differentiated
Threat of entry	High threat; few entry barriers	Low threat; many barriers
Substitutes	Many	Few
Suppliers	Few; high bargaining power	Many; low bargaining power
Customers	Few; high bargaining power	Many; low bargaining power

Although forecasts are designed to help executives make predictions about the future, their accuracy varies from application to application. Because they extrapolate from the past to project the future, forecasts tend to be most accurate when the future ends up looking a lot like the past. Of course, we don't need sophisticated forecasts in those instances. Forecasts are most useful when the future will look radically different from the past. Unfortunately, that is when forecasts tend not to be so accurate. The more things change, the less confidence we tend to have in our forecasts. The best advice for using forecasts might include the following:

- Use multiple forecasts and perhaps average their predictions.
- Remember that accuracy decreases the further into the future you are trying to predict.
- Forecasts are no better than the data used to construct them.
- Use simple forecasts (rather than complicated ones) where possible.
- Important events often are surprises and represent a departure from predictions.[19]

Benchmarking

In addition to trying to predict changes in the environment, firms can undertake intensive study of the best practices of various firms to understand their sources of competitive advantage. **Benchmarking** means identifying the best-in-class performance by a company in a given area, say, product development or customer service, and then comparing your processes to theirs. To accomplish this, a benchmarking team would collect information on its own company's operations and those of the other firm in order to determine gaps. These gaps serve as a point of entry to learn the underlying causes of performance differences. Ultimately, the team would map out a set of best practices that lead to world-class performance. We will discuss benchmarking further in Chapter 4.[20]

> **benchmarking**
>
> The process of comparing an organization's practices and technologies with those of other companies.

Responding to the Environment

For managers and organizations, responding effectively to their environments is almost always essential. Clothing retailers who pay no attention to changes in the public's style preferences, or manufacturers who don't make sure they have steady sources of supply, are soon out of business. To respond to their environment, managers and companies have a number of options. These can be grouped into three categories: (1) adapting to the environment, (2) influencing the environment, and (3) selecting a new environment.

Adapting to the Environment: Changing Yourself

To cope with environmental uncertainty, organizations frequently make adjustments in their structures and work processes. In the case of uncertainty arising from environmental complexity, we can say that organizations tend to adapt by *decentralizing* decision making. For example, if a company faces a growing number of competitors in various markets, if different customers want different things, if the characteristics of different products keep increasing, and if production facilities are being built in different regions of the world, it may be impossible for the chief executive (or a small group of top executives) to keep abreast of all activities and understand all the operational details of a business. In these cases, the top management team is likely to give authority to lower-level managers to make decisions that benefit the firm. The term **empowerment** is used frequently today to talk about this type of decentralized authority. We will address empowerment and decision making in more detail in Chapters 3 and 9.

In response to uncertainty caused by change (dynamism) in the environment, organizations tend to establish more flexible structures. In today's business world, the

> **empowerment**
>
> The process of sharing power with employees, thereby enhancing their confidence in their ability to perform their jobs and their belief that they are influential contributors to the organization.

		Stable	Dynamic
Complex		Decentralized	Decentralized
		Bureaucratic (standardized skills)	Organic (mutual adjustment)
Simple		Centralized	Centralized
		Bureaucratic (standardized work processes)	Organic (direct supervision)

TABLE 2.3

Four Approaches for Managing Uncertainty

buffering

Creating supplies of excess resources in case of unpredictable needs.

smoothing

Leveling normal fluctuations at the boundaries of the environment.

flexible processes

Methods for adapting the technical core to changes in the environment.

term *bureaucracy* generally has a bad connotation. Most of us recognize that bureaucratic organizations tend to be formalized and very stable; frequently they are unable to adjust to change or exceptional circumstances that "don't fit the rules." And while bureaucratic organizations may be efficient and controlled if the environment is stable, they tend to be slow-moving and plodding when products, technologies, customers, competitors, and the like start changing over time. In these cases, more *organic* structures tend to have the flexibility needed to adjust to change. Although we will discuss organic structures in more detail in Chapter 9, suffice it to say here that they are less formal than bureaucratic organizations, and so decisions tend to be made through interaction and mutual adjustment among individuals rather than via a set of predefined rules. Table 2.3 shows four different approaches that organizations can take in adapting to environmental uncertainty.

Adapting at the Boundaries   From the standpoint of an open system, organizations create buffers on both the input and output sides of their boundaries with the environment. **Buffering** is one such approach used for adapting to uncertainty. On the input side, organizations establish relationships with employment agencies to hire part-time and temporary help during rush periods when labor demand is difficult to predict. The growth of contingent workers in the U.S. labor force is a good indication of the popularity of this approach to buffering input uncertainties. On the output side of the system, most organizations use some type of ending inventories that allow them to keep merchandise on hand in case a rush of customers decide to buy their products. Auto dealers are a particularly common example of this use of buffers, but we can see similar use of buffer inventories in fast-food restaurants, bookstores, clothing stores, and even real estate agencies.[21]

In addition to buffering, organizations may try **smoothing** or leveling normal fluctuations at the boundaries of the environment. For example, during winter months (up north) when automobile sales drop off, it is not uncommon for dealers to cut the price of their in-stock vehicles to increase demand. At the end of each clothing season, retailers discount their merchandise to clear it out in order to make room for incoming inventories. These are each examples of smoothing environmental cycles in order to level off fluctuations in demand.

Auto dealers typically have a buffer inventory of products but then cut prices to increase demand at the end of the model year.

Adapting at the Core   While buffering and smoothing work to manage uncertainties at the boundaries of the organization, firms also can establish **flexible processes** that allow for adaptation in their technical core. For example, firms increasingly try to customize their products and services to meet the varied and changing demands of customers. Even in manufacturing, where it is difficult to change basic core processes, firms are adopting techniques of mass customization that help them create flexible factories. Instead of mass-producing large quantities of a "one-size-fits-all" product, with mass customization organizations can produce individually customized products at an equally low cost. Whereas Henry Ford used to claim that "you could have a Model T in any color you wanted, as long as it was black," auto companies now offer a wide array of colors and trim lines, with different options and accessories. The process of mass customization involves the use of a network of independent operating units in which each performs a specific process or task such as making a dashboard assembly on an automobile. When an order comes in, different modules join forces to deliver the product or service as specified by the customer. We will discuss mass customization and flexible factories in more depth in Chapter 9.[22]

> The Internet lets customers quickly find products with the cost and quality features they want.

Influencing Your Environment

In addition to adapting or reacting to the environment, managers and organizations can develop proactive responses aimed at changing the environment. Two general types of proactive responses are independent action and cooperative action.

Independent Action   A company uses **independent strategies** when it acts on its own to change some aspect of its current environment.[23] Table 2.4 shows the definitions and uses of these strategies. For example, when Southwest Airlines enters a new market, it demonstrates competitive aggression by cutting fares so that other, less-efficient airlines must follow it down. In contrast, Kellogg Company typically promotes the cereal industry as a whole, thereby demonstrating competitive pacification. Weyerhaeuser Company advertises its reforestation efforts (public relations). First Boston forgoes its Christmas party and donates thousands of dollars to the poor (voluntary action). General Motors sues a Chinese automobile manufacturer for design infringement (legal action). Disney lobbies Congress to extend copyright-protection laws for an additional period of years so

> **independent strategies**
>
> Strategies that an organization acting on its own uses to change some aspect of its current environment.

TABLE 2.4   Independent Action

Strategy	Definition	Examples
Competitive aggression	Exploiting a distinctive competence or improving internal efficiency for competitive advantage.	Aggressive pricing, comparative advertising (e.g., Wal-Mart)
Competitive pacification	Independent action to improve relations with competitors.	Helping competitors find raw materials
Public relations	Establishing and maintaining favorable images in the minds of those making up the environment.	Sponsoring sporting events
Voluntary action	Voluntary commitment to various interest groups, causes, and social problems.	Johnson & Johnson donating supplies to tsunami victims
Legal action	Company engages in private legal battle.	Warner Music lawsuits against illegal music copying
Political action	Efforts to influence elected representatives to create a more favorable business environment or limit competition.	Issue advertising; lobbying at state and national levels

SOURCE: Adapted from *Journal of Marketing*, published by the American Marketing Association. C. Zeithaml and V. Zeithaml, "Environmental Management: Revising the Marketing Perspective," Spring 1984.

it can maintain ownership of its cartoon characters (political action). Each of these examples shows how organizations—on their own—can have an impact on the environment.

Cooperative Action

cooperative strategies

Strategies used by two or more organizations working together to manage the external environment.

Cooperative Action   In some situations, two or more organizations work together using cooperative strategies to influence the environment.[24] Table 2.5 shows several examples of **cooperative strategies.** An example of contracting occurs when suppliers and customers, or managers and labor unions, sign formal agreements about the terms and conditions of their future relationships. These contracts are explicit attempts to make their future relationship predictable. An example of cooptation might occur when universities invite wealthy alumni to join their boards of directors.

Finally, an example of coalition formation might be when local businesses band together to curb the rise of employee health care costs and when organizations in the same industry form industry associations and special-interest groups. You may have seen cooperative advertising strategies, such as when dairy producers, beef producers, orange growers, and the like, jointly pay for television commercials.

At a more organizational level, organizations establish strategic alliances, partnerships, joint ventures, and mergers with competitors to deal with environmental uncertainties. Cooperative strategies such as these make most sense when (1) taking joint action will reduce the organizations' costs and risks and (2) cooperation will increase their power (that is, their ability to successfully accomplish the changes they desire).

Changing the Environment You Are In

strategic maneuvering

An organization's conscious efforts to change the boundaries of its task environment.

domain selection

Entering a new market or industry with an existing expertise.

As we noted previously, organizations can cope with environmental uncertainty by changing themselves (environmental adaptation), changing the environment, or changing the environment they are in. We refer to this last category as **strategic maneuvering.** By making a conscious effort to change the boundaries of its competitive environment, a firm can maneuver around potential threats and capitalize on arising opportunities.[25] Managers can use several strategic maneuvers, including domain selection, diversification, merger and acquisition, and divestiture.[26]

Domain selection is the entrance by a company into another suitable market or industry. For example, the market may have limited competition or regulation, ample

TABLE 2.5
Cooperative Action

Strategy	Definition	Examples
Contraction	Negotiation of an agreement between the organization and another group to exchange goods, services, information, patents, and so on.	Contractual marketing systems
Cooptation	Absorbing new elements into the organization's leadership structure to avert threats to its stability or existence.	Consumer and labor representatives and bankers on boards of directors
Coalition	Two or more groups coalesce and act jointly with respect to some set of issues for some period of time.	Industry associations; political initiatives of the Business Roundtable and the U.S. Chamber of Commerce

SOURCE: Reprinted from *Journal of Marketing*, published by the American Marketing Association. C. Zeithaml and V. Zeithaml, "Environmental Management: Revising the Marketing Perspective," Spring 1984.

suppliers and customers, or high growth. The effort by cable companies to use their existing technology and customer base to enter the telephone market, or Miller's entry into the light-beer market, are examples of domain selection. The firms are using an existing expertise to broaden the products or services they offer.

Diversification occurs when a firm invests in different types of businesses or products or when it expands geographically to reduce its dependence on a single market or technology. Apple Computer's launch of the iPod is a good example of effective diversification. While Apple has struggled in the highly competitive computer industry, where it has only a 3 percent market share, with the iPod it has gained 88 percent of the market for portable high-drive music players.

A **merger** or **acquisition** takes place when two or more firms combine, or one firm buys another, to form a single company. For example, Yahoo has had a strategy in place for several years to acquire other online companies, such as Hotjobs (bought in 2001) and Musicmatch (bought in 2004), to broaden both its ad revenues and customer service.

Divestiture is when a company sells one or more businesses. We gave one example of divestiture in our opening case, when AT&T had to sell its local telephone business. Another example is IBM's sale in 2004 of its personal computer business to Lenovo, China's computer company.

Organizations engage in strategic maneuvering when they move into different environments. Some companies, called **prospectors**, are more likely than others to engage in strategic maneuvering.[27] Aggressive companies continuously change the boundaries of their competitive environments by seeking new products and markets, diversifying, and merging or acquiring new enterprises. In these and other ways, corporations put their competitors on the defensive and force them to react. **Defenders**, on the other hand, stay within a more limited, stable product domain.

Choosing a Response Approach

Three general considerations help guide management's response to the environment. First, organizations should attempt to *change appropriate elements of the environment.* Environmental responses are most useful when aimed at elements of the environment that (1) cause the company problems, (2) provide it with opportunities, and (3) allow the company to change successfully. Thus, automobile companies faced with intense competition from Japanese automakers successfully lobbied (along with labor) for government-imposed ceilings on Japanese imports. And one

diversification

A firm's investment in a different product, business, or geographic area.

merger

One or more companies combining.

acquisition

One firm buying another.

divestiture

A firm selling one or more businesses.

prospectors

Companies that continuously change the boundaries for their task environments by seeking new products and markets, diversifying and merging, or acquiring new enterprises.

defenders

Companies that stay within a stable product domain as a strategic maneuver.

Nokia is a great example of a company that adapted to environment changes. Starting as a pulp and paper company, the company bought into cable wiring in the 1920s, and then electronics in the 1960s, making TVs and computer monitors. Sensing the emerging market for mobile telecommunications Nokia executives invested into that shift in the 1980s. Today, you know them for their sleek, cellular telephones.

charcoal producer, hoping to increase consumers' opportunities to use its product, launched a campaign to increase daylight saving time.

Second, organizations should *choose responses that focus on pertinent elements of the environment.* If a company wants to better manage its competitive environment, competitive aggression and pacification are viable options. Political action influences the legal environment, and contracting helps manage customers and suppliers.

Third, companies should *choose responses that offer the most benefit at the lowest cost.* Return-on-investment calculations should incorporate short-term financial considerations as well as long-term impact. Strategic managers who consider these factors carefully will guide their organizations to competitive advantage more effectively.

Culture and the Internal Environment of Organizations

organization culture

The set of important assumptions about the organization and its goals and practices that members of the company share.

One of the most important factors that influence an organization's response to its external environment is its culture. **Organization culture** is the set of important assumptions about the organization and its goals and practices that members of the company share. It is a system of shared values about what is important and beliefs about how the world works. In this way, a company's culture provides a framework that organizes and directs people's behavior on the job.[28] The culture of an organization may be difficult for an observer to define easily, yet, like an individual's personality, it can often be sensed almost immediately. For example, the way people dress and behave, the way they interact with each other and with customers, and the qualities that are likely to be valued by their managers are usually quite different at a bank than they are at a rock-music company, and different again at a law firm or an advertising agency.

Cultures can be strong or weak; strong cultures can have great influence on how people think and behave. A strong culture is one in which everyone understands and believes in the firm's goals, priorities, and practices. A strong culture can be a real advantage to the organization if the behaviors it encourages and facilitates are appropriate ones. For example, the Walt Disney Company's culture encourages extraordinary devotion to customer service; the culture at Apple Computer encourages innovation. Employees in these companies don't need rule books to dictate how they act, because these behaviors are conveyed as "the way we do things around here"; they are rooted in their companies' cultures.

On the other hand, a strong culture that encourages inappropriate behaviors can severely hinder an organization's ability to deal effectively with its external environment—particularly if the environment is undergoing change, as is almost always the case today. A culture that was suitable and even advantageous in a prior era may become counterproductive in a new environment. IBM, for example, frequently is discussed as an organization that had a very strong culture that served it well for several decades. But the uniformity and conformity established by IBM's culture were ill suited for creating the more dynamic and flexible organization needed today. One of Lou Gerstner's first tasks after taking over as CEO was to transform the culture to focus on creativity, innovation, and radical thinking. One symbolic gesture in that regard was relaxing IBM's traditional dress code of white shirts and blue pin-striped suits. The dress code itself was not important, but it represented the stodgy old IBM that Gerstner wanted to change.

In contrast to strong cultures, weak cultures have the following characteristics: Different people hold different values, there is confusion about corporate goals, and it is not clear from one day to the next what principles should guide decisions. Some managers may pay lip service to some aspects of the culture ("we would never cheat a customer") but behave very differently ("don't tell him about the flaw"). As you can guess, such a culture fosters confusion, conflict, and poor performance. Most managers would agree that they want to create a strong culture that encourages and supports goals and useful behaviors that will make the company more effective. In other words, they want to create a culture that is appropriately aligned with the organization's competitive environment.[29]

At Nordstrom, the fashion retailer, employees are simply given a five-by-eight-inch card with one rule on it.

Diagnosing Culture

Let's say you want to understand a company's culture. Perhaps you are thinking about working there and you want a good "fit," or perhaps you are working there right now and want to deepen your understanding of the organization and determine whether its culture matches the challenges it faces. How would you go about making the diagnosis? A variety of things will give you useful clues about culture:

- *Corporate mission statements and official goals* are a starting point, as they will tell you the firm's desired public image. Most companies have a mission statement—even the CIA, as shown in Figure 2.5. (Your school has one, and you can probably find it online.) But you still need to figure out whether the public statements truly reflect how the firm conducts business.
- *Business practices* can be observed. How a company responds to problems, makes strategic decisions, and treats employees and customers tells a lot about what top management really values.
- *Symbols, rites, and ceremonies* give further clues about culture. For instance, status symbols can give you a feel for how rigid the hierarchy is and for the nature of relationships between lower and higher levels. Who is hired and fired—and why—and the activities that are rewarded indicate the firm's real values.
- *The stories people tell* carry a lot of information about the company's culture. Every company has its myths, legends, and true stories about important past decisions and actions that convey the company's main values. Traditionally, Frito-Lay tells service stories, Johnson & Johnson tells quality stories, and 3M tells innovation stories. The stories often feature the company's heroes: persons once or still active who possessed the qualities and characteristics that the culture especially values and who act as models for others about how to behave.

In general, cultures can be categorized according to whether they emphasize flexibility versus control and whether their focus is internal or external to the organization. By juxtaposing these two dimensions, we can describe four types of organizational cultures (see Figure 2.6):

- *Group culture.* A group culture is internally oriented and flexible. It tends to be based on the values and norms associated with affiliation. An organizational member's compliance with organizational directives flows from trust, tradition, and long-term commitment. It tends to emphasize member development and values participation in decision making. The strategic orientation associated with this cultural type is one of implementation through consensus building. Leaders tend to act as mentors and facilitators.
- *Hierarchical culture.* The hierarchical culture is internally oriented by more focus on control and stability. It has the values and norms associated with a

Vision	We will provide knowledge and take action to ensure the national security of the United States and the preservation of American life and ideals.
Mission	We are the eyes and ears of the nation and at times its hidden hand. We accomplish this mission by: • Collecting intelligence that matters. • Providing relevant, timely, and objective all-source analysis. • Conducting covert action at the direction of the president to preempt threats or achieve United States policy objectives.
Values	In pursuit of our country's interests, we put Nation before Agency, Agency before unit, and all before self. What we do matters. • Our success depends on our ability to act with total discretion and an ability to protect sources and methods. • We provide objective, unbiased information and analysis. • Our mission requires complete personal integrity and personal courage, physical and intellectual. • We accomplish things others cannot, often at great risk. When the stakes are highest and the dangers greatest, we are there and there first. • We stand by one another and behind one another. Service, sacrifice, flexibility, teamwork, and quiet patriotism are our hallmarks.

FIGURE 2.5
CIA Vision, Mission, and Values

Source: CIA Web site accessed March 10, 2005, at www.cia.gov/information/mission.html.

bureaucracy. It values stability and assumes that individuals will comply with organizational mandates when roles are stated formally and enforced through rules and procedures.

• *Rational culture.* The rational culture is externally oriented and focused on control. Its primary objectives are productivity, planning, and efficiency. Organizational members are motivated by the belief that performance that leads to the desired organizational objectives will be rewarded.

• *Adhocracy.* The adhocracy is externally oriented and flexible. This culture type emphasizes change in which growth, resource acquisition, and innovation are stressed. Organizational members are motivated by the importance or ideological appeal of the task. Leaders tend to be entrepreneurial and risk takers. Other members tend to have these characteristics as well.[30]

Managing Culture

We mentioned earlier in this chapter that one important way organizations have of responding to the environment is to *adapt* to it by changing the organization itself. One of the most important tools managers have for implementing such a change lies in their management of their organization's culture. A culture that is inwardly instead of customer focused, for example, when the new competitive environment requires excellence in customer service, can delay or even defeat a manager's efforts to effect change. Simple directives alone will often be ineffective; the underlying values of the organization also have to be shifted in the desired direction. Most companies today know that adopting a customer orientation, improving quality, and making other moves necessary to remain competitive are so essential that they require deep-rooted cultural changes. When that kind of change occurs, organization members may then begin to internalize the new values and display the appropriate behaviors on their own.

**Flexible
Processes**

Type: Group
Dominant Attribute:
  Cohesiveness, participation,
  teamwork, sense of family
Leadership Style: Mentor,
  facilitator, parent figure
Bonding: Loyalty, tradition,
  interpersonal cohesion
Strategic Emphasis: Toward
  developing human resources,
  commitment, and morale

Type: Adhocracy
Dominant Attribute:
  Entrepreneurship, creativity,
  adaptability, dynamism
Leadership Style: Innovator,
  entrepreneur, risk taker
Bonding: Flexibility, risk,
  entrepreneur
Strategic Emphasis: Toward
  innovation, growth, new
  resources

**Internal
Maintenance**

**External
Positioning**

Type: Hierarchy
Dominant Attribute: Order, rules
  and regulations, uniformity,
  efficiency
Leadership Style: Coordinator,
  organizer, administrator
Bonding: Rules, policies and
  procedures, clear expectations
Strategic Emphasis: Toward
  stability, predictability, smooth

Type: Rational
Dominant Attribute: Goal
  achievement, environment
  exchange, competitiveness
Leadership Style: Production–
  & achievement–oriented,
  decisive
Bonding: Goal orientation,
  production, competition
Strategic Emphasis: Toward
  competitive advantage and
  market superiority

**Control—Oriented
Processes**

SOURCE: Kim S. Cameron and Robert E. Quinn, *Diagnosing and Changing Organizational Culture* (Englewood Cliffs, NJ; Addison-Wesley, 1988).

FIGURE 2.6
Competing Values Model of
Culture

Top managers can take several approaches to managing culture. First, they should espouse lofty ideals and visions for the company that will inspire organization members. (We will be discussing vision more fully in Chapter 4, on strategy, and in Chapter 12, on leadership.) That vision—whether it concerns quality, integrity, innovation, or whatever—should be articulated over and over until it becomes a tangible presence throughout the organization.

Second, executives must give constant attention to the mundane details of daily affairs such as communicating regularly, being visible and active throughout the company, and setting examples. The CEO not only should talk about the vision, he or she should embody it day in and day out. This makes the CEO's pronouncements credible, creates a personal example others can emulate, and builds trust that the organization's progress toward the vision will continue over the long run.

A culture aligned
with its
environment
helps the
organization
succeed.

Important here are the moments of truth when hard choices must be made. Imagine top management trumpeting a culture that emphasizes quality and then discovering that a part used in a batch of assembled products is defective. Whether to replace the part at great expense in the interest of quality or to ship the defective part just to save time and money is a decision that will go a long way toward reinforcing or destroying a quality-oriented culture.

All along, it is essential that the CEO and other executives celebrate and reward those who exemplify the new values. Another key to managing culture involves hiring, socializing newcomers, and promoting on the basis of the new corporate values. In this way, the new culture will begin to permeate the organization. While this may seem a time-consuming approach to building a new culture, effective managers recognize that replacing a long-term culture of traditional values with one that embodies the competitive values needed in the future can take years. But the rewards of that effort will be an organization much more effective and responsive to its environmental challenges and opportunities.

EPILOGUE

TELECOM MANAGERS FIGHT FOR MARKET SHARE

At the opening of this chapter, and throughout, we reviewed some of the environmental challenges faced by telecom managers. We will now close our discussion by mentioning that at the end of 2004 Sprint and Nextel announced that they would merge, turning the newly named Sprint Nextel into the country's third-largest wireless company.

Why did the management of these two companies decide to merge? The main answer lies in the difficult competitive environment they faced. Earlier that year, Cingular had acquired AT&T Wireless, making it the number 1 wireless operator, with 47 million subscribers. Verizon, with 42 million, was number 2. Compared to these two giants, Sprint and Nextel top managers feared that on their own they would be too small to compete. In addition, Nextel's main focus was on the business market. Its top managers felt that would leave the company vulnerable, as bigger companies offering a fuller range of services achieved higher revenues and economies of scale. By combining Sprint's consumer market and Nextel's business market, the merger strengthened both companies.

The merger was also driven by the technological environment the companies faced. Left on its own, Nextel would have had to upgrade its entire network to meet the demand for higher speed and other services. Now it can upgrade both more quickly and less expensively, by building on Sprint's more advanced technol-

ogy. In turn, Nextel offered Sprint access to newer and faster parts of the broadcast spectrum to which it had negotiated access from government regulators. Sprint also announced that it had entered into a deal with Time Warner Cable, allowing that company to offer Sprint's cell phone service on a trial basis.

The merger represented one response to the complex regulatory, competitive, and technological environment faced by telecom managers. But many uncertainties and challenges remain. Cable companies have already wired almost all American households and are in a very strong position to provide communication and entertainment options for the home. The Baby Bells have landlines installed and also own wireless companies; they have also begun to build high-speed fiber lines to compete with cable. And technological improvements may eventually allow wireless companies like Sprint Nextel to hold their own against their cable and Baby Bell competitors. Watching over it all are federal regulators, with the job of protecting consumers and maintaining a level playing field while at the same time encouraging competition and innovation. Telecom managers will need considerable skill to navigate the challenging external environment they confront.

SOURCES: Steve Rosenbush, "Nextel and Sprint: The Big Little Guy," *BusinessWeek online*, December 15, 2004; Roger O. Crockett and Catherine Yang, "Why Sprint and Nextel Got Hitched," *BusinessWeek online*, December 27, 2004

KEY TERMS

Acquisition, p. 65

Barriers to entry, p. 53

Benchmarking, p. 61

Buffering, p. 62

Competitive environment, p. 46

Competitive intelligence, p. 60

Cooperative strategies, p. 64

Customer service, p. 58

Defenders, p. 65

Demographics, p. 50

Diversification, p. 65

Divestiture, p. 65

Domain selection, p. 64

Empowerment, p. 61

Environmental scanning, p. 59

Environmental uncertainty, p. 59

External environment, p. 46

Final consumer, p. 58

Flexible processes, p. 62

Forecasting, p. 60

Independent strategies, p. 63

Inputs, p. 46

Intermediate consumer, p. 58

Macroenvironment, p. 46

Merger, p. 65

Open systems, p. 46

Organizational culture, p. 66

Outputs, p. 46

Prospectors, p. 65

Scenario, p. 60

Smoothing, p. 62

Strategic maneuvering, p. 64

Supply chain management, p. 57

Switching costs, p. 57

SUMMARY OF LEARNING OBJECTIVES

Now that you have studied Chapter 2, you should know:

How environmental forces influence organizations, as well as how organizations can influence their environments.

Organizations are open systems that are affected by, and in turn affect, their external environments. Organizations receive financial, human, material, and information resources from the environment; transform those resources into finished goods and services; and then send those outputs back into the environment.

How to make a distinction between the macroenvironment and the competitive environment.

The macroenvironment is composed of international, legal and political, economic, technological, and social forces that influence strategic decisions. The competitive environment is composed of forces closer to the organization, such as current competitors, threat of new entrants, threat of substitutes, suppliers, and customers. Perhaps the simplest distinction between the macroenvironment and the competitive environment is in the amount of control a firm can exert on external forces. Macroenvironmental forces such as the economy and social trends are much less controllable than are forces in the competitive environment such as suppliers and customers.

Why managers should attend to economic and social developments in the environment.

Developments outside the organization can have a profound effect on the way managers and their companies operate. For example, higher energy costs or increased spending on security may make it harder for managers to keep their prices low. The growing diversity of the labor force gives managers access to a much broader range of talent but also requires them to make sure different types of employees are treated equally. The worldwide increase in free trade can open up overseas markets, but it may also encourage more foreign competition in the domestic market. Effective managers stay aware of trends like these and respond to them effectively.

How to analyze the competitive environment.

Environments can range from favorable to unfavorable. To determine how favorable a competitive environment is, managers should consider the nature of the competitors, potential new entrants, threat of substitutes, suppliers, and customers. Analyzing how these five forces influence the organization provides an indication of potential threats and opportunities. Effective management of the firm's supply chain is one way to achieve a competitive advantage. Attractive environments tend to be those which have high industry growth, few competitors, products that can be differentiated, few potential entrants, many barriers to entry, few substitutes, many suppliers (none with much power), and many customers. After identifying and analyzing competitive forces, managers must formulate a strategy that minimizes the power external forces have over the organization (a topic discussed more fully in Chapter 5).

How organizations respond to environmental uncertainty.

Responding effectively to the environment often requires devising proactive strategies to change the environment. Strategic maneuvering, for example, involves changing the boundaries of the competitive environment through domain selection, diversification, mergers, and the like. Independent strategies, on the other hand, do not require moving into a new environment but rather changing some aspect of the current environment through competitive aggression, public relations, legal action, and so on. Finally, cooperative strategies, such as contracting, cooptation, and coalition building, involve the working together of two or more organizations.

How an organization's culture affects its response to its environment.

The shared values and practices of an organization—its culture—influence how well the organization responds to its environment. A culture may be strong or weak and may be one of four types: group, hierarchical, rational, or adhocracy. Managing and changing the culture to align it with the organization's environment will require strong, long-term commitment by the CEO and other managers.

DISCUSSION QUESTIONS

1. This chapter's opening quote by Peter Drucker said, "The essence of a business is outside itself." What do you think this means? Do you agree?

2. What are the most important forces in the macroenvironment facing companies today?

3. Review the telecom example in the Prologue and the rest of the chapter. What other organizations or industries have faced or are facing similar circumstances in their external environments?

4. What are the main differences between the macroenvironment and the competitive environment?

5. What kinds of changes do companies make in response to environmental uncertainty?

6. We outlined several proactive responses that organizations can make to the environment. What examples have you seen recently of an organization's responding effectively to its environment? Did the effectiveness of the response depend on whether the organization was facing a threat or an opportunity?

7. Can you think of cultural differences in the organizations with which you are familiar? Were there cultural differences in the campuses you might have visited before selecting the one you are attending? Did these help you decide which college to attend?

CONCLUDING CASE

Butch's Box Shop: A Dying Business

THE PAST

Up until the 1970s–1980s, the forest products industry was the largest employer throughout the northern New England area. Though it has been overtaken by high-tech and other service industries, it remains a significant component of the area's economy. The major categories of the industry include paper and paper products, lumber and wood products, Christmas trees, fuel, maple syrup, and miscellaneous others, not to mention the related areas of recreation, wildlife, soils, and water. The wood business is a tough business with tough margins. It is strenuous and dangerous work and many of its products fall into the commodity category, thus creating an economically tough challenge.

Art and Butch Van Delay are brothers and working partners. Their business began with a pine sawmill that converts logs into boards. Bark mulch, sawdust, and wood chips are the by-products of that manufacturing process. Given the nature of the pine, that grows in New England, about one-third of the lumber generated is high quality that is relatively easy to sell at high prices. The other two-thirds is lower quality, knotty lumber that is much more difficult to market given both its large knots and other natural characteristics and its overabundance of supply/inventory. The oversupply and commodity factors combine to drive prices down, sometimes to levels lower than the cost of raw materials (logs) and manufacturing (sawmill).

From a profit perspective, the challenge to all pine sawmills therefore is marketing. Sawmills must find and/or create markets for wood products that will sell for higher than commodity prices. The major strategy in fact is to convert the commodity (piece of lumber) into products (hundreds of examples and opportunities).

For many years, Art and Butch were able to run a very profitable operation thanks to the addition of a box-making factory. A large percentage of their lower-quality lumber was converted into wooden boxes and containers. Their markets included apple boxes, cranberry boxes, potato bins, fish boxes, novelty boxes, and even caskets. Fish boxes evolved as the major product line. One stretch of years saw the factory produce and sell an average of 12,000–15,000 fish boxes per week.

In addition to adding significant value to the lower-quality lumber, the box-making factory greatly benefited the sawmill by enhancing the quality and value of its overall product mix thanks to the absence of much of the low-end lumber.

THE PRESENT

Art and Butch's cozy and profitable world is diminishing as cardboard boxes and plastic containers substitute for and sometimes even replace the demand for wooden boxes. Cardboard containers are cheaper, and plastic containers are reusable even though they cost more. Wooden fish boxes may only be used once due to health and sanitation factors.

Art and Butch's problems are compounded by smaller and smaller catches of fish and new competitor sawmills that are attempting the same product mix and marketing strategy as the Van Delays.

The Van Delays have studied the situation closely and determined and predicted that their fish-box business will essentially become extinct within a few years. They also know that in the meantime, demand for boxes will steadily decline to the point of jeopardizing profitability. The markets for other wooden boxes and containers are low volume or insignificant in terms of being able to sustain profitability and make up the difference.

The brothers know that they have a perfectly good wood products factory. They also know that some of their existing machinery and production lines could be converted to other uses. Their current setup allows them to rip and crosscut lumber into smaller pieces and to facilitate some fastening and gluing of wooden pieces along with a packaging and truck-loading process. Lumber (the raw material) comes in lengths ranging from 4 to 16 feet, in widths ranging from 3 to 12 inches, and in thicknesses ranging from 1 to 6 inches. The current equipment is capable of ripping and crosscutting pieces down to 6 inches long, 1 inch wide and 1/2 inch thick.

The brothers currently employ about 45 people in the factory. Most of those employees are locals who have been with the company for a long time. Art and Butch feel strongly about their responsibilities as employers beyond just a paycheck. They would love nothing more than to transform their box-making plant into another category of wood products without having to lay anyone off. They also know that some of the success of their sawmill and its people is attributable to the existence of the factory.

THE FUTURE

As is the case in many forest products and other manufacturing companies, the owner-operators are primarily production people, not marketing people. Their goals, however, are to simultaneously leave the wooden box business and shift their market and product mix into one with a brighter and more profitable future without missing a beat, meaning continued dedication and service to their suppliers and employees.

QUESTIONS

1. Success in a commodity industry is usually achieved by controlling costs (internal operations). What are the major challenges facing industries that choose marketing as their success option (external environment)?

2. Given the company's existing raw materials and manufacturing capabilities, what new product lines might the principals consider?

3. What steps must be taken by management over time to effect a smooth transition of operations with respect to the competitive environment discussed in the text chapter?

EXPERIENTIAL EXERCISES
2.1 External Environment Analysis

OBJECTIVE

1. To give you the experience of performing an analysis of a company's external environment

INSTRUCTIONS

1. Select a company you like in the music industry. Using online and/or library resources, including Web sites on the music industry and your company's Web site and annual report, fill out the following External Environment Worksheet for that company:

External Environment Worksheet

Laws and regulations

What are some key laws and regulations under which this company and the music industry must operate?

_____

_____

The economy

How does the state of the economy influence the sales of this company's products?

_____

_____

Technology

What new technologies strongly affect the company you have selected?

_____

_____

Demographics

What changes in the population might affect the company's customer base?

_____

_____

Social issues

What changes in society affect the market for your company's music products?

_____

_____

Suppliers

How does your company's relationship with suppliers affect its profitability?

_____

_____

Competitors

What companies compete with the firm you have selected? Do they compete on price, on quality, or on other factors?

_____

_____

New entrants

Are new competitors to the company likely? possible?

_____

_____

Substitutes

Is there a threat of substitutes for the music industry's existing products?

_____

_____

Customers

What characteristics of the company's customer base influence the company's competitiveness?

_____

_____

Discussion Questions

1. What has the company done to adapt to its environment?

2. How does the company attempt to influence its environment?

2.2 Corporate Culture Preference Scale

OBJECTIVE

This self-assessment is designed to help you to identify a corporate culture that fits most closely with your personal values and assumptions.

INSTRUCTIONS

Read each pair of the statements in the Corporate Culture Preference Scale and circle the statement that describes the organization you would prefer to work in. This exercise is completed alone so students assess themselves honestly without concerns of social comparison. However, class discussion will focus on the importance of matching job applicants to the organization's dominant values.

Corporate Culture Preference Scale

I would prefer to work in an organization:

1a.	Where employees work well together in teams.	**OR**	1b.	That produces highly respected products or services.
2a.	Where top management maintains a sense of order in the workplace.	**OR**	2b.	Where the organization listens to customers and responds quickly to their needs.
3a.	Where employees are treated fairly.	**OR**	3b.	Where employees continuously search for ways to work more efficiently.
4a.	Where employees adapt quickly to new work requirements.	**OR**	4b.	Where corporate leaders work hard to keep employees happy.
5a.	Where senior executives receive special benefits not available to other employees.	**OR**	5b.	Where employees are proud when the organization achieves its performance goals.
6a.	Where employees who perform the best get paid the most.	**OR**	6b.	Where senior executives are respected.
7a.	Where everyone gets their jobs done like clockwork.	**OR**	7b.	That is on top of new innovations in the industry.
8a.	Where employees receive assistance to overcome any personal problems.	**OR**	8b.	Where employees abide by company rules.
9a.	That is always experimenting with new ideas in the marketplace.	**OR**	9b.	That expects everyone to put in 110 percent for peak performance.
10a.	That quickly benefits from market opportunities.	**OR**	10b.	Where employees are always kept informed of what's happening in the organization.
11a.	That can quickly respond to competitive threats.	**OR**	11b.	Where most decisions are made by the top executives.
12a.	Where management keeps everything under control.	**OR**	12b.	Where employees care for each other.

Source: Steven L. McShane and Mary Ann Von Glinow, _Organizational Behavior,_ 3rd ed. (New York: McGraw-Hill/Irwin, 2005), p. 499.

Scoring Key for the Corporate Culture Preference Scale

Scoring Instructions: In each space below, write in a "1" if you circled the statement and "0" if you did not. Then add up the scores for each subscale.

Control Culture   _____ + _____ + _____ + _____ + _____ + _____ = _____
              (2a)   (5a)   (6b)   (8b)   (11b)   (12a)

Performance Culture   _____ + _____ + _____ + _____ + _____ + _____ = _____
              (1b)   (3b)   (5b)   (6a)   (7a)   (9b)

Relationship Culture   _____ + _____ + _____ + _____ + _____ + _____ = _____
              (1a)   (3a)   (4b)   (8a)   (10b)   (12b)

Responsive Culture   _____ + _____ + _____ + _____ + _____ + _____ = _____
              (2b)   (4a)   (7b)   (9a)   (10a)   (11a)

Interpreting your Score: These corporate cultures may be found in many organizations, but they represent only four of many possible organizational cultures. Also, keep in mind none of these subscales is inherently good or bad. Each is effective in different situations. The four corporate cultures are defined below, along with the range of scores for high, medium, and low levels of each dimension based on a sample of MBA students:

Corporate Culture Dimension and Definition	Score Interpretation
Control Culture: This culture values the role of senior executives to lead the organization. Its goal is to keep everyone aligned and under control.	High: 3 to 6 Medium: 1 to 2 Low: 0
Performance Culture: This culture values individual and organizational performance and strives for effectiveness and efficiency.	High: 5 to 6 Medium: 3 to 4 Low: 0 to 2
Relationship Culture: This culture values nurturing and well-being. It considers open communication, fairness, teamwork, and sharing a vital part of organizational life.	High: 6 Medium: 4 to 5 Low: 0 to 3
Responsive Culture: This culture values its ability to keep in tune with the external environment, including being competitive and realizing new opportunities.	High: 6 Medium: 4 to 5 Low: 0 to 3

Chapter **3**

CHAPTER 3

Managerial Decision Making

The business executive is by profession a decision maker.
Uncertainty is his opponent. Overcoming it is his mission.

—John McDonald

LEARNING OBJECTIVES

After studying Chapter 3, you will know:

1. The kinds of decisions you will face as a manager.

2. How to make "rational" decisions.

3. The pitfalls you should avoid when making decisions.

4. The pros and cons of using a group to make decisions.

5. The procedures to use in leading a decision-making group.

6. How to encourage creative decisions.

7. The processes by which decisions are made in organizations.

8. How to make decisions in a crisis.

MERCK AND VIOXX

Merck has long been known as an outstanding company, a leader in the pharmaceutical industry. Over the years it has enjoyed an excellent reputation, both as an investment and as a company that sometimes sacrifices the bottom line in order to do the right thing ethically in the service of public health.

One of Merck's greatest success stories was the pain reliever Vioxx. It was a true blockbuster product, bringing in $2.5 billion in annual sales. But in late 2004, CEO Raymond Gilmartin decided to pull the drug off the market. The reason: In September 2004, a long-term Merck study indicated that the drug raised the risk of heart attack and stroke after 18 months of continuous use. Some researchers said the risk occurs much sooner than that.

Some doctors and other critics said that Merck had enough information by 2000 to conclude that the drug was risky. Merck said the studies then available were statistically insignificant or ambiguous. One of the original researchers who suspected a problem, a prominent cardiologist, said that the warning signs were subtle and based only on soft data. He and others suspected a problem, but he said that in 2000 their suspicions lacked hard data and were merely speculative, and they could have been wrong.

New drugs have unknown and unpredictable side effects. To speed up the introduction of potential new blockbusters is to risk lawsuits and regulatory proceedings. On the other hand, too much caution makes bottom lines suffer, and patients are unable to benefit from potentially helpful drugs. Merck executives faced difficult decisions throughout the development and marketing processes leading up to the Vioxx crisis, and face difficult decisions going forward.

Arthur Caplan, chairman of medical ethics at the University of Pennsylvania Medical School, in considering the Merck crisis in conjunction with a subsequent similar problem faced by Pfizer for its Celebrex drug, stated, "No matter what strategy these companies take, this is one of the great drug-company disasters of all time."

Sources for Prologue, Connections, Epilogue: "The Best & Worst Managers," *BusinessWeek*, January 10, 2005, pp. 74–86; M. Mandel, "Candor Can Immunize Big Pharma," *BusinessWeek Online*, December 24, 2004; A. Tsao, "Pfizer and Merck, Different Strokes," *BusinessWeek Online*, December 21, 2004; A. Barrett, "At Merck, There Are No Easy Answers," *BusinessWeek Online*, December 15, 2004; A. Barrett, "On the Firing Line at Embattled Merck," *BusinessWeek*, December 13, 2004, pp. 92–94; A. Barrett, "Minimizing the Mess at Merck," *BusinessWeek Online*, November 15, 2004; A. Barrett, "A New World of Pain for Merck," *BusinessWeek Online*, October 1, 2004; "Early Twinges over Vioxx," *BusinessWeek Online*, October 1, 2004; M. Kaufman, "New Study Criticizes Painkiller Marketing," *The Washington Post*, January 25, 2005, p. A6.

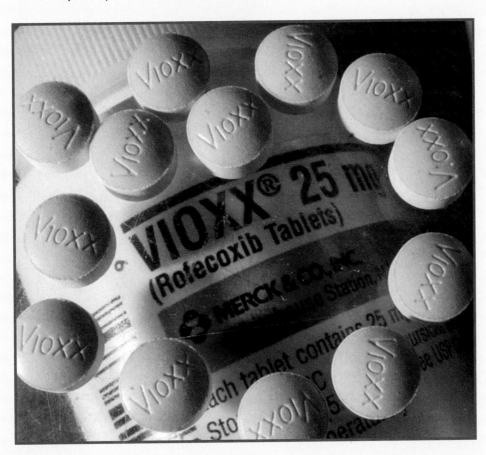

The best managers make decisions constantly, and make them well. At CNN, the president makes critical decisions every minute or two, all day long, while standing eye-to-eye with reporters, editors, and others. Executive producers may make a hundred decisions during a live one-hour show. And these instantaneous decisions have lasting impact. It is no task for the indecisive or squeamish. As CNN's vice chairman said, "Nobody is going to tell you what to do. It's up to you to figure out what to do, then do it. Always take the proactive path. Ask for advice, sure, but don't sit on your hands waiting for an order."[1]

Decisions. If you can't make them, you won't be an effective manager. This chapter discusses the kinds of decisions managers face, how they are made, and how they *should* be made.

Characteristics of Managerial Decisions

Managers face problems constantly. Some problems that require a decision are relatively simple; others seem overwhelming. Some demand immediate action, while others take months or even years to unfold.

Actually, managers often ignore problems.[2] For several reasons, they avoid taking action.[3] First, managers can't be sure how much time, energy, or trouble lies ahead once they start working on a problem. Second, getting involved is risky; tackling a problem but failing to solve it successfully can hurt a manager's track record. Third, because problems can be so perplexing, it is easier to procrastinate or to get busy with less demanding activities.

A moderate ego demonstrates wisdom.
Lao-tzu

You'll be making decisions constantly. It may seem obvious, but it's worth stating: If you know how to make good decisions, you'll deliver good results.

It is important to understand why decision making can be so challenging. Figure 3.1 illustrates several characteristics of managerial decisions that contribute to their difficulty and pressure. Most managerial decisions lack structure and entail risk, uncertainty, and conflict.

Lack of Structure

Lack of structure is the usual state of affairs in managerial decision making.[4] Although some decisions are routine and clear-cut, for most there is no automatic procedure to follow. Problems are novel and unstructured, leaving the decision maker uncertain about how to proceed.

An important distinction illustrating this point is between programmed and nonprogrammed decisions. **Programmed decisions** have been encountered and made be-

FIGURE 3.1
Characteristics of Managerial Decisions

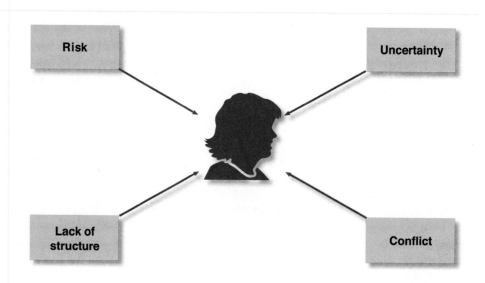

	Programmed Decisions	**Nonprogrammed Decisions**
Problem	Frequent, repetitive, routine. Much certainty regarding cause-and-effect relationships.	Novel, unstructured. Much uncertainty regarding cause-and-effect relationships.
Procedure	Dependence on policies, rules, and definite procedures.	Necessity for creativity, intuition, tolerance for ambiguity, creative problem solving.
Examples		
Business firm	Periodic reorders of inventory.	Diversification into new products and markets.
University	Necessary grade-point average for good academic standing.	Construction of new classroom facilities.
Health care	Procedure for admitting patients.	Purchase of experimental equipment.
Government	Merit system for promotion of state employees.	Reorganization of state government agencies.

TABLE 3.1
Comparison of Types of Decisions

SOURCE: J. Gibson, J. Ivancevich, and J. Donnelly Jr., *Organizations: Behavior, Structure, Processes,* 10th ed. Copyright ©2000 by The McGraw-Hill Companies. Reproduced with permission of The McGraw-Hill Companies.

fore. They have objectively correct answers and can be solved by using simple rules, policies, or numerical computations. If you face a programmed decision, there exists a clear procedure or structure for arriving at the right decision. For example, if you are a small-business owner and must decide the amounts for your employees' paychecks, you can use a formula—and if the amounts are wrong, your employees will prove it to you. Table 3.1 gives some other examples.

If most important decisions were programmed, managerial life would be much easier. But managers typically face **nonprogrammed decisions:** new, novel, complex decisions having no certain outcomes. They have a variety of possible solutions, all of which have merits and drawbacks. The decision maker must create or impose a method for making the decision; there is no predetermined structure on which to rely. As Table 3.1 suggests, important, difficult decisions tend to be nonprogrammed, and they demand creative approaches.

Uncertainty and Risk

If you have all the information you need, and can predict precisely the consequences of your actions, you are operating under a condition of **certainty.**[5] Managers are expressing their preference for certainty when they are not satisfied hearing about what *might have* happened or *may* happen, and insist on hearing what *did* or *will* happen.[6] But perfect certainty is rare. For important, nonprogrammed managerial decisions, uncertainty is the rule.

Uncertainty means the manager has insufficient information to know the consequences of different actions. Decision makers may have strong opinions—they may feel sure of themselves—but they are still operating under conditions of uncertainty if they lack pertinent information and cannot estimate accurately the likelihood of different results of their actions.

When you can estimate the likelihood of various consequences, but still do not know with certainty what will happen, you are facing **risk.** Risk exists when the probability of an action being successful is less than 100 percent, and losses may occur. If

programmed decisions

Decisions encountered and made before, having objectively correct answers, and solvable by using simple rules, policies, or numerical computations.

nonprogrammed decisions

New, novel, complex decisions having no proven answers.

certainty

The state that exists when decision makers have accurate and comprehensive information.

uncertainty

The state that exists when decision makers have insufficient information.

risk

The state that exists when the probability of success is less than 100 percent, and losses may occur.

the decision is the wrong one, you may lose money, time, reputation, or other important assets.

Risk, like uncertainty, is a fact of life in managerial decision making. But this is not the same as *taking* a risk. Whereas it sometimes seems as though risk takers are admired, and that entrepreneurs and investors thrive on taking risks, the reality is that good decision makers prefer to *manage* risk. This means that while they accept the fact that consequential decisions entail risk, they do everything they can to anticipate the risk, minimize it, and control it.

Managerial Risk Taking

When and why do managers make risky decisions? Many factors affect risk taking and risk avoidance. Some are conscious, coming from rational analysis, and some are more subtle and subjective. For example, performance affects risk: Managers take more risks when their companies perform poorly, particularly as they approach bankruptcy. Managers at better-performing firms, especially those that perform up to their aspirations, take fewer, lower risks.

In addition, the business climate affects risk taking, sometimes in surprising ways. Corporate profits were up more than 70 percent by December 2004 since their low in 2001. Normally high profits lead to higher risk taking in the form of business investment; cash provides the means to exploit investment opportunities in new products, technology, factories, people, and markets. But business investment during this period went up only 18 percent. The explanation may be a return to risk aversion (read: "caution"). In the 1990s, it seemed that stocks would always rise; with nothing to worry about, managers often felt that they could do anything, take any chance. But when the tech bubble burst, the recession came, the terrorists attacked, and corporate scandals hit the news, everything changed. Managers in this new risk-averse climate did not make the risky new investments that they would have made in past business climates.

Amgen CEO Kevin Sharer has in his office a portrait of General George Custer, to remind him not to underestimate his opponents when he makes important decisions. Sharer's role model is Horatio Nelson, the English naval hero famous for taking huge risks, often against orders. But unlike Custer, Nelson didn't rush headlong into danger. Sharer wants Amgen to be like Nelson: acting boldly and swiftly, but with consensus—taking risks, but calculated risks having big potential payoffs.

SOURCES: K. Miller and W. Chen, "Variable Organizational Risk Preferences: Tests of the March-Shapira Model," *Academy of Management Journal* 47, (2004) pp. 105–115; R. J. Samuelson, "Cautious Capitalist," *The Washington Post*, December 22, 2004, p. A27; M. Boyle, "Growing against the Grain," *Fortune*, May 3, 2004, pp. 148–156.

Managers prefer certainty to uncertainty. For example, Jim Rogers, CEO of Cinergy, an electric and gas supplier, would be happy to have one major regulation about carbon dioxide emissions passed now.[7] That would be better than multiple, unpredictable regulations over the coming years; he prefers certainty now to the uncertainties created by "death by 1,000 cuts," which makes long-term planning impossible.

As another example, a company called Surface Systems (SSI) profits by specifying probabilities, thereby reducing (but by no means eliminating) uncertainty for decision makers.[8] SSI forecasts the weather as it pertains to particular business problems. More than $1 trillion of the U.S. economy—including orchards, construction, airline travel, clothing and ice cream sales—is affected by temperature, precipitation, wind, and humidity. Forty-four state departments of transportation pay SSI to tell them when to salt their highways, because roads require just one-tenth the amount of salt if it's applied just before the snowfall rather than afterward. Amusement parks, if they know the odds of rain during the hours when customers might make detours to movie theaters instead, can save on labor and food costs. Reducing uncertainty isn't merely psychologically comforting; it has real value.

George Conrades, the chairman and CEO of Akamai Technologies, says, "We operate in an environment—the Internet—where there's an enormous amount of uncertainty. You can't be sure what's going to happen tomorrow, never mind next year. The danger is that the uncertainty can lead to paralysis. You spend so much time trying to nail down all the possibilities and risks, you never get around to taking action. And if that happens—if you become indecisive—you're dead" (p. 120).[9]

The effects of weather on business can be extremely uncertain.

Conflict

Important decisions are even more difficult because of the conflict managers face. **Conflict,** which exists when the manager must consider opposing pressures from different sources, occurs at two levels.

First, individual decision makers experience psychological conflict when several options are attractive, or when none of the options is attractive. For instance, a manager may have to decide whom to lay off, when she doesn't want to lay off anyone. Or she may have three promising job applicants for one position—but choosing one means she has to reject the other two.

Second, conflict arises between people. The chief financial officer argues in favor of increasing long-term debt to finance an acquisition. The chief executive officer, however, prefers to minimize such debt and find the funds elsewhere. The marketing department wants more product lines to sell, and the engineers want higher-quality products. But the production people want to lower costs by having longer production runs of fewer products with no changes. Few decisions are without conflict.

> **conflict**
>
> Opposing pressures from different sources. Two levels of conflict are psychological conflict and conflict that arises between individuals or groups.

The Stages of Decision Making

Faced with these challenges, how can you make good decisions? The ideal decision-making process moves through six stages. At companies that have institutionalized the process, these stages are intended to answer the following questions:[10] What do we want to change? What's preventing us from reaching the "desired state"? How *could* we make the change? What's the *best* way to do it? Are we following the plan? and How well did it work out?

More formally, as Figure 3.2 illustrates, decision makers should (1) identify and diagnose the problem, (2) generate alternative solutions, (3) evaluate alternatives, (4) make the choice, (5) implement the decision, and (6) evaluate the decision.

Identifying and Diagnosing the Problem

The first stage in the decision-making process is to recognize that a problem exists and must be solved. Typically, a manager realizes some discrepancy between the current state (the way things are) and a desired state (the way things ought to be). Such discrepancies— say, in organizational or unit performance—may be detected by comparing current

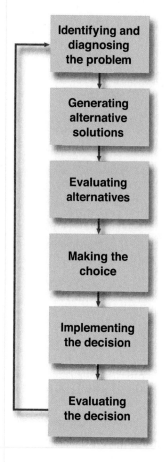

FIGURE 3.2
The Stages of Decision Making

performance against (1) *past* performance, (2) the *current* performance of other organizations or units, or (3) *future* expected performance as determined by plans and forecasts.[11]

Recognizing that a problem exists is only the beginning of this stage. The decision maker also must want to do something about it and must believe that the resources and abilities necessary for solving the problem exist.[12] Then the decision maker must dig in deeper and attempt to *diagnose* the true cause of the problem symptoms that surfaced.

For example, a sales manager knows that sales have dropped drastically. If he is leaving the company soon or believes the decreased sales volume is due to the economy (which he can't do anything about), he won't take action. But if he does try to solve the problem, he should not automatically reprimand his sales staff, add new people, or increase the advertising budget. He must analyze *why* sales are down and then develop a solution appropriate to his analysis. Asking why, of yourself and others, is essential to understanding the real problem.

Useful questions to ask and answer in this stage include[13]

- Is there a difference between what is actually happening and what should be happening?
- How can you describe the deviation, as specifically as possible?
- What is/are the cause(s) of the deviation?
- What specific goals should be met?
- Which of these goals are absolutely critical to the success of the decision?

Generating Alternative Solutions

The second stage links problem diagnosis to the development of alternative courses of action aimed at solving the problem. Managers generate at least some alternative solutions based on past experiences.[14]

Solutions range from ready made to custom made.[15] Decision makers who search for **ready-made solutions** use ideas they have tried before or follow the advice of others who have faced similar problems. **Custom-made solutions,** by contrast, must be designed for specific problems. This technique often combines ideas into new, creative solutions. For example, the Sony Walkman was created by combining two existing products: earphones and a tape player.[16] Potentially, custom-made solutions can be devised for any challenge. Later in the chapter, we will discuss how to generate creative ideas.

Importantly, there are potentially many more alternatives available than managers may realize. For example, what would you do if one of your competitors reduced prices? An obvious choice would be to reduce your own prices. But when American Airlines, Northwest Airlines, and other carriers engaged in fare wars in the early 1990s, the result was record volume of air travel and record losses for the industry.[17]

Fortunately, cutting prices in response to a competitor's price cuts is not the only alternative available, although sometimes it is assumed to be. If one of your competitors cuts prices, don't automatically respond with the initial, obvious response. Generate multiple options, and thoroughly forecast the consequences of these different options. Options other than price cuts include nonprice responses such as emphasizing consumer risks to low-priced products, building awareness of your products' features and overall

ready-made solutions

Ideas that have been seen or tried before.

custom-made solutions

New, creative solutions designed specifically for the problem.

quality, and communicating your cost advantage to your competitors so they realize that they can't win a price war. Winn-Dixie used that last strategy against Food Lion, and the stores stopped competing on price. If you do decide to cut your price as a last resort, do it fast—if you do it slowly, your competitors will gain sales in the meantime, which may embolden them to employ the same tactic again in the future.[18]

Evaluating Alternatives

The third stage involves determining the value or adequacy of the alternatives that were generated. Which solution will be the best?

Too often, alternatives are evaluated with little thought or logic. After Walter P. Chrysler died, Chrysler's lawyer sometimes contacted the ghost of Walter P. for advice. The lawyer would excuse himself from the meeting, go into Chrysler's office, close the door and drapes, turn off the lights, and conjure up Chrysler's spirit. Then the lawyer would return to the meeting and reveal his findings, which the Chrysler executives would use to make the final decision.[19]

Obviously, alternatives should be evaluated more carefully than this. Fundamental to this process is to predict the consequences that will occur if the various options are put into effect.

Managers should consider several types of consequences. Of course, they must attempt to predict the effects on financial or other performance measures. But there are other, less clear-cut consequences to address.[20] Decisions set a precedent; will this precedent be a help or a hindrance in the future? Also, the success or failure of the decision will go into the track records of those involved in making it.

Refer again to your original goals, defined in the first stage. Which goals does each alternative meet, and fail to meet? Which alternatives are most acceptable to you and to other important stakeholders? If several alternatives may solve the problem, which can be implemented at the lowest cost? If no alternative achieves all your goals, perhaps you can combine two or more of the best ones.

Key questions here are:[21]

- Is our information about alternatives complete and current? If not, can we get more and better information?
- Does the alternative meet our primary objectives?
- What problems could we have if we implement the alternative?

Companies that housed operations in and around the World Trade Center had to rely on contingency plans after 9/11. Many were key players in the financial markets. Those that could, reassured clients and the world that operations would continue. Many took out patriotic, inspirational ads such as this one from Standard & Poor's.

Of course, results cannot be forecast with perfect accuracy. But sometimes decision makers can build in safeguards against an uncertain future by considering the potential consequences of several different scenarios. Then they generate **contingency plans**—alternative courses of action that can be implemented depending on how the future unfolds.

For example, scenario planners making decisions about the future might consider four alternative views of the future state of the U.S. economy.[22] (1) An economic boom with 5 to 6 percent annual growth and the United States much stronger than its global competitors; (2) a moderately strong economy with 2 to 3 percent growth;

contingency plans

Alternative courses of action that can be implemented based on how the future unfolds.

(3) a pessimistic outlook with no growth, rising unemployment, and recession; or (4) a worse scenario with global depression, massive unemployment, and widespread social unrest.

Some scenarios will seem more likely than others, and some may seem highly improbable. Ultimately, one of the scenarios will prove to be more accurate than the others. The process of considering multiple scenarios raises important "what if?" questions for decision makers and highlights the need for preparedness and contingency plans.

As you read this, what economic scenario is unfolding? What are the important current events and trends? What scenarios could evolve six or eight years from now? How will *you* prepare?

Making the Choice

Once you have considered the possible consequences of your options, it is time to make your decision. Important concepts here are maximizing, satisficing, and optimizing.[23]

Maximizing is making the best possible decision. The maximizing decision realizes the greatest positive consequences and the fewest negative consequences. In other words, maximizing results in the greatest benefit at the lowest cost, with the largest expected total return. Maximizing requires searching thoroughly for a complete range of alternatives, carefully assessing each alternative, comparing one to another, and then choosing or creating the very best.

Satisficing is choosing the first option that is minimally acceptable or adequate; the choice appears to meet a targeted goal or criterion. When you satisfice, you compare your choice against your goal, not against other options. Satisficing means that a search for alternatives stops at the first one that is okay. Commonly, people do not expend the time or energy to gather more information. Instead, they make the expedient decision based on readily available information. Satisficing is sometimes a result of laziness; other times, there is no other option because time is short, information is unavailable, or other constraints make maximizing impossible.

Let's say you are purchasing new equipment and your goal is to avoid spending too much money. You would be maximizing if you checked out all your options and their prices, and then bought the cheapest one that met your performance requirements. But you would be satisficing if you bought the first one you found that was within your budget and failed to look for less expensive options.

Optimizing means that you achieve the best possible balance among several goals. Perhaps, in purchasing equipment, you are interested in quality and durability as well as price. So, instead of buying the cheapest piece of equipment that works, you buy the one with the best combination of attributes, even though there may be options that are better on the price criterion and others that are better on the quality and durability criteria.

The same idea applies to achieving business goals: One marketing strategy could maximize sales, while a different strategy might maximize profit. An optimizing strategy is the one that achieves the best balance among multiple goals.

Implementing the Decision

The decision-making process does not end once a choice is made. The chosen alternative must be implemented.

Sometimes the people involved in making the choice must put it into effect. At other times, they delegate the responsibility for implementation to others, such as when a top management team changes a policy or operating procedure and has operational managers carry out the change. Unfortunately, sometimes people make decisions but don't take action.

---

maximizing

A decision realizing the best possible outcome.

---

satisficing

Choosing an option that is acceptable, although not necessarily the best or perfect.

---

optimizing

Achieving the best possible balance among several goals.

It's easy to become so focused on maximizing on one goal that you lose sight of other important goals. You're optimizing if you make sure that no important result suffers too much, unnecessarily.

Implementing decisions may fail to occur when talking a lot is mistaken for doing a lot; if people just assume that a decision will "happen"; when people forget that merely making a decision changes nothing; when meetings, plans, and reports are seen as "actions," even if they have no effect on what people actually do; and if managers don't check to ensure that what was said was actually done.[24]

Those who implement the decision must *understand* the choice and why it was made. They also must be *committed* to its successful implementation. These needs can be met by involving those people in the early stages of the decision process. At Steelcase, the world's largest manufacturer of office furniture, new product ideas are put through simultaneous design, engineering, and marketing scrutiny.[25] This is in contrast to an approach in which designers design and the concept is later relayed to other departments for implementation. In the latter case, full understanding and total commitment of all departments are less likely.

Managers should plan implementation carefully. Adequate planning requires several steps.[26]

1. Determine how things will look when the decision is fully operational.
2. Chronologically order, perhaps with a flow diagram, the steps necessary to achieve a fully operational decision.
3. List the resources and activities required to implement each step.
4. Estimate the time needed for each step.
5. Assign responsibility for each step to specific individuals.

Decision makers should assume that things will *not* go smoothly during implementation. It is very useful to take a little extra time to *identify potential problems* and *identify potential opportunities*. Then, you can take actions to prevent problems and also be ready to seize on unexpected opportunities. Useful questions are:

- What problems could this action cause?
- What can we do to prevent the problems?
- What unintended benefits or opportunities could arise?
- How can we make sure they happen?
- How can we be ready to act when the opportunities come?

Many of the chapters in this book are concerned with implementation issues: how to implement strategy, allocate resources, organize for results, lead and motivate people, manage change, and so on. View the chapters from that perspective, and learn as much as you can about how to implement properly.

Evaluating the Decision

The final stage in the decision-making process is evaluating the decision. This means collecting information on how well the decision is working. Quantifiable goals—a 20 percent increase in sales, a 95 percent reduction in accidents, 100 percent on-time deliveries—can be set before the solution to the problem is implemented. Then objective data can be gathered to accurately determine the success (or failure) of the decision.

Decision evaluation is useful whether the conclusion is positive or negative. Feedback that suggests the decision is working implies that the decision should be continued and perhaps applied elsewhere in the organization. Negative feedback means that either (1) implementation will require more time, resources, effort, or thought or (2) the decision was a bad one.

If the decision appears inappropriate, it's back to the drawing board. Then the process cycles back to the first stage: (re)definition of the problem. The decision-making process begins anew, preferably with more information, new suggestions, and an approach that attempts to eliminate the mistakes made the first time around.

Connections: MERCK AND VIOXX

You already know that Merck withdrew Vioxx from the market late in 2004. Here's a little more background. In 2000, when the research hinted that Vioxx had possible cardiovascular side effects, Merck quickly issued a press release to make the findings public. But about a month later, it issued another release confirming the drug's cardiovascular safety and rebutting "speculative news reports." Merck scientists argued that Vioxx didn't hurt the heart; they said that the other medication against which it was compared in the study helped the heart.

Some doctors said that Merck had ignored their concerns about Vioxx for years. Merck traditionally has cared deeply about how the medical community perceives it. This may have affected the decision to pull the drug off the market after the more damaging 2004 study became public. The decision came at the expense of many investors, who would have preferred the drug not be withdrawn, and at significant cost to Merck's reputation. Some say it was a mistake, and that it would have been better simply to publicize more widely the potential side effects, despite some reduced sales.

Shortly thereafter, Pfizer's Celebrex came under similar attack. But Pfizer, which had a stronger recent financial record than Merck, kept Celebrex on the market. It did agree to stop advertising to consumers, but it increased its advertising spending for the medical community. Keeping Celebrex on the market placed the responsibility for decision making on doctors and patients. Pfizer management considered this decision carefully, and decided it was a risk worth taking.

The Best Decision

How can managers tell whether they have made the best decision? One approach is to wait until the results are in. But what if the decision has been made but not yet implemented? What if it takes years before the decision's impact is fully understood?

While nothing can guarantee a "best" decision, managers should at least be confident that they followed proper *procedures* that will yield the best possible decision under the circumstances. This means that the decision makers were appropriately vigilant in making the decision. **Vigilance** occurs when the decision makers carefully and conscientiously execute all six stages of decision making, including making provisions for implementation and evaluation.[27]

> **vigilance**
>
> A process in which a decision maker carefully executes all stages of decision making.

Even if managers reflect on these decision-making activities and conclude that they were executed conscientiously, they still will not know whether the decision will work; after all, nothing guarantees a good outcome. But they *will* know that they did their best to make the best possible decision.

Most of the causes of business failures described in the following section are a result of inadequate vigilance. Consider them decision traps; if you find yourself thinking in the following ways, you may be making poor decisions.

Failed Decision Making

Why do companies, and managers, fail? They fail because of poor decisions, often stemming from poor decision-making processes. Entrepreneurs and corporate managers may throw their hearts into their work, but sometimes fail to use their heads. Entrepreneurs often fall prey to the following mistaken beliefs:

- *I need to make the decisions myself.* When you start your own business, you are responsible for everything. But over time, you need to bring in good people and let go a bit. Stay in touch with what's happening, but you have to delegate more, give other people more responsibility, and let them do what they do best.

- *E-commerce is easy and cheap.* It's easy to construct a Web site that can handle transactions. But most e-commerce efforts have failed, and many big companies have had to try many times before getting it close to right. The strategic, technological, and organizational issues should not be underestimated.
- *My forecasts are conservative.* You may think you can make your plan work because you have made cautious predictions. But you'd better have contingency plans in case your forecasts prove wrong. A rule of thumb is that start-ups take twice as long or need three times as much money as their founders predict. Sales projections are almost never met.
- *With this much money to work with, we can't miss.* It's tough to have to pinch pennies. But too much money may make for risky or poorly thought-out decisions, and you will lose control of costs.

Among failed corporate executives, some common faulty decision processes include:

- *Mistaken perceptions of reality.* Roger Smith of General Motors wasted billions of dollars on robotics, thinking that automating work was essential when the real need was to improve processes.
- *Delusional attitudes.* Any executive may go down a destructive path, even when the evidence says it's not working. When young consumers said that their products weren't hip, Levi Strauss executives paid no attention, refusing to change.
- *Breakdowns in communication.* Important information doesn't get to the top or is ignored. The most powerful example of this may be 9/11.
- *Failing to correct mistakes.* Rubbermaid's CEO in the 1990s, Wolfgang Schmidt, apparently thought he "knew everything about everything." But he was wrong. Before Schmidt, Rubbermaid was Number 1 on *Fortune*'s list of the most highly admired companies. It's no longer anywhere on the list, and Schmidt is gone.

SOURCES: B. G. Posner, "Why Companies Fail," *Inc.*, June 1993, pp. 102–6; R. Balu (Ed.), "Starting your Startup," *Fast Company*, January–February 2000, pp. 81–114; A. Segars, "The Seven Myths of E-Commerce," *Financial Times Mastering Management Review*, January 2000, pp. 28–35; S. Finkelstein, *Why Smart Executives Fail* (New York: Portfolio, 2003), reviewed by H. Beam in *Academy of Management Executive*, May 2004, pp. 157–58.

Barriers to Effective Decision Making

Vigilance and full execution of the six-stage decision-making process are the exception rather than the rule. But research shows that when managers use such rational processes, better decisions result.[28] Managers who make sure they engage in these processes are more effective.

Why don't people automatically invoke such rational processes? It is easy to neglect or improperly execute these processes. The problem may be improperly defined, or goals misidentified. Not enough solutions may be generated, or they may be evaluated incompletely. A satisficing rather than maximizing choice may be made. Implementation may be poorly planned or executed, or monitoring may be inadequate or nonexistent. And decisions are influenced by subjective psychological biases, time pressures, and social realities.

Psychological Biases

Decision makers are far from objective in the way they gather, evaluate, and apply information toward making their choices. People have biases that interfere with objective rationality. The examples that follow represent only a few of the many documented subjective biases.[29]

The **illusion of control** is a belief that one can influence events even when one has no control over what will happen. Gambling is one example: Some people believe they

illusion of control

People's belief that they can influence events, even when they have no control over what will happen.

87

have the skill to beat the odds even though most people, most of the time, cannot. In business, such overconfidence can lead to failure because decision makers ignore risks and fail to objectively evaluate the odds of success. Relatedly, they may have an unrealistically positive view of themselves or their companies,[30] believe they can do no wrong, or hold a general optimism about the future that can lead them to believe they are immune to risk and failure.[31] For example, overconfidence was one contributor to the fall of Enron. Professor Jeffrey Pfeffer of Stanford described Enron's saga as one of "unmitigated pride and arrogance. My impression is that they thought they knew everything, which always is the fatal flaw" (p. A11).[32]

Framing effects refer to how problems or decision alternatives are phrased or presented, and how these subjective influences can override objective facts. In one example, managers indicated a desire to invest more money in a course of action that was reported to have a 70 percent chance of profit than in one said to have a 30 percent chance of loss.[33] The choices were equivalent in their chances of success; it was the way the options were framed that determined the managers' choices.

The Merrill Lynch CEO used framing effectively to advance an idea at an important meeting.[34] He went around the room getting comments from each executive. Each identified one or more problems with the proposal. After all had spoken, the CEO did not dismiss the problems—they were potentially genuine obstacles. But instead of saying "There's too many problems, let's drop the idea," he said that the idea was too important to drop, so the question is, how do we solve the problems? He didn't frame the issue as a choice of whether to proceed; he framed it as a challenge of how to overcome the obstacles.

Often decision makers **discount the future.** That is, in their evaluation of alternatives, they weigh short-term costs and benefits more heavily than longer-term costs and benefits. Consider your own decision about whether to go for a dental checkup. The choice to go poses short-term financial costs, anxiety, and perhaps physical pain. The choice not to go will inflict even greater costs and more severe pain if dental problems worsen. How do you choose? Many people decide to avoid the short-term costs by not going for regular checkups, but end up facing much greater pain in the long run.

The same bias applies to students who don't study, weight watchers who sneak dessert or skip an exercise routine, and working people who take the afternoon off to play golf when they really need to work. It can also affect managers who hesitate to invest funds in research and development programs that may not pay off until far into the future. In all these cases, the avoidance of short-term costs or the seeking of short-term rewards results in negative long-term consequences.

In contrast, CEO George David of United Technologies likes to move early to fund new technologies like fuel cells. These investments drain millions from the annual bottom line, but he believes that they are the seeds of company growth for the long haul. A colleague explains, "George looks at a 20- to 50-year time frame"[35] (p. 77).

When U.S. companies sacrifice present value to invest for the future—such as when Weyerhaeuser incurs enormous costs for its reforestation efforts that won't lead to harvest until 60 years in the future—it seems the exception rather than the rule. Discounting the future partly explains governmental budget deficits, environmental destruction, and decaying urban infrastructure.[36]

framing effects

A psychological bias influenced by the way in which a problem or decision alternative is phrased or presented.

discounting the future

A bias weighting short-term costs and benefits more heavily than longer-term costs and benefits.

Professional gambling establishments count on people's willingness to try to beat the odds. Their illusion of control contributes to the high profits earned by most casinos.

Time Pressures

In today's rapidly changing business environment, the premium is on acting quickly and keeping pace. The most conscientiously made business decisions can become irrelevant and even disastrous if managers take too long to make them.

How can managers make decisions quickly? Some natural tendencies, at least for North Americans, might be to skimp on analysis (not be too vigilant), suppress conflict, and make decisions on one's own without consulting other managers.[37] These strategies may speed up decision making, but they reduce decision *quality*.

In fact, the "speed trap" can be as dangerous as moving too slowly.[38] In an Internet start-up that went bankrupt, fast decisions initially helped the firm achieve its growth objectives. Early on, the founders did everything they could to create a sense of urgency: They planned a meeting to "light a fire under the company," calling it a "state-of-emergency address" with the purpose of creating "the idea of panic with an emerging deadline." They used a metaphor of climbing a big mountain, being only so far up and having too far to go to make it at their current pace. They frequently accelerated the timetable for decisions. They went from fast to too fast, and speed became more important than content. They failed to consider multiple alternatives, used little information, didn't fully acknowledge competing views, and didn't consult outside advisers. They never considered slowing down to be an option. This speed trap syndrome is a potential pathology for organizations under pressure to make fast decisions.

Can managers under time pressure make both timely and high-quality decisions? A recent study of decision-making processes in microcomputer firms—a high-tech, fast-paced industry—showed some important differences between fast-acting and slower-acting firms.[39] The fast-acting firms realized significant competitive advantages without sacrificing the quality of their decisions.

What tactics do such companies use? First, instead of relying on old data, long-range planning, and futuristic forecasts, they focus on *real-time information*: current information obtained with little or no time delay. For example, they constantly monitor daily operating measures like work in process rather than checking periodically the traditional accounting-based indicators such as profitability.

Second, they *involve people more effectively and efficiently* in the decision-making process. They rely heavily on trusted experts, and this yields both good advice and the confidence to act quickly despite uncertainty. They also take a *realistic view of conflict*: They value differing opinions, but they know that if disagreements are not resolved, the top executive must make the final choice in the end. Slow-moving firms, in contrast, are stymied by conflict. Like the fast-moving firms they seek consensus, but when disagreements persist, they fail to come to a decision.

You'll feel pressure to make quick decisions, but that makes it easier to make mistakes. Fortunately, you can be vigilant while moving quickly, and you can avoid the "speed trap."

Social Realities

As the description of decision making in the microcomputer industry implies, many decisions are made by a group rather than by an individual manager. In slow-moving firms, interpersonal factors decrease decision-making effectiveness. Even the manager acting alone is accountable to the boss and to others and must consider the preferences and reactions of many people. Important managerial decisions are marked by conflict among interested parties. Therefore, many decisions are the result of intensive social interactions, bargaining, and politicking.

The remainder of this chapter focuses on the social context of decisions, including decision making in groups and the realities of decision making in organizations.

Decision Making in Groups

Sometimes a manager finds it necessary to convene a group of people for the purpose of making an important decision. Some advise that in today's complex business

Potential Advantages	Potential Disadvantages
1. Larger pool of information.	1. One person dominates.
2. More perspectives and approaches.	2. Satisficing.
3. Intellectual stimulation.	3. Groupthink.
4. People understand the decision.	4. Goal displacement.
5. People are committed to the decision.	

TABLE 3.2
Pros and Cons of Using a Group to Make Decisions

environment, significant problems should *always* be tackled by groups.[40] Managers therefore must understand how groups operate and how to use them to improve decision making. You will learn much more about how groups work later in the book.

The basic philosophy behind using a group to make decisions is captured by the adage "two heads are better than one." But is this statement really valid? Yes, it is—potentially.

If enough time is available, groups usually make higher-quality decisions than most individuals acting alone. However, groups often are inferior to the *best* individual.[41] How well the group performs depends on how effectively it capitalizes on the potential advantages and minimizes the potential problems of using a group. Table 3.2 summarizes these issues.

Potential Advantages of Using a Group

If other people have something to contribute, using groups to make a decision offers at least five potential advantages.[42]

1. More *information* is available when several people are making the decision. If one member doesn't have all the facts or the pertinent expertise, another member might.
2. A greater number of *perspectives* on the issues, or different *approaches* to solving the problem, are available. The problem may be new to one group member but familiar to another. Or the group may need to consider other viewpoints—financial, legal, marketing, human resources, and so on—to achieve an optimal solution.
3. Group discussion provides an opportunity for *intellectual stimulation*. It can get people thinking and unleash their creativity to a far greater extent than would be possible with individual decision making.

These three potential advantages of using a group improve the chance that a more fully informed, higher-quality decision will result. Thus, managers should involve people with different backgrounds, perspectives, and access to information. They should not involve only their cronies who think the same way they do.

Using a group may seem to slow down decision making. If one person dominates the discussion, it may feel like you're speeding up the decision making. But one dominant person reduces decision quality, and most of you will have wasted your time.

4. People who participate in a group discussion are more likely to *understand* why the decision was made. They will have heard the relevant arguments both for the chosen alternative and against the rejected alternatives.
5. Group discussion typically leads to a higher level of *commitment* to the decision. Buying into the proposed solution translates into high motivation to ensure that it is executed well.

The last two advantages improve the chances that the decision will be implemented successfully. Therefore, managers should involve the people who will be responsible for implementing the decision as early in the deliberations as possible.

Potential Problems of Using a Group

Things *can* go wrong when groups make decisions. Most of the potential problems concern the process through which group members interact with one another.[43]

1. Sometimes one group member *dominates* the discussion. When this occurs—such as when a strong leader makes his or her preferences clear—the result is the same as it would be if the dominant individual made the decision alone. Individual dominance has two disadvantages. First, the dominant person does not necessarily have the most valid opinions, and may even have the most unsound ideas. Second, even if that person's preference leads to a good decision, convening as a group will have been a waste of everyone else's time.

2. *Satisficing* is more likely with groups. Most people don't like meetings and will do what they can to end them. This may include criticizing members who want to continue exploring new and better alternatives. The result is a satisficing rather than an optimizing or maximizing decision.

3. *Pressure to avoid disagreement* can lead to a phenomenon called *groupthink*. **Groupthink** occurs when people choose not to disagree or raise objections because they don't want to break up a positive team spirit. Some groups want to think as one, tolerate no dissension, and strive to remain cordial. Such groups are overconfident, complacent, and perhaps too willing to take risks. Pressure to go along with the group's preferred solution stifles creativity and the other behaviors characteristic of vigilant decision making.

4. *Goal displacement* often occurs in groups. The goal of group members should be to come up with the best possible solution to the problem. But when **goal displacement** occurs, new goals emerge to replace the original ones. It is common for two or more group members to have different opinions and present their conflicting cases. Attempts at rational persuasion become heated disagreement. Winning the argument becomes the new goal. Saving face and defeating the other person's idea become more important than solving the problem.

> **groupthink**
>
> A phenomenon that occurs in decision making when group members avoid disagreement as they strive for consensus.
>
> **goal displacement**
>
> A condition that occurs when a decision-making group loses sight of its original goal and a new, less important goal emerges.

Effective managers pay close attention to the group process; they manage it carefully. You have just read about the pros and cons of using a group to make decisions, and you are about to read *how* to manage the group's decision-making process. Chapter 12, on leadership, helps you decide *when* to use groups to make decisions.

Managing Group Decision Making

Figure 3.3 illustrates the requirements for effectively managing group decision making: (1) an appropriate leadership style; (2) the constructive use of disagreement and conflict; and (3) the enhancement of creativity.

Leadership Style

The leader of a decision-making body must attempt to minimize process-related problems. The leader should avoid dominating the discussion or allowing another individual to dominate. This means encouraging less vocal group members to air their opinions and suggestions and asking for dissenting viewpoints.

At the same time, the leader should not allow the group to pressure people into conforming. The leader should be alert to the dangers of groupthink and satisficing. Also, she should be attuned to indications that group members are losing sight of the primary objective: to come up with the best possible solution to the problem.

This implies two things. First, don't lose sight of the problem. Second, make a decision! Keep in mind the slow-moving microcomputer firms that were paralyzed when group members couldn't come to an agreement.

Constructive Conflict

Total and consistent agreement among group members can be destructive. It can lead to groupthink, uncreative solutions, and a waste of the knowledge and diverse viewpoints

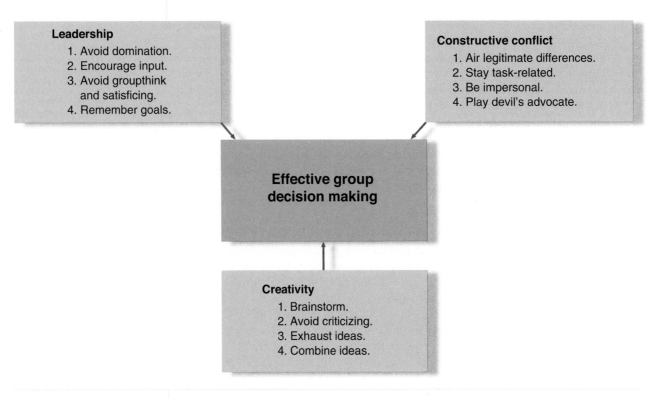

FIGURE 3.3
Managing Group Decision Making

cognitive conflict

Issue-based differences in perspectives or judgments.

affective conflict

Emotional disagreement directed toward other people.

that individuals bring to the group. Therefore, a certain amount of *constructive* conflict should exist.[44] Some companies, including Sun Microsystems and United Parcel Service, take steps to ensure that conflict and debate are generated within their management teams.[45]

The most constructive type of conflict is **cognitive conflict,** or differences in perspectives or judgments about issues. In contrast, **affective conflict** is emotional and directed at other people. Affective conflict is likely to be destructive to the group because it can lead to anger, bitterness, goal displacement, and lower-quality decisions. Cognitive conflict, in contrast, can air legitimate differences of opinion and develop better ideas and problem solutions. Conflict, then, should be task related rather than personal.[46] But even task-related conflict can hurt performance;[47] disagreement is good only when managed properly.

Managers can increase the likelihood of constructive conflict by assembling teams of different types of people, by creating frequent interactions and active debates, and by encouraging multiple alternatives to be generated from a variety of perspectives.[48] Conflict also can be generated formally through structured processes.[49] Two techniques that purposely program cognitive conflict into the decision-making process are devil's advocacy and the dialectic method.

A **devil's advocate** has the job of criticizing ideas. The group leader can formally assign people to play this role. Requiring people to point out problems can lessen inhibitions about disagreeing and make the conflict less personal and emotional.

An alternative to devil's advocacy is the dialectic. The **dialectic** goes a step beyond devil's advocacy by requiring a structured debate between two conflicting courses of action.[50] The philosophy of the dialectic stems from Plato and Aristotle, who advocated synthesizing the conflicting views of a thesis and an antithesis. Structured debates between plans and counterplans can be useful prior to making a strategic decision. For example, one team might present the case for acquiring a firm while another team advocates not making the acquisition.

Generating constructive conflict does not need to be done on such a formal basis, and is not solely the leader's responsibility. Any team member can introduce cognitive

devil's advocate

A person who has the job of criticizing ideas to ensure that their downsides are fully explored.

dialectic

A structured debate comparing two conflicting courses of action.

conflict by being honest with opinions; by not being afraid to disagree with others; by pushing the group to action if it is taking too long, or making the group slow down if necessary; and by advocating long-term considerations if the group is too focused on short-term results. Introducing constructive conflict is a legitimate and necessary responsibility of all group members interested in improving the group's decision-making effectiveness.

Encouraging Creativity

As you've already learned, ready-made solutions to a problem can be inadequate or unavailable. In such cases, custom-made solutions are necessary. This means the group must be creative in generating ideas.

Some say we are in the midst of the next great business revolution: the "creative revolution."[51] Said to transcend the agricultural, industrial, and information revolutions, the most fundamental unit of value in the creativity revolution is ideas. Creativity is more than just an option; it is essential to survival. Allowing people to be creative may be one of the manager's most important and challenging responsibilities.

You might be saying to yourself, "I'm not creative." But even if you are not an artist or a musician, you do have potential to be creative in countless other ways. You are being creative if you (1) bring a new thing into being (*creation*); (2) join two previously unrelated things (*synthesis*); or (3) improve something or give it a new application

> "I invented nothing new. I simply assembled into a car the discoveries of other men behind whom were centuries of work."
>
> Henry Ford

(*modification*). You don't need to be a genius in school, either—Thomas Edison and Albert Einstein were not particularly good students. Nor does something need to change the world to be creative; the "little things" can always be done in new, creative ways that add value to the product and the customer.

How do you "get" creative?[52] Recognize the almost infinite "little" opportunities to be creative. Assume you can be creative if you give it a try. Escape from work once in a while. Read widely, and try new experiences. Take a course or find a good book about creative thought processes; plenty are available. And be aware that creativity is social; your creativity will be affected by your social relationships at work, including your connections with other people outside your immediate close network.[53] Talk to people, often, about the issues and ideas with which you are wrestling.

How do you "get" creativity out of other people?[54] Give creative efforts the credit they are due, and don't punish creative failures. Avoid extreme time pressure if possible.[55] If deadlines are necessary, help people understand why. Support some innovative ideas without heeding projected returns. Stimulate and challenge people intellectually, and give people some creative freedom. Allow enough time to explore different ideas. Put together groups of people with different styles of thinking and behaving. Get your people in touch with customers, and let them bounce ideas around. Protect your people from managers who demand immediate payoffs, who don't understand the importance of creative contributions, or who try to take credit for others' successes. And strive to be creative yourself—you'll set a good example. People also are likely to be more creative if they believe they are capable, if they know that their co-workers expect creativity, and if they believe that their employer values creativity.[56]

Most creative ideas come not from the lone genius in the basement laboratory, but from people talking and working together.

Brainstorming is a technique used to generate as many ideas as possible to solve a problem. You have probably engaged in brainstorming sessions for various class or work projects.

Brainstorming

brainstorming

A process in which group members generate as many ideas about a problem as they can; criticism is withheld until all ideas have been proposed

A commonly used technique is brainstorming. In **brainstorming**, group members generate as many ideas about a problem as they can. As the ideas are presented, they are posted so that everyone can read them, and people can use the ideas as building blocks. The group is encouraged to say anything that comes to mind, with one exception: No criticism of other people or their ideas is allowed. This rule was violated at the Walt Disney Company when, during a brainstorming session for the design of Euro Disneyland, two architects began shoving each other and almost came to blows.[57]

In the proper brainstorming environment—free of criticism—people are less inhibited and more likely to voice their unusual, creative, or even wild ideas. By the time people have exhausted their ideas, a long list of alternatives has been generated. Only then does the group turn to the evaluation stage. At that point, many different ideas can be considered, modified, or combined into a creative, custom-made solution to the problem.

Brainstorming isn't necessarily as effective as some people think. Sometimes in a brainstorming session people are inhibited and anxious, they conform to others' ideas, they set low standards, and they engage in noncreative behaviors including cocktail party–type conversations that are nice but don't help creativity (complimenting one another, repeating ideas, telling stories). Fortunately, there are techniques that help, including brainwriting (taking time to silently write down ideas), using trained facilitators, setting high performance goals, brainstorming electronically so people aren't competing for air time, and even building a playground with fun elements that can foster creativity.[58]

Play and IDEO

"Play" is the name of a small but fast-growing marketing agency gaining attention for its playful work environment and its productive brainstorming sessions for companies including Calvin Klein, PricewaterhouseCooper, Oscar Mayer, and Disney. A typical recent session generated more than 70 ideas for a Weather Channel marketing campaign.

The most carefully studied examples of brainstorming come from IDEO, a firm that has contributed to the design of thousands of products in dozens of industries.

A "brainstormer" at IDEO is a scheduled, face-to-face meeting called to generate ideas. The rules of brainstorming are stenciled on the wall, and enforced. The rules include "Build on the ideas of others—no 'buts,' only 'ands' " and "Go for quantity." A good session generates about 100 ideas per hour.

Examples of the many product designs that IDEO has developed.

Several benefits of brainstorming accrue to IDEO. First, the company generates more solutions to design products. Second, brainstorming adds variety and fun to the job. Third, it helps designers acquire wisdom, to be both confident and humble, as they learn what they know and also what they don't know. Fourth, it encourages people to respect others and work to gain others' respect, so they go out of their way to contribute and to help one another. Fifth, it impresses clients ("We really wow 'em!"). Sixth, it provides income. Clients are billed for the brainstorming sessions. And whereas clients in all industries complain about their bills, complaints about these charges are rare because clients see the value.

Procter & Gamble's CEO Arthur Lafley calls IDEO a world-class strategic partner. *BusinessWeek* says that IDEO's clients don't just like it, they love it. And the design results? Examples are the original Apple computer mouse, Crest Toothpaste's Neat Squeeze tubes, bike helmets, an electric guitar, Nike sunglasses, part of the Jaminator toy guitar, an angioplasty device, fishing equipment, Smith ski goggles, and a combination beach chair and cooler. IDEO has won more *BusinessWeek* Design Excellence Awards, for several years running, than any other product design firm. IDEO was selected by Scott Adams, creator of Dilbert, to redesign, on behalf of office workers everywhere, the bane of Dilbert's work life: the office cubicle.

SOURCES: R. Sutton and A. Hargadon, "Brainstorming Groups in Context: Effectiveness in a Product Design Firm," *Administrative Science Quarterly* 41 (1996), pp. 685–718; B. Nussbaum, "Winners: The Best Product Designs of the Year," *BusinessWeek*, June 2, 1997, pp. 38–41; B. Nussbaum, "The Power of Design," *BusinessWeek*, May 17, 2004, pp. 86–xx.

Organizational Decision Making

Individuals and groups make decisions constantly, throughout organizations. To understand decision making in organizations, a manager must consider (1) the constraints decision makers face, (2) organizational decision processes, and (3) decision making during a crisis.

Constraints on Decision Makers

Organizations—or, more accurately, the people who make important decisions—cannot do whatever they wish. They face various constraints—financial, legal, market, human, and organizational—that inhibit certain actions. Capital or product markets may make an expensive new venture impossible. Legal restrictions may restrain the kinds of international business activities in which a firm can participate. Labor unions may defeat a contract proposed by management, contracts may prevent certain managerial actions, and managers and investors may block a takeover attempt. Even brilliant ideas must take into account the practical matters of implementation.[59]

Suppose you have a great idea that will provide a revolutionary service for your bank's customers. You won't be able to put your idea into action immediately. You will have to sell it to the people who can give you the go-ahead and also to those whose help you will need to carry out the project. You might start by convincing your boss of your idea's merit. Next, the two of you may have to hash it out with a vice president. Then maybe the president has to be sold. At each stage, you must listen to these individuals' opinions and suggestions and often incorporate them into your original concept. Ultimately, you will have to derive a proposal acceptable to others.

In addition, ethical and legal considerations must be thought out carefully. You will have plenty of opportunity to think about ethical issues in Chapter 5. Decision makers must consider ethics and the preferences of many constituent groups—the realities of life in organizations.

> You may be an innovator if you come up with a creative idea. But you're not yet, until you implement it.

Models of Organizational Decision Processes

Just as with individuals and groups, organizational decision making historically was described with rational models like the one depicted earlier in Figure 3.2. But Nobel laureate Herbert Simon challenged the rational model and proposed an important alternative called *bounded rationality*. According to Simon's **bounded rationality**, decision makers cannot be truly rational because (1) they have imperfect, incomplete information about alternatives and consequences; (2) the problems they face are so complex; (3) human beings simply cannot process all the information to which they are exposed; (4) there is not enough time to process all relevant information fully; and (5) people, including managers within the same firm, have conflicting goals.

When these conditions hold—and they do for most consequential managerial decisions—perfect rationality will give way to more biased, subjective, messier decision processes. For example, the **incremental model** of decision making occurs

bounded rationality

A less-than-perfect form of rationality in which decision makers cannot be perfectly rational because decisions are complex and complete information is unavailable.

incremental model

Model of organizational decision making in which major solutions arise through a series of smaller decisions.

when decision makers make small decisions, take little steps, move cautiously, and move in piecemeal fashion toward a bigger solution. The classic example is the budget process, which traditionally begins with the budget from the previous period and makes incremental decisions from that starting point.

The **coalitional model** of decision making arises when people disagree on goals or compete with one another for resources. The decision process becomes political, as groups of individuals band together and try collectively to influence the decision. Two or more coalitions form, each representing a different preference, and each tries to use power and negotiations to sway the decision.

coalitional model
Model of organizational decision making in which groups with differing preferences use power and negotiations to influence decisions.

Organizational politics, in which people try to influence organizational decisions so that their own interests will be served can reduce decision-making effectiveness.[60] One of the best ways to reduce such politics, and to make sure that constructive cognitive conflict does not degenerate into affective conflict, is to *create common goals* for members of the team—that is, make the decision-making process a collaborative, rather than a competitive, exercise by establishing a goal around which the group can rally. In one study, top management teams with stated goals like "build the biggest financial war chest" for an upcoming competitive battle, or "create *the* computer firm of the decade," or "build the best damn machine on the market" were less likely to have dysfunctional conflict and politics between members.[61]

The **garbage can model** of decision making occurs when people aren't sure of their goals, or disagree about the goals, and likewise are unsure of or in disagreement about what to do. This occurs because some problems are so complex that they are not well understood, and also because decision makers move in and out of the decision process because they have so many other things to attend to as well. This model implies that some decisions are chaotic, and almost random. You can see that this is a dramatic departure from rationality in decision making.

garbage can model
Model of organizational decision making depicting a chaotic process and seemingly random decisions.

Advantages of Collaboration

If you find yourself in a conflict, you and your adversary may be focused on the wrong goals. Work to find common ground in the form of an important goal that you both want to achieve.

Decision Making in a Crisis

In crisis situations, managers must make decisions under a great deal of pressure.[62] You may know some of the most famous recent crises: the *Exxon Valdez* and other oil spills; Barings Bank's collapse; airline crashes and bankruptcies; the Firestone Tire recall; and of course the terrorist attacks. Union Carbide's gas leak in Bhopal, India, killed thousands of people; several people were killed in the cyanide poisonings using Johnson & Johnson's Tylenol. As outlined in Table 3.3, Union Carbide and J & J handled their crises in very different ways. To this day, J&J is known for its effective handling of the crisis, as outlined in the table.

Information technology (IT) will be a new source of crisis.[63] IT is always on; it's ubiquitous; it's instantaneous; it packages information according to the user's personal preference; and it increases the sources and spreaders of rumor. More online users across the globe will create more outlets, and users have less time and inclination to check sources. IT will create crises via technical failure, sometimes accidental, sometimes maliciously intentional.

The response to IT-related crises must include involving senior-level execs in online communication, both to protect the firm's reputation and to communicate with outside experts, news sources, and key external and internal stakeholders. Managers can use IT to monitor and respond immediately to problems including scandals, boycotts, rumors, cyber attacks, and other crises.[64]

Union Carbide	Johnson & Johnson
Failed to identify as a crisis the public perception that the company was a negligent, uncaring killer.	Identified the crisis of public perception that Tylenol was unsafe and J&J was not in control.
No planning before reacting:	Planned before reacting:
CEO immediately went to India to inspect damage.	CEO picked one executive to head crisis team.
All executives involved.	Rest of company involved only on a need-to-know basis.
Set no goals.	Set goals to:
	Stop the killings.
	Find reasons for the killings.
	Provide assistance to the victims.
	Restore Tylenol's credibility.
Action: Damage control/stonewalling.	Action: Gave complete information.
Distanced itself.	Worked with authorities.
Misrepresented safety conditions.	Pulled Tylenol from shelves (first-year cost: $150 million).
Did not inform spokespeople.	Used strong marketing program.
Adopted bunker mentality.	Reissued Tylenol with tamper-proof packaging.
Chronic problems continued:	Crisis resolved:
Public confidence low.	Public confidence high.
Costly litigation.	Sales high again.
No formal crisis plan resulted.	Well-documented crisis management plan.

TABLE 3.3
Two Disasters

Your organization should prepare for crises in advance. However, many *Fortune* 1000 firms have no crisis-management plan at all.[65] Table 3.4 lists some common, mistaken beliefs and assumptions about crisis management. They prevent managers from anticipating crises and managing them effectively. Effective managers do not allow these evasions to prevent them from preparing carefully for crises.

Although many companies don't concern themselves with crisis management, it is imperative that it be on management's agenda. An effective plan for crisis management (CM) should include the following elements.[66]

1. *Strategic actions* such as integrating CM into strategic planning and official policies.
2. *Technical and structural actions* such as creating a CM team and dedicating a budget to CM.
3. *Evaluation and diagnostic actions* such as conducting audits of threats and liabilities, and establishing tracking systems for early warning signals.
4. *Communication actions* such as providing training for dealing with the media, local communities, and police and government officials.
5. *Psychological and cultural actions* such as showing a strong top management commitment to CM and providing training and psychological support services regarding the human and emotional impacts of crises.

We don't have a crisis.
We can handle a crisis.
Crisis management is a luxury we can't afford.
If a major crisis happens, someone else will rescue us.
Accidents are just a cost of doing business.
Most crises are the fault of bad individuals; therefore, there's not much we can do to prevent them.
Only executives need to be aware of our crisis plans; why scare our employees or members of the community?
We are tough enough to react to a crisis in an objective and rational manner.
The most important thing in crisis management is to protect the good image of the organization through public relations and advertising campaigns.

TABLE 3.4
Common but Mistaken
Beliefs: How Not to
Handle Crisis Management

SOURCE: From C. M. Pearson and I. I. Mitroff. "From Crisis Prone to Crisis Prepared: A Framework for Crisis Management," *The Executive*, February 1993, pp. 48–59. Reprinted by permission of the Academy of Management.

Ultimately, management should be able to answer the following questions:[67]

- What kinds of crises could your company face?
- Can your company detect a crisis in its early stages?
- How will it manage a crisis if one occurs?
- How can it benefit from a crisis after it has passed?

✳ Meg Whitman of eBay believes fundamentally in the free market, but she does draw the line, occasionally censoring items traded.[69] She banned firearms, alcohol, and tobacco. A difficult decision came when Starbucks chairman and then-eBay-director Howard Schultz returned from a visit to Auschwitz and urged Whitman to take Nazi items off the site. What would you do? Whitman's decision is on the next page.

The last question makes an important point: A crisis, managed effectively, can have *benefits*. For example, when eBay's Web site crashed for 22 hours, CEO Meg Whitman called the event a "near-death experience."[68] The company could have lost all of its customer and transaction data. The crash exposed a glaring company weakness: no in-house talent who could fix the site. Whitman hired a great new technology chief, Maynard Webb, at more than double her own salary. He built an infrastructure that handles more transactions per day than Nasdaq, and it had no major outages after four years.

Thus, with effective crisis management, old as well as new problems can be resolved, new strategies and competitive advantages may appear, and positive change can emerge. And if someone steps in and manages the crisis well, a hero is born.

As a leader during a crisis,[70] don't pretend that nothing happened (as did managers at one firm after a visitor died in the hallway despite employees' efforts to save him). Communicate and reinforce the organization's values. Try to find ways for people to support one another, and remember that people will take cues from your behavior. You should be optimistic but brutally honest. Show emotion, but not fear. "You have to be cooler than

Despite negotiations over the salary cap, the National Hockey League (NHL) decided to cancel the 2004–2005 hockey season, creating a crisis for players, owners, and vendors. Could either party have done anything differently to avoid this?

cool," says Gene Krantz of Apollo 13 ground control fame. But don't ignore the problems, or downplay them and reassure too much; don't create false hopes. Give people the bad news straight—you'll gain credibility, and when the good news comes, it will really mean something.[71]

> An intense debate ensued within eBay, with some arguing strongly to let the free market operate. Whitman banned all Nazi items except coins, documents, and historical books including *Mein Kampf.* "It's a judgment call. There has to be one person making the decision, and it's the CEO."[72]

EPILOGUE

MERCK AND VIOXX

The negative effects of the Vioxx debacle on the company's revenues and stock price, the potential cost of lawsuits, and the impact on Merck's reputation mean that the company will be paying the price for years to come. In early 2005, estimates of the legal liability ran as high as $38 billion.

Also in early 2005, a new study indicated that arthritis patients using Merck's Vioxx and Pfizer's Celebrex would have done just as well with older, cheaper, over-the-counter medications. The aggressive direct-to-consumer marketing played an important role in leading doctors and patients to overuse the new prescription drugs. Direct-to-consumer drug advertising is a $3.5 billion business, legal (as of 2005) only in the United States and New Zealand. One interesting uncertainty for the future: how the courts dealing with the lawsuits will view the different routes in managing their crises taken by Merck and Pfizer.

Merck CEO Gilmartin was preparing to retire in the spring of 2006. Some shareholders demanded that he step down early. The next CEO will step into a huge crisis, and will need to (1) deal with the Vioxx problem and (2) develop strategies for moving forward. Major needs for going forward include cutting costs to help deal with lost revenues (Merck laid off some employees; it was considering cutting dividends and other options). Merck also was looking to strike deals with other companies to strengthen its drug-development pipeline. Merger talk was in the air, and some observers considered a weakened Merck to be ripe for a takeover.

KEY TERMS

SUMMARY OF LEARNING OBJECTIVES

Now that you have studied Chapter 3, you should know:

The kinds of decisions you will face as a manager.

Most important managerial decisions are ill structured and characterized by uncertainty, risk, and conflict. Yet managers are expected to make rational decisions in the face of these challenges.

How to make "rational" decisions.

The ideal decision-making process involves six stages. The first, identifying and diagnosing the problem, requires recognizing a discrepancy between the current state and a desired state and then delving below surface symptoms to uncover the underlying causes of the problem. The second stage, generating alternative solutions, requires adopting ready-made or designing custom-made solutions. The third, evaluating alternatives, means predicting the consequences of different alternatives, sometimes through building scenarios of the future. Fourth, a solution is chosen; the solution might maximize, satisfice, or optimize. Fifth, people implement the decision; this stage requires more careful planning than it often receives. Finally, managers should evaluate how well the decision is working. This means gathering objective, valid information about the impact the decision is having. If the evidence suggests the problem is not getting solved, either a better decision or a better implementation plan must be developed.

The pitfalls you should avoid when making decisions.

Situational and human limitations lead most decision makers to satisfice rather than maximize. Psychological biases, time pressures, and the social realities of organizational life may prevent rational execution of the six decision-making stages. But vigilance and an understanding of how to manage decision-making groups and organizational constraints will improve the process and result in better decisions.

The pros and cons of using a group to make decisions.

Advantages include more information, perspectives, and approaches brought to bear on problem solving; intellectual stimulation; greater understanding by all of the final decision; and higher commitment to the decision once it is made. Potential dangers or disadvantages of using groups include individual domination of discussions, satisficing, groupthink, and goal displacement.

The procedures to use in leading a decision-making team.

Effective leaders in decision-making teams avoid dominating the discussion; encourage people's input; avoid groupthink and satisficing; and stay focused on the group's goals. They encourage constructive conflict via devil's advocacy and the dialectic, posing opposite sides of an issue or solutions to a problem. They also encourage creativity through a variety of techniques.

How to encourage creative decisions.

When creative ideas are needed, leaders should set a good example by being creative themselves. They should recognize the almost infinite "little" opportunities for creativity and have confidence in their own creative abilities. They can inspire creativity in others by pushing for creative freedom, rewarding creativity, and not punishing creative failures. They should encourage interaction with customers, stimulate discussion, and protect people from managers who might squelch the creative process. Brainstorming is one of the most popular techniques for generating creative ideas.

The processes by which decisions are made in organizations.

Decision making in organizations is often a highly complex process. Individuals and groups are constrained by a variety of factors and constituencies. In practice, decision makers are boundedly rational rather than purely rational. Some decisions are made on an incremental basis. Coalitions form to represent different preferences. The process is often chaotic, as depicted in the garbage can model. Politics enter the process, decisions are negotiated, and crises come and go.

How to make decisions in a crisis.

Crisis conditions make sound, effective decision making more difficult. However, it is possible for crises to be managed well. A strategy for crisis management can be developed beforehand, and the mechanisms put into readiness, so that if crises do arise, decision makers are prepared.

DISCUSSION QUESTIONS

1. Discuss Merck and Pfizer in terms of risk, uncertainty, and how each handled its crisis. What is the current news on these companies?

2. Identify some risky decisions you have made. Why did you take the risks? How did they work out? Looking back, what did you learn?

3. Identify a decision you made that had important unexpected consequences. Were the consequences good, bad, or both? Should you, and could you, have done anything differently in making the decision?

4. What effects does time pressure have on your decision making? In what ways do you handle it well and not so well?

5. Recall a recent decision that you had difficulty making. Describe it in terms of the characteristics of managerial decisions.

6. What do you think are some advantages and disadvantages to using computer technology in decision making?

7. Do you think that when managers make decisions they follow the decision-making steps as presented in this chapter? Which steps are apt to be overlooked or given inadequate attention? What can people do to make sure they do a more thorough job?

8. Discuss the potential advantages and disadvantages of using a group to make decisions. Give examples from your experience.

9. Suppose you are the CEO of a major corporation and one of your company's oil tanks has ruptured, spilling thousands of gallons of oil into a river that empties into the ocean. What do you need to do to handle the crisis?

10. Look at the mistaken assumptions described in Table 3.4. Why do such assumptions arise, and what can be done to overcome these biases?

11. Identify some problems you want to solve. Brainstorm with others a variety of creative solutions.

CONCLUDING CASE
The Wallingford Bowling Center

A group of twelve lifelong friends put together $1,200,000 of their own funds and built a $6,000,000, 48-lane bowling alley, near Norfolk, Virginia. Two of the investors became employees of the corporation. Ned Flanders works full-time as General Manager and James Ahmad, a licensed CPA, serves as Controller on a part-time basis.

The beautiful, modern-day facility features a multilevel spacious interior with three rows of 16 lanes on two separate levels of the building, a full-service bar, a small restaurant, a game room (pool, video games, pinball), and two locker rooms. The facility sits on a spacious lot with plenty of parking and room to grow.

The bowling center is located in the small blue-collar town of Wallingford. There is no direct competition within the town. The surrounding communities include a wide-ranging mix of ethnic groups, professionals, middle- to upper-middle-class private homes, and apartment and condominium complexes ranging from singles to young married couples to senior citizen retirement units. Nearly 200,000 people live within 15 miles of Wallingford.

The bowling center is open 24 hours per day and has a staff of 27 part- and full-time employees. After four years of operation, the partners find themselves frustrated with the low profit performance of the business. While sales are covering expenses, the partners are not happy with the end-of-year profit sharing pool. The most recent income statement follows:

Sales	$ 1,844,000
CGS	315,000
GM	$ 1,529,000
Operating expenses	$ 1,466,000
Mortgage	$ 460,000
Depreciation	95,000
Utilities	188,000
Maintenance	70,000
Payroll	490,000
Supplies	27,000
Insurance	136,000
Taxable income	$ 63,000
Taxes	19,000
Net income	$ 44,000

The bowling center operates at 100 percent capacity on Sunday through Thursday nights from 6:00 P.M. until midnight. Two sets of men's leagues come and go on each of those nights, occupying each lane with mostly five-person teams. Bowlers from each league consistently spend money at both the bar and restaurant. In fact, the men's leagues combine to generate about 60 percent of total current sales.

The bowling center operates at about 50 percent capacity on Friday and Saturday nights and on Saturday morning. The Friday and Saturday "open bowling" nights include mostly teenagers, young couples, and league members who come to practice in groups of two or three. The Saturday morning group is a kid's league, ages 10 through 14.

There are four ladies leagues that bowl on Monday and Wednesday afternoons.

Business is extremely slow at the bowling center on Monday through Friday and Sunday mornings, and on the afternoons of Tuesday, Thursday, Friday, Saturday, and Sunday. It is not uncommon to have just three or four lanes in operation during those time periods.

The owners have taken a close look at the cost side of their business as a way to improve profitability. They concluded that while the total operating expense of $1,466,000 might appear to be high, there was in fact little room for expense cutting.

At a recent meeting of the partners, James Ahmad reported on the results of his three-month-long investigation into the operating cost side of other bowling alleys and discovered that the Wallingford Bowling Center was very much in keeping with their industry. James went on to report that bowling alleys were considered to be "heavy fixed cost operations" and that the key to success and profitability lies in maximizing capacity and sales dollars.

QUESTIONS

1. Apply the decision-making process described in the chapter to this case. What is the major problem facing Wallingford? List five specific alternative solutions that could be implemented to solve that major problem.

2. As general manager of this company, how could you utilize and manage the group decision-making process and technique to improve company profits? Which employees would you include in the group?

EXPERIENTIAL EXERCISES
3.1 Competitive Escalation: The Dollar Auction

OBJECTIVE

To explore the effects of competition on decision making.

INSTRUCTIONS

Step 1: 5 Minutes.   The instructor will play the role of auctioneer. In this auction, the instructor will auction off $1 bills (the in-

structor will inform you whether this money is real or imaginary). All members of the class may participate in the auction at the same time.

The rules for this auction are slightly different from those of a normal auction. In this version, *both the highest bidder and the next highest bidder will play their last bids* even though the dollar is awarded only to the highest bidder. For example, if Bidder A bids 15 cents for the dollar and Bidder B bids 10 cents, and there is no further bidding, then A pays 15 cents for the dollar and receives the dollar, while B pays 10 cents and receives nothing. The auctioneer will lose 75 cents on the dollar just sold.

Bids must be made in multiples of 5 cents. The dollar will be sold when there is no further bidding. If two individuals bid the same amount at the same time, ties are resolved in favor of the bidder located physically closest to the auctioneer. *During each round, there is to be no talking except for making bids.*

Step 2: 15 Minutes.   The instructor (auctioneer) will auction off five individual dollars to the class. Any student may bid in an effort to win the dollar. A record sheet of the bidding and winners can be kept in the worksheet that follows.

DISCUSSION QUESTIONS

1. Who made the most money in this exercise—one of the bidders or the auctioneer? Why?

2. As the auction proceeded, did bidders become more competitive or more cooperative? Why?

3. Did two bidders ever pay more for the money being auctioned than the value of the money itself? Explain how and why this happened.

4. Did you become involved in the bidding? Why?

   a. If you became involved, what were your motivations? Did you accomplish your objectives?

   b. If not, why didn't you become involved? What did you think were the goals and objectives of those who did become involved?

5. Did people say things to one another during the bidding to influence their actions? What was said, and how was it influential?

Dollar Auction Worksheet

	Amount paid by winning bidder	Amount paid by second bidder	Total paid for this dollar
First dollar			
Second dollar			
Third dollar			
Fourth dollar			
Fifth dollar			

SOURCE: Excerpted from R. Lewicki, *Experiences in Management and Organizational Behavior,* 3rd ed. Copyright © 1991 John Wiley & Sons, Inc. This material is used by permission of John Wiley and Sons, Inc.

3.2 Group Problem-Solving Meeting at the Community Agency

OBJECTIVE

To understand the interactions in group decision making through role playing a meeting between a chairman and his subordinates.

INSTRUCTIONS

1. Gather role sheets for each character and instructions for observers.

2. Set up a table in front of the room with five chairs around it arranged in such a way that participants can talk comfortably and have their faces visible to observers.

3. Read the introduction and cast of characters.

4. Five members from the class are selected to role play the five characters. All other members act as observers. The participants study the roles. All should play their roles without referring to the role sheets.

5. The observers read the instructions for observers.

6. When everyone is ready, John Cabot enters his office, joins the others at the table, and the scene begins. Allow 20 minutes to complete the meeting. The meeting is carried to the point of completion unless an argument develops and no progress is evident after 10 or 15 minutes of conflict.

DISCUSSION QUESTIONS

1. Describe the group's behavior. What did each member say? Do?

2. Evaluate the effectiveness of the group's decision making.

3. Did any problems exist in leadership, power, motivation, communication, or perception?

4. How could the group's effectiveness be increased?

INTRODUCTION

The Community Agency is a role-play exercise of a meeting between the chairman of the board of a social service agency and four of his subordinates. Each character's role is designed to recreate the reality of a business meeting. Each character comes to the meeting with a unique perspective on a major problem facing the agency as well as some personal impressions of the other characters developed over several years of business and social associations.

THE CAST OF CHARACTERS

John Cabot, the Chairman, was the principal force behind the formation of the Community Agency, a multiservice agency. The agency employs 50 people, and during its 19 years of operations has enjoyed better client relations, a better service record, and a better reputation than other local agencies because of a reputation for high-quality service at a moderate cost to funding agencies. Recently, however, competitors have begun to overtake the Community Agency, resulting in declining contracts. John Cabot is expending every possible effort to keep his agency comfortably at the top.

Ron Smith, Director of the agency, reports directly to Cabot. He has held this position since he helped Cabot establish the agency 19 years ago.

Joan Sweet, Head of Client Services, reports to Smith. She has been with the agency 12 years, having worked before that for HEW as a contracting officer.

Tom Lynch, Head Community Liaison, reports to Joan Sweet. He came to the Community Agency at Sweet's request, having worked with Sweet previously at HEW.

Jane Cox, Head Case Worker, also works for Joan Sweet. Cox was promoted to this position two years ago. Prior to that time. Jane had gone through a year's training program after receiving an MSW from a large urban university.

TODAY'S MEETING

John Cabot has called the meeting with these four managers in order to solve some problems that have developed in meeting service schedules and contract requirements. Cabot must catch a plane to Washington in half an hour; he has an appointment to negotiate a key contract that means a great deal to the future of the Community Agency. He has only 20 minutes to meet with his managers and still catch the plane. Cabot feels that getting the Washington contract is absolutely crucial to the future of the agency.

SOURCE: Judith R. Gordon, *A Diagnostic Approach to Organizational Behavior.* Copyright © 1983 Pearson Education, Inc. Reprinted by permission of Pearson Education, Inc., Upper Saddle River, NJ.

PART I SUPPORTING CASE
SSS Software In-Basket Exercise

One way to assess your own strengths and weaknesses in management skills is to engage in an actual managerial work experience. The following exercise gives you a realistic glimpse of the tasks faced regularly by practicing managers. Complete the exercise, and then compare your own decisions and actions with those of classmates.

SSS Software designs and develops customized software for businesses. It also integrates this software with the customer's existing systems and provides system maintenance. SSS Software has customers in the following industries: airlines, automotive, finance/banking, health/hospital, consumer products, electronics, and government. The company has also begun to generate important international clients. These include the European Airbus consortium and a consortium of banks and financial firms based in Kenya.

SSS Software has grown rapidly since its inception just over a decade ago. Its revenue, net income, and earnings per share have all been above the industry average for the past several years. However, competition in this technologically sophisticated field has grown very rapidly. Recently, it has become more difficult to compete for major contracts. Moreover, although SSS Software's revenue and net income continue to grow, the rate of growth declined during the last fiscal year.

SSS Software's 250 employees are divided into several operating divisions with employees at four levels: nonmanagement, technical/professional, managerial, and executive. Nonmanagement employees take care of the clerical and facilities support functions. The technical/professional staff perform the core technical work for the firm. Most managerial employees are group managers who supervise a team of technical/professional employees working on a project for a particular customer. Staff who work in specialized areas such as finance, accounting, human resources, nursing, and law are also considered managerial employees. The executive level includes the 12 highest-ranking employees at SSS Software. There is an organization chart in Figure A that illustrates SSS Software's structure. There is also an Employee Classification Report that lists the number of employees at each level of the organization.

In this exercise, you will play the role of Chris Perillo, Vice President of Operations for Health and Financial Services. You learned last Wednesday, October 13, that your predecessor, Michael Grant, has resigned and gone to Universal Business Solutions, Inc. You were offered his former job, and you accepted it. Previously, you were the Group Manager for a team of 15 software developers assigned to work on the Airbus consortium project in the Airline Services Division. You spent all of Thursday and Friday and most of the weekend finishing up parts of the project, briefing your successor, and preparing for an interim report you will deliver in Paris on October 21.

It is now 7 A.M. Monday, and you are in your new office. You have arrived at work early so you can spend the next two hours reviewing material in your in-basket (including some memos and messages to Michael Grant), as well as your voice mail and e-mail. Your daily planning book indicates that you have no appointments today or tomorrow but will have to catch a plane for Paris early Wednesday morning. You have a full schedule for the remainder of the week and all of next week.

ASSIGNMENT

During the next two hours, review all the material in your in-basket, as well as your voice mail and e-mail. Take only two hours. Using the following response form as a model, indicate how you want to respond to each item (that is, via letter/memo, e-mail, phone/voice mail, or personal meeting). If you decide not to respond to an item, check "no response" on the response form. All of your responses must be written on the response forms. Write your precise, detailed response (do not merely jot down a few notes). For example, you might draft a memo or write out a message that you will deliver via phone/voice mail. You may also decide to meet with an individual (or individuals) during the limited time available on your calendar today or tomorrow. If so, prepare an agenda for a personal meeting and list your goals for the meeting. As you read through the items, you may occasionally observe some information that you think is relevant and want to remember (or attend to in the future) but that you decide not to include in any of your responses to employees. Write down such information on a sheet of paper titled "note to self."

SOURCE: D. Whetten and K. Cameron, *Developing Management Skills,* 3rd ed. (New York: Harper Collins, 1995).

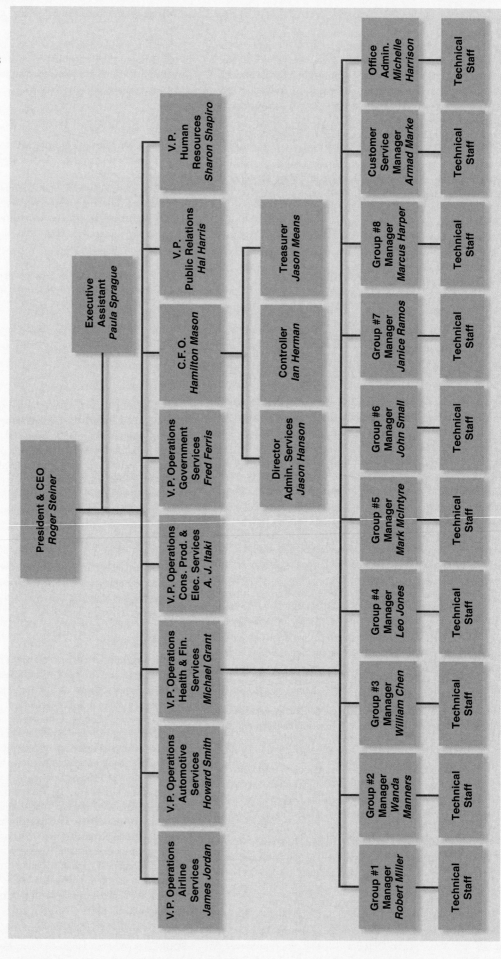

FIGURE A
Partial Organization
Chart of the Health
and Financial Services
Division

SAMPLE RESPONSE FORM

Relates To:

Memo # _____   E-mail # _____   Voice mail # _____

Response form:

_____ Letter/Memo   _____ Meet with person (when, where)

_____ E-mail   _____ Note to self

_____ Phone call/Voice mail _____ No response

ITEM 1 MEMO

TO: All Employees
FROM: Roger Steiner, Chief Executive Officer
DATE: October 15

I am pleased to announce that Chris Perillo has been appointed as Vice President of Operations for Health and Financial Services. Chris will immediately assume responsibility for all operations previously managed by Michael Grant. Chris will have end-to-end responsibility for the design, development, integration, and maintenance of custom software for the health and finance/banking industries. This responsibility includes all technical, financial, and staffing issues. Chris will also manage our program of software support and integration for the recently announced merger of three large health maintenance organizations (HMOs). Chris will be responsible for our recently announced project with a consortium of banks and financial firms operating in Kenya. This project represents an exciting opportunity for us, and Chris's background seems ideally suited to the task.

Chris comes to this position with an undergraduate degree in Computer Science from the California Institute of Technology and an M.B.A. from the University of Virginia. Chris began as a member of our technical/professional staff six years ago and has most recently served for three years as a Group Manager supporting domestic and international projects for our airlines industry group, including our recent work for the European Airbus consortium.

I am sure you all join me in offering congratulations to Chris for this promotion.

ITEM 2 MEMO

TO: All Managers
FROM: Hal Harris, Vice President, Community and Public Relations
DATE: October 15

For your information, the following article appeared on the front page of the business section of Thursday's *Los Angeles Times*.

In a move that may create problems for SSS Software, Michael Grant and Janice Ramos have left SSS Software and moved to Universal Business Solutions Inc. Industry analysts see the move as another victory for Universal Business Solutions Inc. in their battle with SSS Software for share of the growing software development and integration business. Both Grant and Ramos had been with SSS Software for over 7 years. Grant was most recently Vice President of Operations for all SSS Software's work in two industries: health and hospitals, and finance and banking. Ramos brings to Universal Business Solutions Inc. her special expertise in the growing area of international software development and integration.

Hillary Collins, an industry analyst with Merrill Lynch, said "the loss of key staff to a competitor can often create serious problems for a firm such as SSS Software. Grant and Ramos have an insider's understanding of SSS Software's strategic and technical limitations. It will be interesting to see if they can exploit this knowledge to the advantage of Universal Business Solutions Inc."

ITEM 3 MEMO

TO: Chris Perillo

FROM: Paula Sprague, Executive Assistance to Roger Steiner

DATE: October 15

Chris, I know that in your former position as a Group Manager in the Airline Services Division, you probably have met most of the group managers in the Health and Financial Services Division, but I thought you might like some more personal information about them. These people will be your direct reports on the management team.

Group #1: Bob Miller, 55-year-old white male, married (Anne) with two children and three grandchildren. Active in local Republican politics. Well regarded as a "hands-off" manager heading a high-performing team. Plays golf regularly with Mark McIntyre, John Small, and a couple of V.P.s from other divisions.

Group #2: Wanda Manners, 38-year-old white female, single with one school-age child. A fitness "nut," has run in several marathons. Some experience in Germany and Japan. Considered a hard-driving manager with a constant focus on the task at hand. Will be the first person to show up every morning.

Group #3: William Chen, 31-year-old male of Chinese descent, married (Harriet), two young children from his first marriage. Enjoys tennis and is quite good at it. A rising star in the company, he is highly respected by his peers as a "man of action" and a good friend.

Group #4: Leo Jones, 36-year-old white male, married (Janet), with an infant daughter. Recently returned from paternity leave. Has traveled extensively on projects, since he speaks three languages. Has liked hockey ever since the time he spent in Montreal. Considered a strong manager who gets the most out of his people.

Group #5: Mark McIntyre, 45-year-old white male, married (Mary Theresa) to an executive in the banking industry. No children. A lot of experience in Germany and Eastern Europe. Has been writing a mystery novel. Has always been a good "team player," but several members of his technical staff are not well respected and he hasn't addressed the problem.

Group #6: John Small, 38-year-old white male, recently divorced. Three children living with his wife. A gregarious individual who likes sports. He spent a lot of time in Mexico and Central America before he came to SSS Software. Recently has been doing mostly contract work with the federal government. An average manager, has had some trouble keeping his people on schedule.

Group #7: This position vacant since Janice Ramos left. Roger thinks we ought to fill this position quickly. Get in touch with me if you want information on any in-house candidates for any position.

Group #8: Marcus Harper, 42-year-old black male, married (Tamara) with two teenage children. Recently won an award in a local photography contest. Considered a strong manager who gets along with peers and works long hours.

Customer Services: Armand Marke, 38-year-old Armenian male, divorced. A basketball fan. Originally from Armenia. Previously a Group Manager. Worked hard to establish the Technical Services Phone Line, but now has pretty much left it alone.

Office Administrator: Michelle Harrison, 41-year-old white female, single. Grew up on a ranch and still rides horses whenever she can. A strict administrator.

There are a number of good folks here, but they don't function well as a management team. I think Michael played favorites, especially with Janice and Leo. There are a few cliques in this group and I'm not sure how effectively Michael dealt with them. I expect you will find it a challenge to build a cohesive team.

ITEM 4 MEMO

TO: Chris Perillo

FROM: Wanda Manners, Group 2 Manager

DATE: October 15, 1998

CONFIDENTIAL AND RESTRICTED

Although I know you are new to your job, I feel it is important that I let you know about some information I just obtained concerning the development work we recently completed for First National Investment. Our project involved the development of asset management software for managing their international funds. This was a very complex project due to the volatile exchange rates and the forecasting tools we needed to develop.

As part of this project, we had to integrate the software and reports with all their existing systems and reporting mechanisms. To do this we were given access to all of their existing software (much of which was developed by Universal Business Solutions Inc.). Of course, we signed an agreement acknowledging that the software to which we were given access was proprietary and that our access was solely for the purpose of our system integration work associated with the project.

Unfortunately, I have learned that some parts of the software we developed actually "borrow" heavily from complex application programs developed for First National Investment by Universal Business Solutions Inc. It seems obvious to me that one or more of the software developers from Group 5 (that is, Mark McIntyre's group) inappropriately "borrowed" algorithms developed by Universal Business Solutions Inc. I am sure that doing so saved us significant development time on some aspects of the project. It seems very unlikely that First National Investment or Universal Business Solutions Inc. will ever become aware of this issue.

Finally, First National Investment is successfully using the software we developed and is thrilled with the work we did. We brought the project in on time and under budget. You probably know that they have invited us to bid on several other substantial projects.

I'm sorry to bring this delicate matter to your attention, but I thought you should know about it.

ITEM 5A MEMO

TO: Chris Perillo

FROM: Paula Sprague, Executive Assistant to Roger Steiner

DATE: October 15

RE: Letter from C.A.R.E. Services (copies attached)

Roger asked me to work on this C.A.R.E. project and obviously wants some fast action. A lot of the staff are already booked solid for the next couple of weeks. I knew that Elise Soto and Chu Hung Woo have the expertise to do this system, and when I checked with them, they were relatively free. I had them pencil in the next two weeks and wanted to let you know. Hopefully, it will take a "hot potato" out of your hands.

ITEM 5B COPY OF FAX

C.A.R.E.
Child and Adolescent Rehabilitative and Educational Services
A United Way Member Agency
200 Main Street
Los Angeles, California 90230

DATE: October 11

Mr. Roger Steiner, CEO
SSS Software
13 Miller Way
Los Angeles, California 90224

Dear Roger,

This letter is a follow-up to our conversation after last night's board meeting. I appreciated your comments during the board meeting about the need for sophisticated computer systems in nonprofit organizations and I especially appreciate your generous offer of assistance to have SSS Software provide assistance to deal with the immediate problem with our accounting system. Since the board voted to fire the computer consultant, I am very worried about getting our reports done in time to meet the state funding cycle.

Thanks again for your offer of help during this crisis.

Sincerely yours,

Janice Polocizwic

Janice Polocizwic
Executive Director

ITEM 5C COPY OF LETTER

SSS SOFTWARE
13 Miller Way
Los Angeles, CA 90224
213-635-2000

DATE: October 12

Janice Polocizwic
Executive Director, C.A.R.E. Services
200 Main Street
Los Angeles, California 90230

Dear Janice,

I received your fax of October 11. I have asked Paula Sprague, my executive assistant, to line up people to work on your accounting system as soon as possible. You can expect to hear from her shortly.

Sincerely,

Roger Steiner

Roger Steiner

cc: Paula Sprague, Executive Assistant

ITEM 6 MEMO

TO: Michael Grant

FROM: Harry Withers, Group 6 Technical Staff

DATE: October 12

PERSONAL AND CONFIDENTIAL

Our team is having difficulty meeting the submission deadline of November 5 for the Halstrom project. Kim, Fred, Peter, Kyoto, Susan, Mala, and I have been working on the project for several weeks, but are experiencing some problems and may need additional time. I hesitate to write this letter, but the main problem is that our group manager, John Small, is involved in a relationship with Mala. Mala gets John's support for her ideas and brings them to the team as required components of the project. Needless to say, this has posed some problems for the group. Mala's background is especially valuable for this project, but Kim and Fred, who have both worked very hard on the project, do not want to work with her. In addition, one member of the team has been unavailable recently because of child-care needs. Commitment to the project and team morale have plummeted. However, we'll do our best to get the project finished as soon as possible. Mala will be on vacation the next two weeks, so I'm expecting that some of us can complete it in her absence.

ITEM 7 VOICE MAIL

Hello, Michael. This is Jim Bishop of United Hospitals. I wanted to talk with you about the quality assurance project that you are working on for us. When José Martinez first started talking with us, I was impressed with his friendliness and expertise. But recently, he doesn't seem to be getting much accomplished and has seemed distant and on-edge in conversations. Today, I asked him about the schedule and he seemed very defensive and not entirely in control of his emotions. I am quite concerned about our project. Please give me a call at 213-951-1234.

ITEM 8 VOICE MAIL

Hi, Michael. This is Armand. I wanted to talk with you about some issues with the Technical Services Phone Line. I've recently received some complaint letters from Phone Line customers whose complaints have included: long delays while waiting for a technician to answer the phone; technicians who are not knowledgeable enough to solve problems; and, on occasion, rude service. Needless to say, I'm quite concerned about these complaints.

I believe that the overall quality of the phone line staff is very good, but we continue to be understaffed, even with the recent hires. The new technicians look strong, but are working on the help line before being fully trained. Antolina, our best tech, often brings her child to work, which is adding to the craziness around here.

I think you should know that we're feeling a lot of stress here. I'll talk to you soon.

ITEM 9 VOICE MAIL

Hi Chris, it's Pat. Congratulations on your promotion. They definitely picked the right person. It's great news—for me, too. You've been a terrific mentor so far, so I'm expecting to learn a lot from you in your new position. How about lunch next week?

ITEM 10 VOICE MAIL

> *Chris, this is Bob Miller. Just thought you'd like to know that John's joke during our planning meeting has disturbed a few of the women in my group. Frankly, I think the thing's being blown out of proportion, especially since we all know this is a good place for both men and women to work. Give me a call if you want to chat about this.*

ITEM 11 VOICE MAIL

> *Hello. This is Lorraine Adams from Westside Hospital. I read in today's Los Angeles Times that you will be taking over from Michael Grant. We haven't met yet, but your division has recently finished two large million-dollar projects for Westside. Michael Grant and I had some discussion about a small conversion of a piece of existing software to be compatible with the new systems. The original vendor had said that they would do the work but has been stalling, and I need to move quickly. Can you see if Harris Wilson, Chu Hung Woo, and Elise Soto are available to do this work as soon as possible? They were on the original project and work well with our people. You can call me at 213-555-3456.*
>
> *Um ... (long pause) I guess I should tell you that I got a call from Michael offering to do this work. But I think I should stick with SSS Software. Give me a call.*

ITEM 12 VOICE MAIL

> *Hi, Chris. This is Roosevelt Moore calling. I'm a member of your technical/professional staff. I used to report to Janice Ramos, but since she left the firm, I thought I'd bring my concerns directly to you. I'd like to arrange some time to talk with you about my experience since returning from six weeks of paternity leave. Some of my major responsibilities have been turned over to others. I seem to be out of the loop and wonder if my career is at risk. Also, I am afraid that I won't be supported or seriously considered for the opening created by Janice's departure. Frankly, I feel I'm being screwed for taking my leave. I'd like to talk with you this week.*

ITEM 13 E-MAIL

To:	Michael Grant
From:	José Martinez, Group 1 Technical Staff
Date:	October 12

I would like to set up a meeting with you as soon as possible. I suspect that you will get a call from Jim Bishop of United Hospitals and want to be sure that you hear my side of the story first. I have been working on a customized system design for quality assurance for them using a variation of the J-3 product we developed several years ago. They had a number of special requirements and some quirks in their accounting systems, so I have had to put in especially long hours. I've worked hard to meet their demands, but they keep changing the ground rules. I keep thinking, this is just another J-3 I'm working on, but they have been interfering with an elegant design I have developed. It seems I'm not getting anywhere on this project. Then Mr. Bishop asked me if the system was running yet. I was worn out from dealing with the Controller, and I made a sarcastic comment to Mr. Bishop. He gave me a funny look and just walked out of the room.

I would like to talk with you about this situation at your earliest convenience.

ITEM 14 E-MAIL

TO: Chris Perillo

FROM: John Small, Group 6 Manager

DATE: October 15

Welcome aboard, Chris. I look forward to meeting with you. I just wanted to put a bug in your ear about finding a replacement for Janice Ramos. One of my technical staff, Mala Abendano, has the ability and drive to make an excellent group manager. I have encouraged her to apply for the position. I'd be happy to talk with you further about this, at your convenience.

ITEM 15 E-MAIL

TO: Chris Perillo

FROM: Paula Sprague, Executive Assistant to Roger Steiner

DATE: October 15

Roger asked me to let you know about the large contract we have gotten in Kenya. It means that a team of four managers will be making a short trip to determine current needs. They will assign their technical staff the task of developing a system and software here over the next six months, and then the managers and possibly some team members will be spending about 10 months on site in Kenya to handle the implementation. Roger would appreciate an email of your thoughts about the issues to be discussed at this meeting, additional considerations about sending people to Kenya, and about how you will put together an effective team to work on this project. The October 15 memo I sent to you will provide you with some information you'll need to start making these decisions.

ITEM 16 E-MAIL

TO: Chris Perillo

FROM: Sharon Shapiro, V. P. of Human Resources

DATE: October 15

RE: Upcoming meeting

I want to update you on the rippling effect of John Small's sexual joke at last week's planning meeting. Quite a few women have been very upset and have met informally to talk about it. They have decided to call a meeting of all the people concerned about this kind of behavior throughout the firm. I plan to attend, so I'll keep you posted.

ITEM 17 E-MAIL

TO: All SSS-Software Managers
FROM: Sharon Shapiro, Vice President, Human Resources
DATE: October 14
RE: Promotions and External Hires

Year-to-date (January through September) promotions and external hires

Level	Race					Sex		Total
	White	Black	Asian	Hispanic	Native American	M	F	
Hires into Executive Level	0 (0%)	0 (0%)	0 (0%)	0 (0%)	0 (0%)	0 (0%)	0 (0%)	0
Promotions to Executive Level	0 (0%)	0 (0%)	0 (0%)	0 (0%)	0 (0%)	0 (0%)	0 (0%)	0
Hires into Management Level	2 (67%)	1 (33%)	0 (0%)	0 (0%)	0 (0%)	2 (67%)	1 (33%)	3
Promotions to Management Level	7 (88%)	0 (0%)	1 (12%)	0 (0%)	0 (0%)	7 (88%)	1 (12%)	8
Hires into Technical/ Professional Level	10 (36%)	6 (21%)	10 (36%)	2 (7%)	0 (0%)	14 (50%)	14 (50%)	28
Promotions to Technical/ Professional Level	0 (0%)	0 (0%)	0 (0%)	0 (0%)	0 (0%)	0 (0%)	0 (0%)	0
Hires into Non-Management Level	4 (20%)	10 (50%)	2 (10%)	4 (20%)	0 (0%)	6 (30%)	14 (70%)	20
Promotions to Non-Management Level	NA	NA	NA	NA	NA	NA	NA	NA

SSS Software employee (EEO) classification report as of June 30

Level	Race					Sex		Total
	White	Black	Asian	Hispanic	Native American	M	F	
Executive Level	11 (92%)	0 (0%)	1 (8%)	0 (0%)	0 (0%)	11 (92%)	1 (8%)	12
Management Level	43 (90%)	2 (4%)	2 (4%)	1 (2%)	0 (0%)	38 (79%)	10 (21%)	48
Technical/ Professional Level	58 (45%)	20 (15%)	37 (28%)	14 (11%)	1 (1%)	80 (62%)	50 (38%)	130
Non-Management Level	29 (48%)	22 (37%)	4 (7%)	4 (7%)	1 (2%)	12 (20%)	48 (80%)	60
Total	141 (56%)	44 (18%)	44 (18%)	19 (8%)	2 (1%)	141 (56%)	109 (44%)	250

CRITICAL INCIDENTS

Employee Raiding

Litson Cotton Yarn Manufacturing Company, located in Murray, New Jersey, decided as a result of increasing labor costs to relocate its plant in Fairlee, a southern community of 4,200. Plant construction was started, and a human resources office was opened in the state employment office, located in Fairlee.

Because of ineffective HR practices in the other three textile mills located within a 50-mile radius of Fairlee, Litson was receiving applications from some of the most highly skilled and trained textile operators in the state. After receiving applications from approximately 500 people, employment was offered to 260 male and female applicants. These employees would be placed immediately on the payroll with instructions to await final installation of machinery, which was expected within the following six weeks.

The managers of the three other textile companies, faced with resignations from their most efficient and best-trained employees, approached the Litson managers with the complaint that their labor force was being "raided." They registered a strong protest to cease such practices and demanded an immediate cancellation of the employment of the 260 people hired by Litson.

Litson managers discussed the ethical and moral considerations involved in offering employment to the 260 people. Litson clearly faced a tight labor market in Fairlee, and management thought that if the 260 employees were discharged, the company would face cancellation of its plans and large construction losses. Litson management also felt obligated to the 260 employees who had resigned from their previous employment in favor of Litson.

The dilemma was compounded when the manager of one community plant reminded Litson that his plant was part of a nationwide chain supplied with cotton yarn from Litson. He implied that Litson's attempts to continue operations in Fairlee could result in cancellation of orders and the possible loss of approximately 18 percent market share. It was also suggested to Litson managers that actions taken by the nationwide textile chain could result in cancellation of orders from other textile companies. Litson's president held an urgent meeting of his top subordinates to (1) decide what to do about the situation in Fairlee, (2) formulate a written policy statement indicating Litson's position regarding employee raiding, and (3) develop a plan for implementing the policy.

How would you prepare for the meeting, and what would you say at the meeting?

SOURCE: J. Champion and J. James, *Critical Incidents in Management: Decision and Policy Issues,* 6th ed. (Burr Ridge, IL: Richard D. Irwin, 1989).

Effective Management

Dr. Sam Perkins, a graduate of the Harvard University College of Medicine, had a private practice in internal medicine for 12 years. Fourteen months ago, he was persuaded by the Massachusetts governor to give up private practice to be director of the State Division of Human Services.

After one year as director, Perkins recognized he had made little progress in reducing the considerable inefficiency in the division. Employee morale and effectiveness seemed even lower than when he had assumed the position. He realized his past training and experiences were of a clinical nature with little exposure to effective management techniques. Perkins decided to research literature on the subject of management available to him at a local university.

Perkins soon realized that management scholars are divided on the question of what constitutes effective management. Some believe people are born with certain identifiable personality traits that make them effective managers. Others believe a manager can learn to be effective by treating subordinates with a personal and considerate approach and by giving particular attention to their need for favorable working conditions. Still others emphasize the importance of developing a management style characterized by either authoritarian, democratic, or laissez-faire approaches. Perkins was further confused when he learned that a growing number of scholars advocate that effective management is contingent on the situation.

Since a state university was located nearby, Perkins contacted the dean of its college of business administration. The dean referred him to the director of the college's management center, Professor Joel McCann. Discussions between Perkins and McCann resulted in a tentative agreement that the management center would organize a series of management training sessions for the State Division of Human Services. Before agreeing on the price tag for the management conference, Perkins asked McCann to prepare a proposal reflecting his thoughts on the following questions:

1. How will the question of what constitutes effective management be answered during the conference?

2. What will be the specific subject content of the conference?

3. Who will the instructors be?

4. What will be the conference's duration?

5. How can the conference's effectiveness be evaluated?

6. What policies should the State Division of Human Services adopt regarding who the conference participants should be and how they should be selected? How can these policies be best implemented?

SOURCE: J. Champion and J. James, *Critical Incidents in Management: Decision and Policy Issues,* 6th ed. (Burr Ridge, IL: Richard D. Irwin, 1989).

PART
TWO

Foundations of Management
- Managing
- The External Environment and Organizational Culture
- Managerial Decision Making

Planning: Delivering Strategic Value
- Planning and Strategic Management
- Ethics and Corporate Responsibility
- International Management
- Entrepreneurship

Strategy Implementation

Organizing: Building a Dynamic Organization
- Organization Structure
- Organizational Agility
- Human Resources Management
- Managing the Diverse Workforce

Leading: Mobilizing People
- Leadership
- Motivating for Performance
- Teamwork
- Communicating

Controlling: Learning and Changing
- Managerial Control
- Managing Technology and Innovation
- Creating and Managing Change

Planning: Delivering Strategic Value

Part Two introduces key concepts of planning and strategy. The topics emphasize the decisions made by top managers and their implications for the entire organization. Chapter 4 presents a summary of the planning process and an overview of how senior executives manage strategically. The next three chapters treat subjects that have emerged recently as vital considerations for modern managers. Chapter 5 examines the impact of ethical concerns and social and political factors on major decisions. Chapter 6 addresses the pressing reality of managing in a global competitive environment. Finally, Chapter 7 describes entrepreneurs and the new ventures they create. These chapters will provide the reader with a clear understanding of the strategic directions that effective organizations pursue.

Chapter **4**

CHAPTER 4

Planning and Strategic Management

Manage your destiny, or someone else will.
—**Jack Welch, former CEO, General Electric**

LEARNING OBJECTIVES

After studying Chapter 4, you will know:

1. How to proceed through the basic steps in any planning process.

2. How strategic planning integrates with tactical and operational planning.

3. Why it is important to analyze both the external environment and the internal resources of the firm before formulating a strategy.

4. The choices available for corporate strategy.

5. How companies can achieve competitive advantage through business strategy.

6. How core competencies provide the foundation for business strategy.

7. The keys to effective strategy implementation.

To imagine Delta Air Lines, or any organization, dealing with the significant challenges it faces without developing a plan for doing so is almost impossible. Planning is a formal expression of managerial intent. It describes what managers decide to do and how they will do it. It provides the framework, focus, and direction a meaningful effort requires. Without planning, any improvements in an organization's innovation, speed, quality, and cost will be accidental, if they occur at all. This chapter examines the most important concepts and processes involved in planning and strategic management. By learning these concepts, and reviewing the steps outlined, you will be on your way to understanding the current approaches to the strategic management of today's organizations.

An Overview of Planning Fundamentals

The importance of formal planning in organizations has grown dramatically. Until the mid-1900s, most planning was unstructured and fragmented, and formal planning was restricted to a few large corporations. Although management pioneers such as Alfred Sloan of General Motors instituted formal planning processes, planning became a widespread management function only during the last few decades. While larger organizations adopted formal planning initially, even small firms operated by aggressive, opportunistic entrepreneurs now engage in formal planning.[1]

Planning is the conscious, systematic process of making decisions about goals and activities that an individual, group, work unit, or organization will pursue in the future. Planning is not an informal or haphazard response to a crisis; it is a purposeful effort that is directed and controlled by managers and often draws on the knowledge and experience of employees throughout the organization. Planning provides individuals and work units with a clear map to follow in their future activities; at the same time this map may allow for individual circumstances and changing conditions.

The Basic Planning Process

Because planning is a decision process—you're deciding what to do and how to go about doing it—the important steps followed during formal planning are similar to the basic decision-making steps we discussed in Chapter 3. You can see the similarities between decision making and planning summarized in Figure 4.1—including the fact that both move not just in one direction but in a *cycle*. The outcomes of decisions and plans are evaluated, and if necessary they are revised.

We will now describe the basic planning process in more detail. Later in this chapter, we will discuss how managerial decisions and plans fit into the larger purposes of the organization—its ultimate strategy, mission, vision, and goals.

Step 1: Situational Analysis   As the contingency approach advocates, planning begins with a **situational analysis.** Within their time and resource constraints, planners should gather, interpret, and summarize all information relevant to the planning issue in question. A thorough situational analysis studies past events, examines current conditions, and attempts to forecast future trends. It focuses on the internal forces at work in the organization or work unit and, consistent with the open-systems approach, examines influences from the external environment. The outcome of this step is the identification and diagnosis of planning assumptions, issues, and problems.

A thorough situational analysis will point toward the planning decisions you will need to make. For example, if you are a manager in a magazine company considering the launch of a sports publication for the teen market, your analysis will include such factors as the number of teens who subscribe to magazines, the appeal of this market to advertisers, your firm's ability to serve this market effectively, current economic conditions, the level of teen interest in sports, and any sports magazines already serving this market and how successful they are. Such a detailed analysis will help you decide whether or not to proceed with the next step in your magazine launch.

situational analysis

A process planners use, within time and resource constraints, to gather, interpret, and summarize all information relevant to the planning issue under consideration.

DELTA AIR LINES GOES FOR BROKE

On January 1, 2004, Gerald Grinstein, age 71, assumed his job as CEO of Delta Air Lines, the nation's third largest carrier. Grinstein was once CEO of Western Airlines and had made that money-losing operation profitable before Delta bought it in 1987. Since that time he had been a member of Delta's board of directors. Now the board hoped that he could turn Delta around, too. A turnaround was badly needed. Over the last three years Delta had lost a total of $3.2 *billion*. A loss of another $2 billion or more was being forecast for 2004. At this rate, the airline would eventually run out of cash and have to file for bankruptcy.

Could the company, with some 70,000 employees, be saved? The board asked Grinstein to develop a comprehensive strategic plan for Delta, covering every part of the airline's operation. The goal of the plan was to set a new direction for the company, one that would slow down and eventually reverse its downward spiral. To achieve this goal, Grinstein's strategic plan would have to take on some very difficult challenges:

- The events of September 11, 2001, had caused air travel to decline sharply.
- Low-cost carriers like Jet Blue were driving prices downward and taking market share. And these carriers were competing in over 70 percent of Delta's routes.
- Fuel prices were rising, and in fact had increased 32 percent over the previous year.
- Delta's pilots were the highest paid in the industry. In fact, a lucrative agreement had been struck with the pilots' union only months before 9/11. Other airlines had gotten concessions from pilots since 9/11, but Delta hadn't.
- Many of Delta's scheduled flights, particularly to Dallas–Ft. Worth, were unprofitable. On the other hand, several of its profitable locations, like Boston, were doing well but didn't have enough flights.
- The Internet had transformed many online ticket buyers into aggressive bargain hunters. In this market, Delta's airfares were too high. And many customers had been turned off by Delta's complicated fee structure and so-so customer service.
- Delta also had many financial liabilities, including high debt and a rich pension plan for retirees.

Clearly, Grinstein would have to cut Delta's costs significantly, find a way to compete with the low-cost carriers, eliminate unprofitable routes, and increase customer satisfaction. The company could not afford to continue losing passengers and money. A lot depended on Grinstein's ability to quickly develop a plan that would work.

Sources for Prologue, Connections, Epilogue: Brian Grow, "Delta: A Wing, a Prayer, a Revamp," *BusinessWeek*, August 23, 2004, online; Mary Jane Credeur, "Delta CEO Maps Epic Overhaul," *Atlanta Business Chronicle*, September 10, 2004; "Delta Dodges Bankruptcy with Labor Deal," *cnnmoney.com*, October 28, 2004; Philip Baggaley, "Inside Delta's Low-Fare Strategy," *BusinessWeek*, January 6, 2005, online.

Planning: Delivering Strategic Value

Part Two introduces key concepts of planning and strategy. The topics emphasize the decisions made by top managers and their implications for the entire organization. Chapter 4 presents a summary of the planning process and an overview of how senior executives manage strategically. The next three chapters treat subjects that have emerged recently as vital considerations for modern managers. Chapter 5 examines the impact of ethical concerns and social and political factors on major decisions. Chapter 6 addresses the pressing reality of managing in a global competitive environment. Finally, Chapter 7 describes entrepreneurs and the new ventures they create. These chapters will provide the reader with a clear understanding of the strategic directions that effective organizations pursue.

Chapter **4**

CHAPTER 4
Planning and Strategic Management

Manage your destiny, or someone else will.
—**Jack Welch, former CEO, General Electric**

CHAPTER OUTLINE

LEARNING OBJECTIVES

After studying Chapter 4, you will know:

1. How to proceed through the basic steps in any planning process.

2. How strategic planning integrates with tactical and operational planning.

3. Why it is important to analyze both the external environment and the internal resources of the firm before formulating a strategy.

4. The choices available for corporate strategy.

5. How companies can achieve competitive advantage through business strategy.

6. How core competencies provide the foundation for business strategy.

7. The keys to effective strategy implementation.

**General
decision-making stages**

**Specific
formal planning steps**

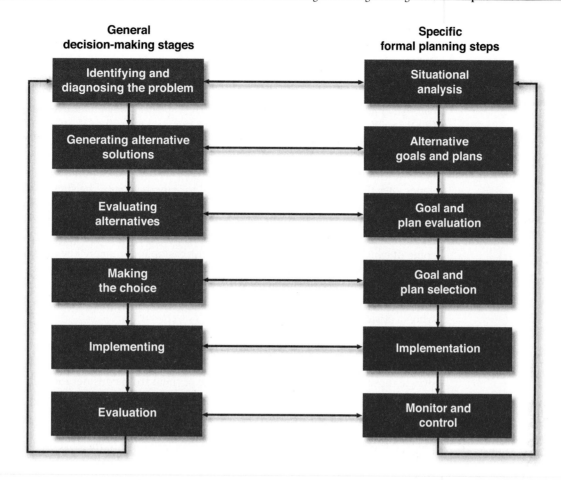

FIGURE 4.1

Decision-Making Stages (Chapter 3) and Formal Planning Steps (Chapter 4)

Step 2: Alternative Goals and Plans Based on the situational analysis, the planning process should generate alternative goals that may be pursued in the future and the alternative plans that may be used to achieve those goals. This step in the process should stress creativity and encourage managers and employees to assume a broad perspective on their jobs. Once a range of alternatives has been developed, the merits of these alternative plans and goals will be evaluated. Continuing with our magazine publishing example, the alternatives you might want to consider could include whether the magazine should be targeted at young men, young women, or both groups, and whether it should be sold mainly through subscriptions or on newsstands.

Goals are the targets or ends the manager wants to reach. Goals should be specific, challenging, and realistic. For example, General Electric's goal of being first or at least second in all its markets is specific and challenging. When appropriate, goals also should be quantified and linked to a time frame. They should be acceptable to the managers and employees charged with achieving them, and they should be consistent both within and among work units.

Plans are the actions or means the manager intends to use to achieve goals. At a minimum, this step should outline alternative actions that may lead to the attainment of each goal, the resources required to reach the goal through those means, and the obstacles that may develop. Aramark's plan to become the premier provider of corporate services outlines the company's activities designed to expand business in catering, food services, and uniform services, as well as health and education. This plan is focused on the company's goals of 10 percent annual growth in sales and profitability.[2]

In this chapter we will talk about various types of plans. Some plans, called *single-use plans,* are designed to achieve a set of goals that are not likely to be repeated in the future. For example, city planners might prepare for an upcoming sesquicentennial

goal

A target or end that management desires to reach.

plans

The actions or means managers intend to use to achieve organizational goals.

celebration by putting in place a plan for parades, festivities, speeches, and the like. Other plans, called *standing plans*, focus on ongoing activities designed to achieve an enduring set of goals. For example, many companies have standing plans for their efforts to recruit minority group members and women. Frequently, standing plans become more permanent policies and rules for running the organization. Finally, *contingency plans* might be referred to as "what if" plans. They include sets of actions to be taken when a company's initial plans have not worked well or if events in the external environment require a sudden change. For example, despite the fact that major financial firms in or near the World Trade Center were severely affected by the 9/11 attacks, within hours many of those firms were able to restart operations from contingency sites that had been specially prepared for emergencies. The sites duplicated the essential information and equipment of their home offices. Some of these contingency plans had been made because of Y2K concerns in 1999, but they found their real use after 9/11. Nevertheless, the events of 9/11 revealed many shortcomings in these plans, some of which have since been upgraded. For example, too many key operations were concentrated in one geographic area. Most major corporations now have contingency plans in place to respond to a major disaster—to make sure vital data are backed up and can be recovered in an emergency, for instance, or that employees know what to do when a crisis occurs.[3]

Step 3: Goal and Plan Evaluation   Next, managers will evaluate the advantages, disadvantages, and potential effects of each alternative goal and plan. They will prioritize those goals and even eliminate some of them from consideration. In our magazine publishing example, your evaluation may determine that newsstand sales alone wouldn't be sufficiently profitable to justify the launch. At the same time, managers will consider carefully the implications of alternative plans for meeting high-priority goals. For example, they will pay a great deal of attention to the cost of any initiative and the investment return that is likely to result.

Advantages of Collaboration

In some companies, teams of managers with diverse backgrounds conduct a goal or plan evaluation. For example, during manager planning efforts at Atlantic Richfield Company (ARCO), senior executives meet with planning groups from strategic planning, operations, marketing, government affairs, and other areas. The different perspectives and ideas such groups generate lead to a more balanced and comprehensive review of the company's goals and plans. This kind of collaboration will also create more support for the plan that eventually emerges, as everyone has contributed to the planning process. In addition, communication of the plan is made easier, as key players throughout the organization are now familiar with some of the assumptions under which the plan was developed.

Step 4: Goal and Plan Selection   Once managers have assessed the various goals and plans, they will select the one that's most appropriate and feasible. The evaluation process will identify the priorities and trade-offs among the goals and plans. For example, if your plan is to launch a number of new publications, and you're trying to choose among them, you might weigh the different up-front investment each requires, the size of each market, which one fits best with your existing product line or company image, and so on. Experienced judgment always plays an important role in this process.

> "Most discussions of decision making assume that only senior executives make decisions or that only senior executives' decisions matter. This is a dangerous mistake."
>
> Peter Drucker

However, as you will discover later in the chapter, relying on judgment alone may not be the best way to proceed.

Typically, a formal planning process leads to a written set of goals and plans that are appropriate and feasible within a predicted set of circumstances. In some organizations, the alternative generation, evaluation, and selection steps generate planning **scenarios,** as discussed in Chapter 2. A different contingency plan is attached to each scenario. The manager pursues the goals and implements the plans associated with the most likely scenario. However, the manager will be prepared to switch to another set of plans if the situation changes and another scenario becomes relevant. This approach helps the firm avoid crises and allows greater flexibility and responsiveness.

The Hard Rock Café carries its strategy—to be identified with rock 'n' roll—through to its hotel signs.

Step 5: Implementation   Once managers have selected the goals and plans, they must implement the plans designed to achieve the goals. The best plans are useless unless they are implemented properly. Managers and employees must understand the plan, have the resources necessary to implement it, and be motivated to do so. If both managers and employees have participated in the previous steps of the planning process, the implementation phase probably will be more effective and efficient. As we suggested earlier, employees usually are better informed, more committed, and more highly motivated when a goal or plan is one that they helped develop.

scenario

A narrative that describes a particular set of future conditions.

Connections: **DELTA AIR LINES**

One of the key requirements in CEO Grinstein's strategic plan was the need to lower Delta's labor costs. In October 2004, Delta and its pilots union announced that they had reached agreement to cut flight-crew wages by a third. This change would save Delta $1 billion a year. The pilots also agreed to work-rule changes that would save still more. In return, the pilots were given the option to buy a 15 percent stake in the company. Grinstein had been helped in his efforts to reach a deal by being candid with the union about Delta's financial condition and about the very real threat of bankruptcy. In a series of "town hall" meetings with pilots and other employees, he discussed the details of the company's new plan, its goals, and why change was necessary. He also postponed high top-executive bonuses, including his own, until Delta became profitable. This sent a signal to the organization that sacrifices would be shared.

Finally, successful implementation requires that the plan be linked to other systems in the organization, particularly the budget and reward systems. If the budget does not provide the manager with sufficient financial resources to execute the plan, the plan is probably doomed. Similarly, goal achievement must be linked to the organization's reward system. Many organizations use incentive programs to encourage employees to achieve goals and to implement plans properly. Commissions, salaries, promotions, bonuses, and other rewards are based on successful performance.

Tying plans to a firm's financials is a key element of success.

Step 6: Monitor and Control   Although it is sometimes ignored, this step in the formal planning process is essential. Without it, you would have no way of knowing whether your plan is succeeding. As we mentioned earlier, planning works in a cycle;

it is an ongoing, repetitive process. Managers must continually monitor the actual performance of their work units according to the unit's goals and plans. They will also need to develop control systems that measure that performance and allow them to take corrective action when the plans are implemented improperly or when the situation changes. In our magazine publishing example, newsstand and subscription sales reports are essential for letting you how well your new magazine launch is going. If subscription sales aren't doing as well as expected, you may need to revise your marketing plan. We will discuss the important issue of control systems in greater detail later in this chapter and in Chapter 16.

Levels of Planning

In Chapter 1 you learned about the three major types of managers: top-level (*strategic* managers), middle-level (*tactical* managers), and frontline (*operational* managers). Because planning is an important management function, managers at all three levels use it. However, the scope and activities of the planning process at each level of the organization often differ.

Strategic Planning

strategic planning

A set of procedures for making decisions about the organization's long-term goals and strategies.

Strategic planning involves making decisions about the organization's long-term goals and strategies. Strategic plans have a strong external orientation and cover major portions of the organization. Senior executives are responsible for the development and execution of the strategic plan, although they usually do not formulate or implement the entire plan personally.

Strategic goals are major targets or end results that relate to the long-term survival, value, and growth of the organization. Strategic managers—top-level managers—usually establish goals that reflect both effectiveness (providing appropriate outputs) and efficiency (a high ratio of outputs to inputs). Typical strategic goals include various measures of growth, market share, profitability, return on investment, quantity and quality of outputs, productivity, customer service, and contribution to society. Organizations will usually have a number of mutually reinforcing strategic goals at the same time. For example, a computer manufacturer may have as its strategic goals the launch of a specified number of new products in a particular time frame, of a higher quality, with a targeted increase in market share.

How does one of the world's most respected news sources, *The New York Times*, continue to succeed after a year (2004) of journalistic scandal, a quick-as-lightning and dynamic media world, and (gasp) weak earnings? A new strategy—that promises to deliver top-notch journalism in any way, shape, or form—anywhere in the world. Will it work?

A **strategy** is a pattern of actions and resource allocations designed to achieve the goals of the organization. The strategy an organization implements is an attempt to match the skills and resources of the organization to the opportunities found in

	Managerial Level	Level of Detail	Time Horizon
Strategic	Top	Low	Long
Tactical	Middle	Medium	Medium
Operational	Frontline	High	Short

FIGURE 4.2
Hierarchy of Goals and Plans

the external environment; that is, every organization has certain strengths and weaknesses. The actions, or strategies, the organization implements should be directed toward building strengths in areas that satisfy the wants and needs of consumers and other key factors in the organization's external environment. Also, some organizations may implement strategies that change or influence the external environment, as discussed in Chapter 2.

Tactical and Operational Planning

Once the organization's strategic goals and plans are identified, they become the basis of planning done by middle-level and frontline managers. As you can see in Figure 4.2, goals and plans become more specific and involve shorter periods of time as they move from the strategic level to the tactical level and then to the operational level. A strategic plan will typically have a time horizon of from three to seven years—but sometimes even decades, as with the successful plan to land a probe on Titan, Saturn's moon. Tactical plans may have a time horizon of a year or two, and operational plans may cover a period of months. **Tactical planning** translates broad strategic goals and plans into specific goals and plans that are relevant to a definite portion of the organization, often a functional area like marketing or human resources, as discussed in Chapter 10. Tactical plans focus on the major actions a unit must take to fulfill its part of the strategic plan. For example, if the strategy calls for the rollout of a new product line, the tactical plan for the manufacturing unit might involve the design, testing, and installation of the equipment needed to produce the new line.

Operational planning identifies the specific procedures and processes required at lower levels of the organization. Frontline managers usually focus on routine tasks such as production runs, delivery schedules, and human resources requirements, as we discuss in Chapters 16 and 17.

The planning model we have been describing is a hierarchical one, with top-level strategies flowing down through the levels of the organization into more specific goals and plans and an ever more limited timetable. But in today's complex organizations, the planning sequence is often not as rigid as this traditional view. As we will see later, managers throughout an organization may be involved in developing the strategic plan and contributing critical elements to it.

Aligning Tactical, Operational, and Strategic Planning

To be fully effective, the organization's strategic, tactical, and operational goals and plans must be *aligned*—that is, they must be consistent, mutually supportive, and focused on achieving the common purpose and direction. Whole Foods Market, for example, links its tactical and operational planning directly to its strategic planning. The firm describes itself on its Web site as a mission-driven company that aims to set the standards for excellence for food retailers. The firm measures its success in fulfilling its vision by "customer satisfaction, Team Member excellence and happiness, return on capital investment, improvement in the state of the environment, and local and larger community support."

strategic goals

Major targets or end results relating to the organization's long-term survival, value, and growth.

strategy

A pattern of actions and resource allocations designed to achieve the organization's goals.

tactical planning

A set of procedures for translating broad strategic goals and plans into specific goals and plans that are relevant to a distinct portion of the organization, such as a functional area like marketing.

operational planning

The process of identifying the specific procedures and processes required at lower levels of the organization.

Ideally, strategic plans integrate all the bottom-line practices of the firm.

Whole Foods' strategic goal is "to sell the highest-quality products that also offer high value for our customers." Its operational goals focus on ingredients, freshness, taste, nutritive value, safety, and appearance that meet or exceed its customers' expectations, including guaranteeing product satisfaction. Tactical goals include store environments that are "inviting, fun, unique, informal, comfortable, attractive, nurturing and educational" and safe and inviting work environments for its employees.

Starbucks has built its strategy of growth and profitability around the notion of excellent service and a "feel-good" ambience. The company continues to expand at a frenetic pace, but it nonetheless strives to be a homey oasis of calm for its customers.

In addition to striving to serve great coffee, Starbucks believes that the customer's experience is everything—that customers immediately absorb the "the good, the bad, and the ugly" about a company. Consequently, the coffee-house giant strives to manage that feel-good experience on all fronts—tactically, operationally, and strategically. Toward that end, Starbucks offers both its full-time and part-time employees (or "partners," as the company calls them) full benefits, and all employees are given an opportunity to own shares in the company as part of its "Bean Stock" program. Starbucks has also beefed up its human resource policies to protect the jobs, pay, and health care benefits of its employees called into military action. As far as its suppliers go, the company

Starbucks's emphasis on customer and service quality is a key element in its success.

FIGURE 4.3

The Strategy Map: Creating Value by Aligning Goals

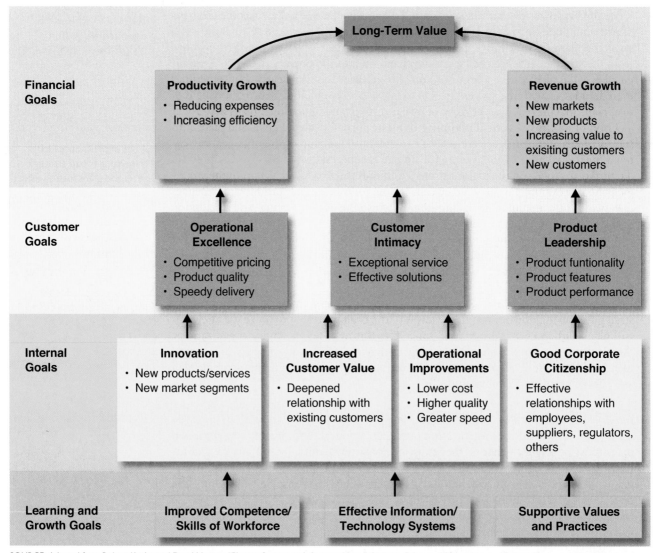

SOURCE: Adapted from Robert Kaplan and David Norton, "Plotting Success with Strategy Maps," *Optimize*, February 2004, online; and Robert Kaplan and David Norton, "Having Trouble with Your Strategy? Then Map It," *Harvard Business Review*, September–October 2000.

champions the interests of its coffee growers, guaranteeing them a coffee price above the prevailing market price. It certifies that its coffee is grown organically, and it is in the process of converting its hot beverage cups to 10 percent recycled. The goal is to never sour people on Starbucks.[4]

One method for aligning the organization's strategic and operational goals is the *strategic map.* The strategic map provides a tool managers can use to communicate their strategic goals and enable members of the organization at every level to understand the parts they will play in helping to achieve them. The map illustrates the four key drivers (or "balanced scorecard") of a firm's long-term success: the skills of its people and their ability to grow and learn; the effectiveness of its internal processes; its ability to deliver value to customers; and, ultimately, its ability to grow its financial assets. The map shows how specific plans and goals in each area link to the others and can generate real improvements in an organization's performance.

> The strategic map shows the relationship between a firm's practices and its long-term success.

Figure 4.3 shows how a strategic map might be built, and how the various goals of the organization relate to each other to create long-term value for the firm. As an example, let us assume that a company's primary *financial goal* is "to increase revenues by enhancing the value we offer to existing customers by making our prices the lowest available." (Target and Wal-Mart might be good examples of companies with this kind of strategy.) The company will then have appropriate goals and plans in the other sections of the map to support that strategy. Its *learning and growth goals* might include bringing in the most efficient production technologies or work processes and training the staff to use them. These in turn will lead to the *internal goals* of improved production speed and lower cost, which in turn leads to the *customer goal* of competitive pricing, making the original financial goal feasible. On the other hand, a financial strategy of revenue growth through new products might lead to people and technology goals that speed up product design, to internal processes that lead to innovation, and to a customer goal of perceived product leadership. Whatever the strategy, the strategic map can be used to develop the appropriate measures and standards in each operational area for that strategy and to show how they are all linked.[5]

Strategic Planning

Strategic decision making is one of the most exciting and controversial topics in management today. In fact, many organizations currently are changing the ways they develop and execute their strategic plans.

Traditionally, strategic planning emphasized a top-down approach—senior executives and specialized planning units developed goals and plans for the entire organization. Tactical and operational managers received those goals and plans, and their own planning activities were limited to specific procedures and budgets for the units.

> New ideas from managers throughout the organization can contribute to a plan's effectiveness.

Over the years, managers and consulting firms innovated a variety of analytical techniques and planning approaches, many of which have been critical for analyzing complex business situations and competitive issues. In many instances, however, senior executives spent too much time with their planning specialists to the exclusion of line managers in the rest of the organization. As a result, a gap often developed between strategic managers and tactical and operational managers, and managers and employees throughout the organization became alienated and uncommitted to the organization's success.[6]

Today, however, senior executives increasingly are involving managers throughout the organization in the strategy formation process.[7] The problems just described and the rapidly changing environment of the last 25 years have forced executives to look to all levels of the organization for ideas and innovations to make their firms more competitive. Although the CEO and other top managers continue to furnish the strategic direction, or "vision," of the organization, tactical and even operational managers often provide valuable inputs to the organization's strategic plan. In some cases, these

Tactical planning at the Gap, including marketing, was important in reinforcing the firm's strategy of commitment to basic fashion for its core group of customers.

managers also have substantial autonomy to formulate or change their own plans. This increases flexibility and responsiveness, critical requirements for success in the modern organization.

Because of this trend, a new term for the strategic planning process has emerged: *strategic management.* **Strategic management** involves managers from all parts of the organization in the formulation and implementation of strategic goals and strategies. It integrates strategic planning and management into a single process. Strategic planning becomes an ongoing activity in which all managers are encouraged to think strategically and focus on long-term, externally oriented issues as well as short-term tactical and operational issues.

Figure 4.4 shows the six major components of the strategic management process: (1) establishment of mission, vision, and goals; (2) analysis of external opportunities and threats; (3) analysis of internal strengths and weaknesses; (4) SWOT (strengths, weaknesses, opportunities, and threats) analysis and strategy formulations; (5) strategy implementation; and (6) strategic control. Because this process is a planning and decision process, it is similar to the planning framework discussed earlier. Although organizations may use different terms or emphasize different parts of the process, the components and concepts described in this section are found either explicitly or implicitly in every organization. As you can see from the accompanying box on page 128, even a small entrepreneurial firm can benefit from the kind of planning framework we will describe here.

Step 1: Establishment of Mission, Vision, and Goals

The first step in strategic planning is establishing a mission, a vision, and goals for the organization. The **mission** is a clear and concise expression of the basic purpose of the organization. It describes what the organization does, who it does it for, its basic product or service, and its values. Here are some current or former mission statements from firms you will recognize:

> *McDonald's:* "To be the world's best quick service restaurant experience. Being the best means providing outstanding quality, service, cleanliness and value, so that we make every customer in every restaurant smile."

---

strategic management

A process that involves managers from all parts of the organization in the formulation and implementation of strategic goals and strategies.

mission

An organization's basic purpose and scope of operations.

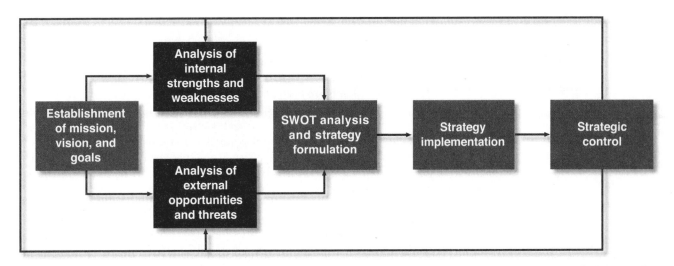

FIGURE 4.4
The Strategic Management
Process

Levi Strauss: "We will market the most appealing and widely worn casual clothing in the world. We will clothe the world."

Wal-Mart: "To give ordinary folk the chance to buy the same thing as rich people."

Microsoft: "To enable people and businesses throughout the world to realize their full potential."

Smaller organizations, of course, may have missions that aren't as broad as these. For example, the local bar found next to most campuses has this implicit mission: "To sell large quantities of inexpensive beer to college students in a noisily enjoyable environment."

The mission describes the organization as it currently operates. The **strategic vision** points to the future—it provides a perspective on where the organization is headed and what it can become. Ideally, the vision statement clarifies the long-term direction of the company and its *strategic intent.* Here are some actual vision statements:

> **strategic vision**
>
> The long-term direction and strategic intent of a company.

General Electric (under then-CEO Jack Welch): "To become the most competitive enterprise in the world by being number one or number two in market share in every business the company is in."

Kodak: "To grow more rapidly than our competitors by providing customers with the solutions they need to capture, store, process, output, and communicate images—anywhere, anytime."

John F. Kennedy: "To land a man on the moon and safely return him to earth by the end of this decade."

The most effective vision statements inspire organization members. They offer a worthwhile target for the entire organization to work together to achieve. Often, these statements are not strictly financial, because financial targets alone may not motivate all organization members. For example, an early vision statement by Pepsi was "to beat Coke." There is little ambiguity in such a statement. It provides a very clear and motivating target for employees at every level of the organization.

Strategic goals evolve from the mission and vision of the organization. The chief executive officer of the organization, with the input and approval of the board of directors, establishes the mission, vision, and major strategic goals. The concepts and information within the mission statement, vision statement, and strategic goals statement may not be identified as such, but they should be communicated to everyone who has contact with the organization. Large firms generally provide public formal statements of their missions, visions,

> "There is no more powerful engine driving an organization toward excellence and long-term success than an attractive, worthwhile, and achievable vision of the future."
>
> Burt Nanus
>
> SOURCE: *Visionary Leadership* (San Francisco: Jossey-Bass, 1992).

An Entrepreneur Gets Advice

Q: I am the owner, operator, designer, and builder of a 7-year-old construction outfit that is in the process of moving into a new market 50 miles from our present location. It is a very big, busy, and competitive construction market. How do I set my company apart from the competition? I want to show that we are well versed in building custom homes with exquisite, high-end detail, and that we are old and experienced enough.

A: Making a move into a new market is a big step, one that will require careful research and strategic planning if you are to be successful in this new and more competitive environment. Simply moving into the area and taking out ads advertising the fact that you are the new kid on the block won't be enough. If you hope to position your firm in the niche you desire, now is the time to do some serious homework.

Start by taking stock of your own company and identifying what makes it unique. You mention "exquisite detail," for instance—well, that's a possible selling point. Analyze what worked for you in the smaller market you are leaving, and how those factors and qualities helped you achieve success. Unless there are reasons to believe that your early strategy won't transfer to this new market, you should take a cue from your own beginnings.

Next, collect and assemble hard data pertaining to your soon-to-be home turf. How does the market you are entering differ from your former locale, and what do those differences suggest that you should do differently? For example, do homeowners value the size of a home more than the materials that go into it? Do they favor originality in design or are they happy with the cookie-cutter approach? If you find that size matters most in this marketplace, then you can focus your efforts accordingly.

You seem concerned about the size and competitive environment you will be facing. Will that be an obstacle to your success, or an opportunity? Look into which builders have been successful, and try to find out why. Identifying where and how you are strong and weak relative to the established builders in town is the first step in determining what your message will be, and how you will position the company.

Once you have a firm handle on the market, your competitors, and how your outfit meshes with the broader picture, then you will be ready to craft and execute your plan. As a small player, the key to building your presence in a new market will be to create strategic alliances that are likely to refer business to you.

Next, figure out who wields the most influence when it comes to residential development and find ways to engage them. You will need to establish yourself as a reliable and quality builder with these people, as well as with homeowners directly. Photos of some of your best homes, referrals, and testimonial letters from happy customers will be most effective in establishing credibility.

And don't forget to make the best use of technology when selling your services. I would make sure my capabilities are well-conveyed through the use of informational literature and/or a Web site, as is conventional with a firm of your size in your industry. Possibly, a professionally produced CD that can . . . highlight your strengths and expertise will help. This is a low-cost method and can be a very efficient way for you to communicate your capabilities to these referral sources.

Finally, there are other, tried-and-true ways to make a name for yourself, such as joining the local Chamber of Commerce. Each option can help you gain visibility and generate the goodwill that will go a long way toward achieving your goals.

SOURCE: Adapted from Karen E. Klein, "The Right Foundation for a Fresh Start," *BusinessWeek*, January 29, 2004, online.

goals, and even values. For example, recall the Microsoft mission on page 127. Here are some of the goals that Microsoft lists on its Web site in support of that mission:

- Connecting with customers, understanding their needs and how they use technology, and providing value through information and support to help them realize their potential
- Thinking and acting globally, enabling a diverse workforce that generates innovative decision-making for a broad spectrum of customers and partners, innovating to lower the costs of technology, and showing leadership in supporting the communities in which we live
- Excellence in everything we do
- Deepening customer trust through the quality of our products and services.

Kodak on its Web site includes these goals and values:

- We will derive our competitive advantage by delivering differentiated, cost-effective solutions—including consumables, hardware, software, systems, and services—quickly and with flawless quality.
- By consistently delivering on our commitments (and even admitting to the occasional mistake), we earn the credibility of those around us.[8]

Such lofty statements of purpose cannot be meaningful without strong leadership support. For example, Enron's listed values included respect, integrity, and communication. The failure of its management to act in accordance with these principles helped destroy the company. But where they have strong leadership support, statements like these of visions and goals clarify the organization's purpose to key constituencies outside the organization. They also help employees focus their talent, energy, and commitment in pursuit of the organization's goals. When the time comes for you to seek employment with a firm, reviewing the firm's statements of mission, vision, and goals is a good first step in determining whether the firm's purposes and values will be compatible with your own.

Step 2: Analysis of External Opportunities and Threats

The mission and vision drive the second component of the strategic management process: analysis of the external environment. Successful strategic management depends on an accurate and thorough evaluation of the environment. The various components of the environment were introduced in Chapter 2.

Table 4.1 lists some of the important activities in an environmental analysis. The analysis begins with an examination of the industry. Next, organizational stakeholders are examined. **Stakeholders** are groups and individuals who affect and are affected by

stakeholders

Groups and individuals who affect and are affected by the achievement of the organization's mission, goals, and strategies.

Advantages of Collaboration

Collaborating with key stakeholders will often be a significant factor in helping organizations successfully execute their strategic plan. For example, working with potential buyers about product or service improvements will often give managers useful, profitable ideas they wouldn't otherwise have considered. Managers who develop nonadversarial relationships with unions may well find that necessary work flow changes are easier to achieve when a new product is launched. Cooperating with community organizations before a new plant is built will often speed up the approval process and may even lead to other beneficial outcomes, such as improvements in local transportation. And, as we described in Chapter 2, working closely with suppliers can lead to significant improvements in the efficiency of an organization's supply chain.

Industry and Market Analysis
• *Industry profile:* major product lines and significant market segments in the industry.
• *Industry growth:* growth rates for the entire industry, growth rates for key market segments, projected changes in patterns of growth, and the determinants of growth.
• *Industry forces:* threat of new industry entrants, threat of substitutes, economic power of buyers, economic power of suppliers, and internal industry rivalry (recall Chapter 2).
Competitor Analysis
• *Competitor profile:* major competitors and their market shares.
• *Competitor analysis:* goals, strategies, strengths, and weaknesses of each major competitor.
• *Competitor advantages:* the degree to which industry competitors have differentiated their products or services or achieved cost leadership.
Political and Regulatory Analysis
• *Legislation and regulatory activities* and their effects on the industry.
• *Political activity:* the level of political activity that organizations and associations within the industry undertake (see Chapter 5).
Social Analysis
• *Social issues:* current and potential social issues and their effects on the industry.
• *Social interest groups:* consumer, environmental, and similar activist groups that attempt to influence the industry (see Chapters 5 and 6).
Human Resources Analysis
• *Labor issues:* key labor needs, shortages, opportunities, and problems confronting the industry (see Chapters 10 and 11).
Macroeconomic Analysis
• *Macroeconomic conditions:* economic factors that affect supply, demand, growth, competition, and profitability within the industry.
Technological Analysis
• *Technological factors:* scientific or technical methods that affect the industry, particularly recent and potential innovations (see Chapter 17).

TABLE 4.1
Environmental Analysis

the achievement of the organization's mission, goals, and strategies. They include buyers, suppliers, competitors, government and regulatory agencies, unions and employee groups, the financial community, owners and shareholders, and trade associations. The environmental analysis provides a map of these stakeholders and the ways they influence the organization.[9]

The environmental analysis also should examine other forces in the environment, such as macroeconomic conditions and technological factors. One critical task in environmental analysis is forecasting future trends. As noted in Chapter 2, forecasting techniques range from simple judgment to complex mathematical models that examine systematic relationships among many variables. Even simple quantitative techniques outperform the intuitive assessments of experts. Judgment is susceptible to bias, and man-

Financial Analysis
Examines financial strengths and weaknesses through financial statements such as a balance sheet and an income statement and compares trends to historical and industry figures (see Chapter 18).
Human Resources Assessment
Examines strengths and weaknesses of all levels of management and employees and focuses on key human resources activities, including recruitment, selection, placement, training, labor (union) relationships, compensation, promotion, appraisal, quality of work life, and human resources planning (see Chapters 10 and 11).
Marketing Audit
Examines strengths and weaknesses of major marketing activities and identifies markets, key market segments, and the competitive position (market share) of the organization within key markets.
Operations Analysis
Examines the strengths and weaknesses of the manufacturing, production, or service delivery activities of the organization (see Chapters 9, 16, and 17).
Other Internal Resource Analyses
Examine, as necessary and appropriate, the strengths and weaknesses of other organizational activities, such as research and development (product and process), management information systems, engineering, and purchasing.

TABLE 4.2
Internal Resource Analysis

agers have a limited ability to process information. Managers should use subjective judgments as inputs to quantitative models or when they confront new situations.

Frequently, the difference between an opportunity and a threat depends on how a company positions itself strategically. For example, Southwest Airlines' original base of operations at Love Field (outside of Dallas, Texas) was seen as a problem for the company. Other major competitors were permitted to fly into the larger and state-of-the-art Dallas–Fort Worth Airport, but Southwest was not. However, given this apparent threat, Southwest built its strategy around point-to-point flights into smaller airports that catered to business travelers. Other airlines soon found that they could not compete with Southwest in its niche. What was originally seen as a threat turned into an opportunity for Southwest.[10]

Step 3: Analysis of Internal Strengths and Weaknesses

As managers conduct an external analysis, they will also assess the strengths and weaknesses of major functional areas inside their organization. Table 4.2 lists some of the major components of this internal resource analysis. For example, is your firm strong enough financially to handle the lengthy and costly investment new projects often require? Can your existing staff carry out its part of the plan, or will additional training or hiring be needed? Is your firm's image compatible with the strategy, or will it have to persuade key stakeholders that a change in direction makes sense? This kind of internal analysis

> "We wanted Nike to be the world's best sports and fitness company. Once you say that, you have a focus. You don't end up making wing tips or sponsoring the next Rolling Stone world tour."
> Philip Knight, Nike Founder

provides strategic decision makers with an inventory of the organization's existing functions, skills, and resources as well as its overall performance level. Many of your other business courses will prepare you to conduct an internal analysis.

Amazon's key customer benefits are speed and excellence of service.

Resources and Core Competencies Without question, strategic planning has been strongly influenced in recent years by a focus on internal resources. **Resources** are inputs to production (recall systems theory) that can be accumulated over time to enhance the performance of a firm. Resources can take many forms, but tend to fall into two broad categories: (1) *tangible assets* such as real estate, production facilities, raw materials, and so on, and (2) *intangible assets* such as company reputation, culture, technical knowledge, and patents, as well as accumulated learning and experience. The Walt Disney Company, for example, has developed its strategic plan on combinations of tangible assets (e.g., hotels and theme parks) as well as intangible assets (brand recognition, talented craftspeople, culture focused on customer service).[11]

Effective internal analysis provides a clearer understanding of how a company can compete through its resources. Resources are a source of competitive advantage only under certain circumstances. First, if the resource is instrumental for creating customer *value*—that is, if it increases the benefits customers derive from a product or service relative to the costs they incur—the resource can lead to a competitive advantage. For example, Amazon's powerful search technology and its ability to track customer preferences and offer personalized recommendations each time its site is accessed, as well as its quick product-delivery system, are clearly valuable resources that enhance Amazon's competitiveness.

Second, resources are a source of advantage if they are *rare* and not equally available to all competitors. Even for extremely valuable resources, if all competitors have equal access, the resource cannot provide a source of competitive advantage. For example, when long-distance telephone service was deregulated, AT&T no longer had exclusive use of its telecommunications infrastructure. For companies such as Merck, DuPont, Dow Chemical, and others, patented formulas represent important resources that are both rare and valuable.

Third, if resources are *difficult to imitate*, they provide a source of competitive advantage. In the office supply business, superstores like Office Depot, Staples, and Office Max have found it difficult to set themselves apart from their competitors. When one competitor makes a move—like guaranteeing printer cartridges will be in stock—the others immediately follow suit. For many years, Xerox believed no one could duplicate its capabilities. Kodak and Canon soon proved Xerox wrong. McDonald's brand name recognition, in contrast, has been more difficult for competitors such as Burger King, Wendy's, and others to duplicate.[12]

Finally, resources can enhance a firm's competitive advantage when they are well *organized*. For example, Coca-Cola's well-organized and global network of bottlers allows the company to quickly introduce a new soft drink worldwide and to distribute it more efficiently than any competitor. IBM, now out of the personal-computer business, has organized its staff and systems to efficiently produce a consolidated technology product for its corporate clients—hardware, software, and service in one package. This spares its clients the cost of managing technology on their own.

As shown in Figure 4.5, when resources are valuable, rare, inimitable, and organized, they can be viewed as a company's core competencies. Simply stated, a **core competence** is something a company does especially well relative to its competitors. Honda, for example, has a core competence in small engine design and manufacturing; Sony has a core competence in miniaturization; Federal Express has a core competence in logistics and customer service. Typically, a core competence refers to a set of skills or expertise in some activity, rather than physical or financial assets. For example, among U.S. automobile manufacturers, General Motors has traditionally been viewed as having a core competence in marketing, while Ford has established quality as its number one strength. Recently Chrysler redefined its core competence around design and engineering. And as you can see from the accompanying article, GE is trying to redefine its core competence to include strategic partnerships with customers and has changed its employee compensation practices to align with that goal.

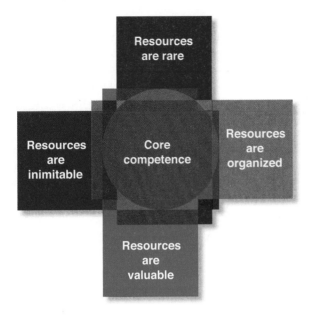

FIGURE 4.5
Resources and Core
Competence

Strategic Partnerships at GE

▼ **FROM THE PAGES OF**

BusinessWeek

Since Chairman and CEO Jeffrey R. Immelt ascended to GE's top job two years ago, he has tried to turn the $132 billion giant into a truly customer-focused organization, in part by sharing its best practices. But the revolution dubbed "At the Customer, For the Customer" isn't just fuzzy feel-good rhetoric. Immelt's push is changing how GE operates, including how its different units interact and how its profit-driven salespeople are measured.

The logic is simple: In an age when products can fast become commodities and service contracts go to the lowest bidder, companies are desperate to differentiate themselves and add more value in serving their customers. So why not make yourself indispensable by bringing your best people, resources, and skills to bear on customers' problems?

Immelt says that improving customer productivity is now a critical part of performance evaluations. But even he concedes that there has been some resistance to offering any help that doesn't immediately boost GE's bottom line. "It's taken me a couple of years to say: 'This is your day job, and it can help you grow faster and it can make you more money.' "

Making money, after all, is what this is all about. Tapping into the knowledge base of GE is a negotiating tool or benefit of doing business, not an end in itself. Bringing customers to GE's research and development centers or famed training facilities in Crotonville, for example, is meant to improve productivity, not provide free field trips. "We have to make sure they understand it has value to them," says J. Jeffrey Schaper, GE's chief commercial officer.

Despite a leadership position in most of its businesses, GE didn't crack the double-digit earnings-growth bar last year, growing 7 percent, to $15.1 billion, while revenues inched up just 5 percent, to $131.7 billion. This year has been worse. The answer, says Adrian Slywotzky of Mercer Management Consulting Inc., is to grab extra share in slow-growth businesses by enhancing one's value to customers. "It's not enough to be customer-centric," says Slywotzky. "You need to become sophisticated about your customers' activities and internal processes."

Few CEOs understand that like Immelt. He tested those customer skills most notably in GE Medical Systems, where he first pushed the notion of tapping the corporation's resources to give customers more bang for their buck. During his tenure there from 1997 to 2000, Immelt increased the service portion of the medical business from 25 percent to 42 percent of revenues and increased profits threefold.

Not surprisingly, GE Medical has been a showcase for the customer-centric approach. Take University Community Health System in Tampa, which had long bought medical equipment from GE. When the organization decided to build a state-of-the-art heart hospital and research center last year, GE joined in the bidding with some extra enticements. Not only did GE execs offer the usual equipment and services, they helped build a system around technology GE is developing that isn't even on the market yet. Hospital execs also got advice on leadership development, workplace design, and coordination with other units of GE to help build the facility.

The payoff for GE? It will supply all of the new hospital's clinical information technology and over 80 percent of its diagnostic and imaging gear. The contract will also run up to seven years, vs. the usual one to five years for normal pacts. Other bidders didn't come close in trying to forge a strategic partnership, says hospital COO Brigitte Shaw, adding: "We don't have the intellectual capital and resources to make this happen on our own."

SOURCE: Adapted from Diane Brady, "Will Jeff Immelt's New Push Pay Off for GE?" *BusinessWeek*, October 13, 2003, online.

Benchmarking   Benchmarking is the process of assessing how well one company's basic functions and skills compare to those of some other company or set of companies. The goal of benchmarking is to thoroughly understand the "best practices" of other firms, and to undertake actions to achieve both better performance and lower costs. For example, Xerox Corporation, a pioneer in benchmarking, established a program to study 67 of its key work processes against "world-class" companies. Many of these companies were not in the copier business. For example, in an effort to improve its order fulfillment process, Xerox studied L. L. Bean, the clothing mail-order company. Benchmarking programs have helped Xerox and a myriad of other companies, such as Ford, Corning, Hewlett-Packard, and Anheuser-Busch, make great strides in eliminating inefficiencies and improving competitiveness. Perhaps the only downside of benchmarking is that it only helps a company perform as well as its competitors; strategic management ultimately is about surpassing those companies.[13] Some companies attempt to overcome this problem, in part, by engaging in internal benchmarking—that is, benchmarking their different internal operations and departments against one another to disseminate the company's best practices throughout the organization and thereby gain a competitive advantage.

Aligning a firm's bottom line practices with "best practices" can improve its competitiveness.

Step 4: SWOT Analysis and Strategy Formulation

Once they have analyzed the external environment and the internal resources of the organization, managers will have the information they need to assess the organization's strengths, weaknesses, opportunities, and threats. Such an assessment normally is referred to as a **SWOT analysis.** For example, organization *strengths* might include skilled management, positive cash flow, and well-known and highly regarded brands. *Weaknesses* might be lack of spare production capacity and the absence of reliable suppliers. *Opportunities* might include a market niche that is currently underserved. And *threats* might include the possibility that competitors will enter that niche once it has been shown to be profitable.

SWOT analysis helps managers summarize the relevant, important facts from their external and internal analyses. They can then identify the primary and secondary strategic issues their organization faces. The strategy managers then formulate will build on the SWOT analysis to take advantage of available opportunities by capitalizing on the organization's strengths, neutralizing its weakness, and countering potential threats. To continue our example, the marketing plan for a new product might include reference to the firm's existing products; the production plan would call for an increase

SWOT analysis

A comparison of strengths, weaknesses, opportunities, and threats that helps executives formulate strategy.

in capacity; and the pricing strategy could be designed to make the market less attractive to competitors. In short, strategy formulation moves from analysis to devising a coherent course of action. The organization's corporate, business, and functional strategies will begin to take shape.

Connections: DELTA AIR LINES

In addition to its wage cuts, the strategic plan CEO Grinstein put into place addressed all the threats and challenges Delta faced. Over 50 percent of the airline's routes were changed, with unprofitable ones reduced and profitable ones expanded. For example, flights at the costly Dallas–Ft. Worth location were cut from 254 to 21. Delta also persuaded its lenders to accept an extended payment period for outstanding loans. This allowed the airline to lower its annual expense. The company also arranged for additional outside financing. To appeal to its most frequent flyers, Delta installed more kiosks at airport check-ins and improved its Web site, so ticket purchasing would be easier. It also simplified its frequent-flyer program. And in certain locations Delta began testing lower-priced fares and improved customer service to see if the public as a whole would respond. Early results indicated that they would.

Before we continue our strategy discussion, we note that many individuals seeking a job or a career change can find a "self-SWOT analysis" helpful. What are you particularly good at? What weaknesses might you need to overcome to improve your employment chances? What firms offer the best opportunity to market your skills to full advantage? Will you have a lot of competition from other job seekers? As with companies, this kind of analysis can be the beginning of a plan of action and can improve the plan's effectiveness.

Corporate Strategy   **Corporate strategy** identifies the set of businesses, markets, or industries in which the organization competes and the distribution of resources among those businesses. Figure 4.6 shows four basic corporate strategy alternatives, ranging from very specialized to highly diverse. A **concentration** strategy focuses on a single business competing in a single industry. In the food-retailing industry, Kroger, Safeway, and A&P all pursue concentration strategies. Frequently companies pursue concentration strategies to gain entry into an industry when industry growth is good, or when the company has a narrow range of competencies.

A **vertical integration** strategy involves expanding the domain of the organization into supply channels or to distributors. At one time, Henry Ford had fully integrated his company from the ore mines needed to make steel all the way to the showrooms where his cars were sold. Vertical integration generally is used to eliminate uncertainties and reduce costs associated with suppliers or distributors. A strategy of **concentric diversification** involves moving into new businesses that are related to the company's original core business. William Marriott expanded his original restaurant business outside Washington, D.C., by moving into airline catering, hotels, and fast food. Each of these businesses within the hospitality industry is related in terms of the services it provides, the skills necessary for success, and the customers it attracts. Often companies such as Marriott pursue a strategy of concentric diversification to take advantage of their strengths in one business to gain advantage in another. Because the businesses are related, the products, markets, technologies, or capabilities used in one business can be transferred to another.

In contrast to concentric diversification, **conglomerate diversification** is a corporate strategy that involves expansion into unrelated businesses. For example, General Electric Corporation has diversified from its original base in electrical and home appliance products to such wide-ranging industries as health, finance, insurance, truck

---

corporate strategy

The set of businesses, markets, or industries in which an organization competes and the distribution of resources among those entities.

concentration

A strategy employed for an organization that operates a single business and competes in a single industry.

vertical integration

The acquisition or development of new businesses that produce parts or components of the organization's product.

concentric diversification

A strategy used to add new businesses that produce related products or are involved in related markets and activities.

Companies that integrate vertically often do so to reduce their costs.

conglomerate diversification

A strategy used to add new businesses that produce unrelated products or are involved in unrelated markets and activities.

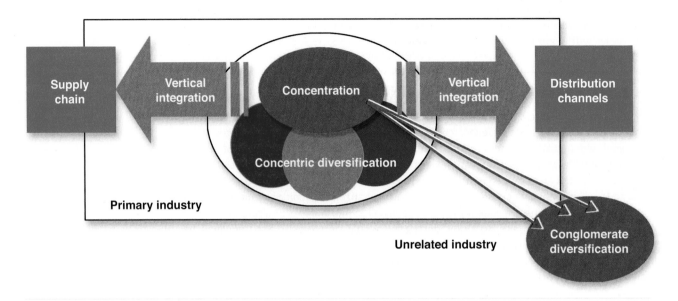

FIGURE 4.6
Summary of Corporate
Strategies

and air transportation, and even media, with its ownership of NBC. Typically, companies pursue a conglomerate diversification strategy to minimize risks due to market fluctuations in one industry.

The diversified businesses of an organization are sometimes called its business *portfolio*. One of the most popular techniques for analyzing a corporation's strategy for managing its portfolio is the BCG matrix, developed by the Boston Consulting Group. The BCG matrix is shown in Figure 4.7. Each business in the corporation is plotted on the matrix on the basis of the growth rate of its market and the relative strength of its competitive position in that market (market share). The business is represented by a circle whose size depends on the business's contribution to corporate revenues.

High-growth, weak-competitive-position businesses are called *question marks*. They require substantial investment to improve their position; otherwise, divestiture is rec-

FIGURE 4.7
The BCG Matrix

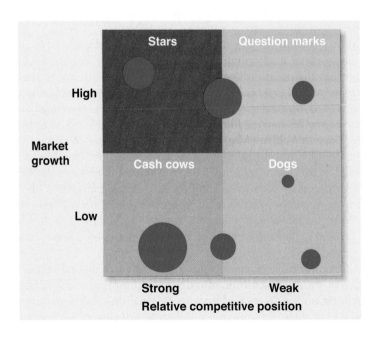

ommended. High-growth, strong-competitive-position businesses are called *stars*. These businesses require heavy investment, but their strong position allows them to generate the needed revenues. Low-growth, strong-competitive-position businesses are called *cash cows*. These businesses generate revenues in excess of their investment needs and therefore fund other businesses. Finally, low-growth, weak-competitive-position businesses are called *dogs*. The remaining revenues from these businesses are realized, and then the businesses are divested.

The BCG matrix is not intended as a substitute for management judgment, creativity, insight, or leadership. But it is a tool that can, along with other techniques, help managers of the firm as a whole and of its individual business evaluate their strategy alternatives.[14]

Trends in Corporate Strategy   In recent years, corporate America has been swept by a wave of mergers and acquisitions, such as AOL and Time Warner, Walt Disney and ABC, Procter & Gamble and Gillette, and Kmart and Sears. Such mergers and acquisitions often reflect the organization's corporate strategy, either by concentrating in one industry or by diversifying its portfolio.

The value of implementing a diversified corporate strategy depends on individual circumstances. Many critics have argued that unrelated diversification hurts a company more often than it helps it. In recent years, a number of diversified companies have sold their peripheral businesses so that they could concentrate on a more focused portfolio. For example, Merck & Company sold its consumer products business to focus on the application of biotechnology in the pharmaceutical industry. Sears sold Allstate Insurance to concentrate more on the core business of retail merchandising. Kodak sold off Eastman Chemical to boost profitability and concentrate more on its imaging business.[15]

In contrast, the diversification efforts of an organization competing in a slow-growth, mature, or threatened industry often are applauded. Many recent bank mergers, like that which occurred between J. P. Morgan Chase and Bank One, were designed to yield greater efficiencies and increased market share in the banking industry.

Although the merits of diversification are an issue for continued study, most observers agree that organizations usually perform better if they implement a more concentric diversification strategy in which businesses are somehow related or similar to one another. Disney, for example, spent $19 billion to merge with ABC/Cap Cities. While the two companies are somewhat different, their businesses are complementary. Disney's success in movies and videos is matched by ABC's network TV as well as its production capabilities in Cap Cities. Though Disney has a cable channel (the Disney Channel), its ability to reach millions of viewers has been enhanced by ABC's presence in network television.[16]

Business Strategy   After the top management team and board make the corporate strategic decisions, executives must determine how they will compete in each business area. **Business strategy** defines the major actions by which an organization builds and strengthens its competitive position in the marketplace. A competitive advantage typically results from one of two generic business strategies introduced here and elaborated in Chapter 7.[17]

First, organizations such as Wal-Mart and Southwest Airlines (mentioned earlier) pursue competitive advantage through **low-cost strategies.** Businesses using a low-cost strategy attempt to be efficient and offer a standard, no-frills product. They often are large and try to take advantage of economies of scale in production or distribution. In many cases, the large size allows them to sell their products and services at a lower price, which leads to higher market share, volume, and, ultimately, profits. To succeed, an organization using this strategy often must be the cost leader in its industry or market segment. However, even a cost leader must offer a product that is acceptable to customers compared to competitors' products. As Gordon Bethune, CEO of Continental Airlines, said, "You can make a pizza so cheap that no one will buy it." In the end, organizations

Low-price strategies usually require low production costs.

business strategy

The major actions by which a business competes in a particular industry or market.

low-cost strategy

A strategy an organization uses to build competitive advantage by being efficient and offering a standard, no-frills product.

A high-quality strategy is often more difficult for competitors to imitate.

differentiation strategy

A strategy an organization uses to build competitive advantage by being unique in its industry or market segment along one or more dimensions.

need to use a cost strategy to increase value to customers, rather than take it away.[18] You can see an example of this approach in action in the accompanying material on Apple's new strategy.

Second, an organization may pursue a **differentiation strategy.** With a differentiation strategy, a company attempts to be unique in its industry or market segment along some dimensions that customers value. This unique or differentiated position within the industry often is based on high product quality, excellent marketing and distribution, or superior service. Nordstrom's commitment to quality and customer service in the retail apparel industry is an excellent example of a differentiation strategy. While it perhaps is not as fancy as competitors such as Saks Fifth Avenue and Neiman Marcus, Nordstrom focuses on providing a full assortment of clothing and accessories to customers and ensuring that they get personal attention. The company's personal shopper program has become a hit in all of the company's 90-some full-line stores. Customers can come in and enjoy a refreshing beverage in a private room while a tireless assistant brings them endless wardrobe options. Customers can also access personal shoppers by phone or on the company's Web site. Nordstrom's personal shoppers reinforce efficiency, speed, and individual service. Better still for the customer, there is absolutely no charge for the service. In an otherwise impersonal and at times overwhelming department store or Web site, Nordstrom's differentiates itself by returning to the days when service was more genteel and individualized.[19]

Whatever strategy managers adopt, *the most effective strategy is one that competitors are unwilling or unable to imitate.* If the organization's strategic plan is one that could well be adopted by other organizations in the same industry, it may not be sufficiently distinctive or, in the long run, contribute significantly to the organization's competitiveness.

Aiming High by Aiming Low

FROM THE PAGES OF ▼

BusinessWeek

Apple Computer CEO Steven P. Jobs always has gobs of new products to unveil to the Mac faithful at the Macworld trade show each January, and this year he showed up with a more startling bag of tricks than usual. The company that has become synonymous with high-end style in computers and music players unveiled not one but two new products aimed at Joe Mainstream.

Taking clear aim at the low end of its two core markets, Jobs first announced the Mac mini, an impossibly small $499 PC that is Apple's first entry into the sub-$700 market that now accounts for almost 70 percent of all home PC sales. Then he brought out the iPod shuffle, which is smaller than a pack of Wrigley's gum and starts at just $99—a far cry from the $249 the Cupertino (Calif.) company now gets for its cheapest music player, the iPod mini. "I think we're going to bring in a lot of new customers to Apple," said Jobs in a post-keynote interview.

Still, the new strategy is not without risk. Chief among the fears: that by moving into crowded entry-level sectors, Apple could cannibalize its higher-priced products, putting at risk the strong profits it needs to finance innovation.

Clearly, Jobs & Co. believe the time is right to broaden out: Thanks to the phenomenal popularity of the iPod, the company is riding high. On January 12, Apple announced that its fiscal first-quarter net earnings quadrupled, to $295 million, over the previous year, on revenues up 74 percent, to $3.49 billion. Sales of the red-hot iPod alone hit 4.5 million units, a 500 percent increase. With iPod mania running full tilt, Jobs figures there's an opening to grab PC market share by drawing in users who want Apple's famous style and ease-of-use.

Until now, Apple products have been too expensive for most PC users, but Jobs is betting that the $499 mini could make Apple a viable contender at the core of the market. To simplify things even further, Apple made sure PC users can plug their existing display, keyboard, and mouse into the unit. "This is the most affordable Mac ever," Jobs told the crowd. "People who are thinking of switching will have no more excuses."

Low cost isn't the only lure. Jobs is also betting that once PC users finally get a chance to use Apple's highly regarded operating system and software suites, there'll be no turning back.

What Jobs has done is deliberately undercut the competition. The base model of the new shuffle costs $99 and holds 120-plus songs. To get to that low price, however, he has designed a barebones player that may not appeal to everyone. Unlike many other flash players, Apple's gadget boasts no screen—meaning users can't see or control what they're playing.

Apple is betting that there are plenty of low-budget buyers out there who will find the shuffle enough gadget for their needs. It also hopes they'll be tempted to move up into a pricier iPod, especially if they get hooked buying music from the company's iTunes Music Store, which currently plays solely on Apple products.

But couldn't the cheaper products prompt some customers to shun the higher-priced ones? Apple has done what it can to prevent that from happening by segmenting its lineup. With its far greater storage and better controls, the original iPod is a very different gadget from the shuffle. Likewise, Jobs, who shrugs off fears of cannibalization, has made sure the new mini lacks the power and many features found in the iMac and the company's higher-priced computers.

Still, Apple will have to tread carefully as it enters the low end of the PC market if it is to avoid succumbing to the profitless prosperity that has dogged so many others. To beat the odds, Apple will keep its costs low so it can maintain its profit margins and thereby have the resources to keep innovating.

SOURCE: Adapted from Peter Burrows, "Apple's Bold Swim Downstream," *BusinessWeek*, January 13, 2005, online.

Functional Strategy   The final step in strategy formulation is to establish the major functional strategies. **Functional strategies** are implemented by each functional area of the organization to support the business strategy. The typical functional areas include production, human resources, marketing, research and development, finance, and distribution. For example, American Express's expansion plans will require separate marketing plans for issuing banks, participating retailers, and current and potential cardholders. It will also require plans for expanding its customer database and technology to manage the new card offers it is planning. And it will need plans to test

> **functional strategies**
>
> Strategies implemented by each functional area of the organization to support the organization's business strategy.

> **Nordstrom differentiates itself from its competitors with superior customer service and broad product selection.**

and roll out new payment and charging options. All these functional plans will need to be in sync with the company's overall business strategy.

Functional strategies typically are put together by functional area executives with the input and approval of the executives responsible for business strategy. Senior strategic decision makers review the functional strategies to ensure that each major department is operating in a manner consistent with the business strategies of the organization. For example, automated production techniques—even if they saved money—would not be appropriate for a piano company like Steinway, whose products are strategically positioned (and priced) as high-quality and hand-tooled.

Step 5: Strategy Implementation

As with any plan, formulating the appropriate strategy is not enough. Strategic managers also must ensure that the new strategies are implemented effectively and efficiently. Recently corporations and strategy consultants have been paying more attention to implementation. They realize that clever techniques and a good plan do not guarantee success. This greater appreciation is reflected in two major trends.

First, organizations are adopting a more comprehensive view of implementation. The strategy must be supported by decisions regarding the appropriate organization structure, technology, human resources, reward systems, information systems, organization culture, and leadership style. Just as the strategy of the organization must be matched to the external environment, it must fit the multiple factors responsible for its implementation. The remainder of this section discusses these factors and the ways in which they can be used to implement strategy.

Second, many organizations are extending the more participative strategic management process to implementation. Managers at all levels are involved with strategy formulation and the identification and execution of the means to implement the new strategies. Senior executives still may orchestrate the overall implementation process, but they place much greater responsibility and authority in the hands of others in the organization. In general, strategy implementation involves four related steps:

- *Step 1: Define strategic tasks.* Articulate in simple language what must be done in a particular business to create or sustain a competitive advantage. Define strategic tasks to help employees understand how they contribute to the organization. This also can redefine relationships among the parts of the organization.
- *Step 2: Assess organization capabilities.* Evaluate the organization's ability to implement the strategic tasks. A task force (typically) interviews employees and managers to identify specific issues that help or hinder effective implementation. Results are summarized for top management. In the course of your career you are likely to be asked to participate in a task force. We discuss working effectively in teams in Chapter 14.
- *Step 3: Develop an implementation agenda.* Management decides how it will change its management pattern, how critical interdependencies will be managed, what skills and individuals are needed in key roles, and what structures, measures, information, and rewards might ultimately support specified behavior. A philosophy statement, communicated in value terms, is the natural outcome of this process.
- *Step 4: Create an implementation plan.* The top management team, the employee task force, and others develop the implementation plan. The top management team monitors progress. The employee task force is charged with providing feedback about how others in the organization are responding to the changes.

This process, though straightforward, does not always go smoothly. Figure 4.8 shows six different barriers to strategy implementation and provides a description of some key principles for overcoming these "silent killers." By paying closer attention to the

Change starts with the leader

The Silent Killers	Principles for Engaging and Changing the Silent Killers
Top-down or laissez-faire senior management style	With the top team and lower levels, the CEO/ general manager creates a partnership built around the development of a compelling business direction, the creation of an enabling organizational context, and the delegation of authority to clearly accountable individuals and teams.
Unclear strategy and conflicting priorites	The top team, as a group, develops a statement of strategy, and priorities that members are willing to stand behind are developed.
An ineffective senior management team	The top team, as a group, is involved in all steps in the change process so that its effectiveness is tested and developed.
Poor vertical communication	An honest, fact-based dialogue is established with lower levels about the new strategy and the barriers to implementing it.
Poor coordination across functions, businesses, or borders	A set of businesswide initiatives and new organizational roles and responsibilities are defined that require "the right people to work together on the right things in the right way" to implement the strategy.
Inadequate down-the-line leadership skills and development	Lower-level managers develop skills through newly created opportunities to lead change and drive key business initiatives. They are supported with just-in-time coaching, training, and targeted recruitment. Those who still are not able to make the grade must be replaced.

SOURCE: Reprinted from M. Beer and R. A Eisenstat, "The Silent Killers of Strategy Implementation and Learning," *MIT Sloan Management Review* (Summer 2000), 4 (4), pp. 29–40, by permission of the publisher. Copyright © 2000 by MIT. All rights reserved.

FIGURE 4.8
Attacking the Six Barriers to Strategy Implementation

processes by which strategies are implemented, executives, managers, and employees can play an important role in making sure that strategic plans are actually carried out.[20]

Step 6: Strategic Control

The final component of the strategic management process is strategic control. A **strategic control system** is designed to support managers in evaluating the organization's progress with its strategy and, when discrepancies exist, taking corrective action. The system must encourage efficient operations that are consistent with the plan while allowing the flexibility to adapt to changing conditions. As with all control systems, the organization must develop performance indicators, an information system, and specific mechanisms to monitor progress.

Most strategic control systems include some type of budget to monitor and control major financial expenditures. In fact, the aspect of your organization's strategic plan you will most likely confront in your first job as a manager is your work unit's budget. Your upper management may give you budget assumptions and targets for your area, reflecting your part in the overall plan, and you may be asked to revise your budget once all the budgets in your organization have been consolidated and reviewed.

The dual responsibilities of a control system— efficiency and flexibility—often seem contradictory with respect to budgets. The budget usually establishes limits on spending, but changing conditions or innovation may require different financial commitments

strategic control system

A system designed to support managers in evaluating the organization's progress regarding its strategy and, when discrepancies exist, taking corrective action.

during the budgetary period. To solve this dilemma, some companies have responded with two separate budgets: strategic and operational. For example, managers at Texas Instruments Incorporated control two budgets under the OST (objectives-strategies-tactics) system. The strategic budget is used to create and maintain long-term effectiveness, and the operational budget is tightly monitored to achieve short-term efficiency. The topic of control in general, and budgets in particular, will be discussed in more detail in Chapter 16.

EPILOGUE:

DELTA AIR LINES GOES FOR BROKE

On January 5, 2005, Delta Air Lines announced a complete change in its entire rate structure. Its new plan, called "Simpli-Fares," cut fares in the continental United States by up to 50 percent. The announcement also said that no one-way coach ticket in the 48 contiguous states would cost more than $499 and no first-class ticket more than $599. The company also simplified and lowered the cost of changing tickets or upgrading. And it removed certain restrictions, like requiring a Saturday-night stay to gain the reduced rate. The intent, CEO Grinstein said, was to improve the airline's relationship with its customers and give them what they say they want: simpler and more affordable rates.

The company expected that, at these rates, business flyers could afford to travel more. And all passengers would welcome the fact that they could get low rates without having to buy tickets well in advance. Delta's strategy was now clear. It intended to move in the direction of the low-fare airlines that had become the major threat to traditional carriers. Early indications were that it had achieved a bump in tickets sold, as

some passengers returned to Delta because its prices were no longer an issue.

The deals Delta struck with its union and outside creditors, the route changes it made, and these latest price cuts were necessary to ensure Delta's survival. But a period of turbulence was expected, and the effectiveness of the new strategy wasn't certain. For example, Delta might not gain enough new travelers to offset the revenue it will lose because of its price cuts. Other airlines might match Delta's price reductions, and in fact several airlines announced that they would do so in some markets. Other concerns were raised as well. Another terrorist attack could cause another sharp drop in air travel. And fuel prices might continue to rise, because worldwide demand for oil remained strong. That would put additional pressure on Delta's bottom line. In fact, despite the company's bold and aggressive new strategy, Delta was forced to declare bankruptcy in September 2005, in part because of continuing jumps in fuel costs due to Hurricane Katrina. But CEO Gruenstein may have given the company the ability to survive even under conditions of bankruptcy on a sounder basis.

KEY TERMS

SUMMARY OF LEARNING OBJECTIVES

Now that you have studied Chapter 4, you should know:

How to proceed through the basic steps in any planning process.

The planning process begins with a situation analysis of the external and internal forces affecting the organization. This will help

identify and diagnose issues and problems and may bring to the surface alternative goals and plans for the firm. Next, the advantages and disadvantages of these goals and plans should be evaluated against one another. Once a set of goals and a plan have been selected, implementation involves communicating the plan to employees, allocating resources, and making certain that other systems such as rewards and budgets are supporting the plan. Finally, planning requires that control systems be put in place to monitor progress toward the goals.

How strategic planning integrates with tactical and operational planning.

Strategic planning is different from operational planning in that it involves making long-term decisions about the entire organization. Tactical planning translates broad goals and strategies into specific actions to be taken within parts of the organization. Operational planning identifies the specific short-term procedures and processes required at lower levels of the organization.

Why it is important to analyze both the external environment and the internal resources of the firm before formulating a strategy.

Strategic planning is designed to leverage the strengths of a firm while minimizing the effects of its weaknesses. It is difficult to know the potential advantage a firm may have unless external analysis is done well. For example, a company may have a talented marketing department or an efficient production system. However, there is no way to determine whether these internal characteristics are sources of competitive advantage until something is known about how well the competitors stack up in these areas.

The choices available for corporate strategy.

Corporate strategy identifies the breadth of a firm's competitive domain. Corporate strategy can be kept narrow, as in a concen- tration strategy, or can move to suppliers and buyers via vertical integration. Corporate strategy also can broaden a firm's domain via concentric (related) diversification or conglomerate (unre- lated) diversification.

How companies can achieve competitive advantage through business strategy.

Companies gain competitive advantage in two primary ways. They can attempt to be unique in some way by pursuing a differ- entiation strategy, or they can focus on efficiency and price by pursuing a low-cost strategy.

How core competencies provide the foundation for business strategy.

A core competence is something a company does especially well relative to its competitors. When this competence, say, in engi- neering or marketing, is in some area important to market success, it becomes the foundation for developing a competitive advantage.

The keys to effective strategy implementation.

Many good plans are doomed to failure because they are not im- plemented correctly. Strategy must be supported by structure, technology, human resources, rewards, information systems, cul- ture, leadership, and so on. Ultimately, the success of a plan de- pends on how well employees at low levels are able and willing to implement it. Participative management is one of the more pop- ular approaches used by executives to gain employees' input and ensure their commitment to strategy implementation.

DISCUSSION QUESTIONS

1. This chapter opened with a quote from former CEO of GE Jack Welch: "Manage your destiny, or someone else will." What does this mean for strategic management? What does it mean when Welch adds, "or someone else will"?

2. How do strategic, operational, and tactical planning differ? How might the three levels complement one another in an organization?

3. What accounts for the shift from strategic planning to strategic management? In which industries would you be most likely to observe these trends?

4. In your opinion, what are the core competencies of compa- nies in the auto industry such as General Motors, Ford, and Daimler Chrysler? How do these competencies help them compete against foreign competitors such as Honda, Toyota, Nissan, BMW, and others?

5. What are the key challenges in strategy implementation? What barriers might prevent strategy implementation?

CONCLUDING CASE

The Computer Guru: A One-Man Show or an Empire?

Juan De Jesus of San Antonio, Texas, was the first in his family to attend college. He earned a computer science degree from the University of Texas in 1994. Upon graduation, Juan was hired as a sales and service technician for one of the large national com- puter corporations. That job provided him with a tremendous amount of experience in the small-business sales and service sec- tor. Four years later he left the company, deciding to go it alone as an independent computer consultant.

Juan set up an office and computer-testing lab in his home and worked hard to grow the business. He was able to take advantage of some of the relationships and contacts that he had established during his tenure at his last job, which resulted in attracting sev- eral immediate clients. His wife Conchita helps out with some of the office work on a part-time basis.

The business grew rapidly thanks to Juan's excellent work and reputation. He has the ability to install hardware and software systems, including industry-specific software, is very effective at training, can fix almost any computer, and is readily available by phone to answer questions and solve problems that occur after the installation and training.

Four years into the business, Juan finds himself charging $100 per hour and earning nearly $150,000 per year for his services. He is good at what he does and people want him—his phone is ringing off the hook. He also feels that the time has come to take a step back to reevaluate his current position, his business options, and his personal goals.

Juan recalled the internship program that is offered at his alma mater and arranged to have three current business students conduct a feasibility study on his behalf. The project began with an interview at his home office. The highlights and key points of that interview follow.

Juan reported that he is making a good living, currently billing about 1,500 hours per year at $100 per hour. He actually works about 60 hours per week, however, with the addition of travel time, seemingly endless phone calls, searching for and ordering parts, completing office paperwork, and attending classes and seminars to remain current with new technology. Conchita works about 20 hours per week in the office. She indicated this to be her limit, as she has another part-time job and is expecting the couple's first child in a few months. She plans to give up the second job and to continue working with Juan at their home office.

Juan is concerned about the fact that his entire business is just Juan. He gets paid only when he works. If he is sick or if he takes a vacation, he earns nothing. He wondered out loud whether he had already reached his maximum potential. He is worried about the fact that there are no growth opportunities under his current setup. He is not sure whether he should just keep doing what he is doing or make a change.

The conversation then turned to "the building of an empire," as Juan put it. He wants to take a close look at some other business options, which is the purpose of retaining the student interns. Those options include:

- Hiring an additional computer technician or two and grow the existing business.
- Opening a retail computer store as a complement to his current services (and, if he were to establish a retail store, determining whether he should rent, lease, or buy the building).
- Hiring an outside salesperson or two to generate new business (either as part of the retail store or as an extension of his current business).
- Establishing a Web site (rather than a retail store) as a complement to his current services.
- Considering new and related ideas generated by the student team.
- Doing nothing, just continuing to do what he is doing.

Juan indicated to the students that he likes the idea of building an empire, but that he feels like he is swimming into new waters that he is unfamiliar with. For example, if he were to open a retail store, could he possibly compete with Circuit City and Best Buy? He wants his success story to continue, and he wants to make more money while working fewer hours. He also wants to earn money when he is not working.

QUESTIONS

1. Form small groups and brainstorm to develop a strategic plan for Juan. Compare and contrast each group's plan and gain consensus as to the best.

2. Using that best plan, return to your original group and develop a tactical plan for Juan.

3. Having now developed a tactical plan, what major challenges face Juan if he were to go forward with your plan? Include a SWOT analysis as part of your assessment.

EXPERIENTIAL EXERCISES
4.1 Strategic Planning

OBJECTIVE

To study the strategic planning of a corporation recently in the news.

INSTRUCTIONS

BusinessWeek magazine frequently has articles on the strategies of various corporations. Find a recent article on a corporation in an industry of interest to you. Read the article and answer the following questions.

Strategic Planning Worksheet

1. Has the firm clearly identified what business it is in and how it is different from its competitors? Explain.

_____

2. What are the key assumptions about the future that have shaped the firm's new strategy?

_____

_____

_____

_____

_____

3. What key strengths and weaknesses of the firm influenced the selection of the new strategy?

_____

_____

_____

_____

_____

_____

_____

4. What specific objectives has the firm set in conjunction with the new strategy?

_____

_____

_____

_____

_____

_____

SOURCE: R. R. McGrath Jr., _Exercises in Management Fundamentals,_ p. 15. Copyright © 1984. Reprinted by permission of Pearson Education, Inc., Upper Saddle River, NJ.

4.2 Formulating Business Strategy

OBJECTIVES

1. To illustrate the complex interrelationships central to the formulation of business strategy.
2. To demonstrate the use of SWOT (strengths, weaknesses, opportunities, and threats) analysis in a business situation.

INSTRUCTIONS

1. Your instructor will divide the class into small groups and assign each group a well-known organization for analysis.
2. Each group will
   a. Study the SWOT Introduction and the SWOT Worksheet to understand the work needed to complete the assignment.
   b. Obtain the needed information about the organization under study through library research, interviews, and so on.
   c. Complete the SWOT Worksheet.
   d. Prepare group responses to the discussion questions.

3. After the class reconvenes, group spokespersons will present group findings.

DISCUSSION QUESTIONS

1. Why would most organizations not develop strategies for matches between opportunities and strengths?
2. Why would most organizations not develop strategies for matches between opportunities and weaknesses?
3. Why do most organizations want to deal from strength?

SWOT INTRODUCTION

One of the more commonly used strategy tools is SWOT (strengths, weaknesses, opportunities, and threats) analysis, which is accomplished in four steps:

Step 1: Analyze the organization's internal environment, identifying its strengths and weaknesses.

Step 2: Analyze the organization's external environment, identifying its opportunities and threats.

Step 3: Match (a) strengths with opportunities, (b) weaknesses with threats, (c) strengths with threats, and (d) weaknesses with opportunities.

Step 4: Develop strategies for those matches which appear to be of greatest importance to the organization. Most organizations give top priority to strategies that involve the matching of strengths with opportunities and second priority to strategies that involve the matching of weaknesses with threats. The key is to exploit opportunities in areas where the organization has a strength and to defend against threats in areas where the organization has a weakness.

SWOT Worksheet

Organization being analyzed: _____

Internal Analysis	External Analysis
Strengths	Opportunites
_____	_____
_____	_____
_____	_____
_____	_____
_____	_____
_____	_____
_____	_____
_____	_____
_____	_____
_____	_____

Weaknesses	Threats
_____	_____
_____	_____
_____	_____
_____	_____
_____	_____
_____	_____
_____	_____
_____	_____
_____	_____
_____	_____

Strategies that Match Strengths with Opportunites

_____
_____
_____
_____
_____
_____
_____
_____
_____
_____
_____
_____
_____
_____
_____

Strategies that Match Weaknesses with Threats

_____
_____
_____
_____
_____
_____
_____
_____
_____
_____
_____
_____
_____
_____
_____

Strategies that Match Strengths with Threats

_____
_____
_____
_____
_____
_____
_____
_____
_____
_____
_____
_____
_____
_____

Strategies that Match Weaknesses with Opportunites

_____
_____
_____
_____
_____
_____
_____
_____
_____
_____
_____
_____
_____
_____

Chapter **5**

CHAPTER 5
Ethics and Corporate Responsibility

It is truly enough said that a corporation has no conscience; but a corporation of conscientious men is a corporation with a conscience.

—Henry David Thoreau

LEARNING OBJECTIVES

After studying Chapter 5, you will know:

1. How different ethical perspectives guide decision making.

2. How companies influence the ethics environment.

3. A process for making ethical decisions.

4. The important issues surrounding corporate social responsibility.

5. How important the natural environment is to business.

6. Actions managers can take to manage with the environment in mind.

ETHICS AT CITIGROUP

On August 2, 2004, Citigroup's London bond traders were high-fiving one another. They had just made profits of over $20 million by dumping European government bonds onto the market, and then within minutes buying back a third of them at lower prices. It wasn't illegal, but it broke an unwritten code: don't whipsaw markets or take advantage of thin summer trading. When a rival trader called to find out what was happening, the Citi traders laughed and hung up.

In the following months, Citi made headlines in several other ways that hurt its reputation. New CEO Chuck Prince is trying to inject ethics into the Citi culture, and stay out of the headlines. Some say it's not possible. A Wall Street analyst says of Citi, "It's one of the most aggressive corporate cultures in banking . . . These people grow up with claws and fangs."

Sources for Prologue, Connections, Epilogue: M. Der Hovanesian, P. Dwyer, and S. Reed, "Can Chuck Prince Clean Up Citi?" *BusinessWeek*, October 4, 2004, pp. 32–35; T. L. O'Brien and L. Thomas Jr., "It's Cleanup Time at Citi," *The New York Times*, November 7, sec. 3, pp. 1, 7; M. Pacelle, "Citigroup CEO Makes 'Values' a Key Focus," *The Wall Street Journal*, October 1, 2004, pp. C1, C5.

It's not a good thing. Martha Stewart, former CEO of Martha Stewart Living Omnimedia, was sentenced to five months in prison for obstruction of justice in a stock sale.

Public opinion pollster Daniel Yankelovich stated recently, "There's an increased readiness to believe negative things about corporations today, which makes it a dangerous time for companies. Executives haven't had to worry about social issues for a generation, but there's a yellow light flashing now, and they better pay attention."[1] The news is actually worse than that: Yankelovich said that in 2000—*before* a series of high-profile scandals rocked the business world.

Enron and WorldCom became shorthand for business scandal. Enron was the biggest and fastest corporate bankruptcy in U.S. history, and a number of its officers have been indicted. Its auditor, Arthur Anderson, destroyed its own reputation. Illegalities at WorldCom brought it down shortly thereafter. Tyco, Global Crossing, Imclone—these companies and others made the news for illegal or unethical business practices.

When Ed Breen took over scandal-ridden Tyco—during the era when Enron, Adelphia, Worldcom, Qwest, and Healthsouth were all making headlines for their transgressions—he got rid of the entire board and fired 290 of the top 300 executives. He also refused to pay bonuses to the managers until he fully understood the way they did business. Tyco is the only success story out of that string of corporate embarrassments, and Ed Breen is widely lauded for doing the right thing.[2]

It's a Big Issue

The business scandals engulfed company executives, independent auditors, politicians and regulators, and shareholders and employees. Other public companies as well have given in to the pressure to inflate stock prices by all possible means, undermining the public's trust in the integrity of the financial markets. Often, the scandals are perpetrated by a number of people cooperating with one another, and many of the guilty parties had been otherwise upstanding individuals.[3]

What other recent cases of legal and ethical transgressions (at least, arguably unethical) come to your mind? Martha Stewart? Napster providing free downloads, but now forced to charge? Dan Rather at CBS News, reporting on unauthenticated documents that discredited President Bush's National Guard service? Radio commentator and TV pundit Armstrong Williams, being paid $240,000 by the Department of Education to praise the No Child Left Behind Act? Business actions that harm the environment . . . Internet scams . . . people in undeveloped parts of the world deprived of the value of local resources? The list goes on, and the cases continue to have repercussions. Ordinary companies and businesspeople are increasingly distrusted by the public simply because they're in business.[4]

And when corporations behave badly, it's often not the top executives but the rank-and-file employees who suffer most. By the time the world's biggest insurance brokerage firm, Marsh & McLennan, was sued for bid rigging, price fixing, and accepting payoffs from insurance companies, chief executive Jeffrey W. Greenberg had earned more than $20 million in pay and bonuses over five years. The company's 60,000 employees around the world saw their retirement accounts decimated. Many had been pushed by the company to put most of their retirement money in Marsh shares, which cratered after the lawsuit.[5]

Using Enron and most other famous cases as examples of lax company ethics presents a problem: It's too easy. It's perfectly clear that there are "bad guys" in these cases, and the ethical lapses are obvious. Saying "I would never do things like that" becomes too easy. But in reality, many of the decisions you will face will pose ethical dilemmas, and the right thing to do is not always evident.[6]

In a recent worldwide survey ranking nations from most honest to least honest, the United States came in 17th (the top rankings went to small economies like Finland and New Zealand). On the 10-point scale, 106 countries scored less than 5, and the overall mean was 4.2.[7]

It's a Personal Issue

"Answer true or false: 'I am an ethical manager.' If you answered 'true,' here's an uncomfortable fact: You're probably not."[8] These are the first sentences in a recent *Harvard Business Review* article called "How (Un) Ethical Are You?" The point is that most of us think we are good decision makers, ethical, and unbiased. But the fact is, most people have unconscious biases that favor themselves and favor their own group. For example, managers often hire people who are like them, think they are immune to conflicts of interest, take more credit than they deserve, and blame others when they deserve some blame themselves. To know that you have biases may help you try to overcome them, but usually that's not enough.

Ethics issues are not easy, and they are not just for newsworthy corporate CEOs. You will face them; no doubt, you already have. You've got your own examples, but consider this one:[9] Imagine being in your first job, working at a local hamburger joint. Your boss is teaching you how to put ice into cups. You take a scoop, pack it to the brim. Nope, says the boss, try again. This time the cup is three-quarters full. Getting better, says the boss. "We want to get as much ice as possible in the cups without making it look like we're overfilling them." He then explains: "Ice is cheaper than cola syrup. But you don't want people to see that you are giving them too much ice. When it's hot, people would really rather have ice anyway, don't you think?" He winks.

What do you think? What would you do? Is this example too small to worry about? Could it be the beginning of a slippery slope to more serious transgressions? This chapter will help you think through decisions with ethical ramifications.

> **ethics**
>
> The system of rules that governs the ordering of values.

Ethics

The aim of ethics is to identify both the rules that should govern people's behavior and the "goods" that are worth seeking. Ethical decisions are guided by the underlying values of the individual. Values are principles of conduct such as caring, honesty, keeping of promises, pursuit of excellence, loyalty, fairness, integrity, respect for others, and responsible citizenship.[10]

Most people would agree that all of these values are admirable guidelines for behavior. However, ethics becomes a more complicated issue when a situation dictates that one value overrules others. **Ethics** is the system of rules that governs the ordering of values.

An **ethical issue** is a situation, problem, or opportunity in which an individual must choose among several actions that must be evaluated as morally right or wrong.[11] Ethical issues arise in every facet of life; we concern ourselves here with business ethics in particular. **Business ethics** comprises the moral principles and standards that guide behavior in the world of business.[12]

> **ethical issue**
>
> Situation, problem, or opportunity in which an individual must choose among several actions that must be evaluated as morally right or wrong.
>
> **business ethics**
>
> The moral principles and standards that guide behavior in the world of business.

Ethical Systems

Moral philosophy refers to the principles, rules, and values people use in deciding what is right or wrong. This is a simple definition in the abstract, but often terribly complex and difficult when facing real choices. How do you decide what is right and wrong? Do you know what criteria you apply, and how you apply them?

Ethics scholars point to various major ethical systems as guides.[13] The first ethical system, **universalism,** states that all people should uphold certain values, such as honesty and other values that society needs to function. Universal values are principles so fundamental to human existence that they are important in all societies—for example, rules against murder, deceit, torture, and oppression.

Some efforts have been made to establish global, universal ethical principles for business. The Caux Roundtable, a group of international executives based in Caux, Switzerland, worked with business leaders from Japan, Europe, and the United States to create the **Caux Principles.** Two basic ethical ideals underpin the Caux Principles: *kyosei* and human dignity. *Kyosei* means living and working together for the common good, allowing cooperation and mutual prosperity to coexist with healthy and fair competition. Human dignity concerns the value of each person as an end, not a means to the fulfillment of others' purposes. You can read the Caux Principles in Appendix B.

Universal principles can be powerful and useful, but what people say, hope, or think they would do is often different from what they *really* do, faced with conflicting demands in real situations. Before we describe other ethical systems, consider the following example, and think about how you or others would resolve it.

moral philosophy

Principles, rules, and values people use in deciding what is right or wrong.

universalism

The ethical system stating that all people should uphold certain values that society needs to function.

Caux Principles

Ethical principles established by international executives based in Caux, Switzerland, in collaboration with business leaders from Japan, Europe, and the United States.

An Example

Suppose that Sam Colt, a sales representative, is preparing a sales presentation on behalf of his firm, Midwest Hardware, which manufactures nuts and bolts. Colt hopes to obtain a large sale from a construction firm that is building a bridge across the Missouri River near St. Louis. The bolts manufactured by Midwest Hardware have a 3 percent defect rate, which, although acceptable in the industry, makes them unsuitable for use in certain types of projects, such as those that might be subject to sudden, severe stress. The new bridge will be located near the New Madrid Fault line, the source of a major earthquake in 1811. The epicenter of that earthquake, which caused extensive damage and altered the flow of the Missouri, is about 190 miles from the new bridge site.

Bridge construction in the area is not regulated by earthquake codes. If Colt wins the sale, he will earn a commission of $25,000 on top of his regular salary. But if he tells the contractors about the defect rate, Midwest may lose the sale to a competitor whose bolts are slightly more reliable. Thus, Colt's ethical issue is whether to point out to the bridge contractor that in the event of an earthquake, some Midwest bolts could fail.

SOURCE: O. C. Ferrell and J. Fraedrich, *Business Ethics: Ethical Decision Making and Cases*, 3rd ed. Copyright © 1997 by Houghton Mifflin Company. Used with permission.

Not everyone would behave the same in this scenario. Different individuals would apply different moral philosophies. Consider each of the following moral philosophies and the actions to which they might lead in the bridge example.[14]

Egoism and Utilitarianism   **Egoism** defines acceptable behavior as that which maximizes benefits for the individual. "Doing the right thing," the focus of moral philosophy, is defined by egoism as "do the act that promotes the greatest good for oneself." If everyone follows this system, according to its proponents, the well-being of

egoism

An ethical system defining acceptable behavior as that which maximizes consequences for the individual.

society as a whole should increase. This notion is similar to Adam Smith's concept of the invisible hand in business. Smith argued that if every organization follows its own economic self-interest, the total wealth of society will be maximized.

Unlike egoism, **utilitarianism** directly seeks the greatest good for the greatest number of people. For example, Lance Morgan is a driven businessman who literally changed the fate of his people. Morgan is a Native American from the Winnebago reservation in Nebraska.[15] The community was poverty-stricken, and people needed work. Morgan build Ho-Chunk ("the people," loosely translated) into a $100 million tribe-owned corporation employing hundreds of people in a variety of businesses. Ho-Chunk created an economy and is building a strong community.

Relativism   Perhaps it seems that the individual makes ethical choices on a personal basis, applying personal perspectives. But this is not necessarily the case. **Relativism** defines ethical behavior based on the opinions and behaviors of relevant other people. This perspective acknowledges the existence of different ethical viewpoints. For example, *norms*, or standards of expected and acceptable behavior, vary from one culture to another. A study of Russian versus U.S. managers[16] found that all followed norms of informed consent about chemical hazards in work situations and paying wages on time. But in Russia more than in the United States, businesspeople were likely to consider the interests of a broader set of stakeholders (in this study, keeping factories open for the sake of local employment), to keep double books to hide information from tax inspectors and criminal organizations, and to make personal payments to government officials in charge of awarding contracts. Relativism defines ethical behavior according to how others behave.

Virtue Ethics   The moral philosophies just described apply different types of rules and reasoning. **Virtue ethics** is a perspective that goes beyond the conventional rules of society by suggesting that what is moral must also come from what a mature person with good "moral character" would deem right. Society's rules provide a moral minimum, and then moral individuals can transcend rules by applying their personal virtues such as faith, honesty, and integrity.

Individuals differ in this regard. **Kohlberg's model of cognitive moral development** classifies people into categories based on their level of moral judgment.[17] People in the *preconventional* stage make decisions based on concrete rewards and punishments and immediate self-interest. People in the *conventional* stage conform to the expectations of ethical behavior held by groups or institutions such as society, family, or peers. People in the *principled* stage take a broader perspective in which they see beyond authority, laws, and norms and follow their self-chosen ethical principles.[18] Some people forever reside in the preconventional stage, some move into the conventional stage, and some develop further yet into the principled stage. Over time, and through education and experience, people may change their values and ethical behavior.

Returning to the bolts-in-the-bridge example, *egoism* would result in keeping quiet about the bolts' defect rate. *Utilitarianism* would dictate a more thorough cost-benefit analysis and possibly the conclusion that the probability of a bridge collapse is so low compared to the utility of jobs, economic growth, and company growth that the defect rate is not worth mentioning. The *relativist* perspective might prompt the salesperson to look at company policy and general industry practice, and to seek opinions from colleagues and perhaps trade journals and ethics codes. Whatever is then perceived to be a consensus or normal practice would dictate action. And finally, *virtue ethics*, applied by people in the principled stage of moral development, would likely lead to full disclosure

utilitarianism

An ethical system stating that the greatest good for the greatest number should be the overriding concern of decision makers.

relativism

Bases ethical behavior on the opinions and behaviors of relevant other people.

virtue ethics

A perspective that what is moral comes from what a mature person with "good" moral character would deem right.

Kohlberg's model of cognitive moral development

Classifies people based on their level of moral judgment.

The average CEO earned $13.1 million in 2001, according to the results of *BusinessWeek*'s 51st annual Executive Pay Scoreboard, compiled with Standard & Poor's Institutional Market Services. Steve Jobs, of Apple Computer Inc., landed the mother of all bonuses after three years of working for free: his own $90 million jet, a Gulfstream V. Outrageous, some would say. Perfectly ethical, say others.

about the product and risks, and perhaps suggestions for alternatives that would reduce the risk.[19]

These major ethical systems underlie personal moral choices and ethical decisions in business.

Business Ethics

Insider trading, illegal campaign contributions, bribery, famous court cases, and other scandals have created a perception that business leaders use illegal means to gain competitive advantage, increase profits, or improve their personal positions. Until the Enron scandal, shareholders tended to ignore fraudulent financial reporting, as long as profits and market share didn't suffer.[20] In a recent survey of 200 professionals, 35 percent admitted lying to customers and colleagues. By the way, you might find it interesting that surveys suggest that males are more likely to behave unethically than females.[21]

Neither young managers[22] nor consumers[23] believe top executives are doing a good job of establishing high ethical standards. Some even joke that *business ethics* has become a contradiction in terms.

> Imagine a manager of a used-car dealership working hard to personify ethical business practices, for and with both his customers and his employees.[24] This would create a powerful competitive advantage compared to the industry's reputation (or at least the common stereotype) for shady practices.

Most business leaders believe they uphold ethical standards in business practices.[25] But many managers and their organizations must deal frequently with ethical dilemmas, and the issues are becoming increasingly complex. For example, many people seek spiritual renewal in the workplace, in part reflecting a broader religious awakening in America, while others argue that this trend violates religious freedom and the separation of church and boardroom.[26] Tables 5.1 and 5.2 show some other important examples of ethical dilemmas in business.

TABLE 5.1
Some Current Ethical Issues

ARTISTIC CONTROL Rock musicians, independent filmmakers, and other artists are rebelling against control by big media and retail companies.
BRANDS In-your-face marketing campaigns have sparked antibrand attitudes among students.
CEO PAY Nearly three-fourths of Americans see executive pay packages as excessive.
COMMERCIALISM IN SCHOOLS Parent groups have mounted battles in hundreds of communities against advertising in the public schools.
CONSUMERISM Anger and frustration are mounting over high gasoline and drug prices, poor airline service, and HMOs that override doctors' decisions.
FRANKENFOODS Europeans' skepticism about genetically modified food is taking hold in the United States, making targets of companies such as Monsanto.
GLOBALIZATION Environmentalists, students, and unionists charge that global trade and economic bodies operate in the interests of multinational companies.
POLITICS Public revulsion over the corporate bankrolling of politicians has energized campaign-finance reform activists.
SWEATSHOPS Anti-sweatshop groups have sprung up on college campuses; they routinely picket clothing manufacturers, toymakers, and retailers.
URBAN SPRAWL Groups in more than 100 cities have blocked big-box superstores by Wal-Mart and other chains.
WAGES Some 56 percent of workers feel they are underpaid, especially as wages since 1992 have topped inflation by 7.6 percent, while productivity is up 17.9 percent.

SOURCE: A. Bernstein, "Too Much Corporate Power?" *BusinessWeek*, September 11, 2000, pp. 146–47.

What would you do in each of these true-life situations, and why?
• You are a sales representative for a construction company in the Middle East. Your company wants very much to land a particular project. The cousin of the minister who will award the contract informs you that the minister wants $20,000 in addition to the standard fees. If you do not make this payment, your competition certainly will—and will get the contract.
• You are international vice president of a multinational chemical corporation. Your company is the sole producer of an insecticide that will effectively combat a recent infestation of West African crops. The minister of agriculture in a small, developing African country has put in a large order for your product. Your insecticide is highly toxic and is banned in the United States. You inform the minister of the risks of using your product, but he insists on using it and claims it will be used "intelligently." The president of your company believes you should fill the order, but the decision ultimately is yours.
• You are a new marketing manager for a large automobile tire manufacturer. Your company's advertising agency has just presented plans for introducing a new tire into the Southeast Asia market. Your tire is a truly good product, but the proposed advertising is deceptive. For example, the "reduced price" was reduced from a hypothetical amount that was established only so it could be "reduced," and claims that the tire was tested under the "most adverse" conditions ignore the fact that it was not tested in prolonged tropical heat and humidity. Your superiors are not concerned about deceptive advertising, and they are counting on you to see that the tire does extremely well in the new market. Will you approve the ad plan?

TABLE 5.2
Ethical Decision Making in the International Context

SOURCE: N. Adler, *International Dimensions of Organizational Behavior*, 2nd ed. (Boston: Kent, 1997).

The Ethics Environment

Responding to the series of corporate scandals (particularly Enron and WorldCom), Congress passed the **Sarbanes-Oxley Act** in 2002 to improve and maintain investor confidence. The law requires companies to have more independent board directors (not just company insiders), to adhere strictly to accounting rules, and to have senior managers personally sign off on financial results. Violations could result in heavy fines and criminal prosecution. One of the biggest impacts of the new law is the requirement for companies and their auditors to provide reports to financial statement users about the effectiveness of internal controls over the financial reporting process.

Some executives say that the new law distracts from their real work and makes them more risk-averse. Some complain about the time and money needed to comply with the internal control reporting (for example, some large companies are spending $2 million annually for technology upgrades). At this writing, the SEC is examining whether to modify the rules for smaller companies, because the cost to them is proportionately larger.[27]

CEO Jim Goodnight of SAS knows that where some managers see problems, other see opportunity: "Smart business will turn Sarbanes-Oxley into an opportunity to learn more and improve their business processes . . . The corporate transparency that Sarbanes-Oxley requires will give CEOs a bigger picture of their organizations. They can then use that information to make intelligent business decisions, reduce costs, and improve the top line."[28] Regardless of managers' attitudes toward Sarbanes-Oxley, it creates legal requirements intended to improve ethical behavior.

Ethics are not shaped only by laws and by individual development and virtue. They also may be influenced by the company's work environment. The **ethical climate** of an organization refers to the processes by which decisions are evaluated and made on the basis of right and wrong.[29]

For example, Marsh & McLennan, the insurance broker mentioned earlier for its fraudulent practices, was known for having a secretive culture. CEO Jeff Greenberg's

Sarbanes-Oxley Act

An act passed into law by Congress in 2002 to establish strict accounting and reporting rules in order to make senior managers more accountable and to improve and maintain investor confidence.

ethical climate

In an organization it refers to the processes by which decisions are evaluated and made on the basis of right and wrong.

Employees sometimes feel that "borrowing" a few office supplies from their company helps compensate for any perceived inequities in pay or other benefits.

defenders claim that he inherited problems when he took over. But he did not change the arrogant culture that encouraged the aggressive pursuit of profit and allowed problems to fester. As long as you "made your numbers," his style was detached and hands-off. But when people missed their targets, heads rolled.[30] This creates an environment that allows and even encourages unethical behavior.

When people make decisions that are judged by ethical criteria, these questions always seem to get asked: Why did she do it? Good motives or bad ones? His responsibility or someone else's? Who gets the credit, or the blame? So often, responsibility for unethical acts is placed squarely on the individual who commits them. But the work environment has a profound influence, as well.

Consider the question of responsibility in the case of illegal, unneeded automotive service at Sears Roebuck in the early 1990s. When the company instituted high-pressure, unrealistic quotas and incentives, people's judgment was affected. Management did not make clear the distinction between unnecessary service and legitimate preventive maintenance. A vast gray area of repair options was exaggerated, overinterpreted, and misrepresented. The company may not have intended to deceive customers, but the result of the work environment was that consumers and attorneys general in more than 40 states accused the company of fraud. The total cost of the settlement was an estimated $60 million.[31]

As illustrated by the Marsh & McLennan and Sears examples, unethical corporate behavior may be the responsibility of an unethical individual; but it often also reveals a company culture that is ethically lax.[32]

Danger Signs In organizations, maintaining consistent ethical behavior by all employees is an ongoing challenge. What are some danger signs that an organization may be allowing or even encouraging unethical behavior? Many factors create a climate conducive to unethical behavior, including (1) excessive emphasis on short-term revenues over longer-term considerations; (2) failure to establish a written code of ethics; (3) a desire for simple, "quick fix" solutions to ethical problems; (4) an unwillingness to take an ethical stand that may impose financial costs; (5) consideration of ethics solely as a legal issue or a public relations tool; (6) lack of clear procedures for handling ethical problems; and (7) responding to the demands of shareholders at the expense of other constituencies.[33]

To understand your organization's ethics climate, think about things from the employees' perspective (actually, it's better to ask than just think about it). What do people think is required to succeed? Do they think that ethical people "finish last" and that the "bad guys win"? Or vice versa, that the company rewards ethical behavior and won't tolerate unethical behavior?[34]

Lockheed Martin gives an annual "Chairman's Award" to the person who displayed the most exemplary ethical behavior during the year.[35] All senior managers make nominations from their business units. The award ceremony is attended by all 250 senior executives. That sends a positive signal about the importance of ethics.

Corporate Ethical Standards People often give in to what they perceive to be the pressures or preferences of powerful others. States Professor Arthur Brief of Tulane University, "If the boss says, 'Achieve a specific sales or profit target, period,' I think people will do their very best to achieve those directions even if it means sacrificing their own values. They may not like it, but they define it as part of the job."[36]

To create a culture that encourages ethical behavior, managers must be more than ethical people. They also should lead others to behave ethically.[37]

It's been said that your reputation is your most precious asset. Here's a suggestion: Set a goal for yourself to be seen by others as both a "moral person" and also as a "moral manager," someone who influences others to behave ethically. When you are both personally moral and a moral manager, you will truly be an **ethical leader.**[38] You can have strong personal character, but if you pay more attention to other things, and ethics is "managed" by "benign neglect," you won't have a reputation as an ethical leader.

It's easy to find excuses for unethical behavior, but the excuses are often bogus.[39] "I was told to do it" implies no thought and blind obedience. "Everybody's doing it" often really means that someone is doing it, but it's rarely everybody; regardless, conventional doesn't mean correct. "Might equals right" is a rationalization. "It's not my problem" is sometimes a wise perspective, if it's a battle you can't win, but sometimes it's just a cop-out. "I didn't mean for that to happen, it just felt right at the time" can be prevented with more forethought and analysis.

IBM uses a guideline for business conduct that asks employees to determine whether under the full glare of examination by associates, friends, and family, they would remain comfortable with their decisions. One suggestion is to imagine how you would feel if you saw your decision and its consequences on the front page of the newspaper.[40] This "light of day" or "sunshine" ethical framework can be powerful.[41]

Such fear of exposure compels people more strongly in some cultures than in others. In Asia, anxiety about losing face often makes executives resign immediately if they are caught in ethical transgressions, or if their companies are embarrassed by revelations in the press. By contrast, in the United States, exposed executives might respond with indignation, intransigence, pleading the 5th amendment, stonewalling, an everyone-else-does-it self-defense, or by not admitting wrongdoing and giving no sign that resignation ever crossed their minds. Partly because of legal tradition, the attitude often is: Never explain, never apologize, don't admit the mistake, do not resign, even if the entire world knows exactly what happened.[42]

> **ethical leader**
>
> One who is both a moral person and a moral manager influencing others to behave ethically.

> Here's a small but potentially powerful suggestion.[43] Change your vocabulary: The word "ethics" is too loaded, even trite. Substitute "responsibility" or "decency." And act accordingly.

Ethics Codes   The Sarbanes-Oxley Act, described earlier, requires that public companies periodically disclose whether they have adopted a code of ethics for senior financial officers—and if not, why not. Many more companies have such codes today than in 2002.[44] Often, the statements are just for show, but when implemented well they can change a company's ethical climate for the better and truly encourage ethical behavior.

Ethics codes must be carefully written and tailored to individual companies' philosophies. Aetna Life & Casualty believes that tending to the broader needs of society is essential to fulfilling its economic role. Johnson & Johnson has one of the most famous ethics codes (see Table 5.3). J&J consistently receives high rankings for community and social responsibility in *Fortune*'s annual survey of corporate reputations.

Most ethics codes address subjects such as employee conduct, community and environment, shareholders, customers, suppliers and contractors, political activity, and technology. Often the codes are drawn up by the organizations' legal departments and begin with research into other companies' codes. The Ethics Resource Center in Washington assists companies interested in establishing a corporate code of ethics.[45]

To make an ethics code effective, do the following:[46] (1) involve those who have to live with it in writing the statement; (2) have a corporate statement, but also allow separate statements by different units throughout the organization; (3) keep it short and therefore easily understood and remembered; (4) don't make it too corny—make it something important that people really believe in; and (5) set the tone at the top, having executives talk about and live up to the statement. When reality differs from the statement—as when a motto says people are our most precious asset or a product is the

TABLE 5.3
Johnson & Johnson's Ethics Code

> *We believe our first responsibility is to the doctors, nurses, and patients, to mothers and all others who use our products and services.* In meeting their needs everything we do must be of high quality. We must constantly strive to reduce our costs in order to maintain reasonable prices. Customers' orders must be serviced promptly and accurately. Our suppliers and distributors must have an opportunity to make a fair profit.
>
> *We are responsible to our employees:* the men and women who work with us throughout the world. Everyone must be considered as an individual. We must respect their dignity and recognize their merit. They must have a sense of security in their jobs. Compensation must be fair and adequate, and working conditions clean, orderly, and safe. Employees must feel free to make suggestions and complaints. There must be equal opportunity for employment, development, and advancement for those qualified. We must provide competent management, and their actions must be just and ethical.
>
> *We are responsible to the communities in which we live and work and to the world community as well.*
>
> *We must be good citizens*—support good works and charities and bear our fair share of taxes. We must encourage civic improvements and better health and education.
>
> *We must maintain in good order the property we are privileged to use, protecting the environment and natural resources.*
>
> *Our final responsibility is to our stockholders.* Business must make a sound profit. We must experiment with new ideas. Research must be carried on, innovative programs developed, and mistakes paid for. New equipment must be purchased, new facilities provided, and new products launched. Reserves must be created to provide for adverse times.
>
> When we operate according to these principles, the stockholders should realize a fair return.

SOURCE: Reprinted with permission of Johnson & Johnson.

finest in the world, but in fact people are treated poorly or product quality is weak—the statement becomes a joke to employees rather than a guiding light.[47]

Ethics Programs Corporate ethics programs commonly include formal ethics codes articulating the company's expectations regarding ethics; ethics committees that develop policies, evaluate actions, and investigate violations; ethics communication systems giving employees a means of reporting problems or getting guidance; ethics officers or ombudspersons who investigate allegations and provide education; ethics training programs; and disciplinary processes for addressing unethical behavior.[48]

Ethics programs can range from compliance-based to integrity-based.[49] **Compliance-based ethics programs** are designed by corporate counsel to prevent, detect, and punish legal violations. Compliance-based programs increase surveillance and controls on people and impose punishments on wrongdoers. Program elements include establishing and communicating legal standards and procedures, assigning high-level managers to oversee compliance, auditing and monitoring compliance, reporting criminal misconduct, punishing wrongdoers, and taking steps to prevent offenses in the future.

Such programs should reduce illegal behavior and help the company stay out of court. But they do not create a moral commitment to ethical conduct; they merely ensure moral mediocrity. As Richard Breeden, former chairman of the SEC, said, "It is not an adequate ethical standard to aspire to get through the day without being indicted."[50]

compliance-based ethics programs

Company mechanisms typically designed by corporate counsel to prevent, detect, and punish legal violations.

Integrity-based ethics programs go beyond the mere avoidance of illegality; they are concerned with the law but also with instilling in people a personal responsibility for ethical behavior. With such a program, companies and people govern themselves through a set of guiding principles that they embrace.

For example, the Americans with Disabilities Act (ADA) requires companies to change the physical work environment so it will allow people with disabilities to function on the job. Mere compliance would involve making the changes necessary to avoid legal problems. Integrity-based programs would go further by training people to understand and perhaps change attitudes toward people with disabilities, and sending clear signals that people with disabilities also have valued abilities. This goes far beyond taking action to stay out of trouble with the law.

When top management has more personal commitment to responsible ethical behavior, programs tend to be better integrated into operations, thinking, and behavior. For example, at a meeting of about 25 middle managers at a major financial services firm, every one of them told the company's general counsel that they had never seen or heard of the company's ethics policy document.[51] The policies existed but were not a part of the everyday thinking of managers. In contrast, one health care products company bases one-third of managers' annual pay raises on how well they carry out the company's ethical ideals. Their ethical behavior is assessed by superiors, peers, and subordinates—making ethics a thoroughly integrated aspect of the way the company and its people do business.

Companies with strong integrity-based programs include NovaCare (a provider of rehabilitation services to hospitals and nursing homes) and Wetherill Associates (a supplier of electrical parts to the automotive market). These companies believe that their programs contribute to competitiveness, higher morale, and sustainable relationships with key stakeholders.[52]

> **integrity-based ethics programs**
>
> Company mechanisms designed to instill in people a personal responsibility for ethical behavior.

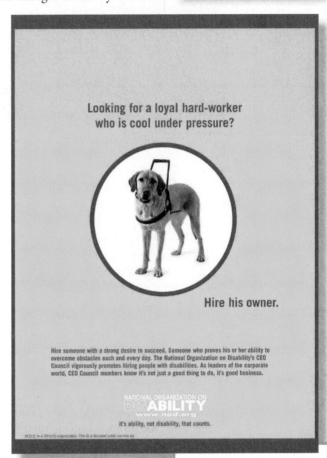

Looking for a loyal hard-worker who is cool under pressure?

Hire his owner.

Hire someone with a strong desire to succeed. Someone who proves his or her ability to overcome obstacles each and every day. The National Organization on Disability's CEO Council vigorously promotes hiring people with disabilities. As leaders of the corporate world, CEO Council members know it's not just a good thing to do, it's good business.

NATIONAL ORGANIZATION ON **DISABILITY** www.nod.org

It's ability, not disability, that counts.

N.O.D. is a 501(c)(3) organization. This is a donated public service ad.

> **This ad from the National Organization on Disability is a public service message. Its intent is to break down the stereotypes that often cause companies to overlook or not hire people with disabilities.**

Connections: CITI

When Japan ordered Citigroup to close its private banking unit there, in part for misleading regulators and failing to guard against money laundering, CEO Charles Prince fired the employees who were accountable—including three prominent senior executives who were close colleagues of his.

Citigroup, under new CEO Prince, overhauled its internal codes of conduct and systems for monitoring compliance. For example, the bank's senior risk officer now oversees global compliance, superceding the legal department. This centralized approach is favored by regulators. But "You can't think of [ethics and values] in terms of control."

Senior risk officer David Bushnell is writing a new set of compliance standards for the firm. The board's audit committee will receive up to seven compliance reports a year; previously it received none. New rules separating research from investment banking, to prevent conflict of interest, will be strictly enforced. And every Citi employee will receive ethics training.

Ethical Decision Making

We've said that it's not easy to make ethical decisions. Such decisions are complex. For starters, you may face pressures that are difficult to resist. Furthermore, it's not always

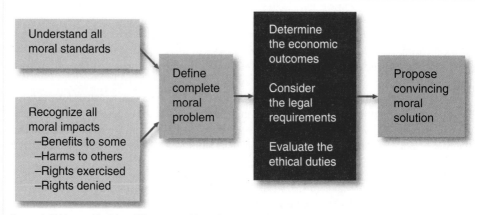

Philosopher John Rawls maintained that only a person ignorant of his identity can make a truly ethical decision.

clear that a problem has ethical dimensions; they don't hold up signs that say "Hey, I'm an ethical issue, so think about me in moral terms!"[53] Making ethical decisions takes *moral awareness* (realizing the issue has ethical implications), *moral judgment* (knowing what actions are morally defensible), and *moral character* (the strength and persistence to act in accordance with your ethics despite the challenges).[54]

Moral awareness begins with considering whether a decision has ramifications that disadvantage employees, the environment, or other stakeholders. Then the challenge is to apply moral judgment.

The philosopher John Rawls created a thought experiment based on the "veil of ignorance."[55] Imagine that you are making a decision about a policy that will benefit and/or disadvantage some groups more than others. For example, a policy might provide extra vacation time for all employees but eliminate flex time, which allows parents of young children to balance their work and family responsibilities. Or you're a university president considering raising tuition or cutting financial support for study abroad.

Now pretend that you belong to one of the affected groups, but you don't know which one—for instance, those who can afford to study abroad or those who can't, or a young parent or a young single person. You won't find out until after the decision is made. How would you decide? Would you be willing to risk being in the disadvantaged group? Would your decision be different if you were in a group other than your own? Rawls maintained that only a person ignorant of his own identity can make a truly ethical decision. A decision maker can tactically apply the veil of ignorance to help minimize personal bias.

Figure 5.1 provides a process for resolving ethical problems. Understand the various moral standards (universalism, relativism, etc.), as described on pp. 154–155. Go through the problem-solving model from Chapter 3, and recognize the impacts of your alternatives: Which people do they benefit and harm, which are able to exercise their rights, and whose rights are denied? You now know the full scope of the moral problem.

You must also consider legal requirements to ensure full compliance, and the economic outcomes of your options, including costs and potential profits. Figure 5.2 shows some of the costs associated with unethical behavior.[56] Some are obvious: fines

FIGURE 5.1
A Process for Ethical Decision Making

Understand all moral standards

Recognize all moral impacts
—Benefits to some
—Harms to others
—Rights exercised
—Rights denied

Define complete moral problem

Determine the economic outcomes

Consider the legal requirements

Evaluate the ethical duties

Propose convincing moral solution

Source: L. T. Hosmer, *The Ethics of Management*, 4th ed. (New York: McGraw-Hill/Irwin, 2003), p. 32.

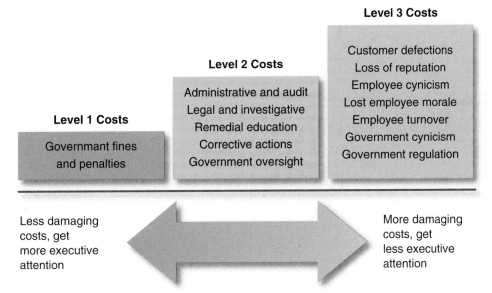

Source: T. Thomas, J. Schermerhorn Jr., and J. Dienhart, "Strategic Leadership of Ethical Behavior in Business," *Academy of Management Executive*, May 2004, p. 58.

FIGURE 5.2
The Business Costs of Ethical Failures

and penalties. Others, like administrative costs and corrective actions, are less obvious. Ultimately, the effects on customers, employees, and government reactions can be huge. Being fully aware of the potential costs can help prevent people from straying into unethical terrain.

Evaluating your ethical duties requires identifying the action(s) that (1) you would be proud to see widely reported in newspapers; (2) would build a sense of community among those involved; (3) will generate the greatest social good; (4) you would be willing to see others take when you might be the victim; (5) doesn't harm the "least among us," and (6) doesn't interfere with the right of everyone to develop their skills to the fullest.[57] As you can see, it's complex, but considering all these factors will help you develop the most convincing moral solution.

Courage

Behaving ethically requires not just moral awareness and moral judgment, but also moral character, including the courage to take actions consistent with your ethical decisions. Think about how hard it can be to do the right thing.[58] Growing up, there's plenty of peer pressure to conform to others' behavior, and it's not cool to be a snitch. On the job, how hard would it be to walk away from lots of money in order to "stick to your ethics"? To tell colleagues or your boss that you believe they've crossed an ethical line? To disobey a boss's order? To go over your boss's head to someone in senior management with your suspicions about accounting practices? To go outside the company to alert others to unethical acts you've witnessed?

At the beginning of the chapter, we mentioned Ed Breen eliminating Tyco's entire board and 290 of its top 300 executives. His actions took tremendous courage. So does *whistleblowing*—telling others, inside or outside the organization, of wrongdoing. For example, Sherron Watkins warned Enron's then-chairman, Kenneth Lay, of major irregularities in the company's accounting practices months before the corporation collapsed.[59] "I am incredibly nervous that we will implode in a wave of accounting scandals," she wrote directly to Lay after her first, anonymous memo was ignored. Ultimately she became something of a hero, but the road for whistleblowers is a very tough one.[60]

"Costs" aren't exactly synonymous with "ethics." But by considering all costs to all parties, you can make high-quality ethics decisions that you can more convincingly "sell" to others who might otherwise balk.

corporate social responsibility
Obligation toward society assumed by business.

People decide whether to blow the whistle based on their perceptions of the wrongful act, their emotions (anger, resentment, fear), and a (sometimes informal) cost-benefit analysis.[61] Courage plays a role in the moral awareness involved in identifying an act as unethical, the moral judgment to fully consider the repercussions, and the moral character to take the ethical action.

Corporate Social Responsibility

economic responsibilities
To produce goods and services that society wants at a price that perpetuates the business and satisfies its obligations to investors.

legal responsibilities
To obey local, state, federal, and relevant international laws.

ethical responsibilities
Meeting other social expectations, not written as law.

philanthropic responsibilities
Additional behaviors and activities that society finds desirable and that the values of the business support.

Should business be responsible for social concerns lying beyond its own economic well-being? Do social concerns affect a corporation's financial performance? The extent of business's responsibility for noneconomic concerns has been hotly debated. In the 1960s and 1970s, the political and social environment became more important to U.S. corporations as society turned its attention to issues like equal opportunity, pollution control, energy and natural resource conservation, and consumer and worker protection.[62] Public debate addressed these issues and how business should respond to them. This controversy focused on the concept of corporate social responsibility.

Corporate social responsibility is the obligation toward society assumed by business. The socially responsible business maximizes its positive effects on society and minimizes its negative effects.[63]

Social responsibilities can be categorized more specifically,[64] as shown in Figure 5.3. The **economic responsibilities** of business are to produce goods and services that society wants at a price that perpetuates the business and satisfies its obligations to investors.

Legal responsibilities are to obey local, state, federal, and relevant international laws. **Ethical responsibilities** include meeting other societal expectations, not written as law. Finally, **philanthropic responsibilities** are additional behaviors and activities that society finds desirable and that the values of the business support. Examples include supporting community projects and making charitable contributions.

Robert Giacalone, who teaches business ethics at Temple University, believes that a 21st-century education must help students think beyond self-interest and profitability.

FIGURE 5.3
Pyramid of Global Corporate Social Responsibility and Performance

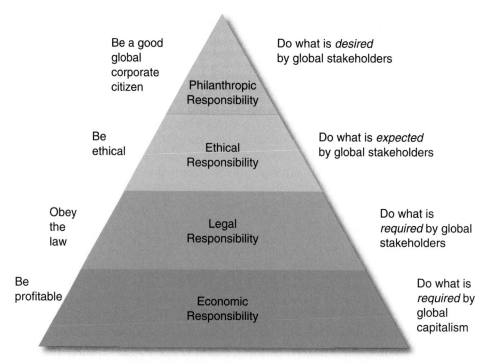

Source: A. Carroll, "Managing Ethically with Global Stakeholders: A Present and Future Challenge," *Academy of Management Executive*, May 2004, pp. 116, 114–20.

A real education, he says, teaches students to leave a legacy that extends beyond the bottom line—a transcendent education.[65] A **transcendent education** has five higher goals that balance self-interest with responsibility to others: *empathy* (feeling your decisions as potential victims might feel them, in order to gain wisdom); *generativity* (learning how to give as well as take, to others in the present as well as to future generations); *mutuality* (viewing success not merely as personal gain, but a common victory); *civil aspiration* (thinking not just in terms of "don'ts" (lie, cheat, steal, kill), but also in terms of positive contributions); and *intolerance of ineffective humanity* (speaking out against unethical actions.)

> **transcendent education**
>
> An education with five higher goals that balance self-interest with responsibility to others.

Business Tackles AIDS

AIDS is, of course, one of humanity's most serious and difficult problems. The Global Business Coalition on HIV/AIDS (GBC) considers AIDS to be one of the most serious problems faced by business, as well. In heavily infected countries, company spending continues to rise for health insurance, sick leave, funerals, and recruiting and training replacement workers.

Business can play a major role in fighting AIDS. Says GBC president Richard Holbrooke, "We're getting the message out and saying to companies, 'AIDS is your business.'" GBC now has 150 members doing business in more than 138 countries. One focus is small- and medium-sized companies in Africa. Says Holbrooke, "If South Africa falls apart, it will have a ripple effect throughout the rest of the world."

GBC believes that awareness and education are powerful tools in the battle against AIDS. Money and knowing how to get information out to remote regions are essential. Holbrooke says the biggest contribution a company can make is to convince its employees to get tested, because a person can have the disease and spread it without knowing it. Although a company can't require testing, it can encourage testing and reassure workers that they will keep their jobs and get treatment if they test positive. Joining the GBC costs a company $25,000; Coca-Cola, one company leading the crusade in Africa, provides more information at www.aidsprogramsinafrica.coca-cola.com.

SOURCE: "Turning the Tide," special advertising section, *Fortune*, July 26, 2004, pp. S1–S5.

Contrasting Views

Two basic and contrasting views describe principles that should guide managerial responsibility. The first holds that managers act as agents for shareholders and, as such, are obligated to maximize the present value of the firm. This tenet of capitalism is widely associated with the early writings of Adam Smith in *The Wealth of Nations*, and more recently with Milton Friedman, the Nobel Prize–winning economist of the University of Chicago. With his now-famous dictum "The social responsibility of business is to increase profits," Friedman contended that organizations may help improve the quality of life as long as such actions are directed at increasing profits.

Some considered Friedman to be "the enemy of business ethics," but his position was ethical: He believed that it was unethical for unelected business leaders to decide what was best for society, and unethical for them to spend shareholders' money on projects unconnected to key business interests.[66]

The second perspective, different from the profit maximization perspective, is that managers should be motivated by principled moral reasoning. Followers of Friedman and *The Wealth of Nations* might sneer at such soft-headed propaganda. But Adam Smith wrote about a world different from the one we are in now, driven in the 18th century by the self-interest of small owner-operated farms and craft shops trying to generate a living income for themselves and their families. This self-interest was quite different from that of top executives of modern corporations.[67] It is interesting to note that Adam

Smith also wrote *A Theory of Moral Sentiments*, in which he argued that "sympathy," defined as a proper regard for others, is the basis of a civilized society.[68]

Advocates of corporate social responsibility argue that organizations have a wider range of responsibilities that extend beyond the production of goods and services at a profit. As members of society, organizations should actively and responsibly participate in the community and in the larger environment.

How would these perspectives apply to the following example?

American Cigarettes, Overseas and at Home

Some people argue that U.S. tobacco companies should not promote tobacco abroad. The tobacco companies disagree. The Chinese already manufacture and consume well over 1 trillion cigarettes annually, and the U.S. tobacco industry wants part of that market. U.S. tobacco companies argue that Asians complain about the menace of American cigarette conglomerates but historically have done little in terms of requiring warning labels, prohibiting sales to minors, or banning smoking.

Asian women and adolescents smoke, and U.S. companies have promised not to court those markets. Nevertheless, a Taiwanese official complained that U.S. manufacturers handed out cigarettes to 12-year-olds at amusement parks. Critics claim that saturation marketing, depicting smoking as glamorous, rugged, and very Western, is designed to entice the enormous, untapped market of Asian women and teens.

Antismoking activists maintain that an unbridled pursuit of profit is fueling an anti-American backlash and hostility toward other U.S. exports. But the global market is vast: $300 billion in sales, roughly half of which goes to taxes. Public health officials would be pleased if the number of smokers held steady at 1.25 billion. However, the World Bank predicts that 10 million people per year will die of tobacco-related deaths by 2030, more than by any other killer. But tobacco interests counter that taxes on their products go directly into the coffers of poor countries that need the money. As the industry sees it, the economic future lies in the developing world.

The U.S. Justice Department sought $280 billion in a civil lawsuit for conspiring since 1953 to cloud the dangers of smoking. That amount is almost the entire profits of the six defendant companies over five decades. Meanwhile, the FDA may gain the power to regulate the manufacturing and contents of cigarettes, which the industry thus far has successfully avoided. But at least one cigarette company, Altria, supports FDA regulation, thinking it will bring in an era of better public relations.

In June 2005, the Justice Department dropped its demand to $10 billion. Critics charged that the motive was political, and demanded an investigation.

SOURCES: S. Mallaby, "Trade and Trade-Offs on Tobacco," *The Washington Post*, January 14, 2002, p. A17; E. Brown, "The World Health Organization Takes on Big Tobacco," *Fortune*, September 17, 2001, pp. 117–24; M. Levin, "U.S. Tobacco Firms Push Eagerly into the Asian Market," *Marketing News*, January 21, 1991, pp. 2, 14; P. Schmeiser, "Pushing Cigarettes Overseas," *New York Times Magazine*, July 10, 1988, pp. 16 ff; A. Bernstein, "Too Much Corporate Power?" *BusinessWeek*, September 11, 2000, pp. 145–58; N. Byrnes and J. Carey, "Double Danger for Big Tobacco," *BusinessWeek*, September 13, 2004, pp. 76–78; Leonnig, C. D. "Tobacco Escapes Huge Penalty," Washington Post, June 8, 2005, A1, A8.

Reconciliation

It used to be that profit maximization and corporate social responsibility were regarded as antagonistic, leading to opposing policies. But now, in a more "ethicized" business climate, the two views can converge.[69] For example, Stella Ogiale, formerly of Nigeria but now living in Seattle, founded Chesterfield Health Services to give home care to people who would otherwise be institutionalized because of physical or mental disabilities.[70] She has about 1,000 clients and has helped hundreds more stay out of institutions. Such work is generally done by government agencies and nonprofits, but Ogiale says she can help more people with her for-profit company because of her entrepreneurial skill and efficiency. "We can be humane and still make money," she says, calling her approach "socio-capitalism."

Earlier attention to corporate social responsibility focused on alleged wrongdoing and how to control it. More recently, attention has also been on the possible competitive advantage of socially responsible actions. CEO Jeff Immelt of GE told *Fortune* that he and GE's people "want to work for a company that makes a difference, a company that's doing great things in the world . . . Good leaders give back. The era we live in belongs to people who believe in themselves but are focused on the needs of others . . . The world's changed. Businesses today aren't admired . . . There's a bigger gulf today between haves and have-nots than ever before. It's up to us to use our platform to be a good citizen. Because not only is it a nice thing to do, it's a business imperative."[71]

Socially responsible actions can have long-term advantages. Companies can avoid unnecessary and costly regulation if they are socially responsible. Honesty and fairness may pay great dividends to the conscience, to the personal reputation, and to the public image of the company as well as in the market response.[72] In addition,

society's problems can offer business opportunities, and profits can be made from systematic and vigorous efforts to solve these problems. Firms can perform a cost-benefit analysis to identify actions that will maximize profits while satisfying the demand for corporate social responsibility from multiple stakeholders.[73] In other words, managers can treat corporate social responsibility as they would treat all investment decisions.

Companies can integrate social responsibility with corporate strategy.[74] Pfizer makes Zithromax, an antibiotic that treats trachoma, the world's leading cause of preventable blindness. Most of the 150 million people in need of the treatment live in remote parts of the world. Pfizer teamed up with world health organizations and spent millions of dollars on distribution. It also provided some of the medicine for free. While "doing good," Pfizer created a low-cost distribution infrastructure that it now uses to promote and sell other products. In another win-win situation, Cisco systems opened an academy in Afghanistan to teach IT skills. Afghanistan has one of the world's least developed telecommunications infrastructures, but Cisco is helping developing countries, training local populations, increasing future demand for its products, and creating a higher-quality, worldwide workforce.

Should pharmaceutical companies be allowed to advertise directly to the consumer if the medicine can be obtained only with a prescription from a doctor? When patients request a particular product, doctors are more likely to prescribe it—even if the patients haven't reported the corresponding symptoms.

Advantages of Collaboration

Global corporations teaming with nongovernment organizations, as in the Pfizer example, can create a powerful combination yielding high-impact, win-win results, tackling even the most daunting of challenges.

Global Warming as a Business Issue

Global climate change is a controversial business issue. Some believe the future of the Winter Olympics is endangered, because winter itself is in danger. Others believe that the doom and gloom talk about the state of the planet is bogus and exaggerated.

ExxonMobil CEO Lee Raymond is skeptical about global warming and blasts the critics of Big Oil. But the number of companies with this perspective is dwindling. Most (not all) scientists fear serious consequences of global warming. And consider this: According to business leaders at the World Economic Forum in Davos, Switzerland, global warming is the most pressing issue facing the business world today.

Many industries and companies are planning now for the potential consequences of climate change. For example, insurance companies need to adapt their predictive models regarding financial losses. The tourism industry should anticipate how demand will change for different vacation locations, including depressed demand for affected tropical areas and ski resorts. Agricultural companies may need to abandon investments in regions that become too warm, and invest heavily in new areas where farming becomes more viable. Timber operations may need to spend more money on fire management.

Environmental shifts create business opportunities as well. Seed sellers can develop crops that deliver higher yields in drier conditions. ABB and Honeywell are investing in sophisticated thermostats and other products whose value will increase as energy costs increase. Ford and GM are investing in cars that do not produce carbon dioxide (a greenhouse gas), and may be able to dominate a new market.

BP Amoco has been a leader in working to reduce global warming. In 1997, CEO Sir John Browne became the first oilman to declare the serious possibility of global warming, and clashed with others in the industry. When Browne split from the industry, one industry official complained that he "left the church." Browne loves it. His outspokenness has forced other oil companies to adjust their public stance on climate change.

ExxonMobil's Raymond has become the energy executive everyone blames for the industry's PR problems. Europeans have boycotted ExxonMobil brands over oil spills and emissions, whereas BP has not been targeted. In the United States, BP's prominent "Beyond Petroleum" campaign brands it as the green energy company. Greenpeace research director Kert Davies isn't convinced, saying "their marketing effort is amazing, but the investment better be equal to the rhetoric." Browne is emphatic that the campaign is not cosmetic, citing BP's results and projects, including its installation of solar panels at some gas stations.

SOURCES: K. O'Neill Packard and F. Reinhardt, "What Every Executive Needs to Know about Global Warming," *Harvard Business Review*, July–August 2000, pp. 129–35; "A Big-Oil Man Gets Religion," *Fortune*, March 6, 2000, pp. F87–F89; "Defending Science," *The Economist*, February 2, 2002, pp. 15–16; R. C. Anderson and B. McKibben, "Winterless Olympics?" *The Washington Post*, February 8, 2002, p. A31; N. D. Schwartz, "Inside the Head of BP," *Fortune*, July 26, 2004, pp. 68–76.

The Natural Environment

Most large corporations developed in an era of abundant raw materials, cheap energy, and unconstrained waste disposal.[75] Many of the technologies developed during this era are contributing to the destruction of ecosystems. Industrial-age systems follow a linear flow of extract, produce, sell, use, and discard—what some call a "take-make-waste" approach.[76] But perhaps no time in history has offered greater possibilities for a change in business thinking.

Business used to look at environmental issues as a no-win situation: You either help the environment and hurt your business, or help your business at a cost to the environment. But now a paradigm shift is taking place in corporate environmental management: the deliberate incorporation of environmental values into competitive strategies and into the design and manufacturing of products.[77] Why? In addition to philosophical reasons, companies "go green" to satisfy consumer demand, to react to a competitor's greening actions, to meet requests from customers or suppliers, to comply with guidelines, and to create competitive advantage.

CEO Jeff Immelt of GE used to view environmental rules as a burden and a cost. Now he sees that cleaning up the planet is a growth opportunity, and he wants GE to be known as a company capable of tackling the world's toughest problems.[78] GE recently purchased a water-purification company, a maker of solar-energy equipment, and a wind-energy business. Also embracing the green philosophy, BP spent about $80 million adding environmental safeguards to a facility in Scotland. CEO John Browne said, "Unlike in the U.S., there was no regulatory pressure at all to do that in Scotland, but we did it voluntarily. It's our way of saying to people, we're here to stay."[79]

Even China, widely considered an environmental disaster, is adopting a "greener" agenda on global warming.[80] It is implementing tough policies on, among other things, auto fuel efficiency, and may enact a law that would make it one of the world's biggest consumers of renewable energy sources. Historically China hasn't enforced tough-sounding environmental rules, but the country badly wants to attract foreign investment in alternative-energy projects.

A Risk Society

We live in a risk society. That is, the creation and distribution of wealth generate by-products that can cause injury, loss, or danger to people and the environment. The fundamental sources of risk in modern society are the excessive production of hazards and ecologically unsustainable consumption of natural resources.[81] Risk has proliferated through population explosion, industrial pollution, and environmental degradation.[82]

Industrial pollution risks include air pollution, smog, global warming, ozone depletion, acid rain, toxic waste sites, nuclear hazards, obsolete weapons arsenals, industrial accidents, and hazardous products. Over 30,000 uncontrolled toxic waste sites have been documented in the United States alone, and the number is increasing by perhaps 2,500 per year. The situation is far worse in other parts of the world. The pattern, for toxic waste and many other risks, is one of accumulating risks and inadequate remedies.

The institutions that create environmental and technological risk (corporations and government agencies) also are responsible for controlling and managing the risks.[83] For example, in December 2001, GE was ordered by the EPA to spend $460 million to dredge PCBs it had dumped into the Hudson River in earlier decades. It fought bitterly against the decision because of the cost and because the actions had been taken decades earlier, when they were legal. In 2002, Monsanto faced the same problem from a facility in Mississippi that had dumped PCBs, legally, from the 1930s to the 1970s.[84]

The world's worst environment problems are in China.[85] At least 6 of the 10 most polluted cities in the world are in China, and the water in five of the country's largest rivers is dangerous to touch. Living in some Chinese cities causes more lung damage than smoking two packs of cigarettes a day. Meanwhile, China is the top emerging market for most automakers, and emissions standards, while tough, are not tightly enforced. The number of cars in the country will rise sevenfold by 2020. At least the problem is recognized: whereas Beijing has cracked down hard on evangelical churches, the China Democracy party, and unofficial labor unions because it views these groups as political, green organizations that criticize the government have been allowed to grow.

Ecocentric Management

Ecocentric management has as its goal the creation of sustainable economic development and improvement of quality of life worldwide for all organizational stakeholders.[86] **Sustainable growth** is economic growth and development that meets the organization's present needs without harming the ability of future generations to meet their needs.[87] Sustainability is fully compatible with the natural ecosystems that generate and preserve life.

ecocentric management

Its goal is the creation of sustainable economic development and improvement of quality of life worldwide for all organizational stakeholders.

sustainable growth

Economic growth and development that meets present needs without harming the needs of future generations.

OUR PROCESS TO REDUCE SULFUR IN GASOLINE HELPS THOSE WHO DON'T EVEN DRIVE.

Sulfur is a naturally occurring element in gasoline and contributes to air pollution. But until recently, the methods used to remove sulfur from gasoline weren't very efficient. So Phillips is developing a new process that removes more than 90% of the sulfur in standard gasoline without significant loss of octane or volume. It's an innovation that will help us reduce harmful emissions from cars, improve air quality and meet proposed sulfur regulations for years to come. And it's just one of the many ways we live up to the name The Performance Company.

PHILLIPS PETROLEUM COMPANY 66

For a copy of our annual report, call 918-661-3700, write to: Phillips Annual Report, B-41, Adams Bldg., Bartlesville, OK 74004, or visit us at www.phillips66.com.

Conoco Phillips Petroleum lauded its environmental achievements by highlighting its development of a new process to reduce sulfur in gasoline without reducing performance. By showing its concern for the environment, Conoco Phillips can create a competitive advantage over other oil companies, especially in the minds of environmentally conscious consumers.

Life-cycle analysis (LCA)

A process of analyzing all inputs and outputs, though the entire "cradle-to-grave" life of a product, to determine total environmental impact.

Some believe that the concept of sustainable growth offers (1) a framework for organizations to use in communicating to all stakeholders; (2) a planning and strategy guide; and (3) a tool for evaluating and improving the ability to compete.[88] The principle can begin at the highest organizational levels and be made explicit in performance appraisals and reward systems.

Increasingly, firms are paying attention to the total environmental impact throughout the life cycle of their products.[89] **Life-cycle analysis (LCA)** is a process of analyzing all inputs and outputs, through the entire "cradle-to-grave" life of a product, to determine the total environmental impact of the production and use of a product. LCA quantifies the total use of resources and the releases into the air, water, and land.

LCA considers the extraction of raw materials, product packaging, transportation, and disposal. Consider packaging alone. Goods make the journey from manufacturer to wholesaler to retailer to customer; then they are recycled back to the manufacturer. They may be packaged and repackaged several times, from bulk transport, to large crates, to cardboard boxes, to individual consumer sizes. Repackaging not only creates waste—it costs time. The design of initial packaging in sizes and formats adaptable to the final customer can minimize the need for repackaging, cut waste, and realize financial benefits.

Profitability need not suffer and may be positively affected by ecocentric philosophies and practices. Some, but not all, research has shown a positive relationship between corporate environmental performance and profitability.[90] Of course, whether the relationship is positive, negative, or neutral depends on the strategies chosen and the effectiveness of implementation. And managers of profitable companies may feel more comfortable turning their attention to the environment than are managers of companies in financial difficulty.

For those interested in reading more about this subject, Appendix C on page 177 discusses in greater detail the reasons for managing with the environment in mind, some history of the environmental movement, economic issues, and a wide array of "green" examples pertaining to strategy, public affairs, legal issues, operations, marketing, accounting, and finance.

Environmental Agendas for the Future

In the past, most companies were oblivious to their negative environmental impact. More recently, many began striving for low impact. Now, some strive for positive impact, eager to sell solutions to the world's problems. For example, the next big boom may be "e-waste," garbage composed of defunct computers, TV sets, and cell phones.[91] Hewlett-Packard, for example, ships 1,500 metric tons a year to Citiray Industries of Singapore, the world's biggest processor of corporate e-waste. In the United States only one of nine retired computers currently is recycled, but the European Union now requires manufacturers to get rid of many of the hazardous chemicals in electronic products by 2006.

P&G believes that it can most effectively contribute to sustainable development through the products and services it provides. P&G talks not just of corporate social responsibility, but of corporate social opportunity.[92] It doesn't want to be just "less bad" than its competitors. P&G focuses on sustainability in three areas: water, health, and hygiene. One of its "millennium goals" is to halve by 2015 the proportion of people in the world without access to safe drinking water and basic sanitation. This translates into delivering safe water to 125,000 new people every day—in part by supplying water purification technology to relief agencies and nongovernment organization partners.

In Sweden, an organization called The Natural Step works with business leaders to create operational strategies with both environmental and economic benefits.[93] The Natural Step works with scientists to create sustainability guidelines and has a board of governors that includes nine business leaders. Its methods are collaborative rather than adversarial. Swedish companies that have worked with The Natural Step include IKEA International, Scandic Hotels, and Electrolux International.

At least 20 U.S.-based organizations are now working with The Natural Step. Ray Anderson, CEO of Interface, a $1 billion carpet manufacturer based in Atlanta that works with The Natural Step principles, said his realization of the importance of sustainability came "as a spear in the chest for me, and I determined almost in an instant to change my company . . . it began in the heart . . . that's where the next industrial revolution has to begin—in the hearts of people—to do the right thing."[94]

Webs of companies with a common ecological vision can combine their efforts into high-leverage, impactful action.[95] In Kalundborg, Denmark, such a collaborative alliance exists among an electric power generating plant, an oil refiner, a biotech production plant, a plasterboard factory, cement producers, heating utilities, a sulfuric acid producer, and local agriculture and horticulture. Chemicals, energy (for both heating and cooling), water, and organic materials flow among companies. Resources are conserved, "waste" materials generate revenues, and water, air, and ground pollution all are reduced.

Companies not only have the *ability* to solve environmental problems; they are coming to see and acquire the *motivation* as well. Some companies now believe that solving environment problems is one of the biggest opportunities in the history of commerce.[96]

Packaging isn't the most glamorous of business topics, but it holds great potential for reducing costs and increasing speed while helping the environment. You can always find opportunities to improve results in unexpected places, where others haven't tried.

EPILOGUE

ETHICS AT CITIGROUP

Were Citi's ethical transgressions worth the immediate payoffs? London bankers say the August 2, 2004, profits described in the Prologue don't cover the reputation costs. Corporate and government clients may be less likely to do business with Citi. Regulators around the globe may block the firm's efforts to do business in their countries. Not good, at a time when CEO Prince wanted to dramatically increase its global presence.

The new CEO Chuck Prince stated, "We should be doing ethical activities where we can do them again tomorrow and next week and next month and next year. We should be building a long-term franchise. We're not in this to make some special thing this quarter or this year." He also said, "We have to have the right moral compass that steers us."

KEY TERMS

Business ethics, p. 151

Caux Principles, p. 152

Compliance-based ethics programs, p. 158

Corporate Social Responsibility, p. 162

Ecocentric management, p. 167

Economic responsibilities, p. 162

SUMMARY OF LEARNING OBJECTIVES

Now that you have studied Chapter 5, you should know:

How different ethical perspectives guide decision making.

The purpose of ethics is to identify the rules that govern human behavior and the "goods" that are worth seeking. Ethical decisions are guided by the individual's values or principles of conduct such as honesty, fairness, integrity, respect for others, and responsible citizenship. Different ethical systems include universalism; egoism and utilitarianism; relativism; and virtue ethics. These philosophical systems, as practiced by different individuals according to their level of cognitive moral development and other factors, underlie the ethical stances of individuals and organizations.

How companies influence the ethics environment.

Different organizations apply different ethical perspectives and standards. Ethical codes sometimes are helpful, although they must be implemented properly. Ethics programs can range from compliance-based to integrity-based. An increasing number of organizations are adopting ethics codes. Such codes address employee conduct, community and environment, shareholders, customers, suppliers and contractors, political activity, and technology.

A process for making ethical decisions.

Making ethical decisions requires moral awareness, moral judgment, and moral character. When faced with ethical dilemmas, the veil of ignorance is a useful metaphor. More precisely, you can know various moral standards (universalism, relativism, and so on), use the problem-solving model described in Chapter 3, identify the positive and negative effects of your alternatives on different parties, consider legal requirements and the costs of unethical actions, and then evaluate your ethical duties using criteria specified in the chapter.

The important issues surrounding corporate social responsibility.

Corporate social responsibility is the extension of the corporate role beyond economic pursuits. It includes not only economic but also legal, ethical, and philanthropic responsibilities. Advocates believe managers should consider societal and human needs in their business decisions because corporations are members of society and carry a wide range of responsibilities. Critics of corporate responsibility believe managers' first responsibility is to increase profits for the shareholders who own the corporation. The two perspectives are potentially reconcilable.

The importance to business of our natural environment.

In the past, most companies viewed the natural environment as a resource to be used for raw materials and profit. But consumer, regulatory, and other pressures arose. Executives often viewed these pressures as burdens, constraints, and costs to be borne. Now, more companies view the interface between business and the natural environment as a potential win-win opportunity. Some are adopting a "greener" agenda for philosophical reasons and personal commitment to sustainable development. Many also are recognizing the potential financial benefits of managing with the environment in mind, and are integrating environmental issues into corporate and business strategy. Some see entering businesses that help rather than harm the natural environment as one of the great commercial opportunities in history.

Actions managers can take to manage with the environment in mind.

Organizations have contributed risk to society and have some responsibility for reducing risk to the environment. They also have the capability to help solve environmental problems. Ecocentric management attempts to minimize negative environment impact, create sustainable economic development, and improve the quality of life worldwide. Relevant actions are described in the chapter, including strategic initiatives, life-cycle analysis, and interorganizational alliances. A chapter appendix provides a wide variety of specific examples of strategic, operations, finance, legal and public affairs, marketing, and accounting practices that are environmentally friendly.

DISCUSSION QUESTIONS

1. Has Citi made headlines recently for any ethical or legal transgressions? Has it made progress in this regard? What other actions has Citi taken?

2. Consider the various ethical systems described early in the chapter. Identify concrete examples from your own past decisions or the decisions of others you have seen or read about.

3. Choose one or more topics from Table 5.1 and discuss the ethical issues surrounding them.

4. What would you do in each of the scenarios described in Table 5.2, "Ethical Decision Making in the International Context"?

5. Identify and discuss illegal, unethical, and socially responsible business actions in the current news.

6. Does your school have a code of ethics? If so, what does it say? Is it effective? Why or why not?

7. You have a job you like at which you work 40 to 45 hours per week. How much off-the-job volunteer work would you do? What kinds of volunteer work? How will you react if your boss makes it clear he or she wants you to cut back on the outside activities and devote more hours to your job?

8. What are the arguments for and against the concept of corporate social responsibility? Where do you stand, and why? Give your opinions, specifically, with respect to the text examples.

9. What do you think of the concept of a transcendent education, as described in the chapter? What can be done to implement such a vision for education?

10. What is the current status of the Sarbanes-Oxley Act? Have there been any changes? What do executives think of it now? What impact has it had?

11. A company in England slaughters 70,000 baby ostrich chicks each year for their meat. It told a teen magazine that it would stop if it received enough complaints. Analyze this policy, practice, and public statement using the concepts discussed in the chapter.

12. A Nike ad in the U.S. magazine *Seventeen* shows a picture of a girl, aged perhaps 8 or 9. The ad reads,

> If you let me play . . .
> I will like myself more.
> I will have more self-confidence.
> I will suffer less depression.
> I will be 60 percent less likely to get breast cancer.
> I will be more likely to leave a man who beats me.
> I will be less likely to get pregnant before I want to.
> I will learn what it means to be strong.
> If you let me play sports.

Assess this ad in terms of chapter concepts surrounding ethics and social responsibility. What questions would you ask in doing this analysis?

13. Should companies like GE and Monsanto be held accountable for actions of decades past, then legal but since made illegal as their harmful effects became known? Why or why not?

14. Discuss courage as a requirement for ethical behavior. What personal examples can you offer, either as an actor or as an observer? What examples are in the news?

CONCLUDING CASE

J & G Garden Center: Lawn Care Services Division

John and Gloria Weed started a new business in 1986 on the outskirts of Columbus, Ohio. Their original retail store with greenhouse attachment featured fresh-cut flowers, annuals, vegetables, and perennials. The building is on the grounds of Gloria's family farm, enabling the Weeds to grow some of their retail products from scratch. Gloria's parents gave the couple several acres of commercially zoned land as a wedding gift in 1982. The building and greenhouse construction were completed by John with a little help from his brothers. This combination of land acquisition and building construction resulted in a very low-overhead situation, which contributed to their start-up success.

An addition to the building completed in 1991 included several new and related product lines such as garden tools, soils and mulch products, gifts, seeds, and related accessories.

Gloria had earned a horticulture degree at the local community college prior to the establishment of the business. In 1997 she was able to fulfill a lifelong dream of starting a landscape design and installation service that became the company's next and newest product line. Gloria set up a small studio and office in the couple's nearby home and was able to acquire some new clients. Her timing was good, as the Columbus area experienced a housing boom during that period. New houses and new developments sprang up in every direction from the city. Their garden center was able to supply the plant materials that each new job required. Soon after, the Weeds expanded their product lines to include a new and wider variety of trees, shrubs, landscape terraces, patios, and walkways as a means to generate new sales and to complement Gloria's new service line.

The original start-up business and each expansion project (building addition, new products, design and installation service) have more than covered their costs, but they have generated only fair to moderate profit margins. The Weeds attribute this mostly to the presence of their competition, which always seems to be growing. As a result, they have been reluctant to raise prices even though some product costs have risen.

One year later, the Weeds completed the final phase of their original long-range business plan with the addition of another new service—Big John, The Lawn & Garden Doctor. This new product line was added because of its very high profit projections.

This new division specializes in the treatment and eradication of lawn and garden pests. Many insects and diseases affect plant life, some of which are fatal. In spite of the fact that the Weeds and other local garden centers offer high-quality plants to consumers, nature has a way of wreaking havoc on lawns, gardens, shrubs, and trees over time.

The start-up of this division required a tremendous amount of time, effort, and expense as a result of the environmental and safety-related hazards of some of the products such as insecticides and fungicides. The Weeds were required to train and license two of their employees as certified applications technicians. A custom-built, high-security storage facility was required and built to house all hazardous materials. The building was secured with a locked, barbed-wire fence, an alarm system, and a hazardous material runoff-proof partition. A special liability insurance policy was purchased as well.

As expected, the new division turned out to be very profitable. Demand was strong and the technician's work was professional and effective. In fact, at the end of its first full year of existence, Big John, The Lawn & Garden Doctor turned a profit that almost matched that of all other divisions combined. At the company's monthly staff meeting, it therefore came as quite a surprise to everyone when John announced that he was seriously considering dropping the division entirely.

John Weed is a local native of the area. He was very strong family and community values, and has always felt responsible for the welfare and happiness of his friends, neighbors, and especially his customers. From the start, he was nervous and apprehensive that something bad would happen as a result of the pesticide or fungicide applications.

And then it happened. A customer's dog became ill, possibly as a result of eating some grass from a recently treated lawn. Big John's technician had taken every precaution. The area was properly treated, marked, and roped off and the customer was instructed as to the after-care safety precautions, which included a well-written handout and a signed liability waiver form. Although the company was clearly not negligent. John was upset.

Two months later, a lawsuit was filed against the company, claiming that the water runoff from the property of one of their customers had tainted a neighbor's well. The Weeds were forced to hire an attorney. Following a full and costly investigation, they were found not guilty of the charge.

Gloria feels that John is overreacting. She points out that the company is in full compliance with every regulation, and that John has gone out of his way to ensure the safety of all. Gloria also noted that no business can control the behavior or be responsible for its customers or the population in general; incidents beyond their control will naturally and always occur. In addition, the high profitability of the division will allow the Weed's to embark upon an aggressive advertising campaign aimed at improving the sales and profits of their other divisions.

John is losing sleep over all of this and is not sure what to do. He is worried about the image and reputation of his family and their business. He feels that the lawn and garden doctor business provides a useful service, but his conscience is bothering him.

QUESTIONS

1. Present an argument in favor of retaining the new division that considers and incorporates the ethical conflicts that Mr. Weed is experiencing.

2. Present an argument in favor of eliminating or changing the new division, and make recommendations to improve overall company profits through means that will be acceptable to Mr. Weed.

3. Aside from compliance with the law, how much additional responsibility does a business owner have to his or her customer base, employees, suppliers, and the community at large? How do you feel about the old saying "buyer beware"?

EXPERIENTIAL EXERCISES

5.1 Assessing Yourself

Circle the response that most closely correlates with each item below.

	Agree	Neither		Disagree
1. I am able to make decisions and stick to them.	1	2 3	4	5
2. I am able to make simple decisions quickly.	1	2 3	4	5
3. I am able to scan a wide array of information and distill the information I need when making a complex decision.	1	2 3	4	5
4. I clarify my purpose before making a decision.	1	2 3	4	5
5. I clarify what process I will be using before making a decision.	1	2 3	4	5
6. I take the time necessary when making complex decisions.	1	2 3	4	5
7. I consider several options before making a decision.	1	2 3	4	5
8. I invite multiple perspectives before making a decision.	1	2 3	4	5
9. I gather the information necessary before making a decision.	1	2 3	4	5
10. I consider the advantages and limitations of each option before choosing a course of action.	1	2 3	4	5
11. I weigh the possible ramifications of each choice before making a decision.	1	2 3	4	5
12. I list and prioritize the factors that are important to me and use these factors when making a decision.	1	2 3	4	5
13. I take time to reflect on how a decision feels to me intuitively before acting on the decision.	1	2 3	4	5

14. I communicate the rationale for my decisions to those who are affected by them.	1	2	3	4	5
15. When I seek outside counsel, I involve internal group members when making the final decision.	1	2	3	4	5
16. I seek input from those involved in a decision.	1	2	3	4	5
17. Those with whom I work feel safe in raising ideas that contradict my own.	1	2	3	4	5
18. I don't dominate meetings and ensure that all present have a chance to speak before decisions are made.	1	2	3	4	5
19. I establish checkpoints and specify who's accountable for decisions made by my group.	1	2	3	4	5
20. I have a set of guidelines I use when faced with an ethical dilemma.	1	2	3	4	5
21. I take into account the needs of all relevant stakeholders before making a decision.	1	2	3	4	5
22. I make decisions that make sense and are consistent with my "best" self-concept.	1	2	3	4	5
23. I take responsibility for my actions.	1	2	3	4	5

If your score is 69 or higher, you might consider creating a plan for increasing your skills in making effective and ethical decisions.

SOURCE: Suzanne C. de Janasz, Karen O. Dowd, and Beth Z. Schneider, *Interpersonal Skills in Organizations* (New York: McGraw-Hill/Irwin, 2002), p. 388.

5.2 Measuring Your Ethical Work Behavior

OBJECTIVES

1. To explore a range of ethically perplexing situations.
2. To understand your own ethical attitudes.

INSTRUCTIONS

Make decisions in the situations described in the Ethical Behavior Worksheet. You will not have all the background information on each situation, and, instead, you should make whatever assumptions you feel you would make if you were actually confronted with the decision choices described. Select the decision choice that most closely represents the decision you feel you would make personally. You should choose decision options even though you can envision other creative solutions that were not included in the exercise.

Ethical Behavior Worksheet

Situation 1. You are taking a very difficult chemistry course, which you must pass to maintain your scholarship and to avoid damaging your application for graduate school. Chemistry is not your strong suit, and, because of a just-below-failing average in the course, you will have to receive a grade of 90 or better on the final exam, which is two days away. A janitor, who is aware of your plight, informs you that he found the master for the chemistry final in a trash barrel and has saved it. He will make it available to you for a price, which is high but which you could afford. What would you do?

_____ (a) I would tell the janitor thanks, but no thanks.

_____ (b) I would report the janitor to the proper officials.

_____ (c) I would buy the exam and keep it to myself.

_____ (d) I would not buy the exam myself, but I would let some of my friends, who are also flunking the course, know that it is available.

Situation 2. You have been working on some financial projections manually for two days now. It seems that each time you think you have them completed your boss shows up with a new assumption or another "what-if" question. If you only had a copy of a spreadsheet software program for your personal computer, you could plug in the new assumptions and revise the estimates with ease. Then, a colleague offers to let you make a copy of some software that is copyrighted. What would you do?

_____ (a) I would accept my friend's generous offer and make a copy of the software.

_____ (b) I would decline to copy it and plug away manually on the numbers.

_____ (c) I would decide to go buy a copy of the software myself, for $300, and hope I would be reimbursed by the company in a month or two.

_____ (d) I would request another extension on an already overdue project date.

Situation 3. Your small manufacturing company is in serious financial difficulty. A large order of your products is ready to be delivered to a key customer when you discover that the product is simply not right. It will not meet all performance specifications, will cause problems for your customer, and will require rework in the field; however, this, you know, will not become evident until after the customer has received and paid for the order. If you do not ship the order and receive the payment as expected, your business may be forced into bankruptcy. And if you delay the shipment or inform the customer of these problems, you may lose the order and also go bankrupt. What would you do?

_____ (a) I would not ship the order and place my firm in voluntary bankruptcy.

_____ (b) I would inform the customer and declare voluntary bankruptcy.

_____ (c) I would ship the order and inform the customer, after I received payment.

_____ (d) I would ship the order and not inform the customer.

Situation 4. You are the cofounder and president of a new venture, manufacturing products for the recreational market. Five months after launching the business, one of your suppliers informs you it can no longer supply you with a critical raw material since you are not a large-quantity user. Without the raw material, the business cannot continue. What would you do?

_____ (a) I would grossly overstate my requirements to another supplier to make the supplier think I am a much larger potential customer in order to secure the raw material from that supplier, even though this would mean the supplier will no longer be able to supply another, noncompeting small manufacturer who may thus be forced out of business.

_____ (b) I would steal raw material from another firm (noncompeting) where I am aware of a sizable stockpile.

_____ (c) I would pay off the supplier, since I have reason to believe that the supplier could be "persuaded" to meet my needs with a sizable "under the table" payoff that my company could afford.

_____ (d) I would declare voluntary bankruptcy.

Situation 5. You are on a marketing trip for your new venture for the purpose of calling on the purchasing agent of a major prospective client. Your company is manufacturing an electronic system that you hope the purchasing agent will buy. During the course of your conversation, you notice on the cluttered desk of the purchasing agent several copies of a cost proposal for a system from one of your direct competitors. This purchasing agent has previously reported mislaying several of your own company's proposals and has asked for additional copies. The purchasing agent leaves the room momentarily to get you a cup of coffee, leaving you alone with your competitor's proposals less than an arm's length away. What would you do?

_____ (a) I would do nothing but await the man's return.

_____ (b) I would sneak a quick peek at the proposal, looking for bottom-line numbers.

_____ (c) I would put the copy of the proposal in my briefcase.

_____ (d) I would wait until the man returns and ask his permission to see the copy.

SOURCE: Jeffry A. Timmons, _New Venture Creation,_ 3rd ed. pp. 285–86. Copyright © 1994 by Jeffry A. Timmons. Reproduced with permission of the author.

5.3 Ethical Stance

Are the following ethical or unethical in your opinion? Why or why not? Consider individually and discuss in small groups.

- Calling in sick when you really are not.
- Taking office supplies home for personal use.
- Cheating on a test.
- Turning someone in for cheating on a test or paper.
- Overcharging on your company expense report.
- Trying to flirt your way out of a speeding ticket.
- Splicing cable from your neighbor.
- Surfing the net on company time.
- Cheating on income tax.
- Lying (exaggerating) about yourself to influence someone of the opposite sex.
- Looking at pornographic sites on the Web through the company network.
- Lying about your education on a job application.
- Lying about experience in a job interview.
- Making a copy of a rental DVD before returning it to the store.

SOURCE: Suzanne C. de Janasz, Karen O. Dowd, and Beth Z. Schneider, _Interpersonal Skills in Organizations_ (New York: McGraw-Hill/Irwin, 2002), p. 391.

The Caux Round Table Principles of Ethics (see p. 154 for general description)

PRINCIPLE 1. THE RESPONSIBILITIES OF BUSINESSES: BEYOND SHAREHOLDERS TOWARD STAKEHOLDERS

The value of a business to society is the wealth and employment it creates and the marketable products and services it provides to consumers at a reasonable price commensurate with quality. To create such value, a business must maintain its own economic health and viability, but survival is not a sufficient goal.

Businesses have a role to play in improving the lives of all their customers, employees, and shareholders by sharing with them the wealth they have created. Suppliers and competitors as well should expect businesses to honor their obligations in a spirit of honesty and fairness. As responsible citizens of the local, national, regional, and global communities in which they operate, businesses share a part in shaping the future of those communities.

PRINCIPLE 2. THE ECONOMIC AND SOCIAL IMPACT OF BUSINESS: TOWARD INNOVATION, JUSTICE, AND WORLD COMMUNITY

Businesses established in foreign countries to develop, produce, or sell should also contribute to the social advancement of those countries by creating productive employment and helping to raise the purchasing power of their citizens. Businesses also should contribute to human rights, education, welfare, and vitalization of the countries in which they operate.

Businesses should contribute to economic and social development not only in the countries in which they operate, but also in the world community at large, through effective and prudent use of resources, free and fair competition, and emphasis upon innovation in technology, production, methods, marketing, and communications.

PRINCIPLE 3. BUSINESS BEHAVIOR: BEYOND THE LETTER OF LAW TOWARD A SPIRIT OF TRUST

While accepting the legitimacy of trade secrets, businesses should recognize that sincerity, candor, truthfulness, the keeping of promises, and transparency contribute not only to their own credibility and stability but also to the smoothness and efficiency of business transactions, particularly on the international level.

PRINCIPLE 4. RESPECT FOR RULES

To avoid trade friction and to promote freer trade, equal conditions for competition, and fair and equitable treatment for all participants, businesses should respect international and domestic rules. In addition, they should recognize that some behavior, although legal, may still have adverse consequences.

PRINCIPLE 5. SUPPORT FOR MULTILATERAL TRADE

Businesses should support the multilateral trade systems of GATT/World Trade Organization and similar international agreements. They should cooperate in efforts to promote the progressive and judicious liberalization of trade, and to relax those domestic measures that unreasonably hinder global commerce, while giving due respect to national policy objectives.

PRINCIPLE 6. RESPECT FOR THE ENVIRONMENT

A business should protect and, where possible, improve the environment, promote sustainable development, and prevent the wasteful use of natural resources.

PRINCIPLE 7. AVOIDANCE OF ILLICIT OPERATIONS

A business should not participate in or condone bribery, money laundering, or other corrupt practices; indeed, it should seek cooperation with others to eliminate them. It should not trade in arms or other materials used for terrorist activities, drug traffic, or other organized crime.

PRINCIPLE 8. CUSTOMERS

We believe in treating all customers with dignity, irrespective of whether they purchase our products and services directly from us or otherwise acquire them in the market. We therefore have a responsibility to:

- provide our customers with the highest quality products and services consistent with their requirements;
- treat our customers fairly in all respects of our business transactions, including a high level of service and remedies for their dissatisfaction;

- make every effort to ensure that the health and safety of our customers, as well as the quality of their environment, will be sustained or enhanced by our products and services;
- assure respect for human dignity in products offered, marketing, and advertising; and respect the integrity of the culture of our customers.

PRINCIPLE 9. EMPLOYEES

We believe in the dignity of every employee and in taking employee interests seriously. We therefore have a responsibility to:

- provide jobs and compensation that improve workers' living conditions;
- provide work conditions that respect each employee's health and dignity;
- be honest in communications with employees and open in sharing information, limited only by legal and competitive restraint;
- listen to and, where possible, act on employee suggestions, ideas, requests, and complaints;
- engage in good faith negotiations when conflict arises;
- avoid discriminatory practices and guarantee equal treatment and opportunity in areas such as gender, age, race, and religion;
- promote in the business itself the employment of differently abled people in places of work where they can be genuinely useful;
- protect employees from avoidable injury and illness in the workplace;
- encourage and assist employees in developing relevant and transferable skills and knowledge; and
- be sensitive to serious unemployment problems frequently associated with business decisions, and work with the government, employee groups, other agencies and each other in addressing these dislocations.

PRINCIPLE 10. OWNERS/INVESTORS

We believe in honoring the trust our investors place in us. We therefore have a responsibility to:

- apply professional and diligent management in order to secure a fair and competitive return on our owners' investment;
- disclose relevant information to owners/investors subject only to legal requirements and competitive constraints;
- conserve, protect, and increase the owners/investors' assets; and
- respect owners/investors' requests, suggestions, complaints, and formal resolutions.

PRINCIPLE 11. SUPPLIERS

Our relationship with suppliers and subcontractors must be based on mutual respect. We therefore have a responsibility to:

- seek fairness and truthfulness in all of our activities, including pricing, licensing, and rights to sell;

- ensure that business activities are free from coercion and unnecessary litigation;
- foster long-term stability in the supplier relationship in return for value, quality, competitiveness, and liability;
- share information with suppliers and integrate them into our planning processes;
- pay suppliers on time and in accordance with agreed terms of trade; and
- seek, encourage, and prefer suppliers and subcontractors whose employment practices respect human dignity.

PRINCIPLE 12. COMPETITORS

We believe that fair economic competition is one of the basic requirements for increasing the wealth of the nations and, ultimately, for making possible the just distribution of goods and services. We therefore have a responsibility to:

- foster open markets for trade and investments;
- promote competitive behavior that is socially and environmentally beneficial and demonstrates mutual respect among competitors;
- refrain from either seeking or participating in questionable payments of favors to secure competitive advantages;
- respect both tangible and intellectual property rights; and
- refuse to acquire commercial information by dishonest or unethical means, such as industrial espionage.

PRINCIPLE 13. COMMUNITIES

We believe that as global corporate citizens, we can contribute to such forces of reform and human rights as are at work in the communities in which we operate. We therefore have a responsibility in those communities to:

- respect human rights and democratic institutions, and promote them wherever practicable;
- recognize government's legitimate obligation to the society at large and support public policies and practices that promote human development through harmonious relations between business and other segments;
- collaborate with those forces in the community dedicated to raising standards of health, education, workplace safety, and economic well-being;
- promote and stimulate sustainable development and play a leading role in preserving and enhancing the physical environment and conserving the earth's resources;
- support peace, security, diversity, and social integration;
- respect the integrity of local cultures; and
- be a good corporate citizen through charitable donations, educational and cultural contributions, and employee participation in community and civic affairs.

SOURCE: Caux Round Table in Switzerland, "Principles for Business," special advertising supplement contributed as a public service by Canon, *Business Ethics*, May–June 1995, p. 35.

Managing in Our Natural Environment

BUSINESS AND THE ENVIRONMENT: CONFLICTING VIEWS

Some people believe everyone wins when business tackles environmental issues.[1] Others disagree.

The Win-Win Mentality Business used to look at environmental issues as a no-win situation: You either help the environment and hurt your business, or help your business only at a cost to the environment. Fortunately, things have changed. "When Americans first demanded a cleanup of the environment during the early 1970s, corporations threw a tantrum. Their response ran the psychological gamut from denial to hostility, defiance, obstinacy, and fear. But today, when it comes to green issues, many U.S. companies have turned from rebellious underachievers to active problem solvers."[2] Table C.1 gives just a few examples of things U.S. corporations are doing to help solve environmental problems.

The Earth Summit in Rio in 1992 helped increase awareness of environmental issues. This led to the Kyoto Protocol, an international effort to control global warming that included an unsuccessful meeting in the Hague in November 2000.[3] "There has been an evolution of most groups—whether industry, governments, or nongovernmental organizations—toward a recognition that everyone plays a part in reaching a solution."[4]

Being "green" is potentially a catalyst for innovation, new market opportunities, and wealth creation. Advocates believe that this is truly a win-win situation; actions can be taken that benefit both business and the environment. For example, Procter & Gamble in a span of five years reduced disposable wastes by over 50 percent while increasing sales by 25 percent.[5] Win-win companies will come out ahead of those companies that have an us-versus-them, we-can't-afford-to-protect-the-environment mentality.

Is the easy part over?[6] Companies have found a lot of easy-to-harvest, "low-hanging fruit"—that is, overly costly practices that were made environmentally friendlier and that saved money at the same time. Many big companies have made these easy changes, and reaped benefits from them. Many small companies still have such low-hanging fruit to harvest,[7] and plenty remains to be done.

The Dissenting View The critics of environmentalism in business are vocal. Some economists maintain that not a single empirical analysis supports the "free lunch view" that spending money on environmental problems provides full payback to the firm.[8] Skepticism should continue, they say; the belief that everyone will come out a winner is naive.

What really upsets many businesspeople is the financial cost of complying with environmental regulations.[9] Consider a few examples:

- GM spent $1.3 billion to comply with California requirements that 10 percent of the cars sold there be emission-free. European automakers spent $7 billion to install pollution-control equipment in all new cars during a five-year period.
- At Bayer, 20 percent of manufacturing costs were for the environment. This is approximately the same amount spent for labor.
- The Clean Air Act alone was expected to cost U.S. petroleum refiners $37 billion, more than the book value of the entire industry.
- California's tough laws are a major reason why manufacturers moved to Arkansas or Nevada.

In industries like chemicals and petroleum, environmental regulations were once considered a threat to their very survival.[10]

Balance A more balanced view is that business must weigh the environmental benefits of an action against value destruction. The advice here is: Don't obstruct progress, but pick your environmental initiatives carefully. Compliance and remediation efforts will protect, but not increase, shareholder value.[11] And it is shareholder value, rather than compliance, emissions, or costs, that should be the focus of objective cost-benefit analyses. Such an approach is environmentally sound but also hard-headed in a business sense, and is the one approach that is truly sustainable over the long term.

Johan Piet maintains, "Only win-win companies will survive, but that does not mean that all win-win ideas will be successful."[12] In other words, rigorous analysis is essential. Thus, some companies maintain continuous improvement in environmental performance, but fund only projects that meet financial objectives.

Most people understand that business has the resources and the competence to bring about constructive change, and that this creates great opportunity—if well managed—for both business and the environment.

TABLE C.I
What Companies Are Doing to Enhance the Environment

- Toyota established an "ecotechnologies" division both for regulatory compliance and to shape corporate direction, including the development of hybrid electric-combustion automobiles.

- Interface Corporation's new Shanghai carpet factory circulates liquid through a standard pumping loop like those used in most industries. But simply by using fatter pipes and short, straight pipes instead of long and crooked pipes, it cut the power requirements by 92 percent.

- Xerox used "zero-waste-to-landfill" engineering to develop a new remanufacturable copier. AT&T cut paper costs by 15 percent by setting defaults on copiers and printers to double-sided mode.

- Electrolux uses more environmentally friendly water-based and powder paints instead of solvent-based paints, and introduced the first refrigerators and freezers free of chlorofluorocarbons.

- Many chemical and pharmaceutical companies, including Novo Nordisk and Empresas La Moderna, are exploring "green chemistry" and seeking biological substitutes for synthetic materials.

- Anheuser-Busch saved 21 million pounds of metal a year by reducing its beer-can rims by 1/8 of an inch (without reducing its contents).

- Nissan enlisted a group of ecologists, energy experts, and science writers to brainstorm about how an environmentally responsible car company might behave. Among the ideas: to produce automobiles that snap together into electrically powered trains for long trips and then detach for the dispersion to final destinations.

SOURCES: P. M. Senge and G. Carstedt, "Innovating Our Way to the Next Industrial Revolution," *Sloan Management Review*, Winter 2001, pp. 24–38; M. P. Polonsky and P. J. Rosenberger III, "Reevaluating Green Marketing: A Strategic Approach," *Business Horizons*, September–October, 2001, pp. 21–30; C. Garfield, *Second to None: How Our Smartest Companies Put People First* (Burr Ridge, IL; Business One-Irwin, 1992); H. Bradbury and J. A. Clair, "Promoting Sustainable Organizations with Sweden's Natural Step," *Academy of Management Executive*, November 1999, pp. 63–74; A. Loving, L. Hunter Lovins, and P. Hawken, "A Road Map for Natural Capitalism, " *Harvard Business Review*, May–June 1999, pp. 145–58; P. Hawken, A. Lovings, and L. Hunter Lovins, *Natural Capitalism* (Boston: Little Brown, 1999); S. L. Hart and M. B. Milstein, "Global Sustainability and the Creative Destruction of Industries," *Sloan Management Review*, Fall 1999, pp. 23–32.

WHY MANAGE WITH THE ENVIRONMENT IN MIND?

Business is turning its full attention to environmental issues for many reasons, including legal compliance, cost effectiveness, competitive advantage, public opinion, and long-term thinking.

Legal Compliance   Table C.2 shows just some of the most important U.S. environmental laws. Government regulations and liability for damages provide strong economic incentives to com-

TABLE C.2
Some U.S Environmental Laws

Superfund [Comprehensive Environmental Response, Compensation, and Liability Act (CERCLA)]: Establishes potential liability for any person or organization responsible for creating an environmental health hazard. Individuals may be prosecuted, fined, or taxed to fund cleanup.

Clean Water Act [Federal Water Pollution Control Act]: Regulates all discharges into surface waters, and affects the construction and performance of sewer systems. The Safe Drinking Water Act similarly protects groundwaters.

Clean Air Act: Regulates the emission into the air of any substance that affects air quality, including nitrous oxides, sulfur dioxide, and carbon dioxide.

Community Response and Right-to-Know Act: Mandates that all facilities producing, transporting, storing, using, or releasing hazardous substances provide full information to local and state authorities and maintain emergency-action plans.

Federal Hazardous Substances Act: Regulates hazards to health and safety associated with consumer products. The Consumer Product Safety Commission has the right to recall hazardous products.

Hazardous Materials Transportation Act: Regulates the packaging, marketing, and labeling of shipments of flammable, toxic, and radioactive materials.

Resource Conservation and Recovery Act: Extends to small-quantity generators the laws regulating generation, treatment, and disposal of solid and hazardous wastes.

Surface Mining Control and Reclamation Act: Establishes environmental standards for all surface-mining operations.

Toxic Substances Control Act: Addresses the manufacture, processing, distribution, use, and disposal of dangerous chemical substances and mixtures.

SOURCE: Dennis C. Kinlaw, *Competitive and Green: Sustainable Performance in the Environmental Age* (Amsterdam: Pfeiffer & Co., 1993). Reprinted by permission of the author.

ply with environmental guidelines. Most industries already have made environmental protection regulation and liability an integral part of their business planning.[13] The U.S. Justice Department has handed out tough prison sentences to executives whose companies violate hazardous-waste requirements.

Some businesspeople consider the regulations to be too rigid, inflexible, and unfair. In response to this concern, regulatory reform may become more creative. The Aspen Institute Series on the Environment in the Twenty-First Century is trying to increase the cost-effectiveness of compliance measures through more flexibility in meeting standards and relying on market-based incentives. Such mechanisms, including tradable permits, pollution charges, and deposit refund systems, provide positive financial incentives for good environmental performance.[14]

Cost Effectiveness   Environmentally conscious strategies can be cost-effective.[15] In the short run, company after company is realizing cost savings from repackaging, recycling, and other approaches. Union Carbide faced costs of $30 a ton for disposal of solid wastes and $2,000 a ton for disposal of hazardous wastes. By recycling, reclaiming, or selling its waste, it avoided $8.5 million in costs *and* generated $3.5 million in income during a six-month period. Dow Chemical launched a 10-year program to improve its environmental, health, and safety performance worldwide. Dow projected savings of $1.8 billion over the 10-year period.[16]

Environmentally conscious strategies offer long-run cost advantages as well. Companies that are functioning barely within legal limits today may incur big costs—being forced to pay damages or upgrade technologies and practices—when laws change down the road.

A few of the other cost savings include fines, cleanups, and litigation; lower raw materials costs; reduced energy use; less expensive waste handling and disposal; lower insurance rates; and possibly higher interest rates.

Competitive Advantage   Corporations gain a competitive advantage by channeling their environmental concerns into entrepreneurial opportunities and by producing higher-quality products that meet consumer demand. Business opportunities abound in pollution protection equipment and processes, waste cleanup, low-water-use plumbing, new lightbulb technology, and marketing of environmentally safe products like biodegradable plastics. With new pools of venture capital, government funding, and specialized investment funds available, environmental technology has become a major sector of the venture-capital industry.[17]

In addition, companies that fail to innovate in this area will be at a competitive *disadvantage*. Environmental protection is not only a universal need; it is also a major export industry. U.S. trade suffered as other countries—notably Germany—took the lead in patenting and exporting anti–air pollution and other environmental technologies. If the United States does not produce innovative, competitive new technologies, it will forsake a growth industry and see most of its domestic spending for environmental protection go to imports.[18]

In short, competitive advantage can be gained by maintaining market share with old customers, and by creating new products for new market opportunities. And if you are an environmental leader, you may set the standards for future regulations—regulations that you are prepared to meet, while your competitors are not.

Public Opinion   The majority of the U.S. population believes business must clean up; few people think it is doing its job well. Gallup surveys show that more than 80 percent of U.S. consumers consider environmentalism in making purchases. An international survey of 22 countries found that majorities in 20 countries gave priority to environmental protection even at the risk of slowing economic growth. Consumers seem to have reached the point of routinely expecting companies to come up with environmentally friendly alternatives to current products and practices.[19]

Companies also receive pressure from local communities and from their own employees. Sometimes the pressure is informal and low key, but much pressure is exerted by environmental organizations, aroused citizen groups, societies and associations, international codes of conduct, and environmentally conscious investors.[20]

Another important reason for paying attention to environmental impact is TRI, the Toxic Release Inventory.[21] Starting in 1986, the EPA required all the plants of approximately 10,000 U.S. manufacturers to report annual releases of 317 toxic chemicals into the air, ground, and water. The substances include freon, PCBs, asbestos, and lead compounds. Hundreds of others have been added to the list. The releases are not necessarily illegal, but they provide the public with an annual environmental benchmark. TRI provides a powerful incentive to reduce emissions.

Finally, it is useful to remember that companies recover very slowly in public opinion from the impact of an environmental disaster. Adverse public opinion may affect sales as well as the firm's ability to attract and retain talented people. You can see why companies like P&G consider concern for the environment a consumer need, making it a basic and critical business issue.

Long-Term Thinking   Long-term thinking about resources helps business leaders understand the nature of their responsibilities with regard to environmental concerns. For example, you read about sustainable growth in the chapter.[22] Economic arguments and the tragedy of the commons also highlight the need for long-term thinking.

Economic Arguments   In Chapter 3, we discussed long-term versus short-term decision making. We stated that it is common for managers to succumb to short-term pressure for profits and to avoid spending now when the potential payoff is years down the road. In addition, some economists maintain that it is the responsibility of management to maximize returns for shareholders, implying the preeminence of the short-term profit goal.

But other economists argue that such a strategy caters to immediate profit maximization for stock speculators and neglects serious investors who are with the company for the long haul. Attention to environmental issues enhances the organization's long-term viability because the goal is the long-term creation of wealth for the patient, serious investors in the company[23]—not to mention the future state of our planet and the new generations who will inhabit it.

The Tragedy of the Commons   In a classic article in *Science*, Garrett Hardin described a situation that applies to all business decisions and social concerns regarding scarce resources like clean water, air, and land.[24] Throughout human history, a commons was a tract of land shared by communities of people on which they grazed their animals. A commons has limited **carrying capacity,** or the ability to sustain a population, because it is a finite resource. For individual herders, short-term interest lies in adding as many animals to the commons as they can. But problems develop as more herders add more animals to graze the commons. This leads to tragedy: As each herder acts in his short-term interest, the long-run impact is the destruction of the commons. The solution is to make choices according to long-run rather than short-run consequences.

In many ways, we are witnessing this **tragedy of the commons.** Carrying capacities are shrinking as precious resources, water chief among them, become scarcer. Inevitably, conflict arises—and solutions are urgently needed.

The Environmental Movement   The 1990s were labeled the "earth decade" when a "new environmentalism" with new features emerged.[25] For example, proponents of the new environmentalism asked companies to reduce their wastes, use resources prudently, market safe products, and take responsibility for past damages. These requests were formalized in the CERES principles (see Table C.3).

The new environmentalism combined many diverse viewpoints, but initially it did not blend easily with traditional business values. Some of the key aspects of this philosophy are noted in the following discussion of the history of the movement.[26]

Conservation and Environmentalism   A strand of environmental philosophy that is not at odds with business management is **conservation.** The conservation movement is anthropocentric (human centered), technologically optimistic, and concerned chiefly with the efficient use of resources. The movement seeks to avoid waste, promote the rational and efficient use of natural resources, and maximize long-term yields, especially of renewable resources.

The **environmental movement,** in contrast, historically has posed dilemmas for business management. Following the lead of early thinkers like George Perkins Marsh (1801–1882), it has shown that the unintended negative effects of human economic activities on the environment often are greater than the benefits. For example, there are links between forest cutting and soil erosion and between the draining of marshes and lakes and the decline of animal life.

Other early environmentalists, such as John Muir (1838–1914) and Aldo Leopold (1886–1948), argued that humans are not above nature but a part of it. Nature is not for humans to subdue but is sacred and should be preserved not simply for economic use but for its own sake—and for what people can learn from it.

Science and the Environment   Rachel Carson's 1962 best-selling book, *The Silent Spring,* helped ignite the modern environmental movement by alerting the public to the dangers of unrestricted pesticide use.[27] Carson brought together the findings of toxicology, ecology, and epidemiology in a form accessible to the public. Blending scientific, moral, and political arguments, she connected environmental politics and values with scientific knowledge.

Barry Commoner's *Science and Survival* (1963) continued in this vein. Commoner expanded the scope of ecology to include everything in the physical, chemical, biological, social, political, economic, and philosophical worlds.[28] He argued that all of these elements fit together, and have to be understood as a whole. According to Commoner, the symptoms of environmental problems are in the biological world, but their source lies in economic and political organizations.

Economics and the Environment   Economists promote growth for many reasons: to restore the balance of payments, to make nations more competitive, to create jobs, to reduce the deficit, to provide for the elderly and the sick, and to reduce poverty. Environmentalists criticize economics for its notions of efficiency and its emphasis on economic growth.[29] For example, environmentalists argue that economists do not adequately consider the unintended side effects of efficiency. Environmentalists hold that economists need to supplement estimates of the economic costs and benefits of growth with estimates of other factors that historically were not measured in economic terms.[30]

Economists and public policy analysts argue that the benefits of eliminating risk to the environment and to people must be balanced against the costs. Reducing risk involves determining how effective the proposed methods of reduction are likely to be and how much they will cost. There are many ways to consider cost factors. Analysts can perform cost-effectiveness analyses, in which they attempt to figure out how to achieve a given goal with limited resources, or they can conduct more formal risk-benefit and cost-benefit analyses, in which they quantify both the benefits and the costs of risk reduction.[31]

TABLE C.3
The CERES Principles

- **Protection of the biosphere:** Minimize the release of pollutants that may cause environmental damage.

- **Sustainable use of natural resources:** Conserve nonrenewable resources through efficient use and careful planning.

- **Reduction and disposal of waste:** Minimize the creation of waste, especially hazardous waste, and dispose of such materials in a safe, responsible manner.

- **Wise use of energy:** Make every effort to use environmentally safe and sustainable energy sources to meet operating requirements.

- **Risk reduction:** Diminish environmental, health, and safety risks to employees.

- **Marketing of safe products and services:** Sell products that minimize adverse environmental impact and are safe for consumers.

- **Damage compensation:** Accept responsibility for any harm the company causes the environment; conduct bioremediation; and compensate affected parties.

- **Disclosure of environmental incidents:** Public dissemination of accidents relating to operations that harm the environment or pose health or safety risks.

- **Environmental directors:** Appoint at least one board member who is qualified to represent environmental interests; create a position of vice president for environmental affairs.

- **Assessment and annual audit:** Produce and publicize each year a self-evaluation of progress toward implementing the principles and meeting all applicable laws and regulations worldwide. Environmental audits will also be produced annually and distributed to the public.

SOURCES: *Chemical Week,* September 20, 1989, copyright permission granted by *Chemical Week* magazine. *CERES Coalition Handbook.*

Qualitative Judgments in Cost-Benefit Analysis

Formal, quantitative approaches to balancing costs and benefits do not eliminate the need for qualitative judgments. For example, how does one assess the value of a magnificent vista obscured by air pollution? What is the loss to society if a particular genetic strain of grass or animal species becomes extinct? How does one assess the lost opportunity costs of spending vast amounts of money on air pollution that could have been spent on productivity enhancement and global competitiveness?

Fairness cannot be ignored when doing cost-benefit analysis.[32] For example, the costs of air pollution reduction may have to be borne disproportionately by the poor in the form of higher gasoline and automobile prices. Intergenerational fairness also plays a role.[33] Future generations have no representatives in the current market and political processes. To what extent should the current generation hold back on its own consumption for the sake of posterity? This question is particularly poignant because few people in the world today are well off. To ask the poor to reduce their life's chances for the sake of a generation yet to come is asking for a great sacrifice.

International Perspectives

Environmental problems present a different face in various countries and regions of the world. The United States and Great Britain lag behind Germany and Japan in mandated emissions standards.[34] In Europe, the Dutch, the Germans, and the Danes are among the most environmentally conscious. Italy, Ireland, Spain, Portugal, and Greece are in the early stages of developing environmental policies. Poland, Hungary, the Czech Republic, and former East Germany are the most polluted of the world's industrialized nations.[35]

U.S. companies need to realize that there is a large growth market in western Europe for environmentally "friendly" products. U.S. managers also need to be fully aware of the environmental movement in western Europe. Environmentalists in Europe have been successful in halting many projects.[36] China has been paying a high ecological price for its rapid economic growth. But the government has begun recognizing the problem and is creating some antipollution laws.[37]

Industries that pollute or make polluting products will have to adjust to the new reality, and companies selling products in certain parts of the world must take into account a growing consumer consciousness about environmental protection. Manufacturers may even be legally required to take products and packaging back from customers after use, to recycle or dispose of. In order to meet these requirements in Germany, and be prepared for similar demands in other countries, Hewlett-Packard redesigned its office-machine packaging worldwide.

WHAT MANAGERS CAN DO

To be truly "green"—that is, a cutting-edge company with respect to environmental concerns—legal compliance is not enough. Progressive companies stay abreast *and* ahead of the laws by going beyond marginal compliance and anticipating future requirements and needs.[38] But companies can go further still by experimenting continually with innovations that protect the environment. McDonald's, for example, conducted tests and pilot projects in composting food scraps and in offering refillable coffee mugs and starch-based (biodegradable) cutlery.[39]

Systems Thinking

The first thing managers can do to better understand environmental issues in their companies is to engage in systems thinking. Environmental considerations relate to the organization's inputs, processes, and outputs.[40] *Inputs* include raw materials and energy. Environmental pressures are causing prices of some raw materials, such as metals, to rise. This greatly increases the costs of production. Higher energy costs are causing firms to switch to more fuel-efficient sources.

Firms are considering new *processes* or methods of production that will reduce water pollution, air pollution, noise and vibration, and waste. They are incorporating technologies that sample and monitor (control) these by-products of business processes. Some chemical plants have a computerized system that flashes warnings when a maximum allowable pollution level is soon to be reached. Many companies keep only minimal stocks of hazardous materials, making serious accidents less likely.

Outputs have environmental impact, whether the products themselves or the waste or by-products of processes. To reduce the impact of its outputs, Herman Miller recycles or reuses nearly all waste from the manufacturing process. It sells fabric scraps to the auto industry, leather trim to luggage makers, and vinyl to stereo and auto manufacturers. It buys back its old furniture, refurbishes it, and resells it. Its corporatewide goal is to send zero waste to landfills. Environmental manager Paul Murray says, "There is never an acceptable level of waste at Miller. There are always new things we can learn."[41]

The environmental movement is a worldwide phenomenon. The "Greens," pictured here demonstrating in LePuy, France, are an important growing European political party.

Strategic Integration Systems thinking reveals that environmental issues permeate the firm, and therefore should be addressed in a comprehensive, integrative fashion. Perhaps the first step is to create the proper mindset. Does your firm see environmental concerns merely in terms of a business versus environment trade-off, or does it see in it a potential source of competitive advantage and an important part of a strategy for long-term survival and effectiveness? The latter attitude, of course, is more likely to set the stage for the following strategic actions.

These ideas help to strategically integrate environmental considerations into the firm's ongoing activities:[42]

1. *Develop a mission statement and strong values supporting environmental advocacy.* Table C.4 shows Procter & Gamble's environmental quality policy.

2. *Establish a framework for managing environmental initiatives.* Some industries have created voluntary codes of environmental practice, for example, the chemical industry's Responsible Care Initiative. Not all standard practices are adopted by all companies, however.[43] At J&J, Environmental Regulatory

TABLE C.4
Procter & Gamble's Environmental Quality Policy

Procter & Gamble is committed to providing products of superior quality and value that best fill the needs of the world's consumers. As part of this, Procter & Gamble continually strives to improve the environmental quality of its products, packaging, and operations around the world. To carry out this commitment, it is Procter & Gamble's policy to:

- Ensure our products, packaging, and operations are safe for our employees, consumers, and the environment.

- Reduce or prevent the environmental impact of our products and packaging in their design, manufacture, distribution, use, and disposal whenever possible.

- Meet or exceed the requirements of all environmental laws and regulations.

- Continually assess our environmental technology and programs, and monitor programs toward environmental goals.

- Provide our consumers, customers, employees, communities, public interest groups, and others with relevant and appropriate factual information about the environmental quality of P&G products, packaging, and operations.

- Ensure every employee understands and is responsible and accountable for incorporating environmental quality considerations in daily business activities.

- Have operating policies, programs, and resources in place to implement our environmental quality policy.

SOURCE: K. Dechant and B. Altman, "Environmental Leadership: From Compliance to Competitive Advantage," *The Academy of Management Executive,* August 1994, p. 10. Reprinted by permission.

Affairs uses external audit teams to conduct environmental audits.[44] The Community Environmental Responsibility Program includes strategy and planning, and the development of products and processes with neutral environmental impact.

3. *Engage in "green" process and product design.* The German furniture maker Wilkhahn uses an integrated strategic approach that minimizes the use of virgin resources and uses recycled materials in an environmentally designed plant.[45]

4. *Establish environmentally focused stakeholder relationships.* Many firms work closely with the EPA and receive technical assistance to help convert to more energy-efficient facilities. And to defray costs as well as develop new ideas, small companies like WHYCO Chromium Company establish environmental management partnerships with firms like IBM and GM.[46]

5. *Provide internal and external education.* Engage employees in environmental actions. Dow's WRAP program has cut millions of pounds of hazardous and solid waste and emissions, and achieved annual cost savings of over $10 million, all through employee suggestions.[47] At the same time, inform the public of your firm's environmental initiatives. For example, eco-labeling can urge consumers to recycle and communicate the environmental friendliness of your product. And BP/Amoco redesigned its logo (BP's logo has always been green) as a sun-based emblem, reflecting its strategic vision of a hydrogen/solar-based energy future.[48]

Implementation How can companies implement "greening" strategies? One tactic you read about in the chapter is life-cycle analysis.[49] That and other approaches begin with a commitment by top management. Specific actions could include commissioning an environmental audit in which an outside company checks for environmental hazards, drafting (or reviewing) the organization's environmental policy, communicating the policy and making it highly visible throughout the organization, having environmental professionals within the company report directly to the president or CEO, allocating sufficient resources to support the environmental effort, and building bridges between the organization and other companies, governments, environmentalists, and local communities.

Ultimately, it is essential to make employees accountable for any of their actions that have environmental impact.[50] Texaco, Du Pont, and other companies evaluate managers on their ideas for minimizing pollution and for new, environment-friendly products. Kodak ties some managers' compensation to the prevention of chemical spills; the company attributes to this policy a dramatic reduction in accidents.[51]

Companies can employ all areas of the organization to meet the challenges posed by pollution and environmental challenges. A variety of companies have responded creatively to these challenges[52] and may serve as models for other organizations. The following sections describe more specific actions companies can take to address environmental issues.

Strategy Actions companies can take in the area of strategy include the following:

1. *Cut back on environmentally unsafe businesses.* Du Pont, the leading producer of CFCs, voluntarily pulled out of this $750 million business.[53]

2. *Carry out R&D on environmentally safe activities.* GM is spending millions to develop hydrogen-powered cars that don't emit carbon dioxide. GE is doing research on earth-friendly hydrogen and lower-emission locomotives and jet engines.[54]

3. *Develop and expand environmental cleanup services.* Building on the expertise gained in cleaning up its own plants, Du Pont formed a safety and environmental resources division to help industrial customers clean up their toxic wastes.[55] Global Research Technologies LLC is trying to use solvents to grab carbon dioxide out of the air to isolate it for disposal.[56]

4. *Compensate for environmentally risky projects.* AES has a long-standing policy of planting trees to offset its power plants' carbon emission.[57]

5. *Make your company accountable to others.* Royal Dutch Shell and Bristol-Myers Squibb are trendsetters in green reporting.[58] Danish health care and enzymes company Novo Nordisk purposely asked for feedback from environmentalists, regulators, and other interested bodies from around Europe. Its reputation has been enhanced, its people have learned a lot, and new market opportunities have been identified.[59]

6. *Make every new product environmentally better than the last.* Intel is developing ultra-energy-efficient chips.[60] IBM aims to use recyclable materials, reduce hazardous materials, reduce emissions, and use natural energy and resources in packaging.[61]

7. *Invest in green businesses.* American Electric Power Co. is investing in renewable energy in Chile, as well as retrofitting Bulgarian schools for greater efficiency.[62]

Public Affairs   In the area of public affairs, companies can take a variety of actions:

1. *Attempt to gain environmental legitimacy and credibility.* The cosponsors of Earth Day included Apple Computer, Hewlett-Packard, and the Chemical Manufacturers Association. McDonald's has tried to become a corporate environmental "educator." Ethel M. Chocolates, in public tours of its Las Vegas factory, showcases effective handling of its industrial wastes.[63]

2. *Try to avoid losses caused by insensitivity to environmental issues.* As a result of Exxon's apparent lack of concern after the *Valdez* oil spill, 41 percent of Americans polled said they would consider boycotting the company.[64] MacMillan Bloedel lost a big chunk of sales almost overnight when it was targeted publicly as a clear-cutter and chlorine user.[65]

3. *Collaborate with environmentalists.* Executives at Pacific Gas & Electric seek discussions and joint projects with any willing environmental group, and ARCO has prominent environmentalists on its board of directors.

The Legal Area   Actions companies can take in the legal area include the following:

1. *Try to avoid confrontation with state or federal pollution control agencies.* W. R. Grace faced expensive and time-consuming lawsuits as a result of its toxic dumps. Browning-Ferris, Waste Management Inc., and Louisiana-Pacific were charged with pollution control violations, damaging their reputations.

2. *Comply early.* Because compliance costs only increase over time, the first companies to act will have lower costs. This will enable them to increase their market share and profits and win competitive advantage. 3M's goal was to meet government requirements to replace or improve underground storage tanks five years ahead of the legally mandated year.

3. *Take advantage of innovative compliance programs.* The EU started a carbon-cutting and trading system in 2005.[66] Instead of source-by-source reduction, the EPA's bubble policy allows factories to reduce pollution at different sources by different amounts, provided the overall result is equivalent. Therefore, 3M installed equipment on only certain production lines at its tape-manufacturing facility in Pennsylvania, thereby lowering its compliance costs.[67] Today, there is greater use of economic instruments like tradable pollution permits, charges, and taxes to encourage improvements.[68] *Joint implementation* involves companies in industrialized nations working with businesses in developing countries to help them reduce greenhouse gas emissions. The company lending a hand then receives credit toward fulfilling its environmental obligations at home. The developing country receives investment, technology, and jobs; the company giving a lending hand receives environmental credits; and the world gets cleaner air.[69]

4. *Don't deal with fly-by-night subcontractors for waste disposal.* They are more likely to cut corners, break laws, and do a poor job. Moreover, the result for you could be bad publicity and legal problems.[70]

Operations   The actions companies can take in the area of operations include the following:

1. *Promote new manufacturing technologies.* Louisville Gas and Electric took the lead in installing smokestack scrubbers, Consolidated Natural Gas pioneered the use of clean-burning technologies, and Nucor developed state-of-the-art steel mills.

2. *Practice reverse logistics.* Firms move packaging and other used goods from the consumer back up the distribution channel to the firm. Make them not just costs, but a source of revenue—inputs to production. Fuji Australia believes that remanufacturing has generated returns in the tens of millions of dollars.[71]

3. *Encourage technological advances that reduce pollution from products and manufacturing processes.* Cinergy and AEP are working on technologies that capture carbon as coal is burned and pump it deep into the ground to be stored for thousands of years.[72] 3M's "Pollution Prevention Pays" program is based on the premise that it is too costly for companies to employ add-on technology; instead, they should attempt to eliminate pollution at the source.[73] Pollution prevention, more than pollution control, is related to both better environmental performance and better manufacturing performance, including cost and speed.[74]

4. *Develop new product formulations.* The Chicago Transit Authority and Union Pacific Corporation are replacing traditional wood railroad ties with plastic ties. Other companies are experimenting with making recycled cross-ties of old tires, grocery bags, milk jugs, and Styrofoam cups.[75] Weyerhaeuser,

recognizing the decreasing supply of timber and growing demand, is working to produce high-quality wood on fewer, continuously regenerated acres.[76] Electrolux has developed a sun-powered lawn mower and a chainsaw that runs on vegetable oil.[77] Many companies are developing green pesticides.

5. *Eliminate manufacturing wastes.* 3M replaced volatile solvents with water-based ones, thereby eliminating the need for costly air pollution control equipment. BPAmoco implemented a similar program.

6. *Find alternative uses for wastes.* When DuPont halted ocean dumping of acid iron salts, it discovered that the salts could be sold to water treatment plants at a profit. A Queensland sugarcane facility powers production via sugarcane waste.[78]

7. *Insist that your suppliers have strong environmental performance.* Chiquita Banana had a spotty environmental record, but now its plantations are certified by the Rainforest Alliance, and Wal-Mart has named Chiquita its most environmentally conscious supplier.[79] Scott Paper discovered that many of its environmental problems were "imported" through the supply chain. Initially focusing on pulp suppliers, the company sent questionnaires asking for figures on air, water, and land releases, energy consumption, and energy sources. Scott was astonished at the variance. For example, carbon dioxide emissions varied by a factor of 17 among different suppliers. Scott dropped the worst performers and announced that the best performers would in the future receive preference in its purchasing decisions.[80]

8. *Assemble products with the environment in mind.* Make them easy to snap apart, sort, and recycle, and avoid glues and screws.

Marketing   Companies can also take action in the marketing area:

1. *Cast products in an environment-friendly light.* Most Americans believe a company's environmental reputation influences what they buy.[81] Wal-Mart has made efforts to provide customers with recycled or recyclable products. A Chinese entrepreneur is making underwear out of soybean by-products.[82] Spiegel plans to offer soybean-fiber halter-top dresses in pink and mocha.[83] Other eco-friendly fibers are made from hemp and bamboo, which require little pesticide.

2. *Avoid attacks by environmentalists for unsubstantiated or inappropriate claims.* When Hefty marketed "biodegradable" garbage bags, that claim was technically true, but it turned out that landfill conditions didn't allow decomposition to occur.[84] The extensive public backlash affected not only Hefty bags but also other Hefty products. Hefty didn't lie, but it did exaggerate. Its tactics overshadowed well-intentioned greening actions.

3. *Differentiate your product via environmental services.* ICI takes back and disposes of customers' waste as a customer service.

Companies like Toyota use advertising to convey to consumers their efforts to become more environmentally friendly.

Disposal is costly, but the service differentiates the firm's products. Teach customers how to use and dispose of products; for instance, farmers inadvertently abuse pesticides. Make education a part of a firm's after-sales service.

4. *Take advantage of the Net.* The EcoMall (www.ecomall.com/biz/) promotes a number of environmentally oriented firms in 68 product categories. Firms using the Net target green consumers globally, effectively, and efficiently.[85]

Accounting   Actions companies can take in the accounting area include the following:

1. *Collect useful data.* The best current reporters of environmental information include Dow Europe, Danish Steel Works, BSO/Origin, 3M, and Monsanto. BSO/Origin has begun to explore a system for corporate environmental accounting.[86]

2. *Make polluters pay.* CIBA-GEIGY has a "polluter pays principle" throughout the firm, so managers have the incentive to combat pollution at the sources they can influence.[87]

3. *Demonstrate that antipollution programs pay off.* 3M's Pollution Prevention Pays program is based on the premise that only if the program pays will there be the motivation to carry it out. Every company needs to be cost-effective in its pollution reduction efforts.

4. *Use an advanced waste accounting system.* Do this in addition to standard management accounting, which can hinder investment in new technologies. Waste accounting makes sure all costs are identified and better decisions can be made.

5. *Adopt full-cost accounting.* This approach, called for by Frank Popoff, Dow's chairman, ensures that the price of a product reflects its full environmental cost.[88]

6. *Show the overall impact of the pollution reduction program.* Companies have an obligation to account for the costs and benefits of their pollution reduction programs. 3M claims half a billion dollars in savings from pollution prevention efforts.[89]

Finance   In the area of finance, companies can do the following:

1. *Gain the respect of the socially responsible investment community.* Many investment funds in the United States and Europe take environmental criteria into account. A study by ICF Kaiser concluded that environmental improvements could lead to significant reduction in the perceived risk of a firm, with a possible 5 percent increase in the stock price.[90] Socially responsible rating services and investment funds try to help people invest with a "clean conscience."[91]

2. *Recognize true liability.* Investment houses often employ environmental analysts who search for companies' true environmental liability in evaluating their potential performance. Bankers look at environmental risks and environmental market opportunities when evaluating a company's credit rating.[92] The Securities and Exchange Commission in New York requires some companies to report certain environmental costs. The Swiss Bank Corp. has specialized Environmental Performance Rating Units to include environmental criteria in order to improve the quality of financial analysis.[93]

3. *Fund and then assist green companies.* Ann Winblad of Hummer Winblad Venture Partners was one of the first venture capitalists to coach green entrepreneurs to increase their business skills and chances of success.[94]

4. *Recognize financial opportunities.* Worldwide, one of these great opportunities is water. Water must be purified and delivered reliably to everyone worldwide. Billions of people lack sanitary sewage facilities and have poor access to drinking water. Infrastructures in big cities, including those in the United States, are seriously deteriorating. Supplying clean water to people and companies is a $400 billion-a-year industry—one-third larger than the global pharmaceutical industry. Companies are aggressively pursuing this market. They are betting that water in the 21st century will be like oil in the 20th century. A Bear Stearns analyst calls water the best sector for the next century.[95]

KEY TERMS

carrying capacity   The ability of a finite resource to sustain a population. p. 179

conservation   An environmental philosophy that seeks to avoid waste, promote the rational and efficient use of natural resources, and maximize long-term yields, especially of renewable resources. p. 180

environmental movement   An environmental philosophy postulating that the unintended negative effects of human eco-

nomic activities on the environment are often greater than the benefits, and that nature should be preserved. p. 180

tragedy of the commons   The environmental destruction that results as individuals and businesses consume finite resources (the "commons") to serve their short-term interests without regard for the long-term consequences. p. 179

DISCUSSION QUESTIONS

1. To what extent can and should we rely on government to solve environmental problems? What are some of government's limitations? Take a stand on the role and usefulness of government regulations on business activities.

2. To what extent should managers today be responsible for cleaning up mistakes from years past that have hurt the environment?

3. How would you characterize the environmental movement in western Europe? How does it differ from the U.S. movement? What difference will this make to a multinational company that wants to produce and market goods in many countries?

4. What business opportunities can you see in meeting environmental challenges? Be specific.

5. You are appointed environmental manager of XYZ Company. Describe some actions you will take to address environmental challenges. Discuss obstacles you are likely to encounter in the company and how you will manage them.

6. Interview a businessperson about environmental regulations and report your findings to the class. How would you characterize his or her attitude? How constructive is his or her attitude?

7. Interview a businessperson about actions he or she has taken that have helped the environment. Report your findings to the class and discuss.

8. Identify and discuss some examples of the tragedy of the commons. How can the tragedies be avoided?

9. Discuss the status of recycling efforts in your community or school, your perspectives on it as a consumer, and what business opportunities could be available.

10. What companies currently come to mind as having the best and worst reputations with respect to the environment? Why do they have these reputations?

11. Choose one product and discuss its environmental impact through its entire life cycle.

12. What are you, your college or university, and your community doing about the environment? What would you recommend doing?

Chapter **6**

CHAPTER 6

International Management

It was once said that the sun never sets on the British Empire. Today, the sun does set on the British Empire, but not on the scores of global empires, including those of IBM, Unilever, Volkswagen, and Hitachi.

—**Lester Brown**

CHAPTER OUTLINE

LEARNING OBJECTIVES

After studying Chapter 6, you will know:

1. Why the world economy is becoming more integrated than ever before.

2. What integration of the global economy means for individual companies and their managers.

3. The strategies organizations use to compete in the global marketplace.

4. The various entry modes organizations use to enter overseas markets.

5. How companies can approach the task of staffing overseas operations.

6. The skills and knowledge managers need to manage globally.

7. Why cultural differences across countries influence management.

STARBUCKS BREWS OVERSEAS EXPANSION

Starbucks's domestic market is not yet saturated. Its over 6,000 owned or licensed U.S.-based stores are still delivering annual sales growth of 8–10 percent, and several hundred new stores are opening throughout the country every year. But some of Starbucks's recent sales growth is based on price increases, not just volume. And while the company has set a long-term target to at least double its number of stores in the United States, some analysts believe that the company, already well represented in urban locations, will find it tougher to expand in rural markets, where potential consumers may be more resistant to Starbucks's prices.

To maintain its strong growth for the foreseeable future, Starbucks has been expanding aggressively overseas. It already operates or licenses about 2,600 stores abroad, in 30 countries throughout Latin America, Europe, the Middle East, and the Pacific Rim. And it projects that half of the 25,000–30,000 stores it eventually plans to have will be located outside the United States and Canada. But Starbucks is finding that these ambitious expansion plans are running into difficulties the company didn't experience in its growth in the United States.

In the domestic market, Starbucks has faced little competition—no national chain has reached even remotely comparable size. But overseas competition is stiff, and rising. In England, for example, a coffee chain rival offers drinks that are comparable to Starbucks's but at lower prices. In Germany, a wave of imitators has sprung up, undercutting Starbucks's formerly unique high-end market position. Start-up and prime-real-estate costs are also higher overseas, and in some countries, like France, labor costs are considerably higher. Starbucks's overseas operations became profitable for the first time only as recently as 2004, but only marginally. Though its overseas locations accounted for more than 25 percent of its stores worldwide, they contributed only about 6 percent of the company's total operating profit.

Starbucks also has to overcome cultural barriers in its international expansion. In many parts of Asia, especially China, the preferred drink is still tea. The company as a whole is seen as a representative of American culture, and there have been anti-American protests at some Mideast locations. In New Zealand, protesters have demanded that the company raise the payments it makes to coffee farmers. And in many European countries, Starbucks still must overcome the tendency of locals to frequent well-established coffee bars and family-run cafés. Yet expansion is essential if Starbucks is to continue its robust long-term growth.

Sources for Prologue, Connections, Epilogue: Monte Burke, "Coffee to Go, Overseas," *Forbes.com*, April 15, 2002; Troy Wolverton, "Can Starbucks Stay Hot?" *TheStreet.com*, November 10, 2003; Helen Jung, "Starbucks Backlash," *The Associated Press*, April 16, 2003, online; Stanley Holmes, "For Starbucks, There's No Place Like Home," *BusinessWeek.com*, June 9, 2003; Shirley Leung, "It's a Grand-Latte World," *The Wall Street Journal*, December 15, 2003, online; Eric Wahlgren, "Will Europe Warm to Starbucks?" *BusinessWeek.com*, January 24, 2005.

As Starbucks's experience suggests, today's managers constantly must make decisions about whether and how to pursue global opportunities. Of course, these opportunities need to be evaluated carefully, not just from a competitive or financial standpoint but from a cultural and managerial standpoint as well. Global opportunities that look good on paper frequently don't pan out if managers are unable to work in a different international context.

This chapter reviews the reasons for the globalization of competition, examines why international management differs from domestic management, considers how companies expand globally, and sees how companies can develop individuals to manage across borders.

The Global Environment

The global economy is becoming more integrated than ever before. For example, in January 1995, the World Trade Organization (WTO) was formed and now has 148 member countries, including China. (The International Monetary Fund, set up by the United Nations in 1945, serves a similar purpose and includes 191 countries.) WTO rules apply to over 90 percent of international trade. Recently the WTO has become controversial, as its role has expanded from reducing tariffs to eliminating nontariff barriers. The controversy stems from the fact that the WTO can be used to challenge environmental, health, and other regulations. These regulations often serve legitimate social goals but may be regarded as impediments to international trade. You can see the importance—and stickiness—of this issue at http://www.wto.org/. Three areas, North America, Europe, and Asia, are the most dominant in the global economy. However, other developing countries and regions represent important areas for economic growth as well. Figure 6.1 shows the major international trade areas and countries of the world.

European Unification

Europe is integrating economically to form the biggest market in the world. Under the Maastricht Treaty, which formally established the European Union (EU), the euro was adopted as a common currency in 2001. Currencies with a long history like the franc and the mark are now relics of the past. The EU is also working on a common constitution, and it allows most goods, services, capital, and human resources to flow freely across its national borders. The goal of unification is to strengthen Europe's position as an economic superpower, particularly vis-à-vis the United States. And the EU may have good prospects for eventually doing so, with 25 members and counting, a population of more than 450 million and a GDP (gross domestic product) roughly equivalent to that of the United States.[1]

The pace of European unification accelerated in 2004, with the addition of formerly Eastern-bloc countries like Poland and Hungary. Many of these new members offer a particular challenge to full integration, because as former Communist countries they do not have extensive experience as modern market economies. Other even less wealthy countries, like Turkey, are also interested in joining the EU.

In addition to the difficulty of integrating widely divergent economies, certain structural issues within Europe need to be corrected for the EU to function effectively. In particular, western Europeans on average work fewer hours, earn more pay, take longer vacations, and enjoy far more social entitlements than do their counterparts in North America and Asia. To be competitive in a global economy, Europeans must increase their level of productivity. In the past, powerful trade unions fiercely defended social benefits, and local governments regulated the labor markets. Both of these actions have encouraged companies such as Siemens and ABB Asea Brown Boveri Ltd. to move operations abroad. Some high-tech companies like Novartis have shifted their R&D operations to the United States, and labor costs have also caused Daimler-

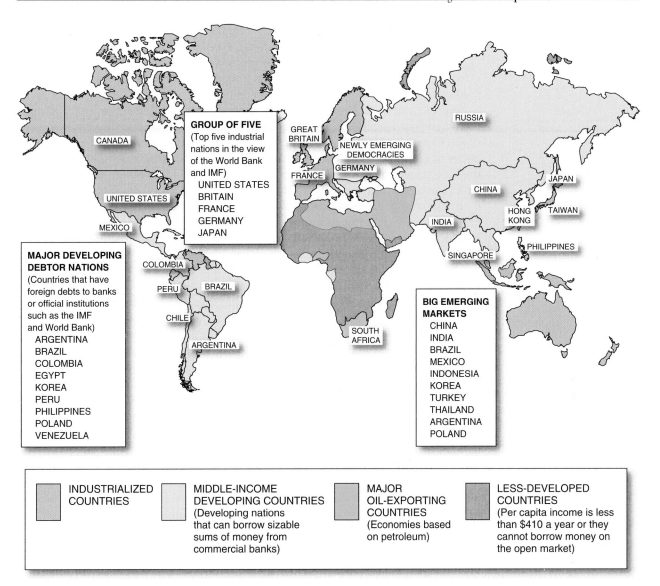

GROUP OF FIVE
(Top five industrial
nations in the view
of the World Bank
and IMF)
UNITED STATES
BRITAIN
FRANCE
GERMANY
JAPAN

MAJOR DEVELOPING
DEBTOR NATIONS
(Countries that have
foreign debts to banks
or official institutions
such as the IMF
and World Bank)
ARGENTINA
BRAZIL
COLOMBIA
EGYPT
KOREA
PERU
PHILIPPINES
POLAND
VENEZUELA

BIG EMERGING
MARKETS
CHINA
INDIA
BRAZIL
MEXICO
INDONESIA
KOREA
TURKEY
THAILAND
ARGENTINA
POLAND

INDUSTRIALIZED
COUNTRIES

MIDDLE-INCOME
DEVELOPING COUNTRIES
(Developing nations
that can borrow sizable
sums of money from
commercial banks)

MAJOR
OIL-EXPORTING
COUNTRIES
(Economies based
on petroleum)

LESS-DEVELOPED
COUNTRIES
(Per capita income is less
than $410 a year or they
cannot borrow money on
the open market)

SOURCE: Michael R. Czinkota and Ilkka A. Ronkainen, *International Marketing,* 7th ed. (Mason, OH: Thomson/South-Western, 2004), p. 91. Adapted and updated from "The Global Economy," *The Washington Post,* January 19, 1986, H1. Reprinted with permission.

FIGURE 6.1
The Global Economy

Globalization
requires
improvements in
all bottom-line
practices.

Chrysler to look at relocating much of its production line. Some labor markets are slowly being deregulated and more incentives are being offered to create jobs. But other problems will present even greater challenges, such as Europe's aging population, low birth rates, and low immigration, all of which are threatening to cause Europe's population to drop, even as America's is increasing.[2]

Nevertheless, it is very likely that unification will create a more competitive Europe, one that U.S. managers will increasingly have to take into account. The EU's share of the world's top 100 industrial firms is rising, and the sharp increase in the value of the euro against the dollar suggests rising demand for European products and currency. The community is pursuing an active industrial policy to enhance its competitiveness in information technology. It is also making fast gains in semiconductors and is restructuring in defense and aerospace.

The EU is also presenting a regulatory challenge to the United States. For example, several years ago the EU blocked the merger of General Electric and Honeywell, two American companies whose merger had already been approved in the United States.

The EU has firmly excluded genetically engineered food products from American firms. And at the end of 2004 Microsoft was forced by EU antitrust officials to unbundle programs from its Windows operating system that would play digital music and video. The EU wanted local media-player companies to have a chance to market their products as well.[3]

The EU's more competitive and regulatory environment clearly will present new challenges to managers and their employees. Managers in U.S. companies that wish to export to that market will have to become more knowledgeable about the new business environment the EU is creating. Management and labor will have to work cooperatively to achieve high levels of quality that will make U.S. products and services attractive to consumers in Europe and other markets across the world. The United States needs not only managers who will stay on top of worldwide developments and manage high-quality, efficient organizations but a well-educated, well-trained, and continually *retrained* labor force to remain competitive with the Europeans, the Chinese, and other formidable competitors.[4]

China and the Pacific Rim

Among the Pacific Rim countries, and in the United States itself, Japan dominated world attention toward the end of the last century. And Japan is still America's third-largest export market, after Canada and Mexico. Nevertheless, it has become clear that the rising economic power to watch is China. That country is on its way to becoming the largest producer and consumer of many of the world's goods. Its large and rising demand for oil helps keep the price of that commodity high, a new cost factor managers everywhere will need to take into account in their long-range planning. The country has also become the world's largest consumer of basic resources like steel and cement, as well as the world's largest cell-phone market. And as you can see in Figure 6.2, when imports are included China has now surpassed Japan as America's third-largest trading partner and will soon pass Mexico as well.[5]

As a consuming nation, China's appeal to managers lies in its large population of 1.3 billion people and its extremely rapid economic growth. Per capita growth has averaged 8 percent a year since 1980, far higher than any other large country in that period, and in recent years its imports have grown by over 30 percent a year. At current

FIGURE 6.2

Top U.S. Trading Partners, Based on Total Imports and Exports in 2003, in Billions

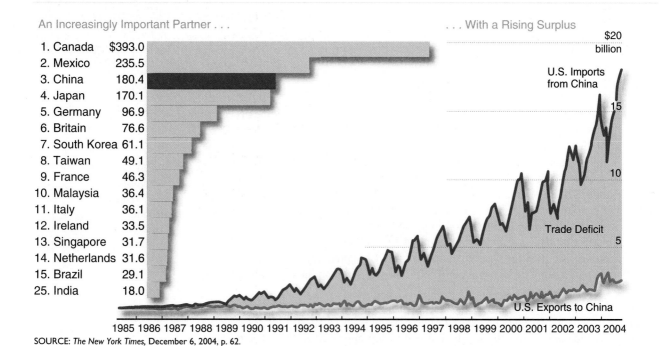

1. Canada	$393.0
2. Mexico	235.5
3. China	180.4
4. Japan	170.1
5. Germany	96.9
6. Britain	76.6
7. South Korea	61.1
8. Taiwan	49.1
9. France	46.3
10. Malaysia	36.4
11. Italy	36.1
12. Ireland	33.5
13. Singapore	31.7
14. Netherlands	31.6
15. Brazil	29.1
25. India	18.0

An Increasingly Important Partner . . .   . . . With a Rising Surplus

1985 1986 1987 1988 1989 1990 1991 1992 1993 1994 1995 1996 1997 1998 1999 2000 2001 2002 2003 2004

SOURCE: *The New York Times*, December 6, 2004, p. 62.

rates of expansion, in only about 10 years China will be the world's largest economy, followed by the United States and India.[6] Several American companies have invested heavily in the Chinese market, with some success. For example, car sales by General Motors in China helped GM earn more than three times as much in the Asian region than in its three other regions combined. General Electric ships $3.5 billion of engines and other products to China each year. Wal-Mart already has 40 stores and more than 20,000 employees in China, with many more store openings scheduled.[7]

But it is in its role as an exporting nation that China has had an even greater global impact. The enormous size of its labor force, combined with its extremely low labor costs, have given it a huge competitive advantage in manufacturing. One study found that labor costs are about 92 cents an hour in China, compared to $1.70 in Mexico and over $21 in the United States. These low prices have led many managers to relocate operations in China or to import an increasing number and variety of products from China instead of continuing to do business with local manufacturers. For example, U.S. exports to China (including Hong Kong) totaled about $50 billion in 2004, but U.S. imports were almost four times as high. In certain industries this trade imbalance may even grow. For example, China currently provides about 16 percent of U.S. apparel imports, but with the elimination in 2005 of most clothing import quotas, China's estimated share of U.S. apparel imports will rise to 50 percent or more.[8]

This kind of trade imbalance may well have contributed to the loss of manufacturing jobs in the United States and Europe. But it has also led to the continuing availability of comparatively low-priced goods, helping consumers everywhere and leading to overall economic and job growth at home. Nevertheless, there is little question that jobs in certain industries, like textiles, may be permanently transferred abroad to lower-cost producers like China and India, creating real hardship for affected workers and communities, even as overall job growth continues. We will be discussing the effects of *outsourcing* or *offshoring* in more detail later in this chapter.

Threats to China's growing dominance include political instability, as the growing prosperity of its cities and industrial enclaves leave millions of poor rural residents further behind. Moreover, countries that have experienced job loss may face growing pressure to restrict Chinese imports, particularly in the EU, with its strong labor unions. But for the foreseeable future, China's growing presence in the world economy, as an importer *and* exporter, is likely to be one that you as a manager will increasingly have to take into account.

Other rapidly growing countries in the region with strong trade relationships with the United States include South Korea, Taiwan, and Singapore. These countries, along with the United States, China and other countries in the region like Australia and Russia, are part of the 21-member Asia-Pacific Economic Cooperation (APEC) trade group. In recent years the United States and the other APEC countries have been working to establish policies that encourage international commerce and reduce trade barriers.[9]

One of China's concerns, especially if it wants more foreign investment in its economy, is the prevalent counterfeiting business. Domestic industries such as film, music, publishing, and software have been heavily affected. Renowned director Zhang Yimou, at the preview of his movie *Hero*, reportedly had all bags, cell phones, and other electronic devices checked to keep guests from secretly recording the film.

China supplies over a third of the world's socks and over half the world's buttons.

SOURCE: *The New York Times*, December 24, 2004, p. C1.

North America

The **North American Free Trade Agreement (NAFTA)** combined the economies of the United States, Canada, and Mexico into the world's largest trading bloc with more than 390 million U.S., Canadian, and Mexican consumers and a total output of $10 trillion. By 2008, virtually all U.S. industrial exports into Mexico and Canada will be duty-free. Although the United States has had a longer-standing agreement with Canada, Mexico has quickly emerged as the United States' second largest trading partner as a result of NAFTA. U.S. industries that have benefited in the short run include capital-goods suppliers, manufacturers of consumer durables, grain producers and distributors, construction equipment manufacturers, the auto industry, and the financial industry, which now has privileged access into a previously protected market. There has also been considerably increased investment in Mexico itself. For example, with its almost 700 stores there, Wal-Mart is now the country's largest private employer.[10]

Economic growth and the easing of import restrictions have also caused trade to rise in other South American countries, particularly in agricultural products. For example, Brazil has become the world's largest exporter of orange juice, coffee, and tobacco, and by 2015 expects to replace the United States as the largest agricultural producer overall. The growing exports of Brazil, Argentina, and other countries are having an increasing impact on U.S. agriculture; farms that can't become or stay competitive may go out of business. On the other hand, these countries also provide a rapidly growing market for American exports of tractors, combines, and other related products.[11]

Efforts are under way to go beyond NAFTA and create a Central American Free Trade Agreement (CAFTA) and a Free Trade Area of the Americas (FTAA) from Canada to Chile. For example, the United States and Chile signed an agreement in 2003 eliminating tariffs on almost all the goods traded between the two countries and also guaranteeing patent protection for American software and prescription drug exports. Similar discussions are currently under way with other countries in the region, with the long-term goal of a hemispherewide free-trade pact.[12]

The Rest of the World

We can't begin to fully discuss all the important developments, markets, and competitors shaping the global environment. India, for example, has become an important provider of online computer and software support and other services, as you can see in the accompanying item. But huge and promising areas of the world—the Middle East, Africa, and parts of South America and the old Soviet Union—have not participated in globalization. These regions account for a major share of the world's natural resources, and their potential has not yet been realized.[13]

Advantages of Collaboration

Some of the reasons managers will collaborate with their overseas counterparts on trade are obvious. Other countries offer expanded markets for one's own products. In turn, they might have natural resources, products, or cost structures that managers need but that aren't available in the home country. But there are other, perhaps less obvious benefits to collaborating with other countries on trade. Because trade allows each country to obtain more efficiently what it cannot as easily produce on its own, it lowers prices overall and makes more goods more widely available. This in turn raises living standards—and may broaden the market for a manager's own products, both locally and abroad. Trade also makes new technologies and methods more widely available, again raising the standard of living and improving efficiency. Finally, collaborating with others on trade creates links between people and cultures that, particularly over the long run, can lead to cooperation in other areas.

The Rise of India

As you pull into General Electric's John F. Welch Technology Center, a uniformed guard waves you through an iron gate. Except for the female engineers wearing saris and the soothing Hindi pop music wafting through the open-air dining pavilion, this could be GE's giant research-and-development facility in the upstate New York town of Niskayuna.

It's more like Niskayuna than you might think. The center's 1,800 engineers are engaged in fundamental research for most of GE's 13 divisions. In one lab, they tweak the aerodynamic designs of turbine-engine blades. In another, they're scrutinizing the molecular structure of materials to be used in next-generation DVDs. In another, technicians have rigged up a working model of a GE plastics plant in Spain and devised a way to boost output there by 20 percent.

Plenty of Americans know of India's inexpensive software writers and have figured out that the nice clerk who booked their air ticket is in Delhi. But these are just superficial signs of India's capabilities. Quietly but with breathtaking speed, India and its millions of world-class engineering, business, and medical graduates are becoming enmeshed in America's New Economy in ways most of us barely imagine.

This techno take-off is wonderful for India—but terrifying for many Americans. In fact, India's emergence is fast turning into the latest Rorschach test on globalization. Many see India's digital workers as bearers of new prosperity to a deserving nation and vital partners of Corporate America. Others see them as shock troops in the final assault on good-paying jobs.

Tech luminary Andrew S. Grove, CEO of Intel Corp., warns that "it's a very valid question" to ask whether America could eventually lose its overwhelming dominance in IT, just as it did in electronics manufacturing. But there's also a far more positive view—that harnessing Indian brainpower will greatly boost American tech and services leadership by filling a big projected shortfall in skilled labor as baby boomers retire. Companies from GE Medical Systems to Cummins to Microsoft to enterprise-software firm PeopleSoft that are hiring in India say they aren't laying off any U.S. engineers. Instead, by augmenting their U.S. R&D teams with the 260,000 engineers pumped out by Indian schools each year, they can afford to throw many more brains at a task and speed up product launches, develop more prototypes, and upgrade quality.

Old economy companies are benefiting, too. Engine maker Cummins plans to use its new R&D center in Pune to develop the sophisticated computer models needed to design upgrades and prototypes electronically. Says International Vice-President Steven M. Chapman: "We'll be able to introduce five or six new engines a year instead of two" on the same $250 million R&D budget—without a single U.S. layoff.

To be sure, many corporations have run into myriad headaches, ranging from poor communications to inconsistent quality. Dell Inc. recently said it is moving computer support for corporate clients back to the U.S. Still, a raft of studies find that companies shifting work to India have cut costs by 40 to 60 percent. Predicts Nandan M. Nilekani, managing director of Bangalore-based Infosys Technologies Ltd.: "Just like China drove down costs in manufacturing and Wal-Mart in retail," he says, "India will drive down costs in services."

But deflation will also mean plenty of short-term pain for U.S. companies and workers who never imagined they'd face foreign rivals. Consider America's IT services industry. Indians still have less than 3 percent of the market. But by undercutting giants such as Accenture, IBM, and Electronic Data Services by a third or more, they've altered the industry's pricing. In other industries, the shift of low-cost production work to East Asia was followed by engineering. Now, South Korea and Taiwan are global leaders in notebook PCs, wireless phones, memory chips, and digital displays. As companies rely more on IT engineers in India and elsewhere, the argument goes, the U.S. could cede control of other core technologies.

Throughout U.S. history, workers have been pushed off farms, textile mills, and steel plants. In the end, the workforce has managed to move up to better-paying, higher-quality

jobs. That could well happen again. There will still be a crying need for U.S. engineers, for example. But what's called for are engineers who can work closely with customers, manage research teams, and creatively improve business processes.

Adapting to the India effect will be traumatic, but there's no sign Corporate America is turning back. Yet the India challenge also presents an enormous opportunity for the U.S. If America can handle the transition right, the end result could be a brain gain that accelerates productivity and innovation.

SOURCE: Adapted from Manjeet Kripalani and Pete Engardio, "The Rise of India," *BusinessWeek*, December 8, 2003, online.

Consequences of a Global Economy

The increasing integration of the global economy has had many consequences. First, over the last few decades, world output and trade have grown at a dramatic pace. But the volume of world trade has grown at a faster rate that has the volume of world output.[14] Years of emphasis on international commerce by major industrial countries, recent liberalized trading brought about by NAFTA, EU, and APEC, as well as market reforms in China, have resulted in lowering the barriers to the free flow of goods, services, and capital among nation-states. The impact of these trends is staggering. The dollar value of international trade (merchandise exports and commercial services) is approximately $9.09 trillion—up from just a few hundred billion dollars 30 years ago. For example, Figure 6.3 shows how the trade of the United States (particularly for goods) has increased relative to the country's output over the course of the last decade-and-a-half. The dollar value of trade in goods has grown from 30 percent to over 50 percent of the country's total output, even as total U.S. output has also grown. Most experts expect competition to increase as trade is liberalized, and as is often the case, the more efficient players will survive. To succeed in this industrial climate, managers need to study opportunities in existing markets, as well as work to enhance the competitiveness of their firms.

FIGURE 6.3
Trade and Output of Goods and Services in the United States, 1990–2003

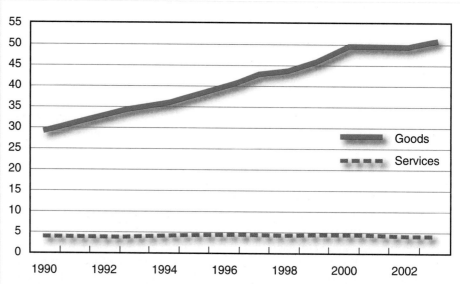

Note: Ratios of goods and of services trade to the output of the goods and the services industries in the United States. Trade (average of exports and imports) and output are measured at constant 2000 prices.
SOURCE: United States, Department of Commerce, Bureau of Economic Analysis.

A second consequence of increased global integration is that *foreign direct investment (FDI)* is playing an ever-increasing role in the global economy as companies of all sizes invest overseas. In particular, the foreign direct investment flows to less-developed countries by firms in developed countries has risen substantially.[15]

A third consequence of an increasingly integrated global economy is that imports are penetrating deeper into the world's largest economies. For example, manufactured goods rather than raw materials now account for more than half of Japan's imports.[16] Nearly two-thirds of the radio and television sets, watches, and motorcycles purchased in the United States are produced abroad. A high percentage of the clothing and textile products, paper, cut diamonds, and VCRs consumed in the United States are also imported. Figure 6.4 shows how the world trade of manufactured merchandise has grown relative to other product groups. The growth of imports is a natural by-product of the growth of world trade and the trend toward the manufacture of component parts, or even entire products, overseas before shipping them back home for final sale.

Finally, the growth of world trade, FDI, and imports implies that companies around the globe are finding their home markets under attack from foreign competitors. This is true in Japan, where IBM has become the market leader in Japan's business software and computer server market, taking share from local companies like Fujitsu; in the United States, where Japanese automakers have captured market share from General Motors (GM), Ford, and DaimlerChrysler; and in western Europe, where the once-dominant Dutch company Philips N. V. has lost market share in the consumer electronics industry to Japan's JVC, Matsushita, and Sony.

What does all this mean for the manager? Compared with only a few years ago, *opportunities are greater* because the movement toward free trade has opened up many formerly protected national markets. The potential for export, and for making direct investments overseas, is greater today than ever before. *The environment is more complex* because today's manager often has to deal with the challenges of doing business in countries with radically different cultures and coordinating globally dispersed operations. *The*

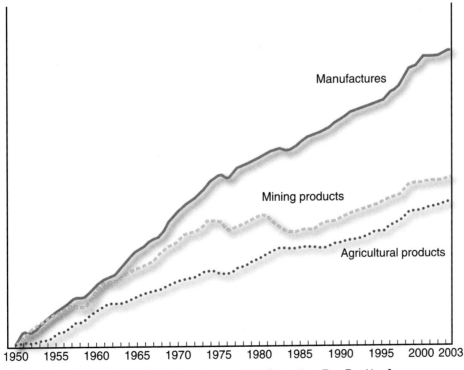

FIGURE 6.4
Relative Growth in World Merchandise Trade by Major Product Group, 1950–2003

Manufactures

Mining products

Agricultural products

1950   1955   1960   1965   1970   1975   1980   1985   1990   1995   2000   2003

SOURCE: World Trade Organization, *International Trade Statistics,* 2004 (Selected Long-Term Trends), p. 2.

environment is more competitive because in addition to domestic competitors, the manager must deal with cost-efficient overseas competitors.

Companies both large and small now view the world, rather than a single country, as their marketplace. As Table 6.1 shows, the United States has no monopoly on international business. Nine of the top 25 corporations in the world are based in countries outside the United States. Also, companies have dispersed their manufacturing, marketing, and research facilities to those locations around the globe where cost and skill conditions are most favorable. This trend is now so pervasive in industries such as automobiles, aerospace, and electronics that it is becoming increasingly irrelevant to talk about "American products" or "British products" or "Japanese products."

TABLE 6.1   The *Business Week* Global 1000

Rank 2004	Rank 2003	Firm	Country	Market Value, Billions of U.S.$
1	1	General Electric	U.S.	328.11
2	2	Microsoft	U.S.	284.43
3	3	Exxon Mobil	U.S.	283.61
4	4	Pfizer	U.S.	269.66
5	5	Wal-Mart Stores	U.S.	241.19
6	6	Citigroup	U.S.	239.43
7	9	BP	Britain	193.05
8	10	American International Group	U.S.	191.18
9	13	Intel	U.S.	184.66
10	8	Royal Dutch/Shell Group	Neth./Britain	174.83
11	21	Bank of America	U.S.	169.84
12	7	Johnson & Johnson	U.S.	165.32
13	14	HSBC Holdings	Britain	163.09
14	12	Vodafone Group	Britain	159.15
15	18	Cisco Systems	U.S.	152.23
16	11	International Business Machines	U.S.	150.55
17	17	Procter & Gamble	U.S.	139.35
18	22	Berkshire Hathaway	U.S.	136.86
19	26	Toyota Motor	Japan	130.65
20	20	Coca-Cola	U.S.	125.56
21	19	Novartis	Switzerland	125.51
22	16	GlaxoSmith Kline	Britain	124.05
23	24	Total	France	122.94
24	15	Merck	U.S.	105.21
25	31	Nestlé	Switzerland	104.87

SOURCE: "The *Business Week* 1000," *BusinessWeek,* July 26, 2004, p. 75.

For example, Chrysler's PT Cruiser is built in Mexico, and the company itself is now owned by DaimlerChrysler, a German automaker. Another German automaker, BMW, builds that quintessential British car, the Rolls-Royce. Toyotas are now built in Kentucky, Hondas are being built in Ohio, and Nissans in Mississippi. And a Dodge Caravan may well have an engine built by Japan's Mitsubishi. Increasingly, a car may be designed in one country and built in another, from parts purchased or made in a variety of other countries. As worldwide trade barriers drop, not national identity but economic considerations, like cost or proximity to markets, increasingly determine where products are made.[17]

Such internationalization in not limited to the largest corporations. An increasing number of medium-size and small firms also engage in international trade. Some companies have limited their involvement to exporting, while others set up production facilities overseas. Even the smallest firms can make arrangements with overseas suppliers and, with the aid of the Internet, communicate with customers worldwide. For example, a tiny company like SpringHill Greenhouses in Lodi, Ohio, with only six employees, operates internationally. SpringHill works with wholesale growers in the Netherlands (for tulips and lilies) and Colombia (for roses) to get the best value for flowers. Then, working through global associations such as FTD and Teleflora, SpringHill networks with other florists to send and receive orders virtually anywhere around the world.[18]

The Role of Outsourcing

In recent years the issue of outsourcing, or offshoring, has become a source of controversy. **Outsourcing** occurs when the organization contracts with an outside provider to produce one or more of an organization's products or services. **Offshoring** occurs when the outside provider is located abroad. It is really offshoring that people mean when they express concern about "outsourcing," because of what they see as the loss of high-paying U.S. jobs to low-cost countries overseas. The concern is prompted by widespread reports of major corporations relocating assembly lines, computer programming, help centers, and other parts of their operation to India or China. One study has estimated that by 2015 more than 3 million U.S. jobs will be sent abroad.[19]

The decline in manufacturing employment in the United States is evident. Almost 3 million manufacturing jobs were lost from 2000 to 2003 alone. But considerable evidence suggests that the cause of this job decline is not offshoring, but innovation. Because of new technology and processes, managers simply need fewer workers to produce the same quantity of goods. For example, since 1970 the steel industry has lost 70 percent of its workers, but domestic steel production has not declined at all.[20]

In addition, the statistics on offshoring often overlook that these job transfers represent a small fraction of the 135 million jobs in the United States. Most jobs require workers to be close to their markets—people still shop at their local supermarket and appliance dealer, visit their doctors, and attend a neighborhood school. Perhaps most important, where offshoring increases efficiency, it frees funds for expansion and additional employment. Despite the jobs moving overseas, overall U.S. employment and productivity have continued to rise, and while individual workers are deeply affected when their jobs are lost,

outsourcing

Contracting with an outside provider to produce one or more of an organization's products or services.

offshoring

Outsourcing to an overseas provider.

These New Delhi white-collar workers at Wipro Spectramind cost 60 percent less than their U.S. counterparts.

retraining and other programs, like Trade Adjustment Assistance, are increasingly available to workers whose jobs have been displaced.[21]

The controversy over offshoring also overlooks the extent to which jobs are often *insourced*—that is, brought to the United States by foreign companies. We mentioned earlier some of the Japanese companies that have built plants in the United States. Even China, a prime offshoring location, decided to move the headquarters of Lenovo, its computer company, to IBM's headquarters in Armonk, New York, when it purchased IBM's personal-computer business.[22] One study has estimated that insourcing companies employ about 5.4 million U.S. workers.[23] These job movements are one inevitable result of the effects of globalization, as companies everywhere seek to become more efficient or move closer to their markets and customers.

One less positive effect of offshoring has been wage stagnation in industries where offshoring is common, as workers in those areas compete with their lower-wage counterparts abroad. On the other hand, wages in some of those other countries have started to rise, reducing the benefits of offshoring. Some firms in India have actually begun to offshore some of *their* work, in order to stay competitive.[24]

In recent years automation has reduced the percentage of product costs that can be attributed to labor, making it less necessary to consider moving jobs overseas. For example, one apparel company located in Los Angeles pays its 1,500 workers well above the minimum wage but has become so efficient that the time and expense of shipping goods from offshore locations would more than offset any wage savings.[25] Managers who offshore to achieve wage savings alone often incur unexpected additional costs in travel, training, quality control, language barriers, and the resistance of some customers who prefer to deal with local personnel.

In short, in deciding whether to offshore, managers should not start out with the assumption that it will be cheaper for them to do so. Instead, here are some of the factors they might take into account:

What is the competitive advantage of the products they offer? If, say, rapid delivery, reliability, and customer contact are paramount, then offshoring is a less attractive option. But if the product is widely available and standardized, like a calculator, and the only competitive advantage is price, the lowest possible production cost becomes essential and offshoring becomes something managers will consider.

Is the business in its early stages? If so, offshoring may well be inappropriate, as managers need to stay close to the business and its customers to solve problems and make sure everything is going according to plan. When the business is more mature, managers can afford to consider moving some operations overseas.

Can production savings be achieved locally? Automation can often achieve significant labor-cost savings and eliminate the advantage of moving production abroad. Where automation savings are not feasible, as with computer call centers, then offshoring becomes a more attractive option.

Distribution of tulips from the Netherlands can be managed by tiny Springhill Greenhouses in Lodi, Ohio.

Can the entire supply chain be improved? As we discussed in Chapter 2, enormous productivity savings are possible when managers develop an efficient supply chain, from suppliers to manufacturing to customers. These improvements permit both lower cost and high customer responsiveness. If the supply chain is not a major consideration, or is already highly efficient or routine, and more savings are needed, then offshoring may be one way for managers to achieve additional efficiencies.[26]

Two Executives Discuss Offshoring

STAYING CLOSE TO HOME: THE MEXICAN OPTION

Ed Trevis *is president and chief executive of* **American Predator,** *a manufacturer of industrial circuit boards, in Morgan Hill, California.*

Our controllers are used in medical equipment like CAT scans and M.R.I.'s. We started outsourcing about 30 percent of our products to a company in Mexico six months ago. They buy the necessary components from United States companies and then assemble our boards. I'm starting slowly, with our higher-volume lines, but eventually I plan to outsource half our products.

Outsourcing will allow us to compete against Asian and European companies overseas, as well as those companies that export to the United States. We will be able to expand our services, increase our revenue, and create more jobs in the United States. I'm hiring now, and I plan to increase the workforce 20 percent in 2005.

The lesson I learned from outsourcing is that business models in other countries are continuing to evolve, which is something American companies can take advantage of.

If you have a product that can be produced routinely and consistently, it pays to have it produced less expensively elsewhere and use the savings to obtain the latest technology here. Few countries can compete with us in that area.

Mexico has its own way of doing business, like all countries, and that has been a challenge. For instance, there are restrictions on how long components can remain in Mexico before a company incurs duties or taxes, and the logistics of handling that can be quite involved.

I'd advise other companies to look at their long-term business-development goals and consider outsourcing to Mexico rather than to Asia. The North American Free Trade Agreement and other agreements have been good for my business and will open up even more markets in the Western Hemisphere. I'd also tell them that increasing profits is not the only reason to outsource. It offers the ability to gain market share and expand services, too.

—As told to Patricia R. Olsen

THE VIDEOCONFERENCE JOB INTERVIEW

Chetan Shah *is executive vice president of technology of* **Synygy Inc.** *in Conshohocken, Pennsylvania.*

We enacted an offshoring model about two years ago and it's been a challenge. Synygy provides solutions to help organizations provide compensation software and services, and we were looking for a way to be able to build more products faster and cheaper. Our clients were demanding more products, but they didn't want to pay top dollar.

So we opened up offices in India and Romania to handle software development and business processes. We have about 500 employees, and 35 percent of them are offshore.

The hardest part of setting this up was finding the right candidates. The hiring process begins in the United States. Everybody has to apply through a Web site, and the applications go to our hiring managers here in the United States. They had to have a lot of training to learn how to look at a foreign résumé. For instance, technical degrees vary from country to country, so these managers had to learn how to decipher everyone's credentials.

Once a résumé is approved, candidates receive an e-mail link for taking a couple of tests. Then comes the hard part. There are two rounds of interviews: the first takes place with Synygy employees in the country where the applicant lives; the second is done through a videoconference in which our American managers participate. Everybody speaks English in the interviews, but the accents can be very difficult to understand. For instance, in India, all of the candidates are English-educated, but their accents vary wildly, depending on which part of the country they're from. We always have a local human resources person sitting in the room to clarify any miscommunication.

(continued)

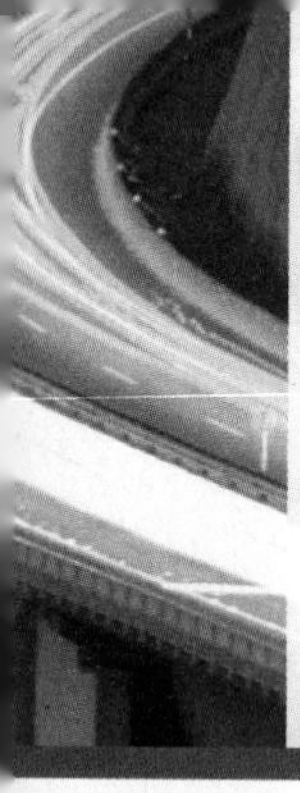

We've been able to handle problems like this by seeding our offshore offices with experienced Synygy people who can bring the company's proven processes and procedures to the offshore operation. We knew going into this that this was going to be the key to doing it right.

—As told to Melinda Ligos

SOURCE: *The New York Times*, December 6, 2004, p. CR.

Global Strategy

One of the critical tasks an international manager faces is to identify the best strategy for competing in a global marketplace. To approach this issue, it is helpful to plot a company's position on an integration-responsiveness grid (see Figure 6.5). The vertical axis measures pressures for *global integration*, and the horizontal axis measures pressures for *local responsiveness*.

Pressures for Global Integration

Managers may have several reasons to want or need a common, global strategy, rather than one tailored to individual markets. These include the existence of universal needs, pressures to reduce costs, or the presence of competitors with a global strategy.

Universal needs create strong pressure for a global strategy. Universal needs exist when the tastes and preferences of consumers in different countries with regard to a product are similar. Products that serve universal needs require little adaptation across national markets; thus, global integration is facilitated. This is the case in many industrial markets. For example, electronic products like semiconductor chips meet universal needs. Certain basic foodstuffs (like colas) and appliances (like can openers) are also increasingly available and regarded in similar ways globally.

Competitive *pressures to reduce costs* may cause managers to seek to integrate manufacturing globally. This can be particularly important in industries in which price is the main competitive weapon and competition is intense (as with hand-held calculators, for example). It is also important if key international competitors are based in coun-

The need to lower costs is a key globalization driver.

FIGURE 6.5
Organizational Models

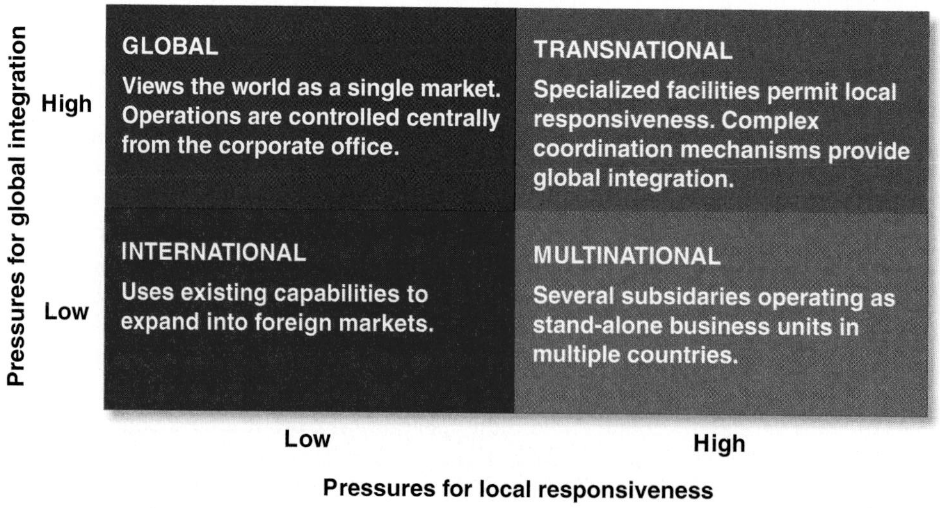

Pressures for global integration

High

GLOBAL
Views the world as a single market. Operations are controlled centrally from the corporate office.

TRANSNATIONAL
Specialized facilities permit local responsiveness. Complex coordination mechanisms provide global integration.

INTERNATIONAL
Uses existing capabilities to expand into foreign markets.

MULTINATIONAL
Several subsidiaries operating as stand-alone business units in multiple countries.

Low

Low   **High**

Pressures for local responsiveness

SOURCES: Christopher A. Bartlett and Sumantra Ghoshal, *Managing across Borders: The Transnational Solution* (Boston: Harvard Business School Press, 1991); and Anne-Wil Harzing. "An Empirical Analysis and Extension of the Bartlett and Ghoshal Typology of Multinational Companies," *Journal of International Business Studies* 31, no. 1 (2000), pp. 101–20.

tries where labor and other operating costs are low. In these cases, products are more likely to be standardized and perhaps produced in a few locations to capture economies of scale.

The presence of competitors engaged in *global strategic coordination* is another factor that creates pressures for global integration. For example, a competitor that centrally coordinates the purchase of raw materials worldwide may achieve significant price reductions compared to firms that allow subsidiaries to handle purchases locally. Global competition can often create pressures to centralize in corporate headquarters certain decisions being made by different national subsidiaries. And once one multinational company adopts global strategic coordination, its competitors may be forced to do the same.

Pressures for Local Responsiveness

In some circumstances, managers need to make sure that their companies are able to adapt to different needs in different locations. Strong pressures for local responsiveness emerge when *consumer tastes and preferences differ significantly* among countries. In such cases, product and/or marketing messages have to be customized.

> "When you travel, remember that a foreign country is not designed to make you comfortable. It is designed to make its own people comfortable."
>
> Clifton Fadiman

In the automobile industry, for example, demand by U.S. consumers for pickup trucks is strong. This is particularly true in the South and West, where many families have a pickup truck as a second or third vehicle. In contrast, in Europe pickup trucks are viewed as utility vehicles and are purchased primarily by companies rather than by individuals. As a result, automakers must tailor their marketing messages to the differences in consumer demand.

Connections: STARBUCKS BREWS EXPANSION

Starbucks's coffees are the same worldwide, and the company even brings overseas managers to its Seattle location for training. Inspection teams visit all locations to maintain uniformity of standards. But the company has also had to tailor some of its operations for the local market. For example, in Taiwan and Japan Starbucks serves green tea Frappuccino—an item that's served nowhere else. A strawberries-and-cream drink was developed for the British market. The company also found that, at least for the short and intermediate term, it does better hiring locals for its stores rather than relocating employees from the United States. Results in the United Kingdom improved when local managers were hired to replace American managers. Local partners and talent also helped Starbucks start up stores more quickly than it otherwise could have—a necessity, as the company attracts imitators who may otherwise move into a location in advance of Starbucks and eliminate the market opportunity.

Pressures for local responsiveness also emerge when there are *differences in traditional practices* among countries. For example, in Great Britain people drive on the left side of the road, creating a demand for right-hand-drive cars, whereas in neighboring France people drive on the right side of the road. Obviously, automobiles must be customized to accommodate this difference in traditional practices.

Differences in distribution channels and sales practices among countries also may create pressures for local responsiveness. In the pharmaceutical industry, the Japanese distribution system differs radically from the U.S. system. Japanese doctors will respond unfavorably to an American-style, high-pressure sales force. Thus, pharmaceutical companies have to adopt different marketing practices in Japan (soft versus hard sell). Similarly, Wal-Mart found that, in Germany, customers were turned off by the

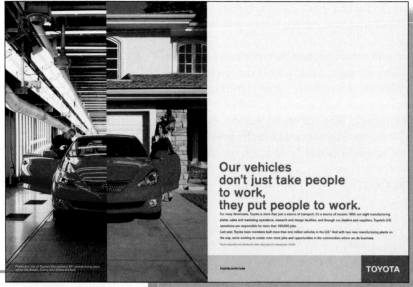

In this ad, Toyota counters the perception that foreign auto companies take jobs from Americans. The production line above is actually its Georgetown, KY, manufacturing plant. According to the organizational model in Figure 6.5, what type of company is Toyota?

international model

An organization model that is composed of a company's overseas subsidiaries and characterized by greater control by the parent company over the research function and local product and marketing strategies than is the case in the multinational model.

The international model helps spread quality standards globally.

overly friendly approach of its store salespeople, preferring a more detached approach that let them do their own shopping.

Finally, *economic and political demands* imposed by host country governments may necessitate a degree of local responsiveness. Most important, threats of protectionism, economic nationalism, and local content rules (rules requiring that a certain percentage of a product be manufactured locally) dictate that international companies manufacture locally.

Choosing a Global Strategy

Figure 6.5 shows that there are four approaches to international competition that managers can use, depending on their company's position on the integration–responsiveness grid: the international model, the multinational model, the global model, and the transnational model. Organizations in each model compete globally, but they differ in the strategy they use and in the structure and systems that drive their operations.

The International Model   The **international model** is one in which managers use their organization's existing core capabilities to expand into foreign markets. As the grid suggests, it is most appropriate when there are few pressures for economies of scale *or* local responsiveness. A company like Pfizer is an example of a company operating in the international model. It is in an industry that doesn't compete on cost, and its drugs obviously don't need to be tailored for local tastes. The international model uses subsidiaries in each country in which the company does business, with ultimate control exercised by the parent company. In particular, while subsidiaries may have some latitude to adapt products to local conditions, core functions such as research and development tend to be centralized in the parent company. Consequently, the dependence of subsidiaries on the parent company for new products, processes, and ideas requires a great deal of coordination and control by the parent company.

The advantage of this model is that it facilitates the transfer of skills and know-how from the parent company to subsidiaries around the globe. For example, IBM, Xerox, and Kodak all profited from the transfer of their core skills in technology and R&D overseas. The overseas successes of Kellogg, Coca-Cola, Heinz, and Procter & Gamble are based more on marketing know-how than on technological expertise. During the late 1900s, many Japanese companies, including Toyota and Honda, successfully penetrated U.S. markets with their core competencies in manufacturing relative to local competitors. Still others have based their competitive advantage on general management skills. These factors explain the growth of international hotel chains such as Hilton International, Intercontinental, and Sheraton.

One disadvantage of the international model is that it does not provide maximum latitude for responding to local conditions. In addition, it frequently does not provide the opportunity to achieve a low-cost position via scale economies.

The Multinational Model   Where global efficiency is not required, but adapting to local conditions offers advantages, the multinational model is appropriate. The **multinational model** uses subsidiaries in each country in which the company does business and provides a great deal of discretion to those subsidiaries to respond to local conditions. Each local subsidiary is a self-contained unit with all the functions required for operating in the host market. Thus, each subsidiary has its own manufacturing, marketing, research, and human resources functions. Because of this autonomy, each multinational subsidiary can customize its products and strategies according to the tastes and preferences of local consumers; the competitive conditions; and political, legal, and social structures.

A good example of a multinational firm is Unilever, a major producer of a wide variety of frozen-food, cooking, and laundry products. Most of the company's worldwide employees are locally trained, and it has a large number of not only global but also regional and local brands. It prides itself on its decentralized structure, which it feels improves its local responsiveness. One advantage of allowing local responsiveness is that there is less need for coordination and direction from corporate headquarters. Since each subsidiary is a self-contained unit, few transfers of goods and services occur among subsidiaries, thus alleviating problems with transfer pricing and the like.

A major disadvantage of the multinational form is higher manufacturing costs and duplication of effort. Although a multinational can transfer core skills among its international operations, it cannot realize scale economies from centralizing manufacturing facilities and offering a standardized product to the global marketplace. Moreover, because a multinational approach tends to decentralize strategy decisions (discussed further in Chapters 8 and 9), launching coordinated global attacks against competitors is difficult. This can be a significant disadvantage when competitors have this ability.

The Global Model

The **global model** is designed to enable a company to market a standardized product in the global marketplace and to manufacture that product in a limited number of locations where the mix of costs and skills is most favorable. The global model has been adopted by companies that view the world as one market and assume that there are no tangible differences among countries with regard to consumer tastes and preferences. Procter & Gamble, for example, has been successful in Europe against Unilever because it has approached the entire continent as a unified whole. Royal Dutch/Shell has been a multinational company for many years, but is now moving to a global model to try to reduce costs, increase integration, and improve efficiency.

Companies that adopt the global model tend to become the low-cost players in any industry. These companies construct global-scale manufacturing facilities in a few selected low-cost locations so that they can realize scale economies. These scale economies come from spreading the fixed costs of investments in new-product development, plant and equipment, and the like, over worldwide sales. By using centralized manufacturing facilities and global marketing strategies, Sony was able to push down its unit costs to the point where it became the low-cost player in the global television market. This enabled Sony to take market share away from Philips, RCA, and Zenith, all of which used traditionally based manufacturing operations in each major national market (a characteristic of the multinational approach). Because operations are centralized, subsidiaries usually are limited to marketing and service functions.

On the downside, because a company pursuing a purely global approach tries to standardize its products and services, it may be less responsive to consumer tastes and demands in different countries. Attempts to lower costs through global product standardization may result in a product that fails to satisfy anyone. For example, while Procter & Gamble has been quite successful using a global approach, the company experienced problems when it tried to market Cheer laundry detergent in Japan. Unfortunately for P&G, the product did not "suds up" as promoted in Japan because the Japanese use a great deal of fabric softener, which suppresses suds. Moreover, the claim that Cheer worked in all water temperatures was irrelevant in Japan, where most washing is done in cold water. The global model also requires a great deal of coordination, with significant additional management and paperwork costs.

The multinational model helps speed up local response.

multinational model

An organization model that consists of the subsidiaries in each country in which a company does business, with ultimate control exercised by the parent company.

global model

An organization model consisting of a company's overseas subsidiaries and characterized by centralized decision making and tight control by the parent company over most aspects of worldwide operations. Typically adopted by organizations that base their global competitive strategy on low cost.

The global model of standardization lowers cost.

transnational model

An organization model characterized by centralization of certain functions in locations that best achieve cost economies; basing of other functions in the company's national subsidiaries to facilitate greater local responsiveness; and fostering of communication among subsidiaries to permit transfer of technological expertise and skills.

The transnational model tries to deliver on all bottom-line practices.

The Transnational Model   In today's global economy, achieving a competitive advantage often requires managers to simultaneously pursue local responsiveness, transfer of know-how, and cost economies.[27] The transnational organization model is designed to help them do just that. It is an approach that enables managers to "think globally but act locally."

In companies that adopt the **transnational model,** functions are centralized where it makes sense to do so, but a great deal of decision making also takes place at the local level. In addition, the experiences of local subsidiaries are shared worldwide, to improve the firm's overall knowledge and capabilities. For example, research, training, and the overall development of the organization's strategy and global brand image tend to be centralized at home. Other functions may be centralized as well, but not necessarily in the home country.

To achieve cost economies, companies may base global-scale production plants for labor-intensive products in low-wage countries such as Mexico and Singapore and locate production plants that require a skilled workforce in high-skill countries such as Germany and Japan.

Other functions, particularly marketing, service, and final-assembly functions, tend to be based in the national subsidiaries to facilitate greater local responsiveness. Thus, major components may be manufactured in centralized production plants to realize scale economies and then shipped to local plants, where the final product is assembled and customized to fit local needs.

Caterpillar Tractor is a transnational company.[28] The need to compete with low-cost competitors such as Komatsu has forced Caterpillar to look for greater cost economies by centralizing global production at locations where the mix of costs and skills is most favorable. At the same time, variations in construction practices and government regulations across countries mean that Caterpillar must be responsive to local needs. On the integration–responsiveness grid in Figure 6.5, therefore, Caterpillar is situated toward the top right-hand corner.

To deal with these simultaneous demands, Caterpillar has designed its products to use many identical components and has invested in a few large-scale component-manufacturing facilities to fill global demand and realize scale economies. But while the company manufactures components centrally, it has assembly plants in each of its major markets. At these plants Caterpillar adds local product features, tailoring the finished product to local needs. Thus, Caterpillar is able to realize many of the benefits of global manufacturing while managing pressure for local responsiveness by differentiating its product among national markets.

Perhaps the most important distinguishing characteristic of the transnational organization is the fostering of communications among subsidiaries and the ability to integrate the efforts of subsidiaries when doing so makes sense. For example, when Caterpillar was engaged in an effort to develop certain medium-size engines, it enlisted the efforts of Caterpillar facilities in the United Kingdom, Mexico, Belgium, and several U.S. locations.[29]

Advantages of Collaboration

When subsidiaries communicate with one another, they can exchange market information, expertise, skills, and new-product ideas among themselves for mutual benefit. The learning and knowledge of the entire organization are significantly increased. Managers in any location, as well as the organization as a whole, can also draw on a much wider base of employees, experience, and customer information to stay ahead of competitors and expand market share. And when centralized manufacturing plants coordinate their production with local assembly plants, they facilitate the smooth operation of an integrated, worldwide production system. This not only results in major economies, but also improves the ability of managers to shift production plans quickly to meet changing market demands. At the same time, regular communication between headquarters and subsidiaries helps the organization maintain common standards of quality and service worldwide.

Achieving such communications across subsidiaries requires elaborate formal mechanisms, such as transnational committees staffed by people from the various subsidiaries who are responsible for monitoring coordination among subsidiaries. Equally important is to transfer managers among subsidiaries on a regular basis. This enables international managers to establish a global network of personal contacts in different subsidiaries with whom they can share information as the need arises. Finally, achieving coordination among subsidiaries requires that the head office play a proactive role in coordinating their activities.

Globalization Hits the Auto Industry

▼ FROM THE PAGES OF

BusinessWeek

Globalization began blurring national auto identities years ago. Today the concept of a purely American carmaker seems quaint. Even the term *Big Three* no longer seems appropriate, since Chrysler Corp. was acquired by Daimler Benz, which has its own transplant factory building Mercedes SUVs in Vance, Alabama. Japan, which had five major independently owned auto companies in 1998, now has only two: Toyota and Honda Motor Co. And just as Asian and European carmakers have been expanding in North America, U.S. companies have been looking for growth overseas. General Motors owns Saab and has stakes in Isuzu, Suzuki, Subaru, Fiat (FIA), and Daewoo. Ford owns Mazda, Volvo, Jaguar, Land Rover, and Aston Martin. DaimlerChrysler owns a controlling stake in Mitsubishi Motors and 10 percent of Hyundai Motor.

The influx of auto factories in the South has been a bonanza for a region ravaged by factory closings and layoffs. Today there are 17 foreign-owned assembly, engine, and transmission factories in the United States, not including American and Japanese joint ventures—an investment of more than $18 billion. Alabama plants alone will be making 600,000 vehicles a year, or 3.5 percent of the U.S. market.

The economic benefits extend far beyond the jobs in those assembly plants. For each auto job created by the transplants, 5.5 additional jobs are created in supplier factories or elsewhere in the community. That multiplier effect is increasing as companies such as Toyota and Honda expand their operations here and use more U.S.-built components. Foreign-based manufacturers, which aren't unionized, pay workers less than their Detroit rivals do. Suppliers to the transplants tend to be nonunionized and pay less too.

Farther north, globalization is working the other way: As Big Three factories use more imported parts from Mexico and other countries, their contribution to the U.S. economy is shrinking. Struggling Ford plans to shutter at least five factories in the United States and Canada and downsize an additional 20. Chrysler already has cut production by eliminating shifts at most of its North American plants. GM, too, will have to close underutilized factories, analysts say.

Detroit automakers have an estimated $1,600-per-vehicle cost disadvantage versus the Japanese. Japanese-owned factories typically build two or more models on a single assembly line, but Big Three factories were designed to build large volumes of a single model.

All the Detroit companies are racing to make their plants more flexible. In 1979, it took GM an average of 41 hours to assemble a vehicle. GM's superefficient modular factory in Lansing, Michigan, has a flexible body shop where robots can be reprogrammed quickly to weld together vehicles ranging from cars to SUVs. It can produce the new Cadillac CTS in just 17 hours—as fast as Nissan's U.S.-best plant in Smyrna, Tennessee.

Detroit has always understood the American auto buyer better than anyone: Witness the minivan and the SUV. Toyota, Honda, and Nissan are pouring more resources into developing and designing vehicles specifically for Americans. After watching consumers flock to striking new foreign models, U.S. automakers have been recruiting hot designers from European rivals and paying fat salaries to design-school graduates. More important, they're giving designers and marketers a stronger voice in developing new models. The result: no more sedans shaped like jelly beans. Detroit is turning out head turners such as the retro Chrysler PT Cruiser, the Euro-styled Ford Focus, and designs that morph into a cargo hauler.

No longer are there just familiar sedans, coupes, and minivans. Consumers can choose from an array of multipurpose vehicles. Moreover, cars keep getting cheaper. Prices have been falling, yet consumers are getting more for their money. Sophisticated safety features such as antilock brakes, side air bags, traction control, and stability-control systems are more widely available. Quality is better too. This is great news for consumers but expensive for automakers pressured to keep product lines fresh even as margins shrink.

Detroit probably will have to settle for a shrinking piece of the pie. The industry that emerges will look very different but may well be stronger. And that will be a good thing for everybody.

SOURCE: Adapted from Joann Muller, "Autos: A New Industry," *BusinessWeek*, July 15, 2002.

Entry Mode

When considering global expansion, international managers must decide on the best means of entering an overseas market. The five basic ways to expand overseas are exporting, licensing, franchising, entering into a joint venture with a host country company, and setting up a wholly owned subsidiary in the host country.[30] Table 6.2 compares the entry modes.

Exporting

Most manufacturing companies begin global expansion as exporters and later switch to one of the other modes for serving an overseas market. The advantages of exporting are that it (1) provides scale economies by avoiding the costs of manufacturing in other countries and (2) is consistent with a pure global strategy. By manufacturing the prod-

TABLE 6.2 Comparison of Entry Modes

Exporting	Licensing	Franchising	Joint Venture	Wholly Owned Subsidiary
Advantages				
Scale economies	Lower development costs	Lower development costs	Local knowledge	Maintains control over technology
Consistent with pure global strategy	Lower political risk	Lower political risk	Shared costs and risk	Maintains control over operations
			May be the only option	
Disadvantages				
No low-cost sites	Loss of control over technology	Loss of control over quality	Loss of control over technology	High cost
High transportation costs			Conflict between partners	High risk
Tariff barriers				

uct in a centralized location and then exporting it to other national markets, the company may be able to realize substantial scale economies from its global sales volume.

However, exporting has a number of drawbacks. First, exporting from the company's home base may be inappropriate if other countries offer lower-cost locations for manufacturing the product. An alternative is to manufacture in a location where the mix of factor costs and skills is most favorable and then export from that location to other markets to achieve scale economies. Several U.S. electronics companies have moved some manufacturing operations to parts of Asia where low-cost, high-skill labor is available, and export from that location to other countries, including the United States.

A second drawback of exporting is that high transportation costs can make it uneconomical, particularly in the case of bulk products. Chemical companies get around this by manufacturing their products on a regional basis, serving several countries in a region from one facility.

A third drawback is that host countries can impose (or threaten to impose) tariff barriers. As was noted earlier, Japanese automakers reduced this risk by setting up manufacturing plants in the United States.

Exporting offers scale economies.

Licensing

International licensing is an arrangement by which a licensee in another country buys the rights to manufacture a company's product in its own country for a negotiated fee (typically, royalty payments on the number of units sold). The licensee then puts up most of the capital necessary to get the overseas operation going. The advantage of licensing is that the company need not bear the costs and risks of opening up an overseas market.

However, a problem arises when a company licenses its technological expertise to overseas companies. Technological know-how is the basis of the competitive advantage of many multinational companies. But RCA Corporation lost control over its color TV technology by licensing it to a number of Japanese companies. The Japanese companies quickly assimilated RCA's technology and then used it to enter the U.S. market. Now the Japanese have a bigger share of the U.S. market than the RCA brand does.

Franchising

In many respects, franchising is similar to licensing. However, whereas licensing is a strategy pursued primarily by manufacturing companies, franchising is used primarily by service companies. McDonald's, Hilton International, and many other companies have expanded overseas by franchising.

In franchising, the company sells limited rights to use its brand name to franchisees in return for a lump-sum payment and a share of the franchisee's profits. However, unlike most licensing agreements, the franchisee has to agree to abide by strict rules as to how it does business. Thus, when McDonald's enters into a franchising agreement with an overseas company, it expects the franchisee to run its restaurants in a manner identical to that used under the McDonald's name elsewhere in the world.

The advantages of franchising as an entry mode are similar to those of licensing. The most significant disadvantage concerns quality control. The company's brand name guarantees consistency in the company's product. Thus, a business traveler booking into a Hilton International hotel in Hong Kong can reasonably expect the same quality of room, food, and service that he or she would receive in New York. But if

A Procter & Gamble ad that appeared in a popular Japanese women's magazine.

Franchising is one way to maintain standards globally.

overseas franchisees are less concerned about quality than they should be, the impact can go beyond lost sales in the local market to a decline in the company's reputation worldwide. If a business traveler has an unpleasant experience at the Hilton in Hong Kong, she or he may decide never to go to another Hilton hotel—and urge colleagues to do likewise. To make matters worse, the geographic distance between the franchisor and its overseas franchisees makes poor quality difficult to detect.

Joint Ventures

Establishing a joint venture (a formal business agreement discussed in more detail in Chapter 11) with a company in another country has long been a popular means for entering a new market. Joint ventures benefit a company through (1) the local partner's knowledge of the host country's competitive conditions, culture, language, political systems, and business systems and (2) the sharing of development costs and/or risks with the local partner. In addition, many countries' political considerations make joint ventures the only feasible entry mode.

Prior to China opening its borders to trade, many U.S. companies like Eastman Kodak, AT&T, Ford, and GM did business in the country via joint ventures. But, as attractive as they sound, joint ventures have their problems. First, as in the case of licensing, a company runs the risk of losing control over its technology to its venture partner. Second, companies may find themselves at odds with one another. For example, one joint-venture partner may want to move production to a country where demand is growing, while the other would prefer to keep its factories at home running at full capacity. Conflict over who controls what within a joint venture is a primary reason many fail.[31] In fact, many of the early joint ventures American and European companies entered into with companies in China lost money or failed precisely because of conflicts over control. To offset these disadvantages, experienced managers strive to iron out technology, control, and other potential conflicts up front, when they first negotiate the joint-venture agreement.

Connections: STARBUCKS BREWS EXPANSION

One method Starbucks used to spark its overseas expansion was to enter into several complicated joint ventures or licensing agreements with local retailers or chains. The joint ventures gave Starbucks immediate access to information about the local market. They also enabled the company to gain access to better locations and to deal smoothly with local tax and licensing issues, and they ensure that the Starbucks stores in each country are sensitive to local consumer tastes. For example, Starbucks in Japan typically has more seating available than in American stores, and the portions served are smaller. But there has been a downside as well. The company has had to give up direct control over costs and is also not receiving all the revenues from each location. Instead, Starbucks receives only a share of revenues, plus licensing fees for its coffee. As a result, the profitability of its joint venture locations, even in successful stores, is substantially reduced.

Wholly Owned Subsidiaries

Establishing a wholly owned subsidiary, that is, an independent company owned by the parent corporation, is the most costly method of serving an overseas market. Companies that use this approach must bear the full costs and risks associated with setting up overseas operations (as opposed to joint ventures, in which the costs and risks are shared, or licensing, in which the licensee bears most of the costs and risks).

Nevertheless, setting up a wholly owned subsidiary offers two clear advantages. First, when a company's competitive advantage is based on technology, a wholly owned subsidiary normally is the preferred entry mode because it reduces the risk of losing control over the technology. This was the case for 3M, which was the first to set up a wholly owned subsidiary in China.[32] The number of wholly owned subsidiaries is at a record high; it is the preferred mode of entry in the semiconductor, electronics, and pharmaceutical industries, for example.

Second, a wholly owned subsidiary gives a company tight control over operations in other countries, which is necessary if it chooses to pursue a global strategy. Establishing a global manufacturing system requires world headquarters to have a high degree of control over the operations of national affiliates. Unlike licensees or joint venture partners, wholly owned subsidiaries usually accept centrally determined decisions about how to produce, how much to produce, and how to price output for transfer among operations.

Managing across Borders

When establishing operations overseas, headquarter executives have a choice among sending **expatriates** (individuals from the parent country), using **host-country nationals** (natives of the host country), and deploying **third-country nationals** (natives of a country other than the home country or the host country). While most corporations use some combination of all three types of employees, there are advantages and disadvantages of each. Colgate-Palmolive and Procter & Gamble, for example, use expatriates to get their products to market abroad more quickly. AT&T and Toyota have used expatriates to transfer their corporate cultures and best practices to other countries—in Toyota's case, to its U.S. plants.

Because sending employees abroad can cost three to four times as much as employing host-country nationals, however, other companies like Texas Instruments have made more limited use of expatriates. Moreover, in many countries—particularly developing countries in which firms are trying to get an economic foothold—the personal security of expatriates is an issue. As a result, more firms are sending their expatriates on shorter assignments and engaging in telecommuting, teleconferencing, and other electronic means to facilitate communications between their international divisions.[33] Indeed, working internationally can be very stressful, even for experienced "globalites." Table 6.3 shows some of the primary stressors for expatriates at different stages of their assignments. It also shows ways for executives to cope with the stress as well as some of the things that companies can do to help with the adjustment.

Clearly, developing a valuable pool of expatriates is important. However, local employees are more available, tend to be familiar with the culture and language, and usually cost less because they do not have to be relocated. In addition, local governments often provide incentives to companies that create good jobs for their citizens (or they may place restrictions on the use of expatriates). Only about a thousand of the roughly 7,000 jobs computer-maker Dell added in 2003 were in the United States. The company directly employs over 20,000 people in Asia, Europe, and South America. Similarly, executives at Allen Bradley, a division of Rockwell International, believe that building a strong local workforce is critical to their success overseas, and they transport key host-country nationals to the United States for skills training. The trend away from using expatriates in top management positions is especially apparent in companies that truly want to create a multinational culture. In Honeywell's European division, for example, many of the top executive positions are held by non-Americans.[34]

Over the years, U.S.-based companies in particular have tended to use more third-country nationals to work in a country different from their own, and different from the parent company's. When Eastman Kodak assembled a management team to devise a launch strategy for its PhotoCD line in Europe, the team members were based in London, but the leader was from Belgium. Because third-country nationals can soften the political tensions between the parent country and the host country, they often represent a convenient compromise.[35]

expatriates

Parent-company nationals who are sent to work at a foreign subsidiary.

host-country nationals

Natives of the country where an overseas subsidiary is located.

third-country nationals

Natives of a country other than the home country or the host country of an overseas subsidiary.

Expatriate hiring lowers cost; training raises quality.

TABLE 6.3 Stressors and Coping Responses in the Developmental Stages of Expatriate Executives

Stage	Primary Stressors	Executive Coping Response	Employer Coping Response
Expatriate selection	Cross-cultural unreadiness.	Engage in self-evaluation.	Encourage expatriate's self- and family evaluation. Perform an assessment of potential and interests.
Assignment acceptance	Unrealistic evaluation of stressors to come. Hurried time frame.	Think of assignment as a growth opportunity rather than an instrument to vertical promotion.	Do not make hard-to-keep promises. Clarify expectations.
Pre- and postarrival training	Ignorance of cultural differences.	Do not make unwarranted assumptions of cultural competence and cultural rules.	Provide pre-, during, and postassignment training. Encourage support-seeking behavior.
Arrival	Cultural shock. Stressor reevaluation. Feelings of lack of fit and differential treatment.	Do not construe identification with the host and parent cultures as mutually exclusive. Seek social support.	Provide postarrival training. Facilitate integration in expatriate network.
Novice	Cultural blunders or inadequacy of coping responses. Ambiguity owing to inability to decipher meaning of situations.	Observe and study functional value of coping responses among locals. Do not simply replicate responses that worked at home.	Provide follow-up training. Seek advice from locals and expatriate network.
Transitional	Rejection of host or parent culture.	Form and maintain attachments with both cultures.	Promote culturally sensitive policies in host country. Provide Internet access to family and friends at home. Maintain constant communication and periodic visits to parent organization.
Mastery	Frustration with inability to perform boundary-spanning role. Bothered by living with a cultural paradox.	Internalize and enjoy identification with both cultures and walking between two cultures.	Reinforce rather than punish dual identification by defining common goals.
Repatriation	Disappointment with unfulfilled expectations. Sense of isolation. Loss of autonomy.	Realistically reevaluate assignment as a personal and professional growth opportunity.	Arrange prerepatriation briefings and interviews. Schedule postrepatriation support meetings.

SOURCE: J. Sanchez, P. Spector, and C. Cooper, *Academy of Management Executive,* 14 no. 2, pp. 96–106. Copyright © 2000 by Academy of Management. Reproduced with permission of Academy of Management via Copyright Clearance Center.

Skills of the Global Manager

failure rate

The number of expatriate managers of an overseas operation who come home early.

It is estimated that nearly 15 percent of all employee transfers are to an international location. However, a recent survey of 1,500 senior executives showed that there is a critical shortage of U.S. managers equipped to run global businesses.[36] Indicative of this fact is the **failure rate** among expatriates (defined as those who come home early), which has been estimated to range from 20 to 70 percent, depending on the country of assignment. The cost of each of these failed assignments ranges from tens of thou-

End-State Dimensions	Sample Items
1. Sensitivity to cultural differences	When working with people from other cultures, works hard to understand their perspective.
2. Business knowledge	Has a solid understanding of the company's products and services.
3. Courage to take a stand	Is willing to take a stand on issues.
4. Brings out the best in people	Has a special talent for dealing with people.
5. Acts with integrity	Can be depended on to tell the truth regardless of circumstances.
6. Is insightful	Is good at identifying the most important part of a complex problem.
7. Is committed to success	Clearly demonstrates commitment to seeing the organization succeed.
8. Takes risks	Takes personal as well as business risks.
Learning-Oriented Dimensions	**Sample Items**
1. Uses feedback	Has changed as a result of feedback.
2. Is culturally adventurous	Enjoys the challenge of working in countries other than his or her own.
3. Seeks opportunities to learn	Takes advantage of opportunities to do new things.
4. Is open to criticism	Does not appear brittle—as if criticism might cause him or her to break.
5. Seeks feedback	Pursues feedback even when others are reluctant to give it.
6. Is flexible	Doesn't get so invested in things that he or she cannot change when something doesn't work.

SOURCE: Gretchen M. Sprietzer, Morgan W. McCall, and Joan D. Mahoney, "Early Identification of International Executive Potential," *Journal of Applied Psychology* 82, no. 1 (1997), pp. 6–29.

TABLE 6.4

Identifying International Executives

sands to hundreds of thousands of dollars.[37] Typically, the causes for failure overseas extend beyond technical capability, and include personal and social issues as well. One of the biggest problems is often a spouse's difficulty in adjusting to his or her surroundings. This problem may be compounded in this era of dual-career couples, where one spouse may have to give up his or her job to accompany the expatriate manager to the new location. For both the expatriate and the spouse, adjustment requires flexibility, emotional stability, empathy for the culture, communication skills, resourcefulness, initiative, and diplomatic skills.[38]

Interestingly, while many U.S. companies have hesitated to send women abroad—believing that women either do not want international assignments or that other cultures would not welcome women—their success rate in some companies and countries has been very good.[39] Ironically, for a country that had been viewed as not welcoming foreign women, in Japan U.S. women are first viewed as foreigners (*gaijin* in Japanese) and only second as women. And because it is unusual for women to be sent on foreign assignments, their distinctiveness and visibility can increase their chances for success.[40]

Companies such as Levi-Strauss, Bechtel, Monsanto, Whirlpool, and Dow Chemical have worked to identify the characteristics of individuals that will predict their success abroad. Table 6.4 shows skills that can be used to identify candidates who are likely to succeed in a global environment. Interestingly, in addition to such things as cultural

Structure assignments clearly: Develop clear reporting relationships and job responsibilities.
Create clear job objectives.
Develop performance measurements based on objectives.
Use effective, validated selection and screening criteria (both personal and technical attributes).
Prepare expatriates and families for assignments (briefings, training, support).
Create a vehicle for ongoing communication with expatriates.
Anticipate repatriation to facilitate reentry when they come back home.
Consider developing a mentor program that will help monitor and intervene in case of trouble.

TABLE 6.5
How to Prevent Failed Global Assignments

sensitivity, technical expertise, and business knowledge, an individual's success abroad may depend greatly on his or her ability to learn from experience.[41]

> "If there is any great secret of success in life, it lies in the ability to put yourself in the other person's place and to see things from his point of view as well as your own."
>
> Henry Ford

Companies such as Amoco, Daimler-Chrysler, Global Hyatt, British Petroleum, and others with large international staffs have extensive training programs to prepare employees for international assignments. Table 6.5 suggests ways to improve their likelihood of success. Other organizations, such as Coca-Cola, Motorola, ChevronTexaco, and Mattel, have extended this training to include employees who may be located in the United States but who nevertheless deal in international markets. These programs focus on areas such as language, culture, and career development.

Managers who are sent on an overseas assignment usually wonder about the effect of such an assignment on their careers. On the one hand, their selection for a post overseas is usually an indication that they are being groomed to become more effective managers in an era of globalization. In addition, they will often have more responsibility, challenge, and operating leeway than they might have at home. On the other hand, they may be concerned that they will soon be "out of the loop" on key developments back home. Good companies and managers address that issue with effective communication between subsidiaries and headquarters and by a program of visitations to and from the home office.

Understanding Cultural Issues

In many ways, cultural issues represent the most elusive aspect of international business. In an era when modern transportation and communication technologies have created a "global village," it is easy to forget how deep and enduring the differences among nations can be. The fact that people everywhere drink Coke, wear blue jeans, and drive Toyotas doesn't mean we are all becoming alike. Each country is unique for reasons rooted in history, culture, language, geography, social conditions, race, and religion. These differences complicate any international activity, and represent the fundamental issues that inform and guide how a company should conduct business across borders.

Ironically, while most of us would guess that the trick to working abroad is learning about the foreign culture, in reality our problems often stem from our being oblivious to our own cultural conditioning. Most of us pay no attention to how culture influences our everyday behavior, and because of this we tend to adapt poorly to situations that are unique or foreign to us. Without realizing it, some managers may even act out of **ethnocentrism**—a tendency to judge foreign peoples or groups by the standards of one's own culture or group, and to see one's own standards as superior. Such tenden-

ethnocentrism

The tendency to judge others by the standards of one's group or culture, which are seen as superior.

cies may be totally unconscious—for example, the assumption that "in England they drive on the *wrong* side of the road," rather than merely on the left. Or they may reflect a lack of awareness of the values underlying a local culture—for example, an assumption that the culture is backward because it does not air American or European television programming, when it is actually focused on maintaining its traditional values and norms.

These kinds of assumptions are one reason why people traveling abroad frequently experience **culture shock**—the disorientation and stress associated with being in a foreign environment. Managers who ignore culture put their organizations at a great disadvantage in the global marketplace. Because each culture has its own norms, customs, and expectations for behavior, success in an international environment depends on one's ability to understand one's own culture and the other culture and to recognize that abrupt changes will be met with resistance.[42]

A wealth of cross-cultural research has been conducted on the differences and similarities among various countries. Geert Hofstede, for example, has identified four dimensions along which managers in multinational corporations tend to view cultural differences:

- *Power distance:* the extent to which a society accepts the fact that power in organizations is distributed unequally.
- *Individualism/collectivism:* the extent to which people act on their own or as a part of a group.
- *Uncertainty avoidance:* the extent to which people in a society feel threatened by uncertain and ambiguous situations.
- *Masculinity/femininity:* the extent to which a society values quantity of life (e.g., accomplishment, money) over quality of life (e.g., compassion, beauty).

> **culture shock**
>
> The disorientation and stress associated with being in a foreign environment.

Figure 6.6 offers a graphic depiction of how 40 different nations differ on the dimensions of individualism/ collectivism and power distance. Of course, this depiction to some extent exaggerates the differences between national traits. Many Americans prefer to act as part of a group, just as many Taiwanese prefer to act individualistically. And globalization may have already begun to blur some of these distinctions. Nevertheless, to suggest no cultural differences exist is equally simplistic. Clearly, cultures such as the United States, which emphasize "rugged individualism," differ significantly from collectivistic cultures such as those of Pakistan, Taiwan, and Colombia. To be effective in cultures that exhibit a greater power distance, managers often must behave more autocratically, perhaps being less participative in decision making. Conversely, in Scandinavian cultures like Sweden's, for instance, where power distance is low, the very idea that management has the prerogative to make decisions on its own may be called into question. Here, managers tend to work more toward creating processes that reflect an "industrial democracy."

In March 2005, Sir Howard Stringer replaced Nobuyuki Idei, becoming the first non-Japanese chairman and CEO of Sony. Stringer had been heading Sony Corporation of America and had been praised for his innovation and management skills. But having no engineering skills and the inability to speak Japanese, Stringer will have his work cut out for him.

Cross-cultural management extends beyond U.S. employees going abroad. It also includes effective management of **inpatriates**—foreign nationals who are brought in to work at the parent company. These employees provide a valuable service to global companies, because they bring with them extensive knowledge about how to operate effectively in their home countries. They will also be in a better position to

> **inpatriate**
>
> A foreign national brought in to work at the parent company.

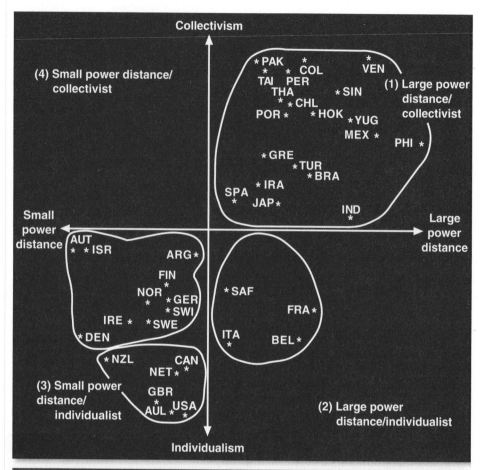

SOURCE: Geert Hofstede, "Motivation, Leadership, and Organization: Do American Theories Apply Abroad?" *Organizational Dynamics* 9, no. 1 (Summer 1980), pp. 42–63. Reprinted by permission.

FIGURE 6.6

The Position of the 40 Countries on the Power Distance and Individualism Scales

communicate their organization's products and values when they return. But they often have the same types of problems as expatriates and may be even more neglected, because parent-company managers either are more focused on their expatriate program or unconsciously see the home country as normal and requiring no period of adjustment. Yet the language, customs, expense, and lack of local community support in the United States will be at least as daunting to inpatriates as the experience of American nationals abroad. Cultural shock works both ways.

Effective managers are sensitive to these issues and take them into account in dealing with foreign-national employees. In addition, when working in the United States, foreign nationals will encounter a number of work-related differences. Alert managers will help their employees adjust to these as well. A few basic categories include the following:

- *Meetings:* Americans tend to have a fairly specific view of the purpose of meetings and how much time can be wasted. International workers may have different preconceptions about the nature and length of meetings, and managers will want to make sure foreign nationals are comfortable with the American approach.
- *Work(aholic) schedules:* Workers from other countries can work long hours but, in countries with strong labor organizations, often get many more weeks of vacation than American workers. And Europeans in particular may balk at working on weekends. Obviously, matters like these are most helpfully raised and addressed at the beginning of the work assignment.
- *E-mail:* Most of the world has not yet embraced e-mail and voicemail the way U.S. workers have. Most others would prefer to communicate face to face. Particularly when potential language difficulties exist, at the outset managers will probably want to avoid using e-mail for important matters.
- *Fast-trackers:* Although U.S. companies may take a young MBA graduate and put him or her on the fast track to management, most other cultures still see no substitute for the wisdom gained through experience. (This is something U.S. managers working abroad will also want to keep in mind.) More experienced managers are often a better choice for mentoring inpatriates.
- *Feedback:* Everyone likes praise, but the use of excessive positive feedback tends to be less prevalent in other cultures than in the United States, a useful fact for managers when they give foreign nationals their performance reviews.[43]

Ethical Issues in International Management

If managers are to function effectively in a foreign setting, they must understand how culture influences both how they are perceived and how others behave. One of the most sensitive issues in this regard is understanding how culture plays out in terms of ethical behavior.[44] Issues of right and wrong get blurred as we move from one culture to another, and actions that may be normal and customary in one setting may be unethical—even illegal—in another. The use of bribes, for example, is an accepted part of commercial transactions in many Asian, African, Latin American, and Middle Eastern cultures.[45] In the United States, of course, such behavior is illegal, but what should a U.S. businessperson do when working abroad? Failure to "sweeten" the deal with bribes can result in lost business. During a 12-month period in 2003–2004, for example, the U.S. Commerce Department estimated that competition for 47 international contracts worth $18 billion was affected by bribes paid by foreign firms to foreign officials. According to a study by Transparency International, a public-interest group dedicated to stamping out bribery, no less than 60 countries around the world are rampant with corruption. Haiti and Bangladesh top the list.[46]

Although the Foreign Corruption Practices Act of 1977 prohibits U.S. employees from bribing foreign officials, one study published in the United States found that less than half of U.S. managers said bribes were unacceptable, and 20 percent actually said they were always acceptable. (Small business gifts or "grease payments" to lower-level officials are permissible under the act, if the dollar amount of the payments would not influence the outcome of the negotiations.) Internationally, countries of the OECD (Organization for Economic Cooperation and Development), including the United States, have also prohibited bribes since 1977.[47]

The enforcement of the antibribery law—if only in the United States—did become more vigorous following the high-profile financial scandals at U.S. corporations like

Enron and WorldCom. The Sarbanes-Oxley Act, passed in 2002, requires CEOs and CFOs to sign off personally on the veracity of their companies' financial statements. It also requires that public companies establish a confidential system for employees to report wrongdoing and create an ethics code for senior financial officers.

Without an understanding of local customs, ethical standards, and applicable laws, an expatriate may be woefully unprepared to work internationally. To safeguard against the problems and mitigate the punishment if an organization should be found guilty of bribery, the U.S. Sentencing Commission has deemed it essential that firms establish effective ethics programs and see that they are enforced. Companies such as Caterpillar, General Dynamics, and United Technologies established official codes of conduct for their employees years ago. But since the recent widely publicized scandals at some U.S. corporations, a large number of other companies have hired official ethics officers and increased their ethics efforts.

To put "teeth" into the corporate ethics initiative, the following additional steps have been suggested:

- *Vigorously oversee corporate ethics and culture.* DuPont distributes periodic "ethics bulletins" to its employees. The bulletins chronicle actual ethics violations within the company, focusing on the consequences of the offenders' actions, what happened to the offenders, and the lessons to be learned from the mistake.
- *Ensure the company has articulated its values.* Starbucks and Levi-Strauss, for example, have posted on their Internet homepages their companies' expectations about the proper behavior of employees when it comes to customers, suppliers, trade, and environmental policies.
- *Let business partners know the standards.* For example, Levi-Strauss has established a set of global sourcing and operating guidelines that detail the terms of engagement for all its partners, including health and safety issues.
- *Include character, integrity, decision making, and other values information in performance reviews and succession-management processes. Show zero tolerance toward breaches of ethics.* H. B. Fuller ties its employees' compensation to their performance evaluations, which include an ethical component. The company also conducts audits of people in key positions subject to difficult moral decisions.[48]

Interestingly, despite some obvious differences across cultures, research suggests that regardless of nationality or religion most people embrace a set of five core values: *compassion, fairness, honesty, responsibility,* and *respect for others.* These values lie at the heart of human rights issues and seem to transcend more superficial differences among Americans, Europeans, and Asians. Finding shared values such as these allows companies to build more effective partnerships and alliances, especially across cultures. It may be the case that as long as people understand that there is a set of core values, they can permit all kinds of differences in strategy and tactics.[49]

To a large extent, the challenge of managing across borders comes down to the philosophies and systems used to manage people. In moving from domestic to international management, managers need to develop a wide portfolio of behaviors along with the capacity to adjust their behavior for a particular situation. This adjustment, however, should not compromise the values, integrity, and strengths of their home country. When managers can transcend national borders, and move among different cultures, they will be in a position to leverage the strategic capabilities of the organization and take advantage of the opportunities that our global economy has to offer.

EPILOGUE:

STARBUCKS BREWS OVERSEAS EXPANSION

Starbucks opened its first overseas store in 1996, in Tokyo, Japan. After years of losses, its international business has turned profitable, and expansion is continuing. Some Japanese stores have twice the sales of comparably sized stores in the United States, and even in China a taste for Starbucks coffee is developing. The company's long-term plan assumes that it will one day have more stores abroad than at home. What are some of the lessons that Starbucks has learned from its international operation? Orin Smith, Starbucks's CEO, offered up these five essential principles for expanding American business overseas:

1. *Don't assume the market is like America, even in an English-speaking country.* Starbucks found that it had to change some of its marketing and operating practices even in Canada, and much more so in the United Kingdom. English-speaking countries or customers are not the same worldwide.

2. *Set up partnerships abroad to grow faster.* Start-ups are a lot easier and faster when assisted by those who understand local conditions and tastes.

3. *Never become better at opening stores than operating them.* In Japan, for example, Starbucks was so busy opening as many as 500 stores that it found itself paying less attention to the business details of each store. It therefore took longer for some of these stores to become profitable.

4. *Hire locally for both managers and rank-and-file employees.* Locals are more attuned to the demands of their marketplace and usually can communicate more effectively with customers.

5. *Adapt to local culture and tastes.* In some ways the world is becoming more alike. But it is a very long way from actually being alike.

KEY TERMS

Culture shock, p. 213

Ethnocentrism, p. 212

Expatriates, p. 209

Failure rate, p. 210

Global model, p. 203

Host-country nationals, p. 209

Inpatriate, p. 213

International model, p. 202

Multinational model, p. 203

North American Free Trade Agreement (NAFTA), p. 192

Offshoring, p. 197

Outsourcing, p. 197

Third-country nationals, p. 209

Transnational model, p. 204

SUMMARY OF LEARNING OBJECTIVES

Now that you have studied Chapter 6, you should know:

Why the world economy is becoming more integrated than ever before.

The gradual lowering of barriers to free trade is making the world economy more integrated. This means that the modern manager operates in an environment that offers more opportunities but is also more complex and competitive than that faced by the manager of a generation ago.

What integration of the global economy means for individual companies and for their managers.

In recent years, rapid growth in world trade, foreign direct investment, and imports has occurred. One consequence is that companies around the globe are now finding their home markets under attack from international competitors. The global competitive environment is becoming a much tougher place in which to do business. However, companies now have access to markets that previously were denied to them.

The strategies organizations use to compete in the global marketplace.

The international corporation builds on its existing core capabilities in R&D, marketing, manufacturing, and so on, to penetrate overseas markets. A multinational is a more complex form that usually has fully autonomous units operating in multiple countries. Subsidiaries are given latitude to address local issues such as consumer preferences, political pressures, and economic trends in different regions of the world. The global organization pulls control of overseas operations back into the headquarters and tends to approach the world market as a "unified whole" by combining activities in each country to maximize efficiency on a global scale. A transnational attempts to achieve both local responsiveness and global integration by utilizing a network structure that coordinates specialized facilities positioned around the world.

The various entry modes organizations use to enter overseas markets.

There are five ways to enter an overseas market: exporting, licensing, franchising, entering into a joint venture, and setting up a wholly owned subsidiary. Each mode has advantages and disadvantages.

How companies can approach the task of staffing overseas operations.

Most executives use a combination of expatriates, host-country nationals, and third-country nationals. Expatriates sometimes are used to quickly establish new country operations, transfer the company's culture, and bring in a specific technical skill. Host-country nationals have the advantages that they are familiar with local customs and culture, may cost less, and are viewed more favorably by local governments. Third-country nationals often are used as a compromise in politically touchy situations or when home-country expatriates are not available.

The skills and knowledge managers need to manage globally.

The causes for failure overseas extend beyond technical capability, and include personal and social issues as well. Success depends on a manager's core skills, such as having a multidimensional perspective; having proficiency in line management and decision making; and having resourcefulness, cultural adaptability, sensitivity, team-building skills, and mental maturity. In addition, helpful augmented skills include computer literacy, negotiating skills, strategic vision, and the ability to delegate.

Why cultural differences across countries influence management.

Culture influences our actions and perceptions as well as the actions and perceptions of others. Unfortunately, we are often unaware of how culture influences us, and this can cause problems. Today managers must be able to change their behavior to match the needs and customs of local cultures. For example, in various cultures, employees expect a manager to be either more or less autocratic or participative. By recognizing their cultural differences, people can find it easier to work together collaboratively and benefit from the exchange.

DISCUSSION QUESTIONS

1. Why is the world economy becoming more integrated? What are the implications of this integration for international managers?

2. Imagine you were the CEO of a major company. What approach to global competition would you choose for your firm: international, multinational, global, or transnational? Why?

3. Why have franchises been so popular as a method of international expansion in the fast-food industry? Contrast this with high-tech manufacturing, where joint ventures and partnerships have been more popular. What accounts for the differences across industries?

4. What are the pros and cons of using expatriates, host-country nationals, and third-country nationals to run overseas operations? If you were expanding your business, what approach would you use?

5. If you had entered into a joint venture with a foreign company but knew that women were not treated fairly in that culture, would you consider sending a female expatriate to handle the start-up? Why or why not?

6. What are the biggest cultural obstacles that we must overcome if we are to work effectively in Mexico? Are there different obstacles in France? Japan?

CONCLUDING CASE

Gordy Goes Global

Gordy La Vertue, a native of Quebec, became a U.S. citizen and now operates a lumber company in Northern Vermont. The company's major product lines include maple and cherry lumber. Logs are converted to lumber through a manufacturing facility. The lumber is then kiln-dried and surface-planed to a moisture content and form suitable for the manufacture of fine furniture and other finished products such as cabinets, musical instruments, fancy boxes, and window and door trim.

Most U.S. markets are flooded with domestically produced lumber. There are many producers of these and similar lumber products throughout the country thus creating a commodity situation and a commodity price.

Gordy wants to go global. Gordy has heard that his beautiful maple and cherry boards are highly sought after by European craftsmen and others. He has learned that those products (trees) simply do not grow or exist in that part of the world. Gordy has also noticed a growing trend and presence of finished consumer wood products that are made in China, Malaysia, and other Asian countries. He suspects that the raw materials for those products (lumber) are produced in the United States, processed overseas, and shipped back as U.S. imports. This seems very wasteful and inefficient to Gordy.

Gordy has also heard about international trade issues such as customs laws and regulations, currency exchange rates, government imposed barriers to trade, international law, shipping through container ports, different systems of measurement and cultural, language and religious influences.

The Northern Vermont lumber manufacturing facility has traditionally operated on a 40- to 50-hour production schedule. Gordy could change his product mix to include a better paying export line and/or could add a second shift. The personnel and raw materials necessary to add a second shift are available. The plant site also includes a small office that houses one secretary and one sales associate. Gordy's company generates $3,000,000 in annual sales revenues with a net-income-to-sales ratio of 8 percent that is considered to be above average for this industry.

Gordy and his salesman have always done business exclusively within the United States, excepting for a few low volume customers just over the border in Canada. Sales are divided equally between wholesalers and direct buyers/users.

Gordy wants to go global, but simply does not know where or how to begin. He wonders if there are better paying markets outside of the United States, and if so, where? Gordy has also heard about the U.S. trade deficit and about some related government support programs that are available to exporters.

QUESTIONS

1. Using what you've learned in this chapter, what additional information will the owner need to obtain in order to develop an effective export plan?

2. Discuss current and future trends in global business. What are your predictions as to the "hot" markets and countries in the years to come?

3. What actions should you take during the next few years to position yourself as a future player in the international marketplace?

EXPERIENTIAL EXERCISES

6.1 Understanding Multinational Corporations

OBJECTIVE

To gain a more thorough picture of how a multinational corporation operates.

INSTRUCTIONS

Perhaps the best way to gain an understanding of multinational corporations is to study a specific organization and how it operates throughout the world. Select a multinational corporation, find several articles on that company, and answer the questions on the Multinational Worksheet.

Multinational Worksheet

1. What is the primary business of this organization?

_____

_____

_____

_____

_____

2. To what extent does the company engage in multinational operations? For example, does it only market its products and/or services in other countries or does it also have overseas manufacturing facilities? What portion of the firm's operating income comes from overseas operations?

_____

_____

_____

_____

_____

3. What percentage of the managers in international activities are American (or from the country the corporation considers home)? Are these managers given any special training before their international assignment?

_____

_____

_____

_____

_____

4. What characteristics of the organization have contributed to its success or lack of success in the international marketplace?

_____

_____

_____

_____

SOURCE: R. R. McGrath Jr., _Exercises in Management Fundamentals_ (Englewood Cliffs, NJ: Prentice-Hall, 1985), p. 177. Reprinted by permission of Prentice-Hall, Inc.

6.2 Cross-Cultural Communication Simulation

In this simulation, you will play the part of a manager employed by one of three firms—a commercial bank, a construction firm, and a hotel development company—which are planning a joint venture to build a new hotel and retail shopping complex in Perth, Australia. They come from three different cultures: Blue, Green, and Red. Each has specific cultural values, traits, customs, and practices.

You are a manager in the company to which you have been assigned. You will attend the kickoff get-together for the three-day meeting during which the three companies will negotiate the details of the partnership. Your management team consists of a vice president and a number of other managers. Consider the types of topics that would be discussed by the various corporations at an initial meeting.

INSTRUCTIONS

Your instructor will provide you with information pertaining to your culture. You will be given about 15 minutes to meet with your fellow corporate members, during which you should:

1. Select a leader.

2. Discuss what your objectives and approaches will be at the opening get-together.

3. Using the description of your assigned culture, practice how you will talk and behave until you are reasonably familiar with your cultural orientation. Be sure to practice conversation distance, greeting rituals, and nonverbal behavior.

You will then return to the kick-off meeting where you will meet with the other firms. As the social proceeds, interact with the managers from the other companies. Maintain the role you have been assigned, but do not discuss it explicitly. Notice how other people react to you and how you react to them. We will discuss the experience after it is over.

Upon completing this activity, answer the following questions:

1. In what ways did your perceptions of others and their differences influence how you interacted with them and your ability to achieve your goals?

_____

_____

_____

_____

_____

_____

_____

2. What did you learn about yourself and others through this activity? Discuss your strengths and weaknesses in cross-cultural interaction.

_____

_____

_____

_____

_____

_____

_____

3. What were things you or others did or said that enabled or hindered you from adjusting to other people and their culture: (1) in this activity? (2) in similar real-life situations?

_____

_____

_____

_____

_____

_____

_____

4. What lessons did you learn from this activity? What steps can you take to improve your ability to understand and appreciate differences?

_____

_____

_____

_____

_____

_____

_____

_____

SOURCE: Daphne A. Jameson, "Using a Simulation to Teach Intercultural Communication in Business Communication Courses," _Bulletin of the Association for Business Communication (Business Communication Quarterly)_ 55, no. 4 (March 1993), pp. 1–10.

Chapter **7**

CHAPTER 7
Entrepreneurship

A man is known by the company he organizes.

—Ambrose Bierce

LEARNING OBJECTIVES

After studying Chapter 7, you will know:

1. Why people become entrepreneurs, and what it takes, personally.

2. How to assess opportunities to start new companies.

3. Common causes of success and failure.

4. Common management challenges.

5. How to increase your chances of success, including good business planning.

6. How to foster intrapreneurship and an entrepreneurial orientation in large companies.

JEFF BEZOS AND AMAZON.COM

Few entrepreneurs have succeeded so greatly despite such great skepticism from others as Jeff Bezos. He moved successfully from visionary of a small start-up to leader of thousands of employees. "It's the long term that matters . . . Half of it was good timing, half of it was luck, and the rest was brains . . . the odds are stacked against any start-up."

In the spring of 1994, Jeff Bezos was driving to California to start a new business. He had just quit a

lucrative Wall Street job and a career path with great potential. But Bezos didn't want to reach the end of his career, look back, and have any regrets about not trying to start his own company. He noticed that Web usage was growing at 2,300 percent per year, and this too was a motivating factor in forming Amazon.com. His early vision was "to create the world's most customer-centric company, the place where you can find and buy anything you want online."

Bezos is far-sighted, intuitive, and smart. He says he's lucky. Moreover, "I believe that optimism is an essential quality for doing anything hard—entrepreneurial endeavors or anything else." That doesn't mean you're blind or unrealistic; it means that you stay focused on eliminating your risks, modifying your strategy, until it is a strategy about which you can be *genuinely* optimistic.

Entrepreneurship, says Bezos, is about being resourceful. It's about problem solving: if something is broken, fix it. Good problem solvers, like good entrepreneurs, are self-reliant.

Sources for Prologue, Connections, Epilogue: R. Walker, "Jeff Bezos, Amazon.com," *Inc.*, April 2004, pp. 148–50; A. Deutschman, "Inside the Mind of Jeff Bezos," *Fast Company*, August 2004, pp. 51–58.

entrepreneurship

The pursuit of lucrative opportunities by enterprising individuals.

Entrepreneurship is inherently about innovation—creating a new venture where one didn't exist before.

small business

A business having fewer than 100 employees, independently owned and operated, not dominant in its field, and not characterized by many innovative practices.

entrepreneurial venture

A new business having growth and high profitability as primary objectives.

As Jeff Bezos and countless others have demonstrated, great opportunity is available to talented entrepreneurs. **Entrepreneurship** occurs when an enterprising individual pursues a lucrative opportunity.[1] To be an entrepreneur is to initiate and build an organization, rather than being only a passive part of one.[2] It involves creating *new* systems, resources, or processes to produce *new* goods or services and/or serve *new* markets.[3]

Entrepreneurship differs from management generally and from small-business management in particular. An entrepreneur *is* a manager, but engages in additional activities that not all managers do.[4] Whereas managers operate in a more formal management hierarchy, with more clearly defined authority and responsibility, entrepreneurs use networks of contacts more than formal authority. And whereas managers usually prefer to own assets, entrepreneurs often rent or use assets on a temporary basis. Some say that managers often are slower to act and tend to avoid risk, whereas entrepreneurs are quicker to act and actively manage risk.

How does entrepreneurship differ from managing a small business?[5] A **small business** is often defined as having fewer than 100 employees, being independently owned and operated, not dominant in its field, and not characterized by many innovative practices. Small business owners tend not to manage particularly aggressively, and they expect normal, moderate sales, profits, and growth. In contrast, an **entrepreneurial venture** has growth and high profitability as primary objectives. Entrepreneurs manage aggressively and develop innovative strategies, practices, and products. They and their financial backers usually seek rapid growth, immediate and high profits, and sometimes a quick sellout with large capital gains.

The Excitement of Entrepreneurship   Consider these recent words from Jeffry Timmons, a leading entrepreneurship scholar and author: "During the past 30 years, America has unleashed the most revolutionary generation the nation has experienced since its founding in 1776. This new generation of entrepreneurs has altered permanently the economic and social structure of this nation and the world . . . It will determine more than any other single impetus how the nation and the world will live, work, learn, and lead in this century and beyond."[6] Timmons had written previously, in 1989, "We are in the midst of a silent revolution—a triumph of the creative and entrepreneurial spirit of humankind throughout the world. I believe its impact on the 21st century will equal or exceed that of the Industrial Revolution on the 19th and 20th."[7]

Overhype? Sounds like it could be, but it's not. Entrepreneurship is transforming economies all over the world, and the global economy in general. In the United States since 1980, more than 95 percent of the wealth has been created by entrepreneurs.[8] It's been estimated that since World War II, small entrepreneurial firms have generated 95 percent of all radical innovation in the United States. An estimated 20 million Americans are running a young business or actively trying to start one.[9]

The self-employed love the entrepreneurial process, and they report the highest levels of pride, satisfaction, and income. Importantly, entrepreneurship is not about the privileged descendents of the Rockefellers and the Vanderbilts—it provides opportunity and upward mobility for anyone who performs well.[10]

Myths about Entrepreneurship   Simply put, entrepreneurs generate new ideas and turn them into business ventures.[11] But entrepreneurship is not simple, and it is frequently misunderstood. Read Table 7.1 to start you thinking about the myths and realities of this important career option.

Here is another myth, not in the table: Being an entrepreneur is great because you can "get rich quick" and enjoy a lot of leisure time while your employees run the company. But the reality is much more difficult. As described by Tom Peters,[12] "You must have incredible mental toughness to survive—let alone thrive." During the start-up period, you are likely to have a lot of bad days. It's exhausting. Even if you don't have employees, you should expect "communications breakdowns" and other "people problems" with agents, vendors, distributors, family, subcontractors, lenders,

TABLE 7.1   Some Myths about Entrepreneurs

Myth 1—Anyone can start a business.

Reality—The easiest part is starting up. What is hardest is surviving, sustaining, and building a venture so its founders can realize a harvest.

Myth 2—Entrepreneurs are gamblers.

Reality—Successful entrepreneurs take very careful, calculated risks. They do not deliberately seek to take more risk or to take unnecessary risk, nor do they shy away from unavoidable risk.

Myth 3—Entrepreneurs want the whole show to themselves.

Reality—It is extremely difficult to grow a higher potential venture by working single-handedly. Higher potential entrepreneurs build a team, an organization, and a company.

Myth 4—Entrepreneurs are their own bosses and completely independent.

Reality—Entrepreneurs are far from independent. They have to serve many masters and constituencies, including partners, investors, customers, suppliers, creditors, employees, families, and social and community obligations.

Myth 5—Entrepreneurs work longer and harder than managers in big companies.

Reality—There is no such evidence. Some work more, some less.

Myth 6—Entrepreneurs experience a great deal of stress and pay a high price.

Reality—No doubt about it: Being an entrepreneur is stressful and demanding. But entrepreneurs find their jobs very satisfying. They are healthier, and are much less likely to retire than those who work for others.

Myth 7—Entrepreneurs are motivated solely by the quest for the almighty dollar.

Reality—Entrepreneurs seeking high potential ventures are more driven by building enterprises and realizing long-term capital gains than by instant gratification through high salaries and perks. Feeling in control of their own destinies, and realizing their vision and dreams, are also powerful motivators. Money is viewed as a tool and a way of keeping score.

Myth 8—Entrepreneurs seek power and control over others.

Reality—Successful entrepreneurs are driven by the quest for responsibility, achievement, and results, rather than for power for its own sake. By virtue of their accomplishments, they may be powerful and influential, but these are more the by-products of the entrepreneurial process than a driving force behind it.

Myth 9—If an entrepreneur is talented, success will happen in a year or two.

Reality—An old maxim among venture capitalists says it all: The lemons ripen in two and a half years, but the pearls take seven or eight. Rarely is a new business established solidly in less than three or four years.

Myth 10—Any entrepreneur with a good idea can raise venture capital.

Reality—Of the ventures of entrepreneurs with good ideas who seek out venture capital, only 1 to 3 out of 100 are funded.

Myth 11—If an entrepreneur has enough start-up capital, he or she can't miss.

Reality—Too much money at the outset often leads to lack of discipline and impulsive spending that usually result in serious problems and failure.

Myth 12—Entrepreneurs are lone wolves and cannot work with others.

Reality—The most successful entrepreneurs are leaders who build great teams and effective relationships working with peers, directors, investors, key customers, key suppliers, and the like.

Myth 13—Unless you attained 600+ on your SATs or GMATs you'll never be a successful entrepreneur.

Reality—Entrepreneurial IQ is a unique combination of creativity, motivation, integrity, leadership, team building, analytical ability and ability to deal with ambiguity and adversity.

SOURCE: Adapted from J. A. Timmons and S. Spinelli, *New Venture Creation*, 6th ed., pp. 67–68 Copyright © 2004. Reproduced with permission of the authors.

entrepreneur

An individual who establishes a new organization without the benefit of corporate sponsorship.

intrapreneurs

New venture creators working inside big companies.

whomever. Dan Bricklin, the founder of VisiCalc, advises that the most important thing to remember is this: "You are not your business. On those darkest days when things aren't going so well—and trust me, you will have them—try to remember that your company's failures don't make you an awful person. Likewise, your company's successes don't make you a genius or superhuman"[13] (p. 58)

As you read this chapter, you will learn about two primary sources of new venture creation: independent entrepreneurship and intrapreneurship. **Entrepreneurs** are individuals who establish a new organization without the benefit of corporate support. **Intrapreneurs** are new venture creators working inside big companies; they are corporate entrepreneurs.[14]

Entrepreneurship

Table 7.2 lists some extraordinary entrepreneurs. The companies they founded are famously successful—and all of the founders started in their 20s. A recent young founder of a highly successful business is Jason Olim, who was a student at Brown University when he got his entrepreneurial idea: selling hard-to-find CDs. He didn't have the money to open a real store, so he opened one on the Internet. He and his parents invested $20,000 for a Macintosh, a Unix server, software licenses, engineers to help with programming problems, graphic designers, print advertisements, and a public relations contract. In its first month, his company brought in $387 in revenues. A modest start before things got rolling for CDnow.[15]

Exceptional though these stories may be, the real, more complete story of entrepreneurship is about people you've never heard of unless they're from your hometown. They have built companies, thrived personally, created jobs, and made positive contributions to their communities through their businesses. Or they're just starting out. Laima Tazmin is president of LAVT LLC, a Web consulting company. She's expanding into customizing computers and developing community-based online businesses. Her assistant pores over Internet boards looking for new markets. Laima had 10 clients by age 15—and starts college in 2007. "I want to direct my own life. Entrepreneurship is about planning for the future, and I want to develop my creativity and have freedom. I want to grow myself" (p. 134).[16]

TABLE 7.2

Mega-Entrepreneurs Who Started in Their 20s

Entrepreneurial Company	Founder(s)
Microsoft	Bill Gates and Paul Allen
Netscape	Marc Andressen
Dell Computers	Michael Dell
Gateway 2000	Ted Waitt
McCaw Cellular	Craig McCaw
Apple Computers	Steve Jobs and Steve Wozniak
Digital Equipment Corporation	Ken and Stan Olsen
Federal Express	Fred Smith
Genentech	Robert Swanson
Polaroid	Edward Land
Nike	Phil Knight
Lotus Development Corporation	Mitch Kapor
Ipix.com	Kevin McCurdy

SOURCE: J. Timmons and S. Spinette, *New Venture Creation*, 6th ed. (New York: McGraw-Hill/Irwin, 2004), p. 7.

Why Become an Entrepreneur?

Bill Gross has started dozens of companies.[17] When he was a boy, he devised home-made electronic games and sold candy for a profit to friends. In college, he built and sold plans for a solar heating device, started a stereo equipment company, and sold a software product to Lotus. In 1991, he sold his educational software company for almost $100 million. And in 1996, he started Idealab!, which hatched dozens of start-ups on the Internet.

> **Question:** Is entrepreneurship getting more difficult?
> *Judy Wicks:* (White Dog Enterprises) "It's harder to compete with corporations on price, but consumers increasingly appreciate the high quality, creativity, and authenticity entrepreneurs can offer."[18]

Why do Bill Gross and other entrepreneurs do what they do? Entrepreneurs start their own firms because of the challenge, the profit potential, and the enormous satisfaction they hope lies ahead.[19] People starting their own businesses are seeking a better quality of life than they might have at big companies. They seek independence and a feeling of being part of the action. They feel tremendous satisfaction in building something from nothing, seeing it succeed, and watching the market embrace their ideas and products.

In addition, people start their own companies when they see their progress blocked at big corporations. When people are laid off, they often try to start businesses of their own. And when employed people believe there is no promotion in their future, or are frustrated by bureaucracy or other features of corporate life, they may quit and become entrepreneurs.

Even the legendary Clive Davis was fired from Arista Records, the company he founded in 1974. Davis responded not by retiring but by launching J Records. Within 18 months, Davis filled J's roster with some of the best new artists in the industry, including Alicia Keys. Her debut album *Songs in A Minor* quickly sold 6 million copies and was nominated for four American Music Awards.[20]

Arista Records fired Clive Davis, who turned around and launched J Records by signing a number of new young artists, including Alicia Keys.

Immigrants also may find conventional paths to economic success closed to them and turn to entrepreneurship.[21] For example, the Cuban community in Miami has produced many successful entrepreneurs, as has the Vietnamese community throughout the United States.

Immigrant Entrepreneurs in . . . Maine

When people think of the most diverse states in the United States, or of hotbeds of entrepreneurship, Maine doesn't usually come to mind. But it offers real opportunity for immigrant entrepreneurs. StartSmart is a program run by a Portland not-for-profit economic development agency called Coastal Enterprises. It provides loans, training, and consulting to refugees and immigrants.

Juan Gonzalez wanted to start a specialty grocery store in Portland, but being from the Dominican Republic, he feared "nobody trusts you. It's very difficult to get a loan." His store, La Bodega Latina, was StartSmart's very first business to open—and it now has a popular restaurant as well.

Emile Bizimungu fled the Congo when war erupted, arriving in the United States in 2000. His Revival Carpentry designs, constructs, and repairs furniture, supplies bat, owl, and

bird houses to Mill Stores (a New England chain of furniture stores), and is building a Web site to sell his beds, bookshelves, and cabinets.

Bogumila Pawlaczyck fled Poland because of political oppression in 1986. As a nurse's assistant in Maine, she drove six hours to Manhattan, once a month, to buy Polish bread ("America is a free country and you can do everything you want here. What was missing was Polish bread.") She now owns Bogusha's Deli and Restaurant.

Osman Hersi was a surgeon in Somalia, but he fled in 1991. He speaks four languages (Somali, English, Arabic, and Russian) and now has a successful translation service. Clients include hospitals, doctors' offices, and courtooms.

Other successful business owners in the region fled Africa, Russia, eastern Europe, Vietnam, and Cambodia during the reign of the Khmer Rouge.

Formerly in the Portland area, employment choices for immigrants and refugees were limited to seafood plants or chicken processing. But StartSmart now has helped more than 70 businesses get started, and trained or coached hundreds of refugees and immigrants from dozens of nations.

SOURCE: D. J. Dent, "Coming to America," *Inc.*, November 2004, pp. 100–107.

What Does It Take to Succeed?

What can we learn from the people who start their own companies and succeed? Let's start by considering Russell Simmons and Andra Rush. Russell Simmons is the entrepreneur who brought us Def Jam, Phat Farm, an energy drink, a debit card, and other products. "All of the businesses that I've gotten in, I got in because I didn't know I couldn't." A friend says, "That's key for entrepreneurs—you need to realize it doesn't stop with one idea."[22]

Andra Rush started her trucking company by buying one new and two used trucks with her savings and some help from her parents. She couldn't afford a cell phone, so she forwarded calls to her grandmother's house. When she was home, she made the company seem bigger by using phony voices and pretending to transfer customers to different lines. She learned how to repair the trucks herself. She accepted every job, no matter what, and really started impressing customers. Today Rush Trucking has 1,000 trucks making 1,400 shipments daily.[23]

What do Russell Simmons, Andra Rush, and other successful entrepreneurs have in common? We can begin answering this question with Figure 7.1. Successful entrepreneurs are innovators, and also have good knowledge and skills in management, business, and networking.[25] Inventors may be

 Question: What is the one piece of advice you would give to someone starting out?[24]

Andra Rush (Rush Trucking): "Don't let anyone steal your dream."

Tom Stemberg (Staples): "Do all your planning with the customer firmly in mind."

Rhonda Kallman (New Century Brewing): "Choose a business you love. You may have to live with it forever."

James Goodnight (SAS): "Avoid the mistakes of the dot-bomb era. Those folks mistook an exit strategy for a business plan. Go into it with the idea of running a business for the long term."

FIGURE 7.1
Who Is the Entrepreneur?

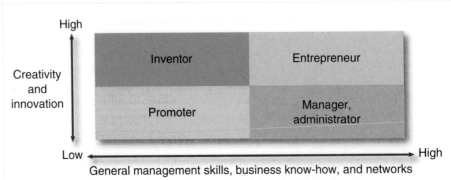

SOURCE: J. Timmons and S. Spivelli, *New Venture Creation*, 6th ed. (New York: McGraw-Hill/Irwin, 2004), p. 65.

highly creative but often lack the skills to turn their ideas into a successful business. Manager-administrators may be great at ensuring efficient operations but aren't necessarily innovators. Promoters have a different set of marketing and selling skills—useful for entrepreneurs, but those skills can be hired whereas innovativeness and business management skills remain the essential combination for successful entrepreneurs.

What Business Should You Start?

You need a good idea, and you need to find or create the right opportunity.

The Idea   Many entrepreneurs and observers say that in contemplating your business, you must start with a great idea. A great product, a viable market, and good timing are essential ingredients in any recipe for success. For example, Tom Stemberg knew that the growing number of small businesses in the 1980s had no one dedicated to sell them needed supplies. Lots of potential customers, in need of service, had no one focused on serving them. He saw his opportunity and attacked it, opening his first Staples in 1986. Staples sales now reach over $11 billion annually.

Many great organizations have been built based on a different kind of idea: the founder's desire to build a great organization, rather than to offer a particular product.[26] The Amos brothers moved from the Florida panhandle to Columbus, Georgia, in 1955 because they knew that Columbus was the largest city in the Southeast without its own insurance company.[27] They knew nothing about insurance. But they wanted to create an organization and saw an opportunity. The brothers were classic strivers who could have started just about any kind of company, and probably would have succeeded, even if it wasn't insurance. The company, by the way, was American Family Life Assurance Co.—now better known as AFLAC.

Similar examples abound. Bill Hewlett and David Packard decided to start a company, and then figured out what to make. J. Willard Marriott knew he wanted to be in business for himself but didn't have a product in mind until he opened an A&W root beer stand. Masaru Ibuka had no specific product idea when he founded Sony in 1945. Sony's first product attempt, a rice cooker, didn't work, and its first product (a tape recorder) didn't sell. The company stayed alive by making and selling crude heating pads.

Many now-great companies had early failures. But the founders persisted; they believed in themselves, and in their dreams of building great organizations. Whereas conventional logic is to see the company as a vehicle for your products, this perspective sees the products as a vehicle for your company. Be prepared to kill or revise an idea, but never give up on your company—this has been a prescription for success for many great entrepreneurs and business leaders.

Think about Sony, Disney, Hewlett-Packard, Procter & Gamble, IBM, and Wal-Mart: Their founders' greatest achievements—their greatest ideas—are their organizations.[28]

After a job in corporate design turned out to be unsatisfying, Jennifer Velande found a creative outlet for herself—designing handbags. Soon, with the help of her friend Robin Newberry, Jennifer turned this "hobby" into a unique business concept. 1154 Lill now gives customers the opportunity to design their own original handbags.

The Opportunity   Entrepreneurs spot, create, and exploit opportunities in a variety of ways.[29] Entrepreneurial companies can explore domains that big companies avoid and introduce goods or services that capture the market because they are simpler, cheaper, more accessible, or more convenient. For example, Jaye Muller spotted an opportunity while touring Europe on a concert tour. The German rock musician missed some important faxes while moving from hotel to hotel. He put his recording career on hold (he still records periodically) and hired some programmers to develop software that can compress faxes into files and send them to Internet e-mail addresses. The company took off.[30]

Java, the Internet programming language, was designed to be safe, and was widely perceived to be safe when it first appeared. But Shlomo Touboul saw it differently. When he talked about his plans to market a Java security product, people scoffed. Alone, he worked to develop a product that would protect companies from hostile programs embedded in the Java code. When some Princeton scientists subsequently found ways in which hackers could exploit Java's weak spots, Touboul was ready and far ahead of any would-be competitors.[31]

To spot opportunities, think carefully about events and trends as they unfold. Consider, for example:[32]

- *Technological discoveries.* Start-ups in biotechnology, microcomputers, and nanotechnology followed. Amber Ratcliffe, Krassen Dimnitrov, Dwayne Dunaway, and Perry Fell founded Nanostring, based on a technology called the molecular bar code, which can digitally count millions of gene transcripts and yield perfectly accurate results in less than half an hour.[33] They are the ultimate specialists, building their company on an idea developed from deep personal expertise.
- *Demographic changes.* All kinds of health care organizations have sprung up to serve an aging population. MinuteClinic places health care kiosks in Target and Cub Food stores—you can get diagnosis and treatment for common conditions including strep throat and ear and sinus infections, as well as blood pressure and cholesterol screenings.[34] It's convenient (15 minutes or less) and cheap ($41 or an insurance copay).
- *Lifestyle and taste changes.* Start-ups have capitalized on new clothing and music trends, desire for fast food, and growing interest in sports.
- *Economic dislocations,* such as booms or failures. The oil boycott spawned new drilling firms. The steel industry collapse was accompanied by minimill start-ups.
- *Calamities* such as wars and natural disasters. Mt. St. Helen's eruption spawned new tourism companies. Andrew Higgins's business expanded from wooden boats for the Louisiana swamps to the design and mass production of the landing vehicles that carried infantry ashore in World War II. Visionics really took off in late 2001; the company makes biometrics software that matches video images to a database of facial measurements in order to identify anyone from runaways to shoplifters to terrorists.[35]
- *Government initiatives and rule changes.* Environmental legislation created opportunities for new consulting firms and cleanup machinery firms. Deregulation spawned new airlines and trucking companies. The top-secret National Security Agency recently announced the opening of a business center dedicated to helping start-up homeland security companies.[36] The message: NSA needs help from the private sector.

franchising

An entrepreneurial alliance between a franchisor (an innovator who has created at least one successful store and wants to grow) and a franchisee (a partner who manages a new store of the same type in a new location.)

Franchises   One important type of opportunity is the franchise. You may know intuitively what franchising is. Or, at least, you can name some prominent franchises: McDonald's, Jiffy Lube, the Body Shop, Dunkin' Donuts, add your favorites here. **Franchising** is an entrepreneurial alliance between two organizations, the franchisor and the franchisee.[37] The franchisor is the innovator who has created at least one successful store and seeks partners to operate the same concept in other local markets. For the franchisee, the opportunity is wealth creation via a proven (but not failureproof) business concept, with the added advantage of the franchisor's expertise. For the franchisor, the opportunity is wealth creation through growth. The partnership is manifest in a trademark or brand, and together the partners' mission is to maintain and build the brand.

If you are contemplating a franchise, consider its market presence (local, regional, or national), market share and profit margins, national programs for marketing and purchasing, the nature of the business, including required training and degree of field support, terms of the license agreement (for example, 20 years with automatic renewal vs. less than 10 years or no renewal), capital required, and franchise fees and royalties.[38] Although some people think that success with a franchise is a no-brainer, there's a lot to consider. Plenty of useful sources are available for learning more, including http://www.bisonl.com/; http://www.franchise-chat.com/; and http://www.businessfranchisedirectory.com/.

The Next Frontiers   The next frontiers for entrepreneurship—where do they lie? Throughout history, aspiring entrepreneurs have asked this question. Currently, Gary Hoover says, "Four of the industries that I think look most exciting over the next 20 to 30 years are financial services, health services and health-related things, travel, and education. And all four are really based on the continuing aging of the baby boomers. I keep a list of new business ideas. Right now there are about 70 ideas on it"[39] (p. 72). Add biotech, eastern Europe, nanotechnology, oceanography . . . make your own list.

One fascinating opportunity for entrepreneurs is outer space.[40] Historically, the space market was driven by the government, and was dominated by big players like Boeing and Lockheed Martin. But now, with huge demand for satellite launches and potential profits skyrocketing, smaller entrepreneurs are entering the field. For example, *Inc.* magazine chose Burt Rutan in 2005 as its entrepreneur of the year.[41] Rutan started the first private business to launch people into space. Ultimately Rutan's goals are (1) to make space flight routinely available to people and (2) to make a big profit. But the new space race has begun, and competition will be fierce from companies including SpaceX, Space Dev, and Zero Gravity Corp.

Other new ventures in space include satellites for automobile navigation, tracking trucking fleets, and monitoring flow rates and leaks in pipelines; testing designer drugs in the near-zero-gravity environment; and using remote sensing to monitor global warming, spot fish concentrations, and detect crop stress for precision farming. And think about this: Instead of the government funding, managing, and implementing Mars travel, one possibility is that it will offer a $20 billion prize to the winner of a private-company race to the red planet.[42]

A flight into space might become as easy as booking a flight to Florida thanks to Burt Rutan. His idea to launch people into space may have opened the door for an entire space tourism industry.

The obstacles for entrepreneurs in the space industry are huge. Space start-ups require hundreds of millions of dollars to ramp up, they are highly unlikely to be profitable, most investors steer clear of them, and most will fail miserably. But the entrepreneurs believe that the challenges are merely financial rather than technical, and that whoever pulls it off will change the world.[43]

Homeland security is another newly burgeoning industry.[44] Before September 11, 2001, the U.S. government was spending about $10 billion on homeland security. Subsequent years averaged $40 billion. But more than 70 percent of the country's crucial infrastructure (oil wells, computer systems, chemical plants) is in private hands. The private sector is expected to spend over $6 billion on security in 2005 and grow up to 10 percent per year. A vast number of companies in a wide range of industries are attempting to benefit—baggage screening, smallpox vaccines, capturing arrival and departure information on travelers, explosives detection systems, sensors for airborne pathogens.

The Internet   A seemingly limitless "new frontier" is the Internet. Shoba Purushothaman knew that TV newsrooms needed information quickly, and that they could get high-quality video footage in only two ways: by tape or by satellite, neither of which is quick or easy.[45] So she distributed footage on the Internet. She offered it free to the press but charged corporate and government clients about $100,000 each to send their news footage to the broadcast media. She was a bit early with her idea: She started in the midst of the dot-com crash, and many newsrooms didn't have the necessary broadband access. But the times have caught up with her idea, and the business is flourishing now.

Clearly, the Internet has radically changed our ability not only to communicate and play but also to conduct commerce. The business opportunities it offered seemed limitless in the mid-to-late 1990s, until the Internet bubble burst and the dot-com era turned into the dot-bomb era. But the fact remains that the Internet is a business frontier that continues to expand. The lesson of the crash is not to avoid Internet commerce but to remember the importance of sound business models and practices. During the heady days of the Internet rush, many entrepreneurs and investors thought revenues and profits were unimportant and all that mattered was to attract visitors to their Web sites ("capture eyeballs"). But it is clear once again that you need to watch costs carefully, and you want to break even and achieve profitability as soon as possible—cash is king.[46]

At least five successful business models have proven successful in the e-commerce market: transaction fee, advertising support, intermediary, affiliate, and subscription models.[47] In the **transaction fee model,** companies charge a fee for goods or services. Amazon.com and online travel agents are prime examples. In the **advertising support model,** advertisers pay the site operator to gain access to the demographic group that visits the operator's site. MSN and Yahoo! have a lot of visitors and host a lot of ads; top online advertisers include Amazon.com, eBaby, Orbitz, Columbia House, and ClassMates.com.

The **intermediary model** has eBay as the premier example, bringing buyers and sellers together and charging a commission for each sale. With the **affiliate model,** sites pay commissions to other sites to drive business to their own sites. And when Web sites charge a monthly or annual fee for site visits, they're using the **subscription model.** Newspapers and magazines are good examples.

What about businesses whose primary focus is not e-commerce? Start-ups and established small companies can create attractive Web sites that add to their professionalism, give them access to more customers, and bring them closer to suppliers, investors, and service providers. Traditional companies can move much more quickly than in the past and save money on activities including customer service/support, technical support, data retrieval, public relations, investor relations, selling, requests for product literature, and purchasing.

Side Streets   There also exists a useful role for trial and error. Some entrepreneurs start their enterprises and then let the market decide whether it likes their ideas or not. This is risky, of course, and should be done only if you can afford the risks. But even if the original idea doesn't work, you may be able to capitalize on the **side street effect.**[48] As you head down a road, you come to unknown places, and unexpected opportunities begin to appear.

And, while you are looking, *prepare* so you are able to act quickly and effectively on the opportunity when it does present itself.

What Does It Take, Personally?

Many people assume there exists an "entrepreneurial personality."[49] There is no single personality type that predicts entrepreneurial success, but you are more likely to succeed as an entrepreneur if you exhibit certain characteristics. The following characteristics contribute to entrepreneurs' success.[50]

1. *Commitment and determination:* Successful entrepreneurs are decisive, tenacious, disciplined, willing to sacrifice, and able to immerse themselves totally in their

---

transaction fee model

Charging fees for goods and services.

advertising support model

Charging fees to advertise on a site.

intermediary model

Charging fees to bring buyers and sellers together.

affiliate model

Charging fees to direct site visitors to other companies' sites.

subscription model

Charging fees for site visits.

---

side street effect

As you head down a road, unexpected opportunities begin to appear.

enterprises. "You have to have a true passion for what you're doing,"[51] says Dan Bricklin, the founder of VisiCalc.

2. *Leadership:* They are self-starters, team builders, superior learners, and teachers. Communicating a vision for the future of the company—an essential component of leadership that you'll learn more about in Chapter 12—has a direct impact on venture growth.[52]

3. *Opportunity obsession:* They have an intimate knowledge of customers' needs, are market driven, and are obsessed with value creation and enhancement.

4. *Tolerance of risk, ambiguity, and uncertainty:* They are calculated risk takers and risk managers, tolerant of stress, and able to resolve problems.

5. *Creativity, self-reliance, and ability to adapt:* They are open-minded, restless with the status quo, able to learn quickly, highly adaptable, creative, skilled at conceptualizing, and attentive to details.

6. *Motivation to excel:* They have a clear results orientation, set high but realistic goals, have a strong drive to achieve, know their own weaknesses and strengths, and focus on what can be done rather than on the reasons things can't be done.

Trial and error can give rise to the side street effect where, like Dorothy in *The Wizard of Oz*, you head down a road and the unexpected begins to appear.

A couple of final quotes on what it takes to be a successful entrepreneur: In the 19th century, Cyrus McCormick said, "Indomitable perseverance in a business properly understood always ensures ultimate success." And in the 21st century, Sir Harold Evans, author of *They Made America*, says that "the principle quality of an innovator lies less in the cortex than in the epidermis."[53] In other words, innovators always are criticized, often in the harshest terms, so thick skins are essential.

Connections: AMAZON.COM

Barnes & Noble launched a Web site in 1997 to rival Amazon. A prominent analyst pronounced Jeff Bezos's company "Amazon.toast." Later, when the tech bubble burst, Amazon stock plummeted from $100 to $6. While some now ridiculed Bezos's Amazon.com vision as naive and impractical, Bezos remained optimistic. He always views challenges as opportunities.

Bezos puts a premium on good people. "I'd rather interview 50 people and not hire anyone than hire the wrong person." He experiments with new ideas when possible. Bezos started the concept of "two-pizza teams" to innovate and test new features: if you can't feed them on two pizzas, the team is too large. But he also gambles on ideas that are too big and long-term to allow experiments. For example, he lets Web surfers search the full texts of hundreds of thousands of books.

When Amazon started publishing customers' reviews of products—some of which were negative—people told Bezos that he didn't understand his business. You can't sell things with negative reviews on your Web site, the critics said. Bezos's point was that they will sell more if they help people make good decisions.

Bezos steals ideas from competitors, unabashedly—for example, he started holding auctions like eBay and started A9, a search engine (à la Google). Those copycats haven't fared as well as the original ideas, but Bezos is tenacious, persistent, and adaptive.

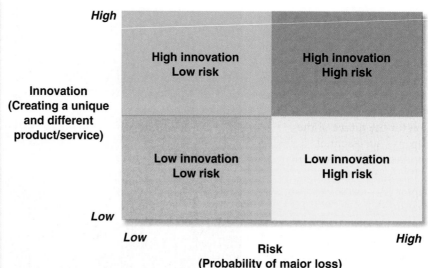

FIGURE 7.2
Entrepreneurial Strategy
Matrix

Making Good Choices   Success is a function not only of personal characteristics, but also of making good choices about the business you start. Figure 7.2 presents a model for conceptualizing entrepreneurial ventures and making the best possible choices. It depicts ventures along two dimensions: innovation and risk. The new venture may involve high or low levels of *innovation*, or the creation of something new and different. It can also be characterized by low or high *risk*. Risk refers primarily to the probability of major financial loss. But it also is more than that; it is psychological risk as perceived by the entrepreneur, including risk to reputation and ego.[54]

The upper-left quadrant, high innovation/low risk, depicts ventures of truly novel ideas with little risk. As examples, the inventors of Lego building blocks and Velcro fasteners could build their products by hand, at little expense. Even some early electronics companies started in this situation. A pioneering product idea from Procter & Gamble might fit here if there are no current competitors and because, for a company of that size, the financial risks of new product investments can seem relatively small.

 You can find a lot of useful hyperlinks at the MIT Enterprise Forum (http://web.mit.edu/entrforum/www/).

In the upper-right quadrant, high innovation/high risk, novel product ideas are accompanied by high risk because the financial investments are high and the competition is great. A new drug or a new automobile would likely fall in this category.

Most small business ventures are in the low innovation/high risk cell (lower right). These are fairly conventional entries in well-established fields. New restaurants, retail shops, and commercial outfits involve high investment for the small business entrepreneur and face direct competition from other similar businesses. Finally, the low innovation/low risk category includes ventures that require minimal investment and/or face minimal competition for strong market demand. Examples are some service businesses having low start-up costs and those involving entry into small towns if there is no competitor and demand is adequate.

How is this matrix useful? It helps entrepreneurs think about their ventures and decide whether they suit their particular objectives. It also helps identify effective and ineffective strategies. You might find one cell more appealing than others. The lower-left cell is likely to have relatively low payoffs but to provide more security. The higher risk/return trade-offs are in other cells, especially the upper right. So you might place your new venture idea in the appropriate cell and determine whether that cell is the one in which you would prefer to operate. If it is, the venture is one that perhaps should be pursued, pending fuller analysis. If it is not, you can reject the idea or take action to move it toward a different cell.

The matrix also can help entrepreneurs remember a useful point: Successful companies do not always require a cutting-edge technology or an exciting new product. Even companies offering the most mundane products—the type that might reside in the lower-left cell—can gain competitive advantage by doing basic things differently from and better than competitors, as the following examples show.

Ordinary Industries, Extraordinary Success

Every year, *Inc.* magazine publishes its list of the 500 fastest-growing companies in the United States. Many companies on recent lists have been in glamour industries. But many are not. Noodles & Co. is a fast-expanding chain built on the premise that everybody loves noodles. Packaging Resources supplies food companies with plastic bags and wrapping. Insulair sells a triple-layer insulated cup to Krispy Kreme and thousands of convenience stores. L.E.M. Products sells meat grinders.

These are not hot-growth industries. But they are industries. And knowing a lot about business and management, in any industry, provides a competitive edge. So your company can grow, even if your industry is not growing.

Larry Harmon of Demar Plumbing, Heating & Air-Conditioning knows that people are not too enamored of plumbing—but would love a plumber who provides world-class customer service. He gives same-day service, trains his staff in customer relations, and makes his customers want to come back to him year after year.

Jim Jeffrey of Pest Control Technologies creates a professional image with white trucks and white uniforms for his employees, while his competitors work in blue jeans and T-shirts. Bear Barnes, a house painter, offers two-year guarantees and maintains a detailed database to target his market, track bids, and record every shade of paint on every house his company services.

A few years ago, *Forbes's* list of the richest people in America included pig farmer Wendell Murphy, who started with one pen and turned it into the biggest hog-farming business in the country. He became a billionaire. He applied computer technology to manage climate control and manure removal, and to help make decisions surrounding when the sows should mate, how to breed, how to feed, and when to sell.

In other words, many highly successful entrepreneurs are in ordinary, dull (on the face of it) businesses, but they manage them extraordinarily well compared to their competitors.

SOURCES: A. Murphy, "Masters of the Ordinary," *Inc.*, October, 1993, pp. 70–71; M. Conlin, "Riding the Revolution," *Forbes*, October 13, 1997, pp. 99–104; "The *Inc.* 500 List 2001," *Inc.*, October 30, 2001, pp. 87–117; "The *Inc.* 500 List 2004," *Inc.*, Fall 2004, pp. 45–155.

Success and Failure

Success or failure lies ahead for entrepreneurs starting their own companies, as well as for those starting new businesses within bigger corporations. Entrepreneurs succeed or fail in private, public, and not-for-profit sectors; in nations of all stages of development; and in all nations, regardless of their politics.[55]

Estimated failure rates for start-ups vary. Most indicate that failure is more the rule than the exception. The failure rate is high for certain businesses like restaurants, and lower for successful franchises. Start-ups have at least two major liabilities: newness and smallness.[56] New companies are relatively unknown and need to learn how to be better than established competitors at something that customers value. Regarding smallness, the odds of surviving improve if the venture reaches a critical mass of at least 10 or 20 people, has revenues of $2 million or $3 million, and is pursuing opportunities with growth potential.[57]

Acquiring venture capital is not essential to the success of most start-up businesses; in fact, it is rare. Only 18 percent of companies in a recent *Inc.* 500 list had raised venture capital, and only 3 percent had it at startup.[58] But overall, less than 1 percent of companies that receive venture capital go bankrupt—not only because of the initial funding, but also through the expertise and additional funds provided later by the investors.[59]

To understand further the factors that influence success and failure, we'll consider risk, the economic environment, various management-related hazards, and initial public stock offerings (IPOs).

Risk   You learned about risk in Chapter 3. It's a given: Starting a new business is risky. Fred Smith of FedEx addresses the importance of realism and of anticipating the risks ahead: "A fundamental problem with most entrepreneurs is they are unrealistic about the market demands or unrealistic about the costs of meeting those demands. It sounds simple, but it's not. It's hard once you're in battle not to be lured by emotion and optimism. You can be the greatest innovator, but if you are not steely-eyed about that you have a problem. Being entrepreneurial doesn't mean jump off a ledge and figure out how to make a parachute on the way down."[60]

Inc. **magazine included actor, director, and producer Mel Gibson in its list of 2004's top entrepreneurs for financing the movie *The Passion of the Christ*. If you had it, would you risk $25 million of your own money on an idea that few believed in?**

Jeff Bezos says this about risk: "People think entrepreneurs are risk-lovers. Really what you find is successful entrepreneurs hate risk" (p. 150).[61] But, says Bezos, they deploy their resources systematically, first eliminating the largest risk, then the second, and so on.

It's hard to imagine a crazier risk than starting a new airline, but David Neeleman saw it as a customer service business, not the aviation industry—and figured out how to deliver great service at low cost.[62] For Neeleman, succeeding despite the risks is "all about being very close to your people." He tries to make sure that the people of JetBlue understand that even though the first few years were immensely successful because of the low costs and great service, their success attracted attention from competitors. As Neeleman describes it, they're now in a dog-fight and they can't get too cocky.[63]

The Role of the Economic Environment   Money is a critical resource for all new businesses. Increases in the money supply and the supply of bank loans, real economic growth, and improved stock market performance lead to both improved prospects and increased sources of capital. In turn, the prospects and the capital increase the rate of business formation. Under favorable conditions, many aspiring entrepreneurs find early success. But economic cycles dictate that favorable conditions will change. To succeed, entrepreneurs must have the foresight and talent to survive when the environment becomes more hostile.

For example, the Internet was called a gold rush and a land grab, with space claimed by whoever got there first.[64] Profits seemed irrelevant. But traditional bricks-and-mortar companies got serious about the Net and started making the transition to bricks-and-clicks companies that took on the upstarts. In 2000, the money for dot-coms dried up, performance pressures rose, and many high-flying dot-coms failed. Strategy, cost, and profit—more generally, good management—became paramount once again.

Although good economic times may make it easier to start a company and to survive, bad times can offer an opportunity to expand.[65] Steve Jobs loves to innovate and introduce new products while competitors cut back. When Howard Schulz had 17 Starbucks stores, he aggressively expanded when the economy started slowing; when the economy came back, his brand was everywhere. It's also easier to recruit talent during down times.

Business Incubators   The need to provide a nurturing environment for fledgling enterprises has led to the creation of business incubators. **Business incubators,** often located in industrial parks or abandoned factories, are protected environments for new, small businesses. Incubators offer benefits such as low rents and shared costs. Shared staff costs, such as for receptionists and secretaries, avoid the expense of a full-time employee but still provide convenient access to services. The staff manager is usually an experienced businessperson or consultant who advises the new business owners. Incubators often are associated with universities, which provide technical and business services for the new companies.

> **business incubators**
> Protected environments for new, small businesses.

The most amazing region for start-ups is Silicon Valley, a 50-mile-long corridor in California where 20 percent of the world's 100 biggest electronics and software companies were born.[66] Local universities (particularly Stanford), great talent, pioneering successes, and then venture capitalists and a complete tech infrastructure characterized by a risk-taking culture have made the Valley an exceptional environment for incubating ideas and companies. Other regions, including Boston, North Carolina's Research Triangle Park, and Austin, have tried to emulate the Valley's success. None has matched it, although Seattle is coming on strong.[67]

Common Management Challenges

As an entrepreneur, you are likely to face several common challenges that you should understand before you face them, and then manage effectively when the time comes. We next discuss several such challenges.

You might not enjoy it   One person who quit a large company to start his own small one stated, "As an executive in a large company, the issues are strategic. You're implementing programs that affect thousands of people. In a small business . . . you worry about inventory every day, because you may not be in business next week if you have negative cash flow." His most unpleasant surprise: "How much you have to sell. You're always out selling . . . I didn't want to be a salesman. I wanted to be an executive."[68]

Survival is difficult   As *Fortune* put it, "Misjudgments are punished ruthlessly. When competition gets tougher, small businesses feel it first. 'In small business there are no small mistakes'—it's a phrase that comes up time and again when you talk to the owners."[69] But, says *Fortune*, most are proud of this description of entrepreneurial hazards.

Under Armor, marketer of performance clothing, provides a good example of how tough competition can get even tougher. Under Armor was No. 2 in 2003's *Inc.* 500. But now, with its success, it's on big companies' radar screens. An industry journalist says, "Under Armor is smack in the middle of Nike's sights. The first time, they [Nike] might miss, but they never miss the second time"[70] (p. 101).

Failure can be devastating. "I remember thinking I was very comfortable financially, and the crystal chandelier hit the floor . . . I remember trying to find enough money to buy groceries. You never forget that."[71] So stated David Pomije of Funco, a chain that he started by buying and reselling used and new Nintendo and Sega videogames. Fortunately, he turned the corner; he now operates more than 100 stores.

Growth Creates New Challenges   Just one in three *Inc.* 500 companies keeps growing fast enough to make the list two years running. The reason: They are facing bigger challenges, competing with bigger firms, stretching the founders' capacities, and probably burning cash. Consultant Doug Tatum calls this phase of a company's growth "No Man's Land."[72] It's a difficult transition.

> **Question:** What sacrifices have you had to make en route to success?
> **Rhonda Kallman:** "I have sacrificed boredom."[73]

In the beginning, the start-up mentality tends to be "we try harder."[74] Entrepreneurs work long hours at low pay, deliver great service, get good word-of-mouth, and their business grows. At first, it's "high performance, cheap labor." But with growth comes the need to pay higher wages to hire more people who are less dedicated than the founders. Then it's time to raise prices or accept lower profits. The founder's talents may not spread to everyone else. You need a unique value proposition that will work as well with 100 employees, because hard work or individual instincts alone no longer will get the job done. Complicating matters is the continuing growth in customers' needs and expectations.[75]

Growth seems like a consuming goal for most entrepreneurs. But some company founders reach the size where they're happy and don't want to grow any further. Reaching a golden mean is possible.[76] Entrepreneurs can stabilize their companies' size, but they still have to keep a high-value business model and provide great customer service. Robert Catlin of Signature Mortgage says, "People tell me all the time, 'You're crazy, pal. You're missing a golden opportunity.' I say, 'Hey, I'm doing just fine. I have control. I have freedom. I have family time and travel time. What more can I ask for?' "[77]

It's Hard to Delegate   As the business grows, entrepreneurs often hesitate to delegate to other people work that they are used to doing. Leadership deteriorates into micromanagement, in which managers monitor too strictly, to the minutest detail. For example, during the Internet craze many company founders with great technical knowledge but little experience became "instant experts" in every phase of business, including branding and advertising.[78] Turns out, they didn't know as much as they thought, and their companies crashed.

Misuse of Funds   Many unsuccessful entrepreneurs blame their failure on inadequate financial resources. Yet failure due to a lack of financial resources doesn't necessarily indicate a real lack of money; it could mean a failure to properly use the money available. A lot of start-up capital is wasted—on expensive locations, great furniture, fancy stationery.[79] Entrepreneurs who fail to use their resources wisely usually make one of two mistakes: They apply financial resources to the wrong uses, or they maintain inadequate control over their resources.

For example, Respond.com spent more than $200,000 on a promotional party (free sushi, circus performers, $50 bottles of champagne as party favors). Pixelon.com spent $10 million for a megaconcert at the MGM Grand Hotel in Las Vegas featuring the Who, Sugar Ray, Tony Bennett, and Natalie Cole. The managers of Boo.com (and their entourages) stayed at the best hotels, set up six luxurious offices in six different cities, and operated with few financial controls. They also tried to build the Mercedes Benz of Web sites, but it wasn't long before they declared bankruptcy.[80]

You probably will pay close attention to costs at the beginning, but success sometimes brings neglect. This story was reversed for a lot of Internet start-up founders who sometimes thought that the future was so bright, they could spend freely without regard to cost and profits. Many went under, learning a lesson the hard way.

Poor Controls   Entrepreneurs, in part because they are very busy, often fail to use formal control systems. One common entrepreneurial malady is an aversion to record keeping. Expenses mount, but records do not keep pace. Pricing decisions are based on intuition without adequate reference to costs. As a result, the company earns inadequate margins to support growth.

The rate at which Internet start-ups burned through cash was stunning; their managers seemed to have a disdain for traditional financial controls.[81] True, implementing their business models was expensive, but the seemingly limitless availability of funds and the lack of pressure for profits created a lack of discipline.

Even in high-growth companies, great numbers can mask brewing problems. Blinded by the light of growing sales, many entrepreneurs fail to maintain vigilance over other aspects of the business. In the absence of controls, the business veers out of control. As the chief financial officer of FTP Software put it, "Success is the worst thing that can happen to a company. You start believing your own headlines. You get sloppy."[82]

Michael Dell observes that people who are too intent on spending money "forget what the fundamentals are in terms of customers and creating value and being disciplined with capital, and you get pretty horrific results."[83] So don't get overconfident; keep asking critical questions. Is our success based on just one big customer? Is our product just a fad that can fade away? Can other companies easily enter our domain and hurt our business? Are we losing a technology lead? Do we really understand the numbers, know where they come from, and have any hidden causes for concern?

Without financial control, entrepreneurs can find their companies in bankruptcy.

Mortality   One long-term measure of an entrepreneur's success is the fate of the venture after the founder's death. The organization can outlive the entrepreneur under one of two conditions: (1) if the company has gone public, or (2) if the entrepreneur has planned an orderly succession, usually to a family member. Both conditions are relatively rare.

Entrepreneurs often fail to seek public capital if equity capital is scarce and expensive or because they want to maintain control. An entrepreneur who is funded with public equity risks losing the business if stockholders are not satisfied. To avoid this risk, the entrepreneur maintains private control over the business. But founding entrepreneurs often fail to plan for succession. When death occurs, estate tax problems and/or the lack of a skilled replacement for the founder can lead to business failure.

> **Question:** What do you want to be known for?[84]
> **Lance Morgan (Ho-Chick, Inc.):** "Always doing what I committed to even if I later didn't want to."
> **Stella Ogiale (Chesterfield Health Services):** "Being a business artist who made a difference for the good of all."

Management guru Peter Drucker offers the following advice to help family-managed businesses survive and prosper.[85] Family members working in the business must be at least as capable and hard-working as other employees; at least one key position should be filled by a nonfamily member; and someone outside the family and the business should help plan succession. Family members who are mediocre performers are resented by others; outsiders can be more objective and contribute expertise the family might not have; and issues of management succession are often the most difficult of all, causing serious conflict and possible breakup of the firm.

Going Public   Sometimes companies reach a point at which the owners want to "go public." **Initial public stock offerings (IPOs)** offer a way to raise capital through federally registered and underwritten sales of shares in the company.[86] You need lawyers and accountants who know current regulations. The reasons for going public include raising more capital, reducing debt or improving the balance sheet and enhancing net worth, pursuing otherwise unaffordable opportunities, and improving credibility with customers and other stakeholders—"you're in the big leagues now." Disadvantages include the expense, time, and effort involved; the tendency to become more interested in the stock price and capital gains than in running the company properly; and the creation of a long-term relationship with an investment banking firm that won't necessarily always be a good one.[87]

initial public offering (IPO)

Sale to the public, for the first time, of federally registered and underwritten shares of stock in the company.

Many entrepreneurs prefer to avoid going public, feeling they'll lose control if they do. States Yvon Chouinard of Patagonia: "There's a certain formula in business where you grow the thing and go public. I don't think it has to be that way. Being a closely held company means being able to take risks and try new things—the creative part of business. If I were owned by a bunch of retired teachers, I wouldn't be able to do what I do; I'd have to be solely concerned with the bottom line. For us to go public would be suicide."[88]

James Goodnight of SAS (a $1.3 billion company) says, "The fact that we're private means that we can make long-range decisions. We don't have to be worried about quarterly profits or about pleasing Wall Street. We just please our employees and our customers."[89]

Executing IPOs and other approaches to acquiring capital is complex, legalistic, and beyond the scope of this chapter. Sources for more information include *The Ernst & Young Guide to Raising Capital*, National Venture Capital Association (www.nvca.org), Venture-One (http://www.ventureone.com), and Venturewire http://www.venturewire.com)

Increasing Your Chances of Success

We discuss here the importance of good planning and nonfinancial resources.

Planning So you think you have identified a business opportunity. And you have the personal potential to make it a success. Now what? Should you act on your idea? Where should you begin?

The Business Plan Your excitement and intuition may convince you that you are on to something. But they might not convince anyone else. You will need more thorough planning and analysis. This will help convince other people to get on board, and help you avoid costly mistakes.

The first formal planning step is to do an opportunity analysis. An **opportunity analysis** includes a description of the product or service, an assessment of the opportunity, an assessment of the entrepreneur (you), a specification of activities and resources needed to translate your idea into a viable business, and your source(s) of capital.[90] Table 7.3 shows the questions you should answer in an opportunity analysis.

The opportunity analysis, or opportunity assessment plan, focuses on the opportunity, not the entire venture. It provides the basis for making a decision on whether to act. Then, the **business plan** describes all the elements involved in starting the new venture.[91] The business plan describes the venture and its market, strategies, and future directions. It often has functional plans for marketing, finance, manufacturing, and human resources.

Table 7.4 shows an outline for a typical business plan. The business plan (1) helps determine the viability of your enterprise; (2) guides you as you plan and organize; and

opportunity analysis

A description of the product or service, an assessment of the opportunity, an assessment of the entrepreneur, specification of activities and resources needed to translate your idea into a viable business, and your source(s) of capital.

business plan

A formal planning step that focuses on the entire venture and describes all the elements involved in starting it.

TABLE 7.3
Opportunity Analysis

What market need does my idea fill?
What personal observations have I experienced or recorded with regard to that market need?
What social condition underlies this market need?
What market research data can be marshaled to describe this market need?
What patents might be available to fulfill this need?
What competition exists in this market? How would I describe the behavior of this competition?
What does the international market look like?
What does the international competition look like?
Where is the money to be made in this activity?

SOURCE: R. Hisrich and M. Peters, *Entrepreneurship: Starting, Developing, and Managing a New Enterprise*, p. 41 Copyright © 1998 by The McGraw-Hill Companies. Reproduced with permission of The McGraw-Hill Companies.

TABLE 7.4   Outline of a Business Plan

I. EXECUTIVE SUMMARY
   A. Description of the Business Concept and the Business.
   B. The Opportunity and Strategy.
   C. The Target Market and Projections.
   D. The Competitive Advantages.
   E. The Economics, Profitability, and Harvest Potential.
   F. The Team.
   G. The Offering.

II. THE INDUSTRY AND THE COMPANY AND ITS PRODUCT(S) OR SERVICE(S)
   A. The Industry.
   B. The Company and the Concept.
   C. The Product(s) or Service(s).
   D. Entry and Growth Strategy.

III. MARKET RESEARCH AND ANALYSIS
   A. Customers.
   B. Market Size and Trends.
   C. Competition and Competitive Edges.
   D. Estimated Market Share and Sales.
   E. Ongoing Market Evaluation.

IV. THE ECONOMICS OF THE BUSINESS
   A. Gross and Operating Margins.
   B. Profit Potential and Durability.
   C. Fixed, Variable, and Semivariable Costs.
   D. Months to Breakeven.
   E. Months to Reach Positive Cash Flow.

V. MARKETING PLAN
   A. Overall Marketing Strategy.
   B. Pricing.
   C. Sales Tactics.
   D. Service and Warranty Policies.
   E. Advertising and Promotion.
   F. Distribution.

VI. DESIGN AND DEVELOPMENT PLANS
   A. Development Status and Tasks.
   B. Difficulties and Risks.
   C. Product Improvement and New Products.
   D. Costs.
   E. Proprietary Issues.

VII. MANUFACTURING AND OPERATIONS PLAN
   A. Operating Cycle.
   B. Geographical Location.
   C. Facilities and Improvements.
   D. Strategy and Plans.
   E. Regulatory and Legal Issues.

VIII. MANAGEMENT TEAM
   A. Organization.
   B. Key Management Personnel.
   C. Management Compensation and Ownership.
   D. Other Investors.
   E. Employment and Other Agreements and Stock Option and Bonus Plans.
   F. Board of Directors.
   G. Other Shareholders, Rights, and Restrictions.
   H. Supporting Professional Advisors and Services.

IX. OVERALL SCHEDULE

X. CRITICAL RISKS, PROBLEMS, AND ASSUMPTIONS

XI. THE FINANCIAL PLAN
   A. Actual Income Statements and Balance Sheets.
   B. Pro Forma Income Statements.
   C. Pro Forma Balance Sheets.
   D. Pro Forma Cash Flow Analysis.
   E. Breakeven Chart and Calculation.
   F. Cost Control.
   G. Highlights.

XII. PROPOSED COMPANY OFFERING
   A. Desired Financing.
   B. Offering.
   C. Capitalization.
   D. Use of Funds.
   E. Investor's Return.

XIII. APPENDICES

SOURCE: J. A. Timmons, *New Venture Creation*, 5th ed., p. 374. Copyright © 1999 by Jeffry A. Timmons. Reproduced with permission of the author.

(3) helps you obtain financing. It is read by potential investors, suppliers, customers, and others. Get help in writing up a sound plan!

Key Planning Elements   Most business plans devote so much attention to financial projections that they neglect other important information—information that matters greatly to astute investors. In fact, financial projections tend to be overly optimistic. Investors know this and discount the figures.[92] In addition to the numbers, the best plans convey—and make certain that the entrepreneurs have carefully thought through—five key factors: the people, the opportunity, the competition, the context, and risk and reward.[93]

The *people* should be energetic and have skills and expertise directly relevant to the venture. For many astute investors, the people are the most important variable, more important even than the idea. Venture capital firms often receive 2,000 business plans per year; many believe that ideas are a dime a dozen and what counts is the ability to execute. Arthur Rock, a legendary venture capitalist who helped start Intel, Teledyne, and Apple, stated, "I invest in people, not ideas. If you can find good people, if they're wrong about the product, they'll make a switch."[94]

The *opportunity* should provide a competitive advantage that can be defended. Customers are the focus here: Who is the customer? How does the customer make decisions? How will the product be priced? How will the venture reach all customer segments? How much does it cost to acquire and support a customer, and to produce and deliver the product? How easy or difficult is it to retain a customer?

It is also essential to fully consider the *competition*. The plan must identify current competitors and their strengths and weaknesses, predict how they will respond to the new venture, indicate how the new venture will respond to the competitors' responses, identify future potential competitors, and consider how to collaborate with actual or potential competitors. Thus, for example, Andrew Busey created ichat, which became the leading provider of software for chat rooms. But then America Online and Microsoft started competing directly with the young entrepreneur. Busey responded by collaborating with IBM; the Lotus division bundled ichat's software with its Internet-ready version of Notes.[95]

The environmental *context* should be a favorable one from regulatory and economic perspectives. Such factors as tax policies, rules about raising capital, interest rates, inflation, and exchange rates will affect the viability of the new venture. The context can make it easier or harder to get backing and to succeed. Importantly, the plan should make clear that you know that the context inevitably will change, how the changes will affect the business, and how you will deal with the changes.

The *risk* must be understood and addressed as fully as possible. The future is always uncertain, and the elements described in the plan will change over time. Although you cannot predict the future, you must contemplate head-on the possibilities of key people leaving, interest rates changing, a key customer leaving, or a powerful competitor responding ferociously. Then describe what you will do to prevent, avoid, or cope with such possibilities. You should also speak to the end of the process: how to get money out of the business eventually. Will you go public? Will you sell or liquidate? What are the various possibilities for investors to realize their ultimate gains?[96]

Selling the Plan   Your goal is to get investors to support the plan. The elements of a great plan, as just described, are essential. It's also important whom you decide to try to convince to back your plan.

Many entrepreneurs want passive investors who will give them money and let them do what they want. Doctors and dentists generally fit this image. Professional venture capitalists do not, as they demand more control and more of the returns. But when a business goes wrong—and chances are, it will—nonprofessional investors are less helpful, and less likely to advance more (needed) money. Sophisticated investors have seen sinking ships before and know how to help. They are more likely to solve problems, provide more money, and also navigate financial and legal waters such as going public.[97]

View the plan as a way for you to figure out how to reduce risk and maximize reward, and to convince others that you understand the entire new venture process. Don't put together a plan built on naïveté or overconfidence or one that cleverly hides major flaws. You might not fool others, and you certainly would be fooling yourself.[98]

Nonfinancial Resources   Also crucial to the success of a new business are nonfinancial resources, including legitimacy in the minds of the public and how other people can help.

Legitimacy   An important resource for the new venture is **legitimacy**—people's judgment of a company's acceptance, appropriateness, and desirability.[99] When the market confers legitimacy, it helps overcome the "liability of newness" that creates a high percentage of new venture failure.[100] Legitimacy helps a firm acquire other resources such as top managers, good employees, financial resources, and government support. A business is legitimate if its goals and methods are consistent with societal values. You can generate legitimacy by visibly conforming to rules and expectations created by governments, credentialing associations, and professional organizations; by visibly endorsing widely held values; and by visibly practicing widely held beliefs.[101]

Networks   The entrepreneur is aided greatly by having a strong *network* of people. *Social capital*—being part of a social network, and having a good reputation—helps entrepreneurs gain access to useful information, gain trust and cooperation from others, recruit employees, form successful business alliances, receive funding from venture capitalists, and become more successful.[102] Social capital provides a lasting source of competitive advantage.[103] Networks are so important that Regis McKenna of the McKenna Group says that how well connected your investors are is more important than how much they invest.[104] Similarly, Andrea Williams of E'Offering Group advises that you sign up with investors with the best track records, because they can open doors for you.[105]

Top Management Teams   The top management team is another crucial resource. The board of directors improves the company's image, develops longer-term plans for expansion, supports day-to-day activities, and develops a network of information sources. Michael Dell, founder of Dell Computer at age 19, knows the importance of surrounding himself with talent. He hired managers who were far more experienced than he, and prominent and powerful board members. By 1995, at age 30, Michael Dell held the longest tenure of any chief executive in the industry.[106]

> **legitimacy**
>
> People's judgment of a company's acceptance, appropriateness, and desirability, generally stemming from company goals and methods that are consistent with societal values.

Advantages of Collaboration

The stereotype of the lone entrepreneur making it against all odds doesn't tell the complete story. You can't do it alone; you need a good reputation and a social network that allows you to mobilize help from talented collaborators.

Advisory Boards   Anita Brattina thought after two or three years of running her own marketing firm she would have lots of cash, no debt, and time to enjoy her independence.[107] Eight years later, she still worked 50 to 60 hours a week and was not making much money. So she got an advisory board. Board members taught her how to do cash-flow analysis, suggested some strategic changes, and encouraged her to cultivate relationships with a banker, an accountant, and an attorney. In addition, they helped her interview salespeople, develop a long-term marketing strategy, and reorganize operations. They also vetoed a number of her ideas. Sales went up, after one year of listening to the board and implementing its ideas.

Partners   Often, two people go into business together as partners. Partners can help one another access capital, spread the workload, share the risk, and share expertise.

Despite the potential advantages of finding a compatible partner, partnerships are not always marriages made in heaven. "Mark" talked three of his friends into joining him in starting his own telecommunications company because he didn't want to try it alone. He learned quickly that while he wanted to put money into growing the business, his three partners wanted the company to pay for their cars and meetings in the Bahamas. The company collapsed. "I never thought a business relationship could overpower friendship, but this one did. Where money's involved, people change."

Question: What was the hardest lesson you've learned?[108]
Tom Stemberg: "Take every competitor seriously."
Judy Wicks: "Put every agreement in writing."

To be successful, partners need to acknowledge one another's talents, let each other do what they do best, communicate honestly, and listen to one another. And they must learn to trust each other by making and keeping agreements. If they must break an agreement, it is crucial that they give early notice and clean up after their mistakes.

Family partnerships don't necessarily work out well, but when they do they are something special. In 2004 Ceja Vineyards shipped nearly 6,000 cases of wine to restaurants and retailers around the world. The unique part of this story is that the vineyard isn't owned by a local Silicon Valley millionaire—the Cejas and their six children used to be migrant grapepickers.[109] One of the sons, Armando, went to U. C. Davis to study winemaking. Three members of the family saved their money, sold their homes, and bought 15 acres of land in 1981. Seven years later came their first grape harvest. In 2001, Ceja was named best new winery by San Francisco's Wine Appreciation Guild.

Intrapreneurship

Recall from chapter 3 that creativity spawns good new ideas, but innovation requires actually implementing those ideas so they become realities. If you work in an organization and have a good idea, you must convince other people to get on board.

Today's large corporations are more than passive bystanders in the entrepreneurial explosion. Even established companies try to find and pursue new and profitable ideas—and they need entrepreneurs to do so. If you work in a company, and are considering launching a new business venture, Table 7.5 can help you decide whether the new idea is worth pursuing.

Building Support for Your Idea

A manager who has a new idea to capitalize on a market opportunity will need to get others in the organization to buy in or sign on. In other words, you need to build a network of allies who support and will help implement the idea.

If you need to build support for a project idea, the first step involves *clearing the investment* with your immediate boss or bosses.[110] At this stage, you explain the idea and seek approval to look for wider support.

Higher executives often want evidence that the project is backed by your peers before committing to it. This involves *making cheerleaders*—people who will support the manager before formal approval from higher levels. Managers at General Electric refer to this strategy as "loading the gun"—lining up ammunition in support of your idea.

Next, *horse trading* begins. You can offer promises of payoffs from the project in return for support, time, money, and other resources that peers and others contribute.

Finally, you should *get the blessing* of relevant higher-level officials. This usually involves a formal presentation. You will need to guarantee the project's technical and political feasibility. Higher management's endorsement of the project and promises of resources help convert potential supporters into an enthusiastic team. At this point, you can go back to your boss and make specific plans for going ahead with the project.

Along the way, expect resistance and frustration—and use passion and persistence, as well as business logic, to persuade others to get on board.[111]

TABLE 7.5   Checklist for Choosing Ideas

Fit with Your Skills and Expertise
Do you believe in the product or service?
Does the need it fits mean something to you personally?
Do you like and understand the potential customers?
Do you have experience in this type of business?
Do the basic success factors of this business fit your skills?
Are the tasks of the enterprise ones you could enjoy doing yourself?
Are the people the enterprise will employ ones you will enjoy working with and supervising?
Has the idea begun to take over your imagination and spare time?

Fit with the Market
Is there a real customer need?
Can you get a price that gives you good margins?
Would customers believe in the product coming from your company?
Does the product or service you propose produce a clearly perceivable customer benefit that is significantly better than that offered by competing ways to satisfy the same basic need?
Is there a cost-effective way to get the message and the product to the customers?

Fit with the Company
Is there a reason to believe your company could be very good at the business?
Does it fit the company culture?
Does it look profitable?
Will it lead to larger markets and growth?

What to Do When Your Idea Is Rejected
As an intrapreneur, you will frequently find that your idea has been rejected. There are a few things you can do.
1. Give up and select a new idea.
2. Listen carefully, understand what is wrong, improve your idea and your presentation, and try again.
3. Find someone else to whom you can present your idea by considering:
a. Who will benefit most if it works? Can they be a sponsor?
b. Who are potential customers? Will they demand the product?
c. How can you get to the people who really care about intrapreneurial ideas?

SOURCE: G. Pinchot III, *Intrapreneuring,* Copyright © 1985 by John Wiley & Sons, Inc. Reprinted by permission of the author, www.pinchot.com.

Building Intrapreneurship

Building an entrepreneurial culture is the heart of the corporate strategy at Acordia, a successful insurance company.[112] Acordia's success in fostering a culture in which intrapreneurs flourish came from making an intentional decision to foster entrepreneurial thinking and behavior, creating new-venture teams, and changing the compensation system so that it encourages, supports, and rewards creative and innovative behaviors. In other words, building intrapreneurship derives from careful and deliberate strategy.

Two common approaches used to stimulate intrapreneurial activity are skunkworks and bootlegging. **Skunkworks** are project teams designated to produce a new product.

skunkworks

A project team designated to produce a new, innovative product.

A team is formed with a specific goal within a specified time frame. A respected person is chosen to be manager of the skunkworks. In this approach to corporate innovation, risk takers are not punished for taking risks and failing—their former jobs are held for them. The risk takers also have the opportunity to earn large rewards.

bootlegging refers to informal efforts—as opposed to official job assignments—in which employees work to create new products and processes of their own choosing and initiative. Informal can mean secretive, such as when a bootlegger believes the company or the boss will frown on those activities. But companies should tolerate some bootlegging, and some even encourage it. To a limited extent, they allow people freedom to pursue pet projects without asking what they are or monitoring progress, figuring bootlegging will lead to some lost time but also to learning and to some profitable innovations.

Merck, desiring entrepreneurial thinking and behavior in R&D, explicitly rejects budgets for planning and control. New product teams don't *get* a budget. They must persuade people to join the team and commit *their* resources. This creates a survival-of-the-fittest process, mirroring the competition in the real world.[113]

At Amgen, R&D chief Roger Perlmutter combines the "command-and-control" approach to drug discovery used by the big, traditional, older pharmaceutical companies with the free-form creativity of small biotech firms. He wanted to "introduce into Amgen the rigor and discipline that characterizes the very best R&D organizations without destroying this entrepreneurial spirit."[114] At both Amgen and Acordia, intrapreneurship derives from deliberate strategic thinking and execution.

Management Challenges

Organizations that encourage intrapreneurship face an obvious risk: The effort can fail. One author noted, "There is considerable history of internal venture development by large firms, and it does not encourage optimism."[115] However, this risk can be managed. In fact, failing to foster intrapreneurship may represent a subtler but greater risk than encouraging it. The organization that resists intrapreneurial initiative may lose its ability to adapt when conditions dictate change.

The most dangerous risk in intrapreneurship is the risk of overreliance on a single project. Many companies fail while awaiting the completion of one large, innovative project.[116] The successful intrapreneurial organization avoids overcommitment to a single project and relies on its entrepreneurial spirit to produce at least one winner from among several projects.

Organizations also court failure when they spread their intrapreneurial efforts over too many projects.[117] If there are many intrapreneurial projects, each effort may be too small in scale. Managers will consider the projects unattractive because of their small size. Or those recruited to manage the projects may have difficulty building power and status within the organization.

The hazards in intrapreneurship, then, are related to scale. One large project is a threat, as are too many underfunded projects. But a carefully managed approach to this strategically important process will upgrade an organization's chances for long-term survival and success.

Entrepreneurial Orientation

Earlier in this chapter, we described the characteristics of individual entrepreneurs. Now we do the same for companies: We describe how companies that are highly entrepreneurial differ from those that are not.

Entrepreneurial orientation is the tendency of an organization to engage in activities designed to identify and capitalize successfully on opportunities to launch new ventures by entering new or established markets with new or existing goods or services.[118] Entrepreneurial orientation is determined by five tendencies: to allow independent action, innovate, take risks, be proactive, and be competitively aggressive.

---

bootlegging

Informal work on projects, other than those officially assigned, of employees' own choosing and initiative.

---

entrepreneurial orientation

The tendency of an organization to identify and capitalize successfully on opportunities to launch new ventures by entering new or established markets with new or existing goods or services.

To *allow independent action* is to grant to individuals and teams the freedom to exercise their creativity, champion promising ideas, and carry them through to completion. *Innovativeness* requires the firm to support new ideas, experimentation, and creative processes that can lead to new products or processes; it requires a willingness to depart from existing practices and venture beyond the status quo. *Risk taking* comes from a willingness to commit significant resources, and perhaps borrow heavily, to venture into the unknown. The tendency to take risks can be assessed by considering whether people are bold or cautious, whether they require high levels of certainty before taking or allowing action, and whether they tend to follow tried-and-true paths.

To be *proactive* is to act in anticipation of future problems and opportunities. A proactive firm changes the competitive landscape; other firms merely react. Proactive firms are forward thinking and fast to act, and are leaders rather than followers. Similarly, some individuals are more likely to be proactive, to shape and create their own environments, than others who more passively cope with the situations in which they find themselves.[119] Proactive firms encourage and allow individuals and teams to *be* proactive.

Finally, *competitive aggressiveness* is the tendency of the firm to challenge competitors directly and intensely in order to achieve entry or improve its position. In other words, it is a competitive tendency to outperform one's rivals in the marketplace. This might take the form of striking fast to beat competitors to the punch, to tackle them head-to-head, and to analyze and target competitors' weaknesses. Michael Dell provides a good example: He can state clearly how each of his competitors is vulnerable and poised to fail.[120]

What makes a firm "entrepreneurial" is its engagement in an effective combination of independent action, innovativeness, risk taking, proactiveness, and competitive aggressiveness.[121] The relationship between these factors and the performance of the firm is a complicated one that depends on many things. Nevertheless, you can imagine how the opposite profile—too many constraints on action, business as usual, extreme caution, passivity, and a lack of competitive fire—will undermine entrepreneurial activities. And without entrepreneurship, how would firms survive and thrive in a constantly changing competitive environment?

Thus, management can create environments that foster more entrepreneurship. If your bosses are not doing this, consider trying some entrepreneurial experiments on your own.[122] Seek out others with an entrepreneurial bent. What can you learn from them, and what can you teach others? Sometimes it takes individuals and teams of experimenters to show the possibilities to those at the top. Ask yourself, and ask others: Between the bureaucrats and the entrepreneurs, who is having a more positive impact? And who is having more fun?

EPILOGUE

JEFF BEZOS AND AMAZON.COM

From the beginning, Amazon.com had operated at a sizable loss, plugging away for years before finally turning its first (miniscule) profit in 2003. But Bezos's conviction never seemed to waiver. By 2004, sales, earnings, share price, market value, and profits were all high.

How will Amazon change as times goes on? It's hard to predict. Bezos loves radical innovation. He also admits he doesn't know what lies ahead. "We have this weirdness in our business. The raw ingredients that make our business—things like CPU processing power, bandwidth, and disk space—get twice as cheap every 12 to 18 months. Disk space is 30 times cheaper than it was five years ago. Thirty times cheaper! So the real question becomes, What can you do with 30 times as much disk space, 20 times as much computing power, and 30 times as much bandwidth? All right, how are you going to make customers happy with that? It turns out that these are not easy questions to answer."

Jeff Bezos is always thinking, wondering, and innovating. Bezos has a grand vision of changing the world over decades, but he also obsesses over finding small, immediate improvements in efficiency. He also is highly customer-centric—the ultimate entrepreneur.

KEY TERMS

Advertising support model, p. 232

Affiliate model, p. 232

Bootlegging, p. 246

Business incubators, p. 237

Business plan, p. 240

Entrepreneur, p. 226

Entrepreneurial orientation, p. 246

Entrepreneurial venture, p. 224

Entrepreneurship, p. 224

Franchising p. 230

Initial public offerings (IPOs), p. 248

Intermediary model, p. 232

Intrapreneurs, p. 226

Legitimacy, p. 243

Opportunity analysis, p. 240

Side street effect, p. 232

Skunkworks, p. 245

Small business, p. 224

Subscription model, p. 232

Transaction fee model, p. 232

SUMMARY OF LEARNING OBJECTIVES

Now that you have studied Chapter 7, you should know:

Why people become entrepreneurs, and what it takes, personally.

People become entrepreneurs because of the profit potential, the challenge, the satisfaction they anticipate (and often receive) from participating in the process, and sometimes because they are blocked from more traditional avenues of career advancement. Successful entrepreneurs are innovators, and they have good knowledge and skills in management, business, and networking. While there is no single "entrepreneurial personality," certain characteristics are helpful: commitment and determination; leadership skills; opportunity obsession; tolerance of risk, ambiguity, and uncertainty; creativity, self-reliance, and the ability to adapt; and motivation to excel.

How to assess opportunities to start new companies.

You should always be on the lookout for new ideas, monitoring the current business environment and other indicators of opportunity. Franchising offers an interesting opportunity, and the potential of the Internet is just beginning to be tapped (after entrepreneurs learned some tough lessons from the dot-bomb era). Trial and error and preparation play important roles. Assessing the business concept on the basis of how innovative and risky it is, combined with your personal interests and tendencies, will also help you make good choices. Ideas should be carefully assessed via opportunity analysis and a thorough business plan.

Common causes of success and failure.

New ventures are inherently risky. The economic environment plays an important role in the success or failure of the business, and the entrepreneur should anticipate and be prepared to adapt in the face of changing economic conditions. How you handle a variety of common management challenges also can mean the difference between success and failure, as can the effectiveness of your planning and your ability to mobilize nonfinancial resources.

Common management challenges.

When new businesses fail, the causes often can be traced to some common challenges that entrepreneurs face and must manage

well. You might not enjoy the entrepreneurial process. Survival—including getting started and fending off competitors—is difficult. Growth creates new challenges, including reluctance to delegate work to others. Funds are put to improper use, and financial controls may be inadequate. Many entrepreneurs fail to plan well for succession. When needing or wanting new funds, initial public offerings provide an option, but they represent an important and difficult decision that must be considered carefully.

How to increase your chances of success, including good business planning.

The business plan helps you think through your idea thoroughly and determine its viability. It also convinces (or fails to convince) others to participate. The plan describes the venture and its future, provides financial projections, and includes plans for marketing, manufacturing, and other business functions. The plan should describe the people involved in the venture, a full assessment of the opportunity (including customers and competitors), the environmental context (including regulatory and economic issues), and the risk (including future risks and how you intend to deal with them). Successful entrepreneurs also understand how to develop social capital, which enhances legitimacy and helps develop a network of others including customers, talented people, partners, and boards.

How to foster intrapreneurship and an entrepreneurial orientation in large companies.

Intrapreneurs work within established companies to develop new goods or services that allow the corporation to reap the benefits of innovation. To facilitate intrapraneurship, organizations use skunkworks—special project teams designated to develop a new product—and allow bootlegging—informal efforts beyond formal job assignments in which employees pursue their own pet projects. Organizations should select projects carefully, have an ongoing portfolio of projects, and fund them appropriately. Ultimately, a true entrepreneurial orientation in a company comes from encouraging independent action, innovativeness, risk taking, proactive behavior, and competitive aggressiveness.

DISCUSSION QUESTIONS

1. On a 1 to 10 scale, what is your level of personal interest in becoming an entrepreneur? Why did you rate yourself as you did?

2. How would you assess your capability of being a successful entrepreneur? What are your strengths and weaknesses? How would you increase your capability?

3. Most entrepreneurs learn the most important skills they need after age 21. How does this affect your outlook and plans?

4. Identify and discuss new ventures that fit each of the four cells in the entrepreneurial strategy matrix.

5. Brainstorm a list of ideas for new business ventures. From where did the ideas come? Which ones are most and least viable, and why?

6. Identify some businesses that recently opened in your area. What are their chances of survival, and why? How would you advise the owners or managers of those businesses to ensure their success?

7. Assume you are writing a story about what it's really like to be an entrepreneur. To whom would you talk, and what questions would you ask?

8. Conduct interviews with two entrepreneurs, asking whatever questions most interest you. Share your findings with the class. How do the interviews differ from one another, and what do they have in common?

9. Read Table 7.1. "Some Myths about Entrepreneurs." Which myths did you believe? Do you still? Why or why not? Interview two entrepreneurs by asking each myth as a true-or-false question. Then ask them to elaborate on their answers. What did they say? What do you conclude?

10. With your classmates, form small teams of skunkworks. Your charge is to identify an innovation that you think would benefit your school, college, or university, and to outline an action plan for bringing your idea to reality.

11. Identify a business that recently folded. What were the causes of the failure? What could have been done differently to prevent the failure?

12. Does franchising appeal to you? What franchises would most and least interest you, and why?

13. The chapter specified some of the changes in the external environment that can provide business opportunity (technological discoveries, lifestyle and taste changes, and so on). Identify some important recent changes or current trends in the external environment and the business opportunities they might offer.

14. Choose an Internet company with which you are familiar and brainstorm ideas for how its services or approach to business can be improved. How about starting a new Internet company altogether—what would be some possibilities?

CONCLUDING CASE

Teachers Turning to Entrepreneurship

Greg, Chris and Nancy are midcareer high school teachers in the Pittsburgh area. They love their jobs, are very dedicated, and plan to stay on until they are eligible for retirement in about fifteen or twenty years. The three teachers and friends have met on several occasions to brainstorm ideas for an outside business venture. With kids approaching college age and a pessimistic outlook towards their state retirement pensions, the three want to test their entrepreneurial skills and start a second career.

Their financial goals are to supplement their annual incomes by $25,000 to $50,000 each per year for college tuition purposes and to build an equity base of about $1,000,000 each for retirement. Following several meetings, some consultation with friends and advisors and some local market research, the new partners are currently thinking about the business of commercial real estate investment, more specifically, multi-unit rental properties.

Pittsburgh and surrounding communities are currently experiencing, and are projected to sustain, above average growth in both jobs and housing. There is a current shortage of both rental units and single-family housing in the area. Interest rates are low at this time and are therefore attractive for borrowing and investing purposes. Greg has learned that local banks will finance commercial properties for up to 25 years at 6 percent interest. In addition, those banks will provide loans for up to 80 percent of assessed property values. Greg, Chris and Nancy have discussed purchasing enough buildings to meet their financial goals. The landlords each have about $150,000 in cash to invest. Each also has about $300,000 in equity borrowing against their homes.

On a more global basis, the new partners continue to have doubts as to whether they have selected the right business. They each have a strong desire, plenty of extra time and a significant amount of money to invest, but each has very little experience in business. They consider themselves to be moderate risk takers. They have thought about bringing in another partner or two to increase capital and to somewhat reduce or at least spread their risk.

QUESTIONS

1. Prepare an outline for a business plan for the teachers.

2. Describe how the three teachers should work together to ensure that they are an effective team and that they remain friends.

3. Identify the key members of a network of partners, allies, and other people that would best ensure success.

4. How should the team proceed to do research on their idea and decide whether to continue or try something else?

EXPERIENTIAL EXERCISES

7.1 Take an Entrepreneur to Dinner

OBJECTIVES

1. To get to know what an entrepreneur does, how she or he got started, and what it took to succeed.

2. To interview a particular entrepreneur in depth about his or her career and experiences.

3. To acquire a feeling for whether you might find an entrepreneurial career rewarding.

INSTRUCTIONS

1. Identify an entrepreneur in your area you would like to interview.

2. Contact the person you have selected and make an appointment. Be sure to explain why you want the appointment and to give a realistic estimate of how much time you will need.

3. Identify specific questions you would like to have answered and the general areas about which you would like information. (See the following suggested interview questions, although there probably won't be time for all of them.) Using a combi-nation of open-ended questions, such as general questions about how the entrepreneur got started, what happened next, and so forth, and closed-ended questions, such as specific questions about what his or her goals were, if he or she had to find partners, and so forth, will help keep the interview fo-cused yet allow for unexpected comments and insights.

4. Conduct the interview. If *both* you and the person you are in-terviewing are comfortable, using a small tape recorder dur-ing the interview can be of great help to you later. Remember, too, that you most likely will learn more if you are an "inter-ested listener."

5. Evaluate what you have learned. Write down the information you have gathered in some form that will be helpful to you later on. Be as specific as you can. Jotting down direct quotes is more effective than statements such as "highly motivated individual." And be sure to make a note of what you did not find out.

6. Write a thank-you note. This is more than a courtesy; it will also help the entrepreneur remember you favorably should you want to follow up on the interview.

Suggested Interview

QUESTIONS FOR GATHERING INFORMATION

- *Would you tell me about yourself before you started your first venture?*

  Were your parents, relatives, or close friends entrepreneurial? How so?

  Did you have any other role models?

  What was your education/military experience? In hindsight, was it helpful? In what specific ways?

  What was your previous work experience? Was it helpful? What particular "chunks of experience" were especially valuable or relevant?

  In particular, did you have any sales or marketing experience? How important was this in starting your company?

- *How did you start your venture?*

  How did you spot the opportunity? How did it surface?

  What were your goals? What were your lifestyle or other personal requirements? How did you fit these factors together?

  How did you evaluate the opportunity in terms of the critical elements for success? The competition? The market?

  Did you find or have partners? What kind of planning did you do? What kind of financing did you have?

  Did you have a start-up business plan of any kind? Please tell me about it.

  How much time did it take from conception to the first day of business? How many hours a day did you spend working on it?

  How much capital did it take? How long did it take to reach a positive cash flow and break-even sales volume? If you did not have enough money at the time, what were some ways in which you "bootstrapped" the venture (i.e., bartering, borrowing, and the like)? Tell me about the pressures and crises during that early survival period.

  What outside help did you get? Did you have experienced advisors? Lawyers? Accountants? Tax experts? Patent experts? How did you develop these networks and how long did it take?

  What was your family situation at the time?

  What did you perceive to be your own strengths? Weaknesses?

  What did you perceive to be the strengths of your venture? Weaknesses?

  What was your most triumphant moment? Your worst moment?

  Did you want to have partners or do it solo? Why?

- *Once you got going then:*

  What were the most difficult gaps to fill and problems to solve as you began to grow rapidly?

  When you looked for key people as partners, advisors, or managers, were there any personal attributes or attitudes you were especially seeking because you knew they would fit with you and were important to success? How did you find them?

Are there any attributes among partners and advisors that you would definitely try to avoid?

Have things become more predictable? Or less?

Do you spend more/same/less time with your business now than in the early years?

Do you feel more managerial and less entrepreneurial now?

In terms of the future, do you plan to harvest? To maintain? To expand?

Do you plan ever to retire? Would you explain?

Have your goals changed? Have you met them?

QUESTIONS FOR CONCLUDING (CHOOSE ONE)

- What do you consider your most valuable asset—the thing that enabled you to "make it"?
- If you had it to do over again, would you do it again, in the same way?

7.2 Starting a New Business

OBJECTIVES

1. To introduce you to the complexities of going into business for yourself.

2. To provide hands-on experience in making new business decisions.

INSTRUCTIONS

1. Your instructor will divide the class into teams and assign each team the task of investigating the start-up of one of the following businesses:
   a. Submarine sandwich shop
   b. Day care service
   c. Bookstore

- Looking back, what do you feel are the most critical concepts, skills, attitudes, and know-how you needed to get your company started and grown to where it is today? What will be needed for the next five years? To what extent can any of these be learned?
- Some people say there is a lot of stress being an entrepreneur. What have you experienced? How would you say it compares with other "hot seat" jobs, such as the head of a big company or a partner in a large law, consulting, or accounting firm?
- What are the things that you find personally rewarding and satisfying as an entrepreneur? What have been the rewards, risks, and trade-offs?
- Who should try to be an entrepreneur? Can you give me any ideas there?
- What advice would you give an aspiring entrepreneur? Could you suggest the three most important "lessons" you have learned? How can I learn them while minimizing the tuition?

SOURCE: Jeffry A. Timmons. *New Venture Creation,* 3rd ed. Copyright © 1994 by Jeffry A. Timmons. Reproduced with permission of the author.

   d. Gasoline service station
   e. Other

2. Each team should research the information necessary to complete the New-Business Start-Up Worksheet. The following agencies or organizations might be of assistance:
   a. Small Business Administration
   b. Local county/city administration agencies
   c. Local chamber of commerce
   d. Local small-business development corporation
   e. U.S. Department of Commerce
   f. Farmer's Home Administration
   g. Local realtors
   h. Local businesspeople in the same or a similar business
   i. Banks and S&Ls

3. Each team presents its findings to the class.

New-Business Start-Up Worksheet

1. *Product*

   What customer need will we satisfy? _____

   How can our product be unique? _____

2. *Customer*

   Who are our customers? What are their profiles? _____

   Where do they live/work/play? _____

   What are their buying habits? _____

   What are their needs? _____

3. *Competition*

   Who/where is the competition? _____

   What are their strengths and weaknesses? _____

   How might they respond to us? _____

4. *Suppliers*

   Who/where are our suppliers?

   What are their business practices?

   What relationships can we expect?

5. *Location*

   Where are our customers/competitors/suppliers?

   What are the location costs?

   What are the legal limitations to location?

6. *Physical Facilities/Equipment*

   Rent/own/build/refurbish facilities?

   Rent/lease/purchase equipment?

   Maintenance?

7. *Human Resources*

   Availability?

   Training?

   Costs?

8. *Legal/Regulatory Environment*

   Licenses/permits/certifications?

   Government agencies?

   Liability?

9. *Cultural/Social Environment*

   Cultural issues?

   Social issues?

10. *International Environment*

    International issues?

11. *Other*

PART 2 SUPPORTING CASE

Global Challenges for Exxon-Mobil

Exxon-Mobil is the largest publicly traded oil company in the world. It conducts business in more than 200 countries and territories. *Fortune* magazine ranked Exxon-Mobil, located in Irving, Texas, Number 2 in its Fortune 500 annual listing. In addition, 2004 also represented a banner year for the company. It earned more than $25 billion for the year, and a record $8.42 billion in the 4th quarter alone. Sales earnings for the year were close to $300 billion, a staggering amount of money for any company by any account.

Despite its stellar financial performance, over the years, Exxon-Mobil has encountered some very serious problems that have in one way or another affected the domestic and international affairs of the company. For example, Exxon, before it merged with Mobil in 1999, has never really erased its image problem as a result of the 1989 *Exxon Valdez* debacle—when an oil tanker, the *Exxon Valdez*, spilled more than 10 million gallons of crude oil into Prince William Sound, Alaska, creating an ecological nightmare that almost destroyed this once pristine Alaskan environment. Instead of owning up to the disaster immediately, company management attempted to shift the blame to third parties—the US Coast Guard and the Alaskan governmental agencies; furthermore, the company took what some observers considered an excessive amount of time before management directly addressed clean up efforts. Incidentally, Exxon paid fines and environmental restoration fees of some $3 billion.

Just last year, Exxon-Mobil was embroiled in a mega oil bribery scandal. Some top executives were charged by the U.S. Federal Government with attempting to bribe leaders in several African, Asian, and newly independent former USSR satellite countries to secure oil rights. At its annual general meeting in May 2005, slightly more than 28 percent of Exxon Mobil shareholders voted on a proposed resolution to force the company to comply with the Kyoto Protocol treaty which calls for the reduction in greenhouse gas emissions. The Kyoto Protocol treaty has been ratified by 140 countries; the United States is one of the countries that has not signed the treaty. Some company critics have openly voiced the opinions that Exxon-Mobil has failed to meet its corporate responsibility.

In addition to these problems, Exxon-Mobil needs to resolve other issues. For example, some conflict-ridden oil rich countries may interrupt the flow of the oil supply and thereby cause the price of oil to fluctuate dramatically. These issues may have an adverse condition on the company's balance sheet, although the recent decline of oil production has not hurt Exxon-Mobil's profits to date. The company has a very strong cash position and is considered cash rich as a result of fiscal prudence of its long-time chairman and CEO Lee Raymond. According to some estimates, cash accumulations approach the $25 billion mark and there are no plans to spend the money. If Exxon-Mobil's profits continue, financial projections suggest a nearly $40 billion cash position by the end of 2006. Yet this enviable financial position has created another problem for Exxon-Mobil. Management has been reluctant to invest in new oil exploration opportunities or to begin the process of building new refineries in the United States.

These current issues present one set of problems for the company. A lesser problem may occur when Chairman and CEO Raymond retires. Rex Tillerson, a 51-year-old civil engineer and 30+ year Exxon employee, who began his career as a production engineer, has been designated as a Raymond's heir apparent. During his tenure at Exxon, Tillerson has worked in a variety of managerial capacities. He possesses intimate knowledge of both domestic and international markets and has had significant experience in countries such as Russia, Thailand, and Yeman. When he assumes the corporate leadership mantle, Tillerson must grapple with these issues. Can Tillerson translate his various international managerial experiences to deal with some of the key issues confronting Exxon-Mobil?

QUESTIONS

1. Assume for a moment that you are Rex Tillerson, CEO/chairman heir apparent. Discuss some corporate strategy initiatives you would take with regard to Exxon-Mobil and the international community.

2. Define corporate responsibility. Do you believe that Exxon-Mobil has failed to meet its corporate responsibility to comply with the Kyoto Protocol? Why? Why not?

3. Are there any other strategies Exxon Mobil can implement to help improve its image?

SOURCES: This case was prepared by Joseph C. Santora, professor, business administration at Essex County College, Newark, New Jersey. Shelia McNulty, Key Issues in the Pipeline for Exxon's Heir Apparent. *Financial Times,* June 1, 2005. Exxon hits Kyoto Storm at Annual Meeting. *Financial Times,* May 26, 2005. http://www.forbes.com/business/services/feeds/ap/2005/01/31ap1793587.html. http://www.exxonmobil.com

Information for Entrepreneurs

If you are interested in starting or managing a small business, you have access to many sources of useful information.

PUBLISHED SOURCES

The first step is a complete search of materials in libraries and on the Internet. You can find a huge amount of published information, databases, and other sources about industries, markets, competitors, and personnel. Some of this information will have been uncovered when you search for ideas. Listed below are additional sources that should help get you started.

Guides and Company Information   Valuable information is available in special issues and the Web sites of *Business Week, Forbes, Inc., The Economist, Fast Company,* and *Fortune* and online, in the following:

- Hoovers.com
- ProQuest.com
- Investext.com
- RDS Bizsuite.com

Valuable Sites on the Internet

- Entreworld (http://www.entreworld.org), the Web site of the Kauffman Center for Entrepreneurial Leadership, Ewing Marion Kauffman Foundation
- *Fast Company* (http://www.fastcompany.com)
- Ernst & Young (http://www.ey.com)
- Global Access—SEC documents through a subscription-based Web site www.primark.com
- *INC.* magazine (http://www.inc.com)
- Entrepreneur.com and magazine (http://www.entrepreneur.com)
- EDGAR Database (http://www.sec.gov)—subscription sources, such as ThomsonResearch (http://www.thomsonfinancial.com), provide images of other filings as well.
- Venture Economics (http://www.ventureeconomics.com)

Journal Articles via Computerized Indexes

- Factiva with Dow Jones, *Reuters, The Wall Street Journal*
- EBSCOhost
- FirstSearch
- Ethnic News Watch
- LEXIS/NEXIS

- *The New York Times*
- InfoTrac from Gale Group
- ABI/Inform and other ProQuest databases
- RDS Business Reference Suite
- *The Wall Street Journal*

Statistics

- Stat-USA (http://www.stat-usa.gov)—U.S. government subscription site for economic, trade and business data, and market research
- U.S. Census Bureau (http://www.census.gov)—the source of many statistical data including:
  - Statistical Abstract of the United States
  - American FactFinder—population data
  - Economic Programs (http://www.census.gov/econ/www/index.html)—data by sector
  - County Business Patterns
  - Zip Code Business Patterns
- Knight Ridder . . . CRB Commodity Year Book
- Manufacturing USA, Service Industries USA, and other sector compilations from Gale Group
- Economic Statistics Briefing Room (http://www.whitehouse.gov/fsbr/esbr.html)
- Federal Reserve Bulletin
- Survey of Current Business
- FedStats (http://www.fedstats.gov/)
- Labstat (http://stats.bls.gov/labstat.htm)
- Global Insight, formerly DRI-WEFA
- International Financial Statistics—International Monetary Fund
- World Development Indicators—World Bank
- Bloomberg Database

Consumer Expenditures

- New Strategist Publications

Projections and Forecasts

- ProQuest
- InfoTech Trends
- Guide to Special Issues and Indexes to Periodicals (*Grey House Directory of Special Issues*)
- RDS Business Reference Suite
- Value Line Investment Survey

Market Studies
- LifeStyle Market Analyst
- MarketResearch.com
- Scarborough Research
- Simmons Market Research Bureau

Consumer Expenditures
- New Strategist Publications
- Consumer Expenditure Survey
- Euromonitor

Other Sources
- Wall Street Transcript
- Brokerage House reports from Investext, Multex, etc.
- Company annual reports and websites

OTHER INTELLIGENCE

Everything entrepreneurs need to know will not be found in libraries because this information needs to be highly specific and current. This information is most likely available from people—industry experts, suppliers, and the like. Summarized below are some useful sources of intelligence.

Trade Associations   Trade associations, especially the editors of their publications and information officers, are good sources of information. Trade shows and conferences are prime places to discover the latest activities of competitors.

Employees   Employees who have left a competitor's company often can provide information about the competitor, especially if the employee departed on bad terms. Also, a firm can hire people away from a competitor. While consideration of ethics in this situation is very important, the number of experienced people in any industry is limited, and competitors must prove that a company hired a person intentionally to get specific trade secrets in order to challenge any hiring legally. Students who have worked for competitors are another source of information.

Consulting Firms   Consulting firms frequently conduct industry studies and then make this information available. Frequently, in such fields as computers or software, competitors use the same design consultants, and these consultants can be sources of information.

Market Research Firms   Firms doing market studies, such as those listed under published sources above, can be sources of intelligence.

Key Customers, Manufacturers, Suppliers, Distributors, and Buyers   These groups are often a prime source of information.

Public Filings   Federal, state, and local filings, such as filings with the Securities and Exchange Commission (SEC), Patent and Trademark Office, or Freedom of Information Act filings, can reveal a surprising amount of information. There are companies that process inquiries of this type.

Reverse Engineering   Reverse engineering can be used to determine costs of production and sometimes even manufacturing methods. An example of this practice is the experience of Advanced Energy Technology, Inc., of Boulder, Colorado, which learned firsthand about such tactics. No sooner had it announced a new product, which was patented, when it received 50 orders, half of which were from competitors asking for only one or two of the items.

Networks   The networks mentioned in this chapter can be sources of new venture ideas and strategies.

Other   Classified ads, buyers' guides, labor unions real estate agents, courts, local reporters, and so on can all provide clues.

J. A. Timmons and S. Spinelli, *New Venture Creation*, 6e, McGraw-Hill/Irwin, 2004, pp. 103–104.

PART THREE

Foundations of Management
- Managing
- The External Environment and Organizational Culture
- Managerial Decision Making

Planning: Delivering Strategic Value
- Planning and Strategic Management
- Ethics and Corporate Responsibility
- International Management
- Entrepreneurship

Strategy Implementation

Organizing: Building a Dynamic Organization
- Organization Structure
- Organizational Agility
- Human Resources Management
- Managing the Diverse Workforce

Leading: Mobilizing People
- Leadership
- Motivating for Performance
- Teamwork
- Communicating

Controlling: Learning and Changing
- Managerial Control
- Managing Technology and Innovation
- Creating and Managing Change

Organizing: Building a Dynamic Organization

Now that you know about planning and strategy, the remaining three parts correspond to the other three functions of management: organizing, leading, and controlling. Parts 3, 4, and 5 discuss issues pertaining to *implementing* strategic plans. In Part 3, we describe how to organize and staff for maximum effectiveness. Chapter 8 introduces you to different organization structures and explains how to group and delegate tasks. Chapter 9 builds on those basic concepts by describing more complex organization designs. This chapter discusses how firms can adapt quickly to rapidly changing environments and how "corporate America" is restructuring. Chapter 10 addresses the management of human resources. Its focus is on staffing the firm with capable employees and the issues surrounding employee reward systems. Finally, Chapter 11 discusses the challenge of managing today's workforce, one composed of diverse groups of people. Chapters 12 and 13 set the stage for Part 4, which further elaborates on how to manage people.

Chapter **8**

CHAPTER 8
Organization Structure

Take my assets—but leave me my organization and in five years I'll have it all back.

—Alfred P. Sloan Jr.

LEARNING OBJECTIVES

After studying Chapter 8, you will know:

1. How differentiation and integration influence an organization's structure.

2. How authority operates.

3. The roles of the board of directors and the chief executive officer.

4. How span of control affects structure and managerial effectiveness.

5. Why effective delegation is important.

6. The difference between centralized and decentralized organizations.

7. The different ways organizations can be structured.

8. The unique challenges of the matrix organization.

9. The nature of important integrative mechanisms.

SONY ORGANIZES FOR CONVERGENCE

Sony Corporation is one of the best-known and most popular companies in the world. It owns a wide variety of businesses at the leading edge of consumer appeal and technology—in music, movies, television, computers, video, and other electronics. Its more than 160,000 employees worldwide create products and services that generate revenues of over $72 billion a year, including more than $20 billion in the United States. The company invented such products as the Trinitron television, Handycam camcorder, Walkman, Walkman CD, and PlayStation2, among many innovations that have transformed the viewing, listening, and game-playing habits of consumers everywhere. Yet even this enormously talented and successful firm found that, in recent years, it has had to make a variety of changes in its structure to remain a high-growth company.

One huge problem facing Sony was the long-standing operating independence of its various divisions. Its many business and product units rarely worked together in a coordinated fashion and at times even competed with each other. For example, in the late 1990s, at least three different units at Sony were independently developing digital cameras, apparently unaware of each other's efforts. Sony's management began to address this issue with a number of structural changes. A high-level management group was created to improve coordination across Sony divisions. And temporary development committees—what Sony called "virtual companies"—made up of representatives from various units of the company were created to develop and launch new products that crossed divisional lines. An

improved version of Sony's MiniDisk player was one result of this effort to create company structures that would help Sony become a more cooperative and coordinated organization.

But management soon realized that these efforts didn't go nearly far enough, and that more fundamental structural changes would be required. With the development of the Internet, broadband, and wireless, the newest electronic products had to be able to link with one another seamlessly. For example, consumers wanted to be able to download music from their computers directly onto handheld devices or to download video on their computers. Companies creating these products, like Sony, had to take these new consumer requirements into account. In addition, entertainment and technology were *converging*—coming together to form a unified product. The software and hardware for videogames, for example, or music and portable audio players, were not independent developments, but had to work together. In this new environment, continuing to operate Sony's divisions as separate fiefdoms would greatly inhibit Sony's ability to bring the right products to market quickly.

Sony also had strong competition to worry about. Companies like Apple, with its successful iPod, Dell in computers, Microsoft in games—all seemed quicker off the mark with new products. Time Warner, with its enormous content businesses in music, publishing, and movies, and its ready access to outlets for that content through its AOL and cable businesses, was also a major

competitive threat. Sony had content assets like music and movies. It had proven technological ability and hardware. To succeed in this new environment of networking, interactivity, and product convergence, Sony managers would have to find new ways to get all the parts of the company working together.

Sources for Prologue, Connections, Epilogue: Jim Davis, "Sony Shifts Gears to Tap Convergence Trend," www.news.com, March 16, 2000; Brenton Schlender, "Asia's Businessman of the Year," Fortune, February 7, 2002, online; Brent Schlender, "Sony Plays to Win," Fortune, May 1, 2000, online; Peter Lewis, "Sony Redreams Its Future," Fortune, November 10, 2002, online; "Sony Energized," Mermigas on Media, November 5, 2003, online; Steven Levy, "Sony Gets Personal," Newsweek International, November 1, 2004, online; Marc Graser, "Sony Shuffles Digital Future," Forbes.com, October 12, 2004; "Sony: More Restructuring Unnecessary," money.cnn.com, February 2, 2005; Adam Lashinsky, "Saving Face at Sony," Fortune, February 7, 2005, online; Phred Dvorak and Merissa Marr, "Can Stringer Tame Sony?" The Wall Street Journal, March 8, 2005, p. B1.

Sony is a company that pretty much all of us know, and would think of as enormously successful. Yet, as the Prologue suggests, the way Sony was structured may not have been ideal for the new consumer and competitive environment it faced. Although the brief description we provided can't provide all the details about Sony's strategy and structure, it does begin to raise a few important issues we want to cover in this chapter. Make no mistake: How a company organizes itself may well be the most important factor in determining whether its strategy will succeed. And Sony, like many other companies, is working hard to make certain that its strategy and structure are aligned with each other.

This chapter focuses on the vertical and horizontal dimensions of organization structure. We begin by covering basic principles of *differentiation* and *integration*. Next, we discuss the vertical structure, which includes issues of *authority*, hierarchy, delegation, and decentralization. We continue on to describe the horizontal structure, which includes functional, divisional, and matrix forms. Finally, we illustrate the ways in which organizations can integrate their structures: coordination by standardization, coordination by plan, and coordination by mutual adjustment.

In the next chapter, we continue with the topic of organization structure but take a different perspective. In that chapter we will focus on the flexibility and responsiveness of an organization, that is, how capable it is of changing its form and adapting to strategy, technology, the environment, and other challenges it confronts.

Fundamentals of Organizing

organization chart

The reporting structure and division of labor in an organization.

To get going, let's start simple. We often begin to describe a firm's structure by looking at its organization chart. The **organization chart** depicts the positions in the firm and how they are arranged. The chart provides a picture of the reporting structure (who reports to whom) and the various activities that are carried out by different individuals. Most companies have official organizational charts drawn up to give people this information.

Figure 8.1 shows the traditional organization chart. Note the various kinds of information that are conveyed in a very simple way:

1. The boxes represent different work.
2. The titles in the boxes show the work performed by each unit.
3. Reporting and authority relationships are indicated by solid lines showing superior-subordinate connections.
4. Levels of management are indicated by the number of horizontal layers in the chart. All persons or units that are of the same rank and report to the same person are on one level.

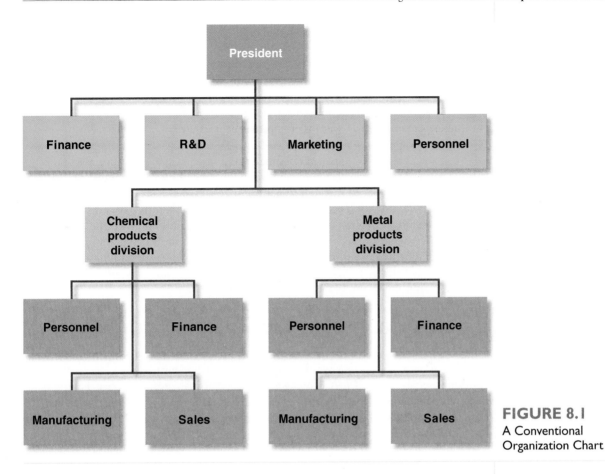

FIGURE 8.1
A Conventional
Organization Chart

Although the organization chart presents some clearly important structural features, other design issues related to structure—while not so obvious—are no less important. Two fundamental concepts around which organizations are structured are differentiation and integration. **Differentiation** means that the organization is composed of many different units that work on different kinds of tasks, using different skills and work methods. **Integration** means that these differentiated units are put back together so that work is coordinated into an overall product.[1]

Differentiation

Several related concepts underlie the idea of structural differentiation. For example, differentiation is created through division of labor and job specialization. **Division of labor** means that the work of the organization is subdivided into smaller tasks. Various individuals and units throughout the organization perform different tasks. **Specialization,** in turn, refers to the fact that different people or groups often perform specific parts of the entire task. The two concepts are, of course, closely related. Secretaries and accountants specialize in, and perform, different jobs; similarly, marketing, finance, and human resources tasks are divided among the respective departments. The numerous tasks that must be carried out in an organization make specialization and division of labor necessities. Otherwise the complexity of the overall work of the organization would be too much for any individual.[2]

Differentiation is high when there are many subunits and many kinds of specialists who think differently. Harvard professors Lawrence and Lorsch found that organizations in complex, dynamic environments (plastics firms in their study) developed a high degree of differentiation in order to cope with the complex challenges. Companies in simple, stable environments (container companies) had low

---

differentiation

An aspect of the organization's internal environment created by job specialization and the division of labor.

integration

The degree to which differentiated work units work together and coordinate their efforts.

division of labor

The assignment of different tasks to different people or groups.

specialization

A process in which different individuals and units perform different tasks.

levels of differentiation. Companies in intermediate environments (food companies) had intermediate differentiation.[3]

Integration

As organizations differentiate their structures, managers must simultaneously consider issues of integration. All the specialized tasks in an organization cannot be performed completely independently. Because the different units are part of the larger organization, some degree of communication and cooperation must exist among them. Integration and its related concept, **coordination,** refer to the procedures that link the various parts of the organization to achieve the organization's overall mission.

Integration is achieved through structural mechanisms that enhance collaboration and coordination. Any job activity that links different work units performs an integrative function. Remember, the more highly differentiated your firm, the greater the need for integration among the different units. Lawrence and Lorsch found that highly differentiated firms were successful if they also had high levels of integration. Organizations are more likely to fail if they exist in complex environments and are highly differentiated, but fail to integrate their activities adequately.[4]

> **coordination**
>
> The procedures that link the various parts of an organization for the purpose of achieving the organization's overall mission.

Connections: SONY ORGANIZES FOR CONVERGENCE

In 2000 Sony announced a major new structure for its corporate management. A dozen or so separate Sony divisions were merged into five major businesses: a Home Network company, merging Sony's TV, VCR, home audio, and Walkman units, to ensure that the same content could be used on all devices; a Personal Network group, combining portable PCs, camcorders, and digital cameras, to eventually allow consumers to edit and e-mail photos and videos; a Core Technology group, to make sure all of Sony's technology was standardized and that its products could be linked to one another; a Broadband unit, combining music and movies, to make Sony artists available online; and Computer Entertainment, combining in one group hardware and software applications for the popular PlayStation. The intent behind this major change in structure, the company said, was to break down barriers between divisions and take advantage of synergies between the company's software, content, and hardware.

These concepts permeate the rest of the chapter. First, we will discuss *vertical differentiation* within organization structure. This includes issues pertaining to authority within an organization, the board of directors, the chief executive officer, and hierarchical levels, as well as issues pertaining to delegation and decentralization. Next, we will discuss *horizontal differentiation* in an organization's structure, including issues of departmentalization that create functional, divisional, and matrix organizations. Finally, we will discuss issues pertaining to structural integration, including coordination, organizational roles, interdependence, and boundary spanning.

The Vertical Structure

In order to understand issues such as reporting relationships, authority, responsibility, and the like, we need to begin with the vertical dimension of a firm's structure.

Corporate governance is a term describing the oversight of the firm by its executive staff and board of directors. In recent years, as a result of a number of corporate scandals, the public's trust in corporate governance has eroded significantly. For example, the Enron board waived its ethics guidelines to allow questionable deals by some of its top officers and ignored warnings of inappropriate activity. WorldCom's board signed off on false financials. Board members at other companies, like ImClone, Global Crossing, and Tyco, also failed their oversight responsibility. Some of these

> **corporate governance**
>
> The role of a corporation's executive staff and board of directors in ensuring that the firm's activities meet the goals of the firm's stakeholders.

firms went bankrupt as a result of executive or board action or inaction, with enormous hardship to employees, pension holders, and investors. As we mentioned in Chapter 5, "Ethics and Corporate Responsibility," in response to these scandals Congress in 2002 passed the Sarbanes-Oxley Act, which along with new SEC requirements imposed much tighter corporate governance rules. For example, company CEOs and CFOs (chief financial officers) now have to personally certify the accuracy of their firm's financial statements.

Corporate Boards: The Worst and the Best

The Corporate Library (www.thecorporatelibrary.com) is an organization that analyzes company boards and also issues Board Effectiveness Ratings, based on a number of criteria, including the independence of compensation committees, outside directors, and auditors. Here are some excerpts from one of its reports on the worst and best corporate boards:

SOME OF THE WORST BOARDS
- **Citigroup, Inc.**   Chairman and CEO Sanford Weill was personally involved in one of the most outrageous scandals of the most scandalous year for American business since the 1929 stock market crash, the infamous exchange of admission [of an analyst's offspring] to the 92nd Street Y preschool for a more favorable analyst report on AT&T. Citi . . . had to pay a massive fine and Weill himself must be accompanied by a lawyer when he speaks to the analysts who work for him. But for Weill and the board, it looks like business as usual . . . The fine was paid by Citi's current shareholders (and the shareholders of Citi's insurers), not by any of the people responsible.
- **Honeywell International, Inc.**   Should former CEOs chair compensation committees? We don't think so: CEOs seem to have a hard time saying no to one another . . . First we learn that former CEO Lawrence Bossidy is entitled to an annual retirement benefit of $3,937,966, and that for the remainder of his life, Mr. Bossidy will be entitled to access to or use of Honeywell facilities and services comparable to those provided to him prior to his retirement . . . And then we learn that incoming CEO David Cote's agreement includes a golden hello worth around $59.5 million, including the grant date value of the more than 2 million stock options he received. None of this, of course, is tied to performance. In the meantime, the full Honeywell board continues to refuse—for three years running—to act on shareholder proposals that have received majority support, including the declassification of board elections.
- **SBC Communications Inc.**   Poor compensation policies and practices loom large at SBC. "Target" bonuses of almost 200 percent of salary were paid out despite targets not actually being met . . . Over-generous post-retirement perks for the CEO have already been approved by the SBC board. And their opposition to a shareholder resolution calling for performance-related stock options contained the following incriminating admission of opposition to "the extraordinary requirement that executives or other employees face 'downside financial risk' beyond loss of the value of the stock options or the decline in the value of stock-based compensation." Extraordinary requirement? Is it the job of the board to shelter their executives from any and all risk based on their performance? On the contrary.

SOME OF THE BEST BOARDS
- **Hershey Foods Corporation (controlled board category)**   . . . Changes in both management and the board appear to have met with considerable success, resulting in an increasingly strong and independent board. CEO compensation levels are also generally conservative, and well aligned with shareholder interests.
- **Cintas Corporation (family board category)**   Father and son Richard T. and Scott D. Farmer, along with with brother-in-law James J. Gardner, all sit on the Cintas

board, and together hold a dominant, though not controlling, percentage of the firm. But the overall board balance and structure here seem exceptionally strong, compensation levels are well considered and appropriate, and the continued sharp focus of the firm on its core business operations . . . makes this an easy board for us to admire in this category.

Other boards that came in for The Corporate Library's censure include Emerson Electric Company, Gemstar-TV Guide International, J. P. Morgan Chase & Co., Loews Corporation, and Disney. Other boards that received praise were Fannie Mae and AMR Corporation.

SOURCE: The Corporate Library, July 2003.

Authority in Organizations

Authority, the legitimate right to make decisions and to tell other people what to do, is fundamental to the functioning of every organization. For example, a boss has the authority to give an order to a subordinate.

Traditionally, authority resides in *positions* rather than in people. Thus, the job of vice president of a particular division has authority over that division, regardless of how many people come and go in that position and who currently holds it.

In private business enterprises, the owners have ultimate authority. In most small, simply structured companies, the owner also acts as manager. Sometimes the owner hires another person to manage the business and its employees. The owner gives this manager some authority to oversee the operations, but the manager is accountable to—that is, reports and defers to—the owner. Thus, the owner still has the ultimate authority.

Formal position authority is generally the primary means of running an organization. An order that a boss gives to a lower-level employee is usually carried out. As this occurs throughout the organization day after day, the organization can move forward toward achieving its goals.[5] We should mention that authority in an organization is not always position-dependent. People with particular expertise, experience, or personal qualities may have considerable *informal* authority—scientists in research companies, for example, or employees who are computer-savvy. Effective managers are aware of informal authority as a factor that can help or hinder their achievement of the organization's goals; we will say more about informal authority in the next chapter. For now, however, we discuss the formal authority structure of the organization from the top down, beginning with the board of directors.

 "Authority without wisdom is like a heavy axe without an edge, fitter to bruise than polish."

Anne Bradstreet

The Board of Directors   In corporations, the owners are the stockholders. But because there are numerous stockholders and these individuals generally lack timely information, few are directly involved in managing the organization. Stockholders elect a board of directors to oversee the organization. The board, led by the chair, makes major decisions affecting the organization, subject to corporate charter and bylaw provisions. Boards perform at least three major sets of duties: (1) selecting, assessing, rewarding, and perhaps replacing the CEO; (2) determining the firm's strategic direction and reviewing financial performance; and (3) assuring ethical, socially responsible, and legal conduct.[6]

Some top executives are likely to sit on the board (they are called *inside directors*). Outside members of the board tend to be executives at other companies. The trend in recent years has been toward reducing the number of insiders and increasing the num-

Retail managers typically meet informally with employees before and after the business day, as at this Staples store.

ber of outsiders. Today most companies have a majority of outside directors. Boards made up of strong, independent outsiders are more likely to provide different information and perspectives and to prevent big mistakes. Successful boards tend to be those which are active, critical participants in determining company strategies. Campbell Soup's board, for example, took control over selecting a new CEO and routinely conducts performance evaluations of board members to make certain they are active contributors.[7]

The Chief Executive Officer　The authority officially vested in the board of directors is assigned to a chief executive officer (CEO), who occupies the top of the organizational pyramid. The CEO is personally accountable to the board and to the owners for the organization's performance.

In some corporations, one person holds all three positions of CEO, chair of the board of directors, and president.[8] More commonly, however, one person holds two of those positions, with the CEO serving also as either the chair of the board or the president of the organization. When the CEO is president, the chair may be honorary and may do little more than conduct meetings. In other cases, the chair may be the CEO and the president is second in command.

In recent years there has been a trend to separate the position of CEO and chairman of the board. A number of high-profile companies, like Microsoft, Disney, and Dell, have moved in this direction. Sometimes this kind of change is related to improved corporate governance; board oversight is easier when the CEO is not quite as dominant a figure. In other cases, the board has acted to reduce an unpopular CEO's power or to help prepare for a successor to the CEO.

The Top Management Team　Increasingly, CEOs share their authority with other key members of the top management team. Top management teams typically are composed of the CEO, president, chief operating officer, chief financial officer, and other key executives. Rather than make critical decisions on their own, CEOs at companies such as Shell, Honeywell, and Merck regularly meet with their top management teams to make decisions as a unit.[9]

Fewer horizontal layers save time and money.

Hierarchical Levels

In Chapter 1, we discussed the three broad levels of the organizational pyramid, commonly called the **hierarchy.** The CEO occupies the top position and is the senior member of top management. The top managerial level also includes presidents and

hierarchy

The authority levels of the organizational pyramid.

Due to financial and creative problems at Disney, Michael Eisner lost his role as chairman of the board but still maintains his position of CEO.

vice presidents. These are the strategic managers in charge of the entire organization. The second broad level is middle management. At this level, managers are in charge of plants or departments. The lowest level is made up of lower management and workers. It includes office managers, sales managers, supervisors, and other first-line managers, as well as the employees who report directly to them. This level is also called the *operational level* of the organization.

An authority structure is the glue that holds these levels together. Generally (but not always), people at higher levels have the authority to make decisions and tell lower-level people what to do. For example, middle managers can give orders to first-line supervisors; first-line supervisors, in turn, direct operative-level workers.

A powerful trend for U.S. businesses over the past few decades has been to reduce the number of hierarchical layers. General Electric used to have 29 levels; today it has only a handful of layers and its hierarchical structure is basically flat. Most executives today believe that fewer layers create a more efficient, fast-acting, and cost-effective organization. This also holds true for the **subunits** of major corporations. A study of 234 branches of a financial services company found that branches with fewer layers tended to have higher operating efficiency than did branches with more layers.[10]

subunits

Subdivisions of an organization.

Span of Control

The number of people under a manager is an important feature of an organization's structure. The number of subordinates who report directly to an executive or supervisor is called the **span of control.** The implications of differences in the span of control for the shape of an organization are straightforward. Holding size constant, narrow spans build a *tall* organization that has many reporting levels. Wide spans create a *flat* organization with fewer reporting levels. The span of control can be too narrow or too wide. The optimal span of control maximizes effectiveness because it is (1) narrow enough to permit managers to maintain control over subordinates but (2) not so narrow that it leads to overcontrol and an excessive number of managers who oversee a small number of subordinates.

span of control

The number of subordinates who report directly to an executive or supervisor.

What is the optimal number of subordinates? Five, according to Napoleon.[11] Some managers today still consider five a good number. At one Japanese bank, in contrast, several hundred branch managers report to the same boss.

Actually, the optimal span of control depends on a number of factors. The span should be wider when (1) the work is clearly defined and unambiguous, (2) subordinates are highly trained and have access to information, (3) the manager is highly capable and supportive, (4) jobs are similar and performance measures are comparable, and (5) subordinates prefer autonomy to close supervisory control. If the opposite conditions exist, a narrow span of control may be more appropriate.[12]

Delegation

As we look at organizations, and recognize that authority is spread out over various levels and spans of control, the issue of delegation becomes paramount. **Delegation** is the assignment of authority and responsibility to a subordinate at a lower level. It often requires that the subordinate report back to his or her boss in regard to how effectively the assignment was carried out. Delegation is perhaps the most fundamental feature of management, because it entails getting work done through others. Thus, delegation is important at all hierarchical levels. The process can occur between any two individuals in any type of structure with regard to any task.

delegation

The assignment of new or additional responsibilities to a subordinate.

Some managers are comfortable fully delegating an assignment to subordinates; others are not. Consider the differences between these two office managers and the ways they gave out the same assignment in the following example.

Are Both of These Examples of Delegation?

Manager A: "Call Tom Burton at Nittany Office Equipment. Ask him to give you the price list on an upgrade for our personal computers. I want to move up to a Pentium 4 with 256 megs of RAM and at least a 80-gigabyte hard drive. Ask them to give you a demonstration of Windows XP and Microsoft Office. I want to be able to establish a LAN for the entire group. Invite Cochran and Snow to the demonstration and let them try it out. Have them write up a summary of their needs and the potential applications they see for the new systems. Then prepare me a report with the costs and specifications of the upgrade for the entire department. Oh, yes, be sure to ask for information on service costs."

Manager B: "I'd like to do something about our personal computer system. I've been getting some complaints that the current systems are too slow, can't run current software, and don't allow for networking. Could you evaluate our options and give me a recommendation on what we should do? Our budget is probably around $3,500 per person, but I'd like to stay under that if we can. Feel free to talk to some of the managers to get their input, but we need to have this done as soon as possible."

Responsibility, Authority, and Accountability   When delegating work, it is helpful to keep in mind the important distinctions among the concepts of authority, responsibility, and accountability.

Responsibility means that a person is assigned a task that he or she is supposed to carry out. When delegating work responsibilities, the manager also should delegate to the subordinate enough authority to get the job done. *Authority*, recall, means that the person has the power and the right to make decisions, give orders, draw upon resources, and do whatever else is necessary to fulfill the responsibility. Ironically, it is quite common for people to have more responsibility than authority; they must perform as best they can through informal influence tactics instead of relying purely on authority. More will be said about informal power and how to use it in Chapter 12.

As the manager delegates responsibilities, subordinates are held accountable for achieving results. **Accountability** means that the subordinate's manager has the right to expect the subordinate to perform the job, and the right to take corrective action if the subordinate fails to do so. The subordinate must report upward on the status and quality of his or her performance of the task.

However, the ultimate responsibility—accountability to higher-ups—lies with the manager doing the delegating. Managers remain responsible and accountable not only for their own actions but for the actions of their subordinates. Thus, managers should not resort to delegation to others as a means of escaping their own responsibilities. In many cases, however, managers refuse to accept responsibility for subordinates' actions. Managers often "pass the buck" or take other evasive action to ensure they are not held accountable for mistakes.[13]

Advantages of Delegation   Delegating work offers important advantages, particularly when it is done effectively. Effective delegation leverages the manager's energy and talent and those of his or her subordinates. It allows managers to accomplish much more than they would be able to do on their own. Conversely, lack of delegation, or ineffective delegation, sharply reduces what a manager can achieve. The manager also saves one of his or her most valuable assets—time—by giving some of his or her responsibility to somebody else. He or she is then free to devote energy to important, higher-level activities such as planning, setting objectives, and monitoring performance.

Another very important advantage of delegation is that it helps develop effective subordinates. Look again at the different ways the two office managers gave out the same assignment. The approach that is more likely to empower subordinates and help

responsibility

The assignment of a task that an employee is supposed to carry out.

accountability

The expectation that employees will perform a job, take corrective action when necessary, and report upward on the status and quality of their performance.

them develop will be obvious to you. (You may also quickly conclude which of the two managers you would prefer to work for.) Delegation essentially gives the subordinate a more important job. The subordinate acquires an opportunity to develop new skills and to demonstrate potential for additional responsibilities and perhaps promotion. In essence, the subordinate receives a vital form of on-the-job training that could pay off in the future.

The organization also receives payoffs. Allowing managers to devote more time to important managerial functions while lower-level employees carry out assignments means that jobs are done in a more efficient and cost-effective manner. In addition, as subordinates develop and grow in their own jobs, their ability to contribute to the organization increases as well.

Effective delegation raises the quality of subordinates.

How Should Managers Delegate?

To achieve the advantages we have just discussed, delegation must be done properly. As Figure 8.2 shows, effective delegation proceeds through several steps.[14]

The first step in the delegation process, defining the goal, requires that the manager have a clear understanding of the outcome he or she wants. Then the manager should select a person who is capable of performing the task.

The person who gets the assignment should be given the authority, time, and resources needed to carry out the task successfully. The required resources will usually involve people, money, and equipment, but often they may also involve critical information that will put the assignment in context. ("Review every cost item carefully, because if we're the low bidder we'll get the account.") Throughout the delegation process, the manager and the subordinate must work together and communicate about the project. The manager

FIGURE 8.2
The Steps in Effective Delegation

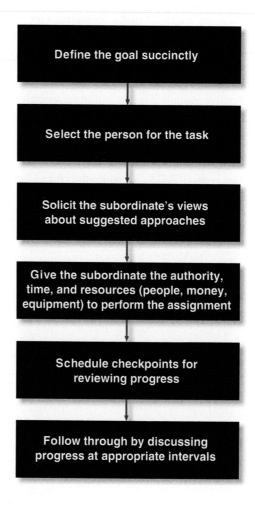

Define the goal succinctly

Select the person for the task

Solicit the subordinate's views about suggested approaches

Give the subordinate the authority, time, and resources (people, money, equipment) to perform the assignment

Schedule checkpoints for reviewing progress

Follow through by discussing progress at appropriate intervals should know the subordinate's ideas at the beginning and inquire about progress or problems at periodic meetings and review sessions. Thus, even though the subordinate performs the assignment, the manager is available and aware of its current status.

Some tasks, such as disciplining subordinates and conducting performance reviews, should not be delegated. But when managers err, it usually is because they delegated too little rather than too much. The manager who wants to learn how to delegate more effectively should remember this distinction: If you are not delegating, you are merely *doing* things; but the more you delegate, the more you are truly *building* and *managing* an organization.[15]

Decentralization

The delegation of responsibility and authority *decentralizes* decision making. In a **centralized organization,** important decisions usually are made at the top. In **decentralized organizations,** more decisions are made at lower levels. Ideally, decision making occurs at the level of the people who are most directly affected and have the most intimate knowledge about the problem. This is particularly important when the business environment is fast-changing and decisions must be made quickly and well.

Sometimes organizations change their degree of centralization, depending on the particular challenges they face. Tougher times often cause senior managements to take charge, whereas in times of rapid growth decisions are pushed further down the chain of command. For example, in the 1980s Harley-Davidson was in great financial difficulty and faced tough competition from Honda, Suzuki, and Yamaha. It needed strong, centralized leadership that could react quickly and decisively to survive. But once the crisis was past, this approach wasn't as effective in gaining the commitment and energy of employees, who were the ones building the products and the relationships with customers. Harley-Davidson made the transition to a flatter, more empowered organization that decentralizes decision making. Today, the traditional hierarchy at the company has been replaced with collaborative leadership, based on the assumption that all employees can make decisions and take responsibility for meeting the organization's goals.[16]

Most American executives today understand the advantages of pushing decision-making authority down to the point of the action. The level that deals directly with problems and opportunities has the most relevant information and can best foresee the consequences of decisions. Executives also see how the decentralized approach allows people to take more timely action.[17] The accompanying news item describes one company's intention to speed decision making through decentralization.

At AES, the world's largest global power company (with revenues in excess of $3 billion), all decisions are pushed down to the lowest levels in the organization. Teams in plants have total responsibility for operations and maintenance. According to Dennis Bakke and Roger Sant, the founders of the company, giving people the power and responsibility to make important decisions has multiple benefits. It leads to better and faster decisions because decisions are made where the action is. Also, it gives employees a chance to learn and get engaged in the business, turning them into "mini-CEOs." An extreme example of this decentralized approach occurred when the plant executives let the maintenance staff take a stab at investing the $12 million cash reserve held at the plant. By three months into the process, the team was actually beating the returns of the people in the home office who were investing money for the company's treasury![18]

centralized organization

An organization in which high-level executives make most decisions and pass them down to lower levels for implementation.

decentralized organization

An organization in which lower-level managers make important decisions.

Decentralization often speeds decision making.

The traditional hierarchy at Harley-Davidson has been replaced with collaborative leadership, based on the assumption that all employees can make decisions and take responsibility for meeting the organizations goals. Why would this be an effective form of decision making?

AOL Split into Four Units

America Online Inc. put new leaders in senior posts and revamped its corporate structure, undertaking a sweeping overhaul.

The far-reaching changes, directed by chief executive Jonathan F. Miller, will result in the departures of three of the Internet firm's most senior executives from its Dulles headquarters. In an e-mail to thousands of employees, Miller made it clear that he intends to shake up an online giant that has been criticized for moving too slowly and not doing enough to foster teamwork.

In addition to making several personnel changes, Miller said he is splitting the company into four divisions and giving each responsibility for its own operations and financial performance. "We are going to try to be much crisper in decision-making," Miller said in an interview. "It is about having clarity of mission and purpose."

AOL veteran Ted Leonsis will head a new division dubbed "Audience." It will focus on profiting mostly by selling advertising that reaches users of AOL's various Web sites and products, including AIM, AOL's free instant messaging service; Moviefone; Mapquest; Netscape.com; and a revamped AOL.com Web site. "I hope to pour a little accelerant on it," Leonsis said of his new responsibility.

Miller said the new team would take charge immediately. In the past, AOL has been a "fractious company" that moved too slowly to make changes, Miller said. The more decentralized structure is aimed at facilitating faster decision making and speedier implementation of initiatives. "In the days ahead, when our transition to a new structure has been completed, we will have a streamlined organization with clear roles and responsibilities," Miller wrote in his e-mail. "It will take some weeks for full organizational detail to fall into place, and I know this will make people uneasy."

Of the other three newly created divisions, the biggest is called "Access." That division encompasses the various services AOL sells to get computer users online, whether it be through dial-up telephone connections or high-speed lines. The unit, to be headed by Neil Smit, who has been overseeing AOL's regional call centers, also includes CompuServe and Netscape ISP, the firm's discount Internet service, as well as Wal-Mart Connect, a partnership between the giant retailer and AOL that offers Internet access at budget prices.

The other two divisions are AOL Europe, headed by Philip Rowley, and Digital Services, headed by AOL's chief technology officer, John McKinley. The Digital Services division will focus on a variety of new premium services, ranging from phone service over the Internet to subscription music services such as MusicNet.

Although advertising at AOL has been improving in recent quarters, the company has continued to suffer subscriber losses, as users depart for cheaper or faster Internet services.

Miller said the organizational and leadership changes stemmed from a report about America Online's strengths and weaknesses that he presented to Time Warner's board of directors last spring. Leonsis said the organization should reduce the number of overlapping responsibilities "which slowed us down in decision making with so many shared resources."

Still, Leonsis cautioned, "You shouldn't interpret this as if we are making four companies in four buildings. It is to get clean shots at success."

The leaders of the four business divisions will report directly to Miller, who plans to meet with them weekly.

SOURCE: Adapted from David A. Vise, "AOL to Be Split into Four Units," *The Washington Post*, November 9, 2004, online.

The Horizontal Structure

Up to this point, we've talked primarily about vertical aspects of organization structure. Issues of authority, span of control, delegation, and decentralization are important in that they give us an idea of how managers and employees relate to one another at different levels. At the same time, separating vertical differentiation from horizontal differentiation is a bit artificial because the elements work simultaneously.

As the tasks of organizations become increasingly complex, the organization inevitably must be subdivided—that is, *departmentalized*—into smaller units or departments. One of the first places this can be seen is in the distinction between line and staff departments. **Line departments** are those which have responsibility for the principal activities of the firm. Line units deal directly with the organization's primary goods or services; they make things, sell things, or provide customer service. At General Motors, for example, line departments include product design, fabrication, assembly, distribution, and the like. Line managers typically have much authority and power in the organization. They have the ultimate responsibility for making major operating decisions. They also are accountable for the "bottom-line" results of their decisions.

Staff departments are those which provide specialized or professional skills that support line departments. These would include research, legal, accounting, public relations, and human resources departments. Each of these specialized units often has its own vice president, and some are vested with a great deal of authority, as when accounting or finance groups approve and monitor budgetary activities. But while staff units formerly focused on monitoring and controlling performance, today most staff units are moving toward a new role focused on strategic support and expert advice.[19]

As organizations divide work into different units, we can detect patterns in the way departments are clustered and arranged. The three basic approaches to **departmentalization** are functional, divisional, and matrix. We will talk about each and highlight some of their similarities and differences.

The Functional Organization

In a **functional organization,** jobs (and departments) are specialized and grouped according to *business functions* and the skills they require: production, marketing, human resources, research and development, finance, accounting, and so forth. Figure 8.3 illustrates a basic functional organization chart.

Functional departmentalization is common in both large and small organizations. Large companies may organize along several different functional groupings, including groupings unique to their businesses. For example, Carmike Cinema, which operates 2,229 screens in 291 theaters in 36 states, has vice presidents of finance, real estate, operations, advertising, information systems, technical, and concessions and a vice president who is the head film buyer.

line departments

Units that deal directly with the organization's primary goods and services.

staff departments

Units that support line departments.

departmentalization

Subdividing an organization into smaller subunits.

functional organization

Departmentalization around specialized activities such as production, marketing, and human resources.

FIGURE 8.3
The Functional Organization

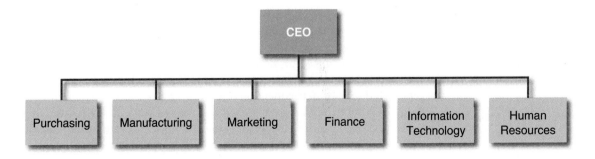

In a functional organization, jobs and departments are specialized and grouped according to business function. For instance, the finance people would only work with those in the finance department. What advantages and disadvantages can you find in a functional organization?

When like functions are grouped, savings often result.

divisional organization

Departmentalization that groups units around products, customers, or geographic regions.

The traditional functional approach to departmentalization has a number of potential advantages for an organization:[20]

1. *Economies of scale can be realized.* When people with similar skills are grouped, more efficient equipment can be purchased, and discounts for large purchases can be used.
2. *Monitoring of the environment* is more effective. Each functional group is more closely attuned to developments in its own field and therefore can adapt more readily.
3. *Performance standards* are better maintained. People with similar training and interests may develop a shared concern for performance in their jobs.
4. People have greater opportunity for *specialized training* and *in-depth skill development*.
5. Technical specialists are relatively *free of administrative work*.
6. *Decision making* and *lines of communication* are simple and clearly understood.

The functional form has disadvantages as well as advantages. People may care more about their own function than about the company as a whole, and their attention to functional tasks may make them lose focus on overall product quality and customer satisfaction. Managers develop functional expertise but do not acquire knowledge of the other areas of the business; they become specialists, but not generalists. Between functions, conflicts arise, and communication and coordination fall off. In short, while functional differentiation may exist, *functional integration* may not.

As a consequence, the functional structure may be most appropriate in rather simple, stable environments. If the organization becomes fragmented (or *dis*integrated), it may be difficult to develop and bring new products to market and to respond quickly to customer demands and other changes. Particularly when companies are growing and business environments are changing, the need arises to integrate work areas more effectively so that the organization can be more flexible and responsive. Other forms of departmentalization can be more flexible and responsive than the functional structure.

Demands for total quality, customer service, innovation, and speed have made clear the shortcomings of the functional form for some firms. Functional organizations are highly differentiated and create barriers to coordination across functions. Cross-functional coordination is essential for total quality, customer service, innovations, and speed. The functional organization will not disappear, in part because functional specialists will always be needed, but functional managers will make fewer decisions. The more important units will be cross-functional teams that have integrative responsibilities for products, processes, or customers.[21]

The Divisional Organization

The discussion of a functional structure's weaknesses leads us to the **divisional organization.** As organizations grow and become increasingly diversified, they find that functional departments have difficulty managing a wide variety of products, customers, and geographic regions. In this case, organizations may restructure in order to group all functions into a single division, and duplicate each of the functions across all the divisions. In the divisional organization chart in Figure 8.4, Division A has its own operations, marketing, and finance department, Division B has its own operations, marketing, and finance department, and so on. In this regard, separate divisions may act almost as separate businesses or profit centers and work autonomously to accomplish the goals of the entire enterprise. Table 8.1 presents examples of how the same tasks would be organized under functional and divisional structures.

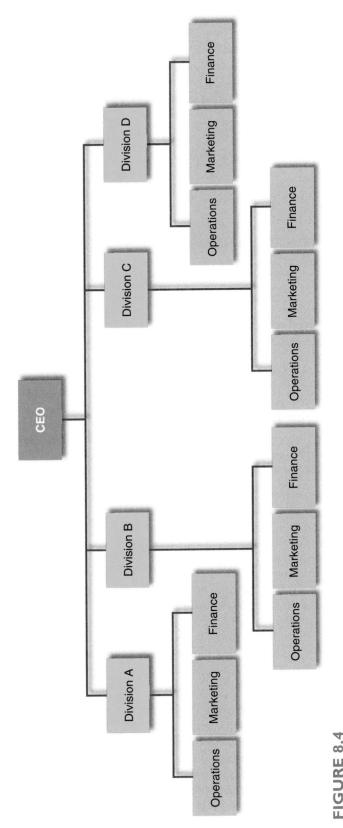

FIGURE 8.4
The Divisional Organization

TABLE 8.1

Examples of Functional and Divisional Organization

Functional Organization	Divisional Organization
A central purchasing department.	Each division has its own purchasing unit.
Separate companywide marketing, production, design, and engineering departments.	Each product group has experts in marketing, design, production, and engineering.
A central-city health department.	The school district and the prison have their own health units.
Plantwide inspection, maintenance, and supply departments.	Production Team Y does its own inspection, maintenance, and supply.
A university statistics department teaches statistics for the entire university.	Each department hires statisticians to teach its own students.

SOURCE: George Strauss and Leonard R. Sayles, *Strauss and Sayles's Behavioral Strategies for Managers,* © 1980, p. 221. Reprinted by permission of Prentice-Hall, Inc., Englewood Cliffs, New Jersey.

There are several ways to create a divisional structure. It can be created around products, customers, or geographic regions. Each of these is described in the following sections.

Product Divisions   In the product organization, all functions that contribute to a given product are organized under one manager. In the product organization, managers in charge of functions for a particular product report to a product manager. Johnson & Johnson is one example of this form. J&J has over 200 independent company divisions, each responsible for a handful of products worldwide.

The product approach to departmentalization offers a number of advantages:[22]

1. *Information needs are managed more easily.* Less information is required, because people work closely on one product and need not worry about other products.
2. *People have a full-time commitment to a particular product line.* They develop a greater awareness of how their jobs fit into the broader scheme.
3. *Task responsibilities are clear.* When things go wrong in a functional organization, functional managers can "pass the buck" ("That other department is messing up, making it harder for us to do our jobs"). In a product structure, managers are more independent and accountable because they usually have the resources they need to perform their tasks. Also, the performances of different divisions can be compared by contrasting their profits and other measures.
4. *People receive broader training.* General managers develop a wide variety of skills, and they learn to be judged by results. Many top executives received crucial early experience in product structures.

Because the product structure is more flexible than the functional structure, it is best suited for unstable environments, when an ability to adapt rapidly to change is important. But the product structure also has disadvantages. It is difficult to coordinate across product lines and divisions. And although managers learn to become generalists, they may not acquire the depth of functional expertise that develops in the functional structure.

Furthermore, functions are not centralized at headquarters, where they can be done for all product lines or divisions. Such duplication of effort is expensive. Also, decision making is decentralized in this structure, and so top management can lose some control over decisions made in the divisions. Proper management of all the issues surrounding decentralization and delegation, as discussed earlier, is essential for this structure to be effective.[23]

Connections: SONY ORGANIZES FOR CONVERGENCE

By 2003 Sony had made considerable progress in integrating its operations—for example, the newer Sony games were now playable on a number of different Sony devices, which wasn't true in the past. But some of the changes Sony's management was making still met resistance within the company. Part of the problem was simply distance: Sony's technologists were concentrated in Japan, the movie business was in California, and the music business was located in New York. To get around that problem, the company put into place regular meetings and videoconferencing so that the technologists would not develop a product without first discussing it with the content creators. More formal structural changes were instituted as well. A new unit was created at a senior level with the sole purpose of ensuring that Sony products and content would work together seamlessly. More company divisions were consolidated under a common management, with the mission of integrating the company's content, electronics, and services in innovative ways. And in Japan, the seniority-based compensation system was all but eliminated and replaced with a pay-for-performance system, more aligned with the compensation structure used in the United States.

Customer and Geographic Divisions   Some companies build divisions around groups of customers or around different geographic areas. Hewlett-Packard, for example, had separate divisions for its personal computer and printer business but saved money by combining them because customers for these products are largely the same.[24] Similarly, a hospital may organize its services around child, adult, psychiatric, and emergency cases. Bank loan departments commonly allocate assignments on the basis of whether customers are requesting consumer, mortgage, small-business, corporate, or agricultural loans.

In contrast to customers, divisions can be structured around geographic regions. Sears, for example, was a pioneer in creating *geographic divisions*. Geographic distinctions include district, territory, region, and country. Seagram International is one of many companies that assign managers to Europe, the Far East, and Latin America and treat those areas as separate lines of business.

The primary advantage of both the product and customer/regional approaches to departmentalization is the ability to focus on customer needs and provide faster, better service. But again, duplication of activities across many customer groups and geographic areas is expensive.

Customer and geographic divisions often service customers faster.

The Matrix Organization

A **matrix organization** is a hybrid form of organization in which functional and divisional forms overlap. Managers and staff personnel report to two bosses—a functional manager and a divisional manager. Thus, matrix organizations have a dual rather than a single line of command. In Figure 8.5, for example, each project manager draws employees from each functional area to form a group for the project. The employees working on those projects report to the individual project manager as well as to the manager of their functional area.

A good example of the matrix structure can be found at Time Inc., the world's largest magazine publisher. At major Time Inc. titles like *Time*, *Sports Illustrated*, and *People*, production managers who are responsible for getting the magazines printed report both to the individual publishers and editors of each title *and* to a senior corporate executive in charge of production. At the corporate level, Time Inc. achieves enormous economics of scale by buying paper and printing in bulk and making sure production activities in the company as a whole are coordinated. At the same time, production managers

> **matrix organization**
>
> An organization composed of dual reporting relationships in which some managers report to two superiors—a functional manager and a divisional manager.

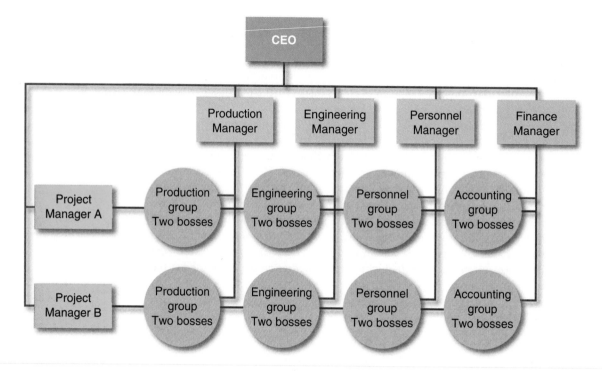

FIGURE 8.5

Matrix Organizational Structure

working at each title make sure the different needs and schedules of their individual magazines are being met. Similar matrix arrangements are in place for other key managers, like circulation and finance. In this way, the company attempts to gain the benefits of both the divisional and functional organization structure.

The matrix form originated in the aerospace industry, first with TRW in 1959 and then with NASA. Applications now occur in hospitals and health care agencies, entrepreneurial organizations, government laboratories, financial institutions, and multinational corporations.[25] Other companies that have used or currently use the matrix form include IBM, Boeing, Xerox, Shell Oil, Texas Instruments, Bechtel, Phillips Petroleum, and Dow Corning.

Pros and Cons of the Matrix Form   Like other organization structures, matrix has both strengths and weaknesses. Table 8.2 summarizes the advantages of using a matrix structure. The major potential advantage is a higher degree of flexibility and adaptability.

TABLE 8.2

Advantages of the Matrix Design

• Decision making is decentralized to a level where information is processed properly and relevant knowledge is applied.
• Extensive communications networks help process large amounts of information.
• With decisions delegated to appropriate levels, higher management levels are not overloaded with operational decisions.
• Resource utilization is efficient because key resources are shared across several important programs or products at the same time.
• Employees learn the collaborative skills needed to function in an environment characterized by frequent meetings and more informal interactions.
• Dual career ladders are elaborated as more career options become available on both sides of the organization.

SOURCE: H. Kolodny, "Managing in a Matrix," *Business Horizons,* March–April 1981, pp. 17–24.

- Confusion can arise because people do not have a single superior to whom they feel primary responsibility.
- The design encourages managers who share subordinates to jockey for power.
- The mistaken belief can arise that matrix management is the same thing as group decision making—in other words, everyone must be consulted for every decision.
- Too much democracy can lead to not enough action.

SOURCE: H. Kolodny, "Managing in a Matrix," *Business Horizons,* March–April 1981, pp. 17–24.

TABLE 8.3
Disadvantages of the Matrix Design

Table 8.3 summarizes the potential shortcomings of the matrix form. Many of the disadvantages stem from the matrix's inherent violation of the **unity-of-command principle,** which states that a person should have only one boss. Reporting to two superiors can create confusion and a difficult interpersonal situation, unless steps are taken to prevent these problems from arising.

Matrix Survival Skills   To a large degree, problems can be avoided if the key managers in the matrix learn the behavioral skills demanded in the matrix structure.[26] These skills vary depending on the job in the four-person diamond structure shown in Figure 8.6.

The *top executive,* who heads the matrix, must learn to balance power and emphasis between the product and functional orientations. *Product or division managers* and *functional managers* must learn to collaborate and manage their conflicts constructively. Finally, the *two-boss managers* or employees at the bottom of the diamond must learn how to be responsible to two superiors. This means prioritizing multiple demands and sometimes even reconciling conflicting orders. Some people function poorly under this ambiguous, conflictual circumstance; sometimes this signals the end of their careers with the company. Others learn to be proactive, communicate effectively with both superiors, rise above the difficulties, and manage these work relationships constructively.

unity-of-command principle

A structure in which each worker reports to one boss, who in turn reports to one boss.

The matrix structure can speed decisions and cut costs.

FIGURE 8.6
The Matrix Diamond

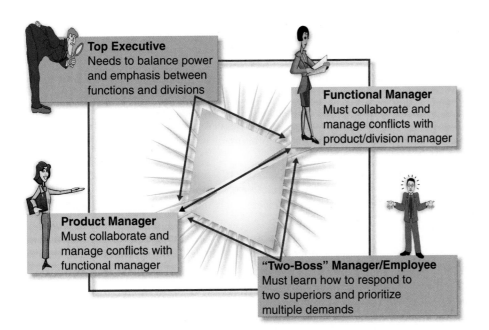

Top Executive
Needs to balance power and emphasis between functions and divisions

Functional Manager
Must collaborate and manage conflicts with product/division manager

Product Manager
Must collaborate and manage conflicts with functional manager

"Two-Boss" Manager/Employee
Must learn how to respond to two superiors and prioritize multiple demands

Advantages of Collaboration

The value of collaboration is particularly pronounced in a matrix organization. For example, in the kind of structure illustrated in Figure 8.5, project group members may not be permanently assigned to the project manager. They will return to their functional area once the project has been completed. For this group to work effectively, the traditional command-and-control management style may not be the most appropriate; it might gain *compliance* from group members, but not their full *commitment,* making it harder to achieve the project's goals. Furthermore, as the matrix organization draws on members of functional groups in order to tap their expertise, it is very important to get their full contribution. A collaborative process, in which the manager and participants develop a shared sense of ownership for the work they are doing, will generate better ideas, participation, and commitment to the project and its outcomes.

Organizations with highly specialized staff, such as NASA astronaut Susan J. Helms (left), shown here with Russian cosmonaut Yury V. Usachev in the International Space Station, typically use a matrix structure.

The Matrix Form Today The popularity of the matrix form waned during the end of the 1980s, when many companies had difficulty implementing it. But lately, it has come back strong. Reasons for this resurgence include pressures to consolidate costs and be faster to market, creating a need for better coordination across functions in the business units, and a need for coordination across countries for firms with global business strategies. Many of the challenges created by the matrix are particularly acute in an international context, mainly because of the distances involved and the differences in local markets.[27]

The key to managing today's matrix is not the formal structure itself but the realization that the matrix is a *process*. Managers who have appropriately adopted the matrix structure because of the complexity of the challenges they confront, but have had trouble implementing it, often find that they haven't changed the employee and managerial relationships within their organizations in ways that make the matrix effective. It is not enough to create a flexible organization merely by changing its structure. To create an environment that allows information to flow freely throughout the organization, managers must also attend to the norms, values, and attitudes that shape how people within their organizations behave.[28] We will address these issues in the next chapter and in Part 4 of the book, which focuses on how to lead and manage people.

The Network Organization

So far, the structures we have been discussing are variations of the traditional, hierarchical organization, within which all the business functions of the firm are performed. In contrast, the **network organization** is a collection of independent, mostly single-function firms that collaborate to produce a product or service. As depicted in Figure 8.7, the network organization describes not one organization but the web of relationships among many firms. Network organizations are flexible arrangements among designers, suppliers, producers, distributors, and customers where each firm is able to pursue its own distinctive competence, yet work effectively with other members of the network. Often members of the network communicate electronically and share information in order to be able to respond quickly to customer demands. In effect, the normal boundary of the organization becomes blurred or porous, as managers within the organization interact closely with network members outside it. The network as a whole, then, can display the technical specialization of the functional structure, the market responsiveness of the product structure, and the balance and flexibility of the matrix.[29]

A very flexible version of the network organization is the **dynamic network**—also called the *modular* or *virtual* corporation. It is composed of temporary arrangements among members that can be assembled and reassembled to meet a changing competi-

network organization

A collection of independent, mostly single-function firms that collaborate on a product or service.

dynamic network

Temporary arrangements among partners that can be assembled and reassembled to adapt to the environment.

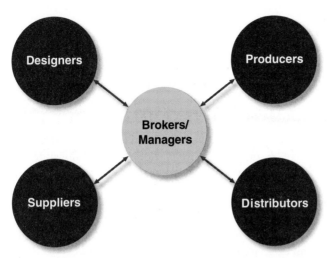

SOURCE: R. Miles and C. Snow, "Organizations: New Concepts for New Forms," *California Management Review*, Spring 1986, p. 65. Copyright © 1986 by The Regents of the University of California. Reprinted from the *California Management Review*, Vol. 28, No. 3 by permission of The Regents.

FIGURE 8.7
A Organization Network

tive environment. The members of the network are held together by contracts that stipulate results expected (market mechanisms) rather than by hierarchy and authority. Poorly performing firms can be removed and replaced.

Such arrangements are common in the electronics, toy, and apparel industries, each of which creates and sells trendy products at a fast pace. For example, Reebok owns no plants; it designs and markets but does not produce. Nike owns only one small factory that makes sneaker parts. Other examples include the Bombay Company, Louis Galoob Toys, Brooks Brothers, and the Registry (which markets the services of independent software engineers, programmers, and technical writers). In biotechnology, smaller firms do research and manufacture, and the drug giants market.[30]

Successful networks potentially offer flexibility, innovation, quick responses to threats and opportunities, and reduced costs and risk. But for these arrangements to be successful, several things must occur:

Networks can improve cost, quality, speed, and innovation.

- The firm must choose the right specialty. This must be something (product or service) that the market needs and which the firm is better at providing than other firms.
- The firm must choose collaborators that also are excellent at what they do and that provide complementary strengths.
- The firm must make certain that all parties fully understand the strategic goals of the partnership.
- Each party must be able to trust all the others with strategic information and also trust that each collaborator will deliver quality products even if the business grows quickly and makes heavy demands.

The role of managers shifts in a network from that of command and control to more like that of a **broker.** Broker/managers serve several important boundary roles that aid network integration and coordination:

- *Designer role.* The broker serves as a network architect who envisions a set of groups or firms whose collective expertise could be focused on a particular product or service.
- *Process engineering role.* The broker serves as a *network co-operator* who takes the initiative to lay out the flow of resources and relationships and makes certain that everyone shares the same goals, standards, payments, and the like.
- *Nurturing role.* The broker serves as a network developer that nurtures and enhances the network (like team building) to make certain the relationships are healthy and mutually beneficial.[31]

broker

A person who assembles and coordinates participants in a network.

Organizational Integration

At the beginning of this chapter, we said that organizations are structured around differentiation and integration. So far, our discussion has focused on *differentiation*—the way the organization is composed of different jobs and tasks, and how these fit on an organization chart. But as organizations differentiate their structures, they also need to be concerned about *integration* and *coordination*—the way all the parts of the organization will work together. Often, the more differentiated the organization, the more difficult integration may be. Because of specialization and the division of labor, different groups of managers and employees develop different orientations. Depending on whether employees are in a functional department or a divisional group, are line or staff, and so on, they will think and act in ways that are geared toward their particular work units. In short, people working in separate functions, divisions, and business units literally tend to forget about one another. When this happens, it is difficult for managers to combine all their activities into an integrated whole.

A variety of approaches are available to managers to help them make certain that interdependent units and individuals will work together to achieve a common purpose. Coordination methods include standardization, plans, and mutual adjustment.[32]

Coordination by Standardization

When organizations coordinate activities by establishing routines and standard operating procedures that remain in place over time, we say that work has been standardized. **Standardization** constrains actions and integrates various units by regulating what people do. People often know how to act—and know how to interact—because standard operating procedures spell out what they should do. For example, managers may establish standards for which types of computer equipment the organization will use. This will simplify the purchasing and computer-training process—everyone will be on a common platform—and make it easier for the different parts of the organization to communicate with each other.

To improve coordination, organizations may also rely on **formalization**—the presence of rules and regulations governing how people in the organization interact. Simple, often written policies regarding attendance, dress, and decorum, for example, may help eliminate a good deal of uncertainty at work. But an important assumption underlying both standardization and formalization is that the rules and procedures should apply to most (if not all) situations. These approaches, therefore, are most appropriate in situations that are relatively stable and unchanging. In some cases, when the work environment requires flexibility, coordination by standardization may not be very effective. Who hasn't experienced a time when rules and procedures—frequently associated with a slow bureaucracy—prevented timely action to address a problem? In these instances, we often refer to rules and regulations as "red tape."[33]

Coordination by Plan

If laying out the exact rules and procedures by which work should be integrated is difficult, organizations may provide more latitude by establishing goals and schedules for interdependent units. **Coordination by plan** does not require the same high degree of stability and routinization required for coordination by standardization. Interdependent units are free to modify and adapt their actions as long as they meet the deadlines and targets required for working with others.

In writing this textbook, for example, we (the authors) sat down with a publication team that included the editors, the marketing staff, the production group, and support staff. Together we ironed out a schedule

standardization

Establishing common routines and procedures that apply uniformly to everyone.

formalization

The presence of rules and regulations governing how people in the organization interact.

coordination by plan

Interdependent units are required to meet deadlines and objectives that contribute to a common goal.

Banks are among the most standardized of organizations, from operating procedures through dress codes, reinforcing to their customers and employees that the organization and their dealings with it are stable and reliable.

for developing this book that covered approximately a two-year period. That development plan included dates and "deliverables" that specified what was to be accomplished and forwarded to the others in the organization. The plan allowed for a good deal of flexibility on each subunit's part, and the overall approach allowed us to work together effectively.

Coordination by Mutual Adjustment

Ironically, the simplest and most flexible approach to coordination may just be to have interdependent parties talk to one another. **Coordination by mutual adjustment** involves feedback and discussions to jointly figure out how to approach problems and devise solutions that are agreeable to everyone. The popularity of teams today is in part due to the fact that they allow for flexible coordination; teams can operate under the principle of mutual adjustment.

But the flexibility of mutual adjustment as a coordination device does not come without some cost. "Hashing out" every issue takes a good deal of time and may not be the most expedient approach for organizing work. Imagine how long it would take to accomplish even the most basic tasks if subunits had to talk through every situation. At the same time, mutual adjustment can be very effective when problems are novel and cannot be programmed in advance with rules, procedures, or plans. Particularly in crisis situations in which rules and procedures don't apply, mutual adjustment is likely to be the most effective approach to coordination.

> **coordination by mutual adjustment**
>
> Units interact with one another to make accommodations in order to achieve flexible coordination.

Coordination and Communication

Today's environments tend to be complex, dynamic, and (therefore) uncertain. Huge amounts of information flow from the external environment to the organization and back to the environment. To cope, organizations must acquire, process, and respond to that information. Doing so has direct implications for how firms organize. To function effectively, organizations need to develop structures for processing information.

Figure 8.8 shows two general strategies that can help managers cope with high uncertainty and heavy information demands. First, management can act to reduce the need for information. Second, it can increase its capacity to handle more information.[34]

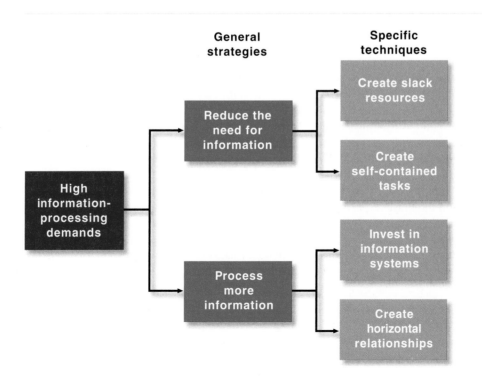

FIGURE 8.8

Managing High Information-Processing Demands

Option 1: Reducing the Need for Information   Managers can reduce the need for information in two ways: (a) creating slack resources and (b) creating self-contained tasks. *Slack resources* are simply extra resources on which organizations can rely "in a pinch" so that if they get caught off guard, they can still adjust. Inventory, for example, is a type of slack resource that provides extra stock on hand in case it is needed. With extra inventory, an organization does not have to have as much information about sales demand, lead time, and the like. Employees also can be a type of slack resource. For example, many companies augment their full-time staffs with part-time and temporary employees. This way, they do not have to perfectly forecast sales peaks, but can rely on supplementary workers to handle irregularities.[35]

Like slack resources, *creating self-contained tasks* allows organizations to reduce the need for some information. Creating self-contained tasks refers to changing from a functional organization to a product or project organization and giving each unit the resources it needs to perform its task. Information-processing problems are reduced because each unit has its own full complement of specialties instead of functional specialties that have to share their expertise among a number of different product teams. Communications then flow within each team rather than among a complex array of interdependent groups.

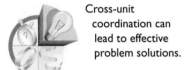

Cross-unit coordination can lead to effective problem solutions.

Option 2: Increasing Information-Processing Capability   Instead of reducing the need for information, an organization may take the approach of increasing its information-processing capability. It can *invest in information systems*, which usually means employing or expanding computer systems. But increasing an organization's information-processing capability also means what we referred to in Chapter 1 as *knowledge management*—capitalizing on the intellect and experience of the organization's human assets to increase collaboration and effectiveness. One way to do that is by creating horizontal relationships between units to foster coordination. Such horizontal relationships are effective because they increase integration, which Lawrence and Lorsch suggest is necessary for managing complex environments. As uncertainty increases, the following horizontal processes may be used, ranging from the simplest to the most complex.[36]

1. *Direct contact (mutual adjustment)* among managers who share a problem. In a university, for example, a residence hall adviser might call a meeting to resolve differences between two feuding students who live in adjacent rooms.
2. *Liaison roles*, or specialized jobs to handle communications between two departments. A fraternity representative is a liaison between the fraternity and the interfraternity council, the university, or the local community.
3. *Task forces*, or groups of representatives from different departments, brought together temporarily to solve a common problem. For example, students, faculty, and administrators may be members of a task force charged with bringing distinguished speakers to campus for a current-events seminar.
4. *Teams*, or permanent interdepartmental decision-making groups. An executive council made up of department heads might meet regularly to make decisions affecting a college of engineering or liberal arts.
5. *Product, program, or project managers* who direct interdisciplinary groups with a common task to perform. In a college of business administration, a faculty administrator might head an executive education program of professors from several disciplines.
6. *Matrix organizations*, composed of dual relationships in which some managers report to two superiors. Your instructors, for example, may report to department heads in their respective disciplines and also to a director of undergraduate or graduate programs.

 "An organization's ability to learn, and translate that learning into action rapidly, is the ultimate competitive advantage."
Jack Welch

Several of these processes are discussed further in Chapter 14, where we examine managing teams and intergroup relations.

Looking Ahead

The organization chart, differentiation, integration, authority, delegation, coordination, and the like, convey fundamental information about an organization's structure. However, the information so far has provided only a snapshot. The real organization is more like a motion picture—it moves! More flexible and innovative—even virtual— forms of organizations are evolving. As you can see from the accompanying table, today's organizations are far removed, in many of their fundamental characteristics, from the traditional forms they once had.

Contrasting Views of the Corporation

FROM THE PAGES OF BusinessWeek

Characteristic	20th Century	21st Century
Organization	The Pyramid	The Web or Network
Focus	Internal	External
Style	Structured	Flexible
Source of strength	Stability	Change
Structure	Self-sufficiency	Interdependencies
Resources	Atoms—physical assets	Bits—information
Operations	Vertical integration	Virtual integration
Products	Mass production	Mass customization
Reach	Domestic	Global
Financials	Quarterly	Real-time
Inventories	Months	Hours
Strategy	Top-down	Bottom-up
Leadership	Dogmatic	Inspirational
Workers	Employees	Employees and free agents
Job expectations	Security	Personal growth
Motivation	To compete	To build
Improvements	Incremental	Revolutionary
Quality	Affordable best	No compromise

SOURCE: "Management by Web," *BusinessWeek*, August 28, 2000, online.

No organization is merely a set of static work relationships. Because organizations are composed of people, they are hotbeds of social relationships. Networks of individuals cutting across departmental boundaries interact with one another. Various friendship groups or cliques band together to form *coalitions*—members of the organization who jointly support a particular issue and try to ensure that their viewpoints determine the outcome of policy decisions.[37]

Thus, the formal organization structure does not describe everything about how the company really works. Even if you know departments and authority relationships, there is still much to understand. How do things really get done? Who influences whom, and how? Which managers are the most powerful? How effective is the top leadership? Which groups are most and which are least effective? What is the nature of communication patterns throughout the organization? These issues are discussed throughout the rest of the book.

Now you are familiar with the basic organizing concepts discussed in this chapter. In the next chapter, we will discuss the current challenges of designing the modern organization with which the modern executive constantly grapples.

EPILOGUE

SONY ORGANIZES FOR CONVERGENCE

By 2005, Sony was under considerable pressure to improve its bottom line. Prices had continued to drop for TVs, DVDs, and other core Sony products, reducing the company's profits significantly. The company also continued to tinker with its organization structure. The company announced that, to speed product development and continue to ensure that all Sony products would link with each other, it was consolidating more of the company's engineers and technology teams. In addition, it formed a new division, called Contact, to compete with Apple's iPod and its iTunes online music service. The head of that division would report to the head of Sony USA as well as the head of Sony's main computer division in Japan. That reporting structure was designed to help link both parts of the company and keep them working together to meet the competitive challenge from Apple.

In the meantime, the changes Sony had already made began to be reflected in its product line. In Japan, the company launched its long-awaited next-generation PlayStation, the PlayStation Portable, or PSP. Japanese sales were robust, and full rollout in the United States was launched in 2005. The PSP reflected the new cooperation between what once were separate and uncoordinated divisions at Sony. For example, some of the technology in the device would also be used in Sony televisions and DVD recorders. And the PSP itself would handle not only games, but a variety of multimedia applications as well: It would record and play high-quality audio and video and accept or send content to and from other Sony devices. It would also come packaged with a DVD of a blockbuster from Sony Pictures, like *Spiderman 2*. This convergence of functionality and content in the PSP was a direct result of Sony's more integrated organization structure. But Sony's need to continue to integrate its different operating units was made clear when Howard Stringer was appointed as the company's new chief executive early in 2005. "The world is not the same place it was just a few years ago," he wrote in a letter to employees. "Our businesses must be restructured so they are much more profitable, and so they can grow."

KEY TERMS

Accountability, p. 267

Authority, p. 264

Broker, p. 279

Centralized organization, p. 269

Coordination, p. 262

Coordination by mutual adjustment, p. 281

Coordination by plan, p. 280

Corporate governance, p. 262

Decentralized organization, p. 269

Delegation, p. 266

Departmentalization, p. 271

Differentiation, p. 261

Division of labor, p. 261

Divisional organization, p. 272

Dynamic network, p. 278

Formalization, p. 280

Functional organization, p. 271

Hierarchy, p. 265

Integration, p. 261

Line departments, p. 271

Matrix organization, p. 275

Network organization, p. 278

Organization chart, p. 260

Responsibility, p. 267

Span of control, p. 266

Specialization, p. 261

Staff departments, p. 271

Standardization, p. 280

Subunits, p. 266

Unity-of-command principle, p. 277

SUMMARY OF LEARNING OBJECTIVES

Now that you have studied Chapter 8, you should know:

How differentiation and integration influence an organization's structure.

Differentiation means that organizations have many parts. Specialization means that various individuals and units throughout the organization perform different tasks. The assignment of tasks to different people or groups often is referred to as the division of labor. But the specialized tasks in an organization cannot all be performed independently of one another. Coordination links the various tasks in order to achieve the organization's overall mission. When there are many different specialized tasks and work units, the organization is highly differentiated; the more differentiated the organization is, the more integration or coordination is required.

How authority operates.

Authority is the legitimate right to make decisions and tell other people what to do. Authority is exercised throughout the hierarchy, as bosses have the authority to give orders to subordinates. Through the day-to-day operation of authority, the organization proceeds toward achieving its goals. Owners or stockholders have ultimate authority.

The roles of the board of directors and the chief executive officer.

Boards of directors report to stockholders. The board of directors controls or advises management, considers the firm's legal and other interests, and protects stockholders' rights. The chief executive officer reports to the board and is accountable for the organization's performance.

How span of control affects structure and managerial effectiveness.

Span of control is the number of people who report directly to a manager. Narrow spans create tall organizations, and wide spans create flat ones. No single span of control is always appropriate; the optimal span is determined by characteristics of the work, the subordinates, the manager, and the organization.

Why effective delegation is important.

Delegation is the assignment of tasks and responsibilities. Delegation has many potential advantages for the manager, the subordinate, and the organization. But to be effective, the process must be managed carefully. The manager should define the goal, select the person, solicit opinions, provide resources, schedule checkpoints, and discuss progress periodically.

The difference between centralized and decentralized organizations.

In centralized organizations, most important decisions are made by top managers. In decentralized organizations, many decisions are delegated to lower levels.

The different ways organizations can be structured.

Organizations can be structured on the basis of function, division (product, customers, or geographic), matrix, and network. Each form has advantages and disadvantages.

The unique challenges of the matrix organization.

The matrix is a complex structure with a dual authority structure. A well-managed matrix enables organizations to adapt to change. But it can also create confusion and interpersonal difficulties. People in all positions in the matrix—top executives, product and function managers, and two-boss managers—must acquire unique survival skills.

The nature of important integrating mechanisms.

Managers can coordinate interdependent units through standardization, plans, and mutual adjustment. Standardization occurs when routines and standard operating procedures are put in place. They typically are accompanied by formalized rules. Coordination by plan is more flexible and allows more freedom in how tasks are carried out but keeps interdependent units focused on schedules and joint goals. Mutual adjustment involves feedback and discussions among related parties to accommodate each other's needs. It is at once the most flexible and simple to administer, but it is time-consuming.

DISCUSSION QUESTIONS

1. Using the concepts in the chapter, discuss the advantages and disadvantages of the various changes in organization structure described in "Sony Organizes for Convergence."

2. What are some advantages and disadvantages of being in the CEO position?

3. Would you like to sit on a board of directors? Why or why not? If you did serve on a board, what kind of organization would you prefer? As a board member, in what kinds of activities do you think you would most actively engage?

4. Interview a member of a board of directors and discuss that member's perspectives on his or her role.

5. Pick a job you have held and describe it in terms of span of control, delegation, responsibility, authority, and accountability.

6. Why do you think managers have difficulty delegating? What can be done to overcome these difficulties?

7. Consider an organization in which you have worked, draw its organization chart, and describe it by using terms in this chapter. How did you like working there, and why?

8. Would you rather work in a functional or divisional organization? Why?

9. If you learned that a company had a matrix structure, would you be more or less interested in working there? Explain your answer. How would you prepare yourself to work effectively in a matrix?

10. Brainstorm a list of methods for integrating interdependent work units. Discuss the activities that need to be undertaken and the pros and cons of each approach.

CONCLUDING CASE

Down East Spud Busters

Down East Spud Busters is part of a conglomerate that represents the potato growers of eastern Canada and northern Maine and that also oversees the collection, processing, and distribution of potatoes and potato products.

For many years, the industry functioned as a local cooperative. The cooperative was simply a collection center where potatoes were weighed and received, washed and graded, bagged and distributed. Potatoes were the only product. Potatoes were distrib-

uted in a variety of bag sizes and weights and were also sold loosely in large bins.

The first phase of Down East Spud Busters' strategic plan resulted in the building of a large manufacturing plant in northern Maine with a focus on value-added products. The major strategy is to process higher-value potato products. Those products include a frozen division line (French fries, home fries, gourmet stuffed potatoes, flavored potato skins, and so on), a dried-food division line (instant mashed potatoes, freeze-dried potatoes, potato pancake mix, and so on), and the traditional potato line (bagged potatoes, loose potatoes, microwave singles, baby potatoes, and so on). The corporate group figures that it can triple sales revenues from the existing yield of potatoes.

The second phase of Down East Spud Busters' strategic plan calls for a nationwide sales and distribution program. A gigantic market in retail food sales has gone untouched by this group of growers and producers. The major strategy is to recruit the appropriate sales force and to set up a system for selling and distributing the products. The major markets are supermarket chains, smaller retail grocers, major hotel chains, and governmental/school institutional kitchens.

Down East Spud Busters is leaning toward the concept of hiring sales associates who will work out of their own homes in strategic locations throughout the United States. Those sales associates will be assigned to specific territories and will be challenged to meet or exceed specific quotas of each of the conglomerate's products. The sales associates will also be responsible for overseeing the distribution and delivery of the products, and for dealing with any and all after-sale problems or issues.

The third and final phase of Down East Spud Busters' strategic plan is to build a second manufacturing plant in Idaho in five years and to possibly facilitate and oversee an increase in crop planting and yield in both territories. The company also plans to expand its market territories into selected locations in Europe and the Pacific Rim.

QUESTIONS

1. Select from the chapter text options and prepare an organizational chart for the national distribution program that this company is about to embark upon. Be sure to incorporate the company's goals into your overall structure.

2. Given the vast geographic expanse and logistical challenges of this new program, what recommendations do you have for the company regarding HR policies and procedures?

3. What other types of industries could use the model from this case as a means to expand sales nationally or internationally?

EXPERIENTIAL EXERCISES

8.1 The Business School Organization Chart

OBJECTIVES

1. To clarify the factors that determine organization structure.
2. To provide insight into the workings of an organization.
3. To examine the working relationships within an organization.

INSTRUCTIONS

1. Draw an organization chart for your school of business. Be sure to identify all the staff and line positions in the school. Specify the chain of command and the levels of administration. Note the different spans of control. Are there any advisory groups, task forces, or committees to consider?

2. Review the chapter material on organization structure to help identify both strong and weak points in your school's organization. Now draw another organization chart for the school, incorporating any changes you believe would improve the quality of the school. Support the second chart with a list of recommended changes and reasons for their inclusion.

DISCUSSION QUESTIONS

1. Is your business school well organized? Why or why not?

2. In what ways is the school's structure designed to suit the needs of students, faculty, staff, the administration, and the business community?

8.2 Designing a Student-Run Organization That Provides Consulting Services

OBJECTIVES

1. To appreciate the importance of the total organization on group and individual behavior.

2. To provide a beginning organization design experience that will be familiar to students.

BACKGROUND

The Industry Advisory Council for your school has decided to sponsor a student-run organization that will provide business consulting services to nonprofit groups in your community. The council has donated $20,000 toward startup costs and has agreed to provide office space, computer equipment, and other materials as needed. The council hopes that the organization will establish its own source of funding after the first year of operation.

Task 1 The dean of the school wants you to develop alternative designs for the new organization. Your task is to identify the main design dimensions or factors to be dealt with in establishing such an organization and to describe the issues that must be resolved for each factor. For example, you might provide an organization chart to help describe the structural issues involved. Before jumping ahead with your design, you may also have to think about (1) groups in the community that could use your help and (2) problems they face. Remember, though, your task is to create the organization that will provide services, not to provide an in-depth look at the types of services provided.

You and your team are to brainstorm design dimensions to be dealt with and to develop a one- or two-page outline that can be shared with the entire class. You have 1 hour to develop the outline. Select two people to present your design. Assume that you will all be involved in the new organization, filling specific positions.

Task 2 After the brainstorming period, the spokespersons will present the group designs or preferred design and answer questions from the audience.

Task 3 The instructor will comment on the designs and discuss additional factors that might be important for the success of this organization.

Source: A. B. (Rami) Shani and James B. Lau, *Behavior in Organizations: An Experimental Approach* (New York: McGraw-Hill/Irwin, 2005), p. 369.

8.3 Decentralization: Pros and Cons

OBJECTIVE

To explore the reasons for, as well as the pros and cons of, decentralizing.

INSTRUCTIONS

The following Decentralization Worksheet contains some observations on decentralization. As you review each of the statements, provide an example that illustrates why this statement is important and related problems and benefits of the situation or condition indicated in the statement.

Decentralization Worksheet

A large number of factors determine the extent to which a manager should decentralize. Clearly, anything that increases a manager's workload creates pressure for decentralization because only a finite level of work can be accomplished by a single person. As with many facets of management, there are advantages and disadvantages to decentralization.

1. The greater the diversity of products, the greater the decentralization.

2. The larger the size of the organization, the more the decentralization.

3. The more rapidly changing the organization's environment, the more decentralization.

4. Developing adequate, timely controls is the essence of decentralizing.

5. Managers should delegate decisions that involve large amounts of time but minimal erosions of their power and control.

    _____

    _____

    _____

    _____

6. Decentralizing involves delegating authority, and therefore, the principles of delegation apply to decentralization. (List the principles of delegation before you start your discussion.)

    _____

    _____

    _____

    _____

SOURCE: R. R. McGrath Jr., *Exercises in Management Fundamentals* (Englewood Cliffs, NJ: Prentice-Hall, 1985) pp. 59–60. Reprinted by permission of Prentice-Hall, Inc.

Chapter **9**

CHAPTER 9
Organizational Agility

It is change, continuing change, inevitable change, that is the dominant fact in society today. No sensible decision can be made any longer without taking into account not only the world as it is, but the world as it will be.

—Isaac Asimov

CHAPTER OUTLINE

LEARNING OBJECTIVES

After studying Chapter 9, you will know:

1. Why it is critical for organizations to be responsive.

2. The advantages of an organic organization structure.

3. The strategies and dynamic organizational concepts that can be used to improve an organization's responsiveness.

4. How a firm can be both big and small.

5. How firms organize to meet customer requirements.

6. How firms organize around different types of technology.

Prologue

CAN AMERICA'S CARMAKERS CATCH TOYOTA?

Yoi kangae, yoi shina! That's Toyota-speak for "Good thinking means good products." The slogan is emblazoned on a giant banner hanging across the company's Takaoka assembly plant. Plenty of good thinking has gone into the high-tech ballet that's performed here 17 hours a day. Six separate car models glide along on a single production line in any of a half-dozen colors. Overhead, car doors flow by on a conveyor belt that descends to floor level and drops off the right door in the correct color for each vehicle. This efficiency means Takaoka workers can build a car in just 20 hours.

The combination of speed and flexibility is world class. A similar dance is happening at 30 Toyota plants worldwide, with some able to make as many as eight different models on the same line. That is leading to a monster increase in productivity and market responsiveness—all part of the company's obsession with what President Fujio Cho calls "the criticality of speed."

Of course, the carmaker has always moved steadily forward: Its executives created the doctrine of *kaizen,* or continuous improvement. But in the past few years Toyota has accelerated these gains, raising the bar for the entire industry. Toyota is closing in on DaimlerChrysler to become the third-biggest carmaker in the United States. Its U.S. share, rising steadily, is now above 11 percent. At its current rate of expansion, Toyota could pass Ford Motor Co. in mid-decade as the world's No. 2 automaker. Toyota is also putting the finishing touches on a plan to create an integrated, flexible, global manufacturing system. In this new network, plants from Indonesia to Argentina will be designed both to customize cars for local markets and to shift production to quickly satisfy any surges in demand from markets worldwide.

In Cambridge, Ontario, Cho is going even further. He's determined to show the world that Toyota can meet its own highest standards of excellence anywhere in its system. Its plant there has introduced "Circle L" stations where workers must double- and triple-check parts that customers have complained about—anything from glove boxes to suspension systems. The Cambridge workers are aided by a radical piece of manufacturing technology being rolled out to Toyota plants worldwide. The system, called the Global Body Line, holds vehicle frames in place while they're being welded, using just one master brace instead of the dozens of separate braces required in a standard factory. Analysts say it lets Toyota save 75 percent of the cost of refitting a production line to build a different car, and it's key to Toyota's ability to make multiple models on a single line.

Cho and his managers are not just reengineering how Toyota makes its cars—they want to revolutionize how it creates products. With the rise of e-mail and teleconferencing, teams of designers, engineers, product planners, workers, and suppliers rarely all convened in the same place. Under Cho, they're again required to work face to face, in a process Toyota calls *obeya*—literally, "big room." This cuts the time it takes to get a car from the drawing board to the showroom. It took only 19 months to develop the Solara. That's better than 22 months for the latest Sienna minivan, and 26 months for the latest Camry—well below the industry average of about three years.

General Motors, Ford Motor, and DaimlerChrysler have diligently studied how the Japanese engineer more cars for less money, using a similar set of chassis and frame parts to create a common vehicle architecture, or "platform." But the U.S.-based carmakers have yet to really master this art, which involves assembling an attractive mix of cars and sport-utility vehicles from components already in the parts bin.

Consumers want the freshest models, and Detroit tries to serve them by redesigning its passenger cars roughly every seven years. But the Japanese have shortened that vehicle life cycle to five years—in part by relying on platform-based development. As a result, U.S. carmakers could see their share of the market drop from 60.2 percent in 2003 to 56.5 percent in 2006. For American carmakers the platform approach is no longer simply an idea to explore. "We have to do this," says Philip R. Martens, Ford's group vice-president for product creation in North America. "The market is hypercompetitive."

Sources for Prologue, Connections, Epilogue: Adapted from Brian Bremner and Chester Dawson, "Can Anything Stop Toyota?" *BusinessWeek*, November 17, 2003, online; Ed Garsten, "Flexible Factories Will Help Dull Japanese Edge," *The Detroit News*, August 5, 2003, online; David Welch, "Detroit Tries It the Japanese Way," *BusinessWeek*, January 26, 2004, online; David Welch, "GM and Daimler Are Stepping on It," *BusinessWeek*, December 27, 2004, online; Danny Hakim, "Building Autos with the Same DNA," *The New York Times*, February 22, 2005, p. C1.

As the Prologue strongly suggests, successful companies do not sit still. If they do, they can all too easily become vulnerable—to new technologies, tougher competitors, shifts in customer preferences, or other changes in their environment. Instead, they use their current successes to continue to build a competitive advantage for the future, constantly seeking new ways to remain flexible, innovative, efficient, and responsive to their customers. One of the most important ways they have of doing that is to make sure that their organization structures and systems remain *adaptable*—prepared to meet the complex and ever-changing challenges that managers and their organizations constantly confront.

In our last chapter, we described the formal structure of the organization. We discussed hierarchical levels, reporting relationships, division of labor, coordination—all the basic, traditional elements of structure that are fundamental for understanding the way organizations work. But a firm's formal structure is only part of the story. Organizations are not static structures but complex systems in which many people do many different things at the same time. The overall behavior of organizations does not just pop out of a chart; it emerges out of all the processes, systems, and relationships within the organization, and how they interact. The task of organizing, then, is a matter of designing not just the appropriate formal structure for the organization but also the appropriate processes, information flows, and technology that make the organization effective. The "structuring" of these elements is critical for the flexibility and agility today's dynamic organizations require. The organization forms that enable that agility are the subject of this chapter.

The Responsive Organization

The formal structure is put in place to *control* people, decisions, and actions. But in today's fast-changing business environment, *responsiveness*—quickness, agility, the ability to adapt to changing demands—is more vital than ever to a firm's survival.[1]

Many years after Max Weber wrote about the concept of bureaucracy, two British management scholars (Burns and Stalker) described what they called the **mechanistic organization**.[2] The common mechanistic structure they described was similar to Weber's bureaucracy, but they went on to suggest that in the modern corporation, the mechanistic structure is not the only option. The **organic structure** stands in stark

Speed is vital to an organization's survival.

mechanistic organization

A form of organization that seeks to maximize internal efficiency.

organic structure

An organizational form that emphasizes flexibility.

contrast to the mechanistic organization. It is much less rigid and, in fact, emphasizes flexibility. The organic structure can be described as follows:

1. Jobholders have broader responsibilities that change as the need arises.
2. Communication occurs through advice and information rather than through orders and instructions.
3. Decision making and influence are more decentralized and informal.
4. Expertise is highly valued.
5. Jobholders rely more heavily on judgment than on rules.
6. Obedience to authority is less important than commitment to the organization's goals.
7. Employees depend more on one another and relate more informally and personally.

Figure 9.1 contrasts the formal structure of an organization—epitomized by the organization chart—to the informal structure, which is much more organic. Astute managers are keenly aware of the network of interactions among the organization's members, and they structure around this network to increase agility. People in organic organizations work more as teammates than as subordinates who take orders from the boss, thus breaking away from the traditional bureaucratic form.[3]

The ideas underlying the organic structure and networks are the foundation for the newer forms of organization described in this chapter. The more organic a firm is, the more responsive it will be to changing competitive demands and market realities. Managers in progressive companies place a premium on being able to act, and act fast. They want to act in accordance with customer needs and other outside pressures. They want to take actions to correct past mistakes and also to prepare for an uncertain future. They want to be able to respond to threats and opportunities. The particular form—and degree—of organic structure the organization adopts to accomplish these goals will depend on its *strategy*, its *size*, its *customers*, and its *technology*. We will consider each of these in turn.

Strategy and Organizational Agility

Certain strategies, and the structures, processes, and relationships that accompany them, seem particularly well suited to improving an organization's ability to respond quickly and effectively to the challenges it faces. They reflect its managers' determination to fully leverage its people and assets to make the firm more agile and competitive. These strategies and structures are based on the firm's core competencies, its strategic alliances, its ability to learn, and its ability to engage all the people in the organization in achieving its objectives.

Organizing around Core Competencies

A recent, different, and important perspective on strategy and organization hinges on the concept of *core competence*.[4] As you learned in Chapter 4, a core competence is the capability—knowledge, expertise, skill—that underlies a company's ability to be a leader in providing a range of specific goods or services. It allows the company to compete on the basis of its core strengths and expertise, not just on what it produces. For example, Barnes & Noble's core competence is book merchandising. A core competence gives value to customers, makes the company's products different from (and better than) those of competitors, and can be used in creating new products. Think of core competencies as the roots of competitiveness and products as the fruits.

Core competence can be a source of quality and innovation.

Successfully developing a world-class core competence opens the door to a variety of future opportunities; failure means being foreclosed from many markets. Thus, a well-understood, well-developed core competence can enhance a company's responsiveness and competitiveness. Strategically, this means that companies should commit to excellence and leadership in competencies, and strengthen those, before they commit to winning market share for specific products. Organizationally, this means that

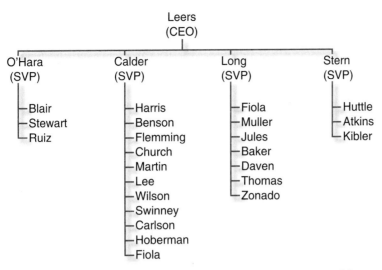

FIGURE 9.1(a)
Organization Chart Shows Who's on Top

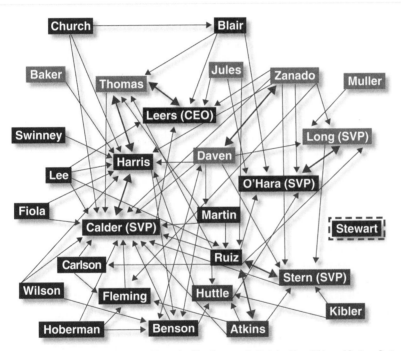

FIGURE 9.1(b)
Advice Network Reveals Knowledge Flow

the corporation should be viewed as a portfolio of competencies, not just a portfolio of specific businesses. Companies should strive for core competence leadership, not just product leadership.

Managers who want to strengthen their firms' competitiveness via core competencies need to focus on several related issues:

- Identify existing core competencies.
- Acquire or build core competencies that will be important for the future.
- Keep investing in competencies so that the firm remains world-class and better than competitors.
- Extend competencies to find new applications and opportunities for the markets of tomorrow.[5]

Connections: AMERICA'S CARMAKERS

Detroit's top brass used to boast that nearly every part in an overhauled model was different from its predecessor—never mind that all those changes drove up costs and took time to engineer. In past decades, only a small percentage of parts were reused from one generation to the next. Now, General Motors Vice-Chairman Robert A. Lutz wants to raise that to 40 percent to 60 percent—about on par with the Japanese. As GM develops the next-generation Chevy Silverado and GMC Sierra pickups for 2008, for example, it aims to reuse much of the existing platform. That should cut development costs in half, to nearly $3 billion. GM also announced that it would be reusing the skeleton beneath its Pontiac Solstice for its Saturn coupe and maybe the sporty Chevrolet wagon called the Nomad. The company is also putting its global resources behind its platforms, mining its European and Asian affiliates for vehicles, engines, and architectures that can deliver new cars to North America in a shorter and less expensive period of time. In so doing, it is seeking to leverage its existing assets to create new value for customers.

Strategic Alliances

As we discussed in Chapter 8, the modern organization has a variety of links with other organizations. These links are more complex than the standard relationships with traditional stakeholders such as suppliers and clients. Today even fierce *competitors* are working together at unprecedented levels to achieve their strategic goals. For example, Federal Express now has drop-off boxes at U.S. Postal Service facilities. And when Microsoft launched its online user ID platform, called Passport, which allowed consumers to handle e-commerce on any Web site, traditional rivals Sony, Hewlett-Packard, and Sun Microsystems formed an alliance to oppose it, eventually forcing Microsoft to abandon its program.[6] In these and other examples, strategic alliances allow participants to respond to customer demands or environmental threats far faster and less expensively than each would be able to do on its own.

Telecom's Next Wave: Alliances

FROM THE PAGES OF ▼

BusinessWeek

Rural wireline carrier CenturyTel has announced that it will return to the wireless market, though on a much smaller scale than before. The telco signed a wireless reseller agreement with Cingular Wireless, with service to be launched within months. The announcement comes on the heels of the partnership formed in August with EchoStar Communication's DISH network to offer satellite-TV service to CenturyTel's customers.

CenturyTel had left the wireless business, selling operations covering some 700,000 subscribers to Alltel, because it couldn't compete against the national wireless carriers. What's different about its latest foray into wireless? Two things: First, CenturyTel is partnering with an industry-leading company rather than running its own network, and second, the company will most likely bundle together wireless service with wireline, DSL, and broadband products to offer to customers.

With growth in traditional wireline services slowing, CenturyTel is going after a larger share of consumer spending on enhanced communications services. Consumer spending on bundled communications services, which includes wireline, wireless, Internet, and cable or satellite TV, has been climbing.

CenturyTel, along with such telcos as Qwest Communications, SBC Communications, and Sprint, is competing fiercely with other local wireline, wireless, and cable-service providers, leading to losses in local-access lines. Looking ahead, competition will only grow with the launch of Internet telephony and the expansion of wireless broadband networks.

But unlike earlier periods, when telcos ratcheted up capital spending to boost growth and gain customer loyalty, partnerships are now the vogue as carriers try to reduce debt.

Indeed, SBC cut its long-term debt by nearly 6 percent. What makes the partnerships appealing is that they let one company provide new services to customers, while allowing its partner to make use of excess capacity to become more efficient.

We're likely to see more of these partnerships in the future. In certain markets, partnerships help wireline carriers compete with cable-TV providers such as Cox Communications or Time Warner for broadband customers. The partnerships also give EchoStar and other satellite providers a chance to lure customers away from cable TV.

To be sure, these partnerships sometimes make strange bedfellows. Before coupling with CenturyTel, Echostar partnered with SBC and Sprint. And in addition to the EchoStar alliance, Sprint has been partnering with outfits in other sectors of the communications industry. For example, Sprint began providing wireless services under the Qwest brand to Qwest's customers in the western United States. And Sprint is teaming up with cable companies in markets where it does not operate as a local carrier. Sprint also signed an agreement with Mediacom Communications, the eighth-largest cable operator in the United States, which will allow the cable company to provide phone service in its markets. Sprint will assist in switching and provide operator and directory services.

We expect more of these communications partnerships as companies seek to offer multiple high-quality services at a reasonable price. For telcos that don't currently offer wireline, wireless, cable/satellite TV, and the Internet services, these alliances are imperative. And while it's too early to say for sure, we think these linkups will lead ultimately to greater revenues and customer loyalty.

SOURCE: Todd Rosenbluth, "Telecom's Next Wave: Alliances," *BusinessWeek*, September 24, 2004, online.

A **strategic alliance** is a formal relationship created with the purpose of joint pursuit of mutual goals. In a strategic alliance, individual organizations share administrative authority, form social links, and accept joint ownership. Such alliances are blurring firms' boundaries. They occur between companies and their competitors, governments, and universities. Such partnering often crosses national and cultural boundaries. Companies form strategic alliances to develop new technologies, enter new markets, and reduce manufacturing costs. Alliances are often the fastest, most efficient way to achieve objectives. Moreover, strategic alliances can pay off not only through the immediate deal, but through creating additional, unforeseen opportunities and opening new doors to the future.[7]

strategic alliance

A formal relationship created among independent organizations with the purpose of joint pursuit of mutual goals.

Connections: AMERICA'S CARMAKERS

At the end of 2004, GM and DaimlerChrysler—normally strong competitors—announced that they would team up to build hybrid systems that will help both companies develop fuel-efficient vehicles faster and more cheaply. Hybrids are fast becoming America's fuel-saver of choice, and the longer these two wait, the further behind technology leader Toyota Motor Corp. they risk falling. While Toyota is already on its second-generation of hybrid offerings, the first models from the GM-Daimler collaboration won't roll off the line until 2007. By then, the Japanese giant will have had two more years to perfect its technology, build up sales volume, and bring down costs for what remains a pricey product. That explains the tie-up with Daimler. It also explains why, in 2005, GM was even rumored to have entered into preliminary discussions with Toyota to cooperate on some hybrid technologies. GM had already planned to sell hybrid SUVs in 2007, but it needed partners to help defray the development outlays. Moreover, by sharing its hybrid technology with Daimler, and possibly Toyota, GM is betting that the more models out there, the cheaper it will be to produce them. Longer term, GM hopes to persuade other carmakers to license its technology.

Alliances can increase speed and innovation and lower costs

An alliance between Starbucks and Pepsico created the popular coffee-flavored drink Frappuccino. The relationship moved Starbucks into the bottled beverage market and Pepsico gained an innovative product. This strategic alliance was a perfect match.

Managers typically devote plenty of time to screening potential partners in financial terms. But for the alliance to work, managers also must foster and develop the human relationships in the partnership. Asian companies seem to be the most comfortable with the nonfinancial, "people" side of alliances; European companies the next so; and U.S. companies the least. Thus, U.S. companies may need to pay extra attention to the human side of alliances. Table 9.1 shows some recommendations for how to do this. In fact, most of the ideas apply not only to strategic alliances but to any type of relationship.[8]

The Learning Organization

Being responsive requires continually changing and learning new ways to act. Some experts have stated that the only sustainable advantage is learning faster than the competition. This has led to a new term that is now part of the vocabulary of most managers: the learning organization.[9] A **learning organization** is an organization skilled at creating, acquiring, and transferring knowledge, and at modifying its behavior to reflect new knowledge and insights.[10]

GE, Corning, and Honda are good examples of learning organizations. Such organizations are skilled at solving problems, experimenting with new approaches, learning from their own experiences, learning from other organizations, and spreading knowledge quickly and efficiently.

How do firms become true learning organizations? There are a few important ingredients.[11]

1. Their people engage in disciplined thinking and attention to details, making decisions based on data and evidence rather than guesswork and assumptions.
2. They search constantly for new knowledge, looking for expanding horizons and opportunities rather than quick fixes to current problems.
3. They carefully review both successes and failures, looking for lessons and deeper understanding.
4. Learning organizations benchmark—they identify and implement the best business practices of other organizations, stealing ideas shamelessly.

learning organization

An organization skilled at creating, acquiring, and transferring knowledge, and at modifying its behavior to reflect new knowledge and insights.

TABLE 9.1
How I's Can Become We's

The best alliances are true partnerships that meet these criteria:
1. *Individual excellence:* Both partners add value, and their motives are positive (pursue opportunity) rather than negative (mask weaknesses).
2. *Importance:* Both partners want the relationship to work because it helps them meet long-term strategic objectives.
3. *Interdependence:* The partners need each other; each helps the other reach its goal.
4. *Investment:* The partners devote financial and other resources to the relationship.
5. *Information:* The partners communicate openly about goals, technical data, problems, and changing situations.
6. *Integration:* The partners develop shared ways of operating; they teach each other and learn from each other.
7. *Institutionalization:* The relationship has formal status with clear responsibilities.
8. *Integrity:* Both partners are trustworthy and honorable.

SOURCE: Adapted and reprinted by permission of *Harvard Business Review*. From R. M. Kanter, "Collaborative Advantage: The Art of Alliances," July–August 1994, pp. 96–108. Copyright © 1994 by the Harvard Business School Publishing Corporation; all rights reserved.

5. They share ideas throughout the organization via reports, information systems, informal discussions, site visits, education, and training.

The High-Involvement Organization

Participative management is becoming increasingly popular as a way to create a competitive advantage. Particularly in high-technology companies facing stiff international competition, such as Microsystems and Compaq Computer, the aim is to generate high levels of commitment and involvement as employees and managers work together to achieve organizational goals.

In a **high-involvement organization,** top management ensures that there is a consensus about the direction in which the business is heading. The leader seeks input from his or her top management team and from lower levels of the company. Task forces, study groups, and other techniques are used to foster participation in decisions that affect the entire organization. Also fundamental to the high-involvement organization is continual feedback to participants regarding how they are doing compared to the competition and how effectively they are meeting the strategic agenda.

Structurally, this usually means that even lower-level employees have a direct relationship with a customer or supplier and thus receive feedback and are held accountable for a product or service delivery. The organizational form is a flat, decentralized structure built around a customer, product, or service. Employee involvement is particularly powerful when the environment changes rapidly, work is creative, complex activities require coordination, and firms need major breakthroughs in innovation and speed—in other words, when companies need to be more responsive.[12]

> **high-involvement organization**
>
> A type of organization in which top management ensures that there is consensus about the direction in which the business is heading.

When companies need to be highly responsive, a high-involvement organization is key. Especially in high-technology companies where competition is tough, it's important for all employees to be on the front line and be able to react quickly to change.

Organizational Size and Agility

One of the most important characteristics of an organization—and one of the most important factors influencing its ability to respond effectively to its environment—is its size. Large organizations are typically less organic and more bureaucratic. For example, at Hewlett-Packard, before the reduction of its stifling bureaucracy, it took over 90 people on nine committees more than seven months to decide what to name some new software.[13]

In large organizations, jobs become more specialized. More distinct groups of specialists get created because large organizations can add a new specialty at lower proportional expense. The complexity these numerous specialties create makes the organization harder to control. Therefore, in the past management added more levels to keep spans of control from becoming too large. To cope with complexity, large companies tend to become more bureaucratic. Rules, procedures, and paperwork are introduced.

Thus, with size comes greater complexity, and complexity brings a need for increased control. In response, organizations adopt bureaucratic strategies of control. The conventional wisdom is that bureaucratization increases efficiency but decreases a company's ability to innovate. So, are larger companies more responsive to competitive demands or not? Let's see.

The Case for Big

Bigger was better after World War II, when foreign competition was limited and growth seemed limitless. To meet high demand for its products, U.S. industry

Large size often leads to scale economies.

embraced high-volume, low-cost manufacturing methods. IBM, General Motors (GM), and Sears all grew into behemoths during those decades.

Alfred Chandler, a pioneer in strategic management, noted that big companies were the engine of economic growth throughout the 20th century.[14] Size creates *scale economies*, that is, lower costs per unit of production. And size can offer specific advantages such as lower operating costs, greater purchasing power, and easier access to capital. For example, Microsoft spent nearly $8 billion in 2004 on research and development, far more than its rivals can afford.[15] Similarly, Wal-Mart, now the largest company in America, has the purchasing power to buy merchandise in larger volumes and sell it at lower prices than its competitors can. Size also creates **economies of scope;** materials and processes employed in one product can be used to make other, related products. With such advantages, huge companies with lots of money may be the best at taking on large foreign rivals in huge global markets.

economies of scope

Economies in which materials and processes employed in one product can be used to make other, related products.

The Case for Small

But a huge, complex organization can find it hard to manage relationships with customers and among its own units. Bureaucracy can run rampant. Too much success can

Efficiency can be greater in a small company, which can cause big businesses to be left in the dust.

breed complacency, and the resulting inertia hinders change. Experts suggest that this is a surefire formula for being "left in the dust" by hungry competitors. As consumers demand a more diverse array of high-quality, customized products supported by excellent service, giant companies have begun to stumble. There is some evidence, for example, that as firms get larger and their market share grows, customers begin to view their products as having lower quality. Larger companies are more difficult to coordinate and control. Thus, while size may enhance efficiency by spreading fixed costs out over more units, it also may create administrative difficulties that inhibit efficient performance. A new term has entered the business vocabulary: *diseconomies of scale*, or the costs of being too big. "Small is beautiful" has become a favorite phrase of entrepreneurial business managers.[16]

Smaller companies can move fast, can provide quality goods and services to targeted market niches, and can inspire greater involvement from their people. Nimble, small firms frequently outmaneuver big bureaucracies. They introduce new and better products, and they steal market share. The premium now is on flexibility and responsiveness—the unique potential strengths of the small firm. For example, in 2000 a group of engineers at Lucent Technologies uncovered a superior technology that delivered wireless data faster and cheaper. But Lucent, fearing that it would cannibalize its own product line, wedded itself to the existing technology. In response, the engineers started their own small, successful competing firm, Flarion Technologies. "The fact that we could come up with our best work and still not have it go anywhere was a clear sign that big company structure was not right for us," says Rajiv Laroia, one of the founding engineers.[17]

Small size may improve speed.

Being Big and Small

Small *is* beautiful for unleashing energy and speed. But in buying and selling, size offers market power. The challenge, then, is to be both big and small to capitalize on the advantages of each.

JetBlue, the highly profitable, low-cost niche airline, started out very small with its concept of low fares and well-received add-ons like on-board TV. With one of the industry's best profit margins, it has been expanding rapidly. Yet the company has put both formal and informal structures into place to ensure that JetBlue retains its small-company feel of information sharing, employee enthusiasm, and intense customer focus. Each top officer of the company is assigned and visits a different location every quarter and works right beside employees there for an entire day. Orientation and training sessions reinforce the small-company culture of the firm, so that the standards and values that have made it successful will continue even as it becomes a larger enterprise.[18]

From a different angle, companies such as Starbucks, AES (mentioned in Chapter 8), Bell, and Amazon are very large companies that work hard to act small and maintain a sense of intimacy with employees and customers. Each is considered among the best-managed companies in the world. To avoid problems of growth and size, they decentralize decision making and organize around small, adaptive, team-based work units.

Downsizing   As large companies attempt to regain the responsiveness of small companies, they often face the dilemma of downsizing. **Downsizing** (or **rightsizing**) is the planned elimination of positions or jobs. Common approaches to downsizing include eliminating functions, hierarchical levels, or even whole units.[19] There has also been a growing trend to replace full-time employees with less-expensive part-time or temporary workers.

In years past, downsizing was most often the result of a company's poor performance—there was a long-term sales decline, for example, and the company no longer needed the same number of employees. But today downsizing has become a normal business practice, as global competition puts pressure on costs, as an increasing number of mergers cause functions to be consolidated, and as new technologies or new ways of doing business continue to emerge. It is hard to pick up a newspaper without seeing announcements of another company downsizing; likewise, it is hard to name a major corporation that has not downsized in recent years. The list includes IBM, Citicorp, AT&T, Kodak, Goodyear, Exxon, Xerox, TRW, and GM.

Historically, layoffs tended to affect manufacturing firms, and operating-level workers in particular. But given that the most recent cycle of downsizing has focused on delayering and eliminating bureaucratic structures, "white-collar" middle managers have been those chiefly affected.

Done appropriately, with inefficient layers eliminated and resources focused more on adding customer value than on wasteful internal processes, downsizing can indeed lead to a more agile, flexible, and responsive firm. But even under the best of circumstances, downsizing can be traumatic for an organization and its employees. What can be done to manage downsizing effectively, to help make it a more effective "rightsizing"?

First of all, firms should avoid excessive (cyclical) hiring to help reduce the need to engage in major or multiple downsizings. But beyond that, firms must avoid common mistakes such as making slow, small, frequent layoffs; implementing voluntary early retirement programs that entice the best people to leave; and laying off so many people that the company's work can no longer be performed. Instead, firms can engage in a number of positive practices to ease the pain of downsizing:

- Choose positions to be eliminated by engaging in careful analysis and strategic thinking.
- Train people to cope with the new situation.
- Identify and protect talented people.
- Give special attention and help to those who have lost their jobs.
- Communicate constantly with people about the process.
- Emphasize a positive future and people's new roles in attaining it.[20]

Interestingly, the people who lose their jobs because of downsizing are not the only ones deeply affected. Those who survive the process—who keep their jobs—tend to exhibit what has become known as **survivor's syndrome**.[21] They struggle with heavier workloads, wonder who will be next to go, try to figure out how to survive, lose com-

downsizing

The planned elimination of positions or jobs.

rightsizing

A successful effort to achieve an appropriate size at which the company performs most effectively.

Even if you are a survivor in a rash of downsizing— how are you still affected?

survivor's syndrome

Loss of productivity and morale in employees who remain after a downsizing.

mitment to the company and faith in their bosses, and become narrow-minded, self-absorbed, and risk-averse. As a consequence, morale and productivity usually drop.

You will learn more about some of these ideas in later chapters on human resources management, leadership, motivation, communication, and managing change. You might also refer back to our discussion in Chapter 1 about some of the things you can do to successfully manage your own career in an era where downsizing is a normal occurrence.

Customers and the Responsive Organization

Today's customers demand new high-quality, low-cost products—fast.

So far, we have discussed how an organization's agility, adaptability, and structure are influenced by its *strategy* and *size*. But, in the end, the point of structuring a responsive, agile organization lies in enabling it to meet and exceed the expectations of its *customers*—the people who it must attract to purchase a good or service and whose continued patronage and involvement with the organization constitute the fundamental driver of sustained, long-term competitiveness and success.

Recall from Chapter 2 that an organization's environment is composed of many different parts (government, suppliers, competitors, and the like). Perhaps no other aspect of the environment has had a more profound impact on organizing in recent years than a focus on customers. Dr. Kenichi Ohmae points out that any business unit must take into account three key players: the *company* itself, the *competition*, and the *customer*. These components form what Ohmae refers to as the *strategic triangle*, as shown in Figure 9.2. Managers need to balance the strategic triangle, and successful organizations use their strengths to create value by meeting customer requirements better than competitors do. In this section, we will discuss in some depth how organizations organize to maintain and extend a competitive advantage with their customers.

Customer Relationship Management

customer relationship management (CRM)

A multifaceted process focusing on creating two-way exchanges with customers to foster intimate knowledge of their needs, wants, and buying patterns.

Customer relationship management (CRM) is a multifaceted process, typically mediated by a set of information technologies, that focuses on creating two-way exchanges with customers so that firms have an intimate knowledge of their needs, wants, and buying patterns. In this way, CRM helps companies understand, as well as anticipate, the needs of current and potential customers. And in that way, it is part of a business strategy for managing customers to maximize their long-term value to an enterprise.[22]

As discussed throughout this book, customers want quality goods and service, low cost, innovative products, and speed. Traditional thinking considered these basic cus-

FIGURE 9.2
The Strategic Triangle

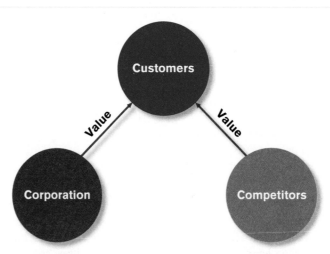

SOURCE: From K. Ohmae et al., *The Mind of the Strategist.* Copyright © 1982 by The McGraw-Hill Companies. Reprinted with permission from The McGraw-Hill Companies.

tomer wants as a set of potential trade-offs. For instance, customers wanted high quality or low costs passed along in the form of low prices. But world-class companies today know that the "trade-off" mentality no longer applies. Customers want it *all*, and they are learning that somewhere an organization exists that will provide it all.

> "Our business is about technology, yes. But it's also about operations and customer relationships."
>
> Michael Dell

But if all companies seek to satisfy customers, how can a company realize a competitive advantage? World-class companies have learned that almost any advantage is temporary, for competitors will strive to catch up. Simply stated—though obviously not simply done—a company attains and retains competitive advantage by continuing to improve. This concept—*kaizen*, or continuous improvement—is an integral part of Japanese operations strategy. Motorola, a winner of the Malcolm Baldrige National Quality Award, operates with the philosophy that "the company that is satisfied with its progress will soon find that its customers are not."

As organizations focus on responding to customer needs, they soon find that traditional meaning of a customer expands to include "internal customers." The word *customer* now refers to the *next process*, or *wherever the work goes next*.[23] This highlights the idea of interdependence among related functions and means that all functions of the organization—not just marketing people—have to be concerned with customer satisfaction. All recipients of a person's work, whether co-worker, boss, subordinate, or external party, come to be viewed as the customer.

A deeper way to understand how organizations can add customer value to their products has been provided by Michael Porter, who popularized the concept of the value chain. A **value chain** is the sequence of activities that flow from raw materials to the delivery of a product or service, with additional value created at each step.

You can see a generic value chain illustrated in Figure 9.3. Each step in the chain adds value to the product or service:

- *Inbound logistics* receive and store raw materials and distribute them to operations.
- *Operations* transform the raw materials into final product.
- *Outbound logistics* warehouse the product and handle its distribution.
- *Marketing and sales* identify customer requirements and get customers to purchase the product.
- *Service* offers customer support, such as repair, after the item has been bought.

value chain

The sequence of activities that flow from raw materials to the delivery of a product or service, with additional value created at each step.

FIGURE 9.3
Generic Value Chain

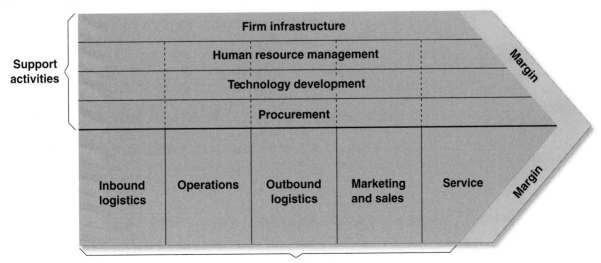

SOURCE: Michael Porter, *Competitive Advantage: Creating and Sustaining Superior Performance* (New York: Free Press, 1985).

When the total value created—that is, *what customers are willing to pay*—exceeds the cost of providing the product or service, the result is the organization's profit *margin*.[24]

Managers can add customer value and build competitive advantage by paying close attention to their organization's value chain—not only each step in it, but the way each step interacts with the others. For example, they can achieve economies of scale, as Wal-Mart has, so that their materials and operations costs are lowered, or they can develop innovative distribution channels, as Amazon has done, and add customer value that way. They can also create structures and systems that link the elements of the value chain in innovative ways.

Advantages of Collaboration

One of the most effective ways to leverage an organization's value chain is to bring together elements of the chain to collaborate to add customer value and build competitive advantage. For example, long-term relationships can be established with suppliers to encourage investment in new technologies and practices that speed product development and turnaround. Nike chooses its suppliers—what it calls its "strategic partners"—to that end, and shares its business plans and strategies with them to reinforce close collaboration. Sales staff can communicate with operations staff, before the manufacturing process even starts, to develop products jointly that customers will value highly. Service managers can constantly report back to operations about defects and work with operations and suppliers to reduce and eliminate them. When managers create that kind of collaboration, their organization's agility and responsiveness are increased significantly.

Total Quality Management

total quality management (TQM)
An integrative approach to management that supports the attainment of customer satisfaction through a wide variety of tools and techniques that result in high-quality goods and services.

High quality requires organizationwide commitment.

Total quality management (TQM) is a way of managing in which everyone is committed to continuous improvement of his or her part of the operation. In business, success depends on having quality products. As described in Chapter 1 and throughout the book, TQM is a comprehensive approach to improving product quality and thereby customer satisfaction. It is characterized by a strong orientation toward customers (external and internal) and has become an umbrella theme for organizing work. TQM reorients managers toward involving people across departments in improving all aspects of the business. Continuous improvement requires integrative mechanisms that facilitate group problem solving, information sharing, and cooperation across business functions. As a consequence, the walls that separate stages and functions of work tend to come down, and the organization operates more in a team-oriented manner.[25]

W. Edwards Deming was one of the founders of the quality management movement. When he started, his work was largely ignored by American companies, but it was adopted eagerly by Japanese firms that wanted to shed their products of their post–World War II reputation for shoddiness. The quality emphasis of Japanese car manufacturing, with which we started this chapter, was one direct result of Deming's work, which has now been adopted by many American and other companies worldwide. Deming's "14 points" of quality emphasized a holistic approach to management that demands intimate understanding of the process—the delicate interaction of materials, machines, and people that determines productivity, quality, and competitive advantage:

1. Create constancy of purpose—strive for long-term improvement rather than short-term profit.
2. Adopt the new philosophy—don't tolerate delays and mistakes.
3. Cease dependence on mass inspection—build quality into the process on the front end.
4. End the practice of awarding business on price tag alone—build long-term relationships.

5. Improve constantly and forever the system of production and service—at each stage.
6. Institute training and retraining—continual updating of methods and thinking.
7. Institute leadership—provide the resources needed for effectiveness.
8. Drive out fear—people must believe it is safe to report problems or ask for help.
9. Break down barriers among departments—promote teamwork.
10. Eliminate slogans, exhortations, and arbitrary targets—supply methods, not buzzwords.
11. Eliminate numerical quotas—they are contrary to the idea of continuous improvement.
12. Remove barriers to pride in workmanship—allow autonomy and spontaneity.
13. Institute a vigorous program of education and retraining—people are assets, not commodities.
14. Take action to accomplish the transformation—provide a structure that enables quality.

One of the most important contributors to total quality management has been the introduction of statistical tools to analyze the causes of product defects, in an approach called *Six Sigma Quality*. Sigma is the Greek letter used to designate the estimated standard deviation or variation in a process. (The higher the "sigma level," the lower the amount of variation.) The product defects analyzed may include anything that results in customer dissatisfaction—for example, late delivery, wrong shipment, or poor customer service, as well as problems with the product itself. When the defect has been identified, managers then engage the organization in a determined, comprehensive effort to eliminate its causes and reduce it to the lowest practicable level. At Six Sigma, a product or process is defect-free 99.99966 percent of the time—less than 3.4 defects or mistakes per million. Reaching that goal almost always requires managers to restructure their internal processes and relationships with suppliers and customers in fundamental ways. For example, managers may have to create teams from all parts of the organization to implement the process improvements that will prevent defects from arising. Many companies, like GE, Motorola, American Express, and 3M, have embraced the Six Sigma program and as a result significantly lowered their costs and increased market share.[26] We will discuss Six Sigma in more detail in Chapter 16.

Commitment to total quality requires a thorough, extensive, integrated approach to organizing. To encourage American companies to make that commitment and achieve quality excellence, The Malcolm Baldrige National Quality Award was established in 1987. Named after the former Secretary of Commerce, the award is given every year to companies and nonprofit organizations that have met certain specified criteria (see box). Recent winners include The Bama Companies, a family-owned manufacturer of frozen foods that, according to the reward citation, implements new product ideas at a rate nearly 10 times the industry average; and the Robert Wood Johnson University Hospital Hamilton, which has cut patient mortality rates for congestive heart failure by almost 70 percent.[27]

The Bama Companies, a family-owned manufacturer of frozen foods, recently won the Malcolm Baldrige National Quality Award.

The Baldrige Criteria and TQM in the United States

The criteria for performance excellence used by the Baldrige Award program are briefly described as follows:

1. *Leadership.* Leaders should set directions and create a customer focus, clear and visible values, and high expectations. They should ensure the creation of strategies, systems, and methods for achieving performance excellence, stimulating innovation, building knowledge and capabilities, and ensuring organizational sustainability. They should encourage all employees to contribute.

2. *Strategic Planning.* Creating a sustainable organization requires a focus on the future. Planning by managers should anticipate the short- and longer-term factors that affect the organization's business and marketplace, such as customers' expectations, new business and partnership opportunities, employee development needs, technological developments, and strategic moves by competitors.

3. *Customer and Market Focus.* Managers must take into account all product and service characteristics and all aspects of customer access that contribute value to their customers. Customer-driven excellence includes understanding today's customer desires and anticipating future customer desires and marketplace potential. It includes differentiating products and services from competing offerings. It also requires *agility*—more rapid product development and faster and more flexible customer response.

4. *Measurement, Analysis, and Knowledge Management.* Organizations depend on the measurement and analysis of performance. Such measurements should provide critical information about key processes, outputs, and results. The measures or indicators selected should best represent the factors that lead to improved customer, operational, financial, and ethical performance. They will provide a clear basis for aligning all processes with the organization's goals.

5. *Human Resource Focus.* Success increasingly depends on the diverse backgrounds, knowledge, skills, creativity, and motivation of employees. Managers who value employees commit to their satisfaction, development, and well-being. This involves more flexible, high-performance work practices; dedication to their employees' success; providing recognition beyond the regular compensation system; sharing knowledge and creating a learning culture so employees can better service customers and the organization's strategic objectives; and creating an environment that encourages risk taking and innovation.

6. *Process Management.* Managers must ensure that key product, service, and other processes create customer and organizational value, such as improved cycle time, productivity, innovation, and cost, as well as overall process improvements in efficiency and effectiveness. In addition, managers align and integrate the organization as a whole. *Alignment* ensures consistency of plans, processes, measures, and actions. *Integration* links the individual units and performance measurement systems so they operate in a fully interconnected manner.

7. *Business Results.* Key results include all product, service, customer, financial, and internal operating performance goals, including market share, new product creation, customer satisfaction, and organizational effectiveness. Results should be used to create value for key stakeholders—customers, employees, stockholders, suppliers and partners, the public, and the community—in proper balance. Performance measures also provide a clear basis for improving results, with the goal of ongoing increases in performance excellence and value.

SOURCE: "2005 Criteria for Performance Excellence," *Baldrige National Quality Program*, www.baldrige.nist.gov/index.html, accessed February 2005.

ISO 9000

The influence of TQM on the organizing process has become even more acute with the emergence of ISO 9000. **ISO 9000** is a series of quality standards developed by a committee working under the International Organization for Standardization. The purpose of the standards is to improve total quality in all businesses for the benefit of producers and consumers alike. ISO 9000 originally was designed for manufacturing; however, most of the standards also can be applied readily to services operations.

U.S. companies first became interested in ISO 9000 because overseas customers, particularly the European Community (EC), embraced it. Companies that comply with the quality guidelines of ISO 9000 can apply for official certification; some countries and companies demand certification as an acknowledgment of compliance before they will do business. Now, some U.S. customers as well are making the same demand.[28]

> "Information technology and business are becomming inextricably interwoven. I don't think anyone can talk meaningfully about one without talking about the other."
>
> Bill Gates

ISO 9000

A series of quality standards developed by a committee working under the International Organization for Standardization to improve total quality in all businesses for the benefit of producers and consumers.

Reengineering

Extending from TQM and a focus on organizing around customer needs, organizations also have embraced the notion of reengineering (introduced in Chapter 1). The principal idea of reengineering is to revolutionize key organizational systems and processes to answer the question: "If you were the customer, how would you like us to operate?" The answer to this question forms a vision for how the organization should run, and then decisions are made and actions are taken to make the organization operate like the vision. Processes such as product development, order fulfillment, customer service, inventory management, billing, and production are redesigned from scratch as if the organization were brand new and just starting out.

After finding out their products were costing their customers more money than other brands, Procter & Gamble completely changed the way its high-cost products were produced. What are the benefits and downfalls of a massive reengineering effort such as this one?

For example: Procter & Gamble learned that the average family buying its products rather than private-label or low-price brands pays an extra $725 per year. That figure, P&G realized, was far too high, and a signal that the company's high prices could drive the company to extinction. Other data also signaled the need for P&G to change. Market shares of famous brands such as Comet, Mr. Clean, and Ivory had been dropping for 25 years. P&G was making 55 price changes *daily* on about 80 brands, and inaccurate billings were common. Its plants were inefficient, and the company had the highest overhead in the business. It was clear that it had to cut prices, and to do that it had to cut costs.

In response, P&G reengineered. The company tore down and rebuilt nearly every activity that contributed to its high costs. It redesigned the way it develops, manufactures, distributes, prices, markets, and sells products. The reengineering was difficult, time-consuming, and expensive. But now, after the changes, price changes are rare, factories are far more efficient, inventory is way down, and sales and profits are up. And P&G brands are now priced comparably to store brands. P&G may have reinvented itself as a leader in the industry once again, and created for itself a long-term competitive advantage that others are scrambling to match.[29]

Effective reengineering can cut costs significantly.

Advantages of Collaboration

The kind of reengineering that P&G undertook requires much more than a management directive from the top, a change in the formal organization structure, the introduction of new technology, or even a well-communicated change in strategy. Rather, to be fully effective and successful, reengineering often requires a fundamental change in the way the parts of the organization work together. They will need to see each other as partners in a common effort rather than as members of a particular department or unit. Teams made up of all levels of the organization may be involved in the reengineering effort, and information on problems and possible solutions needs to be fully shared between them. Customers and other stakeholders may be interviewed to get their contribution. Often several teams will be working simultaneously. In this way, all the information that is available within and outside the organization can be brought to bear on a problem—and the solution developed will have wider acceptance and can be implemented faster.

As you can see, reengineering is not about making minor organizational changes here and there. It is about completely overhauling the operation, in revolutionary ways, in order to achieve the greatest possible benefits to the customer and to the organization.

Technology and Organizational Agility

We have discussed the strategic, size, and customer influences on organizational design and agility. We now turn to one more critical factor affecting an organization's structure and responsiveness: its *technology*.

Broadly speaking, **technology** can be viewed as the methods, processes, systems, and skills used to transform resources (inputs) into products (outputs). Although we will discuss technology—and innovation—more fully in Chapter 17, in this chapter we want to highlight some of the important influences technology has on organizational design.

> **technology**
>
> The systematic application of scientific knowledge to a new product, process, or service.

Types of Technology Configurations

Research by Joan Woodward laid the foundation for understanding technology and structure. According to Woodward, three basic technologies characterize how work is done: small batch, large batch, and continuous process technologies. These three classifications are equally useful for describing either service or manufacturing technologies. Each differs in terms of volume produced and variety of products/services offered. Each also has a different influence on how managers organize and structure the work of their organizations.[30]

Small Batch Technologies

> **small batch**
>
> Technologies that produce goods and services in low volume.

When goods or services are provided in very low volume or **small batches,** a company that does such work is called a *job shop.* A fairly typical example of a job shop is PMF Industries, a small custom metalworking company in Williamsport, Pennsylvania, that produces stainless steel assemblies for medical and other uses. Less formally, in the service industry, restaurants or doctors' offices are examples of job shops, as they provide a high variety of low-volume, customized services.

In a small batch organization, structure tends to be very organic. There tend not to be a lot of rules and formal procedures, and decision making tends to be decentralized. The emphasis is on mutual adjustment among people.

Large Batch Technologies

> **large batch**
>
> Technologies that produce goods and services in high volume.

As volume increases, product variety usually decreases. Companies with higher volumes and lower varieties than a job shop tend to be characterized as **large batch,** or mass production technologies. Examples of large batch technologies include the auto assembly operations of General Motors, Ford, and

DaimlerChrysler. In the service sector, McDonald's and Burger King are good examples. Their production runs tend to be more standardized, and all customers receive similar (if not identical) products. Machines tend to replace people in the physical execution of work. People run the machines.

With a large batch technology, structure tends to be more mechanistic. There tend to be more rules and formal procedures, and decision making tends to be centralized with higher spans of control. Communication tends to be more formal in companies where hierarchical authority is more prominent.

Continuous Process Technologies   At the very-high-volume end of the scale are companies that use **continuous process** technologies, technologies that do not stop and start. Domino Sugar and Shell Chemical, for example, use continuous process technologies where there are a very limited number of products to be produced. People are completely removed from the work itself. It is done entirely by machines and/or computers. In some cases, people run the computers that run the machines.

Ironically, with continuous process technology, structure can return to a more organic form because less monitoring and supervision are needed. Communication tends to be more informal in companies where fewer rules and regulations are established.

> **continuous process**
>
> A process that is highly automated and has a continuous production flow.

Organizing for Flexible Manufacturing

Although issues of volume and variety often have been seen as trade-offs in a technological sense, today organizations are trying to produce both high-volume and high-variety products at the same time. This is referred to as **mass customization**.[31] Automobiles, clothes, computers, and other products are increasingly being manufactured to match each customer's taste, specifications, and budget. While this seemed only a fantasy a few years ago, mass customization is quickly becoming more prevalent among leading firms. You can now buy clothes cut to your proportions, supplements with the exact blend of the vitamins and minerals you like, CDs with the music tracks you choose, and textbooks whose chapters are picked out by your professor.[32]

How do companies organize to pull off this kind of customization at such low cost? As shown in Table 9.2, they organize around a dynamic network of relatively independent operating units.[33] Each unit performs a specific process or task—called a *module*—such as making a component, performing a credit check, or performing a particular welding method. Some modules may be performed by outside suppliers or vendors.

> **mass customization**
>
> The production of varied, individually customized products at the low cost of standardized, mass-produced products.

Today's technologies offer customization at low cost.

Custom clothing for women and men on target.com is just one example of flexible manufacturing. What other companies offer this type of service?

Mass Customization	
Products	High variety and customization
Product design	Collaborative design; significant input from customers
	Short product development cycles
	Constant innovation
Operations and processes	Flexible processes
	Business process reengineering (BPR)
	Use of modules
	Continuous improvement (CI)
	Reduced setup and changeover times
	Reduced lead times
	JIT delivery and processing of materials and components
	Production to order
	Shorter cycle times
	Use of information technology (IT)
Quality management	Quality measured in customer delight
	Defects treated as capability failures
Organizational structure	Dynamic network of relatively autonomous operating units
	Learning relationships
	Integration of the value chain
	Team-based structure
Workforce management	Empowerment of employees
	High value on knowledge, information, and diversity of employee capabilities
	New product teams
	Broad job descriptions
Emphasis	Low-cost production of high-quality, customized products

TABLE 9.2
Key Features in Mass
Customization

SOURCE: Reprinted with permission of APICS—The Educational Society for Resource Management, *Production and Inventory Management,* Volume 41, Number 1, 2000, pp. 56–65.

Different modules join forces to make the good or provide a service. How and when the various modules interact with one another are dictated by the unique requests of each customer. The manager's responsibility is to make it easier and less costly for modules to come together, complete their tasks, and then recombine to meet the next customer demand. The ultimate goal of mass customization is a never-ending campaign to expand the number of ways a company can satisfy customers. The Internet has also made it easy for customers to choose their product preferences online and for companies to take an order straight to the manufacturing floor.

computer-integrated manufacturing (CIM)

The use of computer-aided design and computer-aided manufacturing to sequence and optimize a number of production processes.

Computer-Integrated Manufacturing   **Computer-integrated manufacturing (CIM)** encompasses a host of computerized production efforts linked together. Two examples are computer-aided design and computer-aided manufacturing, which offer the ultimate in computerized process technologies. The magazine-printing industry has also moved to adopt CIM, with editorial and advertising content on publishers' computers linked directly with printing and binding networks at printing plants, producing customized versions of the same magazine for different subscribers.

These systems can produce high-variety and high-volume products at the same time.[34] They may also offer greater control and predictability of production processes, reduced waste, faster throughput times, and higher quality. But managers cannot "buy" their way out of competitive trouble simply by investing in superior technology alone. As the accompanying item on Kodak suggests, they must also ensure that their organization has the necessary strategic and "people" strengths and a well-designed plan for integrating the new technology within the organization.

Shooting Kodak into the Digital Age

↓ **FROM THE PAGES OF**

BusinessWeek

Kodak is desperately trying to reinvent itself for the Digital Age, and President and Chief Operating Officer Antonio M. Perez, who oversaw Hewlett-Packard Co.'s rise to dominance in inkjet printers, was hired to lead the way. The company is in a race against time as its traditional film business disappears. Today, Kodak finds itself in the awkward position of having to establish itself in a field dominated by others.

It's a painful irony for the company. For a century, Kodak enjoyed near-monopoly power—until Fuji Photo Film Co. came along. Kodak even came up with the first digital camera in 1975. But it is only now that the company is starting to capitalize on the technology.

Perez has gotten off to a quick start at a company once known for its destructively slow decision-making. He has made clear what many at the Rochester (N.Y.) headquarters long denied—that Kodak's main business has to be digital imaging. The company announced a sharper focus on digital businesses for its consumer, commercial, and health units that it predicts will increase the company's revenue 23 percent, to $16 billion, in 2006, and to $20 billion by 2010.

Perez helped figure out how to pay for the transition—mostly by reducing investment in film and laying off nearly a quarter of Kodak's 60,000 workforce. He has instilled a new discipline at the company that is speeding product development. And he is uncovering new uses for Kodak's 20,000 patents. "The intellectual property and knowhow is unbelievable in the company," he says. "There is no excuse not to succeed."

But the toughest challenges still lie ahead. Perez has to get Kodak's engineers and marketers to work together to come up with products that will hold their own in areas where the company has little credibility. For example, after rummaging around Kodak's hallowed labs, Perez believes he has found a breakthrough technology that will change the inkjet printer business.

Sounds like wishful thinking to some. "It's not about patents. It's all about commercializing the technology," says Vyomesh Joshi, who worked under Perez at HP and now runs its imaging and printing group. "That's where they're going to have a hard time."

The new Kodak is starting to take shape. Digital products now account for a third of the company's annual revenue but just an estimated 10 percent of operating income. That's the price Kodak will have to pay: The digital business offers much lower margins than film. By 2006, Kodak predicts its gross margins will be about 31 percent, down from a high of nearly double that.

Perez is well aware of the old attitude problems at Big Yellow. The biggest is a strange complacency—some call it arrogance—when it comes to selling what are widely acknowledged to be innovative products. "They tend to bring out one product and think, that's it—that they've now solved all the problems and the world will beat a path to their door," says Frank J. Romano, a professor of printing at Rochester Institute of Technology. The printer dock for the Kodak EasyShare digital camera is a case in point. Introduced in 2003, the dock finally made it easy for digital shutterbugs to print their photos without a computer. If, that is, they used a Kodak camera. Such proprietary standards are a no-no in the digital world. Although the dock topped $100 million in sales in its first year, it could have done much better. Now Kodak is looking for ways to make the dock work with other cameras.

Perez has helped change how Kodak operates to ensure the company doesn't make the same mistake again. He has sharpened the focus of an integrated product-delivery program that helps marketers and gearheads work more closely together. And Perez has sped the reorganization of each Kodak business unit into special product groups. These are teams dedicated to specific areas such as digital cameras, online services, or photo kiosks. By partly tying compensation to each group's performance, he expects better results.

Some employees and customers already note a faster pace. For example, Kodak raced to upgrade 3,300 photo-processing kiosks at CVS Corp. drugstores to wirelessly handle photos from camera phones. The old Kodak might have discouraged the change because it could cut into sales of disposable cameras.

At Kodak Perez has found a company that for all its earlier conceit now sees the need for a change. That gives him a chance to turn Kodak into something it hasn't been for a while: a company whose best years are ahead of it.

SOURCE: Adapted from Faith Arner, " 'No Excuse Not to Succeed,' " *BusinessWeek*, May 10, 2004, online.

---

flexible factories

Manufacturing plants that have short production runs, are organized around products, and use decentralized scheduling.

Flexible Factories   As the name implies, **flexible factories** provide more production options and a greater variety of products. They differ from traditional factories in three primary ways: lot size, flow patterns, and scheduling.[35]

First, the traditional factory has long production runs, generating high volumes of a standardized product. Flexible factories have much shorter production runs, with many different products. Second, traditional factories move parts down the line from one location in the production sequence to the next. Flexible factories are organized around products, in work cells or teams, so that people work closely together and parts move shorter distances with shorter or no delays. Third, traditional factories use centralized scheduling, which is time-consuming, inaccurate, and slow to adapt to changes. Flexible factories use local or decentralized scheduling, in which decisions are made on the shop floor by the people doing the work.

Connections: AMERICA'S CARMAKERS

The ability of Japanese car manufacturers to produce several different vehicles in one factory has been a major reason for their competitive advantage. American carmakers have therefore moved to adopt the same flexible manufacturing approach. DaimlerChrysler's assembly plant in Delaware will now build new car models on the same assembly line as its older model, and the company has cut almost a third of its manufacturing cost for the Dodge Durango SUV by using flexible manufacturing techniques. "The days of one product, one plant are starting to diminish," said one DaimlerChrysler executive. GM, in addition to accelerating its use of common components for different car styles, has also reconfigured its global manufacturing system to more closely match Toyota's. One of the key features of the system—and a defining aspect of the flexible factory—is that it gives workers on the assembly line the authority to report and solve problems on the spot, instead of allowing the car to be delivered to dealers and repaired later.

---

lean manufacturing

An operation that strives to achieve the highest possible productivity and total quality, cost-effectively, by eliminating unnecessary steps in the production process and continually striving for improvement.

Lean Manufacturing   **Lean manufacturing** means an operation that is both efficient and effective; it strives to achieve the highest possible productivity and total quality, cost-effectively, by eliminating unnecessary steps in the production process and continually striving for improvement. Rejects are unacceptable, and staff, overhead, and inventory are considered wasteful. In a lean operation, the emphasis is on quality, speed, and flexibility more than on cost, efficiency, and hierarchy. But with a well-managed lean production process, a company can develop, produce, and distribute products with half or less of the human effort, space, tools, time, and overall cost.[36]

An example of an effective introduction of lean production occurred at Gorton's, the frozen seafood company in Gloucester, Massachusetts. The company's food manufacturing processes were located on different plant floors, with no visual connection between them. Employees did not know what was going on at different stages of the process, and poor work flow, delays, and missed communication were common. Gorton's moved its production system to one floor and rethought and reconfigured every step of the process. The company also worked with its equipment suppliers to design machines with fewer moving parts and more accessible maintenance. Production was significantly speeded up, with far fewer delays, and with the entire operation visible to all employees everyone could spot a problem and contribute to its solution.[37]

For the lean approach to result in more effective operations, the following conditions must be met:[38]

- People are broadly trained rather than specialized.
- Communication is informal and horizontal among line workers.
- Equipment is general purpose.
- Work is organized in teams, or cells, that produce a group of similar products.
- Supplier relationships are long-term and cooperative.
- Product development is concurrent, not sequential, and is done by cross-functional teams.

In recent years, many companies have tried to become more lean by cutting overhead costs, laying off operative-level workers, eliminating layers of management, and utilizing capital equipment more efficiently. But if the move to lean manufacturing is simply a harsh, haphazard cost-cutting approach, the result will be chaos, overworked people, and low morale.

Lean manufacturing strives for high quality, speed, and low cost.

Organizing for Speed: Time-Based Competition

Companies worldwide have devoted so much energy to improving product quality that high quality is now the standard attained by all top competitors. Competition has driven quality to such heights that quality products no longer are enough to distinguish one company from another. *Time* is emerging as the key competitive advantage that can separate market leaders from also-rans.[39]

Companies today must learn what the customer needs and meet those needs as quickly as possible. **Time-based competition (TBC)** refers to strategies aimed at reducing the total time needed to deliver the product or service. TBC has several key organizational elements: logistics, just-in-time (JIT), and simultaneous engineering. JIT production systems reduce the time to manufacture products. Logistics speeds the delivery of products to customers. Both are essential steps toward bringing products to customers in the shortest time possible. In today's world, speed is essential.

Logistics   **Logistics** is the movement of resources into the organization (inbound) and products from the organization to its customers (outbound). Like the supply chain, which we discussed in Chapter 2, an organization's logistics is often a critical element in its responsiveness and competitive advantage.

The world of logistics includes the great mass of parts, materials, and products moving via trucks, trains, planes, and ships from and to every region of the globe. An average box of breakfast cereal can spend more than 100 days getting from the factory to the supermarket, moving through the warehouses of wholesalers, distributors, brokers, and

time-based competition (TBC)

Strategies aimed at reducing the total time it takes to deliver a product or service.

logistics

The movement of the right goods in the right amount to the right place at the right time.

Saturn has earned a reputation for superior customer satisfaction. Some of that reputation is due to Saturn's world-class distribution system. Why is it important that companies have a seamless logistics system in place?

others! If the grocery industry streamlined logistics, it could save an estimated $40 billion annually.[40] Depending on the product, the duplication and inefficiency in distribution can cost far more than making the product itself.

By contrast, Saturn's distribution system is world class. GM has contracted with both Ryder System and Penske Logistics to perform inbound logistics and distribution management for Saturn. Suppliers, factories, and dealers are linked so tightly and efficiently that Saturn barely has any parts inventory.[41]

> **just-in-time (JIT)**
>
> A system that calls for subassemblies and components to be manufactured in very small lots and delivered to the next stage of the production process just as they are needed.

Just-in-Time Operations   An additional element of TBC involves **just-in-time (JIT)** operations. JIT calls for subassemblies and components to be manufactured in very small lots and delivered to the next stage in the process precisely at the time needed, or "just in time." A customer order triggers a factory order and the production process. The supplying work centers do not produce the next lot of product until the consuming work center requires it. Even external suppliers deliver to the company just in time.

Just-in-time is a companywide philosophy oriented toward eliminating waste throughout all operations and improving materials throughout. In this way, excess inventory is eliminated and costs are reduced. The ultimate goal of JIT is to better serve the customer by providing higher levels of quality and service.[42] An example we mentioned earlier in the book of an effective just-in-time operation is provided by Dell, which does not begin production of a computer customized to a consumer's specifications until after the customer's order has been received. Contrast this approach with traditional production methods, which require extremely costly warehousing of inventory and parts, uncertain production runs, considerable waste, no customizing capability, and lengthy delivery times.

 "Big will not beat small any more. It will be the fast beating the slow."
Rupert Murdoch

JIT represents a number of key production and organizational concepts, including the following:

- *Elimination of waste.* Eliminate all waste from the production process, including waste of time, people, machinery, space, and materials.
- *Perfect quality.* Produce perfect parts even when lot sizes are reduced, and produce the product exactly when it is needed in the exact quantities that are needed.
- *Reduced cycle times.* Accomplish the entire manufacturing process more rapidly. Reduce setup times for equipment, move parts only short distances (machinery is placed in closer proximity), and eliminate all delays. The goal is to reduce action to the time spent working on the parts. For most manufacturers today, the percentage of time parts are worked on is about 5 percent of the total production time. JIT seeks to eliminate the other 95 percent, that is, to reduce to zero the time spent not working on the parts.
- *Employee involvement.* In JIT, employee involvement is central to success. The workers are responsible for production decisions. Managers and supervisors are coaches. Top management pledges that there will never be layoffs due to improved productivity.
- *Value-added manufacturing.* Do only those things (actions, work, etc.) that add value to the finished product. If it doesn't add value, don't do it. For example, inspection does not add value to the finished product, so make the product correctly the first time and inspection will not be necessary.
- *Discovery of problems and prevention of recurrence.* Foolproofing, or failsafing, is a key component of JIT. To prevent problems from arising, their cause(s) must be known and acted on. Thus, in JIT operations, people try to find the "weak link in the chain" by forcing problem areas to the surface so that preventive measures may be determined and implemented.

Many believe that only a fraction of JIT's potential has been realized and that its impact will grow as it is applied to other processes, such as service, distribution, and new-product development.[43]

Time-based competition brings speed to all organization processes.

Simultaneous Engineering   JIT is a vital component of TBC, but JIT concentrates on reducing time in only one function: manufacturing. TBC attempts to deliver speed in *all* functions—product development, manufacturing, logistics, and customer service. Customers will not be impressed if you manufacture quickly but it takes weeks for them to receive their products or get a problem solved.

Many companies are turning to simultaneous engineering as the cornerstone of their TBC strategy. **Simultaneous engineering**—also an important component of total quality management—is a major departure from the old development process in which tasks were assigned to various functions in sequence. When R&D completed its part of the project, the work was "passed over the wall" to engineering, which completed its task and passed it over the wall to manufacturing, and so on. This process was highly inefficient, and errors took a long time to correct.

In contrast, simultaneous engineering incorporates the issues and perspectives of all the functions—and customers and suppliers—from the beginning of the process. This team-based approach results in a higher-quality product that is designed for efficient manufacturing *and* customer needs.[44]

Some managers resist the idea of simultaneous engineering. Why should marketing, product planning and design, and R&D "allow" manufacturing to get involved in "their" work? The answer is: because the decisions made during the early, product-concept stage determine most of the manufacturing cost and quality. Furthermore, manufacturing can offer ideas about the product because of its experience with the prior generation of the product and with direct customer feedback. Also, the other functions must know early on what manufacturing can and cannot do. Finally, when manufacturing is in from the start, it is a full and true partner and will be more committed to decisions it helped make.

> **simultaneous engineering**
>
> A design approach in which all relevant functions cooperate jointly and continually in a maximum effort aimed at producing high-quality products that meet customers' needs.

Final Thoughts on Organizational Agility

As we pointed out in the last chapter, *any* approach to organizing has its strengths and limitations. The advantages of even the innovative, leading-edge structures and systems we have discussed in this chapter are likely to be short-lived if they become fixed rather than remain flexible. Smart managers and smart competitors soon catch up. Today's advantages are tomorrow's "table stakes": the minimum requirements that need to be met if an organization expects to be a major player.

To retain, or gain, a competitive edge, managers may want to keep in mind the principle with which we opened this chapter: Successful organizations—and that includes the successful managers within them—do not sit still. They do not follow rigid models but maintain structures, systems, organizational designs, and relationships that are adaptive—always sensitive to changes in their environment and able to respond quickly, efficiently, and effectively to them. Their managers focus constantly on exceeding customer expectations and on continuous quality improvement, designing their systems and structures to help them do just that.

The emphasis on agility, quality, flexibility, learning, and leanness to which you have been exposed in this chapter is likely to be a constant in your managerial career—ideally in your own organization, but perhaps as well in the competition you confront. When Jack Welch was chairman of GE, he saw his goal as the creation of the *boundaryless organization*, one in which there were no meaningful barriers between the organization and its environment. In such an organization, structures, technologies, and systems are perfectly aligned with the external challenges and opportunities it confronts. Increasingly, we hear forward-thinking managers embrace this goal.[45]

EPILOGUE

CAN AMERICA'S CARMAKERS CATCH TOYOTA?

By 2005, Saab's first sports utility vehicle, the 9-7X, was being manufactured by the same General Motors production line in Ohio that delivered four other GM SUVs, including the Trail-Blazer, Envoy, and Ascender. All have similar sizes and shapes, and the same engines, frames, and other parts. GM's savings in manufacturing costs were considerable—an essential first step in making its Saab line profitable. At Ford, the Taurus sedan, Freestar minivan, and crossover SUVs are still on different platforms. But Ford engineers now choose from among just 4 steering wheels instead of contemplating 14, as they did in the past. And six separate vehicle-development groups have been merged into a single team, speeding decision making and encouraging parts sharing. That has helped shave Ford's vehicle-development time to 21 months, down from 29. Ford attributed its new profitability in its European market to the fact that it was using a single architecture for its Ford, Mazda, and Volvo cars. The idea, says Ford's chief operating officer Nicholas V. Scheele: "Engineer it once, use it often."

Over the next eight years, Ford plans to use the Mazda six-sedan platform as the base for 10 new vehicles. This base will spawn the Ford Futura family sedan and different versions for its Lincoln and Mercury divisions, as well as some future SUVs and minivans.

Chrysler is in this game, too. A few years ago, almost every one of its vehicles had its own platform. Even when the company decided to build the PT Cruiser on the Neon chassis, Chrysler couldn't reap the full benefits: Unable to assemble the cars in the same factory without making a huge investment, the company had to build the Cruiser in Mexico and the Neon in Illinois. Now, Chrysler Group CEO Dieter Zetsche wants to base the company's entire fleet of cars, trucks, and SUVs on just four platforms, down from 13. The consolidation will help Chrysler cut its five-year vehicle-development budget from $42 billion to $30 billion, he says.

Can Detroit catch up with Japan on versatile platforms? The big three have shown that they can create attractive models on a budget and spin them into families. That strategy will take years to play out, however. Detroit is getting back in the race, but overtaking Japan on speed and efficiency is still down the road.

KEY TERMS

Computer-integrated manufacturing (CIM), p. 308

Continuous process, p. 307

Customer relationship management, (CRM) p. 300

Downsizing, p. 299

Economies of scope, p. 298

Flexible factories, p. 310

High-involvement organization, p. 297

ISO 9000, p. 305

Just-in-time (JIT), p. 312

Large batch, p. 306

Lean manufacturing, p. 310

Learning organization, p. 296

Logistics, p. 311

Mass customization, p. 307

Mechanistic organization, p. 292

Organic structure, p. 292

Rightsizing, p. 299

Simultaneous engineering, p. 313

Small batch, p. 306

Strategic alliance, p. 295

Survivor's syndrome, p. 299

Technology, p. 306

Time-based competition (TBC), p. 311

Total quality management, (TQM), p. 302

Value chain, p. 301

SUMMARY OF LEARNING OBJECTIVES

Now that you have studied Chapter 9, you should know:

Why it is critical for organizations to be responsive.

Organizations have a formal structure to help control what goes on within them. But to survive today, firms need more than control—they need responsiveness. They must act quickly and adapt to fast-changing demands.

The advantages of an organic organization structure.

The organic form emphasizes flexibility. Organic organizations are decentralized, informal, and dependent on the judgment and expertise of people with broad responsibilities. The organic form is not a single formal structure but a concept that underlies all the new forms discussed in this chapter.

The strategies and dynamic organizational concepts that can be used to improve an organization's responsiveness.

New and emerging organizational concepts and forms include core competencies, strategic alliances, learning organizations, and high-involvement organizations.

How a firm can be both big and small.

Historically, large organizations have had important advantages over small organizations. Today, small size has advantages, including the ability to act quickly, respond to customer demands, and serve small niches. The ideal firm today combines the advantages of both. It creates many small, flexible units, while the corporate levels add value by taking advantage of its size and power.

How firms organize to meet customer requirements.

Firms have embraced principles of continuous improvement and total quality management to respond to customer needs. Baldrige criteria and ISO 9000 standards help firms organize to meet better quality specifications. Extending these, reengineering efforts are directed at completely overhauling processes to provide world-class customer service.

How firms organize around different types of technology.

Organizations tend to move from organic structures to mechanistic structures and back to organic structures as they transition from small batch to large batch and continuous process technologies. To organize for flexible manufacturing, organizations pursue mass customization via computer-integrated manufacturing and lean manufacturing. To organize for time-based competition, firms emphasize their logistics operations, just-in-time operations, and simultaneous engineering.

DISCUSSION QUESTIONS

1. Discuss evidence you have seen of the imperatives for change, flexibility, and responsiveness faced by today's firms.

2. Describe large, bureaucratic organizations with which you have had contact that have not responded flexibly to customer demands. Also describe examples of satisfactory responsiveness. What do you think accounts for the differences between the responsive and nonresponsive organizations?

3. Considering the potential advantages of large and small size, would you describe the "feel" of your college or university as big, small, or small within big? Why? What might make it feel different?

4. What is a core competence? Generate some examples of companies with distinctive competencies, identifying what those competencies are. Brainstorm some creative new products and markets to which these competencies could be applied.

5. If you were going into business for yourself, what would be your core competencies? What competencies do you have now, and what competencies are you going to develop? Describe what your role would be in a network organization, and the competencies and roles of other firms you would want in your network.

6. Identify some recently formed alliances between competitors. What are the goals of the alliance? What brought them together? What have they done to ensure success? How are they doing now?

7. What skills will you need to work effectively in (a) a learning organization and (b) a high-involvement organization? Be specific, generating long lists. Would you enjoy working in these environments? Why or why not? What can you do to prepare yourself for these eventualities?

CONCLUDING CASE

United Trainers, Inc.

United Trainers, Inc., owned and operated by entrepreneur Paul O'Neil, currently operates as a subcontractor to several major auto manufacturers. The company has four facilities in California. The major strategy and niche market of the company is to process recycled and other materials into ready-to-install car and truck parts for a low cost/price.

The major car and truck part product lines include seatback headrests, drink holders, storage containers, and spare tire covers. The low cost/price is the result of the special programs that the company has established with local, state, and federal agencies. The company's workforce consists of disadvantaged and disabled individuals who receive social services benefits. The company also employs a smaller number of prison inmates.

The work is menial and repetitive, requiring minimal skill and dexterity levels. Many of the workers are bussed to their worksite each day and work an average of six hours under close supervision. The workers are very reliable and enthusiastic, and they greatly appreciate the opportunity to become more independent and to earn wages.

Paul O'Neil's vision and goal was and remains to establish the foregoing specific niches in his native California and to later "franchise" the concept around the country and world. Paul feels that a variety of other industries, product line manufacturers, and government agencies will buy into his program and concept.

Paul describes his concept as a win-win program for all parties involved. The process begins by identifying and matching up specific groups of prospective workers who receive partial or total government support with industries in need of manufacturing support services. Programs and partnerships are then established with local, state, and federal agencies. The initial investment of time, training, transportation, facilities, and money by the government agencies provides significant returns through reduced and/or no dependence on social programs by the client workers. The ultimate goal is to see each worker become an independent, taxpaying citizen and for the company to make money. Paul also notes the many intangible benefits to his program as a result of the rehabilitation and change in life that successful clients experience.

The government programs and partnerships typically include, but are not limited to some combination of the following: employee training and cost-share, low- or no-cost facilities, special permits and exemptions, tax incentives, and low-cost loans. Each is briefly described next.

Employee training usually means one-on-one on-site training by social service workers who are familiar with individual clients. The training continues until the client is working up to his or her potential speed and production capability. The government agency will also typically pay a portion of each client's wages for a 6- to 12-month period.

Many cities and towns own land and abandoned or run-down buildings that can be converted into manufacturing facilities. Buildings are built and/or renovated and made available at low or no cost to United Trainers, Inc. Special permits and exemptions are also provided by the appropriate government agencies in cases where current land use regulations would not allow the business to operate.

Under the current program, facilities include 30,000- to 40,000-square foot work areas, containing multiple production lines that easily accommodate the transformation of raw materials into finished products. Transportation and storage are also components of the total production process along with employee break rooms.

Tax incentives are typically provided in the form of federal tax credits, exemptions from local and state taxes, and so on. Low-cost loans are made available through local, state, or federal agencies for purposes of building construction and renovation, equipment and vehicle purchase, and working capital. Paul feels that he has "perfected" the concept and program, and that it is time to "franchise" the business to other parts of the country and to other industries.

QUESTIONS

1. What other industries and product lines would you go after next, as a start to the nationwide expansion of this program?
2. Discuss the ways in which you would utilize the concepts and techniques from this chapter to effectively manage new ventures in new industries.

EXPERIENTIAL EXERCISES

9.1 Mechanistic and Organic Structures

OBJECTIVES

1. To think about your own preferences when it comes to working in a particular organizational structure.
2. To examine aspects of organizations by using as an example this class you are a member of.

INSTRUCTIONS

1. Complete the Mechanistic and Organic Worksheet below.
2. Meet in groups of four to six persons. Share your data from the worksheet. Discuss the reasons for your responses, and analyze the factors that probably encouraged your instructor to choose the type of structure that now exists.

Mechanistic and Organic Worksheet

1. Indicate your general preference for working in one of these two organizational structures by circling the appropriate response:

   Mechanistic   1   2   3   4   5   6   7   8   9   10   **Organic**

2. Indicate your perception of the form of organization that is used in this class by circling the appropriate response for each item:

   A. **Task-role definition**   **Rigid**   1   2   3   4   5   6   7   8   9   10   **Flexible**

   B. **Communication**   **Vertical**   1   2   3   4   5   6   7   8   9   10   **Multidirectional**

   C. **Decision making**   **Centralized**   1   2   3   4   5   6   7   8   9   10   **Decentralized**

   D. **Sensitivity to the environment**   **Closed**   1   2   3   4   5   6   7   8   9   10   **Open**

SOURCE: Keith Davis and John W. Newstrom, *Human Behavior at Work*, 9th ed., p. 358. Copyright © 1993 by The McGraw-Hill Companies. Reprinted by permission of The McGraw-Hill Companies.

9.2 The Woody Manufacturing Company

OBJECTIVE

To apply the concepts learned about structure and agility at the individual, group, and organizational levels in designing the Woody Manufacturing Company.

TASK 1 (INDIVIDUAL ASSIGNMENT)

a. Read the following case study of the Woody Manufacturing Company.

b. Review the chapter carefully, and choose the organizational design orientation that you feel can best guide you in developing the design for Mr. Woody.

c. Write down your thoughts on alternative management structures, pay systems, and allocation of work to individuals and groups.

Designing a New Furniture Company

Mr. Woody, the owner/operator of a small furniture company specializing in the manufacture of high-quality bar stools, has experienced a tremendous growth in demand for his products. He has standing orders for $750,000. Consequently, Mr. Woody has decided to expand his organization and attack the market aggressively. His stated mission is "to manufacture world-class products that are competitive in the world market in quality, reliability, performance, and profitability." He would like to create a culture where "pride, ownership, employment security, and trust" are a way of life. He just finished a set of interviews, and he has hired 32 new workers with the following skills:

Four skilled craftspeople.

Ten people with some woodworking experience.

Twelve people with no previous woodworking experience or other skills.

One nurse.

One schoolteacher.

One bookkeeper.

Three people with some managerial experience in nonmanufacturing settings.

Mr. Woody (with your help) must now decide how to design his new organization. This design will include the management structure, pay system, and the allocation of work to individuals and groups. The bar stool–making process has 15 steps:

1. Wood is selected.
2. Wood is cut to size.
3. Defects are removed.
4. Wood is planed to exact specifications.
5. Joints are cut.

TASK 2 (TEAM ASSIGNMENT)

a. Get together with your team and develop a proposal for Mr. Woody that, if followed, would help him fulfill his vision.

b. Prepare a five-minute presentation. Your typewritten team proposal is due prior to your team presentation in Mr. Woody's conference room.

6. Tops are glued and assembled.
7. Legs/bases are prepared.
8. Legs/bases are attached to tops.
9. Bar stools are sanded.
10. Stain is applied.
11. Varnish is applied.
12. Bar stools are sanded.
13. Varnish is reapplied.
14. Bar stools are packaged.
15. Bar stools are delivered to the customer.

Mr. Woody currently manufactures three kinds of bar stools (pedestal, four-legged corner, and four-legged recessed). There is no difference in the difficulty of making the three types of bar stools. Major cost variations have been associated with defective wood, imprecise cuts, and late deliveries to customers. Mr. Woody must decide how to organize his company to maintain high quality and profits.

He has thought about several options. He could have some individuals perform the first step for all types of bar stools; he could have an individual perform several steps for one type of bar stool; or he could have a team perform some combination of steps for one or more bar stools. He wonders whether how he organized would affect quality or costs. He's also aware that while the demand for all types of bar stools has been roughly equal over the long run, there were short periods where one type of bar stool was in greater demand than the others. Because Mr. Woody wants to use his people effectively, he has committed an expert in work design to help him set up an optimal organization.

SOURCE: A. B. (Rami) Shani and James B. Lau, *Behavior in Organizations: An Experimental Approach* (New York: McGraw-Hill/Irwin, 2005), p. 370.

Chapter **10**

CHAPTER 10
Human Resources Management

You can get capital and erect buildings, but it takes people to build a business.

—**Thomas J. Watson, Founder, IBM.**

LEARNING OBJECTIVES

After studying Chapter 10, you will know:

1. How companies use human resources management to gain competitive advantage.

2. Why companies recruit both internally and externally for new hires.

3. The various methods available for selecting new employees.

4. Why companies spend so much on training and development.

5. How to determine who should appraise an employee's performance.

6. How to analyze the fundamental aspects of a reward system.

7. How unions influence human resources management.

8. How the legal system influences human resources management.

HR AND STRATEGY AT GE

Operating in more than 100 countries with 315,000 employees worldwide, General Electric's business ranges from aircraft engines and power generation to financial services and television programming. With such a diverse range of commercial interests, engendering a homogeneous culture across the company has been made easier largely due to strong leadership support for GE's Human Resource function and a heavy focus on aligning HR with GE's business strategy.

GE's Sam Sheppard says that it's vital to make sure HR initiatives, actions, and priorities are aligned in terms of the business plan, and that HR is integrated into the company's management system. At the beginning of each year GE's management and HR teams sit down to review the template of common goals and objectives for the HR function. The discussion then turns to what are key elements that the HR strategy should drive, relative to business objectives and both internal and external customers. "The aim is to have everybody driving in the same direction with a clear vision of what that business is looking to deliver in that year," she says.

One of GE's core competencies is "energizing the organization" and Sheppard believes leadership is key to this competency. Leaders "can energize others—they can create an environment that propagates vision, and their team will execute on that vision," she says. "But the real difference for the cream of the leadership crop is in those who are prepared to listen to feedback and act on it. Everybody gets feedback within GE, but the people who want to be successful, regardless of their background, are those who actually hear what the organization, employees and peers are telling them, and they change their behavior. This is critical at the senior level, as some people will start with a strength in one particular area and need to grow in another."

GE's global CEO Jeffrey Immelt takes one month out of the organization each year and travels from business to business to assist in the strategic HR planning process. Sheppard believes this is testament to the emphasis that GE places on its people-planning processes and their importance to the management of the company. GE leadership also meets with its top talent pool regularly, and ensures they are monitored and receive the development they need to be successful. Talent within GE is tracked on a variety of layers, from up-and-coming executive talent through promising new hires. "If a person is promoted or is not performing, we know who the right person is to put in their place. We also track who is ready to move to a different business in order to accelerate their career development. We also drive diversity to ensure we have a strong diverse pipeline of future leaders we are developing at every stage of their career," says GE's Steve Bertamini.

To support its succession planning process, GE has set up a comprehensive learning and development program for all employees. The company invests about $1 billion annually on such programs—from assembly lines to corporate classrooms to boardrooms.

It's important to "chart out the process to ensure we have the right development for each person," says Bertamini. He often discusses individual development needs within GE at the HR level, looking at issues such as skills gaps and how to best address them. "For example, should we be sending a person to an outside course to address a specific skill deficiency, or do we take more of a counseling or mentoring type approach to develop them? It's all about developing the individual," he says.

Source for Prologue, Connections, Epilogue: Adapted from "Plugged in HR: the General Electric Strategy," *Human Resources Magazine*, December 3, 2003, online.

human resources management (HRM)

Formal systems for the management of people within an organization.

The opening quote by Thomas Watson, founder of IBM, summarizes our view of the importance of people to any organization. **Human resource management (HRM),** historically known as personnel management, deals with formal systems for managing people at work. For that reason, it is one of the fundamental aspects of organizational and managerial life. Your first formal interaction with an organization you wish to join will likely encounter some aspect of its human resource function, and throughout your career as a manager you will be a part of, as well as being affected by, your organization's human resource management.

We begin this chapter by describing HRM as it relates to strategic management. We will also discuss more of the "nuts and bolts" of HRM: staffing, training, performance appraisal, rewards, and labor relations. Throughout the chapter, we discuss legal issues that influence each aspect of HRM. In the next chapter, we expand this focus to address related issues of managing a diverse workforce.

Strategic Human Resources Management

HRM has assumed a vital strategic role in recent years as organizations attempt to compete through people. Recall from Chapter 4, "Planning and Strategic Management," that firms can create a competitive advantage when they possess or develop resources that are valuable, rare, inimitable, and organized. We can use the same criteria to talk about the strategic impact of human resources:

1. **Creates value.** People can increase value through their efforts to decrease costs or provide something unique to customers or some combination of the two. Empowerment programs, total quality initiatives, and continuous improvement efforts at companies such as Corning, Xerox, and Saturn are intentionally designed to increase the value that employees bring to the bottom line.
2. **Is rare.** People are a source of competitive advantage when their skills, knowledge, and abilities are not equally available to all competitors. Top companies invest a great deal to hire and train the best and the brightest employees in order to gain advantage over their competitors. Dow Chemical went to court to stop General Electric from hiring away its engineers. This case shows that some companies recognize both the value and the rareness of certain employees.
3. **Is difficult to imitate.** People are a source of competitive advantage when their capabilities and contributions cannot be copied by others. Disney, Southwest Airlines, and Mirage Resorts are known for creating unique cultures that get the most from employees (through teamwork) and are difficult to imitate.
4. **Is organized.** People are a source of competitive advantage when their talents can be combined together and deployed rapidly to work on new assignments at a moment's notice. Teamwork and cooperation are two pervasive methods for ensuring an organized workforce. But companies such as Spyglass (a software

Southwest Airlines is known for creating a unique culture that gets the most from employees. Southwest rewards its employees for excellent performance and maintains loyalty by offering free airfare, profit sharing, and other incentives. What benefits would you need to stay motivated?

company) and AT&T have invested in information technology to help allocate and track employee assignments to temporary projects.

These four criteria highlight the importance of people and show the closeness of HRM to strategic management. In a recent survey by *USA Today* and Deloitte & Touche, nearly 80 percent of corporate executives said the importance of HRM in their firms has grown substantially over the last 10 years, and two-thirds said that HR expenditures are now viewed as a strategic investment rather than simply a cost to be minimized.[1] Global competition is intensifying. Rising educational standards and access to technology are increasingly available worldwide. *Innovation*—useful new ideas that emerge from the focused creativity of organization members—has become ever more critical to gaining and maintaining competitive advantage. Because employee skills, knowledge, and abilities are among the most distinctive and renewable resources on which a company can draw, their strategic management is more important than ever. Increasingly, organizations are recognizing that their success depends on what people know, that is, their knowledge and skills. The term **human capital** (or, more broadly, *intellectual capital*) often is used today to describe the strategic value of employee knowledge and abilities.

> "Hire the best. Pay them fairly. Communicate freely. Provide challenges and rewards. Get out of their way. They'll knock your socks off."
> Mary Ann Allison

human capital

The knowledge, skills, and abilities of employees that have economic value.

Managing human capital to sustain competitive advantage is perhaps the most important part of an organization's HR function. But on a day-to-day basis HR managers also have many other concerns regarding their workers and the entire personnel puzzle. These concerns including attracting talent; maintaining a well-trained, highly motivated, and loyal workforce; managing diversity; devising effective compensation systems; managing layoffs; and containing health care and pension costs. Balancing these issues is a difficult task, and the best approach is likely to vary depending on the circumstances of the organization. A steel producer facing a cutback in business may need human resources activities to assist with layoffs, whereas a semiconductor company may need more staff to produce enough microchips to meet the demands of the burgeoning personal computer market. The emphasis on different HR activities depends on whether the organization is growing, declining, or standing still. This leads to the practical issues involved in HR planning.

The HR Planning Process

"Get me the right kind and the right number of people at the right time." It sounds simple enough, but meeting an organization's staffing needs requires strategic human resources planning: an activity with a strategic purpose derived from the organization's plans.

The HR planning process occurs in three stages: planning, programming, and evaluating. First, HR managers need to know the organization's business plans to ensure that the right number and types of people are available—where the company is headed, in what businesses it plans to be, what future growth is expected, and so forth. Few things are more damaging to morale than having to lay off recently hired college graduates because of inadequate planning for future needs. Second, the organization conducts programming of specific human resources activities, such as recruitment, training, and layoffs. In this stage, the company's plans are implemented. Third, human resources activities are evaluated to determine whether they are producing the results needed to contribute to the organization's business plans. Figure 10.1 illustrates the components of the human resources planning process. In this chapter, we focus on human resources planning and programming. Many of the other factors listed in Figure 10.1 are discussed in later chapters.

Connections: HR AND STRATEGY AT GE

At the heart of GE's succession planning process are its annual "Session C" leadership and organizational talent reviews. In these intensive reviews, the CEO and vice president of HR meet with leaders and heads of HR from across different business units. In each session, they review the talent pool and organizational focus of each unit in order to understand the future leadership potential coming through GE. They also develop and review plans to ensure that there are always backups to key management jobs. When the president of GE's U.S. appliance division announced he was leaving to head up another company, GE was able to name his successor on the same day. Furthermore, the company announced at the same time who would take up all the positions created down the line as a result of the promotion.

FIGURE 10.1

An Overview of the HR Planning Process

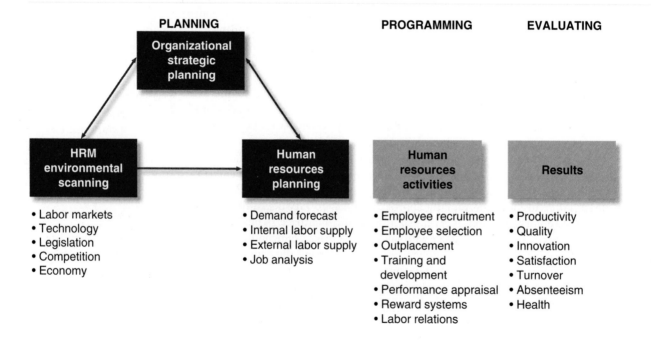

Demand Forecasts   Perhaps the most difficult part of human resources planning is conducting *demand* forecasts, that is, determining how many and what type of people are needed. Demand forecasts for people needs are derived from organizational plans. For example, when the pharmaceutical company Merck developed Propecia, a new drug to cure baldness, managers had to estimate the future size of this market based on demographic projections. Based on current sales and projected future sales growth, managers estimate the plant capacity needed to meet future demand, the sales force required, the support staff needed, and so forth. At this point, the number of labor-hours required to operate a plant, sell the product, distribute it, service customers, and so forth, can be calculated. These estimates are used to determine the demand for different types of workers.

Labor Supply Forecasts   In concert with demand forecasts, the *supply of labor* must be forecast, that is, estimates of how many and what types of employees the organization actually will have. In performing a supply analysis, the organization estimates the number and quality of its current employees as well as the available external supply of workers. To estimate internal supply, the company typically relies on past experiences with turnover, terminations, retirements, or promotions and transfers. A computerized human resources information system assists greatly in supply forecasting.

Externally, organizations have to look at workforce trends to make projections. Worldwide, there is a growing gap between the world's supply of labor and the demand for labor.[2] Most of the well-paid jobs are generated in the cities of the industrialized world, but many skilled and unskilled human resources are in the developing nations. This gap is leading to massive relocation (including immigrants, temporary workers, and retirees) and a reduction of protectionist immigration policies (as countries come to rely on and compete for foreign workers).

In the United States, one of the most important labor-supply issues to emerge in recent years has been the growing shortage of workers with the appropriate skills and education level. Traditional labor-intensive jobs, in agriculture, mining, and assembly-line manufacturing, are making way for jobs in technical, financial, and customized products and service industries. And these jobs often require much more training and schooling than the jobs they are replacing—or that the education system may currently be producing. For example, China now graduates more than three times the number of engineers as the United States. Demand for highly qualified employees continues to outpace supply—one reason some jobs are being transferred overseas. Some demographic trends we discussed in Chapter 2 may worsen this situation. For example, the upcoming retirement of the baby-boomer generation will remove a large number of educated and trained employees from the workforce. One response managers have made to deal with this skills shortage has been to increase significantly the remedial and training budgets within their own organizations.[3]

On the plus side, forecasts of a diverse workforce have become fact, and this has added greatly to the pool of available talent. The business world is no longer the exclusive domain of white males. In fact, two-career families have become the norm. Minorities, women, immigrants, older and disabled workers, and other groups have made the management of diversity a fundamental activity of the modern manager. Because of the importance of managing the "new workforce," the next chapter is devoted entirely to this topic.

Reconciling Supply and Demand   Once managers have a good idea of both the supply of and the demand for various types of employees, they can start developing approaches for reconciling the two. In some cases, organizations find that they need more

In the next couple of years, more and more baby boomers are headed for retirement and will be more inclined to call the shots on a putting green as opposed to the boardroom. How will this affect the dynamics of the workforce?

people than they currently have (i.e., a labor deficit). In such cases, organizations can hire new employees, promote current employees to new positions, or "outsource" work to contractors. In other cases, organizations may find that they have more people than they need (i.e., a labor surplus). If this is detected far enough in advance, organizations can use attrition—the normal turnover of employees—to reduce the surplus. In other instances, the organization may lay off employees or transfer them to other areas.

When managers do need to hire, one tool they have available is their organization's compensation policy. Large companies in particular spend a lot of time gathering information about pay scales for the various jobs they have available, and making sure their compensation system is fair and competitive. We discuss pay issues later in this chapter.

Job Analysis   While issues of supply and demand are fairly "macro" activities that are conducted at an organizational level, HR planning also has a "micro" side called *job analysis*. **Job analysis** does two things.[4] First, it tells the HR manager about the job itself: the essential tasks, duties, and responsibilities involved in performing the job. This information is called a *job description*. For example, the job description for an accounting manager might specify that the position will be responsible for monthly, quarterly, and annual financial reports, getting bills issued and paid, preparing budgets, ensuring the company's compliance with laws and regulations, working closely with line managers on financial issues, and supervising an accounting department of 12 people.

Second, job analysis describes the skills, knowledge, abilities, and other characteristics needed to perform the job. This is called the *job specification*. For our accounting manager example, the job requirements might include a degree in accounting or business, knowledge of computerized accounting systems, prior managerial experience, and excellent communication skills.

Job analysis provides the information that virtually every human resources activity requires. It assists with the essential HR programs: recruitment, training, selection, appraisal, and reward systems. It may also help organizations defend themselves in lawsuits involving employment practices—for example, by clearly specifying what a job requires if someone claims unfair dismissal.[5] Ultimately, job analysis helps increase the value added by employees to the organization because it clarifies what is really required to perform effectively.

> **job analysis**
>
> A tool for determining what is done on a given job and what should be done on that job.

Staffing the Organization

Once HR planning is completed, managers can focus on staffing the organization. The staffing function consists of three related activities: recruitment, selection, and outplacement.

Recruitment

Recruitment activities help increase the pool of candidates that might be selected for a job. Recruitment may be internal to the organization (considering current employees for promotions and transfers) or external. Each approach has advantages and disadvantages.[6]

> **recruitment**
>
> The development of a pool of applicants for jobs in an organization.

Internal Recruiting   The advantages of internal recruiting are that employers know their employees, and employees know their organization. External candidates who are unfamiliar with the organization may find they don't like working there. Also, the opportunity to move up within the organization may encourage employees to remain with the company, work hard, and succeed. Recruiting from outside the company can be demoralizing to employees. Many companies, such as Sears Roebuck and Eli Lilly, prefer internal to external recruiting for these reasons.

Internal staffing has some drawbacks. If existing employees lack skills or talent, internal recruitment yields a limited applicant pool, leading to poor selection decisions.

Also, an internal recruitment policy can inhibit a company that wants to change the nature or goals of the business by bringing in outside candidates. In changing from a rapidly growing, entrepreneurial organization to a mature business with more stable growth, Dell Computer went outside the organization to hire managers who better fit those needs.

Many companies that rely heavily on internal recruiting use a job-posting system. A *job-posting system* is a mechanism for advertising open positions, typically on a bulletin board. Texas Instruments uses job posting. Employees complete a request form indicating interest in a posted job. The posted job description includes a list of duties and the minimum skills and experience required.

External Recruiting   External recruiting brings in "new blood" to a company and can inspire innovation. Among the most frequently used sources of outside applicants are Internet job boards, newspaper advertisements, employee referrals, and college campus recruiting.

Newspaper advertising remains the most popular recruiting source. However, readership bases are declining as more job searchers turn to the Web, which has exploded in popularity as a job-recruitment tool. Most companies with a corporate Web site now let people apply for jobs online, and many even list open positions. Employment agencies are also a common recruitment tool, and for important management positions companies often use specialized executive-search firms. Employee referrals are yet another frequently used source of applicants.[7] Some companies actively encourage employees to refer their friends by offering cash rewards. In fact, surveys show word-of-mouth recommendations are the way most job positions get filled. The advantages of campus recruiting include a large pool of people from which to draw, applicants with up-to-date training, and a source of innovative ideas.[8]

Outside hires often bring new ideas to the organization.

Monster.com's Scary Competition

▼ **FROM THE PAGES OF**

BusinessWeek

For several years now, leading job-search Web site Monster.com has held onto its worldwide dominance with surprising dexterity. Most analysts gave up on the company after it stopped showing its ads through AOL and MSN portals. Still, the outfit has managed to keep traffic coming to its Web site. In one typical month, it grabbed 25.7 percent of all visitors to employment sites, according to research service Hitwise.

But Monster.com may be about to face its toughest battle yet. Yes, the U.S. job-search market is expected to double to $1.9 billion by 2008, according to tech consultancy Forrester Research. But rivals, old and new, are gearing up to give the Monster.com's little green mascot a real run for his money.

New entrants are jumping into job search, with the number of sites having grown by 15 percent in the past year, estimates Bill Tancer, vice-president for research at Hitwise. What's more, many established competitors have access to even greater resources than Monster Worldwide, with its $82 million in cash and equivalents.

Perhaps the biggest threat yet to Monster's supremacy came when auction giant eBay, with $1.4 billion in cash and equivalents, became a 25 percent investor in online billboard Craigslist, which gets 100 percent of its sales from job ads. Craigslist already receives more traffic than Monster's sites, according to Web rankings site Alexa. (Monster is No. 1 in terms of revenues.) Craigslist charges less than Monster, and CEO Jim Buckmaster believes it caters to a more lucrative market—matching job hunters with employers within local markets, rather than by nationwide searches.

Another emerging competitor is Israeli startup Redmatch. Its technology allows newspapers to post their help-wanted ads online. Redmatch's software matches job seekers with employers based on skills and requirements, reducing the time needed to sift through ads and résumés. Already, more than 150 U.S. newspapers have linked to Redmatch's Internet network, which features 85,000 ads. Within six months, CEO Gal Almog expects to quadruple the number of newspapers Redmatch serves.

Redmatch also sells its technology to corporations, many of which are starting their own Web-based job outreach efforts. Many find that keeping in touch with former employees, for example, can help fill vacancies faster—and do so with people who need less training and are familiar with their corporate culture.

Monster.com's longtime rivals are ramping up their efforts as well. Yahoo! is now testing a new version of its sites, offering job postings and other information for local areas, says Dan Finnigan, general manager of the HotJobs.com division of Yahoo! Lately, HotJobs has also aggressively cut its pricing to below that of rivals such as Monster.com, say analysts.

Then there's CareerBuilder.com, which is a joint effort between newspaper chains Gannett, Knight Ridder, and Tribune. CareerBuilder increased its traffic by 8.6 percent year-over-year, gaining at the expense of HotJobs and Monster.com, according to Hitwise. CareerBuilder's revenue has also grown much faster than Monster's, though from a much smaller base.

Not that Monster.com is taking the new challenges sitting down. Andrew McKelvey, Monster Worldwide's chairman and CEO, insists that better revenues and margins will keep Monster.com on top, not traffic numbers. The company increased its marketing and promotion expenses by 20 percent, despite ending relationships with MSN and AOL, which collected millions of dollars in fees for listing Monster.com. Anticipating a robust jobs recovery, Monster also expanded its sales staff and made several acquisitions, even as employment remains soft.

Few think the current lull will last for long, however. That's why this green monster is preparing for battle with some pretty determined adversaries.

SOURCE: Olga Kharif, "Scary Competition for Monster.com," *BusinessWeek*, August 16, 2004, online.

Most companies use some combination of all the methods we have been discussing, depending on the particular job or situation. For example, they might use internal recruiting for existing jobs that need replacements, and external recruiting when the firm is expanding or needs to acquire some new skill.

Selection

Selection builds on recruiting and involves decisions about whom to hire. As important as these decisions are, they are—unfortunately—at times made in very careless or cavalier ways. In this section we describe a number of selection instruments to which you may soon be exposed in your own career.

Applications and Résumés   Application blanks and résumés provide basic information to prospective employers. In order to make a first cut through candidates, employers review the profiles and backgrounds of various job applicants. Applications and résumés typically include information about the applicant's name, educational background, citizenship, work experiences, certifications, and the like. Their appearance and accuracy also say something about the applicant—spelling mistakes, for example, are almost always immediately disqualifying (something to keep in mind when preparing your own). While providing important information, applications and résumés tend not to be extremely useful for making final selection decisions.

The popularity of searching for jobs on the Internet has increased and so has the competition among job-searching Web sites. An Israeli firm "Redmatch" has been in the market for five years with over 500 newspapers in their network. Their unique combination of recruitment sourcing tools and recruitment management tools matches job-seekers with employers based on skills and requirements.

Interviews   *Interviews* are the most popular selection tool, and every company uses some type of interview. However, employment interviewers must be careful about what they ask and how they ask it. Questions that are not job-related are prohibited. In an unstructured (or nondirective) interview, the interviewer asks different interviewees different questions. The interviewer may also use probes, that is, ask follow-up questions to learn more about the candidate.[9]

In a **structured interview,** the interviewer conducts the same interview with each applicant. There are two basic types of structured interview. The first approach—called the *situational interview*—focuses on hypothetical situations. Zale Corporation, a major jewelry chain, uses this type of structured interview to select sales clerks. A sample question is: "A customer comes into the store to pick up a watch he had left for repair. The watch is not back yet from the repair shop, and the customer becomes angry. How would you handle the situation?" An answer that says "I would refer the customer to my supervisor" might suggest that the applicant felt incapable of handling the situation on his or her own. The second approach—called the *behavioral description interview*—explores what candidates have actually done in the past. In selecting college students for an officer training program, the U.S. Army asks the following question to assess a candidate's ability to influence others: "What was the best idea you ever sold to a supervisor, teacher, peer, or subordinate?" A response that described the initial difficulties the applicant had in selling the idea and how he or she overcame them might tell the recruiter something about the applicant's self-confidence and determination. Because behavioral questions are based on real events, they often provide useful information about how the candidate will actually perform on the job.

Each of these interview techniques offers a manager different advantages and disadvantages, and many interviewers use more than one technique during the same interview. Unstructured interviews can help establish rapport and provide a sense of the applicant's personality, but they may not provide the manager with specific information about the candidate's ability. Structured interviews tend to be more reliable predictors of job performance, because they are based on the job analysis that has been done for the position. They are also more likely to be free of bias and stereotypes. And because the same questions are being asked of all candidates for the job, an interview that is at least partially structured allows the manager to compare responses across different candidates.[10]

Reference Checks   *Reference checks* are another commonly used screening device. Virtually all organizations use either a reference or an employment and education record check. Although reference checking makes sense, reference information is becoming increasingly difficult to obtain as a result of several highly publicized lawsuits. In one case, an applicant sued a former boss on the grounds that the boss told prospective employers the applicant was a "thief and a crook." The jury awarded the applicant $80,000.[11] Nevertheless, talking to an applicant's previous supervisor is a common practice, and often does provide useful information, particularly if specific job-related questions are asked ("Can you give me an example of a project candidate X handled particularly well?").

Background Checks.   Following 9/11 and numerous corporate scandals at companies like Enron and World.com, background investigations have become standard procedure for many companies. Some state courts have ruled that companies can be held liable for negligent hiring if they fail to do adequate background checks. Social Security verification, past employment and education verification, and a criminal records check are among the different types of checks. A number of other checks can be conducted if they pertain to the job being hired for, including a motor vehicle record check (for jobs involving driving) and a credit check (for money-handling jobs). Figure 10.2 shows the various screening tools used by many Fortune 1000 companies.

structured interview

Selection technique that involves asking all applicants the same questions and comparing their responses to a standardized set of answers.

During an interview, employers may opt to hold unstructured interviews, where they ask each potential employee different questions, or they may choose to hold structured interviews where the employer asks all potential employees the same questions.

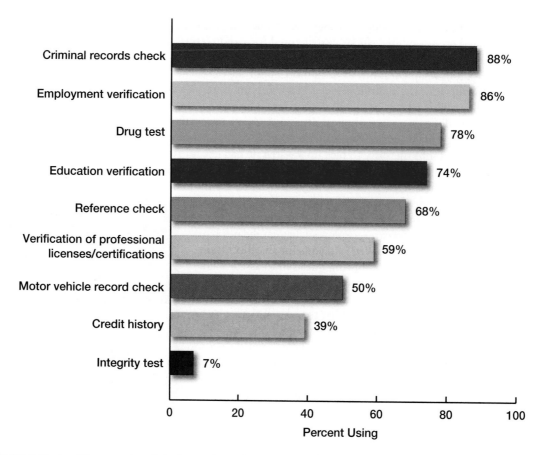

SOURCE: *Top Security Threats and Management Issues Facing Corporate America,* Pinkerton Consulting and Investigations, Inc., 2003.

FIGURE 10.2

Use of Preemployment
Selection Tools (tools that
212 security representative
at Fortune 1000 companies
said their companies use
consistently)

Personality Tests   *Personality tests* are less popular for employee selection, largely because they are hard to defend in court.[12] However, they are regaining popularity, and chances are that at some point in your career you will complete some personality tests. A number of well-known paper-and-pencil inventories measure personality traits such as sociability, adjustment, and energy. Typical questions are "Do you like to socialize with people?" and "Do you enjoy working hard?" Some personality tests try to determine the kind of working conditions that the candidate prefers, to see if he or she would be motivated and productive in the particular job. For example, if the candidate prefers making decisions on his or her own, but the job requires gaining the cooperation of others, another candidate might make for a better fit.

Drug Testing   *Drug testing* is now a frequently used screening instrument. Since the passage of the Drug-Free Workplace Act of 1988, applicants and employees of federal contractors and Department of Defense contractors and those under Department of Transportation regulations have been subject to testing for illegal drugs. Well over half of all U.S. companies conduct preemployment drug tests.

   Genetic testing tries to identify the likelihood of contracting a disease (such as emphysema) on the basis of a person's genetic makeup. It is far less common than drug testing and remains controversial.[13]

Cognitive Ability Tests   *Cognitive ability tests* are among the oldest employment selection devices. These tests measure a range of intellectual abilities, including verbal

Verbal	1. What is the meaning of the word surreptitious?

Verbal

1. What is the meaning of the word surreptitious?
   a. covert
   b. winding
   c. lively
   d. sweet

2. How is the noun clause used in the following sentence: "I hope that I can learn this game."
   a. subject
   b. predicate nominative
   c. direct object
   d. object of the preposition

Quantitative

3. Divide 50 by .5 and add 5. What is the result?
   a. 25
   b. 30
   c. 95
   d. 105

4. What is the value of 144^2?
   a. 12
   b. 72
   c. 288
   d. 20736

Reasoning

5. _____ is to boat as snow is to _____
   a. sail, ski
   b. water, winter
   c. water, ski
   d. engine, water

6. Two women played 5 games of chess. Each woman won the same number of games, yet there were no ties. How can this be so?
   a. There was a forfeit.
   b. One player cheated.
   c. They played different people.
   d. One game was still in progress.

Mechanical

7. If gear A and gear C are both turning counter-clockwise, what is happening to gear B?
   a. It is turning counter-clockwise.
   b. It is turning clockwise.
   c. It remains stationary.
   d. The whole system will jam.

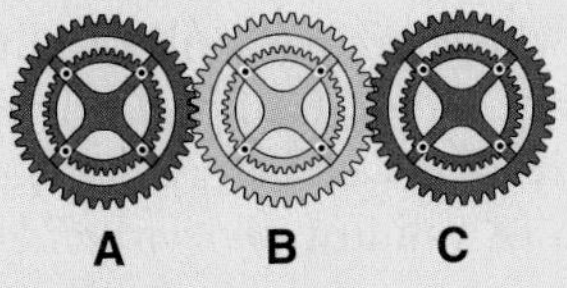

A   B   C

Answers: 1a, 2c, 3d, 4d, 5c, 6c, 7b.

SOURCE: George Bohlander, Scott Snell, and Arthur Sherman, *Managing Human Resources,* 12th ed. Copyright © 2001. Reprinted by permission of South-Western, a division of Thomson Learning, www.thomsonrights.com.

FIGURE 10.3
Sample Measures of Cognitive Ability

comprehension (vocabulary, reading) and numerical aptitude (mathematical calculations). About 20 percent of U.S. companies use cognitive ability tests for selection purposes.[14] Figure 10.3 shows some examples of cognitive ability test questions.

Performance Tests *Performance tests* are procedures in which the test taker performs a sample of the job. Most companies use some type of performance test, typically for secretarial and clerical positions. The most widely used performance test is the typing test. However, performance tests have been developed for almost every occupation, including managerial positions. Assessment centers are the most notable offshoot of the managerial performance test.[15]

Assessment centers originated during World War II. A typical **assessment center** consists of 10 to 12 candidates who participate in a variety of exercises or situations; some of the exercises involve group interactions, and others are performed individually. Each exercise taps a number of critical managerial dimensions, such as leadership, decision-making skills, and communication ability. Assessors, generally line managers

assessment center

A managerial performance test in which candidates participate in a variety of exercises and situations.

from the organization, observe and record information about the candidates' performance in each exercise. AT&T was the first organization to use assessment centers. Since then, a number of large organizations have used or currently are using the assessment center technique, including Bristol-Myers, the FBI, and Sears.

Integrity Tests   *Integrity tests* are used to assess a job candidate's honesty. Two forms of integrity tests are polygraphs and paper-and-pencil honesty tests. Polygraphs, or lie detector tests, have been banned for most employment purposes.[16] Paper-and-pencil honesty tests are more recent instruments for measuring integrity.

These tests include questions such as whether a person has ever thought about stealing and whether he or she believes other people steal ("What percentage of people take more than $1 from their employer?"). Payless ShoeSource, based in Topeka, Kansas, has used an honesty test to reduce employee theft. Within only a year of implementing the program, inventory losses dropped by 20 percent, to less than 1 percent of sales. Despite compelling evidence such as this, the accuracy of these tests is still debatable.[17]

reliability

The consistency of test scores over time and across alternative measurements.

validity

The degree to which a selection test predicts or correlates with job performance.

Reliability and Validity   Regardless of the method used to select employees, two crucial issues that need to be addressed are a test's reliability and its validity. **Reliability** refers to the consistency of test scores over time and across alternative measurements. For example, if three different interviewers talked to the same job candidate but drew very different conclusions about the candidate's abilities, we might suspect that there were problems with the reliability of one or more of the selection tests or interview procedures.

Validity moves beyond reliability to assess the accuracy of the selection test. The most common form of validity, *criterion-related validity*, refers to the degree to which a test actually predicts or correlates with job performance. Such validity is usually established through studies comparing test performance and job performance for a large enough sample of employees to enable a fair conclusion to be reached. For example, if a high score on a cognitive ability test is strongly predictive of good job performance, then candidates who score well will usually be preferred over those who do not. Nevertheless, no test in and of itself perfectly predicts performance. Managers will usually rely on other criteria as well before making a final selection.

Another form of validity, *content validity*, concerns the degree to which selection tests measure a representative sample of the knowledge, skills, and abilities required for the job. The best-known example of a content-valid test is a typing test for secretaries, because typing is a task a secretary almost always performs. However, to be completely content-valid, the selection process also should measure other skills the secretary would be likely to perform, such as answering the telephone, duplicating and faxing documents, and dealing with the public. Content validity is more subjective (less statistical) than evaluations of criterion-related validity, but is no less important, particularly when one is defending employment decisions in court.

Workforce Reductions

Unfortunately, staffing decisions do not simply focus on hiring employees. As organizations evolve and markets change, the demand for certain employees rises and falls. Also, some employees simply do not perform at a level required to justify continued employment. For these reasons, managers sometimes must make difficult decisions to terminate their employment.

Layoffs   As a result of the massive restructuring of American industry brought about by mergers and acquisitions, divestiture, and increased competition, organizations have been *downsizing*—laying off large numbers of managerial and other employees. Dismissing any employee is tough, but when a company lays off a substantial portion of its workforce, the results can rock the foundations of the organization.[18] The victims of restructuring face all the difficulties of being let go—loss of self-esteem, demoralizing job searches, and the stigma of being out of work. **Outplacement** is the process of helping people who have been dismissed from the company to regain employment elsewhere. This can help to some extent, but the impact of layoffs goes further than the employees who leave. For many of the employees who remain with the company, disenchantment, distrust, and lethargy overshadow the comfort of still having a job. In many respects, how management deals with dismissals will affect the productivity and satisfaction of those who remain. A well-thought-out dismissal process eases tensions and helps remaining employees adjust to the new work situation.

All of its employees were laid off after Houston-based Enron collapsed in 2001. What effect does being laid off have on people?

Organizations with strong performance evaluation systems benefit because the survivors are less likely to believe the decision was arbitrary. Further, if care is taken during the actual layoff process—that is, if workers are offered severance pay and help in finding a new job—remaining workers will be comforted. Companies also should avoid stringing out layoffs, that is, dismissing a few workers at a time.

Termination   People sometimes "get fired" for poor performance or other reasons. Should an employer have the right to fire a worker? In 1884, a Tennessee court ruled: "All may dismiss their employee(s) at will for good cause, for no cause, or even for cause morally wrong." The concept that an employee may be fired for any reason is known as **employment-at-will** or *termination-at-will* and was upheld in a 1908 Supreme Court ruling.[19] The logic is that if the employee may quit at any time, the employer is free to dismiss at any time.

Since the mid-1970s, courts in most states have made exceptions to this doctrine. For example, public policy is a policy or ruling designed to protect the public from harm. Under the public policy exception, employees cannot be fired for such actions as refusing to break the law, taking time off for jury duty, or "whistle-blowing" illegal company behavior. For example, if a worker reports an environmental violation to the regulatory agency and the company fires him or her, the courts may argue that the firing was unfair because the employee acted for the good of the community. Union contracts that limit an employer's ability to fire without cause are another major exception to the employment-at-will doctrine.

Employers can avoid the pitfalls associated with dismissal by developing progressive and positive disciplinary procedures.[20] By *progressive*, we mean that a manager takes graduated steps in attempting to correct a workplace behavior. For example, an employee who has been absent receives a verbal reprimand for the first offense. A second offense invokes a written reprimand. A third offense results in employee counseling and probation, and a fourth results in a paid-leave day to think over the consequences of future rule infractions. The employer is signaling to the employee that this is the "last straw." Arbitrators are more likely to side with an employer that fires someone when they believe the company has made sincere efforts to help the person correct his or her behavior.

The **termination interview,** in which the manager discusses the company's position with the employee, is a stressful situation for both parties. Most experts believe that the immediate superior should be the one to deliver the bad news to employees. However, it is often good to have a third party, such as the HR manager, present to serve as a witness, to provide support for an anxious manager, or to diffuse anger by pulling the employee's attention away from the manager. In addition, some suggest that the best time to let someone go is Friday afternoon. However, the research evidence does not support this completely. Finally, it may be a good idea to conduct the termination interview in a neutral location, such as a conference room, so that the

outplacement

The process of helping people who have been dismissed from the company to regain employment elsewhere.

employment-at-will

The legal concept that an employee may be terminated for any reason.

termination interview

A discussion between a manager and an employee about the employee's dismissal.

Do's	Don'ts
• Give as much warning as possible for mass layoffs. • Sit down one on one with the individual, in a private office. • Complete a termination session within 15 minutes. • Provide written explanations of severance benefits. • Provide outplacement services away from company headquarters. • Be sure the employee hears about his or her termination from a manager, not a colleague. • Express appreciation for what the employee has contributed, if appropriate.	• Don't leave room for confusion when firing. Tell the individual in the first sentence that he or she is terminated. • Don't allow time for debate during a termination session. • Don't make personal comments when firing someone; keep the conversation professional. • Don't rush a fired employee offsite unless security is an issue. • Don't fire people on significant dates, like the 25th anniversary of their employment or the day their mother died. • Don't fire employees when they are on vacation or have just returned.

TABLE 10.1
Advice on Termination

SOURCE: S. Alexander, "Firms Get Plenty of Practice at Layoffs, but They Often Bungle the Firing Process," *The Wall Street Journal*, November 14, 1991, p. 31. Copyright © 1991 Dow Jones & Co., Inc. Reproduced with permission of Dow Jones & Co., Inc. via Copyright Clearance Center.

manager and employee can exit gracefully afterward. Table 10.1 provides some other guidelines for conducting a termination interview.[21]

Legal Issues and Equal Employment Opportunity   Many laws have been passed governing employment decisions and practices. A good part of your day-to-day work as a manager, and the human resource function of your organization, will be directly affected by them. Most of these laws are designed to protect job candidates and employees against discrimination or sexual harassment and to establish standards of pay and hours worked for certain classes of employee. For example, the 1938 *Fair Labor Standards Act* (FLSA), among other provisions, creates two employee categories: exempt and nonexempt. Employees are normally exempt from overtime pay if they have considerable discretion in how they carry out their jobs and if their jobs require them to exercise independent judgment. Managers usually fall in this category. Nonexempt employees are usually paid by the hour and must be paid overtime if they work over 40 hours in a week. As a manager you will almost certainly need to specify the exempt or nonexempt status of anyone you hire.

The 1964 *Civil Rights Act* prohibits discrimination in employment based on race, sex, color, national origin, and religion. Title VII of the act specifically forbids discrimination in such employment practices as recruitment, hiring, discharge, promotion, compensation, and access to training.[22] The *Americans with Disabilities Act*, passed in 1990, prohibits employment discrimination against people with disabilities. Recovering alcoholics and drug abusers, cancer patients in remission, and AIDS patients are covered by this legislation. The 1991 *Civil Rights Act* strengthened all these protections and permitted punitive damages to be imposed on companies that violate them.

Failure to comply with any of these laws may expose the organization to charges of unfair practices, expensive lawsuits, and civil and even criminal penalties in some cases. For example, Wal-Mart has been subjected to lawsuits in most states for withholding overtime pay to hourly workers. The company has also been sued for sex discrimination by its female workers, with a potential liability in the billions of dollars. Radio Shack had to pay almost $30 million to store managers who claimed they were improperly classified as exempt employees and should have been paid overtime. Other companies that have been targeted by FLSA lawsuits include State Farm, Pacific Bell, Purdue University, and Taco Bell.[23]

One common reason employers are sued is **adverse impact**—when a seemingly neutral employment practice has a disproportionately negative effect on a group protected by the Civil Rights Act.[24] For example, if equal numbers of qualified men and women apply for jobs but a particular employment test results in far fewer women being hired, the test may be considered to cause an adverse impact, and therefore be subject to challenge on that basis.

> **adverse impact**
>
> When a seemingly neutral employment practice has a disproportionately negative effect on a protected group.

Because of the importance of these issues, many companies have established procedures to ensure compliance with labor and equal-opportunity laws. For example, progressive companies carefully monitor and compare salaries by race, gender, length of service, and other categories to make sure employees across all groups are being fairly paid. Written policies can also help ensure fair and legal practices in the workplace, though the company may also have to demonstrate a record of actually following those procedures and making sure they are implemented. In this sense, smart and effective management practices not only help managers motivate employees to do their best work, but often help provide legal protection as well. For example, managers who provide their employees with regular, specific evaluations can often prevent misunderstandings that can lead to lawsuits. And a written record of those evaluations is often useful in demonstrating fair and objective treatment.

The Americans with Disabilities Act, which was passed in 1990, prohibits employment discrimination against people with disabilities.

Many other important staffing laws affect employment practices. For example, the *Age Discrimination in Employment Act* of 1967 and its amendments in 1978 and 1986 prohibit discrimination against people age 40 and over. One reason for this legislation was the common practice of dismissing older workers to replace them with younger workers who were not as highly paid. The *Worker Adjustment and Retraining Notification Act* of 1989, commonly known as the *WARN Act* or *Plant Closing Bill*, requires covered employers to give affected employees 60 days' written notice of plant closings or mass layoffs. Table 10.2 summarizes many of these major employment laws.

Developing the Workforce

Today's competitive environment requires managers to continually upgrade the skills and performance of employees—and their own. Such constant improvement increases both personal and organizational effectiveness. It makes organization members more useful in their current job and prepares them to take on new responsibilities. And it helps the organization as a whole handle new challenges and take advantage of new methods and technologies that emerge. Developing the workforce in this way involves training and development activities. It also involves appraising employees' performance and giving them effective feedback so they will be motivated to perform at their best. We will discuss each of these activities in turn.

Act	Major Provisions	Enforcement and Remedies
Fair Labor Standards Act (1938)	Creates exempt (salaried) and non-exempt (hourly) employee categories, governing overtime and other rules; sets minimum wage, child-labor laws.	Enforced by Department of Labor, private action to recover lost wages; civil and criminal penalties also possible.
Equal Pay Act (1963)	Prohibits gender-based pay discrimination between two jobs substantially similar in skill, effort, responsibility, and working conditions.	Fines up to $10,000, imprisonment up to 6 months, or both; enforced by Equal Employment Opportunity Commission (EEOC); private actions for double damages up to 3 years' wages, liquidated damages, reinstatement, or promotion.
Title VII of Civil Rights Act (1964)	Prohibits discrimination based on race, sex, color, religion, or national origin in employment decisions: hiring, pay, working conditions, promotion, discipline, or discharge.	Enforced by EEOC; private actions, back pay, front pay, reinstatement, restoration of seniority and pension benefits, attorneys' fees and costs.
Executive Orders 11246 and 11375 (1965)	Requires equal opportunity clauses in federal contracts; prohibits employment discrimination by federal contractors based on race, color, religion, sex, or national origin.	Established Office of Federal Contract Compliance Programs (OFCCP) to investigate violations; empowered to terminate violater's federal contracts.
Age Discrimination in Employment Act (1967)	Prohibits employment discrimination based on age for persons over 40 years; restricts mandatory retirement.	EEOC enforcement; private actions for reinstatement, back pay, front pay, restoration of seniority and pension benefits; double unpaid wages for willful violations; attorneys' fees and costs.
Vocational Rehabilitation Act (1973)	Requires affirmative action by all federal contractors for persons with disabilities; defines disabilities as physical or mental impairments that substantially limit life activities.	Federal contractors must consider hiring disabled persons capable of performance after reasonable accommodations.
Americans with Disabilities Act (1990)	Extends affirmative action provisions of Vocational Rehabilitation Act to private employers; requires workplace modifications to facilitate disabled employees; prohibits discrimination against disabled.	EEOC enforcement; private actions for Title VII remedies.
Civil Rights Act (1991)	Clarifies Title VII requirements: disparate treatment impact suits, business necessity, job relatedness; shifts burden of proof to employer; permits punitive damages and jury trials.	Punitive damages limited to sliding scale only in intentional discrimination based on sex, religion, and disabilities.
Family and Medical Leave Act (1991)	Requires 12 weeks' unpaid leave for medical or family needs: paternity, family member illness.	Private actions for lost wages and other expenses, reinstatement.

TABLE 10.2
U.S. Equal Employment Laws

Training and Development

U.S. businesses spend more than $50 billion to provide each of their employees with an average of 26 hours of formal training annually. By far, most of the money is spent on rank-and-file workers and supervisors versus executives. Technology, transportation, communications, and utilities industries tend to spend the most on training.[25]

Fortune 500 companies such as General Electric and General Motors have invested heavily in training. IBM's annual training costs have at times exceeded Harvard University's annual operating expenses. But many companies are also relying on cheaper methods of training, such as e-learning and Web-based simulations, to train large numbers of workers.

The American Society for Training and Development has argued that as a percentage of total payroll, the average organizational investment in training is too small.[26] This is of great concern in light of the fact that today's jobs require more education but that the education level of U.S. workers has not kept pace. What's more, companies need to ensure that employees who have survived layoffs can lead their organizations through tough times.

Overview of the Training Process   Although we use the general term *training* here, training sometimes is distinguished from development. **Training** usually refers to teaching lower-level employees how to perform their present jobs, while **development** involves teaching managers and professional employees broader skills needed for their present and future jobs. *Phase one* of training usually starts with a **needs assessment.** Managers conduct an analysis to identify the jobs, people, and departments for which training is necessary. Job analysis and performance measurements are useful for this purpose.

Phase two involves the design of training programs. Based on needs assessment, training objectives and content can be established. *Phase three* involves decisions about the training methods to be used (see Figure 10.4), and whether the training will be provided on-the-job or off-the-job. Examples of training methods include lectures, role playing, business simulation, behavior modeling (watching a videotape and imitating what is observed), conferences, vestibule training (practicing in a simulated job environment), and apprenticeships. Job rotation, where employees are assigned to different jobs in the organization to broaden their experience and improve their skills, is another popular training method. It is frequently applied to managers as well as lower-level employees. In fact, smart managers often request assignment to jobs where they can be challenged and their skills broadened. Finally, *phase four* of training should evaluate the program's effectiveness in terms of employee reactions, learning, improved behavior on the job, and bottom-line results.

Training improves employee quality

training

Teaching lower-level employees how to perform their present jobs.

development

Teaching managers and professional employees broad skills needed for their present and future jobs.

needs assessment

An analysis identifying the jobs, people, and departments for which training is necessary.

Connections: HR AND STRATEGY AT GE

GE has set up a comprehensive business-development course designed for its functional and unit business heads. In the course, each head undergoes simulations in running other business units in order to develop broader business skills. The CFO might take up the role of COO in the simulation, for example, while a senior HR executive could be shouldered with the position of CFO. "It forces people to take on different roles and run a fairly sophisticated simulation against other teams. You can see how they interact, make decisions and interpret data. It gives them an idea of what the basic skills are in other functions," GE's Bertamini says. "Fundamentally, we believe we can teach people new skills, or we wouldn't be spending all this time on training. But having said that, some people are naturally better with employees, while some are naturally better with customers." He recounts seeing very senior people early in their careers who didn't perform well in a public forum, yet their skills were highly polished two to three years later after working on particular skill deficiencies.

FIGURE 10.4

Most Frequently Used
Training Methods

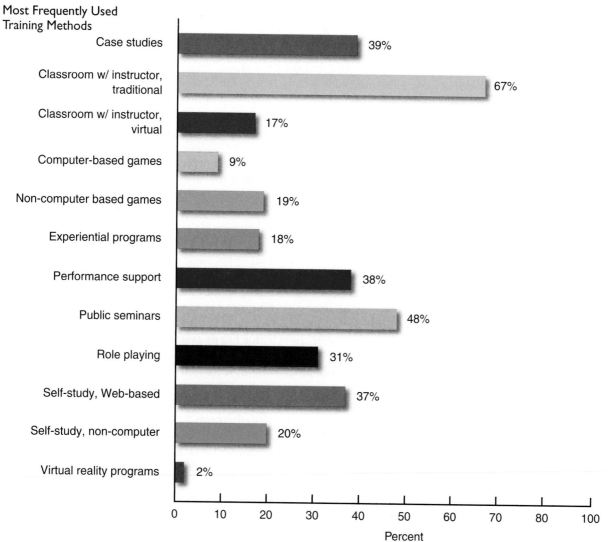

	Percent
Case studies	39%
Classroom w/ instructor, traditional	67%
Classroom w/ instructor, virtual	17%
Computer-based games	9%
Non-computer based games	19%
Experiential programs	18%
Performance support	38%
Public seminars	48%
Role playing	31%
Self-study, Web-based	37%
Self-study, non-computer	20%
Virtual reality programs	2%

SOURCE: Holly Dolezalek, "Industry Report 2004," *Training*, October 2004, p. 32.

orientation training

Training designed to introduce new employees to the company and familiarize them with policies, procedures, culture, and the like.

Types of Training   Companies invest in training to enhance individual performance and organizational productivity. Programs to improve an employee's computer, technical, or communication skills are quite common, and some types of training have become fairly standard across many organizations. **Orientation training** typically is used to familiarize new employees with their new jobs, work units, and the organization in general. Done well, orientation training has a number of reputed benefits, including lower employee turnover, increased morale, better productivity, and lower recruiting and training costs.

Finding Workers Who Fit

Since founders Kip Tindell and Garrett Boone opened the first Container Store in Dallas in 1978, containing growth has turned out to be their most daunting challenge. The privately held company has quietly expanded into a 33-store nationwide chain with projected revenues of $370 million and annual sales growth that has topped 20 percent in all of its 26 years. Behind much of that success, analysts say, aren't just the popular knickknacks the Container Store sells for Type A neat freaks. Just as important is the company's organizing principle for human resources: turning its best customers into loyal, top-performing employees.

In an industry with an average employee turnover rate of more than 70 percent, worker churn at the Container Store is less than 10 percent for full-time employees and 30 to 35 percent for part-timers. And nearly a third of the company's 2,500 workers come from referrals. "To be a great place to shop, you need to be a great place to work," says Doug Fleener, president of Massachusetts-based retail consultancy Dynamic Experiences Group. "This company is in total harmony, from the sales floor to the distribution center." Forget the closet—here's how the Container Store organizes its talent.

1. **In-Store Head-Hunting** Tindell and Boone make recruiting part of everybody's job by offering all staff members handsome bonuses. Workers get $500 for every full-time hire and $200 for every part-timer. All employees, from stockers to managers, carry recruiting cards to pull out when chatting up customers in the aisles. The program is so successful, says Kevin Fuller, director of training and recruiting, that the company often goes six to eight months without placing a single classified ad.

2. **All-Hands Interviews** Applicants who get a call back submit to a group interview with as many as 10 fellow job candidates. There, potential hires often make a pitch for a product that solves an organizational challenge—a key indicator of enthusiasm and sales skills. The group setting offers managers a glimpse of how candidates function as part of a team. "We want to see how people encourage one another, because that's our environment," Fuller says.

3. **Continuous Training** New hires begin a 241-hour training program that stretches out over a year. (The retail-industry average for training new workers is eight hours.) Newbies are paired up with training "buddies" who give them crash courses in everything from sales techniques to the ins and outs of Elfa, the company's best-selling modular storage system. The company won't disclose how much it spends on training, but "we know it's expensive," Fuller says. Still, the training helps ensure better service—which results in fewer lost customers and a lot more sales: The Container Store rings up an average of $400 per square foot, compared with $125 for the rest of the housewares industry.

SOURCE: Vicki Powers, "Finding Workers Who Fit," *Business 2.0*, November 2004, online.

Team training has taken on more importance as organizations reorganize to facilitate individuals working together. Team training teaches employees the skills they need to work together and facilitates their interaction. Coca-Cola's Fountain Manufacturing Operation developed a team training program that focused on technical, interpersonal, and team interaction skills.[27]

Diversity training is now offered in over 50 percent of all U.S. organizations. The programs focus on building awareness of diversity issues as well as providing the skills employees need to work with others who are different from them. This topic is so important that the next chapter is devoted solely to managing diversity.

Today's decentralized and leaner organizations put more demands and responsibility on managers, as has an increasingly competitive environment. And as managers rise in the organization, their technical skills generally become less and less important than their ability to motivate others. For these reasons, *management training programs* have become another widely used development tool. Such programs often seek to improve managers' *people skills*—their ability to delegate effectively, increase the motivation of their subordinates, and communicate and inspire the achievement of organization goals. *Coaching*—being trained by a superior—is usually the most effective and direct management-development tool. Managers may also participate in training programs that are used for all employees, such as job rotation, or attend seminars and courses specifically designed to help them improve their supervisory skills or prepare them for future promotion.

team training

Training that provides employees with the skills and perspectives they need to work in collaboration with others.

diversity training

Programs that focus on identifying and reducing hidden biases against people with differences and developing the skills needed to manage a diversified workforce.

Performance Appraisal

performance appraisal (PA)

Assessment of an employee's job performance.

Performance appraisal (PA) is the assessment of an employee's job performance. It is one of the most important responsibilities you will have as a manager. Done well, it can help employees improve their performance, pay, and chances for promotion; foster communication between managers and employees; and increase the employees' and the organization's effectiveness. Done poorly, it actually can have a negative effect—it can cause resentment, reduce motivation, diminish performance, and even expose the organization to legal action.

Performance appraisal therefore has two basic purposes. First, appraisal serves an *administrative* purpose. It provides managers with the information they need to make salary, promotion, and dismissal decisions; helps employees understand and accept the basis of those decisions; and, if necessary, provides documentation that can justify those decisions in court. Second, and at least as important, appraisal serves a *developmental* purpose. The information gathered in the appraisal can be used to identify and plan the additional training, learning, experience, or other improvement employees require. In addition, the manager's feedback and coaching based on the appraisal help employees improve their day-to-day performance and can help prepare them for greater responsibilities in the future.

What Do You Appraise?

Performance appraisals can assess three basic categories of employee performance: traits, behaviors, and results. *Trait appraisals* involve subjective judgments about employee performance. They contain dimensions such as initiative, leadership, and attitude, and they ask raters to indicate how much of each trait an employee possesses. Usually the manager will use a numerical *ratings scale* to specify the extent to which an employee possesses the particular traits being measured. For example, if the measured trait is "attitude," the employee might be rated anywhere from 1 (very negative attitude) to 5 (very positive attitude). Trait scales are quite common, because they are simple to use and provide a standard measure for all employees. But they are often not valid as performance measures. Because they tend to be ambiguous as well as highly subjective—does the employee really have a bad attitude, or is he or she just shy?—they often lead to personal bias and may not be suitable for providing useful feedback.

> "A leader is best when people barely know he exists. Not so good when people obey and acclaim him. Worse when they despise him. But of a good leader who talks little when his work is done, his aim fulfilled, they will say 'We did it ourselves.'"
>
> Lao-tse

Behavioral appraisals, while still subjective, focus more on observable aspects of performance. They were developed in response to the problems of trait appraisals. These scales focus on specific, prescribed behaviors which can help ensure that all parties understand what the ratings are really measuring. Because they are less ambiguous, they also can help provide useful feedback. Figure 10.5 contains an example of a behaviorally anchored rating scale (BARS) for evaluating quality.

Another common behaviorally focused approach is the *critical incident* technique. In this technique, the manager keeps a regular log and records each significant behavior by the subordinate that reflects the quality of his or her performance. ("Jane impressed the client with her effective presentation today." "Joe was late with his report.") This approach can be subjective as well as time-consuming, and it may give some employees the feeling that everything they do is being recorded. But it does have the advantage of reminding managers in advance of a performance review what the employee actually did.

Results appraisals tend to be more objective and can focus on production data such as sales volume (for a salesperson), units produced (for a line worker), or profits (for a

Performance Dimension: Total Quality Management. This area of performance concerns the extent to which a person is aware of, endorses, and develops proactive procedures to enhance product quality, ensure early disclosure of discrepancies, and integrate quality assessments with cost and schedule performance measurement reports to maximize client's satisfaction with overall performance.

OUTSTANDING	7	Uses measures of quality and well-defined processes to achieve project goals. Defines quality from the client's perspective.
	6	Look for/identifies ways to continually improve the process.
	5	Clearly communicates quality management to others. Develops a plan that defines how the team will participate in quality.
		Appreciates TQM as an investment.
AVERAGE	4	Has measures of quality that define tolerance levels.
	3	Views quality as costly. Legislates quality.
	2	Focuses his/her concerns only on outputs and deliverables, ignoring the underlying processes.
POOR	1	Blames others for absence of quality. Gives lip service only to quality concerns.

SOURCE: Landy, Jacobs, and Associates. Used with permission.

FIGURE 10.5
Example of BARS Used for Evaluating Quality

manager). One approach to results appraisals—called **management by objectives (MBO)**—involves a subordinate and a supervisor agreeing *in advance* on specific performance goals (objectives). They then develop a plan that describes the time frame and criteria for determining whether the objectives have been reached. The aim is to agree on a set of objectives that are clear, specific, and reachable. For example, an objective for a salesperson might be "Increase sales by 25 percent during the following year." An objective for a computer programmer might be "Complete two projects within the next six months."

MBO has several important advantages. First, it avoids the biases and measurement difficulties of trait and behavioral appraisals. At the end of the review period, the employee either has or has not achieved the specified objective. The employee is judged on actual job performance. Second, because the employee and manager have agreed on the objective at the outset, the employee is likely to be more committed to the outcome and there is less chance for misunderstanding. Third, because the employee is directly responsible for achieving the objective. MBO can be useful when managers want to empower employees to adapt their behavior as necessary in order to achieve the desired results. But the approach has disadvantages as well. It can result in unrealistic objectives being set, frustrating the employee and the manager. The objectives can also be too rigid, leaving the employee with insufficient flexibility should circumstances change. Finally, MBO often focuses too much on short-term achievement at the expense of long-term goals.

management by objectives (MBO)

A process in which objectives set by a subordinate and a supervisor must be reached within a given time period.

None of these performance appraisal systems is easy to conduct properly, and all have drawbacks that must be guarded against. In choosing an appraisal method, the following guidelines may prove helpful:

1. Base performance standards on job analysis.
2. Communicate performance standards to employees.
3. Evaluate employees on specific performance-related behaviors rather than on a single global or overall measure.
4. Document the PA process carefully.
5. If possible, use more than one rater (discussed in the next section).
6. Develop a formal appeal process.
7. Always take legal considerations into account.[28]

Who Should Do the Appraisal?

Just as multiple methods can be used to gather performance appraisal information, several different sources can provide PA information. *Managers* and *supervisors* are the traditional source of appraisal information because they are often in the best position to observe an employee's performance. However, companies such as Coors, General Foods, and Digital are turning to peers and team members to provide input to the performance appraisal. *Peers* and *team members* often see different dimensions of performance, and are often best at identifying leadership potential and interpersonal skills.

Advantages of Collaboration

Appraisals are most effective when they are based on an ongoing relationship with employees, and not just a top-down formal judgment issued once a year. Managers of sports teams do not wait until the season is over to perform an appraisal. Instead, they work with team members throughout the season, and with the team as a whole, to improve the team's performance. Similarly, in high-functioning regular organizations informal appraisal and feedback are constantly taking place. Managers discuss the goals of the organization regularly and often to create a shared understanding of the job performance those goals require. They try to create an atmosphere in which they and their employees are working together on a common agenda. And they communicate with their employees on a day-to-day basis, praising or coaching as appropriate and together assessing progress toward goals. When managers and employees have open communication, and employees feel fairly and effectively managed, the kind of appraisal they receive should rarely come as a surprise to them.

One increasingly popular source of appraisal is a person's subordinates. Appraisal by *subordinates* has been used by companies such as Xerox and IBM to give superiors feedback on how their employees view them. Often this information is given in confidence to the manager, and not shared with superiors. Even so, this approach can make managers uncomfortable initially, but the feedback they get is often extremely useful and can help them significantly improve their management style. Because this process gives employees power over their bosses, it is generally used for development purposes only, and not for salary or promotion decisions.

Internal and external customers also are used as sources of performance appraisal information, particularly for companies, such as Ford and Honda, that are focused on total quality management. External customers have been used for some time to appraise restaurant employees, but internal customers can include anyone inside the organization who depends on an employee's work output. Finally, it is usually a good idea for employees to evaluate their own performance. Although *self-appraisals* may be biased upward, the process of self-evaluation helps increase the employee's involvement in the review process and is a starting point for establishing future goals.

Because each source of PA information has some limitations, and since different people may see different aspects of performance, Westinghouse, Eastman Kodak, and many other companies have taken to using approaches that involve more than one source for appraisal information. In a process known as **360 degree appraisal,** feedback is obtained from subordinates, peers, and superiors—every level involved with the employee. Often the person being rated can select the appraisers, subject to a manager's approval, with the understanding that the individual appraisals are kept confidential; returned forms might not include the name of the appraiser, for example, and the results may be consolidated for each level.

The 360 degree appraisal offers many advantages. It provides a much fuller picture of the employee's strengths and weaknesses, and it often captures qualities other appraisal methods miss. For example, an employee may have a difficult relationship with his or her supervisor yet be highly regarded by peers and subordinates. The approach can lead to significant improvement, with employees often very motivated to improve their ratings. On the other hand, employees are often unwilling to rate their colleagues harshly, so a certain uniformity of ratings may result. In addition, the 360 degree appraisal is less useful than more objective criteria, like financial targets, in measuring performance. Its objective is usually the employee's development, not to provide a basis for administrative decisions like raises. For those, appraisal methods like MBO are more appropriate.[29]

In an effort to reach Number 1, Ford has been focused on improving customer satisfaction and quality through customer feedback.

360 degree appraisal

Process of using multiple sources of appraisal to gain a comprehensive perspective on one's performance.

How Do You Give Employees Feedback?

Giving PA feedback can be a stressful task for both managers and subordinates. The purposes of PA conflict to some degree. Providing growth and development requires understanding and support; however, the manager must be impersonal and be able to make tough decisions. Employees want to know how they are doing, but typically they are uncomfortable about getting feedback. Finally, the organization's need to make HR decisions conflicts with the individual employee's need to maintain a positive image.[30] These conflicts often make a PA interview difficult; therefore, managers should conduct such interviews thoughtfully.

Effective feedback raises employee performance.

There is no one "best" way to do a PA interview. In general, appraisal feedback works best when it is *specific* and *constructive*—related to clear goals or behaviors and clearly intended to help the employee rather than simply criticize. Managers have an interest not just in rating performance but in raising it, and effective appraisals take that into account. In addition, the appraisal is likely to be more meaningful and satisfying when the manager gives the employee an opportunity to discuss his or her performance and respond to the appraisal.

"Outstanding leaders go out of their way to boost the self-esteem of their personnel. If people believe in themselves, it's amazing what they can accomplish."

Sam Walton

The most difficult interviews are those with employees who are performing poorly. Here is a useful PA interview format to use when an employee is performing below acceptable standards:

1. Summarize the employee's specific performance. Describe the performance in behavioral or outcome terms, such as sales or absenteeism. Don't say the employee has a poor attitude; rather, explain which employee behaviors indicate a poor attitude.

2. Describe the expectations and standards, and be specific.
3. Determine the causes for the low performance; get the employee's input.
4. Discuss solutions to the problem, and have the employee play a major role in the process.
5. Agree to a solution. As a supervisor, you have input into the solution. Raise issues and questions, but also provide support.
6. Agree to a timetable for improvement.
7. Document the meeting.

Follow-up meetings may be needed. Here are some guidelines for giving feedback to an average employee:

1. Summarize the employee's performance, and be specific.
2. Explain why the employee's work is important to the organization.
3. Thank the employee for doing the job.
4. Raise any relevant issues, such as areas for improvement.
5. Express confidence in the employee's future good performance.

Designing Reward Systems

Organizations today seek new ways to reduce benefits costs.

Reward systems are another major set of HRM activities. Most of this section will be devoted to monetary rewards such as pay and fringe benefits. (We will be discussing other motivational tools in Chapter 13.) Although traditionally pay has been the primary monetary reward considered, in recent years benefits have received increased attention. Benefits currently make up a far greater percentage of the total payroll than they did in past decades.[31] The typical employer today pays nearly 40 percent of payroll costs in benefits, a percentage that is increasing mainly because of the rapidly rising cost of medical care. Accordingly, employers are attempting to reduce these costs, even as their value to employees is rising. Benefits are also receiving more management attention because of their increased complexity. Many new types of benefits are now available, and tax laws affect myriad fringe benefits, such as health insurance and pension plans.

Pay Decisions

Reward systems can serve the strategic purposes of attracting, motivating, and retaining people. The wages paid to employees are based on a complex set of forces. Beyond the body of laws governing compensation, a number of basic decisions must be made in choosing the appropriate pay plan. Figure 10.6 illustrates some of the factors that influence the wage mix.

Three types of decisions are crucial for designing an effective pay plan: pay level, pay structure, and individual pay.

Pay level refers to the choice of whether to be a high-, average-, or low-paying company. Compensation is a major cost for any organization, and so low wages can be justified on a short-term financial basis. But being the high-wage employer—the highest-paying company in the region—ensures that the company will attract many applicants. Being a wage leader may be important during times of low unemployment or intense competition.

The *pay structure* decision is the choice of how to price different jobs within the organization. Jobs that are similar in worth usually are grouped together into job families. A pay grade, with a floor and a ceiling, is established for each job family. Figure 10.7 illustrates a hypothetical pay structure.

Finally, *individual pay decisions* concern different pay rates for jobs of similar worth within the same family. Differences in pay within job families are decided in two ways. First, some jobs are occupied by individuals with more seniority than others. Second, some people may be better performers who are therefore deserving of a higher level of pay.

Internal factors   External factors

SOURCE: George Bohlander, Scott Snell, and Arthur Sherman, *Managing Human Resources*, 12th ed. Copyright © 2001. Reprinted by permission of South-Western, a division of Thomson Learning, www.thomsonrights.com.

FIGURE 10.6
Factors Affecting the Wage Mix

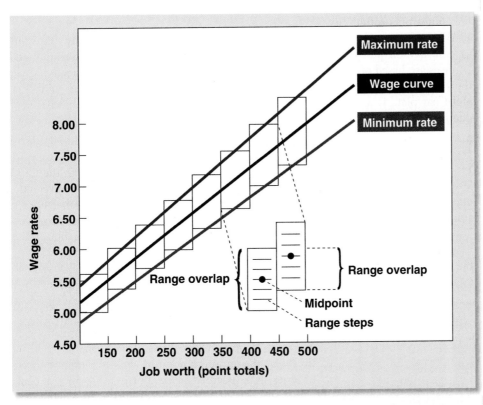

SOURCE: From *Managing Human Resources*, 11th ed., by Sherman/Bohlander/Snell. Copyright © 1998. Reprinted with permission of South-Western, a division of Thomson Learning, www.thomsonrights.com.

FIGURE 10.7
Pay Structure

Incentive Systems and Variable Pay

A number of incentive systems have been devised to encourage and motivate employees to be more productive.[32] (See Chapter 13 for more discussion of rewarding performance.) *Individual incentive plans* are the most common type of incentive plan. An individual incentive system consists of an objective standard against which a worker's performance is compared. Pay is determined by the employee's performance. Individual incentive plans are used frequently in sales jobs—for example, a salesperson will receive extra compensation for exceeding a sales target. Management bonuses are another widely used individual incentive tool. If effectively designed, individual incentive plans

Incentives can help raise all aspects of organization performance.

can be highly motivating. Some companies, like Bank of America, are even beginning to apply them for nonmanagers, using pay-for-performance incentives like bonuses instead of annual pay raises to reward employees.[33]

Several types of group incentive plans, in which pay is based on group performance, are increasingly used today. The idea behind these plans is to give employees a sense of shared participation and even ownership in the performance of the firm. *Gainsharing plans* concentrate on rewarding employees for increasing productivity or saving money in areas under their direct control.[34] For example, if the usual waste allowance in a production line has been 5 percent and the company wants production employees to try to reduce that number, the company may offer to split any savings gained with the employees.

Profit-sharing plans are usually implemented in the division or organization as a whole, though some incentives may still be tailored to unit performance. In most companies, the profit-sharing plan is based on a formula for allocating an annual amount to each employee if the company exceeds a specified profit target. One disadvantage of profit-sharing plans is that they do not reward individual performance. However, they do give all employees a stake in the company's success and motivate efforts to improve the company's profitability.

When objective performance measures are not available but the company still wants to base pay on performance, it uses a *merit pay system*. Individuals' pay raises and bonuses are based on the judgmental merit rating they receive from their boss. Over the years, Lincoln Electric Company has been noted as having a particularly effective merit pay plan. Its employees are reviewed twice a year for a number of specific productivity and other performance goals.[35]

Executive Pay and Stock Options

In recent years the issues of executive pay and stock options, particularly at the CEO level, have become major sources of controversy. One reason is that the gap between the pay of top executives and the average pay of employees has widened considerably. For example, in 1980 CEOs made about 40 times the average wage of a blue-collar employee. Today, average CEO pay is more than 500 times higher than the average blue-collar wage, and about 200 times the average wage overall. This gap is considerably wider in the United States than it is abroad—for example, in Japan the CEO/blue-collar wage ratio is 11, in Germany it is 13, and in Canada it is 20.[36] The sheer size and growth of CEO compensation has also been a factor. Top-earning CEOs today can make over $30 million a year.[37]

A large part of the growth in executive compensation is a result of the increased use of *stock options*. Such options give the options holder the right to purchase shares of stock at a specified price. For example, if the company's stock price is $8 a share, the company may award a manager the right to purchase a specific number of shares of company stock at that price. If the price of the stock rises to, say, $10 a share after a specified holding period—usually three years or more—the manager can *exercise* the option. He or she can purchase the shares from the company at $8 per share, sell the shares on the stock market at $10, and keep the difference. (Of course, if the stock price never rises above $8, the options will be worthless.) For many top managers, large option grants along with sharply rising share prices on the stock market became a major source of additional compensation.

Companies began to issue options to managers to align their interests with those of the company's owners, the shareholders. The

In 2003, Bank of America Corporation paid its CEO, Kenneth Lewis, $20 million while at the some time the company was eliminating 12,500 jobs nationally due to a merger. How might this have affected company morale?

assumption was that managers would become even more focused on making the company successful, leading to a rise in its stock price. However, many critics have suggested that excessive use of options encouraged executives to focus on short-term results to drive up the price of their stock, at the expense of their firm's long-run competitiveness. Others suggested that lucrative options motivated questionable or even unethical behavior, as we mentioned in Chapter 2. Indeed, one recent study found that when CEOs held a large number of valuable options, their companies were more likely to have to issue corrected accounting statements because previous earnings reports were inflated.[38]

Traditionally, companies incurred no expense when they issued options. This was another reason they were considered an attractive incentive tool, and were sometimes even issued to nonmanagers. However, because of corporate scandals, and to curb excessive use of options, the rules were changed in 2004 and options will have to be treated as an expense by companies that issue them. This may reduce the number of options issued.[39] In addition, publicity over some CEO excesses, angry shareholders, and increasingly independent boards are helping to slow the growth rate in CEO compensation.

Employee Benefits

Like pay systems, employee benefit plans are subject to regulation. Employee benefits are divided into those required by law and those optional for an employer.

The three basic required benefits are workers' compensation, social security, and unemployment insurance. *Workers' compensation* provides financial support to employees suffering a work-related injury or illness. *Social Security*, as established in the Social Security Act of 1935, provides financial support to retirees; in subsequent amendments, the act was expanded to cover disabled employees. The funds come from payments made by employers, employees, and self-employed workers. *Unemployment insurance* provides financial support to employees who are laid off for reasons they cannot control. Companies that have terminated fewer employees pay less into the unemployment insurance fund; thus, organizations have an incentive to keep terminations at a minimum.

A large number of benefits are not required to be employer-provided. The most common are pension plans and medical and hospital insurance. Both of these are undergoing significant change. One major reason is that in a global economy they have put U.S. firms at a competitive disadvantage. For example, General Motors spends about $7 billion a year in medical benefits for employees and retirees.[40] Overseas firms generally do not bear these costs, which are usually government-funded, and so are able to compete more effectively on price. As a result, with U.S. medical costs rising rapidly, companies have reduced health benefits or asked employees to share more of their cost. The major change in retirement benefits has been the shift away from guaranteed pensions. While a promised monthly pension used to be the norm, almost no company offers it to new employees today. Instead, in many companies, the employee, the employer, or both may contribute to an individual retirement account, which is invested. When the employee retires, he or she gets the balance that has accumulated in the account.[41]

Because of the wide variety of possible benefits and the considerable differences in employee preferences and needs, companies often use **cafeteria** or **flexible benefit programs.** In this type of program, employees are given credits that they "spend" on benefits they desire. Then employees use their credits toward individualized packages of benefits, including medical and dental insurance, dependent care, life insurance, and so on.

Legal Issues in Compensation and Benefits

A number of laws affect employee compensation and benefits. We have already mentioned the FSLA, which in addition to distinguishing between exempt and nonexempt employees also sets minimum wage, maximum hour, and child labor provisions.[42] *The*

cafeteria benefit program

An employee benefit program in which employees choose from a menu of options to create a benefit package tailored to their needs.

flexible benefit programs

Benefit programs in which employees are given credits to spend on benefits that fit their unique needs.

Equal Pay Act (EPA) of 1963, now enforced by the EEOC, prohibits unequal pay for men and women who perform equal work. Equal work means jobs that require equal skill, effort, and responsibility and are performed under similar working conditions. The law does permit exceptions where the difference in pay is due to a seniority system, a merit system, an incentive system based on quantity or quality of production, or any other factor other than sex, such as market demand. Although equal pay for equal work may sound like common sense, many employers have fallen victim to this law by rationalizing that men, traditionally the "breadwinners," deserve more pay than women or by giving equal jobs different titles (senior assistant versus office manager) as the sole basis for pay differences.

One controversy concerns male and female pay differences within the same company. **Comparable-worth** doctrine implies that women who perform *different* jobs of *equal* worth as those performed by men should be paid the same wage.[43] In contrast to the equal-pay-for-equal-work notion, comparable worth suggests that the jobs need *not* be the same to require the same pay. For example, nurses (predominantly female) were found to be paid considerably less than skilled craftworkers (predominantly male), even though the two jobs were found to be of equal value or worth.[44] Under the Equal Pay Act, this would not constitute pay discrimination because the jobs are very different. But under the comparable-worth concept, these findings would indicate discrimination because the jobs are of equal worth.

> **comparable worth**
>
> Principle of equal pay for different jobs of equal worth.

To date, no federal law requires comparable worth, and the Supreme Court has made no decisive rulings about it. However, some states have considered developing comparable-worth laws, and others already have implemented comparable-worth changes, raising the wages of female-dominated jobs. For example, Minnesota passed a comparable-worth law for public-sector employees after finding that women on average were paid 25 percent less than men. Several other states have comparable-worth laws for public-sector employees, including Iowa, Idaho, New Mexico, Washington, and South Dakota.[45]

Some laws influence mostly benefit practices. The *Pregnancy Discrimination Act* of 1978 states that pregnancy is a disability and qualifies a woman to receive the same benefits that she would with any other disability. The *Employee Retirement Income Security Act (ERISA)* of 1974 protects private pension programs from mismanagement. ERISA requires that retirement benefits be paid to those who vest or earn a right to draw benefits and ensures retirement benefits for employees whose companies go bankrupt or who otherwise cannot meet their pension obligations.

Miners rescued after being trapped 240-feet underground at the Black Wolf Coal Companies' Quecreek Mine in Somerset, Pennsylvania.

Health and Safety

The *Occupational Safety and Health Act (OSHA)* of 1970 requires employers to pursue workplace safety. Employers must maintain records of injuries and deaths caused by workplace accidents and submit to on-site inspections. Large-scale industrial accidents and nuclear power plant disasters worldwide have focused attention on the importance of workplace safety.

Coal mining is one of many industries that benefit from safety laws. Mining is one of the five most dangerous jobs to perform, according to the U.S. Bureau of Labor Statistics. Nearly every coal miner can name a friend or family member who has been killed, maimed, or stricken with black lung disease. "You die quick or you die slow," reports one mine worker. However, according to the Mine Safety and Health Administration, mines have become safer. In 1991, 61 coal miners died in the United States and 14,668 were injured; by 2004, roughly half as many coal miners were killed or injured annually.[46]

Labor Relations

Labor relations is the system of relations between workers and management. Labor unions recruit members, collect dues, and ensure that employees are treated fairly with respect to wages, working conditions, and other issues. When workers organize for the purpose of negotiating with management to improve their wages, hours, or working conditions, two processes are involved: unionization and collective bargaining. These processes have evolved over a 50-year period in the United States to provide important employee rights.[47]

> **labor relations**
>
> The system of relations between workers and management.

Labor Laws

Try to imagine what life would be like with unemployment at 25 percent. Pretty grim, you would say. Legislators in 1935 felt that way too. Therefore, organized labor received its Magna Carta with the passage of the National Labor Relations Act.

The *National Labor Relations Act* (also called the *Wagner Act* after its legislative sponsor) ushered in an era of rapid unionization by (1) declaring labor organizations legal, (2) establishing five unfair employer labor practices, and (3) creating the National Labor Relations Board (NLRB). Prior to the act, employers could fire workers who favored unions, and federal troops were often provided to put down strikes. Today, the NLRB conducts unionization elections, hears unfair labor practices complaints, and issues injunctions against offending employers. The Wagner Act greatly assisted the growth of unions by enabling workers to use the law and the courts to organize and collectively bargain for better wages, hours, and working conditions. Many of the improvements all of us take for granted in the workplace, including minimum wages, health benefits, maternity leave, the 35-hour work week, and worker protections in general were largely the result of collective bargaining over many years by unions.

Public policy began on the side of organized labor in 1935, but over the next 25 years the pendulum swung toward the side of management. The *Labor-Management Relations Act*, or *Taft-Hartley Act* (1947), protected employers' free-speech rights, defined unfair labor practices by unions, and permitted workers to decertify (reject) a union as their representative.

Finally, the *Labor-Management Reporting and Disclosure Act*, or *Landrum-Griffin Act* (1959), swung the public policy pendulum midway between organized labor and management. By declaring a bill of rights for union members, establishing control over union dues increases, and imposing reporting requirements for unions, Landrum-Griffin was designed to curb abuses by union leadership and rid unions of corruption.

Unionization

How do workers join unions? Through a union organizer or local union representative, workers learn what benefits they may receive by joining.[48] The union representative distributes authorization cards that permit workers to indicate whether they want an election to be held to certify the union to represent them. The National Labor Relations Board will conduct a certification election if at least 30 percent of the employees sign authorization cards. Management has several choices at this stage: to recognize the union without an election, to consent to an election, or to contest the number of cards signed and resist an election.

If an election is warranted, an NLRB representative will conduct the election by secret ballot. A simple majority of those voting determines the winner. Thus, apathetic workers who do not show up to vote in effect

The International Brotherhood of Teamsters is the world's most powerful labor union. What are the benefits of being part of a union? What are the drawbacks?

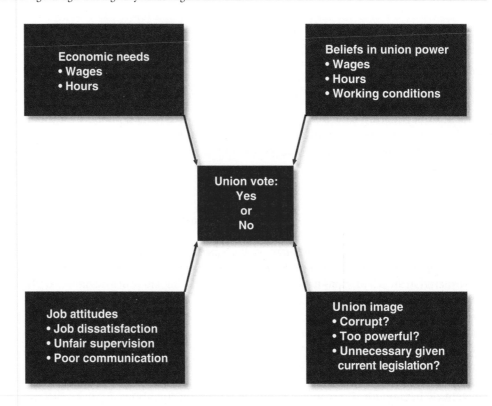

FIGURE 10.8
Determinants of Union
Voting Behavior

support the union. If the union wins the election, it is certified as the bargaining unit representative.

During the campaign preceding the election, efforts are made by both management and the union to persuade the workers how to vote. Most workers, though, are somewhat resistant to campaign efforts, having made up their minds well before the NLRB appears on the scene. If the union wins the election, management and the union are legally required to bargain in good faith to obtain a collective bargaining agreement or contract.

Why do workers vote for a union? Four factors play a significant role (see Figure 10.8).[49] First, economic factors are important, especially for workers in low-paying jobs; unions attempt to raise the average wage rate for their members. Second, job dissatisfaction encourages workers to seek out a union. Poor supervisory practices, favoritism, lack of communication, and perceived unfair or arbitrary discipline and discharge are specific triggers of job dissatisfaction. Third, the belief that the union can obtain desired benefits can generate a pro-union vote. Finally, the image of the union can determine whether a dissatisfied worker will seek out the union. Headline stories of union corruption and dishonesty can discourage workers from unionization.

Collective Bargaining

In the United States, management and unions engage in a periodic ritual (typically every three years) of negotiating an agreement over wages, hours, and working conditions. Two types of disputes can arise during this process. First, before an agreement is reached, the workers may go on strike to compel agreement on their terms. Such an action is known as an *economic strike* and is permitted by law. However, today strikes are less likely to be used as a bargaining tool, though they sometimes do still occur as a last resort. Strikers are not paid if they are on strike, and this is a hardship few workers want to undertake unnecessarily. In addition, managers may legally hire replacement workers during a strike, offsetting some of the strike's effect. Finally, workers are as aware as managers of the tougher competition companies face today, and if treated fairly they will usually share management's interest in coming to an agreement.

Once an agreement is signed, management and the union sometimes disagree over *interpretation* of the agreement. Usually they settle their disputes through arbitration. **Arbitration** is the use of a neutral third party, typically jointly selected, to resolve the dispute. The United States uses arbitration while an agreement is in effect to avoid *wildcat strikes* (in which workers walk off the job in violation of the contract) or unplanned work stoppages.

What does a collective bargaining agreement contain? In a **union shop,** a union security clause specifies that workers must join the union after a set period of time. **Right-to-work** states, through restrictive legislation, do not permit union shops; that is, workers have the right to work without being forced to join a union. The southern United States has many right-to-work states. The wage component of the contract spells out rates of pay, including premium pay for overtime and paid holidays. Individual rights usually are specified in terms of the use of seniority to determine pay increases, job bidding, and the order of layoffs.

A feature of any contract is the grievance procedure. Unions perform a vital service for their membership in this regard by giving workers a voice in what goes on during both contract negotiations and administration through the grievance procedure.[50] In about 50 percent of discharge cases that go to arbitration, the arbitrator overturns management's decision and reinstates the worker.[51] Unions have a legal duty of fair representation, which means they must represent all workers in the bargaining unit and ensure that workers' rights are protected.

> **arbitration**
>
> The use of a neutral third party to resolve a labor dispute.
>
> **union shop**
>
> An organization with a union and a union security clause specifying that workers must join the union after a set period of time.
>
> **right-to-work**
>
> Legislation that allows employees to work without having to join a union.

Advantages of Collaboration

One of the ways management and labor attempt to collaborate, and try to find non-adversarial ways of finding agreement, is through *labor–management committees.* Such committees, usually formed during contract negotiations, are made up of representatives from both sides. Their intent is to explore flexible, creative solutions to long-standing problems outside the formal bargaining process. For example, if managers want to introduce new labor-saving technology, and the union wants to preserve the jobs of its members, a labor–management committee can work out plans for retraining current workers to operate the new equipment. Such a collaborative approach benefits both sides. And the more open atmosphere of the committees, and shared approach to problem solving, may lead to greater trust and cooperation in other areas as well.[52]

What Does the Future Hold?

In recent years union membership has declined to about 12 percent of the U.S. labor force—down from a peak of over 33 percent at the end of World War II. Increased automation eliminated many of the types of manufacturing jobs that used to be union strongholds. Employees in today's white-collar office jobs are less interested in joining unions and are also more difficult to organize. Tough global competition has made managers much less willing to give in to union demands, and as a result the benefits of unionization are less clear to many workers—particularly young, skilled workers who no longer expect to stay with one company all their lives. Some people applaud unions' apparent decline. Others hope for an eventual reemergence based on the potential power of management–union cooperation to help U.S. businesses in the global economy. Unions may play a different role in the future, one that is less adversarial and more cooperative with management. Unions are adapting to changing workforce demographics; they are paying more attention to women, older workers, and people who work at home. Elimination of inefficient work rules, the introduction of profit sharing, and a guarantee of no layoffs were seen as big steps toward a fundamentally different, cooperative long-term relationship. What seems clear is that when companies recognize that their success depends on the talents and energies of employees, the interests of unions and managers begin to converge. Rather than one side exploiting the other, unions and managers find common ground based on developing, valuing, and involving employees. Particularly in knowledge-based companies, the balance of power is shifting toward employees. Individuals, not companies, own their own human capital. And these employees are free, within limits, to leave the organization, taking their human capital with them. This leaves organizations in a particularly vulnerable position if they manage poorly. To establish a strong competitive capability, organizations are searching for ways to obtain, retain, and engage their most valuable resources: human resources.

EPILOGUE

HR AND STRATEGY AT GE

Values play a fundamental role in the running of GE's business and HR operations. This is best illustrated in the "9 Block," one of its key HR tools. The 9 Block is a chart that is divided into nine squares, which are used to plot an employee's ability to meet key performance indicators (KPIs) against their individual demonstration of GE's values. Employees are assessed on how well they perform on both counts, and their position on the chart determines their annual performance rating. If employees don't meet their KPIs but score well on values, they are given a second chance, as opposed to those who get the results but don't exhibit the values.

GE's Sheppard states that the values play an important role in sorting out the managerial chaff from the leadership wheat, as they help pinpoint the behaviors needed to climb up the GE leadership ladder. "They're a good indication as to whether an individual is a genuine leader or a manager who simply gives workers a set task, manages deliverables and gets results," she says. "If a person achieves their results through autocratic management or using bullying, then you have no place in the GE portfolio. So our processes really examine how individuals demonstrate those values to inspire the people that they actually work with. Sure, they can achieve results, but the focus is on how they achieve those results."

Says GE's Bertamini: "You know who these people are in your organization. You might think that you don't have any, but they are there and eventually they are identified via a variety of methods that include 360 reviews and employee surveys. Once we identify and counsel them, if they don't quickly correct their behaviors, they are exited from the organization. I think that really makes a big difference in terms of how you balance the culture with business results."

KEY TERMS

360 degree appraisal, p. 341

Adverse impact, p. 333

Arbitration, p. 349

Assessment center, p. 329

Cafeteria benefit programs, p. 345

Comparable worth, p. 346

Development, p. 335

Diversity training, p. 337

Employment-at-will, p. 331

Flexible benefit programs, p. 345

Human capital, p. 321

Human resources management (HRM), p. 320

Job analysis, p. 324

Labor relations, p. 347

Management by objectives (MBO), p. 339

Needs assessment, p. 335

Orientation training, p. 336

Outplacement, p. 331

Performance appraisal (PA), p. 338

Recruitment, p. 324

Reliability, p. 330

Right-to-work, p. 349

Selection, p. 326

Structured interview, p. 327

Team training, p. 331

Termination interview, p. 331

Training, p. 335

Union shop, p. 349

Validity, p. 330

SUMMARY OF LEARNING OBJECTIVES

Now that you have studied Chapter 10, you should know:

How companies use human resources management to gain competitive advantage.

To succeed, companies must align their human resources to their strategies. Effective planning is necessary to make certain that the right number and kind of employees are available to implement a company's strategic plan. It is clear that hiring the most competent people is a very involved process. Companies that compete on cost, quality, service, and so on also should use their staffing, training, appraisal, and reward systems to elicit and reinforce the kinds of behaviors that underlie their strategies.

Why companies recruit both internally and externally for new hires.

Some companies prefer to recruit internally to make certain that employees are familiar with organizational policies and values. AT&T's Resource Link is an example of a company trying very hard to make certain that available work goes to internal candidates before looking externally. In other instances, companies prefer to recruit externally to find individuals with new ideas and fresh perspectives.

The various methods available for selecting new employees.

There are a myriad of selection techniques from which to choose. Interviews and reference checks are the most common. Personality tests and cognitive ability tests measure an individual's aptitude and potential to do well on the job. Other selection techniques include assessment centers and integrity tests. Regardless of the approach used, any test should be able to demonstrate reliability (consistency across time and different interview situations) and validity (accuracy in predicting job performance).

Why companies spend so much on training and development.

People cannot depend on a set of skills for all of their working lives. In today's changing, competitive world, old skills quickly become obsolete and new ones become essential for success. Refreshing or updating an individual's skills requires a great deal of continuous training. Companies understand that gaining a competitive edge in quality of service depends on having the most talented, flexible workers in the industry.

How to determine who should appraise an employee's performance.

Many companies are using multiple sources of appraisal because different people see different sides of an employee's performance. Typically, a superior is expected to evaluate an employee, but peers and team members are often in a good position to see aspects of performance that a superior misses. Even an employee's subordinates are being asked more often today to give their input in order to get yet another perspective on the evaluation. Particularly in companies concerned about quality, internal and external customers also are surveyed. Finally, employees should evaluate their own performance, if only to get them thinking about their own performance, as well as to engage them in the appraisal process.

How to analyze the fundamental aspects of a reward system.

Reward systems are broken down into three basic components: pay level, pay structure, and individual pay determination. To achieve an advantage over competitors, executives may want to generally pay a higher wage to their company's employees, but this decision must be weighed against the need to control costs (pay-level decisions often are tied to strategic concerns such as these). To achieve internal equity (paying people what they are worth relative to their peers within the company), managers must look at the pay structure, making certain that pay differentials are based on knowledge, effort, responsibility, working conditions, seniority, and so on. Individual pay determination often is based on merit or the different contributions of individuals. In these cases it is important to make certain that men and women receive equal pay for equal work, and managers may wish to base pay decisions on the idea of comparable worth (equal pay for an equal contribution).

How unions influence human resources management.

Labor relations involve the interactions between workers and management. One mechanism by which this relationship is conducted is unions. Unions seek to present a collective voice for workers, to make their needs and wishes known to management. Unions negotiate agreements with management regarding a range of issues such as wages, hours, working conditions, job security, and health care. One important tool that unions can use is the grievance procedure established through collective bargaining. This gives employees a way to seek redress for wrongful action on the part of management. In this way, unions make certain that the rights of all employees are protected.

How the legal system influences human resources management.

The legal system influences managers by placing constraints on the ways potential and actual employees are treated. Equal opportunity laws ensure that companies do not discriminate in their hiring and training practices. The Fair Labor Standards Act and the Equal Pay Act ensure that people earn fair compensation for the contribution they make to the organization. The Occupational Safety and Health Act ensures that employees have a safe and healthy work environment. Labor laws seek to protect the rights of both employees and managers so that their relationship can be productive and agreeable.

DISCUSSION QUESTIONS

1. How will changes in the labor force affect HRM practices for year 2010?
2. Describe the major regulations governing HRM practices.
3. Define job analysis. Why is job analysis relevant to each of the six key HRM activities discussed in the chapter (i.e., planning, staffing, training, performance appraisal, reward systems, labor relations)?
4. What are the various methods for recruiting employees? Why are some better than others? In what sense are they better?
5. What is a "test"? Give some examples of tests used by employers.
6. What purpose does performance appraisal serve? Why are there so many different methods of appraisal?
7. What are some key ideas to remember when conducting a performance interview?
8. How would you define an effective reward system? What role do benefits serve in a reward system?
9. Why do workers join unions? What implications would this have for an organization that wishes to remain nonunion?
10. Discuss the advantages and disadvantages of collective bargaining for the employer and the employee.

CONCLUDING CASE

The University of Dissension

This is a case about unions.

This case involves one of the divisions of the workforce of a state university near you. The personnel of that university are structured like many others around the country, with four distinct divisions of labor. *Administrators* include the president, a number of vice-presidents, and many other executive-level administrative assistants positioned throughout the various departments. *Faculty* make up the second tier, and include assistant, associate, and full professors. *Professional associates* are the "white-collar" support staff; most of these individuals have a college education and work as middle managers, day-to-day operations administrators, technical support staff, and so on. *Operating staffers* are the "blue-collar" workers; they include secretaries, clerical workers, physical plant and grounds maintenance people, and custodians.

Operating staffers represent the largest and lowest paid division of the workforce. Most of those individuals have no education or formal training beyond high school. Their pay scale ranges from minimum wage to $12–$15 per hour. Their benefit package includes some provisions for health and life insurance and retirement. It is far less comprehensive than the other three divisions and is considered to be somewhat comparable to employees in similar positions in the surrounding area.

The operating staffers have always maintained a central committee made up of a cross-representation of the various departments around campus. The committee was originally established to serve as a liaison between labor and management for communication purposes. In reality, it has functioned almost exclusively as a fundraising and community service arm for that group. The operating staffers have always been the most generous division on campus when it comes to community outreach volunteers and for the annual fundraising drives of the traditional nonprofit community service organizations.

For the first time ever, the central committee finds itself talking about unions. Operating staffers have begun to show up for the meetings in growing numbers to voice their displeasure about changes in working conditions and to encourage the committee to go ahead and take a serious look at unionizing.

During the past few years, secretaries, groundskeepers, maintenance workers, and custodians have not been replaced as positions become vacant. Supervisors have simply asked existing workers to "pick up the slack" since "the school cannot afford to fill those vacant positions." In addition, operating staffers have been required to contribute more of their paychecks each year to cover an increasing percentage of their health care costs, while the extent of their health care coverage has diminished.

Administrators claim that "times are tough, outside funding is down, and we must all share in the burden of maintaining our school." In the meantime, wages and benefits of administrators and faculty continue to increase, as do student enrollments. The increase in student enrollments also means more work for operating staffers.

The situation is beginning to "heat up" on both sides. Operating staffers have held public rallies on campus that include speeches by disgruntled workers and posters and banners depicting wages, working conditions, and prounion slogans. The central committee was able to organize a "bitch session" with the president as the result of an aggressive and relentless push for that meeting. The president listened quietly to the concerns and demands of the group and finally thanked them for their dedication to the school.

Supervisors and administrators have "informally encouraged" workers to give up the idea of unionizing. Many conversations are taking place off the record. Those conversations warn workers about the very real possibility of losing their jobs to outside vendors who are eager for the opportunity to provide their services to the school.

QUESTIONS

1. What steps would you take as a school administrator to resolve this issue and avoid unionization of the operating staffers?

2. If unionization appears imminent, what position and actions would you take to work through the process in the most collaborative and least disruptive manner?

3. Consider the labor force/supply in your area. Would subcontracting and/or outside recruiting be a means to quell this union movement?

EXPERIENTIAL EXERCISES

10.1 The "Legal" Interview

OBJECTIVES

1. To introduce you to the complexities of employment law.

2. To identify interview practices that might lead to discrimination in employment.

INSTRUCTIONS

1. Working alone, review the text material on interviewing and discrimination in employment.

2. In small groups, complete the "Legal" Interview Worksheet.

3. After the class reconvenes, group spokespersons present group findings.

"Legal" Interview Worksheet

The employment interview is one of the most critical steps in the employment selection process. It also may be an occasion for discriminating against individual employment candidates. The fol-lowing represents questions that interviewers often ask job applicants. Identify the legality of each question by circling *L* (legal) or *I* (illegal) and briefly explain your decision.

Interview Question	Legality	Explanation
1. Could you provide us with a photo for our files?	L I	_____
2. Have you ever used another name (previous married name or alias)?	L I	_____
3. What was your maiden name?	L I	_____
4. What was your wife's maiden name?	L I	_____
5. What was your mother's maiden name?	L I	_____
6. What is your current address?	L I	_____
7. What was your previous address?	L I	_____
8. What is your social security number?	L I	_____
9. Where was your place of birth?	L I	_____
10. Where were your parents born?	L I	_____
11. What is your national origin?	L I	_____
12. Are you a naturalized citizen?	L I	_____
13. What languages do you speak?	L I	_____
14. What is your religious/church affiliation?	L I	_____
15. What is your racial classification?	L I	_____
16. How many dependents do you have?	L I	_____
17. What are the ages of your dependent children?	L I	_____
18. What is your marital status?	L I	_____
19. How old are you?	L I	_____
20. Do you have proof of your age (birth certificate or baptismal record)?	L I	_____
21. Whom do we notify in case of an emergency?	L I	_____
22. What is your height and weight?	L I	_____
23. Have you ever been arrested?	L I	_____
24. Do you own your own car?	L I	_____
25. Do you own your own house?	L I	_____
26. Do you have any charge accounts?	L I	_____
27. Have you ever had your salary garnished?	L I	_____
28. To what organizations do you belong?	L I	_____
29. Are you available to work on Saturdays and Sundays?	L I	_____
30. Do you have any form of disability?	L I	_____

10.2 The Pay Raise

OBJECTIVES

1. To further your understanding of salary administration.
2. To examine the many facets of performance criteria, performance criteria weighting, performance evaluation, and rewards.

INSTRUCTIONS

1. Working in small groups, complete the Pay Raise Worksheet.
2. After the class reconvenes, group spokespersons present group findings.

Pay Raise Worksheet

April Knepper is the new supervisor of an assembly team. It is time for her to make pay raise allocations for her subordinates. She has been budgeted $30,000 to allocate among her seven subordinates as pay raises. There have been some ugly grievances in other work teams over past allocations, and so April has been advised to base the allocations on objective criteria that can be quantified, weighted, and computed in numerical terms. After she makes her allocations, April must be prepared to justify her decisions. All of the evaluative criteria available to April are summarized as follows:

Employee	Seniority	Output Rating*	Absent Rate	Supervisory Ratings			
				Skills	Initiative	Attitude	Personal
David Bruce	15 yrs.	0.58	0.5%	Good	Poor	Poor	Nearing retirement. Wife just passed away. Having adjustment problems.
Eric Cattalini	12 yrs.	0.86	2.0	Excellent	Good	Excellent	Going to night school to finish his BA degree.
Chua Li	7 yrs.	0.80	3.5	Good	Excellent	Excellent	Legally deaf.
Marilee Miller	1 yr.	0.50	10.0	Poor	Poor	Poor	Single parent with three children.
Victor Munoz	3 yrs.	0.62	2.5	Poor	Average	Good	Has six dependents. Speaks little English.
Derek Thompson	11 yrs.	0.64	8.0	Excellent	Average	Average	Married to rich wife. Personal problems.
Sarah Vickers	8 yrs.	0.76	7.0	Good	Poor	Poor	Women's activist. Wants to create a union.

*Output rating determined by production rate less errors and quality problem.

Chapter **11**

CHAPTER 11

Managing the Diverse Workforce

"e pluribus unum"

CHAPTER OUTLINE

LEARNING OBJECTIVES

After studying Chapter 11, you will know:

1. How changes in the U.S. workforce make diversity a critical organizational and managerial issue.

2. The distinction between affirmative action and managing diversity.

3. How managers can gain a competitive edge by managing diversity effectively.

4. What challenges a manager is likely to encounter with a diverse workforce.

5. How managers and their organizations can take steps to cultivate diversity.

Prologue

EVERYONE KNOWS WOMEN CAN'T PLAY AS WELL AS MEN

The world of classical music—particularly in its European home—was until very recently the preserve of white men. Women, it was believed, simply could not play like men. They didn't have the strength, the attitude, or the resilience for certain kinds of pieces. Their lips were different. Their lungs were less powerful. Their hands were smaller. That did not seem like a prejudice. It seemed like a fact, because when conductors and music directors and maestros held auditions, the men always seemed to sound better than the women. No one paid much attention to how auditions were held, because it was an article of faith that one of the things that made a music expert a music expert was that he could listen to music played under any circumstances and gauge, instantly and objectively, the quality of the performance. Auditions for major orchestras were sometimes held in the conductor's dressing room, or in his hotel room if he was passing through town. Performers played for five minutes or two minutes or ten minutes. What did it matter? Music was music. Rainer Kuchl, the concertmaster of the Vienna Philharmonic, once said he could instantly tell the difference with his eyes closed between, say, a male and female violinist. The trained ear, he believed, could pick up the softness and flexibility of the female style.

But over the past few decades, the classical music world has undergone a revolution. In the United States, orchestra musicians began to organize themselves politically. They formed a union and fought for proper contracts, health benefits, and protections against arbitrary firing, and along with that came a push for fairness in hiring. Many musicians thought that conductors were abusing their power and playing favorites. They wanted the audition process to be formalized. That meant an official audition committee was established instead of a conductor making the decision all by himself. In some places, rules were put in place forbidding the judges from speaking among themselves during auditions, so that one person's opinion would not cloud the view of another. Musicians were identified not by name but by number. Screens were erected between the committee and the auditioner, and if the person auditioning cleared his or her throat or made any kind of identifiable sound—if they were wearing heels, for example, and stepped on a part of the floor that wasn't carpeted—they were ushered out and given a new number. And as these new rules were put in place around the country, an extraordinary thing happened: Orchestras began to hire women.

In the past 30 years, since screens became commonplace, the number of women in the top U.S. orchestras has increased fivefold. "The very first time the new rules for auditions were used, we were looking

for four new violinists," remembers Herb Weksleblatt, a tuba player for the Metropolitan Opera in New York, who led the fight for blind auditions at the Met in the mid-1960s. "And all the winners were women. That would simply never have happened before. Up until that point, we had maybe three women in the whole orchestra. I remember that after it was announced that the four women had won, one guy was absolutely furious at me. He said, 'You're going to be remembered as the SOB who brought women into this orchestra.' "

What the classical music world realized was that what they thought was a pure and powerful first impression—listening to someone play—was in fact hopelessly corrupted. "Some people look like they sound better than they actually sound, because they look confident and have good posture," one musician, a veteran of many auditions, says. "Other people look awful when they play but sound great. Other people have that belabored look when they play, but you can't hear it in the sound. There is always this dissonance between what you see and hear. The audition begins the first second the person is in view. You think, Who is this nerd? Or, Who does this guy think he is?—just by the way they walk out with their instrument."

In Washington, D.C., the National Symphony Orchestra hired Sylvia Alimena to play the French horn. Would she have been hired before the advent of the screen? Of course not. The French horn—like the trombone—is a "male" instrument. More to the point, Alimena is tiny. She's five feet tall. In truth, that's an irrelevant fact. As another prominent horn player says, "Sylvia can blow a house down." But if you were to look at her before you really listened to her, you would not be able to hear that power, because what you saw would so contradict what you heard. There is only one way to make a proper snap judgment of Sylvia Alimena, and that's from behind a screen.

Source for Prologue and Epilogue: Malcolm Gladwell, *blink* (New York: Little, Brown and Company, 2005). Reprinted with permission. Source for first Connection: Claudia Goldin and Cecilia Rouse, "Orchestrating Impartiality: The Impact of 'Blind' Auditions on Female Musicians," NBER Working Paper No. 5903, January 1997.

In our last chapter, we discussed in some detail the laws that require equal opportunity and fair treatment in the workplace. In this chapter, we discuss why a proactive approach to developing and managing a diverse workforce has become not only a legal or moral obligation, but a fundamental business requirement as well. Managers who lack the skills to work with and effectively manage men and women of different colors, cultures, and backgrounds will be at a significant disadvantage in their careers. And organizations that do not take the issue of managing diversity seriously will leave their organizations not only open to legal challenge, but also far less able to compete effectively, at home and abroad.

In the United States, as we shall see, the number of minorities is increasing at a far faster rate than the growth in the white, nonminority population, and women are making up an ever-larger percentage of the workforce. American workers, customers, and markets are already highly diverse and becoming even more so every day. In addition, as we discussed in Chapter 6, businesses are increasingly global. Managers need to be much more aware of, and sensitive to, cultural differences to succeed in a world economy. We have also discussed throughout this book how vital creativity and innovation have become for organization success. These qualities are fostered in an atmosphere where different perspectives and bright people from all walks of life are celebrated. Few societies have access to the range of talents available in the United States, with its immigrant tradition and racially and ethnically diverse population. Yet getting people from widely divergent backgrounds to work together effectively is not easy. For this reason, managing diversity is one of America's biggest challenges—and opportunities.

Managing diversity involves, first, such basic activities as recruiting, training, promoting, and utilizing to full advantage individuals with different backgrounds, beliefs, capabilities, and cultures. But it means more than just hiring women and minorities

> **managing diversity**
>
> Managing a culturally diverse workforce by recognizing the characteristics common to specific groups of employees while dealing with such employees as individuals and supporting, nurturing, and utilizing their differences to the organization's advantage.

and making sure they are treated equally and encouraged to succeed. It also means understanding and deeply valuing employee differences to build a more effective and profitable organization.

This chapter examines the meaning of diversity and the management skills and organizational processes involved in managing the diverse workforce effectively. We also explore the social and demographic changes and economic and employment shifts that are creating this changing U.S. workforce.

Diversity: A Brief History

Managing diversity is not a new or futuristic management issue. From the late 1800s to the early 1900s, most of the groups that immigrated to the United States were from Italy, Poland, Ireland, and Russia. Members of those groups were considered outsiders because most did not speak English and had different customs and work styles. They struggled, often violently, to gain acceptance in industries such as steel, coal, automobile manufacturing, insurance, and finance. In the 1800s, it was considered poor business practice for white Protestant–dominated insurance companies to hire Irish, Italians, Catholics, or Jews. As late as the 1940s, and in some cases even later than that, colleges routinely discriminated against immigrants, Catholics, and Jews, establishing strict quotas that limited their number, if any were admitted at all. The employment prospects of these groups were severely diminished by this kind of discrimination, and it wasn't until the 1960s that the struggle for acceptance by the various white ethnic and religious groups had on the whole succeeded.

Women's struggle for acceptance in the workplace was in some ways even more difficult. When the Women's Rights Movement was launched in Seneca Falls in 1848, most occupations were off-limits to women, and colleges and professional schools were totally closed to them. Women could not vote and lost all property rights once they were married. In the first part of the 20th century, when women began to be accepted into professional schools, they were subject to severe quotas. There was also a widespread, persistent assumption that certain jobs were done only by men, and other jobs only by women. Even into the 1970s, less than 40 years ago, classified ad sections in newspapers listed different jobs by sex, with sections headed "Help Wanted—Males" and "Help Wanted—Females." Women who wanted a bank loan needed a male cosigner, and married women were not issued credit cards in their own name.[1] Only when the Civil Rights Act of 1964 (see Chapter 10) and other legislation began to be enforced was this kind of sex discrimination gradually eliminated. As we shall see, women are still underrepresented at the most senior levels of corporate life, and major disparities in other areas, like pay, still exist. But most jobs today once considered the exclusive province of men—including front-line military units as well as the executive suite—are now open to and occupied by increasing numbers of women.

The most difficult and wrenching struggle for equality involved America's nonwhite minorities. Rigid racial segregation remained a fact of American life for 100 years after the end of the Civil War. Black voting rights, particularly in the South, were often viciously suppressed, and racial discrimination in education, employment, and housing throughout the United States was a harsh, daily reality. Years of difficult, courageous protest and struggle gradually began to eat away at both legal and social barriers to equality. Organizations like the NAACP, formed by a group of blacks and whites, began to use America's court sys-

Many of the rights all of us take for granted today— equal opportunity, fair treatment in housing, the illegality of religious, racial, and sex discrimination— received their greatest impetus from the Civil Rights movement.

tem and the Constitution to bring equality to African-Americans and other people of color. The unanimous *Brown v. Board of Education* Supreme Court decision in 1954 declared segregation unconstitutional, setting the stage for other legislation we discussed in the last chapter, like the Civil Rights Act of 1964. The consequences of America's bitter racial legacy are still with us; the struggle for equality is far from complete. But many of the rights all of us take for granted today—equal opportunity, fair treatment in housing, the illegality of religious, racial, and sex discrimination—received their greatest impetus from the Civil Rights movement.

Today, more than half the U.S. workforce consists of people other than white, U.S.-born males, a trend that is almost certain to continue. Two-thirds of all global migration is into the United States. One-third of all businesses in the United States are owned by women, employing about 20 percent of America's workers.[2]

The traditional American image of diversity has been one of assimilation. The United States was considered the "melting pot" of the world, a country in which ethnic and racial differences were blended into an American purée. In real life, many ethnic and most racial groups retained their identities, but they did not express them at work. Employees often abandoned most of their ethnic and cultural distinctions while at work to keep their jobs and get ahead. Many Europeans came to the United States, Americanized their names, perfected their English, and tried to enter the mainstream as quickly as possible.

Today's immigrants are willing to be part of an integrated team, but they no longer are willing to sacrifice their cultural identities to get ahead. Nor will they have to do so. Companies are finding that they should be more accommodating of differences, and that doing so pays off in business. Managers are also beginning to realize that their customers have become increasingly diverse and that retaining a diversified workforce can provide a significant competitive advantage in the marketplace.

Diversity Today

Today *diversity* refers to far more than skin color and gender. It is a broad term used to refer to all kinds of differences, as summarized in Figure 11.1. These differences include religious affiliation, age, disability status, military experience, sexual orientation, economic class, educational level, and lifestyle in addition to gender, race, ethnicity, and nationality.

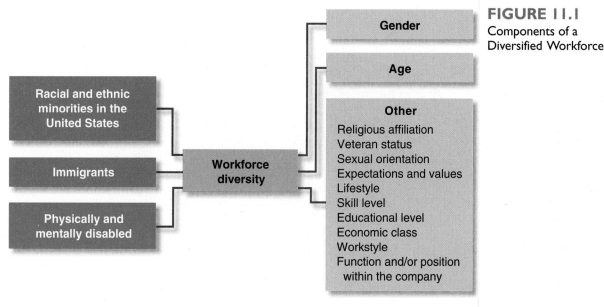

FIGURE 11.1
Components of a Diversified Workforce

Although members of different groups (white males, people born during the Depression, homosexuals, Vietnam veterans, Hispanics, Asians, women, blacks, etc.) share within their groups many common values, attitudes, and perceptions, there is also much diversity within each of these categories. Every group is made up of individuals who are unique in personality, education, and life experiences. There may be more differences among, say, three Asians from Thailand, Hong Kong, and Korea than among a white, an African-American, and an Asian all born in Chicago. And not all white males share the same personal or professional goals and values or behave alike.

Thus, managing diversity may seem a contradiction within itself. It means being acutely aware of characteristics *common* to a group of employees, while also managing these employees as *individuals*. Managing diversity means not just tolerating or accommodating all sorts of differences, but supporting, nurturing, and utilizing these differences to the organization's advantage. Borders Books, for example, tries to match up the demographics of its workforce with the demographics of the communities in which its stores operate. Top managers at the company say that sales are better as a result. U.S. businesses will not have a choice of whether to have a diverse workforce; if they want to survive, they must learn to manage a diverse workforce sooner or better than their competitors do.

As Figure 11.2 shows, the number of HR executives who say their companies need to or are planning to expand their diversity training programs is sizable. Although many companies initially instituted diversity programs to prevent discrimination, more are beginning to see such programs as a crucial way to expand their customer bases both domestically and worldwide. In fact, two out of three companies said they had broadened their diversity programs because of increasing globalization, according to a survey of 1,780 HR and training executives by the Boston-based consulting firm Novations/J. Howard and Associates. A separate survey by Korn/Ferry International showed that approximately 85 percent of European recruiters, 88 percent of recruiters in Asia, and 95 percent of recruiters in Latin America either "strongly agreed" or "somewhat agreed" that being at least bilingual is critical to succeed in today's business environment.

The Size of the Workforce

During most of its history, the United States experienced a surplus of workers. But that is now expected to change. Lower birthrates in the United States and other developed countries are resulting in a smaller labor force. An even more substantial slowdown in the pace of growth of the labor force is projected for the 2015–2025 period, as the baby-boom generation retires.[3]

FIGURE 11.2
The Expansion of Diversity Programs in U.S. Companies

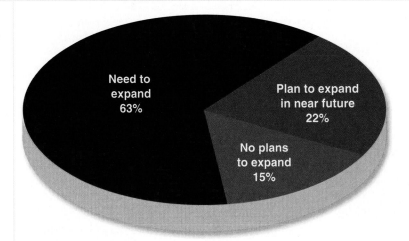

SOURCE: Gail Johnson, "Time to Broaden Diversity, *Training*, September 2004, p. 16.

Employers are likely to outsource some work to factories and firms in developing nations where birthrates are high and the labor supply is more plentiful. But they will have to compete for the best candidates from a relatively smaller and more diverse U.S. labor pool. Employers will need to know who these new workers are—and must be prepared to meet their needs.

The Workers of the Future

Until recently, white American-born males dominated the U.S. workforce. Businesses catered to their needs. However, while this group still constitutes the largest percentage of workers—at about 38 percent of the workforce—it accounts for only 15 percent of the net growth (those entering minus those leaving). The remaining 85 percent of workforce growth is accounted for by U.S.-born white females, immigrants, and minorities. And this growth is accelerating: The Census Bureau has predicted that between the years 2000 and 2020, the number of African-American, Hispanics, Asians, and Native Americans will grow by 42 million, while the number of Caucasians will grow by only 10 million.[4] As the accompanying news item suggests, this significant demographic change will affect not only the nature of the workforce, but also the new and varied customers and markets managers will have to attract.

> "Human diversity makes tolerance more than a virtue; it makes it a requirement for survival."
>
> Rene Dubos

Seeking Growth, Ski Areas Target Minorities

When Karl Kapuscinski took over management of the Mountain High ski resort in Southern California six years ago he sought to revive the slopes by courting the youth market—and not just any youths. He advertised on radio stations popular among black teenagers, sponsored skateboard contests that drew Hispanics, and hired Asian ski instructors.

Last year, Mountain High had 500,000 visits, three times as many as in 1997. About 40 percent of the skiers were African-American, Hispanic and Asian. For a resort that is just a 75-minute drive from Los Angeles, to target minorities was "natural," Mr. Kapuscinski says. "They're our demographic; they're our market."

The small resort appears to be on to something. For a sport deemed whiter than snow, targeting minorities is a revolutionary concept. But after more than two decades of stagnation, the ski industry is starting to realize that it has to go multicultural to grow.

This realization has reached the world's ski mecca, Colorado, thanks to Roberto Moreno, once the only minority ski patroller in the "entire state of Colorado," he says. Five years ago, he and his wife, Louise, started a nonprofit organization, Alpino, with a mission of creating ways for minority youngsters to gain better access to snow sports. "We all know that we are the least inclusive sport in the United States," Mr. Moreno says.

The U.S. ski industry exploded on the back of white baby boomers, who took to the sport in the late 1960s and '70s. But growth has been flat for the past two decades, averaging 54 million visits annually. Despite the stagnation, Mr. Moreno's message has been a tough sell to an industry used to luring mainly deep-pocketed destination skiers. Executives of ski companies initially "looked at me puzzled and rejected the notion that we should become more diverse," Mr. Moreno recalls. He attributes this to the fact that many ski-industry people live in the mountains, out of touch with changes sweeping through urban America. So Mr. Moreno took his cause to ski publications, ski-industry conferences and even officials of the U.S. Forest Service, which oversees the mountains where many ski resorts operate. "I went anyplace I could get an audience," Mr. Moreno says.

He had some success: Over five years, he introduced 5,000 Denver minority youths to the slopes, thanks to small ski operators, local banks and private companies that contributed

items such as $200 of lift tickets or a bus rental for the day. Last year, he set a new, ambitious goal of taking 10,000 minority youths to the Colorado slopes by 2006.

In May, Mr. Moreno took the stage at the national ski convention in Savannah, Ga., armed with irrefutable data: 70 percent of the U.S. population is black or Hispanic; minorities together now outnumber whites in many metropolitan areas; the minority-participation rate for skiing and snowboarding is less than 8 percent; and the average multicultural teen spends $320 a month, 4 percent more than the average non-minority counterpart. Then Mr. Moreno asked the packed auditorium of industry leaders: "How white do you think your resort can be in 35 years and still be in business?"

At Mountain High, the California resort where most guests visit for the day, 60 percent of the clientele come from families whose annual income is $75,000 or less. "These kids borrow equipment from each other and teach each other how to ski and snowboard," Mr. Kapuscinski says. "They save money from a part-time job to buy gear and come."

Marketing with messages that resonate with minorities will be vital. The brochure for Mountain High features photos of Latinos, Asians and blacks on the slopes. The resort also has minorities in front-line positions, as ski instructors, ski patrollers and lift operators.

With a view to making skiing multicultural and less elitist, the Aspen Valley Ski Club, a nonprofit group that runs programs for local children, recently started targeting Latinos. The club will provide scholarships for about 400 low-income children, half of them Hispanic. "It will be fantastic to see these kids start [outshining] white kids on the hill," says Curtis Kaufman, a Californian who had the idea to start the program after moving there. Meanwhile, Mr. Moreno plans to launch Alpino projects in New Hampshire, Vermont and Massachusetts next season. He has received inquiries from ski operators in other states, including Utah, New Mexico, Oregon and Washington. "We need to make sure [snow sports] are not just for the wealthiest Americans," he says.

SOURCE: Miriam Jordan, "Seeking Growth, Ski Areas Target Minorities," *The Wall Street Journal*, December 22, 2004, p. B1.

Gender Issues   One of the most important developments in the U.S. labor market has been the growing number of women working outside the home. Social changes during the 1960s and 1970s coupled with financial necessity caused women to enter the workforce and redefine their roles. Consider this:

- Women make up about 47 percent of the workforce.
- Ninety-nine of 100 women will work for pay at some point in their lives.
- The overall labor force participation rate of women continues to increase while the participation rate of men declines.
- About 60 percent of all marriages are dual-earner marriages.
- One of every five married women who works outside the home earns more than her husband does.[5]

For many women, as well as their spouses, balancing work life with family responsibilities and parenting presents an enormous challenge. Although men's roles in our society have been changing, women still adopt the bulk of family responsibilities, including homemaking, child care, and care of elderly parents. Yet some companies may still expect their employees, particularly at the managerial level, to put in long hours and sacrifice their personal lives for the sake of their jobs, organizations, and careers. These expectations may not only put many women at a disadvantage in the workplace; they may cause companies to lose valuable talent. For example, consulting firm Booz Allen Hamilton found that it was losing too many highly trained women consultants because of the amount of travel its jobs required. The company reorganized many of its jobs to give its male and female employees the ability to choose work projects that would not demand as much travel.[6] Companies that offer their employees the opportunity to balance work and family commitments are better able to recruit and retain women. These companies are offering family-friendly benefits like on-site child care, in-home care for elderly family members, and flexible work schedules, and they are taking advantage of newer technologies to permit more work from home.

Nevertheless, major pay disparities still exist. The average full-time working woman earns only about 77 percent as much as men in the same job (recall the discussion in Chapter 10 about equal pay and comparable worth). At the level of vice-president, the average woman earns over 40 percent less than a man in the same job. And at the very top, the disparities are even greater: The 20 highest-paid male executives in the United States average 10 times the total compensation of the 20 best-paid women. However, this situation is getting somewhat better. The median earnings of young women (ages 16 to 24) are 95 percent of those of young men, and over the last decade the average total compensation of women executives has more than doubled.[7]

Single working-parent families face a tough challenge in balancing work and home life. Single moms—divorced, widowed, or never married—account for over 9 million of single-parent households. For single parents, business travel and other routine demands of a corporate career—including overtime and interoffice transfers—can turn life upside down. Sometimes single parents decline promotions or high-profile assignments to preserve time with their children. In some organizations, experts say, it may be incorrectly assumed single-mom staffers can't handle new duties because of the responsibilities they're shouldering at home.

Some of the discrepancy in compensation is the consequence of both the level and types of jobs women receive. As women—along with minorities—move up the corporate ladder, they encounter a "glass ceiling." The **glass ceiling** is an invisible barrier that makes it difficult for women and minorities to move beyond a certain level in the corporate hierarchy. For example, women make up only about 16 percent of top-ranking corporate executives. But even this percentage is double the percentage that existed as recently as 1995.[8] Only about 10 percent of Fortune 100 companies have a women CEO. Across all management levels, the picture is more encouraging—over 40 percent of middle managers in the United States are women.[9] Nonetheless, evidence persists that women who climb the corporate ladder are faced with making choices between their careers and their families. According to the General Accounting Office, nearly 60 percent of male managers have children at home, compared with 40 percent of female managers.[10] Table 11.1. lists top women executives and the companies for which they work. Table 11.2 shows the best companies for women executives according to the National Association of Female Executives.

One persistent concern for both men and women is the problem of **sexual harassment**. Sexual harassment falls into two different categories. The first, *quid pro quo harassment*, occurs when "submission to or rejection of sexual conduct is used as a basis for employment decisions." The second type of harassment, *hostile environment*, occurs when unwelcome sexual conduct "has the purpose or effect of unreasonably interfering with job performance or creating an intimidating, hostile, or offensive working environment." Behaviors that can cause a hostile work environment include persistent or pervasive displays of pornography, lewd or suggestive remarks, or demeaning taunts or jokes. This type of harassment is now more typical than quid pro quo harassment. But because it may involve more subjective standards of behavior, it puts an extra burden on managers to maintain an appropriate work environment. In fact, managers who do not themselves engage in harassment, but who do not prevent it, or who do not take appropriate action after receiving legitimate complaints about it, may still be held liable along with their companies if a lawsuit is filed. It is also important for managers to know that the "hostile work environment" standard applies to male-on-male harassment, as well as to non-gender-related cases, such as a pattern of racial or ethnic slurs.

glass ceiling

An invisible barrier that makes it difficult for certain groups, such as minorities and women, to move beyond a certain level in the organizational hierarchy.

sexual harassment

Conduct of a sexual nature that has negative consequences for employment.

TABLE 11.1   The A-List: Top Women Executives

Rank	Name	Company	Title
1	Meg Whitman	eBay	President and CEO
2	Andrea Jung	Avon Products	Chairman and CEO
3	Anne Mulcahy	Xerox	Chairman and CEO
4	Marjorie Magner	Citigroup	Chairman and CEO, Global Consumer Group
5	Oprah Winfrey	Harpo	Chairman
6	Sallie Krawcheck	Citigroup	CFO
7	Abigail Johnson	Fidelity Management & Research	President
8	Pat Woertz	Chevron Texaco	EVP, Global Downstream
9	Karen Katen	Pfizer	EVP; President, Global Pharmaceuticals
10	Judy McGrath	Viacom	Chairman and CEO MTV Networks
11	Indra Nooyi	PepsiCo	President and CFO
12	Ann Moore	Time Warner	Chairman and CEO, Time Inc.
13	Pat Russo	Lucent Technologies	Chairman and CEO
14	Christine Poon	Johnson & Johnson	Worldwide Chairman, Medicines and Nutritionals
15	Zoe Cruz	Morgan Stanley	Worldwide Head, Fixed Income, For. Ex., & Commodities
16	Doreen Toben	Verizon	EVP and CFO
17	Anne Sweeney	Walt Disney	Co-Chairman, Disney Media; President, Disney–ABC Television
18	Amy Woods Brinkley	Bank of America	Chief Risk Officer
19	Susan Arnold	Procter & Gamble	Vice Chairman; Global Beauty Care
20	Amy Pascal	Sony	Vice Chairman; Chairman of Motion Picture Group
21	Ann Livermore	Hewlett-Packard	EVP, Technology Solutions Group
22	Myrtle Potter	Genentech	President, Commercial Operations
23	Susan Desmond-Hellmann	Genentech	President, Product Development
24	Gail Berman	News Corp.	President, Entertainment, Fox Broadcasting Co.
25	Shelly Lazarus	WPP	Chairman and CEO, Ogilvy & Mather Worldwide

SOURCE: http://www.fortune.com/fortune/powerwomen/subs/fulllist, accessed March 19, 2005.

One way managers can help their companies prevent harassment from arising, or avoid punitive damages if a lawsuit is filed, is to make sure their organizations have an effective and comprehensive policy on harassment in place. Table 11.3 shows the basic components of such a policy. Companies such as Avon, Corning, and Metro-Goldwyn-Mayer have found that a strong commitment to diversity leads to fewer problems with sexual harassment.[11]

Before moving on, it is important to note that gender issues and the changing nature of work do not apply just to women. In some ways, the changing status of women has given men the opportunity to redefine their roles, expectations, and lifestyles. Some men are deciding that there is more to life than corporate success and are choosing to scale back work hours and commitments in order to spend time with their families. Worker values are shifting toward personal time, quality of life, self-fulfillment,

TABLE 11.2
The 2005 Top 30
Companies for Executive
Women

Aetna, Hartford, CT
Allstate Insurance, Northbrook, IL
American Express, New York, NY
Avon Products Inc., New York, NY
Bristol-Myers Squibb Co., New York, NY
Charming Shoppes, Bensalem, PA
Colgate-Palmolive, New York, NY
Compuware Corporation, Detroit, MI
DuPont, Wilmington, DE
Federated Department Stores, Cincinnati, OH
Gannett Co. Inc., McLean, VA
Gap Inc., San Francisco, CA
Hewlett-Packard, Palo Alto, CA
IBM Corporation, Armonk, NY
Knight Ridder, San Jose, CA
Liz Claiborne, Inc., North Bergen, NJ
Lucent Technologies, Murray Hill, NJ
Manpower Inc., Milwaukee, WI
Merck & Co. Inc., Whitehouse Station, NJ
Nordstrom Inc., Seattle, WA
The New York Times Co., New York, NY
PepsiCo Inc., Purchase, NY
The Phoenix Companies, Enfield, CT
The Principal Financial Group, Des Moines, IA
The Procter & Gamble Companies, Cincinnati, OH
Prudential Financial, Newark, NJ
Scholastic Inc., New York, NY
Target, Minneapolis, MN
WellPoint, Indianapolis, IN
Xerox Corporation, Stamford, CT

SOURCE: www.nafe.com.

and family. Workers today, both men and women, are looking to achieve a balance between career and family.

Minorities and Immigrants   In addition to gender issues, the importance and scope of diversity are evident in the growth of racial minorities and immigrants in the workforce. Consider these facts:

- Minorities and immigrants hold approximately one of every four jobs in the United States.
- Asian and Hispanic workforces are growing the fastest in the Unite States, followed by the African-American workforce.
- Three in ten college enrollees are people of color.
- By 2020, most of California's entry-level workers will be Hispanic.
- English has become the second language for much of the population in California, Texas, and Florida.
- Foreign-born workers make up 14 percent of the U.S. civilian labor force.

1. Develop a comprehensive organizationwide policy on sexual harassment and present it to all current and new employees. Stress that sexual harassment will not be tolerated under any circumstances. Emphasis is best achieved when the policy is publicized and supported by top management.

2. Hold training sessions with supervisors to explain Title VII requirements, their role in providing an environment free of sexual harassment, and proper investigative procedures when charges occur.

3. Establish a formal complaint procedure in which employees can discuss problems without fear of retaliation. The complaint procedure should spell out how charges will be investigated and resolved.

4. Act immediately when employees complain of sexual harassment. Communicate widely that investigations will be conducted objectively and with appreciation for the sensitivity of the issue.

5. When an investigation supports employee charges, discipline the offender at once. For extremely serious offenses, discipline should include penalties up to and including discharge. Discipline should be applied consistently across similar cases and among managers and hourly employees alike.

6. Follow up on all cases to ensure a satisfactory resolution of the problem.

TABLE 11.3
Basic Components of an Effective Sexual Harassment Policy

SOURCE: George Bohlander, Scott Snell, and Arthur Sherman, *Managing Human Resources,* 12th ed. Copyright © 2001. Reprinted by permission of South-Western, a division of Thomson Learning, www.thomsonrights.com.

- The younger Americans are, the more likely they are to be persons of color.
- One in 40 people in the United States identifies himself or herself as multiracial,[12] and the number could soar to 1 in 5 by 2050.

These numbers indicate that the term *minority*, as it is used typically, may soon become outdated. Particularly in urban areas where white males do not predominate, managing diversity means more than eliminating discrimination; it means capitalizing on the wide variety of skills available in the labor market. Organizations that do not take full advantage of the skills and capabilities of minorities and immigrants are severely limiting their potential talent pool and their ability to understand and capture minority markets. And those markets are growing rapidly. For example, minority households now account for over 19 percent of consumer spending, up from only 12 percent as recently as 1990.[13]

Advantages of Collaboration

In many urban areas, with large Asian, Hispanic, or African-American populations, banks have deliberately increased the diversity of their managers and tellers to reflect the population mix in the community and attract additional business. If they did not, customers would readily notice and switch to other banks in the area where they would feel more welcome and comfortable. Such diversity, and collaboration between employees, permits increased customer service, helping banks maintain their competitiveness. For example, tellers approached by new immigrants who do not yet speak English immediately call on the appropriate bilingual colleagues for help. The bilingual colleagues are also in a better position to assist the bank customers with special problems, such as income transfers from abroad.

Even so, the evidence shows some troubling disparities in employment and earnings. Black unemployment is double that of whites, and black men earn about 74 percent as much as white men. This disparity may exist even for similar jobs. African-Americans are also significantly underrepresented in higher management, accounting for less than 1 percent of senior-level managers in the top 1,000 corporations.[14] The Bureau of Labor Statistics has also found that African-Americans and Hispanics are significantly underrepresented in all executive, administrative, and managerial positions. This underrepresentation may itself help perpetuate the problem, as it can leave many aspiring young minorities with fewer role models or mentors that are so helpful in an executive career.[15]

There is also considerable evidence that discrimination may account for at least some of these disparities. For example, in one recent study fictitious résumés were used to respond to help-wanted ads in Boston and Chicago newspapers. Each résumé used either African-American names like Lakisha and Jamal or white-sounding names like Emily and Greg. The résumés with white-sounding names were 50 percent more likely to get a callback for an interview than the same résumés with African-American names. Despite equivalence in credentials, the often unconscious assumptions about different racial groups are very difficult to overcome.[16]

Nevertheless, significant progress has been made. For example, as you can see in Table 11.4, of the largest 1,000 domestic and international corporations, 18 are now headed by an African-American CEO. This is not a large number, but in 1988 there were none, and as recently as 2000 there were only six. In addition, virtually every large organization today has policies and programs dedicated to increasing minority representation—including compensation

Women like Anne M. Mulcahy, President and CEO of Xerox, are taking their place on the top rung of the corporate ladder.

TABLE 11.4 African-American Chief Executive Officers

Name	Company	Title
Kenneth I. Chenault	American Express	Chairman and CEO
Erroll B. Davis Jr.	Alliant Energy	Chairman and CEO
Reginald E. Davis	Wachovia	CEO
W. H. "Bill" Easter III	Duke Energy Field Services	Chairman, CEO, and President
Ann M. Fudge	Young & Rubicam Brands	Chairman and CEO
Arthur "Art" H. Harper	GE Equipment Services	CEO and President
Carl Horton	The Absolut Spirit Company Inc.	CEO and President
Aylwin Lewis	Kmart	President and CEO
Renetta McCann	Starcom Americas	CEO
E. Stanley O'Neal	Merrill Lynch & Co.	Chairman, CEO, and President
Clarence Otis Jr.	Darden Restaurants	CEO
Dan Packer	Entergy New Orleans	CEO and President
Richard D. Parsons	Time Warner	Chairman and CEO
Franklin D. Raines	Fannie Mae	Former Chairman and CEO
Pamela Thomas-Graham	CNBC	CEO and President
John W. Thompson	Symantec Corp.	Chairman and CEO
Lloyd G. Trotter	GE Consumer and Industrial	CEO and President
R. L. "Bob" Wood	Crompton Corp.	Chairman, CEO, and President

SOURCE: Reprinted with permission from Black Enterprise magazine, February 2005.

TABLE 11.5

Top 10 Companies for Diversity Recruitment and Retention

1. Ford
2. Fannie Mae
3. American Express
4. Verizon
5. IBM
6. Safeco
7. Deloitte & Touche
8. Eastman Kodak
9. Bank of America
10. Xerox

SOURCE: Copyright © 2004, DiversityInc.com. Reproduced with permission.

systems that reward managers for increasing the diversity of their operations. Major companies like FedEx, Xerox, Motorola, Shell, and Sun Microsystems have corporate diversity officers who assist organization managers in their efforts to attract, retain, and promote minority and women executives. Many organizations are also working to ensure a continuing supply of minority candidates by supporting minority internships and MBA programs. Dunn and Bradstreet, for example, sponsors summer internship programs for minority MBA students. Lockheed Martin has partnered the American Management Association's Operation Enterprise to establish two-week paid summer internship programs for high school and college students. These internship programs help students and organizations learn about one another and, ideally, turn into full-time employment opportunities. Table 11.5 shows the top 10 companies for diversity according to DiversityInc.com. For all these companies, developing, hiring, and retaining minority executives is critical for their ability to manage an ever-more-diverse workforce and to serve an increasing number of clients and customers with varied backgrounds.

Mentally and Physically Disabled   The largest unemployed minority population in the United States is people with disabilities. It is composed of people of all ethnic backgrounds, cultures, and ages. According to the U.S. Census Bureau, in the last decade the number of Americans with disabilities increased 25 percent, outpacing any other subgroup of the U.S. population. According to the National Organization on Disability, 32 percent of Americans with disabilities, ages 18–64, are working. But 66 percent of those who are unemployed would rather have a job.[17]

The Americans with Disabilities Act (ADA), mentioned in Chapter 10, defines a disability as a physical or mental impairment that substantially limits one or more major life activities. Examples of such physical or mental impairments include those resulting from conditions such as orthopedic, visual, speech, and hearing impairments; cerebral palsy; epilepsy; muscular dystrophy; multiple sclerosis;

A lot of great employees come with their own office chair.

Hiring workers with disabilities doesn't just mean they bring their own office chair—they are likely to be more dependable, miss fewer days of work, and exhibit low turnover.

HIV infections; cancer; heart disease; diabetes; mental retardation; emotional illness; specific learning disabilities; drug abuse; and alcoholism.[18]

New assistive technologies are making it easier for companies to comply with the ADA and for the disabled to be productive on the job.[19] In many cases, state governments will pay for special equipment or other accommodations that workers need. Companies are discovering that making these accommodations can result in unanticipated fringe benefits, too. The National Industries for the Blind (NIB), a Wisconsin company that markets products under the Skilcraft brand name, is a case in point. Seventy-five percent of NIB employees are visually impaired. Because the company's warehouse pickers have trouble reading instructions on paper, NIB installed a voice technology system that conveys instructions to workers through headsets. An added benefit is that the technology has raised the productivity of the entire operation. Accuracy has improved, and workers—both blind and sighted—are able to pick and ship orders faster using the headsets.

For most businesses, mentally and physically disabled people represent an unexplored but fruitful labor market. Frequently, employers have found that disabled employees are more dependable than other employees, miss fewer days of work, and exhibit lower turnover. Tax credits are also available to companies who hire disabled workers. In addition, managers who hire and support employees with disabilities are signaling to other employees and outside stakeholders their strong interest in creating an inclusive organization culture.

The Age of the Workforce

The baby-boom generation (born between 1946 and 1964) is aging. Today, one in three workers is over age 45, and by 2006 the median age of America's workforce will rise to 40.6, up from 30 in the early 1960s. Industries such as nursing and manufacturing are already facing a tremendous loss of expertise as a result of downsizing and a rapidly aging workforce. Other industries will soon be in similar straits.[20] As a result of these trends, the Bureau of Labor Statistics projects that entry-level workers will be in short supply.

On the plus side, 68 percent of workers between the ages of 50 and 70 plan to work in retirement or never retire, the Association for the Advancement of Retired People (AARP) reports. Retirees often return to the workforce at the behest of their employers, who can't afford to lose the knowledge accumulated by longtime employees, their willingness to work nontraditional shifts, and their reliable work habits, which have a positive effect on the entire work group. Eighty percent of respondents in a Society of Human Resources Management found that recruiting managers have little or no hesitancy about hiring older workers.[21]

Nonetheless, to prevent an exodus of talent, employers will need strategies to help retain and attract the talent older workers have to offer. Phased retirement plans that allow older employees to work fewer hours per week is one such strategy. Almost one-third of retiring faculty members at 16 University of North Carolina campuses take advantage of phased retirement, and the concept is slowly catching on in many other public and private organizations. Other strategies include making workplace adaptations to help older workers cope with the physical problems they will experience as they age, like poorer vision, hearing, mobility, and so forth. This is a significant change from the practice in recent decades, when older workers were given incentives to leave in order to allow companies to reduce overhead and perhaps hire less-expensive replacements.

To attract older, experienced employees, executives at Procter & Gamble and Eli Lilly created a separate company that will supply them with retired professionals who want to return to work on a part-time basis. Home Depot offers jobs in Florida for the winter and summer jobs in Maine, and Borders bookstores offer discounts to encourage retired teachers to take sales jobs. Managers in companies like these are forecasting a worker shortage, and want to be prepared.[22] Table 11.6 shows how creative companies are rethinking their retirement policies and solving their skilled-labor shortage by finding ways

Approaches to More Fully Utilizing Older Employees	Approaches Considered Very or Moderately Effective	Businesses that Have Implemented the Approach
Benefit packages targeted toward older employees	68%	18%
Part-time work arrangements with continuation of benefits	64	30
Educating managers about ways to utilize older employees	60	25
Increased availability of part-time work for older employees (regardless of benefits)	55	36
Skill training for older employees	55	44

TABLE 11.6
Top Five Approaches for More Fully Utilizing Older Employees

SOURCE: "American Business and Older Employees: A Survey of Findings," American Association of Retired Persons (AARP). Copyright © 2002 AARP (www.aarp.org). Reprinted with permission.

to attract and retain people over 55. These companies save on turnover and training costs and capitalize on the experience of their older employees.

FROM THE PAGES OF ↓ # Hispanic Nation

BusinessWeek

Baby boomers, move over—the *bebé* boomers are coming. They are 39 million strong—bilingual, bicultural, mostly younger Hispanics who will drive growth in the U.S. population and workforce as far out as statisticians can project. Coming from across Latin America, but predominantly Mexico, these immigrants are creating what experts are calling a "tamale in the snake," a huge cohort of kindergarten to thirty-something Hispanics created by the sheer velocity of their population growth—3 percent a year, vs. 0.8 percent for everyone else.

It's not just that Latinos, as many prefer to be called, officially passed African-Americans last year to become the nation's largest minority. Their numbers are so great that, like the postwar baby boomers before them, the Latino Generation is becoming a driving force in the economy, politics, and culture.

It amounts to no less than a shift in the nation's center of gravity. Hispanics made up half of all new workers in the past decade, a trend that will lift them from roughly 12 percent of the workforce today to nearly 25 percent two generations from now. Despite low family incomes, Hispanics' soaring buying power increasingly influences the food Americans eat, the clothes they buy, and the cars they drive. Companies are scrambling to revamp products and marketing to reach the fastest-growing consumer group.

The United States has never faced demographic change quite like this before. Certainly, the Latino boom brings a welcome charge to the economy at a time when others' population growth has slowed to a crawl. Without a steady supply of new workers and consumers, a graying United States might see a long-term slowdown along the lines of aging Japan, says former Housing and Urban Development chief Henry Cisneros. Already, Latinos are a key catalyst of economic growth. Their disposable income has jumped 29 percent since 2001, to $652 billion, double the pace of the rest of the population. Similarly, the ranks of Latino entrepreneurs have jumped by 30 percent since 1998.

What's not yet clear is whether Hispanic social cohesion will be so strong as to actually challenge the idea of the American melting pot. Throughout the country's history, successive waves of immigrants eventually surrendered their native languages and cultures and melted into the middle class. Hispanics may be different, and not just because many are nonwhites. Hispanics today may have more choice than other immigrant groups to remain within their culture. With national TV networks such as Univision Communications Inc. and hundreds of mostly Spanish-speaking enclaves like Cicero, Hispanics may find it practical to remain bilingual. Today, 78 percent of U.S. Latinos speak Spanish, even if they also know English.

In its eagerness to tap the exploding Hispanic market, Corporate America itself is helping to reinforce Hispanics' bicultural preferences. Last year, Procter & Gamble Co. spent $90 million on advertising directed at Latinos for 12 products such as Crest and Tide— 10 percent of its ad budget for those brands and a 28 percent hike in just a year. "Hispanics are a cornerstone of our growth in North America," says Graciela Eleta, vice-president of P&G's multicultural team in Puerto Rico.

Other companies are making similar assumptions. A new unit of Cypress (Calif.)-based PacifiCare Health Systems Inc. began marketing health insurance in Spanish, directing Hispanics to Spanish-speaking doctors, and translating documents into Spanish for Hispanic workers. "We knew we had to remake the entire company, linguistically and culturally, to deal with this market," says PacifiCare's Russell A. Bennett.

As the ranks of Spanish speakers swell, Spanish-language media are transforming from a niche market into a stand-alone industry. Ad revenues on Spanish-language TV should climb by 16 percent this year, more than other media segments, according to TNS Media Intelligence/CMR. The audience of Univision, the No. 1 Spanish-language media conglomerate in the United States, has soared by 44 percent since 2001, and by 146 percent in the 18- to 34-year-old group. Many viewers have come from English-language networks, whose audiences have declined in that period.

For more than 200 years, the nation has succeeded in weaving the foreign-born into the fabric of U.S. society, incorporating strands of new cultures along the way. With their huge numbers, Hispanics are adding all kinds of new influences. Cinco de Mayo has joined St. Patrick's Day as a public celebration in some neighborhoods, and burritos are everyday fare. More and more, Americans hablan Español. Will Hispanics be absorbed just as other waves of immigrants were? It's possible, but more likely they will continue to straddle two worlds, figuring out ways to remain Hispanic even as they become Americans.

SOURCE: Adapted from Brian Grow, "Hispanic Nation," *BusinessWeek*, March 15, 2004, online.

Managing Diversity versus Affirmative Action

For many organizations, the original impetus to diversify their workforces was social responsibility and legal necessity (recall Chapters 5 and 10). To correct the past exclusion of women and minorities, companies introduced **affirmative action**—special efforts to recruit and hire qualified members of groups that have been discriminated against in the past. The intent was not to prefer these group members to the exclusion of others, but to correct for the long history of discriminatory practices and exclusion. Morally, ethically, and legally, amending these wrongs was simply the right thing to do.

affirmative action

Special efforts to recruit and hire qualified members of groups that have been discriminated against in the past.

Legal remedies to end discrimination have had a powerful impact, transforming our society and organizations in positive ways that would have been unimaginable only a few decades ago. Today the immigrant nature of American society is virtually taken for granted, and even seen as a source of pride. And women, African-Americans, Hispanics, and other minorities routinely occupy positions that in years past would have been totally closed to them.

Connections: EVERYONE KNOWS WOMEN CAN'T PLAY

Until 1965 no more than 5 percent of the musicians in the best orchestras in the United States were women, and even until about 1980 the figure never rose above 10 percent. Some major orchestras had no women at all. (In Europe, even until quite recently, some major orchestras actually had formal policies *forbidding* the hiring of women.) Many conductors were quoted as saying that women were more temperamental, needed special attention, would be more likely to quit, or would make the orchestra sound worse. Today, despite the fact that turnover in orchestras is quite low, women often make up about a third of orchestra musicians. In several orchestras almost half of new hires are women. Some of the same conductors who complained about women musicians ended up hiring many once auditions took place behind a screen. By hiring strictly on the basis of demonstrated talent, not appearance, sex, or race, orchestras were able to eliminate the influence of discrimination. They were also able to increase significantly the talent pool available to them. The result was an immediate and sharp increase in orchestra diversity.

Nevertheless, as we have seen, a legislated approach tends to result in fragmented effort that have not yet achieved fully the integrative goals of diversity. Employment discrimination still persists, and even after three decades of government legislation, equal employment opportunity (EEO) and affirmative action laws have not adequately improved the upward mobility of women and minorities. To move beyond correction of past wrongs to truly inclusive organizations requires a change in organization culture—one in which diversity is seen as contributing directly to the attainment of organization goals.

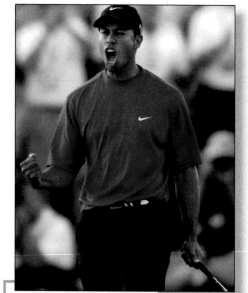

Pro golfer Tiger Woods can be credited with single-handedly advancing the image of golf for many new spectators.

Seen in this way, affirmative action and diversity are complementary, not the same. In contrast to EEO and affirmative action programs, managing diversity means moving beyond legislated mandates to embrace a proactive business philosophy that sees differences as a positive value. In the end, *all* employees are different. These differences may include the fundamental attributes of race, ethnicity, age, and gender we have been discussing, but they also may include less obvious attributes like employees' place of origin, their education, or their life experience. All these elements add to the richness of talents and perspectives managers can draw on. Managing diversity in this broader sense involves organizations making changes in their systems, structures, and practices in order to eliminate barriers that may keep people from reaching their full potential. It means treating people as individuals—*equally*, but not necessarily the *same*—recognizing that each employee has different needs and will need different things to succeed. But it also asks managers to recognize and value the uniqueness of each employee, and to see the different ideas and perspectives each brings to the organization as a source of competitive advantage. In short, managing diversity is not only about getting more minorities and women into the organization. It is about creating an environment in which employees from *every* background listen to each other and work better together so the organization as a whole will become more effective.

Competitive Advantage through Diversity

Today many organizations are approaching diversity from a more practical, business-oriented perspective. Increasingly, diversity can be a powerful tool for building competitive advantage. A study by the Department of Labor's Glass Ceiling Institute showed that the stock performance of firms that were high performers on diversity-related goals was over twice as high as that of other firms. Another recent study found that companies with the highest percentage of women among senior managers had a significantly higher return to shareholders than companies with the lowest percentage. Conversely, announcements of damage awards from discrimination lawsuits frequently have had a negative effect on stock returns.[23]

There are many advantages—and some obvious challenges—to managing a diverse workforce. We discuss some of them in the following section.

Ability to Attract and Retain Motivated Employees   For companies facing changing demographics and business needs, diversity makes good sense. Companies with a reputation for providing opportunities for diverse employees will have a competitive advantage in the labor market and will be sought out by the most qualified employees. In addition, when employees believe their differences are not merely tolerated but valued, they may become more loyal, productive, and committed.

Better Perspective on a Differentiated Market   Companies such as Avon, Prudential, Eastman Kodak, and Toys "R" Us are committed to diversity because as the composition of the American workforce changes, so does the customer base of these companies. Just as women and minorities may prefer to work for an employer that values diversity, they may prefer to patronize such organizations.

Diversity can help the organization succeed in new markets.

Many Asian-Americans, African-Americans, Mexican-Americans, and women have entered the middle class and now control consumer dollars. A multicultural workforce can provide a company with greater knowledge of the preferences and consuming habits of this diversified marketplace. This knowledge can assist companies in designing products and developing marketing campaigns to meet those consumers' needs. In addition, for at least some products and services, a multicultural sales force may help an organization sell to diverse groups. A diverse workforce also can give a company a competitive edge in a global economy by facilitating understanding of other customs, cultures, and marketplace needs.

Ability to Leverage Creativity and Innovation in Problem Solving   Work team diversity promotes creativity and innovation, because people from different backgrounds hold different perspectives on issues. Diverse groups have a broader base of experience from which to approach a problem; when effectively managed, they invent more options and create more solutions than homogeneous groups do. In addition, diverse work groups are freer to deviate from traditional approaches and practices. The presence of diversity also can help minimize "groupthink" (recall Chapter 3).[24]

Diversity can bring new ideas to the organization.

Advantages of Collaboration

Many law firms will now routinely have diverse legal teams working together on a case. Fresh "out of the box" ideas are often required in complex cases, and a group of lawyers from the same background who all think the same way may not be able to be as innovative as a team that is more diverse. In addition, in jury trials, the kind of impression a legal team makes on a jury can help or badly hurt the client, and diverse jurors are more likely to be receptive to a visibly diverse team, with different kinds of lawyers participating. The increased importance of legal-team diversity has caused some law firms to form alliances with minority firms, so they can collaborate on cases.

Enhancement of Organizational Flexibility   A diverse workforce can enhance organizational flexibility, because managing diversity successfully requires a corporate culture that tolerates many different styles and approaches. Less restrictive policies and procedures and less standardized operating methods enable organizations to become more flexible and thus better able to respond quickly to environmental changes (recall

A diverse workforce can lead to greater responsiveness.

Chapters 2 and 9). Executives at PepsiCo, Verizon, Kodak, and Prudential are so convinced of the competitive potential of a diverse workforce that they tie a portion of management compensation to success in recruiting and promoting minorities and women.[25]

Challenges of a Diverse Workforce

We have discussed the laws guaranteeing equal opportunity, and the significant and growing business advantages of diversity. Yet every year thousands of lawsuits are filed over issues of discrimination and fair treatment, some involving even the largest and most respected firms.[26] And even when there is no overt discrimination in hiring and pay, managing diversity can be difficult. Often minorities and women who have been hired find themselves in an organization culture or environment that does not give them the opportunity to do their best work. And managers with all the goodwill in the world find it harder than they expected to get people from different backgrounds to work together for a common goal.[27]

To become effective managers of the diverse organization, we first have to identify and overcome a number of challenges. These include unexamined assumptions, lower cohesiveness, communication problems, mistrust and tension, and stereotyping.

Unexamined Assumptions   For must of us, seeing the world from someone else's perspective is difficult, because our own assumptions and viewpoints seem so normal and familiar. For example, heterosexuals may not even think about whether to put a picture of their loved ones on their desks; it is a routine, even automatic decision, repeated in a million workplaces across the country. But for gay employees in many companies, displaying such a picture may cause considerable anxiety—if they feel able to consider it at all. White employees in most U.S. organizations rarely feel a sense of difference or isolation, because they are usually surrounded by people who look much like themselves. The perspective of minorities in largely white organizations may be quite different. In an organization that is oblivious to these different perspectives and does not take an active role in making people from diverse backgrounds feel welcome, managers may find it more difficult to develop an enthusiastically shared sense of purpose.

Lower Cohesiveness   Diversity can create a lack of cohesiveness. *Cohesiveness* refers to how tightly knit the group is and the degree to which group members perceive, interpret, and act on their environment in similar or mutually agreed-upon ways. Because of their lack of similarity in language, culture, and/or experience, diverse groups typically are less cohesive than homogeneous groups. Often mistrust, miscommunication, stress, and attitudinal differences reduce cohesiveness, which in turn can diminish productivity. Group cohesiveness will be discussed in greater detail in Chapter 14.

Communication Problems   Perhaps the most common negative effect of diversity is communication problems. These difficulties include misunderstandings, inaccuracies, inefficiencies, and slowness. Speed is lost when not all group members are fluent in the same language or when additional time is required to explain things. Sometimes diversity may decrease communication, as when white male managers feel less comfortable giving feedback to women or minorities, for fear of how criticism may be received. The result may be employees who do not have a clear idea of what they need to do to improve their performance.

Diversity can also lead to errors and misunderstandings. Group members may assume they interpret things similarly when they in fact do not, or they may disagree because of their different frames of reference.[28] For example, if managers do not actively encourage and accept the expression of different points of view, some employees may be afraid to speak up at meetings, leaving the manager with a false impression that consensus has been reached. We discuss other problems in communication and how to avoid them in Chapter 15.

Mistrust and Tension   People prefer to associate with others who are like themselves. This is a normal, understandable tendency. But it can often lead to misunderstanding, mistrust, and even fear of those who are different, because of a lack of contact and low familiarity. For example, if women and minority-group members are routinely excluded, as they sometimes are, from joining white male colleagues at business lunches or after-hour gatherings, they may come to feel isolated from their colleagues. This can cause stress, tension, and even resentment, making it more difficult to reach agreement on solutions to problems.

Stereotyping   We learn to see the world in a certain way on the basis of our backgrounds and experiences. Our interests, values, and cultures act as filters and distort, block, and select what we see and hear. We see and hear what we expect to see and hear. Group members often inappropriately stereotype their "different" colleagues rather than accurately perceiving and evaluating those individuals' contributions, capabilities, aspirations, and motivations. Such stereotypes are usually negative or condescending. Women may be stereotyped as not dedicated to their careers, older workers as unwilling to learn new skills, minority-group members as less educated or capable. But even so-called positive stereotypes can be burdensome. For example, the common stereotype that Asians are good at math may well leave unrecognized other attributes that a particular Asian employee might have. Many women and minorities even dislike being stereotyped as members of groups that need special help or support, very much preferring to be treated as individuals.

> "Among CEO's of Fortune 500 companies, 58 percent are six feet or taller . . . Most of us, in ways we are not entirely aware of, automatically associate leadership with imposing physical stature."
>
> Malcolm Gladwell

Unless managers are aware of these stereotypes, either their own or those held by others, the stereotypes can directly affect how people in their organizations are treated. Employees stereotyped as unmotivated or emotional will be given less-stress-provoking (and perhaps less important) jobs than their co-workers. Those job assignments will create frustrated employees, perhaps resulting in lower commitment, higher turnover, and underused skills.[29]

The Challenge Ahead   For all these reasons, and more, managing diversity is not easy. U.S. organizations are not isolated from the continuing effects of America's racial legacy or the barriers to equal opportunity that remain. Nor are managers immune to the biases, stereotypes, lack of experience, and tensions that make communication, teamwork, and leadership in a diverse workforce much more challenging. Yet managers very much need to confront these issues. They need to develop the skills and strategies diversity requires if they and their organizations are to succeed in our increasingly multicultural business environment. We address some of the ways they might do that in the remainder of the chapter.

Multicultural Organizations

To capitalize on the benefits and minimize the costs of a diverse workforce, perhaps one of the first things managers need to do is examine their organization's prevailing assumptions about people and cultures. Table 11.7 shows some of the fundamental assumptions that may exist. Based on these assumptions, we can classify organizations as one of three types and describe their implications for managers.

Some organizations are **monolithic.** This type of organization has very little *cultural integration;* in other words, it employs few women, minorities, or any other groups that differ from the majority. The organization is highly homogeneous in terms of its employee population. In monolithic organizations, if groups other than the norm are employed, they are found primarily in low-status jobs. Minority group members

monolithic organization

An organization that has a low degree of structural integration—employing few women, minorities, or other groups that differ from the majority—and thus has a highly homogeneous employee population.

TABLE 11.7 Diversity Assumptions and Their Implications for Management

Common and Misleading Assumptions		Less Common and More Appropriate Assumptions	
Homogeneity	*Melting pot myth:* We are all the same.	Heterogeneity	*Image of cultural pluralism:* We are not all the same; groups within society differ across cultures.
Similarity	*Similarity myth:* "They" are all just like me.	Similarity and difference	*They are not just like me:* Many people differ from me culturally. Most people exhibit both cultural similarities and differences when compared to me.
Parochialism	*Only-one-way myth:* Our way is the only way. We do not recognize any other way of living or working.	Equifinality	*Our way is not the only way:* There are many culturally distinct ways of reaching the same goal, of working, and of living one's life.
Ethnocentrism	*One-best-way myth:* Our way is the best way. All other approaches are inferior versions of our way.	Culture contingency	*Our way is one possible way:* There are many different and equally good ways to reach the same goal. The best way depends on the culture of the people involved.

SOURCE: From "Diversity Assumptions and Their Implications for Management" by Nancy J. Adler, *Handbook of Organization,* 1996. Reprinted courtesy of Marcel Dekker, Inc. NY.

pluralistic organization

An organization that has a relatively diverse employee population and makes an effort to involve employees from different gender, racial, or cultural backgrounds.

multicultural organization

An organization that values cultural diversity and seeks to utilize and encourage it.

must adopt the norms of the majority to survive. This fact, coupled with small numbers, keeps conflicts among groups low. Discrimination and prejudice typically prevail, informal integration is almost nonexistent, and minority group members do not identify strongly with the company.

Most large U.S. organizations made the transition from monolithic to *pluralistic* organizations in the 1960s and 1970s because of changing demographics as well as societal forces such as the civil rights and women's movements. **Pluralistic organizations** have a more diverse employee population and take steps to involve persons from different gender, racial, or cultural backgrounds. These organizations use an affirmative action approach to managing diversity: They actively try to hire and train a diverse workforce and to ensure against any discrimination against minority group members. They typically have much more integration than do monolithic organizations, but like monolithic organizations, they often have minority group members clustered at certain levels or in particular functions within the organization.

Because of greater cultural integration, affirmative action programs, and training programs, the pluralistic organization has some acceptance of minority group members into the informal network, much less discrimination, and less prejudice. Improved employment opportunities create greater identification with the organization among minority group members. Often the resentment of majority group members, coupled with the increased number of women and minorities, creates more conflict than exists in the monolithic organization.

The pluralistic organization fails to address the cultural aspects of integration. In contrast, in **multicultural organizations** diversity not only exists but is valued. These organizations fully integrate gender, racial, and minority group members both formally and informally. But managers in such organizations do not focus prima-

The U.S. military has, for years, made a deliberate effort to diversify throughout its ranks.

rily on the visible differences between employees, like race or sex. Rather, managers value and draw on the different *experience* and *knowledge* employees bring to the organization and help it achieve agreed-upon strategies and goals.[30] The multicultural organization is marked by an absence of prejudice and discrimination and by low levels of intergroup conflict. Such an organization creates a *synergistic* environment in which all members contribute to their maximum potential and the advantages of diversity can be fully realized.[31]

How Organizations Can Cultivate a Diverse Workforce

An organization's plans for becoming multicultural and making the most of its diverse workforce should include (1) securing top management leadership and commitment, (2) organizational assessment, (3) attracting employees, (4) training employees in diversity, and (5) retaining employees. But beyond an organizationwide effort, each of these elements will also require the personal commitment of individual managers, who will address the issues involved as seriously as they do other management challenges. They will actively seek to develop the skills, understanding, and practices that enable people of every background to do their best work in the common pursuit of the organization's goals.

Top Management Leadership and Commitment

Obtaining top management leadership and commitment is critical for diversity programs to succeed. Otherwise, the rest of the organization will not take the effort seriously. One way to communicate this commitment to all employees—as well as to the external environment—is to incorporate the organization's attitudes toward diversity into the corporate mission statement and into strategic plans and objectives. Managerial compensation can be linked directly to accomplishing diversity goals. Adequate funding must be allocated to the diversity effort to ensure its success. Also, top management can set an example for other organization members by participating in diversity programs and making participation mandatory for all managers.

As we mentioned earlier, some organizations have established corporate offices or committees to coordinate the companywide diversity effort and provide feedback to top management. Digital Equipment Corporation hired a "director of valuing differences," Honeywell, a "director of workforce diversity," and Avon, a "director of multicultural planning and design." Other companies prefer to incorporate diversity management into the function of director of affirmative action or EEO.

> "Diversity: The art of thinking independently together."
> Malcolm Forbes

The work of managing diversity cannot be done by top management or diversity directors alone. Many companies rely on minority advisory groups or task forces to monitor organizational policies, practices, and attitudes; assess their impact on the diverse groups within the organization; and provide feedback and suggestions to top management.

For example, at Digital Equipment Corporation employees from different backgrounds form small groups to address stereotypes and other relevant issues. At Equitable Life Assurance Society, employee groups meet regularly with the CEO to discuss issues pertaining to women, African-Americans, and Hispanics and make recommendations for improvement. At Honeywell, disabled employees formed a council to discuss their needs. They proposed and accepted an accessibility program that went beyond federal regulations for accommodations of disabilities.

As you can see, progressive companies are moving from asking managers what they think minority employees need to asking the employees themselves what they need.

Organizational Assessment

The next step in managing diversity is to establish an ongoing assessment of the organization's workforce, culture, policies, and practices in areas such as recruitment, promotions, benefits, and compensation. As part of this assessment, managers may evaluate whether they are attracting their share of diverse candidates from the labor pool and whether the needs of their customers are being addressed by the current composition of their workforce. The objective is to identify problem areas and make recommendations where changes are needed.

For example, many women and Asians can be at a disadvantage when aggressiveness is a valued part of an organization's culture. Analysis might reveal that this value exists and that it excludes employees who do not share it from full participation. Managers can then decide that the organizational values need to be changed so other styles of interacting are equally acceptable. Managers can also change their own behaviors to reflect this change—for example, by calling on all individuals in a meeting for their ideas instead of letting more assertive participants dominate. Corporate values and norms should be identified and critically evaluated regarding their necessity and their impact on the diverse workforce.

Attracting Employees

Companies can attract a diverse, qualified workforce by using effective recruiting practices, accommodating employees' work and family needs, and offering alternative work arrangements.

Recruitment   A company's image can be a strong recruiting tool. Companies with reputations for hiring and promoting all types of people have a competitive advantage. Xerox gives prospective minority employees reprints of an article that rates the company as one of the best places for African-Americans to work. Hewlett-Packard ensures that its female candidates are familiar with its high rating by *Working Woman* magazine. Many employers are implementing policies to attract more women, ensure that women's talents are used to full advantage, and avoid losing their most capable female employees.

Many minorities and economically disadvantaged people are physically isolated from job opportunities. Companies can bring information about job opportunities to

Pictured here is Anja Mansfield, corporate recruiter with Howard Industries. Smart companies strive to beat their competitors by hiring a more diverse workforce, believing the move will ultimately result in broader market share.

the source of labor, or they can transport the labor to the jobs. Polycast Technology in Stamford, Connecticut, contracts with a private van company to transport workers from the Bronx in New York City to jobs in Stamford. Days Inn recruits homeless workers in Atlanta and houses them in a motel within walking distance of their jobs. Burger King has done a lot to recruit and hire immigrants in its fast-food restaurants.

Connections: EVERYONE KNOWS WOMEN CAN'T PLAY

For African-American musicians, the use of blind auditions also eliminated the direct effect of discrimination. U.S. symphony orchestras were made up exclusively of white musicians until the late 1950s, when the Cleveland Orchestra first broke the color line by hiring an African-American cellist. Still, discrimination continued until the use of audition screens gave African-American, Hispanic, and other minority musicians the opportunity to be evaluated by their talent alone.

Minority musicians have remained underrepresented in symphony orchestras, but less because of discrimination than because of their lack of access to the world of classical music, instruments, and training. To increase the available pool of classical minority musicians, many orchestras have launched outreach and scholarship programs. For example, the Chicago Symphony Orchestra offers a Diversity Fellowship Program for young string players. The intent of the program is to increase the number of minority musicians who qualify for auditions. In addition, the Sphinx Organization, founded in the late 1990s by Aaron Dworkin, an African-American violinist and composer, holds national competitions for young African-American instrumentalists and works to attract more minorities to the classical music profession.

Seeing the Benefits of Hiring the Blind

For blind people, finding a job is likely to involve a lot of search effort. Even the simplest things, such as filling out a job application, can pose problems; not very many applications come in a Braille version.

Barry Honig heads the executive-placement firm Riskon in New York City. Honig takes a special interest in helping people with disabilities find jobs, especially the blind. Why? Because he is blind. He says clients want to hire people with disabilities but often are confused about the steps they need to take and the accommodations they need to make.

In recent years, assistive technology has been the key to putting many visually impaired people into the marketplace by allowing them to do things such as operate computers. Low-tech and high-tech solutions both exist. Low-tech solutions include something as simple as putting silicon on a knob to let blind employees know if an operating switch is on or off or putting Braille labels on vending machines in break rooms. High-tech devices enlarge type on computers, produce a synthesized voice that reads the content aloud, and translate the output into Braille. "Window-Eyes," a Windows-based screen reader, is a top-selling enlargement product. JAWS (Job Access with Speech) for Windows speaks the letters on the keyboard as a blind person types them. Using Scan N Talk, a person who is blind can simply push a button and the device will read aloud a book, newspaper, magazine, mail, and so forth. Scan N Talk can also save the copy as text (which can then be enlarged and read) or as Braille. Products like these can range in cost from just a couple of hundred to thousands of dollars.

But the issue isn't just about companies having the right technology and the money to spend on it—it's about having the right mindset for hiring the blind. Honig says that during the first meeting with a candidate, an interviewer should ask if the blind person needs help—but not insist on giving it. He or she also should realize that visually impaired persons

Technology solutions allow the visually impaired to operate computers, making the workplace more diverse.

won't be familiar with the layout of the office and should ask them if extending an arm for guidance would help. And, of course, don't pet or distract seeing-eye dogs. As for applicants, Honig advises: "Be up-front and be comfortable about your disability. Ask the question, 'How am I going to do my job?' And be very honest with the answer."

Honig, who worked on Wall Street for several years, says that the financial services industry is a good hunting ground for the blind: "It's rough and tumble, especially on Wall Street, but people have no problem hiring the disabled as long as they can make them money." Technology industries are also good because people working in that field are used to thinking of technology as a "barrier-breaking tool."

The tech industry is where Margaret Redman and her husband, David, work. Both are visually impaired and are employed by Earthlink in technology support. David was the first visually impaired person in the company. "My husband and I showed them that a blind person could be a [tech assistant] on the phones, so they hired more blind people, who we both trained," Margaret Redman explains.

At any time, any one of us can become temporarily or permanently disabled. As the baby boomers in the workforce age, for example, many of them will experience diminished sight or other disabilities. Honig says that companies want to do the right thing but sometimes need a little push to understand the benefits of hiring the blind. "I know having a disability is a life of being told what your limits are by employers and co-workers," says Margaret Redman. "But my husband and I have been working to push the limits people and companies think of."

SOURCE: "Mobile Speech Software to Benefit Blind Users," *Computer Weekly,* January 25, 2005, p. 8; Suzanne Robitaille, "Bringing the Blind into the Workplace," *Business Week Online,* January 23, 2002.

Accommodating Work and Family Needs   More job seekers are putting family needs first. Corporate work and family policies are now one of the most important recruiting tools.

Employers that have adopted on-site child care report decreased turnover and absenteeism and improved morale. In addition to providing child care, many companies now assist with care for elderly dependents, offer time off to care for sick family members, provide parental leaves of absence, and offer a variety of benefits that can be tailored to individual family needs. Some companies are accommodating the needs and concerns of dual-career couples by limiting relocation requirements or providing job search assistance to relocated spouses.

Alternative Work Arrangements   Another way managers accommodate diversity is to offer flexible work schedules and arrangements. When the New Haven region of People's Bank based in Bridgeport, Connecticut, was having difficulty recruiting part-time tellers, the region's employee relations specialist initiated the Working Parent Program. The program allowed part-timers to schedule their hours to coincide with their children's: home by 3 P.M., with summers and school holidays off. Staffing problems were solved by being flexible, using part-timers to cover peak hours, and hiring college students to fill in during holidays and summers.[32]

Other creative work arrangements include compressed workweeks (for example, four 10-hour days) and job sharing, in which two part-time workers share one full-time job. Another option to accommodate working mothers and the disabled is teleworking (working from home) or telecommuting (working from home via computer hookup to the main work site). This option has been slow to catch on, but the organizations that have tried it report favorable results.

Training Employees

As you learned in Chapter 10, employees can be developed in a variety of ways. Traditionally, most management training has been based on the unstated assumption that "managing" means managing a homogeneous, often white-male, full-time workforce. But gender, race, culture, and other differences create an additional layer of complexity.[33] Diversity training programs attempt to identify and reduce hidden biases and develop the skills needed to manage a diversified workforce effectively.

More than 50 percent of all U.S. organizations sponsor some sort of diversity training. Typically, diversity training has two components: awareness building and skill building.

Awareness Building   *Awareness building* is designed to increase awareness of the meaning and importance of valuing diversity.[34] Its aim is not to teach specific skills but to sensitize employees to the assumptions they make about others and how those assumptions affect their behaviors, decisions, and judgment. For example, male managers who have never reported to a female manager may feel awkward the first time they are required to do so. Awareness-building can reveal this concern in advance and help the managers address it.

To build awareness, people are taught to become familiar with myths, stereotypes, and cultural differences as well as the organizational barriers that inhibit the full contributions of all employees. They develop a better understanding of corporate culture, requirements for success, and career choices that affect opportunities for advancement.

In most companies, the "rules" for success are ambiguous, unwritten, and perhaps inconsistent with written policy. A common problem for women and minorities is that they are unaware of many of the rules that are obvious to people in the mainstream. For example, organizations often have informal networks and power structures that may not be apparent or readily available to women and minority-group members. As a result, they are less likely to know where to go when they need to get something approved or when they want to build support and alliances. For managers, valuing diversity means teaching the unwritten "rules" or cultural values to those who need to know them and changing the rules when necessary to benefit employees and hence the organization. It also requires inviting "outsiders" in and giving them access to information and meaningful relationships with people in power.

Skill Building   Diversity training that merely identifies problems without giving participants the tools they need to be able to act on what they have learned may leave participants feeling that the training was not useful or worthwhile. For this reason, many organizations include skill building as part of a diversity program. *Skill building* is designed to allow all employees and managers to develop the skills they need to deal effectively with one another and with customers in a diverse environment. Most of the skills taught are interpersonal, such as active listening, coaching, and giving feedback. Ideally, the skills taught are based on the organizational assessment, so the training can be tailored to the specific business issues managers have identified. For example, if too many women and minorities feel they are not getting enough helpful feedback, the skills-building program can be designed to address that issue. Tying the training to specific, measurable business goals increases its usefulness and also allows managers to assess whether it is working.

Hewlett-Packard and Wisconsin Power and Light are examples of companies that provide both awareness and skill building. These companies attempt to transfer the training to the job by asking managers to develop personal action plans before they leave the program. For example, a manager may recognize from training that his record of retaining African-American sales representatives is poor and plan to spend more time coaching these salespeople.[35]

Experiential exercises and videotapes, DVDs, and software often are used in the training programs to help expose stereotypes and encourage employees to discuss fears, biases, and problems. Again, the best exercises will be related to the actual problems employees are likely to encounter in the workplace. For example, employees in a hospital diversity-training program may practice how to handle a white patient who asks to be treated only by a white doctor, or a male patient who only wants to be treated by a male doctor. Training ABC, Advanced Training Source, and American Training Resources are among the companies that offer such products. Table 11.8 provides a set of guidelines for designing effective diversity training.

TABLE 11.8
Guidelines for Diversity Training

1. **Position training in your broad diversity strategy.** Training is one important element of managing diversity, but on its own it will probably fail. Culture change means altering underlying assumptions and systems that guide organizational behavior. Training programs must be internally consistent with, and complement, other initiatives focused on culture change.

2. **Do a thorough needs analysis.** Do not start training prematurely. As with any training program, eagerness to "do something" may backfire unless you have assessed what specific aspects of diversity need attention first. Focus groups help identify what employees view as priority issues.

3. **Distinguish between education and training.** Education helps build awareness and understanding but does not teach usable skills. Training involves activities that enhance skills in areas such as coaching, conducting performance appraisals, and adapting communications styles. Education and training are both important but they're not the same.

4. **Use a participative design process.** Tap a multitude of parties to ensure that the content and tone of the program are suitable to everyone involved. Outsider consultants often provide fresh perspectives, and have credibility. Insiders have specific company knowledge, sensitivity to local issues, and long-standing relationships with company members. Balance these various sources.

5. **Test the training thoroughly before rollout.** Given the sensitivity, even volatility, of diversity issues, use diversity councils and advocacy groups to pilot the programs. Build in ample feedback time to allow these groups to address sensitive concerns, and refine the training.

6. **Incorporate diversity programs into the core training curriculum.** One-time programs do not have a lasting impact. Blend the program's content into other training programs such as performance appraisal, coaching, and so on.

Retaining Employees

As replacing qualified and experienced workers becomes more difficult and costly, retaining good workers will become much more important. Aetna estimates its annual turnover expense at more than $100 million—largely money spent on training new employees and the costs of their lower productivity during the learning period. When Deloitte & Touche had problems retaining minorities and women, top executives moved quickly. The firm not only ameliorated its problems; it created a more positive environment for all employees. A number of policies and strategies, like the following, can be used to increase retention of all employees, especially those who are "different" from the norm.[36]

> Retaining qualified employees increases workforce quality.

Support Groups   Companies can help form minority networks and other support groups to promote information exchange and social support. Support groups provide emotional and career support for members who traditionally have not been included in the majority's informal groups. They also can help diverse employees understand work norms and the corporate culture.

At Apple headquarters in Cupertino, California, support groups include a Jewish cultural group, a gay/lesbian group, an African-American group, and a technical women's group. Avon encourages employees to organize into African-American, Hispanic, and Asian networks by granting them official recognition and assigning a senior manager to provide advice. These groups help new employees adjust and provide direct feedback to management on problems that concern the groups. Avon once had a women's network, but that group disbanded years ago. With women holding a large majority percentage of management positions, female employees at Avon believed the group was no longer necessary.

> **mentors**
>
> Higher level managers who help ensure that high-potential people are introduced to top management and socialized into the norms and values of the organization.

Mentoring   Many people have been puzzled at the inability of women and minorities to move up beyond a certain point on the corporate ladder (the glass ceiling). To help these groups enter the informal network that provides exposure to top management and access to information about organizational politics, many companies have implemented formal mentoring programs. **Mentors** are higher-level managers who help ensure that high-potential people are introduced to top management and socialized into the norms and values of the organization.

Procter & Gamble's "Mentor Up" program has been working very successfully. The number of women at the general manager/vice-president level has more than tripled in the last decade. General Electric has formed a 10,000-strong women's network whose goal is to foster professional development and facilitate women's advancement.[37]

Career Development and Promotions   Because they are hitting a glass ceiling, many of the most talented women and minority group members are leaving their organizations in search of better opportunities elsewhere. In response, companies such as Mobil Oil and Honeywell have established teams to evaluate the career progress of women, minorities, and employees with disabilities and to devise ways to move them up through the ranks. One extremely important step is to make sure deserving employees get a chance at line positions. Women in particular are often relegated to staff positions, like Human Resources, with less opportunity to demonstrate they can earn money for their employers. Career

Bill Wear, a program manager for security at Hewlett-Packard, started out hacking into phone lines at the age of 10. At 14, he hacked into his school computer using a password he'd stolen from his guidance counselor. The counselor knew Wear had stolen the password, so he left this message for him: "I know that you're using my account. I also know about your father. I know he abuses you. I also know that we can do something. Call me. Let me help." The counselor helped get him into a private school, and through two engineering degrees. Wear today is a mentor. He even wrote a handbook for the company's e-mail-mentoring program.

development programs that give a wide range of employees exposure and experience in line jobs can make senior management positions more available to them.

Systems Accommodation   Managers can support diversity by recognizing cultural and religious holidays, differing modes of dress, and dietary restrictions, as well as accommodating the needs of individuals with disabilities. One important disabling condition is AIDS. Under the ADA, organizations must accommodate employees with AIDS as they would persons with any other disability, permitting and even encouraging them to continue working for as long as they are able and, if warranted, allowing flexible scheduling.

Accountability   For diversity efforts to succeed, managers must be held accountable for workforce development. Organizations must ensure that their performance appraisal and reward systems reinforce the importance of effective diversity management. Baxter Health Care, Coca-Cola, and Merck (as well as Prudential and Kodak, mentioned earlier) all tie compensation to managers' performance in diversity efforts.[38]

For 25 years, U.S. corporations were striving to integrate their workforces because of regulatory and social responsibility pressures. Today globalization, changing demographics, and the expansion of ethnic markets at home have made managing a diverse workforce a bottom-line issue. Managers and their companies now realize that to remain competitive in the coming years, they will have to make managing diversity a strategic priority to attract top talent.

EPILOGUE

EVERYONE KNOWS WOMEN CAN'T PLAY

The fact that women now play for symphony orchestras is not a trivial change. It matters because it has opened up a world of possibility for a group that had been locked out of opportunity. It also matters because by fixing the first impression at the heart of the audition—by judging purely on the basis of ability—orchestras now hire better musicians, and better musicians mean better music.

When Julie Landsman auditioned for the role of principal French horn at the Met, the screens had just gone up in the practice hall. At the time, there were no women in the brass section of the orchestra, because everyone "knew" that women could not play the horn as well as men. But Landsman came and sat down and played—and she played well. "I knew in my last round

that I had won before they told me," she says. "It was because of the way I performed the last piece. I held on to the last high C for a very long time, just to leave no doubt in their minds. And they started to laugh, because it was above and beyond the call of duty." But when they declared her the winner and she stepped out from behind the screen, there was a gasp. It wasn't just that she was a woman, and female horn players were rare. And it wasn't just that bold, extended high C, which was the kind of macho sound that they expected from a man only. It was because they *knew* her. Landsman had played for the Met before as a substitute. Until they listened to her with just their ears, however, they had no idea she was so good. The screen created a small miracle: They saw her for who she truly was.

KEY TERMS

Affirmative action, p. 371

Glass ceiling, p. 363

Managing diversity, p. 357

Mentors, p. 383

Monolithic organization, p. 375

Multicultural organization, p. 376

Pluralistic organization, p. 376

Sexual harassment, p. 363

SUMMARY OF LEARNING OBJECTIVES

Now that you have studied Chapter 11, you should know:

How changes in the U.S. workforce are making diversity a critical organizational and managerial issue.

The labor force is getting older and more ethnic, with a higher proportion of women. And while the absolute number of workers is increasing, the growth in jobs is outpacing the numerical growth of workers. In addition, the jobs that are being created frequently require higher skills than the typical worker can provide; thus, we are seeing a growing skills gap. To be competitive, organizations can no longer take the traditional approach of depending on white males to form the core of the workforce. Today, managers must look broadly to make use of talent wherever it can be found. As the labor market changes, organizations that can recruit, develop, motivate, and retain a diverse workforce will have a competitive advantage.

The distinction between affirmative action and managing diversity.

Affirmative action is designed to correct past exclusion of women and minorities from U.S. organizations. But despite the accomplishments of affirmative action, it has not eliminated barriers that prevent individuals from reaching their full potential. Managing diversity goes beyond hiring people who are different from the norm and seeks to support, nurture, and use employee differences to the organization's advantage.

How managers can gain a competitive edge by managing diversity effectively.

Managing diversity is a bottom-line issue. If managers are effective at managing diversity, they will have an easier time attracting, retaining, and motivating the best employees. They will be more effective at marketing to diverse consumer groups in the United States and globally. They will have a workforce that is more creative, more innovative, and better able to solve problems. In addition, they are likely to increase the flexibility and responsiveness of the organization to environmental change.

What challenges a manager is likely to encounter with a diverse workforce.

The challenges for managers created by a diverse workforce include decreased group cohesiveness, communication problems, mistrust and tension, and stereotyping. These challenges can be turned into advantages by means of training and effective management.

How managers and their organizations can take steps to cultivate diversity.

To be successful, organizational efforts to manage diversity must have top management support and commitment. Organizations should first undertake a thorough assessment of their cultures, policies, and practices, as well as the demographics of their labor pools and customer bases. Only after this diagnosis has been completed is a company in position to initiate programs designed to attract, develop, motivate, and retain a diverse workforce.

DISCUSSION QUESTIONS

1. What opportunities do you see as a result of changes in our nation's workforce?

2. Is prejudice declining in our society? In our organizations? Why or why not?

3. What distinctions can you make between affirmative action and managing diversity?

4. How can we overcome obstacles to diversity such as mistrust and tension, stereotyping, and communication problems?

5. How can organizations meet the special needs of different groups (e.g., work and family issues) without appearing to show favoritism to those particular sets of employees?

6. How can diversity give a company a competitive edge? Can diversity really make a difference in the bottom line? How?

CONCLUDING CASE

The New Guys Take Over

The inland Mid-Atlantic State region of the country is a rural area that includes a large number of isolated population centers. Small towns of 5,000 to 15,000 people are separated by ten- to thirty-mile stretches of woods and mountains. These "pockets of people" are viewed as "captive audiences of employees" in some business circles. Because of the travel distance between towns, these small population centers offer a finite number of job opportunities. There tends to be a relatively large number of small employers (the local post office, bank, convenience store, pizza/sub shop and so on) and a very small number of large employers (one or two in-town factories).

Jim Brennan returned to his rural Virginia birthplace following the Vietnam conflict to achieve his goal of building and owning his own business and being his own boss. Jim was raised with an iron fist in the conservative old traditions of post World War II America. "The boss is the boss. Do what you're told and don't ask questions. Men hunt, fish, work, bring home the bacon and rule the roost." These are just a few of Jim's beliefs.

Jim saw the opportunity to capitalize on the captive audience of employees in his hometown. The community never seemed to have enough jobs to feed the people. It is a rather dreary town characterized by high unemployment, old trailer parks, buildings that resemble shacks rather than houses, an average education level of 11th grade, a high level of alcoholism, lots of very old cars and not much hope for the future.

The population is very diverse and includes a mix of ethnic races, education levels and social classes. Most of the towns include pockets of immigrants—new neighborhoods where many of the people do not speak English. All of this made Jim's eyes light up. He saw this as a way to build an enterprise, hire cheap help, work them hard, give them little or no benefits, make a lot of money and rule the roost of his business as well as his home. Jim purchased a deserted old warehouse and transformed it into a factory that processed, packaged and shipped smoked and dried fish specialty products to retailers and consumers nationwide. Jim hired a few of the "bright folks," as he put it, to act as foremen and to run the office. The production and shipping process was set up with 33 workstations.

Jim's attitude towards his workers and the workforce in general is that "they are all lazy, will only work out of necessity and need to be constantly watched and yelled at to stay in line." In fact, Jim typically carried about 45 production people on the payroll, figuring that it takes that many in order for 33 to actually show up for work. On those rare occasions when more than 33 did show up, Jim would either have them sweep the floor or would just send them home for the day.

Production workers were paid minimum wage with no benefits. The hours varied depending on the number of orders on file. Jim would run the plant for upwards of 60 or 70 hours per week during the busy periods and for as little as 25 or 30 hours during slow times. He simply hired and fired people as needed.

Over time, Jim found himself with "a steady bunch of about 15 or 20 good help," as he put it, who were paid a higher wage—the rest just came and went, bouncing between unemployment, welfare and the other factory in town. Jim's factory is a depressing place. There is no lunch- or break-room and the bathroom looks and smells as if it has never been cleaned. The floor is concrete—hard and cold on the feet. The inside of the building is a sweatbox in the summer and an icebox in the winter; it's poorly lit and it smells.

Jim is quite proud of himself. He's making lots of money and comes and goes as he pleases. He has even found the time to eliminate most of his wholesale suppliers by dealing directly with fishermen. He has set up a number of "cash and other private arrangements" to buy raw materials without having to work through proper channels. On the sales side, he has learned that he can "get away with murder by shorting certain customers 'cause they're too stupid to weigh the stuff." Jim has also been known to add weight to some shipments by soaking them with water and/or adding ice. Jim avoids paying overtime to his workers by shifting wages from one week to the next when someone exceeds forty hours.

The company has been cited and fined a number of times by state and federal agencies for assorted other violations such as overweight trucks, workplace safety hazards and delinquent taxes, but Jim simply views this as "the cost of being in business." He figures that the money he's made on the side far outweighs the fines that he has paid.

Shortly after Jim's 15th year in business, he was approached by a Canadian fishing conglomerate that has been buying up small businesses throughout the Eastern U.S. and Canada as part of a plan to expand their production and sales capabilities.

This is a first-class company and group of people that run a very successful and professional operation. In fact, the company's slogan is "our success is the result of our most important resource—our people." The purchase included a no competition clause that Jim was required to sign, whereby he agreed to cease all related business operations for a period of five years within 100 miles of the plant.

QUESTIONS

1. The new owners have inherited a very diverse group of workers, suppliers and customers, and a long history of questionable business practices. What transition strategies would you implement in both the short- and long-term?

2. Given the wide-ranging age and mix of employees, how would you expand this operation over time using the chapter's personnel-management concepts and techniques?

EXPERIENTIAL EXERCISES

11.1 Being Different

OBJECTIVES

1. To increase your awareness of the feeling of "being different."

2. To better understand the context of "being different."

INSTRUCTIONS

1. Working alone, complete the Being Different Worksheet.

2. In small groups, compare worksheets and prepare answers to the discussion questions.

3. When the class reconvenes, group spokespersons present group findings.

DISCUSSION QUESTIONS

1. Were there students who experienced being different in situations that surprised you?

2. How would you define "being different"?

3. How can this exercise be used to good advantage?

Being Different Worksheet

Think back to a recent situation in which you experienced "being different" and answer the following questions:

1. Describe the situation in which you experienced "being different."

_____

_____

2. Explain how you felt.

_____

_____

3. What did you do as a result of "being different"? (That is, in what way was your behavior changed by the feeling of "being different"?)

_____

_____

4. What did others in the situation do? How do you think they felt about the situation?

_____

_____

_____

5. How did the situation turn out in the end?

_____

_____

6. As a result of that event, how will you probably behave differently in the future? In what way has the situation changed you?

_____

_____

11.2 Gender Stereotypes

PART I

Your instructor will divide the group into smaller groups based on gender, resulting in male-only and female-only groups. Groups are to brainstorm a list in response to the following statements. It is not necessary for all members to agree with everything the group generates. Add all inputs to the list.

Female groups complete the following:
- All men are _____
- Men think all women are _____

Male groups complete the following:
- All women are _____
- Women think all men are _____

PART II

After generating your lists, your groups will present a role-play to the class based on the following scenarios by switching gender roles (females portray males, and males portray females):

Two friends (of the same gender) meeting each other back at school for the first time this year.

A person flirting with a member of the opposite sex at a party. (Females play a male flirting with a female; males play a female flirting with a male.)

Questions:
1. What aspects of the role-plays were accurate, distorted, or inaccurate?
2. How did you feel portraying the opposite gender and how did it feel to see your gender portrayed?
3. On what stereotypes or experiences were these role-plays based?

PART III

Your group will now write its brainstorm lists on the board for discussion. Remember that these lists are a product of a group effort and are generally based on stereotypes and not necessarily the view of any one individual.

Analyze the lists for positive and negative results in both personal and professional settings. Generate a list of ways to dispel, reduce, or counter negative stereotypes.

Questions:
1. What similarities, patterns, or trends developed from the groups?
2. How do you feel about the thoughts presented about your gender?
3. What implications do these thoughts have on actions and situations in the work environment?
4. What can you do to reduce the negative affects of these stereotypes? What can you do to help dispel these stereotypes? (Brainstorm with your group or class.)

SOURCE: Portions of this exercise are adapted from concepts in Susan F. Fritz, William Brown, Joyce Lunde, and Elizabeth Banset, *Interpersonal Skills for Leadership* (Englewood Cliffs, NJ: Prentice Hall, 1999); and A. B. Shani and James B. Lau, *Behavior in Organizations: An Experiential Approach,* Sixth Ed. (Chicago: Irwin, 1996).

11.3 He Works, She Works

INSTRUCTIONS

1. Complete the He Works, She Works Worksheet. In the appropriate spaces, write what you think the stereotyped responses would be. Do not spend too much time considering any one item. Rather, respond quickly and let your first impression or thought guide your answer.

2. Compare your individual responses with those of other class members or participants. It is interesting to identify and discuss the most frequently used stereotypes.

He Works, She Works Worksheet

The family picture is on *his* desk: *He's a solid, responsible family man.*

His desk is cluttered: _____
_____

He's talking with co-workers: _____
_____

He's not at his desk: _____
_____

He's not in the office: _____
_____

The family picture is on *her* desk: *Her family will come before her career.*

Her desk is cluttered: _____
_____

She's talking with co-workers: _____
_____

She's not at her desk: _____
_____

She's not in the office: _____
_____

The family picture is on *his* desk: *He's a solid, responsible family man.*

He's having lunch with the boss: _____
_____

The boss criticized *him:* _____
_____

He got an unfair deal: _____
_____

He's getting married: _____
_____

He's going on a business trip: _____
_____

He's leaving for a better job: _____
_____

The family picture is on *her* desk: *Her family will come before her career.*

She's having lunch with the boss: _____
_____

The boss criticized *her:* _____

_____

She got an unfair deal: _____

_____

She's getting married: _____

_____

She's going on a business trip: _____

_____

She's leaving for a better job: _____

_____

SOURCE: F. Luthans, *Organizational Behavior.* Copyright © 1989 by The McGraw-Hill Companies. Reproduced with the permission of The McGraw-Hill Companies.

PART 3 SUPPORTING CASE

Pension Benefits Guaranty Corporation to the Rescue: Is It Time for Pension Reform?

On September 2, 1974, President Gerald R. Ford signed The Employee Retirement Income Security Act (ERISA) into law, and created the Pension Benefits Guaranty Corporation (PBGC), a "government-sponsored insurer of private pension plans," to protect the pensions of workers. When participating companies declare bankruptcy or face other pension-related problems, PBGC races to the rescue and guarantees employees will continue to receive a pension. PBGC covers retirees who receive "defined" or "fixed" benefits. Under this pension scheme, retirees are paid a monthly payout based on their salary and years of service to a company.

PBGC offers two types of pension insurance: 1) a single employer program which includes some 35 million working and retired people enrolled in nearly 30,000 pension plans, and 2) a multi-employer program which includes almost 10 million working and retired people enrolled in more than 1,500 pension plans. It pays more than 500,000 retired people in nearly 3,500 terminated pension funds. PBGC generates revenues from several sources: insurance premiums paid by participating employers, its investments, and when it absorbs failing pension plans.

In recent years, the airline industry has caused PBGC to work overtime. Some airline companies have inadequately funded their pension plans and they are unable to continue paying pensions to their retirees. For example, when Pan Am went bankrupt some 15 years ago and many employees who worked at the company for 20 to 30 years lost their pensions, PBGC came to the rescue and bailed out Pan Am's pension program. More recently, two major airlines, US Airways and United Airlines, have fallen into serious financial troubled times. In 2003, PBGC took over US Airways' pilots' pension obligations. In December 2004, PBGC took over United Airlines pilots' pension program to the tune of about $1.4 billion. In 2005, PBGC took over US Airways' flight attendants' and mechanics' pension plan. All told, the bailouts of these two airlines cost PBGC approximately $4 billion and have placed a tremendous financial strain on the government-sponsored agency's resources. Recent financial analyses of Delta Airlines suggest that it too may be headed down the same path as US Airways and United Airlines.

According to The Center on Federal Financial Institution (CFFI), a nonprofit Washington, DC policy institute, all is not well at PBGC. This nonpartisan organization has raised serious concerns about the financial health of PBGC, and its continued ability to bail out failing pension plans. In 2003, PBGC had an $11 billion deficit which has more than doubled in 2004 to $23 billion. The agency's current and future financial obligations to pensioners are projected to include more than one million retired people. Moreover, one projection by CFFI suggests that PBGC may not have enough money to support payments to pensioners in 15 years. Such gloomy projections have caused Elaine Chao, the US Secretary of Labor, in January 2005, to develop a plan so that the government-sponsored agency can survive. Perhaps it is time for companies to change defined benefits pension plans in favor of other plans, such as a defined contribution plans that provide benefits based on employee and employer contributions rather than a monthly guarantee.

QUESTIONS

1. As a future full-time employee, would you prefer a defined pension benefit or a defined contribution plan? Why?

2. Pension benefits are costly; yet, workers need them desperately. Are there any ways managers can ensure employee pension plans are protected?

3. When a company goes bankrupt, should the federal government bail out pension funds? Why? Why not?

SOURCES: This case was prepared by Joseph C. Santora who is a professor of business administration at Essex County College, Newark, New Jersey. N. Byrnes. 2004. "The coming pension crunch," *BusinessWeek Online,* September 15, 2004; D. Elliot, "PBGC: Effects of US Air and UAL Terminations," Center on Federal Financial Institutions, 2004, *http://www.coffi.org;* A Newman, ed., "Pension Reform: Next?" *BusinessWeek,* January 24, 2005, p. 46; *http://www.pbgc.gov/about/default.htm.*

PART
FOUR

Foundations of Management
- Managing
- The External Environment and Organizational Culture
- Managerial Decision Making

Planning: Delivering Strategic Value
- Planning and Strategic Management
- Ethics and Corporate Responsibility
- International Management
- Entrepreneurship

Strategy Implementation

Organizing: Building a Dynamic Organization
- Organization Structure
- Organizational Agility
- Human Resources Management
- Managing the Diverse Workforce

Leading: Mobilizing People
- Leadership
- Motivating for Performance
- Teamwork
- Communicating

Controlling: Learning and Changing
- Managerial Control
- Managing Technology and Innovation
- Creating and Managing Change

Leading: Mobilizing People

Now that you know about planning and organizing, Part 4 elaborates on managing people by discussing the third function of management: leading. Effective managers know how to lead others toward unit and organizational success. Chapter 12 explores the essential components of leadership, including the use of power in the organization. Chapter 13 focuses on motivating people, with implications for enhancing performance. Chapter 14 examines teamwork, including the management of relationships between teams. Finally, Chapter 15 addresses a vital management activity: communication. Here, you will learn how to maximize your effectiveness in communicating with other people throughout the organization.

Chapter **12**

CHAPTER 12
Leadership

Every soldier has a right to competent command.

—Julius Caesar

CHAPTER OUTLINE

LEARNING OBJECTIVES

After studying Chapter 12, you will know:

1. What it means to be a leader.

2. What people want and organizations need from leaders.

3. How a good vision helps you be a better leader.

4. How to understand and use power.

5. The personal traits and skills of effective leaders.

6. The behaviors that will make you a better leader.

7. What it means to be a charismatic and transformational leader.

8. The many types of opportunities to be a leader in an organization.

9. How to further your own leadership development.

ANDREA JUNG AND AVON'S EXTREME MAKEOVER

Andrea Jung took over as CEO of Avon in 1999, and she gave the company an extreme makeover. The first woman CEO in Avon history (think about that, given the company's products and customers), she tackled what may have been the toughest turnaround challenge in consumer products. Avon's traditional door-to-door, direct sales model, begun in the 19th century, now seemed antiquated. It was up to Jung to make sure the old company with an old business model survived in the modern era.

After becoming CEO, Jung sold Avon products door to door, learning in the process about the customers and the challenges facing her sales force. Once she knew Avon's shortcomings, she established a turnaround plan. The plan was highly ambitious, and most people thought she couldn't pull it off. One analyst reported that the plan had "a high probability of disappointment." But Jung has, in fact, succeeded.

Sources for Prologue, Connections, Epilogue: R. Setoodeh, "Andrea Jung," *Newsweek*, December 27, 2004, pp. 98–100; N. Byrnes, "Avon: The New Calling," *BusinessWeek*, September 18, 2000, pp. 137–148; A. Harrintong and P. Bartosiewicz, "Who's Up? Who's Down?" *Fortune*, October 18, 2004, pp. 181–90; K. Brooker, "It Took a Lady to save Avon," *Fortune*, October 15, 2001, pp. 202–8.

People get excited about the topic of leadership. They want to know: What makes a great leader? Executives at all levels in all industries are interested in this question. They believe the answer will bring improved organizational performance and personal career success. They hope to acquire the skills that will transform an "average" manager into a true leader.

Fortunately, leadership can be taught—and learned. Companies annually spend about $50 billion on leadership training.[1] According to one source, "Leadership seems to be the marshaling of skills possessed by a majority but used by a minority. But it's something that can be learned by anyone, taught to everyone, denied to no one."[2]

What is leadership? To start, a leader is one who influences others to attain goals. The greater the number of followers, the greater the influence. And the more successful the attainment of worthy goals, the more evident the leadership. But we must explore beyond this bare definition to capture the excitement and intrigue that devoted followers and students of leadership feel when they see a great leader in action, to understand what organizational leaders really do, and to learn what it really takes to become a truly outstanding leader.

Outstanding leaders combine good strategic substance and effective interpersonal processes to formulate and implement strategies that produce results and sustainable competitive advantage.[3] They may launch enterprises, build organization cultures, win wars, or otherwise change the course of events.[4] They are strategists who seize opportunities others overlook, but "they are also passionately concerned with detail—all the small, fundamental realities that can make or mar the grandest of plans."[5]

What Do We Want from Our Leaders?

What do people want from their leaders? Broadly speaking, they want help in achieving their goals.[6] This includes not just more pay and promotions, but support for their development, clearing obstacles so they can perform at high levels, and treatment that is respectful, fair, and ethical. Leaders serve people best when they help them develop their own initiative and good judgment, enable them to grow, and help them become better contributors. People want the kinds of things you will read about in this chapter and that are found in other chapters in this book.

What do organizations need? Organizations need people at all levels to be leaders. Leaders throughout the organization are needed to do the things that their people want, but also to help create and implement strategic direction.

These two perspectives—what people want and what organizations need—are neatly combined in a set of five key behaviors identified by James Kouzes and Barry Posner, two well-known authors and consultants.[7] The best leaders (1) *challenge the process*—they challenge conventional beliefs and practices, and they create change; (2) *inspire a shared vision*—they appeal to people's values and motivate them to care about an important mission; (3) *enable others to act*—they give people access to information and give them the power to perform to their full potential; (4) *model the way*—they don't just tell people what to do, they are living examples of the ideals they believe in; and (5) *encourage the heart*—they show appreciation, provide rewards, and use various approaches to motivate people in positive ways.

You will read about these and other aspects of leadership in this and the following chapters. The things we discuss will not only help you become a better leader; they'll give you benchmarks that will help you assess the competence and fairness with which your boss manages you.

Vision

"The leader's job is to create a vision," stated Robert L. Swiggett, former chair of Kollmorgen Corporation.[8] Until a few years ago, *vision* was not a word one heard managers utter. But today, having a vision for the future and communicating that vision to others are known to be essential components of great leadership. "If there is no vision, there is no business," maintains entrepreneur Mark Leslie.[9] Joe Nevin, an MIS director, described leaders as "painters of the vision and architects of the journey."[10] Practicing businesspeople are not alone in this belief; academic research shows that a clear vision and communication of that vision lead to higher venture growth in entrepreneurial firms.[11]

A **vision** is a mental image of a possible and desirable future state of the organization. It expresses the leader's ambitions for the organization.[12] A leader can create a vision that describes high performance aspirations, the nature of corporate or business strategy, or even the kind of workplace worth building. The best visions are both ideal and unique.[13] If a vision conveys an *ideal*, it communicates a standard of excellence and a clear choice of positive values. If the vision is also *unique*, it communicates and inspires pride in being different from other organizations. The choice of language is important; the words should imply a combination of realism and optimism, an action orientation, and resolution and confidence that the vision will be attained.[14]

Visions can be small or large and can exist throughout all organizational levels as well as at the very top. The important points are that (1) a vision is necessary for effective leadership; (2) a person or team can develop a vision for any job, work unit, or organization; and (3) many people, including managers who do not develop into strong leaders, do not develop a clear vision—instead, they focus on performing or surviving on a day-by-day basis.

Put another way, leaders must know what they want.[15] And other people must understand what that is. The leader must be able to articulate the vision, clearly and often. Other people throughout the organization should understand the vision and be able to state it clearly themselves. That's a start. But the vision means nothing until the leader and followers take action to turn the vision into reality.[16]

A metaphor reinforces the important concept of vision.[17] Putting a jigsaw puzzle together is much easier if you have the picture on the box cover in front of you. Without the picture, or vision, the lack of direction is likely to result in frustration and failure. That is what communicating a vision is all about: making it clear where you are heading.

Not just any vision will do. Visions can be inappropriate, and even fail, for a variety of reasons.[18] First, an inappropriate vision may reflect merely the leader's personal needs. Such a vision can be unethical, or it may fail because of lack of acceptance by the market or by those who must implement it.

Second (and related to the first), an inappropriate vision may ignore stakeholder needs. Third, the leader must stay abreast of environmental changes. Although effective leaders maintain confidence and persevere despite obstacles, the time may come when the facts dictate that the vision must change. You will learn more about change and how to manage it later in the text.

Where do visions come from?[19] Leaders should be sensitive to emerging opportunities, develop the right capabilities or worldviews, and not be overly invested in the status quo. You also can capitalize on networks of insightful individuals who have ideas about the future. Some visions are accidental; a company may stumble into an opportunity, and the leader may get credit for foresight. And some leaders and companies launch many new initiatives and, through trial and error, occasional home runs occur. If the company learns from these successes, the "vision" emerges.

vision

A mental image of a possible and desirable future state of the organization.

You can't perform in the long run if you don't have a vision of what you want to accomplish.

Imagine trying to complete a challenging jigsaw puzzle without the "vision" of what you're working toward.

Leading and Managing

Effective managers are not necessarily true leaders. Many administrators, supervisors, and even top executives execute their responsibilities successfully without being great leaders. But these positions afford opportunity for leadership. The ability to lead effectively, then, will set the excellent managers apart from the average ones.

Whereas management must deal with the ongoing, day-to-day complexities of organizations, true leadership includes effectively orchestrating important change.[20] While managing requires planning and budgeting routines, leading includes setting the direction (creating a vision) for the firm. Management requires structuring the organization, staffing it with capable people, and monitoring activities; leadership goes beyond these functions by inspiring people to attain the vision. Great leaders keep people focused on moving the organization toward its ideal future, motivating them to overcome whatever obstacles lie in the way.

Many observers decry the rarity of good leadership.[21] While many managers focus on superficial activities and worry about short-term profits and stock prices, too few have emerged as leaders who foster innovation and the attainment of long-term goals. And whereas many managers are overly concerned with "fitting in" and not rocking the boat, those who emerge as leaders are more concerned with making important decisions that may break with tradition but are humane, moral, and right. The leader puts a premium on substance rather than on style.

It is important to be clear here about several things. First, management and leadership are both vitally important. To highlight the need for more leadership is not to minimize the importance of management or managers. It is to say that leadership involves unique processes that are distinguishable from basic management processes.[22] Moreover, just because they involve different processes does not mean that they require different, separate people. The same individual can exemplify effective managerial processes, leadership processes, both, or neither.

Some people dislike the idea of distinguishing between management and leadership, maintaining it is artificial or derogatory toward the managers and the management processes that make orgnizations run. Perhaps a better or more useful distinction is between supervisory and strategic leadership.[23] **Supervisory leadership** is behavior that provides guidance, support, and corrective feedback for day-to-day activities. **Strategic leadership** gives purpose and meaning to organizations. Strategic leadership involves anticipating and envisioning a viable future for the organization, and working with others to initiate changes that create such a future.[24]

supervisory leadership

Behavior that provides guidance, support, and corrective feedback for day-to-day activities.

strategic leadership

Behavior that gives purpose and meaning to organizations, envisioning and creating a positive future.

Sports teams, like leaders, have followers. When the father-and-son team of Cablevision Systems Corporation, Chairman Charles F. Dolan and CEO James L. Dolan, decided not to include the New York Yankees Entertainment & Sports Network as part of its basic offerings, diehard Yankees fans said, "Na na, hey hey, goodbye." As the Dolans found out, a leader's decisions clearly affect the attitudes and behaviors of followers.

Leading and Following

Organizations succeed or fail not only because of how well they are led but because of how well followers follow. Just as managers are not necessarily good leaders, people are not always good followers. As one leadership scholar puts it, "Executives are given subordinates; they have to earn followers" (p. 240).[25] But it's also true that good followers help produce good leaders.

As a manager, you will be asked to play the roles of both leader and follower. As you lead the people who report to you, you will report to your boss. You will be a member of some teams and committees, and you may head others. While the leadership roles get the glamour and therefore are the roles that many people covet, followers must perform their responsibilities conscientiously and well.

Good followership doesn't mean merely obeying orders (although some bosses may view it that way). The most effective followers are capable of independent thinking and at the same time are actively committed to organizational goals.[26] Robert Townsend, who led a legendary turnaround at Avis, says that the most important characteristic of a follower may be the willingness to tell the truth.[27]

Effective followers also distinguish themselves from ineffective ones by their enthusiasm and commitment to the organiza-
tion and to a person or purpose—an idea, a
product—other than themselves or their own
interests. They master skills that are useful to
their organizations, and they hold perform-
ance standards that are higher than required. Effective followers may not get the glory,
but they know their contributions to the organization are valuable. And as they make
those contributions, they study leaders in preparation for their own leadership roles.[29]

> What are the failures of followership? Here's one answer: apathy, passivity,
> cynicism, and noninvolvement that invite leaders' abuse of power.[28]

Advantages of Collaboration

Imagine the potential of reframing the boss–subordinate relationship as a true collaboration in which leader and follower both try to help one another improve their effectiveness.

Connections: ANDREA JUNG AND AVON

Andrea Jung had very little operating experience when she took over at Avon. Suddenly
she was running a company with 3 million sales reps and operations in 137 countries. She
vowed to make Avon as big in the women's beauty business as Disney is in entertainment.
She wants Avon to be the "ultimate relationship marketer of products and services for
women."

She knew the Internet was key to implementing her vision, but she faced a big challenge:
figuring out how the traditional Avon reps would fit in. The reps produced 98 percent of
the company's revenues, acting as the backbone of the company and epitomizing its brand
image throughout Avon's history. Jung said, "If we don't include them in everything we do,
then we're just another retail brand, just another Internet site, and I don't see the world
needing more of those." Jung surveyed the reps about the Web site and created incentives
for them to get involved. She involved both the computer-savvy and the computer-illiterate
in the process. Among other things, the site asked customers if they want a personal eRep-
resentative in their zip code. "What we do is about relationships, affiliations, being with
other people. That is never going to go out."

Jung needed the support of those millions of independent sales reps and employees to
get today's women to buy an old brand. Addressing 13,000 reps at a sales convention, she
stated, "Avon is first and foremost about you. I stand here before you and promise you that
that will never change." To women in a Chinese factory, she said "We will change the future of women around the world!"

Power and Leadership

Central to effective leadership is **power**—the ability to influence other people. In organizations, this often means the ability to get things done or accomplish one's goals
despite resistance from others.

power

The ability to influence
others.

Sources of Power

One of the earliest and still most useful approaches to understanding power, offered by
French and Raven, suggests that leaders have five important potential sources of power
in organizations.[30] Figure 12.1 shows those power sources.

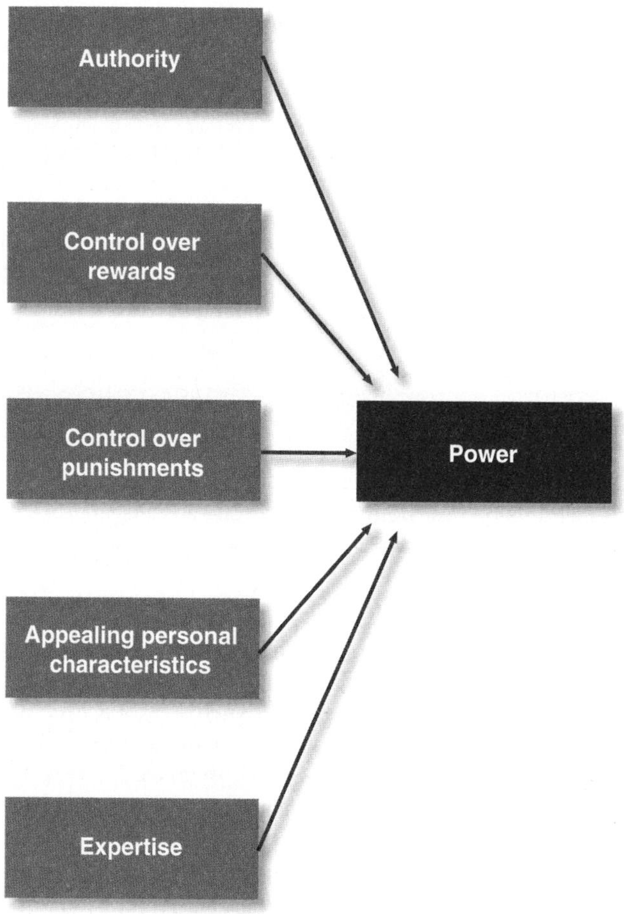

FIGURE 12.1
Sources of Power

SOURCE: Adapted from J. R. P. French and B. Raven, "The Bases of Social Power," in *Studies in Social Power,* ed. D. Cartwright (Ann Arbor, MI: Institute for Social Research, 1959).

Legitimate Power   The leader with *legitimate power* has the right, or the authority, to tell others what to do; employees are obligated to comply with legitimate orders. For example, a supervisor tells an employee to remove a safety hazard, and the employee removes the hazard because he has to obey the authority of his boss. In contrast, when a staff person lacks the authority to give an order to a line manager, the staff person has no legitimate power over the manager. As you might guess, managers have more legitimate power over their direct reports than they do over their peers, bosses, and others inside or outside their organizations.[31]

Reward Power   The leader who has *reward power* influences others because she controls valued rewards; people comply with the leader's wishes in order to receive those rewards. For example, a manager works hard to achieve her performance goals to get a positive performance review and a big pay raise from her boss. On the other hand, if company policy dictates that everyone receive the same salary increase, a leader's reward power decreases because he or she is unable to give higher raises.

Coercive Power   The leader with *coercive power* has control over punishments; people comply to avoid those punishments. For instance, a manager implements an absenteeism policy that administers disciplinary actions to offending employees. A manager has less coercive power if, say, a union contract limits her ability to punish. In general, lower-level managers have less legitimate, coercive, and reward power than do middle- and higher-level managers.[32]

Referent Power   The leader with *referent power* has personal characteristics that appeal to others; people comply because of admiration, a desire for approval, personal liking, or a desire to be like the leader. For example, young, ambitious managers emulate the work habits and personal style of a successful, charismatic executive. An executive who is incompetent, disliked, and commands little respect has little referent power.

Expert Power   The leader who has *expert power* has certain expertise or knowledge; people comply because they believe in, can learn from, or can otherwise gain from that expertise. For example, a sales manager gives her salespeople some tips on closing a deal. The salespeople then alter their sales techniques because they respect the manager's expertise. On the other hand, this manager may lack expert power in other areas, such as finance; thus, her salespeople may ignore her advice concerning financial matters.

People who are in a position that gives them the right to tell others what to do, who can reward and punish, who are well liked and admired, and who have expertise on which other people can draw will be powerful members of the organization. All of these sources of power are potentially important. Although it is easy to assume that the most powerful bosses are those who have high legitimate power and control major rewards and punishments, it is important not to underestimate the more "personal" sources like expert and referent power. These personal sources of power are the ones most closely related to people's motivation to perform to their managers' expectations.[33]

Traditional Approaches to Understanding Leadership

Three traditional approaches to studying leadership are the trait approach, the behavioral approach, and the situational approach.

Leader Traits

The **trait approach** is the oldest leadership perspective; it focuses on individual leaders and attempts to determine the personal characteristics (traits) that great leaders share. What set Winston Churchill, Alexander the Great, Gandhi, and Martin Luther King apart from the crowd? The trait approach assumes the existence of a leadership personality and assumes that leaders are born, not made.

> **trait approach**
>
> A leadership perspective that attempts to determine the personal characteristics that great leaders share.

From 1904 to 1948, over 100 leadership trait studies were conducted.[34] At the end of that period, management scholars concluded that no particular set of traits is necessary for a person to become a successful leader. Enthusiasm for the trait approach diminished, but some research on traits continued. By the mid-1970s, a more balanced view emerged: Although no traits ensure leadership success, certain characteristics are potentially useful. The current perspective is that some personality characteristics—many of which a person need not be born with but can strive to acquire—do distinguish effective leaders from other people.[35]

1. *Drive.* *Drive* refers to a set of characteristics that reflect a high level of effort. Drive includes high need for achievement, constant striving for improvement, ambition, energy, tenacity (persistence in the face of obstacles), and initiative. In several countries, the achievement needs of top executives have been shown to be related to the growth rates of their organizations.[36] But the need to achieve can be a drawback if leaders focus on personal achievement and get so personally involved with the work that they do not delegate enough authority and responsibility. And whereas need for achievement has been shown to predict organizational effectiveness in entrepreneurial firms, it does not predict success for division heads in larger and more bureaucratic firms.[37]

2. *Leadership motivation.* Great leaders not only have drive; they *want to lead*. In this regard, it helps to be *extraverted*—extraversion is consistently related to both leadership emergence and leadership effectiveness.[38] Also important is a high need for power, a preference to be in leadership rather than follower positions. A high power need induces people to attempt to influence others, and sustains interest and satisfaction in the

process of leadership. When the power need is exercised in moral and socially constructive ways, rather than to the detriment of others, leaders inspire more trust, respect, and commitment to their vision.

3. *Integrity. Integrity* is the correspondence between actions and words. Honesty and credibility, in addition to being desirable characteristics in their own right, are especially important for leaders because these traits inspire trust in others.

4. *Self-confidence. Self-confidence* is important for a number of reasons. The leadership role is challenging, and setbacks are inevitable. Self-confidence allows a leader to overcome obstacles, make decisions despite uncertainty, and instill confidence in others.

> ✳ A senior partner in a law firm told his attorneys about the importance of trust. When a young, ambitious lawyer asked how one can gain trust, the senior partner replied, "Try being trustworthy."[39]

Of course, you don't want to overdo this; arrogance and cockiness have triggered more than one leader's downfall.

5. *Knowledge of the business.* Effective leaders have a high level of *knowledge* about their industries, companies, and technical matters. Leaders must have the intelligence to interpret vast quantities of information. Advanced degrees are useful in a career, but ultimately less important than acquired expertise in matters relevant to the organization.[40]

Finally, there is one personal skill that may be the most important: the ability to perceive the needs and goals of others and to adjust one's personal leadership approach accordingly.[41] Effective leaders do not rely on one leadership style; rather, they are capable of using different styles as the situation warrants.[42] This quality is the cornerstone of the situational approaches to leadership, which we will discuss shortly.

Men and Women Leaders: (How) Do They Differ?

Admiral Louise Wilmot was the highest-ranking woman in the U.S Navy when she retired.

On the average, men and women are equally effective as leaders. However, the situation may make a difference: Male leaders tend to be more effective in military settings, and women are usually more effective in educational, social service, and government organizations. Why this is so is not completely clear.

Is there a "male" leadership style, and if so, does it differ from the "female" style? Some think so. According to an article in *Harvard Business Review*, women are moving into top management by drawing on unique skills and attitudes that men are less likely to possess. Men, says author Judy Rosener, are more likely to rely on their formal authority and on rewards and punishments (legitimate, reward, and coercive powers), whereas women tend to use their charisma, interpersonal skills, hard work, and personal contacts. In Rosener's study, women leaders claimed to encourage participation, share power and information, and enhance other people's self-worth. Additional academic research confirms that women managers tend to be more participative than males.

Admiral Louise Wilmot was the highest-ranking woman in the U.S. Navy when she retired. Her leadership style emphasized teamwork and interpersonal relationships. When asked if her style arose because she is a woman, she replied that as a leader you should "preserve your person and preserve whatever you are that is good and wholesome and makes you interesting and different from everyone else. There is no reason in the world to surrender your soul, your person, or your spirit."

Dame Margaret Anstee, head of the United Nations peacekeeping mission in Angola in the early 1990s, strongly advocates risk-taking. "I was the first woman to head a military mission for the UN, and I didn't want someone saying: 'We did try to get a woman there, but she wouldn't take the challenge.' " Political analyst David Gergen, addressing the Women in Leadership Summit, said that in the political world it's time for the United States to advance women to positions of leadership. "We had the year of the woman, but that was not enough. We had the decade of the woman, and that was not enough. We now need the century of the woman."

Cisco's John Chambers believes that great female leadership talent is waiting to be tapped, and is about to explode onto the Silicon Valley scene. Support for this comes from Harvard's Rosabeth Moss Kanter's comment, "Women get high ratings on exactly those skills needed to succeed in the global Information Age, where teamwork and partnering are so important."

SOURCES: J. B. Rosener, "Ways Women Lead," *Harvard Business Review* 68 (May–June 1990), pp. 103–11; A. Eagly, S. Karom, and M. Makhijani, "Gender and the Effectiveness of Leaders: A Meta-Analysis," *Psychological Bulletin*, 1995, pp. 125–45; V. H. Vroom, "Leadership and the Decision-Making Process," *Organizational Dynamics*, Spring 2000, pp. 82–93; P. Sellers, "The 50 Most Powerful Women in Business," *Fortune*, October 16, 2000, pp. 131–16, E. Fagenson-Eland and P. J. Kidder, "A Conversation with Rear Admiral Louise Wilmot: Taking the Lead and Leading the Way," *Organizational Dynamics*, Winter 2000, pp. 80–91; R. Sharpe, "As Leaders, Women Rule," *BusinessWeek*, November 20, 2000, pp. 74–84; A. Stanley, "For Women, to Soar Is Rare, to Fall Is Human," *The New York Times*, January 13, 2002, sec. 3, pp. 1, 10; A. Maitland, "A Bandit Peacekeeper Who Thrived on Risk," *Financial Times*, August 2, 2004, p. 9; David Gergen, "Political Analyst, on Leadership," *The Boston Globe*, September 26, 2004, p. E2.

Leader Behaviors

The **behavioral approach** to leadership attemps to identify what good leaders do. Should leaders focus on getting the job done or on keeping their followers happy? Should they make decisions autocratically or democratically? In the behavioral approach, personal characteristics are considered less important than the actual behaviors leaders exhibit.

Three general categories of leadership behavior have received particular attention: behaviors related to task performance, group maintenance, and employee participation in decision making.

Task Performance   Leadership requires getting the job done. **Task performance behaviors** are the leader's efforts to ensure that the work unit or organization reaches its goals. This dimension is variously referred to as *concern for production, directive leadership, initiating structure,* or *closeness of supervision.* It includes a focus on work speed, quality and accuracy, quantity of output, and following the rules.[43] This type of leader behavior improves leader job performance and group and organizational performance.[44]

Group Maintenance   In exhibiting **group maintenance behaviors,** leaders take action to ensure the satisfaction of group members, develop and maintain harmonious work relationships, and preserve the social stability of the group. This dimension is sometimes referred to as *concern for people, supportive leadership,* or *consideration.* It includes a focus on people's feelings and comfort, appreciation of them, and stress reduction.[45] This type of leader behavior has a strong positive impact on follower satisfaction, motivation, and leader effectiveness.[46]

What *specific* behaviors do performance- and maintenance-oriented leadership imply? To help answer this question, assume you are asked to rate your boss on these two

behavioral approach

A leadership perspective that attempts to identify what good leaders do— that is, what behaviors they exhibit.

task performance behaviors

Actions taken to ensure that the work group or organization reaches its goals.

group maintenance behaviors

Actions taken to ensure the satisfaction of group members, develop and maintain harmonious work relationships, and preserve the social stability of the group.

TABLE 12.1

Questions Assessing Task Performance and Group Maintenance Leadership

Task performance behaviors focus on achieving work goals.

Task Performance Leadership
1. Is your superior strict about observing regulations?
2. To what extent does your superior give you instructions and orders?
3. Is your superior strict about the amount of work you do?
4. Does your superior urge you to complete your work by a specified time?
5. Does your superior try to make you work to your maximum capacity?
6. When you do an inadequate job, does your superior focus on the inadequate way the job is done?
7. Does your superior ask you for reports about the progress of your work?
8. How precisely does your superior work out plans for goal achievement each month?

Group Maintenance Leadership
1. Can you talk freely with your superior about your work?
2. Does your superior generally support you?
3. Is your superior concerned about your personal problems?
4. Do you think your superior trusts you?
5. Does your superior give you recognition when you do your job well?
6. When a problem arises in your workplace, does your superior ask your opinion about how to solve it?
7. Is your superior concerned about your future benefits, such as promotions and pay raises?
8. Does your superior treat you fairly?

SOURCE: Reprinted from J. Misumi and M. Peterson, "The Performance-Maintenance (PM) Theory of Leadership: Review of a Japanese Research Program," *Administrative Science Quarterly* 30, no. 2 (June 1985), by permission of *Administrative Science Quarterly*, © 1985 by Johnson Graduate School of Management, Cornell University.

Leader-Member Exchange (LMX) theory

Highlights the importance of leader behaviors not just toward the group as a whole but toward individuals on a personal basis.

participation in decision making

Leader behaviors that managers perform in involving their employees in making decisions.

autocratic leadership

A form of leadership in which the leader makes decisions on his or her own and then announces those decisions to the group.

democratic leadership

A form of leadership in which the leader solicits input from subordinates.

dimensions. If a leadership study were conducted in your organization, you would be asked to fill out a questionnaire similar to the one in Table 12.1. The behaviors indicated in the first set of questions represent performance-oriented leadership; those indicated in the second set represent maintenance-oriented leadership.

Leader-Member Exchange (LMX) theory[47] highlights the importance of leader behaviors not just toward the group as a whole but toward individuals on a personal basis. The focus is primarily on the leader behaviors historically considered group maintenance.[48] According to LMX theory, and as supported by research evidence, maintenance behaviors such as trust, open communication, mutual respect, mutual obligation, and mutual loyalty form the cornerstone of relationships that are satisfying and perhaps more productive.[49]

Remember, though, the potential for cross-cultural differences. Maintenance behaviors are important everywhere, but the specific behaviors can differ from one culture to another. For example, in the United States, maintenance behaviors include dealing with people face-to-face; in Japan, written memos are preferred over giving directions face-to-face, thus avoiding confrontation and permitting face-saving in the event of disagreement.[50]

Participation in Decision Making   How should a leader make decisions? More specifically, to what extent should leaders involve their people in making decisions?[51] The **participation-in-decision-making** dimension of leadership behavior can range from autocratic to democratic. **Autocratic leadership** makes decisions and then announces them to the group. **Democratic leadership** solicits input from others. Democratic leadership seeks information, opinions, and preferences, sometimes to the point of meeting with the group, leading discussions, and using consensus or majority vote to make the final choice.

The Effects of Leader Behavior   How the leader behaves influences people's attitudes and performance. Studies of these effects focus on autocratic versus democratic decision styles or on performance- versus maintenance-oriented behaviors.

Decision Styles   The classic study comparing autocratic and democratic styles found that a democratic approach resulted in the most positive attitudes, whereas an autocratic approach resulted in somewhat higher performance.[52] A **laissez-faire** style, in which the leader essentially made no decisions, led to more negative attitudes and lower performance. These results seem logical and probably represent the prevalent beliefs among managers about the general effects of these decision-making approaches.

> **laissez-faire**
>
> A leadership philosophy characterized by an absence of managerial decision making.

Democratic styles, appealing though they may seem, are not always the most appropriate. When speed is of the essence, democratic decision making may be too slow, or people may want decisiveness from the leader.[53] Whether a decision should be made autocratically or democratically depends on the characteristics of the leader, the followers, and the situation.[54] Thus, a situational approach to leader decision styles, discussed later in the chapter, is appropriate.

Performance and Maintenance Behaviors   The performance and maintenance dimensions of leadership are independent of each other. In other words, a leader can behave in ways that emphasize one, both, or neither of these dimensions. Some research indicates that the ideal combination is to engage in both types of leader behaviors.

A team of Ohio State University researchers investigated the effects of leader behaviors in a truck manufacturing plant of International Harvester.[55] Generally, supervisors who were high on *maintenance behaviors* (which the researchers termed *consideration*) had fewer grievances and less turnover in their work units than supervisors who were low on this dimension. The opposite held for *task performance behaviors* (which the research team called *initiating structure*). Supervisors high on this dimension had more grievances and higher turnover rates.

When maintenance and performance leadership behaviors were considered together, the results were more complex. But one conclusion was clear: When a leader is high on performance-oriented behaviors, he or she should *also* be maintenance oriented. Otherwise the leader will have employees with high rates of turnover and grievances.

At about the same time the Ohio State studies were being conducted, a research program at the University of Michigan was studying the impact of the same leader behaviors on groups' job performance.[56] Among other things, the researchers concluded that the most effective managers engaged in what they called *task-oriented behavior*: planning, scheduling, coordinating, providing resources, and setting performance goals. Effective managers also exhibited more *relationship-oriented behavior*: demonstrating trust and confidence, being friendly and considerate, showing appreciation, keeping people informed, and so on. As you can see, these dimensions of leader behavior are essentially the task performance and group maintenance dimensions.

After the Ohio State and Michigan findings were published, it became popular to talk about the ideal leader as one who is always both performance and maintenance oriented. The best-known leadership training model to follow this style is Blake and Mouton's Leadership Grid.®[57] In grid training, managers are rated on their performance-oriented behavior (called *concern for production*) and maintenance-oriented behavior (*concern for people*). Then their scores are plotted on the grid shown in Figure 12.2. The highest score is a 9 on both dimensions.

As the figure shows, joint scores can fall at any point on the grid. Managers who did not score a 9,9—for example, those who were high on concern for people but low on concern for production—would then receive training on how to become a 9,9 leader.

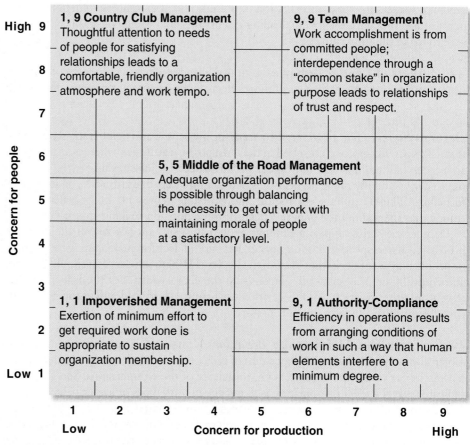

Figure from The Leadership Grid. Axes: vertical axis "Concern for people" ranging from Low 1 to High 9; horizontal axis "Concern for production" ranging from 1 Low to 9 High.

1, 9 Country Club Management
Thoughtful attention to needs of people for satisfying relationships leads to a comfortable, friendly organization atmosphere and work tempo.

9, 9 Team Management
Work accomplishment is from committed people; interdependence through a "common stake" in organization purpose leads to relationships of trust and respect.

5, 5 Middle of the Road Management
Adequate organization performance is possible through balancing the necessity to get out work with maintaining morale of people at a satisfactory level.

1, 1 Impoverished Management
Exertion of minimum effort to get required work done is appropriate to sustain organization membership.

9, 1 Authority-Compliance
Efficiency in operations results from arranging conditions of work in such a way that human elements interfere to a minimum degree.

FIGURE 12.2
The Leadership Grid®

For a long time, grid training was warmly received by U.S. business and industry. Later, however, it was criticized for embracing a simplistic, one-best-way style of leadership and ignoring the possibility that 9,9 is not best under all circumstances. For example, even 1,1 can be appropriate if employees know their jobs (and therefore don't need to receive directions). Also, they may enjoy their jobs and their co-workers enough that whether the boss shows personal concern for them is not very important. Nonetheless, if the manager is uncertain how to behave, it probably is best to exhibit behaviors that are related to both task performance and group maintenance.[58]

In fact, a wide range of effective leadership styles exists. Organizations that understand the need for diverse leadership styles will have a competitive advantage in the modern business environment over those that believe there is only "one best way."

Situational Approaches to Leadership

situational approach

Leadership perspective proposing that universally important traits and behaviors do not exist, and that effective leadership behavior varies from situation to situation.

According to proponents of the **situational approach** to leadership, universally important traits and behaviors don't exist. They believe effective leader behaviors vary from situation to situation. *The leader should first analyze the situation and then decide what to do.* In other words, look before you lead.

A head nurse in a hospital described her situational approach to leadership:[59] "My leadership style is a mix of all styles. In this environment I normally let people participate. But in a code blue situation where a patient is dying I automatically become very autocratic: 'You do this; you do that; you, out of the room; you all better be quiet; you, get Dr. Mansfield.' The staff tell me that's the only time they see me like that. In an emergency like that, you don't have time to vote, talk a lot, or yell at each other. It's time for someone to set up the order.

"I remember one time, one person saying, 'Wait a minute, I want to do this.' He wanted to do the mouth-to-mouth resuscitation. I knew the person behind him did it better, so I said, 'No, he does it.' This fellow told me later that I hurt him so badly to yell that in front of all the staff and doctors. It was like he wasn't good enough. So I explained it to him: that's the way it is. A life was on the line. I couldn't give you warm fuzzies. I couldn't make you look good because you didn't have the skills to give the very best to that patient who wasn't breathing anymore."[60]

This nurse has her own intuitive situational approach to leadership. She knows the potential advantages of the participatory approach to decision making, but she also knows that in some circumstances she must make decisions herself.

The first situational model of leadership was proposed in 1958 by Tannenbaum and Schmidt. In their classic *Harvard Business Review* article, these authors described how managers should consider three factors before deciding how to lead: forces in the manager, forces in the subordinate, and forces in the situation.[61] Forces in the manager include the manager's personal values, inclinations, feelings of security, and confidence in subordinates. Forces in the subordinate include his or her knowledge and experience, readiness to assume responsibility for decision making, interest in the task or problem, and understanding and acceptance of the organization's goals. Forces in the situation include the type of leadership style the organization values, the degree to which the group works effectively as a unit, the problem itself and the type of information needed to solve it, and the amount of time the leader has to make the decision.

Consider which of these forces makes an autocratic style most appropriate and which dictates a democratic, participative style. By engaging in this exercise, you are constructing a situational theory of leadership.

Although the Tannenbaum and Schmidt article was published almost a half century ago, most of its arguments remain valid. Since that time, other situational models have emerged. We will focus here on two of them: the Vroom model for decision making and path-goal theory. Others are summarized in the appendix to this chapter.

Nurses experience situational leadership on a daily basis. How would you handle a leadership role under pressure?

The Vroom Model of Leadership

This situational model follows in the tradition of Tannenbaum and Schmidt. The **Vroom model** emphasizes the participative dimension of leadership: how leaders go about making decisions. The model uses the basic situational approach of assessing the situation before determining the best leadership style.[62]

Table 12.2 shows the situational factors used to analyze problems. Each is based on an important attribute of the problem the leader faces and should be assessed as either high or low.

The Vroom model, shown in Figure 12.3, operates like a funnel. You answer the questions one at a time, choosing high or low for each, sometimes skipping questions as you follow the appropriate path. Eventually, you reach one of 14 possible endpoints. For each endpoint, the model states which of five decision styles is most appropriate. Several different decision styles may work, but the style recommended is the one that takes the least amount of time.

Table 12.3 defines the five leader decision styles. The five styles indicate that there are several shades of participation, not just autocratic or democratic.

The boxed example on pages 407 and 408 presents a managerial decision for you to work through using the model.

> **Vroom model**
>
> A situational model that focuses on the participative dimension of leadership.

Situational Factors for Problem Analysis	
Decision significance:	The significance of the decision to the success of the project or organization.
Importance of commitment:	The importance of team members' commitment to the decision.
Leader's expertise:	Your knowledge or expertise in relation to this problem.
Likelihood of commitment:	The likelihood that the team would commit itself to a decision that you might make on your own.
Group support for objectives:	The degree to which the team supports the organization's objectives at stake in this problem.
Group expertise:	Team members' knowledge or expertise in relation to this problem.
Team competence:	The ability of team members to work together in solving problems.

TABLE 12.2
Situational Factors for Problem Analysis

SOURCE: V. Vroom, "Leadership and the Decision-Making Process," *Organizational Dynamics*, Spring 2000, pp. 82–94. Copyright © 2000 with permission from Elsevier Science.

Time-Driven Model

Instructions: The Matrix operates like a funnel. You start at the left with a specific decision problem in mind. The column headings denote situational factors which may or may not be present in that problem. You progress by selecting High or Low (H or L) for each relevant situational factor. Proceed down from the funnel, judging only those situational factors for which a judgement is called for, until you reach the recommended process.

Problem Statement	Decision Significance	Importance of Commitment	Leader Expertise	Likelihood of Commitment	Group Support	Group Expertise	Team Competence	Recommended process
	H	H	H	H	-	-	-	Decide
				L	H	H	H	Delegate
							L	Consult (Group)
						L	-	Consult (Group)
					L	-	-	Consult (Group)
			L	H	H	H	H	Facilitate
							L	Consult (Individually)
						L	-	Consult (Individually)
					L	-	-	Consult (Individually)
				L	H	H	H	Facilitate
							L	Consult (Group)
						L	-	Consult (Group)
					L	-	-	Consult (Group)
		L	H	-	-	-	-	Decide
			L	-	H	H	H	Facilitate
							L	Consult (Individually)
						L	-	Consult (Individually)
					L	-	-	Consult (Individually)
	L	H	-	H	-	-	-	Decide
				L	-	-	H	Delegate
							L	Facilitate
		L	-	-	-	-	-	Decide

FIGURE 12.3
Vroom's Model of Leadership Style

SOURCE: V. Vroom, "Leadership and the Decision-Making Process," *Organizational Dynamics*, Spring 2000, pp. 82–94. Copyright © 2000 with permission from Elsevier Science.

Decide: You make the decision alone and either announce or "sell" it to the group. You may use your expertise in collecting information that you deem relevant to the problem from the group or others.

Consult individually: You present the problem to the group members individually, get their suggestions, and then make the decision.

Consult the group: You present the problem to the group members in a meeting, get their suggestions, and then make the decision.

Facilitate: You present the problem to the group in a meeting. You act as a facilitator, defining the problem to be solved and the boundaries within which the decision must be made. Your objective is to get concurrence on a decision. Above all, you take care to ensure that your ideas are not given any greater weght than those of others simply because of your position.

Delegate: You permit the group to make the decision within prescribed limits. The group undertakes the identification and diagnosis of the problem, developing alternative procedures for solving it, and deciding on one or more alternative solutions. While you play no direct role in the group's deliberations unless explicity asked, your role is an important one behind the scenes, providing needed resources and encouragement.

TABLE 12.3
Vroom's Leader Decision Styles

SOURCE: V. Vroom, "Leadership and the Decision-Making Process," *Organizational Dynamics*, Spring 2000, pp. 82–94. Copyright © 2000 with permission from Elsevier Science.

Of course, not every managerial decision warrants this complicated analysis. But the model becomes less complex after you work through it a couple of times. Also, using the model for major decisions ensures that you consider the important situational factors and alerts you to the most appropriate style to use.

Path-Goal Theory   Perhaps the most comprehensive and generally useful situational model of leadership effectiveness is path-goal theory. (Two additional situational models are described in Appendix E.) Developed by Robert House, **path-goal theory** gets its name from its concern with how leaders influence followers' perceptions of their work goals and the paths they follow toward goal attainment.[63]

> **path-goal theory**
>
> A theory that concerns how leaders influence subordinates' perceptions of their work goals and the paths they follow toward attainment of those goals.

Applying the Vroom Model of Leadership

Setting: Banking
Your Position: President & Chief Executive Officer

The bank examiners have just left, insisting that many of your commercial real estate loans be written off, thereby depleting already low capital. Along with many other banks in your region, your bank is in serious danger of being closed by the regulators. As the financial problems surfaced, many of the top executives left to pursue other interests, but fortunately, you were able to replace them with three highly competent younger managers. While they had no prior acquaintance with one another, each is a product of a fine training program with one of the money center banks in which they rotated through positions in each of the banking functions.

Your extensive experience in the industry leads you to the inevitable conclusion that the only hope is a two-pronged approach involving reduction of all but the most critical expenses and the sale of assets to other banks. The task must be accomplished quickly since further deterioration of the quality of the loan portfolio could result in a negative capital position, forcing regulators to close the bank.

The strategy is clear to you, but you have many details that will need to be worked out. You believe that you know what information will be needed to get the bank on a course for future prosperity. You are fortunate in having three young executives to help you. While they have had little experience in working together, you know that each is dedicated to the survival of the bank. Like you, they know what needs to be done and how to do it.

SOURCE: V. Vroom, "Leadership and the Decision-Making Process," *Organizational Dynamics*, Spring 2000, pp. 82–94.

The key situational factors in path-goal theory are (1) personal characteristics of followers and (2) environmental pressures and demands with which followers must cope to attain their work goals. These factors determine which leadership behaviors are most appropriate.

The four pertinent leadership behaviors are (1) *directive leadership*, a form of task performance-oriented behavior; (2) *supportive leadership*, a form of group maintenance-oriented behavior; (3) *participative leadership*, or decision style; and (4) *achievement-oriented leadership*, or behaviors geared toward motivating people, such as setting challenging goals and rewarding good performance.

These situational factors and leader behaviors are merged in Figure 12.4. As you can see, appropriate leader behaviors—as determined by characteristics of followers and the work environment—lead to effective performance.

The theory also specifies *which* follower and environmental characteristics are important. There are three key follower characteristics. *Authoritarianism* is the degree to which individuals respect, admire, and defer to authority. *Locus of control* is the extent to which individuals see the environment as responsive to their own behavior. People with an *internal* locus of control believe that what happens to them is their own doing; people with an *external* locus of control believe that it is just luck or fate. Finally, *ability* is people's beliefs about their own abilities to do their assigned jobs.

Path-goal theory states that these personal characteristics determine the appropriateness of various leadership styles. For example, the theory makes the following propositions:

- A directive leadership style is more appropriate for highly authoritarian people, because such people respect authority.

FIGURE 12.4
The Path-Goal Framework

- A participative leadership style is more appropriate for people who have an internal locus of control, because these individuals prefer to have more influence over their own lives.
- A directive style is more appropriate when subordinates' ability is low. The directive style helps people understand what has to be done.

Appropriate leadership style is also determined by three important environmental factors: people's tasks, the formal authority system of the organization, and the primary work group.

answer to the boxed Vroom banker problem:

Answers are H H H L H H L. The preferred decision style is to consult your group.

- Directive leadership is inappropriate if tasks already are well structured.
- If the task and the authority or rule system are dissatisfying, directive leadership will create greater dissatisfaction.
- If the task or authority system is dissatisfying, supportive leadership is especially appropriate, because it offers one positive source of gratification in an otherwise negative situation.
- If the primary work group provides social support to its members, supportive leadership is less important.

Path-goal theory offers many more propositions. In general, the theory suggests that the functions of the leader are to (1) make the path to work goals easier to travel by providing coaching and direction; (2) reduce frustrating barriers to goal attainment; and (3) increase opportunities for personal satisfaction by increasing payoffs to people for achieving performance goals.

How best to do these things depends on your people and on the work situation. Again: Analyze, then adapt your style accordingly.

Whether you're the **CEO** of a company or the coach of a basketball team, a leader should make the team goals easier to obtain by providing coaching and direction.

Substitutes for Leadership   Sometimes leaders don't have to lead, or situations constrain their ability to lead effectively. The situation may be one in which leadership is unnecessary or has little impact. **Substitutes for leadership** can provide the same influence on people that leaders otherwise would have.

Certain follower, task, and organizational factors are substitutes for task performance and group maintenance leader behaviors.[64] For example, group maintenance behaviors are less important and have less impact if people already have a closely knit group, they have a professional orientation, the job is inherently satisfying, or there is great physical distance between leader and followers. Physicians who are strongly concerned with professional conduct, enjoy their work, and work independently do not need social support from hospital administrators.

substitutes for leadership

Factors in the workplace that can exert the same influence on employees that leaders would provide.

Task performance leadership is less important and will have less of a positive effect if people have a lot of experience and ability, feedback is supplied to them directly from the task or by computer, or the rules and procedures are rigid. If these factors are operating, the leader does not have to tell people what to do or how well they are performing.

The concept of substitutes for leadership does more than indicate when a leader's attempts at influence will and will not work. It provides useful and practical prescriptions for how to manage more efficiently.[65] If the manager can develop the work situation to the point where a number of these substitutes for leadership are operating, less time will need to be spent in direct attempts to influence people. The leader will be free to spend more time on other important activities.

Research indicates that substitutes for leadership may be better predictors of commitment and satisfaction than of performance.[66] These substitutes are helpful, but you can't put substitutes in place and think you've completed your job as leader. And as a follower, consider this: If you're not getting good leadership, and if these substitutes are not in place, create your own "substitute" for leadership—self-leadership. Take the initiative to motivate yourself, lead yourself, create positive change, and lead others.

Contemporary Perspectives on Leadership

So far, you have learned the major classic approaches to understanding leadership. Now we will discuss a number of new developments that are revolutionizing our understanding of this vital aspect of management.

Charismatic Leadership

Like many great leaders, Ronald Reagan had charisma. Thomas Watson, Alfred Sloan, Steve Jobs, and Richard Branson are good examples of charismatic leaders in industry.

Charisma is a rather elusive concept; it is easy to spot but hard to define. When executive recruiter Korn/Ferry International advised CEO wannabes to "develop charisma," *BusinessWeek* responded sarcastically, "What's next? Grow a third eye? Master telekinesis?" (p. 86).[67]

What *is* charisma, and how does one acquire it? According to one definition, "Charisma packs an emotional wallop for followers above and beyond ordinary esteem, affection, admiration, and trust . . . The charismatic is an idolized hero, a messiah and a savior."[68] As you can see from this quotation, many people, particularly North Americans, value charisma in their leaders. But some people don't like the term charisma;[69] it can be associated with the negative charisma of evil leaders whom people follow blindly.[70]

Charismatic leaders are dominant, exceptionally self-confident, and have a strong conviction in the moral righteousness of their beliefs.[71] They strive to create an aura of competence and success and communicate high expectations for and confidence in followers.

The charismatic leader articulates ideological goals and makes sacrifices in pursuit of those goals.[72] Martin Luther King had a dream for a better world, and John F. Kennedy spoke of landing a human on the moon. In other words, such leaders have a compelling vision. The charismatic leader also arouses a sense of excitement and adventure. He or she is an eloquent speaker who exhibits superior verbal skills, which helps communicate the vision and motivate followers. Walt Disney mesmerized people with his storytelling, had enormous creative talent, and instilled in his organization strong values of good taste, risk taking, and innovation.[73]

Leaders who possess these characteristics or do these things inspire in their followers trust, confidence, acceptance, obedience, emotional involvement, affection, admiration, and higher performance.[74] Evidence for the positive effects of charismatic leadership has been found in a wide variety of groups, organizations, and management levels, and in countries including India, Singapore, the Netherlands, China, Japan, and Canada.[75]

Charisma has been shown to improve corporate financial performance, particularly under conditions of uncertainty[76]—

> **charismatic leader**
>
> A person who is dominant, self-confident, convinced of the moral righteousness of his or her beliefs, and able to arouse a sense of excitement and adventure in followers.

Martin Luther King was a brilliant, charismatic leader who had a compelling vision, a dream for a better world.

that is, in risky circumstances or when environments are changing and people have difficulty understanding what they should do. Uncertainty is stressful, and makes people more receptive to the ideas and actions of charismatic leaders.

Transformational Leadership

Charisma contributes to transformational leadership. **Transformational leaders**[77] get people to transcend their personal interests for the sake of the larger community.[78] They generate excitement and revitalize organizations. At Hewlett-Packard, the ability to generate excitement is an explicit criterion for selecting managers. In the United Kingdom, Richard Branson of Virgin Group is a transformational leader who built a global business empire.[79]

The transformational process moves beyond the more traditional *transactional* approach to leadership. **Transactional leaders** view management as a series of transactions in which they use their legitimate, reward, and coercive powers to give commands and exchange rewards for services rendered. Unlike transformational leadership, transactional leadership is dispassionate; it does not excite, transform, empower, or inspire people to focus on the interests of the group or organization. However, transactional approaches may be more effective for individualists than for collectivists[80] (recall Chapter 6).

Generating Excitement   Transformational leaders generate excitement in several ways.[81] First, they are *charismatic*, as described earlier. Second, they give their followers *individualized attention*. Transformational leaders delegate challenging work to deserving people, keep lines of communication open, and provide one-on-one mentoring to develop their people. They do not treat everyone alike, because not everyone *is* alike.

Third, transformational leaders are *intellectually stimulating*. They arouse in their followers an awareness of problems and potential solutions. They articulate the organization's opportunities, threats, strengths, and weaknesses. They stir the imagination and generate insights. Therefore, problems are recognized and high-quality solutions are identified and implemented with the full commitment of followers.

Skills and Strategies   At least four skills or strategies contribute to transformational leadership.[82] First, transformational leaders *have a vision*—a goal, an agenda, or a results orientation that grabs people's attention. Second, they *communicate their vision;* through words, manner, or symbolism, they relate a compelling image of the ultimate goal. Third, transformational leaders *build trust* by being consistent, dependable, and persistent. They position themselves clearly by choosing a direction and staying with it, thus projecting integrity. Finally, they have a *positive self-regard.* They do not feel self-important or complacent; rather, they recognize their personal strengths, compensate for their weaknesses, nurture and continually develop their talents, and know how to learn from failure. They strive for success rather than merely try to avoid failure.

Transformational leadership has been identified in industry, the military, and politics.[83] Examples of transformational leaders in business include Henry Ford, Herb Kelleher, Jeff Bezos, David Neeleman, Lee Iacocca, and Jan Carlzon.[84] As with studies of charisma, transformational leadership and its positive impact on follower satisfaction and performance[85] have been demonstrated in countries the world over, including Egypt, Germany, China, England, and Japan.[86] A study in Korean companies found that transformational leadership predicted employee motivation, which in turn predicted creativity.[87]

Transforming Leaders   Importantly, transformational leadership is not the exclusive domain of presidents and chief executives. In the military, leaders who received transformational leadership training had a positive impact on followers' personal development. They also were successful as *indirect* leaders: military recruits under the transformational leaders' direct reports were stronger performers.[88] Don't forget, though:

transformational leader

A leader who motivates people to transcend their personal interests for the good of the group.

transactional leaders

Leaders who manage through transactions, using their legitimate, reward, and coercive powers to give commands and exchange rewards for services rendered.

Transformational leadership is good for people and good for the bottom line.

the best leaders are those who can display both transformational and transactional behaviors.[89]

Ford Motor Company, in collaboration with the University of Michigan School of Business, put thousands of middle managers through a program designed to stimulate transformational leadership.[90] The training included analysis of the changing business environment, company strategy, and personal reflection and discussion about the need to change. Participants assessed their own leadership styles and developed a specific change initiative to implement after the training—a change that would make a needed and lasting difference for the company.

Over the next six months, the managers implemented change on the job. Almost half of the initiatives resulted in transformational changes in the organization or work unit; the rest of the changes were smaller, more incremental, or more personal. Whether managers made small or transformational changes depended on their attitude going into the training, their level of self-esteem, and the amount of support they received from others on the job for their efforts. Thus, some managers did not respond as hoped. But almost half embraced the training, became more transformational in orientation, and tackled significant transformational changes for the company.[91]

Level 5 leadership, a term well-known among executives, is considered by some the ultimate leadership style. Level 5 leadership is a combination of strong professional will (determination) and personal humility that builds enduring greatness.[92] But Level 5 requires first that the leader exhibit a combination of transactional and transformational styles.[93]

Authenticity

In general, consider **authentic leadership** to be rooted in the ancient Greek philosophy "To thine own self be true."[94] In your own leadership, strive for authenticity in the form of honesty, genuineness, reliability, integrity, and trustworthiness. Authentic transformational leaders care about public interests (community, organizational, or group), not just their own.[95] They are willing to sacrifice their own interests for others, and they can be trusted. They are ethically mature; people view leaders who exhibit moral reasoning as more transformational than leaders who do not.[96]

Pseudotransformational leaders are the opposite: they talk a good game, but they ignore followers' real needs as their own self-interests (power, prestige, control, wealth, fame) take precedence.[97]

Opportunities for Leaders

A common view of leaders is that they are heroes. Phenomenally talented, they step forward in difficult times and save the day. But in these complex times, it is foolhardy to assume that a great top executive can solve all problems alone.[98] Arnold Schwarzenegger isn't going to step in and make things right.

Effective leadership must permeate the organization, not reside in one or two superstars at the top. The leader's job becomes one of spreading leadership abilities throughout the firm.[99] Make people responsible for their own performance. Create an environment in which each person can figure out what needs to be done and then do it well. Point the way and clear the path so that people can succeed. Give them the credit they deserve. Make heroes out of *them*.

Thus, what is now required of leaders is less the efficient management of resources, and more the effective unleashing of people and their intellectual capital.

This perspective uncovers a variety of nontraditional leadership roles that are emerging as vitally important.[100] The term **servant-leader** was coined by Robert Greenleaf, a retired AT&T executive. The term is paradoxical in the sense that "leader" and "servant" are usually opposites. Uniting the two is highly meaningful. For the individual who wants to both lead and serve others, servant-leadership is a way of relating to others to serve their needs and enhance their personal growth while strengthening the organization.

---

level 5 leadership

A combination of strong professional will (determination) and humility that builds enduring greatness.

---

authentic leadership

A style in which the leader is true to himself or herself while leading.

pseudotransformational leaders

Leaders who talk about positive change but allow their self interest to take precedence over followers' needs.

---

servant-leader

A leader who serves others' needs while strengthening the organization.

A number of other nontraditional roles provide leadership opportunities. **Bridge leaders** are those who leave their cultures for a significant period of time.[101] They live, go to school, travel, or work in other cultures. Then they return home, become leaders, and through their expanded repertoire they serve as bridges between conflicting value systems within their own cultures or between their culture and other cultures.

With work often being team-based (see Chapter 14), **shared leadership** occurs when leadership rotates to the person with the key knowledge, skills, and abilities for the issue facing the team at a particular time.[102] Shared leadership is most important when tasks are interdependent, are complex, and require creativity. High-performing teams engaged in such work exhibit more shared leadership than poor-performing teams. The role of vertical leader remains important—the formal leader still designs the team, manages its external boundaries, provides task direction, emphasizes the importance of the shared leadership approach, and engages in the transactional and transformational activities described in this chapter. But at the same time, the metaphor of geese in V-formation adds strength to the group: the lead goose periodically drops to the back, and another goose "steps up" and takes its place at the forefront.

Lateral leadership does not involve a hierarchical, superior–subordinate relationship, but instead invites colleagues at the same level to solve problems together.[103] You alone can't provide a solution to every problem, but you can create processes through which people work collaboratively. If you can get people working to improve methods collaboratively, you can help create an endless stream of innovations. In other words, it's not about you providing solutions to problems; it's about creating better interpersonal processes for finding solutions. Strategies and tactics can be found throughout this book, including the chapters on decision making, organization structure, teams, communication, and change.

A single leader can't "save the day" alone. However, one can give people in the firm the opportunity to become the heros.

bridge leaders

A leader who bridges conflicting value systems or different cultures.

shared leadership

Rotating leadership, in which people rotate through the leadership role based on which person has the most relevant skills at a particular time.

lateral leadership

Style in which colleagues at the same hierarchical level are invited to collaborate and facilitate joint problem solving.

A Note on Courage

To be a good leader, you need the courage to create a vision of greatness for your unit; identify and manage allies, adversaries, and fencesitters; and execute your vision, often against opposition. This does not mean you should commit career suicide by alienating too many powerful people; it does mean taking reasonable risks, with the good of the firm at heart, in order to produce constructive change.

For example, Ed Breen showed great courage when, immediately upon being hired, he replaced the entire board of directors at Tyco. This had never been done before at a company of that size. Breen believed that Tyco "needed a clean sweep to send a message to the market that this was going to be a different company."[104]

Specifically, some acts of courage required to fulfill your vision will include:[105] (1) seeing things as they are and facing them head-on, making no excuses and harboring no wishful illusions; (2) saying what needs to be said to those who need to hear it; and (3) persisting despite resistance, criticism, abuse, and setbacks. Courage includes stating the realities, even when they are harsh, and publicly stating what you will do to help and what you want from others. This means laying the cards on the table honestly: Here is what I want from you . . . What do you want from me?[106]

Advantages of Collaboration

You don't have to be the boss to initiate new collaborative processes among colleagues.

Senator John McCain is considered courageous not only because of his years as a POW in Vietnam, but also for his willingness to speak the truth.[107] According to Senator McCain, anyone can have a vision, but courage means fighting for it passionately, sometimes against opposition and the odds, being accountable for your mistakes, and seeing your vision through. Additional aspects of courage, for McCain, are optimism in the face of big challenges; seeking solutions instead of just announcing or complaining about problems; sharing credit; admitting when you're wrong; and going for the shared success, not the easy personal victory.

Developing Your Leadership Skills

As with other things, you must work at *developing* your leadership abilities. Great musicians and great athletes don't become great on natural gifts alone. They also pay their dues by practicing, learning, and sacrificing. Leaders in a variety of fields, when asked how they became the best leader possible, offered the following comments:[108]

- "I've observed methods and skills of my bosses that I respected."
- "By taking risks, trying, and learning from my mistakes."
- "Reading autobiographies of leaders I admire to try to understand how they think."
- "Lots of practice."
- "By making mistakes myself and trying a different approach."
- "By purposely engaging with others to get things done."
- "By being put in positions of responsibility that other people counted on."

Donald Trump and his team supposedly select "the best of the best" to be in *The Apprentice*. Based on what you have seen, do you believe these contestants possess the best leadership skills?

FROM THE PAGES OF ↓

BusinessWeek

Leadership Development: What Would You Learn Through This Experience?

You're working for PricewaterhouseCoopers and the firm decides that you are ripe for leadership development. Your assignment: helping village leaders in Africa deal with the AIDS crisis. You face language barriers, cultural differences, and a lack of electricity. You actually have to talk with people instead of just give a PowerPoint presentation. Tahir Ayub was in this situation; one lesson he learned was "You better put your beliefs and biases to one side and figure out new ways to look at things."

PwC sends its top talent on eight-week service projects in the developing world. The goals are to test the talent and expand the worldview of the firm's future leaders. The programs are well outside the expertise of the participants; they reveal how people handle pressure, and what people can accomplish without their usual resources at hand. Ayub now favors face-to-face conversation over e-mail because it builds trust. Jennifer Chang, whose assignment was in Belize, became a better listener and more flexible. "Once you see how slowly decisions are made in other places, you gain patience for the people you work with."

Cisco, J&J, and other companies are considering programs similar to PwC's. In fact, many companies use social-responsibility initiatives to develop leaders. A big challenge for professional service firms is finding leaders who can find unconventional answers to seemingly impossible problems.

SOURCE: J. Hempel and S. Porges, "It Takes a Village—And a Consultant," *BusinessWeek*, September 6, 2004, pp. 76–77.

How Do I Start?

How do you go about developing your leadership abilities? Start by thinking about your potential employer. Look for how it develops leadership talent. Best practices include paying close executive-level attention to the development of people, providing assignments that stretch the abilities of up-and-coming talent, creating individualized development plans, and providing multirater feedback.[109] Companies best at leadership development include Johnson & Johnson, Hewlett-Packard, Shell International, General Electric, and the World Bank.[110]

More specifically, here are some developmental experiences you should seek:[111]

- *Assignments:* Building something from nothing; fixing or turning around a failing operation; taking on project or task force responsibilities; accepting international assignments.
- *Other people:* Having exposure to positive role models; increasing visibility to others; working with people of diverse backgrounds.
- *Hardships:* Overcoming ideas that fail and deals that collapse; confronting others' performance problems; breaking out of a career rut.
- *Other events:* Formal courses; challenging job experiences; supervision of others; experiences outside work.

What Are the Keys?

The most effective developmental experiences have three components: assessment, challenge, and support.[112] *Assessment* includes information that gives you an understanding of where you are now, what your strengths are, your current levels of performance and leadership effectiveness, and your primary development needs. You can think about past feedback, previous successes and failures, how people have reacted to your ideas and actions, what your personal goals are, and what strategies you should implement to make progress. You can seek answers from your peers at work, bosses, family, friends, customers, and anyone else who knows you and how you work. The information you collect will help clarify what you need to learn, improve, or change.

The most potent developmental experiences provide *challenge*—they stretch you. We all think and behave in habitual, comfortable ways. This is natural, and perhaps sufficient to survive. But you've probably heard people say how important it can be to get out of your comfort zone—to tackle situations that require new skills and abilities, that are confusing or ambiguous, or that you simply would rather not deal with. Sometimes the challenge comes from lack of experience; other times, it requires changing old habits. It may be uncomfortable, but this is how great managers learn. Remember, some people don't bother to learn or refuse to learn. Make sure you think about your experiences along the way and reflect on them afterward, introspectively and in discussion with others.

You receive *support* when others send the message that your efforts to learn and grow are valued. Without support, challenging developmental experiences can be overwhelming. With support, it is easier to handle the struggle, stay on course, open up to learning, and actually learn from experiences. Support can come informally from other people, more formally through the procedures of the organization, and through learning resources in the forms of training, constructive feedback, talking with others, and so on.

What develops in leadership development? Through such experiences, you can acquire more self-awareness and self-confidence, a broader perspective on the organizational system, creative thinking, the ability to work more effectively in complex social systems, and the ability to learn from experience.

EPILOGUE

ANDREA JUNG AND AVON

In four years, Avon's stock price went up 174 percent. Jung now leads more than 4 million sales reps, selling a truly global brand. Revenues from China and Russia, for instance, are growing dramatically. The long term looks extremely bright for Avon.

Avon's board members named Andrea Jung chairman, a title they had been withholding until they saw how she performed. By October 2004, she was ranked number 3 in *Fortune's* list of America's 50 most powerful women in business. By 2005, she was appearing on the short list of potential CEOs for many big companies in need of a turnaround.

KEY TERMS

Authentic leadership, p. 412

Autocratic leadership, p. 402

Behavioral approach. p. 401

Bridge leaders, p. 413

Charismatic leader, p. 410

Democratic leadership, p. 402

Group maintenance behaviors, p. 401

Laissez-faire, p. 403

Lateral leadership, p. 413

Leader-Member Exchange (LMX) theory, p. 402

Level 5 leadership, p. 412

Participation in decision making, p. 402

Path-goal theory, p. 407

Power, p. 397

Pseudotransformational leaders, p. 412

Servant leader, p. 412

Shared leadership, p. 413

Situational approach, p. 404

Strategic leadership, p. 396

Substitutes for leadership, p. 409

Supervisory leadership, p. 396

Task performance behaviors, p. 401

Trait approach, p. 399

Transactional leaders, p. 411

Transformational leader, p. 411

Vision, p. 395

Vroom model, p. 405

SUMMARY OF LEARNING OBJECTIVES

Now that you have studied Chapter 12, you should know:

What it means to be a leader.

A leader is one who influences others to attain goals. Leaders orchestrate change, set direction, and motivate people to overcome obstacles and move the organization toward its ideal future.

What people want and organizations need from their leaders.

People want help in achieving their goals, and organizations need leaders at all levels. The best leaders challenge the process, inspire a shared vision, enable others to act, model the way, and encourage the heart.

How a good vision helps you be a better leader.

Outstanding leaders have vision. A vision is a mental image that goes beyond the ordinary and perhaps beyond what others thought possible. The vision provides the direction in which the leader wants the organization to move.

How to understand and use power.

Having power and using it appropriately are essential to effective leadership. Managers have five potential sources of power: legitimate, reward, coercive, referent, and expert. These power sources are potentially available to managers at all organizational levels and should be used appropriately.

The personal traits and skills of effective leaders.

The old idea that leaders have certain traits or skills fell into disfavor but lately has been resurrected. Important leader characteristics include drive, leadership, motivation, integrity, self-confidence, and knowledge of the business. Perhaps the most important skill is the ability to accurately perceive the situation and then change behavior accordingly.

The behaviors that will make you a better leader.

Important leader behaviors include task performance behaviors, group maintenance, and participation in decision making. The Vroom model helps a leader decide how much participation to use in making decisions. Path-goal theory assesses characteristics of the followers, the leader, and the situation; it then indicates the appropriateness of directive, supportive, participative, or achievement-oriented leadership behaviors.

What it means to be a charismatic and transformational leader.

To have charisma is to be dominant and self-confident, to have a strong conviction of the righteousness of your beliefs, to create an aura of competence and success, and to communicate high expectations for and confidence in your followers. Charisma is one component of transformational leadership. Transformational leaders translate a vision into reality by getting people to transcend their individual interests for the good of the larger community. They do this through charisma, individualized attention to followers, intellectual stimulation, formation and communication of their vision, building of trust, and positive self-regard.

The many types of opportunities to be a leader in an organization.

There's plenty of opportunity to be a leader; being a manager of others who report to you is just the traditional one. You can also take or create opportunities to be a servant-leader or bridge leader and engage in shared leadership and lateral leadership.

How to further your own leadership development.

You can develop your own leadership skills not only by understanding what effective leadership is all about, but also by seeking challenging developmental experiences. Such important life experiences come from taking challenging assignments, through exposure in working with other people, by overcoming hardships and failures, by taking formal courses, and by other actions. The most important elements of a good developmental experience are assessment, challenge, and support.

DISCUSSION QUESTIONS

1. What do you want from your leader?

2. Is there a difference between effective management and effective leadership? Explain your views and learn from others' views.

3. Identify someone you think is an effective leader. What traits and skills does this person possess that make him or her effective?

4. Do you think most managers can be transformational leaders? Why or why not?

5. In your own words, define courage. What is the role of courage in leadership? Give examples of acts of leadership you consider courageous.

6. Do you think men and women differ in their leadership styles? If so, how? Do men and/or women prefer different styles in their bosses? What evidence do you have for your answers?

7. Who are your heroes? What makes them heroes, and what can you learn from them?

8. Assess yourself as a leader based on what you have read in this chapter. What are your strengths and weaknesses?

9. Identify the developmental experiences you have had that may have strengthened your ability to lead. What did those experiences teach you? Also identify some developmental experiences you need to acquire, and how you will seek them. Be specific.

10. Consider a couple of decisions you are facing that could involve other people. Use the Vroom model to decide what approach to use to make the decisions.

11. Consider a job you hold or held in the past. Consider how your boss managed you. How would you describe him or her as a leader? What substitutes for leadership would you have enjoyed seeing put into place?

12. Consider an organization of which you are a leader or a member. What could great transformational leadership accomplish in the organization?

13. Name some prominent leaders who you would describe as authentic and inauthentic and discuss.

14. Name some leaders you consider servant-leaders, and discuss.

15. Identify some opportunities for you to exhibit shared leadership and lateral leadership.

CONCLUDING CASE

The Law Offices of Jeter, Jackson, Guidry, and Boyer

THE EVOLUTION OF THE FIRM

David Jeter and Nate Jackson started a small general law practice in 1992 near Sacramento, California. Prior to that, the two had spent five years in the district attorney's office after completing their formal schooling. What began as a small partnership—just the two attorneys and a paralegal–secretary—had now grown into a practice that employs more than 27 people in three separate towns. The current staff includes 18 attorneys (three of whom have become partners), three paralegals, and six secretaries.

For the first time in the firm's existence, the partners feel that they are losing control of their overall operation. The firm's current caseload, number of employees, number of clients, travel requirements, and facilities management needs have grown far beyond anything that the original partners had ever imagined.

Attorney Jeter called a meeting of the partners to discuss the matter. Before the meeting, opinions about the pressing problems of the day and proposed solutions were sought from the entire staff. The meeting resulted in a formal decision to create a new position, general manager of operations. The partners proceeded to compose a job description and job announcement for recruiting purposes.

Highlights and major responsibilities of the job description include:

- Supervising day-to-day office personnel and operations (phones, meetings, word processing, mail, billings, payroll, general overhead, and maintenance).
- Improving customer relations (more expeditious processing of cases and clients).
- Expanding the customer base.
- Enhancing relations with the local communities.
- Managing the annual budget and related incentive programs.
- Maintaining an annual growth in sales of 10 percent while maintaining or exceeding the current profit margin.

The general manager will provide an annual executive summary to the partners along with specific action plans for improvement and change. A search committee was formed and two months later the new position was offered to Brad Howser, a long-time administrator from the insurance industry seeking a final career change and a return to his California roots. Howser made it clear that he was willing to make a five-year commitment to the position and would then likely retire.

Things got off to a quiet and uneventful start as Brad spent the first few months just getting to know the staff, observing day-to-day operations, and reviewing and analyzing assorted client and attorney data and history, financial spreadsheets and so on.

About six months into the position, Brad became more outspoken and assertive with the staff and established several new operational rules and procedures. He began by changing the regular working hours. The firm previously had a flex schedule in place that allowed employees to begin and end the workday at their choosing within given parameters. Brad did not care for such a "loose schedule" and now required that all office personnel work from 9:00 to 5:00 each day. A few staff members were unhappy about this and complained to Brad who matter-of-factly informed them that "this is the new rule that everyone is expected to follow, and that anyone who could or would not comply should probably look for another job." Sylvia Bronson, a secretary who had been with the firm for several years, was particularly unhappy about this change. She arranged for a private meeting with Brad to discuss her child care circumstances and the difficulty that the new schedule presented. Brad seemed to listen half-heartedly and at one point told Sylvia that "secretaries are essentially a-dime-a-dozen and are readily available." Sylvia was seen leaving the office in tears that day.

Brad was not happy with the average length of time that it took to receive payments for services rendered to the firm's clients (accounts receivables). A closer look showed that 30 percent of the clients paid their bills in thirty days or less, 60 percent paid in thirty to sixty days and the remaining 10 percent stretched it out to as many as one hundred twenty days. Brad composed a letter that was sent to all clients whose outstanding invoices exceeded thirty days. The strongly worded letter demanded immediate payment in full, and went on to indicate that legal action might be taken against anyone who did not respond in a timely fashion. While a small number of "late" payments were received soon after the mailing, the firm received an even larger number of

letters and phone calls from angry clients, some of whom had been with the firm since its inception.

Brad was given an advertising and promotion budget for purposes of expanding the client base. One of the paralegals suggested that those expenditures should be carefully planned and that the firm had several attorneys who knew the local markets quite well and could probably offer some insight and ideas on the subject. Brad thought about this briefly and then decided to go it alone, reasoning that most attorneys know little or nothing about marketing.

In an attempt to "bring all of the people together to form a team," Brad established weekly staff meetings. These mandatory, hour-long sessions were run by Brad, who presented a series of overhead slides, handouts and lectures about "some of the proven management techniques that were successful in the insurance industry." The meetings typically ran past the allotted time frame and rarely if ever covered all of the agenda items.

Brad spent some of his time "enhancing community relations." He was very generous with many local groups such as the historical society, the garden clubs, the recreational sports programs, the middle- and high-school band programs, and others.

In less than six months he had written checks and authorized donations totaling more than $25,000. Brad was delighted about all of this and was certain that such gestures of goodwill would pay off handsomely in the future.

As for the budget, Brad carefully reviewed each line item in search of ways to increase revenues and cut expenses. He then proceeded to increase the expected base or quota for attorney's monthly billable hours, thus directly affecting their profit sharing and bonus program. On the cost side, Brad significantly reduced the attorney's annual budget for travel, meals, and entertainment. He considered these to be frivolous and unnecessary. Brad decided that one of the two full-time secretarial positions in each office should be reduced to part-time with no benefits. He saw no reason why the current workload could not be completed within this model. Brad wrapped up his initial financial review and action plan by posting notices throughout each office with new rules regarding the use of copy machines, phones, and supplies.

Brad completed the first year of his tenure with the required executive summary report to the partners that included his analysis of the current status of each department and his action plan. The partners were initially impressed with both Brad's approach to the new job and with the changes that he made. They all seemed to make sense and were directly in line with the key components of his job description. At the same time, "the office rumor mill and grape vine" had "heated up" considerably. Company morale, which had always been quite high, was now clearly waning. The water coolers and hallways became the frequent meeting place of disgruntled employees.

As for the marketplace, while the partners did not expect to see an immediate influx of new clients, they certainly did not expect to see shrinkage in their existing client base. A number of individual and corporate clients took their business elsewhere, still fuming over the letter they had received.

The partners met with Brad to discuss the situation. Brad urged them to "sit tight and ride out the storm." He had seen this happen before and had no doubt that in the long run the firm would achieve all of its goals. Brad went on to point out that people in general are resistant to change. The partners met for drinks later that day and looked at each other with a great sense of uncertainty. Should they ride out the storm as Brad suggested? Had they done the right thing in creating the position and in hiring Brad? What had started as a seemingly wise, logical, and smooth sequence of events had now become a crisis.

QUESTIONS

1. Do you agree with Brad's suggestion to "sit tight and ride out the storm," or should the partners take some action immediately? If so, what actions specifically?

2. Assume that the creation of the GM-Operations position was a good decision. What leadership style and type of individual would you try to place in this position?

3. Consider your own leadership style. What types of positions and situations should you seek? What types of positions and situations should you seek to avoid? Why?

EXPERIENTIAL EXERCISES
12.1 Power and Influence

OBJECTIVE

To explore the nature of power and influence, and your attitudes toward different kinds of power and influence.

INSTRUCTIONS

Read the introductions and complete sections A, B, and C.

Power and Influence Worksheet

A. Power

A number of people have made statements about power and winning (e.g., P. T. Barnum, Mao Tse-tung, Leo Durocher, Lord Acton, Vince Lombardi). Some of these statements are listed in the table that follows. Indicate how you feel about each of the statements by circling number 1 if you strongly disagree, number 5 if you strongly agree, and so on.

	Strongly Disagree	Disagree	Neutral	Agree	Strongly Agree
Winning is everything.	1	2	3	4	5
Nice guys finish last.	1	2	3	4	5
There can only be one winner.	1	2	3	4	5
There's a sucker born every minute.	1	2	3	4	5
You can't completely trust anyone.	1	2	3	4	5
All power rests at the end of the gun.	1	2	3	4	5
Power seekers are greedy and can't be trusted.	1	2	3	4	5
Power corrupts; absolute power corrupts absolutely.	1	2	3	4	5
You get as much power as you pay for.	1	2	3	4	5

B. Influence

During the past week or so you have come in contact with many people. Some have influenced you positively, some negatively. Try to recall recent experiences with employers, peers, teachers, parents, clergy, and the like who may have influenced you in some way. Then try to think about how and why they influenced you as they did.

1. On the following table, list the names of all those who influenced you during the past week or so according to the kind of power that person used. The same person's name may appear under more than one type of power if that person used multiple power bases. Also, indicate whether the influence was positive (+) or negative (−).

Power Base	Names and Whether (+) or (−)
Legitimate authority	_____
Reward	_____
Coercive	_____
Referent	_____
Expert	_____

2. After examining your list, check (√) the following questions.

	Yes	No
a. Was there one person who had + marks appearing under several power bases?	_____	_____
b. Was there one person who had − marks appearing under several power bases?	_____	_____
c. Did you find that most of the people with + marks tended to fall under the same power bases?	_____	_____
d. Did you find that most of the people with − marks tended to fall under the same power bases?	_____	_____

3. From your answers to the last two questions, list which power bases you found to be positive (+) and which you found to be negative (−).

+	−
_____	_____
_____	_____
_____	_____
_____	_____
_____	_____

Do you think you personally prefer to use those power bases you listed under + when you try to influence people? Do you actually use them?

C. Power and influence

From the table in Part B, find the one person who you think had the strongest positive influence on you (Person 1), and the one who had the strongest negative influence (Person 2). These are most likely the persons whose names appear most frequently.

In the following table, place a 1 on the line for each statement that best indicates how you think Person 1 would respond to that statement. Put a 2 on the line for each statement that reflects how you think Person 2 would respond to that item.

	Strongly Disagree	Disagree	Neutral	Agree	Strongly Agree
Winning is everything.					
Nice guys finish last.					
There can only be one winner.					
There's a sucker born every minute.					
You can't completely trust anyone.					
All power rests at the end of the gun.					
Power seekers are greedy and can't be trusted.					
Power corrupts; absolute power corrupts absolutely.					
You get as much power as you pay for.					

Now compare your responses in Part A to those in Part C. Do you more closely resemble Person 1 or Person 2? Do you prefer to use the kinds of power that person uses? Which kinds of power do you use most frequently? Which do you use least frequently? When do you feel you have the greatest power? When do you have the least power? How do these answers compare to what you found in Part B3?

SOURCE: Excerpted from Lawrence R. Jauch, Arthur G. Bedeian, Sally A. Coltin, and William F. Glueck, *The Managerial Experience: Cases, Exercises, and Readings*, 5th ed. Copyright © 1989. Reprinted with permission of South-Western, a division of Thomson Learning, www.thomsonrights.com.

12.2 Evaluating Your Leadership Style

OBJECTIVES

1. To examine your personal style of leadership.
2. To study the nature of the leadership process.
3. To identify ways to improve or modify your leadership style.

INSTRUCTIONS

1. Working alone, complete and score the Leadership Style Survey.
2. In small groups, exchange scores, compute average scores, and develop responses to the discussion questions.
3. After the class reconvenes, group spokespersons present group findings.

DISCUSSION QUESTIONS

1. In what ways did your experience or lack of experience influence your responses to the survey?
2. In what ways did student scores and student responses to survey test items converge? In what ways did they diverge?
3. What do you think accounts for differences in student leadership attitudes?
4. How can students make constructive use of the survey results?

Leadership Style Survey

This survey describes various aspects of leadership behavior. To measure your leadership style, respond to each statement according to the way you would act (or think you would act) if you were a work group leader.

	Always	Frequently	Occasionally	Seldom	Never
1. I would allow team members the freedom to do their jobs in their own way.	5	4	3	2	1
2. I would make important decisions on my own initiative without consulting the workers.	5	4	3	2	1
3. I would allow the team members to make their own decisions.	5	4	3	2	1
4. I would not try to socialize with the workers.	5	4	3	2	1
5. I would allow team members to do their jobs as they see fit.	5	4	3	2	1
6. I would consider myself to be the group's spokesperson.	5	4	3	2	1
7. I would be warm, friendly, and approachable.	5	4	3	2	1
8. I would be sure that the workers understand and follow all the rules and regulations.	5	4	3	2	1
9. I would demonstrate a real concern for the workers' welfare.	5	4	3	2	1
10. I would be the one to decide what is to be done and how it is to be done.	5	4	3	2	1
11. I would delegate authority to the workers.	5	4	3	2	1
12. I would urge the workers to meet production quotas.	5	4	3	2	1
13. I would trust the workers to use good judgment in decision making.	5	4	3	2	1
14. I would assign specific tasks to specific people.	5	4	3	2	1
15. I would let the workers establish their own work pace.	5	4	3	2	1
16. I would not feel that I have to explain my decisions to workers.	5	4	3	2	1
17. I would try to make each worker feel that his or her contribution is important.	5	4	3	2	1
18. I would establish the work schedules.	5	4	3	2	1
19. I would encourage workers to get involved in setting work goals.	5	4	3	2	1
20. I would be action oriented and results oriented.	5	4	3	2	1
21. I would get the workers involved in making decisions.	5	4	3	2	1
22. I would outline needed changes and monitor action closely.	5	4	3	2	1
23. I would help the group achieve consensus on important changes.	5	4	3	2	1
24. I would supervise closely to ensure that standards are met.	5	4	3	2	1
25. I would consistently reinforce good work.	5	4	3	2	1
26. I would nip problems in the bud.	5	4	3	2	1
27. I would consult the group before making decisions.	5	4	3	2	1

APPENDIX E

APPENDIX E

Classic Contingency Models of Leadership

Many situational theories of leadership have been offered over the years. We elected to focus on two in this chapter: the Vroom model of decision making, and path-goal theory, the most comprehensive. Here are two more, presented in an appendix in the interest of preserving chapter space.

FIEDLER'S CONTINGENCY MODEL

Fiedler's contingency model of leadership effectiveness states that effectiveness depends on two factors: the personal style of the leader and the degree to which the situation gives the leader power, control, and influence over the situation.[1] Figure E.1 illustrates the contingency model. The upper half of the figure shows the situational analysis, and the lower half indicates the appropriate style. In the upper portion, three questions are used to analyze the situation:

1. Are leader–member relations good or poor? (To what extent is the leader accepted and supported by group members?)
2. Is the task structured or unstructured? (To what extent do group members know what their goals are and how to accomplish them?)
3. Is the leader's position power strong or weak (high or low)? (To what extent does the leader have the authority to reward and punish?)

These three sequential questions create a decision tree (from top to bottom, in the figure) in which a situation is classified into

FIGURE E.1

Fiedler's Analysis of Situations in Which the Task- or Relationship-Motivated Leader is More Effective

Leader–member relations	Good				Poor			
Task structure	Structured		Unstructured		Structured		Unstructured	
Leader position power	High	Low	High	Low	High	Low	High	Low
	1	2	3	4	5	6	7	8
Favorable for leader →								Unfavora for leade
Type of leader most effective in the situation	Task-motivated	Task-motivated	Task-motivated	Relation-ship-motivated	Relation-ship-motivated	Relation-ship-motivated	Relation-ship-motivated	Task-motivat

SOURCE: D. Organ and T. Bateman, *Organizational Behavior,* 4th ed. Copyright © 1990 by The McGraw-Hill Companies. Reproduced with permission of The McGraw-Hill Companies.

one of eight categories. The lower the category number, the more favorable the situation is for the leader; the higher the number, the less favorable the situation. Originally, Fiedler called this variable "situational favorableness" but now calls it "situational control." Situation 1 is the best: Relations are good, task structure is high, and power is high. In the least favorable situation (8), in which the leader has very little situational control, relations are poor, tasks lack structure, and the leader's power is weak.

Different situations dictate different leadership styles. Fiedler measured leadership styles with an instrument assessing the leader's *least preferred co-worker* (LPC); that is, the attitude toward the follower the leader liked the least. This was considered an indication more generally of leaders' attitudes toward people. If a leader can single out the person she likes the least, but her attitude is not all that negative, she received a high score on the LPC scale. Leaders with more negative attitudes toward others would receive low LPC scores.

Based on the LPC score, Fiedler considered two leadership styles. **Task-motivated leadership** places primary emphasis on completing the task and is more likely exhibited by leaders with low LPC scores. **Relationship-motivated leadership** emphasizes maintaining good interpersonal relationships and is more likely from high-LPC leaders. These leadership styles correspond to task performance and group maintenance leader behaviors, respectively.

The lower part of Figure E.1 indicates which style is situationally appropriate. For situations 1, 2, 3, and 8, a task-motivated leadership style is more effective. For situations 4 through 7, relationship-motivated leadership is more appropriate.

Fiedler's theory was not always supported by research. It is better supported if three broad rather than eight specific levels of situational control are assumed: low, medium, and high. It was quite controversial in academic circles; among other arguable things, it assumed that leaders cannot change their styles but must be assigned to situations that suit their styles. However, the model has withstood the test of time and still receives attention. Most important, it initiated and continues to emphasize the importance of finding a fit between the situation and the leader's style.

HERSEY AND BLANCHARD'S SITUATIONAL THEORY

Hersey and Blanchard developed a situational model that added another factor the leader should take into account before deciding whether task performance or maintenance behaviors are more important. Originally called the *life cycle theory of leadership*, their **situational theory** highlights the maturity of the follow-

ers as the key situational factor.[2] **Job maturity** is the level of the follower's skills and technical knowledge relative to the task being performed; **psychological maturity** is the follower's self-confidence and self-respect. High-maturity followers have both the ability and the confidence to do a good job.

The theory proposes that the more mature the followers, the less the leader needs to engage in task performance behaviors. The required amount of maintenance behaviors is a bit more complex: Maintenance behaviors are not important with followers of low or high levels of maturity but are important for followers of moderate maturity. For low-maturity followers, the emphasis should be on performance-related leadership; for moderate-maturity followers, performance leadership is somewhat less important and maintenance behaviors become more important; and for high-maturity followers, neither dimension of leadership behavior is important.

Little academic research has been done on this situational theory, but the model is popular in management training seminars. Regardless of its scientific validity, Hersey and Blanchard's model provides a reminder that it is important to treat different people differently. Moreover, it suggests the importance of treating the same individual differently from time to time as he or she changes jobs or acquires more maturity in her or his particular job.[3]

APPENDIX KEY TERMS

Fiedler's contingency model of leadership effectiveness A situational approach to leadership postulating that effectiveness depends on the personal style of the leader and the degree to which the situation gives the leader power, control, and influence over the situation, p. 423

Hersey and Blanchard's situational theory A life cycle theory of leadership postulating that a manager should consider an employee's psychological and job maturity before deciding whether task performance or maintenance behaviors are more important, p. 424

job maturity The level of the employee's skills and technical knowledge relative to the task being performed, p. 424

psychological maturity An employee's self-confidence and self-respect, p. 424

relationship-motivated leadership Leadership that places primary emphasis on maintaining good interpersonal relationships, p. 424

task-motivated leadership Leadership that places primary emphasis on completing a task, p. 424

Chapter 13

CHAPTER 13
Motivating for Performance

The worst mistake a boss can make is not to say well done.
—**John Ashcroft, Business Executive**
The reward of a thing well done is to have done it.
—**Ralph Waldo Emerson**

CHAPTER OUTLINE

LEARNING OBJECTIVES

After studying Chapter 13, you will know:

1. The kinds of behaviors managers need to motivate in people.

2. How to set challenging, motivating goals.

3. How to reward good performance properly.

4. The key beliefs that affect people's motivation.

5. The ways in which people's individual needs affect their behavior.

6. How to create a motivating, empowering job.

7. How people assess fairness and how to achieve fairness.

8. The causes and consequences of a satisfied workforce.

Prologue

ROCKY FLATS

Rocky Flats, located a few miles outside Denver, used to be a nuclear weapons plant. It ceased production in 1989. *Nightline* once called a building on the site the "most dangerous building in America."

Kaiser-Hill is the company running the cleanup, and Denny Ferrara is managing the teardown of the "cold" (nonnuclear) buildings. He has worked there for 30 years, as has his brother. Their father worked there starting in 1953. Other family members work there still. Through most of its history, Rocky Flats was seen as a place offering lifetime employment—a very good thing for employees.

Rocky Flats workers were treated like heroes during the Cold War, when they made plutonium-based triggers for nuclear bombs. Then a 1989 FBI raid shut the place down, and the workers became pariahs as their public image went from being patriots to being polluters. They had to clean up the place, and morale was low. Even in late 2000, after much had been accomplished, management at Kaiser-Hill thought it just 15 percent likely that the job could be completed by 2006.

The work now is no more or less dangerous than traditional construction work, and this is the kind of work the Ferraras and their co-workers do. But they are working as hard and as fast as they can to finish the job and put themselves out of work.

Initial estimates were that it would take 70 years and $36 billion to complete the job. Kaiser-Hill set goals of 10 years and less than $7 billion. At the current pace, the Rocky Flats facility will cease to exist in 2006—decades ahead of what most people thought possible.

Source: For Prologue, Connections, Epilogue J. McGregor, "Rocky Mountain High," *Fast Company*, July 2004, pp. 58–63.

This chapter tackles an age-old question: How can a manager motivate people to work hard and perform at their best levels?

A sales manager in one company had a unique approach to this question. Each month, the person with the worst sales performance took home a live goat for the weekend. The manager hoped the goat-of-month employee would be so embarrassed that he or she would work harder the next month to increase sales.[1]

This sales manager may get high marks for creativity. But if he is graded by results, as he grades his salespeople, he will fail. He may succeed in motivating a few of his people to increase sales, but some good people will be motivated to quit the company.

Motivating for Performance

Understanding why people do the things they do on the job is not an easy task for the manager. *Predicting* their response to management's latest productivity program is harder yet. Fortunately, enough is known about motivation to give the thoughtful manager practical, effective techniques for increasing people's effort and performance.

Motivation refers to forces that energize, direct, and sustain a person's efforts. All behavior, except involuntary reflexes like eye blinks (which have little to do with management), is motivated. A highly motivated person will work hard toward achieving performance goals. With adequate ability and understanding of the job, such a person will be highly productive.

motivation

Forces that energize, direct, and sustain a person's efforts.

To be effective motivators, managers must know what behaviors they want to motivate people to exhibit. Although productive people appear to do a seemingly limitless number of things, most of the important activities can be grouped into five general categories.[2] Managers must motivate people to (1) *join the organization*; (2) *remain in the organization*; and (3) *come to work regularly*. On these points, you should reject the common recent notion that loyalty is dead, and accept the challenge of creating an environment that will attract and energize people so that they commit to the organization.[3]

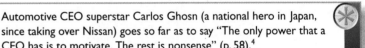

Automotive CEO superstar Carlos Ghosn (a national hero in Japan, since taking over Nissan) goes so far as to say "The only power that a CEO has is to motivate. The rest is nonsense" (p. 58).[4]

Of course, companies also want people to (4) *perform*—that is, once employees are at work, they should work hard to achieve high *output* (productivity) and high *quality*. Finally, managers want employees to (5) *exhibit good citizenship*. Good citizens of the organization are committed, satisfied employees who perform above and beyond the call of duty by doing extra things that can help the company. The importance of citizenship behaviors may be less obvious than productivity, but these behaviors help the organization function smoothly. They also make managers' lives easier.

Many ideas have been proposed to help managers motivate people to engage in these constructive behaviors. The most useful of these ideas are described in the following pages. We start with the most fundamental *processes* that influence the motivation of all people. These processes—described by goal-setting, reinforcement, and expectancy theories—suggest basic and powerful actions for managers to take. Then we discuss the *content* of what people want and need from work, how individuals differ from one another, and how understanding people's needs leads to powerful prescriptions about designing motivating jobs and empowering people to perform at the highest possible levels. Finally, we discuss the most important beliefs and perceptions about fairness that people hold toward their work, and the implications for motivation.

Setting Goals

Providing work-related goals for people is an extremely effective way to stimulate motivation. In fact, it is perhaps the most important, valid, and useful single approach to motivating performance. Therefore, we discuss it first.

goal-setting theory

A motivation theory stating that people have conscious goals that energize them and direct their thoughts and behaviors toward a particular end.

Goal-setting theory states that people have conscious goals that energize them and direct their thoughts and behaviors toward a particular end.[5] With the principle that goals matter in mind, managers set goals for employees. For example, a cable-TV company might set goals for increasing the number of new subscribers, or the number of current subscribers who pay for premium channels, or the timeliness of responses to customer inquiries.[6] Goal setting works for any job in which people have control over their performance.[7] You can set goals for performance quality and quantity, plus behavioral goals like cooperation or teamwork.[8] In fact, you can set goals for whatever is important.[9]

Goals that Motivate

You can set goals for cost, quality, speed, innovation—anything that's important.

The most powerful goals are *meaningful*—noble purposes that appeal to people's "higher" values add extra motivating power.[10] Johnson & Johnson pursues profit, but it's also about improving health care. Ben & Jerry's makes great ice cream but also is socially responsible. ServiceMaster, the cleaning and maintenance company, has a religious commitment that appeals to its employees, and Huntsman Chemical has goals of paying off corporate debt but also relieving human suffering—it sponsors cancer research and a number of charities. This point is not just about the values companies espouse and the lofty goals they pursue; it's also about leadership at a more personal level. Followers of transformational leaders view their work as more important and as highly congruent with their personal goals[11] as compared with transactional leaders[11] (recall Chapter 12).

More specifically, much is known about how to manage goals in ways that motivate high job performance. Goals should be *acceptable* to employees. This means, among other things, that they should not conflict with people's personal values and that people have reasons to pursue the goals. Allowing people to participate in setting their work goals—as opposed to having the boss set goals for them—is often a great way to generate goals that people accept and pursue willingly.

Ben & Jerry's is known for making some of the world's best ice cream. But its social responsibility, especially its dedication to making people more environmentally aware, is also highly important to many employees and customers.

Acceptable, maximally motivating goals are *challenging but attainable*. In other words, they should be high enough to inspire better performance but not so high that people can never reach them. One team of consultants to an international corporation created more than 40 programs aimed at increasing quality. The company announced it did not expect significant quality improvement until the *fourth year* of the program. Such a goal is not nearly demanding enough.[12]

Microsoft uses the acronym SMART to create motivating goals: specific, measurable, achievable, results-based, and time-specific.[13] Ideal goals do not merely exhort employees to improve performance, start doing their best, increase productivity, or decrease the length of time customers must wait to receive service. Goals should be more like Caterpillar Tractor's guaranteed parts delivery within 24 hours or JetBlue's 20-minute goal for unloading luggage.[14]

Such deadlines, and measurable performance goals, are specific, quantifiable goals that employees are motivated to achieve. By the way, data about competitors can also provide good goals, stoking people's competitive spirit and desire to succeed in the marketplace.[15]

Stretch Goals

stretch goals

Targets that are particularly demanding, sometimes even thought to be impossible.

Top firms today set **stretch goals**—targets that are exceptionally demanding, and that some people would never even think of. There are two types of stretch goals:[16] vertical stretch goals, aligned with current activities including productivity and financial results; and horizontal stretch goals, which involve people's professional development like attempting and learning new, difficult things. Impossible though stretch goals may seem to some, they often are in fact attainable.

Stretch goals can generate a major shift away from mediocrity and toward tremendous achievement. But if someone tries in good faith but doesn't meet their stretch goals, don't punish—remember how difficult they are! Base your assessment on how much performance has improved, how the performance compares to others, and how much progress has been made.[17]

Stretch Goals in Practice

Some legendary business leaders motivated themselves and their people via stretch goals. In the 1950s, when the label "Made in Japan" conveyed to Americans that the product was cheap junk, Sony's Akio Morita set out to change the world's perception of Japanese quality. At the time, he had fewer than 1,000 employees, with no significant overseas presence. Yet he succeeded. In the United States, Sam Walton started out in 1945 by wanting to make his store in Newport the best variety store in Arkansas. Later, in 1977, he declared that Wal-Mart would double in size and become a $1 billion company within four years. Even in 1990, when Wal-Mart seemed to be everywhere and sales had reached $30 billion, he set targets of doubling the number of stores and achieving sales volume of $125 billion.

More recent examples abound. In 2000, when revenues were $431 million, Meg Whitman of eBay announced that eBay would reach $3 billion in 2005. Scott Cook, Intuit founder and an eBay board member, said "I thought it was nuts." eBay flew past $3 billion, ahead of schedule. Schwab people don't view their company as a leader in discount brokerage; they view it as having captured only 1 percent of the savings of investors in the United States. In other words, they aim at landing the available 99 percent.

Boeing's stretch goals were to cut the cost of manufacturing an airplane 25 percent, and then it reduced the time needed to build one from 18 months to 8 months. States Boeing's CEO, "We're doing things we didn't think were possible."

Sony's Akio Morita's goal to change the world's perception of Japanese quality was achieved with products like the Sony "boom box," VCR, and the Walkman. Most people think high quality when they think of a Sony TV, and are willing to pay the higher prices Sony is able to charge.

SOURCES: J. Collins and J. Porras, *Built to Last* (London: Century Business, 1996); S. Tully, "Why to Go for Stretch Targets," *Fortune*, November 4, 1994, pp. 145–58; K. Thompson, W. Hochwarter, and N. Mathys, "Stretch Targets: What Makes Them Effective?" *Academy of Management Executive* 11 (1997), pp. 48–60; G. Hamel, "Reinvent Your Company," *Fortune*, June 12, 2000, pp. 98–118; P. Sellers, "eBay's Secret," *Fortune*, October 18, 2004, pp. 160–78.

Limitations of Goal Setting

Goal setting is an extraordinarily powerful management technique. But even specific, challenging, attainable goals work better under some conditions than others. For example, if people lack relevant ability and knowledge, a better course to follow might be simply urging them to do their best or setting a goal to learn rather than a goal to achieve a specific performance level.[18] Also, people focused on their own goals may not help others attain their goals. Individual performance goals can be dysfunctional if people work in a group and cooperation among team members is essential to team performance.[19] Individualized goals can create competition and reduce cooperation. If cooperation is important, performance goals should be established *for the team*.

Goals can generate manipulative game-playing and unethical behavior. For example, people can sometimes find ingenious ways to set easy goals and convince their bosses that they are difficult.[20] People who don't meet their goals are more likely to engage in unethical behavior than are people who are trying to do their best but have no specific performance goals. This is true regardless of whether they have financial incentives, and is particularly true when people fall just short of reaching their goals.[21] During the tech boom years, continually "raising the bar" for growth in stock values created "ever-higher expectations [that] could not be met without financial and accounting practices that were the equivalent of steroids."[22]

As another important example, some executives have mastered the art of "earnings management," precisely meeting Wall Street analysts' earnings estimates or beating them by a single penny.[23] The media trumpet, and investors reward, meeting or beating the estimates. People meet this goal by either manipulating the numbers or initiating whispering campaigns to persuade analysts to lower their estimates, making them more attainable. The marketplace wants quarterly measurement, but long-term viability is ultimately more important.

It is important *not* to establish a single productivity goal if there are other important dimensions of performance.[24] For instance, productivity goals will likely enhance productivity, but they may also cause employees to neglect other things like tackling new projects or developing creative solutions to job-related problems. The manager who wants to motivate creativity should establish creativity goals along with productivity goals. Even the prestigious Baldrige award for quality was criticized for generating such zealous pursuit that companies focus single-mindedly on winning the award at the expense of other key elements of business success.[25]

Set Your Own Goals

Goal setting works for yourself, as well—it's a powerful tool for self-management. Set goals for yourself; don't just try hard or hope for the best. Create a statement of purpose for yourself comprised of three elements: an inspiring distant vision, a mid-distant goal along the way (worthy in its own right), and near-term objectives to start working on immediately.[26] So, if you are going into business, you might articulate your goal for the type of businessperson you want to be in five years, the types of jobs that could create the opportunities and teach you what you need to know to become that businessperson, and the specific schoolwork and job search activities that can get you moving in those directions. And on the job, apply SMART and other goal-setting advice for yourself.

Reinforcing Performance

law of effect

A law formulated by Edward Thorndike in 1911 stating that behavior that is followed by positive consequences will likely be repeated.

reinforcers

Positive consequences that motivate behavior.

organizational behavior modification (OB Mod)

The application of reinforcement theory in organizational settings.

Goals are universal motivators. So are the processes of reinforcement described in this section. In 1911, psychologist Edward Thorndike formulated the **law of effect:** Behavior that is followed by positive consequences probably will be repeated.[27] This powerful law of behavior laid the foundation for countless investigations into the effects of the positive consequences, called **reinforcers,** that motivate behavior. **Organizational behavior modification** attempts to influence people's behavior, and improve performance,[28] by systematically managing work conditions and the consequences of people's actions.

Four key consequences of behavior either encourage or discourage people's behavior (see Figure 13.1):

1. **Positive reinforcement**—applying a consequence that increases the likelihood that the person will repeat the behavior that led to it. Examples of positive reinforcers include compliments, letters of commendation, favorable performance evaluations, and pay raises. For example, North American Tool & Die provided monthly cash awards for creativity.[29] At Immunex, employees received on-the-spot Applause Awards worth from $250 to $2,500.[30] But it is important to remember that positive feedback and social reinforcers, including recognition for a job well done, are as powerful as monetary reinforcers.[31]

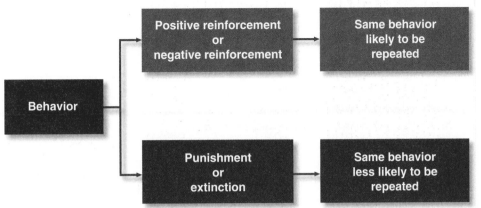

FIGURE 13.1
The Consequences of Behavior

2. **Negative reinforcement**—removing or withholding an undesirable consequence. For example, a manager takes an employee (or a school takes a student) off probation because of improved performance. A few years ago, Nordstrom, the prominent retailer, received a great deal of negative publicity about its overreliance on negative reinforcement as a motivational tool. Frequent threatening memos admonished people to achieve every one of their many performance goals: "If any of these areas are not met to our expectations, you will be terminated." Another memo reminded employees that calling in sick once every three months is "a lot" and enough to "question your dedication."[32] Negative reinforcement in these examples occurs when people perform well and avoid punishment.

3. **Punishment**—administering an aversive consequence. Examples include criticizing or shouting at an employee, assigning an unappealing task, and sending a worker home without pay. Negative reinforcement can involve the *threat* of punishment, but not delivering it when employees perform satisfactorily. Punishment is the actual delivery of the aversive consequence. Managers use punishment when they think it is warranted or when they believe others expect them to, and they usually concern themselves with following company policy and procedure.[33]

4. **Extinction**—withdrawing or failing to provide a reinforcing consequence. When this occurs, motivation is reduced and the behavior is *extinguished*, or eliminated. For higher-level managers at P&G, failure to share creative ideas means failure to get promoted.[34] Other examples include not giving a compliment for a job well done, forgetting to say thanks for a favor, and setting impossible performance goals so that the person never experiences success.

The first two consequences, positive and negative reinforcement, are positive for the person receiving them—the person either gains something or avoids something negative. Therefore, the person who experiences these consequences will be motivated to behave in the ways that led to the reinforcement. The last two consequences, punishment and extinction, are negative outcomes for the person receiving them: Motivation to repeat the behavior that led to the undesirable results will be reduced.

(Mis)Managing Rewards and Punishments

You've learned about the positive effects of a transformational leadership style, but giving rewards to high-performing people is also essential.[35] Unfortunately, sometimes organizations and managers reinforce the wrong behaviors.[36] Whereas executive stock options were intended to motivate executives to care more about the company's stock price, they have motivated executives to engage in inappropriate behaviors to manipulate the stock price rather than create real value.[37] The company that bases performance reviews on short-term results is reinforcing a short-run perspective in decision

positive reinforcement

Applying consequences that increase the likelihood that a person will repeat the behavior that led to it.

negative reinforcement

Removing or withholding an undesirable consequence.

punishment

Administering an aversive consequence.

extinction

Withdrawing or failing to provide a reinforcing consequence.

"The things that get rewarded get done" is what one author called The Greatest Management Principle in the World. With this in mind, Michael LeBoeuf offered prescriptions for effectively motivating high performance. Companies, and individual managers, should reward the following:

1. *Solid solutions* instead of quick fixes.
2. *Risk taking* instead of risk avoiding.
3. *Applied creativity* instead of mindless conformity.
4. *Decisive action* instead of paralysis by analysis.
5. *Smart work* instead of busywork.
6. *Simplification* instead of needless complication.
7. *Quietly effective behavior* instead of squeaky wheels.
8. *Quality work* instead of fast work.
9. *Loyalty* instead of turnover.
10. *Working together* instead of working against.

TABLE 13.1

The Greatest Management Principle in the World

Source: From The Greatest Management Principel in the Worldy by Michael LeBoeuf. Copyright © 1985 by Michael Le Boeuf. Used by permission of Berkeley Publishing Group, a division of Penquin Putnam, Inc.

making. At the same time, it is discouraging behaviors that will pay off in the long run. Programs that punish employees for absenteeism beyond a certain limit may actually encourage them to be absent. People may use up all their allowable absences and fail to come to work regularly until they reach the point where their next absence will result in punishment.

Managers must identify which kinds of behaviors they reinforce and which they discourage (see Table 13.1). The reward system has to support the firm's strategy, defining people's performance in ways that pursue strategic objectives.[38] Reward employees for developing themselves in strategically important ways—for building new skills that are critical to strengthening core competencies and creating value.

SAS employees get free M&Ms on Wednesdays. This tradition was started in its early days as an inexpensive, fun way to tell employees they mattered. Now, with over 10,000 employees, SAS spends $45,000 annually on 22 tons of M&Ms.[40]

Managers should be creative in their use of reinforcers.[39] Some companies awarded Palm Pilots to employees who recruited good, new talent. CEO A. G. Lafley of P&G gave rank-and-file employees 50 stock options for creative ideas and celebrates innovators on the company's internal Web site.[41] Donald Trump rewards loyalty with trips to his Florida estate Mar-a-Lago or golf club memberships, and he remembers birthdays.[42] Other companies have used as rewards private rodeos with mechanical bulls, flights in a fighter plane, lifetime supplies of Ben & Jerry's ice cream, fly fishing trips, and sabbaticals.[43]

Innovative managers use nonmonetary rewards, including intellectual challenge, greater responsibility, autonomy, recognition, flexible benefits, and greater influence over decisions. These and other rewards for high-performing employees, when creatively devised and applied, can continue to motivate when pay and promotions are scarce.[44]

Managing Mistakes

How a manager reacts to people's mistakes has a big impact on motivation. Punishment is sometimes appropriate, as when people violate the law, ethical standards, important safety rules, or standards of interpersonal treatment, or when they fail to attend or perform like a slacker. But sometimes managers punish people when they shouldn't—as when poor performance isn't the person's fault, or managers take out their frustrations on the wrong people.

Managers who overuse punishment or use it inappropriately create a climate of fear in the workplace.[45] Fear causes people to focus on the short term, sometimes creating problems in the longer run. Fear also creates a focus on oneself, rather than on the group and the organization. The key is how to think about and handle mistakes.

Recognize that everyone makes mistakes, and that mistakes can be dealt with constructively by discussing and learning from them. Don't punish, but praise people who deliver bad news to their bosses. Treat failure to act as a failure but don't punish unsuccessful, good-faith efforts. If you're a leader, talk about your failures with your people, and show how you learned from them. Give people second chances, and maybe third chances (Trump claims to give second chances, but never third). Encourage people to try new things, and don't punish them if they don't work out.

Providing Feedback

Most managers don't provide enough useful feedback, and most people don't receive or ask for feedback enough.[46] As a manager, you should consider all potential causes of poor performance, pay full attention when employees ask for feedback or want to discuss performance issues, and give feedback according to the guidelines you read about in Chapter 10.

Feedback can be offered in many ways.[47] Customers sometimes give feedback directly: you also can request customer feedback and give it to the employee. You can provide statistics on work that the person has directly influenced. A manufacturing firm—high-tech or otherwise—can put the phone number of the production team on the product so customers can call the team directly. Performance reviews, described in Chapter 11, should be conducted regularly. And bosses should give more regular, ongoing feedback—it helps correct problems immediately, provides immediate reinforcement for good work, and prevents surprises when the formal review comes.

For yourself, try not to be afraid of receiving feedback; in fact, you should actively seek it. And when you get it, try to avoid negative emotions like anger, hurt, defensiveness, or resignation. Think: It's up to me to get the feedback I need; I need to know these things about my performance and my behavior; learning what I need to know about myself will help me identify needs and create new opportunities; it serves my interest best to know rather than not know; taking initiative on this gives me more power and influence over my career.[48]

How would your attitude toward work be affected if your manager overreacted by yelling at you over an honest mistake?

Make sure that you reward the right things, not the wrong things. Sound obvious? You'd be surprised how often this principle is violated!

Connections: ROCKY FLATS

Remember from the Prologue how hard Denny Ferrara and his family and colleagues are working to clean up and close down Rocky Flats? How did Kaiser-Hill get employees to commit to working so hard, so fast, so well?

The company needed to convince employees to strive for results that most thought impossible, to stretch themselves like they never had before, and to create new ways of working faster, safer, and smarter.

Workers had not had a clear performance goal since 1989. Kaiser-Hill created performance goals that could be measured, reached, and celebrated. CEO Nancy Tuor said "We had to reinstate the pride and accomplishment that they'd had during the production days." In meetings, newsletters, and announcements, she praised workers' progress—a rare event in previous years.

Kaiser-Hill worked with the union to eliminate narrow job responsibilities and create flexible teams of workers. This led to countless innovations and improved productivity. On the other hand, when workers mishandled a fire, management realized it had given workers too much freedom and provided more training and guidance.

The company offered overtime pay and financial incentives linked to performance, contributing to the overall effort and ultimately to finishing the job. Kaiser-Hill also asked employees to envision a wildlife refuge in place of the Rocky Flats facility, and challenged them to accomplish something that had never been done before.

Performance-Related Beliefs

Reinforcement theory describes the processes by which factors in the work environment affect people's behavior. Expectancy theory adds to that some of the cognitive processes that go on in people's heads. According to **expectancy theory,** the person's work *efforts* lead to some level of *performance*.[49] Then performance results in one or more *outcomes* for the person (see Figure 13.2). People develop two important beliefs linking these three events: expectancy, which links effort to performance, and instrumentality, which links performance to outcomes.

The Effort-to-Performance Link

The first belief, **expectancy,** is people's perceived likelihood that their efforts will enable them to attain their performance goals. An expectancy can be high (up to 100 percent), such as when a student is confident that if she studies hard she can get a good grade on the final. An expectancy can also be low (down to a 0 percent likelihood), such as when a suitor is convinced that his dream date will never go out with him.

All else equal, high expectancies create higher motivation than do low expectancies. In the preceding examples, the student is more likely to study for the exam than the suitor is to pursue the dream date, even though both want their respective outcomes.

Expectancies can vary among individuals, even in the same situation. For example, a sales manager might initiate a competition in which the top salesperson wins a free trip to Hawaii. In such cases, the few top people, who have performed well in the past, will be more motivated by the contest than will the historically average and below-average performers. The top people will have higher expectancies—stronger beliefs that their efforts can help them turn in the top performance.

The Performance-to-Outcome Link

The example about the sales contest illustrates how performance results in some kind of **outcome,** or consequence, for the person. Actually, it often results in several outcomes. For example, turning in the best sales performance could lead to (1) a competitive victory, (2) the free trip to Hawaii, (3) feelings of achievement, (4) recognition from the boss, (5) prestige throughout the company, and (6) resentment from other salespeople.

But how certain is it that performance will result in all of those outcomes? Will winning the contest really lead to resentment? Will it really lead to increased prestige?

These questions address the second key belief described by expectancy theory: instrumentality.[50] **Instrumentality** is the perceived likelihood that performance will be followed by a particular outcome. Like expectancies, instrumentalities can be high (up to 100 percent) or low (approaching 0 percent). For example, you can be fully confident that if you do a good job you'll get a promotion, or you can feel that no matter how well you do, the promotion will go to someone else.

Also, each outcome has an associated valence. **Valence** is the value the person places on the outcome. Valences can be positive, like the Hawaiian vacation, or negative, like the other salespeople's resentment.

FIGURE 13.2

Basic Concepts of Expectancy Theory

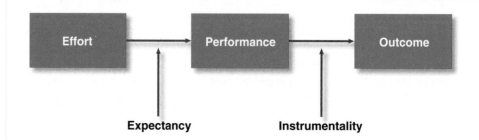

Winning a competition for a free trip to Hawaii would be great, but what about all the losers?

Impact on Motivation

For motivation to be high, expectancy, instrumentalities, and total valence of all outcomes must all be high. A person will not be highly motivated if any of the following conditions exist:

1. He believes he can't perform well enough to achieve the positive outcomes that he knows the company provides to good performers (high valence and high instrumentality but low expectancy).
2. He knows he can do the job, and is fairly certain what the ultimate outcomes will be (say, a promotion and a transfer). However, he doesn't want those outcomes or believes other, negative outcomes outweigh the positive (high expectancy and high instrumentality but low valence).
3. He knows he can do the job, and wants several important outcomes (a favorable performance review, a raise, and a promotion). But he believes that no matter how well he performs, the outcomes will not be forthcoming (high expectancy and positive valences but low instrumentality).

— cognitive evaluation

Managerial Implications of Expectancy Theory

Expectancy theory helps the manager zero in on key leverage points for influencing motivation. Three implications are crucial:

1. *Increase expectancies.* Provide a work environment that facilitates good performance, and set realistically attainable performance goals. Provide training, support, and encouragement so that people are confident they can perform at the levels expected of them. Recall from Chapter 12 that charismatic leaders excel at boosting their followers' confidence.
2. *Identify positively valent outcomes.* Understand what people want to get out of work. Think about what their jobs provide them and what is not, but could be, provided. Consider how people may differ in the valences they assign to outcomes. Know the need theories of motivation, described in the next section, and their implications for identifying important outcomes.
3. *Make performance instrumental toward positive outcomes.* Make sure that good performance is followed by personal recognition and praise, favorable performance reviews, pay increases, and other positive results. Also, make sure

that working hard and doing things well will have as few negative results as possible. It is useful to realize, too, that bosses usually provide (or withhold) rewards, but others do so as well, including peers, direct reports, customers, and others.[51] A division of Wells Fargo distributed Monopoly money to employees, and told them to award it to helpful colleagues. The recipients then converted the play money to real money. Similarly, Northwest Airlines distributed cash-convertible certificates to frequent flyers and invited them to award the certificates to Northwest employees who deserved them.

Understanding People's Needs

So far we have focused on *processes* underlying motivation. The manager who appropriately applies goal-setting, reinforcement, and expectancy theories is creating essential motivating elements in the work environment. But characteristics of the person also affect motivation. The second type of motivation theory, *content theories*, indicates the kinds of needs that people want to satisfy. People have different needs energizing and motivating them toward different goals and reinforcers. The extent to which and the ways in which a person's needs are met or not met at work affect his or her behavior on the job.

The most important theories describing the content of people's needs are Maslow's need hierarchy, Alderfer's ERG theory, and McClelland's needs.

Maslow's Need Hierarchy

Abraham Maslow organized five major types of human needs into a hierarchy, as shown in Figure 13.3.[52] The **need hierarchy** illustrates Maslow's conception of people satisfying their needs in a specified order, from bottom to top. The needs, in ascending order, are:

> **Maslow's need hierarchy**
>
> A conception of human needs organizing needs into a hierarchy of five major types.

1. *Physiological* (food, water, sex, and shelter).
2. *Safety or security* (protection against threat and deprivation).
3. *Social* (friendship, affection, belonging, and love).
4. *Ego* (independence, achievement, freedom, status, recognition, and self-esteem).
5. *Self-actualization* (realizing one's full potential, becoming everything one is capable of being).

FIGURE 13.3
Maslow's Need Hierarchy

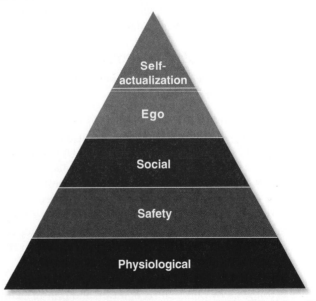

SOURCE: D. Organ and T. Bateman, *Organizational Behavior* 4th ed. Copyright © 1990 by The McGraw-Hill Companies. Reproduced with permission of The McGraw-Hill Companies.

According to Maslow, people are motivated to satisfy the lower needs before they try to satisfy the higher needs. In the modern workplace, safety needs generally are well satisfied, making social, ego, and self-actualization needs preeminent. But safety issues are still very important in manufacturing and other work environments. Moreover, 9/11 affected people everywhere, including the workplace, and not just where the attacks occurred. Surveys show that since the crisis, managers have responded to employees' physical safety concerns although not necessarily to their emotional concerns.[53] Months after the event, employees still felt fear, denial, and anger—especially among people with children, women, and those close to the events. On an emotional level, managers can demonstrate visible leadership, acting as a role model of calmness and reassurance. To deal more directly with safety issues, managers can show what the firm will do to improve security and manage employee risk, including crisis management plans as discussed in Chapter 3.

Once a need is satisfied, it is no longer a powerful motivator. For example, labor unions negotiate for higher wages, benefits, safety standards, and job security. These bargaining issues relate directly to the satisfaction of Maslow's lower-level needs. Only after these needs are reasonably satisfied do the higher-level needs—social, ego, and self-actualization—become dominant concerns.

Maslow's hierarchy, however, is a simplistic and not altogether accurate theory of human motivation.[54] For example, not everyone progresses through the five needs in hierarchical order. But Maslow made three important contributions. First, he identified important need categories, which can help managers create effective positive reinforcers. Second, it is helpful to think of two general levels of needs, in which lower-level needs must be satisfied before higher-level needs become important. Third, Maslow alerted managers to the importance of personal growth and self-actualization.

Self-actualization is the best-known concept arising from this theory. According to Maslow, the average person is only 10 percent self-actualized. In other words, most of us are living our lives and working at our jobs with a large untapped reservoir of potential. The implication is clear: Create a work environment that provides training, resources, autonomy, responsibilities, and challenging assignments. This type of environment gives people a chance to use their skills and abilities in creative ways and allows them to achieve more of their full potential.

So treat people not merely as a cost to be controlled but an asset to be developed. Many companies, including AT&T, Procter & Gamble, Du Pont, General Electric, and Coast Gas of Watsonville, California, have embarked on programs that provide personal growth experiences for their people.[55] An employee at Federal Express said, "The best I can be is what I can be here. Federal Express . . . gave me the confidence and self-esteem to become the person I had the potential to become" (p. 63).[56]

Organizations gain by making full use of their human resources. Employees also gain by capitalizing on opportunities to meet their higher-order needs on the job. At Du Pont, managers set personal growth goals along with performance goals. "In the past," says one executive, "[people asked] what job am I getting next? Now, it's more, how can I be developed as a person?"[57]

Federal Express treats employees not as a cost to be controlled but as an asset to be developed.

Alderfer's ERG Theory

A theory of human needs that is more advanced than Maslow's is Alderfer's ERG theory.[58] Maslow's theory has general applicability, but Alderfer aims his theory expressly at understanding people's needs at work.

ERG theory postulates three sets of needs: existence, relatedness, and growth. *Existence* needs are all material and physiological desires. *Relatedness* needs involve relationships with other people and are satisfied through the process of mutually sharing thoughts and feelings. *Growth* needs motivate people to productively or creatively

Alderfer's ERG theory

A human needs theory developed by Alderfer postulating that people have three basic sets of needs which can operate simultaneously.

change themselves or their environment. Satisfaction of the growth needs comes from fully utilizing personal capacities and developing new capacities.

What similarities do you see between Alderfer's and Maslow's needs? Roughly speaking, existence needs subsume physiological and security needs, relatedness needs are similar to social and esteem needs, and growth needs correspond to self-actualization.

ERG theory proposes that several different needs can be operating at once. Thus, whereas Maslow would say that self-actualization is important to people only after other sets of needs are satisfied, Alderfer maintains that people—particularly working people in our postindustrial society—can be motivated to satisfy both existence and growth needs at the same time.

Maslow's theory is better known to American managers than Alderfer's, but ERG theory has more scientific support.[59] Both have practical value in that they remind managers of the types of reinforcers or rewards that can be used to motivate people. Regardless of whether the manager prefers the Maslow or the Alderfer theory of needs, he or she can motivate people by helping them satisfy their needs, and particularly by offering opportunities for self-actualization and growth.

McClelland's Needs

David McClelland also identified a number of basic needs that guide people. The most important needs for managers, according to McClelland, are the needs for achievement, affiliation, and power.[60] Different needs predominate for different people. As you read about these needs, think about yourself—which one(s) are most and least important to you?

The need for *achievement* is characterized by a strong orientation toward accomplishment and an obsession with success and goal attainment. Most managers and entrepreneurs in the United States have high levels of this need and like to see it in their employees.

The need for *affiliation* reflects a strong desire to be liked by other people. Individuals who have high levels of this need are oriented toward getting along with others and may be less concerned with performing at high levels.

The need for *power* is a desire to influence or control other people. This need can be a negative force—termed *personalized power*—if it is expressed through the aggressive manipulation and exploitation of others. People high on the personalized-power need want power purely for the pursuit of their own goals. But the need for power also can be a positive motive—called *socialized power*—because it can be channeled toward the constructive improvement of organizations and societies.

Low need for affiliation and moderate to high need for power are associated with managerial success for both higher- and lower-level managers.[61] One reason the need for affiliation is not necessary for leadership success is that people high on this need have difficulty making tough but necessary decisions that will make some people unhappy.

Need Theories: International Perspectives

The Japanese are more group oriented while Americans are more individually oriented when it comes to motivation. How do you think this affects how these two countries do business together?

How do the need theories apply abroad?[62] Whereas managers in the United States care most strongly about achievement, esteem, and self-actualization, managers in Greece and Japan are motivated more by security. Social needs are most important in Sweden, Norway, and Denmark. "Doing your own thing"—the phrase from the 1960s that describes an American culture oriented toward self-actualization—is not even translatable into Chinese. "Achievement" too is difficult to translate into most other languages. Researchers in France, Japan, and Sweden would have been unlikely to even conceive of McClelland's achievement motive, because people of those countries are more group-oriented than individually oriented.

Clearly, achievement, growth, and self-actualization are profoundly important in the United States, Canada, and Great Britain. But these needs are not universally important. Every manager must remember that need importance varies from country to country and that people may not be motivated by the same needs. Generally, no single way is best, and managers can customize their approaches by considering how individuals differ.[63]

Designing Motivating Jobs

Here's an example of a company that gave a "reward" that didn't motivate. One of Mary Kay Ash's former employers gave her a sales award: a flounder fishing light. Unfortunately, she doesn't fish. Fortunately, she later was able to design her own organization around both *intrinsic* as well as *extrinsic* motivators that *mattered* to her people.[64] **Extrinsic rewards** are given to people by the boss, the company, or some other person. An **intrinsic reward** is reward the person derives directly from performing the job itself. An interesting project, an intriguing subject that is fun to study, a completed sale, and the discovery of the perfect solution to a difficult problem all can give people the feeling that they have done something well. This is the essence of the motivation that comes from intrinsic rewards.

Intrinsic rewards are essential to the motivation underlying creativity.[65] A challenging problem, a chance to create something new, and work that is exciting in and of itself can provide intrinsic motivation that inspires people to devote time and energy to the task. So do managers who allow people some freedom to pursue the tasks that interest them most. The opposite situations result in routine, habitual behaviors which interfere with creativity.[66] A study in manufacturing facilities found that employees initiated more applications for patents, made more novel and useful suggestions, and were rated by their managers as more creative when their jobs were challenging and their managers did not control their activities closely.[67] On the other hand, some jobs and organizations create environments that quash creativity and motivation.[68]

The classic example of a demotivating job is the highly specialized assembly line job; each worker performs one boring operation before passing the work along to the next worker. Such specialization, or the "mechanistic" approach to job design, was the prevailing practice through most of the 20th century.[69]

But jobs that are too simple and routine result in employee dissatisfaction, absenteeism, and turnover. Moreover, people at many successful firms have become millionaires, leading to turnover problems. The only way to keep such employees is to let them design their own jobs so that their work is more interesting than it would be elsewhere.[70] Increasingly, jobs are being designed in the following ways to increase intrinsic rewards and therefore motivation.

Job Rotation, Enlargement, and Enrichment

With **job rotation**, workers who spend all their time in one routine task can instead move from one task to another. Rather than dishing out the pasta in a cafeteria line all day, a person might work the pasta, then the salads, and then the vegetables, or desserts. Job rotation is intended to alleviate boredom by giving people different things to do at different times.

As you may guess, however, the person may just be changing from one boring job to another. But job rotation can benefit everyone when done properly, with people's input and career interests in mind. At G.S.I. Transcomm Data Systems of Pittsburgh, people often voice their preferences and rotate laterally to new assignments. Examples include an operations manager who moved into sales management, a programmer who moved into service for longtime customers, and a receptionist who moved

> **extrinsic rewards**
>
> Rewards given to a person by the boss, the company, or some other person.

> **intrinsic reward**
>
> Reward a worker derives directly from performing the job itself.

Intrinsic rewards and the freedom to be creative are keys to innovation.

> **job rotation**
>
> Changing from one routine task to another to alleviate boredom.

into sales.[71] The result of the rotation policy often is a reenergized worker who stays with the company.

Job enlargement is similar to job rotation in that people are given different tasks to do. But whereas job rotation involves doing one task at one time and changing to a different task at a different time, job enlargement means that the worker has multiple tasks at the same time. Thus, an assembly worker's job is enlarged if he or she is given two tasks rather than one to perform. In a study of job enlargement in a financial services organization, enlarged jobs led to higher job satisfaction, better error detection by clerks, and improved customer service.[72]

With job enlargement, the person's additional tasks are at the same level of responsibility. More profound changes occur when jobs are enriched. **Job enrichment** means that jobs are restructured or redesigned by adding higher levels of responsibility. This includes giving people not only more tasks but higher-level ones, such as when decisions are delegated downward and authority is decentralized. Efforts to redesign jobs by enriching them are now common in American industry. Herzberg's two-factor theory was the first approach to job enrichment, followed by the Hackman and Oldham model.

Herzberg's Two-Factor Theory

Frederick Herzberg's **two-factor theory** distinguished between two broad categories of factors that affect people working on their jobs.[73] The first category, **hygiene factors,** are *characteristics of the workplace:* company policies, working conditions, pay, co-workers, supervision, and so forth. These factors can make people unhappy if they are poorly managed. If they are well managed, and viewed as positive by employees, the employees will no longer be dissatisfied. However, no matter how good these factors are, they will not make people truly satisfied or motivated to do a good job.

According to Herzberg, the key to true job satisfaction and motivation to perform lies in the second category: the motivators. The **motivators** describe the *job itself,* that is, what people *do* at work. Motivators are the nature of the work itself, the actual job responsibilities, opportunity for personal growth and recognition, and the feelings of achievement the job provides. When these factors are present, jobs are presumed to be both satisfying and motivating for most people.

Herzberg's theory has been criticized by many scholars, and for that reason we will not go into more detail about his original theory. But Herzberg was a pioneer in the area of job design and still is a respected name among American managers. Furthermore, even if the specifics of his theory do not hold up to scientific scrutiny, he made several very important contributions. First, Herzberg's theory highlights the important distinction between extrinsic rewards (from hygiene factors) and intrinsic rewards (from motivators). Second, it reminds managers not to count solely on extrinsic rewards to motivate workers but to focus on intrinsic rewards as well. Third, it set the stage for later theories, such as the Hackman and Oldham model, that explain more precisely how managers can enrich people's jobs.

---

job enlargement

Giving people additional tasks at the same time to alleviate boredom.

job enrichment

Changing a task to make it inherently more rewarding, motivating, and satisfying.

two-factor theory

Herzberg's theory describing two factors affecting people's work motivation and satisfaction.

hygiene factors

Characteristics of the workplace, such as company policies, working conditions, pay, and supervision, that can make people dissatisfied.

motivators

Factors that make a job more motivating, such as additional job responsibilities, opportunities for personal growth and recognition, and feelings of achievement.

Motivator, Hygiene, or Distractor?

In the early 1900s, cigar makers paid people to read stories to employees working boring jobs. In the textile industry during the same period, managers allowed kittens to play on the floor, also to help workers fight boredom.

Now, bored employees wear iPods. Some employers prohibit them, maintaining they interfere with concentration and communication. But others see benefits. A Banc One executive sees people developing rhythmic work patterns, and believes the music improves concentration and quality. A study of assembly-line workers found that headphones had no impact on job performance, and that people wearing them reported higher job satisfaction.

Other people bored at work spend time in chatrooms, engage in other non-work-related Internet activities, and play computer games. At a nuclear power plant, employees became hooked to the multiuser game Doom. The information technology manager claimed that safety wasn't compromised directly, but the Doom files are huge and can slow down the PC network.

One company believed that perhaps 60 percent to 70 percent of Web site visits by its employees are unrelated to business. Many companies are cracking down. Kraft Foods installed a system preventing employees from visiting Web sites unrelated to their jobs, with the chief information officer saying, "We're here for business purposes, not for individual entertainment." Meanwhile, employees are finding ways to resist management's attempts to monitor and control. Don's Boss Page on the Web featured "Stealth Surfing: secret tips and tricks from the pros on how to look busy at work while you're cruising the Internet."

Wearing an iPod while working—how does this affect motivation?

Some managers claim that these activities rob the company of productivity, others claim no effect, and still others maintain that people need a break once in a while. Many executives engage in the same activities, whereas some executives insist on firing anyone caught doing these things when he or she is supposed to be working. Unfortunately for Hong Kong's education secretary, Professor Arthur Li, he was caught playing a video game on his PDA during a Legislative Council debate. The council was cutting university budgets and declaring that educators need to increase their efficiency.

What do you think? What do these activities have to do with job design, motivation, and job satisfaction? If you were a manager, how would you handle policy on this issue, and what would you do with people engaging in these activities?

SOURCES: C. Powell, "When Workers Wear Walkmans on the Job," *The Wall Street Journal*, July 11, 1994, pp. B1, B8; J. Stuller, "Games Workers Play," *Across the Board*, July–August 1997, pp. 16–22; and C. Harmon, "Goofing Off at Work: First You Log On," *International Herald Tribune*, September 23, 1997, pp. 1, 10; "Game Theory," *Financial Times* (Japan edition), March 1, 2004, p. 12.

The Hackman and Oldham Model of Job Design

Following Herzberg's work, Hackman and Oldham proposed a more complete model of job design.[74] Figure 13.4 illustrates their model. As you can see, well-designed jobs lead to high motivation, high-quality performance, high satisfaction, and low absenteeism and turnover. These outcomes occur when people experience three critical psychological states (noted in the middle column of the figure): (1) They believe they are doing something meaningful because their work is important to other people; (2) they feel personally responsible for how the work turns out; and (3) they learn how well they performed their jobs.

These psychological states occur when people are working on enriched jobs, that is, jobs that offer the following five core job dimensions:

1. *Skill variety*—different job activities involving several skills and talents. For example, at Ashton Photo in Salem, Oregon, employees decide what skills they need and grade themselves on their performance. Rewards are also based on the ability to teach others new skills.[75]
2. *Task identity*—the completion of a whole, identifiable piece of work. People at Prospect Associates of Rockville, Maryland, market their ideas, and create new business.[76] At State Farm Insurance, agents are independent contractors who

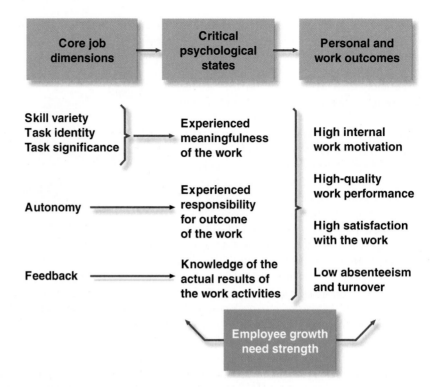

SOURCE: From "A New Strategy for Job Enrichment" by J. Richard Hackman, et al., *California Management Review*. Copyright © 1975 by the Regents of the University of California. Reprinted from the *California Management Review*, vol. 17, no. 4. By permission of The Regents.

FIGURE 13.4

The Hackman and Oldham Model of Job Enrichment

sell and service State Farm products exclusively. They have built and invested in their own businesses. Agent retention and productivity are far better than industry norms.[77]

3. *Task significance*—an important, positive impact on the lives of others. At Medtronic, employees know their product saves lives.[78] Odwall is a maker of fruit and vegetable juices; its employees are proud of the nutritional value of their products. At Schwab, employees consider themselves not as mere discount brokers, but as the guardians of their customers' financial dreams.[79] At Harley, the pay is good but it's the product that binds people to the company. Says one employee, "When you work here, you feel like you are part of what makes America great."[80] Even at companies with mundane products, individuals can believe in the significance of their work if customers like the product, if the company has a good reputation, or if their work is appreciated by others inside the company.[81]

4. *Autonomy*—independence and discretion in making decisions. At Action Instruments of San Diego, employees are urged to "make it happen": discover problems and solve them.[82] At Childress Buick in Phoenix, lot salespeople can finalize deals; they don't have to check with the sales manager.[83] In a research hospital, a department administrator told her people to do the kinds of research they wanted as long as it was within budget (and legal!). With no other guidelines—that is, complete autonomy—productivity increased sixfold in a year.[84]

5. *Feedback*—information about job performance. Many companies post charts or provide computerized data indicating productivity, number of rejects, and other data. At Aspect Communications in San Jose, employees pay constant attention to customer feedback on their performance.[85] At Great Plains

Software, programmers are expected to spend time with customers.[86] This way, they learn what customers think of their products, and what kind of impact they are having.

The most effective job enrichment increases all five core dimensions.

A person's growth need strength will help determine just how effective a job enrichment program might be. **Growth need strength** is the degree to which individuals want personal and psychological development. Job enrichment would be more successful for people with high growth need strength. But very few people respond negatively to job enrichment.[87]

Empowerment

Today one frequently hears managers talk about "empowering" their people. Individuals may (or may not) feel empowered, and groups can have a "culture" of empowerment which predicts work-unit performance.[88] **Empowerment** is the process of sharing power with employees, thereby enhancing their confidence in their ability to perform their jobs and their belief that they are influential contributors to the organization. Unfortunately, empowerment doesn't always live up to its hype. One problem is that managers undermine it by sending mixed messages like "Do your own thing— the way we tell you."[89] But empowerment can be profoundly motivating when done properly.[90]

Empowerment results in changes in employees' beliefs—from feeling powerless to believing strongly in their own personal effectiveness.[91] The result is that people take more initiative and persevere in achieving their goals and their leader's vision even in the face of obstacles.[92] Specifically, empowerment encourages the following beliefs among employees.[93] First, they perceive *meaning* in their work: their job fits their values. Second, they feel *competent*, or capable of performing their jobs with skill. Third, they have a sense of *self-determination*, of having some choice in regard to the tasks, methods, and pace of their work. Fourth, they have an *impact*—that is, they have some influence over important strategic, administrative, or operating decisions or outcomes on the job.

When speaking of times when they felt empowered, people mentioned:[94]

- I had no input into a hiring decision of someone who was to report directly to me. I didn't even get to speak to the candidate.
- They treated us like mushrooms. They fed us and kept us in the dark.
- I worked extremely hard—long hours and late nights—on an urgent project, and then my manager took full credit for it.
- My suggestions, whether good or bad, were either not solicited or, worse, ignored.
- The project was reassigned without my knowledge or input.

In contrast, people felt empowered in the following examples:

- I was able to make a large financial decision on my own. I got to write a large check without being questioned.
- After having received a memo that said, "Cut travel," I made my case about why it was necessary to travel for business reasons, and I was told to go ahead.
- I was five years old, and my dad said, "You'll make a great mechanic one day." He planted the seed. Now I'm an engineer.
- My president supported my idea without question.
- All the financial data were shared with me.

To foster empowerment, management must create an environment in which all the employees feel they have real influence over performance standards and business effectiveness within their areas of responsibility.[95] An empowering work environment provides people with *information* necessary for them to perform at their best, *knowledge* about how to use the information and how to do their work, *power* to make decisions that give them control over their work, and the *rewards* they deserve for the contributions they make.[96] Such an environment reduces costs, because fewer people are needed to supervise, monitor, and coordinate. It improves quality and service, because high performance is inspired at the source, the people who do the work. It also allows quick action, because people on the spot see problems, solutions, and opportunities for innovation on which they are empowered to act.

It is essential to give people clear strategic direction, but to leave some room for flexibility and calculated risk taking. For example, Southwest Airlines' strategic principle of "meet customers' short-haul travel needs at fares competitive with the cost of automobile travel" helps employees keep strategic objectives in mind and use their discretion in making complicated decisions about service offerings, route selection, cabin design, ticketing procedures, and pricing.[97] More specific actions include increasing signature authority at all levels; reducing the number of rules and approval steps; assigning nonroutine jobs; allowing independent judgment, flexibility, and creativity; defining jobs more broadly as projects rather than tasks; and providing more access to resources and people throughout the organization .[98]

Empowerment does not mean allowing people to decide trivial things like what color to paint the lunchroom. For empowerment to make a difference, people must have an impact on things about which they care, such as quality and productivity.[99] Companies including Lord Corporation in Dayton, Ohio (which produces engine mounts for aircraft), Herman Miller (the Michigan-based furniture manufacturer), Johnsonville Foods, and Goodyear all were highly successful and received great acclaim for their empowerment programs.[100]

You should not be surprised when empowerment causes some problems, at least in the short term. This is the case with virtually any change, including changes for the better. It's important to remember that with empowerment comes responsibility, and employees don't necessarily like the accountability at first.[101] People may make mistakes at first, especially until they have had adequate training. And because more training is needed, costs are higher. Also, because people acquire new skills and make greater contributions, they may demand higher wages. But if they are well-trained and truly empowered, they will deserve them—and both they and the company will benefit.

> Job enrichment and empowerment don't work magic overnight; people may resist the new approaches and make mistakes along the way. But done right, their potential to achieve real results is undeniable.

Achieving Fairness

Ultimately, one of the most important issues in motivation surrounds how people view their contributions to the organization and what they receive from the organization. Ideally, they will view their relationship with their employer as a well-balanced, mutually beneficial exchange. As people work and realize the outcomes or consequences of their actions, they assess how fairly the organization treats them.

The starting point for understanding how people interpret their contributions and outcomes is equity theory.[102] **Equity theory** proposes that when people assess how fairly they are treated, they consider two key factors: outcomes and inputs. *Outcomes*, as in expectancy theory, refer to the various things the person receives on the job: recognition, pay, benefits, satisfaction, security, job assignments, punishments, and so forth. *Inputs* refer to the contributions the person makes to the organization: effort, time, talent, performance, extra commitment, good citizenship, and so forth. People have a general expectation that the outcomes they receive will reflect, or be proportionate to, the inputs they provide—a fair day's pay (and other outcomes) for a fair day's work (broadly defined by how people view all their contributions).

equity theory

A theory stating that people assess how fairly they have been treated according to two key factors: outcomes and inputs.

But this comparison of outcomes to inputs is not the whole story. People also pay attention to the outcomes and inputs others receive. At salary review time, for example, most people—from executives on down—try to pick up clues that will tell them who got the high raises. As described in the following section, they compare ratios, restore equity if necessary, and derive more or less satisfaction based on how fairly they believe they have been treated.

Assessing Equity

Equity theory suggests that people compare the ratio of their own outcomes to inputs against the outcome-to-input ratio of some comparison person. The comparison person can be a fellow student, a co-worker, a boss, or an average industry pay scale. Stated more succinctly, people compare:

$$\text{Their own } \frac{\text{Outcomes}}{\text{Inputs}} \text{ versus Others' } \frac{\text{Outcomes}}{\text{Inputs}}$$

If the ratios are equivalent, people believe the relationship is equitable, or fair. Equity causes people to be satisfied with their treatment. But the person who believes his or her ratio is lower than another's will feel inequitably treated. Inequity causes dissatisfaction and leads to an attempt to restore balance to the relationship.

Inequity and the negative feelings it creates may appear anywhere. For example, some CEOs receive astronomical pay despite poor company performance. According to *Fortune*, "The American public isn't angered by big pay. It's angered by perceived injustice" (p. 70).[103] As a student, perhaps you have been in the following situation. You stay up all night and get a C on the exam. Meanwhile another student studies a couple of hours, goes out for the rest of the evening, gets a good night's sleep, and gets a B on the exam. You perceive your inputs (time spent studying) as much greater than the other student's, but your outcomes are lower. You are displeased at the seeming unfairness.

In business, the same thing happens with pay raises. One manager puts in 60-hour weeks, has a degree from a prestigious university, and believes she is destined for the top. When her archrival—whom she perceives as less deserving ("she never comes into the office on weekends, and all she does when she is here is butter

> Equity theory suggests that people compare the ratio of their outcomes-to-inputs against the outcome-to-input ratio of some comparison person. How would you deal with someone you perceive to be a slacker who gets promoted over you?

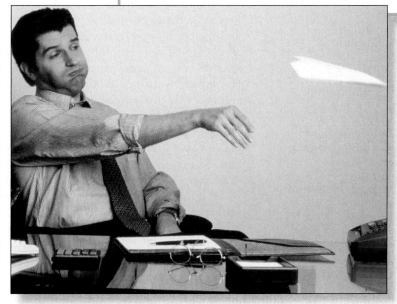

up the boss")—gets the higher raise or the promotion, she experiences severe feelings of inequity. Perceived pay inequities may be the reason major league baseball teams that have great differences in their player salaries tend to win fewer games.[104]

Assessments of equity are not made objectively. They are subjective perceptions or beliefs. In the preceding examples, the person who got the higher raise probably felt she deserved it. Even if she admits she doesn't put in long workweeks, she may convince herself she doesn't need to because she's so talented. The student who got the higher grade may believe it was a fair, equitable result because (1) she kept up all semester, while the other student did not, and (2) she's smart (ability and experience, not just time and effort, can be seen as inputs).

Restoring Equity

People who feel inequitably treated and dissatisfied are motivated to do something to restore equity. They have a number of options that they carry out by actually doing something to change the ratios, or by reevaluating the situation and deciding it is equitable after all.

The equity equation shown earlier indicates a person's options for restoring equity. People who feel inequitably treated can *reduce their inputs* by giving less effort, performing at lower levels, or quitting ("Well, if that's the way things work around here, there's no way I'm going to work that hard [or stick around]"). Or they can attempt to *increase their outcomes* ("My boss [or teacher] is going to hear about this. I deserve more; there must be some way I can get more").

Other ways of restoring equity focus on changing the other person's ratio. A person can *decrease others' outcomes*. For example, an employee may sabotage work to create problems for his company or his boss.[105] A person can also change her perceptions of inputs or outcomes ("That promotion isn't as great a deal as he thinks. The pay is not that much better, and the headaches will be unbelievable"). It is also possible to *increase others' inputs*, particularly by changing perceptions ("The more I think about it, the more he deserved it. He's worked hard all year, he's competent, and it's about time he got a break").

Thus, a person can restore equity in a number of ways by behaviorally or perceptually changing inputs and outcomes.

Procedural Justice

Inevitably, managers make decisions that have outcomes more favorable for some than for others. Those with favorable outcomes will be pleased; those with worse outcomes, all else equal, will be more displeased. But managers desiring to put salve on the wounds—say, of people they like or respect or want to keep and motivate—still can take actions to reduce the dissatisfaction. The key is for people to believe that managers provide **procedural justice**—using fair process in decision making and helping others know that the process was as fair as possible. When people perceive procedural fairness, they are more likely to support decisions and decision makers.[106] For example, one year after layoffs, managers' use of procedural justice (in the form of employee participation in decisions) still predicted survivors' organizational commitment, job satisfaction, and trust toward management.[107]

Even if people believe that their *outcome* was inequitable and unfair, they are more likely to view justice as having been served if the *process* was fair. You can increase people's beliefs that the process was fair by making the process open and visible; stating decision criteria in advance rather than after the fact; making sure that the most appropriate people—those who have valid information and are viewed as trustworthy— make the decisions; giving people a chance to participate in the process: and providing an appeal process that allows people to question decisions safely and receive complete answers.[108]

> **procedural justice**
>
> Using fair process in decision making and making sure others know that the process was as fair as possible.

For example, at an elevator plant in the United States, an army of consultants arrived one day, unexplained and annoying.[109] The rumor mill kicked in; employees thought that the plant was to be shut down, or that some of them would be laid off. Three months later, management unveiled its new plan, involving a new method of manufacturing based on teams. As the changes were implemented, management did not adequately answer questions about the purpose of the changes, employees resisted, conflicts arose, and the formerly popular plant manager lost the trust of his people. Costs skyrocketed, and quality plummeted.

Advantages of Collaboration

People feeling that their outcomes are fair (equity) and the processes used were fair (procedural justice) may represent the ultimate in true collaboration.

Concerned, management conducted an employee survey. Employees were skeptical that the survey results would lead to any positive changes and were worried that management would be angry that people had voiced their honest opinions. But management reacted by saying, "We were wrong, we screwed up, we didn't use the right process." They went on to share with employees critical business information, the limited options available, and the dire consequences if the company didn't change. Employees saw the dilemma and came to view the business problem as theirs as well as management's, but they were scared that some of them would lose their jobs. Management retained the right to lay people off if business conditions grew worse but also made several promises: no layoffs as a result of changes made; cross-training programs for employees; no replacements of departing people until conditions improved; a chance for employees to serve in new roles, as consultants on quality issues; and sharing of sales and cost data on a regular basis.

The news was bad, but people understood it and began to share responsibility with management. This was the beginning of the restoration of trust and commitment, and of steady improvements in performance.[110]

In Need of Motivation, and More, at Toys 'R' Us

FROM THE PAGES OF

BusinessWeek

In 1998, Toys 'R' Us was the number one U.S. toy seller. In 2000, Wal-Mart was number one. Toys 'R' Us was in the middle of a string of sales and earnings disappointments, wrestling with management problems, and described as "long-troubled" and the store of "unhelpful sales clerks, warehouse-length aisles done in dismal gray and blue, and Christmas-eve frustration." CEO John H. Eyler Jr. wanted to change all that.

Eyler's analysis showed inventory and delivery problems that the company worked to remedy. But another huge challenge was the opinion of U.S. shoppers. Many customers griped about unhelpful sales staff. One woman, trying to buy an infant bathtub, couldn't find one and finally went to the customer-service booth for help. She was told that if the store had one, it was on the floor, and if it didn't have one, she was out of luck. When she convinced the clerk to check by computer, they found five bathtubs in stock. The clerk said it would be several hours before someone could take one down for the customer, who then left without the bathtub. This was no isolated incident. A study of 15 big retailers ranked Toys 'R' Us 14th in customer service.

In 2005, Toys 'R' Us was still struggling, and its executives agreed to be bought by two private equity firms and Vornado Realty Trust, one of the country's largest owners of re-

tail and office property. Some were worried that the partnership would liquidate the stores to cash in on the real estate, but early indications were that they were committed to the toy business and wanted to turn the company around. Eyler said, "Toys 'R' Us is going to be here for years and years to come."

In the short term, some 20 percent of the stores are expected to close, and the remaining stores (at least 500 in the United States) will have to provide a friendly alternative to Wal-Mart and other discounters.

One advantage Toys 'R' Us has is its wide assortment of products. But customers have wide selections online and at some other stores as well, and Toys 'R' Us does not have the same cost advantage that it used to enjoy. Moreover, all that product in-store means that a lot of space is required, customers may have questions or not know about all of their options, and employees need product knowledge and the willingness to share that knowledge with customers.

Striving to get customers to return, Toys 'R' Us must perform as well or better than the competition.

So, like so many companies, Toys 'R' Us must do a lot of things as well as its competitors, and also find its distinctive competitive advantage. Strategically, the company no longer wants to battle discounters like Wal-Mart on their turf, preferring to narrow its product assortments and add more exclusive items. Perhaps, too, it can create a unique shopping environment. And perhaps it can somehow motivate its staff to provide great service.

SOURCES: N. Byrnes, "Toy 'R' Us: Can CEO John Eyler Fix The Chain?" *BusinessWeek*, December 4, 2000, pp. 128–40; L. Braham and R. Berner, "The Wrong Time for REITs?" *BusinessWeek Online*, p. 88 March 11, 2002; R. Berner and G. Khermouch, "Retail Reckoning," *BusinessWeek Online*, December 10, 2001, pp. 72–77; "Managers to Watch 2002," *BusinessWeek Online*, January 14, 2002, pp. 52–72. J. Verdon, The Record (Bergen County, NJ), March 18, 2005, p. A01.

Job Satisfaction

If people feel fairly treated from the outcomes they receive, or the processes used, they will be satisfied. A satisfied worker is not necessarily more productive than a dissatisfied one; sometimes people are happy with their jobs because they don't have to work hard! But job dissatisfaction, aggregated across many individuals, creates a workforce that is more likely to exhibit (1) higher turnover; (2) higher absenteeism; (3) less good citizenship among employees;[111] (4) more grievances and lawsuits; (5) strikes; (6) stealing, sabotage, and vandalism; (7) poorer mental and physical health (which can mean higher job stress, higher insurance costs, and more lawsuits);[112] (8) fewer injuries;[113] (9) poor customer service;[114] and (10) lower productivity and profits.[115] All of these consequences of dissatisfaction, either directly or indirectly, are costly to organizations.

Job satisfaction is especially important for relationship-oriented service employees such as realtors, hair stylists, and stockbrokers. Customers develop (or don't develop) a commitment to a specific service provider. Satisfied service providers are less likely to quit the company and more likely to provide an enjoyable customer experience.[116]

Quality of Work Life

Quality of work life (QWL) programs create a workplace that enhances employee well-being and satisfaction. The general goal of QWL programs is to satisfy the full range of employee needs. People's needs apparently are well met at Wegman's Food Markets, which was number one in *Fortune*'s top 100 companies to work for in 2005. Wegman's creates a work environment in which people can reach their full potential and feel part of the social fabric rather than just workers in a bureaucratic hierarchy.[117] At SAS, which has been on the *Fortune* list every year since it began (1998), employees receive plenty of great perks: a 35-hour workweek, day care, unlimited sick leave, deeply discounted country club memberships, car detailing, a 77,000-square-foot fitness center, soccer and softball fields, a dining hall with a pianist, an on-site medical clinic, an eldercare referral service, and a masseuse who visits several times a week.[118]

QWL has eight categories:[120]

1. Adequate and fair compensation.
2. A safe and healthy environment.
3. Jobs that develop human capacities.
4. A chance for personal growth and security.
5. A social environment that fosters personal identity, freedom from prejudice, a sense of community, and upward mobility.
6. Constitutionalism, or the rights of personal privacy, dissent, and due process.
7. A work role that minimizes infringement on personal leisure and family needs.
8. Socially responsible organizational actions.

Organizations differ drastically in their attention to QWL. Critics claim that QWL programs don't necessarily inspire employees to work harder if the company does not tie rewards directly to individual performance. Advocates of QWL claim that it improves organizational effectiveness and productivity. The term *productivity*, as applied by QWL programs, means much more than each person's quantity of work output.[121] It also includes turnover, absenteeism, accidents, theft, sabotage, creativity, innovation, and especially the quality of work.

Psychological Contracts

The relationship between individuals and employing organizations typically is formalized by a written contract. But in employees' minds there also exists a **psychological contract**—a set of perceptions of what they owe their employers, and what their employers owe them.[122] This contract, whether it is seen as being upheld or violated—and whether the parties trust one another or not—has important implications for employee satisfaction and motivation and the effectiveness of the organization.

Wal-Mart, under the legendary Sam Walton, offered a psychological contract to its people: We'll pay less-than-top wages, but we'll care about you and be fair with you, and you'll work hard for us in return. Fairness included many small but important things: "an open door" policy in which workers could share concerns with managers at any level, a real chance for hourly workers to earn promotions into salaried management positions, scheduling work hours with family needs in mind, and other acts of personal consideration. Unfortunately, some say that this "contact" is now frayed, in large part because of Wal-Mart's incredible growth, mammoth size, 24/7 store hours, and a narrower focus on the bottom line. The psychological contract that generated committed employees and a culture that provided a real competitive advantage is, say some, in danger of becoming an extinct legend.[123]

Historically, in many companies the employment relationship was stable and predictable. Now, mergers and layoffs and other disruptions have thrown asunder the

---

quality of work life (QWL) programs

Programs designed to create a workplace that enhances employee well being.

"If we keep our employees happy, they do a good job of keeping our customers happy."[119]

James Goodnight of SAS

A single, satisfied person doesn't necessarily produce well on every performance dimension. But an organization full of people with high job satisfaction will likely perform well in countless ways.

---

psychological contract

A set of perceptions of what employees owe their employers, and what their employers owe them.

You should expect Allstate to:

1. Offer work that is meaningful and challenging.
2. Promote an environment that encourages open and constructive dialogue.
3. Recognize you for your accomplishments.
4. Provide competitive pay and rewards based on your performance.
5. Advise you on your performance through regular feedback.
6. Create learning opportunities through education and job assignments.
7. Support you in defining career goals.
8. Provide you with information and resources to perform successfully.
9. Promote an environment that is inclusive and free from bias.
10. Foster dignity and respect in all interactions.
11. Establish an environment that promotes a balance of work and personal life.

Allstate expects you to:

1. Perform at levels that significantly increase our ability to outperform the competition.
2. Take on assignments critical to meeting business objectives.
3. Continually develop needed skills.
4. Willingly listen to and act upon feedback.
5. Demonstrate a high level of commitment to achieving company goals.
6. Exhibit no bias in interactions with colleagues and customers.
7. Behave consistently with Allstate's ethical standards.
8. Take personal responsibility for each transaction with our customers and for fostering their trust.
9. Continually improve processes to address customers' needs.

TABLE 13.2
Allstate Employability
Contract

SOURCE: Courtesy of Allstate Insurance Company. Cited in E. E. Lawler III, *Treat People Right!* (San Francisco: Jossey-Bass, 2003).

"old deal."[124] As a McGraw-Hill executive put it, "The 'used-to-be's' must give way to the realities of 'What is and what will be.' "[125] The fundamental "used-to-be" of traditionally managed organizations was that employees were expected to be loyal and employers would provide secure employment. Today, the implicit contract goes something like this:[126] If people stay, do their own job plus someone else's (who has been downsized), and do additional things like participating in task forces, the company will try to provide a job (if it can), provide gestures that it cares, and keep providing more or less the same pay (with periodic small increases). The likely result of this not-very-satisfying arrangement: uninspired people and a business trying to survive.

But a better deal is possible, for both employers and employees.[127] Allstate's general employment contract (Table 13.2) provides an example.[128] Ideally, your employer will provide continuous skill updating and an invigorating work environment in which you can use your skills and are motivated to stay even though you may have other job options.[129] You could work for a company that provides the following deal: If you develop the skills we need, apply them in ways that help the company succeed, and behave consistently with our values, we will provide for you a challenging work environment, support for your development, and full, fair rewards for your contributions. The results of such a "contract" are much more likely to be a mutually beneficial and satisfying relationship and a high-performing, successful organization.

EPILOGUE

ROCKY FLATS

On a negative note, some at Rocky Flats maintained that the motivation to finish the cleanup is so intense that safety management has suffered. Management made improvements and now uses safety records to decide executive bonuses.

Speaking of the big picture, Denny Ferrara says "I think it's great. Not great to work myself out of a job, but it's great to be able to say I've been there through production and I was here to see the closure of the gate." He hopes to get a new assign-

ment from the company as it competes for other nuclear cleanup contracts.

By 2006, some 3,000 workers will lose their jobs as a consequence of their own productivity. Kaiser-Hill has an elaborate program to ease the transition and help people find new jobs, including advertising workers' skills, funding grants for entrepreneurs, and sponsoring an online job bank. And, The Rocky Flats site will be managed by the Fish and Wildlife Service as a wildlife refuge.

KEY TERMS

Empowerment, p. 443

Equity theory, p. 444

ERG theory, p. 437

Expectancy, p. 434

Expectancy theory, p. 434

Extinction, p. 431

Extrinsic rewards, p. 439

Goal-setting theory, p. 428

Growth need strength, p. 443

Hygiene factors, p. 446

Instrumentality, p. 434

Intrinsic reward, p. 439

Job enlargement, p. 440

Job enrichment, p. 440

Job rotation, p. 439

Law of effect, p. 430

Maslow's need hierarchy, p. 436

Motivation, p. 427

Motivators, p. 440

Negative reinforcement, p. 431

Organizational behavior modification (OB Mod), p. 430

Outcome, p. 434

Positive reinforcement, p. 431

Procedural justice, p. 446

Psychological contract, p. 449

Punishment, p. 431

Quality of work life (QWL) programs, p. 449

Reinforcers, p. 430

Stretch goals, p. 428

Two-factor theory, p. 440

Valence, p. 434

SUMMARY OF LEARNING OBJECTIVES

Now that you have studied Chapter 13, you should know:

The kinds of behaviors managers need to motivate in people.

All important work behaviors are motivated. Managers need to motivate employees to join and remain in the organization and to exhibit high attendance, job performance, and citizenship.

How to set challenging, motivating goals.

Goal setting is a powerful motivator. Specific, quantifiable, and challenging but attainable goals motivate high effort and performance. Goal setting can be used for teams as well as for individuals. Care should be taken that single goals are not set to the exclusion of other important dimensions of performance. Managers also should not lose sight of the other potential downsides of goals.

How to reward good performance properly.

Organizational behavior modification programs influence behavior at work by arranging consequences for people's actions. Most programs use positive reinforcement as a consequence, but other important consequences are negative reinforcement, punishment,

and extinction. Care must be taken to reinforce appropriate, not inappropriate, behavior. Innovative managers use a wide variety of rewards for good performance. They also understand how to "manage mistakes" and provide useful feedback.

The key beliefs that affect people's motivation.

Expectancy theory describes three important work-related beliefs. That is, motivation is a function of people's (1) expectancies, or effort-performance links; (2) instrumentalities, or performance-outcome links; and (3) the valences people attach to the outcomes of performance. In addition, equity theory addresses important beliefs about fairness.

The ways in which people's individual needs affect their behavior.

Maslow's five most important needs are physiological, safety, social, ego, and self-actualization. Alderfer's ERG theory describes three sets of needs: existence, relatedness, and growth. McClelland emphasizes three different needs: achievement, affiliation, and power. Because people are inclined to satisfy their various needs, these theories help to suggest to managers the kinds of rewards that motivate people.

How to create a motivating, empowering job.

One approach to satisfying needs and motivating people is to create intrinsic motivation through the improved design of jobs. Jobs can be enriched by building in more skill variety, task identity, task significance, autonomy, and feedback. Empowerment is the most recent development in the creation of motivating jobs. Empowerment includes the perceptions of meaning, competence, self-determination, and impact, and comes from an environment in which people have necessary information, knowledge, power, and rewards.

How people assess fairness, and how to achieve fairness.

Equity theory states that people compare their inputs and outcomes to the inputs and outcomes of others. Perceptions of equity (fairness) are satisfying; feelings of inequity (unfairness) are dissatisfying and motivate people to change their behavior or their perceptions to restore equity. In addition to fairness of outcomes, as described in equity theory, fairness is also appraised and managed through procedural justice.

The causes and consequences of a satisfied workforce.

A satisfied workforce has many advantages for the firm, including lower absenteeism and turnover; fewer grievances, lawsuits, and strikes; lower health costs; and higher-quality work. One general approach to generating higher satisfaction for people is to implement a quality of work life program. QWL seeks to provide a safe and healthy environment, opportunity for personal growth, a positive social environment, fair treatment, and other improvements in people's work life. These and other benefits from the organization, exchanged for contributions from employees, create a psychological contract. Over time, how the psychological contract is upheld or violated, and changed unfairly or fairly, will influence people's satisfaction and motivation.

DISCUSSION QUESTIONS

1. Think of a significant mistake made by someone on a job. How did the boss handle it, and what was the effect?

2. Why do you think it is so difficult for managers to empower their people?

3. Think of a job you hold currently or held in the past. How would you describe the psychological contract? How does (did) this affect your attitudes and behaviors on the job?

4. If a famous executive or sports figure were to give a passionate motivational speech, trying to persuade people to work harder, what do you think the impact would be? Why?

5. Give some examples of situations in which you wanted to do a great job but were prevented from doing so. What was the impact on you, and what would this suggest to you in your efforts to motivate other people to perform?

6. Discuss the similarities and differences between setting goals for other people and setting goals for yourself. When does goal setting fail, and when does it succeed?

7. Identify four examples of people inadvertently reinforcing the wrong behaviors, or punishing or extinguishing good behaviors.

8. Assess yourself on McClelland's three needs. On which need are you highest, and on which are you lowest? What are the implications for you as a manager?

9. Identify a job you have worked and appraise it on Hackman and Oldham's five core job dimensions. Also describe the degree to which it made you feel empowered. As a class, choose one job and discuss together how it could be changed to be more motivating and empowering.

10. Using expectancy theory, analyze how you have made and will make personal choices, such as a major area of study, a career to pursue, or job interviews to seek.

11. Describe a time when you felt unfairly treated and explain why. How did you respond to the inequity? What other options might you have had?

12. Provide examples of how outcomes perceived as unfair can decrease motivation. Then discuss how procedural justice, or fair process, can help overcome the negative effects.

13. What are the implications for your career of, and how will you prepare for, the psychological contracts described at the end of the chapter?

14. Set some goals for yourself, considering the discussion about goal setting in the chapter.

CONCLUDING CASE

Big Ray's Custom Chairs

BUSINESS OVERVIEW AND HISTORY

After a successful career in sales with a large national department store chain, Ray Malone, known as "Big Ray," started a small business that manufactures and distributes a line of outdoor leisure chairs. The company employs 11 people—9 work in manufacturing (see detailed breakdown of work assignments in Figure 1), one is assigned to outside sales, and one to the office and general administration area. Big Ray works as general manager.

The business has been in existence for seven years. Sales and profits grew steadily (averaging about 10 percent per year) until Big Ray experienced his first setback. During 2003, the company generated sales of $2,300,000, with a net profit of $253,000. The year 2004 generated a small increase in sales to $2,415,000, but yielded a lower profit of $217,350.

Demand for Ray's chairs remains strong; indeed, the staff has not been able to keep up with orders and shipments. The major problem appears to be in the production area, with a chronic shortage and frequent turnover of production help, along with diminishing skill levels and abilities of those workers. Production costs have increased as a percentage of sales for both labor and raw materials.

Big Ray's region has grown tremendously during the past decade. This has resulted in the establishment of many new businesses that are able to offer higher wages and better working conditions. Most of the staff have families to support, so the opportunity for higher wages and better fringe benefits is hard to pass up.

Big Ray usually has no problem securing the necessary raw materials for his products, especially during moderate to slow economic times. When markets and the economy in general are strong, raw material availability and cost are an issue. Big Ray has many excellent contacts and relationships on the sales side. He sells to his former employer's East Coast stores and to a wide variety of midwestern establishments. Along with his outside sales associate, Big Ray is able to maintain his existing order file and consistently develop new markets. His plant has the capacity to produce enough volume/units to generate upwards of $3,500,000 in sales, which is his long-term goal.

Big Ray finds himself in a quandary. The production staff is slowly falling behind while the orders keep coming. Deadlines are not being met, and for the first time ever, Big Ray finds himself receiving phone calls from unhappy customers.

THE PRODUCTION PROCESS

Lumber and fabric are the two primary raw materials. Lumber is delivered in packages containing 1,000 board feet that cost $1,000. The boards come in varying sizes, ranging from 3 to 12 inches wide and from 4 to 12 feet in length. All boards are the same thickness. The fabric comes in rolls that range from 30 to 36 inches wide and from 50 to 100 yards in length, costing $2.50 per square foot. All material is the same thickness.

Big Ray has never cared much for these material specifications, as they seem to greatly affect the cost of producing the finished product. For example, one bolt of fabric that is 36 inches by 50 feet (150 square feet) may yield just 120 square feet of finished product. This 20 percent waste factor results in an actual finished product material cost of $ 3.13 per square foot ($2.50/0.8). The remaining 30 square feet of fabric is too narrow and/or too short for use in any of the product lines, and is currently discarded.

The same holds true for the lumber. On average, 1,000 board feet of lumber yields just 700 board feet of finished product stock. This increases the actual finished product material cost to $1,428.57 per 1,000 feet ($1,000/0.7). The remaining 300 board feet is waste, since it is too short and/or too narrow for use in any of the product lines as well.

Over the course of producing thousands of units of chairs, this greatly impacts raw material production costs. In addition, the yield and waste figures seem to always vary by as much as 10 percent to 40 percent, depending on the particular shipment of materials and on the personnel who are cutting the material into finished product-size pieces. Some people seem to have the knack for generating the higher yields, others do not. Some shipments also generate higher yields than others.

Figure 1 sketches the production process: The forklift operator, who also serves as production foreman, manages the flow of inventory. This includes input to the primary processing ma-

FIGURE 1
Sketch of the Production Process (nine employees)

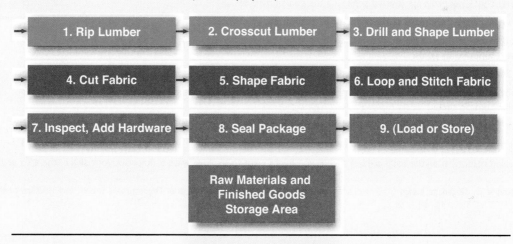

chines, output of finished goods, and loading of trucks and storage. Two workers rip and crosscut the wood, while a third oversees the final shaping and drilling of holes. Two workers cut and shape the fabric, while a third oversees the looping and stitching process. Two workers inspect and package the final product, which is then shipped or stored in the warehouse.

Wages of the production staff range from $7 to $15 per hour. Position numbers 2, 3, 5, and 6 in the sketch are at the low end of the wage range. The rest of the staff, who have been with the company for several years, are at the higher end of the wage scale according to seniority.

Most of the turnover has occurred in the primary production area (material handling, cutting, and processing). This is the most labor-intensive and physically demanding aspect of the production process and is also the loudest and most dangerous area of the shop. Seven of the eleven workers have been with the company from the start, and they appear to be very happy and content in their positions. The remaining four positions seem to experience an almost continuous turnover.

QUESTIONS

1. Given Big Ray's labor situation and the nature of the work, what specific motivational techniques would you recommend to resolve the problem at hand?

2. How would you incorporate the text concepts to help Big Ray achieve his long-term production and sales goals?

EXPERIENTIAL EXERCISES

13.1 Assessing Yourself

Circle the response that most closely correlates with each item below.

	Agree		Neither		Disagree
1. I have developed a written list of short- and long-term goals I would like to accomplish.	1	2	3	4	5
2. When setting goals for myself, I give consideration to what my capabilities and limits are.	1	2	3	4	5
3. I set goals that are realistic and attainable.	1	2	3	4	5
4. My goals are based on my hopes and beliefs, not on those of my parents, friends, or significant other.	1	2	3	4	5
5. When I fail to achieve a goal, I get back on track.	1	2	3	4	5
6. My goals are based on my personal values.	1	2	3	4	5
7. I have a current mission statement and have involved those closest to me in formulating it.	1	2	3	4	5
8. I regularly check my progress toward achieving the goals I have set.	1	2	3	4	5
9. When setting goals I strive for performance, not outcomes.	1	2	3	4	5
10. I have a support system in place—friends, family members, and/or colleagues who believe in me and support my goals.	1	2	3	4	5
11. I apply SMART characteristics to my goals.	1	2	3	4	5
12. I prioritize my goals, focusing only on the most important or valuable ones at a particular point in time.	1	2	3	4	5
13. I reward myself when I achieve a goal, or even when I reach a particular milestone.	1	2	3	4	5
14. I revisit my goals periodically, and add and modify goals as appropriate.	1	2	3	4	5

Sum your circled responses. If your total is 42 or higher, you might want to explore ways to improve your skill in the area of goal setting.

SOURCE: Suzanne C. de Janasz, Karen O. Dowd, and Beth Z. Schneider, *Interpersonal Skills in Organizations* (New York: McGraw-Hill/Irwin, 2002), pp. 56–61.

13.2 Personal Goal Setting

1. In the space below, brainstorm your goals in the following categories. Write down as many as you wish, including goals that are short-, mid-, and long-term.

   Academic, intellectual

   Health, fitness

   Social: family, friends, significant other, community

   Career, job

   Financial

   Other

2. Of the goals you have listed, select from each of the six categories the two most important goals that you would like to pursue in the short term (next 6–12 months). Write these below.

   a. _____

   b. _____

   c. _____

   d. _____

   e. _____

   f. _____

   g. _____

   h. _____

   i. _____

   j. _____

   k. _____

   l. _____

3. From the twelve goals listed above, choose the three that are the most important to you at this time: the three you commit to work on in the next few months. Write a goal statement for each one, using the following guidelines:

   Begin each with the word "To . . ."

   Be specific.

   Quantify the goal if possible.

   Each goal statement should be realistic, attainable, and within your control.

   Each goal statement should reflect your aspirations—not those of others such as parents, roommates, significant others, and the like.

   a. _____
   _____

   b. _____
   _____

   c. _____
   _____

4. On a separate sheet of paper, develop an action plan for each goal statement. For each action plan:

   List the steps you will take to accomplish the goal.

   Include dates (by when) and initials (who's responsible) for each step.

   Visualize completing the goal and, working backwards, specify each step necessary between now and then to reach the goal.

   Identify any potential barriers you might experience in attaining the goal. Problem-solve around these obstacles and convert them into steps in your action plan.

   Identify the resources you will need to accomplish these goals, and build in steps to acquire the necessary information into your action plan.

5. Transfer the dates of each step for each goal in your action plan to a daily calendar.

6. Keep an ongoing daily or weekly record of the positive steps you take toward meeting each goal.

SOURCE: Suzanne C. de Janasz, Karen O. Dowd, and Beth Z. Schneider, *Interpersonal Skills in Organizations* (New York: McGraw-Hill/Irwin, 2002), pp. 56–61.

13.3 Job Satisfaction and Job Performance: A Debate Exercise

OBJECTIVE

The objective of this exercise is to explore the relationship between job satisfaction and job performance.

INSTRUCTIONS

This in-class exercise takes the form of a nontraditional four-way debate. Students will be divided by the instructor into four debating teams, each having four or five members. The remaining students will then be divided into judging teams consisting of three to six members each. The debate itself will focus on the relationship between job satisfaction and job performance.

DEBATING POSITIONS

Each debating team will be assigned one of the following four positions:

1. There is a direct positive relationship between job satisfaction and job performance. The higher an employee's job satisfaction, the higher will be her or his job performance and vice versa.

2. Job satisfaction is related to job performance in only the following way: A slight amount of job dissatisfaction is a prerequisite to high job performance. Thus, employees who are somewhat dissatisfied with their jobs will have higher productivity than those who are very dissatisfied or those who are completely satisfied with their jobs.

3. Job performance ultimately causes an employee's job satisfaction (high or low). If employees achieve high job performance, they will receive high rewards and this, in turn, will result in high job satisfaction. If employees perform poorly on their jobs, resulting rewards will be low as will the employees' job satisfaction.

4. This position will be provided by the instructor.

The debate consists of two rounds. In round one each team first states its position and then tries to convince the judges, through the use of examples and other evidence, that its position is fully legitimate. During round two of the debate, each debating team counters the position of the other teams, that is, team one criticizes teams two, three, and four; team two criticizes teams one, three, and four, and so on. The group being countered may not rebut the criticisms made by the other teams during the debate unless specifically told to do so by the instructor. Group members just listen.

Round two, the last round of the debate, ends when team four has finished criticizing the positions of the other three teams. All debaters will be given a 10-minute recess between rounds one and two in order to finalize their criticisms of the other teams.

The judging teams' role during the debate is to "search for the truth," not select a "winner." They are to listen to all of the different arguments presented during the debate and, after it has ended, discuss the different positions among themselves until a consensus is reached regarding the "true" relationship between job satisfaction and job performance. There are no constraints placed on the judges; they are free to disagree with all of the positions presented, to agree with parts of two or more of them, and so forth. After their deliberations are complete (usually about 10 minutes), each judging team presents its conclusions to the class. Judges should hold preliminary discussions of the four positions during the intermission between rounds one and two.

SOURCE: R. Bruce McAfee and Paul J. Champagne, *Organizational Behavior: A Manager's View.* Copyright © 1987. Reprinted with permission of South-Western College Publishing, a division of Thomson Learning.

13.4 What Do Students Want from Their Jobs?

OBJECTIVES

1. To demonstrate individual differences in job expectations.

2. To illustrate individual differences in need and motivational structures.

3. To examine and compare extrinsic and intrinsic rewards.

INSTRUCTIONS

1. Working alone, complete the "What I Want from My Job" survey.

2. In small groups, compare and analyze differences in the survey results and prepare group responses to the discussion questions.

3. After the class reconvenes, group spokespersons present group findings.

DISCUSSION QUESTIONS

1. Which items received the highest and lowest scores from you. Why?

2. On which items was there most and least agreement among students? What are the implications?

3. Which job rewards are extrinsic, and which are intrinsic?

4. Were more response differences found in intrinsic or in extrinsic rewards?

5. In what ways do you think blue-collar workers' responses would differ from those of college students?

What I Want from My Job Survey

Determine what you want from a job by circling the level of importance of each of the following job rewards.

	Very Important	Moderately Important	Indifferent	Moderately Unimportant	Very Unimportant
1. Advancement opportunities	5	4	3	2	1
2. Appropriate company policies	5	4	3	2	1
3. Authority	5	4	3	2	1
4. Autonomy and freedom on the job	5	4	3	2	1
5. Challenging work	5	4	3	2	1
6. Company reputation	5	4	3	2	1
7. Fringe benefits	5	4	3	2	1
8. Geographic location	5	4	3	2	1
9. Good co-workers	5	4	3	2	1
10. Good supervision	5	4	3	2	1
11. Job security	5	4	3	2	1
12. Money	5	4	3	2	1
13. Opportunity for self-development	5	4	3	2	1
14. Pleasant office and working conditions	5	4	3	2	1
15. Performance feedback	5	4	3	2	1
16. Prestigious job title	5	4	3	2	1
17. Recognition for doing a good job	5	4	3	2	1
18. Responsibility	5	4	3	2	1
19. Sense of achievement	5	4	3	2	1
20. Training programs	5	4	3	2	1
21. Type of work	5	4	3	2	1
22. Working with people	5	4	3	2	1

Chapter **14**

CHAPTER 14
Teamwork

No one can whistle a symphony. It takes an orchestra to play it.

—**Halford E. Luccock**

CHAPTER OUTLINE

LEARNING OBJECTIVES

After studying Chapter 14, you will know:

1. How teams contribute to your organization's effectiveness.

2. What makes the new team environment different from the old.

3. How groups become teams.

4. Why groups sometimes fail.

5. How to build an effective team.

6. How to manage your team's relationships with other teams.

7. How to manage conflict.

JOHN MACKEY AND WHOLE FOODS

Whole Foods is the largest organic- and natural-foods grocer in the world. The fundamental operating unit is not the regional offices, or the stores, but teams.

Every store is divided into about eight functional teams. If you're hired there, you join the seafood team, or the cashier/front-end team, or the bakery team. Each team at each store meets monthly to make decisions, most of which are based on a consensus of team members. The National Leadership Team makes decisions by majority vote, rarely overruled by CEO John Mackey.

The core philosophy about decision making at Whole Foods is that decisions should be made closest to the action, involving only the people who are affected and who carry out the decisions. John Mackey's favorite decisions, and those which he says are most common, are "decisions that are not my decision." Thus, local managers are empowered to make decisions based on their knowledge of local products and local tastes. Individual team leaders decide what to stock, in consultation with store team leaders. Regional or corporate offices don't make those decisions.

John Mackey describes Whole Foods as a social system, not a hierarchy. He doesn't hand down a lot of rules from headquarters. Self-examination and peer pressure substitute for bureaucracy. It's better for loyalty, he firmly believes.

Sources for Prologues, Connections, Epilogue: K. Hammonds, "Is Your Company Up to Speed?" *Fast Company*, June 2003, pp. 81–86; C. Fishman, "The Anarchist's Cookbook," *Fast Company*, July 2004, pp. 70–78.

Sometimes teams "work," and sometimes they don't. The goal of this chapter is to help make sure that your work teams succeed rather than fail.

Teams are transforming the ways in which companies do business.[1] Almost all companies now use teams to produce goods and services, to manage projects, and to make decisions and run the company.[2] Stated the CEO of Texas Instruments, "No matter what your business, these teams are the wave of the future."[3]

For you, this has two vital implications. First, you *will* be working in and perhaps managing teams. Second, the *ability* to work in and lead teams is valuable to your employer and important to your career. Fortunately, coursework focusing on team training can enhance students' teamwork knowledge and skills.[4]

The Contributions of Teams

Well-managed teams are powerful forces that can deliver all desired results.

It is no wonder that team-based approaches to work have generated such excitement. Used appropriately, teams can be powerfully effective as a *building block for organization structure*. Organizations like Semco, Whole Foods, and Kollmorgen, manufacturer of printed circuits and electro-optic devices, are structured entirely around teams. A team-oriented structure was also in place at Kyocera Corporation, when it was voted the best-managed company in Japan. 3M's breakthrough products emerge through the use of teams that are small entrepreneurial businesses within the larger corporation.[5]

Teams also can increase *productivity*, improve *quality*, and reduce *costs*. Shenandoah Life Insurance Company credited its new team organization with a 50 percent increase in the handling of applications and customer service requests, with fewer people.[6] Quality rose 50 percent in a Nortel facility, and Federal Express reduced billing errors and lost packages by 13 percent. Honeywell's teams saved over $11 million after reducing production times and shipping over 99 percent of orders on time.[7] Boeing's engineering teams built its new 777 passenger jet with far fewer design errors than occurred in earlier programs,[8] and Boeing received the fastest flight certification ever for a new commercial aircraft.[9] Boeing management claims that it could not have developed the 777 without cross-functional teams; it would have been prohibitively expensive.[10]

Teams also can enhance *speed* and be powerful forces for *innovation* and *change*. 3M, DaimlerChrysler, and many other companies are using teams to create new products faster. Lenders cut home mortgage approval times from weeks to hours, and life insurance companies cut time to issue new policies from six weeks to one day.[11] Some companies have become more entrepreneurial in part through the creation of client service groups.[12] At KPMG Netherlands, a strategic integration team of 12 partners, with 100 other professionals divided into 14 task forces, led strategic and cultural changes by studying future trends and scenarios, defining core competencies, and dealing with organizational challenges.[13] The auto industry relies on project teams to develop new vehicles, including Ford's great success with its Taurus project.[14] At 3M, work teams turned around one division by tripling the number of new products.[15] Amgen hadn't launched a new drug in almost a decade, but it created better-integrated teams from clinical science and marketing, and new-product development is now proceeding nicely.[16]

Teams also provide many *benefits for their members*.[17] The team is a very useful learning mechanism. Members learn about the company and themselves, and they acquire new skills and performance strategies. The team can satisfy important personal needs, such as affiliation and esteem. Other needs are met as team members receive tangible organizational rewards that they could not have achieved working alone.

Team members can provide one another with feedback; identify opportunities for growth and development; and train, coach, and mentor.[18] A marketing representative can learn about financial modeling from a colleague on a new-product development team, and the financial expert can learn about consumer marketing. Experience working together in a team, and developing strong problem-solving capabilities, is a vital supplement to specific job skills or functional expertise. And the skills are transferable to new positions.

The New Team Environment

The words *group* and *team* often are used interchangeably.[19] Modern managers sometimes use the word *teams* to the point that it has become cliche; they talk about teams while skeptics perceive no real teamwork. Thus, making a distinction between groups and teams can be useful. A *working group* is a collection of people who work in the same area or have been drawn together to undertake a task but do not necessarily come together as a unit and achieve significant performance improvements. A real **team** is formed of people (usually a small number) with complementary skills who trust one another and are committed to a common purpose, common performance goals, and a common approach for which they hold themselves mutually accountable.[20] A real team is committed to working together successfully to achieve high performance.

Organizations have been using groups for a long time, but things are different today.[21] Teams are used in many different ways, and to far greater effect, than in the past. Table 14.1 highlights just a few of the differences between the traditional work environment and the way true teams work today. Ideally, people are far more involved, they are better trained, cooperation is higher, and the culture is one of learning as well as producing.

Relay teams are built with people of varying skill levels who work toward a common goal—to win. Teams in a business are often formed with the same mindset.

Traditional Environment	Team Environment
Managers determine and plan the work.	Managers and team members jointly determine and plan the work.
Jobs are narrowly defined.	Jobs require broad skills and knowledge.
Cross-training is viewed as inefficient.	Cross-training is the norm.
Most information is "management property."	Most information is freely shared at all levels.
Training for nonmanagers focuses on technical skills.	Continuous learning requires interpersonal, administrative, and technical training for all.
Risk taking is discouraged and punished.	Measured risk taking is encouraged and supported.
People work alone.	People work together.
Rewards are based on individual performance.	Rewards are based on individual performance and contributions to team performance.
Managers determine "best methods."	Everyone works to continuously improve methods and processes.

TABLE 14.1
The New Team Environment

team

A small number of people with complementary skills who are committed to a common purpose, set of performance goals, and approach for which they hold themselves mutually accountable.

SOURCE: From *Leading Teams* by J. Zenger and Associates. Reprinted by permission.

Types of Teams

work teams
Teams that make or do things like manufacture, assemble, sell, or provide service.
project and development teams
Teams that work on long-term projects but disband once the work is completed.
parallel teams
Teams that operate separately from the regular work structure, and exist temporarily.
management teams
Teams that coordinate and provide direction to the subunits under their jurisdiction and integrate work among subunits.
transnational teams
Work groups composed of multinational members whose activities span multiple countries.
virtual teams
Teams that are physically dispersed and communicate electronically more than face-to-face.

There may be hundreds of groups and teams in your organization, but there are just a few primary types.[22] **Work teams** make or do things such as manufacture, assemble, sell, or provide service. These typically are well defined, a clear part of the formal organizational structure, and composed of a full-time, stable membership. These are what most people think of when they think of teams in organizations.[23]

Project and development teams work on long-term projects, often over a period of years. They have specific assignments, such as research or new-product development, and members usually must contribute expert knowledge and judgment. These teams work toward a one-time product, disbanding once their work is completed. Then new teams are formed for new projects.

Parallel teams operate separately from the regular work structure of the firm on a temporary basis. Members often come from different units or jobs and are asked to do work that is not normally done by the standard structure. Their charge is to recommend solutions to specific problems. They usually do not have authority to act, however. Examples include task forces and quality or safety teams formed to study a particular problem.

Management teams coordinate and provide direction to the subunits under their jurisdiction and integrate work among subunits.[24] The management team is based on authority stemming from hierarchical rank and is responsible for the overall performance of the business unit. Managers responsible for different subunits form a team together, and at the top of the organization resides the executive management team that establishes strategic direction and manages the firm's overall performance.

Transnational teams are work teams composed of multinational members whose activities span multiple countries.[25] Such teams differ from other work teams not only by being multicultural, but also by often being geographically dispersed, being psychologically distant, and working on highly complex projects having considerable impact on company objectives.

Transnational teams tend to be **virtual teams,** communicating electronically more than face-to-face, although other types of teams may operate virtually as well. Virtual teams create difficult challenges: building trust, cohesion, and team identity, and overcoming the isolation of virtual team members.[26]

Legendary Teams

To ensure the safety of themselves and each other, Boots & Coots firefighters need to maintain trust and communicate under some of the toughest circumstances.

The Navy Seals, it seems, can do anything; they have an overriding drive to excel and succeed. The Tokyo String Quartet is one of the world's finest, excelling at putting egos aside to become "one with the music." The University of North Carolina women's soccer team won nine NCAA championships in a row—some say the greatest team ever, in any sport, at any level. Emergency room staff at Massachusetts General Hospital can handle anything: Team members all know their roles, someone takes charge, people rotate in and out of leadership roles as circumstances ebb and flow. And when there's an oil well blowout, from Texas to the Middle East, the Boots & Coots firefighters can usually handle it based on their expertise, trust, and mutual loyalty.

Some of the all-time great work teams include the Walt Disney studio in the 1930s, the Apple Macintosh team, the Manhattan Project, the engineering teams at Xerox's legendary Palo Alto Research Center (PARC), and the elite corps of aeronautical engineers and fabricators who built radically new planes at Lockheed's top-secret Skunk Works. A team now working at Lockheed Martin may achieve similar legendary status.

Tom Burbage's Joint Strike Fighter (JSF) team was charged with winning a five-year battle with Boeing in the most lucrative competition in Pentagon history. The company that won the contract—potentially worth $200 billion—would develop a radar-evading, sound-barrier-busting aircraft that would serve as the combat jet of the future for the U.S. Air Force, Navy, and Marines and the United Kingdom's Royal Air Force and Royal Navy.

To meet the expectations of the U.S. armed services, Burbage's team had to solve seemingly impossible technical problems. The plane needed to be able to take off in tight places and make vertical landings on aircraft carriers and lighter ships. Think about that: Among so many other challenges, they needed to defy gravity by generating enough thrust to vertically lift a 30,000-pound plane. Guess what? They pulled it off. After 10 years of work, the Marine version of the aircraft took its first-ever vertical flight in the high desert of California. And Lockheed won the contract.

At a ribbon-cutting ceremony in August 2004, a spokesperson announced, "We have transitioned from design to the first flyable hardware and software." Testing began in 2005.

SOURCE: W. Bennis and P. Ward Biederman, *Organizing Genius: The Secrets of Creative Collaboration* (Reading, MA: Addison-Wesley, 1997); B. Breen, "High Stakes, High Bets," *Fast Company*, April 2002, pp. 66–78; B. Breen, "From Postmortems to Premortems," *Fast Company*, April 2002, p. 76; K. Labich, "Elite Teams Get the Job Done," *Fortune*, February 19, 1996, pp. 90–99; "F-35 Joint Strike Fighter Electronic Warfare Suite 'Ready to Fly,' " *Business Wire*, August 27, 2004.

Self-Managed Teams

Today there exist many different types of work teams with many different labels. The terms can be confusing, and sometimes are used interchangeably out of a lack of awareness of actual differences. Figure 14.1 shows the different types according to how much autonomy they have.[27] To the left, teams are more traditional with little decision-making authority, being under the control of direct supervision. To the right there is more autonomy, decision-making power, and self-direction.

The trend today is toward **self-managed teams,** in which workers are trained to do all or most of the jobs in the unit, they have no immediate supervisor, and they make decisions previously made by first-line supervisors.[28] Self-managed teams are most frequently found in manufacturing. People often resist self-managed work teams,[29] in part because they don't want so much responsibility and the change is difficult. In addition, people often don't like to do performance evaluation of teammates, or to fire people. But compared to traditionally managed teams, self-managed teams appear to be more productive, have lower costs, provide better customer service, provide higher quality, have better safety records, and are more satisfying for members.

Referring to Figure 14.1, **traditional work groups** have no managerial responsibilities. The first-line manager plans, organizes, staffs, directs, and controls them, and other groups provide support activities, including quality control and maintenance. **Quality circles** are voluntary groups of people drawn from various production teams who make suggestions about quality but have no authority to make decisions or execute. **Semiautonomous work groups** make decisions about managing and carrying out major production activities, but still get outside support for quality control and maintenance. **Autonomous work groups,** or *self-managing teams*, control decisions about and execution of a complete range of tasks—acquiring raw materials and performing operations, quality control, maintenance, and shipping. They are fully responsible for an entire product or an entire part of a production process. **Self-designing teams** do all of that and go one step further—they also have control over the design of the team. They decide themselves whom to hire, whom to fire, and what tasks the team will perform.

self-managed teams

Autonomous work groups in which workers are trained to do all or most of the jobs in a unit, have no immediate supervisor, and make decisions previously made by first-line supervisors.

traditional work groups

Groups that have no managerial responsibilities.

quality circles

Voluntary groups of people drawn from various production teams who make suggestions about quality.

semiautonomous work groups

Groups that make decisions about managing and carrying out major production activities, but still get outside support for quality control and maintenance.

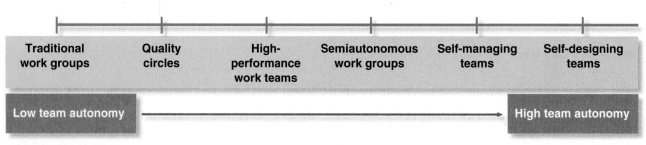

SOURCE: R. Banker, J. Field, R. Schroeder, and K. Sinha, "Impact of Work Teams on Manufacturing Performance: A Longitudinal Field Study," *Academy of Management Journal*. Copyright © 1996 by Academy of Management. Reproduced with permission of Academy of Management via Copyright Clearance Center.

FIGURE 14.1
Team Autonomy
Continuum

---

autonomous work groups

Groups that control decisions about and execution of a complete range of tasks.

self-designing teams

Teams with the responsibilities of autonomous work groups, plus control over hiring, firing, and what tasks members perform.

Movement from left to right on the continuum corresponds with more and more worker participation. Toward the right, the participation is not trivial and not merely advisory. It has real substance, including not just suggestions but action and impact. When companies have introduced teams that reach the point of being truly self-managed, results have included lower costs and greater levels of team productivity, quality, and customer satisfaction.[30] Overall, semiautonomous and autonomous teams are known to improve the organization's financial and overall performance, at least in North America.[31]

Such results are inspiring U.S.-based multinational firms to use self-managed teams in their foreign facilities. For example, Goodyear Tire & Rubber has initiated self-managed work teams in Europe, Latin America, and Asia; Sara Lee in Puerto Rico and Mexico; and Texas Instruments in Malaysia. These companies are learning—and other companies should be forewarned—of the different ways different cultures might respond to self-managed teams, and to customize implementation according to cultural values.[32]

How Groups Become Real Teams

As a manager, you will want your group to become an effective team. To accomplish this, you will need to understand how groups can become true teams, and why groups sometimes fail to become teams. Groups become true teams via basic group activities, the passage of time, and team development activities.

Group Activities

Assume you are the leader of a newly formed group—actually a bunch of people. What will you face as you attempt to develop your group into a high-performing team? If groups are to develop successfully, they will engage in various activities, including:[33]

- *Forming*—group members attempt to lay the ground rules for what types of behavior are acceptable.
- *Storming*—hostilities and conflict arise, and people jockey for positions of power and status.
- *Norming*—group members agree on their shared goals, and norms and closer relationships develop.
- *Performing*—the group channels its energies into performing its tasks.

Groups that deteriorate move to a *declining* stage, and temporary groups add an *adjourning* or terminating stage. Groups terminate when they complete their task or when they disband due to failure or loss of interest and new groups form, as the cycle continues.

Virtual teams go through these stages of group development.[34] The forming stage is characterized by unbridled optimism: "I believe we have a great team and will work

Self-managed teams can have a positive effect on productivity. But people often resist self-managed teams in part because they don't want so much responsibility and the change is difficult.

well together. We all understand the importance of the project and intend to take it seriously." Optimism turns into reality shock in the storming stage: "No one has taken a leadership role. We have not made the project the priority that it deserves." The norming stage comes at about the halfway point in the project life cycle, in which people refocus and recommit: "You must make firm commitments to a specific time schedule." The performing stage is the dash to the finish, as teammates show the discipline needed to meet the deadline.

The Passage of Time

A key aspect of group development is the passage of time. Groups pass through critical periods, or times when they are particularly open to formative experiences.[35] The first such critical period is in the forming stage, at the first meeting, when rules and roles are established that set long-lasting precedents. A second critical period is the midway point between the initial meeting and a deadline (e.g., completing a project or making a presentation). At this point, the group has enough experience to understand its work; it comes to realize that time is becoming a scarce resource and it must "get on with it"; and there is enough time left to change its approach if necessary.

In the initial meeting, the group should establish desired norms, roles, and other determinants of effectiveness considered throughout this chapter. At the second critical period (the midpoint), groups should renew or open lines of communication with outside constituencies. The group can use fresh information from its external environment to revise its approach to performing its task and ensure that it meets the needs of customers and clients. Without these activities, groups may get off on the wrong foot from the beginning, and members may never revise their behavior in the appropriate direction.[36]

A Developmental Sequence: From Group to Team

As a manager or group member, you should expect the group to engage in all the activities just discussed at various times. But groups are not always successful. They do not always engage in the developmental activities that turn them into effective, high-performing teams.

A useful developmental sequence is depicted in Figure 14.2. The figure shows the various activities as the leadership of the group moves from traditional supervision, through a more participative approach, to true team leadership.[37]

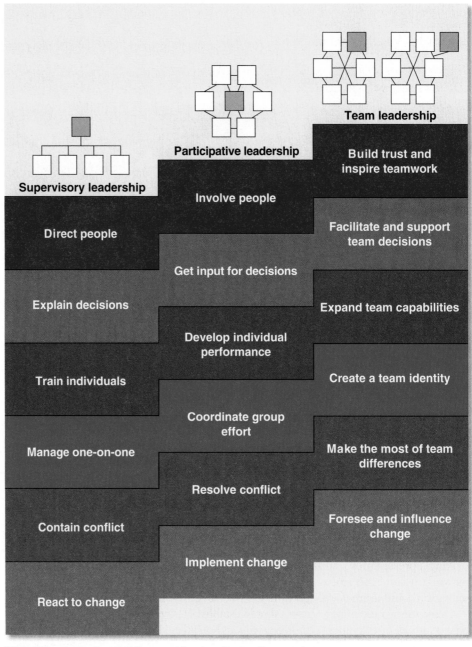

FIGURE 14.2
Stepping up to Team
Leadership

SOURCE: From *Leading Teams* by J. Zenger and Associates. Reprinted by permission.

It is important to understand a couple of things about this model. Groups do not necessarily keep progressing from one "stage" to the next; they may remain permanently in the supervisory level, or become more participative but never make it to true team leadership. Therefore, progress on these dimensions must be a conscious goal of the leader and the members, and all should strive to meet these goals. Your group can meet these goals, and become a true team, by engaging in the activities in the figure.

Why Groups Sometimes Fail

Team building does not necessarily progress smoothly through such a sequence, culminating in a well-oiled team and superb performance.[38] Some groups never do work out. Such groups can be frustrating for managers and members, who may feel they are a waste of time, and that the difficulties outweigh the benefits.

It is not easy to build high-performance teams. *Teams* is often just a word used by management to describe merely putting people into groups. "Teams" sometimes are launched

"Teams are the Ferraris of work design. They're high performance but high maintenance and expensive."[39]

with little or no training or support systems. For example, managers as well as group members need new skills to make the group work. These skills include learning the art of diplomacy, tackling "people issues" head on, and walking the fine line between encouraging autonomy and rewarding team innovations without letting the team get too independent and out of control.[40] Giving up some control is very difficult for managers from traditional systems; they have to realize they will gain control in the long run by creating stronger, better-performing units.

Teams should be truly empowered, as discussed in Chapter 13. The benefits of teams are reduced when they are not allowed to make important decisions—in other words, when management doesn't trust them with important responsibilities. If teams must acquire permission for every innovative idea, they will revert to making safe, traditional decisions.[41]

Empowerment enhances team performance even among virtual teams. Empowerment for virtual teams includes thorough training in using the technologies and strong technical support from management. Some virtual teams have periodic face-to-face interactions, which help performance; empowerment is particularly helpful for virtual teams that don't often meet face-to-face.[42]

Failure lies in not knowing and doing what makes teams successful. To be successful you must apply clear thinking and appropriate practices.[43] That is what the rest of the chapter is about.

Building Effective Teams

All the considerations just described form the building blocks of an effective work team. But what does it really mean for a team to be effective? What, precisely, can a manager do to design a truly effective team? Team effectiveness is defined by three criteria.[44]

First, the *productive output* of the team meets or exceeds the standards of quantity and quality; the team's output is acceptable to those customers, inside or outside the organization, who receive the team's products or services. As examples, Procter & Gamble's business teams are effective at reducing costs and at developing new products.[45] Clarence L. "Kelly" Johnson's group designed, built, and flew the first U.S. tactical jet fighter, XP80, in 143 days.[46] Tom West's legendary Eclipse Group at Data General worked overtime for a year and a half to create the 32-bit superminicomputer that heralded the next generation of minicomputers.[47]

Second, team members realize *satisfaction* of their personal needs. P&G's team members enjoy the opportunity to participate creatively. Johnson and West gave their teams the freedom to innovate and stretch their skills. Team members were enthusiastic and realized great pride and satisfaction in their work.

Third, team members remain *committed* to working together again; that is, the group doesn't burn out and disintegrate after a grueling project. Looking back, the members are glad they were involved. In other words, effective teams remain viable and have good prospects for repeated success in the future.[48]

Teams, with guidance from internal and external customers, should identify the nature of the results they want to achieve.

A Performance Focus

The key element of effective teamwork is commitment to a common purpose.[49] The best teams are ones that have been given an important performance challenge by management, and then come to a common understanding and appreciation of their purpose. Without such understanding and commitment, a group will be just a bunch of individuals.

The best teams also work hard at developing a common understanding of how they will work together to achieve their purpose.[50] They discuss and agree upon such things as how tasks and roles will be allocated and how they will make decisions. The team should develop norms for examining its performance strategies and be amenable to changing when appropriate. With a clear, strong, motivating purpose, and effective performance strategies, people will pull together into a powerful force that has a chance to achieve extraordinary things.

The team's general purpose should be translated into specific, measurable performance goals.[51] You learned in Chapter 13 about how goals motivate individual performance. Performance can be defined by collective end products instead of a bunch of individual products.[52] Team-based performance goals help define and distinguish the team's product, encourage communication within the team, energize and motivate team members, provide feedback on progress, signal team victories (and defeats), and ensure that the team focuses clearly on results. Teams with both difficult goals and incentives to attain them achieve the highest performance levels.[53]

The best team-based measurement systems will inform top management of the team's performance and help the team understand its own processes and gauge its own progress. Ideally, the team will play the lead role in designing its own measurement system. This is a great indicator of whether the team is truly empowered.[54]

Teams, like individuals, need feedback on their performance. Feedback from customers is crucial. Some customers for the team's products are inside the organization. Teams should be responsible for satisfying them, and should be given or should seek performance feedback. Better yet, wherever possible, teams should interact directly with external customers who make the ultimate buy decisions about their products and services. This will be the most honest, and most crucial and useful, performance feedback of all.[55]

Motivating Teamwork

social loafing
Working less hard and being less productive when in a group.

social facilitation effect
Working harder when in a group than when working alone.

Sometimes individuals work less hard and are less productive when they are members of a group. Such **social loafing** occurs when individuals believe that their contributions are not important, others will do the work for them, their lack of effort will go undetected, or they will be the lone sucker if they work hard but others don't. On the other hand, sometimes individuals work harder when they are members of a group than when they are working alone. This **social facilitation effect** occurs because individuals usually are more motivated when others are present, they are concerned with what others think of them, and they want to maintain a positive self-image.

A social facilitation effect is maintained, and a social loafing effect can be avoided, when group members know each other, they can observe and communicate with one an-

How well is teamwork motivated on *Survivor* and *The Apprentice*?

other, clear performance goals exist, the task is meaningful to the people working on it, they believe that their efforts matter and others will not take advantage of them, and the culture supports teamwork.[56] Thus, ideally it will be clear that everyone works hard, contributes in concrete ways to the team's work, and is accountable to other team members. Accountability to one another, rather than just to "the boss," is an essential aspect of good teamwork. Accountability inspires mutual commitment and trust.[57] Trust in your teammates—and their trust in you—may be the ultimate key to effectiveness.

Team effort is also generated by designing the team's task to be motivating. Techniques for creating motivating tasks appear in the guidelines for job enrichment discussed in Chapter 13. Tasks are motivating when they use a variety of member skills and provide high task variety, identity, significance, autonomy, and performance feedback.

Ultimately, teamwork is best motivated by tying rewards to team performance.[58] If team performance can be measured validly, team-based rewards can be given accordingly. It is not easy to move from a system of rewards based on individual performance to one based on team performance. It also may not be appropriate, unless people are truly interdependent and must collaborate to attain true team goals.[59] Sometimes team-based rewards can be added to existing rewards already based on individual performance. In the case of a financial services firm, year 1 of a new team system included pay increases based 15 percent on team performance, increasing to 50 percent by year 3.[60]

If team performance is difficult to measure validly, then desired behaviors, activities, and processes that indicate good teamwork can be rewarded. Individuals within teams can be given differential rewards based on teamwork indicated by active participation, cooperation, leadership, and other contributions to the team.

If team members are to be rewarded differentially, such decisions are better *not* left only to the boss.[61] They should be made by the team itself, via peer ratings or multi-rater evaluation systems. Team members are in a better position to observe, know, and make valid reward allocations. Finally, the more teams the organization has, and the more a full team orientation exists, the more valid and effective it will be to distribute rewards via gainsharing and other organizationwide incentives.

Connections: JOHN MACKEY AND WHOLE FOODS

As noted in the Prologue, when you join Whole Foods you join a team—the bakery, seafood, whatever. You're not fully hired yet, though: After four weeks, your team votes on whether to keep you. You need a two-thirds yes vote to join permanently. As a team member, your rewards are both social and financial. For example, before each business meeting is adjourned, participants engage in a round of "appreciations," commending things said or done by others in attendance. Financial rewards are based on performance. Because some pay is team-based (after base wages), teams care about whom they keep; they want people who will produce. Every four weeks, work teams' productivity is assessed, and profit sharing is awarded in every other paycheck.

Member Contributions

Team members should be selected and trained so they become effective contributors to the team. Teams often hire their new members.[62] Miller Brewing Company and Eastman Chemical teams select members on the basis of tests designed to predict how well they will contribute to team success in an empowered environment. At Texas Instruments, Human Resources screens applicants; then team members interview them and make selection decisions.

Some companies have computer systems combining PC networks with databases and videoconferencing to help teams identify and find the right new people. Generally, the skills required by the team include technical or functional expertise, problem-solving and

Many teams undergo training exercises to learn team-building techniques. This is the classic "trust fall." The blindfolded person falls backwards, trusting that his teammates will catch him and not let him fall. Trust must be earned, not demanded.

decision-making skills, and interpersonal skills. Some managers and teams mistakenly overemphasize some skills, particularly technical or functional, and underemphasize the others. It is vitally important that all three types of skills be represented, and developed, among team members.

Development Dimensions International provides people with 300 hours of training, mostly about how to work in teams, but also technical cross-training. K Shoes, Ltd., trains team members in teamwork, overall business knowledge, supplier partnership development, and retail management. Kodak provides 150 hours of first-year training on team effectiveness, including teaching people to cross-train others, and 120 more hours subsequently on the same team skills plus business and financial skills.[63]

Norms

norms

Shared beliefs about how people should think and behave.

Norms are shared beliefs about how people should think and behave. From the organization's standpoint, norms can be positive or negative. In some teams, everyone works hard; in other groups, employees are antimanagement and do as little work as possible. Some groups develop norms of taking risks, others of being conservative.[64] A norm could dictate that employees speak either favorably or critically of the company. Team members may show concern about poor safety practices, drug and alcohol abuse, and employee theft, or they may not care about these issues (or may even condone such practices). Health consciousness is the norm among executives at some companies, but smoking is the norm at tobacco companies. Some groups have norms of distrust and of being closed toward one another, but as you might guess, norms of trust and open discussion about conflict can improve group performance.[65]

A professor described his consulting experiences at two companies that exhibited different norms in their management teams.[66] At Federal Express Corporation, a young manager interrupted the professor's talk by proclaiming that a recent decision by top management ran counter to the professor's point about corporate planning. He was challenging top management to defend its decision. A hot debate ensued, and after an hour everyone went to lunch without a trace of hard feelings. But at another corporation, the professor opened a meeting by asking a group of top managers to describe the company's culture. There was silence. He asked again. More silence. Then someone passed him an unsigned note that read, "Dummy, can't you see that we can't speak our minds? Ask for the input anonymously, in writing." As you can see, norms are important, and can vary greatly from one group to another.

Roles

Roles are different sets of expectations for how different individuals should behave. Whereas norms apply generally to all team members, different roles exist for different members within the norm structure.

Two important sets of roles must be performed.[67] **Task specialist** roles are filled by individuals who have particular job-related skills and abilities. These employees keep the team moving toward task accomplishment. **Team maintenance specialists** develop and maintain harmony within the team. They boost morale, give support, provide humor, soothe hurt feelings, and generally exhibit a concern with members' well-being.

Note the similarity between these roles and the important task performance and group maintenance leadership behaviors you learned about in Chapter 12. As suggested in that chapter, some of these roles will be more important than others at different times and under different circumstances. But these behaviors need not be carried out only by one or two leaders; any member of the team can carry out these roles at any time. Over time, both types of roles can be performed by different individuals to maintain an effectively functioning work team.

What roles should leaders perform? Superior team leaders are better at relating, scouting, persuading, and empowering than are average team leaders.[68] *Relating* includes exhibiting more social and political awareness, caring for team members, and trust-building. *Scouting* means seeking information from managers, peers, and specialists, and investigating problems systematically. *Persuading* means not only influencing the team, but also obtaining external support. *Empowerment* includes delegating authority, being flexible regarding team decisions, and coaching. Moreover, leaders should roll up their sleeves and do real work, not just supervise.[69]

Self-managed teams report to a management representative who sometimes is called the coach. In true self-managed teams, the coach is not a true member of the team.[70] This is because the group is supposed to make its own decisions, and because the power of the management representative can have a dampening effect on the team's openness and autonomy.

The role of the coach, then, is to help the team understand its role in the organization, and to act as a resource for the team. The coach can provide information, resources, and opinions that team members do not or cannot acquire on their own. And the coach should be an advocate for the team in the rest of organization.

Cohesiveness

One of the most important properties of a team is cohesiveness.[71] **Cohesiveness** refers to how attractive the team is to its members, how motivated members are to remain in the team, and the degree to which team members influence one another. In general, it refers to how tightly knit the team is.

The Importance of Cohesiveness   Cohesiveness is important for two primary reasons. First, it contributes to *member satisfaction*. In a cohesive team, members communicate and get along well with one another. They feel good about being a part of the team. Even if their jobs are unfulfilling or the organization is oppressive, people gain some satisfaction from enjoying their co-workers.

Second, cohesiveness has a major impact on *performance*. A recent study of manufacturing teams led to a conclusion that performance improvements in both quality and productivity occurred in the most cohesive unit, whereas conflict within another team prevented any quality or productivity improvements.[72] Sports fans read about this all the time. When teams are winning, players talk about the team being close, getting

---

roles

Different sets of expectations for how different individuals should behave.

task specialist

An individual who has more advanced job-related skills and abilities than other group members possess.

team maintenance specialist

Individual who develops and maintains team harmony.

cohesiveness

The degree to which a group is attractive to its members, members are motivated to remain in the group, and members influence one another.

Cohesive groups are better than noncohesive groups at attaining the goals they want to attain; as a manager you need to ensure that your team's goals represent good business results.

along well, and knowing one another's games. In contrast, losing is attributed to infighting and divisiveness. Generally, cohesiveness clearly can and does have a positive effect on performance.[73]

But this interpretation is simplistic; exceptions to this intuitive relationship occur. Tightly knit work groups can be disruptive to the organization, such as when they sabotage the assembly line, get their boss fired, or enforce low performance norms.

When does high cohesiveness lead to good performance, and when does it result in poor performance? This depends on (1) the task, and (2) whether the group has high or low performance norms.

The Task   If the task is to make a decision or solve a problem, cohesiveness can lead to poor performance. Groupthink (discussed in Chapter 3) occurs when a tightly knit group is so cooperative that agreeing with one another's opinions and refraining from criticizing others' ideas become norms. For a cohesive group to make good decisions, it should establish a norm of constructive disagreement. This is important for groups up to the level of boards of directors;[74] in top management teams it has been shown to improve the financial performance of companies.[75]

Group Meetings: Love 'em or Hate 'em

A lot of people hate meetings. A lot of companies are overrun by too many unproductive, morale-sapping meetings. But some meetings are just too good to miss. Here are a few, as described by the people who love them:

• MaMaMedia.com holds weekly meetings called Thought Provoking Sessions that provide a creative refuge from the daily work. Rebecca Randall never misses them because "it's a great way for me to step outside of the day-to-day routine and come up with new approaches to doing my job." The company provides Web-based "playful learning" for kids 12 and under, and the meetings "approximate the way children learn through exploration, fun, surprise, and imagination." Each week, a different work team plans and hosts the meeting.

As a company that provides innovative Web site-based learning tools for children, MaMaMedia.com understands the need for holding meetings that produce creative thinking.

• At Kaufman and Broad Home Corp., one of the top home builders in the United States, the monthly After 5 meeting of the marketing and communications staff is usually held in the Marketing War Room, although one was held in a moving bus. The meetings are brainstorming sessions aimed a taking the company's brand image into fun new territory. One meeting led to a major promotional campaign that used a full-scale replica of Marge and Homer Simpson's home. The norm at the meetings is that anything goes: "Think The McLaughlin Group, only nicer. The best ideas sound absolutely insane at first, so we don't want people to be editing their thoughts. The unspoken rule: If you think it, say it."

• Nortel's Caribbean and Latin American division airs its Virtual Leadership Academy live, once a month. Using teleconferencing technologies, the Leadership Academy educates geographically dispersed employees about important strategic issues. Emma Carrasco never misses it because the networked meetings "let us tap into leadership ability and expertise throughout the company . . . We leverage and showcase Nortel's technology as well as its culture . . . and reinforce a core cultural tenet: that groundbreaking technology is about elevating, not replacing, human interaction."

• Terry Pope, Operations Manager for Motorola, never misses the daily morning production meeting with 30-plus managers, engineers, and technicians. The purpose is to communicate the last 24 hours' problems that need to be addressed during the next 24 hours. If a problem is identified, the person responsible says, "Here's what's wrong, and here's what we're doing now to make sure that it doesn't happen again." He never misses the meeting because it "sets the pace for the entire factory and defines its culture. It's a daily demonstration of our ability to perform."

- Peter Kirwan has regular "Fireside Chats" with his engineers, programmers, and technical writers. The norms of the meetings are relaxed honesty and constructive criticism. "This is a chance to discuss tough issues in a friendly, informal setting . . . Business issues are always changing, and so are personal and organizational issues." He starts the meeting by opening a homemade cardboard "fireplace" and pulling up chairs. It's silly, on purpose. It loosens people up, and they talk. He learns, and helps them to learn.
- Entrepreneur Craig Forman never misses Sunday nights with his family. "This 'meeting' brings us together and gives us the motivation to attack the week. It's an anchor for all three of us." He wants to make sure his family's priorities don't get lost in the frenzy of Silicon Valley's start-up culture.

Can you identify common themes among, and differences between, these group gatherings? When you are a manager, what regular meetings will you have, and how will you (a) avoid having people dread them, and (b) get people to "not want to miss" them?

SOURCES: C. Olofson, "Play Hard, Think Big," *Fast Company Online*, January 2001, p. 64; C. Olofson, "Can We Talk? Put Another Log on the Fire," *Fast Company Online*, October 1999, p. 86; A. Wilson, "All in the Family," *Fast Company Online*, March 2000, p. 72; M. Goldberg, "At Motorola, the Meeting Is the Network," *Fast Company Online*, October 1997, p. 70; C. Olofson, "Global Reach, Virtual Leadership," *Fast Company Online*, September 1999, p. 80; C. Olofson, "Open Minds after Closing Time," *Fast Company Online*, June 1999, p. 72.

Cohesiveness can enhance performance, particularly if the task is to produce some tangible output. In day-to-day work groups for which decision making is not the primary task, the effect of cohesiveness on performance can be positive. But that depends on the group's performance norms.[76]

Performance Norms   Some groups are better than others at ensuring that their members behave the way the group prefers. Cohesive groups are more effective than noncohesive groups at norm enforcement. But the next question is: Do they have norms of high or low performance?

As Figure 14.3 shows, the highest performance occurs when a cohesive team has high performance norms. But if a highly cohesive group has low performance norms, that group will have the worst performance. In the group's eyes, however, it will have succeeded in achieving its goal of poor performance. Noncohesive groups with high performance norms can be effective from the company's standpoint. However, they won't be as productive as they would be if they were more cohesive. Noncohesive groups with low performance norms perform poorly, but they will not ruin things for management as effectively as can cohesive groups with low performance norms.

Building Cohesiveness and High Performance Norms

As Figure 14.3 suggests, managers should build teams that are cohesive and have high performance norms. The following actions can help create such teams:[77]

1. *Recruit members with similar attitudes, values, and backgrounds.* Similar individuals are more likely to get along with one another. Don't do this, though, if the team's task requires heterogeneous skills and inputs. For example, a homogeneous committee or board might make poor decisions, because it will lack different information and viewpoints and may succumb to groupthink.

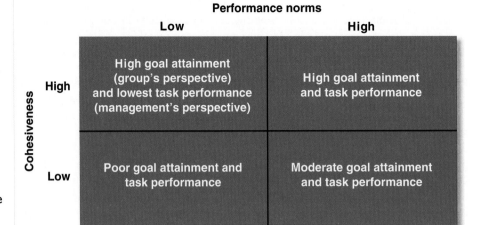

FIGURE 14.3
Cohesiveness, Performance Norms, and Group Performance

2. *Maintain high entrance and socialization standards.* Teams and organizations that are difficult to get into have more prestige. Individuals who survive a difficult interview, selection, or training process will be proud of their accomplishment and feel more attachment to the team.

3. *Keep the team small* (but large enough to get the job done). The larger the group, the less important members may feel. Small teams make individuals feel like large contributors.

4. *Help the team succeed, and publicize its successes.* You read about empowerment in the last chapter; you can empower teams as well as individuals.[78] Be a path-goal leader who facilitates success; the experience of winning brings teams closer together. Then, if you inform superiors of your team's successes, members will believe they are part of an important, prestigious unit. Teams that get into a good performance track continue to perform well as time goes on; groups that don't often enter a downward spiral in which problems compound over time.[79]

5. *Be a participative leader.* Participation in decisions gets team members more involved with one another and striving toward goal accomplishment. Too much autocratic decision making from above can alienate the group from management.

6. *Present a challenge from outside the team.* Competition with other groups makes team members band together to defeat the enemy (witness what happens to school spirit before the big game against an archrival). Some of the greatest teams in business and in science have been completely focused on winning a competition.[80] But don't *you* become the outside threat. If team members dislike you as a boss, they will become more cohesive—but their performance norms will be against you, not with you.

7. *Tie rewards to team performance.* To a large degree, teams are motivated just as individuals are—they do the things that are rewarded. Make sure that high-performing teams get the rewards they deserve and that poorly performing groups get fewer rewards. You read about this earlier. Bear in mind that not just monetary rewards but also recognition for good work are powerful motivators. Recognize and celebrate team accomplishments. The team will become more cohesive and perform better to reap more rewards. Performance goals will be high, the organization will benefit from higher team motivation and productivity, and the individual needs of team members will be better satisfied. Ideally, being a member of a high-performing team, recognized as such throughout the organization, will become a badge of honor.[81]

But keep in mind that strong cohesiveness encouraging "agreeableness" can be dysfunctional. For problem solving and decision making, the team should establish norms promoting an open, constructive atmosphere including honest disagreement over issues without personal conflict and animosity.[82]

Managing Lateral Relationships

Teams do not function in a vacuum; they are interdependent with other teams. For example, at Miller Brewing Company, major team responsibilities include coordinating with other teams and policy groups. At Texas Instruments, teams are responsible for interfacing with other teams to eliminate production bottlenecks and implement new processes, and also for working with suppliers on quality issues.[83] Thus, some activities crucial to the team are those that entail dealing with people *outside* the group.

Advantages of Collaboration

Teams don't produce results in a vacuum; they perform best by collaborating with other teams.

Managing Outward

Several vital roles link teams to their external environments, that is, to other individuals and groups both inside and outside the organization. A specific type of role that spans team boundaries is the **gatekeeper,** a team member who stays abreast of current information in scientific and other fields and informs the group of important developments. Information useful to the group can also include information about resources, trends, and political support throughout the corporation or the industry.[84]

The team's strategy dictates the team's mix of internally versus externally focused roles and how the mix changes over time. General team strategies include informing, parading, and probing.[85] The **informing** strategy entails making decisions with the team and then telling outsiders of the team's intentions. **Parading** means the team's strategy is to simultaneously emphasize internal team building and achieve external visibility. **Probing** involves a focus on external relations. This strategy requires team members to interact frequently with outsiders; diagnose the needs of customers, clients, and higher-ups; and experiment with solutions before taking action.

The appropriate balance between an internal and external strategic focus and between internal and external roles depends on how much the team needs information, support, and resources from outside. When teams have a high degree of dependence on outsiders, probing is the best strategy. Parading teams perform at an intermediate level, and informing teams are likely to fail. They are too isolated from the outside groups on which they depend.

Informing or parading strategies may be more effective for teams that are less dependent on outside groups, for example, established teams working on routine tasks in stable external environments. But for most important work teams of the future—task forces, new-product teams, and strategic decision-making teams tackling unstructured problems in a rapidly changing external environment—effective performance in roles that involve interfacing with the outside will be vital.

Lateral Role Relationships

Managing relationships with other groups and teams means engaging in a dynamic give-and-take that ensures proper coordination throughout the management system. To many managers, this process often seems like a chaotic free-for-all. It is useful to identify the different types of lateral role relationships and take a strategic approach to building constructive relationships.

Different teams, like different individuals, have roles to perform. As teams carry out their roles, several distinct patterns of working relationships develop.[86]

1. *Work-flow relationships* emerge as materials are passed from one group to another. A group commonly receives work from one unit, processes it, and sends it to the next unit in the process. Your group, then, will come before some groups and after others in the process.

---

gatekeeper

A team member who keeps abreast of current developments and provides the team with relevant information.

informing

A team strategy that entails making decisions with the team and then informing outsiders of its intentions.

parading

A team strategy that entails simultaneously emphasizing internal team building and achieving external visibility.

probing

A team strategy that requires team members to interact frequently with outsiders, diagnose their needs, and experiment with solutions.

2. *Service relationships* exist when top management centralizes an activity to which a large number of other units must gain access. Common examples are technology services, libraries, and clerical staff. Such units must service other people's requests.

3. *Advisory relationships* are created when teams with problems call on centralized sources of expert knowledge. For example, staff members in the human resources or legal department advise work teams.

4. *Audit relationships* develop when people not directly in the chain of command evaluate the methods and performances of other teams. Financial auditors check the books, and technical auditors assess the methods and technical quality of the work.

5. *Stabilization relationships* involve auditing before the fact. In other words, teams sometimes must obtain clearance from others—for example, for large purchases—before they take action.

6. *Liaison relationships* involve intermediaries between teams. Managers often are called upon to mediate conflict between two organizational units. Public relations people, sales managers, purchasing agents, and others who work across organizational boundaries serve in liaison roles as they maintain communications between the organization and the outside world.

Public relations people serve in liaison roles as they maintain communications between the organization and the outside world.

By assessing each working relationship with another unit ("From whom do we receive, and to whom do we send work? What permissions do we control, and to whom must we go for authorizations?"), teams can better understand whom to contact and when, where, why, and how to do so. Coordination throughout the working system improves, problems are avoided or short-circuited before they get too serious, and performance improves.[87]

Managing Conflict

The complex maze of interdependencies throughout organizations provides boundless opportunity for conflict to arise among groups and teams. Some conflict is constructive for the organization, as we discussed in Chapter 3. Michael Eisner, former CEO and chairman of Disney, said that the key to ideas and innovation is to create an environment of supportive conflict, or what he called "appropriate friction."[88] But many things cause great potential for destructive conflict: the sheer number and variety of contacts; ambiguities in jurisdiction and responsibility; differences in goals; intergroup competition for scarce resources; different perspectives held by members of different units; varying time horizons in which some units attend to long-term considerations and others focus on short-term needs; and other factors.

Tensions and anxieties are likely to arise in demographically diverse teams, or teams from different parts of the organization, or teams composed of contrasting personalities. Both demographic[89] and crossfunctional[90] heterogeneity initially lead to problems such as stress, lower cooperation, and lower cohesiveness. But over time and with communication, diverse groups tend to become more cooperative and perform better than do homogeneous groups. Norms of cooperation can improve performance,[91] as does the fact that cross-functional teams engage in more external communication with more areas of the organization.[92]

Conflict Styles

Teams inevitably face conflicts and must decide how to manage them. The aim should be to make the conflict productive, that is, to make those involved believe they have benefited rather than lost from the conflict.[93] People believe they have benefited from a conflict when (1) a new solution is implemented, the problem is solved, and it is unlikely to emerge again, and (2) work relationships have been strengthened and people believe they can work together productively in the future.

People handle conflict in different ways. You have your own style; others' styles may be similar or may differ. Their styles depend in part on their country's cultural norms. For example, Chinese people are more concerned with collective than with individual interests, and are more likely than managers in the United States to turn to higher authorities to make decisions rather than resolve conflicts themselves.[94] But culture aside, any team or individual has several options regarding how they deal with conflicts.[95] These personal styles of dealing with conflict, shown in Figure 14.4, are distinguished based on how much people strive to satisfy their own concerns (the assertiveness dimension) and how much they focus on satisfying the other party's concerns (the cooperation dimension).

For example, a common reaction to conflict is **avoidance.** In this situation, people do nothing to satisfy themselves or others. They either ignore the problem by doing nothing at all or address it by merely smoothing over or deemphasizing the disagreement. This, of course, fails to solve the problem or clear the air.

Accommodation means cooperating on behalf of the other party but not being assertive about one's own interests. **Compromise** involves moderate attention to both parties' concerns, being neither highly cooperative nor highly assertive. This style results in satisficing but not optimizing solutions. **Competing** is a highly competitive response in which people focus strictly on their own wishes and are unwilling to recognize the other person's concerns. Finally, **collaboration** emphasizes both cooperation and assertiveness. The goal is to maximize satisfaction for both parties.

So, imagine you and a friend want to go to a movie together, and you have different movies in mind. If he insists that you go to his movie, he is showing the competing style. If you agree, even though you prefer another movie, you are accommodating. If one of you mentions a third movie that neither of you is excited about but you both are willing to live with it, you are compromising. If you realize you don't know all the options, do some research and find another movie that you're both enthusiastic about, you are collaborating.

Different approaches are necessary at different times.[96] For example, competing can be necessary when cutting costs or dealing with other scarce resources. Compromise may be useful when people are under time pressure, when they need to achieve a temporary solution, or when collaboration fails. People should accommodate when they learn they are wrong or to minimize loss when they are outmatched. Even avoiding may be appropriate if the issue is trivial or resolving the conflict should be someone else's responsibility.

But when the conflict concerns important issues, when both sets of concerns are valid and important, when a creative solution is needed, and when commitment to the solution is vital to implementation, collaboration is the ideal approach. Collaboration can be achieved by airing feelings and opinions, addressing all concerns, and avoiding goal displacement by not letting personal attacks interfere with problem solving. An important technique is to invoke **superordinate goals**—higher-level organizational goals toward which everyone should be striving and that ultimately need to take precedence over personal or unit preferences.[97] Collaboration offers the best chance of

Conflicts can arise for any team—the trick is to make them productive. This ad promotes the American Arbitration Association's mission to train professionals on how to effectively minimize and manage conflict—"before the mud starts flying."

avoidance

A reaction to conflict that involves ignoring the problem by doing nothing at all, or deemphasizing the disagreement.

accommodation

A style of dealing with conflict involving cooperation on behalf of the other party but not being assertive about one's own interests.

compromise

A style of dealing with conflict involving moderate attention to both parties' concerns.

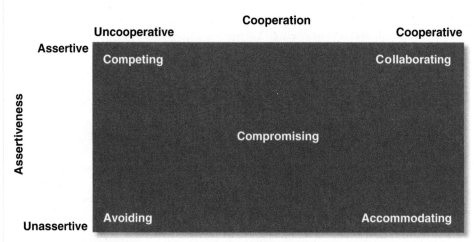

FIGURE 14.4
Conflict Management Strategies

SOURCE: K. Thomas, "Conflict and Conflict Management." In *Handbook of Industrial and Organizational Psychology*, ed. M. D. Dunnette. Copyright © 1976. Reprinted by permission of the editor.

competing

A style of dealing with conflict involving strong focus on one's own goals, and little or no concern for the other person's goals.

collaboration

A style of dealing with conflict emphasizing both cooperation and assertiveness in order to maximize both parties' satisfaction.

superordinate goals

Higher-level goals taking priority over specific individual or group goals.

mediator

A third party who intervenes to help others manage their conflict.

reaching mutually satisfactory solutions based on the ideas and interests of all parties, and of maintaining and strengthening work relationships.

Being a Mediator

Managers spend a lot of time trying to resolve conflict between *other* people. You already may have served as a **mediator:** a "third party" intervening to help settle a conflict between other people. Third-party intervention, done well, can improve working relationships and help the parties improve their own conflict-management, communication, and problem-solving skills.[98]

A study of human resource (HR) managers and the conflicts with which they deal provides some insight.[99] HR managers deal with every type of conflict imaginable: interpersonal difficulties from minor irritations to jealousy to fights; operations issues, including union issues, work assignments, overtime, and sick leave; discipline over infractions ranging from drug use and theft to sleeping on the job; sexual harassment and racial bias; pay and promotion issues; and feuds or strategic conflicts among divisions or individuals at the highest organizational levels.

In the study, the HR managers successfully settled most of the disputes. These managers typically follow a four-stage strategy. They *investigate* by interviewing the disputants and others and gathering more information. While talking with the disputants, they seek both parties' perspectives, remaining as neutral as possible. The discussion should stay issue-oriented, not personal. They *decide* how to resolve the dispute, often in conjunction with the disputants' bosses. In preparing to decide what to do, blame should not be assigned prematurely; at this point they should be exploring solutions. They *take action* by explaining their decisions and the reasoning, and advise or train the disputants to avoid future incidents. And they *follow up* by making sure everyone understands the solution, documenting the conflict and the resolution, and monitoring the results by checking back with the disputants and their bosses. Throughout, the objectives of the HR people are to be fully informed so they understand the conflict; to be active and assertive in trying to resolve it; to be as objective, neutral, and impartial as humanly possible; and to be flexible by modifying their approaches according to the situation.[100]

Here are some other recommendations for more effective conflict management.[101] Don't allow dysfunctional conflict to build, or hope or assume that it will go away. Address it before it escalates. Try to resolve it, and if the first efforts don't work, try others. And remember the earlier discussion (Chapter 13) of procedural justice. Even if disputants are not happy with your decisions, there are benefits to providing fair treatment, making a good-faith effort, giving them a voice in the proceedings, and so on. Remember, too, that you may be able to ask HR specialists to help with difficult conflicts.

Advantages of Collaboration

The collaborative approach to managing conflict involves caring about others' goals as well as your own. As a mediator, you should remember this to help ensure a collaborative process between others.

Electronic and Virtual Conflict

Conflict management affects the success of virtual teams.[102] In a recent study, avoidance hurt performance. Accommodation—conceding to others in order to maintain harmony rather than assertively attempting to negotiate integrative solutions—had no effect on performance. Collaboration had a positive effect on performance. The researchers also uncovered two surprises: Compromise hurt performance, and competition helped performance. Compromises hurt because they often are watered-down, middle-of-the-road, suboptimal solutions. Competitive behavior was useful because the virtual teams were temporary and under time pressure, so that having some individuals behave dominantly and impose decisions in order to achieve efficiency was useful rather than detrimental.

When people have problems in B2B e-commerce (for example, costly delays), they tend to behave competitively and defensively rather than collaboratively.[103] Technical problems, and recurring problems, test people's patience. The conflict will escalate unless people use more cooperative, collaborative styles. Try to prevent conflicts before they arise; for example, make sure your information system is running smoothly before linking with others. Monitor and reduce or eliminate problems as soon as possible. When problems arise, express your willingness to cooperate, and then *actually be* cooperative. Even technical problems require the social skills of good management.

EPILOGUE

JOHN MACKEY AND WHOLE FOODS

In a recent two-year period, Whole Foods cleared $188 million in profits. As comparisons, Safeway lost $1 billion and Food Lion made $150 million in profits—but Food Lion had seven times as many stores and five times the revenue. While grocery sales in the United States grew 13 percent over five years through 2004, Whole Foods grew more than that in *each* of those five years—

overall, and on a per-store basis. Comparable-store sales growth was nearly twice that of Wal-Mart, the nation's largest grocer.

You can't attribute all this success to teamwork—strategy, leadership, human resources management, and countless other things contribute to any company's success and failure. But without a doubt, teams form the basis of Whole Foods, and they do work well.

KEY TERMS

SUMMARY OF LEARNING OBJECTIVES

Now that you have studied Chapter 14, you should know:

How teams can contribute to your organization's effectiveness.

Teams are building blocks for organization structure and forces for productivity, quality, cost savings, speed, change, and innovation. They have the potential to provide many benefits for both the organization and individual members.

What makes the new team environment different from the old.

Compared to traditional work groups that were closely supervised, today's teams have more authority and often are self-managed. Teams now are used in many more ways, for many more purposes, than in the past. Generally, types of teams include work teams, project and development teams, parallel teams, management teams, transnational teams, and virtual teams. Types of work teams range from traditional groups with low autonomy to self-designing teams with high autonomy.

How groups become teams.

Groups carry on a variety of important developmental activities, including forming, storming, norming, and performing. For a group to become a team, it should move beyond traditional supervisory leadership, become more participative, and ultimately enjoy team leadership. A true team has members who complement one another; who are committed to a common purpose, performance goals, and approach; and who hold themselves accountable to one another.

Why groups sometimes fail.

Teams do not always work well. Some companies underestimate the difficulties of moving to a team-based approach. Teams require training, empowerment, and a well-managed transition to make them work. Groups may fail to become effective teams unless managers and team members commit to the idea, understand what makes teams work, and implement appropriate practices.

How to build an effective team.

Create a team with a high-performance focus by establishing a common purpose; by translating the purpose into measurable team goals; by designing the team's task so it is intrinsically motivating; by designing a team-based performance measurement system; and by providing team rewards.

Work to develop a common understanding of how the team will perform its task. Make it clear that everyone has to work hard and contribute in concrete ways. Establish mutual accountability and build trust among members. Examine the team's strategies periodically and be willing to adapt.

Make sure members contribute fully by selecting them appropriately, training them, and checking that all important roles are carried out. Take a variety of steps to establish team cohesiveness and high performance norms.

And don't just manage inwardly. Manage the team's relations with outsiders, too.

How to manage your team's relationships with other teams.

Perform important roles such as gatekeeping, informing, parading, and probing. Identify the types of lateral role relationships you have with outsiders. This can help coordinate efforts throughout the work system.

How to manage conflict.

Managing lateral relationships well can prevent some conflict. But conflict arises because of the sheer number of contacts, ambiguities, goal differences, competition for scarce resources, and different perspectives and time horizons. Depending on the situation, five basic interpersonal approaches to managing conflict can be used: avoidance, accommodation, compromise, competition, and collaboration. Superordinate goals offer a focus on higher-level organizational goals that can help generate a collaborative relationship. Techniques for managing conflict between other parties include acting as a mediator and managing virtual conflict.

DISCUSSION QUESTIONS

1. Why do you think some people resist the idea of working in teams? How would you deal with their resistance?

2. Consider a job you have held, and review Table 14.1 about the traditional and new team environment. Which environment best describes your job? Assess your job on each of the dimensions described in the table.

3. Assess your job as in question 2, using Figure 14.2, "Stepping Up to Team Leadership." Which leadership "stage" characterized your job environment?

4. Identify some things from a previous job that could have been done differently to move your work group closer toward the "team leadership" depicted in Figure 14.2.

5. Experts say that teams are a means, not an end. What do you think they mean? What do you think happens in a company that creates teams just for the sake of having teams because it's a fad or just because it sounds good? How can this pitfall be avoided?

6. Choose a sports team with which you are familiar. Assess its effectiveness and discuss the factors that contribute to its level of effectiveness.

7. Assess the effectiveness, as in question 6, of a student group with which you have been affiliated. Could anything have been done to make it more effective?

8. Consider the various roles members have to perform for a team to be effective. Which roles would play to your strengths, and which to your weaknesses? How can you become a better team member?

9. Discuss personal examples of virtual conflict and how they were managed, well or poorly.

10. What do you think are your own most commonly used approaches to handling conflict? Least common? What can you do to expand your repertoire and become more effective at conflict management?

11. Generate real examples of how superordinate goals have helped resolve a conflict. Identify some current conflicts and provide some specific ideas for how superordinate goals could be used to help.

12. Have you ever been part of a group that was "self-managed"? What was good about it, and what not so good? Why do many managers resist this idea? Why do some people love the idea of being a member of such a team, while others don't?

13. How might self-managed teams operate differently in different cultures? What are the advantages, disadvantages, and implications of homogeneous versus highly diverse self-managed teams?

CONCLUDING CASE

Rocky Gagnon, General Contractor

Rocky Gagnon is a 50-year old journeyman carpenter, laborer, and craftsman. Over the past 30 years, Rocky has worked in almost every job and phase of the house building process. Rocky is getting older and his back is getting sore. He loves the construction business and feels that now is the time for him to start working more with his mind than his back. Rocky wants to become a general contractor.

Some general contractors have their own facilities, equipment and employees. Others simply work out of their homes and subcontract all of the work required to complete a particular project.

Rocky has an idea and a vision for something a little different. He wants to put together a team of tradespeople who will agree to work together toward the successful completion of about eight to fifteen homes per year. At the same time, each individual will be able to continue to operate as an independent contractor during off hours.

One of the results of working for 30 years in the local building trades is a large and varied network of friends and acquaintances. Rocky has enjoyed many a drink with the local plumbing and heating contractors, roofers, insulation people, land surveyors, and others. Rocky wants to take advantage of those relationships. The general profile of local contractors, according to Rocky, is that of a highly skilled, very independent group of people with poor communication skills. The workmanship is generally very good—when it finally gets done.

Many jobs and phases of the house building process take place in a logical sequence. For example, insulation people cannot do their work until the "rough" electrical, plumbing and heating work is completed. If any of those contractors falls behind schedule or does not complete their task, the process is disrupted. Outside factors such as weather, availability of materials, and overlapping schedules and deadlines with other jobs further complicates the challenge of meeting deadlines. Rocky wants to coordinate all of this and make house building more efficient.

The spirit of cooperation is also severely lacking, according to Rocky. It seems that many contractors could not care less about the crew that will follow them in the building process. For example, a framing crew should know about the exact plans for the fireplace, hearth, and chimney on each job, and should leave the site properly set up for that contractor. According to Rocky, the all too typical response of the framer (as well as others) is that, "that's not my job, so don't tell me about it." Independent contractors are also notorious for leaving their messes behind for someone else to clean up, such as the general contractor or next crew.

Rocky wants to change all of this by bringing together a group of tradespeople who will agree to work together as a team for the common good. If done right, Rocky sees this as a win-win situation for all parties.

Rocky knows that the opportunity for success clearly exists. New home construction is very strong in his area, and is expected to stay that way for a long time. Rocky also knows that the key to his success will be the presence of strong organizational and communication skills. Rocky feels that all of the pieces of the puzzle are there for the taking, and that all he needs is some help in setting up the right team and an organizational structure and work process that will achieve the desired results.

During the past few months, Rocky put together a list, and has met separately with individuals who he considers to be the best craftsmen in the area, and most importantly who he knows have the potential and willingness to form the team and working relationship that he envisions. The first of several meetings has been set up in order for the entire group to meet and work through the particulars. Rocky has hired a well-known and respected business professor from the local community to serve as an advisor and mediator for the group.

QUESTIONS

1. What type of team would work best in this situation? Support your answer with concepts from the text that apply to this proposed venture.

2. What kinds of problems would you expect this group to encounter? What is the best way to work through those?

3. What are the likely keys to success in motivating these individuals to cooperate and communicate as a team?

EXPERIENTIAL EXERCISES

14.1 Prisoners' Dilemma: An Intergroup Competition

INSTRUCTIONS

1. The instructor explains what will take place in this exercise and assigns people to groups. Two types of teams are formed and named Red and Blue (with no more than eight per group) and are not to communicate with the other team in any way, verbally or nonverbally, except when told to do so by the instructor. Groups are given time to study the Prisoner's Dilemma Tally Sheet.

2. (3 min.) Round 1. Each team has three minutes to make a team decision. Write your decisions when the instructor says time is up.

3. (2 min.) The choices of the teams are announced for Round 1. The scores are entered on the Tally Sheet.

4. (4–5 min.) Round 2 is conducted in the same manner as Round 1.

5. (6 min.) Round 3 is announced as a special round, for which the payoff points are doubled. Each team is instructed to send one representative to chairs in the center of the room. After representatives have conferred for three minutes, they return to their teams. Teams then have three minutes, as before, in which to make their decisions. When recording their scores, they should be reminded that points indicated by the payoff schedule are doubled for this round only.

6. (8–10 min.) Rounds 4, 5, and 6 are conducted in the same manner as the first three rounds.

7. (6 min.) Round 7 is announced as a special round, in which the payoff points are "squared" (multiplied by themselves: e.g., a score of 4 would be $4^2 = 16$). A minus sign would be retained: e.g., $-(3)^2 = -9$. Team representatives meet for three minutes; then the teams meet for three minutes. At the instructor's signal, the teams write their choices; then the two choices are announced.

8. (6 min.) Round 8 is handled exactly as Round 7 was. Payoff points are squared.

9. (10–20 min.) The point total for each team is announced, and the sum of the two team totals is calculated and compared to the maximum positive or negative outcomes ($+108$ or -108 points).

Prisoners' Dilemma Tally Sheet

Instructions: For 10 successive rounds, the Red team will choose either an A or a B and the Blue team will choose either an X or a Y. The score each team receives in a round is determined by the pattern made by the choices of both teams, according to the schedule below.

Payoff Schedule:

AX—Both teams win 3 points.

AY—Red team loses 6 points; Blue team wins 6 points.

BX—Red team wins 6 points; Blue team loses 6 points.

BY—Both teams lose 3 points.

Scorecard:

Round	Minutes	Choice		Cumulative Points	
		Red Team	**Blue Team**	**Red Team**	**Blue Team**
1	3				
2	3				
3*	3 (reps.) 3 (teams)				
4	3				
5	3				
6*	3 (reps.) 3 (teams)				
7**	3 (reps.) 3 (teams)				
8**	3 (reps.) 3 (teams)				

*Payoff points are doubled for this round. **Payoff points are squared for this round. (Retain the minus sign.)

SOURCE: Dorothy Hai, "Prisoner's Dilemma," in *Organizational Behavior: Experiences and Cases.* Copyright © 1986. Reprinted with permission of South-Western College Publishing, a division of Thomson Learning.

14.2 The Traveler's Check Scam Group Exercise

INSTRUCTIONS

1. (3 min.) Group selects an observer. The observer remains silent during the group problem-solving process, recording the activities of the group on the Observer's Report Form.

2. (15 min.) Group members read the following problem and proceed to solve it.

3. (2 min.) When the group has a solution to the problem upon which all members agree, it will be written on a note and handed to the instructor.

4. (5 min.) The observer briefs the group on the problem-solving processes observed during the exercise.

5. (25 min.) The small group discusses the following topics:
   a. Did the group decide on a problem solution process before it attempted to solve the problem? If so, what was it?
   b. Was the solution of the problem hindered in any way by the lack of an appropriate agreed-upon group problem-solving process? Explain.
   c. Who were the leaders of the group during the exercise? What did they do? Critique their leadership activities.
   d. What communications patterns were used by the group during the exercise? Who participated the most? Who participated the least? Describe individual behaviors.
   e. Did the group solve the problem? How many members of the group discovered the correct answer on their own?
   f. Was using the group to solve this problem better than assigning the problem to one person? Explain the rationale for your answer.

THE CASE OF MICKEY THE DIP

Mickey the Dip, an expert pickpocket and forger, liked to work the Los Angeles International Airport on busy days. His technique was to pick the pockets of prosperous-looking victims just before they boarded planes to the East Coast. This gave Mickey five hours to use stolen credit cards before the owners could report their losses.

One morning Mickey snatched a fat wallet from a traveler and left the airport to examine his loot. To his surprise he found no credit cards but instead $500 in traveler's checks. After 20 minutes of practice, Mickey could sign a perfect imitation of the victim's signature. He then proceeded to a large department store where all suits were being sold for 75 percent of the regular price. Mickey purchased a suit for $225 and paid for it with $300 in stolen traveler's checks. After the clerk who served him went to lunch, he bought another suit for $150 and paid for it with the remaining $200 of stolen traveler's checks. Later, Mickey switched the labels on the two suits and, using the receipt from the $225 suit, returned the $150 suit at a centralized return desk for a refund. The refund clerk took the suit and gave Mickey eleven $20 bills, which he stuffed into his pocket and disappeared.

When the department store deposited the traveler's checks, they were returned as forgeries. Assuming the store normally sold suits at twice their wholesale price and used 10 percent of sales as an overhead cost figure, what was the cash value of the loss suffered by the store as a result of Mickey's caper? Do not consider taxes in your computations.

THE TRAVELER'S CHECK SCAM EXERCISE OBSERVER'S REPORT

1. What happened during the first few minutes the group met after members finished reading the problem? (List behaviors of specific group members.)

2. Identify the group role played by each group member during the exercise. Give examples of the behavior of each.

3. Were there any conflicts within or among group members during the exercise? Explain the nature of the conflicts and the behavior of the individual(s) involved.

4. How were decisions made in the group? Give specific examples.

5. How could the group improve its problem-solving skills?

SOURCE: Peter P. Dawson, *Fundamentals of Organizational Behavior*. Copyright © 1985 Pearson Education, Inc. Reprinted by permission of Pearson Education, Inc., Upper Saddle River, NJ.

Chapter **15**

CHAPTER 15
Communicating

The single biggest problem with communication is the illusion that it has taken place.

— **G. B. Shaw**

CHAPTER OUTLINE

LEARNING OBJECTIVES

After studying Chapter 15, you will know:

1. The important advantages of two-way communication.

2. Communication problems to avoid.

3. When and how to use the various communication channels.

4. Ways to become a better "sender" and "receiver" of information.

5. How to improve downward, upward, and horizontal communication.

6. How to work with the company grapevine.

7. The advantages and characteristics of the boundaryless organization.

DAVID NEELEMAN OF JETBLUE

When JetBlue's CEO David Neeleman walks through the terminal, ticket agents call out, "Hey, David!" Neeleman talks constantly with employees, many of whom (there are thousands of them) he knows by name. He asks about their work and their families.

He used to receive alerts if any plane was one minute late, until his president and COO Dave Barger said that was too much information and made him stop. But he still checks out JetBlue's Web site to make sure the right things are being communicated to potential customers. He makes phone calls to find out what's being done for passengers whose flights are delayed. He calls a flight attendant who was ill on a flight to make sure she's feeling better.

When he's on a plane, he walks down the aisle talking to the people on board. He collects business cards. He asks people what they like and dislike, and writes down suggestions.

Neeleman and Dave Barger spend as much time as possible on the front lines, rather than in executive suites. Both men appear at nearly every orientation for new hires, on the first day. They have monthly informal Q&A meetings with employees. They also make sure they visit cities every quarter, and work alongside crew members. David Neeleman believes the best leaders practice servant leadership—helping others do their jobs better.

Sources for Prologue, Connections, Epilogue: C. Salter, "And Now the Hard Part," *Fast Company*, May 2004, pp. 66–75; W. Zellner, "Is JetBlue's Flight Plan Flawed?" *BusinessWeek*, February 16, 2004, pp. 72–75.

Effective communication is a fundamental aspect of job performance and managerial effectiveness.[1] In this chapter, we will present important communication concepts and some practical guidelines for improving your effectiveness. We will discuss both interpersonal and organizational communication.

Interpersonal Communication

communication

The transmission of information and meaning from one party to another through the use of shared symbols.

Communication is the transmission of information and meaning from one party to another through the use of shared symbols. Figure 15.1 shows a general model of how one person communicates with another.

The *sender* initiates the process by conveying information to the *receiver*—the person for whom the message is intended. The sender has a *meaning* he or she wishes to communicate and *encodes* the meaning into symbols (e.g., the words chosen for the message). Then the sender *transmits*, or sends, the message through some *channel*, such as a verbal or written medium.

The receiver *decodes* the message (e.g., reads it) and attempts to *interpret* the sender's meaning. The receiver may provide *feedback* to the sender by encoding a message in response to the sender's message.

The communication process often is hampered by *noise*, or interference in the system, that blocks perfect understanding. Noise could be anything that interferes with accurate communication: ringing telephones, thoughts about other things, or simple fatigue or stress.

one-way communication

A process in which information flows in only one direction—from the sender to the receiver, with no feedback loop.

two-way communication

A process in which information flows in two directions—the receiver provides feedback, and the sender is receptive to the feedback.

The model in Figure 15.1 is more than a theoretical treatment of the communication process: It points out the key ways in which communications can break down. Mistakes can be made at each stage of the model. A manager who is alert to potential problems can perform each step carefully to ensure more effective communication. The model also helps explain the topics discussed next: the differences between one-way and two-way communication, communication pitfalls, misperception, and the various communication channels.

One-Way versus Two-Way Communication

In **one-way communication,** information flows in only one direction—from the sender to the receiver, with no feedback loop. A manager sends a memo to a subordinate without asking for a response. A boss gives an order over the phone. A father scolds his son and then storms out of the room.

When receivers respond to senders—Person B becomes the sender and Person A the receiver— **two-way communication** has occurred. One-way communication in situations like those just described can become two-way if the manager follows up her memo with a phone call and asks the receiver if he has any questions, the boss on the telephone listens to alternative suggestions for carrying out her order, and the father calms down and listens to his son's side of the story.

Don't expect to deliver results without communicating effectively in all directions of the compass.

True two-way communication means not only that the receiver provides feedback but also that the sender is receptive to the feedback. In these constructive exchanges, information is shared between both parties rather than merely delivered from one person to the other.

FIGURE 15.1
A Model of One-Way Communication

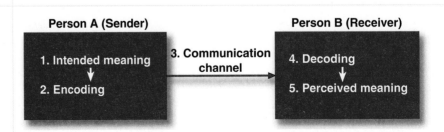

One-way communication is much more common than it should be because it is faster and easier for the sender. The busy executive finds it easier to dash off a memo than to discuss the issue with the subordinate. Also, he doesn't have to deal with questions or be challenged by someone who disagrees.

Two-way communication is more difficult and time-consuming than one-way communication. However, it is more accurate; fewer mistakes occur, and fewer problems arise. Receivers have a chance to ask questions, share concerns, and make suggestions or modifications, and consequently understand more precisely what is being communicated and what they should do with the information.[2]

Communication Pitfalls

The sender's intended message does not always "get across" to the receiver. You are operating under an illusion if you think there is a perfect correlation between what you say and what people hear.[3]

Errors can occur in all stages of the communication process. In the encoding stage, words can be misused, decimal points entered in the wrong places, facts left out, or ambiguous phrases inserted. In the transmission stage, a memo gets lost on a cluttered desk, the words on the screen are too small to read from the back of the room, or words are spoken with ambiguous inflections.

Decoding problems arise when the receiver doesn't listen carefully or reads too quickly and overlooks a key point. And, of course, receivers can misinterpret the message, as a reader draws the wrong conclusion from an unclear memo, a listener takes a general statement by the boss too personally, or a sideways glance is taken the wrong way.

More generally, people's perceptual and filtering processes create misinterpretations. **Perception** is the process of receiving and interpreting information. As you know, such processes are not perfectly objective. They are subjective, as people's self-interested motives and attitudes toward the sender and toward the message create biased interpretations. People often assume that others share their views, and naturally pay more attention to their own views than to those of others.[5] But perceptual differences get in the way of shared consensus. It helps to see others' viewpoints as legitimate, and incorporate others' perspectives into your interpretation of issues.[6] Generally, adopting another person's viewpoint is fundamental to working collaboratively. And, your ability to take others' perspectives—say, to really understand the viewpoints of customers or suppliers—can result in higher assessments of your performance.[7]

Filtering is the process of withholding, ignoring, or distorting information. Senders do this, for example, when they tell the boss what they think the boss wants to hear, or give unwarranted compliments rather than honest criticism. Receivers also filter information; they may fail to recognize an important message, or attend to some aspects of the message but not others.

Filtering and subjective perception pervade one interesting aspect of the communications dynamic: how men and women differ in their communicating styles. A manager at

One example of one-way communication is the employee receiving a "pink slip" from the manager without notice. Why do you think this might not be the best form of communication?

A chef interviewing for a job with a high-end steakhouse answered all the questions perfectly, until the restaurant owner asked, "What do you know about me?" Not knowing the owner, he replied "Next to nothing." End of interview. The chef was out the door and halfway down the street when he realized the question had been, "What do you know about meat?"[4]

perception

The process of receiving and interpreting information.

filtering

The process of withholding, ignoring, or distorting information.

a magazine who tended to phrase the assignments she gave her reporters as questions—"How would you like to do the X project with Y?" and "I was thinking of putting you on the X project; is that okay?"—was criticized by her male boss, who told her she did not assume the proper demeanor with her staff.[8] Another, the owner of a retail operation, told one of her store managers to do something by saying, "The bookkeeper needs help with the billing. How would you feel about helping her out?" He said fine, but didn't do it. Whereas the boss thought he meant he would do it, he said he meant how he would feel about helping. He decided he had better things to do.[9]

Advantages of Collaboration

Being able to see the other person's viewpoint is one of the ultimate keys to effective collaboration.

Q & A with the President

President George W. Bush has had fewer press conferences than his predecessors. With opportunities so rare, reporters try to take full advantage when they do have a chance to communicate directly with the president.

Reporters' goals are to ask good questions that will be answered with specificity, will be informative or controversial, and will "make news" (get them on TV or the front page). The reporters want President Bush to reflect on choices that he has made, explore alternatives that he might have chosen, or shed light on how he reaches decisions.

President Bush's goal is to be disciplined: keep things brief and stay "on message," often repeating things that have been previously stated.

The reporters have developed opinions about the forms of questions that will get the best and worst responses. Most know that hostile wording has zero chance of eliciting news, because the president will shut down and move on. Several shared their thoughts on how to address the president.

CNN's John King says that it's a rookie mistake to ask convoluted questions, to which the president can answer the part he chooses. King makes sure his questions have only one element, two at most.

John Dickerson of *Time* magazine's objective is to get the president to think out loud. He considers "how Bush will react, what might shut him down, what might bore him, what might smell like a trap to him." Dickerson says, "There are a lot of hurdles with a president who doesn't particularly like the press and thinks we're there only to 'peacock,' as he calls it."

John Roberts of CBS News notes that President Bush uses stern looks to shoot down any questions he doesn't want to take. "It's all part of the message-control regime at the White House, but it's not something the White House press corps should roll over and play dead for."

Terry Moran of ABC News says, "Don't let yourself be intimidated. Don't let yourself be charmed. Bush likes to try to do both. Just remember that he is a public servant, and part of his job is to take your questions . . . Focused, forceful, and direct questions work best with Bush—the shorter the better . . . He responds sharply to sharp challenges. He gives better answers to fact-based queries than to open-ended invitations to muse or reflect on events or policies."

President Bush poked fun at NBC's David Gregory at a joint press conference with President Jacques Chirac of France, when Gregory posed a question in French. Ann Compton of ABC News: "Questions to Bush get the best answers when they are tough but respectful. And not in French."

SOURCE: M. Allen, "Next Question," *The Washington Post*, December 1, 2004, pp. C1–C8.

Any interpersonal situation holds potential for perceptual errors, filtering, and other communication breakdowns.

Because of such filtering and perceptual differences, you cannot assume the other person means what you think he means, or understands the meanings you intend. Managers need to excel at reading interactions and adjusting their communication styles and perceptions to the people with whom they interact.[10] The very human tendencies to filter and perceive subjectively underlie much of the ineffective communication, and the need for more effective communication practices, that you will read about in the rest of this chapter.

Mixed Signals and Misperception

A common thread underlying the discussion so far is that people's perceptions can undermine attempts to communicate. People do not pay attention to everything going on around them. They inadvertently send mixed signals that can undermine the intended messages. Different people attend to different things, and people interpret the same thing in different ways. All of this creates problems in communication.

If the communication is between people from different cultures, these problems are magnified.[11] Communication "breakdowns" often occur when business transactions take place between people from different countries. Chapter 6 introduced you to the importance of these cultural issues. Table 15.1 offers suggestions for communicating effectively with someone who speaks a different language.

The following example further highlights the operation of mixed signals and misperceptions. A bank CEO knew that to be competitive he had to downsize his organization, and the employees who remained would have to commit to customer service, become more empowered, and really *earn* customer loyalty.[12] Knowing that his employees would have doubts and concerns about the coming reorganization, he decided to make a promise to them that he would do his best to guarantee employment to the survivors.

What signals did the CEO communicate to his people by his promises? One positive signal was that he cared about his people. But he also signaled that *he* would take care of *them*, thus undermining his goal of giving them more responsibility and empowering them. The employees wanted management to take responsibility for the market challenge that *they* needed to face—to handle things for them when *they* needed to learn the new ways of doing business. Inadvertently, the CEO spoke to their backward-looking need for security when he had meant to make them see that the bank's future depended on *their* efforts.

Verbal Behavior
• *Clear, slow speech*. Enunciate each word. Do not use colloquial expressions.
• *Repetition*. Repeat each important idea using different words to explain the same concept.
• *Simple sentences*. Avoid compound, long sentences.
• *Active verbs*. Avoid passive verbs.

Nonverbal Behavior
• *Visual restatements*. Use as many visual restatements as possible, such as pictures, graphs, tables, and slides.
• *Gestures*. Use more facial and appropriate hand gestures to emphasize the meaning of words.
• *Demonstrations*. Act out as many themes as possible.
• *Pauses*. Pause more frequently.
• *Summaries*. Hand out written summaries of your verbal presentation.

Accurate Interpretation
• *Silence*. When there is a silence, wait. Do not jump in to fill the silence. The other person is probably just thinking more slowly in the nonnative language or translating.
• *Intelligence*. Do not equate poor grammar and mispronunciation with lack of intelligence; it is usually a sign of nonnative language use.
• *Differences*. If unsure, assume difference, not similarity.

Comprehension
• *Understanding*. Do not just assume that they understand; assume that they do not understand.
• *Checking comprehension*. Have colleagues repeat their understanding of the material back to you. Do not simply ask if they understand or not. Let them explain what they understand to you.

Design
• *Breaks*. Take more frequent breaks. Second language comprehension is exhausting.
• *Small modules*. Divide the material to be presented into smaller modules.
• *Longer time frame*. Allocate more time for each module than you usually need for presenting the same material to native speakers of your language.

Motivation
• *Encouragement*. Verbally and nonverbally encourage and reinforce speaking by nonnative language participants.
• *Drawing out*. Explicitly draw out marginal and passive participants.
• *Reinforcement*. Do not embarrass novice speakers.

TABLE 15.1
What Do I Do If They Do Not Speak My Language?

SOURCE: N. Adler, *International Dimensions of Organizational Behavior.* Copyright © 1986. Reprinted with permission of South-Western College Publishing, a division of Thomson Learning.

Consider how many problems could be avoided—and how much more effective communication could be—if people took the time to (1) ensure that the receivers attend to the message they are sending; (2) consider the other party's frame of reference and attempt to convey the message with that viewpoint in mind; (3) take concrete steps to minimize perceptual errors and improper signals in both sending and receiving; and (4) send *consistent* messages. You should make an effort to predict people's interpretations of your messages and think in terms of how they could *misinterpret* your messages. It helps to say not only what you mean but also what you *don't* mean. Every time you say, "I am not saying X, I am saying Y," you eliminate a possible misinterpretation.[13]

Oral and Written Channels

Communication can be sent through a variety of channels (step 3 in the Figure 15.1 model), including oral, written, and electronic. Each channel has advantages and disadvantages.

Oral communication includes face-to-face discussion, telephone conversations, and formal presentations and speeches. Advantages are that questions can be asked and answered; feedback is immediate and direct; the receiver(s) can sense the sender's sincerity (or lack thereof); and oral communication is more persuasive and sometimes less expensive than written. However, oral communication also has disadvantages: It can lead to spontaneous, ill-considered statements (and regret), and there is no permanent record of it (unless an effort is made to record it).

Written communication includes memos, letters, reports, computer files, and other written documents. Advantages to using written messages are that the message can be revised several times, it is a permanent record that can be saved, the message stays the same even if relayed through many people, and the receiver has more time to analyze the message. Disadvantages are that the sender has no control over where, when, or if the message is read; the sender does not receive immediate feedback; the receiver may not understand parts of the message; and the message must be longer to contain enough information to answer anticipated questions.[14]

You should weigh these considerations when deciding whether to communicate orally or in writing. Also, sometimes use both channels, such as following up a meeting with a confirming memo or writing a letter to prepare someone for your phone call.

Electronic Media

A vital category of communication channels is electronic media. Managers use computers not only to gather and distribute quantitative data but to "talk" with others electronically. In electronic decision rooms, software supports simultaneous access to shared files, and allows people to share views and do work collectively.[15] Other means of electronic communication include *teleconferencing*, in which groups of people in different locations interact over telephone lines, and perhaps also see one another on television monitors as they participate in group discussions (*videoconferencing*). And you probably are intimately familiar with e-mail, instant messaging, and blogging.

Most companies use instant messaging, although most people do it without their boss's consent, and many put it to personal use. Some companies hope and pretend that employees don't use it (they're wrong, of course), and some ban it outright.[16] Nonetheless, IMing will soon surpass e-mailing.[17]

Blogging—posting text to a Web site—also has arrived in the business world. Jonathan Schwartz, president and CEO of Sun Microsystems, may have been the first top executive to embrace blogging and encourage it among his employees. He thinks managers need both e-mail and blogs to be effective.

Advantages *Advantages* of electronic communication are numerous and dramatic. Within firms, the advantages include the sharing of more information, and speed and efficiency in delivering routine messages to large numbers of people across vast geographic areas. It can reduce time spent traveling, talking, and photocopying. It's also cheap. Alcoa reduced its cost base by over $1 billion by installing a system that enables it to manage in real time—that is, making decisions immediately, on the basis of accurate information communicated "live," as it happens.[18]

Some companies, including Boeing, use brainstorming software that allows anonymous contributions, presuming this will add more honesty to internal discussions. Some research indicates more data sharing and critical argumentation, and higher-

Imagine how much time you would lose if you couldn't communicate electronically; imagine the savings you could create if your company and its people sought and used the most cost-effective ways to communicate.

E-mail is one of the most convenient forms of communication, but what are some of the pitfalls? How often have you sent an e-mail, whether personal or professional, and found someone had misinterpreted the message?

quality decisions, with a group decision support system than is found in face-to-face meetings.[19] But anonymity also offers great potential for lies, gossip, insults, threats, harassment, and the release of confidential information.[20]

Disadvantages   *Disadvantages* of electronic communication include the difficulty of solving complex problems that require more extended, face-to-face interaction, and the inability to pick up subtle, nonverbal, or inflectional clues about what the communicator is thinking or conveying. In online bargaining—even before it begins—negotiators distrust one another more than in face-to-face negotiations. After the negotiation (compared to face-to-face negotiators), people usually are less satisfied with their outcomes, even when the outcomes are economically equivalent.[21]

Although organizations rely heavily on computer-aided communication for group decision making, face-to-face groups generally take less time, make higher-quality decisions, and are more satisfying for members.[22] E-mail is most appropriate for routine messages that do not require the exchange of large quantities of complex information. It is less suitable for confidential information, resolving conflicts, or negotiating.[23]

IMs, as well, can help people work together productively, but they also leak sensitive information. Companies are worried about leaks and negative portrayals, and they may require employees to agree to specific guidelines before starting blogs. The bottom line for most managers: Reading blogs is more important than writing them.[24]

One inevitable consequence of electronic communication is "flaming": hurling insults, sending "nastygrams," venting frustration, snitching on co-workers to the boss, and otherwise breaching protocol.[25] E-mail liberates people to send things they would not say to a person's face. The lack of nonverbal cues can result in "kidding" remarks being taken seriously, causing resentment and regret. It is not unheard of for confidential messages, including details about people's personal lives and insulting, embarrassing remarks, to become public knowledge through electronic leaks.

Other downsides to electronic communication are important to know.[26] Different people and sometimes different working units latch onto different channels as their medium of choice. For example, an engineering division might use e-mail most, but a design group might rely primarily on voice mail or printed faxes, and neglect e-mail.[27] Another disadvantage is that e-mail messages sometimes are monitored or seen inadvertently by those for whom they are not intended. Deleting messages does not destroy them; they are saved elsewhere. Recipients can forward them to others, unbeknownst to the original sender. And they can be used in court cases to indict individuals or companies. E-mail messages are private property—but the private property of the system's owner, not of the sender.[28]

Managing the Electronic Load   Electronic communication media seem essential these days, and people wonder how they ever worked without them. But the sheer volume of communication can be overwhelming.[29]

Fortunately, a few rules of thumb can help you in your electronic communications.[30] For the problem of information overload, the challenge is to separate the truly important from the routine. Effective managers find time to think about bigger business issues, and don't get too bogged down in responding to every message that seems urgent but may be trivial. Essential here is to think strategically about your goals, identify the things that are most important, and prioritize your time around those goals. This is easier said than done, of course, but it is essential, and it helps. And then, by the way, you can apply technical solutions: software that, based on the most important information needs you identify for yourself, can help protect you from the electronic information quagmire.[31]

Be careful with your IMs: Make sure you don't accidentally send them to the wrong person and that they don't pop up on the screen during a PowerPoint presentation.[32] A few more specific suggestions:[33] With e-mail, don't hit "reply to all" when you should hit just "reply." Don't think of e-mail as secure and private; it's not. Don't call a customer an idiot in internal e-mail; it can be sent to the customer, accidentally or otherwise. Get organized by creating lots of folders, sorted by subject, priority, or sender, and flag messages that require follow-up. If you receive a copy, you don't need to respond, it's just an FYI. And don't forget to have real, face-to-face conversations sometimes.

When Monster Cable Products developed clogged company inboxes, the culprit was too many employee mass e-mails ("Can someone watch my dog this weekend?").[34]

An e-mail golden rule (like the sunshine rule in the ethics chapter): Don't hit "send" unless you'd be comfortable having the contents on the front page of a newspaper, being read by your mother or a competitor.[35] And it's not a bad idea to have a colleague read nonroutine e-mails before sending.

Some companies are recognizing the downsides of electronic media overuse. GlaxoSmith-Kline, the Philadelphia-based pharmaceutical firm, charges business units fees based on the number and length of e-mail messages. Computer Associates shuts down the e-mail system every day for two hours. Many firms, and individuals and teams, set aside time every day, free from e-mails and phones, to work on their primary tasks. They often report this to be the most productive part of the day.[36]

The Virtual Office   Many entrepreneurs conduct business via open "offices" on the Internet, working off their computers from wherever they happen to be. Simi-

virtual office

A mobile office in which people can work anywhere, as long as they have the tools to communicate with customers and colleagues.

larly, major companies like IBM, GE, and Chiat/Day are slashing office space and giving people laptops or powerful notebook computers, telecommunications software, voice mail, and other communications technologies so they can work virtually anywhere, anytime.[37] Based on the philosophy that management's focus should be on what people do, not where they are, the **virtual office** is a mobile office in which people can work anywhere— their home, car, airport, customers' offices—as long as they have the tools to communicate with customers and colleagues.[38] One observer calls the virtual office "the most radical redefinition of the workplace since the Industrial Revolution."[39]

In the short run, at least, the benefits appear substantial. Compaq reduced sales costs and administrative expenses from 22 percent of revenue to 12 percent. Perkin-Elmer, which makes scientific equipment, was able to close 35 branch offices. Mobile offices can allow salespeople to spend 15 to 20 percent more time with customers.[40] And most people like the flexibility it gives them.

But what will be the longer-term impact on productivity and morale? We may be in danger of losing too many "human moments," those authentic encounters that happen only when two people are physically together.[41] Some people hate being forced to work at home. Some valuable people have quit. Some send faxes, e-mail, and voice mail in the middle of the night—and others receive them. Some work around the clock and still feel they are not doing enough. The long hours of being constantly close to the technical tools of work can cause burnout. And some companies are learning that direct supervision at the office is necessary to maintain the quality of work, especially when employees are

Spacious corner office, redefined.

SIEMENS
Global network of innovation

The virtual office nowadays can be as close as the deck on the back of your lake house. This Siemens ad promotes their ability to help with information exchange solutions from cellular phones to optical networks. What problems do you think might occur with virtual offices, besides the lack of in-office interaction?

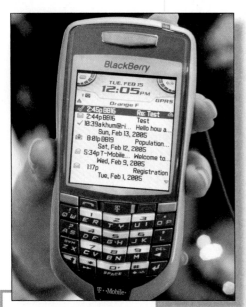

Technology has greatly affected communication both in and out of the office. Blackberry created a handheld device that offers a tri-band phone, e-mail, Internet access, and text messaging, which enables us to communicate 24 hours a day. What kind of problems do you think might occur with such capabilities?

media richness

The degree to which a communication channel conveys information.

inexperienced and need guidance. One company president says, "As soon as I separate my supervisors from the people they're supposed to be developing, I make it difficult for effective coaching to occur."[42]

The "virtual office" proved its value in 2001 through its ability to keep businesses going despite the terrorist attacks. But the virtual office requires changes in human beings and presents technical challenges.[43] The virtual office is much hyped and useful, but it will not replace real offices and face-to-face work.

As overwhelming as electronic communications can be, you can take steps to simplify them. For example, a global customer-account-management team established two ground rules: (1) whenever a member communicated with a customer, the member was to send a briefing to all team members; and (2) they designated a primary contact on the team for each customer, with no one else on the team authorized to discuss or decide strategies or policies with the customer. If contacted by a customer, team members would direct the customer to the appropriate contact person. These steps simplified communication channels and greatly reduced contradictory and confusing messages.[44]

Media Richness

Some communication channels convey more information than others. The amount of information a medium conveys is called **media richness**.[45] The more information or cues a medium sends to the receiver, the "richer" the medium is.[46] The richest media are more personal than technological, provide quick feedback, allow lots of descriptive language, and send different types of cues. Thus, face-to-face communication is the richest medium because it offers a variety of cues in addition to words: tone of voice, facial expression, body language, and other nonverbal signals. It also allows more descriptive language than, say, a memo does. In addition, it affords more opportunity for the receiver to give feedback to and ask questions of the sender, turning one-way into two-way communication.

The telephone is less rich than face-to-face communication, electronic mail is less rich yet, and memos are the least rich medium. In general, you should send difficult and unusual messages through richer media, transmit simple and routine messages through less rich media like memos, and use multiple media for important messages that you want to ensure people attend to and understand.[47] You should also consider factors such as which medium your receiver prefers, the preferred communication style in your organization, and cost.[48] Table 15.2 gives some sample situations for choosing channels based on the message and the audience.

Situation 1: A midsize construction firm wants to announce a new employee benefit program.

Situation 2: A manager wishes to confirm a meeting time with 10 employees.

Situation 3: Increase enthusiasm in a midsize insurance company for a program that asks employees from different departments to work on the same project team.

Situation 4: A group of engineers who are geographically dispersed want to exchange design ideas with one another.

Situation 5: Describe a straightforward but somewhat detailed and updated version of a voice mail system to 1,000 employees who are geographically dispersed.

TABLE 15.2
What Communication Channel Would You Use? (Compare your answers with those in Table 15.3)

SOURCE: From *Communicating for Managerial Effectiveness* by P.G. Clampitt. Copyright © 1991 by Sage Publications, Inc. Reprinted by permission of Sage Publications, Inc.

TABLE 15.3
Suggested Media Choices
for Scenarios in Table 15.2

Situation	Poor Choice	Better Choice
1	Memo	Small group meetings

Rationale: The memo does not offer the feedback potential necessary to explain what may be seen as obscure information. Moreover, with these employees there is a possibility of literacy problems. A group meeting will allow for an oral explanation after which participants can more easily ask questions about any of the complex materials.

2	Phone	Voice mail or e-mail

Rationale: For a simple message like this, there is no need to use a rich medium when a lean one will do the job.

3	E-mail, voice mail	Face-to-face, telephone

Rationale: In situations requiring persuasion the sender must be able to quickly adapt the message to the receiver in order to counter objections. This is not a feature of either e-mail or voice mail. Face-to-face communication offers the sender the greatest flexibility. The phone is the next best alternative.

4	Teleconference	Fax, computer conference

Rationale: A teleconference is apt to overly accentuate the status and personality differences among the engineers. Fax or computer conferencing would allow the quality of the ideas to be the central focus of interaction. Moreover, quick feedback is still possible with these media.

5	Newsletter	Video

Rationale: If employees are already persuaded of the updated system's merit, you can probably use the newsletter. But a videotape graphically conveys information that requires demonstration, and will educate people about procedures.

Improving Communication Skills

In recent years, employers have been dismayed by college graduates' poor communication skills. A demonstrated ability to communicate effectively makes a job candidate more attractive and distinguishes him or her from others. You can do many things to improve your communication skills, both as a sender and as a receiver.

Improving Sender Skills

To start, be aware that honest, direct, straight talk is important but all too rare. CEOs are often coached on how to slant their messages for different audiences—the investment community, employees, or the board. That's not likely to be straight talk. The focus of the messages can differ, but they can't be inconsistent. People should be able to identify your perspective, your reasoning, and your intentions.[49]

Beyond this basic point, senders can improve their skills in making persuasive presentations, writing, language use, and sending nonverbal messages. Table 15.4 offers some useful tips on formal presentations; the following discussion focuses more on other keys to persuasion.

Presentation and Persuasion Skills
You will be called upon to "state your case" on a variety of issues. You will have information and perhaps an opinion or proposal to present to others. Typically, your goal will be to "sell" your idea. In other words, your chal-

One small-company president began charging his employees $1 every time they utter a grammatical error or use unprofessional language. Don't (over)use: y'know; like; "He goes" instead of "He said"; wimpy words like "I just wanted to say that . . .;" and "uptalk," the singsong pattern where sentences end with a rising inflection.

A publisher routinely rejects sales and editorial candidates for grammatically incorrect speech. "It's as if they pulled out a baseball cap and put it on backward. It simply reflects a low level of professionalism," he says.[50]

TABLE 15.4
Ten Ways to Add Power to Your Presentations

"All the great speakers were bad speakers at first." Ralph Waldo Emerson

1. *Spend adequate time on the* **content** *of your presentation.* It's easy to get so distracted with PowerPoint slides or concern about delivery skills that the actual content of a presentation is neglected. Know your content inside and out; you'll be able to discuss it conversationally and won't be tempted to memorize. If you believe in what you're saying and *own* the material, you will convey enthusiasm and will be more relaxed.

2. *Clearly understand the* **objective** *of your presentation.* Answer this question with one sentence: "What do I want the audience to believe following this presentation?" Writing down your objective will help you focus on your *bottom line.* Everything else in a presentation—the structure, the words, the visuals—should support your objective.

3. **Tell** *the audience the* **purpose** *of the presentation.* As the saying goes, "Tell them what you're going to tell them, then tell them, then tell them what you've told them." Use a clear preview statement early on to help the audience know where you're taking them.

4. *Provide* **meaning,** *not just data.* Today, information is widely available; you won't impress people by overloading them with data. People have limited attention spans and want presenters to help *clarify the meaning* of data.

5. **Practice, practice, practice.** Appearing polished and relaxed during a presentation requires rehearsal time. Practice making your points in a variety of ways. Above all, don't memorize a presentation's content.

6. *Remember that a presentation is more like a* **conversation** *than a speech.* Keep your tone conversational, yet professional. Audience members will be much more engaged if they feel you are talking *with* them rather than *at* them. Rely on PowerPoint slides or a broad outline to jog your memory.

7. *Remember the incredible power of* **eye contact.** Look at individual people in the audience. Try to have a series of one-on-one conversations with people in the room. This will calm you and help you connect with your audience.

8. **Allow imperfection**. If you forget what you were going to say, simply pause, look at your notes, and go on. Don't "break character" and effusively apologize or giggle or look mortified. Remember that an audience doesn't know your material nearly as well as you do and won't notice many mistakes.

9. *Be prepared to* **answer tough questions.** Try to anticipate the toughest questions you might receive. Plan your answers in advance. If you don't have an answer, acknowledge the fact and offer to get the information later.

10. *Provide a* **crisp wrap-up** *to a question-and-answer session.* Whenever possible, follow the Q&A period with a brief summary statement. Set up the Q&A session by saying, "We'll take questions for 10 minutes and then have a few closing remarks." This prevents your presentation from just winding down to a weak ending. Also, if you receive hostile or hard-to-answer questions, you'll have a chance to have the final word.

SOURCE: Lynn Hamilton, class handout (with permission)

lenge will be to persuade others to go along with your personal recommendation. As a leader, some of your toughest challenges will arise when people do not want to do what has to be done. Leaders have to be persuasive to get people "on board."[51]

Your attitude is very important here. Persuasion is not what a lot of people think it is: merely selling an idea or convincing others to see things your way. Don't assume that it takes a "my-way-or-the-highway" approach, with a one-shot effort to make an up-front hard sell, and resisting compromise.[52] It usually is more constructive to consider persuasion a process of learning from each other and negotiating a shared solution. It requires credibility, which comes from expertise and relationships in which people know you are trustworthy. Effective persuasion is an attempt to find an emotional connection with the other person and a common ground on which mutual interests meet.[53]

The most powerful and persuasive messages are simple and informative, are told with stories and anecdotes, and convey excitement.[54] GE's Jack Welch had tremendous success with his simple message to all employees of speed, simplicity, and self-confidence. Lawrence Bossidy of AlliedSignal took a similar approach by talking frequently about the three P's: performance (meeting the numbers), portfolio (getting the right product mix), and people (attracting and motivating employees).[55] And the credible communicator backs up the message with actions consistent with the words.

Writing Skills   Effective writing is more than correct spelling, punctuation, and grammar (although these help!). Good writing above all requires clear, logical thinking.[56] The act of writing can be a powerful aid to thinking, because you have to think about what you really want to say and what the logic is behind your message.[57]

You want people to find your memos and reports readable and interesting. Strive for clarity, organization, readability, and brevity.[58] Brevity is much appreciated by readers who are overloaded with documents, including wordy memos. Use a dictionary and a thesaurus, and avoid fancy words. Charles Krauthammer, the newspaper columnist, praises brevity in a column titled "Make it Snappy."[59] He notes that Ian Wilmut, the scientist who cloned the sheep Dolly, announced his findings to the scientific community in a three-page journal article. Two of the greatest speeches in American history fit on part of one wall at the Lincoln Memorial. The Truman doctrine, which set the course of American foreign policy for half a century, took only 18 minutes to deliver. Watson and Crick's article announcing the discovery of the structure of DNA was just over one page.

> "When [cultivated people] look, they see clearly. When they listen, they think of how to hear keenly … In their demeanor, they think of how to be respectful. In their speech, they think of how to be truthful … When in doubt, they think of how to pose questions."
>
> Confucius

Your first draft rarely is as good as it could be. If you have time, revise it. Take the reader into consideration. Go through your entire letter, memo, or report and delete all unnecessary words, sentences, and paragraphs. Use specific, concrete words rather than abstract phrases. Instead of saying, "A period of unfavorable weather set in," say, "It rained every day for a week."

Be critical of your own writing. If you want to improve, start by reading *The Elements of Style* by William Strunk and E. B. White and the most recent edition of *The Little, Brown Handbook*.[60]

Language   Word choice can enhance or interfere with communication effectiveness. For example, jargon is actually a form of shorthand and can make communication more effective when both the sender and the receiver know the buzzwords. But when the receiver is unfamiliar with the jargon, misunderstandings result. When people from different functional areas or disciplines communicate with one another, misunderstandings often occur because of "language" barriers. As in writing, simplicity usually helps.

Therefore, whether speaking or writing, you should consider the receiver's background and adjust your language accordingly. When you are receiving, don't assume that your understanding is the same as the speaker's intentions. Japanese people use the simple word *hai* (yes) to convey that they understand what is being said; it does not necessarily mean that they agree. Asian businesspeople rarely use the direct "no," using more subtle or tangential ways of disagreeing.[61]

Global teams fail when members have difficulty communicating because of language, cultural, and geographic barriers. What could you do to overcome these barriers?

Global teams fail when members have difficulties communicating because of language, cultural, and geographic barriers. Heterogeneity harms team functioning at first. But when they develop ways to interact and communicate, teams develop a common identity and perform well.[62]

When conducting business overseas, try to learn something about the other country's language and customs. Americans are less likely to do this than people from some other cultures; most Americans do not consider a foreign language necessary for doing business abroad, and a significant majority of U.S. firms do not require employees sent abroad to know the local language.[63] But those who do will have a big edge over their competitors who do not.[64] Making the effort to learn the local language builds rapport, sets a proper tone for doing business, aids in adjustment to culture shock, and especially can help you "get inside" the other culture.[65] You will learn more about how people think, feel, and behave, both in their lives and in their business dealings.

Language Differences

In Korea, few ground controllers speak English, so American pilots are required by law to be paired with a Korean first officer. But what if a crisis arises, and the American and the Korean have trouble understanding each other? The problem goes beyond language to cultural norms. Korea's rigid hierarchical, authoritarian culture means that those of lower rank or younger age hesitate to volunteer information, ask questions, or make suggestions.

Lewis and Clark needed Charbonneau and Sacagawea to help them communicate with the Indian tribes they encountered on their expedition. Lewis spoke English to Charbonneau's partner, who translated into French, which Charbonneau then translated into Hidatsu, the language spoken throughout the Upper Midwest. But when they reached the Pacific, the Indians there spoke only Walla Walla, a language not known to any of them. Fortunately, they had captured a Shoshone warrior who spoke both Hidatsu and Walla Walla. Without this chain of translators, Lewis and Clark might not have rewritten American history.

Today, army units' readiness for war is judged not just by traditional standards but also by the number of foreign speakers, their awareness of the local culture where they will fight, and their ability to train local security forces. In a training exercise, a lieutenant asked a soldier pretending to be an Iraqi mayor where the insurgents were hiding. The mock mayor just shrugged and demanded water and food for his townspeople. A colonel told the lieutenant, "Be a little more personable. Ask about the mayor's family. Build a relationship before you ask him where the bad guys are." The same colonel said that the U.S. Army's modernization program was overlooking the human and psychological dimensions of war. Now, the army's Command and General Staff College offers a course taught by cultural anthropologists and marketing experts who sell to foreign audiences. They want to learn how companies like Pepsi sell on the streets of Baghdad.

English appears to be accepted everywhere and to be spoken by almost everyone. But English is the mother tongue of only 5 percent of the world's population, and people much prefer to speak their own languages. Many businesspeople from other countries are tired of native English speakers assuming it is their responsibility to make the extra effort and speak English. They will respond better to those who don't insist on English. As the examples above should make clear, sometimes knowing other languages and having skilled interpreters are nothing short of essential.

SOURCES: S. Glain, "Language Barrier Proves Dangerous in Korea's Skies," *The Wall Street Journal*, October 4, 1994, pp. B1, B16; M. Posner, "Beating the Language Barrier," *Credit Management*, October 2001, p. 16; G. Jaffe, "As Chaos Mounts in Iraq, U.S. Army Rethinks Its Future," *The Wall Street Journal*, December 8, 2004, pp. A1, A9.

Nonverbal Skills

As you know, people send and interpret signals other than those that are spoken or written. Nonverbal messages can support or undermine the stated message. Often, nonverbal cues make a greater impact than other signals. In employees' eyes, managers' actions often speak louder than the words managers choose.

In conversation, except when you intend to convey a negative message, you should give nonverbal signals that express warmth, respect, concern, a feeling of equality, and a willingness to listen. Negative nonverbal signals show coolness, disrespect, lack of interest, and a feeling of superiority.[66] The following suggestions can help you send positive nonverbal signals.

First, use *time* appropriately. Avoid keeping your employees waiting to see you. Devote sufficient time to your meetings with them, and communicate frequently with them to signal your interest in their concerns. Second, make your *office arrangement* conducive to open communication. A seating arrangement that avoids separation of people helps establish a warm, cooperative atmosphere (in contrast, an arrangement in which you sit behind your desk and your subordinate sits before you creates a more intimidating, authoritative environment).[67] Third, remember your *body language*. Research indicates that facial expression and tone of voice can account for 90 percent of the communication between two people.[68] Several nonverbal body signals convey a positive attitude toward the other person: assuming a position close to the person; gesturing frequently; maintaining eye contact; smiling; having an open body orientation, such as facing the other person directly; uncrossing the arms; and leaning forward to convey interest in what the other person is saying.

Silence is an interesting nonverbal situation. The average American is said to spend about twice as many hours per day in conversation as the average Japanese.[69] North Americans tend to talk to fill silences. Japanese allow long silences to develop, believing they can get to know people better. Japanese believe that two people with good rapport will know each other's thoughts. The need to use words implies a lack of understanding.

Nonverbal Signals in Different Countries   Here are just a few nonverbal mistakes that Americans might make in other countries.[70] Nodding the head up and down in Bulgaria means no. The American thumb-and-first-finger circular A-OK gesture is vulgar in Brazil, Singapore, Russia, and Paraguay. The head is sacred in Buddhist cultures, so you must never touch someone's head. In Muslim cultures, never touch or eat

Are you shocked by Jenna Bush's gesture? The Norwegians were. Jenna was innocently gesturing the sign of love for the University of Texas Longhorns, but in Norway the gesture carries a different meaning. To the Norwegians, this symbol is a sign for Satan.

with the left hand, which is thought unclean. Crossing your ankle over your knee is rude in Indonesia, Thailand, and Syria. Don't point your finger toward yourself in Germany or Switzerland—it insults the other person.

You also need to correctly interpret the nonverbal signals of others. Chinese scratch their ears and cheeks to show happiness. Greeks puff air after they receive a compliment. Hondurans touch their fingers below their eyes to show disbelief or caution. Japanese indicate embarrassment or "no" by sucking in air and hissing through their teeth. Vietnamese look to the ground with their heads down to show respect. Compared to Americans, Russians use fewer facial expressions, and Scandinavians fewer hand gestures, whereas people in Mediterranean and Latin cultures may gesture and touch more. Brazilians are more likely than Americans to interrupt, Arabs to speak loudly, and Asians to respect silence.

Use these examples not to stereotype but to remember that people have different styles and to aid in communication accuracy.

Improving Receiver Skills

Once you become effective at sending oral, written, and nonverbal messages, you are halfway home toward becoming a complete communicator. However, you must also develop adequate receiving capabilities. Receivers need good listening, reading, and observational skills.

Listening   In today's demanding work environment, managers need better listening skills.[71] Although it is easy to assume that good listening is easy and natural, in fact it is difficult and not nearly as common as needed.

> **reflection**
> Process by which a person states what he or she believes the other person is saying.

A basic technique called *reflection* will help a manager listen effectively.[72] **Reflection** is a process by which a person states what he or she believes the other person is saying. This technique places a greater emphasis on listening than on talking. When both parties actively engage in reflection, they get into each other's frame of reference rather than listening and responding from their own. The result is more accurate two-way communication.

The best-known corporate effort to heighten managers' listening skills was based on an advertising theme—"We understand how important it is to listen"—that reflected a basic philosophy and way of doing business.[73] The company's senior management development specialists created listening training seminars for company personnel, drawing from a study of the 100 best and 100 worst listeners in the freshman class at the University of Minnesota. Table 15.5 summarizes these effective listening techniques.

Listening begins with personal contact. Staying in the office, keeping the door closed, and eating lunch at the desk are sometimes necessary to get pressing work done, but that is no way to stay on top of what's going on. Better to walk the halls, initiate conversations and go to lunch even with people outside your area, have coffee in a popular gathering place, and maybe even move your desk onto the factory floor.[74]

When a manager takes time to really listen to and get to know people, they think, "She's showing an interest in me" or "He's letting me know that I matter" or "She values my ideas and contributions." Trust develops. Listening and learning from others are even more important for innovation than for routine work. Successful change and innovation come through lots of human contact.

Advantages of Collaboration

Could you really be an effective collaborator if you don't know how to really listen?

Reading   Illiteracy is a significant problem in the United States. Even if illiteracy is not a problem in your organization, reading mistakes are common and costly. As a re-

TABLE 15.5
Ten Keys to Effective Listening

1. *Find an area of interest.* Even if you decide the topic is dull, ask yourself, "What is the speaker saying that I can use?"

2. *Judge content, not delivery.* Don't get caught up in the speaker's personality, mannerisms, speaking voice, or clothing. Instead, try to learn what the speaker knows.

3. *Hold your fire.* Rather than getting immediately excited by what the speaker seems to be saying, withhold evaluation until you understand the speaker's message.

4. *Listen for ideas.* Don't get bogged down in all the facts and details; focus on central ideas.

5. *Be flexible.* Have several systems for note taking, and use the system best suited to the speaker's style. Don't take too many notes or try to force everything said by a disorganized speaker into a formal outline.

6. *Resist distraction.* Close the door, shut off the radio, move closer to the person talking, or ask him or her to speak louder. Don't look out the window or at papers on your desk.

7. *Exercise your mind.* Some people tune out when the material gets difficult. Develop an appetite for a good mental challenge.

8. *Keep your mind open.* Many people get overly emotional when they hear words referring to their most deeply held convictions, for example, *union, subsidy, import, Republican* or *Democrat,* and *big business.* Try not to let your emotions interfere with comprehension.

9. *Capitalize on thought speed.* Take advantage of the fact that most people talk at a rate of about 125 words per minute, but most of us think at about four times that rate. Use those extra 400 words per minute to think about what the speaker is saying rather than turning your thoughts to something else.

10. *Work at listening.* Spend some energy. Don't just pretend you're paying attention. Show interest. Good listening is hard work, but the benefits outweigh the costs.

SOURCE: Ralph G. Nichols, "Listening Is a 10-Part Skill," *Nation's Business* 45 (July 1957), pp. 56–60. Cited in R. C. Huseman, C. M. Logue, and D. L. Freshley, eds., *Readings in Interpersonal and Organizational Communication* (Boston: Allyn & Bacon, 1977).

ceiver, for your own benefit, read memos as soon as possible, before it's too late to respond. You may skim most of your reading materials, but read important memos, documents, and passages slowly and carefully. Note important points for later referral. Consider taking courses to increase your reading speed and comprehension skills. Finally, don't limit your reading to items about your particular job skill or technical expertise; read materials that fall outside your immediate concerns. You never know when a creative idea that will help you in your work will be inspired by a novel, a biography, a sports story, or an article about a problem in another business or industry.

Observing Effective communicators are also capable of observing and interpreting nonverbal communications. (As Yogi Berra said, "You can observe a lot by watching.") For example, by reading nonverbal cues a presenter can determine how her talk is going and adjust her approach if necessary. Some companies train their sales forces to interpret the nonverbal signals of potential customers. People can also decode nonverbal signals to determine whether a sender is being truthful or deceitful. Deceitful communicators maintain less eye contact, make either more or fewer body movements than usual, and smile either too much or too little. Verbally, they offer fewer specifics than do truthful senders.[75]

A vital source of useful observations comes from personally visiting people, plants, and other locations to get a firsthand view.[76] Many corporate executives rely heavily on reports from the field and don't travel to remote locations to observe firsthand what is going on. Reports are no substitute for actually seeing things happen in practice. Frequent visits to the field, and careful observation, can help a manager develop deep understanding of current operations, future prospects, and ideas for how to fully exploit capabilities.[77]

States Michael Eisner former CEO of Disney, "Sometimes you just have to be there with your people. You have to be in the same room with them, look them in the eyes, hear their voices. I'll tell you one thing. Most of the bad decisions I've made I've made while teleconferencing. In creative companies, you have to be able to read body language—see the look in people's eyes when an idea is launched, see whether they fall asleep" (p. 122).[78]

Of course, you must *accurately interpret* what you observe. A Canadian conducting business with a high-ranking official in Kuwait was surprised that the meeting was held in an open office and was interrupted constantly.[79] He interpreted the lack of a big, private office and secretary to mean that the Kuwaiti was of low rank and uninterested in doing business, and he lost interest in the deal. The Canadian observed the facts accurately, but his perceptual biases and lack of awareness regarding how norms differ across cultures caused him to misinterpret what he saw.

The Japanese are particularly skilled at interpreting every nuance of voice and gesture, putting most Westerners at a disadvantage.[80] When one is conducting business in Asian or other countries, local guides can be invaluable not only to interpret language but to "decode" behavior at meetings, subtle hints and nonverbal cues, who the key people are, and how the decision-making process operates.

Connections: DAVID NEELEMAN AT JETBLUE

At JetBlue, David Neeleman teaches every new employee how the company makes money and how each person contributes to the bottom line. He works, literally, with the flight crews. He says he wants them to know that he values their contributions—values their work so much that he's not too much of a big shot to chip in.

Thus he helps flight attendants serve the customers. He cleans planes. So do pilots. The messages: Everyone is a complete contributor, and everyone's work transcends job titles. Neeleman knows that actions speak louder than words: Talk of teamwork is meaningless if he doesn't demonstrate it.

Organizational Communication

Being a skilled communicator is essential to being a good manager and team leader. But communication must also be managed throughout the organization. Every minute of every day, countless bits of information are transmitted through an organization. We will discuss downward, upward, horizontal, and informal communication in organizations.

Downward Communication

downward communication

Information that flows from higher to lower levels in the organization's hierarchy.

Downward communication refers to the flow of information from higher to lower levels in the organization's hierarchy. Examples include a manager giving an assignment to a secretary, a supervisor making an announcement to his subordinates, and a company president delivering a talk to her management team. Downward communication that provides relevant information enhances employee identification with the company, supportive attitudes, and decisions consistent with the organization's objectives.[81]

People must receive the information they need to perform their jobs and become (and remain) loyal members of the organization. But they often lack adequate information.[82] One problem is *information overload:* They are bombarded with so much information that they fail to absorb everything. Much of the information is not very important, but its volume causes a lot of relevant information to be lost.

A second problem is a *lack of openness* between managers and employees. Managers may believe "No news is good news," "I don't have time to keep them informed of everything they want to know," or "It's none of their business, anyway." Some managers withhold information even if sharing it would be useful.

100%
Board

63%
Vice presidents

56%
General managers

40%
Plant managers

30%
Supervisors

20%
Workers

FIGURE 15.2
Information Loss in
Downward Communication

A third problem is *filtering*, introduced earlier in the chapter. When messages are passed from one person to another, some information is left out. When a message passes through many people, each transmission may cause further information losses. The message can also be distorted as people add their own words or interpretations.

Filtering poses serious problems in organizations. As messages are communicated downward through many organizational levels, much information is lost. The data in Figure 15.2 suggest that by the time messages reach the people for whom they are intended, the receivers may get very little useful information.

The fewer the number of authority levels through which communications must pass, the less information will be lost or distorted. Flatter organization offers the advantage of fewer problems caused by filtering of information as it cascades through many layers.

Coaching   Some of the most important downward communications occur when managers give performance feedback to their direct reports. We discussed earlier the importance of giving feedback and positive reinforcement when it is deserved. It is also important to explicitly discuss poor performance and areas that can be improved.

Coaching is dialogue with a goal of helping another be more effective and achieve his or her full potential on the job.[83] When done properly, coaching develops executives and enhances performance.[84] When people have performance problems, or exhibit behaviors that need to be changed, coaching is often the best way to help a person change and succeed. And coaching is not just for poor performers; as even the greatest athletes know, it is for anyone who is good and aspires to excellence. Although coaches for executives sometimes are hired from the outside, coaches from outside your organization may not understand fully the context in which you are working.[85] So don't take advice automatically. The best use of coaches is as sounding boards, helping you think through the potential impact of your ideas, generate new options, and learn from experience.

Companies such as Coca-Cola use coaching as an essential part of their executive development process. When done well, coaching is true dialogue between two committed people engaged in joint problem solving. Thus, it is far more than an occasion for highlighting poor performance, delivering reprimands, or giving advice. Good coaching requires achieving real understanding of the problem, the person, and the situation; jointly generating ideas for what to do; and encouraging the person to improve. Good coaches ask a lot of questions, listen well, provide input, and also encourage others to think for themselves. Effective coaching requires honesty, calmness, and supportiveness—all aided by a sincere desire to help. The ultimate and longest-lasting form of help is to help people think through and solve their own problems.

> **coaching**
>
> Dialogue with a goal of helping another be more effective and achieve his or her full potential on the job.

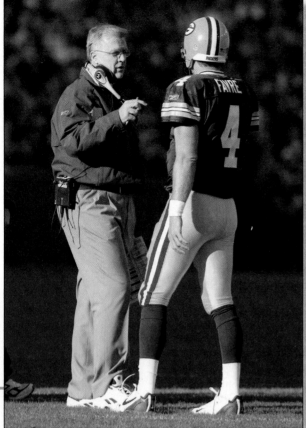

Even the greatest athletes know that coaching is not just for poor performers; it is for anyone who is good and aspires to excellence. Effective coaching can lead to achievement; but what makes a coach ineffective?

Downward Communication in Difficult Times

Adequate downward communication can be particularly valuable during difficult times. During corporate mergers and acquisitions, employees are anxious as they wonder how the changes will affect them. Ideally—and ethically—top management communicates with employees about the change as early as possible.

But some argue against that approach, maintaining that informing employees about the reorganization might cause them to quit too early. Then too, top management often cloisters itself, prompting rumors and anxiety. CEOs and other senior execs are surrounded by lawyers, investment bankers, and so on—people who are paid merely to make the deal happen, not to make it work. Yet with the people who are affected by the deal, you must increase, not decrease, communication.[86]

In a merger of two Fortune 500 companies, two plants received very different information.[87] All employees at both plants received the initial letter from the CEO announcing the merger. But after that, one plant was kept in the dark while the other was continually filled in on what was happening. Top management gave employees information about layoffs, transfers, promotions and demotions, and changes in pay, jobs, and benefits.

Which plant do you think fared better as the difficult transitional months unfolded? In both plants, the merger decreased employees' job satisfaction and commitment to the organization and increased their belief that the company was untrustworthy, dishonest, and uncaring. In the plant whose employees got little information, these problems persisted for a long time. But in the plant where employees received complete information, the situation stabilized and attitudes improved toward their normal levels. Full communication not only helped employees survive an anxious period; it served a symbolic value by signaling care and concern for employees. Without such communications, employee reactions to a merger or acquisition may be so negative as to undermine the corporate strategy.

Open-Book Management   Executives often are proud of their newsletters, staff meetings, videos, and other vehicles of downward communication. More often than not, the information provided concerns company sports teams, birthdays, and new copy machines. But today a more unconventional philosophy is gathering steam. **Open-book management** is the practice of sharing with employees at all levels of the organization vital information previously meant for management's eyes only. This includes financial goals, income statements, budgets, sales, forecasts, and other relevant data about company performance and prospects. This is dramatically different from the traditional closed-book approach in which people may or may not have a clue about how the company is doing, may or may not believe the things that management tells them, and may or may not believe that their personal performance makes a difference. Open-book management is controversial, as many managers prefer to keep such information to themselves. Sharing strategic plans and financial information with employees could lead to leaks to competitors or to employee dissatisfaction with compensation. But the companies that share this information claim a favorable impact on motivation and productivity. Cecil Ursprung, president and CEO of Reflexite Corporation in New Britain, Connecticut, said, "Why would you tell 5 percent of the team what the score was and not the other 95 percent?"[88]

Father of scientific management Frederick Taylor early in the 20th century would have considered opening the books to all employees "idiotic."[89] But then Jack Stack

---

open-book management

Practice of sharing with employees at all levels of the organization vital information previously meant for management's eyes only.

tried it at Springfield ReManufacturing Corporation, which was on the brink of collapse.[90] The results?[91] A reporter calls Jack Stack's SRC "the most highly motivated and business-savvy work force I ever encountered." Further, "I met fuel-injection-pump rebuilders who knew the gross margins of every nozzle and pump they produced. I met crankshaft grinders and engine assemblers who could discuss the ROI of their maching tools." The rewards they deserve are part of the picture here, too: "I met a guy who worked on turbochargers and ran his area as if it were his own small business. Then again, why shouldn't he? Like the other employees, he was an owner of SRC."

Other small companies joined the movement. Now, bigger companies like Amoco Canada, R. R. Donnelley, Wabash National, and Baxter Healthcare use open-book management.

Opening the books, done properly, is a complete communications system that makes sense to people on the shop floor just as it does to the top executives. The basic steps toward open-book management include:[92] (1) provide the information; (2) teach basic finance and the basics of the business; (3) empower people to make decisions based on what they know; and (4) make sure everyone shares directly in the company's success (and risks), such as through stock ownership and bonuses.

> The more management communicates cost, quality, and other data, the more people will care about and pay attention to performance and find new ways to improve.

Would You Really Do It?

Imagine that you own and manage a small or midsize company. You pick the industry; you pick the location. Imagine that the firm is all yours.

You read in *Inc.* or *Fast Company* or *Harvard Business Review* about the latest management innovation: open-book management. You read about a number of companies that realized great results through opening the books, and understand the reasons why from taking a management course. But there are downsides, as you learn when you get home and read another article. Your company has been around for a while, and the operating norms are pretty well established. How will people respond to this idea of opening the books? Will they understand? What will they think of the numbers? Will they want higher pay? Do they want a more active role in the company affairs?

Importantly, you will need to train them. You will need to commit to a lengthy, time-consuming learning period. Some of your managers and accountants, who had been privy to the confidential information, might not like the idea. They might fear they will lose power and status, or they might not trust the workers with the information. Possibly some confidential information will leak to competitors.

An intriguing issue here is pay. Pay is just about the only thing kept secret at AES, where financial and market data, and even the details of potential acquisition decisions, are widely circulated even though some people worry that information will be leaked to competitors. However, even the topic of pay secrecy may be open for debate. CEO Dennis Bakke said, "Personal compensation issues are confidential, but we're not even sure why that has to be the case."

You are not naive about the potential downsides of opening your books, or the implementation challenges. Can your managers really share the financial information? Can they really delegate decisions they used to make? What if outsiders learn our costs and other data? (Customers and suppliers would renegotiate prices; competitors might gain advantage.) How much information is enough, or too much? Is open-book management suitable for only certain kinds of businesses?

You have the sole authority to make this decision for your company. Would you implement an open-book system? And, what do you think about the issue of pay secrecy? What is your opinion—both as an employee and as company president? If you were president, what would you do about it?

SOURCES: J. Case, "Opening the Books," *Harvard Business Review*, March–April 1997, pp. 118–27; R. T. V. Davis, "Open-Book Management: Its Promise and Pitfalls," *Organizational Dynamics*, Winter 1997, pp. 7–20; S. Wetlaufer, "Organizing for Empowerment: An Interview with AES's Roger Sant and Dennis Bakke," *Harvard Business Review*, January–February 1999, pp. 110–23; R. Aggarwal and B. Simkins, "Open Book Management: Optimizing Human Capital," *Business Horizons* 44 (2001), pp. 5–13.

Upward Communication

upward communication

Information that flows from lower to higher levels in the organization's hierarchy.

Upward communication travels from lower to higher ranks in the hierarchy. Adequate upward communication is important for several reasons.[93] First, managers learn what's going on. Management gains a more accurate picture of subordinates' work, accomplishments, problems, plans, attitudes, and ideas. Second, employees gain from the opportunity to communicate upward. People can relieve some of their frustrations, achieve a stronger sense of participation in the enterprise, and improve morale. Third, effective upward communication facilitates downward communication as good listening becomes a two-way street.

Boeing's engineers went on strike in 2000 with nearly disastrous consequences for the company. At Boeing, the emphasis had been on downward communication, without much upward communication.[94] But even the downward communications were inadequate, failing to include explanations about major changes, or plans for the future. Upper management failed to listen to or respond to the perceptions, needs, and suggestions of the company's engineers. The lack of attention to upward communication meant that management didn't know about the engineers' low morale, and then was blindsided by the strike. Of course, strikes usually have multiple causes, but poor communications were critical. After the strike, Boeing's new president, Phil Condit, said, "All of us have a greater understanding of what is meant by the issue of "respect." One day I hope we can all look back on this as a turning point, a time when we more clearly recognized the importance of listening to and seeking to understand one another."[96]

At a town hall meeting with 400 employees, one suggested the installation of a traffic light to ease congestion in the parking lot at the end of the day.[95] The CEO said, "I don't ever have trouble in the parking lot, but then I leave at 8 P.M. Maybe if you didn't leave at 6 P.M., you wouldn't have trouble either." Later, the CEO said he was joking—but only after the employee turned deep red, left the room, and never came back.

The problems common in upward communication are similar to those for downward communication. Managers, like their subordinates, are bombarded with information and may neglect or miss information from below. Furthermore, some employees are not always open with their bosses; in other words, filtering occurs upward as well as downward. People tend to share only good news with their bosses and suppress bad news, because they (1) want to appear competent; (2) mistrust their boss and fear that if he or she finds out about something they have done they will be punished; (3) fear the boss will punish the messenger, even if the reported problem is not that person's fault; or (4) believe they are helping their boss if they shield him or her from problems.

For these and other reasons, managers may not learn about important problems. As one leadership expert put it, "If the messages from below say you are doing a flawless job, send back for a more candid assessment."[97]

Managing Upward Communication Generating useful information from below requires that managers both *facilitate* and *motivate* upward communication. For example, they could have an open-door policy and encourage people to use it, have lunch or coffee with employees, use surveys, institute a program for productivity suggestions, or have town-hall meetings. They can ask for employee advice, make informal visits to plants, really think about and respond to employee suggestions, and distribute summaries of new ideas and practices inspired by employee suggestions and actions.[98]

Some executives practice MBWA (management by wandering around). That term, coined by Ed Carlson of United Airlines, refers simply to getting out of the office, walking around, and talking frequently and informally with employees.[99] Thus Nissan's CEO, Carlos Ghosn, makes constant and often unannounced visits to every part of his organization, from plants to parts suppliers to dealerships to test tracks.[100] Donald Trump doesn't use e-mail—his office has only one computer, unplugged. He calls employees constantly and walks the floor of his casinos, asking doormen, table operators, and everyone else what's going on.[101]

When Kevin Sharer became CEO of Amgen, he interviewed the top 100 executives— even though he had been Amgen's president for eight years.[102] He wanted a new perspective, including what was on their minds. He asked, "What do you want to keep? What do you want to change? What do you want me to do? What are you afraid I'll do? What else do you want to ask me?" Of course, you don't want to come across as clueless (which he didn't), but you do want to learn what's on their minds and convey that you care. One thing Sharer learned was that the executives aspired to accomplish more than higher profits; they agreed to try to make Amgen the very best therapeutic company.

Useful upward communication must be reinforced and not punished. The person who tries to talk to the manager about a problem must not be brushed off consistently. An announced open-door policy must truly be open-door. Also, people must trust their supervisor and know that the manager will not hold a grudge if they deliver negative information.

In a recent town-hall meeting that received worldwide media attention, a soldier asked Defense Secretary Donald Rumsfeld why the soldiers in Iraq didn't have the armor and other protection they needed. Mr. Rumsfeld's answer wasn't very satisfying, and he was publicly criticized. The good news is that, unlike in most armies, the soldier could directly ask a question like that. The bad news is, in many companies, employees are afraid to be honest with the boss. A career coach, Dory Hollander, says "The drug of choice in most workplaces is avoid, avoid, avoid."[103] To get honesty, managers must truly listen, not punish the messenger for being honest, and act on valid comments.

Horizontal Communication

Much information needs to be shared among people on the same hierarchical level. Such **horizontal communication** can take place among people in the same work team, or in different departments. For example, a purchasing agent discusses a problem with a production engineer and a task force of department heads meets to discuss a particular concern. Communicating with others outside the firm, including Wall Street,[104] is another vital type of horizontal communication.

Horizontal communication has several important functions.[105] First, it allows sharing of information, coordination, and problem solving among units. Second, it helps solve conflicts. Third, by allowing interaction among peers, it provides social and emotional support to people. All these factors contribute to morale and effectiveness.

> **horizontal communication**
>
> Information shared among people on the same hierarchical level.

Managing Horizontal Communication   The need for horizontal communication is similar to the need for integration, discussed in Chapter 8. Particularly in complex environments, in which decisions in one unit affect another, information must be shared horizontally. As examples of good horizontal communication, Motorola holds an annual conference for sharing best learnings across functional and business groups throughout the company. NASA co-locates scientists from different disciplines. Hewlett-Packard uses common databases for different product groups to share information and ideas.[106]

GE offers a great example of how to use productive horizontal communication as a competitive weapon.[107] GE's businesses could operate independently, but each is supposed to help the others. They transfer technical resources, people, information, ideas, and money among themselves. GE accomplishes this high level of communication and cooperation through easy access between divisions and to the CEO; a culture of openness, honesty, trust, and mutual obligation; and quarterly meetings in which all the top executives get together to share information and ideas. The same kinds of things are done at lower levels as well.

Informal Communication

Organizational communications differ in formality. *Formal communications* are official, organization-sanctioned episodes of information transmission. They can move upward, downward, or horizontally and often are prearranged and necessary for performing some task.

Informal communication is more unofficial. People gossip;[108] employees complain about their boss; people talk about their favorite sports teams; work teams tell newcomers how to get by.

The **grapevine** is the social network of informal communications. Informal networks provide people with information, help them solve problems, and teach them how to do their work successfully. You should develop a good network of people willing and able to help.[109] However, the grapevine can be destructive when irrelevant or erroneous gossip and rumors proliferate and harm operations.[110]

What does this mean for you personally? Don't engage in e-gossip. Embarrassing things become public, and lawsuits based on defamation of character and invasion of privacy have used e-mail evidence. But don't avoid the grapevine, either.[111] Listen, but evaluate before believing what you hear. Who is the source? How credible is he or she? Does the rumor make sense? Is it consistent or inconsistent with other things you know or have heard? Seek more information. Don't stir the pot.

grapevine

Informal communication network.

No one knows how rumors get started, but we do know they happen. The so-called grapevine can be managed if you talk to the key people involved, suggest ways to prevent the rumors, and neutralize rumors once they've started.

Managing Informal Communication   Rumors start over any number of topics, including who's leaving, who's getting a promotion, salaries, job security, and costly mistakes. Rumors can destroy people's faith and trust in the company—and in each other. But the grapevine cannot be eliminated. Therefore, managers need to *work with* the grapevine.

The grapevine can be managed in several ways.[112] First, if a manager hears a story that could get out of hand, he or she should *talk to the key people* involved to get the facts and their perspectives. Don't allow malicious gossip.

Second, suggestions for *preventing* rumors from starting include explaining things that are important but have not been explained; dispelling uncertainties by providing facts; and working to establish open communications and trust over time.[113] Be a role model; don't malign people or the company in front of others. Participate in a positive way by spreading good news about people and the firm.[114]

Third, *neutralize* rumors once they have started: disregard the rumor if it is ridiculous; openly confirm any parts that are true; make public comments (no comment is seen as a confirmation of the rumor); deny the rumor, if the denial is based in truth (don't make false denials); make sure communications about the issue are consistent; select a spokesperson of appropriate rank and knowledge; and hold town meetings if needed.[115]

Boundarylessness

Many executives and management scholars today consider free access to information in all directions to be an organizational imperative. Jack Welch of GE coined the term *boundarylessness*. A **boundaryless organization** is one in which there are no barriers to information flow. Instead of boundaries separating people, jobs, processes, and places, ideas, information, decisions, and actions move to where they are most needed.[116] This does not imply a random free-for-all of unlimited communication and information overload. It implies information available *as needed* moving quickly and easily enough so that the organization functions far better as a whole than as separate parts.[117]

> **boundaryless organization**
> Organization in which there are no barriers to information flow.

As GE's chief learning officer said to managers, "I bet every one of you goes home at night with stuff in your head that would help the company . . . and you don't tell your boss" because "it's awkward or risky. Imagine if you could just unleash the power of the collective knowledge right in this room; imagine the good it would do."[118] The chief learning officer uses the metaphor of the organization as a house having three kinds of boundaries: the floors and ceilings, the walls that separate the rooms, and the outside walls. These barriers[119] correspond in organizations to the boundaries between different organizational levels, different units and departments, and the organization and its external stakeholders—for example, suppliers and customers. GE adds a fourth wall: global boundaries separating domestic from global operations.

Advantages of Collaboration

What could be more collaborative than organizations in which people and information are not confined by vertical and horizontal boundaries?

GE's famous Workout program is a series of meetings for business members across multiple hierarchical levels, characterized by extremely frank, tough discussions that break down vertical boundaries. Workout has involved over 222,000 GE people; in any given week thousands may be participating in a Workout program.[120] Workout is also done with customers and suppliers, breaking down outside boundaries.

GE uses plenty of other techniques to break down boundaries, as well. It relentlessly benchmarks competitors and companies in other industries to learn best practices all over the world. GE places different functions together physically, such as engineering and manufacturing. It shares services across units. And it sometimes shares physical locations with its customers.

Boundaryless organizations intentionally create dialogue across boundaries, turning barriers into permeable membranes. As the GE people put it, people from different parts of the organization need to learn "how to talk."[121] They must also learn "how to walk." That is, dialogue is essential, but it must be followed by commensurate action.

EPILOGUE

DAVID NEELEMAN OF JETBLUE

JetBlue has been phenomenally successful. In 2005 it still was growing like crazy, but some observers wondered whether it will survive. In the 1980s, upstart airline PeopleExpress was as successful and at least as famous as JetBlue today. But, like so many companies that grow too quickly, it didn't cope well. It failed.

For JetBlue, the low costs that have given it such a competitive advantage are going up as the company grows and ages—employees will start demanding more, and new planes will need repairs.

And JetBlue's success and visibility have attracted attention—competitors are learning from JetBlue and are taking direct aim.

A pilot sees Neeleman in the jetway and says, kiddingly, "So, you really do exist." The pilot had been with JetBlue for two and a half years, and was only now meeting the CEO. Neeleman rolls with the joking, but it worries him—with phenomenal growth, can JetBlue maintain its culture and its personal touch with both employees and customers?

KEY TERMS

Boundaryless organization, p. 509

Coaching, p. 503

Communication, p. 486

Downward communication, p. 502

Filtering, p. 487

Grapevine, p. 508

Horizontal communication, p. 507

Media richness, p. 494

One-way communication, p. 486

Open-book management, p. 504

Perception, p. 487

Reflection, p. 500

Two-way communication, p. 486

Upward communication, p. 506

Virtual office, p. 493

SUMMARY OF LEARNING OBJECTIVES

Now that you have studied Chapter 15, you should know:

The important advantages of two-way communication.

One-way communication flows from the sender to the receiver, with no feedback loop. In two-way communication, each person is both a sender and a receiver as both parties provide and react to information. One-way communication is faster and easier but less accurate than two-way; two-way communication is slower and more difficult, but is more accurate and results in better performance.

Communication problems to avoid.

The communication process involves a sender who conveys information to a receiver. Problems in communication can occur in all stages: encoding, transmission, decoding, and interpreting. Noise in the system further complicates communication, creating more distortion. Moreover, feedback may be unavailable or misleading. Subjective perceptions and filtering add to the possibility of error.

When and how to use the various communications channels.

Communications are sent through oral, written, and electronic channels. All have important advantages and disadvantages that should be considered before choosing a channel. Electronic media have a huge impact on interpersonal and organizational communications and make possible the virtual office. Key advantages of electronic media are speed, cost, and efficiency, but the downsides are also significant, including information overload. Media richness, or how much and what sort of information a channel conveys, is one factor to consider as you decide which channels to use and how to use them both efficiently and effectively.

Ways to become a better "sender" and "receiver" of information.

Practice writing, be critical of your work, and revise. Train yourself as a speaker. Use language carefully and well, and work to overcome cross-cultural language differences. Be alert to the nonverbal signals that you send, including your use of time as perceived by other people. Know the common bad listening habits, and work to overcome them. Read widely, and engage in careful, firsthand observation and interpretation.

How to improve downward, upward, and horizontal communication.

Actively manage communications in all directions. Engage in two-way communication more than one-way. Make information available to others. Useful approaches to downward communication include coaching, special communications during difficult periods, and open-book management. You should also both facilitate and motivate people to communicate upward. Many mechanisms exist for enhancing horizontal communications.

How to work with the company grapevine.

The informal flow of information can contribute as much as formal communication can to organizational effectiveness and morale. Managers must understand that the grapevine cannot be eliminated, and should be managed actively. Many of the suggestions for managing formal communications apply also to managing the grapevine. Moreover, managers can take steps to prevent rumors or neutralize the ones that do arise.

The advantages and characteristics of the boundaryless organization.

Boundaries—psychological if not physical—exist between different organizational levels, units, and organizations and external stakeholders. The ideal boundaryless organization is one in which there are no barriers to information flow. Ideas, information, decisions, and actions move to where they are most needed. Information is available as needed, freely accessible, so the organization as a whole functions far better than as separate parts.

DISCUSSION QUESTIONS

1. Think of an occasion when you faced a miscommunication problem. What do you think caused the problem? How do you think it should have been handled better?

2. Have you ever *not* given someone information or opinions that perhaps you should have? Why? Was it the right thing to do? Why or why not? What would cause you to be glad that you provided (or withheld) negative or difficult information? What would cause you to regret providing/ withholding it?

3. Think back to discussions you have heard or participated in. Consider the differences between one-way and two-way communication. How can two "one-ways" be turned into a true "two-way"?

4. Share with the class some of your experiences—both good and bad—with electronic media.

5. Report examples of mixed signals you have received (or sent). How can you reduce the potential for misunderstanding and misperception as you communicate with others?

6. What makes you want to say to someone, "You're not listening!"?

7. What do you think about the practice of open-book management? What would you think about it if you were running your own company?

8. Discuss organizational rumors you have heard: what they were about, how they got started, how accurate they were, and how people reacted to them. What lessons can you learn from these episodes?

9. Refer to the section on "The Virtual Office." What do you think will be the long-term impact of the mobile office on job satisfaction and performance? If you were a manager, how would you maximize the benefits and minimize the drawbacks? If you worked in this environment, how would you manage yourself to maximize your performance and avoid burnout?

10. Have you ever made or seen mistakes due to people not speaking a common language well? How do you or will you deal with others who do not speak the same language as you?

11. Have you ever tried to coach someone? What did you do well, and what mistakes did you make? How can you become a better coach?

12. Have you ever been coached by someone? What did he or she do well, and what mistakes were made? How was it for you to be on the receiving end of the coaching, and how did you respond? What is required to be successful as the "receiver" of someone else's coaching attempts?

13. Think about how companies communicate with Wall Street and the media, and how analysts on TV communicate with viewers. What concepts from the chapter apply, and how can you become a more astute "consumer" of such information?

CONCLUDING CASE

Rock On

A small coastal New England town is home to a group of dedicated musicians who practice hard and play regularly to enthusiastic audiences. The band Rock On has been together for more than 10 years, has completed three successful tours around the United States, and has produced and distributed three CDs.

The group wants to become famous. They want to get on MTV and other shows with high visibility. They want to enter into a lucrative big-name recording contract. They want to be heard regularly on radio shows nationwide. They also want to tour again, but this time before large audiences with big name groups.

The band members are all pushing 30 and feel as though their time is running out. They are discouraged to constantly see bands of obviously lesser talent achieving the goals that they are after.

The group consists of Dave on vocals and rhythm guitar, Big Nate on lead guitar, Nomar on bass, and The Animal on drums. Most of the songs they play are originals. Unlike many other bands, they offer a wide range of music that greatly enhances audience appeal. With the exception of Big Nate, a full-time musician who performs solo and with another smaller group, all other band members hold full-time jobs on the outside.

Historically, the band has reinvested almost all of the money it has earned back into recording fees, CD production, equipment upgrades, radio, and benefit performances and travel.

The group recently used college interns as marketing/consulting agents. Those students made phone connections with radio station people nationwide, and followed up on those calls with the mailing of press kits that included sample CD's, posters of the band, biographical information, and a sample stack of press clippings. The student team also researched different aspects of the music business in search of ways to help the band achieve it goals.

The band plays in many venues between Portland, Maine, and New York City, including both the small towns and the larger cities such as Boston, Hartford, and New Haven. They are well known in Boston and well-networked throughout the entire region. They are often part of a show that includes two or three other bands. They use a combination of booking agents and direct selling to club owners to get gigs.

Most agree that they are a great band of great people who play great music. All of their press releases and reviews are excellent.

They seem to be doing all of the right things but have yet to achieve their goals.

QUESTIONS

1. What specific communication techniques from the text should this group begin to incorporate into their activities, both on and off stage?

2. Effective communication with the right people could lead this group to the achievement of its goals. Once these meetings

and opportunities are established, how would you recommend that the group proceed?

3. What forms of non-verbal communication should this group incorporate into its efforts to achieve success?

EXPERIENTIAL EXERCISES

15.1 Nonverbal Communication

OBJECTIVE

To become more conscious of nonverbal messages.

INSTRUCTIONS

Following is a list of nonverbal communication "methods." Pick a day on which you will attempt to keep track of these meth-

ods. Think back at the end of the day to three people with whom you communicated in some way. Record how you responded to these people in terms of their nonverbal communication methods. Identify those that had the greatest and least effect on your behavior.

Nonverbal Communication Worksheet

Medium	What Was the Message?	How Did You Respond?	Which Affected Your Behavior Most and Least?
How they shook hands			
Their posture			
Their facial expressions			
Their appearance			
Their voice tones			
Their smiles			
The expressions in their eyes			
Their confidence			
The way they moved			
The way they stood			
How close they stood to you			
How they smelled			
Symbols or gestures they used			
How loudly they spoke			

SOURCE: Excerpted from Lawrence R. Jauch, Arthur G. Bedian, Sally A. Coltrin, and William F. Glueck, *The Managerial Experience* 5th ed. Copyright © 1989. Reprinted with permission of South-Western, a division of Thomson Learning, www.thomsonrights.com.

15.2 Listening Skills Survey

OBJECTIVES

1. To measure your skills as a listener.

2. To gain insight into the factors that determine good listening habits.

3. To demonstrate how you can become a better listener.

INSTRUCTIONS

1. Working alone, complete the Listening Skills Survey.

2. In small groups, compare scores, discuss survey test items, and prepare responses to the discussion questions.

3. After the class reconvenes, group spokespersons present group findings.

DISCUSSION QUESTIONS

1. In what ways did students' responses on the survey agree or disagree?

2. What do you think accounts for the differences?

3. How can the results of this survey be put to practical use?

Listening Skills Survey

To measure your listening skills, complete the following survey by circling the degree to which you agree with each statement.

	Strongly Agree	Agree	Neither Agree nor Disagree	Disagree	Strongly Disagree
1. I tend to be patient with the speaker, making sure she or he is finished speaking before I respond in any fashion.	5	4	3	2	1
2. When listening I don't doodle or fiddle with papers and things that might distract me from the speaker.	5	4	3	2	1
3. I attempt to understand the speaker's point of view.	5	4	3	2	1
4. I try not to put the speaker on the defensive by arguing or criticizing.	5	4	3	2	1
5. When I listen, I focus on the speaker's feelings.	5	4	3	2	1
6. I let a speaker's annoying mannerisms distract me.	5	4	3	2	1
7. While the speaker is talking, I watch carefully for facial expressions and other types of body language.	5	4	3	2	1
8. I never talk when the other person is trying to say something.	5	4	3	2	1
9. During a conversation, a period of silence seems awkward to me.	5	4	3	2	1
10. I want people to just give me the facts and allow me to make up my own mind.	5	4	3	2	1
11. When the speaker is finished, I respond to his or her feelings.	5	4	3	2	1
12. I don't evaluate the speaker's words until she or he is finished talking.	5	4	3	2	1
13. I formulate my response while the speaker is still talking.	5	4	3	2	1
14. I never pretend that I'm listening when I'm not.	5	4	3	2	1
15. I can focus on message content even if the delivery is poor.	5	4	3	2	1
16. I encourage the speaker with frequent nods, smiles, and other forms of body language.	5	4	3	2	1

(continued)

	Strongly Agree	Agree	Neither Agree nor Disagree	Disagree	Strongly Disagree
17. Sometimes I can predict what someone is going to say before she or he says it.	5	4	3	2	1
18. Even if a speaker makes me angry, I hold my temper.	5	4	3	2	1
19. I maintain good eye contact with the speaker.	5	4	3	2	1
20. I try to focus on the speaker's message, not his or her delivery.	5	4	3	2	1
21. If I am confused by a statement someone makes, I never respond until I have asked for and received adequate clarification.	5	4	3	2	1

15.3 Active Listening

This exercise involves triads. Each triad counts off into threes: 1, 2, 3, 1, 2, 3, and so on. In the first round, all the 1s in their respective triads take the pro position (see topics below), all the 2s take the con position, and all the 3s act as observers. After a topic is given, two individuals representing opposing viewpoints have one minute to collect their thoughts, and then five–seven minutes to arrive at a *mutually agreeable position* on that topic.

The observer should use the form below to capture *actual examples* of what the individuals said or did that indicated active and less-than-active listening. When time is called, the pro individuals share their opinion of which listening behaviors they performed well and which ones they'd like to improve. Then the con indi-

viduals do the same. Finally, the observers share their observations and insights, using examples to reinforce their feedback.

If additional rounds are used, rotate the roles so that each person plays a speaking role, and if possible an observing role.

Round 1:
Topic selected:_____
Notes:

Round 2:
Topic selected:_____
Notes:

Listening Feedback Form

Indicators of Active Listening	Pro	Con
1. Asked questions for clarification		
2. Paraphrased the opposing view		
3. Responded to nonverbal cues (e.g., body posture, tone of voice)		
4. Appeared to move toward a mutually satisfying solution		
Indicators of Less-than-Active Listening		
5. Interrupted before allowing the other person to finish		
6. Was defensive about their position		
7. Appeared to dominate the conversation		
8. Ignored nonverbal cues		

Potential topics to be used:

1. Gun control

2. Capital punishment

3. Race as a criterion for college admission

4. Prison reform

5. U.S. intervention in wars outside of the U.S.

6. Legalization of marijuana

7. Mandatory armed forces draft

8. Interracial adoption

9. Premarital and extramarital sex

10. Prayer in schools

11. Diversity in the workplace

12. Pornography on the Internet

QUESTIONS

1. Did you arrive at a mutually agreeable solution? What helped you get there?

2. What were some factors that hindered this process?

3. How comfortable did you feel "arguing" the position you were given? How did this influence your ability to actively listen?

4. If the position you were given was exactly opposite your values or beliefs, did you see this topic differently now than before the exercise?

5. What steps can you take to improve your ability to listen actively to friends or associates, especially when you don't agree with their viewpoint?

PART 4 SUPPORTING CASE

Leadership at AIG: Does Style Matter?

"The King Is Dead, Long Live the King." These indeed may be the very words echoed by employees at American International Group, the world's largest insurance company. Its legendary CEO Maurice "Hank" Greenberg, age 79, has been deposed by AIG's board of directors after Elliot Spitzer, New York State's attorney general, leveled charges against the company for possibly manipulating its earnings.

Headquartered in New York, AIG has been in business for nearly 90 years, has some $170 billion in market capitalization, and has approximately 80,000 employees worldwide. Greenberg, an attorney and a much heralded figure in the insurance business, has worked at AIG for more than four decades. In 1967, he became president, replacing company founder Cornelius Vander Starr. Greenberg transformed the company from a midlevel insurance company into a major international player. With a reputation as an autocratic leader, Greenberg was known to scream at employees. One source likened Greenberg's tenure to a "reign of terror." Another source offered insights to Greenberg's leadership and managerial style: He "calls employees with detailed questions about contracts and other minutiae." At one meeting in the late 1990s, he told a high-ranking manager: "This is one of the worst presentations I've seen in years... Go back, get your stuff and don't come back until you can tell me something I don't already know."

Greenberg also had trouble with his sons, Jeffrey and Evan, when they worked for him at AIG. Jeffrey, the older of the two, worked there for 17 years before quitting in 1995; Evan, who had been designated as his father's successor at AIG, resigned a few years later, in 2000. In some circles people believed their father "pushed" his sons too much by expecting more from them than from other company executives. His sons—Evan, in particular— were concerned about their father's so-called succession plan. Apparently, the senior Greenberg had given only lip service to the idea of succession with no intention of retiring any time soon.

In early March 2005, AIG's board of directors replaced Greenberg with 50-year-old vice chairman and co–chief operating officer (COO) Martin Sullivan, who had worked at the company and for Greenberg in various capacities for more than 30 years. His years in the company make him the consummate insider to lead

the company. However, like Greenberg, he is considered a micromanager, known to get involved in some of the nitty-gritty deal-making instead of enabling subordinates to play that role. If he continues micromanaging instead of delegating, he may create some serious problems for himself and the company. Yet, despite any managerial similarities to his former boss, staff view him as more pleasant and more amicable. One source stated that his "greatest strength is the respect he gets from people who work for him... He doesn't scream and shout like Mr. Greenberg." Sullivan's leadership style may be exactly the breath of fresh air the troubled company needs.

QUESTIONS

1. AIG chairman and CEO Maurice "Hank" Greenberg was considered an autocratic leader and a micromanager by many employees, yet the company grew dramatically during his reign as CEO. Does leadership style matter as long as the company performs well and shareholders are satisfied with their return on investment?

2. AIG's new CEO Sullivan has been labeled a micromanager, but with a more pleasant personality. Can he, as a micromanager, develop a more participative leadership style? How?

3. Greenberg named his son Evan as the heir apparent. Yet Greenberg never set a departure date. Should a good leader set a date for departure? When should he name a successor?

Sources: D. Brady, "AIG Needs New Policies," *BusinessWeek online,* March 1, 2005; E. Kelleher and A. Felsted, "New AIG Chief Has a Softer Touch," *Financial Times,* March 21, 2005, p. 18; I. McDonald, "Insurance Industry's First Family Fades," *The Wall Street Journal* March 15, 2005, p. C13; N. Scheiber, "Sins of the Son," *New York Magazine,* 2004; J. Weil, M. Langley, and N. Deogun, "AIG's Greenberg Plans to Depart as Woes Mount," *The Wall Street Journal,* March 14, 2005, pp. 1, 14.

This case was prepared by Joseph C. Santora, who is a professor of business administration at Essex County College, Newark, New Jersey.

PART FIVE

Foundations of Management
- Managing
- The External Environment and Organizational Culture
- Managerial Decision Making

Planning: Delivering Strategic Value
- Planning and Strategic Management
- Ethics and Corporate Responsibility
- International Management
- Entrepreneurship

Strategy Implementation

Organizing: Building a Dynamic Organization
- Organization Structure
- Organizational Agility
- Human Resources Management
- Managing the Diverse Workforce

Leading: Mobilizing People
- Leadership
- Motivating for Performance
- Teamwork
- Communicating

Controlling: Learning and Changing
- Managerial Control
- Managing Technology and Innovation
- Creating and Managing Change

Controlling: Learning and Changing

In Parts One through Four, you learned about the foundations of management, planning and strategy and how to implement plans by organizing, staffing, and leading. Part Five concludes with three chapters about controlling and changing what the organization and its people are doing. Chapter 16 describes managerial control, including issues related to culture as well as techniques for ensuring that intended activities are carried out and goals are accomplished.

The last two chapters focus on change and renewal. Chapter 17 discussed technology and innovation, including a strategic approach to new technologies and the creation of a culture for innovation. Chapter 18 examines an ongoing challenge for the modern executive: becoming world-class through the management of change. In that chapter, we describe the nature of this challenge and how managers can deal with it. Some of the topics you learned about in earlier chapters play central roles in the change process; Chapter 18 should remind you how your understanding of them will benefit your managerial career.

Chapter   16

CHAPTER 16
Managerial Control

More than at any time in the past, companies will not be able to hold themselves together with the traditional methods of control: hierarchy, systems, budgets, and the like . . . The bonding glue will increasingly become ideological.

— **Collins & Porras**[1]

Use your good judgment in all situations. There will be no additional rules.

— **Nordstrom's employee manual**

CHAPTER OUTLINE

LEARNING OBJECTIVES

After studying Chapter 16, you will know:

1. Why companies develop control systems for employees.

2. How to design a basic bureaucratic control system.

3. The purposes for using budgets as a control device.

4. How to interpret financial ratios and other financial controls.

5. The procedures for implementing effective control systems.

6. The different ways in which market control mechanisms are used by organizations.

7. How clan control can be approached in an empowered organization.

"THE ENVIRONMENT WAS RIPE FOR ABUSE"

Unrelenting stress on growth and absence of controls helped push executives into unethical behavior.

For most of the 1990s, CEOs at Old Economy companies struggled to turn slow-moving organizations into nimbler, more flexible outfits. Failure cost chieftains their jobs at General Motors, Eastman Kodak, Westinghouse, and a host of other behemoths. Truth is, real transformations are the exception rather than the rule. Changing the core values, the attitudes, the fundamental relationships of a vast organization is overwhelmingly difficult. That's why an army of academics and consultants descended on Enron in the late 1990s and held it up as a paragon of management virtue. Enron seemed to have transformed itself from a stodgy regulated utility to a fast-moving enterprise where performance was paramount.

If only that were true. When Enron collapsed at the very end of 2001, after having hidden its deteriorating financial performance through illegal practices, it was the largest bankruptcy in American history. Some 4,000 employees lost their livelihood, many investors lost their life savings, and a number of senior executives came under indictment. The demise of Enron's audit firm, Arthur Andersen, came six months later, after it was accused of helping Enron falsify its financials. Many of the same academics are now scurrying to distill the cultural and leadership lessons from the debacle. Their conclusion so far: Enron didn't fail just because of improper accounting or alleged corruption at the top. It also failed because of its entrepreneurial culture. The unrelenting emphasis on earnings growth and individual initiative, coupled with a shocking absence of the usual corporate checks and balances, tipped the culture from one that rewarded aggressive strategy to one that increasingly relied on unethical corner-cutting. In the end, too much leeway was given to young, inexperienced managers without the necessary controls to minimize failures.

Before 1990, Enron was a sleepy, regulated natural-gas company dominated by engineers and hard assets. But that year, Enron chairman Kenneth L. Lay hired McKinsey & Co. partner Jeffrey K. Skilling, who was eventually promoted to president in 1997 and to CEO in early 2001. Skilling's recipe for changing the company was right out of the New Economy playbook. Layers of management were wiped out. Hundreds of outsiders were recruited and encouraged to bring new thinking to a tradition-bound business. The company abolished seniority-based salaries in favor of more highly leveraged compensation that offered huge cash bonuses and stock option grants to top performers. Young people, many just out of undergraduate or MBA programs, were handed extraordinary authority, able to make $5 million decisions without higher approval.

In the new culture, success or failure came remarkably fast. It was not unusual for execs to change jobs two or three times in as many years. Indeed, turnover from promotions alone was almost 20 percent. "In larger companies like IBM and GE, even though there is a movement toward youth, there are still enough older people around to mentor them," says James O'Toole, professor at the Center for Effective Organizations at the University of Southern California. "At Enron, you had a bunch of kids running loose without adult supervision."

In theory, of course, the kids were closely supervised. Skilling often described the new culture as "loose and

MR. DUNCAN DR. WINOKUR DR. JAEDICKE

In May 2002, members of Enron's board of directors were questioned by the U.S. Senate. Their CEO at the time, Kenneth Lay, chose to invoke the fifth amendment.

tight," one of the eight attributes of the successful companies profiled by McKinsey consultants Thomas J. Peters and Robert H. Waterman Jr. in their best-selling book, *In Search of Excellence*. The idea is to combine tight controls with maximum individual authority to allow entrepreneurship to flourish without the culture edging into chaos.

At Enron, however, the pressure to make the numbers often overwhelmed the pretext of "tight" controls. "The environment was ripe for abuse," says a former

manager in Enron's energy services unit. "Nobody at corporate was asking the right questions. It was completely hands-off management. A situation like that requires tight controls. Instead, it was a runaway train."

Source for Prologue and final Connection: John A. Byrne, "At Enron, 'The Environment Was Ripe for Abuse,' " *BusinessWeek*, February 25, 2002, online; source for first Connection: Kurt Eichenwald, *Conspiracy of Fools* (New York: Broadway Books, 2005); source for Epilogue: Heesun Wee, "Enron in Perfect Hindsight," *BusinessWeek*, December 19, 2001, online.

How do once-respected, widely praised, multi-billion-dollar companies like Enron get out of control? We provided some of the answer in earlier chapters, as in Chapter 5, when we discussed ethics and corporate responsibility, and in Chapters 2 and 10, when we discussed the adverse impact that an excessive preoccupation with the stock market and stock options can have on organization managers. But, as our Prologue suggests, another extremely important part of the answer is often a lack of control—a means or mechanism for regulating the behavior of organization members. Left on their own, people may act in ways that they perceive to be beneficial to them individually but that may work to the detriment of the organization as a whole. Without some means of regulating what people do, an organization can literally fall apart, just as Enron did. In this regard, control is one of the fundamental forces that keep the organization together.[2]

Control is defined as any process that directs the activities of individuals toward the achievement of organizational goals. It is how effective managers make sure that things are going as planned. Some managers don't want to admit it (see Table 16.1), but control problems—the lack of controls or the wrong kinds of controls—frequently cause irreparable damage to organizations. Ineffective control systems result in problems ranging from employee theft to peeling tire tread problems to escalating fuel prices in California. Employees simply wasting time cost U.S. employers billions of dollars each year![3]

Control has been called one of the Siamese twins of management. The other twin is planning. Some means of control are necessary because once managers form plans and strategies, they must ensure that the plans are carried out. This means making sure that other people are doing what needs to be done and not doing inappropriate things. If plans are not carried out properly, management must take steps to correct the problem. This is the primary control function of management. Ensuring creativity, en-

control

Any process that directs the activities of individuals toward the achievement of organizational goals.

Control is essential for the attainment of any management objective.

TABLE 16.1

Symptoms of an Out-of-Control Company

- **Lax top management**—senior managers do not emphasize or value the need for controls, or they set a bad example.

- **Absence of policies**—the firm's expectations are not established in writing.

- **Lack of agreed-upon standards**—organization members are unclear about what needs to be achieved.

- **"Shoot the messenger" management**—employees feel their careers would be at risk if they reported bad news.

- **Lack of periodic reviews**—managers do not assess performance on a regular, timely basis.

- **Bad information systems**—key data are not measured and reported in a timely and easily accessible way.

- **Lack of ethics in the culture**—organization members have not internalized a commitment to integrity.

System Control	Features and Requirements
Bureaucratic control	Uses formal rules, standards, hierarchy, and legitimate authority. Works best where tasks are certain and workers are independent.
Market control	Uses prices, competition, profit centers, and exchange relationships. Works best where tangible output can be identified and market can be established between parties.
Clan control	Involves culture, shared values, beliefs, expectations, and trust. Works best where there is "no one best way" to do a job and employees are empowered to make decisions.

SOURCES: W. G. Ouchi, "A Conceptual Framework for the Design of Organizational Control Mechanisms," *Management Science* 25 (1979), pp. 833–48; W. G. Ouchi, "Markets, Bureaucracies, and Clans," *Administrative Science Quarterly* 25 (1980), pp. 129–41; and Richard D. Robey and C. A. Sales, *Designing Organizations* (Burr Ridge, IL: Richard D. Irwin, 1994).

TABLE 16.2
Characteristics of Controls

hancing quality, reducing costs—managers must figure out ways to control what occurs in their organizations.

Not surprisingly, effective planning facilitates control, and control facilitates planning. Planning lays out a framework for the future and, in this sense, provides a blueprint for control. Control systems, in turn, regulate the allocation and utilization of resources and, in so doing, facilitate the process of planning. In today's complex organizational environment, both functions have become more difficult to implement at the same time that they have become more important in every department of the organization. Managers today must control their people, inventories, quality, and costs, to mention just a few of their responsibilities.

According to William Ouchi of the University of California at Los Angeles, managers can apply three broad strategies for achieving organizational control: bureaucratic control, market control, and clan control.[4] **Bureaucratic control** is the use of rules, regulations, and formal authority to guide performance. It includes such things as budgets, statistical reports, and performance appraisals to regulate behavior and results. **Market control** involves the use of pricing mechanisms to regulate activities in organizations as though they were economic transactions. Business units may be treated as profit centers and trade resources (services or products) with one another via such mechanisms. Managers who run these units may be evaluated on the basis of profit and loss. **Clan control,** unlike the first two types, does not assume that the interests of the organization and individuals naturally diverge. Instead, clan control is based on the idea that employees may share the values, expectations, and goals of the organization and act in accordance with them. When members of an organization have common values and goals—and trust one another—formal controls may be less necessary. Clan control is based on many of the interpersonal processes described in the organization culture section of Chapter 2, in Chapter 12 on leadership, and in Chapter 14 on groups and teams (e.g., group norms and cohesiveness).

Table 16.2 summarizes the main features of bureaucratic, market, and clan controls. We use this framework as a foundation for our discussions throughout the chapter.

bureaucratic control

The use of rules, regulations, and authority to guide performance.

market control

Control based on the use of pricing mechanisms and economic information to regulate activities within organizations.

clan control

Control based on the norms, values, shared goals, and trust among group members.

Bureaucratic Control Systems

Bureaucratic (or formal) control systems are designed to measure progress toward planned performance and, if necessary, to apply corrective measures to ensure that performance is in line with managers' objectives. Control systems detect and correct significant variations, or discrepancies, in the results obtained from planned activities.

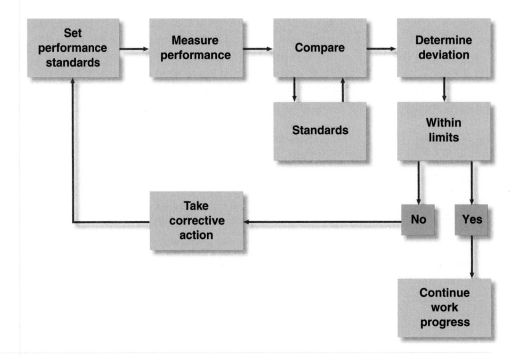

FIGURE 16.1
The Control Process

The Control Cycle

Figure 16.1 shows a typical control system with four major steps: (1) setting performance standards, (2) measuring performance, (3) comparing performance against the standards and determining deviations, and (4) taking corrective action.

Step 1: Setting Performance Standards Every organization has goals: profitability, innovation, satisfaction of constituencies, and so on. A **standard** is the level of expected performance for a given goal. Standards are performance targets that establish desired performance levels, motivate performance, and serve as benchmarks against which to assess actual performance. Standards can be set for any activity—financial activities, operating activities, legal compliance, charitable contributions, and so on.[5]

We have discussed setting performance standards in other parts of the text. For example, employee goal setting for motivation is built around the concept of specific, measurable performance standards. Such standards should be challenging and should aim for improvement over past performance. Typically, performance standards are derived from job requirements. Examples might include increasing market share by 10 percent, reducing costs 20 percent, and answering customer complaints within 24 hours. But performance standards don't apply just to people in isolation—they frequently reflect the integration of human and system performance. BAE Systems, for example, makes control systems for aircraft engines (these controls are essentially computers mounted on the engines to monitor performance, control speed, and optimize fuel efficiency). These controls have to withstand extreme temperatures and vibration. And because they're used on a wide variety of military and commercial aircraft, they must be highly reliable. "Every four seconds, one of our engine controls takes off," noted BAE's director of operations. "At this instant there are a quarter of a million people flying somewhere, trusting our engine control." In producing these controls, workers in BAE's plant set very stringent performance standards for quality and reliability. The failure rate (termed a "shutdown rate") of the engine controls is just 0.7 incident per million hours. That means you'd have to fly 24 hours a day, every day for a century, to experience one in-flight engine shutdown. That's a pretty incredible standard.[6]

Performance standards can be set with respect to (1) quantity, (2) quality, (3) time used, and (4) cost. For example, production activities include volume of output (quantity), de-

standard

Expected performance for a given goal: a target that establishes a desired performance level, motivates performance, and serves as a benchmark against which actual performance is assessed.

Standards must be set for all bottom-line practices.

fects (quality), on-time availability of finished goods (time use), and dollar expenditures for raw materials and direct labor (cost). Many important aspects of performance, such as customer service, can be measured by the same standards—adequate supply and availability of products, quality of service, speed of delivery, and so forth.

One word of caution: The downside of establishing performance targets and standards is that they may not be supported by other elements of the control system. Each piece of the system is important and dependent on the others. Otherwise the system can get terribly out of balance. Let's look at some of the other pieces.

Step 2: Measuring Performance   The second step in the control process is to measure performance levels. For example, managers can count units produced, days absent, papers filed, samples distributed, and dollars earned. Performance data commonly are obtained from three sources: written reports, oral reports, and personal observations.

> "When you confront a problem you begin to solve it."
> Rudy Giuliani

Written reports include computer printouts. Thanks to computers' increasing capabilities and decreasing costs, both large and small companies can gather huge amounts of performance data.

Connections: "THE ENVIRONMENT WAS RIPE FOR ABUSE"

At Enron, these basic controls were not in place. For example, Enron finance managers had no system that would tell them how much cash was going out or coming into the company on a daily basis, or even how much cash the company had on hand. To find out, Enron would have to send inquiries to its various divisions and wait for often delayed replies to come back. One result was that the company often had to borrow to meet obligations, because managers could not immediately find and access the cash they did have. This unnecessarily increased Enron's interest expense. Moreover, many of the company's transactions and the terms of many of its deals were not recorded. As a result, the company did not, and in some cases actually could not, monitor the changing risks of some of the deals to which the company was legally committed. Even at the height of the crisis, when Enron's top management desperately needed to determine where it stood financially, it was unable to do so on a timely basis.

One common example of *oral reports* occurs when a salesperson contacts his or her immediate manager at the close of each business day to report the accomplishments, problems, or customers' reactions during the day. The manager can ask questions to gain additional information or clear up any misunderstandings. When necessary, tentative corrective actions can be worked out during the discussion.

Personal observation involves going to the area of activities and watching what is occurring. The manager can observe work methods, employees' nonverbal signals, and the general operation. Personal observation gives an intimate picture of what is going on, but it also has some disadvantages. It does not provide accurate quantitative data; the information usually is general and subjective. Also, employees can misconstrue personal observation as mistrust or lack of confidence. Nevertheless, many managers believe there is no good substitute for firsthand observation. As you learned in earlier chapters, personal contact can increase leadership visibility and upward communication. It also provides valuable information about performance to supplement written and oral reports.

Regardless of the performance measure used, the information must be provided to managers on a timely basis. For example, consumer-goods companies like General Foods carefully track new-product sales in selected local markets first, so they can make any necessary adjustments well before a national roll-out. Information that is not actionable is of little or no use to managers.

principle of exception

A managerial principle stating that control is enhanced by concentrating on the exceptions or significant deviations from the expected result or standard.

Step 3: Comparing Performance with the Standard   The third step in the control process is comparing performance with the standard. In this process, the manager evaluates the performance. For some activities relatively small deviations from the standard are acceptable, while in others a slight deviation may be serious. Managers who perform the controlling work therefore must analyze and evaluate the results carefully.

The managerial **principle of exception** states that control is enhanced by concentrating on the exceptions, or significant deviations, from the expected result or standard. In comparing performance with the standard, managers need to direct their attention to the exception. For example, controlling the quality of components produced on an assembly line might show that only 5 pieces per 1,000 fall out of line. These five components are the exceptions and should be investigated further.[7]

With the principle of exception, only exceptional cases require corrective action. The manager should not be concerned with performance that equals or closely approximates the expected results. This principle is important in controlling. Managers can save much time and effort if they apply the principle of exception.

Step 4: Taking Corrective Action   The last step in the control process is to take action to correct significant deviations. This step ensures that operations are adjusted where necessary to achieve the initially planned results. Where significant variances are discovered, the manager will usually take immediate and vigorous action.

An alternative approach is for the corrective action to be taken not by higher-ups but by the operator at the point of the problem. In computer-controlled production technology, two basic types of control are feasible: specialist control and operator control. With *specialist control*, operators of computer-numerical-control (CNC) machines must notify engineering specialists of malfunctions. With this traditional division of labor, the specialist takes corrective action. With *operator control*, multiskilled operators can rectify their own problems as they occur. At companies such as Harley-Davidson, not only is this strategy more efficient (because deviations are controlled closer to their source), operators benefit by virtue of a more enriched job.[8]

The appropriate corrective action depends on the nature of the problem. The corrective action may involve a shift in marketing strategy (if, say, the problem is lower-than-expected sales), a disciplinary action, a new way to check the accuracy of manufactured parts, or a major organizational modification. Or it may simply be an inexpensive investment in employee training. At Corning, the source of major quality and production problems was traced to minute drafting errors by the engineering group. One of the solutions was quite simple: An engineer was sent to a proofreading class.[9]

Advantages of Collaboration

When corrective action is needed to solve a systemic problem, such as major delays in work flow, often a team approach is most effective. A corrective action is more likely to have greater acceptance in the organization if it is based on a common effort and takes into account multiple points of view. As we discussed in Chapter 14, teams often bring a greater diversity of resources, ideas, and perspectives to problem solving. Knowledgeable team members can often prevent managers from simplistic solutions that don't address the underlying causes of a problem. They are more likely to take into account the effects of any solution on other parts of the organization, preventing new problems from arising later. And they may well develop solutions that managers might not have considered on their own. As a result, any corrective action that is finally adopted will probably be more effective. An important added benefit of bringing employees together to develop corrective action is that it helps managers build and reinforce an organizationwide culture of high standards.

Approaches to Bureaucratic Control

The three approaches to bureaucratic control are feedforward, concurrent, and feedback. **Feedforward control** takes place before operations begin and includes policies, procedures, and rules designed to ensure that planned activities are carried out properly. Examples include inspection of raw materials and proper selection and training of employees. **Concurrent control** takes place while plans are being carried out. It includes directing, monitoring, and fine-tuning activities as they occur. **Feedback control** focuses on the use of information about results to correct deviations from the acceptable standard after they arise.

Feedforward Control   Feedforward control (sometimes called *preliminary control*) is future-oriented; its aim is to prevent problems before they arise. Instead of waiting for results and comparing them with goals, a manager can exert control by limiting activities in advance. For example, companies have policies defining the scope within which decisions are made. A company may dictate that managers adhere to clear ethical and legal guidelines when making decisions. Formal rules and procedures also prescribe people's actions before they occur. Stating that a financial officer must approve expenditures over $1,000 or that only components that pass all safety tests can be used in a product specifies in advance which actions can and cannot be taken. To prevent loan defaults, banks may require extensive loan documentation, reviews, and approvals by bank officers before authorizing a loan.[10]

Concurrent Control   Concurrent control, which takes place while plans are carried out, is the heart of any control system. On the production floor, all efforts are directed toward producing the correct quantity and quality of the right products in the specified amount of time. In an airline terminal, the baggage must get to the right airplanes before flights depart. In factories, materials must be available when and where needed, and breakdowns in the production process must be repaired immediately. Concurrent control also is in operation when supervisors watch employees to ensure they work efficiently and avoid mistakes. Advances in information technology have created powerful concurrent controls. Computerized systems give managers immediate access to data from the most remote corners of their companies. For example, managers can update budgets continuously based on an ongoing flow of performance data. In production facilities, monitoring systems that track errors per hour, machine speeds, and other measures allow managers to correct small production problems continuously before they become disasters.

Feedback Control   Feedback control implies that performance data were gathered and analyzed and the results were returned to someone (or something) in the process to make corrections. When supervisors monitor behavior, they are exercising concurrent control. When they point out and correct improper performance, they are using feedback as a means of control.

Timing is an important aspect of feedback control. Long time lags often occur between performance and feedback, such as when actual spending is compared with the quarterly budget, instead of weekly or monthly, or when some aspect of performance is compared to the projection made a year earlier. If feedback on performance is not timely, managers cannot quickly identify and eliminate the problem and prevent more serious harm.[11]

Some feedback processes are under real-time (concurrent) control, such as a computer-controlled robot on an assembly

---

feedforward control

The control process used before operations begin, including policies, procedures, and rules designed to ensure that planned activities are carried out properly.

concurrent control

The control process used while plans are being carried out, including directing, monitoring, and fine-tuning activities as they are performed.

feedback control

Control that focuses on the use of information about previous results to correct deviations from the acceptable standard.

In late spring 2005, carmaker General Motors was struggling with legacy costs, a shrinking sales base, and negative cash flow . . . not to mention foreign competition from Honda and Toyota. What control measures might be lacking at GM? Considering what you've read about approaches to control, what method might be beneficial to GM?

line. Such units have sensors that continually determine whether they are in the correct position to perform their functions. If they are not, a built-in control device makes immediate corrections.

How Xerox Got Up to Speed

Xerox Corp. thought it was doing a smart thing when it consolidated 36 administrative centers into 3 back in 1999. But the move came just as Xerox was also reorganizing its sales division. The simultaneous upheaval in two key units unleashed chaos across the company's billing system. Customers received invoices quoting prices they had never agreed to—or detailing equipment they had never ordered. Worse, the mistakes took months to sort out, prompting some longtime customers to defect.

After struggling to fix the problem itself, the company hired General Electric Capital to handle its billing. GE brought more than order to the process: It showed Xerox a whole new way to diagnose and fix its problems. If the company could omit steps from its design, manufacturing, and servicing processes, as well as fine-tune those that remained, it would be able to deliver better printers and copiers to customers far faster and at lower cost.

What did GE have that Xerox didn't? For one, years of experience in applying Six Sigma, the data-driven technique for eliminating defects in any business process. But GE had moved beyond Six Sigma to apply so-called lean manufacturing tools made famous by Toyota Motor Corp. in the 1980s. The combination—known as Lean Six Sigma—has taken root across Corporate America. Companies are using the techniques to analyze and improve tasks ranging from simple processes such as customer credit checks to complex product-design challenges.

Xerox kicked into high gear with training for top execs, including CEO Anne M. Mulcahy, who has spearheaded the effort. And the results are already rolling in: Xerox claims a $6 million return in one year on a $14 million investment in Lean Six Sigma. It expects an even bigger payoff the next year.

One of the strengths of Lean Six Sigma is that it blankets the company. Previous quality initiatives may have addressed a particular factory operation or only a part of it. The point is not to automate complicated processes, but to "lean out" existing processes by removing unnecessary steps and then fix those that remain. Sounds easy, but learning the dozens of analytical methods involved in Lean Six Sigma takes weeks of training. Figuring out what steps to trim or replace chews up time, too. But the hardest task is getting employees to accept that how they've always done things may not be the best way. But consultants say Xerox is succeeding because the CEO has made the program a priority.

One of the "soft" challenges is tearing down walls to get different divisions to work together. This is never easy in a complex, big organization. Yet at Xerox, teams from supply, manufacturing, and research and development pulled it off to resolve a problem with a $500,000 printing press introduced last year. Customers quickly found that the fuser roll (which uses heat and pressure to bond toner to paper) was wearing out sooner than expected. The Xerox team used Lean Six Sigma tools to zero in on the cause in just one month. The oil on the roller was fouling up the works. The team worked with the oilmaker, which changed the chemistry, saving Xerox $2 million and keeping its customers happy.

Ultimately, Xerox' efforts are focused on getting new products to customers faster, which has meant taking steps out of the design process. For its new DocuTech print-on-demand machines, for example, Xerox used software to simulate an early design stage, saving the time and expense of building a prototype. Xerox has gotten so good at applying Lean Six Sigma that, like GE before, it's even helping out its customers. Says one executive: "We've moved from being consciously incompetent to consciously competent." Now, Mulcahy is pushing Xerox to become unconsciously competent—the point where the tools are so ingrained that no one even thinks about them anymore.

Source: Faith Arner, "How Xerox Got Up to Speed," *BusinessWeek*, May 3, 2004, online.

The Role of Six Sigma   One of the most important quality-control tools to emerge is Six Sigma, which we first discussed in Chapter 9. It is a particularly robust and powerful application of feedback control. Six Sigma is designed to reduce defects in all organization processes—not only product defects, but anything that may result in customer dissatisfaction, such as inadequate service, delayed delivery, and excessively high prices due to high costs or inefficiency. The system was developed by Motorola in the late 1980s, when the company found it was being beaten consistently in the competitive marketplace by foreign firms that were able to produce higher-quality products at a lower cost. Since then, the technique has been widely adopted and even improved on by many companies, such as GE, Allied Signal, Ford, and, as you can see from the accompanying news item, Xerox.

Sigma is the Greek letter used in statistics to designate the estimated standard deviation or variation in a process. It indicates how often defects in a process are likely to occur. The lower the sigma number, the higher the level of variation or defects; the higher the sigma number, the lower the level of variation or defects. For example, as you can see in Table 16.3, a two sigma level process has more than 300,000 defects per million opportunities (DPMO)—not a very well-controlled process. A three sigma level process has 66,807 DPMO, which is roughly a 93 percent level of accuracy. Many organizations operate at this level, which on its face does not sound too bad, until we consider its implications—for example, 7 items of airline baggage lost for every 100 processed. The additional costs to organizations of such inaccuracy are enormous. As you can see in the table, even at just above a 99 percent defect-free rate, or 6,210 DPMO, the accuracy level is often unacceptable—the statistical equivalent of about 50 dropped newborn babies a day.[12]

At six sigma level, a process is producing fewer than 3.4 defects per million, which means it is operating at a 99.99966 percent level of accuracy. Six Sigma companies have not only close to zero product or service defects, but also substantially lower production costs and cycle times and much higher levels of customer satisfaction. The methodology isn't just for the factory floor, either. Hospitals that use Six Sigma report that they have lowered the incidence of patients mistakenly given the wrong medications.[13]

The Six Sigma approach is based on an intense statistical analysis of business processes that contribute to customer satisfaction. For example, one of the processes GE measured when it introduced the process was product delivery time. Once the defects or variations are measured, their causes are analyzed. Teams of employees then work on designing and testing new processes that will reduce the causes of the variations. For example, if the team finds that delivery delays are caused by production bottlenecks, it will work on eliminating those. When an improved process is installed, it is analyzed again for remaining defects, and employees then work on reducing those. This cycle continues until the desired quality level is achieved. In this way, the Six Sigma process leads to continuous improvement in an organization's operations.

TABLE 16.3
Relationship between Sigma Level and Defects per Million Opportunities

Sigma Level	DPMO	Is Four Sigma Good Enough?
2σ	308,537	Consider these everyday examples of four sigma quality . . .
3σ	66,807	• 20,000 lost articles of mail per hour
4σ	**6,210**	• Unsafe drinking water 15 minutes per day
5σ	233	• 5,000 incorrect surgical operations per week
6σ	3.4	• 200,000 wrong prescriptions each year
		• No electricity for 7 hours each month

SOURCE: Tom Rancour and Mike McCracken, "Applying 6 Sigma Methods for Breakthrough Safety Performance," *Professional Safety*, October 2000, 45, no. 10, 29–32. Reprinted with permission.

Management Audits

Over the years, **management audits** have developed as a means for evaluating the effectiveness and efficiency of various systems within an organization, from social responsibility to accounting control. Management audits may be external or internal. Managers conduct external audits of other companies and internal audits of their own companies. Some of the same tools and approaches are used for both types of audit.[14]

External Audits An **external audit** occurs when one organization evaluates another organization. Typically an external body such as a CPA firm conducts financial audits of an organization (accounting audits are discussed later). But any company can conduct external audits of competitors or other companies for its own strategic decision-making purposes. This type of analysis (1) investigates other organizations for possible merger or acquisition, (2) determines the soundness of a company that will be used as a major supplier, or (3) discovers the strengths and weaknesses of a competitor to maintain or better exploit the competitive advantage of the investigating organization. Publicly available data usually are used for these evaluations.[15]

External audits were used in feedback control in the discovery and investigation of the savings and loan scandals. They also are useful for preliminary control because they can prevent problems from occurring. If a company gathers adequate, accurate information about acquisition candidates, it is more likely to acquire the most appropriate companies and avoid unsound acquisitions.

Internal Audits **Internal audits** assess (1) what the company has done for itself and (2) what it has done for its customers or other recipients of its goods or services. The company can be evaluated on a number of factors, including financial stability, production efficiency, sales effectiveness, human resources development, earnings growth, public relations, civic responsibility, and other criteria of organizational effectiveness. The audit reviews the company's past, present, and future.[16]

To perform a management audit, a list of desired qualifications is drawn up and weights are attached to each qualification. Among the more common undesirable practices uncovered by a management audit are the performance of unnecessary work, duplication of work, poor inventory control, uneconomical use of equipment and machines, procedures that are more costly than necessary, and wasted resources. At Square D (now a part of Schneider Electric), managers discovered they could throw away four manuals with 760 rules and regulations in favor of 11 simple policy statements. At Heinz, a quality program aimed mostly at eliminating waste and rework is predicted to save $250 million over three years.[17] One recent study found that the stock prices of companies with highly-rated audit committees tended to rise faster than shares of companies with lower-rated internal auditors. It is likely that the higher-rated audit committees do a better job of finding and eliminating undesirable practices.[18]

Budgetary Controls

Budgetary control is one of the most widely recognized and commonly used methods of managerial control. It ties together feedforward control, concurrent control, and feedback control, depending on the point at which it is applied. *Budgetary control* is the process of finding out what's being done and comparing the results with the corresponding budget data to verify accomplishments or remedy differences. Budgetary control commonly is called **budgeting.**

Fundamental Budgetary Considerations In private industry, budgetary control begins with an estimate of sales and expected income. Table 16.4 shows a budget with estimates for sales and expenses for the first three months of the year. There is space to enter the actual accomplishments to expedite a comparison between expected and actual results. Note that the profit estimate is based on the estimate of total sales less the estimate of expenses.

	January		February		March	
	Estimate	**Actual**	**Estimate**	**Actual**	**Estimate**	**Actual**
Sales	$1,200,000		$1,350,000		$1,400,000	
Expenses						
General overhead	310,000		310,000		310,000	
Selling	242,000		275,000		288,000	
Producing	327,000		430,500		456,800	
Research	118,400		118,400		115,000	
Office	90,000		91,200		91,500	
Advertising	32,500		27,000		25,800	
Estimated gross profit	80,100		97,900		112,900	

TABLE 16.4
A Sales-Expense Budget

Budgeting information is supplied to the entire enterprise or to any of its units; it is not confined to financial matters. Units other than dollars typically can be used. For example, industry will often budget production in physical units and labor in skill levels or hours of work required.

A primary consideration of budgeting is the length of the budget period. All budgets are prepared for a definite time period. Many budgets are for one, three, or six months or for one year. The length of time selected depends on the primary purpose of the budgeting. The period chosen should include the enterprise's complete normal cycle of activity. For example, seasonal variations should be included both for production and for sales. The budget period commonly coincides with other control devices, such as managerial reports, balance sheets, and statements of profit and loss. In addition, the extent to which reasonable forecasts can be made should be considered in selecting the length of the budget period.

Budgetary control proceeds through several stages. *Establishing expectancies* starts with the broad plan for the company and the estimate of sales, and it ends with budget approval and publication. The *budgetary operations* stage, then, deals with finding out what is being accomplished and comparing the results with expectancies. The last stage, as in any control process, involves taking corrective action when necessary.

Although practices differ widely, a member of top management often serves as the chief coordinator for formulating and using the budget. Usually the chief financial officer (CFO) has these duties. He or she needs to be less concerned with the details than with resolving conflicting interests, recommending adjustments when needed, and giving official sanction to the budgetary procedures.

Types of Budgets   There are many types of budgets. Some of the more common types are as follows:

- *Sales budget.* Usually data for the sales budget are prepared by month, sales area, and product.
- *Production budget.* The production budget commonly is expressed in physical units. Required information for preparing this budget includes types and capacities of machines, economic quantities to produce, and availability of materials.
- *Cost budget.* The cost budget is used for areas of the organization that incur expenses but no revenue, such as human resources and other support departments. Cost budgets may also be included in the production budget. Costs may be *fixed*, or independent of the immediate level of activity, like rent, or *variable*, rising or falling with the level of activity, like raw materials.

- *Cash budget.* The cash budget is essential to every business. It should be prepared after all other budget estimates are completed. The cash budget shows the anticipated receipts and expenditures, the amount of working capital available, the extent to which outside financing may be required, and the periods and amounts of cash available.
- *Capital budget.* The capital budget is used for the cost of fixed assets like plant and equipment. Such costs are usually treated not as regular expenses but as investments, because of their long-term nature and importance to the organization's productivity.
- *Master budget.* The master budget includes all the major activities of the business. It brings together and coordinates all the activities of the other budgets and can be thought of as a "budget of budgets."

Traditionally, budgets were often imposed *top-down*, with senior management setting specific targets for the entire organization at the beginning of the budget process. In today's more complex organizations, the budget process is much more likely to be *bottom-up*, with top management setting the general direction, but with lower-level and midlevel managers actually developing the budgets and submitting them for approval. When the budgets are consolidated, senior managers can then determine whether the budget objectives of the organization are being met. The budget will then be either approved or sent back down the organization for additional refinement.

Accounting records must be inspected periodically to ensure they were properly prepared and are correct. **Accounting audits,** which are designed to verify accounting reports and statements, are essential to the control process. This audit is performed by members of an outside firm of public accountants. Knowing that accounting records are accurate, true, and in keeping with generally accepted accounting practices (GAAP) creates confidence that a reliable base exists for sound overall controlling purposes.[19]

accounting audits

Procedures used to verify accounting reports and statements.

Connections: "THE ENVIRONMENT WAS RIPE FOR ABUSE"

Of course, to be effective, the accounting audit actually has to follow those accepted practices. The audits at Enron did not. Arthur Andersen, Enron's auditor, violated the rules when it repeatedly allowed Enron to exclude money-losing partnerships from its financial statements. The effect was to make Enron seem much more profitable than it really was. Part of the problem was that Andersen earned not only large audit fees from Enron but also millions in nonaudit consulting fees. Many observers believe that these large fees fatally undermined Andersen's independence and caused it to compromise its professional ethics and standards. In 2002, a jury found the firm guilty of obstruction of justice for shredding thousands of documents and computer printouts related to its Enron audits. While this conviction was overturned by the Supreme Court in 2005, the company had long since lost all its clients as a result of its legal problems and faulty accounting practices. Andersen, a Big Five accounting firm with over $9 billion in annual revenues and 28,000 U.S. employees, went out of business. Even for the largest firms, the failure to maintain high standards of integrity can have severe real-life costs.

Activity-based costing can highlight overspending.

Activity-Based Costing Traditional methods of cost accounting may be inappropriate in today's business environment because they are based on outdated methods of rigid hierarchical organization. Instead of assuming that organizations are bureaucratic "machines" that can be separated into component functions such as human resources, purchasing, and maintenance, companies such as Chrysler, Hewlett-Packard, and GE have begun using **activity-based costing (ABC)** to allocate costs across business processes.

	Salaries	Fringes	Supplies	Fixed costs
Process sales order				$144,846
Source parts				$136,320
Expedite supplier orders				$ 72,143
Expedite internal processing				$ 49,945
Receive supplier quality				$ 47,599
Reissue purchase orders				$ 45,235
Expedite customer orders				$ 27,747
Schedule intracompany sales				$ 17,768
Request engineering change				$ 16,704
Resolve problems				$ 16,648
Schedule parts				$ 15,390

Old way

Old-style accounting identifies costs according to the category of expense. The new math tells you that your real costs are what you pay for the different tasks your employees perform. Find that out and you will manage better.

New way — **Activity-based costing**

Salaries $371,917

Fringes $118,069

Supplies $76,745

Fixed Costs $23,614

Total $590,345

Total $590,345

SOURCE: Courtesy Dana Corporation.

FIGURE 16.2
How Dana Discovers What Its True Costs Are

ABC starts with the assumption that organizations are collections of people performing many different but related activities to satisfy customer needs. The ABC system is designed to identify those streams of activity and then to allocate costs across particular business processes. The basic procedure works as follows (see Figure 16.2): First, employees are asked to break down what they do each day in order to define their *basic activities*. For example, employees in Dana Corporation's material control department engage in a number of activities that range from processing sales orders and sourcing parts to requesting engineering changes and solving problems. These activities form the basis for ABC. Second, managers look at total expenses computed by traditional accounting—fixed costs, supplies, salaries, fringe benefits, and so on—and spread total amounts over the activities according to the amount of time spent on each activity. At Dana, customer service employees spend nearly 25 percent of their time processing sales orders and only about 3 percent scheduling parts. Thus, 25 percent of the total cost ($144,846) goes to order processing and 3 percent ($15,390) goes to scheduling parts. As can be seen in Figure 16.2, both the traditional and ABC systems reach the same bottom line. However, because the ABC method allocates costs across business processes, it provides a more accurate picture of how costs should be charged to products and services.[20]

This heightened accuracy can give managers a more realistic picture of how the organization is actually allocating its resources. It can highlight where wasted activities are occurring or if activities cost too much relative to the benefits provided. Managers can then take action to correct the problem. For example, Dana's most expensive activity is sales-order processing. Its managers might try to find ways to lower that cost, freeing up resources for other tasks. By providing this type of information, ABC has become a valuable method for streamlining business processes.

Financial Controls

In addition to budgets, businesses commonly use other statements for financial control. Two financial statements that help control overall organizational performance are the balance sheet and the profit and loss statement.

The Balance Sheet   The **balance sheet** shows the financial picture of a company at a given time. This statement itemizes three elements: (1) assets, (2) liabilities, and (3) stockholders' equity. **Assets** are the values of the various items the corporation owns. **Liabilities**

activity-based costing (ABC)

A method of cost accounting designed to identify streams of activity and then to allocate costs across particular business processes according to the amount of time employees devote to particular activities.

balance sheet

A report that shows the financial picture of a company at a given time and itemizes assets, liabilities, and stockholders' equity.

assets

The values of the various items the corporation owns.

liabilities

The amounts a corporation owes to various creditors.

stockholders' equity

The amount accruing to the corporation's owners.

are the amounts the corporation owes to various creditors. **Stockholders' equity** is the amount accruing to the corporation's owners. The relationship among these three elements is as follows:

$$\text{Assets} = \text{Liabilities} + \text{Stockholders' equity}$$

TABLE 16.5
A Comparative Balance Sheet

Comparative Balance Sheet for the Years Ending December 31		
	This Year	**Last Year**
Assets		
Current assets:		
Cash	$161,870	$119,200
U.S. Treasury bills	250,400	30,760
Accounts receivable	825,595	458,762
Inventories:		
Work in process and finished products	429,250	770,800
Raw materials and supplies	251,340	231,010
Total current assets	1,918,455	1,610,532
Other assets:		
Land	157,570	155,250
Building	740,135	91,784
Machinery and equipment	172,688	63,673
Furniture and fixtures	132,494	57,110
Total other assets before depreciation	1,202,887	367,817
Less: Accumulated depreciation and amortization	67,975	63,786
Total other assets	1,134,912	304,031
Total assets	$3,053,367	$1,914,563
Liabilities and stockholders' equity		
Current liabilities:		
Accounts payable	$287,564	$441,685
Payrolls and withholdings from employees	44,055	49,580
Commissions and sundry accruals	83,260	41,362
Federal taxes on income	176,340	50,770
Current installment on long-term debt	85,985	38,624
Total current liabilities	667,204	622,021
Long-term liabilities:		
15-year, 9 percent loan, payable in each of the years 2002–2015	210,000	225,000
5 percent first mortgage	408,600	
Registered 9 percent notes payable		275,000
Total long-term liabilities	618,600	500,000
Stockholders' equity:		
Common stock: authorized 1,000,000 shares, outstanding last year 492,000 shares, outstanding this year 700,000 shares at $1 par value	700,000	492,000
Capital surplus	981,943	248,836
Earned surplus	75,620	51,706
Total stockholder's equity	1,757,563	792,542
Total liabilities and stockholders' equity	$3,053,367	$1,914,563

Table 16.5 shows an example of a balance sheet. During the year, the company grew because it enlarged its building and acquired more machinery and equipment by means of long-term debt in the form of a first mortgage. Additional stock was sold to help finance the expansion. At the same time, accounts receivable were increased and work in process was reduced. Observe that Total assets ($3,053,367) = Total liabilities ($677,204 + $618,600) + Stockholders' equity ($700,000 + $981,943 + $75,620).

Summarizing balance sheet items over a long period of time uncovers important trends and gives a manager further insight into overall performance and areas in which adjustments need to be made. For example, at some point the company might decide that it would be prudent to slow down its expansion plans.

The Profit and Loss Statement   The **profit and loss statement** is an itemized financial statement of the income and expenses of a company's operations. Table 16.6 shows a comparative statement of profit and loss for two consecutive years. In this illustration, the operating revenue of the enterprise has increased. Expense also has increased, but at a lower rate, resulting in a higher net income. Some managers draw up tentative profit and loss statements and use them as goals. Then performance is measured against these goals or standards. From comparative statements of this type, a manager can identify trouble areas and correct them.

Controlling by profit and loss is most commonly used for the entire enterprise and, in the case of a diversified corporation, its divisions. However, if controlling is by departments, as in a decentralized organization in which department managers have control over both revenue and expense, a profit and loss statement is used for each department. Each department's output is measured, and a cost, including overhead, is charged to each department's operation. Expected net income is the standard for measuring a department's performance.

Financial Ratios   An effective approach for checking on the overall performance of an enterprise is to use key financial ratios. Ratios help indicate possible strengths and weaknesses in a company's operations. Key ratios are calculated from selected items on the profit and loss statement and the balance sheet. We will briefly discuss three categories of financial ratios: liquidity, leverage, and profitability.

> **profit and loss statement**
>
> An itemized financial statement of the income and expenses of a company's operations.

Comparative Statement of Profit and Loss for the Years Ending June 30			
	This Year	Last Year	Increase or Decrease
Income:			
Net sales	$ 253,218	$ 257,636	$ 4,418*
Dividends from investments	480	430	50
Other	1,741	1,773	32
Total	255,439	259,839	4,400*
Deductions:			
Cost of goods sold	180,481	178,866	1,615
Selling and administrative expenses	39,218	34,019	5,199
Interest expense	2,483	2,604	121*
Other	1,941	1,139	802
Total	224,123	216,628	7,495
Income before taxes	31,316	43,211	11,895*
Provision for taxes	3,300	9,500	6,200*
Net income	$28,016	$33,711	$5,695*

TABLE 16.6
A Comparative Statement of Profit and Loss

*Decrease.

current ratio

A liquidity ratio which indicates the extent to which short-term assets can decline and still be adequate to pay short-term liabilities.

debt-equity ratio

A leverage ratio which indicates the company's ability to meet its long-term financial obligations.

return on investment (ROI)

A ratio of profit to capital used, or a rate of return from capital.

- **Liquidity ratios.** *Liquidity ratios* indicate a company's ability to pay short-term debts. The most common liquidity ratio is *current assets to current liabilities*, called the **current ratio** or *net working capital ratio*. This ratio indicates the extent to which current assets can decline and still be adequate to pay current liabilities. Some analysts set a ratio of 2 to 1, or 2.00, as the desirable minimum. For example, if you refer back to Table 16.5, the liquidity ratio there is about 2.86 ($1,918,455/$667,204). The company's current assets are more than capable of supporting its current liabilities.
- **Leverage ratios.** *Leverage ratios* show the relative amount of funds in the business supplied by creditors and shareholders. An important example is the **debt-equity ratio,** which indicates the company's ability to meet its long-term financial obligations. If this ratio is less than 1.5, the amount of debt is not considered excessive. In Table 16.5, the debt-equity ratio is only .35 ($618,600/$1,757,563). The company has financed its expansion almost entirely by issuing stock rather than by incurring significant long-term debt.
- **Profitability ratios.** *Profitability ratios* indicate management's ability to generate a financial return on sales or investment. For example, **return on investment (ROI)** is a ratio of profit to capital used, or a rate of return from capital (equity plus long-term debt). This ratio allows managers and shareholders to assess how well the firm is doing compared to other investments. For example, if the net income of the company in Table 16.5 was $300,000 this year, its return on capital would be 12.6 percent ($300,000/($1,757,563 + $618,600)), normally a very reasonable rate of return.

Using Financial Ratios   Although ratios provide both performance standards and indicators of what has occurred, exclusive reliance on financial ratios can have negative consequences. Because ratios usually are expressed in compressed time horizons (monthly, quarterly, or yearly), they often cause **management myopia**—managers focus on short-term earnings and profits at the expense of their longer-term strategic obligations.[21] Control systems using long-term (e.g., three- to six-year) performance targets can reduce management myopia and focus attention further into the future.

A second negative outcome of ratios is that they relegate other important considerations to a secondary position. Research and development, management development, progressive human resources practices, and other considerations may receive insufficient attention. Therefore, the use of ratios should be supplemented with other control measures. Organizations can hold managers accountable for market share, number of patents granted, sales of new products, human resources development, and other performance indicators.

management myopia

Focusing on short-term earnings and profits at the expense of longer-term strategic obligations.

The Downside of Bureaucratic Control

So far you have learned about control from a mechanical viewpoint. But organizations are not strictly mechanical; they are composed of people. While control systems are used to constrain people's behavior and make their future behavior predictable, people are not machines that automatically fall into line as the designers of control systems intend. In fact, control systems can lead to dysfunctional behavior. A control system cannot be effective without consideration of how people will react to it. For effective control of employee behavior, managers should consider three types of potential responses to control: rigid bureaucratic behavior, tactical behavior, and resistance.[22]

Rigid Bureaucratic Behavior   Often people act in ways that will help them look good on the control system's measures. This tendency can be useful, because it causes people to focus on the behaviors management requires. But it can result in rigid, inflexible behavior geared toward doing *only* what the system requires.

Rigid bureaucratic behavior occurs when control systems prompt employees to stay out of trouble by following the rules. Unfortunately, such systems often lead to poor customer service and make the entire organization slow to act (recall the discussion of bureaucracy in Chapter 10).

We have all been victimized at some time by rigid bureaucratic behavior. Reflect for a moment on this now classic story of a "nightmare" at a hospital:

> At midnight, a patient with eye pains enters an emergency room at a hospital. At the reception area, he is classified as a nonemergency case and referred to the hospital's eye clinic. Trouble is, the eye clinic doesn't open until the next morning. When he arrives at the clinic, the nurse asks for his referral slip, but the emergency room doctor had forgotten to give it to him. The patient has to return to the emergency room and wait for another physician to screen him. The physician refers him back to the eye clinic and to a social worker to arrange payment. Finally, a third doctor looks into his eye, sees a small piece of metal, and removes it—a 30-second procedure.[23]

Stories such as these have, of course, given bureaucracy a bad name. Some managers will not even use the term *bureaucratic control* because of its potentially negative connotation. That is unfortunate because the control system itself is not the problem. The problems occur when the systems are no longer viewed as tools for running the business, but as rules for dictating rigid behavior.

Tactical Behavior   Control systems will be ineffective if employees engage in tactics aimed at "beating the system." The most common type of tactical behavior is to manipulate information or report false performance data. People may produce two kinds of invalid data: about what *has* been done and about what *can* be done. False reporting about the past is less common, because it is easier to identify someone who misreports what happened than someone who gives an erroneous prediction or estimate of what might happen. Still, managers sometimes change their accounting systems to "smooth out" the numbers. That's what happened at MCI WorldCom. By mischaracterizing expenses, managers were able to distort the bottom line by $4 billion. Also, people may intentionally feed false information into a management information system to cover up errors or poor performance.[24]

More commonly, people falsify their predictions or requests for the future. When asked to give budgetary estimates, employees usually ask for larger amounts than they need. On the other hand, they sometimes submit unrealistically *low* estimates when they believe a low estimate will help them get a budget or a project approved. Budget-setting sessions can become tugs-of-war between subordinates trying to get slack in the budget and superiors attempting to minimize slack. Similar tactics are exhibited when managers negotiate unrealistically low performance standards so that subordinates will have little trouble meeting them; when salespeople project low forecasts so they will look good by exceeding them; and when workers slow down the work pace when time-study analysts are setting work pace standards. In these and other cases, people are concerned only with their own performance figures rather than with the overall performance of their departments or companies.[25]

Resistance to Control   Often people strongly resist control systems. This occurs for several reasons. First, comprehensive control systems increase the accuracy of performance data and make employees more accountable for their actions. Control systems uncover mistakes, threaten people's job security and status, and decrease people's autonomy.

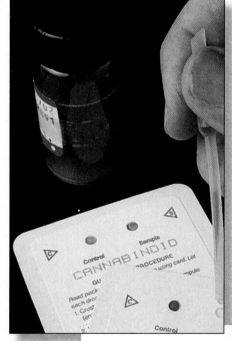

Drug testing is one of the ways organizations monitor employees. Some people favor the control measure but change their minds when personally asked to submit a urine specimen.

Second, control systems can change expertise and power structures. For example, management information systems can make the costing, purchasing, and production decisions previously made by managers. Thus, individuals fear a loss of expertise, power, and decision-making authority.

Third, control systems can change the social structure of an organization. They can create competition and disrupt social groups and friendships. People may end up competing against those with whom they formerly had comfortable, cooperative relationships. Because people's social needs are so important, they will resist control systems that reduce social need satisfaction.

Fourth, control systems may be seen as an invasion of privacy, lead to lawsuits, and cause low morale.

FROM THE PAGES OF ↓

Management by the Numbers

BusinessWeek *"If you could only monitor five metrics to run/steer your business, what would they be and why?"*

We posed the question to John W. Thompson, chairman and CEO of Symantec, a Cupertino, California, Internet security outfit that makes antivirus and firewall technology. Below are edited excerpts from his responses, culled from our conversation:

Q: So what would be your critical metrics and why?
A: Here are five critical metrics I use to manage Symantec:

Customer satisfaction: We use an outside firm to poll customers on a continuous basis to determine their satisfaction with our products and services. Polling is done by product area: firewall, antivirus, services, and other product lines.

Market share: We look at this a couple of ways. We have our own views based on relevant markets. Then we use industry analysts as benchmarks for annualized results on market share. On a quarterly basis, we look at our revenue performance and growth rates, and that of our competitors. We compare against actual, realized growth rates, as compared to growth rates of relevant competitors in similar segments. The objective is to get trending data. That gives us a sense of market changes and market growth.

Revenue growth: You have to consider if revenue is growing at a rate equal to or greater than the market rate. If you look at the antivirus market, for example, industry analysts projected growth in the high teens, while our enterprise antivirus sector grew at a rate of 32 percent. This indicates that we're gaining market share faster than the market growth rate for the industry. We can then assess how we had planned to grow. Did we plan to grow at 32 percent or less—or more? You have to gauge your growth relative to the market for your product or service, and your own internal expectations of your performance.

Expenses: It's important to always plan for how much money will have to be spent to generate a certain level of revenue. This enables you to monitor funds flow in the company. Did I plan to spend $10 or $12, and what did I get for that expense in return? The objective is to keep expenses in equilibrium to revenue generation.

Earnings: Two keys to watch here—operating margins and earnings per share (EPS). A business running efficiently is improving its operating margins. If you are efficient in your operating margins, this should produce a strong EPS, which is a strong metric that Wall Street looks at all the time.

Q: What problems do tracking metrics solve for a corporation?
A: I'm a little old-fashioned—I don't believe you can manage what you don't measure. The importance of metrics becomes more important as the enterprise grows in size and scale. Metrics also serve as an indication for the team about what you're paying attention to. If employees know you're measuring market growth and customer satisfaction, they'll pay attention to those considerations and will behave based on indicators that you, as the leader, provide to the organization. Metrics help the team focus on what's important for an organization.

Q: What do other CEOs and managers need to keep in mind as they consider/ reevaluate the use of metrics for their companies?

A: Live by the adage that you can't manage what you can't measure. The best metrics are simple to understand, simple to communicate, and relatively easy for everyone to get access to the data that represents the results. That makes your metrics an effective management tool. If you make your metrics difficult to gather, manage, or communicate, they won't be effective.

SOURCE: David Liss, "Management by the Numbers," *BusinessWeek*, July 21, 2003, online.

Designing Effective Control Systems

Effective control systems maximize potential benefits and minimize dysfunctional behaviors. To achieve this, management needs to design control systems that (1) are based on valid performance standards, (2) communicate adequate information to employees, (3) are acceptable to employees, (4) use multiple approaches, and (5) recognize the relationship between empowerment and control.

Establish Valid Performance Standards An effective control system must be based on valid and accurate performance standards. The most effective standards, as discussed earlier, tend to be expressed in quantitative terms; they are objective rather than subjective. Also, the measures should not be capable of being easily sabotaged or faked. Moreover, the system must incorporate all important aspects of performance. For example, a company that just focused on sales volume without also looking at profitability might soon go out of business. As you learned earlier, unmeasured behaviors are neglected. But management also must defend against another problem: too many measures that create overcontrol and employee resistance. To make many controls tolerable, managers can devote attention to a few key areas while setting "satisfactory" performance standards in others. Or they can establish simple priorities. The purchasing agent may have to meet targets in the following sequence: quality, availability, cost, inventory level. Finally, managers can set tolerance ranges. For example, in financial budgeting optimistic, expected, and minimum levels sometimes are specified.

Many companies' budgets set cost targets only. This causes managers to control spending, but also to neglect earnings. At Emerson Electric, profit and growth are key measures. If an unanticipated opportunity to increase market share arises, managers can spend what they need to go after it. The phrase "it's not in the budget" is less likely to stifle people at Emerson than it is at most other companies.

This principle applies to nonfinancial aspects of performance as well. At Motorola, the recruiting department used to be measured by how much money it spent for each new hire. Now it is measured by how well its recruits subsequently perform.[26]

Provide Adequate Information Management must communicate to employees the importance and nature of the control system. Then people must receive feedback about their performance. Feedback motivates people and provides information that enables them to correct their own deviations from performance standards. Allowing people to initiate their own corrective action encourages self-control and reduces the need for outside supervision.

Chris Liddell, the chief financial officer for Microsoft, believes in "structured-process discipline," which he defines as "the ability to run internal processes—whether it's control processes, dealing with legislative issues [surrounding] Sarbanes-Oxley, running strategic-planning processes and budgeting—for all of those, the clarity that comes with great structure is fundamental for running a large company well." (*BusinessWeek Online*, April 26, 2005.)

Information should be as accessible as possible, particularly when people must make decisions quickly and frequently. For example, a national food company with its own truck fleet had a difficult problem. The company wanted drivers to go through customer sales records every night, insert new prices from headquarters every morning, and still make their rounds—an impossible set of demands. To solve this control problem, the company installed personal computers (PCs) in more than 1,000 delivery trucks. Now drivers use their PCs for constant communication with headquarters. Each night drivers send information about the stores, and each morning headquarters sends prices and recommended stock mixes.

In general, a manager designing a control system should evaluate the information system in terms of the following questions:

1. Does it provide people with data relevant to the decisions they need to make?
2. Does it provide the right amount of information to decision makers throughout the organization?
3. Does it provide enough information to each part of the organization about how other, related parts of the organization are functioning?[27]

Ensure Acceptability to Employees   Employees are less likely to resist a control system and exhibit dysfunctional behaviors if they accept the system. They are more likely to accept systems that have useful performance standards but are not overcontrolling. One Food Lion (a supermarket chain) store manager said to a *Fortune* reporter about standards he considered unreasonable, "I put in more and more and more time—a hundred hours a week—but no matter . . . I could never satisfy the supervisors . . . They wanted 100 percent conditions, seven days a week, 24 hours a day. And there's no . . . way you could do it."[28] Employees will find systems more acceptable if they believe the standards are possible to achieve.

The control system should emphasize positive behavior rather than focusing on controlling negative behavior alone. As noted earlier, companies such as Emerson look at profits rather than costs. As the former head of CMP Packaging, a leading packaging firm in Europe, Jean-Marie Descarpentries clearly preferred to highlight the positive: He had the heads of 94 profit centers project their best possible performance if everything went perfectly—to "dream the impossible dream"—and he avoided penalizing people who just missed their lofty goals by assessing them based on how they performed in previous years and against the performances of the best managers in the industry.[29] In other words, Descarpentries's approach exhibited the motivational quality we described in Chapter 13—"procedural justice." It gave employees the feeling that they were being evaluated by a fair process and was therefore more likely to be accepted by them.

Advantages of Collaboration

One of the best ways to establish reasonable standards and thus gain employee acceptance of the control system is to set standards participatively. As we discussed in Chapter 4, participation in decision making secures people's understanding and cooperation and results in better decisions. Allowing employees to collaborate in control-system decisions that affect their jobs directly will help overcome resistance and foster acceptance of the system. In addition, employees on the "front line" are more likely to know which standards are most important and practical, and they can inform a manager's judgment on these issues. Finally, if standards are established in collaboration with employees, managers will more easily obtain cooperation on solving the problem when deviations from standards occur.

Maintain Open Communication   When deviations from standards occur, it is important that employees feel able to report the deviations so the problem can be addressed. If employees come to feel that their managers want to hear only good news or, worse, if they fear reprisal for reporting bad news, even if it is not their fault, then any controls that are in place will be much less likely to be effective. Problems may go unreported

"I've learned that mistakes can often be as good a teacher as success."
Jack Welch

or, even worse, may reach the point where they become much more expensive or difficult to solve. But if managers create an environment of openness and honesty, one in which employees feel comfortable sharing even negative information, and are appreciated for doing so in a timely fashion, then the control system is much more likely to work effectively.

Nevertheless, managers may sometimes need to discipline employees who are failing to meet important standards. In such cases, an approach called *progressive discipline* is usually most effective. In this approach, clear standards are established, but failure to meet them is dealt with in a progressive or step-by-step process. For example, the first time an employee's sales performance has been worse than it should have been, the supervising manager may offer verbal counseling or coaching. If problems persist, the next step might be a written reprimand. This type of reasonable and considered approach signals to all employees that the manager is interested in improving their performance, not in punishing them.

Use Multiple Approaches   Multiple controls are necessary. For example, casinos exercise control over card dealers by (1) requiring them to have a card dealer's license before being hired; (2) using various forms of direct scrutiny, including up to three levels of direct supervision, closed-circuit cameras, and observation through one-way mirrors; and (3) requiring detailed paperwork to audit transfers of cash and cash equivalents.[30] As you learned earlier in this chapter, control systems generally should include both financial and nonfinancial performance targets and incorporate aspects of preliminary, concurrent, and feedback control. Effective control will also require managers and organizations to use many of the other techniques and practices of good management. For example, compensation systems will grant rewards for meeting standards and impose consequences if they are not met. And to gain employee acceptance, managers may also rely on many of the other communication and motivational tools that we discussed in earlier chapters, such as persuasion and positive reinforcement.

The Other Controls: Markets and Clans

Although the concept of control has always been a central feature of organizations, the principles and philosophies underlying its use are changing. In the past, control was focused almost exclusively on bureaucratic (and market) mechanisms. Generations of managers were taught that they could maximize productivity by regulating what employees did on the job—through standard operating procedures, rules, regulations, and close supervision. To increase output on an assembly line, for example, managers in the past tried to identify the "one best way" to approach the work and then to monitor employees' activities to make certain that they followed standard operating procedures. In short, they controlled work by dividing and simplifying tasks, a process we referred to in Chapter 1 as *scientific management*.

Although formal bureaucratic control systems are perhaps the most pervasive in organizations (and the most talked about in management textbooks), they are not always the most effective. *Market controls* and *clan controls* may both represent more flexible, though no less potent, approaches to regulating performance.

Market Control

In contrast to bureaucratic controls, market controls involve the use of economic forces—and the pricing mechanisms that accompany them—to regulate performance.

Market controls help maintain low prices.

The system works like this: In cases where output from an individual, department, or business unit has value to other people, a price can be negotiated for its exchange. As a market for these transactions becomes established, two effects occur:

- Price becomes an indicator of the value of the product or service.
- Price competition has the effect of controlling productivity and performance.

The basic principles that underlie market controls can operate at the corporate level, the business unit (or department) level, and the individual level. Figure 16.3 shows a few different ways in which market controls are used in an organization.

Market Controls at the Corporate Level   In large, diversified companies, market controls often are used to regulate independent business units. Particularly in large conglomerate firms that act as holding companies, business units typically are treated as profit centers that compete with one another. Top executives may place very few bureaucratic controls on business unit managers but use profit and loss data for evaluating performance. While decision making and power are decentralized to the business units, market controls ensure that business unit performance is in line with corporate objectives.

Use of market control mechanisms in this way has been criticized by those who insist that economic measures do not reflect the complete value of an organization adequately. Employees often suffer as diversified companies are repeatedly bought and sold based on market controls.

Market Controls at the Business Unit Level   Market control also can be used within business units to regulate exchanges among departments and functions. Transfer pricing is one method that organizations use to try to reflect market forces for internal transactions. A **transfer price** is the charge by one unit in the organization for

transfer price

Price charged by one unit for a product or service provided to another unit within the organization.

FIGURE 16.3
Examples of Market Control

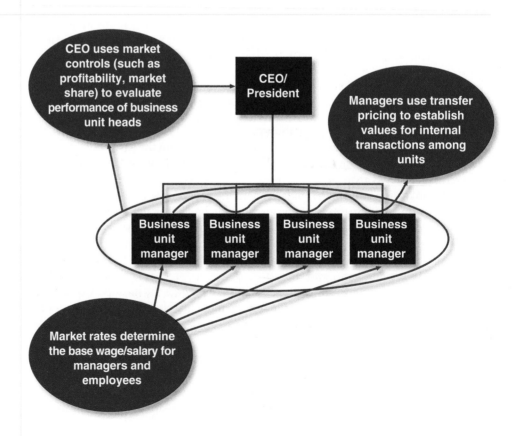

a product or service that it supplies to another unit of the same organization. For example, in automobile manufacturing, a transfer price may be affixed to components and subassemblies before they are shipped to subsequent business units for final assembly. Ideally, the transfer price reflects the price that the receiving business unit would have to pay for that product or service in the marketplace.

As organizations have more options to outsource products and services to external partners, market controls such as transfer prices provide natural incentives to keep costs down and quality up. Managers of such departments stay in close touch with prices in the marketplace to make sure their own costs are in line, and even try to improve the service they provide to increase their department's value to the organization. Consider the situation in which training and development activities can be done internally by the human resources department or outsourced to a consulting firm. If the human resources department cannot supply quality training at a reasonable price, there may be no reason for that department to exist inside the firm. Organizations such as Continental Airlines, IBM, and Corning have placed strict market controls on their human resources functions in order to manage costs and performance.[31]

Market Controls at the Individual Level   Market controls also are used at the individual level. For example, in situations where organizations are trying to hire employees, the supply and demand for particular skills influence the wages employees can expect to receive and the rate organizations are likely to pay. Employees or job candidates who have more valuable skills tend to be paid a higher wage. Of course, wages don't always reflect market rates—sometimes they are based (perhaps arbitrarily) on internal resource considerations—but the market rate is often the best indicator of an employee's potential worth to a firm.

Market-based controls such as these are important in that they provide a natural incentive for employees to enhance their skills and offer them to potential firms. Even after individuals gain employment, market-based wages are important as controls in that persons with higher economic value may be promoted faster to higher positions in the organization.

Market controls often are used by boards of directors to manage CEOs of major corporations. Ironically, CEOs usually are seen as the ones controlling everyone else in the company, but the fact is that the CEO is accountable to the board of directors, and the board must devise ways to ensure that the CEO acts in its interest. Absent board control, CEOs may act in ways that make them look good personally (such as making the company bigger or more diversified) but that do not lead to higher profits for the firm. And as recent corporate scandals have shown, without board control CEOs may also artificially inflate the firm's earnings, or not fully declare expenses, making the firm look much more successful than it really is.

Traditionally, boards have tried to control CEO performance mainly through the use of incentive plans, in addition to base salary. These typically include some type of bonus tied to short-term profit targets. In large U.S. companies, most CEO compensation is now at risk, meaning it depends mainly on the performance of the company. In addition to short-term incentives, boards use some type of long-term incentives linked to the firm's share price, usually through stock options, which we discussed in Chapter 10. However, the widespread fraud and financial scandals at companies like Enron, WorldCom, Adelphia Communications, and HealthSouth, and the indictment of their CEOs, have caused both boards and regulatory agencies to put more controls in place. CEOs can no longer claim ignorance about financial misstatements—they must personally certify in writing that their company's financial reports are accurate. In addition, CEOs are required to establish additional mechanisms and procedures within their companies to ensure that reporting violations are detected.[32]

As much as it would seem that market controls play a significant role in the salary of a professional baseball player or any other professional athlete, are the sometimes ridiculously high salaries that are paid for players today truly indicative of a player's skill—or something else? If the player doesn't live up to the expectation of the previously perceived skill level or, put another way, has a "bad year," should the organization be allowed to cut his pay?

Clan control empowers employees to meet performance standards.

Clan Control: The Role of Empowerment and Culture

Increasingly, managers are discovering that control systems based solely on bureaucratic and market mechanisms are insufficient for directing today's workforce. There are several reasons for this.

- *Employees' jobs have changed.* The nature of work is evolving. Employees working with computers, for example, have more variability in their jobs, and much of their work is intellectual and therefore invisible. Because of this, there is no one best way to perform a task, and programming or standardizing jobs becomes extremely difficult. Close supervision is also unrealistic since it is nearly impossible to supervise activities such as reasoning and problem solving.
- *The nature of management has changed.* The role of managers is evolving, too. It used to be the case that managers knew more about the job than employees did. Today, it is typical for employees to know more about their jobs than anyone else does. We refer to this as the shift from touch labor to knowledge work. When real expertise in organizations exists at the very lowest levels, hierarchical control becomes impractical.[33]
- *The employment relationship has changed.* The social contract at work is being renegotiated. It used to be that employees were most concerned about issues such as pay, job security, and the hours of work. Today, however, more and more employees want to be more fully engaged in their work, taking part in decision making, devising solutions to unique problems, and receiving assignments that are challenging and involving. They want to use their brains.

> "As a manager the important thing is not what happens when you are there, but what happens when you are not there."
>
> Ken Blanchand

For these three reasons, the concept of *empowerment* not only has become more popular in organizations; it has become a necessary aspect of a manager's repertoire of control. With no "one best way" to approach a job and no way to scrutinize what employees do every day, managers must empower employees to make decisions and trust that they will act in the best interests of the firm. But this does not mean giving up control. It means creating a strong culture of high standards and integrity so employees will exercise effective control on their own.

Connections: "THE ENVIRONMENT WAS RIPE FOR ABUSE"

At Enron, a risk-management group was supposed to screen proposals and review deals. But many of the unit's employees had every reason to sign off on deals: Their own performance reviews were partially done by the people whose deals they were approving. The process made honest evaluations virtually impossible. "If your boss was [fudging], and you have never worked anywhere else, you just assume that everybody fudges earnings," said one young Enron control person. "Once you get there and you realized how it was, do you stand up and lose your job? It was easy to get into 'Well, everybody else is doing it, so maybe it isn't so bad.'" The system bred a culture in which people were afraid to get crossways with someone who could screw up their reviews. Anyone who questioned suspect deals quickly learned to accept assurances of outside lawyers and accountants. There was little scrutiny of whether the earnings were real or how they were booked. "That kind of culture has a subtle encouragement to cut corners and to cheat," said one observer. "You can see everyone else moving forward, and you have to keep up." At other companies, by contrast, an emphasis on individual achievement is balanced by a strong focus on process and a set of guiding values.

Recall our extensive discussion of organization culture in Chapter 2. If the organization's culture encourages the wrong behaviors, then an effort to impose effective

1. ***Put control where the operation is.*** Layers of hierarchy, close supervision, and checks and balances are quickly disappearing and being replaced with self-guided teams. For centuries even the British Empire—as large as it was—never had more than six levels of management including the Queen.

2. ***Use "real time" rather than after-the-fact controls.*** Issues and problems must be solved at the source by the people doing the actual work. Managers become a resource to help out the team.

3. ***Rebuild the assumptions underlying management control to build on trust rather than distrust.*** Today's "high-flex" organizations are based on empowerment, not obedience. Information must facilitate decision making, not police it.

4. ***Move to control based on peer norms.*** Clan control is a powerful thing. Workers in Japan, for example, have been known to commit suicide rather than disappoint or lose face within their team. Although this is extreme, it underlines the power of peer influence. The Japanese have a far more homogeneous culture and set of values than we do. In North America, we must build peer norms systematically and put much less emphasis on managing by the numbers.

5. **Rebuild the incentive systems to reinforce responsiveness and teamwork.** The twin goals of adding value to the customer and team performance must become the dominant raison d'être of the measurement systems.

TABLE 16.7
Management Control in an Empowered Setting

SOURCE: Gerald H. B. Ross, "Revolution in Management Control," *Management Accounting*, November 1990, pp. 23–27. Reprinted by permission.

controls will be severely hindered. But if managers create and reinforce a strong culture that encourages correct behavior, one in which everyone understands management's values and expectations and is motivated to act in accordance with them, then clan control can be a very effective control tool.[34] As we noted at the beginning of this chapter, *clan control* involves creating relationships built on mutual respect and encouraging each individual to take responsibility for his or her actions. Employees work within a guiding framework of values, and they are expected to use good judgment. For example, at Nordstrom, the fashion retailer, instead of a thick manual laying out company policies, employees are simply given a five- by eight-inch card that reads: "Use good judgment in all situations. There will be no additional rules." (See page 67.) The emphasis in an empowered organization is on satisfying customers, not on pleasing the boss. Mistakes are tolerated as the unavoidable by-product of dealing with change and uncertainty and are viewed as opportunities to learn. And team members learn together. Table 16.7 provides a set of guidelines for managing in an empowered world.

The resiliency and time investment of clan control are a "double-edged sword." Clan control takes a long time to develop and an even longer time to change. This gives an organization stability and direction during periods of upheaval in the environment or the organization (e.g., during changes in the top management). Yet if managers want to establish a new culture—a new form of clan control—they must help employees unlearn the old values and embrace the new. We will talk about this transition process more in the final chapter of this book (Chapter 18, "Creating and Managing Change").

EPILOGUE

"THE ENVIRONMENT WAS RIPE FOR ABUSE"

In hindsight, Enron's management was asleep at the wheel or had little supervision, as managers crafted private partnerships that allowed the company to move millions of dollars of debt off its balance sheet. But this sad saga has no shortage of culprits—accountants, the company's board, stock analysts, and even shareholders all bear some of the responsibility for not realizing sooner that something untoward was going on at Enron.

- **Where was management?** How many times must it be said: A company chairman needs to stay in touch with his or her company's business. A company board must understand how a company actually works—and ask questions if it doesn't understand. And managers need to manage. There were so many checkpoints at which those involved in managing and monitoring the company should have blown the whistle. Control doesn't work if no one exercises it, or if the culture rewards cutting corners.
- **Where were the auditors?** Financial alchemy was behind Enron's transformation from a staid pipeline company to a giant trader of commodities. Andersen admitted that it didn't make the necessary adjustment in its accounting procedures

to reflect that change. Granted, Enron's financial structure was a labyrinth. But no matter how complex, it's the job of auditors to be vigilant, especially when the numbers don't add up or make sense.
- **Where were the analysts and the shareholders?** Investors also must share some of the blame for Enron's tumble. They were so in awe of the company's stock performance that many didn't seem to care how it worked. Instead, stock analysts and credit-rating agencies remained optimistic until the bitter end. On the day before Enron collapsed on November 28, six Wall Street research analysts had a strong-buy rating on the company. The lesson here is that when a company stock looks too good to be true, it probably is.

KEY TERMS

Accounting audits, p. 530

Activity-based costing (ABC), p. 531

Assets, p. 531

Balance sheet, p. 531

Budgeting, p. 528

Bureaucratic control, p. 521

Clan control, p. 521

Concurrent control, p. 525

Control, p. 520

Current ratio, p. 534

Debt-equity ratio, p. 534

External audit, p. 528

Feedback control, p. 525

Feedforward control, p. 525

Internal audit, p. 528

Liabilities, p. 531

Management audit, p. 528

Management myopia, p. 534

Market control, p. 521

Principle of exception, p. 524

Profit and loss statement, p. 533

Return on investment (ROI), p. 534

Standard, p. 522

Stockholders' equity, p. 532

Transfer price, p. 540

SUMMARY OF LEARNING OBJECTIVES

Now that you have studied Chapter 16, you should know:

Why companies develop control systems for employees.

Left to their own devices, employees may act in ways that do not benefit the organization. Control systems are designed to eliminate idiosyncratic behavior and keep employees directed toward achieving the goals of the firm. Control systems are a steering mechanism for guiding resources, for helping each individual act in behalf of the organization.

How to design a basic bureaucratic control system.

The design of a basic control system involves four steps: (1) setting performance standards, (2) measuring performance, (3) comparing performance with the standards, and (4) eliminating unfavorable deviations by taking corrective action. Performance standards should be valid, and should cover issues such as quantity, quality, time, and cost. Once performance is compared with the standards, the principle of exception suggests that the manager needs to direct attention to the exceptional cases that have significant deviations. Then the manager takes the action most likely to solve the problem.

The purposes for using budgets as a control device.

Budgets combine the benefits of feedforward, concurrent, and feedback controls. They are used as an initial guide for allocating resources, a reference point for using funds, and a feedback mech-

anism for comparing actual levels of sales and expenses to their expected levels. Recently, companies have modified their budgeting processes to allocate costs over basic processes (such as customer service) rather than to functions or departments. By changing the way they prepare budgets, many companies have discovered ways to eliminate waste and improve business processes.

How to interpret financial ratios and other financial controls.

The basic financial statements are the balance sheet and the profit and loss statement. The balance sheet compares the value of company assets to the obligations the company owes to owners and creditors. The profit and loss statement shows company income relative to costs incurred. In addition to these statements, companies look at liquidity ratios (whether the company can pay its short-term debts), leverage ratios (the extent to which the company is funding operations by going into debt), and profitability ratios (profit relative to investment). These ratios provide a goal for managers as well as a standard against which to evaluate performance.

The procedures for implementing effective control systems.

To maximize the effectiveness of controls, managers should (1) design control systems based on valid performance standards, (2) ensure that employees are provided with adequate information about their performance, (3) encourage employees to participate in the control system's design, (4) see that multiple approaches are used (such as bureaucratic, market, and clan control), and (5) recognize the relationship between empowerment and control.

The different ways in which market control mechanisms are used by organizations.

Market controls can be used at the level of the corporation, the business unit or department, or the individual. At the corporate level, business units are evaluated against one another based on profitability. At times less profitable businesses are sold while more profitable businesses receive more resources. Within business units, transfer pricing may be used to approximate market mechanisms to control transactions among departments. At the individual level, market mechanisms control the wage rate of em-

ployees and can be used to evaluate the performance of individual managers.

How clan control can be approached in an empowered organization.

Approaching control from a centralized, mechanistic viewpoint is increasingly impractical. In today's organizations, it is difficult to program "one best way" to approach work, and it is often difficult to monitor performance. To be responsive to customers, companies must harness the expertise of employees and give them the freedom to act on their own initiative. To maintain control while empowering employees, companies should (1) use self-guided teams, (2) allow decision making at the source of the problems, (3) build trust and mutual respect, (4) base control on a guiding framework of norms, and (5) use incentive systems that encourage teamwork.

DISCUSSION QUESTIONS

1. Can you think of an instance in which an organization did not use some form of control? What happened?

2. How are leadership and control different? How are planning and control different? How are structure and control different?

3. Of the four steps in the control process, which is the most important?

4. What are the pros and cons of bureaucratic controls such as rules, procedures, and supervision?

5. How effective is clan control as a control mechanism? What are its strengths? Its limitations? When would a manager rely on clan control the most?

6. Does empowerment imply the loss of control? Why or why not?

CONCLUDING CASE

Parker Mountain Products, Inc.

COMPANY HISTORY

The New England region of the U.S. includes a beautiful coastal stretch that extends from Maine to Rhode Island, through the states of New Hampshire, Massachusetts, and Connecticut. The area is famous for its summer tourism, which includes beaches, quaint villages and towns, restaurants, shops, historic sites and landmarks, and lobsters.

Shortly after World War II, Ernest Parker returned to his hometown of Rochester, New Hampshire, and built a small factory that produces low-end glass and ceramic regional souvenirs. These products include wine glasses, general glassware, ceramic cups and bowls, and small platters. Each of these is decorated with a variety of painted images and words related to the specific coastal tourist towns and markets—pictures of lobsters, gulls, ocean waves, famous towns, and famous sites.

The factory hasn't changed much and still features most of the original, very labor-intensive production equipment. Virtually all of the office and administrative work is done by hand. Ernest has provided steady employment for 35 production and support staff, and has grown the business at a rate of about 5 percent per year (in sales). The most recent profit and loss statement is shown:

Parker Mountain Products, Inc. Profit and Loss Statement—2004	
Sales	$ 2,000,000
Cost of Sales*	990,000
Gross Profit	$ 1,010,000
Expenses	930,000
Net Income	$ 80,000

*Includes direct materials only.

The entire production is sold through a small number of manufacturer's reps, wholesalers, and brokers. While the opportunity was always there to sell direct, Ernest chose to focus all of his efforts on the production side of the business, allowing others to market, sell, and distribute the products to retail shops, hotels, and other vendors. The industry average or norm for profits is between 5 and 7 percent (net income to sales).

CURRENT SITUATION

Having now reached the age of 75, Ernest has decided to retire and turn the business over to his grandsons Chris and Ben, two young and ambitious entrepreneurs who recently graduated with degrees in business and computer science.

Chris and Ben are anxious to modernize the plant and to incorporate many of the new technologies that they have learned about in school. They plan to improve efficiency on the produc-tion side, and to develop a variety of direct niche markets to complement their wholesale distribution on the marketing and sales side. The opportunity to add, drop and/or shift the product mix, and to increase production and sales exists. In order to prop-erly analyze and act on this, they have asked their bookkeeper to provide more specific production and cost data.

This information is presented below:

Product Line	Units Produced	Selling Price per Unit	Cost of Goods Sold per Unit	Total Variable Costs per Year
Platter	300,000	$2.00	$0.60	$240,000
Cups	200,000	2.50	1.50	160,000
Bowls	100,000	2.00	0.20	80,000
General glassware	100,000	1.00	0.70	80,000
Wine glasses	300,000	2.00	1.40	240,000

The total variable costs of $800,000 are assigned or charged to each product line based on the number of units produced. To-tal fixed costs for the factory are $80,000; selling and administra-tive costs for the total company are $50,000. The current factory is operating at about 85 percent of production capacity. While Chris and Ben know that production could be increased without incurring any extra expense beyond direct materials, they are anxious to analyze and possibly invest in computer-aided design and manufacturing software and equipment.

Chris and Ben also know that the selling price could be in-creased by 15 percent as a result of a direct sales program. Their only uncertainty or fear is in disrupting the long-standing rela-tionships that exist with the various manufacturer's reps, whole-salers, and brokers who have been able to sell all of the company's production for many years. They are afraid of 'biting the hand that feeds them' by selling to an end-user that currently buys from one of their own distributors. They are also anxious to analyze and pos-sibly invest in administrative and sales software.

QUESTIONS

1. As a first step, conduct a financial analysis of current operations. (*Hint:* Reformat the income statement to include individual prod-uct lines as well as total company.)

2. Given the information provided, list and briefly describe some of the new production, administrative and selling technologies that the new partners should consider.

3. Advise the new partners as to the specific analysis and decision-making process that they should use regarding investment in new technology. Consider the history of the company and the fact that the majority of the current workforce has little or no knowledge of or experience with computer technology.

EXPERIENTIAL EXERCISES

16.1 Safety Program

OBJECTIVE

To understand some of the specific activities that fall under the management functions *planning, organizing, controlling and staffing,* and *directing.*

INSTRUCTIONS

After reading the following case, briefly describe the kinds of steps you would take as production manager in trying to solve your safety problem. Be sure to relate your answer specifically to the activities of *planning, organizing, controlling and staffing,* and *directing.*

MANAGING THE VAMP CO. SAFETY PROGRAM

If there are specific things that a manager does, how are they done? What does it "look like" when one manages? The follow-ing describes a typical situation in which a manager performs managerial functions:

As production manager of the Vamp Stamping Company, you've become quite concerned over the metal stamping shop's safety record. Accidents that resulted in operators' missing time on the job have increased quite rapidly in the past year. These more serious accidents have jumped from 3 percent of all acci-dents reported to a current level of 10 percent.

Because you're concerned about your workers' safety as well as the company's ability to meet its customers' orders, you want to reduce this downtime accident rate to its previous level or lower within the next six months.

You call the accident trend to the attention of your production supervisors, pointing out the seriousness of the situation and their continuing responsibility to enforce the gloves and safety goggles rules. Effective immediately, every supervisor will review his or her accident reports for the past year, file a report summarizing these accidents with you, and state their intended actions to correct recurring causes of the accidents. They will make out weekly safety reports as well as meet with you every Friday to discuss what is being done and any problems they are running into.

You request the union steward's cooperation in helping the safety supervisor set up a short program on shop safety practices.

Because the machine operators are having the accidents, you encourage your supervisors to talk to their workers and find out what they think can be done to reduce the downtime accident rate to its previous level.

While the program is going on, you review the weekly reports, looking for patterns that will tell you how effective the program is and where the trouble spots are. If a supervisor's operators are not decreasing their accident rate, you discuss the matter in considerable detail with the supervisor and his or her key workers.

SOURCE: From Theodore T. Herbert, *The New Management: Study Guide,* 4th ed., p. 41. Copyright © 1983 Pearson Education. Reprinted by permission of Pearson Education, Inc., Upper Saddle River, NJ.

16.2 Preliminary, Concurrent, and Feedback Control

OBJECTIVES

1. To demonstrate the need for control procedures.
2. To gain experience in determining when to use preliminary, concurrent, and feedback controls.

INSTRUCTIONS

1. Read the text materials on preliminary, concurrent, and feedback control.
2. Read the Control Problem Situation and be prepared to resolve those control problems in a group setting.
3. Your instructor will divide the class into small groups. Each group completes the Preliminary, Concurrent, and Feedback Control Worksheet by achieving consensus on the types of control that should be applied in each situation. The group also develops responses to the discussion questions.
4. After the class reconvenes, group spokespersons present group findings.

DISCUSSION QUESTIONS

1. For which control(s) was it easier to determine application? For which was it harder?
2. Would this exercise be better assigned to groups or to individuals?

CONTROL PROBLEM SITUATION

Your management consulting team has just been hired by Technocron International, a rapidly growing producer of electronic surveillance devices that are sold to commercial and government end users. Some sales are made through direct selling, and some through industrial resellers. Direct-sale profits are being hurt by what seem to be exorbitant expenses paid to a few of the salespeople, especially those who fly all over the world in patterns that suggest little planning and control. There is trouble among the resellers because standard contracts have not been established and each reseller has an entirely different contractual relationship. Repayment schedules vary widely from customer to customer. Also, profits are reduced by the need to specialize most orders, making mass production almost impossible. However, no effort has been made to create interchangeable components. There are also tremendous inventory problems. Some raw materials and parts are bought in such small quantities that new orders are being placed almost daily. Other orders are so large that there is hardly room to store everything. Many of these purchased components are later found to be defective and unusable, causing production delays. Engineering changes are made that make large numbers of old components still in storage obsolete. Some delays result from designs that are very difficult to assemble, and assemblers complain that their corrective suggestions are ignored by engineering. To save money, untrained workers are hired and assigned to experienced "worker-buddies" who are expected to train them on the job. However, many of the new people are too poorly educated to understand their assignments, and their worker-buddies wind up doing a great deal of their work. This, along with the low pay and lack of consideration from engineering, is causing a great deal of worker unrest and talk of forming a union. Last week alone there were nine new worker grievances filed, and the U.S. Equal Employment Opportunity Commission has just announced intentions to investigate two charges of discrimination on the part of the company. There is also a serious cash-flow problem, as a number of long-term debts are coming due at the same time. The cash-flow problem could be relieved somewhat if some of the accounts payable could be collected.

The CEO manages corporate matters through five functional divisions: operations, engineering, marketing, finance, and human resources management and general administration.

Preliminary, Concurrent, and Feedback Control Worksheet

Technocron International is in need of a variety of controls. Complete the following matrix by noting the preliminary, concurrent, and feedback controls that are needed in each of the five functional divisions.

Divisions	Preliminary Controls	Concurrent Controls	Feedback Controls
HRM and general administration	_____	_____	_____
Operations	_____	_____	_____
Engineering	_____	_____	_____
Marketing	_____	_____	_____
Finance	_____	_____	_____

Chapter **17**

CHAPTER 17
Managing Technology and Innovation

The imperatives of technology and organization, not the images of ideology, are what determine the shape of economic society.

— **John Kenneth Galbraith**

CHAPTER OUTLINE

LEARNING OBJECTIVES

After studying Chapter 17, you will know:

1. The processes involved in the development of new technologies.

2. How technologies proceed through a life cycle.

3. How to manage technology for competitive advantage.

4. How to assess technology needs.

5. The key factors to consider when making decisions about technological innovation.

6. The roles different people play in managing technology.

7. How to develop an innovative organization.

8. The key characteristics of successful development projects.

TAKING AIM AT IPOD

Sometimes wanna be your lover /
Sometimes wanna be your friend

Jason Smikle couldn't get the song out of his head. A freshman at Temple University, the 19-year-old hummed the tune by hip-hop impresario Ludacris, in the shower, over breakfast, and as he walked to class. On a recent 80-degree day in Philadelphia, he started singing the lyrics while he and a buddy relaxed on the campus quad. His friend whipped out his LG mobile phone, tapped a couple of keys, and presto, the melody wafted into the air. "So cool," Smikle recalls. He only wished he could download the song to his own phone on the spot.

Jason, your wish may soon be granted. Mobile phones that rock, jam, thunder, and swing are on the way. Wireless operators around the globe are working with music studios, phone makers, and artists such as Sean "P. Diddy" Combs in a sweeping effort to turn the mobile phone into a go-anywhere digital jukebox. Foreign carriers such as Vodafone and SK Telecom are leading the way, and U.S. wireless players are following fast. Verizon Wireless, Sprint, and Cingular Wireless are expected to unveil services for downloading music directly to wireless phones.

With innovative services and snazzier phones, the telecom players figure they can swipe a chunk of the digital music market that Apple Computer Inc. cracked open with its iconic iPod. That sets the stage for a battle between two industries. On one side are Apple and the other tech players concentrated in Silicon Valley that see the computer as central to the future of music. On the other are telecom companies, from Finland to South Korea to the United States, that think the mobile phone can become the center of this emerging world.

The telecom approach has several strengths Apple can't match. For starters, a quarter of the world's population already has a mobile phone. That's 1.4 billion people, compared with 10 million iPods sold to date. Most of those cell-phone toters pay a monthly phone bill, making it a snap to add a music charge. Perhaps most important, wireless technology could provide access anytime, anywhere to millions of songs. "You don't have to be a genius to see that the phone will be your own portable stereo that's with you wherever you go," says Jordan Schur, co-president of Geffen Records, whose artists include Snoop Dogg and Garbage.

To Apple, this threat may look more than a little overblown. After all, the company's elegant iPod and easy-to-use iTunes have been such breakthroughs that they sparked a musical revolution. The carefully crafted combo gives consumers a no-hassle way to buy tunes on the Net and carry every single song they own with them. Plus, Apple has learned from the past. Some 20 years ago it lost its lead in the personal computer industry by insisting on complete control over its technology. But Apple has learned from its mistakes and is showing much more flexibility these days. It

opened up its iTunes store to people using computers with Microsoft Corp.'s operating system and let partner Hewlett-Packard Co. distribute its own version of the iPod. It's also developing an iPod phone with Motorola Inc. that the pair have started marketing to wireless operators. If that happens, the carrier would not build its own music store and instead send its customers to iTunes.

What will come out of all this is not just a battle of sharp words and elbows but also a new round of innovation in digital music. Apple and other MP3 player makers could add wireless technology to their devices or help develop a crop of music phones. As hundreds of millions of mobile devices around the world go musical, there will be an explosion in the possibilities for marketing, distributing, and listening to music. "A lot of people are paying attention to this new frontier and what its potential can be," says Virgin Mobile CEO Daniel H. Schulman.

Source for Prologue, Connections, Epilogue: Roger O. Crockett, "iPod Killers?" *BusinessWeek*, April 25, 2005, online.

Technological innovation is daunting in its complexity and pace of change. And as you have no doubt figured out, it is therefore vital for a firm's competitive advantage. Not long ago, new products took years to plan and develop, were standardized and mass produced, and were pushed onto the market through extensive selling and promotional campaigns. With sales lives for these products measured in decades, production processes used equipment dedicated to making only those standardized products and achieved savings through economies of scale. But today's customers often demand products that have yet to be designed. Product development is now a race to become the first to introduce innovative products—products whose lives often are measured in months as they are quickly replaced by other, even more technologically sophisticated products.

Today's managers and organizations are likely to depend on effective management of technology not only to carry out their basic tasks but, even more important, to ensure the continuing competitiveness of their products or services. In a marketplace where technology and rapid innovation are critical for success, managers must understand how technologies emerge, develop, and affect the ways organizations compete and the ways people work. This chapter discusses how technology can affect an organization's competitiveness and how to integrate technology into the organization's competitive strategy. Then we assess the technological needs of the organization and the means by which these needs can be met.

Technology and Innovation

technology

The systematic application of scientific knowledge to a new product, process, or service.

innovation

A change in method or technology; a positive, useful departure from previous ways of doing things.

In Chapter 9 ("Organizational Agility") we defined **technology** as the methods, processes, systems, and skills used to transform resources into products. More broadly speaking, we can think of technology as the commercialization of science: the systematic application of scientific knowledge to a new product, process, or service. In this sense, technology is embedded in every product, service, and procedure used or produced.[1]

If we find a better product, process, or procedure to accomplish our task, we have an innovation. **Innovation** is a change in method or technology—a positive, useful departure from previous ways of doing things. Two fundamental types of innovation are process and product innovation. *Process innovations* are changes that affect the way outputs are produced. In Chapter 9 we discussed flexible manufacturing practices such as just-in-time, massed customization, and simultaneous engineering. Each of these innovations has changed the way products are manufactured and distributed. In contrast, *product innovations* are changes in the actual outputs (products and services) themselves.[2]

There are definable and predictable patterns in the way technologies emerge, develop, and are replaced. Critical forces converge to create new technologies, which then follow well-defined life-cycle patterns. Understanding the forces driving techno-logical development and the patterns they follow can help a manager anticipate, mon-itor, and manage technologies more effectively.

Innovation is a
key to
competitiveness.

- First, there must be a *need*, or *demand*, for the technology. Without this need driving the process, there is no reason for technological innovation to occur.
- Second, meeting the need must be theoretically possible, and the *knowledge* to do so must be available from basic science.
- Third, we must be able to *convert* the scientific knowledge into practice in both engineering and economic terms. If we can theoretically do something but doing it is economically impractical, the technology cannot be expected to emerge.
- Fourth, the *funding, skilled labor, time, space*, and *other resources* needed to develop the technology must be available.
- Finally, *entrepreneurial initiative* is needed to identify and pull all the necessary elements together.

The Technology Life Cycle

Technological innovations typically follow a relatively predictable pattern called the **technology life cycle.** Figure 17.1 depicts the pattern. The cycle begins with the recognition of a need and a perception of a means by which the need can be satisfied through applied science or knowledge. The knowledge and ideas are brought together and developed, culminating in a new technological innovation. Early progress can be slow in these formative years as competitors experiment a great deal with product de-sign and operational characteristics to meet consumer needs. This is where the rate of product innovation tends to be highest. For example, during the early years of the auto industry, companies tried a wide range of machines, including electric and steam-driven cars, to determine which product would be most effective. Eventually the in-ternal combustion engine emerged as the dominant design, and the number of product innovations leveled off.

Once early problems are resolved and a dominant design emerges, improvements come more from process innovations to refine the technology. At this point managers can gain an advantage by pursuing process efficiencies and cost competitiveness. In the auto example, as companies settled on a product standard, they began leveraging the benefits of mass production and vertical integration to improve productivity. These

technology life cycle

A predictable pattern followed by a technological innovation, from its inception and development to market saturation and replacement.

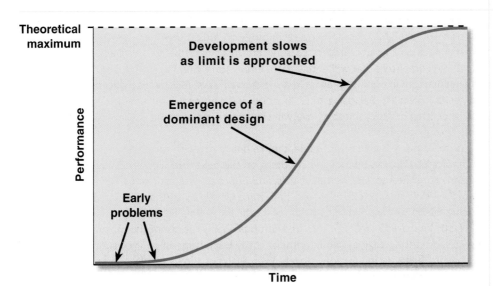

FIGURE 17.1
The Technology Life Cycle

> "I think there is a world market for maybe five computers."
> Thomas Watson, IBM Chairman, in 1943

process innovations were instrumental in lowering production costs and bringing the price of automobiles in line with consumer budgets.[3]

Eventually the new technology begins to reach the upper limits of both its performance capabilities and the spread of its usage. Development slows and becomes increasingly costly, and the market becomes saturated (i.e., there are few new customers). The technology can remain in this mature stage for some time—as in the case of autos—or can be replaced quickly by another technology offering superior performance or economic advantage. The evolution of life cycles can take decades or even centuries, as in the case of iron and steelmaking technologies. A dramatic example of technology evolution can be found in the recorded-music industry, which moved from the relatively primitive device Thomas Edison invented through the vinyl record to the cassette tape to the digitally recorded CD and then to highly miniaturized but memory-intensive music players like iPod. And as we discussed in our chapter opening, the iPod is now being challenged in turn by cell phone manufacturers, with new wireless phones that will download a large number of songs directly, even without a PC.

As this example shows, a technology life cycle can be made up of many individual *product* life cycles. Each of these products performs a similar task—delivering recorded music to a listener—yet each product is an improvement over its predecessors. In this way, technological development involves significant innovations, often representing entirely new technologies, followed by a large number of small, incremental innovations. Ongoing development of a technology increases the benefits gained through its use, makes the technology easier to use, and allows more applications, as the accompanying item on e-commerce suggests. In the process, the use of the technology expands to new adopters.

Taking E-Commerce to the Next Level

FROM THE PAGES OF ▼

BusinessWeek

This summer, Chester Yeum was watching Tom Cruise's sci-fi thriller *Minority Report*, set in the year 2054, when he realized he was helping make an element of it a reality today. The epiphany came as Cruise strode through a shopping concourse and impromptu, personalized advertising pitches buffeted him from all sides—just the kind of location-based marketing Yeum is trying to bring to market.

Yeum's first step to a 2054-like world is SpotMeeting.com, a location-based online dating service. Romance seekers are linked to others near them through software that identifies their location. Today the site maps each member's Internet address, but an upcoming version will use global positioning technology to locate members on the go. Eventually, Yeum hopes to sign up retailers to send his customers pitches via their cell phones or handheld computers that will entice them into a store they're approaching. "I don't believe the mainstream market is ready for that right now," says Yeum, who thinks people first have to get comfortable disclosing their location and personal information. Once his site establishes itself in dating, he says, "we will stream in supplemental applications that will plug right into e-commerce."

With so many e-tailers profitable, they're finally ready to move ahead with adding new technologies that can take online shopping to the next level. For shoppers, the next level means more interactivity, better visuals, and improved search results with more product information. It also means being watched more closely by sites and receiving personalized pitches based on past browsing behavior—which can be a little creepy.

Vastly improved search and site navigation probably represent the most important sales drivers for cutting-edge e-commerce sites today. But cutting-edge Web sites are also tracking buyers' behavior much more closely. Web analytics allows retailers to predict what customers might want to buy next by looking at their past purchasing history, as well as data generated from other shoppers. With so much data available at their fingertips, more retailers will be using Web analytics to personalize e-mail. For example, customers might get an e-mail letting them know that a sweater they perused but never bought is now available for 10 percent off. Also important, if less whizzy, retailers' Web sites are finally achieving long-promised levels of interactivity. HomeDepot.com recently added a new application that allows customers to preview color selections on an assortment of sample walls.

Creating a richer, more realistic online shopping experience is just one way retailers are getting customers to buy more. They're also employing so-called smart-pricing technology to optimize how much they charge for items on their sites. Plus, they're learning they can generate more sales by adding more information, such as customer ratings and reviews.

Too much computer-driven personalization can backfire, though, as Tom Cruise's character learned in the Big Brother–style world of *Minority Report.* "Retailers have to be careful to make sure shoppers don't feel they're being watched a little too closely," says one analyst. That's why Yeum is happy to take a slow and steady pace in bringing his brand of e-commerce to the next level. Your favorite clothing retailer won't be broadcasting a personalized message to you as you walk by for a while yet. But Yeum, for one, is confident that'll happen sooner than you might think.

SOURCE: Amey Stone, "Taking E-Commerce to the Next Level," *BusinessWeek*, August 31, 2004, online

E-tailer Red Envelope focuses on providing customers with items they can't find anywhere else. How does this strategy benefit a company? In an age of e-commerce, what might be the drawbacks to this strategy?

The Diffusion of Technological Innovations

Like the technology life cycle we discussed earlier, the adoption of new technology over time follows an S-shaped pattern (see the top line in Figure 17.2). The percentage of people using the technology is small in the beginning but increases dramatically as the technology succeeds and spreads through the population. Eventually the number of users peaks and levels off when the market for the technology is saturated. This pattern, first observed in 1903, has been verified with many new technologies and ideas in a wide variety of industries and settings.[4]

The adopters of a new technology fall into five groups (see the bottom line in Figure 17.2). Each group presents different challenges and opportunities to managers who want to market a new technology or product innovation.

The first group, representing approximately 2.5 percent of adopters, consists of the *innovators.* Typically, innovators are adventurous and willing to take risks. They are willing to pay a premium for the latest and newest technology or product to come along, and to champion it if it meets with their approval. The enthusiasm of innovator-adopters is no guarantee of success—for example, the product may still turn out to be too expensive for the general market. But a lack of enthusiasm among this group is often a sign that the new technology has serious problems and more development is needed.

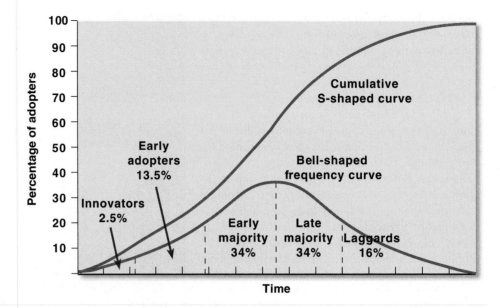

FIGURE 17.2
Technology Dissemination Pattern and Adopter Categories

The next 13.5 percent of adopters are *early adopters*. This group is critical to the success of a new technology, because its members include well-respected opinion leaders. Early adopters often are the people or organizations to which others look for leadership, ideas, and up-to-date technological information. Innovators and early adopters are extremely important in new-product launches, and marketing managers often spend heavily in promotion among these groups to generate a groundswell of enthusiasm.

The next group, representing 34 percent of adopters, is the *early majority*. These adopters are more deliberate and take longer to decide to use something new. Often they are important members of a community or industry, but typically not the leaders. It may take a while for the technology or new product to spread to this group, but once it does, use will begin to proliferate into the mainstream.

Representing the next 34 percent are the *late majority*. Members of this group are more skeptical of technological change and approach innovation with great caution, often adopting only out of economic necessity or increasing social pressure.

The final 16 percent are *laggards*. Often isolated and highly conservative in their views, laggards are extremely suspicious of innovation and change.

Connections: TAKING AIM AT IPOD

Why are telecom players looking to steal some of Apple's thunder now? Technological advances in storage, compression, battery life, and wireless networks are making it easier to receive and store high-quality music on phones. Korea's Samsung Electronics just introduced a phone with a 3-gigabyte hard drive, enough to store 1,000 songs. A 10-gig phone could hit the market within two years. And the future looks wide open. Research firm Strategy Analytics estimates that in 2008 half of the 860 million cell phones sold will be able to store and play songs, up from 8 percent today. Wireless operators have also seen what a gold mine music can be. Ringtones, the snippets of songs you can put on your phone to customize your ring, have become a huge hit. Ringtone revenues have hit $5.8 billion, and that's expected to reach $9.4 billion in 2008. The success of ringtones has given operators the confidence to push digital music even further. Also, because wireless companies already bill mobile customers each month, they have a system in place for handling music charges—one that doesn't require sharing fees with Visa or Master Card.

The speed with which an innovation spreads depends largely on five attributes. An innovation will spread quickly if it:

1. Has a great advantage over its predecessor.
2. Is compatible with existing systems, procedures, infrastructures, and ways of thinking.
3. Has less rather than greater complexity.
4. Can be tried or tested easily without significant cost or commitment.
5. Can be observed and copied easily.

Designing products with these technological considerations in mind can make a critical difference in their success.

Technological Innovation in a Competitive Environment

Discussions about technology life cycles and diffusion patterns may imply that technological change occurs naturally or automatically. Just the opposite; change is neither easy nor natural in organizations (we discuss change more fully in the next chapter). Decisions about technology and innovation are very strategic and managers need to approach them in a systematic way.

In Chapter 4, we discussed two generic strategies a company can use to position itself in the market: low cost and differentiation. With *low-cost* leadership, the company maintains an advantage because it has a lower cost than its competitors. With a *differentiation* strategy, the advantage comes from having a unique product or service for which customers are willing to pay a premium price.[5] Technological innovations can support either of these strategies: They can be used to gain cost advantage through pioneering lower-cost product designs and creating low-cost ways to perform needed operations, or they can support differentiation by pioneering unique products or services that increase buyer value and thus command premium prices.

Innovation can improve any bottom-line practice.

In some cases, a new technology can completely change the rules of competition within an industry.[6] Leading companies that respond ineffectively to technological opportunities can falter while new companies emerge as the dominant competitors. For example, Bill Gates's shrewd decision to make the details of Microsoft's operating system widely available let software writers easily develop products for it, helping Microsoft achieve its dominant position today.

But industries seldom are transformed overnight. Typically, signals of a new technology's impact are visible well in advance, leaving time for companies and people to respond. For example, almost any competitor in the telecommunications industry fully understands the potential value of cellular technology. Often the key issue is not *whether* to adopt a new technology but *when* to adopt it and how to integrate the change with the organization's operating practices and strategies.

Technology Leadership

The adage "timing is everything" is applied to many things, ranging from financial investments to telling jokes. It also applies to the development and exploitation of new technologies. Industry leaders such as Xerox, 3M, Hewlett-Packard, and Merck built and now maintain their competitive positions through early development and application of new technologies. However, technology leadership imposes costs and risks, and it is not the best approach for every organization (see Table 17.1).[7]

Advantages of Technology Leadership
What makes innovators and technology leadership attractive is the potential for high profits and first-mover advantages. Being the first to market with new technologies can provide significant competitive advantage. If technology leadership increases an organization's efficiency relative to competitors, it achieves a cost advantage. The organization can use the advantage to reap

Advantages	Disadvantages
First-mover advantage	Greater risks
Little or no competition	Cost of technology development
Greater efficiency	Costs of market development and customer education
Higher profit margins	
Sustainable advantage	Infrastructure costs
Reputation for innovation	Costs of learning and eliminating defects
Establishment of entry barriers	Possible cannibalization of existing products
Occupying of best market niches	
Opportunities to learn	

TABLE 17.1

Advantages and Disadvantages of Technology Leadership

greater profits than competitors or attract more customers by charging lower prices. Similarly, if a company is first to market with a new technology, it may be able to charge a premium price because it faces no competition. Higher prices and greater profits can defray the costs of developing new technologies.

This one-time advantage of being the technology leader can be turned into a sustainable advantage. Sustainability of a lead depends on competitors' ability to duplicate the technology and the organization's ability to keep building on the lead quickly enough to outpace competitors. It can do this in several ways. The reputation for being an innovator can create an ongoing advantage and even spill over to the company's other products. For example, 3M's reputation for innovation and quality differentiates some of its standard products, such as adhesive tape, and allows a product to command a premium price. A competitor may be able to copy the product but not the reputation. Patents and other institutional barriers also can be used to block competitors and maintain leadership. Polaroid successfully kept industry giant Kodak out of the instant-photography market for years through a series of patents and new products such as Joy-Cam and i-Zone until digital photography changed the market entirely.[8]

The first mover also can preempt competitors by occupying the best market niches. If it can establish high switching costs (recall Chapter 2) for repeat customers, these positions can be difficult for competitors to capture. As we mentioned earlier, Microsoft now dominates the software market with its Windows operating system because of the large library of software that is packaged with it. Although other companies can offer more advanced software, their products are not as attractive because they are not bundled as the Windows-based systems are. (Ironically, this advantage was so intractable that it was viewed as monopolistic in court.)[9]

Technology leadership can provide a significant learning advantage. While competitors may be able to copy or adopt a new technology, ongoing learning by the technology leader can keep a company ahead by generating minor improvements that are difficult to imitate. Many Japanese manufacturers use several small, incremental improvements generated with their *kaizen* programs (recall Chapter 9) to upgrade the quality of their products and processes continuously.

T-Mobile was the first to market a phone with the power of Blackberry e-mail, which provides users access to their e-mail and Internet from anywhere. What are the benefits of being on the cutting edge of technology? What are the pitfalls?

All these minor improvements cannot be copied easily by competitors, and collectively they can provide a significant advantage.[10]

Disadvantages of Technology Leadership   However, being the first to develop or adopt a new technology does not always lead to immediate advantage and high profits. While such potential may exist, technology leadership imposes high costs and risks that followers are not required to bear. Being the leader thus can be more costly than being the follower. These costs include educating buyers unfamiliar with the new technology, building an infrastructure to support the technology, and developing complementary products to achieve the technology's full potential. For example, when the personal computer was first developed in the 1970s, dozens of computer companies entered the market. Almost all of them failed, usually because they lacked the financial, marketing, and sales ability required to attract and service customers. Also, many new products require regulatory approval. For example, the cost of producing a new drug, including testing and the expense of obtaining FDA approval, is estimated at around $200 million. While followers do not get the benefits of being first to market, they can copy the drug for a fraction of this cost once the original patents expire.[11]

Being a pioneer carries other risks. If raw materials and equipment are new or have unique specifications, a ready supply at a reasonable cost may not be available. Or the technology may not be fully developed and may have problems yet to be resolved. In addition, the unproved market for the technology creates uncertainty in demand. Finally, the new technology may have an adverse impact on existing structures or business. It may cannibalize current products or make existing investments obsolete.

Technology Followership

Not all organizations are equally prepared to be technology leaders, nor would leadership benefit each organization equally. In deciding whether to be a technology leader or follower, managers will consider their company's competitive strategy, the benefits gained through use of the technology, and the characteristics of their organization.

Interestingly, technology followership also can be used to support both low-cost and differentiation strategies. If the follower learns from the leader's experience, it can avoid the costs and risks of technology leadership, thereby establishing a low-cost position. Personal computer (PC) manufacturers have been successful with this type of followership strategy. IBM's personal computer market share within the United States has never matched that of its mainframes largely because of low-cost technology followers such as Dell and Gateway. Followership also can support differentiation. By learning from the leader, the follower can adapt the products or delivery systems to fit buyers' needs more closely.

A manager's decision on when to adopt new technology is also dependent on the potential benefits of the new technology, as well as the organization's technology skills. As discussed earlier, technologies do not emerge in their final state; rather, they exhibit *ongoing development* (see Figure 17.3). Such development eventually makes the technology easier to use and more adaptable to various strategies. For example, the development of high-bandwidth communication networks has enabled many more companies to work with suppliers located abroad. At the same time, *complementary products and technologies* may be developed and introduced that make the main technology more useful. For example, the combination of the personal computer with disk drives, printers, e-mail, and other software turned it into an essential business tool.

These complementary products and technologies combine with the *gradual diffusion* of the technology to form a shifting competitive impact from the technology. The appropriate time for an organization to adopt technological innovations is when the costs and risks of switching to the technology are outweighed by the benefits. This point will be different for each organization, with some organizations benefiting from a leadership, early adopter role, and others from a followership role, depending on each organization's characteristics and strategies.[12]

Following the technology leader can save development expense.

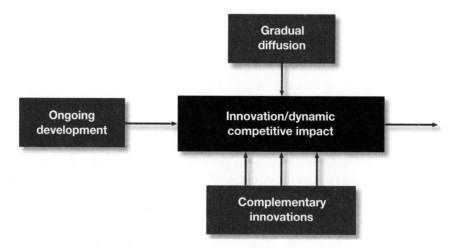

FIGURE 17.3

Dynamic Forces of a Technology's Competitive Impact

SOURCE: D. M. Schroeder, "A Dynamic Perspective on the Impact of Process Innovation upon Competitive Strategies," *Strategic Management Journal* 11 (January 1990), pp. 25–42.

Connections: TAKING AIM AT IPOD

U.S. wireless operators aren't going to cause an overnight sensation in music. Their first offerings are too expensive and clumsy to spark strong demand. Yet within a year or two, the operators have a real chance of giving the MP3 crowd a run for its money. The phone companies have a track record of refining their offerings until they attract the mass market. Verizon and its brethren have traditionally overpriced services such as broadband, long-distance, and even cellular service and then lowered prices. That's likely to be the pattern in music, too. The wireless companies are also coming from far behind in setting up their music stores. Apple spent years refining its iTunes site and already has sold more than 300 million songs. But inside Sprint, execs talk about the mobile phone as if it were a modern-day jukebox. The company is offering wireless customers Music Choice, the same 24/7 service offered by satellite and cable-TV operators. Customers can't pick individual songs yet. But Sprint is working on providing users with hundreds of thousands of songs. It's even considering development of a mobile-phone cradle, attached to top-notch speakers, for home use. "Business models will absolutely change," says Richard S. Siber, CEO of wireless consultant SiberConsulting.

Assessing Technology Needs

Little more than a decade ago, the major U.S. steel companies suffered from significant cost disadvantages relative to non-U.S. producers. Those high costs were due largely to poor productivity resulting from aging plants and obsolete equipment. U.S. companies lagged their European and Japanese counterparts in adopting new, productivity-enhancing process technologies such as the basic oxygen furnace and the continuous-casting process. If the U.S. companies had accurately assessed and adopted these technologies in a timely manner, the massive layoffs (about 60 percent) of the industry's workforce might have been avoided. In today's increasingly competitive environment, failure to correctly assess the technology needs of the organization can fundamentally impair the organization's effectiveness.

Assessing the technology needs of the organization involves measuring current technologies as well as external trends affecting the industry.

Measuring Current Technologies

Before organizations can devise strategies for developing and exploiting technological innovation, they must gain a clear understanding of their current technology base. A

technology audit helps clarify the key technologies on which an organization depends. The most important dimension of a new technology is its competitive value. One technique for measuring competitive value categorizes technologies as emerging, pacing, key, and base.[13]

technology audit

Process of clarifying the key technologies on which an organization depends.

- *Emerging technologies* are still under development and thus are unproved. They may, however, significantly alter the rules of competition in the more distant future. Managers will want to monitor the development of emerging technologies, but may not yet need to invest in them until they have been more fully developed.

- *Pacing technologies* have yet to prove their full value but have the potential to alter the rules of competition by providing significant advantage. For example, when first installed, computer-aided manufacturing (see Chapter 9) was a pacing technology. Its full potential was not yet widely realized, but companies that used it effectively developed significant speed and cost advantages. Managers will want to focus on developing or investing in pacing technologies because of the competitive advantages they can provide.

- *Key technologies* have proved effective, but they also provide a strategic advantage because not everyone uses them. Knowledge and dissemination of these technologies are limited, and they continue to provide some first-mover advantages. For example, a more powerful, proprietary processing chip by Intel is a key technology for that organization. Eventually, alternatives to key technologies can emerge. But until then key technologies can give organization managers a significant competitive edge and make it much more difficult for new entrants to threaten the organization.

- *Base technologies* are those that are commonplace in the industry; everyone must have them to be able to operate. Thus, they provide little competitive advantage. Managers have to invest only to ensure their organization's continued competence in the technology.

Although it is still years away from actual use, Airborne Networks—technology that NASA and the U.S. Air Force are developing—will create an "Internet in the sky" that could let planes fly safely without ground controllers.

Technologies can evolve rapidly through these categories. For example, electronic word processing was considered an emerging technology in the late 1970s. By the early 1980s, it could have been considered pacing. While promising advantages, the technology's cost and capabilities restricted its usefulness to a limited number of applications. With continued improvements and more powerful computer chips, electronic word processing quickly became a key technology. Its costs dropped, its usage spread, and it demonstrated the capacity to enhance productivity. By the late 1980s, it was considered a base technology in most applications. Word processing technology is now used so widely that it is viewed as a routine activity in almost every office.

Assessing External Technological Trends

Just as with any planning, decisions about technology must balance internal capabilities (strengths and weaknesses) with external opportunities and threats. There are several techniques that managers use to better understand how technology is changing within an industry.

Benchmarking   As mentioned in Chapter 4, benchmarking is the process of comparing the organization's practices and technologies with those of other companies. The ability to benchmark technologies against those of competitors can vary among industries. While competitors understandably are reluctant to share their secrets, information trading for benchmarking is not uncommon and can prove highly valuable. For example, Harley-Davidson's recovery of its reputation for manufacturing quality

Japanese companies, such as Nissan, are often willing to show U.S. competitors their operations because they believe the U.S. companies are unwilling or unable to use what they have learned.

Benchmarking can lower cost and raise speed and quality.

motorcycles began only after company executives toured Honda's plant and witnessed firsthand the weaknesses of Harley's manufacturing technologies and the vast potential for improvement. In fact, Japanese companies often are willing to show U.S. competitors their operations because they believe the U.S. companies won't use the information!

Benchmarking against potential competitors in other nations is important. Companies may find key or pacing technologies in use that can be imported easily and offer significant advantage. Also, overseas firms may be more willing to share their knowledge if they are not direct competitors and if they are eager to exchange information for the benefit of both companies.

Scanning   Whereas benchmarking focuses on what is being done currently, scanning focuses on what can be done and what is being developed. In other words, benchmarking examines key and perhaps some pacing technologies, while scanning seeks out pacing and emerging technologies—those just being introduced and still in development.

Scanning typically involves a number of tactics, many of them the same as those used in benchmarking. However, scanning places greater emphasis on identifying and monitoring the sources of new technologies for an industry. It also may dictate that executives read more cutting-edge research journals and attend research conferences and seminars. The extent to which scanning is done depends largely on how close to the cutting edge of technology an organization needs to operate.

Key Factors to Consider in Technology Decisions

Once managers have done a thorough job of analyzing their organization's current technological position, they can begin to make decisions about how to proceed into the future to either develop or exploit emerging technological innovations. Decisions about technological innovations must balance many interrelated factors. The most effective approach to technology depends not only on the technology's potential to support the organization's strategic needs but also on the organization's skills and capabilities to exploit the technology successfully. The organization's competitive strategy, the technical abilities of its employees to deal with the new technology, the fit of the technology with the company's operations, and the company's ability to deal with the risks and ambiguities of adopting a new technology all must be timed to coincide with the dynamic forces of a developing technology. This does not always mean waiting for the technology to develop. Often it requires changing the capabilities and strategies of the organization to match the needs of the technology. This could include hiring new people, training existing employees, changing internal policies and procedures, and changing strategies. These considerations are discussed next.

Anticipated Market Receptiveness

The first consideration that needs to be addressed in developing a strategy around technological innovation is market potential. In many cases, innovations are stimulated by external demand for new products and services. For example, current work to develop low earth-orbiting satellites (LEOs) for wireless Internet access is motivated by a clear understanding of its worldwide market potential. Telecommunications companies such as AT&T, Motorola, TRW, and Loral are working diligently to develop innovative technologies in this arena.[14]

In assessing market receptiveness, executives need to make two determinations. In the short run, there should be an immediate application that demonstrates the value of the new technology. In the long run, there needs to be a set of applications that show the technology is the proven means to satisfy a market need. For example, despite the recent dominant use of audio compact discs (CDs), the shift to technologies such as MP3 may result in CDs becoming less attractive. LPs, cassettes, and eight-tracks (does anyone remember them?) are virtually nonexistent today.

Motorcycles Ride High on Hydrogen

▼ FROM THE PAGES OF

BusinessWeek

The new, hydrogen-powered ENV prototype doesn't look like a typical motorbike or scooter. Sleeker and taller than a scooter, with thinner wheels and a noticeable lack of exhaust pipes, the ENV looks more like an ordinary bicycle that has been fitted out with a hefty, futuristic body. But even more unusual than its appearance are its capabilities. Intelligent Energy's ENV (for emissions-neutral vehicle) is emission-free, quiet, has a top speed of 50 mph, and can travel up to 100 miles between refills.

Like the broader auto industry, makers of motorcycles and scooters have been working to develop a hydrogen-powered ride that runs without producing polluting carbon emissions. Honda and Aprilia are among the other companies that have developed such prototypes. So far, none of the other experimental models are close to being commercially produced. But London-based Intelligent Energy says its ENV bike could be on the road in 2006.

The bikes are all powered by fuel cells, in which hydrogen and oxygen are combined to produce electricity, with water as the only by-product. But Intelligent Energy officials contend that the ENV bike is a step forward, since it has been designed from scratch around the fuel-cell technology. More important, Intelligent Energy's fuel cell is simpler and more compact than its competitors, which means it's less expensive to make. While hand-making the bike would cost around $28,285, a production run of 10,000 would bring the retail price down to about $5,660. That's still considerably more expensive than an ordinary low-speed scooter designed for urban commuting. But it's within the range of more powerful models, which can run to $5,000.

Experts in the fuel-cell industry say hydrogen-powered motorbikes may ultimately be easier to bring to the market than cars and trucks. The bikes need less power, for one. While a car needs 50 to 100 kilowatts, a light motorcycle, like the ENV bike, can depend on as little as one. Since fuel cells become more expensive the more powerful they are, a one-kilowatt version is relatively affordable. Further, because a motorbike's fuel cell is small, it can be air-cooled rather than water-cooled, which eliminates one of the difficulties of making large vehicles.

Consumer expectations are lower, too. Motorbikes made for driving around urban areas are often designed to be refilled every 60 miles or so, while cars are expected to be able to drive 300 miles without a refill. Moreover, a large potential market exists for relatively inexpensive, nonpolluting bikes. Intelligent Energy sees the immediate market for the ENV bike in environmentally conscious commuters or recreational motorcyclists who are drawn to the distinctive design. The long-term market for the bike would be in Asian cities such as Hong Kong, Bangkok, and Beijing, where people rely far more on motorbikes and where pollution is a serious problem.

Of course, a major drawback is the lack of infrastructure for supplying hydrogen. Although fueling stations are cropping up in some areas, the United States has no national hydrogen-supply system, which may make manufacturers reluctant to risk producing the bikes. And although Intelligent Energy hasn't ruled out producing the bike itself, the business is looking for a partner to handle manufacturing.

Niche marketing is another possibility. The ENV bike could be launched in one of the areas committed to building hydrogen highways, such as California, where 16 hydrogen fueling stations have been built. Another alternative would be to try "micro-retailing" the bike in specific cities or regions where hydrogen is now produced as an industrial by-product. Whatever happens, Intelligent Energy doesn't plan to produce the ENV on a massive scale, as the key to its appeal is "the novelty of having an environmentally friendly and quiet vehicle," says the company's CEO.

SOURCE: Beth Carney, "Motorcycles Ride High on Hydrogen," *BusinessWeek*, April 14, 2005, online.

> **Intelligent Energy sees the immediate market for the ENV bike in environmentally conscious commuters and recreational motorcyclists who are drawn to the distinctive design.**

Technological Feasibility

In addition to market receptiveness, managers must consider the feasibility of technological innovations. Visions can stay unrealized for a long time. Technical obstacles may represent barriers to progress. For example, limitations on battery miniaturization and storage continue to hinder the development of battery-powered vehicles. The data-carrying limitations of telephone wires prevented the full development of videophones, even though the basic technology was understood decades ago. And companies like Intel face continual hurdles in developing newer and faster computer chips.

> "I have not failed. I've just found 10,000 ways that don't work."
> Thomas Edison

Since Intel brought the first microprocessor to market in 1971, chip makers have made dramatic advances in computing. The number of transistors on a chip, and its resulting performance, has doubled nearly every 18 to 24 months, upholding what has become known as Moore's Law (Gordon Moore is the cofounder of Intel).

But the frontier of microprocessor technology is being restricted by the combined forces of physics and economics. The wires that run between transistors right now are 400 times thinner than a human hair. Can they be made skinnier yet? Yes, but the task of continually doubling the speed of electrons passing wires of near-zero width will be tricky—and maybe impossible—at some point. Even if it's technically feasible, can companies afford the massive investments needed to do this?[15]

Other industries face similar technological hurdles. In the oil industry, for example, technological barriers prevent exploration and drilling in the deepest parts of the ocean. In medicine, scientists and doctors work continuously to identify the causes of and cures for diseases such as cancer and AIDS. In aviation and aeronautics, researchers are working to refine technologies that allow pilots to "see" through clouds. Each of these potentially valuable innovations is slowed by the technical limits of currently available technologies.[16]

Economic Viability

Closely related to technological feasibility is economic viability. Apart from whether a firm can "pull off" a technological innovation, executives must consider whether there is a good financial incentive for doing so. For example, the use of solar fusion to generate electricity has been technically feasible for years. However, its cost remains prohibitively higher than the cost of fossil fuels. Similarly, the use of hydrogen-powered fuel-cell technology for automobiles is almost feasible technically, but its costs are still too high. And even if those costs were brought down to more acceptable levels, the lack of a supporting infrastructure in the society as a whole—for example, the lack of hydrogen refueling stations, as in the previous news item—would represent another barrier to economic viability.

Innovation requires financial feasibility.

Less futuristic innovations also require a careful assessment of economic viability and costs. New technologies often represent an expensive and long-term commitment of resources. And integrating them effectively within the organization can require a great deal of management time. Once an organization commits to a technological innovation, a change in direction becomes extremely difficult and costly. For these reasons, a careful, objective analysis of technology costs versus benefits is essential.

The issue of economic viability takes us back to our earlier discussion of adoption timing. Earlier adopters may have first-mover advantages, but there are costs associated with this strategic approach. The development costs of a particular technological innovation may be quite high, as in pharmaceuticals, chemicals, and software. Patents and copyrights often help organizations recoup the costs of their investments in technological innovations. Without such protection, the investments in research and development might not be justifiable.

Handheld computers continue to grow more powerful and spawn a host of peripherals.

Unfortunately, the exploding growth in piracy or even fakery of patented pharmaceuticals, software, and other products has added new barriers to economic viability. Globalization has created a worldwide market for goods produced by low-cost counterfeiters and pirates overseas, who have the added advantage that they do not have to incur research and development expense. In addition, technology has made it easy to copy software without paying for it. Pfizer's cholesterol-lowering drug Lipitor, Hewlett-Packard inkjet cartridges, Intel computer chips, GM car designs, Viagra, Callaway golf clubs, Sony Playstations and games—all these and much more have been counterfeited or illegally copied and sold. Worldwide lost sales as a result of this illegal activity—the theft of *intellectual property*—have been estimated at over $500 billion a year. A major contributor to the problem is China, which by some estimates accounts for almost two-thirds of the worldwide production of fake or pirated goods. However, China's own companies are now being victimized by counterfeiting. That fact, plus a growing chorus of complaints from other countries, including the United States, may cause that country to begin to crack down on violators. Some companies have also taken action on their own. For example, GM has seven full-time investigators on staff seeking out copyright violators. Other companies, like battery-manufacturer Nokia, are embedding their products with holographic images or taking other technical measures to make copying more difficult. All these measure are designed to help organizations—and countries—maintain the economic viability of their innovations.[17]

Anticipated Competency Development

We have stated repeatedly in this text that organizations should (and do) build their strategies based on core competencies. This advice applies to technology and innovation strategies as well. Frequently, we can view technological innovations that are the tangible product of intangible—or tacit—knowledge and capabilities that make up a firm's core competence. Merck and Intel are examples of companies in which core competencies in research and development lead to new technological innovations.

By contrast, firms that are not technology-oriented must develop new competencies in order to survive. For example, when Amazon.com changed the face of e-retailing in the 1990s, traditional brick-and-mortar bookstores had to adapt quickly. To regain competitiveness, they had to bolster their information technology competencies, which wasn't always an easy thing to do.

The upshot of this is that while certain technologies may have tremendous market applicability, managers must have (or develop) the internal competencies needed to execute their technology strategies. Without the skills needed to implement an innovation, even promising technological advances may prove disastrous.

Organizational Suitability

The final issues that tend to be addressed in deciding on technological innovations have to do with the culture of the organization, the interests of managers, and the expectations of stakeholders. Companies such as 3M and Sony, which are seen as proactive "technology-push" innovators, tend to have cultures that are more outward-looking and opportunistic. Executives in these *prospector* firms give considerable priority to developing and exploiting technological expertise, and decision makers tend to have bold intuitive visions of the future. Typically there are technology champions who articulate competitively aggressive, first-mover technological strategies. In many cases, executives are more concerned about the opportunity costs of not taking action than they are about the potential to fail.

> "Get your feet off my desk, get out of here, you stink, and we're not going to buy your product." So said the President of Atari in 1976, responding to Steve Jobs's offer to sell him rights to the new personal computer he and Steve Wozniak had developed.

By contrast, *defender* firms such as the car unit of Rolls-Royce tend to adopt a more circumspect posture toward innovation. These firms tend to operate in very stable environments. As a result, their strategies are focused more on deepening their capability base through complementary technologies that extend rather than replace their current ones. Strategic decisions are likely to be based on careful analysis and experience in the industry setting. A hybrid *analyzer* firm like Matsushita, with its Panasonic and other electronics brands, needs to stay technologically competitive but tends to allow others to demonstrate solid demand in new arenas before it responds. As we noted earlier, these types of firms tend to adopt an early-follower strategy to grab a dominant position more from their strengths in marketing and manufacturing than through technological innovation.[18]

Every company has different capabilities to deal with new technology. As discussed previously, early adopters have characteristics different from those of late adopters. Early adopters of new technologies tend to be larger, more profitable, and more specialized. Therefore, they are in an economic position to absorb the risks associated with early adoption while profiting more from its advantages. In addition, the people involved in early adoption are more highly educated, have a greater ability to deal with abstraction, can cope with uncertainty more effectively, and have strong problem-solving capabilities. Thus, early adopters can more effectively manage the difficulties and uncertainty of a less fully developed technology.[19]

One additional consideration managers need to take into account when introducing new technology is the impact the new technology will have on employees. Often, new technology will bring with it work-flow and other changes that will directly affect the organization's work environment. If the organization is not one where innovation is

Considerations	Examples
Market Receptiveness—Assess external demand for the technology (short/long run).	Cell phones, MP3, personal digital assistants (PDAs), HDTV
Technological Feasibility—Evaluate technical barriers to progress.	Deep-sea oil exploration, physical size of PC microprocessors
Economic Viability—Examine any cost considerations and forecast profitability.	Solar fusion, fuel cells for automobiles, missile defense system
Competency Development—Determine if current competencies are sufficient.	Information technology in hospitals, digital technology in cameras
Organizational Suitability—Assess the fit with culture and managerial systems.	Steel companies focusing on creativity and innovation

TABLE 17.2

Framing Decisions about Technological Innovation

commonplace, these changes may create anxiety and even resistance among employees, making integration of the technology within the organization more difficult. When managers communicate well in advance about the new technology, explain its purpose, and provide the necessary training, the process of integrating the new technology into the organization's existing processes becomes easier. The cooperation of employees is often a major factor in determining how difficult and costly the introduction of new technology will be. We discuss the issue of managing change in more detail in the next chapter.

Table 17.2 briefly summarizes the five major factors we have been discussing: market receptiveness, technological feasibility, economic viability, anticipated competency development, and organizational suitability. All of these considerations jointly influence the decisions managers will make about technology innovations. A lack in even one of them can derail an otherwise promising project.

Sourcing and Acquiring New Technologies

Developing new technology may conjure up visions of scientists and product developers working in research and development (R&D) laboratories like that of Bell Labs. However, new technology also can come from many other sources, including suppliers, manufacturers, users, other industries, universities, the government, and overseas companies. While every source of innovation should be explored, each industry usually has specific sources for most of its new technologies. For example, because of the limited size of most farming operations, innovations in farming most often come from manufacturers, suppliers, and government extension services. Seed manufacturers develop and market new, superior hybrids; chemical producers improve pesticides and herbicides; and equipment manufacturers design improved farm equipment. Land-grant universities develop new farming techniques, and extension agents spread their usage.

In many industries, however, the primary sources of new technology are the organizations that use the technology. For instance, over three-fourths of scientific innovations are developed by the users of the scientific instruments being improved and subsequently may be licensed or sold to manufacturers or suppliers.[20]

Essentially, the question of how to acquire new technology is a **make-or-buy decision**. In other words, should the organization develop the technology itself or acquire it from an outside source? However, the decision is not that simple. There are many alternatives, and each has advantages and disadvantages. Some of the more common options are discussed in the following sections.

make-or-buy decision

The question an organization asks itself about whether to acquire new technology from an outside source or develop it itself.

Internal Development

Developing a new technology within the company has the potential advantage of keeping the technology proprietary (exclusive to the organization). This provides an important advantage over competitors. The disadvantage of internal development is that it usually requires additional staff and funding for an extended period. Even if the development succeeds, considerable time may elapse before practical benefits are realized. Managers must carefully weigh the potential benefits of proprietary technology against the cost of developing it.

Purchasing may be faster and cheaper than internal development.

Purchase

Most technology already is available in products or processes that can be purchased openly. For example, a bank that needs sophisticated information-processing equipment need not develop the technology itself. It can simply purchase the technology from manufacturers or suppliers. In most situations, this is the simplest, easiest, and most cost-effective way to acquire new technology. However, in this case the technology itself will not offer a competitive advantage.

Contracted Development

If the technology is not available and a company lacks the resources or time to develop it internally, it may choose to contract the development from outside sources. Possible contractors include other companies, independent research laboratories, and university and government institutions. Usually outside contracting involves an agreed-upon series of objectives and timetables for the project, with payments made as each part of the project is tested and achieved.

The U.S. Army teamed up with Arizona State University to research, develop, and manufacture flexible display technologies. Both parties will benefit from this alliance. ASU received a new state-of-the-art facility and the army will secure emerging technologies.

Licensing

Certain technologies that are not easily purchased as part of a product can be licensed for a fee. Pioneers of the VHS format for videocassette recorders held the critical patents, but they freely licensed the technology and the right to use it to competing manufacturers of video equipment. This practice helped make VHS the dominant format (over Beta) by providing other manufacturers with easy access to the technology, thereby creating an industry standard.

Technology Trading

Technology trading is another way to gain access to new technologies. Ironically, this tactic sometimes is used between rival companies. For example, U.S. steel producers that use the minimill concept freely trade a great deal of know-how among one another. In some cases, this activity extends to training (without charge) a competitor's employees in new process improvements. While not all industries are amenable to technology sharing, trading is becoming increasingly common because of the high cost of developing advanced technologies independently.[21]

Research Partnerships and Joint Ventures

Research partnerships are arrangements designed to jointly pursue specific new-technology development. Typically, each member enters the partnership with different skills or resources needed for development to succeed. An effective combination is an established company and a start-up. Joint ventures are similar in most respects to research partnerships, but they tend to have greater permanence and their outcomes result in entirely new companies.[22] But as we described in our discussion on strategic alliances in Chapter 9, sometimes even powerful competitors collaborate on projects—for example, as when General Motors and DaimlerChrysler announced they would jointly work on developing the next generation of hybrid vehicles.

Advantages of Collaboration

Today, a number of factors are contributing to an increase in technology-related collaboration. Worldwide competition and lower-cost manufacturers abroad are putting pressures on businesses to develop cheaper and more powerful products faster, *and* at a lower cost. At the same time, technology is becoming more complex, and few companies have the human and financial resources to develop new products entirely on their own. Increasingly, companies are working cooperatively with other companies, clients, and customers to accelerate the development of new technologies. For example, IBM recently announced that it would make 500 of its communication-related patents available to others and promised that it would make other patents available as well. Although the company is not sharing its core technologies, it made a strategic decision that sharing some of its proprietary software standards will accelerate growth in the entire industry and also cause other companies and programmers to build applications based on IBM products. The company has deliberately facilitated collaboration to encourage additional innovation—and, in the long run, higher IBM sales.[23]

Acquisition of an Owner of the Technology

If a company lacks the needed technology but wishes to acquire proprietary ownership of it, one option is to purchase the company that owns the technology. This transaction can take a number of forms, ranging from an outright purchase of the entire company to a minority interest sufficient to gain access to the technology. For example, AOL acquired Moviefone and Mapquest, both of which had an existing customer base, rather than go through the expense and effort of re-creating these applications on its own. Sun Microsystems' CEO, Scott McNealy, readily acknowledges that part of his firm's strategy is to acquire companies with emerging technologies. In the fast-paced world of Internet computing, there is no way one firm can do it all itself.[24]

Choosing among these alternatives can be simplified by asking the following basic questions:

1. Is it important (and possible) in terms of competitive advantage that the technology remain proprietary?
2. Are the time, skills, and resources for internal development available?
3. Is the technology readily available outside the company?

As Figure 17.4 illustrates, the answers to these questions guide the manager to the most appropriate technology acquisition option.

If the preferred decision is to acquire a company, managers take additional steps to ensure the acquisition will make sense for the long term. For example, they try to make sure that key employees will remain with the firm, instead of leaving and

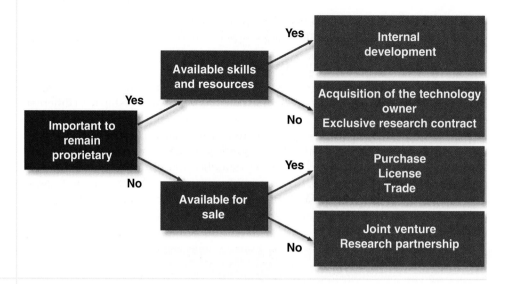

FIGURE 17.4
Technology Acquisition Options

perhaps taking essential technical expertise with them. Similarly, as with any large investment, managers carefully assess whether the financial benefits of the acquisition will justify the purchase price.

Technology and Managerial Roles

chief technology officer (CTO)

Executive in charge of technology strategy and development.

> "Technology is dominated by two types of people: those who understand what they do not manage, and those who manage what they do not understand."
>
> Anonymous

In organizations, technology traditionally has been the responsibility of vice presidents for research and development. These executives are directly responsible for corporate and divisional R&D laboratories. Typically, their jobs have a functional orientation. But increasingly companies are creating the position of **chief technology officer (CTO),** often also called the *chief information officer (CIO).* The CTO is a senior position at the corporate level with broad, integrative responsibilities. CTOs coordinate the technological efforts of the various business units, act as a voice for technology in the top management team, supervise new-technology development, and assess the technological implications of major strategic initiatives such as acquisitions, new ventures, and strategic alliances.[25] They may also manage their organization's *information technology (IT)* group.

Without the CTO's integrative role, different departments in an organization could easily adopt different technology tools and standards, leading to much higher equipment and maintenance expense and difficulties in connecting the different parts of the organization. Also, because organization technologists often have a very specialized expertise, managers without such expertise may have difficulty supervising them effectively. A CTO can help managers ensure that the work that technologists do is aligned with the strategic goals of the organization.

CTOs also perform an important boundary role: They work directly with outside organizations. For example, they work with universities for funding research to stay abreast of technical developments and with regulatory agencies to ensure compliance with regulations, identify trends, and influence the regulatory process.

Other people play a variety of critical roles in developing new technology. Recall from Chapter 7 that it is the *entrepreneur* who, in an effort to exploit untried technologies, invents new products or finds new ways to produce old products. The entrepreneur opens up new possibilities that change the competitive structure of entire industries.[26] For example, Steven Jobs started Apple Computer in his garage and launched the multibillion-dollar personal computer industry.

Key roles in acquiring and developing new technologies are the technical innovator, product champion, and executive champion.[27] The **technical innovator** develops the new technology or has the key skills needed to install and operate the technology. This person possesses the requisite technical skills, but he or she may not have the managerial skills needed to push the idea forward and secure acceptance within the organization. This is where the product champion gets involved. Introducing new technology into an organization requires that someone promote the idea. The **product champion**—often at the risk of his or her position and prestige—promotes the idea throughout the organization, searching for support and acceptance. The champion can be a high-level manager, but often this is not the case. If the champion lacks the power and financial resources to make the required changes independently, she or he must convince people who have such authority to support the innovation. In other words, product champions must get sponsorship.

Sponsorship comes from the **executive champion,** who has the status, authority, and financial resources to support the project and protect the product champion. Without this support and protection, the product champion, and thus the new technology, could not succeed. Resources needed to develop the innovation would be unavailable, and without protection the champion would not be allowed to continue promoting the change.

> **technical innovator**
>
> A person who develops a new technology or has the key skills to install and operate the technology.
>
> **product champion**
>
> A person who promotes a new technology throughout the organization in an effort to obtain acceptance of and support for it.
>
> **executive champion**
>
> An executive who supports a new technology and protects the product champion of the innovation.

Organizing for Innovation

In Chapter 6 we introduced the concept of "learning organizations." These are companies that excel at solving problems, seeking and finding new approaches, and sharing new knowledge with all the members of the organization. Such learning organizations are particularly well-positioned to develop useful innovations. The innovations may involve *exploiting* existing capabilities—to improve production speed or product quality, for example. Or the innovation may involve *exploring* new knowledge—seeking to develop new products or services.[28] Both innovation processes are necessary. Innovative learning organizations use their existing strengths to improve their operations, and improve their bottom lines that way. But they also learn to unleash people's creative energies and capabilities to develop new products and processes that will ensure their long-term competitiveness. In this section we discuss some of the approaches managers use to organize for innovation.

Unleashing Creativity

As discussed in Chapter 7 ("Entrepreneurship"), 3M has a strong orientation toward *intrapreneurship* and derives about one-third of its revenues from new products. 3M, and companies such as Merck, Hewlett-Packard, and Rubbermaid, have well-established histories of producing many successful new technologies and products. What sets these and other continuous innovators apart? The one thing these companies have in common is an organizational culture that encourages innovation.[29]

Consider the 3M legend from the early 1920s of inventor Francis G. Okie. Okie dreamed up the idea of using sandpaper instead of razor blades for shaving. The aim was to reduce the risk of nicks and avoid sharp instruments. The idea failed, but rather than being punished for the failure, Okie was encouraged to champion other ideas, which included 3M's first blockbuster success: waterproof sandpaper. A culture that permits failure is crucial for fostering the creative thinking and risk taking required for innovation.

As strange as it may seem, *celebrating* failure can be vital to the innovation process.[30] Failure is the essence of learning, growing, and succeeding.

A culture that permits failure is crucial for fostering the creative thinking and risk taking required for innovation. If 3M hadn't kept Francis G. Okie on board after a few failed inventions, Okie would never have come up with 3M's first success—waterproof sandpaper.

- **Set goals for innovation.** By corporate decree, 25 to 30 percent of annual sales must come from new products that are five years old or less.

- **Commit to research and development.** 3M invests in R&D at almost double the rate of the average U.S. company. One R&D goal is to cut in half the time it takes to introduce new products.

- **Inspire intrapreneurship.** Champions are encouraged to run with new ideas, and they get a chance to manage their products as if they were running their own businesses. 3Mers are allowed to spend 15 percent of their time pursuing personal research interests unrelated to current company projects.

- **Facilitate, don't obstruct.** Divisions are kept small and are allowed to operate with a great deal of independence but have constant access to information and technical resources. Researchers with good ideas are awarded $50,000 Genesis grants to develop their brainstorms into new products.

- **Focus on the customer.** 3M's definition of quality is to demonstrate that the product can do what the customer—not some arbitrary standard—dictates.

- **Tolerate failure.** 3Mers know that if their ideas fail, they still will be encouraged to pursue other innovative ideas. Management knows that mistakes will be made and that destructive criticism kills initiative.

TABLE 17.3
3M's Rules for an Innovative Culture

SOURCES: Company reports; R. Mitchell, "Masters of Innovation: How 3M Keeps Its New Products Coming," *BusinessWeek*, April 10, 1989, pp. 58–63; T. Katauskas, "Follow-Through: 3M's Formula for Success," *R&D*, November 1990; and Thomas J. Martin, "Ten Commandments for Managing Creative People," *Fortune*, January 16, 1995, pp. 135–36.

Innovative companies have many balls in the air at all times, with many people trying many new ideas. A majority of the ideas will fail, but it is only through this process that the few big "hits" will emerge that make a company an innovative star.

3M uses the simple set of rules listed in Table 17.3 to help foster innovation. These rules can be—and are—copied by other companies. But 3M has an advantage in that it has followed these rules since its inception and ingrained them in its culture. This culture is shared and passed on in part through stories. One such legend is about the 3M engineer who was fired because he refused to stop working on a project that his boss thought was wasting resources. Despite being fired, the engineer came to work as usual, finished the project, and demonstrated the value of his innovation. The engineer eventually was promoted to head a new division created to manufacture and market the innovation.

Bureaucracy Busting

Bureaucracy-busting encourages innovation.

Bureaucracy is an enemy of innovation. While bureaucracy is useful to maintain orderliness and gain efficiencies, it also can work directly against innovativeness. Developing radically different technologies requires a more fluid and flexible (organic) structure that does not restrict thought and action. However, such a structure can be chaotic and disruptive to normal operations. Consequently, companies often establish special temporary project structures that are isolated from the rest of the organization and allowed to operate under different rules. These units go by many names, including "skunkworks" (recall Chapter 7), "greenhouses," and "reserves."

In Japan, *angura* is an "underground research" policy that allows scientists to spend up to 20 percent of their time pursuing projects about which only the immediate supervisor knows.[31] When Apple developed the Macintosh, Steve Jobs took a small group of young engineers and programmers and set up operations apart from the remainder of the plant. They started from scratch, trying to rethink the personal computer completely. A pirate's flag was flown over their operation to demonstrate that they were not part of the regular bureaucratic operating structure and defied conventional rules. The result was a very successful new product.

Advantages of Collaboration

Bureaucracy-busting managerial systems that encourage collaboration can facilitate innovation. At steel companies such as Chaparral and Nucor, for example, employees work in cross-functional teams to solve problems and create innovative solutions. These flat structures help create an environment that encourages creativity and cooperation. Teams focus on present issues and problems as well as future concerns and opportunities. In addition, teams collaborate with outside partners to bring knowledge into the organization so that it can be integrated with existing ideas and information to create innovations. All the while, teams are supported by values of egalitarianism, information sharing, openness to outside ideas, and positive risk. The aim is to destroy the traditional boundaries between functions and departments in order to create collaborative, less bureaucratic "learning laboratories."[32]

Implementing Development Projects

A powerful tool for managing technology and innovations is the **development project**.[33] A development project is a focused organizational effort to create a new product or process via technological advances. For example, several years ago Eastman Kodak launched a development project to create the FunSaver Camera. The concept was simple: to package film in an inexpensive plastic camera body so that after the pictures were taken, the consumer could simply drop off the whole assembly at a photo finisher. While the FunSaver utilized existing design knowledge, it was developed on a unique computer-aided design and manufacturing (CAD/CAM) system. Two years earlier, Hewlett-Packard had initiated a development project of its own to design a new class of low-cost computer printers based on inkjet technology. HP's Deskjet Printer was one of the company's first attempts to integrate manufacturing, marketing, and R&D. The development project allowed the company to achieve an unprecedented advantage in both cost and speed.

> **development project**
>
> A focused organizational effort to create a new product or process via technological advances.

Development projects such as these typically feature a special cross-functional team that works together on an overall concept or idea. Like most cross-functional teams, its success depends on how well individuals work together to pursue a common vision. And in the case of development projects, teams must interact with suppliers and customers frequently, making the complexity of their task that much greater. Because of their urgency and strategic importance, most development projects are conducted under intense time and budget pressures, thus presenting a real-time test of the company's ability to innovate.

Managers should recognize that development projects have multiple benefits. Not only are they useful for creating new products and processes, they frequently cultivate skills and knowledge that can be used for future endeavors. In other words, the capabilities that companies derive from a development project frequently can be turned into a source of competitive advantage. For example, when Ford created a development project to design an air-conditioning compressor to outperform its Japanese rival, executives also discovered that they had laid the foundation for new processes that Ford could use in future projects. Their new capability in integrated design and manufacturing helped Ford reduce the costs and lead times for other product developments. Thus, *organizational learning* had become an equally important criterion for evaluating the success of the project.

The success of a project is determined by how well a cross-functional team can work together. What traits do good team players have?

For development projects to achieve their fullest benefit, they should build on core competencies (recall Chapters 4 and 9); have a guiding vision about what must be accomplished and why (Chapter 12); have a committed team (Chapters 12 and 14); instill a philosophy of continuous improvement (Chapter 9); and generate integrated, coordinated efforts across all units (Chapters 8 and 9).

Technology, Job Design, and Human Resources

Adopting a new technology typically requires changes in the way jobs are designed. Often the way the task is redefined fits people to the demands of the technology to maximize the technology's operation. But this often fails to maximize total productivity, because it ignores the human part of the equation. The social relationships and human aspects of the task may suffer, lowering overall productivity.

sociotechnical systems

An approach to job design that attempts to redesign tasks to optimize operation of a new technology while preserving employees' interpersonal relationships and other human aspects of the work.

The **sociotechnical systems** approach to work redesign specifically addresses this problem. This approach redesigns tasks in a manner that jointly optimizes the social and technical efficiency of work. Beginning with studies on the introduction of new coal-mining technologies in 1949, the sociotechnical systems approach to work design focused on small, self-regulating work groups.[34] Later it was found that such work arrangements could operate effectively only in an environment in which bureaucracy was limited. Today's trends in bureaucracy "bashing," lean and flat organizations, work teams, and an empowered workforce are logical extensions of the sociotechnical philosophy of work design. At the same time, the technologies of the information age— in which people at all organizational levels have access to vast amounts of information— make these leaner and less bureaucratic organizations possible.

Managers face several choices regarding how to apply a new technology. Technology can be used to limit the tasks and responsibilities of workers and "deskill" the workforce, thus turning workers into servants of the technology. Alternatively, managers can select and train workers to master the technology, using it to achieve great accomplishments and improve the quality of their lives. Technology, when managed effectively, can empower workers as it improves the competitiveness of organizations.

However, as managers make decisions about how to design jobs and manage employees, they also need to consider other human resource systems that complement the introduction of new technology. Table 17.4, for example, shows how compensation systems can be changed to facilitate the implementation of advanced manufacturing

TABLE 17.4
Compensation Practices in Traditional and Advanced Manufacturing Firms

Type of Compensation Practice	Traditional Factory	Integrated Manufacturing
Performance-contingent	Focus on *individual incentives* reflects division of labor and separation of stages and functions.	Extensive use of *group incentives* to encourage teamwork, cooperation, and joint problem solving.
Job-contingent	Use of *hourly wage* assumes that the differences in employee contribution are captured in job classifications and that performance is determined largely by the production system.	Use of *salary* assumes that employees' contributions transcend the job per se to substantially affect output. The distinctions between classes of employment are diminished.
Person-contingent	*Seniority pay* rewards experience as a surrogate for knowledge and skill in a stable environment and rewards loyalty to reduce uncertainty within the system.	*Skill-based* pay rewards continuous learning and the value added from increased flexibility in a dynamic environment.

SOURCE: Scott A. Snell and James W. Dean Jr., "Strategic Compensation for Integrated Manufacturing: The Moderating Effects of Jobs and Organizationl Inertia," *Academy of Management Journal* 37 (1994), pp. 1109–40.

technology. In the contemporary setting, the use of group incentives, salary, and skill-based pay systems helps reinforce the collective effort (recall the use of cross-functional teams), professionalism, empowerment, and flexibility required for knowledge work. If a company's pay system is not aligned with the new technologies, it may not reward behavior that is needed to make the changes work. Worse, existing reward systems actually may reinforce old behaviors that run counter to what is needed for the new technology.

Taken as a whole, these ideas provide a set of guidelines for managing the strategic and organizational issues associated with technology and innovation. In Chapter 18, we expand this discussion to focus on how organizations can reshape themselves to adapt to a dynamic marketplace. Managing change and organizational learning are central elements of what it takes to become a world-class organization.

EPILOGUE

TAKING AIM AT IPOD

Going forward, creative thinking inside cellular and music companies will be working on ways to tap into the social appeal of music, too. Right now, a kid sprawled on a college lawn can use his or her phone to let friends hear the latest Green Day song. With the next generation of wireless music technology, called superdistribution, that song could be zipped off to the phone of a friend, who could listen to it one or two times or buy it directly from a wireless carrier's service on the spot. Phone makers, meantime, are now focusing on making their products more music-friendly. Mobile music skeptics argue that only tech geeks will be patient enough to navigate a music playlist on the cumbersome keypads and tiny screens of most phones. But manufacturers from Motorola to Hong Kong contract manufacturer HTC are hustling to make phones easy to use. HTC's SDA has little buttons built into the phone that let the user play, pause, fast-forward, and rewind songs. Sony Ericsson's new Walkman phone and Motorola's new E680i sport built-in FM radio receivers and cables that make it a snap to transfer music from a PC to a phone.

Add it up, and Apple is facing what looks like the most serious threat so far to its digital music dominance. Of its trio of devices, the iPod may be the least affected. Its hard drive of as much as 60 gigabytes, or 15,000 songs, makes it a music aficionado's dream, and no phone can match it. The iPod mini and Shuffle are more vulnerable, since their storage is well within reach of a phone's capabilities. Some experts are convinced mobile phones will become the primary devices for carrying around tunes. "It's not a matter of if, it's a matter of when," says Scott Horn, a senior director at Microsoft Corp., which sells software for phones and music players.

Who would have thought the cell phone would evolve from a brick-sized talking device to a pocket-sized jukebox? In early April 1973, to much fanfare, a Motorola researcher made the first reported call using a handheld wireless phone. Now, Jason Smikle and his buddies not only can talk on one, they can dance to stereo-quality tunes booming from the little gadgets. Music on phones is coming of age. Watch out, Apple.

KEY TERMS

Chief technology officer (CTO), p. 568

Development project, p. 571

Executive champion, p. 569

Innovation, p. 550

Make-or-buy decision, p. 565

Product champion, p. 569

Sociotechnical systems, p. 572

Technical innovator, p. 569

Technology, p. 550

Technology audit, p. 559

Technology life cycle, p. 551

SUMMARY OF LEARNING OBJECTIVES

Now that you have studied Chapter 17, you should know:

The processes involved in the development of new technologies.

Forces that compel the emergence of a new technology include (1) a need for the technology, (2) the requisite scientific knowledge, (3) the technical convertibility of this knowledge, (4) the capital resources to fund development, and (5) the entrepreneurial insight and initiative to pull the components together.

How technologies proceed through a life cycle.

New technologies follow a predictable life cycle. First, a workable idea about how to meet a market need is developed into a product innovation. Early progress can be slow as competitors experiment with product designs. Eventually a dominant design emerges as the market accepts the technology, and further refinements to the technology result from process innovations. As the technology begins to approach both the theoretical limits to its performance potential and market saturation, growth slows and the technology matures. At this point the technology can remain stable or be replaced by a new technology.

How to manage technology for competitive advantage.

Adopters of new technologies are categorized according to the timing of their adoption: innovators, early adopters, the early majority, the late majority, and laggards. Technology leadership has many first-mover advantages but also poses significant disadvantages. The same may be said for followership. After that, technology that helps improve efficiency will support a low-cost strategy, while technologies that help make products more distinctive or unique will support a differentiation strategy. Determining an appropriate technology strategy depends on the degree to which the technology supports the organization's competitive requirements and, if a technology leadership strategy is chosen, the company's ability, in terms of skills, resources, and commitment, to deal with the risks and uncertainties of leadership.

How to assess technology needs.

Assessing the technology needs of a company begins by benchmarking, or comparing, the technologies it employs with those of both competitors and noncompetitors. Benchmarking should be done on a global basis to understand practices used worldwide. Technology scanning helps identify emerging technologies and those still under development in an effort to project their eventual competitive impact.

The key factors to consider when making decisions about technological innovation.

New technologies can be acquired or developed. Options include internal development, purchase, contracted development, licensing, trading, research partnerships and joint ventures, and acquisition. The approach used depends on the existing availability of the technology; the skills, resources, and time available; and the importance of keeping the technology proprietary.

The roles different people play in managing technology.

People play many different roles in managing technology. For example, the chief technology officer is the person with broad, integrative responsibility for technological innovation. In addition, the entrepreneur is the person who recognizes the competitive potential of the technology and finds new ways to exploit opportunities. The technical innovator has the key skills needed to develop or install and operate the technology. The product champion is the person who promotes the new idea(s) in order to gain support throughout the organization. The executive champion is the person with the status and resources to support the project.

How to develop an innovative organization.

Organizing for innovation involves unleashing the creative energies of employees while directing their efforts toward meeting market needs in a timely manner. Culture, structure, development projects, and job design are critical for building an innovative organization.

The key characteristics of successful development projects.

For development projects to achieve the fullest benefit, they should (1) build on core competencies, (2) have a guiding vision about what must be accomplished and why, (3) have a committed team, (4) instill a philosophy of continuous improvement, and (5) generate integrated, coordinated efforts across all teams and units.

DISCUSSION QUESTIONS

1. According to Francis Bacon, "A wise man will make more opportunities than he finds." What does this have to do with technology and innovation? What does it have to do with competitive advantage?

2. What examples of technological innovation can you identify? What forces led to the commercialization of the science behind those technologies? Did the capability exist before the market demand, or was the demand there before the technology was available?

3. Thomas Edison once said that most innovations are 10 percent inspiration and 90 percent perspiration. How does this match what you know about technology life cycles?

4. Why would a company choose to follow rather than lead technological innovations? Is the potential advantage of technological leadership greater when innovations are occurring rapidly, or is it better in this case to follow?

5. If you were in the grocery business, who would you benchmark for technological innovations? Would the companies be inside or outside your industry? Why?

6. How would you see the executive champion, the chief technology officer, and the product champion working together? Could the roles all be played by the same individual? Why or why not?

CONCLUDING CASE

S & Z East Coast Importers

OVERVIEW

Herbie Shapiro has worked as a retail footwear salesman in the New York City area for nearly 20 years. The New York City native has always worked for someone else, but he knows the business and its people very well. Herbie has always felt that the supply side of the retail footwear business is poorly organized, and that few if any distributors provide good service to the hundreds of retail outlets in the metropolitan area.

Mei Zhao, a native of China, is a longtime acquaintance of Herbie, and a manufacturer's rep for several of the Pacific Rim footwear manufacturers. Mei functions primarily as a foreign agent and freight forwarder for the Asian manufacturers, overseeing the unloading and trucking of container ship cargo.

Mei shares many of the same views as Herbie when it comes to the distribution and supply side of the retail footwear business. Both men are at the midpoint of their careers, have built a solid business and personal relationship with one another, and, following several meetings, have decided to form a partnership. S & Z East Coast Importers has the opportunity to lease a 60,000-square-foot warehouse with a buy option in northern New Jersey for purposes of establishing a distribution center for the metropolitan area retail footwear business.

Mei already has many good links and relationships with the major suppliers and shippers of retail footwear. The partners plan to import a wide range of products, including casual shoes, athletic footwear, fashion and outdoor boots, slippers, socks, laces, pads, and inserts. Mei has access to all of the major national brands as well as the bargain-priced no-name lines.

In addition to his long association and membership in local and national footwear organizations, Herbie knows many store owners and employees within the New York–New Jersey metro area. Herbie is well liked and well respected. The partners believe that their strong combination of supply-side and retail experience will provide them with access to many good markets.

As is the case in many industries, retail footwear has a very small number of large suppliers of manufactured products coupled with a very large number of small retail stores. One of the major keys to success therefore is the existence of an efficient, well-organized system of distribution. Herbie and Mei are focusing their efforts on doing a better job than the competition and on filling that niche in the footwear market.

LOGISTICAL ISSUES AND CHALLENGES

Most of the aforementioned footwear products arrive at the West Coast on giant container ships. After clearing customs, the containers are offloaded onto tractors for local (western) delivery and onto railcars for midwestern and East Coast distribution. Herbie and Mei plan to set up their building as a warehouse and distribution center.

Warehouse and distribution centers must purchase virtually all of their products in large quantities. Herbie and Mei will typically be faced with buying shipments of 500,000 pairs of shoes, 1,000,000 pairs of socks, 600,000 pairs of running shoes, and so on. Retailers, on the other hand, typically must purchase very small quantities of mixed loads of products, primarily because of a lack of retail and storage space. Herbie and Mei will typically be faced with orders that call for 50–150 pairs of shoes, 50–100 pairs of socks, 100–300 pairs of running shoes, and so on.

Warehouse and distribution centers must therefore be set up to receive, unload, and store large shipments of product (railroad cars/tractor trailers), to "break bulk" (unpack, count, inventory, and repack), and to load and deliver small mixed loads to retail establishments. Many metro-area retailers are located on cramped and busy streets with limited access.

The financial side of Herbie and Mei's business looks very promising. Thanks to Mei's connections with suppliers and Herbie's connections with the New York–New Jersey metro market, the partners anticipate an average markup of 30 percent for their products. That is nearly twice as much as Mei earns as a manufacturer's rep.

For their business to succeed, several variables and logistics must fall into place and be properly managed. The warehouse and distribution process, quality of service, and financial management must operate at maximum efficiency. In addition to in-house efficiency and cost control, the company must also buy and sell enough volume of product to cover all costs and generate profits.

Retail customers are looking for timely and frequent deliveries of small quantities of specific products. Some of those customers may need merchandising help as well. If products are not selling, the distribution centers and manufacturers will soon be backed up with product as well. Retail sales are the key to avoiding a bottleneck in the process and flow of manufacturing and distribution.

The financial side of this business requires close and careful management of receivables and payables. Manufacturers typically expect and receive payment for their products in about 10 days. This is essential to the sustained cash flow of those operations (primarily for payroll and raw materials purposes). Retailers, on the other hand, expect and receive accounts payable terms ranging from 30 to 60 days. This is essential to the sustained cash flow of those operations, as customer sales are the primary source of funds. So while the prospect of a 30 percent markup is clearly attractive, the cash flow situation and challenge must be met.

Herbie and Mei are unsure about the best way to facilitate and manage trucking and insurance. They have the option of buying or leasing their own trucks on both the supply and delivery side and also have the option of using independent trucking companies. They could select some combination of those two options. In addition, merchandise must be insured, but who exactly is responsible for that coverage and when does that "ownership" change hands?

The partners project monthly warehouse operating expenses of $55,000 (building, payroll, administration, and salaries). This does not include merchandise, trucking, or insurance. Given their 30 percent average markup on products, monthly sales of about $180,000 will be needed to break even. The partners have conservatively projected first-year sales to be $3 million.

Their warehouse inventory capabilities are in excess of $30 million. Herbie and Mei realize that it will take some time to approach that level from both a sales and cash flow perspective. Their facility and market base clearly present the potential to achieve sales of $40 million or more. Cash flow is the current obstacle. They have just over $1 million in working capital for their start-up and believe that that will accommodate first year sales of $3 million given their logistics of inventory purchase, sales, and cash flow.

From a distance, the prospect of success is promising. The partners have the opportunity to buy low and sell high in large volume. A market niche is waiting to be filled. The partners have the experience and the connections on both the supply and sales sides of the business.

QUESTIONS

1. How can the principals use technology to achieve success in their new venture? Be sure to address each of the major categories presented—purchasing, transportation, operations, distribution, and financial management.

2. Select a specific business or industry that you may become a part of; how would you incorporate the technological aspects of the text into your day-to-day operations?

EXPERIENTIAL EXERCISES

17.1 Planning for Innovation

OBJECTIVES

1. To brainstorm innovative ideas for a company that has become stagnant.
2. To explore the elements of a good innovation plan.

INSTRUCTIONS

1. Read the Mason, Inc., scenario.
2. Individually or in small groups, offer a plan for encouraging innovation at Mason, Inc. Discuss staffing, rewards, organizational structure, work design, and any other facets of organizational behavior that apply.
3. In small groups, or with the entire class, share the plans you developed.

MASON, INC., SCENARIO

Mason, Inc., designs, develops, and manufactures personal grooming products. From 1950 to 1980 it was a leader in introducing new, profitable products into the marketplace. Its Research and Development Division grew from 20 to 150 professionals during that time. Since 1980, however, the company has relied on its past successes and has failed to introduce any significant innovative product into the marketplace. Top management wants to reestablish Mason's reputation as the number-one innovator in the industry.

DISCUSSION QUESTIONS

1. What elements do these plans have in common?
2. How well do the plans follow the innovation process?
3. Do the plans incorporate provisions for fulfilling the various roles required for innovation?
4. What are the strengths and weaknesses of each plan?
5. What should be the components of an effective plan?

SOURCE: J. Gordon, *A Diagnostic Approach to Organizational Behavior* (Englewood Cliffs, NJ: Prentice-Hall, 1983), p. 654. Reprinted by permission of Prentice-Hall, Inc., Englewood Cliffs, N.J.

17.2 Innovation for the Future

OBJECTIVE

To look ahead into the future.

INSTRUCTIONS

Choose a partner. Together, develop an innovative product or service that will be popular in the year 2025. As you develop your product or service, ask yourselves the following questions:

1. What trends lead you to believe that this product or service will be successful?
2. What current technologies, services, or products will be replaced by your idea?

Present your idea to the class for discussion.

Operations Management in the New Economy

The business of a company—any company—is to take certain inputs and, by means of a process, transform them into outputs. Bringing these outputs (the product) to market cost-effectively will ensure the company's continued existence and well-being. The methods, systems, and mental framework by which a company transforms its inputs into outputs characterize its *operations*. A company maintains the health of its transformation process through *management* of these operations. *Operations management* is the analysis and implementation of this process.

Many varied factors impinge on a company's operations and managers. As company size increases, so do the number of variables. Effective management of the operation and its variables contributes in no small measure to the company's success, whether the company is small or large, diversified or devoted to core businesses, a network organization or a highly structured, centralized body. It holds true whether the company sells a tangible product (goods) or an intangible one (services), for in both cases, the customer is buying the object of a desire, or the satisfaction of a need.

EFFECTS OF CHANGE

We often read that operations management is in transition today. In actuality, it has always been in transition, because the world is always changing. Changes may take the form of new products (imagine the first traders bringing spices to Europe in the early Middle Ages), new distribution channels (Federal Express completely revamped our expectations about package delivery), alterations in the labor pool (women assumed many factory jobs during World War II, when men were at war), or new technologies (gunpowder altered all the rules of war in 14th-century Europe).

Characteristic of the current age is the quickening *rate* at which change occurs, placing pressure on individuals to adapt quickly and rewarding those able to shift mental gears, personal habits, and priorities easily. Indeed, survival of the fittest applies not only to physical attributes but also to mental agility. Operations managers must be among the most "fit" to function effectively in today's world.

THE CONTEXT OF OPERATIONS MANAGEMENT

What does it mean to be an effective manager of an operation? It means responding to the needs of diverse parties *within* the company, ensuring smooth movement through all stages of the transformation process. We can even take the viewpoint that, within the process, the "customer" is the department receiving the result of the preceding stage. For example, in a printing company, the operator of the press is the customer of the prepress area. An effective manager works with this awareness, ensuring that each area supplies what the next one expects.

Operations management also means satisfying parties in the *larger* arena. For example, investors may want to know how well a new product line is faring in the market or whether a new manufacturing process is delivering as promised. The community may want assurances that wastes from the production process will not cause quality of life to suffer. The government may demand an accounting of any number of activities covered by regulations. Thus, the manager of an operation does not exist in isolation but is part of an ongoing interaction among any number of parties.

In ages past, the world was home to many different societies or cultures, which were mostly different one from another, but each was more homogeneous than is the case today. Buyers in a given community needed the same products. Everyone knew what those products were, and common agreement on quality prevailed. Also prevalent was a common understanding of the entitlements of various social levels (what goods of what quality were the prerogative of the wealthy, for example). Because items were individually made, customization was the norm, for there was no other way to do business.

As the industrial age dawned in the 19th century, this situation changed. Suddenly the "customer" was no longer a few identifiable individuals, but a growing mass of less well-defined persons, any of whom, with money, could have what was formerly the prerogative of the few. With industrialization came mass production, and one product for all buyers became the norm, because there was no other cost-effective way to do business.

The modern-day corporation took shape against this background, and marketing was born. Now in the digital age, we are witnessing a phenomenon that once would have sounded like an oxymoron: mass customization. What are the implications for today's managers?

When the product is static or has few variations, operations management quite justifiably focuses on the product (and its cost). This perspective has produced the orientation of traditional operations management. With the ability to manufacture many variations of the same product, with access to increasing amounts of information, the focus today has shifted to the customer's *experience* of the product: how he or she perceives to have been served by the vendor. The customer assesses whether the product contains the desired characteristics and quality, at the best price. Management of an operation with this awareness probably will spell the success or failure of the company in today's environment.

But is today's customer truly different? Yes and no, for despite the fact that things change, things also stay the same. Human beings still engage in the same activities: They create community; they raise the next generation; they trade; they provide for themselves; and in the process, they learn, fight, and play. And today's managers still shuttle inputs through the transformation process into successful outputs. Most of the traditional notions about human activity still apply.

To explain any activity, however, one may use a variety of lenses (Galileo's lens was different from Ptolemy's, and so he derived a different explanation of the universe). A manager may view the process from the standpoint of product specifications, cost limitations, customer satisfaction, or any number of viewpoints. The lens chosen will reflect a particular view of the world and its priorities, as well as the company's priorities.

Sometimes there are no right or wrong choices, only consequences. The lens that adequately explained a given phenomenon at one time may not serve today. What is reflected through the lens will form the guidelines for decisions, however, and so the choice has far-reaching repercussions.

NEW PERSPECTIVES

From time to time, particular orientations or viewpoints burst onto the stage, altering perceptions and leaving changed priorities in their wake. Such is the case with W. Edward Deming's *total quality management,* now an article of faith for many of today's managers. The Japanese readily embraced Deming's principles, taking an enviable and now imitated approach to customer satisfaction (see Chapter 9 of the text for Deming's 14 points). Western nations paid scant attention until they saw the results of offering quality in a customer-oriented operation.

For most of us, quality is what we see in the end result (does the product meet manufacturing specifications?). In his lengthy essay *Zen and the Art of Motorcycle Maintenance,* Robert Pirsig associated achievement of quality with a state of mind: "Skilled mechanics and machinists of a certain sort . . . have patience, care and attentiveness to what they're doing, a kind of inner peace of mind that isn't contrived but results from a kind of harmony with the work . . ."[1] More characteristic of the Eastern mindset, this statement means that quality (good or bad) is not an attribute of

Streamlined Plane Making

Bitter rivals Airbus and Boeing Co. don't agree on much, but these days their production gurus chant a common mantra: Let's copy Toyota, the company that reinvented car making. The giant jet makers and their suppliers are going back to school to learn about efficient production from companies that churn out vehicles that are just a fraction of a plane's size and complexity.

Cutting production costs and speeding assembly is a vital step in the Airbus–Boeing duel to stay competitive. So airplane people are now designing parts with an eye to how fast they can be assembled. Both Boeing and Airbus have slashed their parts inventories, copied the way carmakers organize factories, and trimmed production times. Boeing has also managed to apply to gargantuan planes a technique long ago adopted by Henry Ford: assembly lines.

Not long ago, the idea of aping a mass-market car manufacturer seemed preposterous. Carmakers churned out millions of light vehicles last year, each priced in the tens of thousands of dollars. Annual output at Boeing and Airbus together was just 605 planes, some priced at almost $200 million. Car models change every few years, while jetliner models change over decades. "We always thought airplanes were different because they had four million parts," says Alan Mulally, head of Boeing's commercial aircraft division. "Well, airplanes aren't different. This is manufacturing."

Airbus aims to build a single-aisle plane from scratch in just six months, half the time taken in 2003. Working faster means Airbus can produce more planes at its existing factories, and it expects to free up more than $1.3 billion in cash by shortening the time it keeps its parts in stock—another economy pioneered by carmakers.

As Boeing prepares to build its proposed fuel-efficient 787 Dreamliner jet, project manager Mike Bair wants to make the plane so modular that the last stage of assembly takes just three days. Its predecessor model, the 767, took up to a month to assemble. Because individuality sends costs soaring, he is also emu-

lating car companies by offering a standard set of features on the 787. Customers can no longer dictate cockpit layouts and have limited choice on items such as electronics and interiors. Airbus and Boeing have also started outsourcing entire components, just as carmakers outsource systems like transmissions.

On shop floors, the plane makers have also learned from carmakers. At an Airbus factory in Wales, production teams used to walk far to the stockroom for bags of bolts and rivets, and frequently left them scattered about because they lacked nearby storage. Using work-analysis methods developed by the auto industry, project teams studied which fasteners were needed where, and when, and then organized racks on the shop floor. Now, carefully labeled bins contain tidy sets of supplies needed for specific tasks. The change has sped up work and saved over $100,000 in rivets and bolts at the Welsh factory alone, Airbus says.

But swapping one production method for another can require huge investments in new equipment and staff training. That's a big reason why aviation manufacturers have moved slowly. Airbus, for example, moves planes through successive stations during assembly but still maintains much of the old piecework approach. Production managers say this gives flexibility because a glitch that slows one plane won't stall a whole assembly line. Boeing, though, made one of the most dramatic production changes yet when it began putting together planes on a huge moving line. Top Boeing executives made multiple visits to Toyota when they were first beginning to study how to convert the production process to a moving line. When many workers initially balked at the production line and unions filed complaints, Boeing took extra pains to win them over. The change paid off: Boeing halved the time it takes to assemble a single-aisle 737, and has started putting its other planes—including its oldest and largest product, the 747—on moving lines.

SOURCE: Daniel Michaels and J. Lynn Lunsford, "Streamlined Plane Making," *The Wall Street Journal,* April 1, 2005, p. B1.

Streamlined Plane Making

Boeing, Airbus Look to Car Companies' Methods to Speed Up Jetliner Production

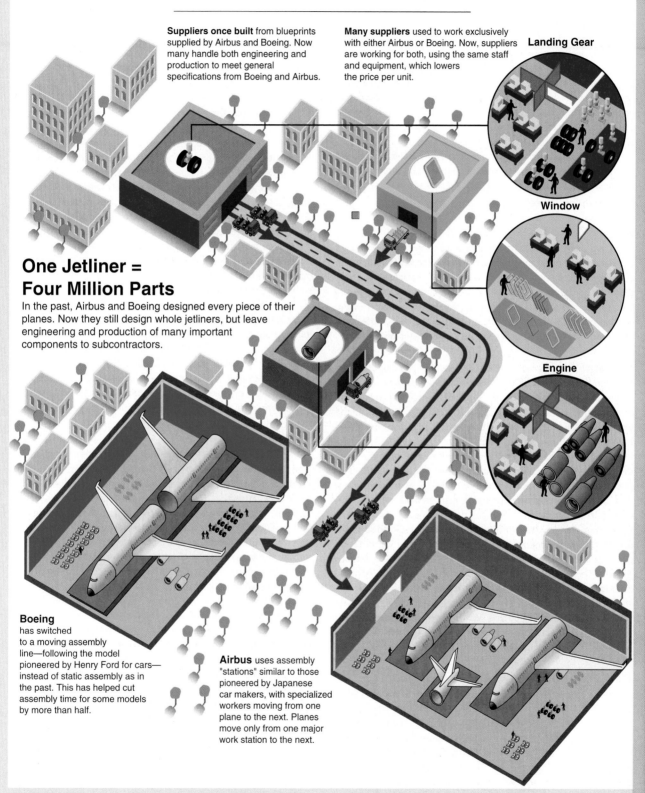

Suppliers once built from blueprints supplied by Airbus and Boeing. Now many handle both engineering and production to meet general specifications from Boeing and Airbus.

Many suppliers used to work exclusively with either Airbus or Boeing. Now, suppliers are working for both, using the same staff and equipment, which lowers the price per unit.

Landing Gear

Window

Engine

One Jetliner = Four Million Parts

In the past, Airbus and Boeing designed every piece of their planes. Now they still design whole jetliners, but leave engineering and production of many important components to subcontractors.

Boeing has switched to a moving assembly line—following the model pioneered by Henry Ford for cars—instead of static assembly as in the past. This has helped cut assembly time for some models by more than half.

Airbus uses assembly "stations" similar to those pioneered by Japanese car makers, with specialized workers moving from one plane to the next. Planes move only from one major work station to the next.

SOURCE: *The Wall Street Journal*, April 1, 2005, p. B1.

the end product, but rather is inherent in the way an individual interacts with the subject of his or her attention.

To achieve good quality requires knowing what is good, and then having the mindset suitable for achieving it. This attentiveness is related to the Japanese *kaizen,* a willingness and desire to improve constantly. Since the 1980s, Japanese business practices have been the object of study and implementation by Westerners, from specific procedures (such as *kanban,* the basis of just-in-time inventory management) to general philosophies (the *kaizen* that is part of Japanese general operations strategy). A manager anywhere today would be ill served by neglect of these concepts. As you can see from the accompanying news item, even airplane manufacturers are finding new relevance in Japan's manufacturing philosophy and techniques.

Likewise, companies that involve employees in the process are on the way to understanding that the people who interface with the product are crucial to its success. We will see how important this view is in a few pages.

CORPORATE ORGANIZATION

There are many ways to structure a company, and some of today's companies have taken their present form as a result of trends in the economy: mergers or acquisitions, diversification, alliances. With all, there are still certain functions identifiable in most corporate organizations. The operation of that function is what commands the attention of its managers. Let us consider how some of these common functions support the operations management system.

Strategic Planning   On the highest level, guiding the corporation from the broadest perspective is strategic, or long-range, planning. The firm's upper-level managers provide the corporation's direction, defining and refining its mission in the process. Management of this function entails answering questions such as: What business are we in? What business should or will we be in? Who are our customers? How can or should we serve them? Do we want to focus on core businesses or diversify? Answers to these questions will help develop corporate goals, which, filtered through the company's management levels, give direction to its operation.

As stated earlier, the world is always changing. Good strategic planning seeks to *anticipate* change and then plan for it. Good planners also foster a feeling of confidence about what is likely to produce success. During the 1990s, when the rallying cry of much of corporate management was to stick to core businesses, GE chief Jack Welch built a successful conglomerate of widely diverse businesses, finding people with the mindset to operate well within that structure, and achieving effective coordination of all functions through its many divisions.

Marketing   Of all the company's functions, marketing is closest to the customer. Its job is to identify customer needs (latent or manifest) and translate them back to the firm for its reaction. Its role in supporting the operations management system is therefore critical. Operations managers must then restate what marketing has communicated in terms that will bring about the needed response from the production mechanism. To support its efforts, marketing works with advertising to state the company's offerings in terms that are attractive to the buyer. Sales is a part of the marketing function also, salespeople being those who take action to sell within an identified market. This is the front line, the

place where information about customer needs and desires penetrates and gains the attention of the company.

A story told in sales circles is about the ABC Company (a shoe manufacturer), whose marketing head visited a remote area of the world to assess the market. He returned to report to his boss, "There's no market; they don't wear shoes." The marketing head of competitor XYZ Company made the same trip for the same purpose, reporting to *his* boss: "It's a terrific market! They've got no shoes!" Marketing's response to a circumstance can take a firm into new areas.

Research and Engineering   Suppose the marketing function has identified a new need or potential market. Enter the design and engineering people, whose function is the development and refinement of the product and the processes that manufacture it. They design, develop, and test the product through all stages until it is ready for market launch. They interact with customers who participate in the testing of a new product prior to launching. They also interact with operations—the product attributes and the processes required to make them will become the responsibility of the operations management system. Even as a product is still on the drawing board, its design may change based on customer response, manufacturing procedures (i.e., what is feasible in the current setup), or prices of material or labor.

As researchers and developers, this part of the company is most in touch with what will be available in the future, and one of its functions is identification and implementation of solutions not currently in use. The end result of the designers' work will affect purchasing (of parts, equipment, materials), inventory management (quantities of items to keep on hand), shop floor operation (equipment may need rearrangement), capacity requirements (maximum rate of production), and human resources (human skills needed and cost of acquisition).

Human Resources   This brings us to the next function: human resources. A company *is* its people. They form the culture, produce the product, and deliver it. The human resources function must seek, attract, and keep individuals having the skills, human qualities, and experience required by the operations management system. Effective management of human resources thus directly affects the entire production process. Any company wishing to build a plant in a geographically desirable area would be foolish not to take into account the human component: educational level, work ethic, habits, and expectations of the labor pool.

Some believe that there are no bad employees, only employees placed in wrong positions. Effective use of employees will provide operations managers with a valuable source of innovation and productivity gains, for the employees are actually in contact with the product (and with the customer, in the case of a service business). They are the interface where quality is born. It cannot be stressed too heavily that one of the most valuable attributes of any employee is the ability to communicate: to articulate what's right about the work experience, what's wrong, and how to improve it. Dissatisfaction unexpressed is potential trouble; ideas not presented represent lost potential.

Purchasing   Just as human inputs matter, so do materials. Selecting inputs that will support the company's orientation and vision is the crucial role played by the purchasing function. Optimally, it is a source of expertise for the operations management system, providing information about the variety of materials and systems available for use by the production process. The performance of any operating division is ultimately dependent on goods and services supplied to it by purchasing. Will the materials produce the result intended by the design of the product? Will they allow themselves to be molded as intended by the production process? Will they support the level of quality promised?

Cost-effective supply of the right materials potentially represents enormous savings for the company. A purchasing manager was once heard to say: "The sales division would have to close $500,000 in new business to produce the money I just saved by changing suppliers."

Logistics   The logistics of moving inputs through transformation may or may not benefit from an overview of the entire process, for the flow may take different names, depending on its location in the process. It may be called *inventory management* as inputs arrive, *scheduling* while in the transformation process, and *distribution* when outputs are en route to the customer. Smooth or poor coordination of the flow from supplier of materials to delivery to the customer has repercussions throughout the channel. If materials are not ready for a specific section of the production apparatus at the right time, equipment and machinery sit idle (a drain on profitability). Delays in delivery to customers mean delays in payment received, and that has an impact on the company's cash flow.

Finance   This brings us to the finance area. This function serves as an interface between the firm's managers and the financial community: banks, investment firms, and stockholders. These entities have a stake in the company's success or failure, and at all times are poised to assist, advise, provide support, or withdraw it. Finance must explain the company's performance adequately to elicit the maximum amount of support from financial institutions. In so doing, it makes use of the accounting department. Not merely a mechanism for tracking costs, the accounting department provides information useful to managers in understanding the cost implications of their decisions. Such cost-monitoring information can help managers understand how their own costs compare with standard costs, for example. Accounting also can help derive the cost implications of introducing new equipment or technologies.

In another of its roles, the finance function must be knowledgeable about the firm's creditworthiness. Any decline in the company's ability to pay its bills will weaken its position vis-à-vis competitors. Finance also must monitor the creditworthiness of suppliers. If suppliers are not financially able to deliver what they promise, the operations management system will feel the impact immediately. The financial community watches the impact of all these decisions, basing its ratings (and therefore support) on the wisdom of the decision makers.

A Team Operation   The fineness with which one breaks down the preceding functions can vary, but it should be clear at this point that the operations management system is only one of those operating within the corporate context. In the best of all possible worlds, operations management works hand in glove with the other functions, alert to any harmful fragmentation or lack of communication. Communication is, of course, a two-way street, and just as operations people must be aware of the workings of the other functions, the latter must know what the operations management system perceives, needs, and expects.

Satisfying customer expectations is a corporate activity, the work of one body (from *corpus,* Latin for "body"), with the whole dependent on how well its parts work individually and how well they work together. Neglect of any one organ affects the body's ability to perform at optimum level.

PREPARING FOR THE FUTURE IN THE NEW ECONOMY

In addition to awareness of how the company is operating at present, every good manager will give thought to what *could* happen, what is likely to happen, and what is possible, both for the company as a whole and for his or her own sphere of influence. Stated another way, an effective manager has a sense of vision. This means being aware of changes or potential changes in customer demands and changes in the company's resources (technology, labor pool, financial support). A good manager must listen, being attentive to all facts, and then select the useful facts from among the many supplied. A manager must constantly ask, "What if . . . ?"

With good vision and a healthy curiosity, a manager will more adequately handle factors impinging on the operations management system. The objective is to develop a sense of vision adequate to anticipate conceivable consequences. Let us consider some of today's challenges in what is often referred to as the **"new economy."**

Globalization   A company's sphere of activity has always been what could be reached easily by current means of communication and transportation. What is reachable has constantly expanded. The entire world is today's operating arena, both for buying inputs and for selling outputs. This circumstance presents the operations management system with a new range of possibilities.

The possibility of *outsourcing* has always been present. That is, do we make a particular component of the product, or do we send it out for manufacture pursuant to our specifications? Today, a manager may outsource locally or to any facility in the world offering the capability of supplying the need. It takes a lot of information, as well as sound judgment, to know which part of the process would benefit from being handled out of house.

The success of producing elsewhere depends in part on the characteristics of the "elsewhere." In the 20th century, U.S. companies based in northern states sometimes would move certain manufacturing operations to the southern part of the country, taking advantage of lower labor costs. While this required some adjustment in expectations, the adjustment is slight compared to manufacturing in Pacific Rim countries or Latin America, for example. The reason is simple: Each culture handles things in a particular way. A wise manager will not assume that a different culture will respond to expectations in the same manner as an American labor force would, and this circumstance may work to one's advantage or to one's detriment. Those who can anticipate potential problem areas are ahead of the game in the decision to manufacture offshore.

Then there is the globe as *marketplace.* To sell globally requires product design that accounts for differing tastes throughout the world's cultures. A small manufacturer of skin-care products based on formulas from India began marketing her line in America some years ago. She reports that she had to make alterations to account for the fact that Americans would not use a product with an unusual smell, no matter how beneficial for the skin.[2] Nescafe markets its products all over the globe, but the instant coffee sold in Brazil does not taste like that sold in the United States—in each instance, the product must satisfy the taste of a different culture.[3]

The ease with which the operations management system can make these alterations has increased dramatically in the last few decades. Digital technology has made flexibility in manufacturing a much more attainable situation than was previously the case, offering enormous potential to vary the product.

Environment Another challenge facing today's manager is the environment, meaning both the world and the milieu in which the company operates. In an earlier time, negative effects from a manufacturing process were absorbed unobtrusively by the surroundings. As population density increased and consumption skyrocketed, particularly in the Western nations, this ceased to be true. What occurs in one place on the planet has an impact on the rest of it. The manager's challenge is to care enough about the future without imperiling today's operations, and the decisions are not simple.

It is unfortunate that the issue of environmental responsibility traditionally has been cast in ethical terms. While this stance is valid, and ultimately *the* reason for being good stewards of the planet, it does not help managers handle all the information required to make good decisions or quantify what is needed for decision making. In addition, consumers are often inconsistent, demanding recycled paper, for instance, and then choosing to buy whiter paper that is not recycled.

Certainly the last few decades have witnessed significant progress in the handling of the most blatantly offensive effects of manufacturing processes (waste streaming, emissions control). But making the right decision is not a clear-cut path. Consider the simple example of the supermarket checkout stand. "Would you like paper or plastic for your groceries?" The environmentally responsible buyer must choose between less than desirable alternatives. Paper (even if recycled) uses trees; plastic uses hydrocarbons and is not as easy to recycle. Decisions faced by operations managers are infinitely more complex.

Furthermore, if managers do not see to their societal responsibility, others will demand compliance. A corporation is not its own island in community waters, for others are affected by its decisions: property owners, investors, the larger public, and tomorrow's adults. Surely we have learned by now that groups that do not police their own ranks effectively are sure targets for policing by others, be they governmental agencies or community organizations.

The alternatives for an operations manager are therefore to react or to take a leadership role, becoming knowledgeable about potential negative effects of the process managed by him or her and proposing ways to handle them. In the long term, if we are to manage our economy's activities for tomorrow rather than today, responsibility for the environment is not a choice.

Knowledge and Information One of the features of the new economy is that in the transformation process, the major input is intellectual property: knowledge, research, information, and design. These inputs have supplanted (in value) the

material inputs required to build physical units. When knowledge is the major raw material, launching the first unit of a product represents millions of dollars; the cost of the second and thereafter is minuscule.

The products themselves are of a different nature, and it often takes greater sophistication to use a new-economy product—thus, for example, people's reluctance to switch from a PC to a Mac, or vice versa. As a result, customers are not as likely to be swayed by advertising, but rather by their increasing knowledge of the product and its technology. Successful companies will be those that increase a customer's knowledge base in general, and skill with their own products in particular.

As the information explosion continues to feed today's consumers and today's workforce, the knowledge acquired gives rise to expectations. As we will discuss later, today's consumers are far from being locked into only a few sources for their information. Rather, they swim in an ocean of facts, figures, perspectives, and opportunities.

Nor are today's employees like those of yesteryear. It is instead the case that, depending on his or her own personal needs or aspirations, an employee is drawn to (and will stay with) a specific job in a given company for two reasons: (1) the possibility of experiencing personal satisfaction or growth and (2) satisfaction in the human interaction prevalent at that company. The balance of these factors varies with the individual, but everyone draws from these two wells. Today's managers therefore must provide more than the means for an employee to put bread on the table. The company must offer ongoing professional development, opportunity for increased responsibility in the firm, and a satisfying place to work. Today's employees do not expect to be *supervised*, but rather *coached* along the path of success. Clearly, the manager also must be knowledgeable and continue to grow, increasing in value as a mentor.

Technology The challenge of technology will occupy us for the rest of these pages. Technology has always existed and has always been neutral. That is, just as a knife serves to feed the family or to kill an adversary, new technologies can be used to help or harm. As with any challenge, managers can view technological innovation as something to react to, something to anticipate, something to plan for, or something from which to derive potential improvements and growth.

Technologies exist in various stages of development; that is, some are ready and available for use by the operations management system, some will be cost-effective in 5 or 10 years, and some are in embryo. Any forward-looking manager will be aware of all three. Technology companies (those which market the latest of a given technology, e.g., cellular phones) must monitor technology on two fronts. They must be aware of similar products on the market, constantly assessing the limits of their own products. They also must be aware of technologies potentially usable by their own operations, just as any nontechnology company would.

In its development, a technology tends to move to the hands of the user. Take the clock as an example. At one time in history, the only clock in the community was the one in the town square. Then wealthier people could purchase large timepieces known as "grandfather clocks." By the middle of the 20th century most adults owned a wristwatch, often a special gift received at graduation. Today children and adults have access to many timepieces, from those on their wrists to the many in the home, office, or car.

We could trace a similar progression for other technologies, such as engines and, of course, computers (where the transition from mainframes to portable PCs occurred within a few decades of the last century).

The shift of a technology to the user is not always smooth. One of the potential stumbling blocks when a company embraces a technology is to discount the human factor involved in its use. We see this in small businesses constantly. The local copy shop brings in the latest copying and finishing equipment, offering everything from double-sided, spiral-bound reports graced with photos to personalized, artistic party invitations. The resulting product, however, is in part dependent on the skill and experience of the operator and the availability of sufficient personnel to work with customers.

Larger industrial equipment offers a similar scenario. At an earlier time in history, the operator of, for example, a multi-story printing press would have 30 years to become familiar with the operation of that equipment before a new generation came on stream. In today's offices, employees barely become proficient at using the current popular software before a new or different version of it comes out. These "improvements" provide fertile ground for inefficiencies, for in the final analysis, technology can advance only at the rate at which human beings can use it effectively.

With this knowledge, any effective operations manager will have some type of formal technology management in place—some means of looking ahead, preparing for the effects of new technologies. When envisioning the potential of new technology (or technology in embryo), the best human characteristics to bring to the table are:

1. Awareness (information plus perspective) and
2. Imagination (the ability to create new scenarios from existing ones).

Awareness is the easiest to acquire. In fact, it can be bought from the many consultants standing ready to assist corporations in preparing for the future. One must cultivate powers of imagination within oneself.

THE INTERNET

That brings us to the current challenge for one's imaginative powers: the Internet. Opportunities and pitfalls abound on the Web. What follows are some noteworthy experiences gained from successful and unsuccessful uses of the Internet. By the time this material sees print, much will have changed.

Several methods have emerged as options for exploiting an Internet operation. A regular "**bricks and mortar**" business can create its own in-house Web group, or it can partner with a dotcom company that will operate the Web end of its business for it. For example, when the three largest retailers in the country decided to jump on the "**e-tailing**" bandwagon in the late 1990s, their strategies differed: JC Penney and Sears formed their own in-house Web site divisions; Kmart, in contrast, contracted with a subsidiary, bluelight.com, to get its site up and running. Last, a business can elect to sell its products only on the Internet.

Amazon.com was slow to make a profit because of its initial start-up costs—for product and warehouses, for example. However, e-tailers offering travel products, software, and financial services have low overhead and can see a profit much faster.

Internet-only companies are referred to as "**pure-play**" operations. Amazon.com is an example.

Managers also have to figure out how to integrate Web activities seamlessly into their operations. Poorly integrated systems can wreak havoc within an organization. For instance, the first Christmas Toys 'R' Us did business on the Web, the company had to turn away customers because it couldn't fill the number of orders the site generated. To solve the problem, Toys 'R' Us formed an alliance with Amazon.com. Amazon handled the Web site and the online ordering process, and Toys 'R' Us managed inventory and shipping. Each company had expertise the other needed to sell toys online.

Alongside Web sales, retailers are in various stages of deploying new technologies to offer the benefits of online shopping at the retail site. For example, a kiosk on the shopping floor can make information available electronically, providing shoppers the information they need to make a buying decision. Lamps Plus gives its customers access to high-resolution images they can zoom in on and manipulate to review fabric textures and sample different colors and products in a 360-degree view. Pacific Sunwear lets its customers search for and display clothing for boys or girls by item, color, and price. Other sites, like Circuit City, eBags, and Amazon, offer online guides or customer reviews to help buyers make decisions.

These retailers, along with others such as Nordstrom, Eddie Bauer, and Radio Shack, are building on brand-name presence and a familiarity already created at the mall, in the dealership, and through catalog sales—an advantage not enjoyed by companies operating exclusively on the Web.

Not long ago, the online auctioneer eBay and a few companies that built e-stores for other firms were the only ones operating in the black. However, pure-play companies can be successful. Approximately one-quarter of the 200 public Internet companies that survived the dot-bomb shakeout are profitable now under standard accounting rules. The biggest moneymakers are online travel, software, and financial services. Why? Because they sell pure information products—there are no products to store or ship. But even Amazon.com, which has long operated in the red, is finally showing a profit despite the fact that every time some-one buys a book on Amazon, the company must turn around and purchase a copy from the publisher. Also, once pure-play compa-nies recoup their initial start-up costs, they don't need to spend much more money as sales rise. No additional stores need to be built to reach consumers, for example.[4]

Nonetheless, technology tricks and novel business ideas are not enough. Customers still want speed, convenience, quality, and good service. In this regard, the Web is no different from con-ventional stores and catalogs. Customers ultimately will cast their votes for the companies that provide the best product experi-ence whether they see the product on the Web or can touch it in stores.

COMPANYWIDE RESONANCE

Sales and marketing data collection is turned on its head by the Internet, as companies record information about a user's habits during a Web site visit. For instance, if you buy a product on Ama-zon.com, during future visits, the site will make suggestions about similar products in which you might be interested. Many retailers are of the opinion that this type of **data mining** will make or break the operation in the future. That is, the ability to collect and use information from online customers will be crucial to suc-cessful marketing decisions.

Moreover, a company's Web page can make it easy or hard for the customer to get the information leading to a purchase. As some have learned the hard way, it is not enough to simply take images that are successful in print and place them on the Web, for each medium has its own characteristics.

The design of the company's Web site has a companywide im-pact. For example, if a customer on the Web can verify that an item is available, the chances of closing the sale are increased. If a customer can find out the expected delivery date of the product and the means, the chances of a sale are increased even more. In this scenario, front- and back-end operations touch, and deliver-ing the goods is still key to success.

Mountains of Data   The purchasing function benefits from the Web through sheer availability of information, as well as ease of response to questions. Today, a purchasing manager need not wait for a visit from a sales representative. In fact, under the im-pact of the Web, businesses are seeing a realignment of the tra-ditional relationships among producers, wholesalers, distributors, and retailers. In the business-to-business world, buyers previously faced a number of obstacles to getting the best deal: Suppliers were distant, research time was scarce, and intermediaries con-trolled most of the information. Enter Ariba, a Web-based mar-ketplace for industrial goods. Purchasing need only put out a contract on the Web, and a flood of bids from suppliers may be the response. In a sense, Web-based companies are becoming the new intermediaries, the conduit between producers and buyers.

Purchasing managers can go online to Ariba for industrial goods, National Transportation Exchange for trucking, Chemdex for biochemical supplies, and IMX Exchange for mortgage brokers to find loans, and this is only the start.

The Internet has also become the intermediary between em-ployers and employees. Human resources departments can avail themselves of numerous Web-based tools to find candidates. Not only are there gigantic job exchanges such as Monster.com, but intranets exist to keep job searches within companies. Job seek-

Companies can easily track their shipments by downloading the information directly from FedEx.

ers and potential employers can access one another's information based on geographic preference, salary range, or skill sets.

Logistics, scheduling, and distribution tasks increasingly are plugged into Web-based networks, benefiting from the ease of gathering weather data, traffic patterns, and late-breaking news. Tracking information about shipments can be downloaded from Federal Express. Zip codes are available online from the U.S. Postal Service. These factors affect the company's ability to de-liver the product on time and the availability of materials from suppliers, effects ultimately felt by the operations management system.

Changing Information Patterns   To reduce printing costs and make documents widely available, companies are digi-tizing information. In some instances, they are posting it on the Web. Different people residing in distant places can view the same information this way. Still, digitizing information is not without its obstacles. Not all people have the same hardware and software used for viewing and printing out information. Additionally, mis-communications can occur that otherwise might not if all em-ployees were working under one roof.

Corporations must take these circumstances into account when deciding how to make use of the Web, for the decisions af-fect each of the company's functioning units. Posting certain kinds of information does not usually cause problems. For example, providing company address(es), phone numbers, hours of opera-tion, and the like, is more economically done on the Web than by a live employee answering the telephone. Many inquiries that in the print age were handled by mailing out an annual report, for example, may be handled more cost-effectively on the Web.

Supplying other types of information, however, might not be as free of repercussions as in the preceding examples. Depending on whether the company is a business-to-business or a business-to-consumer operation, buyers will want product information, forms and terms of payment, special sales, return policies, status of an order, shipping rates and turnaround, possibility of changing a cur-rent order, tracking information, or status of an order.

Providing and maintaining only one piece of this information—for example, change in an order—affects at least three departments: accounting, distribution, and marketing. Each department supplying the information must be aware of the consequences of making the information available and have a mechanism for handling changes. Coordination becomes an issue as well. For example, charges to a credit-card account must not occur before the merchandise is shipped. Whether selling to another business or to consumers, online operation requires new networks. Companies forge ahead nonetheless in this burgeoning technology, realizing that the potential advantages are well worth the temporary discomforts.

INTELLECTUAL PROPERTY

We have mentioned that a characteristic of the new economy is the nature of the product: knowledge, design, and engineering, rather than hard manufacturing. Let us look at an environmental engineering firm and how the Web affects its operation. The business of such a firm might include devising solutions to improve power-plant operation. The activities of firms involved in the planning of any such industrial facility are subject to compliance with government regulations. Handling engineering projects, for example, a new power plant, requires submission of an enormous amount of data to demonstrate that the firm has complied with and planned for all impacts on the community. A requirement might be, for example, that notification be given to every property owner within a certain radius of the plant. Downloading that information from title companies and then monitoring the notification process is only one of a multitude of tasks potentially manageable on the Web.

The firm must provide the information to the various parties in certain forms, which gives rise to new information needs. For example, one way to verify that it has indeed shipped the requisite print or CD-ROM copies is by downloading tracking information from Federal Express. It also can make its compliance documentation available in a read-only format on the Web, allowing printing of sections by those who wish to do so.

In preparing to build a plant, all federal, state, and local regulations must be accounted for. The firm must provide information on how its power plant will affect traffic patterns, cultural resources, schools, water supply, flora and fauna, and air quality. It also must state its plans for handling hazardous materials generated during the construction and operation of the plant.

Managing the enormous body of information to respond in the ways illustrated would have been a near impossibility before computer management of data.

PITFALLS

What have been the experiences of those who have succeeded in e-commerce and those who have failed, and what can we learn from them? We already mentioned Toys 'R' Us and its inability to fill its orders on the Web. In addition to losing business, it, along with other retailers such as Macys.com and CDNow, was subject to Federal Trade Commission investigation and fines regarding rules for order fulfillment. The FTC regulation states that if retailers cannot meet promised deadlines, they must notify customers, giving them the option of canceling the order. Could the management of these companies have foreseen the inability to fill orders, and if so, how?

Confidentiality of information is an issue. A recent Gallup poll revealed that 66 percent of Americans favor new laws to protect

their privacy amid the high-tech revolution.[5] Amazon.com found itself under fire after it began charging different consumers different prices on the basis of information it had collected on them. Toys 'R' Us was hit with a class-action lawsult claiming that it allowed market researchers to access consumer data from its Web site. The retailer responded that it had hired the firm to analyze customers' data in order to improve their shopping experience. Although breach of confidentiality predates the Web, the enormity of any breach is compounded by the staggering amounts of digital data available for tapping. The Federal Trade Commission and Congress are attempting to pass laws and institute regulations to protect consumers.

Customer familiarity with the Web is another issue. Despite what seems to be a flurry of online buying, media reports suggest that many customers are not buying online at all, or only infrequently, or only certain products. As with catalog shopping, the online industry will mature as consumers become more familiar with offerings and as Web retailers improve in presentation and fulfillment.

Some customers are concerned about credit-card data transmitted online and are therefore hesitant to shop. The misuse of credit-card data is present, however, every time a clerk in a store records the data during a purchase. Although this is more a perception than a real problem, perception motivates people's actions, preventing some from making the leap into cybershopping.

Circumstances such as these are forcing the formation of new business models as companies grapple with all the variables, spurred on by the potential benefits.

NEW NEEDS AND DESIRES

Customers themselves are changing as it becomes possible to satisfy latent needs or desires. We have alluded to mass customization. Here are some specific examples of varying product features.

Setting up an assembly line or installing production equipment is part of the cost of manufacturing. Speaking of color choice in automobiles, Henry Ford once said: "They can have any color they want, as long as it's black." Alteration of a manufacturing process to vary a product feature was very costly. With the flexible manufacturing available in the digital age, manufacturers have the option of producing multiple flavors of bottled water, blue jeans tailored for different bodies, and a veritable artist's palette for automobile colors. Levi Strauss and Brooks now offer machine-customized garments, accommodating a vast array of body measurements. Barbie's friends can have hair and skin color, clothing, and even personalities picked by their young owners. Digital technology fuels the manufacturing capability; the Web spurs demand.

The result is that customers' desire for customization and personalization has been moved to a new level. Shoppers previously settled for a product that was mostly, or approximately, what they wanted. They are now beginning to see that sometimes they can have a product endowed with *precisely* the features they want. The experience of product acquisition is therefore changing.

THE VALUE OF HUMAN ATTRIBUTES

What are the implications of all this change for traditional operations management? Changes are remembered as negative or positive, depending on how well one has survived them. There is no reason to believe that technological change is any more threatening than other kinds of change. Traditional human qualities still serve: vision, awareness, alertness, imagination, courage, steadfastness, persistence, flexibility, attentiveness, and goodwill.

Today's managers must be aware, noticing shifts in trends, habits and customs, possibilities, and ground rules. They must have or develop the vision to foresee the range of possibilities, and then the imagination to create solutions. They must have the courage to strike out in new directions and be alert to adjustments required by the new direction. An effective manager will be flexible enough to make an adjustment and steadfast in the face of misunderstandings and mistakes. A manager will need to be persistent in following the chosen path, with attentiveness to all facets of the surroundings. Chances of success in any challenge are enhanced by goodwill.

Finally, he or she will need luck. Some say "it comes to you," and some say "you make your own." Most think that both are true.

KEY TERMS

bricks and mortar, p. 583
data mining, p. 584
e-tailing, p. 583
new economy, p. 581
pure-play, p. 583

DISCUSSION QUESTIONS

1. What is "mass customization"? How can products be mass-produced yet still be differentiated to appeal to individual market sectors? How has mass customization affected management's focus on the product?

2. Why was Deming's "total quality management" embraced by the Japanese long before Deming's philosophy became key to U.S. operations management? How does it relate to operations management?

3. How has the new economy changed operations management? What is the major input in the operations process as a result?

4. What must businesses consider in deciding to take advantage of new technology? How does new technology affect operations management decisions?

5. Why were many dot-com companies so short-lived at the end of the 20th century? Why would Amazon and Toys 'R' Us form an alliance? Which firm is likely to benefit more? Explain.

6. How can the Internet improve a firm's operations management?

7. What are the implications for operations management of customers being able to satisfy purchasing needs immediately by using the Internet? Have e-business functions fundamentally changed the way firms do business? Explain.

Chapter **18**

CHAPTER 18

Creating and Managing Change

The world hates change, yet that is the only thing that has brought progress.

— **Charles Kettering**

My interest is in the future because I am going to spend the rest of my life there.

— **Charles Kettering**

CHAPTER OUTLINE

LEARNING OBJECTIVES

After studying Chapter 18, you will know:

1. What it takes to be world class.

2. How to manage change effectively.

3. How to create a successful future.

Prologue

GE AND JEFFREY IMMELT

GE is often featured in *Fortune*'s poll of U.S. corporate executives as the country's "Most Admired Company" and named by London's *Financial Times* as the "Most Respected Company in the World." You read about GE's HR practices in Chapter 10. Another key to GE's extraordinary success is its ability to change, as orchestrated by its top leaders as well as people throughout the organization.

GE began on the basis of new discoveries and inventions—Thomas Edison founded the company in 1898. In the 20th century, it was a bellwether of new management practices. In the 1930s, it was the classic highly centralized, tightly controlled corporation. In the 1950s, GE delegated responsibility to department managers and led the trend toward decentralization. In the 1960s and 1970s, it reorganized into 43 strategic business units overseeing groups, divisions, and departments and was famous for its sophisticated strategic planning process.

When Jack Welch became CEO in 1981, he envisioned an entrepreneurial company that was highly diversified and had world-class leadership in every product line. He set stretch goals, downsized, sold off underperforming businesses, and then set about changing the corporate culture. Despite having hundreds of thousands of employees, he wanted to create the nonbureaucratic, open, fast-moving culture of a small company. He succeeded, creating more wealth than any CEO in business history and being named *Fortune*'s "Manager of the Century." (For more on how Welch accomplished what he did, see the case at the end of this part of the book, "The Transformation at General Electric.")

Welch retired in 2001, choosing Jeffrey Immelt as his successor. One observer remarked on the difficulty of the task ahead: "Who wants to follow Babe Ruth?" Immelt was following a legend.

Despite GE's long run of incredible success, Immelt couldn't just ride the wave. His first full day in office was September 10, 2001—one day before the world changed. GE had to change as well. In 2002, earnings growth was below double digits for the first time in 10 years. The stock price dropped by a third during Immelt's first year. Immelt needed to turn what many consider the greatest company of all time into a more nimble, customer-driven company.

Sources for Prologue, Connections, Epilogue: N. Madden, "Beijing, '08: GE Jump-Starts Olympic Push," *Advertising Age*, January 3, 2005, p. 6; J. Useem, "Another Boss Revolution," *Fortune*, April 5, 2004, pp. 112–24; D. Jones, M. McCarthy, and G. Stoller, "Deal Helps Immelt Put His Stamp on GE," *USA Today*, October 9, 2003, p. 1B; "Managers Who Hit Their Marks," *BusinessWeek*, *The America's Intelligence Wire*, January 10, 2005; C. Bartlett and M. Wozny, *GE's Two-Decade Transformation: Jack Welch's Leadership* (Boston, MA: Harvard Business School Press, 2002); J. Gapper and D. Roberts, "Man of the Year Jeffrey Immelt," *Financial Times*, December 27, 2003, p. 11; S. Herera and Bill Griffeth, *CNBC Interview*, *The America's Intelligence Wire*, January 21, 2005.

> Want a tough job? Try leading an organization through major change . . . Almost without exception, executives claim it's the hardest work they've ever done.
>
> **—T. A. Stewart, *Fortune***
>
> Anybody who says it can't be done: Wrong. Anybody who says it's easy: Also wrong.
>
> **—Charles Lee, Verizon**
>
> We're on a journey that never ends. And the day we think we've got it made, that's the day we'd better start worrying about going out of business.
>
> **—Rich Teerlink, Harley-Davidson**
>
> In a world that keeps changing, perhaps the most valuable capability of all—for a company, for a team, for an individual—is the capacity for leading change.
>
> **—Fast Company**

These executives—and Chris Rock below—are all talking about the same things: the difficulties and challenges of creating change, and the need to improve constantly in order to achieve world-class excellence and competitive advantage for the future.

Change happens—constantly and unpredictably. Whatever competitive advantage you may have depends on particular circumstances at a particular time, but circumstances change.[1] The economic environment shifts; competitors pop up everywhere; markets emerge and disappear. The challenge for organizations is not just to produce innovative new products—it is to balance a culture that is innovative and that builds a sustainable business.[2] And for individuals, the ability to cope with change is related to their job performance and the rewards they receive.[3]

> "You know how it is in the music business. Fickle! Here today, gone today!"
>
> Chris Rock

Becoming World Class

Managers today want, or *should* want, their organizations to become world class.[4] To some people, striving for world-class excellence seems a lofty, impossible, unnecessary goal. But it is a goal that is essential to survival and success in today's intensely competitive business world.

Being world class requires applying the best and latest knowledge and ideas, and having the ability to operate at the highest standards of any place anywhere.[5] Thus, becoming world class does not mean merely improving. It means becoming one of the very best in the world at what you do. A few years ago, some estimated that for most companies, becoming world class required increasing quality by 100 to 1,000 times, decreasing costs by 30 percent to 50 percent, increasing productivity by two to four times, decreasing order-to-delivery time by a factor of 5 to 10, and decreasing new-product development times by 30 percent to 60 percent. And even if a firm realized these dramatic improvements, it still had to keep getting better![6]

World-class companies create high-value products and earn superior profits over the long run. They demolish the obsolete methods, systems, and cultures of the past that impeded their competitive progress, and apply more effective and competitive organizational strategies, structures, processes, and management of human resources. The result is an organization capable of competing successfully on a global basis.[7]

It's a worthy aspiration: becoming world class at every one of your competitive goals.

Sustainable, Great Futures

Two Stanford professors, James Collins and Jerry Porras, studied 18 corporations that had achieved and maintained greatness for half a century or more.[8] The companies included Sony, American Express, Motorola, Marriott, Johnson & Johnson, Disney, 3M, Hewlett-Packard, Citicorp, and Wal-Mart. Over the years, these companies have been widely admired, been considered the premier institutions in their industries, and made a real *impact on the world*. Although every company goes through periodic downturns—

3M	Innovation; "Thou shalt not kill a new product idea"
	Absolute integrity
	Respect for individual initiative and personal growth
	Tolerance for honest mistakes
	Product quality and reliability
	"Our real business is solving problems"
American Express	Heroic customer service
	Worldwide reliability of services
	Encouragement of individual initiative
Boeing	Being on the leading edge of aeronautics; being pioneers
	Tackling huge challenges and risks
	Product safety and quality
	Integrity and ethical business
	To "eat, breathe, and sleep the world of aeronautics"
Sony	To experience the sheer joy that comes from the advancement, application, and innovation of technology that benefits the general public
	To elevate the Japanese culture and national status
	Being pioneers—not following others, but doing the impossible
	Respecting and encouraging each individual's ability and creativity
Wal-Mart	"We exist to provide value to our customers"—to make their lives better via lower prices and greater selection; all else is secondary
	Swim upstream, buck conventional wisdom
	Be in partnership with employees
	Work with passion, commitment, and enthusiasm
	Run lean
	Pursue ever-higher goals
Walt Disney	No cynicism allowed
	Fanatical attention to consistency and detail
	Continuous progress via creativity, dreams, and imagination
	Fanatical control and preservation of Disney's "magic" image
	"To bring happiness to millions" and to celebrate, nurture, and promulgate "wholesome American values"

TABLE 18.1

Core Ideologies in
Built-to-Last Companies

SOURCE: From *Built to Last* by James C. Collins and Jerry I. Porras, Copyright © 1997 by James C. Collins and Jerry I. Porras. Reprinted by permission of HarperCollins Publishers, Inc and Random House Group Limited.

and these companies are no exceptions over their long histories—these companies have consistently prevailed across the decades. They turn in extraordinary performance *over the long run*, rather than fleeting greatness. This study is reported in the book called *Built to Last*—which is what these great organizations were and are.

The researchers sought to identify the essential characteristics of enduringly great companies. These great companies have strong core values in which they believe deeply, and they express and live the values consistently. They are driven by goals—not just incremental improvements or business-as-usual goals, but stretch goals (recall Chapter

13). They change continuously, driving for progress via adaptability, experimentation, trial and error, entrepreneurial thinking, and fast action. And they do not focus on beating the competition; they focus primarily on beating themselves. They continually ask, "How can we improve ourselves to do better tomorrow than we did today?"

But underneath the action and the changes, the core values and vision remain steadfast and uncompromised. Table 18.1 displays the core values of several of the companies that were "built to last." Note that the values are not all the same. In fact, there was no set of common values that consistently predicted success. Instead, the critical factor is that the great companies *have* core values, *know* what they are and what they mean, and *live* by them—year after year after year.

The Tyranny of the "*Or*"

Many companies, and individuals, are plagued by what the authors of *Built to Last* call the **"tyranny of the *or*."** This refers to the belief that things must be either A or B, and cannot be both. The authors provide many common examples:[9] beliefs that you must choose either change or stability; be conservative or bold; have control and consistency or creative freedom; do well in the short term or invest for the future; plan methodically or be opportunistic; create shareholder wealth or do good for the world; be pragmatic or idealistic. Such beliefs, that only one goal but not another can be attained, often are invalid and certainly are constraining—unnecessarily so.

> **tyranny of the "or"**
> The belief that things must be either A or B, and cannot be both; that only one goal and not another can be attained.

The Genius of the "*And*"

In contrast to the "tyranny of the *or*," the **"genius of the *and*"**—more academically, **organizational ambidexterity**—refers to being able to achieve multiple things at the same time.[10] It develops via the actions of many individuals throughout the organization. We discussed earlier in the book the importance of delivering multiple competitive values to customers; performing all the management functions; reconciling hard-nosed business logic with ethics; leading and empowering; and others. Authors Collins and Porras have their own list,[11] which includes:

> **genius of the "and";**
> **organizational**
> **ambidexterity**
> Ability to achieve multiple things simultaneously.

- Purpose beyond profit *and* pragmatic pursuit of profit.
- Relatively fixed core values *and* vigorous change and movement.
- Conservatism with the core values *and* bold business moves.
- Clear vision and direction *and* experimentation.
- Stretch goals *and* incremental progress.
- Control based on values *and* operational freedom.
- Long-term thinking and investment *and* demand for short-term results.
- Visionary, futuristic thinking *and* daily, nuts-and-bolts execution.

You have learned about all of these things throughout this course and should not lose sight of any of them—either in your mind or in your actions. To achieve them requires the continuous and effective management of change.

Organization Development

How do organizations become more ambidextrous and move in the other positive directions described throughout this book? This chapter discusses several general approaches that will create positive change. We begin here with an umbrella concept called organization development.

Organization development (OD) is a systemwide application of behavioral science knowledge to develop, improve, and reinforce the strategies, structures, and processes that lead to organization effectiveness.[12] Throughout this course, you have acquired knowledge about behavioral science and the strategies, structures, and processes that help organizations become more effective. The "systemwide" component of the definition means that OD is not a narrow improvement in technology or operations, but a broader approach to changing organizations, units, or people. The "behavioral science" component

> **organization**
> **development (OD)**
> The systemwide application of behavioral science knowledge to develop, improve, and reinforce the strategies, structures, and processes that lead to organizational effectiveness.

To more effectively and efficiently reach their customers, Entenmann's teamed up with AT&T to set up a network to "receive detailed sales information from thousands of retail stores, utilize that information to identify the products needed, transmit the data to regional bakeries, and dispatch trucks to fill the shelves with fresh pastry even before it has a chance to cool." These things don't just happen; they require a concerted, intensive set of change efforts.

means that OD is not directly about economic, financial, or technical aspects of the organization—although they may benefit, through changes in the behavior of the people in the organization. The other key part of the definition—to develop, improve, and reinforce—refers to the actual process of changing, for the better and for the long term.

Two features of organization development are important to note.[13] First, it aims to increase organizational effectiveness—it improves the organization's ability to respond to external groups like customers, stockholders, governments, employees, and other stakeholders, resulting in better quality products, higher financial returns, and high quality of work life. Second, OD has an important underlying value orientation: It supports human potential, development, and participation in addition to performance and competitive advantage.

Many specific OD techniques fit under this philosophical umbrella.[14] The basic types are *strategic interventions*, including helping organizations conduct mergers and acquisitions, change their strategies, and develop alliances; *technostructural interventions* relating to organization structure and design, employee involvement, and work design; *human resources management interventions*, including attracting good people, setting goals, and appraising and rewarding performance; and *human process interventions*, including conflict resolution, team-building, communication, and leadership. As you can see, you learned about these topics throughout your management course. You also will learn more about the process of creating change through the rest of this chapter.

Achieving Greatness

A recent study of 200 management techniques employed by 160 companies over 10 years identified the specific management practices that lead to sustained, superior performance.[15] The authors boiled their findings down to four key factors: (1) *strategy*—focused on customers, continually fine-tuned based on marketplace changes, and clearly communicated to employees; (2) *execution*—good people, with decision-making authority on the front lines, doing quality work and cutting costs; (3) *culture*—one that motivates, empowers people to innovate, rewards people appropriately (psychologically as well as economically), entails strong values, challenges people, and provides a satisfying work environment; and (4) *structure*—making the organization easy to work in and easy to work with, characterized by cooperation and the exchange of information and knowledge throughout the organization. You have been learning about these things throughout this course.

Becoming world class doesn't apply only to the private sector. People worry about globalization's negative effects on local communities, as plants shut down and people lose their jobs overseas. But local communities do have options—not easy ones, but doable. A locality can strive to become a world-class center of *thinkers, makers,* or *traders*.[16] Thus, Boston creates new ideas and technologies that often dominate world markets; Spartanville–Greenville, South Carolina, is a world-class manufacturing region that has attracted direct foreign investment from more than 200 companies in 18 countries; and Miami, Florida, connects Latino and Anglo cultures the way Hong Kong and Singapore have historically bridged Chinese and British cultures. The keys to creating world-class local communities: visionary leadership, a climate friendly to business, a commitment to training workers, and collaboration among businesses and between business and local government.[17]

Advantages of Collaboration

Imagine the power and the impact on local communities when businesses work together with one another and with local governments.

People are the key to successful change.[18] For an organization to be great, or even just to survive, people have to care about its fate and know how they can contribute. But typically, leadership lies with only a few people at the top. Too few take on the burden of change; the number of people who care deeply, and who make innovative contributions, is too small. People throughout the organization need to take a greater interest and a more active role in helping the business as a whole. They have to identify with the entire organization, not just with their unit and close colleagues.

Managing Change

Shared leadership is crucial to the success of most change efforts—people must be not just *supporters* of change, but also *implementers*.[19]

This is not unusual in start-ups and very small organizations. But too often it is lost with growth and over time. In large, traditional corporations, it is all too rare. There needs to be a permanent rekindling of individual creativity and responsibility, a true change in the behavior of people throughout the organization. The essential task is to motivate people fully to keep changing in response to new business challenges.

Change agent: Ken Kutaragi

Change agents are, as the name implies, people who create change. Throughout this chapter, you will read highlighted profiles of change agents—in some cases what they have created, in other cases what they have learned.

Ken Kutaragi of Sony knew that his company was behind in three hot new digital markets: videogames, personal computers, and cell phones. Sony's historical strengths were in the analog technologies found in TVs, VCRs, and tape players. He went on a mission to convince senior management of the importance of computer entertainment and to persuade them that Sony had to convert to digital. After threatening to quit if Sony didn't fund his R&D efforts in a videogame project, he promised he could create a platform for Sony's future growth. Two years later, the PlayStation was born. By 2005, Kutaragi had several successful innovations to his name.

SOURCES: I. M. Kunii, C. Edwards, and J. Greene, "Can Sony Regain the Magic?" *BusinessWeek*, March 11, 2002, pp. 72–80; A. Lashinsky, "Sony: Getting Back Its Music Mojo," *Fortune*, February 21, 2005, pp. 79–86.

Motivating People to Change

People must be *motivated* to change. But often they resist changing. Some people resist change more than others,[20] but managers tend to underestimate the amount of resistance they will encounter.

People everywhere—customers, top executives, employees—resist change. Microsoft struggled to get people to change to its search engine from Google and Yahoo![21] Schwinn knew about mountain bikes, but stayed too long with traditional products.[22] Not long ago, "experts" said that satellite radio would never work—no one would ever pay for it. Now a competitive battle is raging between XM and Sirius, with huge growth opportunities at stake, and the established radio companies will have to change or die off.[23]

Many people settle for mediocrity rather than aspire to world-class status. They resist the idea of striving mightily for excellence. When told by their managers, "We have to become world class," they say things like the following:

- "Those world-class performance numbers are ridiculous! I don't believe them, they are impossible! Maybe in some industries, some companies . . . but ours is unique . . ."
- "Sure, maybe some companies achieve those numbers, but there's no hurry . . . We're doing all right. Sales were up 5 percent this year, costs were down 2 percent. And we've got to keep cutting corners . . ."
- "We can't afford to be world class like those big global companies; we don't have the money or staff . . ."
- "We don't believe this stuff about global markets and competitors. We don't need to expand internationally. One of our local competitors tried that a few years ago and lost its shirt."
- "It's not a level playing field . . . the others have unfair advantages . . ."

To deal with such reactions, and successfully implement positive change, managers must understand why people often resist change. Figure 18.1 shows the common reasons for resistance. Some reasons are general and arise in most change efforts. Other reasons for resistance relate to the specific nature of a particular change.

General Reasons for Resistance   Several reasons for resistance arise regardless of the actual content of the change.[24]

- *Inertia.* Usually people don't want to disturb the status quo. The old ways of doing things are comfortable and easy, so people don't want to shake things up and try something new. For example, it is easier to keep living in the same apartment or house than to move to another.
- *Timing.* People often resist change because of poor timing. Maybe you would like to move to a different place to live, but do you want to move this week? Even if a place were available, you probably couldn't take the time. If managers

FIGURE 18.1

Reasons for Resistance to Change

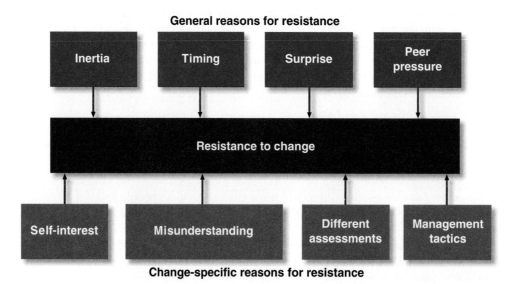

Fear of the unknown and mistrust can prompt resistance to change.

or employees are unusually busy or under stress, or if relations between management and workers are strained, the timing is wrong for introducing new proposals. Where possible, managers should introduce change when people are receptive.

- *Surprise.* One key aspect of timing and receptivity is surprise. If the change is sudden, unexpected, or extreme, resistance may be the initial—almost reflexive—reaction. Suppose your university announced an increase in tuition, effective at the beginning of next term. Resistance would be high. At the very least, you would want to know about this change far enough in advance to have time to prepare for it.
- *Peer pressure.* Sometimes work teams resist new ideas. Even if individual members do not strongly oppose a change suggested by management, the team may band together in opposition. If a group is highly cohesive and has antimanagement norms (recall Chapter 14), peer pressure will cause individuals to resist even reasonable changes.

Change-Specific Reasons for Resistance   Other causes of resistance arise from the specific nature of a proposed change. Change-specific reasons for resistance include:[25]

- *Self-interest.* Most people care less about the organization's best interest than they do about their own best interests. They will resist a change if they think it will cause them to lose something of value.

What could people fear to lose? At worst, their jobs, if management is considering closing down a plant. A merger or reorganization, or technological change, could create the same fear. Despite assurances that no one will be laid off or fired, people might fear a cut in pay or loss of power and status under the new arrangement.

- *Misunderstanding.* Even when management proposes a change that will benefit everyone, people may resist because they don't fully understand it. People may not see how the change fits with the firm's strategy, or they simply may not see the change's advantage over current practices.[26] One company met resistance to the idea of introducing flexible working hours, a system in which workers have some say regarding the hours they work. This system can benefit employees, but a false rumor circulated among plant employees that people would have to work evenings, weekends, or whenever their supervisors wanted. The employees' union demanded that management drop the flexible-hours idea. The president was caught completely off guard by this unexpected resistance, and complied with the union's demand.

- *Different assessments.* Employees receive different—and usually less—information than management receives. Even within top management ranks, some executives know more than others do. Such discrepancies cause people to develop different assessments of proposed changes. Some may be aware that the benefits outweigh the costs, while others may see only the costs and not perceive the advantages. This is a common problem when management announces a change, say, in work procedures, and doesn't explain to employees why the change is needed. Management expects advantages in terms of increased efficiency, but workers may see the change as another arbitrary, ill-informed management rule that causes headaches for those who must carry it out.

- *Management tactics.* Sometimes a change that is successful elsewhere is undertaken in a new location, and problems may arise during the transfer.[27] Management may attempt to force the change and may fail to develop employee commitment. Or it may fail to provide the necessary resources, knowledge, or leadership to help the change succeed. Sometimes a change receives so much exposure and glorification that employees resent it, and resist.

It is important to recognize that employees' assessments can be more accurate than management's; they may know a change won't work even if management doesn't. In this case, resistance to change is beneficial for the organization. Thus, even though management typically considers resistance a challenge to be overcome, it may actually represent an important signal that a proposed change requires further, more open-minded scrutiny.[28]

Change agents: Nick Moon and Martin Fisher

At Appro TEC, Nick Moon and Martin Fisher developed a human-powered irrigation pump that sells for $80. The pump allows subsistence farmers in sub-Saharan Africa to grow through the dry season, increasing their incomes as much as tenfold. The pump, called the MoneyMaker, is now produced and distributed by independent, for-profit companies. Appro TEC is expanding into other markets in the region, developing other products, expanding sales to wholesalers worldwide, and helping to reduce world poverty.

SOURCE: C. Dahle, "The Change Masters," *Fast Company,* January 2005, pp. 47–58.

A General Model for Managing Resistance

Figure 18.2 shows that motivating people to change often requires three basic stages: unfreezing, moving to institute the change, and refreezing.[29]

unfreezing

Realizing that current practices are inappropriate and that new behavior must be enacted.

Unfreezing   In the **unfreezing** stage, management realizes that its current practices are no longer appropriate and the company must break out of (unfreeze) its present mold by doing things differently. People must come to recognize that some of the past ways of thinking, feeling, and doing things are obsolete.[30] Perhaps the most effective way to do this is to communicate to people the negative consequences of the old ways by comparing the organization's performance to its competitors'. As discussed in Chapter 15, management can share with employees data about costs, quality, and prof-

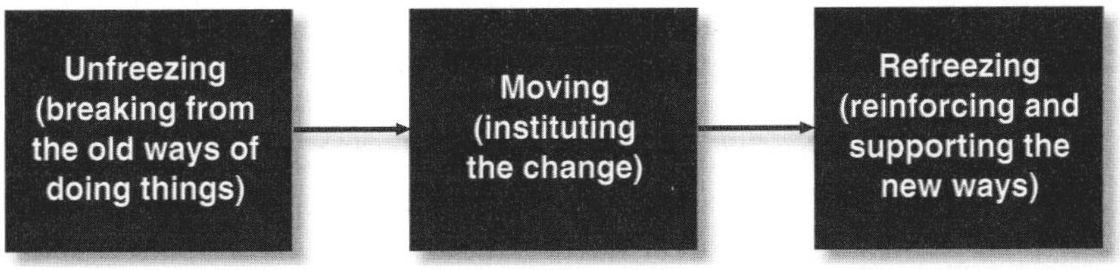

Unfreezing (breaking from the old ways of doing things) → Moving (instituting the change) → Refreezing (reinforcing and supporting the new ways)

FIGURE 18.2
Motivating People to Change

its.[31] However, care must be taken not to arouse people's defensiveness by pinning the blame directly and entirely on them.[32]

An important contributor to unfreezing is the recognition of a performance gap, which can be a precipitator of major change. A **performance gap** is the difference between actual performance and the performance that should or could exist.[33] A gap typically implies poor performance; for example, sales, profits, stock price, or other financial indicators are down. This situation attracts management's attention, and management introduces changes to try to correct things.

Another, very important form of performance gap can exist. This type of gap can occur when performance is good but someone realizes that it could be better. Thus, the gap is between what is and what *could be*. This is where entrepreneurs seize opportunities and where companies that engage in strategic maneuvering gain a competitive edge. Whereas many change efforts begin with the negative, it often is more valuable to identify strengths and potential and then develop new modes of operating from that positive perspective.[34]

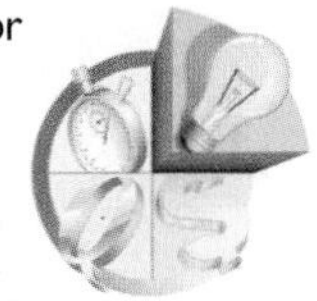

As an impetus for change, a performance gap can apply to the organization as a whole; it also can apply to departments, groups, and individuals. If a department or work group is not performing as well as others in the company, or if it sees an opportunity that it can exploit, that unit will be motivated to change. Similarly, an individual may receive negative performance feedback or see a personal opportunity on which to capitalize. Under these circumstances, unfreezing begins, and people can be more motivated to change than if they identify no such gap.

Moving   The next step, **moving** to institute the change, begins with establishing a vision of where the company is heading. You learned about vision in the leadership chapter. The vision can be realized through strategic, structural, cultural, and individual change. Strategic ideas are discussed throughout the book. Changes in structure may involve moving to the divisional, matrix, or some other appropriate form (discussed in Chapters 8 and 9). Cultural changes (Chapter 2) are institutionalized through effective leadership (Chapters 12 through 15). Individuals will change as new people join the company (Chapters 10 and 11) and as people throughout the organization adopt the leader's new vision for the future.

One technique that helps to manage the change process, **force-field analysis,** involves identifying the specific forces that prevent people from changing and the specific forces that will drive people toward change.[35] Eliminating the restraining forces helps people unfreeze, and increasing the driving forces helps and motivates them to move forward. An exercise at the end of the chapter provides an example and takes you through this process.

Refreezing   Finally, **refreezing** means strengthening the new behaviors that support the change. The changes must be diffused and stabilized throughout the company. Refreezing involves implementing control systems that support the change (Chapter 16), applying corrective action when necessary, and reinforcing behaviors and performance (Chapter 13) that support the agenda. Management should consistently support and reward all evidence of movement in the right direction.[36]

In today's organizations, refreezing is not always the best third step, if it creates new behaviors that are as rigid as the old ones. The ideal new culture is one of continuous

performance gap

The difference between actual performance and desired performance.

A useful tactic for innovating toward a positive future is to imagine the difference between what *is* and what *could be.*

moving

Instituting the change.

force-field analysis

An approach to implementing Lewin's unfreezing/moving/refreezing model, involving identifying the forces that prevent people from changing and those that will drive people toward change.

refreezing

Strengthening the new behaviors that support the change.

In response to Apple's über-successful iPod, cell phone makers like Motorola, and its iTunes download-capable E1060, are changing cell phones into phones *and* music players. A competitor's success creates a performance gap that can unfreeze a company and its people, prompting a move toward new product development.

change. Refreezing is appropriate when it permanently installs behaviors that maintain essential core values, such as a focus on important business results and those values maintained by the companies that are "built to last." But refreezing should not create new rigidities that might become dysfunctional as the business environment continues to change.[37] The behaviors that should be refrozen are those that promote continued adaptability, flexibility, experimentation, assessment of results, and continuous improvement. In other words, lock in key values, capabilities, and strategic mission, but not necessarily specific management practices and procedures.

Specific Approaches to Enlist Cooperation

You can try to command people to change, but the key to long-term success is to use other approaches.[38] Developing true support is better than "driving" a program forward.[39] How, specifically, can management motivate people to change?

Most managers underestimate the variety of ways they can influence people during a period of change.[40] Several effective approaches to managing resistance and enlisting cooperation are available, as described in Table 18.2:

1. **Education and communication.** Management should educate people about upcoming changes before they occur. It should communicate not only the *nature* of the change but its *logic.* This process can include one-on-one discussions, presentations to groups, or reports and memos. For Amy Radin of Citibank, "Getting buy-in across the organization takes a lot of education. If you have a core group of people who are focused only on e-commerce, then you've got to keep everyone else informed about what you're doing on the e-commerce front" (p. 363).[41]

2. **Participation and involvement.** Change requires reflection and dialogue,[42] as discussed in Chapter 15. It is important to listen to the people who are affected by the change. They should be involved in the change's design and implementation. For major, organizationwide change, participation in the process can extend from the top to the very bottom of the organization.[43] When feasible, management should use the advice of people throughout the organization.

    As you learned in Chapter 3, people who are involved in decisions understand them more fully and are more committed to them. People's understanding and commitment are important ingredients in the successful implementation of a change. Participation also provides an excellent opportunity for education and communication.

3. **Facilitation and support.** Management should make the change as easy as possible for employees and be supportive of their efforts. Facilitation involves providing the training and other resources people need to carry out the change and perform their jobs under the new circumstances. This step often includes decentralizing authority and empowering people, that is, giving them the power to make the decisions and changes needed to improve their performance.

    Offering support involves listening patiently to problems, being understanding if performance drops temporarily or the change is not perfected immediately, and generally being on the employees' side and showing consideration during a difficult period.

4. **Negotiation and rewards.** When necessary, management can offer concrete incentives for cooperation with the change. Perhaps job enrichment is

Approach	Commonly used in situations	Advantage	Drawbacks
Education and communication	Where there is a lack of information or inaccurate information and analysis.	Once persuaded, people will often help with the implementation of the change.	Can be very time-consuming if lots of people are involved.
Participation and involvement	Where the initiators do not have all the information they need to design the change, and where others have considerable power to resist.	People who participate will be committed to implementing change, and any relevant information they have will be integrated into the change plan.	Can be very time-consuming if participators design an inappropriate change.
Facilitation and support	Where people are resisting because of adjustment problems.	No other approach works as well with adjustment problems.	Can be time-consuming and expensive, and still fail.
Negotiation and rewards	Where someone or some group will clearly lose out in a change, and where that group has considerable power to resist.	Sometimes it is a relatively easy way to avoid major resistance.	Can be too expensive in many cases if it alerts others to negotiate for compliance.
Manipulation and cooptation	Where other tactics will not work, or are too expensive.	It can be a relatively quick and inexpensive solution to resistance problems.	Can lead to future problems if people feel manipulated.
Explicit and implicit coercion	Where speed is essential, and the change initiators possess considerable power.	It is speedy and can overcome any kind of resistance.	Can be risky if it leaves people angry at the initiators.

SOURCE: Reprinted by permission of the *Harvard Business Review.* An exhibit from "Choosing Strategies for Change" by John P. Kotter and Leonard A. Schlesinger (March–April 1979). Copyright © 1979 by the President and Fellows of Harvard College; all rights reserved.

TABLE 18.2
Methods for Managing Resistance to Change

acceptable only with a higher wage rate, or a work rule change is resisted until management agrees to a concession on some other rule (say, regarding taking breaks). Even among higher-level managers, one executive might agree to another's idea for a policy change only in return for support on some other issue of more personal importance. Rewards such as bonuses, wages and salaries, recognition, job assignments, and perks can be examined and perhaps restructured to reinforce the direction of the change.[44]

When people trust one another, change is easier. But change is further facilitated by demonstrating its benefits to people.[45] Janiece Webb, who creates change at Motorola, says that nobody wins unless everybody wins, and that you must demonstrate to others how your work benefits them.[46] Amy Radin of

Citibank says, "One lesson that I've learned is to create a financial incentive so that business units will support an Internet initiative. We are planning to create a shadow P&L for our e-commerce efforts to track how everything is going. But the benefits, all of the revenues created, will be allocated to the operating units . . . You're helping people meet their own goals."

5. **Manipulation and cooptation.** Sometimes managers use more subtle, covert tactics to implement change. One form of manipulation is cooptation, which involves giving a resisting individual a desirable role in the change process. The leader of a resisting group often is coopted. For example, management might invite a union leader to be a member of an executive committee, or ask a key member of an outside organization to join the company's board of directors. As a person becomes involved in the change, he or she may become less resistant to the actions of the coopting group or organization.

6. **Explicit and implicit coercion.** Some managers apply punishment or the threat of punishment to those who resist change. With this approach, managers use force to make people comply with their wishes. For example, a boss might insist that subordinates cooperate with the change and threaten them with job loss, denial of a promotion, or an unattractive work assignment. Sometimes you just have to lay down the law: The game is changing, and you need to play by the new rules or play somewhere else.[47]

Each approach to managing resistance has advantages and drawbacks and, like many of the other situational management approaches described in this book, each is useful in different situations. Table 18.2 summarizes the advantages, drawbacks, and appropriate circumstances for these approaches to managing resistance to change. As the table implies, managers should not use just one or two general approaches, regardless of the circumstances. Effective change managers are familiar with the various approaches and know how to apply them according to the situation.

Throughout the process, change leaders need to build in stability. Recall from the companies that were "built to last" that they all have essential core characteristics of which they don't lose sight. In the midst of change, turmoil, and uncertainty, people need anchors onto which they can latch.[48] This means keeping some things constant and visible, such as the organization's values and mission. In addition, strategic principles can be important anchors during change.[49] It can help further to maintain the visibility of key people, continue key assignments and projects, and make announcements about which organizational components will not change. Such anchors will reduce anxiety and help overcome resistance.

Change agents: Jordan Kassalow and Scott Berrie

The Scojo Foundation was established by Jordan Kassalow and Scott Berrie, using profits from their commercial eyewear company. As a student visiting Colombia, Kassalow saw villagers travel for days to see an eye doctor. He also saw many people with vision so poor they couldn't read or get good jobs. He and Berrie now distribute affordable eyewear through a network of women entrepreneurs. Women, they say, are more likely to reinvest their incomes into their families and communities, creating a platform for tackling other health problems. In 2005, at least 100 women started businesses through Scojo, and they will sell 30,000 pairs of glasses in their communities.

SOURCE: C. Dahle, "The Change Masters," *Fast Company*, January 2005, pp. 47–58.

Harmonizing Multiple Changes

There are no "silver bullets" or single-shot methods of changing organizations successfully. Single shots rarely hit a challenging target. Usually, many issues need simultaneous attention, and any single, small change will be absorbed by the prevailing culture and disappear. **Total organization change** involves introducing and sustaining multiple policies, practices, and procedures across multiple units and levels.[50] Such change affects the thinking and behavior of everyone in the organization, can enhance the organization's culture and success, and can be sustained over time.

A survey at a Harvard Business School conference found that the average attendee's company had five major change efforts going on at once.[51] The most common change programs were the things you have studied in this course: continuous improvement, quality programs, time-based competition, and creation of a learning organization, a team-based organization, a network organization, core competencies, and strategic alliances. The problem is, these efforts usually are simultaneous but not coordinated. Things get muddled; people lose focus.[52] The result for the people involved is confusion, frustration, low morale, and low motivation.

Because companies introduce new changes constantly, many people complain about their companies' "flavor-of-the-month" approach to change. That is, employees often see many change efforts as just the company's jumping on the latest bandwagon or fad. The more these change fads come and go, the more cynical people become, and the more difficult it is to get them committed to making the change a success.[53]

So an important question is, Which change efforts are really worth undertaking? Here are some specific questions to ask before embarking on a change project.[54] What is the evidence that the approach really can produce positive results? Is the approach relevant to your company's strategies and priorities? Can you assess the costs and potential benefits? Does it really help people add value through their work? Does it help the company focus better on customers and the things they value? Can you go through the decision-making process described in Chapter 3, understand what you're facing, and feel that you are taking the right approach?

Management also needs to "connect the dots"—that is, integrate the various efforts into a coherent picture that people can see, understand, and get behind.[55] You connect the dots by understanding each change program and what its goals are, by identifying similarities among the programs and identifying their differences, and by dropping programs that don't meet priority goals with a clear results orientation. Most important, you do it by communicating to everyone concerned the common themes among the various programs: their common rationales, objectives, and methods. You show them how the various parts fit the strategic big picture, and how the changes will make things better for the company and its people. You must communicate these things thoroughly, honestly, and frequently.[56]

> **total organization change**
>
> Introducing and sustaining multiple policies, practices, and procedures across multiple units and levels.

Change agent: Terry Semel

Jerry Yang founded Yahoo in 1995 and hired Terry Semel as CEO in 2001. Semel has improved the business and morale, despite being a highly controversial choice. Why was he controversial? Because he came from Hollywood (Warner Bros.) and had barely used a PC or surfed the Net. He read e-mail by having his assistant print messages out, and he replied by scribbling notes on the pages and having his secretary retype them. He asked questions like "What's a server? What's a protocol?" But he listened, and he learned. He showed great patience and stamina. One of his biggest admirers is Jeff Mallett, who wanted the job that Semel got. But Mallett stayed with the company for a year, helping to teach Semel, saying later "I think he learned three years of information in six months."

SOURCE: F. Vogelstein, "Bringing Up Yahoo," *Fortune,* April 5, 2004, pp. 220–28.

Leading Change

Successful change requires managers to actively lead it. The essential activities of leading change are summarized in Figure 18.3.

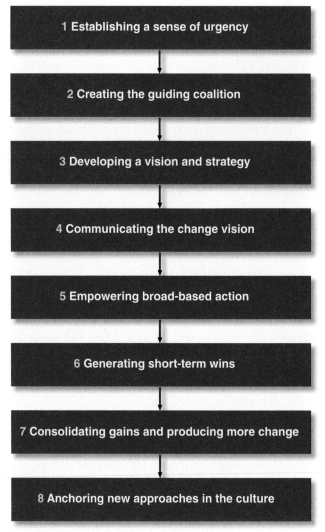

FIGURE 18.3
Leading Change

A useful start for change leaders is to *establish a sense of urgency.*[57] This requires examining current realities and pressures in the marketplace and the competitive arena, identifying both crises and opportunities, and being frank and honest about them. This is an important component, in part because so many large companies grow complacent.

Figure 18.4 shows some of the common reasons for complacency. To stop complacency and create urgency, the manager can talk candidly about weaknesses compared to competitors, making a point of backing up statements with data. Other tactics include setting stretch goals, putting employees in direct contact with unhappy customers and shareholders, distributing worrisome information to all employees instead of merely engaging in management "happy talk," eliminating excessive perks, and highlighting to everyone the future opportunities that exist but that the organization so far has failed to pursue.

Ultimately, urgency is driven by compelling business reasons for change. Survival, competition, and winning in the marketplace are compelling; they provide a sense of direction and energy around change. Change becomes not a hobby, a luxury, or something nice to do, but a business necessity.[58]

To *create a guiding coalition* means putting together a group with enough power to lead the change. Change efforts fail when a sufficiently powerful coalition is not formed.[59] Major organization change requires leadership from top management,

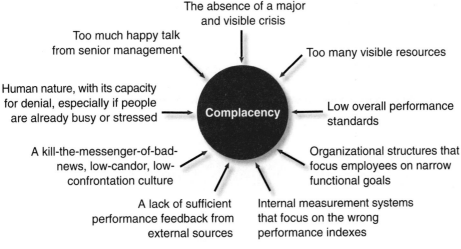

FIGURE 18.4
Sources of Complacency

working as a team. But over time, the support must gradually expand outward and downward throughout the organization. Middle managers and supervisors are essential. Groups at all levels are the glue that can hold change efforts together, the medium for communicating about the changes, and the means for enacting new behaviors.[60]

Developing a vision and strategy, as discussed in earlier chapters, will direct the change effort. This process involves determining the idealized, expected state of affairs after the change is implemented. Because confusion is common during major organizational change, the clearest possible image of the future state must be developed and conveyed to everyone.[61] This image, or vision, will be a target or guideline that can clarify expectations, dispel rumors, and mobilize people's energies. The portrait of the future also should communicate how the transition will occur, why the change is being implemented, and how people will be affected by the change. The power of a compelling vision is one of the most important aspects of change, and should not be underestimated or underutilized.

Change agent: Tim Berners-Lee

The "father of the World Wide Web," Tim Berners-Lee, now envisions the next generation that will replace today's Web. The Semantic Web will structure all the random information on Web pages and elsewhere to make it more intelligible to machines. It will be a smart network that understands human languages and will make working with computers very similar to working with other humans. Computers already are better than people at number crunching, of course. What if they were also better at language and reason? The Semantic Web "will foster global collaboration among people with diverse cultural perspectives, so we have a better chance of finding the right solutions to the really big issues—like the environment and climate warming." Many doubt his vision, but John Patrick, a retired IBM senior exec and a founder of the World Wide Web Consortium, says that "Tim has a gift for seeing the future and making it happen."

SOURCES: O. Port, "Special Report: The Next Web," *BusinessWeek*, March 4, 2002, pp. 96–102; R. Waters, "In Search of More: The 'Friendly' Engines that Will Manage the Data of Daily Life," *Financial Times*, February 1, 2005, p. 17.

Communicating the change vision requires using every possible channel and opportunity to talk up and reinforce the vision and required new behaviors. It is said that aspiring change leaders undercommunicate the vision by a factor of 10, or even 100 or 1,000, seriously undermining the chances of success.[62] Chris Crosby, senior VP and director of Internet at Dain Rauscher Corp., advises you to "Draw pictures that take people where they want to go. Make the idea as tangible as possible. I had to take management out 18 months and say, 'Here's what the Web site will look like in a year and a half.' Once people could see it and touch it, they could understand it" (p. 358).[63]

Empowering broad-based action means getting rid of obstacles to success, including systems and structures that constrain rather than facilitate. Encourage risk taking and experimentation, and empower people by providing information, knowledge, authority, and rewards, as described in Chapter 13.

Advantages of Collaboration

Will the Semantic Web become a reality and foster global collaboration to solve the biggest problems of our time?

Connections: GE AND JEFFREY IMMELT

Jeff Immelt started making changes with the support and active participation of people throughout GE. He made a variety of changes, sometimes in contrast to his legendary predecessor. Welch had gotten GE into financial services; Immelt started getting out. Immelt placed heavy emphasis on technology, service, and globalization and entered businesses like wind energy, security, water services, and personalized medicine. Welch had made Wall Street happy by setting specific earnings targets and hitting them; Immelt gives higher priority to long-term demands. Welch had grown GE through acquisitions; Immelt is acquiring companies but wants more growth through innovation.

Immelt decided that the new environment, marked by low growth, low inflation, geopolitical volatility, and the rise of China and India, required that he reshape the company. His goal was (and is) to build a company that can outperform in a slow-growth world. With this in mind, Immelt's first initiative was R&D. He revitalized the research center and opened new centers around the world. Research is proceeding in nanotechnology, hydrogen power, advanced propulsion, and many other areas. When Immelt does acquire companies, it's not necessarily because they're growing—it's because they have the ability to grow, in the long run.

During Immelt's first couple of years as GE's CEO, the world and the business environment were not the only things that were changing; Jack Welch's reputation changed in some ways. Welch's public divorce revealed aspects of his personal life and his retirement package. Immelt renounced the stock options packages that made Welch and so many other CEOs wealthy and tied his compensation to his performance. Highly sensitive to the demise of the corporate image, Immelt called upon himself and other CEOs to repair it through not just words but actions, over the long haul. You read earlier, in the ethics chapter, about Immelt's changes in the moral culture of GE and his push toward greater corporate social responsibility.

Generate short-term wins. Don't wait for the ultimate grand realization of the vision. You need results. As small victories accumulate, you make the transition from an isolated initiative to an integral part of the business.[64] Plan for and create small victories that indicate to everyone that progress is being made. Recognize and reward the people who made the wins possible, doing it as visibly as you can so people notice and the positive message permeates the organization.

Make sure you *consolidate gains and produce more change.* With the well-earned credibility of previous successes, keep changing things in ways that support the vision. Hire, promote, and develop people who will further the vision. Reinvigorate the organization and your change efforts with new projects and change agents.

Finally, *anchor new approaches in the culture.*[65] Highlight positive results, communicate the connections between the new behaviors and the improved results, and keep

The emergence of online shopping has made many retailers fearful about the future. Instead of simply worrying, some have reconceived the shopping experience. Now, instead of a typical bricks-and-mortar shopping mall, consumers can drive to their local "lifestyle center"—open-air centers that evoke the small-town shopping of previous generations. Because stores are outdoors and have parking usually directly in front of or next to them, they offer the perception of getting in and out quickly – speed being one of the original, and still valid, reasons for shopping at a dot-com.

developing new change agents and leaders. Continually increase the number of people joining you in taking responsibility for change.[66]

Shaping the Future

A newspaper reporter talking to people at think tanks in Washington, D.C., found a variety of forecasts about the global future, but clear agreement on two things: "First, that a very different world is roaring up on us. Second, that the history of our times will be the story of how we prepared for this different world—which, so far, is mostly a story of how we have failed to prepare" (p. 20).[67] While he was writing primarily about geopolitics, the same statements can be made about business.

Most change is reactive. A better way to change is to be proactive. **Reactive change** means responding to pressure, after the problem has arisen. It also implies being a follower. **Proactive change** means anticipating and preparing for an uncertain future. It implies being a leader and *creating* the future you want.

The road to the future includes drivers, passengers, and road kill. Put another way: On the road to the future, who will be the windshield, and who will be the bug?[68]

Needless to say, it's best to be a driver.[69] How do you become a driver? By being proactive more than merely reactive, by really thinking about the future, and by *creating* futures.

reactive change

A response that occurs under pressure; problem-driven change.

proactive change

A response that is initiated before a performance gap has occurred.

Thinking about the Future

If you think only about the present, or wallow in the uncertainties of the future, your future is just a roll of the dice. It is far better to exercise foresight, set an agenda for the future, and pursue it with everything you've got. So, contemplate and envision the future.

As of 75 years ago, we had no safe and effective antibiotics, no TV, no computers, and no commercial air travel. In recent years we have gone to the moon, created the Internet, and read the human genome. *BusinessWeek* asks, Will the next 75 years bring the same mega-transformations? Or will progress be more incremental, elaborating on current knowledge more than creating new technologies and industries?[70]

BusinessWeek answers its own question: "The global economy could be on the cusp of an age of innovation equal to that of the past 75 years. All the right factors are in place: Science is advancing rapidly, more countries are willing to devote resources to research and development and education, and corporate managers, too, are convinced of the importance of embracing change" (p. 93).[71] *BusinessWeek* cites nanotechnology, energy technologies, and the biological sciences as examples. Innovation will be key to the world's future.

Shoshana Zuboff and Jim Maxim, authors of *The Support Economy*,[72] claim that the era of industrial capitalism is over, traditional business enterprises are disappearing, vast new markets exist, new kinds of companies are ready to be created, and the new business model hasn't yet emerged.[73] But new business models are interesting to contemplate, as exemplified in the box, Companies of the Future.

Companies of the Future?

Fortune asked futurist Peter Schwarz to look ahead 50 years and describe the top companies as they might appear then. Among his imaginary (but feasible) great companies of the future (and the worlds in which they operate):

AmazonBay—Most shopping is virtual; using low prices to lure shoppers into stores is passé. People make instant wireless purchases of anything and everything, from home loans to micropayments for pieces of information. You'll have a digital shopper—a cross between a butler and an accountant—that knows everything about you and either makes purchases for you or gives you choices. The battle for customers is multigenerational; all data since birth are embedded in your parents' system, so it's hard to switch.

Toyota—Schwarz predicts that Toyota will win the hydrogen fuel race to become the undisputed king of the automobile business. More affluent workers in Asia can afford cars. Smart cars, which combined with smart highways will prevent accidents, are a prerequisite for life insurance.

Sinobiocorp—The world leader in life science (drugs, agriculture, and bioindustrial processing). It was formed by a state-driven roll-up of Chinese biotech start-ups. Life extension is the fastest-growing business.

IBM—Its quantum computers solve amazingly complicated problems like missile defense, traffic management, and climate forecasting. Nearly all technology works via voice recognition. Offices, homes, and automobiles not only respond to voice commands, but often anticipate our needs and act on them before we ask.

Nestlé—Nutriceuticals are foods that bridge the gap between agriculture and drugs, and Nestlé dominates the market. Products are tailored to local cultures. Chocolates contain stem-cell memory boosters, frozen foods reduce cholestrerol, and lipstick provides daily doses of vitamins.

Pattelco—Because security problems and disease make air travel unattractive, people use telepresence (TP) devices to travel virtually. Some is leisure travel, including outer space, but most is business travel. The operating system for TP devices is constantly being upgraded, following the old Microsoft business model.

SOURCE: P. Schwarz, "Future Shock," *Fortune*, April 5, 2004, pp. 260–66.

Creating the Future

Companies can try different strategic postures to prepare to compete in an uncertain future. **Adapters** take the current industry structure and its future evolution as givens. They choose where to compete. This posture is taken by most companies by conducting standard strategic analysis and choosing how to compete within given environments. In contrast, **shapers** try to change the structure of their industries, creating a future competitive landscape of their own design.[74]

In a recent 10-year period, but prior to the recession, 17 companies in the *Fortune* 1000 grew total shareholder return by 35 percent or more per year.[75] How did they do it? They completely reinvented industries. Harley-Davidson turned around by selling not just motorcycles, but nostalgia. Amgen broke the rules of the biotech industry by focusing not on what customers wanted, but on great science. Starbuck's took a commodity and began selling it in trendy stores. CarMax and other companies reinvented the auto industry.[76]

adapters

Companies that take the current industry structure and its evolution as givens, and choose where to compete.

shapers

Companies that try to change the structure of their industries, creating a future competitive landscape of their own design.

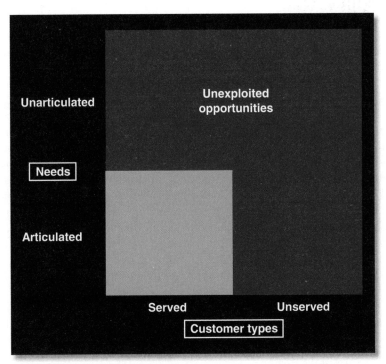

FIGURE 18.5
Vast Opportunity

You need to create advantages. The challenge is not to maintain your position in the current competitive arena, but to create new competitive arenas, transform your industry, and imagine a future that others don't see. Creating advantage is better than playing catch-up. At best, doing things to catch up buys time; it cannot get you out ahead of the pack or buy world-class excellence.[77] To create new markets or transform industries—these are perhaps the ultimate forms of proactive change.[78]

Figure 18.5 illustrates the vast opportunity to create new markets. Articulated needs are those that customers acknowledge and try to satisfy. Unarticulated needs are those that customers have not yet experienced. Served customers are those to whom your company is now selling, and unserved customers are untapped markets.

Business-as-usual concentrates on the lower-left quadrant. The leaders who recreate the game are constantly trying to create new opportunities in the other three quadrants.[79]

For example, you can pursue the upper-left quadrant by imagining how you can satisfy a larger proportion of your customers' total needs.[80] Nike realized its customers didn't want only shoes and running apparel, but also specialized sunglasses, watches, and wearable MP3 music players. GE's Power Systems business learned that major electric utilities would pay not only for turbines and transformers, but also for a wide range of consulting and maintenance services, which have much higher margins.

Jim Stengel, P&G's chief marketing officer, believes that P&G and its competitors have already met consumers' obvious needs.[81] So P&G has cut way back on focus groups, the traditional approach to consumer research. P&G must create opportunity out of needs that consumers don't currently articulate. It now has marketers spending time in consumers' homes, watching how they diaper their babies, wash clothes, and clean their floors, and asking them about their habits and frustrations.

Shawn Fanning and nanotechnology provide two other current examples. Shawn Fanning, founder of Napster, is now trying to reshape the digital music landscape with Snocap.[82] His goal is to increase the amount of legally available music and create an automated central clearinghouse for music files online. This would ensure that labels get paid when their files are downloaded or shared. Fanning says, "There's an interest in creating the world we are describing, but no one can take the first step." He plans to break the deadlock. The big labels initially fought against file-sharing—more resistance to change!—but they may have to become more flexible as the music industry continues to evolve. Converts are signing on. One CEO of a small start-up calls Snocap "one giant experiment" in which "we're all playing around with a lot of different ideas."[83]

The nanometer—one-billionth of a meter, about the size of 10 hydrogen atoms in a row—is the building block of a new-and-future industry, nanotechnology. Why is the nanometer so important?[84] Because matter of this size often behaves differently—transmitting light or electricity, or becoming harder than diamonds, or becoming powerful chemical catalysts. Large and small companies are beginning to rush nano-based products into the marketplace. The first products will be modest but fun: golf balls that fly straight, tennis racquets with more bounce. But many nanotech applications appear ultimately to lie in health care, and Hewlett-Packard announced a breakthrough that could move computing beyond silicon and transistors. An HP senior fellow, Stan Williams, says, "We are reinventing the computer at the molecular scale."[85]

Is nanotech—for that matter, are most "industries of the future"—being overhyped? The science is in its infancy. Researchers at SMU reported brain damage in a large-mouth bass that had been in an aquarium with common nanoparticles known as buckey-balls.[86] Can the industry convince consumers of its safety, or will there be a global backlash, as with genetically modified foods in Europe? What regulations will appear? Which nanotechnologies will create what new industries? Which companies will go the way of the dot-bombs? Who will emerge as winners? And what will it take to do so?

As you've read, technological change is a central part of the changing landscape, and competition often arises between newcomers and established companies. Consider the example in the following box.

Blogging and the Changing Competitive Landscape

The mainstream media are facing a competitive onslaught, public backlash, and eroding market share. They are being battered continually in the blogosphere, and they are losing public trust. Some forecast that the mainstream media will disappear.

Millions of people blog, and many of them are entrepreneurs practicing a new brand of journalism. Some do a good job, some do not. Some are careful and fair, while others care mainly about speed to market, with less concern about accuracy.

A traditional journalist described bloggers as a "lynch mob" of "salivating morons." A blogger replied that "you aren't higher beings" and "no one in print or on TV deserves free passes [from criticism] because you call yourself 'journalists.' " Duncan Riley of the Blog Herald: "The battles are . . . based on hatred of the blogosphere by the old media as it continues to lose readership and the revenues a large readership attracts." Another blogger told old media to stop whining and "appreciate the fact that, after generations of stagnation, something new has arrived."

Blogs also are affecting corporate culture. Some companies—IBM, Dr. Pepper, Verizon, DaimlerChrysler, and others—use Web log software to let employees post comments, generate upward communication, provide information, discuss problems, and record solutions. Blogging is sometimes seen as a knowledge-management tool, as people tap into a company's knowledge base. It's also a great way to learn from customers.

But blogs are so open and anarchic that they can be unsettling. Managers sometimes don't want employees to post what they post. They worry about what employees might say—not just complaining to each other about their bosses, or criticizing the company or its products to customers, but also revealing secrets, sending faulty information, and creating potential for legal trouble. One employee blogger says, "I know I'm playing with dynamite."

On the other hand, Jonathan Carson, president and CEO of BuzzMetrics, says that "if companies focus in on what's going on in the blog world, it's an amazing leading indicator of what's going to break in the real world."

Back to the mainstream media: Through blogs, their mistakes have been publicized and criticized more widely than ever before. What should they do to restore or create new competitive advantages?

SOURCES: J. McGregor, "It's a Blog World After All," *Fast Company*, April 2004, pp. 84–86; H. Kurtz, "The Forecast: Overheated, Gusty and Increasingly Bloggy," *The Washington Post*, February 21, 2005, pp. C1, C2.

All things considered, which should you and your firm do?

- Preserve old advantages, or create new advantages?
- Lock in old markets, or create new markets?
- Take the path of greatest familiarity, or the path of greatest opportunity?
- Be only a benchmarker, or a pathbreaker?
- Place priority on short-term financial returns, or on making a real, long-term impact?
- Do only what seems doable, or what is difficult and worthwhile?
- Change what is, or create what isn't?
- Look to the past, or live for the future?[87]

Shaping Your Own Future

If you are an organizational leader, and your organization operates in traditional ways, your key goal should be to create a revolution, genetically reengineering your company before it becomes a dinosaur of the modern era.[88] What should be the goals of the revolution? You've been learning about them throughout this course.

But maybe you are not going to lead a revolution. Maybe you just want a successful career and a good life. You still must be able to deal with an economic environment that is increasingly competitive and fast-moving.[89] Creating the future you want for yourself requires setting high personal standards. Don't settle for mediocrity; don't assume that "good" is necessarily good enough—for yourself or for your employer. Think about how to not just meet expectations but exceed them; to not merely "live with" apparent constraints but break free of the unimportant, arbitrary, or imagined ones; and to seize opportunities instead of let them pass by.[90]

At Stanford, students take two required courses even before school starts: one about self-assessment, and one about managing your career. Stanford's placement director, Andy Chan, says, "We call it career self-reliance. You have to do it yourself" (p. 61).[91] Table 18.3 helps you think about how you can continually add value to your employer,

TABLE 18.3
Adding Value, Personally

Go beyond your job description: • Volunteer for projects. • Identify problems. • Initiate solutions.
Seek out others and share ideas and advice.
Offer your opinions and respect those of others.
Take an inventory of your skills every few months.
Learn something new every week.
Discover new ways to make a contribution.
Engage in active thought and deliberate action.
Take risks based on what you know and believe.
Recognize, research, and pursue opportunity.
Differentiate yourself.

SOURCE: Compiled from C. Hakim, *We Are All Self-Employed* (San Francisco: Barrett-Koehler, 1994).

and also to yourself, as you upgrade your skills, your ability to contribute, your security with your current employer, and your ability to find alternative employment if necessary. The most successful individuals will take charge of their own development just like an entrepreneur takes charge of a business.[92]

Change agent: Heather White

Heather White of Verité founded a consulting firm promoting fair labor conditions for factory workers. Verité provides high-quality audits that identify violations and works as a partner with companies to develop better working conditions. The firm has directly improved the working conditions and lives of hundreds of thousands of people. What inspired her to start Verité? Absolute disgust—but not over factory conditions per se. When a guest speaker in her MBA class described conditions in Asian factories—forced pregnancy tests, child labor, harassment, and beating—her students were surprisingly and frustratingly unmoved.

Source: C. Dahle, "The Change Masters," *Fast Company,* January 2005, pp. 47–58.

More advice from the leading authors on career management:[93] Consciously and actively manage your own career. Develop marketable skills, and keep developing more. Make career choices based on personal growth, development, and learning opportunities. Look for positions that stretch you, and for bosses who develop their protégés. Seek environments that provide training and opportunity to experiment and innovate. And know yourself: Assess your strengths and weaknesses, your true interests, and ethical standards. If you are not already thinking in these terms and taking commensurate action, you should start now.

Additionally: Become indispensable to your organization. Be happy and enthusiastic in your job, and committed to doing great work, but don't be blindly loyal to one company. Be prepared to leave if necessary. View your job as an opportunity to prove what you can do and increase what you can do, not as a comfortable niche for the long term.[94] Go out on your own if it meets your skills and temperament.

This points out the need to maintain your options. More and more, contemporary careers can involve leaving behind the large organization and going entrepreneurial, becoming self-employed in the "postcorporate world."[95] In such a career, independent individuals are free to make their own choices. They can flexibly and quickly respond to demands and opportunities. Developing start-up ventures, consulting, accepting temporary employment, doing project work for one organization and then another, working in professional partnerships, being a constant deal maker—these can be the elements of a successful career.

Don't think taking risks and being fearless is only for companies; think of your own quest for *personal* competitive advantage in the same way. Ultimately, where you go, what you do, who you become all are up to you. So, be fearless.

Ideally, this self-employed model can help provide a balanced approach to working and to living life at home and with family, because people have more control over their work activities and schedules.

This can sound like the ideal world. It also has downsides. The independence can be frightening, the future unpredictable. It can isolate "road warriors" who are always on the go, working from their cars and airports, and interfere with social and family life.[96] Effective self-management is needed to keep things in perspective and in control.

Learning and Leading

Continuous learning is a vital route to renewable competitive advantage.[97] People in your organization—and you, personally—should constantly explore, discover, and take action, as illustrated in Figure 18.6. With this approach, you can learn what is effective and what is not, and adjust and improve accordingly. The philosophy of continuous learning helps your company achieve lower cost, higher quality, innovation, and speed—and helps you grow and develop on a personal level.

Commit to lifelong learning. Lifelong learning includes being willing to seek new challenges and to reflect honestly on successes and failures.[98] Lifelong learning requires occasionally taking risks; moving outside of your "comfort zone"; honestly assessing the reasons behind your successes and failures; asking for and listening to other people's information and opinions; and being open to new ideas.

Figure 18.7 illustrates a hierarchy of stages a person can "inhabit" and grow into through a career. The descriptions in the hierarchy suggest not only that you do these things, but do them *well*. Your first job may not include managerial responsibilities, but it will require you to be an individual contributor and probably to be part of a team. Level 3 is where managerial competencies are required, while Level 4 distinguishes true leadership from competent management. Level 5 represents a leadership style that you read about briefly in Chapter 12, which combines strong will and determination

Continuous learning provides a fundamental competitive advantage by helping you and your organization achieve difficult goals.

FIGURE 18.6
Learning Cycle: Explore, Discover, Act

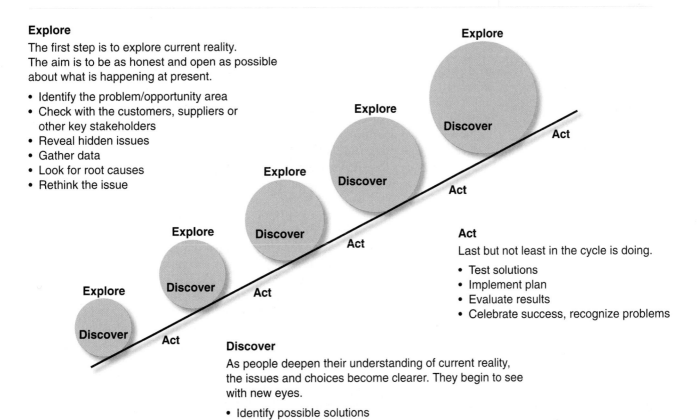

Explore

The first step is to explore current reality.
The aim is to be as honest and open as possible about what is happening at present.

- Identify the problem/opportunity area
- Check with the customers, suppliers or other key stakeholders
- Reveal hidden issues
- Gather data
- Look for root causes
- Rethink the issue

Act

Last but not least in the cycle is doing.

- Test solutions
- Implement plan
- Evaluate results
- Celebrate success, recognize problems

Discover

As people deepen their understanding of current reality, the issues and choices become clearer. They begin to see with new eyes.

- Identify possible solutions
- Plan
- Anticipate problems

SOURCE: From *Leaning into the Future: Changing the Way People Change Organizations* by George Binney and Colin Williams; published by Nicholas Brealey Publishing Ltd., 1997. Tel: (0171) 430-0224, Fax: (0171) 404-8311. Reprinted by permission.

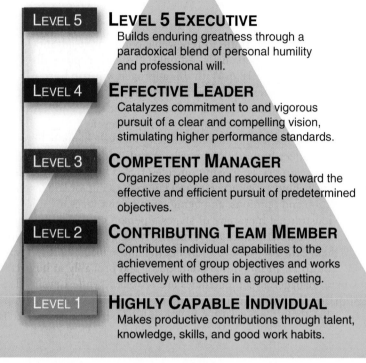

FIGURE 18.7
Level 5 Hierarchy

SOURCE: J. Collins, *Good to Great* (New York: Harper Business 2001).

with personal humility. The figure shows that Level 5 leadership represents a peak achievement: It is the ultimate contribution of a leader who can turn a good company into a great one.[99] You might ask yourself, What is my level now (or where will I be after graduation)? What do I aspire to? What have I learned to this point that can help me progress, and what do I need to learn to develop myself further?

A leader—and this could include you—should be able to create an environment in which "others are willing to learn and change so their organizations can adapt and innovate [and] inspire diverse others to embark on a collective journey of continual learning and leading" (p. 125).[100] *Learning leaders*[101] exchange knowledge freely; commit to their own continuous learning as well as to others'; are committed to examining their own behaviors and defensiveness that may inhibit their learning; devote time to their colleagues, suspending their own beliefs while they listen thoughtfully; and develop a broad perspective, recognizing that organizations are an integrated system of relationships.

Honored as one of the best management books of the year in Europe, *Leaning into the Future* gets its title from a combination of the words *leading* and *learning*.[102] The two perspectives, on the surface, appear very different. But they are powerful and synergistic when pursued in complementary ways. A successful future derives from adapting to the world *and* shaping the future; being responsive to others' perspectives *and* being clear about what you want to change; encouraging others to change *while* recognizing what you need to change about yourself; understanding current realities *and* passionately pursuing your vision; learning *and* leading.

> GM's CEO, Rick Wagoner, working to turn around a struggling GM, says, "Don't ever think you've got it licked, because you probably don't. This is not a one-step game. This is a multiple [year] thing, and it's hard, and you learn as you go along. The key thing is to remember what you've learned so you don't have to relearn it."[103]

This is another example of an important concept from the beginning of the chapter. For yourself, as well as for your organization, be ambidextrous: recognize and live the genius of the *and.*

Change agents: Helena Luczywo and Wanda Rapaczynski

Helena Luczywo and Wanda Rapaczynski turned a small underground newspaper in Poland into a local media empire, Agora SA. Theirs is one of the most remarkable success stories in postcommunist Europe. Says Luczywo, "I believe that our newspaper should stand for important things and should not avoid difficult topics. It should tell the truth, even when the truth goes against the popular grain, the government, or advertisers." Says Rapaczynski, "We aren't liked by everybody . . . We take seriously our role in this country as an institution of democracy." They both believe that the way to guarantee their independence as an agent of democracy is to become highly profitable, so as not to be vulnerable to outside economic pressure. States Luczywo, "If you want to be independent, then you must be financially independent." CEO Rapaczynski was recently named one of the most powerful women in international business.

SOURCES: P. Kruger, "Helena Luczywo & Wanda Rapaczynski," *Fast Company,* November 2000, pp. 152–66; J. Guyon, "Worldly Women," *Fortune,* October 18, 2004, p. 193.

EPILOGUE

GE AND JEFFREY IMMELT

Jeff Immelt clearly learned a lot from Manager-of-the-Century Jack Welch, but he also was highly capable of going his own way, successfully. He has turned GE into a truly global enterprise. Immelt said that in 1981 about half of GE's top 600 executives didn't have passports. He now spends about half of his time traveling, much of it abroad. He sees heavy growth prospects in China, Russia, and India. In early 2005 GE started its first-ever global campaign revolving around the Olympics, anticipating the 2008 Games in Beijing.

Despite spending Immelt's first 18 months in crisis mode, GE returned to double-digit growth and Immelt was named the *Financial Times* Man of the Year. A Merrill Lynch portfolio manager said, "To pull this off has taken a lot of guts, a lot of discipline, and a lot of thoughtfulness. It has not come without short-term costs . . . But if he was looking for a way to make people forget about Jack Welch, he couldn't have done much better."

Immelt is self-confident but not overbearing or imperialistic. A *Fortune* article, singing Immelt's praises, concludes, "Confidence breeds conviction. And conviction breeds something that, had we not grown so cynical, would look suspiciously like . . . well, courage."

Immelt doesn't want GE to be at the mercy of the economy; he wants GE to control its own fate.

KEY TERMS

Adapters, p. 606

Force-field analysis, p. 597

Genius of the "and", p. 591

Moving, p. 597

Organization development (OD), p. 591

Organizational ambidexterity, p. 591

Performance gap, p. 597

Proactive change, p. 605

Reactive change, p. 605

Refreezing, p. 597

Shapers, p. 606

Total organization change, p. 601

Tyranny of the "or," p. 591

Unfreezing, p. 596

SUMMARY OF LEARNING OBJECTIVES

Now that you have studied Chapter 18, you should know:

What it takes to be world class.

You should strive for world-class excellence, which means using the very best and latest knowledge and ideas to operate at the highest standards of any place anywhere. Sustainable greatness comes from, among other things, having strong core values, living those values constantly, striving for continuous improvement, experimenting, and always trying to do better tomorrow than today. It is essential to not fall prey to the tyranny of the *or;* that is, the belief that one important goal can be attained only at the expense of another. The genius of the *and* is that multiple important goals can be achieved simultaneously and synergistically.

How to manage change effectively.

Effective change management occurs when the organization moves from its current state to a desired future state without excessive cost to the organization or its people. People resist change for a variety of reasons, including inertia, poor timing, surprise, peer pressure, self-interest, misunderstanding, different information about (and assessments of) the change, and management's tactics.

Motivating people to change requires a general process of unfreezing, moving, and refreezing, with the caveat that appropriate and not inappropriate behaviors be "refrozen." More specific techniques to motivate people to change include education and communication, participation and involvement, facilitation and support, negotiation and rewards, manipulation and cooptation,

and coercion. Each approach has strengths, weaknesses, and appropriate uses, and multiple approaches can be used. It is important to harmonize the multiple changes that are occurring throughout the organization.

Effective change requires active leadership, including creating a sense of urgency, forming a guiding coalition, developing a vision and strategy, communicating the change vision, empowering broad-based action, generating short-term wins, consolidating gains and producing more change, and anchoring the new approaches in the culture.

Ideas for how to create a successful future.

Preparing for an uncertain future requires a proactive approach. You can proactively forge the future by being a shaper more than an adapter, creating new competitive advantages, actively managing your career and your personal development, and becoming an active leader and a lifelong learner.

DISCUSSION QUESTIONS

1. Review the quotes on page 586, describing "resistance to becoming world class." Why do some people resist the goal of becoming world class? What lies behind the quotes? How can this resistance be overcome?

2. Generate specific examples of world-class business that you have seen as a consumer. Also, generate examples of poor business practice. Why and how do some companies inspire world-class practices, while others do not?

3. How might blogging affect the process of managing change? What are the professional and career implications of blogging for you?

4. Generate and discuss examples of problems and opportunities that have inspired change, both in businesses and in you, personally.

5. Review the methods for dealing with resistance to change. Generate specific examples of each that you have seen,

and analyze the reasons why they worked or failed to work.

6. Choose some specific types of changes you would like to see happen in groups or organizations with which you are familiar. Imagine that you were to try to bring about these changes. What sources of resistance should you anticipate? How would you manage the resistance?

7. Develop a specific plan for becoming a "continuous learner."

8. In your own words, what does the idea of "creating the future" mean to you? How can you put this concept to good use? Again, generate some specific ideas that you can really use.

9. Consider the great companies of 50 years hence, described by futurist Peter Schwartz on page 606. How far-fetched, or realistic, do they seem? What new business ideas do they suggest for entrepreneurs? What do they suggest about your own preparation for the future?

CONCLUDING CASE

Barbara's World of Windows, Fabrics, and Accessories—Home Consultant Division

BUSINESS OVERVIEW AND PERSPECTIVE

Shortly after World War II, Barbara and Jerry Klein opened a small retail store in the northern New Jersey metropolitan area. Their major product lines included cotton, wool, and other fabrics that Jerry was able to buy from a few of his old war buddies who worked in mills located throughout the southeastern United States. The fabrics were purchased by an almost exclusively female clientele from the local area for use in making curtains, clothing, slipcovers, pillows, and other related home furnishings. The store also sold curtain rods, hardware, zippers, sewing supplies, and related accessories.

The store was a great success throughout the 1950s, 1960s, and 1970s. During that time, sales grew from $150,000 to more than $2,500,000 annually. The store employed 30 people, mostly homemakers from the local area who were sewers and clothing makers themselves. The warm, cozy, and friendly atmosphere made the store a favorite of the local and surrounding townspeople. Several competitors came and went over the years—those that survived were very small, posing little threat to Barbara and Jerry, who essentially enjoyed the fruits of a monopoly.

Barbara's (comfortable) World came crashing down during the 1980s, as sales steadily declined to less than $1,800,000 by the decade's end. Their original clientele had gradually retired, moved away, or passed on by that time. The modern-day women from the area were now going to college and establishing professional careers rather than staying at home sewing curtains or making clothes. At the same time, a number of new and more diversified competitors had come onto the scene, capturing more and more market share.

Those new stores carried a much wider range of products, including bridal wear, tablecloths and napkins, miniblinds and assorted shades, quilts, blankets, and limited lines of furniture, lamps, candles, and complementary products.

Barbara and Jerry's daughter Sandy, a recent business school graduate who grew up working part-time in the business, came on board as assistant manager of operations. Sandy was being trained and groomed to eventually take over the business. Given her many years of direct work experience and her newly acquired business management skills, Sandy was given some freedom and encouragement to effect change and turn things around.

A NEW ERA

The store's entire merchandise inventory was counted, assessed, and reorganized. Sandy got rid of slow-moving and stagnant inventory. High-turnover, high-profit merchandise was given more and better shelf space. A number of new products were added to challenge the competition and better reflect the buying trends and needs of the modern-day consumer.

The most significant change was the addition of a new Home Consultant Division. Recognizing the needs and characteristics of today's professional woman shopper, Sandy proceeded to bring the business to the customer in the comfort of her own home. During evening and weekend hours, sales associates visited the homes of working women. Offered a variety of full-color catalogs and fabric samples, customers could simply select the blinds, shades, draperies, wall coverings, slipcovers, and so on of their choosing and write a check for one-half of the total invoice as a deposit. The sales associate took the necessary measurements while on site. The finished products were delivered and installed in approximately two to four weeks. The remaining balance was paid at the time of delivery and installation.

The Home Consultant Division was a huge start-up success. Sales reached $1,000,000 during the first year of operation and $1,500,000 during year two. As the division grew, so too did a number of problems and inefficiencies. A shortage of qualified installers caused the lag time between orders and installations to grow from to as much as 6 to 12 weeks. On the home appointment side, where a customer could once expect to have a sales associate visit within a week or two of inquiring, the wait for an appointment had grown to average about one month. On top of all of this, Sandy knew that there was a lot more business out there to capture.

Customers became impatient and unhappy, as Sandy now faced her first serious problem that needed to be fixed fast. The complacency and lack of marketing savvy of her parents had allowed a number of able competitors to come onto the scene, two of which were gearing up to offer their own home shopping divisions.

Sandy asked Barbara Johnson, one of the sales associates, to document the complete and exact process that takes place from the time an inquiry is received to the time that an installation is completed, in hopes of identifying specific inefficiencies and production bottlenecks. Barbara's report can be summarized as follows:

- The process begins with a phone call from people responding to newspaper ads or from in-store shoppers. No programs are currently in place to actively solicit prospective customers.
- The secretary, or whoever happens to answer the phone, records the information (name, address, phone number, nature of inquiry) and places a note in the sales associate's mailbox.
- A sales associate (currently two full-time, one part-time) places a phone call to set up an appointment in the order in which the inquiry was received. Most clients are within a 25 mile radius of the store.
- A typical day for a sales associate might include a 4:00 P.M. appointment in one town followed by a 7:30 P.M. appointment in another town. On Saturdays, the sales associate typically has a 9:00 A.M. appointment in one town followed by a 12:00 P.M. appointment in another town.
- The associate then meets with the client, equipped with catalogs and samples, order forms, and measuring equipment. Most appointments result in a sale. The sales associate takes the necessary measurements (window sizes, sofa dimensions, and so on), and leaves with a check for an estimated 50 percent deposit.
- The sales associates spend about one day per week processing orders (calculating the yardage and best source of material, locating the appropriate curtain rod, tabulating the exact invoice total, and so on).
- When all of the materials arrive at the store for a particular order, the sales associate is notified and then proceeds to contact and schedule an installer; this also includes a scheduling call to the client.
- The installer completes the delivery and installation and collects the final payment for the store.

Barbara also provided the following breakdown of each sales associate's average distribution of time spent on the job:

- 40 percent of the time is spent selling at the client's home.
- 30 percent of the time is spent processing orders.
- 30 percent of the time is spent traveling between appointments.

Barbara's report concluded with a summary from the installation side of the division: "Most deliveries and installations are made by two independent subcontractors that have been with the company since the start-up of the division. They have a reputation for doing good work. Several others have come and gone—this due to either poor workmanship or lack of availability or reliability.

Several customers have complained about the appearance and presentation of the installers and their equipment. Many of the clients are women who live in suburban neighborhoods. These women are often home alone when the deliveries and installations are made. They are apprehensive and fearful when they see unshaven young men with old clothes pull up to their home in a battered old van. A few customers have actually refused to let the installer into their home without first speaking with someone at the store.

The two primary installers are working hard and are steadily falling further and further behind the order file."

As for the many untapped markets and additional new business that is out there, Sandy wants her staff to become more proactive—to go after orders rather than just waiting for the phone to ring or for a shopper to inquire while in the store.

Sandy feels that the company is making a big mistake by completely ignoring the local industrial and governmental markets. For example, on the industrial side, hotels, restaurants, banks, offices, and many other establishments regularly purchase and update their furniture, window coverings, and other interior decor. The same is true for prospective governmental customers such as schools, city and town offices, and federal buildings. Sandy also notes that all of the customers, both in the store and in the home, continue to be almost exclusively women.

QUESTIONS

1. You have inherited a company that must make several internal changes in order to survive and thrive. How would you plan for and manage each of the changes that must occur? Be sure to address both strategic and tactical aspects of your plan.

2. The text lists and describes a number of operational aspects and components; select each of those that are relevant to this case and provide a specific example of a technique that you would incorporate into the new operation?

3. In general, what interpersonal skills and management techniques will you use to successfully effect change?

EXPERIENTIAL EXERCISES

18.1 A Force-Field Analysis

OBJECTIVE

To introduce you to force-field analysis for managing organizational change.

INSTRUCTIONS

Read the following force-field analysis, and come up with an organizational problem of your own to analyze.

Force-Field Analysis

A force-field analysis is one way to assess change in an organization. This concept reflects the forces, driving and restraining, at work at a particular time. It helps assess organizational strengths and select forces to add or remove in order to create change. The theory of change suggested by Kurt Lewin, who developed the force-field analysis, is that while driving forces may be more easily affected, shifting them could increase opposition (tension and/or conflict) within the organization and add restraining

forces. Therefore, it may be more effective to remove restraining forces to create change.

The use of the force-field analysis will demonstrate the range of forces pressing on an organization at a particular time. This analysis can increase people's optimism that it is possible to strategize and plan for change.

Example—Trying to increase student participation in student government.

Driving Forces	Restraining Forces
More money allocated for student government activities. ⟶	⟵ High emphasis on grades—a need to study more.
Better publicity and public relations programs for student government. ⟶	⟵ Other activities—cultural, social, sports— divert interest.
Student government representatives go to classes and explain positive effects of student decisions. ⟶	⟵ Not much public relations work in the past.
Special career programs offered for student government participants. ⟶	⟵ Students do not see student government as effective or helping them get a job.

Present balance point

Force-Field Analysis Worksheet

1. (10–15 min.) Choose an organizational change in process, complete the Problem Analysis section, and fill in the model.

2. (20 min.) In groups of three or four, discuss the driving and restraining forces in each person's problem.

3. (10 min.) Class discussion

   a. Why is it useful to break a problem situation up into driving and restraining forces?

   b. Would the model be used any differently whether applied to an individual or organizational problem?

PROBLEM ANALYSIS

1. Describe the problem in a few words.

_____

_____

_____

_____

_____

_____

2. A list of forces *driving* toward change would include:

   a. _____

   b. _____

   c. _____

   d. _____

   e. _____

   f. _____

3. A list of forces *restraining* change would include:

   a. _____

   b. _____

   c. _____

   d. _____

   e. _____

   f. _____

4. Put the driving and restraining forces of the problem on this force-field analysis, according to their degree of impact on change.

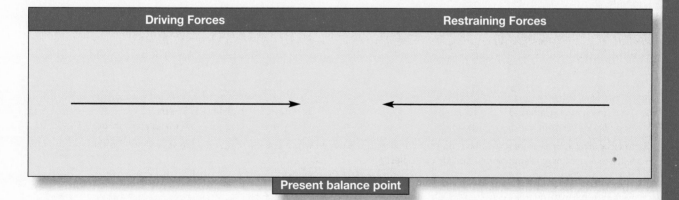

SOURCE: Dorothy Hai, "Force-Field Analysis" in *Organizational Behavior: Experiences and Cases* (St. Paul, MN: West, 1986), pp. 259–61. Copyright © 1986. Reprinted by permission by South-Western College Publishing, a division of Thomson Learning.

18.2 Values Inventory

1. From the list below, choose five items that are most important to you. Rank the top five items according to your current values, in the "Current" column. This is only a partial list; fill in the (other) blanks with items that are of personal value to you. Give the most important item a 1, the next most important a 2, and so on.

Values	Current	5 years	10 years	20 years	30 years
Security					
Financial independence					
Having children					
Owning a home					
Free time					
Recognition or fame					
Friendships					
Helping others less fortunate than you					
Family					
Travel					
Having the respect of others					
Playing sports					
Having an interesting job or career					
Having good physical health					
Being a knowledgeable, informed person					
Having a sense of accomplishment					
Spiritual fulfillment					
Doing well in school					
(other)					
(other)					

2. From the same list, indicate in the columns which values would comprise your top five ranking in 5 years, 10 years, 20 years, 30 years. Look back over your rankings. Does anything surprise you? Were there any drastic changes from the present through 30 years?

3. In examining your current values, how do these fit in with the way in which you currently allocate your time? Do these values fit in with your dreams, goals, ambitions, and life principles?

4. What major, unanticipated event could cause you to modify your rankings (serious illness, business failure, marriage, etc.)? Discuss how this event would impact your rankings.

SOURCE: Suzanne C. de Janasz, Karen O. Dond, and Beth Z. Schneider, *Interpersonal Skills in Organizations* (New York: Mcgraw-Hill/Irwin, 2002), p. 57.

18.3 Networking Scenarios

1. Working on your own, develop a networking strategy for the following three scenarios. (10 min.)

2. Working with your partner or small group, collaborate on identifying the best strategy for dealing with each of the three scenarios. Each group should develop one best strategy for each scenario. (20 min.)

3. Each group reports, sharing its best strategies for each of the three scenarios (or at least one if not enough time is available). (2–3 min. per group per strategy).

4. The large group or class engages in discussion, using the questions at the end. (10 min.)

SCENARIOS

I. You are running for Student Government President. What steps would you take to make your candidacy a success?

1. _____
2. _____
3. _____
4. _____
5. _____
6. _____

II. You are in an internship and are interested in becoming a permanent full-time employee at the organization. What people would you approach and what steps could you take to obtain an offer?

1. _____
2. _____
3. _____
4. _____
5. _____
6. _____

III. You just moved to a new community and your company's business growth relies heavily on referrals. How do you make contacts in a place where you don't know anyone? How can you build a client base?

1. _____
2. _____
3. _____
4. _____
5. _____
6. _____

QUESTIONS

1. What was difficult about this exercise?
2. What creative means were devised to build networks of contacts in these scenarios?
3. Which of these ideas would be easy to implement? Which would be difficult? What makes some strategies easier to do than others?
4. What personal qualities are needed to actually use these strategies?
5. How can someone who is shy about approaching new people use (some or all of) these strategies successfully?
6. What did you learn about yourself and others from this exercise?

SOURCE: Suzanne C. de Janasz, Karen O. Dowd, and Beth Z. Schneider, *Interpersonal Skills in Organizations* (New York: Mcgraw-Hill/Irwin, 2002), p. 212.

PART 5 SUPPORTING CASE

The Transformation at General Electric

Jack Welch Jr. was appointed chairman and chief executive officer of General Electric in April 1981. Recently, Welch retired. His tenure in the job was characterized by constant strategic and organizational change at GE. Among the initiatives with which Welch is associated are

1. *Changing the shape of the business portfolio.* Welch established two sets of criteria for redefining the business portfolio of GE. The first was to declare, "We will only run businesses that are number one or number two in their global markets—or, in the case of services, that have a substantial position—and are of a

scale and potential appropriate to a $50 billion enterprise." Second, Welch defined three broad areas of business for GE: core, high-technology, and service businesses. As a result of these criteria, during the 1980s GE sold or closed businesses accounting for $10 billion in assets and acquired businesses amounting to $18 billion in assets. Divestment included Utah International, housewares and small appliances, consumer electronics, and semiconductors. Additions included RCA; Employers Reinsurance Corp.; Kidder Peabody Group; Navistar Financial; several new plastics ventures; Thomson's medical electronics business; and joint ventures with Fanuc (factory automation), Robert Bosch (electric motors), GEC (major appliances and electrical equipment), and Ericsson (mobile communications).

2. *Changing strategic planning.* Welch largely dismantled the highly elaborate strategic planning system that had been built up at GE over the previous decade. Documentation was drastically reduced, and the planning review process was made more informal—the central element was a meeting between Welch, his two vice chairmen, and top management of each SBU (Strategic Business Unit), which focused on identifying and discussing a few key themes. By 1984 the 200-strong corporate planning staff had been halved. The broad objective was "to get general managers talking to general managers about strategy rather than planners talking to planners."

3. *Delayering.* The changes in planning were one aspect of a more general change in the role of headquarters staff from being "checker, inquisitor, and authority figure to facilitator, helper, and supporter." This change involved a substantial reduction in reporting and paper generation and an increase in individual decision-making authority. These changes permitted a substantial widening of spans of control and the removal of several layers of hierarchy. In most of GE, levels of management were reduced from nine to four.

4. *Destaffing.* Divesting pressures, removing management layers, reducing corporate staffs, and increasing productivity resulted in enormous improvements. Between 1980 and 1990, GE's sales more than doubled while its numbers of employees fell from 402,000 to 298,000.

5. *Values.* A persistent theme in Welch's leadership was a commitment to values. Welch continually emphasized the importance of the company's "software" (values, motivation, and commitment) over its "hardware" (businesses and management structure). Welch's philosophy was articulated in 10 key principles and values:

Being number one or two in each business.

Becoming and staying lean and agile.

"Ownership"—individuals taking responsibility for decisions and actions.

"Stewardship"—individuals ensuring that GE's resources were leveraged to the full.

"Entrepreneurship."

"Excellence"—the highest personal standards.

"Reality."

"Candor."

"Open communications"—both internally and externally.

Financial support—earning a return needed to support success.

This emphasis on values was supported by a type of leadership that put a huge emphasis on communicating and disseminating these values throughout the company. Welch devoted a large portion of his time to addressing meetings of employees and management seminars at GE's Crotonville Management Development Institute.

NEW CULTURE, NEW SYSTEMS

During his first 5 years in office, Welch's priorities were strategy and structure. GE's business portfolio was radically transformed, and within its main businesses GE's strategies gave a much greater emphasis to local presence and global success and to the development and application of new technology. In terms of organizational structure, Welch's crusade against excess costs, complacency, and administrative inefficiencies resulted in a drastic pruning of the corporate hierarchy and a much flatter organization.

At the root of the "new culture" what Welch sought to build at GE was a redefinition of the relational contract between GE and its employees:

> "Like many other large companies in the United States, Europe and Japan, GE has had an implicit psychological contract based upon perceived lifetime employment . . . This produced a paternal, feudal, fuzzy kind of loyalty. You put in your time, worked hard, and the company took care of you for life. That kind of loyalty tends to focus people inward . . . The psychological contract has to change. People at all levels have to feel the risk-reward tension.
>
> My concept of loyalty is not "giving time" to some corporate entity and, in turn, being shielded and protected from the outside world. Loyalty is an affinity among people who want to grapple with the outside world and win . . . The new psychological contract, if there is such a thing, is that jobs at GE are the best in the world for people who are willing to compete. We have the best training and development resources and an environment committed to providing opportunities for personal and professional growth."[1]

Creating a new attitude requires a shift from an internal focus to an external focus:

> "What determines your destiny is not the hand you're dealt, it's how you play your hand. The best way to play your hand is to face reality—see the world as it is and act accordingly . . . For me, the idea is: to shun the incremental and go for the leap. Most bureaucracies—and ours is no exception—unfortunately still think in incremental terms rather than in terms of fundamental change. They think incrementally because they think internally. Changing the culture—opening it up to quantum change—means constantly asking, not how fast am I going, how well am I doing versus how well I did a year or two before, but rather, how fast and how well am I doing versus the world outside."[2]

Critical to building a new culture and changing the "old ways" of GE was not just the bureaucracy itself, but the habits and attitudes that had been engendered by bureaucracy:

"The walls within a big, century-old company don't come down like Jericho's when management makes some organizational changes or gives a speech. There are too many persistent habits propping them up. Parochialism, turf battles, status, "functionalities" and, most important, the biggest sin of a bureaucracy, the focus on itself and its inner workings, are always in the background."[3]

THE WORK-OUT PROGRAM— A GENERIC VIEW

GE's Work-Out Program was a response to the desire to speed the process of organizational change in GE. Welch conceived the idea of Work-Out in September 1988. Welch conducted a session at every class of GE managers attending Management Development Institute at Crotonville, New York. He was impressed by the energy, enthusiasm, and flow of ideas that his open discussion sessions with managers were capable of generating. At the same time, he was frustrated by the resilience of many of GE's bureaucratic practices and the difficulty of transferring the ideas that individual managers possessed into action. After a particularly lively session at Crotonville, Welch and GE's education director, James Braughman, got together to discuss how the interaction in these seminars could be replicated throughout the company in a process that would involve all employees and would generate far-reaching changes within GE. In the course of a helicopter ride from Crotonville to GE's Fairfield headquarters, Welch and Braughman sketched the concept and the framework for the Work-Out process.

A model for GE's Work-Out was a traditional New England town hall meeting where citizens gather to vent their problems, frustrations, and ideas, and people eventually agree on certain civic actions. Welch outlined the goals of Work-Out as follows:

> "Work-Out has a practical and an intellectual goal. The practical objective is to get rid of thousands of bad habits accumulated since the creation of General Electric ... The second thing we want to achieve, the intellectual part, begins by putting the leaders of each business in front of 100 or so of their people, eight to ten times a year, to let them hear what their people think. Work-Out will expose the leaders to the vibrations of their business opinions, feelings, emotions, resentments, not abstract theories of organization and management."[4]

A generic summary of the Work-Out Program reveals three interrelated purposes: to fuel a process of continuous improvement and change; to foster cultural transformation characterized by trust, empowerment, elimination of unnecessary work, and a boundaryless organization; and to improve business performance.

THE STRUCTURE OF THE WORK-OUT PROCESS

The central idea of the Work-Out process was to create a forum where a cross-section of employees in each business could speak their minds about how their business was managed without fear of retribution. Because those doing the work were often the best people to recommend improvements in how their work should be managed, such interaction was seen as a first step in taking actions to remove unnecessary work and improve business processes. In January 1989, Welch announced Work-Out at an annual meeting of GE's 500 top executives. A broad framework was set out, but considerable flexibility was given to each of GE's 14 core businesses in how they went about the program. The key elements of Work-Out were

- *Off-site meetings.* Work-Out was held as a forum and to get away from the company environment. Two-to-three-day Work-Out events were held off-site.
- *Focus on issues and key processes.* There was a strong bias toward action-oriented sessions. The initial Work-Out events tended to focus on removing unnecessary work. This is what Braughman referred to as the "low-hanging fruit." As the programs developed, Work-Out focused more on more complex business processes. For example, in GE Lighting, groupwide sessions were held to accelerate new product development, improve fill rates, and increase integration between component production and assembly. In plastics the priorities were quality improvement, lower cycle times, and increased cross-functional coordination.
- *Cross-sectional participation.* Work-Out sessions normally involved between 50 and 100 employees drawn from all levels and all functions of a business. Critical to the process was the presence of the top management of the particular business.
- *Small groups and town meetings.* Work-Out events normally involved a series of small group meetings that began with a brainstorming session followed by a plenary session (or "town meeting") in which the suggestions developed by the small groups were put to senior managers and then openly debated. At the end of each discussion, the leader was required to make an immediate decision: to adopt, reject, or defer for further study.
- *Follow-up.* A critical element of Work-Out was a follow-up process to ensure that what had been decided was implemented.

THE RESULTS OF WORK-OUT

The results from Work-Out were remarkable. During its first 4 years, more than 3,000 Work-Out sessions had been conducted in GE, resulting in thousands of small changes eliminating "junk work" as well as much more complex and further-reaching changes in organizational structure and management processes. The terms *rattlers* and *pythons* were introduced to describe the two types of problem. Rattlers were simple problems that could be "shot" on sight. Pythons were more complex issues that needed unraveling.

As well as tangible structural changes and performance gains, some of the most important effects were changes in organizational culture. In GE Capital, one of the most centralized and bureaucratized of GE's businesses, one employee described the changes as follows: "we've been suppressed around here for a long time. Now that management is finally listening to us, it feels like the Berlin Wall is coming down.[5]

In 5 years, more than 300,000 employees, customers, and suppliers went through Work-Out sessions. A large variety of impressive and significant performance and efficiency improvements are reported in GE's internal documents, following introduction of the Work-Out processes. For example, the Gas Engine Turbines business unit at Albany, New York, reported an 80 percent decrease in production time to build gas engine turbines; Aircraft Engines at Lynn, Massachusetts, reduced jet engine production time from 30 weeks to 4 weeks. GE's Financial Services Operation reported a reduction in operating costs from $5.10 to $4.55 per invoice, invoices paid per employee were up 34 percent, costs per employee paid fell 19 percent, and employees paid per payroll worker rose 32 percent. The Aerospace plant at Syracuse, New York, reported that as a result of the Work-Out Program, beyond achieving 100 percent compliance with pollution regulations, the production of hazardous waste materials was reduced from 759 tons in 1990 to 275 tons in 1992.

MANAGING WORK-OUT

Work-Out was intended as a bottom-up process in which (1) employees throughout each business would be free to challenge their leaders and (2) management's role was primarily to perpetuate the program and to ensure that decisions, once made, were implemented. But Work-Out could not be just a populist movement within the corporation. It needed to be directed toward creating the kind of corporation that GE needed to be to survive and prosper. To this extent Jack Welch saw his role as communicating and disseminating the principles, values, and themes that would permit GE's continued success.

In 1989 Welch crystallized his ideas about GE's management around three themes: speed, simplicity, and self-confidence:

> "We found in the 1980s that becoming faster is tied to becoming simpler. Our businesses, with tens of thousands of employees, will not respond to visions that have sub-paragraphs and foot-notes. If we're not simple we can't be fast ... and if we're not fast, we can't win.

> Simplicity, to an engineer, means clean, functional, winning designs, no bells and whistles. In marketing it might manifest itself as clear, unencumbered proposals. For manufacturing people it would produce a logical process that makes sense to every individual on the line. And on an individual, interpersonal level it would take the form of plain speaking, directness, honesty.

> But as surely as speed flows from simplicity, simplicity is grounded in self-confidence. Self-confidence does not grow in someone who is just another appendage on the bureaucracy; whose authority rests on little more than a title. People who are freed from the confines of their box on the organization chart, whose status rests on real world achievement—those are the people who develop the self-confidence to be simple, to share every bit of information available to them, to listen to those above, below and around them and then move boldly.

> But a company cannot distribute self-confidence. What it can do—what we must do—is to give our people an opportunity to win, to contribute, and hence earn self-confidence themselves. They don't get that opportunity, they can't taste winning if they spend their days wandering in the muck of a self-absorbed bureaucracy.

> Speed ... simplicity ... self-confidence. We have it in increasing measure. We know where it comes from ... and we have plans to increase it in the 1990s."[6]

BEST PRACTICES

One of the Work-Out Program's many impressive outcomes is that it's a catalyst for new improvement programs. One such pro-

gram, Best Practices, is aimed at increasing productivity. The GE business-development staff focused on 24 credible companies from an initial pool of 200 that had achieved faster productivity growth than GE and sustained it for at least 10 years. From this list, one dozen companies agreed to take part in GE's proposal to send its employees to their companies to learn their secrets to success. In exchange, GE offered to share the results of the study as well success stories with the participating companies. This learning for the Best Practices program involved companies such as Ford, Hewlett-Packard, Xerox, and Chaparral Steel plus three Japanese firms.

GE was less concerned with the actual work done at the companies than with management practices and attitudes of the employees. The difference between Best Practices and traditional benchmarking is that the former does not require keeping score. The focus on learning alternative successful management practices and managing processes was identified as the most critical component for long-term productivity improvements. The basic assumption that through multiple exposure to alternative management practices, managers and employees will be stimulated to continuously improve their own practices, continues to guide the program. Best Practices has evolved into a formal course taught to at least one dozen employees and managers per month in each business unit.

QUESTIONS

1. Based on the information presented, describe the overall planned change approach and phases led by Jack Welch.

2. Identify and briefly describe the major characteristics of the Work-Out Program.

3. Discuss how the organizational culture changed. What caused the change? What effects did the culture change have on human behavior and organizational performance and effectiveness?

4. Assess the case using the models and concepts presented in the last chapter and other parts of the book.

SOURCE: This case was written by R. Grant and A. B. (Rami) Shani for classroom use. The case draws heavily on the following sources: N. M. Tichy and S. Sherman, *Control Your Destiny or Someone Else Will* (New York: Doubleday, 1992); R. Slater, *The New GE: How Jack Welch Revived an American Institution* (Burr Ridge, IL: Irwin, 1993); R. N. Ashkenas and T D. Jick, "From Dialogue to Action in GE Work-Out," in W. A. Pasmore and R. Woodman (eds.), *Research in Organization Change and Development*, vol. 6. (Greenwich. CT: JAI Press, 1993), pp. 267–87; "Jack Welch's Lessons for Success," *Fortune*, February 25, 1993, pp. 86–90.

CASE INCIDENTS

Robot Repercussion

Victor Principal, vice president of industrial relations for General Manufacturing, Inc., sat in his office reviewing the list of benefits the company expected to realize from increasing its use of industrial robots. In a few minutes, he would walk down to the labor-management conference room for a meeting with Ralph McIntosh, president of the labor union local representing most of the company's industrial employees. The purpose of this meeting would be to informally exchange views and positions preliminary

to the opening for formal contract negotiations later in the month, which would focus on the use of computer-integrated robotics systems and the resulting impact on employment, workers, and jobs.

Both Principal and McIntosh had access to similar information flows relevant to industrial robots, including the following. Unlike single-task machines, installed in earlier stages of automation, robots can be programmed to do one job and then reprogrammed to do another one. The pioneering generation of robots was mainly programmed to load machines, weld, forge, spray paint, handle materials, and inspect auto bodies. The latest generation of robots includes vision-controlled robots, which enable the machines to approximate the human ability to recognize and size up objects by using laser-beam patterns recorded by television cameras and transmitted to "smart" computers. The computer software interprets and manipulates the images relayed by the camera in a "smart" or artificially intelligent way.

Experts concluded that the impact of robot installation on employment would be profound, although the extent of the worker replacement was not clear. The inescapable conclusion was that robot usage had the capacity to increase manufacturing performance and to decrease manufacturing employment.

Principal walked down to the conference room. Finding McIntosh already there, Principal stated the company's position regarding installation of industrial robots: "The company needs the cooperation of the union and our workers. We don't wish to be perceived as callously exchanging human workers for robots." Then Principal listed the major advantages associated with robots: (1) improved quality of product as a result of the accuracy of robots; (2) reduced operating costs, as the per-hour operational cost of robots was about one-third of the per-hour cost of wages and benefits paid to an average employee; (3) reliability improvements, as robots work tirelessly and don't require behavioral support; and (4) greater manufacturing flexibility, because robots are readily reprogrammable for different jobs. Principal concluded that these advantages would make the company more competitive, which would allow it to grow and increase its workforce.

McIntosh's response was direct and strong: "We aren't Luddites racing around ruining machines. We know it's necessary to increase productivity and that robotic technology is here. But we can't give the company a blank check. We need safe-guards and protection." McIntosh continued, "We intend to bargain for the following contract provisions:

1. Establishment of labor–management committees to negotiate *in advance* about the labor impact of robotics technology and, of equal importance, to have a voice in deciding how and whether it should be used.

2. Rights to advance notice about installation of new technology.

3. Retraining rights for workers displaced, to include retraining for new positions in the plant, the community, or other company plants.

4. Spreading the work among workers by use of a four-day workweek or other acceptable plan as an alternative to reducing the workforce."

McIntosh's final sentence summed up the union's position: "We in the union believe the company is giving our jobs to robots to reduce the labor force."

Their meeting ended amiably, but Principal and McIntosh each knew that much hard bargaining lay ahead. As Principal returned to his office, the two opposing positions were obvious. On his yellow tablet, Principal listed the requirements as he saw them: (1) A clearly stated overall policy was needed to guide negotiation decisions and actions; (2) it was critical to decide on a company position regarding each of the union's announced demands and concerns; and (3) a plan had to be developed.

As Principal considered these challenges, he idly contemplated a robot possessing artificial intelligence and vision capability that could help him in his work. Immediately a danger alarm sounded in his mind. A robot so constructed might be more than helpful and might take over this and other important aspects of his job. Slightly chagrined, Principal returned to his task. He needed help—but not from any "smart" robot.

SOURCE: J. Champion and J. James, *Critical Incidents in Management: Decision and Policy Issues,* 6th ed. The McGraw-Hill Companies, 1989).

Implementing Strategic Change

James Fulmer, chief executive officer of Allied Industries, reviewed three notes he had exchanged with Frank Curtis, director of fiscal affairs, now president of a company owned by Allied. The two executives were going to meet in a few minutes to discuss problems that had recently surfaced. During the past decade, Allied had aggressively pursued a growth objective based on a conglomerate strategy of acquiring companies in distress. CEO Fulmer's policy was to appoint a new chief operating officer for each acquisition with instructions to facilitate a turnaround. Fulmer reviewed two of the notes he had written to Curtis.

Date: January 15, 2003.

Memorandum

To: Frank Curtis, Director of Fiscal Affairs, Allied Industries

From: James Fulmer, Chairman, Allied Industries

Subject: Your Appointment as President, Lee Medical Supplies

You are aware that Allied Industries recently acquired Lee Medical Supplies. Mr. John Lee, founder and president of the company, has agreed to retire, and I am appointing you to replace him. Our acquisitions group will brief you on the company, but I want to warn you that Lee Medical Supplies has a history of mismanagement. As a distributor of medical items, the company's sales last year totaled approximately $300 million, with net earnings of only $12 million. Your job is to make company sales and profits compatible with Allied standards. You are reminded that it is my policy to call for an independent evaluation of company progress and your performance as president after 18 months.

Date: September 10, 2004.

Memorandum

To: Frank Curtis, President, Lee Medical Supplies

From: James Fulmer, Chairman, Allied Industries

Subject: Serious Problems at Lee Medical Supplies

In accord with corporate policy, consultants recently conducted an evaluation of Lee Medical Supplies. In a relatively short period of time, you have increased sales and profits to meet Allied's standards, but I am alarmed at other aspects of your performance. I am told that during the past 18 months, three of your nine vice presidents have resigned and that you have terminated four others. An opinion survey conducted by the consultants indicates that a low state of morale exists and that your managerial appointees are regarded by their subordinates as hard-nosed perfectionists obsessed with quotas and profits. Employees report that ruthless competition now exists between divisions, regions, and districts. They also note that the collegial, family-oriented atmosphere fostered by Mr. Lee has been replaced by a dog eat-dog situation characterized by negative management attitudes toward employee feelings and needs. After you have studied the enclosed report from the consultants, we will meet to discuss their findings. I am particularly concerned with their final conclusion that "a form of corporate cancer seems to be spreading throughout Lee Medical Supplies."

As Fulmer prepared to read the third note, written by Frank Curtis, he reflected on his interview with the consultants. While Fulmer considered Curtis a financial expert and a turnaround specialist, his subordinates characterized Curtis as an autocrat and better suited to be a Marine boot camp commander.

Date: September 28, 2004.

Memorandum

To: James Fulmer

From: Frank Curtis

Subject: The So-Called Serious Problems at Lee Medical Supplies

I have received your memorandum dated September 10, and reviewed the consultants' report. When you appointed me to my present position I was instructed to take over an unprofitable company and make it profitable. I have done so in 18 months, although I inherited a family-owned business that by your own admission had been mismanaged for years. I found a group of managers and salespeople with an average company tenure of 22 years. Mr. Lee had centralized all personnel decisions so that only he could terminate an employee. He tolerated mediocre performance. All employees were paid on a straight salary basis, with seniority the sole criterion for advancement. Some emphasis was given to increasing sales each year, but none was given to reducing costs and increasing profits. Employees did indeed find the company a fun place to work, and the feeling of being a part of a family did permeate the company. Such attitudes were, however, accompanied by mediocrity, incompetence, and poor performance.

I found it necessary to implement immediate strategic changes in five areas: the organization's structure, employee rewards and incentives, management information systems, allocation of resources, and managerial leadership style. As a result, sales areas were reorganized into divisions, regions,

and districts. Managers who I felt were incompetent and/or lacking in commitment to my objectives and methods were replaced. Unproductive and mediocre employees were encouraged to find jobs elsewhere. Authority for staffing and compensation decisions was decentralized to units at the division, region, and district levels. Managers of those units were informed that along with their authority went responsibility for reducing costs and for increasing sales and profits. Each unit was established as a profit center. A new department was established and charged with reviewing performance of those units. Improved accounting and control systems were implemented. A management-by-objectives program was developed to establish standards and monitor performance. Performance appraisals are now required for all employees. To encourage more aggressive action, bonuses and incentives are offered to managers of units showing increased profits. A commission plan based on measurable sales and profit performances has replaced straight salaries. Resources are allocated to units based on their performance.

My own leadership style has probably represented the most traumatic change for employees. Internal competition is a formally mandated policy throughout the company. It has been responsible for much of the progress achieved to date. Progress, however, is never made without costs, and I recognize that employees are not having as much fun as in the past. I was employed to achieve results and not to ensure that employees remain secure and happy in their work. Don't let a few crybabies unable to adjust to changes lead you to believe that problems take precedence over profits. Does it mean that I am not people oriented if I believe it is unlikely that a spirit of aggressiveness and competitiveness can coexist with an atmosphere of cooperativeness and family orientation? Do you feel that we are obligated to employees because of past practices? Frankly, I thought I had your support to do whatever was necessary to get this company turned around. In our meeting, tell me if you think my approaches have been wrong and, if so, tell me what I should have done differently.

Just as Fulmer finished reviewing the third memorandum, his secretary informed him that Curtis had arrived for their scheduled meeting. He realized he was undecided about how to communicate to Curtis his ideas and beliefs regarding how changes in an organization can best be implemented. One thing he did know: He didn't appreciate how Curtis had expressed his views in his memorandum, but he recognized that he probably should set aside emotions and respond to the questions Curtis posed.

SOURCE: J. Champion and J. James, *Critical Incidents in Management: Decision and Policy Issues,* 6th ed. (Burr Ridge, IL.: Richard D. Irwin, 1989).

Glossary

A

accommodation A style of dealing with conflict involving cooperation on behalf of the other party but not being assertive about one's own interests.

accountability The expectation that employees will perform a job, take corrective action when necessary, and report upward on the status and quality of their performance.

accounting audits Procedures used to verify accounting reports and statements.

acquisition One firm buying another.

activity-based costing (ABC) A method of cost accounting designed to identify streams of activity and then to allocate costs across particular business processes according to the amount of time employees devote to particular activities.

adapters Companies that take the current industry structure and its evolution as givens, and choose where to compete.

adverse impact When a seemingly neutral employment practice has a disproportionately negative effect on a protected group.

advertising support model Charging fees to advertise on a site.

affective conflict Emotional disagreement directed toward other people.

affiliate model Charging fees to direct site visitors to other companies' sites.

affirmative action Special efforts to recruit and hire qualified members of groups that have been discriminated against in the past.

Alderfer's ERG theory A human needs theory developed by Alderfer postulating that people have three basic sets of needs which can operate simultaneously.

Applying the Vroom Model of Leadership path-goal theory A theory that concerns how leaders influence subordinates' perceptions of their work goals and the paths they follow toward attainment of those goals.

arbitration The use of a neutral third party to resolve a labor dispute.

assessment center A managerial performance test in which candidates participate in a variety of exercises and situations.

assets The values of the various items the corporation owns.

authentic leadership A style in which the leader is true to himself or herself while leading.

authority The legitimate right to make decisions and to tell other people what to do.

autocratic leadership A form of leadership in which the leader makes decisions on his or her own and then announces those decisions to the group.

autonomous work groups Groups that control decisions about and execution of a complete range of tasks.

avoidance A reaction to conflict that involves ignoring the problem by doing nothing at all, or deemphasizing the disagreement.

B

balance sheet A report that shows the financial picture of a company at a given time and itemizes assets, liabilities, and stockholders' equity.

barriers to entry Conditions that prevent new companies from entering an industry.

behavioral approach A leadership perspective that attempts to identify what good leaders do—that is, what behaviors they exhibit.

benchmarking The process of comparing an organization's practices and technologies with those of other companies.

bootlegging Informal work on projects, other than those officially assigned, of employees' own choosing and initiative.

boundaryless organization Organization in which there are no barriers to information flow.

bounded rationality A less-than-perfect form of rationality in which decision makers cannot be perfectly rational because decisions are complex and complete information is unavailable.

brainstorming A process in which group members generate as many ideas about a problem as they can; criticism is withheld until all ideas have been proposed

bridge leaders A leader who bridges conflicting value systems or different cultures.

broker A person who assembles and coordinates participants in a network.

budgeting The process of investigating what is being done and comparing the results with the corresponding budget data to verify accomplishments or remedy differences. Also called budgetary controlling.

buffering Creating supplies of excess resources in case of unpredictable needs.

bureaucratic control The use of rules, regulations, and authority to guide performance.

business ethics The moral principles and standards that guide behavior in the world of business.

business incubators Protected environments for new, small businesses.

business plan A formal planning step that focuses on the entire venture and describes all the elements involved in starting it.

business strategy The major actions by which a business competes in a particular industry or market.

C

cafeteria benefit program An employee benefit program in which employees choose from a menu of options to create a benefit package tailored to their needs.

Caux Principles Ethical principles established by international executives based in Caux, Switzerland, in collaboration with business leaders from Japan, Europe, and the United States.

centralized organization An organization in which high-level executives make most decisions and pass them down to lower levels for implementation.

certainty The state that exists when decision makers have accurate and comprehensive information.

charismatic leader A person who is dominant, self-confident, convinced of the moral righteousness of his or her beliefs, and able to arouse a sense of excitement and adventure in followers.

chief technology officer (CTO) Executive in charge of technology strategy and development.

clan control Control based on the norms, values, shared goals, and trust among group members.

coaching Dialogue with a goal of helping another be more effective and achieve his or her full potential on the job.

coalitional model Model of organizational decision making in which groups with differing preferences use power and negotiations to influence decisions.

cognitive conflict Issue-based differences in perspectives or judgments.

cohesiveness The degree to which a group is attractive to its members, members are motivated to remain in the group, and members influence one another.

collaboration A style of dealing with conflict emphasizing both cooperation and assertiveness in order to maximize both parties' satisfaction.

communication The transmission of information and meaning from one party to another through the use of shared symbols.

comparable worth Principle of equal pay for different jobs of equal worth.

competing A style of dealing with conflict involving strong focus on one's own goals, and little or no concern for the other person's goals.

competitive environment The immediate environment surrounding a firm; includes suppliers, customers, competitors, and the like.

competitive intelligence Information that helps managers determine how to compete better.

compliance-based ethics programs Company mechanisms typically designed by corporate counsel to prevent, detect, and punish legal violations.

compromise A style of dealing with conflict involving moderate attention to both parties' concerns.

computer-integrated manufacturing (CIM) The use of computer-aided design and computer-aided manufacturing to sequence and optimize a number of production processes.

concentration A strategy employed for an organization that operates a single business and competes in a single industry.

concentric diversification A strategy used to add new businesses that produce related products or are involved in related markets and activities.

conceptual and decision skills Skills pertaining to the ability to identify and resolve problems for the benefit of the organization and its members.

concurrent control The control process used while plans are being carried out, including directing, monitoring, and fine-tuning activities as they are performed.

conflict Opposing pressures from different sources. Two levels of conflict are psychological conflict and conflict that arises between individuals or groups.

conglomerate diversification A strategy used to add new businesses that produce unrelated products or are involved in unrelated markets and activities.

contingency plans Alternative courses of action that can be implemented based on how the future unfolds.

continuous process A process that is highly automated and has a continuous production flow.

control Any process that directs the activities of individuals toward the achievement of organizational goals.

controlling The management function of monitoring performance and making needed changes.

cooperative strategies Strategies used by two or more organizations working together to manage the external environment.

coordination The procedures that link the various parts of an organization for the purpose of achieving the organization's overall mission.

coordination by mutual adjustment Units interact with one another to make accommodations in order to achieve flexible coordination.

coordination by plan Interdependent units are required to meet deadlines and objectives that contribute to a common goal.

core competencies The unique skills and/or knowledge an organization possesses that give it an edge over competitors.

corporate governance The role of a corporation's executive staff and board of directors in ensuring that the firm's activities meet the goals of the firm's stakeholders.

corporate social responsibility Obligation toward society assumed by business.

corporate strategy The set of businesses, markets, or industries in which an organization competes and the distribution of resources among those entities.

cost competitiveness Keeping costs low in order to achieve profits and be able to offer prices that are attractive to consumers.

culture shock The disorientation and stress associated with being in a foreign environment.

current ratio A liquidity ratio which indicates the extent to which short-term assets can decline and still be adequate to pay short-term liabilities.

custom-made solutions New, creative solutions designed specifically for the problem.

customer relationship management (CRM) A multifaceted process focusing on creating two-way exchanges with customers to foster intimate knowledge of their needs, wants, and buying patterns.

customer service The speed and dependability with which an organization can deliver what customers want.

D

debt-equity ratio A leverage ratio which indicates the company's ability to meet its long-term financial obligations.

decentralized organization An organization in which lower-level managers make important decisions.

defenders Companies that stay within a stable product domain as a strategic maneuver.

delegation The assignment of new or additional responsibilities to a subordinate.

democratic leadership A form of leadership in which the leader solicits input from subordinates.

demographics Measures of various characteristics of the people who comprise groups or other social units.

departmentalization Subdividing an organization into smaller subunits.

development Teaching managers and professional employees broad skills needed for their present and future jobs.

development project A focused organizational effort to create a new product or process via technological advances.

devil's advocate A person who has the job of criticizing ideas to ensure that their downsides are fully explored.

dialectic A structured debate comparing two conflicting courses of action.

differentiation An aspect of the organization's internal environment created by job specialization and the division of labor.

differentiation strategy A strategy an organization uses to build competitive advantage by being unique in its industry or market segment along one or more dimensions.

discounting the future A bias weighting short-term costs and benefits more heavily than longer-term costs and benefits.

diversification A firm's investment in a different product, business, or geographic area.

diversity training Programs that focus on identifying and reducing hidden biases against people with differences and developing the skills needed to manage a diversified workforce.

divestiture A firm selling one or more businesses.

division of labor The assignment of different tasks to different people or groups.

divisional organization Departmentalization that groups units around products, customers, or geographic regions.

domain selection Entering a new market or industry with an existing expertise.

downsizing The planned elimination of positions or jobs.

downward communication Information that flows from higher to lower levels in the organization's hierarchy.

dynamic network Temporary arrangements among partners that can be assembled and reassembled to adapt to the environment.

E

ecocentric management Its goal is the creation of sustainable economic development and improvement of quality of life worldwide for all organizational stakeholders.

economic responsibilities To produce goods and services that society wants at a price that perpetuates the business and satisfies its obligations to investors.

economies of scope Economies in which materials and processes employed in one product can be used to make other, related products.

egoism An ethical system defining acceptable behavior as that which maximizes consequences for the individual.

emotional intelligence The skills of understanding yourself, managing yourself, and dealing effectively with others.

employment-at-will The legal concept that an employee may be terminated for any reason.

empowerment The process of sharing power with employees, thereby enhancing their confidence in their ability to perform their jobs and their belief that they are influential contributors to the organization.

entrepreneur An individual who establishes a new organization without the benefit of corporate sponsorship.

entrepreneurial orientation The tendency of an organization to identify and capitalize successfully on opportunities to launch new ventures by entering new or established markets with new or existing goods or services.

entrepreneurial venture A new business having growth and high profitability as primary objectives.

entrepreneurship The pursuit of lucrative opportunities by enterprising individuals.

environmental scanning Searching for and sorting through information about the environment.

environmental uncertainty Lack of information needed to understand or predict the future.

equity theory A theory stating that people assess how fairly they have been treated according to two key factors: outcomes and inputs.

ethical climate In an organization it refers to the processes by which decisions are evaluated and made on the basis of right and wrong.

ethical issue Situation, problem, or opportunity in which an individual must choose among several actions that must be evaluated as morally right or wrong.

ethical leader One who is both a moral person and a moral manager influencing others to behave ethically.

ethical responsibilities Meeting other social expectations, not written as law.

ethics The system of rules governing the ordering of values.

ethnocentrism The tendency to judge others by the standards of one's group or culture, which are seen as superior.

executive champion An executive who supports a new technology and protects the product champion of the innovation.

expatriates Parent-company nationals who are sent to work at a foreign subsidiary.

expectancy Employees' perception of the likelihood that their efforts will enable them to attain their performance goals.

expectancy theory A theory proposing that people will behave based on their perceived likelihood that their effort will lead to a certain outcome and on how highly they value that outcome.

external audit An evaluation conducted by one organization, such as a CPA firm, on another.

external environment All relevant forces outside a firm's boundaries, such as competitors, customers, the government, and the economy.

extinction Withdrawing or failing to provide a reinforcing consequence.

extrinsic rewards Rewards given to a person by the boss, the company, or some other person.

F

failure rate The number of expatriate managers of an overseas operation who come home early.

feedback control Control that focuses on the use of information about previous results to correct deviations from the acceptable standard.

filtering The process of withholding, ignoring, or distorting information.

final consumer Those who purchase products in their finished form.

flexible benefit programs Benefit programs in which employees are given credits to spend on benefits that fit their unique needs.

flexible factories Manufacturing plants that have short production runs, are organized around products, and use decentralized scheduling.

flexible processes Methods for adapting the technical core to changes in the environment.

force-field analysis An approach to implementing Lewin's unfreezing/moving refreezing model, involving identifying the forces that prevent people from changing and those that will drive people toward change.

forecasting Method for predicting how variables will change the future.

formalization The presence of rules and regulations governing how people in the organization interact.

framing effects A psychological bias influenced by the way in which a problem or decision alternative is phrased or presented.

franchising An entrepreneurial alliance between a franchisor (an innovator who has created at least one successful store and wants to grow) and a franchisee (a partner who manages a new store of the same type in a new location.)

frontline managers Lower-level managers who supervise the operational activities of the organization.

functional organization Departmentalization around specialized activities such as production, marketing, and human resources.

functional strategies Strategies implemented by each functional area of the organization to support the organization's business strategy.

G

garbage can model Model of organizational decision making depicting a chaotic process and seemingly random decisions.

gatekeeper A team member who keeps abreast of current developments and provides the team with relevant information.

glass ceiling An invisible barrier that makes it difficult for certain groups, such as minorities and women, to move beyond a certain level in the organizational hierarchy.

global model An organization model consisting of a company's overseas subsidiaries and characterized by centralized decision making and tight control by the parent company over most aspects of worldwide operations. Typically adopted by organizations that base their gl

goal A target or end that management desires to reach.

goal displacement A condition that occurs when a decision-making group loses sight of its original goal and a new, less important goal emerges.

goal-setting theory A motivation theory stating that people have conscious goals that energize them and direct their thoughts and behaviors toward a particular end.

grapevine Informal communication network.

group maintenance behaviors Actions taken to ensure the satisfaction of group members, develop and maintain harmonious work relationships, and preserve the social stability of the group.

groupthink A phenomenon that occurs in decision making when group members avoid disagreement as they strive for consensus.

growth need strength The degree to which individuals want personal and psychological development.

H

hierarchy The authority levels of the organizational pyramid.

high-involvement organization A type of organization in which top management ensures that there is consensus about the direction in which the business is heading.

horizontal communication Information shared among people on the same hierarchical level.

host-country nationals Natives of the country where an overseas subsidiary is located.

human capital The knowledge, skills, and abilities of employees that have economic value.

human resources management (HRM) Formal systems for the management of people within an organization.

hygiene factors Characteristics of the workplace, such as company policies, working conditions, pay, and supervision, that can make people dissatisfied.

I

illusion of control People's belief that they can influence events, even when they have no control over what will happen.

incremental model Model of organizational decision making in which major solutions arise through a series of smaller decisions.

independent strategies   Strategies that an organization acting on its own uses to change some aspect of its current environment.

informing   A team strategy that entails making decisions with the team and then informing outsiders of its intentions.

initial public offering (IPO)   Sale to the public, for the first time, of federally registered and underwritten shares of stock in the company.

innovation   A change in method or technology; a positive, useful departure from previous ways of doing things.

innovation   The introduction of new goods and services.

inpatriate   A foreign national brought in to work at the parent company.

inputs   Goods and services organizations take in and use to create products or services.

instrumentality   The perceived likelihood that performance will be followed by a particular outcome.

integration   The degree to which differentiated work units work together and coordinate their efforts.

integrity-based ethics programs   Company mechanisms designed to instill in people a personal responsibility for ethical behavior.

intermediary model   Charging fees to bring buyers and sellers together.

intermediate consumer   A customer who purchases raw materials or wholesale products before selling them to final customers.

internal audit   A periodic assessment of a company's own planning, organizing, leading, and controlling processes.

Internal Development chief technology officer (CTO)   Executive in charge of technology strategy and development.

international model   An organization model that is composed of a company's overseas subsidiaries and characterized by greater control by the parent company over the research function and local product and marketing strategies than is the case in the multinational model.

interpersonal and communication skills   People skills; the ability to lead, motivate, and communicate effectively with others.

intrapreneurs   New venture creators working inside big companies.

intrinsic reward   Reward a worker derives directly from performing the job itself.

ISO 9000   A series of quality standards developed by a committee working under the International Organization for Standardization to improve total quality in all businesses for the benefit of producers and consumers.

J

job analysis   A tool for determining what is done on a given job and what should be done on that job.

job enlargement   Giving people additional tasks at the same time to alleviate boredom.

job enrichment   Changing a task to make it inherently more rewarding, motivating, and satisfying.

job rotation   Changing from one routine task to another to alleviate boredom.

just-in-time (JIT)   A system that calls for subassemblies and components to be manufactured in very small lots and delivered to the next stage of the production process just as they are needed.

K

Kohlberg's model of cognitive moral development   Classifies people based on their level of moral judgment.

L

labor relations   The system of relations between workers and management.

laissez-faire   A leadership philosophy characterized by an absence of managerial decision making.

large batch   Technologies that produce goods and services in high volume.

lateral leadership   Style in which colleagues at the same hierarchical level are invited to collaborate and facilitate joint problem solving.

law of effect   A law formulated by Edward Thorndike in 1911 stating that behavior that is followed by positive consequences will likely be repeated.

Leader-Member Exchange (LMX) theory   Highlights the importance of leader behaviors not just toward the group as a whole but toward individuals on a personal basis.

leading   The management function that involves the manager's efforts to stimulate high performance by employees.

lean manufacturing   An operation that strives to achieve the highest possible productivity and total quality, cost-effectively, by eliminating unnecessary steps in the production process and continually striving for improvement.

learning organization   An organization skilled at creating, acquiring, and transferring knowledge, and at modifying its behavior to reflect new knowledge and insights.

legal responsibilities   To obey local, state, federal, and relevant international laws.

legitimacy   People's judgment of a company's acceptance, appropriateness, and desirability, generally stemming from company goals and methods that are consistent with societal values.

Level 5 leadership   A combination of strong professional will (determination) and humility that builds enduring greatness.

liabilities   The amounts a corporation owes to various creditors. Activity-based costing can highlight overspending.

Life-cycle analysis (LCA)   A process of analyzing all inputs and outputs, though the entire "cradle-to-grave" life of a product, to determine total environmental impact.

line departments   Units that deal directly with the organization's primary goods and services.

logistics   The movement of the right goods in the right amount to the right place at the right time.

low-cost strategy   A strategy an organization uses to build competitive advantage by being efficient and offering a standard, no-frills product.

M

macroenvironment   The most general environment; includes governments, economic conditions, and other fundamental factors that generally affect all organizations.

make-or-buy decision   The question an organization asks itself about whether to acquire new technology from an outside source or develop it itself.

management   The process of working with people and resources to accomplish organizational goals.

management audits   An evaluation of the effectiveness and efficiency of various systems within an organization.

management by objectives (MBO)   A process in which objectives set by a subordinate and a supervisor must be reached within a given time period.

management myopia   Focusing on short-term earnings and profits at the expense of longer-term strategic obligations.

management teams   Teams that coordinate and provide direction to the subunits under their jurisdiction and integrate work among subunits.

managing diversity   Managing a culturally diverse workforce by recognizing the characteristics common to specific groups of employees while dealing with such employees as individuals and supporting, nurturing, and utilizing their differences to the organization's advantage.

market control   Control based on the use of pricing mechanisms and economic information to regulate activities within organizations.

Maslow's need hierarchy   A conception of human needs organizing needs into a hierarchy of five major types.

mass customization   The production of varied, individually customized products at the low cost of standardized, mass-produced products.

matrix organization   An organization composed of dual reporting relationships in which some agers report to two superiors—a functional manager and a divisional manager.

maximizing   A decision realizing the best possible outcome.

mechanistic organization   A form of organization that seeks to maximize internal efficiency.

media richness   The degree to which a communication channel conveys information.

mediator   A third party who intervenes to help others manage their conflict.

mentors Higher level managers who help ensure that high-potential people are introduced to top management and socialized into the norms and values of the organization.

merger One or more companies combining.

middle-level managers Managers located in the middle layers of the organizational hierarchy, reporting to top-level executives.

mission An organization's basic purpose and scope of operations.

monolithic organization An organization that has a low degree of structural integration—employing few women, minorities, or other groups that differ from the majority—and thus has a highly homogeneous employee population.

moral philosophy Principles, rules, and values people use in deciding what is right or wrong.

motivation Forces that energize, direct, and sustain a person's efforts.

motivators Factors that make a job more motivating, such as additional job responsibilities, opportunities for personal growth and recognition, and feelings of achievement.

moving Instituting the change.

multicultural organization An organization that values cultural diversity and seeks to utilize and encourage it.

multinational model An organization model that consists of the subsidiaries in each country in which a company does business, with ultimate control exercised by the parent company.

N

needs assessment An analysis identifying the jobs, people, and departments for which training is necessary.

negative reinforcement Removing or withholding an undesirable consequence.

network organization A collection of independent, mostly single-function firms that collaborate on a product or service.

nonprogrammed decisions New, novel, complex decisions having no proven answers.

norms Shared beliefs about how people should think and behave.

North American Free Trade Agreement (NAFTA) An economic pact that combined the economies of the United States, Canada, and Mexico into the world's largest trading bloc.

O

offshoring Outsourcing to an overseas provider.

one-way communication A process in which information flows in only one direction—from the sender to the receiver, with no feedback loop.

open-book management Practice of sharing with employees at all levels of the organization vital information previously meant for management's eyes only.

open systems Organizations that are affected by, and that affect, their environment.

operational planning The process of identifying the specific procedures and processes required at lower levels of the organization.

opportunity analysis A description of the product or service, an assessment of the opportunity, an assessment of the entrepreneur, specification of activities and resources needed to translate your idea into a viable business, and your source(s) of capital.

optimizing Achieving the best possible balance among several goals.

organic structure An organizational form that emphasizes flexibility.

organization chart The reporting structure and division of labor in an organization.

organization culture The set of important assumptions about the organization and its goals and practices that members of the company share.

organizational ambidexterity Ability to achieve multiple things simultaneously; the genius of the and.

organizational behavior modification (OB Mod) The application of reinforcement theory in organizational settings.

organizational development (OD) The systemwide application of behavioral science knowledge to develop, improve, and reinforce the strategies, structures, and processes that lead to organizational effectiveness.

organizing The management function of assembling and coordinating human, financial, physical, informational, and other resources needed to achieve goals.

orientation training Training designed to introduce new employees to the company and familiarize them with policies, procedures, culture, and the like.

outcome A consequence a person receives for his or her performance.

outplacement The process of helping people who have been dismissed from the company to regain employment elsewhere.

outputs The products or services organizations create.

outsourcing Contracting with an outside provider to produce one or more of an organization's products or services.

P

parading A team strategy that entails simultaneously emphasizing internal team building and achieving external visibility.

parallel teams Teams that operate separately from the regular work structure, and exist temporarily.

participation in decision making Leader behaviors that managers perform in involving their employees in making decisions.

path-goal theory A theory that concerns how leaders influence subordinates' perceptions of their work goals and the paths they follow toward attainment of those goals.

perception The process of receiving and interpreting information.

performance appraisal (PA) Assessment of an employee's job performance.

performance gap The difference between actual performance and desired performance.

philanthropic responsibilities Additional behaviors and activities that society finds desirable and that the values of the business support.

planning The management function of systematically making decisions about the goals and activities that an individual, a group, a work unit, or the overall organization will pursue.

plans The actions or means managers intend to use to achieve organizational goals.

pluralistic organization An organization that has a relatively diverse employee population and makes an effort to involve employees from different gender, racial, or cultural backgrounds.

positive reinforcement Applying consequences that increase the likelihood that a person will repeat the behavior that led to it.

power The ability to influence others.

principle of exception A managerial principle stating that control is enhanced by concentrating on the exceptions or significant deviations from the expected result or standard.

proactive change A response that is initiated before a performance gap has occurred.

probing A team strategy that requires team members to interact frequently with outsiders, diagnose their needs, and experiment with solutions.

procedural justice Using fair process in decision making and making sure others know that the process was as fair as possible.

product champion A person who promotes a new technology throughout the organization in an effort to obtain acceptance of and support for it.

profit and loss statement An itemized financial statement of the income and expenses of a company's operations.

programmed decisions Decisions encountered and made before, having objectively correct answers, and solvable by using simple rules, policies, or numerical computations.

project and development teams Teams that work on long-term projects but disband once the work is completed.

prospectors Companies that continuously change the boundaries for their task environments by seeking new products and markets, diversifying and merging, or acquiring new enterprises.

pseudotransformational leaders Leaders who talk about positive change but allow their self interest to take precedence over followers' needs.

psychological contract A set of perceptions of what employees owe their employers, and what their employers owe them.

punishment Administering an aversive consequence.

Q

quality circles Voluntary groups of people drawn from various production teams who make suggestions about quality.

quality of work life (QWL) programs Programs designed to create a workplace that enhances employee well being.

quality The excellence of your product (goods or services).

R

reactive change A response that occurs under pressure; problem-driven change.

ready-made solutions Ideas that have been seen or tried before.

recruitment The development of a pool of applicants for jobs in an organization.

reflection Process by which a person states what he or she believes the other person is saying.

refreezing Strengthening the new behaviors that support the change.

reinforcers Positive consequences that motivate behavior.

relativism Bases ethical behavior on the opinions and behaviors of relevant other people.

reliability The consistency of test scores over time and across alternative measurements.

resources Inputs to a system that can enhance performance.

responsibility The assignment of a task that an employee is supposed to carry out.

return on investment (ROI) A ratio of profit to capital used, or a rate of return from capital.

rightsizing A successful effort to achieve an appropriate size at which the company performs most effectively.

right-to-work Legislation that allows employees to work without having to join a union.

risk The state that exists when the probability of success is less than 100 percent, and losses may occur.

roles Different sets of expectations for how different individuals should behave.

S

Sarbanes-Oxley Act An act passed into law by Congress in 2002 to establish strict accounting and reporting rules in order to make senior managers more accountable and to improve and maintain investor confidence.

satisficing Choosing an option that is acceptable, although not necessarily the best or perfect.

scenario A narrative that describes a particular set of future conditions.

selection Choosing from among qualified applicants to hire into an organization.

self-designing teams Teams with the responsibilities of autonomous work groups, plus control over hiring, firing, and what tasks members perform.

self-managed teams Autonomous work groups in which workers are trained to do all or most of the jobs in a unit, have no immediate supervisor, and make decisions previously made by first-line supervisors.

semiautonomous work groups Groups that make decisions about managing and carrying out major production activities, but still get outside support for quality control and maintenance.

servant-leader A leader who serves others' needs while strengthening the organization.

sexual harassment Conduct of a sexual nature that has negative consequences for employment.

shapers Companies that try to change the structure of their industries, creating a future competitive landscape of their own design. Methods for adapting the technical core to changes in the environment.

shared leadership Rotating leadership, in which people rotate through the leadership role based on which person has the most relevant skills at a particular time.

side street effect As you head down a road, unexpected opportunities begin to appear.

simultaneous engineering A design approach in which all relevant functions cooperate jointly and continually in a maximum effort aimed at producing high-quality products that meet customers' needs.

situational analysis A process planners use, within time and resource constraints, to gather, interpret, and summarize all information relevant to the planning issue under consideration.

situational approach Leadership perspective proposing that universally important traits and behaviors do not exist, and that effective leadership behavior varies from situation to situation.

skunkworks A project team designated to produce a new, innovative product.

small batch Technologies that produce goods and services in low volume.

small business A business having fewer than 100 employees, independently owned and operated, not dominant in its field, and not characterized by many innovative practices.

smoothing Leveling normal fluctuations at the boundaries of the environment.

social capital Goodwill stemming from your social relationships.

social facilitation effect Working harder when in a group than when working alone.

social loafing Working less hard and being less productive when in a group.

sociotechnical systems An approach to job design that attempts to redesign tasks to optimize operation of a new technology while preserving employees' interpersonal relationships and other human aspects of the work.

span of control The number of subordinates who report directly to an executive or supervisor.

specialization A process in which different individuals and units perform different tasks.

speed Fast and timely execution, response, and delivery of results.

staff departments Units that support line departments.

stakeholders Groups and individuals who affect and are affected by the achievement of the organization's mission, goals, and strategies.

standard Expected performance for a given goal: a target that establishes a desired performance level, motivates performance, and serves as a benchmark against which actual performance is assessed.

standardization Establishing common routines and procedures that apply uniformly to everyone.

stockholders' equity The amount accruing to the corporation's owners.

strategic alliance A formal relationship created among independent organizations with the purpose of joint pursuit of mutual goals.

strategic control system A system designed to support managers in evaluating the organization's progress regarding its strategy and, when discrepancies exist, taking corrective action.

strategic goals Major targets or end results relating to the organization's long-term survival, value, and growth.

strategic leadership Behavior that gives purpose and meaning to organizations, envisioning and creating a positive future.

strategic management A process that involves managers from all parts of the organization in the formulation and implementation of strategic goals and strategies.

strategic maneuvering An organization's conscious efforts to change the boundaries of its task environment.

strategic planning A set of procedures for making decisions about the organization's long-term goals and strategies.

strategic vision The long-term direction and strategic intent of a company.

strategy A pattern of actions and resource allocations designed to achieve the organization's goals.

stretch goals Targets that are particularly demanding, sometimes even thought to be impossible.

structured interview Selection technique that involves asking all applicants the same questions and comparing their responses to a standardized set of answers.

subscription model Charging fees for site visits.

substitutes for leadership Factors in the workplace that can exert the same influence on employees that leaders would provide.

subunits Subdivisions of an organization.

superordinate goals Higher-level goals taking priority over specific individual or group goals.

supervisory leadership Behavior that provides guidance, support, and corrective feedback for day-to-day activities.

supply chain management The managing of the network of facilities and people that obtain materials from outside the organization, transform them into products, and distribute them to customers.

survivor's syndrome Loss of productivity and morale in employees who remain after a downsizing.

sustainable growth Economic growth and development that meets present needs without harming the needs of future generations.

switching costs Fixed costs buyers face when they change suppliers.

SWOT analysis A comparison of strengths, weaknesses, opportunities, and threats that helps executives formulate strategy.

T

tactical planning A set of procedures for translating broad strategic goals and plans into specific goals and plans that are relevant to a distinct portion of the organization, such as a functional area like marketing.

task performance behaviors Actions taken to ensure that the work group or organization reaches its goals.

task specialist An individual who has more advanced job-related skills and abilities than other group members possess.

team A small number of people with complementary skills who are committed to a common purpose, set of performance goals, and approach for which they hold themselves mutually accountable.

team maintenance specialist Individual who develops and maintains team harmony.

team training Training that provides employees with the skills and perspectives they need to work in collaboration with others.

technical innovator A person who develops a new technology or has the key skills to install and operate the technology.

technical skill The ability to perform a specialized task involving a particular method or process.

technology The systematic application of scientific knowledge to a new product, process, or service.

technology audit Process of clarifying the key technologies on which an organization depends.

technology life cycle A predictable pattern followed by a technological innovation, from its inception and development to market saturation and replacement.

termination interview A discussion between a manager and an employee about the employee's dismissal.

third-country nationals Natives of a country other than the home country or the host country of an overseas subsidiary.

360 degree appraisal Process of using multiple sources of appraisal to gain a comprehensive perspective on one's performance.

time-based competition (TBC) Strategies aimed at reducing the total time it takes to deliver a product or service.

top-level managers Senior executives responsible for the overall management and effectiveness of the organization.

total organization change Introducing and sustaining multiple policies, practices, and procedures across multiple units and levels.

total quality management (TQM) An integrative approach to management that supports the attainment of customer satisfaction through a wide variety of tools and techniques that result in high-quality goods and services.

traditional work groups Groups that have no managerial responsibilities.

training Teaching lower-level employees how to perform their present jobs.

trait approach A leadership perspective that attempts to determine the personal characteristics that great leaders share.

transaction fee model charging fees for goods and services.

transactional leaders Leaders who manage through transactions, using their legitimate, reward, and coercive powers to give commands and exchange rewards for services rendered.

transcendent education An education with five higher goals that balance self-interest with responsibility to others.

transfer price Price charged by one unit for a product or service provided to another unit within the organization.

transformational leader A leader who motivates people to transcend their personal interests for the good of the group.

transnational model An organization model characterized by centralization of certain functions in locations that best achieve cost economies; basing of other functions in the company's national subsidiaries to facilitate greater local responsiveness; and fostering of communication among subsidiaries to permit transfer of technological expertise and skills.

transnational teams Work groups composed of multinational members whose activities span multiple countries.

two-factor theory Herzberg's theory describing two factors affecting people's work motivation and satisfaction.

two-way communication A process in which information flows in two directions—the receiver provides feedback, and the sender is receptive to the feedback.

tyranny of the "or" The belief that things must be either A or B, and cannot be both; that only one goal and not another can be attained.

U

uncertainty The state that exists when decision makers have insufficient information.

unfreezing Realizing that current practices are inappropriate and that new behavior must be enacted.

union shop An organization with a union and a union security clause specifying that workers must join the union after a set period of time.

unity-of-command principle A structure in which each worker reports to one boss, who in turn reports to one boss.

universalism The ethical system stating that all people should uphold certain values that society needs to function.

upward communication Information that flows from lower to higher levels in the organization's hierarchy.

utilitarianism An ethical system stating that the greatest good for the greatest number should be the overriding concern of decision makers.

V

valence The value an outcome holds for the person contemplating it.

validity The degree to which a selection test predicts or correlates with job performance.

value chain The sequence of activities that flow from raw materials to the delivery of a product or service, with additional value created at each step.

vertical integration The acquisition or development of new businesses that produce parts or components of the organization's product.

vigilance A process in which a decision maker carefully executes all stages of decision making.

virtual teams Teams that are physically dispersed and communicate electronically more than face-to-face.

virtue ethics A perspective that what is moral comes from what a mature person with "good" moral character would deem right.

vision A mental image of a possible and desirable future state of the organization.

Vroom model A situational model that focuses on the participative dimension of leadership.

W

work teams Teams that make or do things like manufacture, assemble, sell, or provide service.

Notes

Chapter 1

1. Special Report, "The Fallen," *BusinessWeek*, January 14, 2002, pp. 78–79.
2. S. Finkelstein, "The Myth of Managerial Superiority in Internet Startups: An Autopsy," *Organizational Dynamics*, Fall 2001, pp. 172–85.
3. P. Coy, "The Creative Economy," *BusinessWeek*, August 21–28, 2000, pp. 76–82.
4. W. J. Holstein, "The Stateless Corporation," *BusinessWeek*, May 14, 1990, pp. 98–105.
5. D. Eisenberg, "Judy McGrath: MTV Networks," *Time*, December 20, 2004, p. 141.
6. J. Lippman, "Hollywood Report: Bombs—Away," *The Wall Street Journal*, November 19, 2004, p. W12.
7. S. Green, F. Hassan, J. Immelt, M. Marks, and D. Meiland, "In Search of Global Leaders," *Harvard Business Review*, August 2003, pp. 38–45.
8. P. Sellers, "eBay's Secret," *Fortune*, October 18, 2004, pp. 160–78.
9. C. Bartlett and S. Ghoshal, "What Is a Global Manager?" *Harvard Business Review*, August 2003, pp. 101–8.
10. N. King Jr., "A Whole New World," *The Wall Street Journal*, September 27, 2004, pp. R1, R3.
11. T. Bisoux, "Corporate CounterCulture," *BizEd*, November/December 2004, pp. 16–20.
12. G. Huber, *The Necessary Nature of Future Firms* (Thousand Oaks, CA: Sage, 2004).
13. Special Report: "The Best & Worst Managers of the Year," *BusinessWeek*, January 10, 2005, pp. 55–86.
14. F. Cairncross, *The Company of the Future* (Cambridge, MA: Harvard Business School Press, 2002).
15. T. J. Mulaney, "Break Out the Black Ink," *BusinessWeek*, May 13, 2002, pp. 74–76.
16. Ibid.
17. Ibid.
18. D. Rynecki, "Make Their Pain Your Gain," *Fortune*, July 9, 2001, pp. 158–159.
19. R. Hof and S. Hamm, "How E-Biz Rose, Fell, and Will Rise Anew," *BusinessWeek*, May 13, 2002, pp. 64–72.
20. Ibid.
21. J. Useem, "Dot-coms: What Have We Learned?" *Fortune*, October 30, 2000, pp. 82–104.
22. Coy, "The Creative Economy."
23. C. Edwards, "Keeping You Glued to the Couch," *BusinessWeek*, May 17, 2004, p. 58.
24. N. Gross, "Mining a Company's Mother Lode of Talent," *BusinessWeek*, August 28, 2000, pp. 135–37.
25. S. Cranor, *The Management Century* (San Francisco: Jossey-Bass, 2000).
26. M. Hansen and B. von Oetinger, "Introducing T-Shaped Managers: Knowledge Management's Next Generation," *Harvard Business Review*, March 2001, pp. 106–16.
27. P. Sellers, "P&G: Teaching an Old Dog New Tricks," *Fortune* May 31, 2004, pp. 166–80.
28. B. Schlender, "The New Soul of a Wealth Machine," *Fortune*, April 5, 2004, pp. 102–10.
29. R. Standifer and J. A. Wall Jr., "Managing Conflict in B2B Commerce," *Business Horizons*, March–April 2003, pp. 65–70.
30. L. Willcocks and R. Plant, "Pathways to E-Business Leadership: Getting from Bricks to Clicks," *Sloan Management Review*, Spring 2001, pp. 50–59.
31. C. Loomis (Ed.), "Mr. Buffet on the Stock Market," *Fortune*, November 22, 2000, pp. 212–20.
31. Bisoux, "Corporate CounterCulture."
32. Ibid.
33. M. Maynard, "Why the Big Airlines Can't Get Off the Ground," *New York Times*, September 19, 2004, sec. 4, p. 4.
34. Ibid.
35. Loomis, "Mr. Buffet on the Stock Market."
36. P. Sellers, "P&G: Teaching an Old Dog New Tricks," *Fortune*, May 31, 2004, pp. 166–80.
37. L. M. Bellman, "Bricks and Mortar: 21st Century Survival," *Business Horizons*, May–June, 2001, pp. 21–28.
38. M. Boyle, "Kraft's Arrested Development," *Fortune*, November 15, 2004, p. 44.
39. G. Hamel, "Avoiding the Guillotine," *Fortune*, April 2, 2001, pp. 139–44.
40. Ibid., p. 140.
41. R. I. Sutton, "The Weird Rules of Creativity," *Harvard Business Review*, September, 2001, pp. 94–103.
42. Hamel, "Avoiding the Guillotine."
43. C. Yang and R. Grover, "He's Not in Kansas Anymore," *BusinessWeek*, September 27, 2004, pp. 78–79.
44. Ibid.
45. Edwards, "Keeping You Glued to the Couch."
46. O. Port, "The Kings of Quality," *BusinessWeek*, August 30, 2004, p. 20.
47. A. Merrick, G. McWilliams, E. Byron, and K. Stringer, "Targeting Wal-Mart," *The Wall Street Journal*, December 1, 2004, pp. B1–B2.
48. D. Feeny, "Making Business Sense of the E-Opportunity," *Sloan Management Review*, Winter 2001, pp. 41–51.
49. H. L. Lee and S. Whang, "Winning the Last Mile of E-Commerce," *Sloan Management Review*, Summer 2001, pp. 54–62.
50. D. A. Garvin, "Manufacturing Strategic Planning," *California Management Review*, Summer 1993, pp. 85–106.
51. F. Vogelstein, "Goggle @ 165," Fortune, December 13, 2004, pp. 98–110.
52. S. Gray, "On the Menu: Speed and Variety," *The Wall Street Journal*, November 22, 2004, p. R4.
53. T. Agins, "Plain Is Out. Vibrant Is In," *The Wall Street Journal*, November 22, 2004, p. R7.
54. Merrick, McWilliams, Byron, and Stringer, "Targeting Wal-Mart."
55. C. Lu-Lien Tan, "U.S. Response: Speedier Delivery," *The Wall Street Journal*, November 18, 2004, pp. D1, D3.
56. Byrne, "Management by Web."
57. Ibid., p. D3.
58. Merrick, McWilliams, Byron, and Stringer, "Targeting Wal-Mart," p. B1.
59. Maynard, "Why the Big Airlines Can't Get Off the Ground."
60. I. Mount, "David Neeleman, JetBlue," *Inc.*, April 2004, p. 144.
61. J. Simons, "Internet Survivors," *Fortune*, July 9, 2001, pp. 155–56.
62. E. Brown, "Heartbreak Hotel?" *Fortune*, November 26, 2001, pp. 161–65.
63. N. Brodsky, "Street Smarts," *Inc.*, December 2004, pp. 57–58.
64. M. Boyle, "What We Learned," *Fortune*, December 24, 2001, pp. 179–80.
65. Useem, "Dot-Coms: What Have We Learned?"
66. Merrick, McWilliams, Byron, and Stringer, "Targeting Wal-Mart."
67. B. Bremmer, G. Edmondson, and C. Dawson, "Nissan's Boss," *BusinessWeek*, October 4, 2004, pp. 50–58.
68. T. Burt, "Pumping Up the Volume," *The Financial Times*, December 7, 2004, pp. 12–13.

69. K. Hammonds, "Is Your Company Up to Speed?" *Fast Company*, June 2003, pp. 81–86.

70. Edwards, "Keeping You Glued to the Couch."

71. D. Kirkpatrick, "Now Everyone in PCs Wants to Be Like Mike," *Fortune*, September 8, 1997, pp. 47–48.

72. Special Report: "The Best & Worst Managers of the Year," *BusinessWeek*, January 10, 2005, pp. 55–86.

73. J. W. Cortada, *21st Century Business* (London: Financial Times/Prentice Hall, 2001).

74. J. Collins, "Don't Rewrite the Rules of the Road." *BusinessWeek*, August 28, 2000, pp. 206–8.

75. Ibid.

76. P. Shenon, "U.S. Agencies Seen as Slow to Move on Terrorism Risk," *New York Times*, May 12, 2002, pp. 1, 6.

77. J. Kahn and B. O'Keefe, "Best & Worst 2001," *Fortune*, December 24, 2001, pp. 139–44.

78. R. Webber, "General Management Past and Future," *Financial Times Mastering Management*, 1997.

79. P. Capelli and M. Hamori, "The New Road to the Top," *Harvard Business Review*, January 2005.

80. Q. N. Huy, "In Praise of Middle Managers," *Harvard Business Review*, September 2001, pp. 72–79.

81. L. A. Hill, "New Manager Development for the 21st Century," *Academy of Management Executive*, August 2004, pp. 121–26.

82. C. Bartlett and S. Goshal, "The Myth of the Generic Manager: New Personal Competencies for New Personal Competencies for New Management Roles," *California Management Review*, 40, no. 1, (1997), pp. 92–116.

83. L. R. Sayles, "Doing Things Right: A New Imperative for Middle Managers," *Organizational Dynamics*, Spring 1993, pp. 5–14.

84. H. Mintzberg, *The Nature of Managerial Work* (New York: Harper & Row, 1973).

85. R. Katz, "Skills of an Effective Administrator," *Harvard Business Review* 52 (September–October), pp. 90–102.

86. Hill, "New Manager Development for the 21st Century."

87. H. Mintzberg, "The Manager's Job: Folklore and Fact," *Harvard Business Review* 53 (July–August 1975), pp. 49–61.

88. M. Goldsmith, "Nice Guys Can Finish First," *Fast Company*, November 2004, p. 123.

89. A. Deutschman, "The Trouble with MBAs," *Fortune*, July 29, 1991, pp. 67–79.

90. S. Lehrman, "Putting Management Potential to the Test," *Bryan-College Station Eagle*, December 8, 1985; p. 3F.

91. M. W. McCall Jr., *High Flyers: Developing the Next Generation of Leaders* (Boston: Harvard Business School Press, 1997).

92. G. Anders, "How Traits that Helped Executive Climb Ladder Came to Be Fatal Flaws," *The Wall Street Journal*, February 10, 2005, pp. A1, A8.

93. Hill, "New Manager Development for the 21st Century."

94. D. Goleman, R. Boyatzis, and A. McKee, *Primal Leadership: Realizing the Power of Emotional Intelligence* (Boston: Harvard Business School Press, 2002).

95. A. Jung, "Seek Frank Feedback," *Harvard Business Review*, January 2004, p. 31.

96. R. Boyatzis, "Get Motivated," *Harvard Business Review*, January 2004, p. 30.

97. W. George, "Find Your Voice," *Harvard Business Review*, January 2004, p. 35.

98. W. Kiechel III, "A Manager's Career in the New Economy," *Fortune*, April 4, 1994, pp. 68–72.

99. Ibid.

100. K. Inkson and M. B. Arther, "How to Be a Successful Career Capitalist," *Organizational Dynamics*, Summer 2001, pp. 48–60.

101. Kiechel, "A Manager's Career in the New Economy."

102. E. W. Morrison, "Newcomers' Relationships: The Role of Social Network Ties During Socialization," *Academy of Management Journal* 45 (2002), pp. 1149–60.

103. P. Adler and S. Kwon, "Social Capital: Prospects for a New Concept," *Academy of Management Review* 27 (2002), pp. 17–40.

104. B. O'Brian, and G. Stern, "Nonstop Networking Propels an Accountant into U.S. Big Leagues," *The Wall Street Journal*, March 20, 1997, pp. 1, 2.

105. T. Peters, *Liberation Management* (New York: Alfred A. Knopf, 1992).

106. D. Brady, "Wanted: Eclectic Visionary with a Sense of Humor," *BusinessWeek*, August 21–28, 2000, pp. 143–44.

107. T. Peters, "The New Wired World of Work," *BusinessWeek*, August 21–28, 2000, p. 172–74.

108. F. Drucker, "What Makes an Effective Executive?" *Harvard Business Review*, June 2004, pp. 58–63.

109. J. Kotter, *The New Rules: How to Succeed in Today's Post-Corporate World* (New York: The Free Press, 1995).

110. Ibid.

Appendix A

1. C. George, *The History of Management Thought* (Englewood Cliffs, NJ: Prentice-Hall, 1972).

2. Ibid.

3. A. D. Chandler, *Scale and Scope: The Dynamic of Industrial Capitalism* (Cambridge, MA: Belknap Press of Harvard University Press, 1990).

4. Ibid.

5. J. Schlosser and E. Florian, "*Fortune* 500 Amazing Facts!" *Fortune*, April 5, 2004, pp. 152–59.

6. J. Baughman, *The History of American Management* (Englewood Cliffs, NJ: Prentice-Hall, 1969), chap. 1.

7. George, *The History of Management Thought* chaps. 5–7; F. Taylor *The Principles of Scientific Management* (New York: Harper & Row, 1911).

8. J. Case, "A Company of Businesspeople," *Inc.*, April 1993, pp. 70–93.

9. Schlosser and Florian, "*Fortune* 500 Amazing Facts!"

10. H. Kroos and C. Gilbert, *The Principles of Scientific Management* (New York: Harper & Row, 1911).

11. H. Fayol, *General and Industrial Management*, trans. C. Storrs (Marshfield, MA: Pitman Publishing, 1949).

12. George, *The History of Management Thought*, chap. 9; J. Massie, "Management Theory," in *Handbook of Organizations*, ed. J. March (Chicago: Rand McNally, 1965), pp. 387–422.

13. C. Barnard, *The Functions of the Executive* (Cambridge, MA: Harvard University Press, 1938).

14. George, *The History of Management Thought*: Massie, "Management Theory."

15. Schlosser and Florian, "*Fortune* 500 Amazing Facts!"

16. E. Mayo, *The Human Problems of Industrial Civilization* (New York: Macmillan, 1933): F. Roethlisberger and W. Dickson, *Management and the Worker* (Cambridge, MA: Harvard University Press, 1939).

17. A. Maslow, "A Theory of Human Motivation," *Psychological Review*, 50 (July 1943), pp. 370–96.

18. A. Carey, "The Hawthorne Studies: A Radical Criticism," *American Sociological Review* 32, no.3 (1967), pp. 403–16.

19. M. Weber, *The Theory of Social and Economic Organizations*, trans. T. Parsons and A. Henderson (New York: Free Press, 1947).

20. George, *The History of Management Thought*, chap. 11.

21. D. McGregor, *The Human Side of Enterprise* (New York: McGraw-Hill, 1960).

22. C. Argyris, *Personality and Organization* (New York: Harper & Row, 1957).

23. R. Likert, *The Human Organization* (New York: McGraw-Hill, 1967).

24. L. von Bertalanffy, "The History and Status of General Systems Theory," *Academy of Management Journal* 15 (1972), pp. 407–26; D. Katz and R. Kahn, *The Social Psychology of Organizations*, 2nd ed. (New York: John Wiley & Sons, 1978).

25. J. Thompson, *Organizations in Action* (New York: McGraw-Hill, 1967); J. Galbraith, *Organization Design* (Reading, MA: Addison-Wesley, 1977); D. Miller and P. Friesen, *Organizations: A Quantum View* (Englewood Cliffs, NJ: Prentice-Hall, 1984).

26. Schlosser and Florian, "*Fortune* 500 Amazing Facts!"

Chapter 2

1. Amy Tsao, "This Time, Tech Will Follow, Not Lead," *BusinessWeek Online*, November 12, 2001,

www.businessweek.com; D. Kadlec, "The Nasdaq: What a Drag!" *Time*, October 23, 2000, 156, no. 17, pp. 72–73.

2. Joseph Fuller and Michael C. Jensen, "Just Say No to Wall Street," *Journal of Applied Corporate Finance* 14, no. 4 (Winter 2002), pp. 41–46.

3. "Labor Force (Demographic) Data," U.S. Department of Labor, Bureau of Labor Statistics Web site, accessed February 2, 2005, www.bls.gov/emp/emplabl.htm; Judith J. Friedman and Nancy DiTomaso, "Myths about Diversity: What Managers Need to Know about Changes in the U.S. Labor Force," *California Management Review* 38, no. 4 (Summer 1996), pp. 54–77.

4. "NRDC Report Finds Improved Fuel Efficiency Expands Consumer Choice," National Resources Defense Council press release, July 30, 2001, www.nrdc.org, accessed at ww.nrdc.org/media/pressrel eases/0107300aso.

5. "Wal-Mart Tired of Critics' Complaints," *MSNBC.com*, February 1, 2004.

6. Johnathan R. Laing, "Just Spiffy," *Barron's* 77, no. 12 (March 24, 1997), pp. 37–42; Matthew J. Kiernan, "Get Innovative or Get Dead," *Business Quarterly* 61, no. 1 (Autumn 1996), pp. 51–58.

7. David J. Collis and Cynthis A. Montgomery, *Corporate Strategy: Resources and Scope of the Firm* (New York: McGraw-Hill/Irwin, 1997).

8. Roger Hallowell, "Southwest Airlines: A Case Study Linking Employee Needs, Satisfaction, and Organizational Capabilities to Competitive Advantage," *Human Resource Management* 35, no. 4 (Winter 1996), pp. 513–34: Wendy Zeller, "Greyhound Is Limping Badly," *BusinessWeek*, August 22, 1994, p. 32.

9. Brian K. Schimmoller, "Magicians Wanted," *Power Engineering*, August 2000, 104, no. 8, p. 3.

10. "Woods Is Fined By Actors' Union," *New York Times*, November 11, 2000, p. 7; Arthur Sherman, George Bohlander, and Scott Snell, *Managing Human Resources*, 11th ed. (Cincinnati, OH: Southwestern Publishing, 1998).

11. Brent Schlender, "The Adventures of Scott McNealy: Javamtan," *Fortune* 136, no. 7 (October 13, 1997), pp. 70–78.

12. Adapted from Hau L. Lee and Corey Billington, "The Evolution of Supply-Chain-Management Models and Practice at Hewlett-Packard," *Interfaces* 25, no. 5 (September–October 1995), pp. 42–63.

13. Rune Teigen, "Supply Chain Management," retrieved from eil.utoronto.ca/profiles/rune/node5.html, May 27, 1997; Steve Palagyi, "Making the Supply Chain a Strategic Asset," *Worldtrademag.com*, October 1, 2004; Arthi Ramesh, "Web Enabling Supply Chain Management," retrieved from web-enable.com; "Built-to-Order Model For Success (Part II)," retrieved from

themanagementor.com/kuniverse/kmailers, 2003; Gary Rivlin, "Who's Afraid of China?" *New York Times*, December 19, 2004.

14. P. Kotler, *Marketing Management: Analysis, Planning, Implementation and Control*, 9th ed. (Englewood Cliffs, NJ: Prentice Hall, 1990).

15. Aaron A. Buchko, "Conceptualization and Measurement of Environmental Uncertainty: An Assessment of the Miles and Snow Perceived Environmental Uncertainty Scale," *Academy of Management Journal* 37, no. 2 (April 1994), pp. 410–25.

16. Abdalla F. Hagen, "Corporate Executives and Environmental Scanning Activities: An Empirical Investigation." *SAM Advanced Management Journal* 60, no. 2 (Spring 1995), pp. 41–47; Richard L. Daft. "Chief Executive Scanning, Environmental Characteristics, and Company Performance: An Empirical Study," *Strategic Management Journal* 9, no. 2 (March/April 1988), pp. 123–39; Masoud Yasai-Ardekani, "Designs for Environmental Scanning Systems: Tests of a Contingency Theory," *Management Science* 42, no. 2 (February 1996), pp. 187–204.

17. Sumantra Ghoshal, "Building Effective Intelligence Systems for Competitive Advantage," *Sloan Management Review* 28, no. 1 (Fall 1986), pp. 49–58; Kenneth D. Cory, "Can Competitive Intelligence Lead to a Sustainable Competitive Advantage?" *Competitive Intelligence Review* 7, no. 3 (Fall 1996), pp. 45–55.

18. Paul J. H. Schoemaker, "Multiple Scenario Development: Its Conceptual and Behavioral Foundation," *Strategic Management Journal* 14, no. 3 (March 1993), pp. 193–213.

19. Robin R. Peterson, "An Analysis of Contemporary Forecasting in Small Business," *Journal of Business Forecasting Methods & Systems* 15, no. 2 (Summer 1996), pp. 10–12; Spyros Makridakis. "Business Forecasting for Management: Strategic Business Forecasting," *International Journal of Forecasting* 12, no. 3 (September 1996), pp. 435–37.

20. Irving DeToro, "The 10 Pitfalls of Benchmarking," *Quality Progress* 28, no. 1 (January 1995), pp. 61–63.

21. Martin B. Meznar, "Buffer or Bridge? Environmental and Organizational Determinants of Public Affairs Activities in American Firms," *Academy of Management Journal* 38, no. 4 (August 1995), pp. 975–96.

22. David Lei, "Advanced Manufacturing Technology: Organizational Design and Strategic Flexibility," *Organization Studies* 17, no. 3 (1996), pp. 501–23; James W. Dean Jr. and Scott A. Snell, "The Strategic Use of Integrated Manufacturing: An Empirical Examination," *Strategic Management Journal* 17, no. 6 (June 1996), pp. 459–80.

23. C. Zeithaml and V. Zeithaml, "Environmental Management: Revising the Marketing Perspective," *Journal of Marketing* 48 (Spring 1984), pp. 46–53.

24. Willem P. Burgers, "Cooperative Strategy in High Technology Industries," *International Journal of Management* 13, no. 2 (June 1996), pp. 127–34; Jeffrey E. McGee, "Cooperative Strategy and New Venture Performance: The Role of Business Strategy and Management Experience," *Strategic Management Journal* 16, no. 7 (October 1995), pp. 565–80.

25. Richard A. D'Aveni, *Hypercompetition—Managing the Dynamics of Strategic Maneuvering* (New York, Free Press 1994); Michael A. Cusumano, "Strategic Maneuvering and Mass-Market Dynamics: The Triumph of VHS over Beta," *Business History Review* 66, no. 1 (Spring 1992), pp. 51–94.

26. Model adapted from C. Zeithami and V. Zeithami, "Environmental Management: Revising the Marketing Perspective," *Journal of Marketing*, Spring 1984. Published by the American Marketing Association.

27. R. Miles and C. Snow, *Organizational Strategy, Structure, and Process* (New York: McGraw-Hill, 1978).

28. Ralph H. Kilmann, Mary J. Saxton, and Roy Serpa, *Gaining Control of the Corporate Culture* (San Francisco: Jossey-Bass, 1985); Kim S. Cameron and Robert E. Quinn, *Diagnosing and Changing Organizational Culture: Based on the Competing Values Framework* (Englewood Cliffs, NJ: Addison-Wesley, 1998).

29. Cameron and Quinn, *Diagnosing and Changing Organizational Culture*.

30. R. Leifer and P. K. Mills, "An Information Processing Approach for Deciding upon Control Strategies and Reducing Control Loss in Emerging Organizations," *Journal of Management* 22, no. 1 (1996), pp. 113–37; Scott A. Dellana and Richard D. Hauser, "Toward Defining the Quality Culture," *Engineering Management Journal* 11, no. 2 (June 1999), pp. 11–15; Don Cohen and Lawrence Prusak, *In Good Company: How Social Capital Makes Organizations Work* (Cambridge, MA: Harvard Business School Press, 2001).

Chapter 3

1. T. Peters, *Liberation Management* (New York: Alfred A. Knopf, 1992).

2. M. Magasin and F. L. Gehlen, "Unwise Decisions and Unanticipated Consequences," *Sloan Management Review* 41 (1999), pp. 47–60.

3. M. McCall and R. Kaplan, *Whatever It Takes: Decision Makers at Work* (Englewood Cliffs, NJ: Prentice-Hall, 1985).

4. B. Bass, *Organizational Decision Making* (Homewood, IL: Richard D. Irwin, 1983).

5. J. March, "Bounded Rationality, Ambiguity, and the Engineering of Choice," *Bell Journal of Economics* 9 (1978), pp. 587–608.

6. D. Messick and M. Bazerman, "Ethical Leadership and the Psychology of Decision Making," *Sloan Management Review*, Winter 1996, pp. 9–22.

7. J. Kahn, "Stop Me Before I Pollute Again," *Fortune*, January 21, 2002, pp. 87–90.

8. D. Jones, "Playing the Weather Game," *USA Today*, December 11, 2001, pp. 1B–2B.

9. N. Carr, "On the Edge: An Interview with Akamai's George Conrades," *Harvard Business Review*, May–June 2000, pp. 118–25.

10. G. A. Garvin, "Building a Learning Organization," *Harvard Business Review*, July–August 1993, pp. 78–91.

11. McCall and Kaplan, *Whatever It Takes.*

12. K. MacCrimmon and R. Taylor, "Decision Making and Problem Solving," in *Handbook of Industrial and Organizational Psychology*, ed. M. D. Dunnette (Chicago: Rand McNally, 1976).

13. Q. Spitzer and R. Evans, *Heads, You Win! How the Best Companies Think* (New York: Simon & Schuster, 1997).

14. C. Gettys and S. Fisher, "Hypothesis Plausibility and Hypotheses Generation," *Organizational Behavior and Human Performance* 24 (1979), pp. 93–110.

15. E. R. Alexander, "The Design of Alternatives in Organizational Contexts: A Pilot Study," *Administrative Science Quarterly* 24 (1979), pp. 382–404.

16. P. Nayak and J. Ketteringham, *Breakthroughs* (New York: Rawson Associates, 1986).

17. A. R. Rao, M. E. Bergen, and S. Davis, "How to Fight a Price War," *Harvard Business Review*, March–April 2000, pp. 107–16.

18. Ibid.

19. J. O'Toole, *Vanguard Management: Redesigning the Corporate Future* (Garden City, NY: Doubleday, 1985).

20. McCall and Kaplan, *Whatever It Takes.*

21. Spitzer and Evans, *Heads, You Win!*

22. K. Labich, "Four Possible Futures," *Fortune*, January 25, 1993, pp. 40–48.

23. McCall and Kaplan, *Whatever It Takes.*

24. J. Pfeffer and R. Sutton, *The Knowing–Doing Gap* (Boston: Harvard Business School Press, 2000).

25. M. B. Stein, "Teaching Steelcase to Dance," *New York Times Magazine*, April 1, 1990, pp. 22ff.

26. D. Siebold, "Making Meetings More Successful," *Journal of Business Communication* 16 (Summer 1979), pp. 3–20.

27. I. Janis and L. Mann, *Decision Making* (New York: Free Press, 1977); Bass, *Organizational Decision Making.*

28. J. W. Dean Jr. and M. Sharfman, "Does Decision Process Matter? A Study of Strategic Decision-Making Effectiveness," *Academy of Management Journal* 39 (1996), pp. 368–96.

29. R. Nisbett and L. Ross, *Human Inference: Strategies and Shortcomings* (Englewood Cliffs, NJ: Prentice-Hall, 1980).

30. R. Lowenstein, *When Genius Failed* (New York: Random House, 2000).

31. Messick and Bazerman, "Ethical Leadership."

32. S. Pearlstein, and P. Behr, "At Enron, the Fall Came Quickly," *The Washington Post*, December 2, 2001, pp. A1–A11.

33. T. Bateman and C. Zeithaml, "The Psychological Context of Strategic Decisions: A Model and Convergent Experimental Findings," *Strategic Management Journal* 10 (1989), pp. 59–74.

34. Pfeffer and Sutton, *The Knowing–Doing Gap.*

35. D. Brady, "The Unsung CEO," *BusinessWeek*, October 25, 2004, pp. 74–84.

36. Messick and Bazerman, "Ethical Leadership."

37. N. Adler, *International Dimensions of Organizational Behavior* (Boston: Kent, 1990).

38. L. Perlow, G. Okhuysen, and N. Repenning, "The Speed Trap: Exploring the Relationship between Decision Making and Temporal Context," *Academy of Management Journal* 45 (2002), pp. 931–55.

39. K. M. Esenhardt, "Speed and Strategic Choice: How Managers Accelerate Decision Making," *California Management Review* 32 (Spring 1990), pp. 39–54.

40. Q. Spitzer and R. Evans, "New Problems in Problem Solving," *Across the Board*, April 1997, pp. 36–40.

41. G. W. Hill, "Group versus Individual Performance: Are n + 1 Heads Better than 1?" *Psychological Bulletin* 91 (1982), pp. 517–39.

42. N. R. F. Maier, "Assets and Liabilities in Group Problem Solving: The Need for an Integrative Function," *Psychological Review* 74 (1967), pp. 239–49.

43. Ibid.

44. D. A. Garvin and M. A. Roberto, "What You Don't Know about Making Decisions," *Harvard Business Review*, September 2001, pp. 108–16.

45. R. Cosier and C. Schwenk, "Agreement and Thinking Alike: Ingredients for Poor Decisions," *The Executive*, February 1990, pp. 69–74.

46. A. Amason, "Distinguishing the Effects of Functional and Dysfunctional Conflict on Strategic Decision Making: Resolving a Paradox for Top Management Teams," *Academy of Management Journal* 39 (1996), pp. 123–48; R. Dooley and G. Fyxell, "Attaining Decision Quality and Commitment from Dissent: The Moderating Effects of Loyalty and Competence in Strategic Decision-Making Teams," *Academy of Management Journal*, August 1999, pp. 389–402.

47. C. De Dreu and L. Weingart, "Task versus Relationship Conflict, Team Performance, and Team Member Satisfaction: A Meta-Analysis," *Journal of Applied Psychology* 88 (2003), pp. 741–49.

48. K. Eisenhardt, J. Kahwajy, and L. J. Bourgeois III, "Conflict and Strategic Choice: How Top Management Teams Disagree," *California Management Review*, Winter 1997, pp. 42–62.

49. Cosier and Schwenk, "Agreement and Thinking Alike."

50. Ibid.

51. P. LaBerre, "The Creative Revolution," *Industry Week*, May 16, 1994, pp. 12–19.

52. J. V. Anderson, "Weirder Than Fiction: The Reality and Myths of Creativity," *Academy of Management Executive*, November 1992, pp. 40–47; J. Krohe Jr., "Managing Creativity," *Across the Board*, September 1996, pp. 17–21; R. I. Sutton, "The Weird Rules of Creativity," *Harvard Business Review*, September 2001, pp. 94–103.

53. J. Perry-Smith and C. Shalley, "The Social Side of Creativity: A Static and Dynamic Social Network Perspective," *Academy of Management Review* 28 (2003), pp. 89–106.

54. A. Farnham, "How to Nurture Creative Sparks," *Fortune*, January 10, 1994, pp. 94–100; T. M. Amabile, "A Model of Creativity and Innovation in Organizations," in *Research in Organizational Behavior*, ed. B. Straw and L. Cummings, vol. 10 (Greenwich, CT: JAI press, 1988), pp. 123–68.

55. T. Amabile, C. Hadley, and S. Kramer, "Creativity under the Gun," *Harvard Business Review*, August 2002, pp. 52–61.

56. S. Farmer, P. Tierney, and K. Kung-McIntyre, "Employee Creativity in Taiwan: An Application of Role Identity Theory," *Academy of Management Journal* 46 (2003), pp. 618–30.

57. C. Knowlton, "How Disney Keeps the Magic Going," *Fortune*, December 4, 1989, pp. 115–32.

58. L. Thompson, "Improving the Creativity of Organizational Work Groups," *Academy of Management Executive* 17 (2003), pp. 96–109.

59. T. Levitt, "Creativity Is Not Enough," *Harvard Business Review*, August 2002, pp. 137–44.

60. Dean and Sharfman, "Does Decision Process Matter?"

61. K. Eisenhardt, J. Kahwajy, and L. J. Bourgeois III, "How Management Teams Can Have a Good Fight," *Harvard Management Review*, July–August 1997, pp. 77–85.

62. C. M. Pearson and I. I. Mitroff, "From Crisis Prone to Crisis Prepared: A Framework for Crisis Management," *Academy of Management Executive*, February 1993, pp. 48–59.

63. S. Moore, "Disaster's Future: The Prospects for Corporate Crisis Management and Communication," *Business Horizons*, January–February 2004, pp. 29–36.
64. Ibid.
65. J. Hickman and W. Crandall, "Before Disaster Hits: A Multifaceted Approach to Crisis Management," *Business Horizons*, March–April 1997, pp. 75–79.
66. G. Meyers with J. Holusha, *When It Hits the Fan: Managing the Nine Crises of Business* (Boston: Houghton Mifflin, 1986).
67. McCall and Kaplan, *Whatever It Takes.*
68. P. Sellers, "eBay's Secret," *Fortune*, October 18, 2004, pp. 160–78.
69. Ibid.
70. J. Dutton, P. Frost, M. Worline, J. Lilius, and J. Kanov, "Leading in Times of Trauma," *Harvard Business Review*, January 2002, pp. 54–61.
71. J. Useem, "What It Takes," *Fortune*, November 12, 2001, pp. 126–32.
72. Sellers, "eBay's Secret," pp. 173–74.

Chapter 4

1. J. Bracker and J. Pearson, "Planning and Financial Performance of Small Mature Firms," *Strategic Management Journal* 7 (1986), pp. 503–22; Philip Waalewijn and Peter Segaar, "Strategic Management: The Key to Profitability in Small Companies," *Long Range Planning* 26, no. 2 (April 1993), pp. 24–30.
2. Aramark annual report, 1997.
3. Roger W. Ferguson Jr., "Implications of 9/11 for the Financial Services Sector," *BIS Review*, 2002, online; Scott Leibs, "Lesson from 9/11," *CFO Magazine*, September 1, 2002, online.
4. Abraham Lustgarten, "A Hot Steaming Cup of Customer Awareness," *Fortune*, November 15, 2004, p. 192; V. Viswanath and D. Harding, "The Starbuck Effect," *Harvard Business Review*, March–April, 2000; M. Hornblower, "Wake Up and Smell the Protest," *Time*, April 17, 2000; M. Gimein, "Right On: Starbucks Makes a Net Play," *Fortune*, March 6, 2000; L. Lee, "Now, Starbucks Uses Its Bean," *Business Week*, February 14, 2000; R. Papiernik, "Starbucks Starts Fiscal 2000 with 30% Profit Growth in 1st Q," *Nation's Restaurant News*, February 7, 2000; K. Holland, "Starbucks Thinks It Will Travel Well," *BusinessWeek*, November 16, 1998; N. Weiss, "How Starbucks Impassions Workers to Drive Growth," *Workforce*, August 1998, K. Strauss, "Howard Schultz: Starbucks' CEO Serves a Blend of Community, Employee Commitment," *Nation's Restaurant News*, January 2000; "Interview with Howard Schultz: Sharing Success," *Executive Excellence*, November 1999; N. D. Schwartz, "Still Perking after All These Years," *Fortune*, May 24, 1999.
5. Robert Kaplan and David Norton, "Plotting Success with Strategy Maps," *Optimize Magazine*, February 2004, online; Robert S. Kaplan and David P. Norton, "Having Trouble with Your Strategy? Then Map It," *Harvard Business Review*, September–October 2000.
6. "Business: Fading Fads," *The Economist*, April 22, 2000, 355, no. 8167, pp. 60–61.
7. Steven W. Floyd and Peter J. Lane, "Strategizing throughout the Organization: Management Role Conflict in Strategic Renewal," *Academy of Management Review*, 25, no. 1, (January 2000) pp. 154–77; Don MacRae, "Seeing beyond Monday Morning," *BusinessWeek*, November 22, 2000, online.
8. www.microsoft.com and www.kodak.com, accessed January 2005.
9. Arthur A. Thompson and A. J. Strickland III, *Strategic Management: Concepts and Cases*, 8th ed. (Burr Ridge, IL: Richard D. Irwin, 1995), p. 23.
10. Roger Hallowell, "Southwest Airlines: A Case Study Linking Employee Needs Satisfaction and Organizational Capabilities to Competitive Advantage," *Human Resource Management* 35, no. 4 (Winter 1996), pp. 513–34.
11. William C. Symons, "Can Office Depot Clip Staples?" *BusinessWeek Online*, July 2004; David J. Collis and Cynthia A. Montgomery, *Corporate Strategy: A Resource-Based Approach*, 2nd ed. (New York, McGraw-Hill/Irwin, 2005).
12. Collis and Montgomery, *Corporate Strategy*.
13. Robert C. Camp. "A Bible for Benchmarking, by Xerox," *Financial Executive* 9, no. 4 (July/August 1993) pp. 23–27. See also Dawn Anfuso, "At L. L. Bean, Quality Starts with People," *Personnel Journal* 73, no. 1 (January 1994), p. 60; Ken Stork, "Benchmarking: Analyze as You Go about Planning," *Purchasing*, October 19, 2000, 129, no. 7, p. 33; "Finding Best Practices in Your Own B.A.C.K.Y.A.R.D." *Supply Chain Management*, January–February 2005, pp. 54–59.
14. P. Haspeslagh, "Portfolio Planning: Uses and Limits," *Harvard Business Review* 60, no.1 (1982), pp. 58–67; R. Hamermesh, *Making Strategy Work* (New York: John Wiley & Sons, 1986); R. A. Proctor, "Toward a New Model for Product Portfolio Analysis," *Management Decision* 28, no. 3 (1990), pp. 14–17.
15. Robert E. Hoskisson, "Corporate Divestiture Intensity in Restructuring Firms: Effects of Governance, Strategy, and Performance," *Academy of Management Journal* 37, no. 5 (October 1994), pp. 1207–51; S. Gannes, "Merck Has Made Biotech Work," *Fortune*, January 19, 1987, pp. 58–64; Mark Maremont. "Why Kodak's Dazzling Spin-Off Didn't Bedazzle," *BusinessWeek*, June 28, 1993, p. 34; Emily S. Plishner, "Eastman Chemical Spins Out of the Kodak Family Portrait," *Chemical Week* 152, no. 24 (June 23, 1993), p. 7.
16. Stratford Sherman, "Why Disney Had to Buy ABC," *Fortune* 132, no. 5 (September 4, 1995), p. 80.
17. M. Porter, *Competitive Advantage* (New York: Free Press, 1985), pp. 11–14.
18. John Huey, "Outlaw Flyboy CEOs," *Fortune* 142, no. 11 (November 13, 2000) pp. 237–50; Kristin Young, "Nordstrom's Full-Service Formula," *Women's Wear Daily*, December 11, 2003, p. 12.
19. Anne Faircloth, "One-on-One Shopping," *Fortune*, July 7, 1997, pp. 235–36; Melanie Wells, "Are Dynasties Dying?" *Forbes*, March 6, 2000, p. 126.
20. R. A. Eisenstat, "Implementing Strategy: Developing a Partnership for Change," *Planning Review*, September–October 1993, pp. 33–36.

Chapter 5

1. A. Bernstein, "Too Much Corporate Power?" *BusinessWeek*, September 11, 2000, pp. 145–58.
2. S. Tully, "Mr. Cleanup," *Fortune*, November 15, 2004, pp. 151–63.
3. V. Anand, B. Ashforth, and M. Joshi, "Business as Usual: The Acceptance and Perpetuation of Corruption in Organizations," *Academy of Management Executive*, May 2004, pp. 39–53.
4. G. Colvin, "The Verdict on Business: Presumed Guilty," *Fortune*, November 15, 2004, p. 78.
5. G. Morgenson, "Who Loses the Most at Marsh? Its Workers," *New York Times*, October 24, 2004, sec. 3, pp. 1, 9.
6. A. Bernstein, "Too Much Corporate Power?" *BusinessWeek*, September 11, 2000, pp. 145–58.
7. O. Ryan, "By the Numbers," *Fortune*, November, 15, 2004, p. 40.
8. M. Banaji, M. Bazerman, and D. Chugh, "How (Un)Ethical Are You?" *Harvard Business Review*, December 2003, pp. 56–64.
9. A. Hudgins, "First Job," *Washington Post Magazine*, March 3, 2002 pp. 19–31.
10. M. E. Guy, *Ethical Decision Making in Everyday Work Situations* (New York: Quorum Books, 1990).
11. O. C. Ferrell and J. Fraedrich, *Business ethics: Ethical Decision Making and Cases*, 3rd ed. (Boston: Houghton Mifflin, 1997).
12. Ibid.
13. Guy, *Ethical Decision Making.*
14. Ferrell and Fraedrich, *Business Ethics.*
15. P. J. Sauer, "Lance Morgan, Ho-Chunk," *Inc.*, April 2004, p. 116.

16. A. Spicer, T. Dunfee, and W. Biley, "Does National Context Matter in Ethical Decision Making? An Empirical Test of Integrative Social Contracts Theory," *Academy of Management Journal* 47 (2004), pp. 610–20.

17. L. Kohlberg and D. Candee, "The Relationship of Moral Judgment to Moral Action" in *Morality, Moral Behavior, and Moral Development*, ed. W. M. Kurtines and J. L. Gerwitz (New York: John Wiley & Sons, 1984).

18. L. K. Trevino, "Ethical Decision Making in Organizations: A Person-Situation Interactionist Model," *Academy of Management Review*, 1992, pp. 601–17.

19. Ferrell and Fraedrich, *Business Ethics.*

20. J. Krohe Jr., "Ethics Are Nice, but Business Is Business," *Across the Board*, April 1997, pp. 16–22.

21. Ibid.

22. J. Badarocco Jr. and A. Webb, "Business Ethics: A View from the Trenches," *California Management Review*, Winter 1995, pp. 8–28.

23. G. Laczniak, M. Berkowitz, R. Brookes, and J. Hale, "The Business of Ethics: Improving or Deteriorating?" *Business Horizons*, January–February 1995, pp. 39–47.

24. S. Brenner and E. Molander, "Is the Ethics of Business Changing?" in *Ethics in Practice: Managing the Moral Corporation*, ed. K. Andrews (Cambridge, MA: Harvard Business School Press, 1989).

25. M. Gunther, "God & Business," *Fortune*, July 9, 2001, pp. 58–80.

26. Anand, Ashforth, and Joshi, "Business as Usual."

27. J. Calmes and D. Solomon, "Snow Says 'Balance' is Needed in Enforcing Sarbanes-Oxley Law," *The Wall Street Journal*, December 17, 2004, pp. A1, A7.

28. T. Bisoux, "Corporate CounterCulture," *BizEd*, November/December 2004, pp. 16–20.

29. R. T. De George, *Business Ethics*, 3rd ed. (New York: Macmillan, 1990).

30. M. Vickers, "The Secret World of Marsh Mac," *BusinessWeek*, November 1, 2004, pp. 78–89.

31. J. B. Ciulla, "Why Is Business Talking about Ethics? Reflections on Foreign Conversations," *California Management Review*, Fall 1991, pp. 67–80.

32. R. E. Allinson, "A Call for Ethically Centered Management," *Academy of Management Executive*, February 1995, pp. 73–76.

33. R. A. Cooke, "Danger Signs of Unethical Behavior: How to Determine if Your Firm Is at Ethical Risk," *Journal of Business Ethics*, April 1991, pp. 249–53.

34. L. K. Trevino and M. Brown, "Managing to Be Ethical: Debunking Five Business Ethics Myths," *Academy of Management Executive*, May 2004, pp. 69–81

35. Ibid.

36. Krohe, "Ethics Are Nice."

37. Trevino and Brown, "Managing to Be Ethical."

38. Ibid.

39. K. Gibson, "Excuses, Excuses: Moral Slippage in the Workplace," *Business Horizons*, November–December 2000, pp. 65–72.

40. D. Messick and M. Bazerman, "Ethical Leadership and the Psychology of Decision Making," *Sloan Management Review*, Winter 1996, pp. 9–22.

41. Krohe, "Ethics Are Nice."

42. C. Handy, *Beyond Uncertainty: The Changing Worlds of Organizations* (Boston: Harvard Business School Press, 1996).

43. B. L. Toffler, "Five Ways to Jump-Start Your Company's Ethics," *Fast Company*, October 2003, p. 36

44. Anand, Ashforth, and Joshi, "Business as Usual."

45. Ciulla, "Why Is Business Talking about Ethics?"

46. A. Farnham, "State Your Values, Hold the Hot Air," *Fortune*, April 19, 1993, pp. 117–24.

47. Ibid.

48. G. R. Weaver, L. K. Trevino, and P. L. Cochran, "Corporate Ethics Programs as Control Systems: Influences of Executive Commitment and Environmental Factors," *Academy of Management Journal* 42 (1999), pp. 41–57.

49. L. S. Paine, "Managing for Organizational Integrity," *Harvard Business Review*, March–April 1994, pp. 106–17.

50. F. Hall and E. Hall, "The ADA: Going beyond the Law," *Academy of Management Executive*, February 1994, pp. 7–13; A. Farnham, "Brushing Up Your Vision Thing," *Fortune*, May 1, 1995, p. 129.

51. G. R. Weaver, L. K. Trevino, and P. L. Cochran, "Integrated and Decoupled Corporate Social Performance: Management Commitments, External Pressures, and Corporate Ethics Practices" *Academy of Management Journal* 42 (1999), pp. 539–52.

52. Paine, "Managing for Organizational Integrity."

53. Trevino and Brown, "Managing to Be Ethical," p. 70.

54. Ibid.

55. Banaji, Bazerman, and Chugh, "How (Un)Ethical Are You?"

56. T. Thomas, J. Schermerhorn Jr., and J. Dienhart, "Strategic Leadership of Ethical Behavior in Business," *Academy of Management Executive*, May 2004, pp. 56–66.

57. L. T. Hosmer, *The Ethics of Management*, 4th ed. (New York: McGraw-Hill/Irwin, 2003).

58. Trevino and Brown, "Managing to Be Ethical."

59. J. Frey, "The Woman Who Saw Red," *The Washington Post*, January 25, 2002, p. C8.

60. C. E. Mayer and A. Joyce, "Blowing the Whistle," *The Washington Post*, February 10, 2002, pp. H1, H5.

61. M. Gundlach, S. Douglas, and M. Martinko, "The Decision to Blow the Whistle: A Social Information Processing Framework," *Academy of Management Review*, 28 (2003), pp. 107–23.

62. L. Preston and J. Post, eds., *Private Management and Public Policy* (Englewood Cliffs, NJ: Prentice-Hall, 1975).

63. Ferrel and Fraedrich, *Business Ethics.*

64. A. Carroll, "Managing Ethically with Global Stakeholders: A Present and Future Challenge," *Academy of Management Executive*, May 2004, pp. 114–20.

65. R. Giacalone, "A Transcendent Business Education for the 21st Century," *Academy of Management Learning & Education*, 2004, pp. 415–20.

66. M. Witzel, "Not for Wealth Alone: The Rise of Business Ethics," *Financial Times Mastering Management Review*, November 1999, pp. 14–19.

67. D. C. Korten, *When Corporations Ruled the World* (San Francisco: Berrett-Kochler, 1995).

68. Handy, *Beyond Certainty.*

69. D. Quinn and T. Jones, "An Agent Morality View of Business Policy," *Academy of Management Review* 20 (1995), pp. 22–42.

70. B. Gossage, "Stella Ogiale," *Inc.* April 2004, p. 121.

71. M. Gunther, "Money and Morals at GE," *Fortune*, November, 15, 2004, pp. 176–82.

72. D. Turban and D. Greening, "Corporate Social Performance and Organizational Attractiveness to Prospective Employees," *Academy of Management Journal* 40 (1997), pp. 658–72.

73. A. McWilliams and D. Siegel, "Corporate Social Responsibility: A Theory of the Firm Perspective," *Academy of Management Review* 26 (2001), pp. 117–27.

74. Z. Navoth, "Verve! Newsletter," February 2004, http://www.verve.nu/articles/verve newsletter February2004. html.

75. S. L. Hart and M. B. Milstein, "Global Sustainability and the Creative Destructions of Industries," *Sloan Management Review*, Fall 1999, pp. 23–33.

76. P. M. Senge and G. Carstedt, "Innovating Our Way to the Next Industrial Revolution," *Sloan Management Review*, Winter 2001, pp. 24–38.

77. C. Holliday, "Sustainable Growth, the DuPont Way," *Harvard Business Review*, September 2001, pp. 129–34.

78. M. Gunther, "Money and Morals at GE," *Fortune*, November 15, 2004, pp. 176–82.
79. A. Fisher, "The World's Most Admired Companies," *Fortune*, October 27, 1997, pp. 40–58.
80. J. Ball, "China Talks Up 'Green' Agenda on Energy Policy," *The Wall Street Journal*, December 16, 2004, pp. A14, A15.
81. P. Shrivastava, "Ecocentric Management for a Risk Society," *Academy of Management Review* 20 (1995), pp. 118–37.
82. Ibid.
83. Ibid.
84. M. Grunwald, "Monsanto Hid Decades of Pollution," *The Washington Post*, January 1, 2002, pp. A1–A17.
85. J. Kurlantzick, "China's Blurred Horizon," *The Washington Post*, September 19, 2004, pp. B1–B2.
86. Shrivastava, "Ecocentric Management."
87. F. Rice, "Who Scores Best on the Environment," *Fortune*, July 26, 1993, pp. 114–22.
88. J. O'Toole, "Do Good, do Well: The Business Enterprise Trust Awards," *California Management Review*, Spring 1991, pp. 9–24.
90. M. Russo and P. Fouts, "A Resource-Based Perspective on Corporate Environmental Performance and Profitability," *Academy of Management Journal* 40 (1997), pp. 534–59; R. D. Klassen and D. Clay Whybark, "The Impact of Environmental Technologies on Manufacturing Performance," *Academy of Management Journal* 42 (1999), pp. 599–615.
91. C. Prystay, "Recycling 'E-Waste,' " *The Wall Street Journal*, September, 23, 2004, pp. B1, B6.
92. P&G Perspectives Web site, http://www/pgperspectives.com
93. H. Bradbury and J. A. Clair, "Promoting Sustainable Organizations with Sweden's Natural Step," *Academy of Management Executive*, November 1999, pp. 63–74.
94. Ibid., p. 72.
95. G. Pinchot and E. Pinchot, *The Intelligent Organization* (San Francisco: Berrett-Koehler, 1996).
96. S. L. Hart, "Beyond Greening: Strategies for a Sustainable World," *Harvard Business Review*, January–February 1997, pp. 66–76.

Appendix C

1. P. Hawken, A. Lovins, and L. Hunter Lovins, *Natural Capitalism* (Boston: Little Brown, 1999).
2. F. Rice, "Who Scores Best on the Environment?" *Fortune*, July 26, 1993, p. 114–22.
3. J. K. Hammitt, "Climate Change Won't Wait for Kyoto," *The Washington Post*, November 29, 2000, p. A39.
4. A. Brown, "Business Leaders Respond to Rio with Self-Regulation,"

International Herald Tribune, June 23, 1997, p. 17.
5. Ibid.
6. K. W. Chilton, "Reengineering U.S. Environmental Protection," *Business Horizons*, March–April 2000, pp. 7–16.
7. K. Dechant and B. Altman, "Environmental Leadership: From Compliance to Competitive Advantage," *Academy of Management Executive*, August 1994, pp. 7–20.
8. R. Stavins, letter in "The Challenge of Going Green," *Harvard Business Review*, July–August 1994, pp. 37–50.
9. N. Walley and B. Whitehead, "It's Not Easy Being Green," *Harvard Business Review*, May–June 1994, pp. 46–51; C. J. Corbett and L. N. Van Wassenhove, "The Green Fee: Internationalizing and Operationalizing Environmental Issues," *California Management Review*, Fall 1993, pp. 116–33.
10. Walley and Whitehead, "It's Not Easy Being Green."
11. Stavins, "The Challenge of Going Green."
12. Ibid.
13. F. B. Cross, "The Weaning of the Green: Environmentalism Comes of Age in the 1990s," *Business Horizons*, September–October 1990, pp. 40–46.
14. Stavins, "The Challenge of Going Green."
15. J. Singh, "Making Business Sense of Environmental Compliance," *Sloan Management Review*, Spring, 2000, pp. 91–100.
16. H. Ellison, "Saving Nature While Earning Money," *International Herald Tribune*, June 23, 1997, p. 18.
17. E. Smith and V. Cahan, "The Greening of Corporate America," *BusinessWeek*, April 23, 1990, pp. 96–103.
18. M. E. Porter, "America's Green Strategy," *Science*, April 1991, p. 168.
19. A. Kleiner, "What Does It Mean to Be Green?" *Harvard Business Review*, July–August 1991, pp. 38–47.
20. D. C. Kinlaw, *Competitive and Green: Sustainable Performance in the Environmental Age* (Amsterdam: Pfeiffer & Co., 1993).
21. Rice, "Who Scores Best on the Environment?"
22. Rice, "Who Scores Best on the Environment?"; J. O'Toole, "Do Good, Do Well: The Business Enterprise Trust Awards," *California Management Review*, Spring 1991, pp. 9–24.
23. O'Toole, "Do Good, Do Well."
24. G. Hardin, "The Tragedy of the Commons," *Science* 162 (1968), pp. 1243–48.
25. D. Kirkpatrick, "Environmentalism: The New Crusade," *Fortune*, February 12, 1990, pp. 44–55.
26. Ibid.
27. R. Carson, *The Silent Spring* (Boston: Houghton Mifflin, 1962); R. Paehlke, *Environmentalism and the Future of Progressive Politics* (New Haven, CT: Yale University Press, 1989), pp. 13–41,

76–143; R. Nash, ed., *The American Environment* (Reading, MA: Addison-Wesley, 1968); R. Revelle and H. Landsberg, eds., *America's Changing Environment* (Boston: Beacon Press, 1970); L. Caldwell, *Environment: A Challenge to Modern Society* (Garden City, NY: Anchor Books, 1971); J. M. Petulla, *Environmental Protection in the United States* (San Francisco: San Francisco Study Center, 1987).
28. B. Commoner, *Science and Survival* (New York: Viking Press, 1963); B. Commoner, *The Closing Circle: Nature, Man and Technology* (New York: Bantam Books; 1971).
29. R. Paehlke, *Environmentalism and the Future of Progressive Politics* (New Haven: Yale University Press, 1989).
30. P. Shrivastava, "Ecocentric Management for a Risk Society," *Academy of Management Review* 20 (1995), pp. 118–37.
31. Commoner, *The Closing Circle*.
32. Paehlke, *Environmentalism*.
33. Ibid.
34. Ibid.
35. P. Hawken, J. Ogilvy, and P. Schwartz, *Seven Tomorrows: Toward a Voluntary History* (New York: Bantam Books, 1982); Paehlke, *Environmentalism*.
36. Porter, "America's Green Strategy."
37. R. Y. K. Chan, "An Emerging Green Market in China: Myth or Reality?" *Business Horizons*, March–April 2000, pp. 55–60.
38. S. Waddock and N. Smith, "Corporate Responsibility Audits: Doing Well by Doing Good," *Sloan Management Review*, Winter 2000, pp. 75–83.
39. C. Morrison, *Managing Environmental Affairs: Corporate Practices in the U.S., Canada, and Europe* (New York: Conference Board, 1991).
40. Ibid.
41. Kleiner, "What Does It Mean to Be Green?"
42. K. Fischer and J. Schot, *Environmental Strategies for Industry* (Washington, DC: Island Press, 1993).
43. J. Howard, J. Nash, and J. Ehrenfeld, "Standard or Smokescreen? Implementation of a Voluntary Environmental Code," *California Management Review*, Winter 2000, pp. 63–82.
44. Rice, "Who Scores Best on the Environment?"
45. M. P. Polonsky and P. J. Rosenberger III, "Reevaluating Green Marketing: A Strategic Approach," *Business Horizons*, September–October 2001, pp. 21–30.
46. Rice, "Who Scores Best on the Environment?"
47. Ibid.
48. Polansky and Rosenberger, "Reevaluating Green Marketing."
49. S. Hart and M. Milstein, "Global Sustainability and the Creative Destruction of Industries," *Sloan Management Review*, Fall 1999,

pp. 23–32; Ellison, "Saving Nature While Earning Money."

50. Dechant and Altman, "Environment Leadership."

51. Smith and Cahan, "The Greening of Corporate America."

52. J. Elkington and T. Burke, *The Green Capitalists* (London: Victor Gullanez, 1989); M. Zetlin, "The Greening of Corporate America," *Management Review*, June 1990, pp. 10–17.

53. Smith and Cahan, "The Greening of Corporate America."

54. J. Carey, "Global Warming," *BusinessWeek*, August 16, 2004, pp. 60–69.

55. J. Stevens, "Assessing the Health Risks of Incinerating Garbage," *EURA Reporter*, October 1989, pp. 6–10.

56. Carey, "Global Warming."

57. A. Lovins, L. Hunter Lovins, and P. Hawken, "A Road Map for Natural Capitalism," *Harvard Business Review*, May–June 1999, pp. 145–58.

58. A. Kolk, "Green Reporting," *Harvard Business Review*, January–February 2000, pp. 15–16.

59. L. Blumberg and R. Gottlieb, "The Resurrection of Incineration" and "The Economic Factors," in *War on Waste*, ed. L. Blumberg and R. Gottlieb (Washington, DC: Island Press, 1989).

60. Carey, "Global Warming."

61. L. Blumberg and R. Gottlieb, "Recycling's Unrealized Promise," in Blumberg and Gottlieb; *War on Waste*, pp. 191–226.

62. Carey, "Global Warming."

63. Lovins, Lovins, and Hawken, "A Road Map for Natural Capitalism."

64. J. Elkington, "Towards the Sustainable Corporation: Win-Win-Win Business Strategies for Sustainable Development," *California Management Review*, Winter 1994, pp. 90–100.

65. Lovins, Lovins, and Hawken, "A Road Map for Natural Capitalism."

66. Carey, "Global Warming."

67. Dechant and Altman, "Environmental Leadership."

68. Brown, "Business Leaders Respond to Rio with Self-Regulation."

69. H. Ellison, "Joint Implementation Promotes Cooperation on World Climate," *International Herald Tribune*, June 23, 1997, p. 21.

70. Corbett and Van Wassenhove, "The Green Fee."

71. Polansky and Rosenberger, "Reevaluating Green Marketing."

72. Carey, "Global Warming."

73. Corbett and Van Wassenhove, "The Green Fee."

74. R. D. Klassen and D. Clay Whybark, "The Impact of Environmental Technologies on Manufacturing Performance," *Academy of Management Journal* 42 (1999), pp. 599–615.

75. D. Machalaba, "New Recyclables Market Emerges: Plastic Railroad Ties," *The Wall Street Journal*, October 19, 2004, p. B1.

76. Hart and Milstein, "Global Sustainability."

77. Ibid.

78. Polansky and Rosenberger, "Reevaluating Green Marketing."

79. N. Stein, "Yes, We Have No Profits," *Fortune*, November 26, 2001, pp. 183–96.

80. Hart and Milstein, "Global Sustainability."

81. Ibid.

82. M. Fong, "Soy Underwear? China Targets Eco-Friendly Clothes Market," *The Wall Street Journal*, December 17, 2004, pp. B1, B4.

83. Ibid.

84. Polansky and Rosenberger, "Reevaluating Green Marketing."

85. Ibid.

86. Elkington, "Towards the Sustainable Corporation."

87. F. S. Rowland, "Chlorofluorocarbons and the Depletion of Stratospheric Ozone," *American Scientist*, January–February 1989, pp. 36–45.

88. Elkington, "Towards the Sustainable Corporation."

89. Corbet and Van Wassenhove, "The Green Fee."

90. Ellison, "Joint Implementation Promotes Cooperation on World Climate."

91. Elkington, "Towards the Sustainable Corporation."

92. H. Ellison, "The Balance Sheet," *International Herald Tribune*, June 23, 1997, p. 21.

93. Ibid.

94. P. B. Gray and D. Devlin, "Heroes of Small Business," *Fortune Small Business*, November 2000, pp. 50–64.

95. S. Tully, "Water, Water Everywhere," *Fortune*, May 15, 2000, pp. 343–54.

Chapter 6

1. europ.eu.int/index_en.htm, accessed February 2005.

2. "EU: MNCs Face New Challenges as Frontiers Merge," *Crossborder Monitor* 2, no. 10 (March 16, 1994), p. 1; Jane Sasseen, "EU Dateline," *International Management* 49, no. 2 (March 1994), p. 5; Andrew Martin and George Ross, *The Brave New World of European Labor: European Trade Unions at the Millennium* (New York: Berghahn, 1999); Robert A. Feldman and C. Maxwell Watson, "Central Europe: From Transition to EU Membership," *Finance & Development* 37, no. 3 (September 2000), pp. 24–27; Lars Perner, "International Marketing," www.consumerpsychologist.com/international.htm; Jeffrey Garten, "Europe: Staring into the Abyss," *BusinessWeek*, August 2, 2004, online; "The US and the EU," professorbainbridge.com/2004.

3. Jonathan Krim, "EU Orders Microsoft to Modify Windows," *Washington Post*, December 23, 2004, online.

4. Robert W. Bednarzik, "The Role of Entrepenuership in U.S. and European Job Growth," *Monthly Labor Review* 123, no. 7 (July 2000), pp. 3–16; Wolf Sauter, *Competition Law and Industrial Policy in the EU* (Oxford, UK: Oxford University Press, 1998).

5. Paul Blustein, "China Passes U.S. in Trade with Japan," *Washington Post*, January 27, 2005, online; Keith Bradsher, "The Two Faces of China," *The New York Times*, December 6, 2004, p. C1.

6. "Commentary: Does It Matter If China Catches Up to the U.S.?" *BusinessWeek*, December 8, 2004, online.

7. Danny Hakim, "U.S. Automakers See China as the Land of Opportunity," *The New York Times*, December 6, 2004, p. C3; David Barboza, "China: A Big Supplier Becomes a Big Consumer, Too," *The New York Times*, December 6, 2004, p. C6; Bradsher, "The Two Faces of China," p. C1.

8. David Barboza, "In Roaring China, Sweaters Are West of Socks City," *The New York Times*, December 24, 2004, p. C1; Blustein, "China Passes U.S."; Barboza, "China: A Big Supplier," p. C3

9. Michael Shari, "Free Trade in Asia: Bogged Down Again," *BusinessWeek*, December 4, 2000, p. 62; "Asia: Smaller Steps," *The Economist*, 357, no. 8197 (November 18, 2000), p. 50.

10. James T. Peach and Richard V. Adkisson, "NAFTA and Economic Activity along the U.S.-Mexico Border," *Journal of Economic Issues* 34, no. 2 (June 2000), pp. 481–89; Elisabeth Malkin, "Mexico: More Sales than Its Three Top Competitors Combined," *The New York Times*, December 6, 2004, p. C6.

11. Larry Rohter, "South America Seeks to Fill the World's Table," *The New York Times*, December 12, 2004, p. 1.

12. Geri Smith, "Chile: A Giant Step toward Free Trade across the Americas?" *BusinessWeek*, June 16, 2003, online.

13. Gail M. Gerhart, "Can Africa Claim the 21st Century?" *Foreign Affairs*, 79, no. 6 (November/December 2000), p. 191; Michael D. White, "Land of Promise," *World Trade* 12, no. 9 (September 1999), pp. 58–60; Evangelos O. Simos, "International Economic Outlook: The World Economy in 2009," *Journal of Business Forecasting Methods & Systems* 19, no. 3 (Fall 2000), pp. 31–35.

14. Roger Ahrens, "Going Global," *International Business* 9, no. (July/August 1996), pp. 26–30; Bill Javetski, "Old World, New Investment," *BusinessWeek*, October 7, 1996, pp. 50–51.

15. *World Investment Report*, 2004 (New York: United Nations, 2004), pp. 1–2.

16. "Current International Trade Position of the U.S.: Imports Outpace Exports: Balance with Japan Improves," *Business America* 117, no. 6 (June 1996), pp. 35–37.

17. Peter Bohr, "American Made?" *aaaworld.com*, January/February 2005, online.

18. James Barron, "Flower Power," *CIO* 13, no. 25 (September 15, 2000), pp. 108–12.

19. Daniel W. Drezner, "The Outsourcing Bogeyman," *Foreign Affairs*, May/June 2004, online.

20. Eduardo Porter, "Factories Rev Up (At Last) in the U.S.," *The New York Times*, January 23, 2005, sect. 10, p. 1; Robert J. Samuelson, "Competition's Anxious Victory," *Washington Post*, February 2, 2005, online.

21. Drezner, "The Outsourcing Bogeyman."

22. David Barboza, "Outsourcing to the U.S.," *The New York Times*, December 25, 2004, p. C1.

23. Matthew J. Slaughter, "Insourcing Jobs," www.offii.org/insourcing/insourcing_study.pdf, October 2004.

24. Mike Yamamoto, "Will India Price Itself Out of Offshore Market?" *CNET News.com*, March 29, 2004.

25. "When Staying Put Trumps Offshoring," *McKinsey Quarterly*, December 7, 2004, online.

26. Ibid.; "The Profits and Pains of Outsourcing," *The New York Times*, December 6, 2004, p. C9.

27. Anne-Wil Harzing, "An Empirical Analysis and Extension of the Bartlett and Ghoshal Typology of Multinational Companies," *Journal of International Business Studies* 31, no. 1 (2000), pp. 101–20; Don E. Schultz and Philip J. Kitchen, "Global Reach," *Adweek* 41, no. 44 (October 30, 2000), p. 51.

28. Steven E. Prokesch, "Making Global Connections at Caterpillar," *Harvard Business Review* 74, no. 2 (March–April 1996), pp. 88–89; Laurie Freeman, "Caterpillar on a Roll," *B to B* 85, no. 14 (September 11, 2000), pp. 3, 44; Ian Buchanan, "The US Experience," *Asian Business* 34, no. 5 (May 1998), pp. 14–16.

29. *Off-Highway Engineering: Technical Innovations*, www.sae.org/ohmag/techinnovations/02-2001/.

30. Chang H. Moon, "The Choice of Entry Modes and Theories of Foreign Direct Investment," *Journal of Global Marketing* 11, no. 2 (1997), pp. 43–64; Isabelle Maignan and Bryan A. Lukas, "Entry Mode Decisions: The Role of Managers' Mental Models," *Journal of Global Marketing* 10, no. 4 (1997), pp. 7–22.

31. Robert C. Beasley, "Reducing the Risk of Failure in the Formation of Commercial Partnerships," *Licensing Journal* 24, no. 4 (April 2004), p. 71.

32. Maureen Nevin Duffy, "3M Lauds China Government Help," *Chemical Marketer Reporter* 251, no. 1 (January 6, 1997), p. 19.

33. "Cendant Mobility Survey Shows Continued Challenges Around Repatriation Management: Focus on Cost Control Also Driving New Approaches to Global Assignments, Say Global Mobility Practitioners," *PR Newswire*, April 28, 2004, online.

34. Nancy J. Adler and Susan Bartholomew, "Managing Globally Competent People," *Academy of Management Executive* 6, no. 3 (1992), pp. 52–65; Cecil G. Howard, "Profile of the 21st-Century Expatriate Manager," *HRMagazine*, June 1992, pp. 93–100.

35. Andrew Park, "Dell's Hiring Binge— Abroad," *BusinessWeek*, April 14, 2004, online.

36. Donald C. Hambrick, James W. Fredrickson, Lester B. Korn, and Richard M. Ferry, "Reinventing the CEO," *21st Century Report* (New York: Korn/Ferry and Columbia Graduate School of Business, 1989).

37. Aaron W. Andreason, "Expatriate Adjustment to Foreign Assignments," *International Journal of Commerce and Management* 13 no. 1 (Spring 2003), pp. 42–61.

38. Reyer A. Swaak, "Expatriate Failures: Too Many, Too Much Cost, Too Little Planning," *Compensation & Benefits Review*, November/December 1995, pp. 50–52.

39. Howard, "Profile of the 21st-Century Expatriate Manager."

40. Nancy Lockwood, "The Glass Ceiling: Domestic and International Perspectives," *HRMagazine* 49, no. 6 (June 2004), pp. S1–11.

41. Gretchen M. Sprietzer, Morgan W. McCall, and Joan D. Mahoney, "Early Identification of International Executive Potential," *Journal of Applied Psychology* 82, no. 1 (1997), pp. 6–29; Ronald Mortensen, "Beyond the Fence Line," *HRMagazine*, November 1997, pp. 100–109; "Expatriate Games," *Journal of Business Strategy*, July/August 1997, pp. 4–5; "Building a Global Workforce Starts with Recruitment," *Personnel Journal* (special supplement), March 1996, pp. 9–11.

42. Gunnar Beeth, "Multicultural Managers Wanted," *Management Review*, May 1997, p. 21.

43. David Stamps, "Welcome to America," *Training*, November 1996, pp. 23–30.

44. Linda K. Trevino and Katherine A. Nelson, *Managing Business Ethics: Straight Talk about How to Do It Right* (New York: John Wiley & Sons, 1995).

45. Patricia Digh, "Shades of Gray in the Global Marketplace," *HRMagazine*, April 1997, pp. 91–98.

46. David M. Katz, "The Bribery Gap: While Foreign Rivals May Make Payoffs Routinely, U.S. Firms Face New Pressure to Root Out Abuses," *CFO* 21, no. 1 (January 2005), pp. 59–62.

47. J. G. Longnecker, J. A. McKinney, and C. W. Moore, "The Ethical Issues of International Bribery: A Study of Attitudes among U.S. Business Professionals," *Journal of Business Ethics* 7 (1988), pp. 341–346.

48. Curtis C. Verschoor, "Survey Shows Need for More Ethics Awareness," *Strategic Finance*, December 2004, pp. 15–17; Andrew E. Reisman, "Spreading Roots: Corporate Culture beyond the Corporation: Today, Ethics Is a Basic Necessity," *Contract Management* 44, no. 9 (September 2004), pp. 26–31; Charlene Marmer Solomon, "Put Your Global Ethics to the Test," *Personnel Journal*, January 1996, pp. 66–74.

49. Digh, "Shades of Gray"; Ashay B. Desai and Terri Rittenburg, "Global Ethics: An Integrative Framework for MNEs," *Journal of Business Ethics* 16 (1997), pp. 791–800; Paul Buller, John Kohls, and Kenneth Anderson, "A Model for Addressing Cross-Cultural Ethical Conflicts," *Business & Society* 36, no. 2 (June 1997), pp. 169–93.

Chapter 7

1. S. Shane and S. Venkataraman, "The Promise of Entrepreneurship as a Field of Research, *Academy of Management Review* 25 (2000), pp. 217–26.

2. J. A. Timmons, *New Venture Creation* (Burr Ridge, IL: Richard D. Irwin, 1994).

3. G. T. Lumpkin and G. G. Dess, "Clarifying the Entrepreneurial Orientation Construct and Linking It to Performance," *Academy of Management Review* 21 (1996), pp. 135–72.

4. R. W. Smilor, "Entrepreneurship: Reflections on a Subversive Activity," *Journal of Business Venturing* 12 (1997), pp. 341–46.

5. W. Megginson, M. J. Byrd, S. R. Scott Jr., and L. Megginson, *Small Business Management: An Entrepreneur's Guide to Success*, 2nd ed. (Boston: Irwin McGraw-Hill, 1997).

6. J. Timmons and S. Spinelli, *New Venture Creation: Entrepreneurship for the 21st Century*, 6th ed. (New York: McGraw-Hill/Irwin, 2004), p. 3.

7. J. A. Timmons, *The Entrepreneurial Mind* (Andover, MA: Brick House, 1989).

8. Timmons and Spinelli, *New Venture Creation*.

9. Ibid.

10. Ibid.

11. Timmons, *New Venture Creation*.

12. T. Peters, "Thrashed by the Real World," *Forbes*, April 7, 1997, p. 100.

13. D. Bricklin, "Natural-Born Entrepreneur," *Harvard Business Review*, September 2001, pp. 53–59.

14. G. Pinchot, "How Intrapreneurs Innovate," *Management Today*, December 1985, pp. 54–61.

15. J. Akasie, "Imaging, No Inventory," *Forbes*, November 17, 1997, pp. 144–46.

16. P. J. Sauer, "Laima Tazmin, LAVT," *Inc.*, April 2004, pp. 133–34.

17. A. Marsh, "Promiscuous Breeding," *Forbes*, April 7, 1997, pp. 74–77.

18. *Inc.*, April 2004, p. 135.

19. B. O'Reilly, "The New Face of Small Business," *Fortune*, May 2, 1994, pp. 82–88.

20. "The Top Entrepreneurs," *BusinessWeek*, January 14, 2002, pp. 74–76.

21. H. Aldrich, *Ethnic Entrepreneurs: Immigrant Business in Industrial Societies* (Newbury Park, CA: Sage, 1990).

22. R. Kurtz, "Russell Simmons, Rush Communications," *Inc.*, April 2004, p. 137.

23. N. Heintz, "Andra Rush, Rush Trucking," *Inc.*, April 2004, p. 128.

24. *Inc.*, April 2004, pp. 146–47.

25. Timmons and Spinelli, *New Venture Creation.*

26. J. Collins and J. Porras, *Built to Last* (London: Century, 1996).

27. J. Nocera, "A Tale of Two Companies," *Fortune*, April 5, 2004, pp. 232–238.

28. Collins and Porras, *Built to Last.*

29. K. H. Vesper, *New Venture Mechanics* (Englewood Cliffs, NJ: Prentice-Hall, 1993).

30. B. Schlender et al., "Cool Companies, Part 1," *Fortune*, July 7, 1997, pp. 50–60.

31. Ibid.

32. Vesper, *New Venture Mechanics.*

33. Nocera, "A Tale of Two Companies."

34. J. Case, "Why 20 Million of You Can't Be Wrong," *Inc.*, April 2004, pp. 100–105.

35. "The Top Entrepreneurs," *BusinessWeek*, January 14, 2002, pp. 74–76.

36. C. Davenport, "Terrorism Fight Prods NSA to Look Beyond Its Fortress," *The Washington Post*, January 3, 2005, pp. A1, A7.

37. Timmons and Spinelli, *New Venture Creation.*

38. Ibid.

39. T. Singer, "What Business Would You Start?" *Inc.*, March 2002, pp. 68–76.

40. E. Schonfeld, "The Space Business Heats Up," *Fortune*, November 24, 1997, pp. 52–60.

41. D. H. Freedman, "Burt Rutan, Entrepreneur of the Year," *Inc.*, January 2005, pp. 58–66.

42. Schonfeld, "The Space Business."

43. E. Schonfeld, "Going Long," *Fortune*, March 20, 2000, pp. 172–92.

44. N. Stein, "The Fruits of Safety," *Fortune*, June 28, 2004, pp. 27–30.

45. N. Heintz, "Shoba Purushothaman," *Inc.*, January 2005, pp. 68–69.

46. J. E. Lange, "Entrepreneurs and the Continuing Internet: The Expanding Frontier," in Timmons and Spinelli, *New Venture Creation*, pp. 183–220.

47. Ibid.

48. Vesper, *New Venture Mechanics.*

49. "Do Universities Stifle Entrepreneurship?" *Across the Board*, July/August 1997, pp. 32–38.

50. Timmons, *New Venture Creation.*

51. Bricklin, "Natural-Born Entrepreneur," p. 54.

52. J. R. Baum and E. A. Locke, "The Relationship of Entrepreneurial Traits, Skill, and Motivation to Subsequent Venture Growth," *Journal of Applied Psychology* 89 (2004), pp. 587–98.

53. H. Evans, "What Drives America's Great Innovators?" *Fortune*, October 18, 2004, pp. 84–86.

54. M. Sonfield and R. Lussier, "The Entrepreneurial Strategy Matrix: A Model for New and Ongoing Ventures," *Business Horizons*, May–June 1997, pp. 73–77.

55. Lange, "Entrepreneurs and the Continuing Internet."

56. S. Venkataraman and M. Low, "On the Nature of Critical Relationships: A Test of the Liabilities and Size Hypothesis," in *Frontiers of Entrepreneurship Research* (Babson Park, MA: Babson College, 1991), p. 97.

57. Timmons and Spinelli, *New Venture Creation.*

58. S. Greco, "The INC.500 Almanac," *Inc.*, October 2001, p. 80.

59. *Venture Xpert*, Thompson Financial Data Service, 2001.

60. M. Boyle, "Absolutely, Positively, Slow the Hell Down," *Fortune*, November 15, 2004, p. 196.

61. R. Walker, "Jeff Bezos, Amazon.com," *Inc.*, April 2004, pp. 148–50.

62. I. Mount, "David Neeleman, JetBlue," *Inc.*, April 2004, p. 144.

63. N. Hira, "Customer Service. In New York. Who Knew?" *Fortune*, November 15, 2004, p. 198.

64. P. Evans and T. S. Wurster, "Getting Real about Virtual Commerce," *Harvard Business Review*, November–December 1999, pp. 85–94.

65. J. Rose, "The New Risk-Takers," *Fortune Small Business*, February 15, 2002, fortune.com.

66. "How It Really Works: Introduction," *BusinessWeek*, August 25, 1997, pp. 48–49.

67. P. Elstron, "It Must Be Something in the Water," *BusinessWeek*, August 25, 1997, pp. 84–87.

68. O'Reilly, "The New Face of Small Business."

69. C. Burck, "The Real World of the Entrepreneur," *Fortune*, April 5, 1993, pp. 62–81.

70. Case, "Why 20 Million of You Can't Be Wrong."

71. A. E. Serwer, "Lessons from America's Fastest-Growing Companies," *Fortune*, August 8, 1994, pp. 42–60.

72. D. McGinn, "Why Size Matters," *Inc.*, Fall 2004, pp. 32–36.

73. *Inc.*, April 2004, p. 112.

74. B. Burlingham, "How Big Is Big Enough?" *Inc.*, Fall 2004, pp. 40–43.

75. Ibid.

76. Ibid.

77. Ibid., p. 40.

78. S. Finkelstein, "The Myth of Managerial Superiority in Internet Startups: An Autopsy," *Organizational Dynamics*, Fall 2001, pp. 172–85.

79. N. Brodsky, "Street Smarts," *Inc.*, January 2005, pp. 47–48.

80. Ibid.

81. Ibid.

82. W. Barrett, "The Perils of Success," *Forbes*, November 3, 1997, p. 137.

83. Singer, "What Business Would You Start?" p. 71.

84. *Inc.*, April 2004, p. 126.

85. P. F. Drucker, "How to Save the Family Business," *The Wall Street Journal*, August 19, 1994, p. A10.

86. D. Gamer, R. Owen, and R. Conway, *The Ernst & Young Guide to Raising Capital* (New York: John Wiley & Sons, 1991).

87. Ibid.

88. A. Lustgarten, "Warm, Fuzzy, and Highly Profitable," *Fortune*, November 15, 2004, p. 194.

89. D. Fenn, "James Goodnight, SAS," *Inc.*, April 2004, p. 126.

90. R. D. Hisrich and M. P. Peters, *Entrepreneurship: Starting Developing, and Managing a New Enterprise* (Burr Ridge, IL: Irwin, 1994).

91. Ibid.

92. W. A. Sahlman, "How to Write a Great Business Plan," *Harvard Business Review*, July–August 1997, pp. 98–108.

93. Ibid.

94. Ibid.

95. Schlender et al., "Cool Companies."

96. Sahlman, "How to Write a Great Business Plan."

97. Ibid.

98. J. A. Fraser, "Do I Need to Plan Differently for a Dot-Com Business?" *Inc.*, July 2000, pp. 142–43.

99. M. Zimmerman and G. Zeitz, "Beyond Survival: Achieving New Venture Growth by Building Legitimacy," *Academy of Management Review*, 27 (2002), pp. 414–21.

100. A. L. Stinchcombe, "Social Structure and Organizations," in J. G. March (Ed.), *Handbook of Organizations* (Chicago: Rand McNally, 1965), pp. 142–93.

101. Ibid.

102. R. A. Baron and G. D. Markman, "Beyond Social Capital: How Social Skills Can Enhance Entrepreneurs' Success," *Academy of Management Executive*, February 2000, pp. 106–16.

103. J. Florin, M. Lubatkin, and W. Schulze, "A Social Capital Model of High-Growth Ventures," *Academy of Management Journal* 46 (2003), pp. 374–84.

104. R. Balu, "Starting Your Startup," *Fast Company*, January–February 2000, pp. 81–112.

105. Ibid.

106. S. McCartney, "Michael Dell—and His Company—Grow Up," *The Wall Street Journal*, January 31, 1995, pp. B1, B4.

107. A. F. Brattina, "The Diary of a Small-Company Owner," *Inc.*, May 1993, pp. 79–89, and June 1993, pp. 117–22.

108. *Inc.*, April 2004, p. 130.
109. N. Gull, "The Ceja Family," *Inc.*, January 2005, p. 72.
110. R. M. Kanter, *The Change Masters* (New York: Simon & Schuster, 1983).
111. D. Clark, "How a Woman's Passion and Persistence Made 'Bob,' " *The Wall Street Journal*, January 10, 1995, pp. B1, B8.
112. D. Kuratko, R. D. Ireland, and J. Hornsby, "Improving Firm Performance through Entrepreneurial Actions: Acordia's Corporate Entrepreneurship Strategy," *Academy of Management Executive* 15 (2001), pp. 60–71.
113. Collins and Porras, *Built to Last*.
114. M. Boyle, "Growing against the Grain," *Fortune*, May 3, 2004, pp. 148–56.
115. Kanter et al., "Driving Corporate Entrepreneurship," *Management Review*, April 1987, pp. 14–16.
116. J. Argenti, *Corporate Collapse: The Causes and Symptoms* (New York: John Wiley & Sons, 1979).
117. Kanter et al., "Driving Corporate Entrepreneurship."
118. G. T. Lumpkin and G. G. Dess, "Clarifying the Entrepreneurial Orientation Construct and Linking It to Performance," *Academy of Management Review* 21 (1996), pp. 135–72.
119. T. Bateman and J. M. Crant, "The Proactive Dimension of Organizational Behavior," *Journal of Organizational Behavior*, 1993, pp. 103–18.
120. A. E. Serwer, "Michael Dell Turns the PC World Inside Out," *Fortune*, September 8, 1997, pp. 38–44.
121. Lumpkin and Dess, "Clarifying the Entrepreneurial Orientation Construct."
122. C. Pinchot and E. Pinchot, *The Intelligent Organization* (San Francisco: Barrett-Koehler, 1996).

Chapter 8

1. Ronald N. Ashkenas and Suzanne C. Francis, "Integration Managers: Special Leaders for Special Times," *Harvard Business Review* 78, no. 6 (November–December 2000), pp. 108–16.
2. Andrew West, "The Flute Factory: An Empirical Measurement of the Effect of the Division of Labor on Productivity and Production Cost," *American Economist* 43, no. 1 (Spring 1999), pp. 82–87.
3. P. Lawrence and J. Lorsch, *Organization and Environment* (Homewood, IL: Richard D. Irwin, 1969).
4. Ibid.; Brad Lee Thompson, *The New Manager's Handbook*, (New York: McGraw-Hill, 1994); Also see S. Sharifi and K. S. Pawar, "Product Design as a Means of Integrating Differentiation," *Technovation* 16, no. 5 (May 1996), pp. 255–64; W. B. Stevenson and J. M. Bartunek, "Power, Interaction, Position, and the Generation of Cultural Agreement in Organizations," *Human Relations* 49, no. 1 (January 1996), pp. 75–104.
5. Abbas J. Ali, Robert C. Camp, and Manton Gibbs, "The Ten Commandments Perspective on Power and Authority in Organizations," *Journal of Business Ethics* 26, no. 4 (August 2000), pp. 351–61; Robert F. Pearse, "Understanding Organizational Power and Influence Systems," *Compensation & Benefits Management* 16, no. 4 (Autumn 2000), pp. 28–38.
6. Susan F. Shultz, *Board Book: Making Your Corporate Board a Strategic Force in Your Company's Success* (New York: AMACOM, 2000); Ralph D. Ward, *Improving Corporate Boards: The Boardroom Insider Guidebook* (New York: John Wiley & Sons, 2000).
7. John A. Byrne, "The Best & the Worst Boards," *BusinessWeek*, January 24, 2000, pp. 142–52.
8. A. J. Michels, "Chief Executives as Idi Ahmin?" *Fortune*, July 1, 1991, p. 13; C. M. Daily and D. R. Dalton, "CEO and Board Chair Roles Held Jointly or Separately: Much Ado about Nothing?" *Academy of Management Executive* 11, no. 3 (August 1997), pp. 11–20.
9. Tony Simons, Lisa Hope Pelled, and Ken A. Smith, "Making Use of Difference: Diversity, Debate, and Decision Comprehensiveness in Top Management Teams," *Academy of Management Journal* 42, no. 6 (December 1999), pp. 662–73; C. Carl Pegels, Yong I Song, and Baik Yang, "Management Heterogeneity, Competitive Interaction Groups, and Firm Performance," *Strategic Management Journal* 21, no. 3 (September 2000), pp. 911–21.
10. Shawnee Vickery, Cornelia Droge, and Richard Germain, "The Relationship between Product Customization and Organizational Structure," *Journal of Operations Management* 17, no. 4 (June 1999), pp. 377–91.
11. D. Van Fleet and A. Bedeian, "A History of the Span of Management," *Academy of Management Review* 2 (1977), pp. 356–72.
12. Philippe Jehiel, "Information Aggregation and Communication in Organizations," *Management Science* 45, no. 5 (May 1999), pp. 659–69; Ahnn Altaffer, "First-Line Managers: Measuring Their Span of Control," *Nursing Management* 29, no. 7 (July 1998), pp. 36–40.
13. "Span of Control vs. Span of Support," *Journal for Quality and Participation* 23, no. 4 (Fall 2000), p. 15; James Gallo and Paul R. Thompson, "Goals, Measures, and Beyond: In Search of Accountability in Federal HRM," *Public Personnel Management* 29, no. 2 (Summer 2000), pp. 237–48; Clinton O. Longenecker and Timothy C. Stansfield, "Why Plant Managers Fail: Causes and Consequences," *Industrial Management* 42, no. 1 (January/February 2000), pp. 24–32.
14. E. Beaubien, "Legendary Leadership," *Executive Excellence* 14, no. 9 (September 1997), p. 20; "How Well Do You Delegate," *Supervision* 58, no. 8 (August 1997), p. 26; J. Mahoney, "Delegating Effectively," *Nursing Management* 28, no. 6 (June 1997), p. 62; J. Lagges, "The Role of Delegation in Improving Productivity," *Personnel Journal*, November 1979, pp. 776–79.
15. G. Matthews, "Run Your Business or Build an Organization?" *Harvard Management Review*, March–April 1984, pp. 34–44.
16. "More Than a Bicycle: The Leadership Journey at Harley-Davidson," *Harvard Business School Working Knowledge*, September 5, 2000, online; Clyde Fessler, "Rotating Leadership and Harley-Davidson: From Hierarchy to Interdependence," *Strategy & Leadership* 25, no. 4 (July/August 1997), pp. 42–43; Jeffrey Young and Kenneth L. Murrell, "Harley-Davidson Motor Company Organizational Design: The Road to High Performance," *Organizational Development Journal* 16, no. 1 (Spring 1998), p. 65.
17. Russ Forrester, "Empowerment: Rejuvenating a Potent Idea," *Academy of Management Executive* 14, no. 3 (August 2000), pp. 67–80; Monica L. Perry, Craig L. Pearce, and Henry P. Sims Jr., "Empowered Selling Teams: How Shared Leadership Can Contribute to Selling Team Outcomes," *Journal of Personal Selling & Sales Management* 19, no. 3 (Summer 1999), pp. 35–51.
18. Suzy Wetlaufer, "Organizing for Empowerment: An Interview with AES's Roger Sant and Dennis Bakke," *Harvard Business Review* 77, no. 1 (January–February 1999), pp. 110–23.
19. E. E. Lawler III, "New Roles for the Staff Function: Strategic Support and Services," in *Organizing for the Future*, J. Galbraith, E. E. Lawler III, & Associates (San Francisco: Jossey-Bass, 1993).
20. Rob Cross and Lloyd Baird, "Technology Is Not Enough: Improving Performance by Building Organizational Memory," *Sloan Management Review* 41, no. 3 (Spring 2000), pp. 69–78; R. Duncan, "What is the Right Organizational Structure?" *Organizational Dynamics* 7 (Winter 1979), pp. 59–80.
21. George S. Day, "Creating a Market-Driven Organization," *Sloan Management Review* 41, no. 1 (Fall 1999), pp. 11–22.
22. R. Boehm and C. Phipps, "Flatness Forays," *McKinsey Quarterly* 3 (1996), pp. 128–43.
23. Bruce T. Lamont, V. Sambamurthy, Kimberly M. Ellis, and Paul G. Simmonds, "The Influence of

Organizational Structure on the Information Received by Corporate Strategists of Multinational Enterprises," *Management International Review* 40, no. 3 (2000), pp. 231–52.

24. Jeff Neal, "Tech Companies Shift to Package Offerings," *Optionics.com*, February 4, 2005.

25. Wilma Bernasco, Petra C. de Weerd-Nederhof, Harry Tillema, and Harry Boer, "Balanced Matrix Structure and New Product Development Process at Texas Instruments Materials and Controls Division," *R&D Management* 29, no. 2 (April 1999), pp. 121–31; J. K. McCollum, "The Matrix Structure: Bane or Benefit to High Tech Organizations?" *Project Management Journal* 24, no. 2 (June 1993), pp. 23–26; R. C. Ford, "Cross-Functional Structures: A Review and Integration of Matrix," *Journal of Management* 18, no. 2 (June 1992), pp. 267–94; H. Kolodny, "Managing in a Matrix," *Business Horizons*, March–April 1981, pp. 17–24.

26. David Cackowski, Mohammad K. Najdawi, and Q. B. Chung, "Object Analysis in Organizational Design: A Solution for Matrix Organizations," *Project Management Journal* 31, no. 3 (September 2000), pp. 44–51; J. Barker, "Conflict Approaches of Effective and Ineffective Project Managers: A Field Study in a Matrix Organization," *Journal of Management Studies* 25, no. 2 (March 1988), pp. 167–78; G. J. Chambers, "The Individual in a Matrix Organization," *Project Management Journal* 20, no. 4 (December 1989), pp. 37–42, 50; S. Davis and P. Lawrence, "Problems of Matrix Organizations," *Harvard Business Review*, May–June 1978, pp. 131–42.

27. Anthony Ferner, "Being Local Worldwide: ABB and the Challenge of Global Management Relations," *Industrielles* 55, no. 3 (Summer 2000), pp. 527–29; C. Bartlett and S. Ghoshal, "Matrix Management: Not a Structure, a Frame of Mind," *Harvard Business Review* 68 (July–August 1990), pp. 138–45.

28. Jasmine Tata, Sameer Prasad, and Ron Thorn, "The Influence of Organizational Structure on the Effectiveness of TQM Programs," *Journal of Managerial Issues* 11, no. 4 (Winter 1999), pp. 440–53; Davis and Lawrence, "Problems of Matrix Organizations."

29. R. E. Miles and C. C. Snow, *Fit, Failure, and the Hall of Fame* (New York: Free Press, 1994); Gillian Symon, "Information and Communication Technologies and Network Organization: A Critical Analysis," *Journal of Occupational and Organizational Psychology* 73, no. 4 (December 2000), pp. 389–95.

30. M. Lynne Markus, Brook Manville, and Carole E. Agres, "What Makes a Virtual Organization Work?" *Sloan Management Review* 42, no. 1 (Fall 2000), pp. 13–26; William M. Fitzpatrick and Donald R. Burke, "Form, Functions, and Financial Performance Realities for the Virtual Organization," *S.A.M. Advanced Management Journal* 65, no. 3 (Summer 2000), pp. 13–20.

31. Miles and Snow, *Fit, Failure, and the Hall of Fame.*

32. J. G. March and H. A. Simon, *Organizations* (New York: John Wiley & Sons, 1958); J. D. Thompson, *Organizations in Action* (New York: McGraw-Hill, 1967).

33. Paul S. Adler, "Building Better Bureaucracies," *Academy of Management Executive* 13, no. 4 (November 1999), pp. 36–49.

34. J. Galbraith, "Organization Design: An Information Processing View," *Interfaces* 4 (Fall 1974), pp. 28–36. See also S. A. Mohrman, "Integrating Roles and Structure in the Lateral Organization," in *Organizing for the Future*, J. Galbraith, E. E. Lawler III, & Associates (San Francisco: Jossey-Bass, 1993); Barbara B. Flynn and F. James Flynn, "Information-Processing Alternatives for Coping with Manufacturing Environment Complexity," *Decision Sciences* 30, no. 4 (Fall 1999), pp. 1021–52.

35. Walden Paddlers, personal communication.

36. Galbraith, "Organization Design," Mohrman, "Integrating Roles and Structure."

Chapter 9

1. Rick Dove, "Agility = Knowledge Management + Response Ability," *Automotive Manufacturing & Production*, 111, no. 3 (March 1999), pp. 16–17; Patrick M Wright, Lee Dyer, and Michael G Takla, "What's Next? Key Findings from the 1999 State-of-the-Art & Practice Study," *Human Resource Planning* 22, no. 4 (1999), pp. 12–20.

2. T. Burns and G. Stalker, *The Management of Innovation* (London: Tavistock, 1961).

3. D. Krackhardt and J. R. Hanson, "Information Networks: The Company behind the Chart," *Harvard Business Review*, July–August 1993, pp. 104–11.

4. G. Hamel and C. K. Prahalad, "Competing for the Future," *Harvard Business Review*, July–August 1994, pp. 122–28.

5. G. Hamel and C. K. Prahalad, *Competing for the Future* (Boston: Harvard Business School Press, 1994).

6. Sherri Singer, "Diesel Engines Burn Leaner and Cleaner," *Machine Design*, 71, no. 19 (October 7, 1999), pp. 64–69; P. P. Balestrini, "Globalization in the Automotive Industry: The Preferred External Growth Path," *Journal of International Marketing and Marketing Research* 25, no. 3 (October 2000), pp. 137–65; Eric Doyle, "Liberty Specifications Released," *Computer Weekly*, July 25, 2002, p. 30; Joseph Menn, "Microsoft's Passport Fails to Travel Far as Web Strategy," *Seattle Times*, December 31, 2004, online.

7. Pamela Harper and D. Vincent Varallo, "Global Strategic Alliances," *Executive Excellence* 17, no. 10 (October 2000), pp. 17–18.

8. R. M. Kanter, "Collaborative Advantage: The Art of Alliances," *Harvard Business Review*, July–August 1999, pp. 96–108; John B. Cullen, Jean L. Johnson, and Tomoaki Sakano, "Success through Commitment and Trust: The Soft Side of Strategic Alliance Management," *Journal of World Business* 35, no. 3 (Fall 2000), pp. 223–40; Prashant Kale, Harbir Singh, and Howard Perlmutter, "Learning and Protection of Proprietary Assets in Strategic Alliances: Building Relational Capital," *Strategic Management Journal* 21, no. 3 (March 2000), pp. 217–37.

9. P. Senge, *The Fifth Discipline* (New York: Doubleday Currency, 1990).

10. D. A. Garvin, "Building a Learning Organization," *Harvard Business Review*, July–August 1993, pp. 78–91; David A. Garvin, *Learning in Action: A Guide to Putting the Learning Organization to Work* (Boston: Harvard Business School Press, 2000); Victoria J. Marsick and Karen E. Watkins, *Facilitating Learning Organizations: Making Learning Count* (Aldershot, Hampshire, Gower Pub. Co, 1999).

11. Ibid.

12. Robert J. Vandenberg, Hettie A. Richardson, and Lorrina J. Eastman, "The Impact of High Involvement Work Process on Organizational Effectiveness: A Second-Order Latent Variable Approach," *Group & Organization Management* 24, no. 3 (September 1999), pp. 300–39; Gretchen M. Spreitzer and Aneil K. Mishra, "Giving Up Control without Losing Control: Trust and Its Substitutes' Effects on Managers' Involving Employees in Decision Making," *Group & Organization Management* 24, no. 2 (June 1999), pp. 155–87; Susan Albers Mohrman, Gerald E. Ledford, and Edward E. Lawler III, *Strategies for High Performance Organizations—The CEO Report: Employee Involvement, TQM, and Reengineering Programs in Fortune 1000 Corporations* (San Francisco: Jossey-Bass, 1998).

13. B. Buell and R. Hof, "Hewlett-Packard Rethinks Itself," *Business Week*, April 1, 1991, pp. 76–79.

14. "Why Big Might Remain Beautiful," *The Economist*, March 24, 1990, p. 79; W. Zellner, "Go-Go Goliaths," *BusinessWeek*, February 13, 1995, pp. 64–70.

15. Steve Rosenbush, "One Small Step for R&D Spending," *BusinessWeek*, November 1, 2004, online.

16. Linda L. Hellofs and Robert Jacobson, "Market Share and Customers' Perceptions of Quality: When Can Firms Grow Their Way to Higher versus Lower Quality?" *Journal of Marketing*, 63, no. 1 (January 1999), pp. 16–25.

17. Keith H. Hammonds, "Size Is Not a Strategy," *Fast Company*, September 2002, pp. 78–82.

18. Chuck Salter, "And Now the Hard Part," *Fast Company*, May 2004, online.

19. W. Cascio, "Downsizing: What Do We Know? What Have We Learned?" *Academy of Management Executive*, February 1993, pp. 95–104; Sarah J. Freeman, "The Gestalt of Organizational Downsizing: Downsizing Strategies as Package of Change," *Human Relations* 52, no. 12 (December 1999), pp. 1505–154.

20. R. E. Stross, "Microsoft's Big Advantage—Hiring Only the Supersmart," *Fortune*, November 25, 1996, pp. 159–62; R. Lieber, "Wired for Hiring: Microsoft's Slick Recruiting Machine," *Fortune*, February 5, 1996, pp. 123–24; Ibid.; M. Hitt, B. Keats, H. Harback, and R. Nixon, "Rightsizing: Building and Maintaining Strategic Leadership and Long-Term Competitiveness," *Organizational Dynamics*, Fall 1994, pp. 18–31.

21. Cascio, "Downsizing"; Jack Ciancio, "Survivor's Syndrome," *Nursing Management* 31, no. 5 (May 2000), pp. 43–45.

22. K. Ohmae, *The Mind of the Strategist: Business Planning for Competitive Advantage* (New York: Penguin Books, 1982), Chap. 8; Harry Stern, "Succeeding in a 'Customer-Centric' Economy," *Foodservice Equipment & Supplies* 53, no. 10 (September 2000), pp. 27–28.

23. K. Ishikawa, *What Is Total Quality Control? The Japanese Way*, trans. David J. Lu (Englewood Cliffs, NJ: Prentice-Hall, 1985); Bob Lewis, "Instead of Focusing Solely on Internal Customers, Look at Customers as Well," *InfoWorld*, 21, no. 4 (October 25, 1999), p. 104.

24. Michael Porter, *Competitive Advantage: Creating and Sustaining Superior Performance* (New York: Free Press, 1985); "The Value Chain," NetMBA.com.

25. Bill Creech, *The 5 Pillars of TQM: How to Make Total Quality Management Work for You* (New York: Plume Publishing, 1995); James R. Evans and William M. Lindsay, *Management and Control of Quality* (Cincinnati: Southwestern College Publishing, 1998).

26. Sunil Thawani, "Six Sigma Quality—Strategy for Organizational Excellence," *Total Quality Management and Business Effectiveness* 15, no. 5, 6 (July/August 2004) p. 655.

27. *Baldrige National Quality Program*, www.baldrige.nist.gov/index.html, accessed February 2005.

28. For more information about ISO 9000 (as well as newer programs such as ISO 14000 for environmental management), see the International Organization for Standardization's Web page: http://www.iso.ch/welcome.html.

29. J. Champy, *Reengineering Management* (New York: HarperBusiness, 1995). See also M. Hammer and J. Champy, *Reengineering the Corporation* (New York: HarperCollins, 1992).

30. Joan Woodward, *Industrial Organization: Theory and Practice* (London: Oxford University Press, 1965).

31. James H. Gilmore and B. Joseph Pine, eds., *Markets of One: Creating Customer-Unique Value through Mass Customization* (Cambridge, MA: Harvard Business Review Press, 2000); B. Joseph Pine, *Mass Customization: The New Frontier in Business Competition* (Cambridge, MA: Harvard Business School Press, 1992).

32. Erick Schonfeld, "The Customized, Digitized, Have-It-Your Way Economy," *Fortune* 138, no. 6 (September 28), pp. 114–20.

33. Funda Sahin, "Manufacturing Competitiveness: Different Systems to Achieve the Same Results," *Production and Inventory Management Journal* 41, no. 1 (First Quarter 2000), pp. 56–65.

34. Subhash Wadhwa and K. Srinivasa Rao, "Flexibility: An Emerging Meta-Competence for Managing High Technology," *International Journal of Technology Management* 19, no. 7–8 (2000), pp. 820–45.

35. Jeff Green, "How Architects Are Giving Jeep New Traction," *BusinessWeek*, October 2, 2000, p. 152H; Jeff Green, "Honda's Independent Streak," *BusinessWeek*, October 2, 2000, pp. 152B–152H; Brett A. Peters and Leon F. McGinnis, "Strategic Configuration of Flexible Assembly Systems: A Single Period Approximation," *IIE Transaction* 31, no. 4 (April 1999), pp. 379–90.

36. A. Taylor III, "How Toyota Defies Gravity," *Fortune*, December 8, 1997, pp. 100–108; Gary S. Vasilash, "How Toyota Does It—Every Day," *Automotive Manufacturing & Production*, 112, no. 8 (August 2000), pp. 48–49; Stephen R. Morrey, "Learning to Think Lean: A Roadmap and Toolbox for the Lean Journey," *Automotive Manufacturing & Production* 112, no. 8 (August 2000), p. 147; Funda Sahin, "Manufacturing Competitiveness: Different Systems to Achieve the Same Results," *Production and Inventory Management Journal* 41, no. 1 (First Quarter 2000), pp. 56–65; "Chrysler's Retooling Pays Off with Increased Productivity," *Knight-Ridder/Tribune Business News*, June 24, 2002, p. ITEM20175006; "Strategic Reconfiguration: Manufacturing's Key Role in Innovation," *Production and Inventory Management Journal*, Summer–Fall 2001, pp. 9–17.

37. Jeff Whiteacre, "Gorton's Keeps Moving: Lean Successes in the Plant, the Supply Chain, and the Office," www.advancedmanufacturing.com/lean manufacturing/casestudy.htm.

38. Sahin, "Manufacturing Competitiveness"; Gary S. Vasilash, "Flexible Thinking: How Need, Innovation, Teamwork & a Whole Bunch of Machining Centers Have Transformed TRW Tillsonburg into a Model of Lean Manufacturing," *Automotive Manufacturing & Production* 111, no. 10 (October 1999), pp. 64–65.

39. Chen H. Chung, "Balancing the Two Dimensions of Time for Time-Based Competition," *Journal of Managerial Issues* 11, no. 3 (Fall 1999), pp. 299–314; Denis R. Towill and Peter McCullen, "The Impact of Agile Manufacturing on Supply Chain Dynamics," *International Journal of Logistics Management* 10, no. 1 (1999), pp. 83–96; see also George Stalk and Thomas M. Hout, *Competing against Time: How Time-Based Competition Is Reshaping Global Markets* (New York: Free Press, 1990).

40. R. Henkoff, "Delivering the Goods," *Fortune*, November 28, 1994, pp. 64–78; Tony Seideman, "A&P Uses Transportation Software to Wring New Efficiency Out of Supply Chain," *Stores* 82, no. 9 (September 2000), pp. 172–74; "Cactus Commerce Launches the Cactus GDS Accelerator for BizTalk Server 2004; Global Data Synchronization Reduces Costs for Manufacturers and Retailers and Provides the Foundation for Successful RFID and CPFR Deployments," *PR Newswire*, May 17, 2004, online.

41. "2001 in Review; Logistics" *Traffic World* 265, no. 1 (January 1, 2001), p. 15; Morris A. Cohen, Carl Cull, Hau L. Lee, and Don Willen, "Saturn's Supply-Chain Innovation: High Value in After-Sales Service," *Sloan Management Review* 41, no. 4 (Summer 2000), pp. 93–101; "Penske Logistics," *Supply Chain Management Review* 8, no. 5 (July–August 2004), p. 12.

42. Tom Stundza, "Buyers Ask Service Centers: 'What Happened to JIT?' . . . and a Few Other Things," *Purchasing* 126, no. 7 (May 6, 1999), pp. 60–70; Damien Power and Amrik S. Sohal, "Human Resource Management Strategies and Practices in Just-in-Time Environments: Australian Case Study Evidence," *Technovation* 20, no. 7 (July 2000), pp. 373–87.

43. M. Tucker and D. Davis, "Key Ingredients for Successful Implementation of Just-in-Time: A System for All Business Sizes," *Business Horizons*, May–June 1993, pp. 59–65; Helen L. Richardson, "Tame Supply Chain Bottlenecks," *Transportation & Distribution* 41, no. 3 (March 2000), pp. 23–28.

44. John E. Ettlie, "Product Development—Beyond Simultaneous Engineering," *Automative*

Manufacturing & Production 112, no. 7 (July 2000), p. 18; Utpal Roy, John M. Usher, and Hamid R. Parsaei, eds. *Simultaneous Engineering: Methodologies and Applications* (Newark, NJ: Gordon and Breach, 1999); Marilyn M. Helms and Lawrence P. Ettkin, "Time-Based Competitiveness: A Strategic Perspective," *Competitiveness Review* 10, no. 2 (2000), pp. 1–14.

45. R. Ashkenas, D. Ulrich, T. Jick, and S. Kerr, *The Boundaryless Organization: Breaking the Chains of Organizational Structure* (San Francisco: Jossey-Bass, 1995); R. W. Keidel, "Rethinking Organizational Design," *Academy of Management Executive*, November 1994, pp. 12–27; Ron Ashkenas, Todd Jick, Dave Ulrich, and Catherine Paul-Chowdhury, *The Boundaryless Organization Field Guide: Practical Tools for Building the New Organization* (San Francisco: Jossey-Bass, 1999).

Chapter 10

1. "The Importance of HR," *HRFocus*, March 1996, p. 14; John McMorrow, "Future Trends in Human Resources," *HR Focus* 76, no. 9 (September 1999), pp. 7–9; Albert A. Vicere, "New Economy, New HR," *Employment Relations Today* 27, no. 3 (Autumn 2000), pp. 1–11.

2. Thomas O. Davenport, "Workers as Assets: A Good Start but . . .," *Employment Relations Today* 27, no. 1 (Spring 2000), pp. 1–18; Bruce Gilley, "Filling the Gap," *Far Eastern Economic Review* 163, no. 37 (September 14, 2000), pp. 44–46; "Filling the Skills Gap," *Business Europe* 40, no. 10 (May 17, 2000), p. 6.

3. David Ellwood, *Grow Together or Grow Slowly Apart*, The Aspen Institute, 2003, online; Stephen Baker and Manjeet Kripalani, "Software," *BusinessWeek*, March 1, 2004, online; www.super-solutions.com/WorkerShortages.asp; John Schmid, "China Engineers Its Next Great Leap," *JSOnline*, December 30, 2003.

4. Darin E. Hartley, *Job Analysis at the Speed of Reality* (Amherst, MA: HRD Press, 1999); Frederick P. Morgeson and Michael A. Campion, "Accuracy in Job Analysis: Toward an Inference-Based Model," *Journal of Organizational Behavior* 21, no. 7 (November 2000), pp. 819–27; Jeffery S. Shippmann, Ronald A. Ash, Linda Carr, and Beryl Hesketh, "The Practice of Competency Modeling," *Personnel Psychology* 53, no. 3 (Autumn 2000), pp. 703–40.

5. Jeffery S. Schippmann, *Strategic Job Modeling: Working at the Core of Integrated Human Resources* (Mahwah, NJ: Lawrence Erlbaum Associates, 1999).

6. David E. Terpstra, "The Search for Effective Methods," *HRFocus*, May 1996, pp. 16–17; Herbert G. Heneman III and

7. Robyn A. Berkley, "Applicant Attraction Practices and Outcomes Among Small Businesses," *Journal of Small Business Management* 37, no. 1 (January 1999), pp. 53–74; Jean-Marie Hiltrop, "The Quest for the Best: Human Resource Practices to Attract and Retain Talent," *European Management Journal* 17, no. 4 (August 1999), pp. 422–30.

7. Alex Daniels, "An Online Job War," *Newsbytes*, February 6, 2002, p. NWSB0203700E; Kerri Koss Morehart, "How to Create an Employee Referral Program that Really Works," *HR Focus* 78, no. 1 (January 2001), pp. 3–5; Keith Swenson, "Maximizing Employee Referrals," *HR Focus* 76, no. 1 (January 1999), pp. 9–10; "Are Your Recruiting Methods Discriminatory?" *Workforce* 79, no. 5 (May 2000), pp. 105–36.

8. "Pop Quiz: How Do You Recruit the Best College Grads?" *Personnel Journal*, August 1995, pp. 12–18; Shannon Peters Talbott, "Boost Your Campus Image to Attract Top Grads," *Personnel Journal*, March 1996, pp. 6–8; Cora Daniels, "Wall Street Says Please," *Fortune* 141, no. 5 (March 6, 2000), p. 420; Jean Buchanan, "Finding and Keeping Talent in a Shrinking Labor Pool," *Office Systems* 16, no. 11 (November 1999), pp. 42–46.

9. Malcolm Wheatley, "The Talent Spotters," *Management Today*, June 1996, pp. 62–64; Michael McDaniel, Deborah L. Whetzel, Frank L. Schmidt, and Steven D. Maurer, "The Validity of Employment Interviews: A Comprehensive Review and Meta-Analysis," *Journal of Applied Psychology* 79, no. 4 (August 1994), pp. 599–616; Michael A. Campion, James E. Campion, and Peter J. Hudson Jr., "Structured Interviewing: A Note on Incremental Validity and Alternative Question Types," *Journal of Applied Psychology* 79, no. 6 (December 1994), pp. 998–1002; R. A. Fear, *The Evaluation Interview* (New York: McGraw-Hill, 1984); Pamela Mendels, "Asking the Right Questions," *BusinessWeek Online*, October 13, 2000; Matthew T. Miklave and A. Jonathan Trafimow, "Ask Them If They Were Fired, but Not When They Graduated," *Workforce* 79, no. 8 (August 2000), pp. 90–93; Olivia Crosby, "Employment Interviewing: Seizing the Opportunity and the Job," *Occupational Outlook Quarterly* 44, no. 2 (Summer 2000), pp. 14–21.

10. U.S. Merit Systems Protection Board, "The Federal Selection Interview: Unrealized Potential," February 2003, mspb.gov/studies/interview.htm.

11. Christopher E. Stenberg, "The Role of Pre-Employment Background Investigations in Hiring," *Human Resource Professional* 9, no. 1 (January/February 1996), pp. 19–21; "The Final Rung: References," *Across*

the Board, March 1996, p. 40; Paul Taylor, "Providing Structure to Interviews and Reference Checks," *Workforce*, May 1999, Supplement, pp. 7–10; "Avoiding 'Truth or Dare' in Reference Checks," *HRFocus* 77, no. 5 (May 2000), pp. 5–6; "Fear of Lawsuits Complicates Reference Checks," *InfoWorld* 21, no. 5 (February 1, 1999), p. 73; D. L. Hawley, "Background Checks on the Rise," *Legal Assistant Today* 17, no. 5 (May/June 2000), pp. 28, 40; David E. Terpstra, R. Bryan Kethley, Richard T. Foley, and Wanthanee Limpaphayom, "The Nature of Litigation Surrounding Five Screening Devices," *Public Personnel Management*, 29, no. 1 (Spring 2000), pp. 43–54.

12. See also M. R. Barrick and M. K. Mount, "The Big Five Personality Dimensions and Job Performance: A Meta-Analysis," *Personnel Psychology*, 44 (1991), pp. 1–26; Daniel P. O'Meara, "Personality Tests Raise Questions of Legality and Effectiveness," *HRMagazine*, January 1994, pp. 97–100; Lynn A. McFarland and Ann Marie Ryan, "Variance in Faking across Noncognitive Measures," *Journal of Applied Psychology* 85, no. 5 (October 2000), pp. 812–21.

13. "Denny's Takes Drug-Free Policy Nationwide," *Employee Benefit Plan Review* 55, no. 4 (October 2000), pp. 34–36; "Fewer Employers Are Currently Conducting Psych & Drug Tests," *HRFocus* 77, no. 10 (October 2000), p. 8; Debra R. Comer, "Employees' Attitudes toward Fitness-for-Duty Testing," *Journal of Managerial Issues* 12, no. 1 (Spring 2000), pp. 61–75; "ACLU Report Debunks Workplace Drug Testing," *HRFocus* 76, no. 4 (November 1999), p. 4.

14. Patrick M. Wright, Michele K. Kacmar, Gary C. McMahan, and Kevin Deleeuw, "P = f(M × A): Cognitive Ability as a Moderator of the Relationship between Personality and Job Performance," *Journal of Management* 21, no. 6 (1995), pp. 1129–2063; Paul R. Sackett and Daniel J. Ostgaard, "Job-Specific Applicant Pools and National Norms for Cognitive Ability Tests: Implications for Range Restriction Corrections in Validation Research," *Journal of Applied Psychology* 79, no. 5 (October 1994), pp. 680–84; F. L. Schmidt and J. E. Hunter, "Tacit Knowledge, Practical Intelligence, General Mental Ability, and Job Knowledge," *Current Directions in Psychological Science* 2, no. 1 (1993), pp. 3–13; Mary Roznowski, David N. Dickter, Linda L. Sawin, Valerie J. Shute, and Sehee Hong, "The Validity of Measures of Cognitive Processes and Generability for Learning and Performance on Highly Complex Computerized Tutors: Is the G Factor of Intelligence Even More

General?" *Journal of Applied Psychology* 85, no. 6 (December 2000), pp. 940–55; Jose M. Cortina, Nancy B. Goldstein, Stephanie C. Payne, H. Krisl Davison, and Stephen W. Gilliland, "The Incremental Validity of Interview Scores over and above Cognitive Ability and Conscientiousness Scores," *Personnel Psychology* 53, no. 2 (Summer 2000), pp. 325–51.

15. Winfred Arthur Jr., David J. Woehr, and Robyn Maldegen, "Convergent and Discriminant Validity of Assessment Center Dimensions: A Conceptual and Empirical Reexamination of the Assessment Center Construct-Related Validity Paradox," *Journal of Management* 26, no. 4 (2000), pp. 813–35; Raymond Randall, Eammon Ferguson, and Fiona Patterson, "Self-Assessment Accuracy and Assessment Center Decisions," *Journal of Occupational and Organizational Psychology* 73, no. 4 (December 2000), p. 443.

16. Lynn A. McFarland and Ann Marie Ryan, "Variance in Faking across Noncognitive Measures," *Journal of Applied Psychology* 85, no. 5 (October 2000), pp. 812–21; Terpstra, Kethley, Foley, and Limpaphayom, "The Nature of Litigation Surrounding Five Screening Devices."

17. D. S. Ones, C. Viswesvaran, and F. L. Schmidt, "Comprehensive Meta-Analysis of Integrity Test Validities: Findings and Implications for Personnel Selection and Theories of Job Performance," *Journal of Applied Psychology* 78 (August 1993), pp. 679–703.

18. Rocki-Lee DeWitt, "The Structural Consequences of Downsizing," *Organization Science* 4, no. 1 (February 1993), pp. 30–40; Priti Pradhan Shah, "Network Destruction: The Structural Implications of Downsizing," *Academy of Management Journal* 43, no. 1 (February 2000), pp. 101–12; Jennifer Laabs, "Has Downsizing Missed Its Mark?" *Workforce* 78, no. 4 (April 1999), pp. 30–38.

19. See *Adair v. United States*, 2078 U.S. 161 (1908); Deborah A. Ballam, "Employment-at-Will; The Impending Death of a Doctrine," *American Business Law Journal* 37, no. 4 (Summer 2000), pp. 653–87.

20. Anne Fisher, "Dumping Troublemakers, and Exiting Gracefully," *Fortune* 139, no. 3 (February 15, 1999), p. 174; Paul Falcone, "Employee Separations: Layoffs vs. Terminations for Cause," *HRMagazine* 45, no. 10 (October 2000), pp. 189–96; Paul Falcone, "A Blueprint for Progressive Discipline and Terminations," *HRFocus* 77, no. 8 (August 2000), pp. 3–5.

21. See also John E. Lyncheski, "Mishandling Terminations Causes Legal Nightmares," *HRMagazine* 40,

no. 5 (May 1995), pp. 25–30. Katherine A. Karl and Barry W. Hancock, "Expert Advice on Employment Termination Practices: How Expert Is It?" *Public Personnel Management* 28, no. 1 (Spring 1999), pp. 51–62.

22. *Employer EEO Responsibilities* (Washington, DC: Equal Employment Opportunity Commission, U.S. Government Printing Office, 1996); Nancy J. Edman and Michael D. Levin-Epstein, *Primer of Equal Employment Opportunity*, 6th ed. (Washington, DC: Bureau of National Affairs, 1994).

23. Arnstein & Lehr LLP, "How to Get Sued in Business without Really Trying," *Employment Law E-Update*, April 2004, online; Wendy Zellner, "A Wal-Mart Settlement: What It Might Look Like," *BusinessWeek*, July 5, 2004, online.

24. Robert Gatewood and Hubert Field, *Human Resource Selection*, 3rd ed. (Chicago: Dryden Press, 1994), pp. 36–49; R. A. Baysinger, "Disparate Treatment and Disparate Impact Theories of Discrimination: The Continuing Evolution of Title VII of the 1964 Civil Rights Act," in *Readings in Personnel and Human Resource Management*, ed. R. S. Schuler, S. A. Youngblood, and V. L. Huber (St. Paul, MN: West Publishing, 1987).

25. Nicole Lee, "Learning How to Make the Best of Workplace Education," *The Financial Times*, August 19, 2002, p. 12; "Career Building Gets Put on Hold," *Crain's New York Business*, August 5, 2002, p. 21; "Industry Report 2000: The Money," *Training* 37, no. 10 (October 2000), pp. 51–55; Skip Corsini, "The Great Training Robbery," *Training* 37, no. 10 (October 2000), p. 160; "Spending on Training Remains Steady in 2004 According to ASTD," *Lifetime Learning Market Report* 10, no. 1 (January 7, 2005), pp. 3–4; "What to Do Now that Training Is Becoming a Major HR Force," *HR Focus*, February 2005, pp. 5–6.

26. A. P. Carnevale, *America and the New Economy: How New Competitive Standards Are Radically Changing American Workplaces* (San Francisco: Jossey-Bass, 1991); Marc Hequet, "Doing More with Less," *Training* 31 (October 1995), pp. 77–82; Robert M. Fulmer, Philip A. Gibbs, and Marshall Goldsmith, "Developing Leaders: How Winning Companies Keep on Winning," *Sloan Management Review* 42, no. 1 (Fall 2000), pp. 49–59; "Most Training Dollars Spent on Trainers, and Not Materials," *HR Focus* 77, no. 12 (December 2000), p. 8.

27. Sandra N. Phillips, "Team Training Puts Fizz in Coke Plant's Future," *Personnel Journal* 75, no. 1 (January 1996), pp. 39–42. See also George Bohlander and Kathy McCarthy, "How to Get the Most from Team Training,"

National Productivity Review, Autumn 1996, pp. 25–35.

28. For more information, see Kenneth Wexley and Gary Latham, *Increasing Productivity through Performance Appraisal* (Reading, MA; Addison-Wesley, 1994).

29. Ginka Toegel and Jay Conger, "360 Degree Assessment: Time for Reinvention," *Academy of Management Learning and Education* 2, no. 3 (September 2003), p. 297; Lauren Keller Johnson, "Retooling 360s for Better Performance," *Harvard Business School Working Knowledge*, February 23, 2004, online.

30. Mark Edwards and Ann J. Ewen, "How to Manage Performance and Pay with 360-Degree Feedback," *Compensation and Benefits Review* 28, no. 3 (May/June 1996), pp. 41–46. Also see Mary N. Vinson, "The Pros and Cons of 360-Degree Feedback: Making It Work," *Training and Development* 50, no. 4 (April 1996), pp. 11–12; John F. Milliman, Robert F. Zawacki, Carol Norman, Lynda Powell, and Jay Kirksey, "Companies Evaluate Employees from All Perspectives," *Personnel Journal* 73, no. 11 (November 1994), pp. 99–103; R. S. Schuler, *Personnel and Human Resource Management* (St. Paul, MN: West Publishing, 1984).

31. G. W. Bohlander, S. A. Snell, and A. W. Sherman Jr., *Managing Human Resources*, 12th ed. (Cincinnati, OH: Southwestern Publishing, 2001).

32. Garry M. Ritzky, "Incentive Pay Programs That Help the Bottom Line," *HRMagazine* 40, no. 4 (April 1995), pp. 68–74; Steven Gross and Jeffrey Bacher, "The New Variable Pay Programs: How Some Succeed, Why Some Don't," *Compensation and Benefits Review* 25, no. 1 (January–February 1993), p. 51; G. T. Milkovich and J. M. Newman, *Compensation* (New York: McGraw-Hill/Irwin, 1999).

33. Jeff D. Opdyke, "Getting a Bonus Instead of a Raise," *The Wall Street Journal*, December 29, 2004, p. D1.

34. Theresa Welbourne and Luis Gomez-Mejia, "Gainsharing: A Critical Review and a Future Research Agenda," *Journal of Management* 21, no. 3 (1995), pp. 559–609; Luis P. Gomez-Mejia, Theresa M. Welbourne, and Robert M. Wiseman, "The Role of Risk Sharing and Risk Taking under Gainsharing," *Academy of Management Review* 25, no. 3 (July 2000), pp. 492–507; Denis Collins, *Gainsharing and Power: Lessons from Six Scanlon Plans* (Ithaca, NY: ILR Press, 1998); P. K. Zingheim and J. R. Schuster, *Pay People Right!* (San Francisco: Jossey-Bass, 2000).

35. Kenneth W. Chilton, "Lincoln Electric's Incentive System: A Reservoir of Trust," *Compensation and Benefits Review* 25, no. 6 (November 1994),

pp. 29–34. See also D. W. Meyers. *Human Management: Principles and Practice* (Chicago: Commerce Clearing House, 1986); James P. Guthrie, "Alternative Pay Practices and Employee Turnover: An Organization Economics Perspective," *Group & Organization Management* 25, no. 4 (December 2000), pp. 419–39.

36. "Executives vs. Workers' Pay—the Gap Widens," *Growth & Success eNews*, no. 105, December 6, 2002, online; Louis Lavelle, "Executive Pay," *BusinessWeek*, April 21, 2003, online.

37. Louis Lavelle, "Executive Pay," *BusinessWeek*, April 19, 2004, online.

38. Louis Lavelle, "Options Today, Restatement Tomorrow?" *BusinessWeek*, May 21, 2004, online.

39. Louis Lavelle, "Time to Start Weighing the Options," *BusinessWeek*, January 17, 2005, online.

40. Ed Garsten, "GM: Repair Health Care," *The Detroit News*, February 10, 2005, online.

41. Nanette Byrnes, "The Benefits Trap," *BusinessWeek*, July 19, 2004, online.

42. Ellen C. Kearns and Monica Gallagher, eds., *The Fair Labor Standards Act* (Washington, DC: BNA, 1999).

43. Charles Fay and Howard W. Risher, "Contractors, Comparable Worth and the New OFCCP; Deja Vu and More," *Compensation and Benefits Review* 32, no. 5 (September/October 2000), pp. 23–33; Gillian Flynn, "Protect Yourself from an Equal-Pay Audit," *Workforce* 78, no. 6 (June 1999), pp. 144–46.

44. Bohlander, Snell, and Sherman, *Managing Human Resources*.

45. Eileen Henry, "Wage-Bias Bill: Study Panel Proposed," *Arizona Business Gazette*, February 28, 2002, pp. 2–4; Susan E. Gardner and Christopher Daniel, "Implementing Comparable Worth/Pay Equity: Experiences of Cutting-Edge States," *Public Personnel Management* 27, no. 4 (Winter 1998), pp. 475–89.

46. Alfred Lubrano, "Miners Live Life of Good Pay for High Danger," *Knight-Ridder/Tribune Business News*, August 13, 2002, p. ITEM02225012; T. Gup, "The Curse of Coal," *Time*, November 4, 1991, pp. 54–64.

47. Linda Kahn, *Primer of Labor Relations*, 25th ed. (Washington, DC: Bureau of National Affairs Books, 1994); A. Sloane and F. Witney, *Labor Relations* (Engle-wood Cliffs, NJ: Prentice-Hall, 1985).

48. S. Premack and J. E. Hunter; "Individual Unionization Decisions," *Psychological Bulletin* 103 (1988), pp. 223–34; Leo Troy, *Beyond Unions and Collective Bargaining* (Armonk, NY: M. E. Sharpe, 1999); John A. McClendon, "Members and Nonmembers: Determinants of Dues-Paying Membership in a Bargaining Unit," *Relations Industrielles* 55, no. 2 (Spring 2000), pp. 332–47.

49. Robert Sinclair and Lois Tetrick, "Social Exchange and Union Commitment: A Comparison of Union Instrumentality and Union Support Perceptions," *Journal of Organizational Behavior* 16, no. 6 (November 1995), pp. 669–79. See also Premack and Hunter, "Individual Unionization Decisions."

50. David Lewin and Richard B. Peterson, *The Modern Grievance Procedure in the United States* (Westport CT: Quorum Books, 1998); Steven E. Abraham and Paula B. Voos, "Right-to-Work Laws: New Evidence from the Stock Market," *Southern Economic Journal* 67, no. 2 (October 2000), pp. 345–62.

51. George Bohlander and Donna Blancero, "A Study of Reversal Determinants in Discipline and Discharge Arbitration Awards: The Impact of Just Cause Standards," *Labor Studies Journal* 21, no. 3 (Fall 1996), pp. 3–18.

52. "The Pivotal Role of Labor-Management Committees," *Workforce Management*, January 2004, online.

Chapter 11

1. Bonnie Eisenberg and Mary Ruthsdotter, "Living the Legacy: The Women's Rights Movement 1848–1998," www.legacy98.org/move-hist.html.

2. Ibid.

3. *2000–2010 Employment Projections* (Washington DC: Bureau of Labor Statistics, U.S. Department of Labor, 2002), http://www.bls.gov/news.release/ecopro.nr0.htm.

4. "Diversity Is about to Get More Elusive," *BusinessWeek*, June 30, 2003, online.

5. *Employment Projections*, Bureau of Labor Statistics; *Highlights of Women's Earnings in 2001* (Washington DC: Bureau of Labor Statistics, U.S. Department of Labor, May 2002); Press release "Ask a Working Woman Survey, 2002," AFL-CIO, copyright 2002; Margaret Steen, "Male–Female Pay Gap Widened, Study Says," *Knight-Ridder/Tribune Business News*, September 1, 2002, pITEM02244014; Jennifer Laabs, "Celebrating National Business Women's Week," *Workforce* 79, no. 10 (October 2000), p. 32; "Statistics—Women," *Break the Glass Ceiling*, www.breaktheglassceiling.com/statistics-women.htm.

6. Lisa Belkin, "Goodbye Doesn't Need to Mean Forever," *The New York Times*, March 13, 2005, Section 10, p. 1.

7. Toddi Gutner, "The Rose-Colored Glass Ceiling," *BusinessWeek*, September 2, 2002; Catalyst's "2001 Census of Women Board Directors of the Fortune 1000"; Tamil Lubhy, "Women Execs Narrowing Salary Gap," *Newsday.com*, June 24, 2002; Nacy Perry, "More Women Are Executive VPs," *Fortune*, July 12, 1993,

p. 16; Jennifer Laabs, "Saturn Gets Female President, but Female Leaders Are Still a Corporate Oddity," *Workforce* 78, no. 2 (February 1999), p. 22.

8. Joann S. Lublin, "Executive Aspirations Abound among Women Professionals," *CareerJournal.com*, June 29, 2004, online.

9. Jon Bonne, "A Gender Split in the Executive Suite," *MSNBC.com*, August 11, 2004, online; "Progress Stalled for Newspaper Women," *Media Report to Women* 30 (Winter 2002), online.

10. "How to Shrink the Pay Gap," *BusinessWeek*, June 24, 2002, p. 15; Tom Dunkel, "The Front Runners," *Working Woman*, April 1996, pp. 30–35, 72, 75; Rosemary Cafasso, "The Diversity Gap," *Computerworld*, June 1996, pp. 35–37; Laabs, "Saturn Gets Female President," p. 22; Rochelle Sharpe, "As Leaders, Women Rule," *BusinessWeek*, November 20, 2000, pp. 74–84.

11. George Bohlander, Scott Snell, and Arthur Sherman, *Managing Human Resources*, 12th ed. (Cincinnati, OH: Southwestern Publishing, 2001); William Petrocelli and Barbar Kate Repa, *Sexual Harassment on the Job: What It Is and How to Stop It* (Berkeley, CA: Nolo Press, 1998).

12. Kipp Cheng, "Beyond Just the Numbers, What Counts as an Emerging Market?" *DiversityInc.com*, July 1, 2002; U.S. Department of Labor; Jennifer Lee and Frank D. Bean, "America's Changing Color Lines," *Annual Review of Sociology*, 2004, pp. 221–43.

13. Jennifer Merritt, "Commentary: B-Schools: A Failing Grade on Minorities," *BusinessWeek*, May 12, 2003, online.

14. Roger O. Crockett, "For Blacks, Progress without Parity," *BusinessWeek*, July 14, 2003, online; "75 Most Powerful African Americans in Corporate America," *Black Enterprise*, February 2005, online.

15. Merritt, "Commentary."

16. Marianne Bertrand and Sendhill Mullainathan, "Are Emily and Greg More Employable than Lakisha and Jamal?" NBER Working Paper No. 9873, July 2003, online.

17. "On the Job," *Paraplegia News*, June 2002, pp. 41–42; "For the Disabled. It's Always a Depression," *BusinessWeek Online*, December 5, 2001; "An ADA Checklist for Implementation and Review," *HR Focus*, July 1994, p. 19; Stephen Overall, "Firms Hire Fewer Disabled People in Unskilled Jobs," *People Management*, November 16, 1995, p. 10; James Jordan, *ADA Americans with Disabilities Act Compliance Manual for California* (Bristol, UK: Jordan Publishing, 1999); "Disabled Workers Have Proportionally Harder Time Finding Jobs in Down Economy," *Denver Post*,

March 1, 2004, online (accessed via *Knight-Ridder/Tribune Business News*).

18. "New ADA Enforcement Guides from the EEOC," *HR Focus* 77, no. 12 (December 2000), p. 2.

19. Gail Dutton, "The ADA at 10," *Workforce* 79, no. 12 (December 2000), pp. 40–46.

20. *Employment Projections*, Bureau of Labor Statistics; Sarah Fister Gale, "Phased Retirement Keeps Employees—and Keeps Them Happy," *Workforce Management*, July 2003, pp. 92–96.

21. *Employment Projections*; "Older Workers Will Be Critical for Workforce Planning, Studies Show," *Human Resource Department Management Report*, September 2003, p. 12.

22. John Leland, "Retirees Return to the Grind, but This Time It's on Their Own Terms," *The New York Times*, December 8, 2004, online; Milt Freudenheim, "More Help Wanted: Older Workers Please Apply," *The New York Times*, March 23, 2005, p. 1.

23. Kenneth Labich, "No More Crude at Texaco," *Fortune* 140, no. 5 (September 6, 1999), pp. 205–12; *Good for Business: Making Full Use of the Nation's Human Capital* (Washington, DC: Federal Glass Ceiling Commission, 1995); Kimberly Weisul, "The Bottom Line on Women at the Top," *BusinessWeek*, January 26, 2004, online.

24. N. Adler, *International Dimensions of Organizational Behavior*, 3rd ed. (Boston: PWS-Kent, 1997); T. Cox and S. Blake, "Managing Cultural Diversity: Implications for Organizational Competitiveness," *Academy of Management Executives* 5 (August 1991), pp. 45–56.

25. "America's 50 Best Companies for Minorities," *Fortune*, July 28, 2002; "Successful Companies Realize That Diversity Is a Long-Term Process, Not a Program," *Personnel Journal*, April 1993, p. 54; Joan Crockett, "Diversity: Winning Competitive Advantage through a Diverse Workforce," *HR Focus* 76, no. 5 (May 1999), pp. 9–10.

26. See, for example, "Morgan Stanley Settles Sex Discrimination Lawsuit for $54 Million," U.S. Equal Opportunity Commission, July 12, 2004, online; "A New Black Eye for Boeing," *BusinessWeek*, April 26, 2004, online; "Wal-Mart Faces Lawsuit over Sex Discrimination," *The New York Times*, February 16, 2003, p. 22; and Steven Greenhouse, "Abercrombie & Fitch Bias Case Is Settled," *The New York Times*, November 17, 2004, p. 16.

27. R. Roosevelt Thomas Jr., "From Affirmative Action to Affirming Diversity," *Harvard Business Review*, March–April 1990.

28. Adler, *International Dimensions of Organizational Behavior*; Cox and Blake, "Managing Cultural Diversity."

29. Adler, *International Dimensions of Organizational Behavior*.

30. Karen A. Jehn, "Workplace Diversity, Conflict, and Productivity: Managing in the 21st Century," www-marketing.wharton.upenn.edu/SEI/diversity.html.

31. Audrey J. Murrell, Faye J. Crosby, and Robin J. Ely, *Mentoring Dilemmas: Developmental Relationships within Multicultural Organizations* (Mahwah, NJ: Lawrence Erlbaum Associates, 1999). See a review of this book by Mark L. Lengnick-Hall, "Mentoring Dilemmas: Developmental Relationships within Multicultural Organizations," *Personnel Psychology*, 53, no. 1 (Spring 2000), pp. 224–27.

32. A. Livingston, "What Your Department Can Do." *Working Woman*, January 1991, pp. 59–60; Mary Dean Lee, Shelley M. MacDermid, and Michelle L. Buck, "Organizational Paradigms of Reduced-Load Work: Accommodation, Elaboration, and Transformation," *Academy of Management Journal* 43, no. 6 (December 2000), pp. 1211–34.

33. Leslie E. Overmyer Day, "The Pitfalls of Diversity Training," *Training and Development* 49, no. 12 (December 1995), pp. 24–29; Sara Rynes and Benson Rosen, "A Field Survey of Factors Affecting the Adoption and Perceived Success of Diversity Training," *Personnel Psychology* 48, no. 2 (Summer 1995), pp. 247–70; Lynda Ford, "Diversity: From Cartoons to Confrontations," *Training & Development* 54, no. 8 (August 2000), pp. 70–71; "Diversity: A 'New' Tool for Retention," *HR Focus* 77, no. 6 (June 2000), pp. 1, 14: Lin Grensing-Pophal, "Is Your HR Department Diverse Enough?" *HR Magazine* 45, no. 9 (September 2000), pp. 46–52; John M. Ivancevich and Jacqueline A. Gilbert, "Diversity Management: Time for a New Approach," *Public Personnel Management* 29, no. 1, (Spring 2000), pp. 75–92.

34. Michael Burkart, "The Role of Training in Advancing a Diversity Initiative," *Diversity Factor* 8, no. 1 (Fall 1999), pp. 2–5.

35. Nancy L. Mueller, "Wisconsin Power and Light's Model Diversity Program," *Training and Development*, March 1996, pp. 57–60; Robert J. Grossman, "Is Diversity Working?" *HR Magazine* 45, no. 3 (March 2000), pp. 46–50.

36. Phyllis Shurn-Hannah, "Solving the Minority Retention Mystery," *The Human Resource Professional* 13, no. 3 (May/June 2000), pp. 22–27; Gillian Flynn, "Firm's Diversity Efforts Even the Playing Field," *Personnel Journal*, (January 1996), p. 56.

37. Barbara Durr, "Clubbing Together to Get Ahead," *Financial Times*, June 17, 2002, p. 11; Margaret Blackburn White, "Organization 2005: New Strategies at P&G," *Diversity Factor* 8, no. 1 (Fall 1999), pp. 16–20.

38. William G. Bowen, Derek Bok, and Glenda Burkhart, "A Report Card on Diversity: Lessons for Business from Higher Education," *Harvard Business Review*, 7, no. 1 (January–February 1999), pp. 38–45; Bryan Gingrich, "Individual and Organizational Accountabilities Reducing Stereotypes and Prejudice within the Workplace," *Diversity Factor* 8, no. 2 (Winter 2000), pp. 14–19; Joan Crockett, "Diversity: Winning Competitive Advantage through a Diverse Workforce," *HR Focus* 76, no. 5 (May 1999), pp. 9–10.

Chapter 12

1. J. A. Raelin, "Don't Bother Putting Leadership into People," *Academy of Management Executive*, August 2004, pp. 131–35.

2. W. Bennis and B. Nanus, *Leaders* (New York: Harper & Row, 1985), p. 27.

3. J. Petrick, R. Schere, J. Brodzinski, J. Quinn, and M. Fall Ainina, "Global Leadership Skills and Reputational Capital: Intangible Resources for Sustainable Competitive Advantage," *Academy of Management Executive*, February 1999, pp. 58–69.

4. Bennis and Nanus, *Leaders*.

5. Ibid., p. 144.

6. E. E. Lawler III, *Treat People Right! How Organizations and Individuals Can Propel Each Other into a Virtual Spiral of Success* (San Francisco: Jossey-Bass, 2003).

7. J. Kouzes and B. Posner, *The Leadership Challenge*, 2nd ed. (San Francisco: Jossey-Bass, 1995).

8. J. Kouzes and B. Posner, *The Leadership Challenge*, 1st ed. (San Francisco: Jossey-Bass, 1987).

9. Ibid.

10. Ibid.

11. J. Baum, E. A. Locke, and S. Kirkpatrick, "A Longitudinal Study of the Relation of Vision and Vision Communication to Venture Growth in Entrepreneurial Firms," *Journal of Applied Psychology* 83 (1998), pp. 43–54.

12. E. C. Shapiro, *Fad Surfing in the Boardroom* (Reading, MA: Addison-Wesley, 1995).

13. Kouzes and Posner, *The Leadership Challenge* (1995).

14. Ibid.

15. W. Bennis and R. Townsend, *Reinventing Leadership* (New York: William Morrow, 1995).

16. Ibid.

17. Kouzes and Posner, *The Leadership Challenge* (1987).

18. J. A. Conger, "The Dark Side of Leadership," *Organizational Dynamics* 19 (Autumn 1990), pp. 44–55.

19. J. Conger, "The Vision Thing: Explorations into Visionary Leadership,"n *Cutting Edge Leadership 2000*, ed. B. Kellerman and L. Matusak (College Park, MD: James MacGregor Burns Academy of Leadership, 2000).

20. J. P. Kotter, "What Leaders Really Do," *Harvard Business Review* 68 (May–June 1990) pp. 103–11.

21. A. Zaleznik, "The Leadership Gap," *The Executive* 4 (February 1990), pp. 7–22.

22. G. Yukl, *Leadership in Organizations*, 3rd ed. (Englewood Cliffs, NJ: Prentice-Hall, 1994).

23. R. House and R. Aditya, "The Social Scientific Study of Leadership: Quo Vadis?" *Journal of Management* 23 (1997), pp. 409–73.

24. R. D. Ireland and M. A. Hitt. "Achieving and Maintaining Strategic Competitiveness in the 21st Century. The Role of Strategic Leadership," *Academy of Management Executive*, February 1999, pp. 43–57.

25. J. Gardner, "The Heart of the Matter: Leader–Constituent Interaction," pp. 239–244. *Leading & Leadership*, ed. T. Fuller (Notre Dame, IN: University of Notre Dame Press, 2000), pp. 38–45.

26. R. E. Kelly, "In Praise of Followers," *Harvard Business Review* 66 (November–December 1988), pp. 142–48.

27. Bennis and Townsend, *Reinventing Leadership*.

28. Gardner, "The Heart of the Matter."

29. Kelly, "In Praise of Followers."

30. J. R. P. French and B. Raven, "The Bases of Social Power," in *Studies in Social Power*, ed. D. Cartwright (Ann Arbor, MI: Institute for Social Research, 1959).

31. G. Yukl and C. Falbe, "Importance of Different Power Sources in Downward and Lateral Relations," *Journal of Applied Psychology* 76 (1991), pp. 416–23.

32. Ibid.

33. Ibid.

34. R. M. Stogdill, "Personal Factors Associated with Leadership: A Survey of the Literature," *Journal of Psychology* 25 (1948), pp. 35–71.

35. S. Kirkpatrick and E. Locke, "Leadership: Do Traits Matter?" *The Executive* 5 (May 1991), pp. 48–60.

36. G. A. Yukl, *Leadership in Organizations*, 2nd ed. (Englewood Cliffs, NJ: Prentice-Hall, 1989).

37. R. Heifetz and D. Laurie, "The Work of Leadership," *Harvard Business Review*, January–February 1997, pp. 124–34.

38. T. Judge, J. Bono, R. Ilies, and M Gerhardt, "Personality and Leadership: A Qualitative and Quantitative Review," *Journal of Applied Psychology* 87 (2002), pp. 765–80.

39. T. Fuller, *Leading & Leadership, 2000*, (Notre Dame, IN: University of Notre Dame Press), p. 243.

40. J. P. Kotter, *The General Managers* (New York: Free Press, 1982).

41. S. Zaccaro, R. Foti, and D. Kenny, "Self-Monitoring and Trait-Based Variance in Leadership: An Investigation of Leader Flexibility across Multiple Group Situations," *Journal of Applied Psychology* 76 (1991), pp. 308–15.

42. D. Goleman, "Leadership that Gets Results," *Harvard Business Review*, March–April 2000, pp. 78–90.

43. J. Misumi and M. Peterson, "The Performance-Maintenance (PM) Theory of Leadership: Review of a Japanese Research Program," *Administrative Science Quarterly* 30 (June 1985), pp. 198–223.

44. T. Judge, R. Piccolo, and R. Ilies, "The Forgotten Ones? The Validity of Consideration and Initiating Structure in Leadership Research," *Journal of Applied Psychology* 89 (2004), pp. 36–51.

45. Misumi & Peterson, "The Performance-Maintenance (PM) Theory."

46. Judge, Piccolo, and Ilies, "The Forgotten Ones?"

47. G. Graen and M. Uhl-Bien, "Relationship-Based Approach to Leadership: Development of Leader-Member Exchange (LMX) Theory of Leadership over 25 Years: Applying a Multi-Level Multidomain Perspective," *Leadership Quarterly* 6, no. 2 (1995), pp. 219–47.

48. House and Aditya, "The Social Scientific Study of Leadership."

49. C. R. Gerstner and D. V. Day, "Meta-Analytic Review of Leader-Member Exchange-Theory: Correlates and Construct Issues," *Journal of Applied Psychology* 82 (1997), pp. 827–44.

50. House and Aditya, "Social Scientific Study."

51. J. Wagner III, "Participation's Effect on Performance and Satisfaction: A Reconsideration of Research," *Academy of Management Review*, April 1994, pp. 312–30.

52. R. White and R. Lippitt, *Autocracy and Democracy: An Experimental Inquiry* (New York: Harper & Brothers, 1960).

53. J. Muczyk and R. Steel, "Leadership Style and the Turnaround Executive," *Business Horizons*, March–April 1999, pp. 39–46.

54. A. Tannenbaum and W. Schmidt, "How to Choose a Leadership Pattern," *Harvard Business Review* 36 (March–April 1958), pp. 95–101.

55. E. Fleishman and E. Harris, "Patterns of Leadership Behavior Related to Employee Grievances and Turnover," *Personnel Psychology* 15 (1962), pp. 43–56.

56. R. Likert, *The Human Organization: Its Management and Value* (New York: McGraw-Hill, 1967).

57. R. Blake and J. Mouton, *The Managerial Grid* (Houston: Gulf, 1964).

58. Misumi and Peterson, "The Performance-Maintenance (PM) Theory."

59. J. Wall, *Bosses* (Lexington, MA: Lexington Books, 1986).

60. Ibid., p. 103.

61. Tannenbaum and Schmidt, "How to Choose a Leadership Pattern."

62. V. H. Vroom, "Leadership and the Decision-Making Process," *Organizational Dynamics*, Spring 2000, pp. 82–93.

63. R. J. House, "A Path Goal Theory of Leader Effectiveness," *Administrative Science Quarterly* 16 (1971), pp. 321–39.

64. J. Howell, D. Bowen, P. Dorfman, S. Kerr, and P. Podsakoff, "Substitutes for Leadership: Effective Alternatives to Ineffective Leadership," *Organizational Dynamics* 19 (Summer 1990), pp. 21–38.

65. R. G. Lord and W. Gradwohl Smith, "Leadership and the Changing Nature of Performance," in *The Changing Nature of Performance*, ed. D. R. Ilgen and E. D. Pulakos (San Francisco: Jossey-Bass, 1999).

66. S. Dionne, F. Yammarino, L. Atwater, and L. James, "Neutralizing Substitutes for Leadership Theory: Leadership Effects and Common-Source Bias," *Journal of Applied Psychology* 87 (2002), pp. 454–64.

67. A. Bianco and L. Lavell, "The CEO Trap," *BusinessWeek*, December 11, 2000, pp. 86–92.

68. B. M. Bass, *Leadership and Performance Beyond Expectations* (New York: Free Press, 1985).

69. Y. A. Nur, "Charisma and Managerial Leadership: The Gift That Never Was," *Business Horizons*, July–August 1998, pp. 19–26.

70. R. J. House, "A 1976 Theory of Charismatic Leadership," in *Leadership: The Cutting Edge*, ed. J. G. Hunt and L. L. Larson (Carbondale, IL: Southern Illinois University Press, 1977).

71. M. Potts and P. Behr, *The Leading Edge* (New York: McGraw-Hill, 1987).

72. S. Yorges, H. Weiss, and O. Strickland, "The Effect of Leader Outcomes on Influence, Attributions, and Perceptions of Charisma," *Journal of Applied Psychology* 84 (1999), pp. 428–36.

73. Potts and Behr, "Leading Edge."

74. D. A. Waldman and F. J. Yammarino, "CEO Charismatic Leadership: Levels-of-Management and Levels-of-Analysis Effects," *Academy of Management Review* 24 (1999), pp. 266–85.

75. House and Aditya, "The Social Scientific Study of Leadership."

76. D. A. Waldman, G. G. Ramirez, R. J. House, and P. Puranam, "Does Leadership Matter? CEO Leadership Attributes and Profitability under Conditions of Perceived Environmental Uncertainty," *Academy of Management Journal* 44 (2001), pp. 134–43.

77. J. M. Howell and K. E. Hall-Merenda, "The Ties that Bind: The Impact of Leader-Member Exchange, Transformational and Transactional Leadership, and Distance on Predicting Follower Performance," *Journal of Applied Psychology* 84 (1999), pp. 680–94.

78. B. M. Bass, "Leadership: Good, Better, Best," *Organizational Dynamics*, Winter 1985, pp. 26–40.

79. F. J. Yammarino, F. Dansereau, and C. J. Kennedy, "A Multiple-Level Multidimensional Approach to Leadership: Viewing Leadership through an Elephant's Eye." *Organizational Dynamics*, Winter 2001, pp. 149–63.

80. D. I. Jung and B. J. Avolio, "Effects of Leadership Style and Followers'

Cultural Orientation on Performance in Group and Individual Task Conditions," *Academy of Management Journal* 42 (1999), pp. 208–18.

81. Bass, *Leadership.*

82. Bennis and Nanus, *Leaders.*

83. B. Bass, B. Avolio, and L. Goodheim, "Biography and the Assessment of Transformational Leadership at the World-Class Level," *Journal of Management* 13 (1987), pp. 7–20.

84. K. Albrecht and R. Zemke, *Service America* (Homewood, IL: Dow Jones Irwin, 1985).

85. T. A. Judge and J. E. Bono, "Five-Factor Model of Personality and Transformational Leadership," *Journal of Applied Psychology* 85 (2000), pp. 751–65.

86. B. Bass, "Does the Transactional-Transformational Paradigm Transcend Organizational and National Boundaries?" *American Psychologist* 22 (1997), pp. 130–42.

87. S. J. Shin and J. Zhou, "Transformational Leadership, Conservation, and Creativity: Evidence from Korea," *Academy of Management Journal* 46 (2003), pp. 703–14.

88. T. Dvir, D. Eden, B. Avolio, and B. Shamir, "Impact of Transformational Leadership on Follower Development and Performance: A Field Experiment," *Academy of Management Journal* 45 (2002), pp. 735–44.

89. B. M. Bass, *Transformational Leadership: Industry, Military, and Educational Impact* (Mahwah, NJ: Lawrence Erlbaum Associates, 1998).

90. G. Spreitzer and R. Quinn, "Empowering Middle Managers to Be Transformational Leaders," *Journal of Applied Behavioral Science* 32 (1996), pp. 237–61.

91. Ibid.

92. J. Collins, "Level 5 Leadership," *Harvard Business Review* 1 (2001), pp. 66–76.

93. D. Vera and M. Crossan, "Strategic Leadership and Organizational Learning," *Academy of Management Review* 29 (2004), pp. 222–40.

94. F. Luthans, *Organizational Behavior,* 10th ed. (New York: McGraw-Hill/Irwin, 2005).

95. B. M. Bass, "Thoughts and Plans," in *Cutting Edge Leadership 2000,* ed. B. Kellerman and L. R. Matusak (College Park, MD: James MacGregor Burns Academy of Leadership, 2000), pp. 5–9.

96. N. Turner, J. Barling, O. Epitropaki, V. Butcher, and C. Milner, "Transformational Leadership and Moral Reasoning," *Journal of Applied Psychology* 87 (2002), pp. 304–11.

97. Bass, "Thoughts and Plans."

98. J. Huey, "The New Post-Heroic Leadership," *Fortune,* February 21, 1994, pp. 42–50.

99. W. Bennis, "The End of Leadership: Exemplary Leadership Is Impossible without Full Inclusion, Initiatives, and Cooperation of Followers," *Organizational Dynamics,* Summer 1999, pp. 71–79.

100. L. Spears, "Emerging Characteristics of Servant Leadership," in *Cutting Edge Leadership 2000,* ed. B. Kellerman and L. Matusak (College Park, MD: James MacGregor Burns Academy of Leadership, 2000).

101. J. Ciulla, "Bridge Leaders," in *Cutting Edge Leadership 2000,* ed. B. Kellerman and L. Matusak (College Park, MD: James MacGregor Burns Academy of Leadership, 2000), pp. 25–28.

102. C. L. Pearce, "The Future of Leadership: Combining Vertical and Shared Leadership to Transform Knowledge Work," *Academy of Management Executive,* February 2004, pp. 47–57.

103. R. Fisher and A. Sharp, *Getting It Done* (New York: HarperCollins, 1998).

104. S. Kirsner, "One Tough Assignment," *Fast Company,* September 2004, pp. 76–77.

105. P. Block, *The Empowered Manager* (San Francisco: Jossey-Bass, 1991).

106. Ibid.

107. D. Lidsky, "How Do You Rate?" *Fast Company,* September 2004, pp. 107–9.

108. Kouzes and Posner, *The Leadership Challenge* (1995).

109. J. Beeson, "Succession Planning: Building the Management Corps," *Business Horizons,* September–October, pp. 61–66.

110. R. Fulmer, P. Gibbs, and M. Goldsmith, "Developing Leaders: How Winning Companies Keep on Winning," *Sloan Management Review,* Fall 2000, pp. 49–59.

111. M. McCall, *High Flyers* (Boston: Harvard Business School Press, 1998).

112. E. Van Velsor, C. D. McCauley, and R. Moxley, "Our View of Leadership Development," in *Center for Creative Leadership Handbook of Leadership Development,* ed. C. D. McCauley, R. Moxley, and E. Van Velsor (San Francisco: Jossey-Bass, 1998), pp. 1–25.

Appendix E

1. F. E. Fiedler, *A Theory of Leadership Effectiveness* (New York: McGraw-Hill, 1967).

2. P. Hersey and K. Blanchard, *The Management of Organizational Behavior* (Englewood Cliffs, NJ: Prentice Hall, 1984)

3. Yukl, *Leadership in Organizations.* G. Yukl, Leadership in Organizations, 3e, Englewood Cliffs, N.J.: Prentice Hall, 1994.

Chapter 13

1. R. Kreitner and F. Luthans, "A Social Learning Approach to Behavioral Management: Radical Behaviorists 'Mellowing Out,'" *Organizational Dynamics,* Autumn 1984, pp. 47–65.

2. D. Katz and R. L. Kahn, *The Social Psychology of Organizations* (New York: John Wiley & Sons, 1966).

3. C. A. Bartlett and S. Ghoshal, "Building Competitive Advantage through People," *Sloan Management Review,* Winter 2002, pp. 34–41.

4. B. Bremmer, G. Edmondson, and C. Dawson, "Nissan's Boss," *BusinessWeek,* October 4, 2004, pp. 50–58.

5. E. Locke, "Toward a Theory of Task Motivation and Incentives," *Organizational Behavior and Human Performance* 3 (1968), pp. 157–89.

6. W. F. Cascio, "Managing a Virtual Workplace," *Academy of Management Executive,* August 2000, pp. 81–90.

7. E. A. Locke, "Guest Editor's Introduction: Goal-Setting Theory and Its Applications to the World of Business," *Academy of Management Executive* 4 (November 2004), pp. 124–25.

8. G. P. Latham, "The Motivational Benefits of Goal-Setting," *Academy of Management Executive* 4 (November 2004), pp. 126–29.

9. E. A. Locke, "Linking Goals to Monetary Incentives," *Academy of Management Executive* 4 (November 2004), pp. 130–33.

10. E. E. Lawler III, *Treat People Right!* (San Francisco: Jossey-Bass, 2003).

11. J. Bono and T. Judge, "Self-Concordance at Work: Toward Understanding the Motivational Effects of Transformational Leaders," *Academy of Management Journal* 46 (2003), pp. 554–71.

12. R. H. Schaffer, "Demand Better Results—and Get Them," *Harvard Business Review* 69 (March–April 1991), pp. 142–49.

13. K. N. Shaw, "Changing the Goal-Setting Process at Microsoft," *Academy of Management Executive* 4 (November 2004), pp. 139–43.

14. I. Mount, "David Neeleman, JetBlue," *Inc.,* April 2004, p. 144.

15. Lawler, *Treat People Right!*

16. S. Kerr and S. Laundauer, "Using Stretch Goals to Promote Organizational Effectiveness and Personal Growth: General Electric and Goldman Sachs," *Academy of Management Executive* 4 (November 2004), pp. 134–38.

17. Ibid.

18. Latham, "Motivational Benefits of Goal-Setting."

19. T. Mitchell and W. Silver, "Individual and Group Goals When Workers Are Interdependent: Effects on Task Strategies and Performance," *Journal of Applied Psychology* 75 (1990), pp. 185–93.

20. Latham, "Motivational Benefits of Goal-Setting."

21. M. Schweitzer, L. Ordonez, and B. Douma, "Goal Setting as a Motivator of Unethical Behavior," *Academy of Management Journal* 47 (2004), pp. 422–32.

22. G. Will, "The Arrogance of Executives," *The Washington Post*, January 17, 2002, p. A23.

23. G. Morgenson, "Pennies that Aren't from Heaven," *The New York Times*, November 7, 2004, sec. 3, pp. 1, 8.

24. P. C. Early, T. Connolly, and G. Ekegren, "Goals, Strategy Development, and Task Performance: Some Limits on the Efficacy of Goal Setting," *Journal of Applied Psychology 74* (1989), pp. 24–33; C. E. Shalley, "Effects of Productivity Goals, Creativity Goals, and Personal Discretion on Individual Creativity," *Journal of Applied Psychology 76* (1991), pp. 179–85.

25. J. Main, "Is the Baldridge Overblown?" *Fortune*, July 1, 1991, pp. 62–65.

26. R. Fisher and A. Sharp, *Getting It Done* (New York: HarperCollins, 1998).

27. E. Thorndike, *Animal Intelligence* (New York: Macmillan, 1911).

28. A. D. Stajkovic and F. Luthans, "Differential Effects of Incentive Motivators on Work Performance," *Academy of Management Journal 44* (2001), pp. 580–90.

29. R. Levering and M. Moskowitz, "The 100 Best Companies to Work For," *Fortune*, January 8, 2001, pp. 148–68.

30. Cascio, "Managing a Virtual Workplace."

31. S. Kerr, "Organizational Rewards: Practical, Cost-Neutral Alternatives That You May Know, But Don't Practice," *Organizational Dynamics*, Summer 1999, pp. 61–70.

32. S. C. Faludi, "At Nordstrom Stores, Service Comes First—but at a Big Price," *The Wall Street Journal*, February 20, 1990, pp. A1, A16.

33. K. Butterfield, L. K. Trevino, and G. Ball, "Punishment from the Manager's Perspective: A Grounded Investigation and Inductive Model," *Academy of Management Review 39* (1996), pp. 1479–512.

34. P. Sellers, "P&G: Teaching an Old Dog New Tricks," *Fortune*, May 31, 2004, pp. 166–80.

35. T. Judge and R. Piccolo, "Transformational and Transactional Leadership: A Meta-Analytic Test of Their Relative Ability," *Journal of Applied Psychology 89* (2004), pp. 755–68.

36. S. Kerr, "On the Folly of Rewarding A While Hoping for B," *Academy of Management Journal 18* (1975), pp. 769–83.

37. S. Pearlstein, "Executive Privilege?" *The Washington Post*, March 24, 2002, pp. H1, H4.

38. E. E. Lawler III, *Rewarding Excellence* (San Francisco: Jossey-Bass, 2000).

39. J. Weber, "Farewell, Fast Track," *BusinessWeek*, December 10, 1990, pp. 192–200.

40. T. Bisoux, "Corporate CounterCulture," *BizEd*, November/December 2004, pp. 16–20.

41. Sellers, "P&G: Teaching an Old Dog New Tricks."

42. D. Roth, "The Trophy Life," *Fortune*, April 19, 2004, pp. 70–83.

43. Lawler, *Treat People Right!*

44. A. Bennett, "When Money Is Tight, Bosses Scramble for Other Ways to Motivate the Troops," *The Wall Street Journal*, October 31, 1990, pp. B1, B5.

45. J. Pfeffer and R. Sutton, *The Knowing–Doing Gap* (Boston: Harvard Business School Press, 2000).

46. S. Moss and J. Sanchez, "Are Your Employees Avoiding You? Managerial Strategies for Closing the Feedback Gap," *Academy of Management Executive* 18, no. 1 (February 2004), pp. 32–44.

47. Lawler, *Treat People Right!*

48. J. Jackman and M. Strober, "Fear of Feedback," *Harvard Business Review*, April 2003, 101–107.

49. V. H. Vroom, *Work and Motivation* (New York: John Wiley & Sons, 1964).

50. R. E. Wood, P. W. B. Atkins, and J. E. H. Bright, "Bonuses, Goals, and Instrumentality Effects," *Journal of Applied Psychology* 84 (1999), pp. 703–20.

51. Kerr, "Organizational Rewards."

52. A. H. Maslow, "A Theory of Human Motivation," *Psychological Review*, July 1943, pp. 370–96.

53. L. Mainicro and D. Gibson, "Managing Employee Trauma: Dealing with the Emotional Fallout from 9–11," *Academy of Management Executive*, August 2003, pp. 130–43.

54. M. Wahba and L. Birdwell, "Maslow Reconsidered: A Review of Research on the Need Hierarchy Theory," *Organizational Behavior and Human Performance* 15 (1976), pp. 212–40.

55. F. Rose, "A New Age for Business?" *Fortune*, October 8, 1990, pp. 156–64.

56. G. Dessler, "How to Earn Your Employees' Commitment," *Academy of Management Executive*, May 1999, pp. 58–67.

57. Weber, "Farewell, Fast Track."

58. C. Alderfer, *Existence, Relatedness, and Growth: Human Needs in Organizational Settings* (Glencoe, IL: Free Press, 1972).

59. C. Pinder, *Work Motivation* (Glenview, IL: Scott, Foresman, 1984).

60. D. McClelland, *The Achieving Society* (New York: Van Nostrand Reinhold, 1961).

61. D. McClelland and R. Boyatzis, "Leadership Motive Pattern and Long-Term Success in Management," *Journal of Applied Psychology* 67 (1982), pp. 737–43.

62. N. Adler, *International Dimensions of Organizational Behavior*, 2nd ed. (Boston: Kent, 1991); G. Hofstede, *Cultures and Organizations* (London: McGraw-Hill, 1991).

63. E. E. Lawler III and D. Finegold, "Individualizing the Organization: Past, Present, and Future," *Organizational Dynamics*, Summer 2000, pp. 1–15.

64. Ibid.

65. T. M. Amabile, "A Model of Creativity and Innovation in Organizations," in *Research in Organizational Behavior*, ed. B. M. Staw and L. L. Cummings

(Greenwich, CT: JAJ Press, 1988), pp. 10, 123–67.

66. C. M. Ford, "A Theory of Individual Creative Action in Multiple Social Domains," *Academy of Management Review* 21 (1996), pp. 1112–42.

67. G. Oldham and A. Cummings, "Employee Creativity: Personal and Comtextual Factors at Work," *Academy of Management Journal* 39 (1996), pp. 607–34.

68. T. Amabile, R. Conti, H. Coon, J. Lazenby, and M. Herron, "Assessing the Work Environment for Creativity," *Academy of Management Journal* 39 (1996), pp. 1154–84.

69. M. Campion and G. Sanborn. "Job Design," in *Handbook of Industrial Engineering*, ed. G. Salvendy (New York: John Wiley & Sons, 1991).

70. Lawler and Finegold, "Individualizing the Organization."

71. B. G. Ponser, "Role Changes," *Inc.*, February 1990, pp. 95–98.

72. M. Campion and D. McClelland, "Interdisciplinary Examination of the Costs and Benefits of Enlarged Jobs: A Job Design Quasi-Experiment," *Journal of Applied Psychology* 76 (1991), pp. 186–98.

73. F. Herzberg, *Work and the Nature of Men* (Cleveland: World, 1966).

74. J. R. Hackman, G. Oldham, R. Janson, and K. Purdy, "A New Strategy for Job Enrichment," *California Management Review* 16 (Fall 1975), pp. 57–71.

75. T. Ehrenfeld, "Cashing In," *Inc.*, July 1993, pp. 69–70.

76. D. Fenn, "Bottoms Up," *Inc.*, July 1993, pp. 58–60.

77. R. Rechheld, "Loyalty-Based Management" *Harvard Business Review*, March-April 1993, pp. 64–73.

78. D. Whitford, "A Human Place to Work," *Fortune*, January 8, 2001, pp. 108–18, 458–59.

79. G. Hamel, "Reinvent Your Company," *Fortune*, June 12, 2000, pp. 98–118.

80. Levering and Moskowitz, "The 100 Best Companies."

81. A. Bianchi, "True Believers," *Inc.*, July 1993, pp. 72–73.

82. J. Finegan, "People Power," *Inc.*, July 1993, pp. 62–63.

83. Ibid.

84. T. Peters and N. Austin, *A Passion for Excellence* (New York: Random House, 1985).

85. Ehrenfeld, "Cashing In."

86. Finegan, "People Power."

87. Campion and Sanborn, "Job Design."

88. S. Seibert, S. Silver, and W. A. Randolph, "Taking Empowerment to the Next Level: A Multiple-Level Model of Empowerment, Performance, and Satisfaction," *Academy of Management Journal* 47 (2004), pp. 332–49.

89. C. Argyris, "Empowerment: The Emperor's New Clothes," *Harvard Business Review*, May–June 1998, pp. 98–105.

90. R. Forrester, "Empowerment: Rejuvenating a Potent Idea," *Academy of Management Executive*, August 2000, pp. 67–80.

91. R. C. Liden, S. J. Wayne, and R. T. Sparrowe, "An Examination of the Mediating Role of Psychological Empowerment on the Relations between the Job, Interpersonal Relationships, and Work Out comes," *Journal of Applied Psychology* 85 (2000), pp. 407–16.

92. Peters and Austin, *A Passion for Excellence*.

93. K. Thomas and B. Velthouse, "Cognitive Elements of Empowerment: An 'Interpretive' Model of Intrinsic Task Motivation," *Academy of Management Review* 15 (1990), pp. 666–81.

94. J. Kouzes and B. Posner, The Leadership Challenge, 2nd ed. Copyright © 1995 Jossey-Bass, Inc. This material is used by permission of Jossey-Bass, Inc. a subsidiary of John Wiley & Sons, Inc.

95. Price Waterhouse Change Integration Team, Better Change (Burr Ridge, IL: Richard D. Irwin, 1995).

96. E. E. Lawler III, *The Ultimate Advantage: Creating the High Involvement Organization* (San Francisco: Jossey-Bass, 1992).

97. O. Gadiesh and J. L. Gilbert, "Transforming Corner-Office Strategy into Frontline Action," *Harvard Business Review*, May 2001, pp. 72–79.

98. J. Kouzes and B. Posner, *The Leadership Challenge* (San Francisco: Jossey-Bass, 1995).

99. Price Waterhouse Change Integration Team, *Better Change*.

100. J. Jasinowski and R. Hamrin, *Making It in America* (New York: Simon & Schuster, 1995).

101. W. A. Randolph and M. Sashkin, "Can Organizational Empowerment Work in Multinational Settings?" *Academy of Management Executive* 16 (2002), pp. 102–15.

102. J. Adams, "Inequality in Social Exchange," in *Advances in Experimental Social Psychology*, ed. L. Berkowitz (New York: Academic Press, 1965).

103. G. Colvin, "The Great CEO Pay Heist," *Fortune*, June 25, 2001, pp. 64–70.

104. M. Bloom, "The Performance Effects of Pay Dispersion of Individuals and Organizations," *Academy of Management Journal* 42 (1999), pp. 25–40.

105. D. Skarlicki, R. Folger, and P. Tesluk, "Personality as a Moderator in the Relationships between Fairness and Retaliation," *Academy of Management Journal* 42 (1999), pp. 100–108.

106. J. Brockner, "Making Sense of Procedural Fairness: How High Procedural Fairness Can Reduce or Heighten the Influence of Outcome Favorability," *Academy of Management Review* 27 (2002), pp. 58–76; D. De Cremer and D. van Knippenberg, "How Do Leaders Promote Cooperation? The Effects of Charisma and Procedural Fairness," *Journal of Applied Psychology* 87 (2002), pp. 858–66.

107. M. Kernan and P. Hanges, "Survivor Reactions to Reorganization: Antecedents and Consequences of Procedural, Interpersonal, and Informational Justice," *Journal of Applied Psychology* 87 (2002), pp. 916–28.

108. Lawler, *Treat People Right!*

109. W. C. Kim and R. Mauborgne, "Fair Process: Managing in the Knowledge Economy," *Harvard Business Review*, July–August 1997, pp. 65–75.

110. Ibid.

111. T. Bateman and D. Organ, "Job Satisfaction and the Good Sold: The Relationship between Affect *Academy of Management Journal*, 1983, 587–595 and Employee 'Citizenship'."

112. D. Henne and E. Locke, "Job Dissatisfaction: What Are the Consequences?" *International Journal of Psychology* 20 (1985), pp. 221–40.

113. J. Barling, E. K. Kelloway, and R. Iverson, "High-Quality Work, Job Satisfaction, and Occupational Injuries," *Journal of Applied Psychology* 88 (2003), pp. 276–83.

114. D. Bowen, S. Gilliland, and R. Folger, "HRM and Service Fairness: How Being Fair with Employees Spills Over to Customers," *Organizational Dynamics*, Winter 1999, pp. 7–23.

115. J. Harter, F. Schmidt, and T. Hayes, "Business-Unit-Level Relationship between Employee Satisfaction, Employee Engagement, and Business Outcomes: A Meta-Analysis," *Journal of Applied Psychology* 87 (2002), pp. 268–79.

116. Bisoux, "Corporate CounterCulture."

117. M. Boyle, "The Wegman's Way," *Fortune*, January 24, 2005, pp. 62–68.

118. D. Fenn, "James Goodnight, SAS," *Inc.*, April 2004, p. 126.

119. Ibid.

120. R. E. Walton, "Improving the Quality of Work Life," *Harvard Business Review*, May–June 1974, pp. 12, 16, 155.

121. E. E. Lawler III, "Strategies for Improving the Quality of Work Life," *American Psychologist* 37 (1982), pp. 486–93; J. L. Suttle, "Improving Life at Work: Problems and Prospects," in *Improving Life at Work*, ed. J. R. Hackman and J. L. Suttle (Santa Monica, CA: Goodyear, 1977).

122. S. L. Robinson, "Trust and Breach of the Psychological Contract," *Administrative Science Quarterly* 41 (1996), pp. 574–99.

123. M. Gimein, "Sam Walton Made Us a Promise," *Fortune*, March 18, 2002, pp. 120–30.

124. D. Rousseau, "Changing the Deal While Keeping the People," *Academy of Management Executive* 10 (1996), pp. 50–58.

125. E. Ridolfi, "Executive Commentary," *Academy of Management Executive* 10 (1996), pp. 59–60.

126. E. E. Lawler III, *From the Ground Up* (San Francisco: Jossey-Bass 1996).

127. Lawler, *From the Ground Up.*

128. Lawler, *Treat People Right!*

129. S. Ghoshal, C. Bartlett, and P. Moran, "Value Creation: The New Management Manifesto," *Financial Times Mastering Management Review*, November 1999, pp. 34–37.

Chapter 14

1. E. C. Wenger and W. M. Snyder, "Communities of Practice: The Organizational Frontier," *Harvard Business Review*, January–February 2000, pp. 139–45.

2. S. Cohen and D. Bailey "What Makes Teams Work: Group Effectiveness Research from the Shop Floor to the Executive Suite," *Journal of Management* 23 (1997), pp. 239–90.

3. B. Dumaine, "Who Needs a Boss?" *Fortune*, May 7, 1990, pp. 52–60.

4. G. Chen, L. Donahue, and R. Klimoski, "Training Undergraduates to Work in Organizational Teams," *Academy of Management Learning and Education* 3 (2004), pp. 27–40.

5. Dumaine, "Who Needs a Boss?"

6. K. Wexley and S. Silverman, *Working Scared* (San Francisco: Jossey-Bass, 1993).

7. Wexley and Silverman, *Working Scared.*

8. B. Dumaine, "The Trouble with Teams," *Fortune*, September 5, 1994, pp. 86–92.

9. E. E. Lawler III, *From the Ground Up* (San Francisco: Jossey-Bass, 1996).

10. Lawler, *From the Ground Up.*

11. Ibid.

12. R. M. Kanter, "Championing Change: An Interview with Bell Atlantic's CEO Raymond Smith," *Harvard Business Review*, January–February 1991, pp. 118–30.

13. R. Heifetz and D. Laurie, "The Work of Leadership," *Harvard Business Review*, January–February 1996, pp. 124–34.

14. Lawler, *From the Ground Up.*

15. Dumaine, "Who Needs a Boss?"

16. M. Boyle, "Growing against the Grain," *Fortune*, May 3, 2004, pp. 148–56.

17. D. Nadler, J. R. Hackman, and E. E. Lawler III, *Managing Organizational Behavior* (Boston: Little, Brown, 1979).

18. M. Cianni and D. Wnuck, "Individual Growth and Team Enhancement: Moving toward a New Model of Career Development," *Academy of Management Executive* 11 (1997), pp. 105–15.

19. Cohen and Bailey, "What Makes Teams Work."

20. J. Katzenback and D. Smith, "The Discipline of Teams," *Harvard Business Review*, March–April 1993, pp. 111–20.

21. J. Zenger and Associates, *Leading Teams* (Burr Ridge, IL: Business One Irwin, 1994).

22. S. Cohen, "New Approaches to Teams and Teamwork," in J. Galbraith,

E. E. Lawler III, and Associates, *Organizing for the Future* (San Francisco: Jossey-Bass, 1993).

23. Cohen and Bailey, "What Makes Teams Work."

24. Ibid.

25. C. Snow, S. Snell, S. Davison, and D. Hambrick, "Use Transnational Teams to Globalize Your Company," *Organizational Dynamics*, Spring 1996, pp. 50–67.

26. B. Kirkman, B. Rosen, C. Gibson, P. Tesluk, and S. McPherson, "Five Challenges to Virtual Team Success: Lessons from Sabre, Inc." *Academy of Management Executive* 16 (2002), pp. 67–80.

27. R. Banker, J. Field, R. Schroeder, and K. Sinha, "Impact of Work Teams on Manufacturing Performance: A Longitudinal Field Study," *Academy of Management Journal* 39 (1996), pp. 867–90.

28. D. Yeatts, M. Hipskind, and D. Barnes, "Lessons Learned from Self-Managed Work Teams," *Business Horizons*, July–August 1994, pp. 11–18.

29. B. Kirkman and D. Shapiro, "The Impact of Cultural Values on Job Satisfaction and Organizational Commitment in Self-Managing Work Teams: The Mediating Role of Employee Resistance," *Academy of Management Journal* 44 (2001), pp. 557–69.

30. B. Kirkman and D. Shapiro, "The Impact of Cultural Values on Employee Resistance to Teams: Toward a Model of Globalized Self-Managing Work Team Effectiveness," *Academy of Management Review* 22 (1997), pp. 730–57.

31. B. Macy and H. Isumi, "Organizational Change, Design, and Work Innovation: A Meta-Analysis of 131 North American Field Studies—1961–1991," *Research in Organizational Change and Development* 7 (1993), pp. 235–313.

32. Ibid.

33. B. W. Tuckman, "Developmental Sequence in Small Groups," *Psychological Bulletin* 63 (1965), pp. 384–99.

34. S. Furst, M. Reeves, B. Rosen, and R. Blackburn, "Managing the Life Cycle of Virtual Teams," *Academy of Management Executive*, May 2004, pp. 6–20. Quotes in this paragraph from pp. 11 and 12.

35. C. J. G. Gersick, "Time and Transition in Work Teams: Toward a New Model of Group Development," *Academy of Management Journal* 31 (1988), pp. 9–41.

36. J. R. Hackman, *Groups That Work (and Those That Don't)* (San Francisco: Jossey-Bass, 1990).

37. Zenger and Associates, *Leading Teams.*

38. R. Cross, "Looking before You Leap: Assessing the Jump to Teams in Knowledge-Based Work," *Business Horizons*, September–October 2000, pp. 29–36.

39. Dumaine, "The Trouble with Teams."

40. J. Case, "What the Experts Forgot to Mention," *Inc.*, September 1993, pp. 66–78.

41. A. Nahavandi and E. Aranda, "Restructuring Teams for the Reengineered Organization," *Academy of Management Executive*, November 1994, pp. 58–68.

42. B. Kirkman, B. Rosen, P. Tesluk, and C. Gibson, "The Impact of Team Empowerment on Virtual Team Performance: The Moderating Role of Face-to-Face Interaction," *Academy of Management Journal* 47 (2004), pp. 175–92.

43. J. Katzenback and D. Smith, *The Wisdom of Teams* (Boston: Harvard Business School Press, 1993).

44. Nadler, Hackman, and Lawler, *Managing Organizational Behavior.*

45. P. Petty, "Behind the Brands at P & G: An Interview with John Smale," *Harvard Business Review*, November–December 1985, pp. 78–80.

46. T. Peters and N. Austin, *A Passion for Excellence* (New York: Random House, 1985).

47. T. Kidder, *The Soul of a New Machine* (Boston: Little, Brown, 1981).

48. Nadler, Hackman, and Lawler, *Managing Organizational Behavior.*

49. Katzenback and Smith, "The Discipline of Teams."

50. Ibid.

51. C. Meyer, "How the Right Measures Help Teams Excel," *Harvard Business Review*, May–June 1994, pp. 95–103.

52. J. R. Katzenbach and J. A. Santamaria, "Firing Up the Front Line," *Harvard Business Review*, May–June 1999, pp. 107–17.

53. D. Knight, C. Durham, and E. Locke, "The Relationship of Team Goals, Incentives, and Efficacy to Strategic Risk, Tactical Implementation, and Performance," *Academy of Management Journal* 44 (2001), pp. 326–38.

54. B. L. Kirkman and B. Rosen, "Powering Up Teams," *Organizational Dynamics*, Winter 2000, pp. 48–66.

55. Lawler, *From the Ground Up.*

56. M. Erez, "Is Group Productivity Loss the Rule or the Exception? Effects of Culture and Group-Based Motivation," *Academy of Management Journal* 39 (1996), pp. 1513–37.

57. Katzenbach and Smith, "The Discipline of Teams."

58. P. Pascarelloa, "Compensating Teams," *Across the Board*, February 1997, pp. 16–22.

59. R. Wageman, "Interdependence and Group Effectiveness," *Administrative Science Quarterly* 40 (1995), pp. 145–80.

60. Cianni and Wnuck, "Individual Growth and Team Enhancement."

61. Lawler, *From the Ground Up.*

62. R. Wellins, R. Byham, and G. Dixon, *Inside Teams* (San Francisco: Jossey-Bass, 1994).

63. Ibid.

64. J. M. Levine, E. T. Higgins, and H. Choi, "Development of Strategic Norms in Groups," *Organizational Behavior and Human Decision Processes* 82 (2000), pp. 88–101.

65. K. Jehn and E. Mannix, "The Dynamic Nature of Conflict: A Longitudinal Study of Intragroup Conflict and Group Performance," *Academy of Management Journal* 44 (2001), pp. 238–51.

66. J. O'Toole, *Vanguard Management: Redesigning the Corporate Future* (New York: Doubleday, 1985).

67. R. F. Bales, *Interaction Process Analysis: A Method for the Study of Small Groups* (Reading, MA: Addison-Wesley, 1950).

68. V. U. Druskat and J. Wheeler, "Managing from the Boundary: The Effective Leadership of Self-Managing Work Teams," *Academy of Management Journal* 46 (2003), pp. 435–57.

69. Katzenback and Smith, *The Wisdom of Teams.*

70. C. Stoner and R. Hartman, "Team Building: Answering the Tough Questions," *Business Horizons*, September–October 1993, pp. 70–78.

71. S. E. Seashore, *Group Cohesiveness in the Industrial Work Group* (Ann Arbor, MI: University of Michigan Press, 1954).

72. Banker et al., "Impact of Work Teams on Manufacturing Performance."

73. B. Mullen and C. Cooper, "The Relation between Group Cohesiveness and Performance: An Integration," *Psychological Bulletin* 115 (1994), pp. 210–27.

74. D. P. Forbes and F. J. Milliken, "Cognition and Corporate Governance: Understanding Boards of Directors as Strategic Decision-Making Groups," *Academy of Management Review* 24 (1999), pp. 489–505.

75. T. Simons, L. H. Pelled, and K. A. Smith, "Making Use of Difference: Diversity, Debate, and Decision Comprehensiveness in Top Management Teams," *Academy of Management Journal* 42 (1999), pp. 662–73.

76. Seashore, *Group Cohesiveness in the Industrial Work Group.*

77. B. Lott and A. Lott, "Group Cohesiveness as Interpersonal Attraction: A Review of Relationships with Antecedent and Consequent Variables," *Psychological Bulletin*, October 1965, pp. 259–309.

78. B. L. Kirkman and B. Rosen, "Beyond Self-Management: Antecedents and Consequences of Team Empowerment," *Academy of Management Journal* 42 (1999), pp. 58–74.

79. Hackman, *Groups That Work.*

80. W. Bennis, *Organizing Genius* (Reading, MA: Addison-Wesley, 1997).

81. Cianni and Wnuck, "Individual Growth and Team Enhancement."

82. K. Jehn, "A Multimethod Examination of the Benefits and Detriments of

83. Intragroup Conflict," *Administrative Science Quarterly* 40 (1995), pp. 245–82.

83. Wellins, Byham, and Dixon, *Inside Teams.*

84. D. G. Ancona, "Outward Bound: Strategies for Team Survival in an Organization," *Academy of Management Journal* 33 (1990), pp. 334–65.

85. Ibid.

86. L. Sayles, *Leadership: What Effective Managers Really Do, and How They Do It* (New York: McGraw-Hill, 1979).

87. Ibid.

88. S. Wetlaufer, "Common Sense and Conflict: An Interview with Disney's Michael Eisner," *Harvard Business Review*, January–February 2000, pp. 114–24.

89. J. Chatman and F. Flynn, "The Influence of Demographic Heterogeneity on the Emergence and Consequences of Cooperative Norms in Work Teams," *Academy of Management Journal* 44 (2001), pp. 956–74.

90. R. T. Keller, "Cross-Functional Project Groups in Research and New Product Development: Diversity, Communications, Job Stress, and Outcomes," *Academy of Management Journal* 44 (2001), pp. 547–55.

91. Chatman and Flynn, "The Influence of Demographic Heterogeneity."

92. Keller, "Cross-Functional Project Groups."

93. D. Tjosvold, *Working Together to Get Things Done* (Lexington, MA: Lexington Books, 1986).

94. C. Tinsley and J. Brett, "Managing Workplace Conflict in the United States and Hong Kong," *Organizational Behavior and Human Decision Processes* 85 (2001), pp. 360–81.

95. K. W. Thomas, "Conflict and Conflict Management," in *Handbook of Industrial and Organizational Psychology*, ed. M. D. Dunnette (Chicago: Rand McNally, 1976).

96. K. W. Thomas, "Toward Multi-Dimensional Values in Teaching: The Example of Conflict Behaviors," *Academy of Management Review*, 1977, pp. 484–89.

97. C. O. Longenecker and M. Neubert, "Barriers and Gateways to Management Cooperation and Teamwork," *Business Horizons*, September–October 2000, pp. 37–44.

98. P. S. Nugent, "Managing Conflict: Third-Party Interventions for Managers," *Academy of Management Executive* 16 (2002), pp. 139–54.

99. M. Blum and J. A. Wall Jr., "HRM: Managing Conflicts in the Firm," *Business Horizons*, May–June 1997, pp. 84–87.

100. Ibid.

101. J. A. Wall Jr., and R. R. Callister, "Conflict and Its Management," *Journal of Management* 21 (1995), pp. 515–58.

102. M. Montoya-Weiss, A. Massey, and M. Song, "Getting It Together: Temporal Coordination and Conflict Management in Global Virtual Teams,"

Academy of Management Journal 44 (2001), pp. 1251–62.

103. R. Standifer and J. A. Wall Jr., "Managing Conflict in B2B Commerce," *Business Horizons*, March–April 2003, pp. 65–70.

Chapter 15

1. L. Penley, E. Alexander, I. E. Jernigan, and C. Henwood, "Communication Abilities of Managers: The Relationship to Performance," *Journal of Management* 17 (1991), pp. 57–76.

2. W. V. Haney, "A Comparative Study of Unilateral and Bilateral Communication," *Academy of Management Journal* 7 (1964), pp. 128–36.

3. M. McCormack, "The Illusion of Communication," *Financial Times Mastering Management Review*, July 1999, pp. 8–9.

4. J. S. Lublin, "Managing Your Career," *The Wall Street Journal*, November 30, 2004, p. B1.

5. R. Cross and S. Brodt, "How Assumptions of Consensus Undermine Decision Making," *Sloan Management Review* 42 (2001), pp. 86–94.

6. S. Mohammed and E. Ringseis, "Cognitive Diversity and Consensus in Group Decision Making: The Role of Inputs, Processes, and Outcomes," *Organizational Behavior and Human Decision Processes* 85 (2001), pp. 310–35.

7. S. Parker and C. Axtell, "Seeing Another Viewpoint: Antecedents and Outcomes of Employee Perspective Taking," *Academy of Management Journal* 44 (2001), pp. 1085–100.

8. D. Tannen, "The Power of Talk: Who Gets Heard and Why," *Harvard Business Review*, September–October 1995, pp. 138–48.

9. Ibid.

10. Ibid.

11. L. K. Larkey, "Toward a Theory of Communicative Interactions in Culturally Diverse Workgroups," *Academy of Management Review*, April 1996, pp. 463–91.

12. C. Argyris, "Good Communication That Blocks Learning," *Harvard Business Review*, July–August 1994, pp. 77–85.

13. C. Deutsch, "The Multimedia Benefits Kit," *The New York Times*, October 14, 1990, sec. 3, p. 25.

14. T. W. Comstock, *Communicating in Business and Industry* (Albany, NY: Delmar, 1985).

15. J. Taylor and W. Wacker, *The 500 Year Delta: What Happens after What Comes Next* (New York: HarperCollins, 1997).

16. M. Totty, "Business Solutions: Firms Get the 'Instant' Message," *The Wall Street Journal*, December 13, 2004, p. R8.

17. A. Joyce, "Never Out of IM Reach," *The Washington Post*, December 26, 2004, p. F5.

18. T. A. Stewart, "How Cisco and Alcoa Make Real Time Work," *Fortune*, May 29, 2000, pp. 284–86.

19. S. S. K. Lam and J. Schaubroeck, "Improving Group Decisions by Better Pooling Information: A Comparative Advantage of Group Decision Support Systems," *Journal of Applied Psychology* 85 (2000), pp. 565–73.

20. M. Schrage, "If You Can't Say Anything Nice, Say It Anonymously," *Fortune*, December 6, 1999, p. 352.

21. C. Naquin and G. Paulson, "Online Bargaining and Interpersonal Trust," *Journal of Applied Psychology* 88 (2003), pp. 113–20.

22. B. Baltes, M. Dickson, M. Sherman, C. Bauer, and J. LaGanke, "Computer-Mediated Communication and Group Decision Making: A Meta-Analysis," *Organizational Behavior and Human Decision Processes* 87 (2002), pp. 156–79.

23. R. Rice and D. Case, "Electronic Message Systems in the University: A Description of Use and Utility," *Journal of Communication* 33 (1983), pp. 131–52; C. Steinfield, "Dimensions of Electronic Mail Use in an Organizational Setting," *Proceedings of the Academy of Management*, San Diego, 1985.

24. D. Kirkpatrick, "It's Hard to Manage if You Don't Blog," *Fortune*, October 4, 2004, p. 46.

25. J. Solomon, "As Electronic Mail Loosens Inhibitions, Impetuous Senders Feel Anything Goes," *The Wall Street Journal*, October 12, 1990, pp. B1, B8.

26. B. Glassberg, W. Kettinger, and J. Logan, "Electronic Communication: An Ounce of Policy Is Worth a Pound of Cure," *Business Horizons*, July–August 1996, pp. 74–80.

27. Ibid.

28. Ibid.

29. J. Stuller, "Overload," *Across the Board*, April 1996, pp. 16–22.

30. Taylor and Wacker, *The 500 year Delta.*

31. R. Tetzeli, "Surviving Information Overload," *Fortune*, July 11, 1994, pp. 32–35.

32. A. Joyce, "Never Out of IM Reach," *The Washington Post*, December 26, 2004, p. F5.

33. Lublin, "Managing Your Career."

34. V. Vara, "Taming the Email Monster," *The Wall Street Journal*, Dec 13, 2004, pp. R8, R11.

35. Ibid.

36. Tetzeli, "Surviving Information Overload."

37. N. B. Kurland and D. E. Bailey, "Telework: The Advantages and Challenges of Working Here. There, Anywhere, Anytime," *Organizational Dynamics*, Autumn 1999, pp. 53–68.

38. K. Edelman "Open Office? Try Virtual Office," *Across the Board*, March 1997, p. 34.

39. S. Shellenbarger, "Overwork, Low Morale Vex Office Staff," *The Wall Street Journal*, August 17, 1994, pp. B1, B4.

40. Ibid.

41. E. M. Hallowell, "The Human Moment at Work," *Harvard Business*

Review, January–February 1999, pp. 58–66.

42. "Home Alone: The Job," *Collections & Credit Risk*, May 1997, p. 23.

43. " 'Virtual Office' Not Yet Common," *Financial Executive*, March/April 2002, p. 10.

44. V. Govindarajan and A. Gupta, "Building an Effective Global Team," *Organizational Dynamics* 42 (2001), pp. 63–71.

45. R. Lengel and R. Daft, "The Selection of Communication Media as an Executive Skill," *Academy of Management Executive* 2 (1988), pp. 225–32.

46. J. R. Carlson and R. W. Zmud, "Channel Expansion Theory and the Experiential Nature of Media Richness Perceptions," *Academy of Management Journal* 42 (1999), pp. 153–70.

47. L. Trevino, R. Daft, and R. Lengel, "Understanding Managers' Media Choices: A Symbolic Interactionist Perspective," in *Organizations and Communication Technology*, ed. J. Fulk and C. Steinfield (London: Sage, 1990).

48. J. Fulk and B. Boyd, "Emerging Theories of Communication in Organizations," *Journal of Management*, 17 (1991), pp. 407–46.

49. L. Bossidy and R. Charan, *Confronting Reality: Doing What Matters to Get Things Right* (New York: Crown Business, 2004).

50. J. S. Lublin, "To Win Advancement, You Need to Clean Up Any Bad Speech Habits," *The Wall Street Journal*, October 5, 2004, p. B1.

51. M. McCall, M. Lombardo, and A. Morrison, *The Lessons of Experience: How Successful Executives Develop on the Job* (Lexington, MA: Lexington, 1988).

52. J. A. Conger, "The Necessary Art of Persuasion," *Harvard Business Review*, May–June 1998, pp. 84–95.

53. D. Sull, "The Rhetoric of Transformation," *Financial Times Mastering Management Review*, December/January 1999/2000, pp. 34–37.

54. N. Nohria and B. Harrington, *Six Principles of Successful Persuasion* (Boston: Harvard Business School Publishing Division, 1993).

55. R. Ashkenas, D. Ulrich, T. Jick, and S. Kerr, *The Boundaryless Organization* (San Francisco: Jossey-Bass, 1995).

56. H. K. Mintz, "Business Writing Styles for the 70's," *Business Horizons*, August 1972. Cited in *Readings in Interpersonal and Organizational Communication*, ed. R. C. Huseman, C. M. Logue, and D. L. Freshley (Boston: Allyn & Bacon, 1977).

57. C. D. Decker, "Writing to Teach Thinking," *Across the Board*, March 1996, pp. 19–20.

58. M. Forbes, "Exorcising Demons from Important Business Letters," *Marketing Times*, March–April 1981, pp. 36–38.

59. C. Krauthammer, "Make It Snappy: In Praise of Short Papers, Short Speeches, and, Yes, the Sound Bite," *Time*, July 21, 1997, p. 84.

60. W. Strunk Jr. and E. B. White, *The Elements of Style*, 3rd ed. (New York: Macmillan, 1979); H. R. Fowler, *The Little Brown Handbook* (Boston: Little, Brown, 1986).

61. G. Ferraro, "The Need for Linguistic Proficiency in Global Business," *Business Horizons*, May–June 1996, pp. 39–46.

62. P. C. Early and E. Mosakowski, "Creating Hybrid Team Cultures: An Empirical Test of Transnational Team Functioning," *Academy of Management Journal* 43 (2000), pp. 26–49.

63. Ferraro, "The Need for Linguistic Proficiency."

64. C. Chu, *The Asian Mind Game* (New York: Rawson Associates, 1991).

65. Ferraro, "The Need for Linguistic Proficiency."

66. Comstock, *Communicating in Business and Industry*.

67. M. Korda, *Power: How to Get It. How to Use It* (New York: Random House, 1975).

68. A. Mehrabian, "Communication without Words," *Psychology Today*, September 1968, p. 52. Cited in M. B. McCaskey, "The Hidden Message Managers Send," *Harvard Business Review*, November–December 1979, pp. 135–48.

69. Ferraro, "The Need for Linguistic Proficiency."

70. *Business Horizons*, May–June 1993. Copyright 1993 by the Foundation for the School of Business at Indiana University. Used with permission.

71. "Too Many in the New Workforce Are Lacking Basic Skills," *Research Alert*, November 15, 1996, p. 5.

72. A. Athos and J. Gabarro, *Interpersonal Behavior* (Englewood Cliffs, NJ: Prentice-Hall, 1978).

73. "Have You Heard about Sperry?" *Management Review* 69 (April 1980), p. 40.

74. J. Kouzes and B. Posner, *The Leadership Challenge* (San Francisco: Jossey-Bass, 1995).

75. G. Graham, J. Unruh, and P. Jennings, "The Impact of Nonverbal Communication in Organizations: A Survey of Perceptions," *Journal of Business Communications* 28 (1991), pp. 45–62.

76. Ibid.

77. D. Upton and S. Macadam, "Why (and How) to Take a Plant Tour," *Harvard Business Review*, May–June 1997, pp. 97–106.

78. S. Wetlaufer, "Common Sense and Conflict: An Interview with Disney's Michael Eisner," *Harvard Business Review*, January–February 2000, pp. 114–24.

79. N. Adler, *International Dimensions of Organizational Behavior*, 2nd ed. (Boston: Kent, 1991).

80. Chu, *The Asian Mind Game*.

81. A. Smidts, A. T. H. Pruyn, and C. B. M. van Riel, "The Impact of Employee Communication and Perceived External Prestige on Organizational Identification," *Academy of Management Journal* 49 (2001), pp. 1051–62.

82. J. W. Koehler, K. W. E. Anatol, and R. L. Applebaum, *Organizational Communication: Behavioral Perspectives* (Orlando, FL: Holt, Rinehart & Winston, 1981).

83. J. Waldroop and T. Butler, "The Executive as Coach," *Harvard Business Review*, November–December 1996, pp. 111–17.

84. D. T. Hall, K. L. Otazo, and G. P. Hollenbeck, "Behind Closed Doors: What Really Happens in Executive Coaching," *Organizational Dynamics*, Winter 1999, pp. 39–53.

85. T. Judge and J. Cowell, "The Brave New World of Coaching," *Business Horizons*, July–August 1997, pp. 71–77; E. E. Lawler III, *Treat People Right!* (San Francisco: Jossey-Bass, 2003); L. A. Hill, "New Manager Development for the 21st Century," *Academy of Management Executive*, August 2004, pp. 121–26.

86. J. Gutknecht and J. B. Keys, "Mergers, Acquisitions, and Takeovers: Maintaining Morale of Survivors and Protecting Employees," *Academy of Management Executive*, August 1993, pp. 26–36.

87. D. Schweiger and A. DeNisi, "Communication with Employees Following a Merger: A Longitudinal Field Experiment," *Academy of Management Journal* 34 (1991), pp. 110–35.

88. J. Case, "The Open-Book Managers," *Inc.*, September 1990, pp. 104–13.

89. J. Case, "Opening the Books," *Harvard Business Review*, March–April 1997, pp. 118–27.

90. T. R. V. Davis, "Open-Book Management: Its Promise and Pitfalls," *Organization Dynamics*, Winter 1997, pp. 7–20.

91. B. Burlingham, "Jack Stack, SRC Holdings," *Inc.*, April 2004, pp. 134–35.

92. R. Aggarwal and B. Simkins, "Open Book Management: Optimizing Human Capital," *Business Horizons* 44 (2001), pp. 5–13.

93. W. V. Ruch, *Corporate Communications* (Westport, CT: Quorum, 1984).

94. W. Imberman, "Why Engineers Strike: The Boeing Story," *Business Horizons* 44 (2001), pp. 35–44.

95. C. Hymowitz, "In the Lead: Like Rumsfeld, CEOs Who Seek Questions May Not Like Them," *The Wall Street Journal*, December 14, 2004, p. B1.

96. S. Verhovek, "Tentative Pact Made to End Boeing Strike," *The New York Times*, March 18, 2000, p. C1. Cited in Imberman, "Why Engineers Strike."

97. J. Gardner, "The Heart of the Matter: Leader-Constituent Interaction," in *Leading & Leadership*, ed. T. Fuller (Notre Dame, IN: Notre Dame University Press, 2000), pp. 239–44.

98. Ashkenas et al., *The Boundaryless Organization*.

99. Ruch, *Corporate Communications*.
100. B. Bremmer, G. Edmondson, and C. Dawson, "Nissan's Boss," *BusinessWeek*, October 4, 2004, pp. 50–58.
101. D. Roth, "The Trophy Life," *Fortune*, April 19, 2004, pp. 70–83.
102. C. Hymowitz, "Some Tips from CEOs to Help You to Make a Fresh Start in 2005," *The Wall Street Journal*, December 28, 2004, p. B1.
103. C. Hymowitz, "In the Lead: Like Rumsfeld, CEOs Who Seek Questions May Not Like Them," *The Wall Street Journal*, December 14, 2004, p. B1.
104. A. Hutton, "Four Rules for Taking Your Message to Wall Street," *Harvard Business Review*, May 2001, pp. 125–32.
105. Koehler, Anatol, and Applebaum, *Organizational Communication*.
106. Ashkenas et al., *The Boundaryless Organization*.
107. D. K. Denton, "Open Communication," *Business Horizons*, September–October 1993, pp. 64–69.
108. N. B. Kurland and L. H. Pelled, "Passing the Word: Toward a Model of Gossip and Power in the Workplace," *Academy of Management Review* 25 (2000), pp. 428–38.
109. L. Abrams, R. Cross, E. Lesser, and D. Levin, "Nurturing Interpersonal Trust in Knowledge-Sharing Networks," *Academy of Management Executive* 17, November 2003, pp. 64–77.
110. R. L. Rosnow, "Rumor as Communication: A Contextual Approach," *Journal of Communication* 38 (1988), pp. 12–28.
111. L. Burke and J. M. Wise, "The Effective Care, Handling, and Pruning of the Office Grapevine," *Business Horizons*, May–June 2003, pp. 71–76.
112. K. Davis, "The Care and Cultivation of the Corporate Grapevine," *Dun's Review*, July 1973, pp. 44–47.
113. N. Difonzo, P. Bordia, and R. Rosnow, "Reining in Rumors," *Organizational Dynamics*, Summer 1994, pp. 47–62.
114. Burke and Wise, "The Effective Care, Handling, and Pruning of the Office Grapevine."
115. Difonzo, Bordia, and Rosnow, "Reining in Rumors."
116. Ashkenas et al., *The Boundaryless Organization*.
117. Ibid.
118. R. M. Hodgetts, "A Conversation with Steve Kerr," *Organizational Dynamics*, Spring 1996, pp. 68–79.
119. Ibid.
120. R. M. Fulmer, "The Evolving Paradigm of Leadership Development," *Organizational Dynamics*, Spring 1997, pp. 59–72.
121. Ashkenas et al., *The Boundaryless Organization*.

Chapter 16

1. James C. Collins, and Jerry I. Porras, *Built to Last: Successful Habits of Visionary Companies* (New York: HarperBusiness, 1994).
2. Keith Naughton, "Spinning Out of Control," *Newsweek* 136, no. 11, (September 11, 2000), p. 58; Christopher Palmeri, "California's Utilities Doth Protest Too Much," *BusinessWeek*, January 15, 2001, pp. 42–43.
3. W. G. Ouchi, "Markets, Bureaucracies, and Clans," *Administrative Science Quarterly* 25 (1980), pp. 129–41.
4. Robert Simons, Antonio Davila, and Robert S. Kaplan, *Performance Measurement & Control Systems for Implementing Strategy* (Englewood Cliffs, NJ: Prentice-Hall, 2000).
5. Elaine D. Pulakos, Sharon Arad, Michelle A. Donovan, and Kevin E. Plamondon, "Adaptability in the Workplace: Development of a Taxonomy of Adaptive Performance," *Journal of Applied Psychology:* 85, no. 4 (August 2000), pp. 12–24; John H. Sheridan, "Lean Sigma Synergy," *Industry Week* 249, no. 17 (October 16, 2000), pp. 81–82.
6. J. T. Burr, "Keys to a Successful Internal Audit," *Quality Progress* 30, no. 4 (April 1997), pp. 75–77; John E. Ettlie, "Surfacing Quality at GE," *Automotive Manufacturing & Production* 112, no. 8 (August 2000), pp. 44–46; Roy A. Maxion and Robert T. Olszewski, "Eliminating Exception Handling Errors with Dependability Cases: A Comparative, Empirical Study," *IEEE Transactions on Software Engineering* 26, no. 9 (September 2000), pp. 888–906.
7. Robert Della, "Harley Rides High on SPC Changes," *Quality* 39, no. 1 (January 2000), pp. 40–43.
8. R. Henkoff, "Make Your Office More Productive," *Fortune*, February 25, 1990, pp. 40–49; R. Buchele, "How to Evaluate a Firm," *California Management Review*, Fall 1962, pp. 5–17.
9. George Ellis, "Feedforward for Faster Control Response," *Control Engineering* 47, no. 11 (October 2000), p. 104.
10. Vanessa Urch Druskat, "Effects and Timing of Developmental Peer Appraisals in Self-Managing Work Groups," *Journal of Applied Psychology* 84, no. 1 (February 1999), p. 58.
11. Sandra Waddock and Neil Smith, "Corporate Responsibility Audits: Doing Well by Doing Good," *Sloan Management Review* 41, no. 2 (Winter 2000), pp. 75–83; Lynn L. Bergeson, "OSHA Gives Incentives for Voluntary Self-Audits," *Pollution Engineering* 32, no. 10 (October 2000), pp. 33–34.
12. Sunil Thawani, "Six Sigma Quality—Linking Customers, Processes and Financial Results," onesixsigma.com, April 20, 2002.
13. Tom Rancour and Mike McCracken, "Applying 6 Sigma Methods for Breakthrough Safety Performance," *Professional Safety* 45, no. 10 (October 2000), pp. 29–32; Michael Arndt, "Where Precision Is Life or Death," *BusinessWeek*, July 22, 2002, online; "Quality Isn't Just for Widgets," *BusinessWeek*, July 22, 2002, online; George Eckes, "Making Six Sigma Last," *Ivey Business Journal*, January–February 2002, p. 77.
14. Janet, L. Colbert, "The Impact of the New External Auditing Standards," *The Internal Auditor* 5, no. 6 (December 2000), pp. 46–50.
15. G. A. Ewert, "How to Sell Internal Auditing," *Internal Auditor* 54, no. 5 (October 1997), pp. 54–57; J. T. Burr, "Keys to a Successful Internal Audit," *Quality Progress* 30, no. 4 (April 1997), pp. 75–77; Satina V. Williams and Benson Wier, "Value-Added Auditing: Where Are the Efficiencies Realized?" *Internal Auditing* 15, no. 4 (July/August 2000), pp. 37–42; David B. Crawford, "Levels of Control," *Internal Auditor* 57, no. 5 (October 2000), pp. 42–45.
16. R. Henkoff, "Cost Cutting: How to Do It Right," *Fortune*, April 9, 1990, pp. 40–49.
17. Carol J. Loomis, "I Pay More in Income Taxes Than Cisco—So Do You," *Fortune* 42, no. 14 (December 18, 2000), pp. 44–46; Thomas G. Donlan, "Bridging the GAAP," *Barron's* 80, no. 45 (November 6, 2000), p. 74.
18. Jonathan D. Glater, "The Better the Audit Panel, the Higher the Stock Price," *The New York Times*, April 8, 2005, p. C4.
19. P. C. Brewer and L. A. Vulinec, "Harris Corporation's Experiences with Using Activity-Based Costing," *Information Strategy: The Executive's Journal* 13, no. 2 (Winter 1997), pp. 6–16; Terence P. Pare, "A New Tool for Managing Costs," *Fortune*, June 14, 1993, pp. 124–29.
20. K. Merchant, *Control in Business Organizations* (Boston: Pitman, 1985); C. W. Chow, Y. Kato, and K. A. Merchant, "The Use of Organizational Controls and Their Effects on Data Manipulation and Management Myopia," *Accounting, Organizations, and Society* 21, nos. 2/3 (February/April 1996), pp. 175–92.
21. E. E. Lawler III and J. Rhode, *Information and Control in Organizations* (Pacific Palisades, CA: Goodyear, 1976); Anthony Ferner, "The Underpinnings of 'Bureaucratic' Control Systems: HRM in European Multinationals," *Journal of Management Studies* 37, no. 4 (June 2000), pp. 521–39; Marilyn S. Fenwick, "Cultural and Bureaucratic Control in MNEs: The Role of Expatriate Performance Management," *Management International Review* 39 (1999), pp. 107–25.
22. J. Veiga and J. Yanouzas, *The Dynamics of Organization Theory*, 2nd ed. (St. Paul, MN: West, 1984).
23. L. Schiff, "Downsizing Workplace Stress," *Business & Health* 15, no. 1 (November 1997), pp. 45–46; S. Albrecht, "Are Your Employees the

Enemy?" *HRFocus* 74, no. 4 (April 1997), p. 21.

24. Michael Scott, "Seven Pitfalls for Managers When Handling Poor Performers and How to Overcome Them," *Manage* 51, no. 3 (February 2000), pp. 12–14.

25. Henkoff, "Make Your Office More Productive"; see also Peggy Anderson and Marica Pulich, "Recruiting Good Employees in Tough Times," *Health Care Manager* 18, no. 3 (March 2000), pp. 32–40.

26. Lawler and Rhode, *Information and Control in Organizations*; J. A. Gowan Jr. and R. G. Mathieu, "Critical Factors in Information System Development for a Flexible Manufacturing System," *Computers in Industry* 28, no. 3 (June 1996), pp. 173–83.

27. T. A. Stewart, "Do You Push Your People Too Hard?" *Fortune*, October 22, 1990, pp. 121–28.

28. S. Tully, "The CEO Who Sees Beyond Budgets," *Fortune*, October 22, 1990, pp. 121–28.

29. Robert W. Rudloff, "Casino Fraud," *The Internal Auditor* 56, no. 3 (June 1999), pp. 44–49; Mike McNamee, "Faster, Cheaper Trading—Can the Regulators Keep Up?" *BusinessWeek*, August 9, 1999, pp. 84; Bill Zalud, "Conquering Digital Marks CCTV Innovations," *Security* 37, no. 4 (April 2000), pp. 43–44.

30. Gillian Flynn, "Out of the Red, into the Blue," *Workforce* 79, no. 3 (March 2000), pp. 50–52; Alison Stein Wellner, "Entrepreneurial HR," *HR Magazine* 45, no. 3 (March 2000), pp. 52–58.

31. Christopher Farrell, "Stock Options for All!" *BusinessWeek Online*, September 20, 2002; Eric Wahlgren, "CEO Pay Tomorrow: Same as Today," *BusinessWeek Online*, August 21, 2002.

32. "Commentary: Corporate America's New Accountability," *BusinessWeek*, July 26, 2004, online.

33. Ken Moores and Joseph Mula, "The Salience of Market, Bureaucratic, and Clan Controls in the Management of Family Firm Transitions: Some Tentative Australian Evidence," *Family Business Review* 13, no. 2 (June 2000), pp. 91–106; Anthony Walker and Robert Newcombe, "The Positive use of Power on a Major—Construction Project," *Construction Management and Economics* 18, no. 1 (January/February 2000), pp. 37–44.

34. Peter H. Fuchs, Kenneth E. Mifflin, Danny Miller, and John O. Whitney, "Strategic Integration: Competing in the Age of Capabilities," *California Management Review* 42, no. 3 (Spring 2000), pp. 118–47; Mary Ann Lando, "Making Compliance Part of Your Organization's Culture," *Healthcare Executive* 15, no. 5 (September/October 1999), pp. 18–22; Kenneth A. Frank and Kyle Fahrbach, "Organization Culture as a Complex System: Balance and Information in Models of Influence and Selection," *Organization Science* 10, no. 3 (May/June 1999), pp. 253–77.

Chapter 17

1. Robert A. Burgelman, Modesto A. Maidique, and Steven C. Wheelwright, *Strategic Management of Technology and Innovation*, (New York: McGraw-Hill Higher Education, 2000).

2. Donna C. L. Prestwood and Paul A. Schumann Jr., "Revitalize Your Organization," *Executive Excellence* 15, no. 2 (February 1998), p. 16; Carliss Y. Baldwin and Kim B. Clark, "Managing in an Age of Modularity," *Harvard Business Review* 75, no. 5 (September–October 1997), pp. 84–93; Shanthi Gopalakrishnan, Paul Bierly, and Eric H. Kessler, "A Reexamination of Product and Process Innovations Using a Knowledge-Based View," *Journal of High Technology Management Research* 10, no. 1 (Spring 1999), pp. 147–66; John Pullin, "Bombardier Commands Top Marks," *Professional Engineering* 13, no. 3 (July 5, 2000), pp. 40–46.

3. Gary P. Pisano. *The Development Factory: Unlocking the Potential of Process Innovation* (Boston: Harvard Business School Press, 1996); Richard Leifer, Christopher M. McDermott, Gina Colarelli O'Connor, Lois S. Peters, Mark Rice, and Robert W. Veryzer, *Radical Innovation: How Mature Companies Can Outsmart Upstarts* (Cambridge MA: Harvard Business School Press, 2000).

4. Hugh M. O'Neill, Richard W. Pounder, and Ann K. Buchholtz, "Patterns in the Diffusion of Strategies across Organizations: Insights from the Innovation, Diffusion Literature," *Academy of Management Review* 23, no. 1 (January 1998), pp. 98–114; Everett M. Rogers, *Diffusion of Innovations* (New York: Free Press, 1995); Bernard Guilhon, ed., *Technology and Markets for Knowledge—Knowledge Creation, Diffusion and Exchange within a Growing Economy* (Economics of Science, Technology and Innovation, Volume 22) (Dordrecht, Netherlands: Kluwer Academic Publishing, 2000).

5. M. E. Porter, *Competitive Strategy* (New York: Free Press, 1980); "Ciba Specialty Chemicals Highlights Sustainable Growth through Innovation," *Chemical Market Reporter* 257, no. 16 (April 17, 2000), p. 5.

6. J. A. Schumpeter, *The Theory of Economic Development* (Boston: Harvard University Press, 1934); Kathleen DesMarteau, "Information Technology Trends Drive Dramatic Industry Change," *Bobbin* 41, no. 12 (August 2000), pp. 48–58.

7. Shaker A. Zahra, Sarah Nash, and Deborah J. Bickford. "Transforming Technological Pioneering in Competitive Advantage," *Academy of Management Executive* 9, no. 1 (1995), pp. 17–31; Michael Sadowski and Aaron Roth, "Technology Leadership Can Pay Off," *Research Technology Management* 42, no. 6 (November/December 1999), pp. 32–33.

8. Todd Wasserman, "Kodak, Polaroid to Duel in Malls over Gen Y Girls," *Brandweek* 41, no. 5 (January 31, 2000), p. 10; Joel Dreyfuss, "Pixel This: How to Choose a Digital Camera," *Fortune*, 141, no. 7 (April 3, 2000), pp. 263–64.

9. Jared Sandberg, "Microsoft's Six Fatal Errors," *Newsweek*, June 19, 2000, pp. 22–28; "Leaders: Breaking Up Microsoft," *The Economist* 355, no. 8174 (June 10, 2000), p. 20.

10. Masaaki Imai and Gemba Kaizen, *A Commonsense, Low-Cost Approach to Management* (New York: McGraw-Hill, 1997); Masaaki Imai and Gemba Kaizen, *The Key to Japan's Competitive Success* (New York: McGraw-Hill, 1986).

11. Marc Bertucco, "FDA under Fire," *Psychology Today* 34, no. 1 (January/February 2001), pp. 10–11; Jill Wechsler, "Carrying a Big Stick," *Pharmaceutic Executive* 20, no. 9 (September 2000), pp. 24–27; Robin Goldwyn Blumenthal, "Next Thing You Know the FDA Will Be Profitable," *Barron's* 79, no. 47 (November 22, 1999), p. 12.

12. P. A. Geroski, "Models of Technology Diffusion," *Research Policy* 29, no. 4/5 (April 2000), pp. 603–25; Louis A. Thomas, "Adoption Order of New Technologies in Evolving Markets," *Journal of Economic Behavior & Organization* 38, no. 4 (April 1999), pp. 453–82.

13. Ronald E. Oligney and Michael I. Economides, "Technology as an Asset," *Hart's Petroleum Engineer International* 71, no. 9 (September 1998), p. 27.

14. Scott Blake Harris, "Fixing Financial Standards," *Satellite Communications* 23, no. 3 (March 1999), p. 22; Lauren E. Burns, "Still Avoiding Flameout, Globalstar Learns Iridium's Lessons," *Aviation Week & Space Technology* 153, no. 1 (July 3, 2000), p. s23.

15. "Computing's Outer Limits," *Popular Science* 252, no. 3 (March 1998), p. 64.

16. Peter G. Neumann, "Missile Defense," *Communications of the ACM* 43, no. 9 (September 2000), p. 128; Nancy Gohring, "New Spectrum Up for Grabs," *Telephony* 236, no. 21 (May 24, 1999), p. 14.

17. Frederik Balfour, "Fakes!" *BusinessWeek*, February 7, 2005, online.

18. Irene M. Kunii, "A Bold Mechanic for a Creaky Machine," *BusinessWeek*, August 7, 2000, p. 58H; Sadanori Arimura, "How Matsushita Electric and Sony Manage Global R&D," *Research Technology Management* 42, no. 2 (March/April 1999), pp. 41–52; Richard Nathan, "Matsushita Hopes Silicon Valley Links Can Boost Its R&D," *Research Technology Management* 42, no. 2 (March/April 1999), pp. 4–5.

19. Rajiv Dewan, Bing Jing, and Abraham Seidmann, "Adoption of Internet-Based Product Customization and Pricing Strategies," *Journal of Management Information Systems* 17, no. 2 (Fall 2000), pp. 9–28; P. A. Geroski, "Models of Technology Diffusion," *Research Policy* 29, no. 4/5 (April 2000), pp. 603–25; Everett M. Rogers, *Diffusion of Innovations* (New York: Free Press, 1995).

20. Eric Von Hippel, *The Sources of Innovation* (Oxford, UK: Oxford University Press, 1994); Dorothy Leonard, *Wellsprings of Knowledge: Building and Sustaining the Sources of Innovation* (Cambridge MA: Harvard Business School Press, 1998).

21. Ibid.

22. John Hagedoorn, Albert N. Link, and Nicholas S. Vonortas, "Research Partnerships," *Research Policy* 29, no. 4/5 (April 2000), pp. 567–86; Sang-Seung Yi, "Entry, Licensing and Research Joint Ventures," *International Journal of Industrial Organization* 17, no. 1 (January 1999), pp. 1–24.

23. Steve Lohr, "Sharing the Wealth at I.B.M.," *The New York Times*, April 11, 2005, p. C1.

24. Joseph F. Kovar, "Readers' Choice: Scott McNealy, Sun," *Computer Reseller News* 920 (November 13, 2000), pp. 129–30; Peter Burrows, Michael Moeller, and Steve Hamm, "Free Software from Anywhere?" *BusinessWeek*, September 13, 1999, pp. 37–38; Gary K. Jones, Aldor Lanctot Jr., and Hildy J. Teegan, "Determinants and Performance Impacts of External Technology Acquisition," *Journal of Business Venturing* 16, no. 3 (May 2000), pp. 255–83.

25. Michael Vizard, "It's the CTOs Who Help to Drive the Changing Role of IT in the World of Business," *InfoWorld* 21, no. 48 (November 29, 1999), p. 91; Gary H. Anthes, "The CIO/CTO Balancing Act," *Computerworld* 34, no. 25 (June 19, 2000), pp. 50–51.

26. Melanie Warner, "The New Way to Start Up in Silicon Valley," *Fortune*, March 2, 1998, pp. 168–74; Leon Richardson, "The Successful Entrepreneur," *Asian Business*, July 1994, p. 71; Charles Burck, "The Real World of the Entrepreneur," *Fortune*, April 5, 1993, pp. 42–55.

27. D. L. Day, "Raising Radicals: Different Processes for Championing Innovative Corporate Ventures," *Organization Science* 5, no. 2 (May 1994), pp. 148–72; Clifford Siporin, "Want Speedy FDA Approval? Hire a 'Product Champion,'" *Medical Marketing & Media*, October 1993, pp. 22–28; Clifford Siporin, "How You Can Capitalize on Phase 3B," *Medical Marketing & Media*, October 1994, pp. 72–72. Eric H. Kessler, "Tightening the Belt: Methods for Reducing Development Costs Associated with

New Product Innovation," *Journal of Engineering and Technology Management* 17, no. 1 (March 2000), pp. 59–92.

28. March, J. G., "Exploration and Exploitation in Organizational Learning," *Organization Science*, 1991, 2:1, 71–87.

29. Edgar Figueroa and Pedro Conceicao, "Rethinking the Innovation Process in Large Organizations: A Case Study of 3M," *Journal of Engineering and Technology Management* 17, no. 1 (March 2000), pp. 93–109; David Howell, "No Such Thing as a Daft Idea," *Professional Engineering* 13, no. 4 (February 23, 2000), pp. 28–29.

30. Lisa K. Gundry, Jill R. Kickul, and Charles W. Prather, "Building the Creative Organization," *Organizational Dynamics* 22, no. 2 (Spring 1994), pp. 22–36; Thomas Kuczmarski, "Inspiring and Implementing the Innovation Mind-Set," *Planning Review*, September–October 1994, pp. 37–48; Robert D. Ramsey, "How an Optimistic Outlook Can Give You an Edge," *Supervision* 61 no. 9 (September 2000), pp. 6–8.

31. R. Neff, "Toray May Have Found the Formula for Luck," *BusinessWeek*, June 15, 1990, p. 110.

32. Dorothy Leonard, *Wellsprings of Knowledge: Building and Sustaining the Sources of Innovation* (Cambridge MA: Harvard Business School Press, 1998); Dorothy Leonard-Barton "The Factory as a Learning Laboratory," *Sloan Management Review*, Fall 1992, pp. 23–38; Anil K. Gupta and Vijay Govindarajan, "Knowledge Management's Social Dimension: Lessons from Nucor Steel," *Sloan Management Review* 42, no. 1 (Fall 2000), pp. 71–80.

33. H. Kent Bowen, Kim B. Clark, Charles A. Holloway, and Steven C. Wheelwright, "Development Projects: The Engine of Renewal," *Harvard Business Review*, September–October 1994, pp. 110–20; C. Eden, T. Williams, and F. Ackermann, "Dismantling the Learning Curve: The Role of Disruptions on the Planning of Development Projects," *International Journal of Project Management* 16, no. 3 (June 1998), pp. 131–38; Mohan V. Tatikonda and Stephen R. Rosenthal, "Technology Novelty, Project Complexity, and Product Development Project Execution Success: A Deeper Look at Task Uncertainty in Product Innovation," *IEEE Transactions on Engineering Management* 47, no. 1 (February 2000), pp. 74–87.

34. E. Trist, "The Evolution of Sociotechnical Systems as a Conceptual Framework and as an Action Research Program," in *Perspectives on Organizational Design and Behavior*, ed. A. Van de Ven and W. F. Joyce (New York: John Wiley & Sons, 1981), pp. 19–75; Alfonso Molina, "Insights

into the Nature of Technology Diffusion and Implementation: The Perspective of Sociotechnical Alignment," *Technovation* 17, nos. 11/12 (November/December 1997), pp. 601–26.

Appendix F

1. Robert M. Pirsig, *Zen and the Art of Motorcycle Maintenance* (New York: William Morrow and Company, 1974).

2. Pratima Raichur, *Absolute Beauty* (New York: HarperPerennial, 1986).

3. Nescafe: Nestle (verified by Terril Haywood via 1/16/01 e-mail that Nescafe and Nesquik flavors are modified for the market in which they are sold).

4. Timothy J. Mullaney and Robert D. Hof, "Information Technology Annual Report," *BusinessWeek Online*, June 24, 2002.

5. Jane Black, "The Fight for Privacy Has Just Begun," *BusinessWeek Online*, January 10, 2002.

Chapter 18

1. C. M. Christensen, "The Past and Future of Competitive Advantage," *Sloan Management Review*, Winter 2001, pp. 105–09.

2. M. Schrage, "Getting Beyond the Innovation Fetish," *Fortune*, November 13, 2000, pp. 225–32.

3. T. A. Judge, C. J. Thoresen, V. Pucik, and T. M. Welbourne, "Managerial Coping with Organizational Change: A Dispositional Perspective," *Journal of Applied Psychology* 84 (1999), pp. 107–22.

4. C. Giffi, A. Roth, and G. Seal, *Competing in World-Class Manufacturing: America's 21st Century Challenge* (Homewood, IL: Business One Irwin, 1990).

5. R. M. Kanter, *World Class: Thriving Locally in the Global Economy* (New York: Touchstone, 1995).

6. T. G. Gunn, *21st Century Manufacturing* (New York: HarperBusiness, 1992).

7. Giffi, Roth, and Seal, *Competing in World-Class Manufacturing*.

8. J. Collins and J. Porras, *Built to Last* (London: Century, 1996).

9. Ibid.

10. C. Gibson and J. Birkinshaw, "The Antecedents, Consequences, and Mediating Role of Organizational Ambidexterity," *Academy of Management Journal* 47 (2004), pp. 209–26.

11. Collins and Porras, *Built to Last*.

12. T. Cummings and C. Worley, *Organization Development and Change* 8th ed. (Mason, OH: Thomson/Southwestern, 2005).

13. Ibid.

14. Ibid.

15. N. Nohria, W. Joyce, and B. Roberson, "What Really Works," *Harvard Business Review*, July 2003, pp. 42–52.

16. R. M. Kanter, "Thriving Locally in the Global Economy," *Harvard Business Review*, August 2003, pp. 119–27.

17. Ibid.
18. R. Teerlink, "Harley's Leadership U-Turn," *Harvard Business Review*, July-August 2000, pp. 43–48.
19. E. E. Lawler, III. *Treat People Right!* (San Francisco: Jossey-Bass, 2003).
20. S. Oreg, "Resistance to Change: Developing an Individual Differences Measure," *Journal of Applied Psychology*, 2003, pp. 680–93.
21. J. Green, "Microsoft's Mission: Search and Destroy," *Business Week Online*, February 2, 2005.
22. S. Finkelstein, *Why Smart Executives Fail* (New York: Portfolio, 2003). Reviewed by H. Beam in *Academy of Management Executive*, May 2004, pp. 157–58.
23. B. Breen, "Written in the Stars," *Fast Company*, February 2005, pp. 54–59.
24. J. Stanislao and B. C. Stanislao, "Dealing with Resistance to Change," *Business Horizons*, July-August 1983, pp. 74–78.
25. J. P. Kotter and L. A. Schlesinger, "Choosing Strategies for Change," *Harvard Business Review*, March-April 1979, pp. 106–14.
26. D. Zell, "Overcoming Barriers to Work Innovations: Lessons Learned at Hewlett-Packard," *Organizational Dynamics*, Summer 2001, pp. 77–85.
27. Ibid.
28. E. B. Dent and S. Galloway Goldberg, "Challenging Resistance to Change," *Journal of Applied Behavioral Science*, March 1999, pp. 25–41.
29. G. Johnson, *Strategic Change and the Management Process* (New York: Basil Blackwell, 1987); K. Lewin, "Frontiers in Group Dynamics," *Human Relations* 1 (1947), pp. 5–41.
30. E. H. Schein, "Organizational Culture: What It Is and How to Change It," in *Human Resource Management in International Firms*, ed. P. Evans, Y. Doz, and A. Laurent (New York: St. Martin's Press, 1990).
31. M. Beer, R. Eisenstat, and B. Spector, *The Critical Path to Corporate Renewal* (Cambridge, MA: Harvard Business School Press, 1990).
32. E. E. Lawler III, "Transformation from Control to Involvement," in *Corporate Transformation*, ed. R. Kilmann and T. Covin (San Francisco: Jossey-Bass, 1988).
33. D. Hellriegel and J. W. Slocum Jr., *Management*, 4th ed. (Reading, MA: Addison-Wesley, 1986).
34. P. Harris, *New World, New Ways, New Management* (New York: American Management Association, 1983).
35. Lewin, "Frontiers in Group Dynamics."
36. Schein, "Organizational Culture."
37. E. E. Lawler III, *From the Ground Up* (San Francisco: Jossey-Bass, 1995).
38. Nguyen Huy, Q., "Time, Temporal Capability, and Planned Change," *Academy of Management Review* 26 (2001), pp. 601–23.

39. B. Sugarman, "A Learning-Based Approach to Organizational Change: Some Results and Guidelines," *Organizational Dynamics*, Summer 2001, pp. 62–75.
40. Kotter and Schlesinger, "Choosing Strategies for Change."
41. P. C. Judge, "It's Lonely on the Edge," *Fast Company*, September 2000, pp. 352–63.
42. Sugarman, "A Learning-Based Approach to Organizational Change."
43. R. H. Miles, "Beyond the Age of Dilbert: Accelerating Corporate Transformations by Rapidly Engaging all Employees," *Organizational Dynamics*, Spring 2001, pp. 313–21.
44. D. A. Nadler, "Managing Organizational Change: An Integrative Approach," *Journal of Applied Behavioral Science* 17 (1981), pp. 191–211.
45. D. Rousseau and S. A. Tijoriwala, "What's a Good Reason to Change? Motivated Reasoning and Social Accounts in Promoting Organizational Change," *Journal of Applied Psychology* 84 (1999), pp. 514–28.
46. P. C. Judge, "Janiece Webb," *Fast Company*, November 2000, pp. 218–26.
47. R. B. Reich, "Your Job Is Change," *Fast Company*, October 2000, pp. 140–60.
48. C. F. Leana and B. Barry, "Stability and Change as Simultaneous Experiences in Organizational Life," *Academy of Management Review 25* (2000), pp. 753–59.
49. O. Gadiesh and J. Gilbert, "Transforming Corner-Office Strategy into Frontline Action," *Harvard Business Review*, May 2001, pp. 72–79.
50. B. Schneider, A. Brief, and R. Guzzo, "Creating a Climate and Culture for Sustainable Organizational Change," *Organizational Dynamics*, Spring 1996, pp. 7–19.
51. The Price Waterhouse Change Integration Team, *Better Change: Best Practices for Transforming Your Organization* (Burr Ridge, IL: Irwin, 1995).
52. M. Beer and N. Nohria, "Cracking the Code of Change," *Harvard Business Review*, May–June 2000, pp. 133–41.
53. N. Nohria and J. Berkley, "Whatever Happened to the Take-Charge Manager?" *Harvard Business Review*, January–February 1994, pp. 128–37.
54. D. Miller, J. Hartwick, and I. Le Breton-Miller, "How to Detect a Management Fad—and Distinguish It from a Classic," *Business Horizons*, July–August 2004, pp. 7–16.
55. The Price Waterhouse Change Integration Team, *Better Change*.
56. Ibid.
57. J. Kotter, *Leading Change* (Boston: Harvard Business School Press, 1996).
58. Lawler, *From the Ground Up*.
59. Kotter, *Leading Change*.
60. Schneider, Brief, and Guzzo, "Creating a Climate and Culture."

61. R. Beckhard and R. Harris, *Organizational Transitions* (Reading, MA: Addison-Wesley, 1977).
62. Kotter, *Leading Change*.
63. Judge, "It's Lonely on the Edge."
64. G. Hamel, "Waking Up IBM" *Harvard Business Review*, July–August 2000, pp. 137–46.
65. Kotter, *Leading Change*.
66. D. Smith, *Taking Charge of Change* (Reading, MA: Addison-Wesley, 1996).
67. D. Von Drehle, "The Yikes Years," *The Washington Post Magazine*, November 21, 2004, pp. 16–31.
68. G. Hamel, "Killer Strategies That Make Shareholders Rich," *Fortune*, June 23, 1997, pp. 22–34.
69. G. Hamel and C. K. Prahalad, *Competing for the Future* (Boston: Harvard Business School Press, 1994).
70. M. J. Mandel, "This Way to the Future," *Business Week*, October 11, 2004, pp. 92–98.
71. Ibid.
72. Zuboff and Maxim, *The Support Economy*.
73. J. Case, "Why 20 Million of You Can't Be Wrong," *Inc.*, April 2004, pp. 100–105.
74. H. Courtney, J. Kirkland, and P. Viguerie, "Strategy under Uncertainty," *Harvard Business Review*, November–December 1997, pp. 66–79.
75. J. O'Shea and C. Madigan, *Dangerous Company: The Consulting Powerhouses and the Business They Save and Ruin* (New York: Times Books, 1997).
76. Ibid.
77. Hamel and Prahalad, *Competing for the Future*.
78. Ibid.
79. Hamel and Prahalad, *Competing for the Future*.
80. R. Charan and G. Colvin, "Managing for the Slowdown," *Fortune*, February 5, 2001, pp. 78–88.
81. P. Sellers, "P&G: Teaching an Old Dog New Tricks," *Fortune*, May 31, 2004, pp. 166–80.
82. H. Green, "Shawn Fanning's New Tune: Snocap," *Business Week Online*, December 6, 2004.
83. Ibid.
84. S. Baker and A. Aston, "The Business of Nanotech," *Business Week Online*, February 14, 2005, pp. 569–70.
85. Ibid.
86. Ibid.
87. Hamel and Prahalad, *Competing for the Future*.
88. J. Kotter, *The New Rules: How to Succeed in Today's Post-Corporate World* (New York: Free Press, 1995).
89. Ibid.
90. T. Bateman and C. Porath, "Transcendent Behavior," in *Positive Organizational Scholarship*, ed. K. Cameron, J. Dutton, and R. Quinn (San Francisco: Barrett-Koehler, 2003).
91. J. Reingold, "What We Learned in the New Economy," *Fast Company*, March 2004, pp. 56–68.

92. L. A. Hill, "New Manager Development for the 21st Century," *Academy of Management Executive*, August 2004, pp. 121–26.

93. Lawler, *From the Ground Up*; Kotter, *The New Rules.*

94. Lawler, *Treat People Right!*

95. M. Peiperl and Y. Baruck, "Back to Square Zero: The Post-Corporate Career," *Organizational Dynamics*, Spring 1997, pp. 7–22.

96. Ibid.

97. J. W. Slocum Jr., M. McGill, and D. Lei, "The New Learning Strategy Anytime, Anything, Anywhere," *Organizational Dynamics*, Autumn 1994, pp. 33–37.

98. Kotter, *The New Rules.*

99. J. Collins, *From Good to Great* (New York: HarperBusiness, 2001).

100. Hill, "New Manager Development for the 21st Century."

101. J. A. Raelin, "Don't Bother Putting Leadership into People," *Academy of Management Executive*, August 2004, pp. 131–35.

102. G. Binney, and C. Williams, *Leaning into the Future* (London: Nicholas Brealey, 1997).

103. A. Taylor III, "GM Gets Its Act Together. Finally," *Fortune*, April 4, 2004, pp. 136–46.

Photo Credits

Chapter 1

Photo 1.1, page 5, © Walt Disney Pictures/Pixar Animation/Bureau L.A.Collections/Corbis.
Photo 1.2, page 7, These materials have been reproduced with the permission of eBay Inc. Copyright © EBAY Inc. All Rights Reserved.
Photo 1.3, page 8, San Francisco Chronicle.
Photo 1.4, page 12, With permission of the Procter & Gamble Co.
Photo 1.5, page 13, Courtesy of Sony Electronics Inc.
Photo 1.6, page 17, Image provided by Columbia Sportswear.
Photo 1.7, page 22, Justin Sullivan/Getty Images.
Photo 1.8, page 24, Reprinted from the Summer 2002/Golf Digest issue of *BusinessWeek* by permission. Copyright 2005 by The McGraw-Hill Companies.

Appendix A

Photo A.1.1, page 36, Martin Rogers/Getty Images.
Photo A.1.2, page 37, Stock Montage.
Photo A.1.3, page 37, Stock Montage

Chapter 2

Photo 2.1, page 45, Scott T. Baxter/Getty Images.
Photo 2.2, page 52, Honda/Getty Images.
Photo 2.3, page 54, Courtesy of Apple.
Photo 2.4, page 62, © Royalty-Free/Corbis.
Photo 2.5, page 65, Courtesy of Nokia.
Photo 2.6, page 67, Nordstrom Employee Handbook, courtesy of Nordstrom, Inc

Chapter 3

Photo 3.1, page 77, AP/Wide World Photos.
Photo 3.2, page 81, © Reuters/Corbis.
Photo 3.3, page 83, Courtesy of Standard & Poors.
Photo 3.4, page 88, Kim Steele/Getty Images.
Photo 3.5, page 93, Keith Brofsky/Getty Images.
Photo 3.6, page 94, Courtesy of IDEO.
Photo 3.7, page 98, Brian Bahr/Getty Images.

Chapter 4

Photo 4.1, page 117, PhotoLink/Getty Images.
Photo 4.2, page 121, © Richard Cummins/Corbis.
Photo 4.3, page 122, AP/Wide World Photos.
Photo 4.4, page 126, © Rob Crandall/Stock Boston, LLC.
Photo 4.5, page 139, © Mark Richards/Photo Edit.

Chapter 5

Photo 5.1, page 149,Roslan Rahman/AFP/Getty Images.
Photo 5.2, page 150, AP/Wide World Photos.
Photo5.3, page 153, © Reuters/Corbis.
Photo5.4, page 156, © Michael Newman/Photo Edit.
Photo 5.5, page 159, Used with permission of the National Organization on Disability; *www.nod.org.*
Photo 5.6, page 160, © *ThinkStock*/SuperStock.
Photo 5.7, page 165, © Jonathan Nourok/Photo Edit.
Photo 5.8, page 168, Photo Courtesy of Conoco Phillips.
Photo 5.9, page 181, © Royalty-Free/Corbis.
Photo 5.10, page 184, Toyota Motor North America, Inc.

Chapter 6

Photo 6.1, page 187, AP/Wide World Photos.
Photo 6.2, page 191, AP/Wide World Photos.
Photo 6.3, page 197, Samuel Zuder/Bilderberg/Aurora.
Photo 6.4, page 198, Royalty-Free/Corbis.
Photo 6.5, page 202, Toyota Motor North America, Inc.
Photo 6.6, page 207, Peter Oxley/Photo Japan.
Photo 6.7, page 213, © Toshiyuki Aizawa/Reuters/Corbis.

Chapter 7

Photo 7.1, page 223, Henny Ray Abrams/AFP/Getty Images.
Photo 7.2, page 227, © Reuters/Corbis.
Photo 7.3, page 229, 1154 LILL Studio.
Photo 7.4, page 231, Courtesy of Scaled Composites.
Photo 7.5, page 233, The Kobal Collection/The Picture Desk, Inc.
Photo 7.6, page 236, Lucky Mat/Getty Images.
Photo 7.7, page 239, Royalty Free/Corbis.

Chapter 8

Photo 8.1, page 259, Peter Kramer/Getty Images.
Photo 8.2, page 265, Spencer Grant/PhotoEdit.
Photo 8.3, page 266, AP/Wide World Photos.
Photo 8.4, page 269, © Steven Rubin/The Image Works.
Photo 8.5, page 272, PhotoLink/Getty Images.
Photo 8.6, page 278, Courtesy of NASA.
Photo 8.7, page 280, Keith Brofsky/Getty Images.

Chapter 9

Photo 9.1, page 290, Toshifumi Kitamura/AFP/Getty Images.
Photo 9.2, page 296, Bill Aron/PhotoEdit.
Photo 9.3, page 297, © Ricki Rosen/Corbis Saba.
Photo 9.4, page 298, Digital Vision/Getty Images.
Photo 9.5, page 299, © Images.com/Corbis.
Photo 9.6, page 303, Courtesy of The Bama Companies, Inc.
Photo 9.7, page 305, David Young-Wolff/PhotoEdit.
Photo 9.8, page 307, Printed with permission by Target, Minneapolis.
Photo 9.9, page 311, © Rhoda Sidney/The Image Works.

Chapter 10

Photo 10.1, page 319, Stan Honda/AFP/Getty Images.
Photo 10.2, page 321, William Thomas Cain/Getty Images.
Photo 10.3, page 323, Royalty Free/Corbis.
Photo 10.4, page 326, © 2005 Used with permission Redmatch Ltd.
Photo 10.5, page 327, Ryan McVay/Getty Images.
Photo 10.6, page 331, © Greg Smith/Corbis.
Photo 10.7, page 333, Keith Brofsky/Getty Images.
Photo 10.8, page 341, Joe Raedle/Getty Images.
Photo 10.9, page 344, AP/Wide World Photos.
Photo 10.10, page 346, Gene J. Puskar-Pool/Getty Images.
Photo 10.11, page 347, AP/Wide World Photos.

Chapter 11

Photo 11.1, page 356, © age footstock.
Photo 11.2, page 358, Library of Congress, Prints and Photographs Division, LC-U9-10364-37.
Photo 11.3, page 363, Keith Brofsky/Getty Images.
Photo 11.4, page 367, Courtesy of Xerox Corporation.
Photo 11.5, page 368, Used with permission of the NationalOrganization on Disability; *www.nod.org.*
Photo 11.6, page 372, Roberto Schmidt/AFP/Getty Images.
Photo 11.7, page 376, Gamma Press.
Photo 11.8, page 378, AP/Wide World Photos.
Photo 11.9, page 380, Michael Newman/PhotoEdit.
Photo 11.10, page 383,© Ann States.

Name Index

Subject Index